The Teachings of Emanuel Swedenborg Vol 1
by Emanuel Swedenborg

Heaven and Hell
Divine Love and Wisdom
Divine Providence

The Teachings of
Emanuel Swedenborg Vol I

Start Publishing PD LLC
Copyright © 2024 by Start Publishing PD LLC

All rights reserved, including the right to reproduce this book or portions thereof in any form whatsoever.

Start Publishing PD is a registered trademark of Start Publishing PD LLC
Manufactured in the United States of America

Cover art: Shutterstock/Taisiya Kozorez

Cover design: Jennifer Do

10 9 8 7 6 5 4 3 2 1

ISBN 979-8-8809-2151-5

Heaven and Hell
Translated by John C. Ager

Section 1

The Lord, speaking in the presence of His disciples of the consummation of the age, which is the final period of the church, 1-1 says, near the end of what He foretells about its successive states in respect to love and faith: 1-2 Immediately after the tribulation of those days the sun shall be darkened, and the moon shall not give her light, and the stars shall fall from heaven, and the powers of the heavens shall be shaken. And then shall appear the sign of the Son of man in heaven; and then shall all the tribes of the earth mourn; and they shall see the Son of man coming in the clouds of heaven with power and great glory. And He shall send forth His angels with a trumpet and a great sound; and they shall gather together His elect from the four winds, from the end to end of the heavens (Matt. 24:29-31). Those who understood these words according to the sense of the letter have no other belief than that during that latest period, which is called the final judgment, all these things are to come to pass just as they are described in the literal sense, that is, that the sun and moon will be darkened and the stars will fall from the sky, that the sign of the Lord will appear in the sky, and He Himself will be seen in the clouds, attended by angels with trumpets; and furthermore, as is foretold elsewhere, that the whole visible universe will be destroyed, and afterwards a new heaven with a new earth will come into being. Such is the opinion of most men in the church at the present day. But those who so believe are ignorant of the arcana that lie hid in every particular of the Word. For in every particular of the Word there is an internal sense which treats of things spiritual and heavenly, not of things natural and worldly, such as are treated of in the sense of the letter. And this is true not only of the meaning of groups of words, it is true of each particular word. 1-3 For the Word is written solely by correspondences, 1-4 to the end that there may be an internal sense in every least particular of it. What that sense is can be seen from all that has been said and shown about it in the Arcana Coelestia; also from quotations gathered from that work in the explanation of The White Horse spoken of in the Apocalypse. It is according to that sense that what the Lord says in the passage quoted above respecting His coming in the clouds of heaven is to be understood. The "sun" there that is to be darkened signifies the Lord in respect to love; 1-5 the "moon" the Lord in respect to faith; 1-6 "stars" knowledges of good and truth, or of love and faith; 1-7 "the sign of the Son of man in heaven" the manifestation of Divine truth; "the tribes of the earth" that shall mourn, all things relating to truth and good or to faith and love; 1-8 "the coming of the Lord in the clouds of heaven with power and glory" His presence in the Word, and revelation, 1-9 "clouds" signifying the sense of the letter of the Word, 1-10 and "glory" the internal sense of the Word; 1-11 "the angels with a trumpet and great voice" signify heaven as a source of Divine truth. 1-12 All this makes clear that these words of the Lord mean that at the end of the church, when there is no longer any love, and consequently no faith, the Lord will open the internal meaning of the Word and reveal arcana of heaven. The arcana revealed in the following pages relate to heaven and hell, and also to the life of man after death. The man of the church at this date knows scarcely anything about heaven and hell or about his life after death, although all these matters are set forth and described in the Word; and yet many of those born within the church refuse to believe in them, saying in their hearts, "Who has come from that world and told us?" Lest, therefore, such a spirit of denial, which especially prevails with those who have much worldly wisdom, should also infect and corrupt the simple in heart and the simple in faith, it has been granted me to associate with angels and to talk with them as man with man, also to see what is in the heavens and what is in the hells, and this for thirteen years; so now from what I have seen and heard it has been granted me to describe these, in the hope that ignorance may thus be enlightened and unbelief dissipated. Such immediate revelation is granted at this day because this is what is meant by the Coming of the Lord. [REFERENCES TO THE AUTHOR'S ARCANA COELESTIA.]

THE GOD OF HEAVEN IS THE LORD First of all it must be known who the God of heaven is, since upon that all the other things depend. Throughout all heaven no other than the Lord alone is acknowledged as the God of heaven. There it is said, as He Himself taught, That He is one with the Father; that the Father is in Him, and He in the Father; that he who sees Him sees the Father; and that everything that is holy goes forth from Him (John 10:30, 35; 14:9-11; 16:13-15). I have often talked with angels on this subject, and they have invariably declared that in heaven they are unable to divide the Divine into three, because they know and perceive that the Divine is One and this One is in the Lord. They also said that those of the church who come from this world having an idea of three Divine beings cannot be admitted into heaven, since their thought wanders from one Divine being to another; and it is not allowable there to think three and say one. 2-1 Because in heaven everyone speaks from his thought, since speech there is the immediate product of the thought, or the thought speaking. Consequently, those in this world who have divided the Divine into three, and have adopted a different idea of each, and have not made that idea one and centered it in the Lord, cannot be received into heaven, because in heaven there is a sharing of all thoughts, and therefore if any one came thinking three and saying one, he would be at once found out and rejected. But let it be known that all those who have not separated what is true from what is good, or faith from love, accept in the other life, when they have been taught, the heavenly idea of the Lord, that He is the God of the universe. It is otherwise with those who have separated faith from life, that is, who have not lived according to the precepts of true faith.

Those within the church who have denied the Lord and have acknowledged the Father only, and have confirmed themselves in that belief, are not in heaven; and as they are unable to receive any influx from heaven, where the Lord alone is worshiped, they gradually lose the ability to think what is true about any subject whatever; and finally they become as if dumb, or they talk stupidly, and ramble about with their arms dangling and swinging as if weak in the joints. Again, those who, like the Socinians, have denied the Divinity of the Lord and have acknowledged His Humanity only, are likewise outside of heaven; they are brought forward a little towards the right and are let down into the deep, and are thus wholly separated from the rest that come from the Christian world. Finally, those who profess to believe in an invisible Divine, which they call the soul of the universe [Ens universi], from which all things originated, and who reject all belief in the Lord, find out that they believe in no God; since this invisible Divine is to them a property of nature in her first principles, which cannot be an object of faith and love, because it is not an object of thought. 3-1 Such have their lot among those called Naturalists. It is otherwise with those born outside the church, who are called the heathen; these will be treated of hereafter.

Infants, who form a third part of heaven, are all initiated into the acknowledgment and belief that the Lord is their Father, and afterwards that He is the Lord of all, thus the God of heaven and earth. That children grow up in heaven and are perfected by means of knowledges, even to angelic intelligence and wisdom, will be seen in the following pages.

Those who are of the church cannot doubt that the Lord is the God of heaven, for He Himself taught, That all things of the Father are His (Matt. 11:27; John 16:15; 17:2). And that He hath all power in heaven and on earth (Matt. 28:18). He says "in heaven and on earth," because He that rules heaven rules the earth also, for the one depends upon the other. 5-1 "Ruling heaven and earth" means to receive from the Lord every good pertaining to love and every truth pertaining to faith, thus all intelligence and wisdom, and in consequence all happiness, in a word, eternal life. This also the Lord taught when He said: He that believeth on the Son hath eternal life; but he that believeth not the Son shall not see life (John 3:36). Again: I am the resurrection and the life; he that believeth on Me, though he die yet shall he live; and whosoever liveth and believeth on Me shall never die (John 11:26, 26). And again: I am the way, the truth, and the life (John 14:6).

There were certain spirits who while living in the world had professed to believe in the Father; but of the Lord they had the same idea as of any other man, and therefore did not believe Him to be the God of heaven. For this reason they were permitted to wander about and inquire wherever they wished whether there were any other heaven than the heaven of the Lord. They searched for several days, but nowhere found any. These were such as place the happiness of heaven in glory and dominion; and as they were unable to get what they desired, and were told that heaven does not consist in such things, they became indignant, and wished for a heaven where they could lord it over others and be eminent in glory like that in the world.

II. IT IS THE DIVINE OF THE LORD THAT MAKES HEAVEN. The angels taken collectively are called heaven, for they constitute heaven; and yet that which makes heaven in general and in particular is the Divine that goes forth from the Lord and flows into the angels and is received by them. And as the Divine that goes forth from the Lord is the good of love and the truth of faith, the angels are angels and are heaven in the measure in which they receive good and truth from the Lord.

Everyone in the heavens knows and believes and even perceives that he wills and does nothing of good from himself, and that he thinks and believes nothing of truth from himself, but only from the Divine, thus from the Lord; also that good from himself is not good, and truth from himself is not truth, because these have in them no life from the Divine. Moreover, the angels of the inmost heaven clearly perceive and feel the influx, and the more of it they receive the more they seem to themselves to be in heaven, because the more are they in love and faith and in the light of intelligence and wisdom, and in heavenly joy therefrom; and since all these go forth from the Divine of the Lord, and in these the angels have their heaven, it is clear that it is the Divine of the Lord, and not the angels from anything properly their own that makes heaven. 8-1 This is why heaven is called in the Word the "dwelling-place" of the Lord and "His throne," and those who are there are said to be in the Lord. 8-2 But in what manner the Divine goes forth from the Lord and fills heaven will be told in what follows.

Angels from their wisdom go still further. They say that not only everything good and true is from the Lord, but everything of life as well. They confirm it by this, that nothing can spring from itself, but only from something prior to itself; therefore all things spring from a First, which they call the very Being [Esse] of the life of all things. And in like manner all things continue to exist, for continuous existence is a ceaseless springing forth, and whatever is not continually held by means of intermediates in connection with the First instantly disperses and is wholly dissipated. They say also that there is but One Fountain of life, and that man's life is a rivulet therefrom, which if it did not unceasingly continue from its fountain would immediately flow away. [2] Again, they say that from this One Fountain of life, which is the Lord, nothing goes forth except Divine good and Divine truth, and that each one is affected by these in accordance with his reception of them, those who receive them in faith and life find heaven in them while those who reject them or stifle them change them into hell; for they change good into evil and truth into falsity, thus life into death. Again, that everything of life is from the Lord they confirm by this: that all things in the universe have relation to good and truth,-the life of man's will, which is the life of his love, to good; and the life of his understanding, which is the life of his faith, to truth; and since everything good and true comes from above it follows that everything of life must come from above. [3] This being the belief of the angels they refuse all thanks for the good they do, and are displeased and withdraw if any one attributes good to them. They wonder how any one can believe that he is wise from himself or does anything good from himself. Doing good for one's own sake they do not call good, because it is done from self. But doing good for the sake of good they call good from the Divine; and this they say is the good that makes heaven, because this good is the Lord.9-1

Such spirits as have confirmed themselves during their life in the world in the belief that the good they do and the truth they believe is from themselves, or is appropriated to them as their own (which is the belief of all who place merit in good actions and claim righteousness to themselves) are not received into heaven. Angels avoid them. They look upon them as stupid and as thieves; as stupid because they continually have themselves in view and not the Divine; and as thieves because they steal from the Lord what is His. These are averse to the belief of heaven, that it is the Divine of the Lord in the angels that makes heaven.

The Lord teaches that those that are in heaven and in the church are in the Lord and the Lord is in them, when He says: Abide in Me and I in you. As the branch cannot bear fruit of itself except it abide in the vine, so neither can ye, except ye abide in Me. I am the Vine, ye are the branches. He that abideth in Me and I in him, the same beareth much fruit; for apart from Me ye can do nothing (John 15:4, 5).

From all this it can now be seen that the Lord dwells in the angels of heaven in what is His own, and thus that the Lord is the all in all things of heaven; and this for the reason that good from the Lord is the Lord in angels, for what is from the Lord is the Lord; consequently heaven to the angels is good from the Lord, and not anything of their own.

III. IN HEAVEN THE DIVINE OF THE LORD IS LOVE TO HIM AND CHARITY TOWARDS THE NEIGHBOR. The Divine that goes forth from the Lord is called in heaven Divine truth, for a reason that will presently appear. This Divine truth flows into heaven from the Lord from His Divine love. The Divine love and the Divine truth therefrom are related to each other as the fire of the sun and the light therefrom in the world, love resembling the fire of the sun and truth therefrom light from the sun. Moreover, by correspondence fire signifies love, and light truth going forth from love. 13-1 From this it is clear what the Divine truth that goes forth from the Lord's Divine love is-that in its essence it is Divine good joined to Divine truth, and being so conjoined it vivifies all things of heaven; just as in the world when the sun's heat is joined to light it makes all things of the earth fruitful, which takes place in spring and summer. It is otherwise when the heat is not joined with the light, that is, when the light is cold; then all things become torpid and lie dead. With the angels this Divine good, which is compared to heat, is the good of love; and Divine truth, which is compared to light, is that through which and out of which good of love comes.

The Divine in heaven which makes heaven is love, because love is spiritual conjunction. It conjoins angels to the Lord and conjoins them to one another, so conjoining them that in the Lord's sight they are all as one. Moreover, love is the very being [esse] of everyone's life; consequently from love both angels and men have life. Everyone who reflects can know that the inmost vitality of man is from love, since he grows warm from the presence of love and cold from its absence, and when deprived of it he dies. 14-1 But it is to be remembered that the quality of his love is what determines the quality of each one's life.

In heaven there are two distinct loves, love to the Lord and love towards the neighbor, in the inmost or third heaven love to the Lord, in the second or middle heaven love towards the neighbor. They both go forth from the Lord, and they both make heaven. How these two loves are distinct and how they are conjoined is seen in heaven in clear light, but in the world only obscurely. In heaven loving the Lord does not mean loving Him in respect to His person, but it means loving the good that is from Him; and to love good is to will and do good from love; and to love the neighbor does not mean loving a companion in respect to his person, but loving the truth that is from the Word; and to love truth is to will and do it. This makes clear that these two loves are distinct as good and truth are distinct, and that they are conjoined as good is conjoined with truth. 15-1 But this can scarcely be comprehended by men unless it is known what love is, what good is, and what the neighbor is. 15-2

I have repeatedly talked with angels about this matter. They were astonished, they said, that men of the church do not know that to love the Lord and to love the neighbor is to love what is good and true, and to do this from the will, when they ought to know that one evinces love by willing and doing what another wishes, and it is this that brings reciprocal love and conjunction, and not loving another without doing what he wishes, which in itself is not loving; also that men should know that the good that goes forth from the Lord is a likeness of Him, since He is in it; and that those who make good and truth to belong to their life by willing them and doing them become likenesses of the Lord and are conjoined to Him. Willing is loving to do. That this is so the Lord teaches in the Word, saying, He that hath My commandments and doeth them, he it is that loveth Me; and I will love him and will make My abode with him (John 14:21, 23). And again: If ye do My commandments ye shall abide in My love (John 15:10).

All experience in heaven attests that the Divine that goes forth from the Lord and that affects angels and makes heaven is love; for all who are in heaven are forms of love and charity, and appear in ineffable beauty, with love shining forth from their faces, and from their speech and from every particular of their life. 17-1 Moreover, there are spiritual spheres of life emanating from and surrounding every angel and every spirit, by which their quality in respect to the affections of their love is known, sometimes at a great distance. For with everyone these spheres flow forth from the life of his affection and consequent thought, or from the life of his love and consequent faith. The spheres that go forth from angels are so full of love as to affect the inmosts of life of those who are with them. They have repeatedly been perceived by me and have thus affected me. 17-2 That it is love from which angels have their life is further evident from the fact that in the other life everyone turns himself in accordance with his love-those who are in love to the Lord and in love towards the neighbor turning themselves always to the Lord, while those who are in love of self turn themselves always away from the Lord. This is so, however their bodies may turn, since with those in the other life spaces conform to the states of their interiors, likewise quarters, which are not constant as they are in this world, but are determined in accordance with the direction of their faces. And yet it is not the angels that turn themselves to the Lord; but the Lord turns to Himself those that love to do the things that are from Him. 17-3 But more on this subject hereafter, where the quarters in the other life are treated of.

The Divine of the Lord in heaven is love, for the reason that love is receptive of all things of heaven, such as peace, intelligence, wisdom and happiness. For love is receptive of each and all things that are in harmony with it; it longs for them, seeks them, and drinks them in as it were spontaneously, for it desires unceasingly to be enriched and perfected by them. 18-1 This, too, man well knows, for with him love searches as it were the stores of his memory and draws forth all things that are in accord with itself, collecting and arranging them in and under itself-in itself that they may be its own, and under itself that they may be its servants; but other things not in accord with it it discards and expels. That there is present in love every capacity for receiving truths in harmony with itself, and a longing to conjoin them to itself, has been made clear also by the fact that some who were simple-minded in the world were taken up into heaven, and yet when they were with the angels they came into angelic wisdom and heavenly blessedness, and for the reason that they had loved what is good and true for its own sake, and had implanted it in their life, and had thereby become capacities for receiving heaven with all that is ineffable there. But those who are in love of self and of the world have no capacity for receiving what is good and true; they loathe and reject it, and at its first touch and entrance they flee and associate themselves with those in hell who are in loves like their own. There were spirits who had doubts about there being such capacities in heavenly love, and who wished to know whether it were true; whereupon they were let into a state of heavenly love, whatever opposed being for the time removed, and were brought forward some distance, where there was an angelic heaven, and from it they talked with me, saying that they perceived a more interior happiness than they could possibly express in words, and they lamented greatly that they must return into their former state. Others also were taken up into heaven; and the higher or more interiorly they were exalted the more of intelligence and wisdom were they admitted into, such as enabled them to perceive what had before been incomprehensible to them. From this it is clear that the love that goes forth from the Lord is receptive of heaven and all things therein.

That love to the Lord and love towards the neighbor include in themselves all Divine truths is made evident by what the Lord Himself said of these two loves: Thou shalt love thy God with all thy heart and with all thy soul. This is the greatest and first commandment. And the second, like unto it, is, Thou shalt love thy neighbor as thyself. On these two commandments hang the law and the prophets (Matt. 22:37-40). "The law and the prophets" are the whole Word, thus all Divine truth.

IV. HEAVEN IS DIVIDED INTO TWO KINGDOMS. As there are infinite varieties in heaven, and no one society nor any one angel is exactly like any other, 20-1 there are in heaven general, specific, and particular divisions. The general division is into two kingdoms, the specific into three heavens, and the particular into innumerable societies. Each of these will be treated of in what follows. The general division is said to be into kingdoms, because heaven is called "the kingdom of God."

There are angels that receive more interiorly the Divine that goes forth from the Lord, and others that receive it less interiorly; the former are called celestial angels, and the latter spiritual angels. Because of this difference heaven is divided into two kingdoms, one called the Celestial Kingdom, the other the Spiritual Kingdom. 21-1

As the angels that constitute the celestial kingdom receive the Divine of the Lord more interiorly they are called interior and also higher angels; and for the same reason the heavens that they constitute are called interior and higher heavens. 22-1 They are called higher and lower, because these terms designate what is interior and what is exterior. 22-2

The love in which those are, who are in the celestial kingdom is called celestial love, and the love in which those are who are in the spiritual kingdom is called spiritual love. Celestial love is love to the Lord, and spiritual love is love towards the neighbor. And as all good pertains to love (for good to any one is what he loves) the good also of the other kingdom is called celestial, and the good of the other spiritual. Evidently, then, the two kingdoms are distinguished from each other in the same way as good of love to the Lord is distinguished from good of love towards the neighbor. 23-1 And as the good of love to the Lord is an interior good, and that love is interior love, so the celestial angels are interior angels, and are called higher angels.

The celestial kingdom is called also the Lord's priestly kingdom, and in the Word "His dwelling-place;" while the spiritual kingdom is called His royal kingdom, and in the Word "His throne." And from the celestial Divine the Lord in the world was called "Jesus," while from the spiritual Divine He was called "Christ."

The angels in the Lord's celestial kingdom, from their more interior reception of the Divine of the Lord, far excel in wisdom and glory the angels that are in His spiritual kingdom; for they are in love to the Lord, and consequently are nearer and more closely conjoined to Him. 25-1 These angels are such because they have received and continue to receive Divine truths at once in their life, and not first in memory and thought, as the spiritual angels do. Consequently they have Divine truths written in their hearts, and they perceive them, and as it were see them, in themselves; nor do they ever reason about them whether they are true or not. 25-2 They are such as are described in Jeremiah: I will put my law in their mind, and will write it in their heart. They shall teach no more everyone his friend and everyone his brother, saying, Know ye Jehovah. They shall know Me, from the least of them even to the greatest of them (31:33, 34). And they are called in Isaiah: Taught of Jehovah (54:13). That the "taught of Jehovah" are those who are taught by the Lord He Himself teaches in John (6:45, 46).

It has been said that these angels have wisdom and glory above others for the reason that they have received and continue to receive Divine truths at once in their life. For as soon as they hear Divine truths, they will and do them, instead of storing them up in the memory and afterwards considering whether they are true. They know at once by influx from the Lord whether the truth they hear is true; for the Lord flows directly into man's willing, but mediately through his willing into his thinking. Or what is the same, the Lord flows directly into good, but mediately through good into truth. 26-1 That is called good which belongs to the will and action therefrom, while that is called truth that belongs to the memory and to the thought therefrom. Moreover, every truth is turned into good and implanted in love as soon as it enters into the will; but so long as truth remains in the memory and in the thought therefrom it does not become good, nor does it live, nor is it appropriated to man, since man is a man from his will and understanding therefrom, and not from his understanding separated from his will. 26-2

Because of this difference between the angels of the celestial kingdom and the angels of the spiritual kingdom they are not together, and have no interaction with each other. They are able to communicate only through intermediate angelic societies, which are called celestial-spiritual. Through these the celestial kingdom flows into the spiritual; 27-1 and from this it comes to pass that although heaven is divided into two kingdoms it nevertheless makes one. The Lord always provides such intermediate angels through whom there is communication and conjunction.

As the angels of these two kingdoms will be fully treated of in what follows, particulars are here omitted.

THERE ARE THREE HEAVENS. There are three heavens, entirely distinct from each other, an inmost or third, a middle or second, and an outmost or first. These have a like order and relation to each other as the highest part of man, or his head, the middle part, or body, and the lowest, or feet; or as the upper, the middle, and the lower stories of a house. In the same order is the Divine that goes forth and descends from the Lord; consequently heaven, from the necessity of order, is threefold.

The interiors of man, which belong to his mind and disposition, are also in like order. He has an inmost, a middle, and an outmost part; for when man was created all things of Divine order were brought together in him, so that he became Divine order in form, and consequently a heaven in miniature. 30-1 For this reason also man, as regards his interiors, has communication with the heavens and comes after death among the angels, either among those of the inmost, or of the middle, or of the outmost heaven, in accordance with his reception of Divine good and truth from the Lord during his life in the world.

The Divine that flows in from the Lord and is received in the third or inmost heaven is called celestial, and in consequence the angels there are called celestial angels; the Divine that flows in from the Lord and is received in the second or middle heaven is called spiritual, and in consequence the angels there are called spiritual angels; while the Divine that flows in from the Lord and is received in the outmost or first heaven is called natural; but as the natural of that heaven is not like the natural of the world, but has the spiritual and the celestial within it, that heaven is called the spiritual-natural and the celestial-natural, and in consequence the angels there are called spiritual-natural and celestial-natural. 31-1 Those who receive influx from the middle or second heaven, which is the spiritual heaven, are called spiritual-natural; and those who receive influx from the third or inmost heaven, which is the celestial heaven, are called celestial-natural. The spiritual-natural angels and the celestial-natural angels are distinct from each other; nevertheless they constitute one heaven, because they are in one degree.

In each heaven there is an internal and an external; those in the internal are called there internal angels, while those in the external are called external angels. The internal and the external in the heavens, or in each heaven, hold the same relation as the voluntary and intellectual in man-the internal corresponding to the voluntary, and the external to the intellectual. Everything voluntary has its intellectual; one cannot exist without the other. The voluntary may be compared to a flame and the intellectual to the light therefrom.

Let it be clearly understood that with the angels it is the interiors that cause them to be in one heaven or another; for as their interiors are more open to the Lord they are in a more interior heaven. There are three degrees of interiors in each angel and spirit, and also in man. Those in whom the third degree is opened are in the inmost heaven. Those in whom the second degree is opened, or only the first, are in the middle or in the outmost heaven. The interiors are opened by reception of Divine good and Divine truth. Those who are affected by Divine truths and admit them at once into the life, thus into the will and into action therefrom, are in the inmost or third heaven, and have their place there in accordance with their reception of good from affection for truth. Those who do not admit truths at once into the will but into the memory, and thence into the understanding, and from the understanding will and do them, are in the middle or second heaven. But those who live morally and who believe in a Divine, and who care very little about being taught, are in the outmost or first heaven. 33-1 From this it is clear that the states of the interiors are what make heaven, and that heaven is within everyone, and not outside of him; as the Lord teaches when He says: The kingdom of God cometh not with observation, neither shall they say, Lo here, or Lo there; for behold the kingdom of God ye have within you (Luke 17:20, 21).

Furthermore, all perfection increases towards interiors and decreases towards exteriors, since interiors are nearer to the Divine, and are in themselves pure, while exteriors are more remote from the Divine and are in themselves grosser. 34-1 Intelligence, wisdom, love, everything good and the resulting happiness, are what constitute angelic perfection; but not happiness apart from these, for such happiness is external and not internal. Because in the angels of the inmost heaven the interiors have been opened in the third degree their perfection immeasurably surpasses the perfection of angels in the middle heaven, whose interiors have been opened in the second degree. So the perfection of these angels exceeds in like measure the perfection of angels of the outmost heaven.

Because of this distinction an angel of one heaven cannot go among the angels of another heaven, that is, no one can ascend from a lower heaven and no one can descend from a higher heaven. One ascending from a lower heaven is seized with a distress even to anguish, and is unable to see those who are there, still less to talk with them; while one descending from a higher heaven is deprived of his wisdom, stammers in his speech, and is in despair. There were some from the outmost heaven who had not yet been taught that the interiors of angels are what constitute heaven, and who believed that they might come into a higher heavenly happiness by simply gaining access to a heaven where higher angels are. These were permitted to enter among such angels. But when they were there they could see no one, however much they searched, although there was a great multitude present; for the interiors of the newcomers not having been opened in the same degree as the interiors of the angels there, their sight was not so opened. Presently they were seized with such anguish of heart that they scarcely knew whether they were alive or not. Therefore they hastily betook themselves to the heaven from which they came, glad to get back among their like, and pledging themselves that they would no longer covet higher things than were in agreement with their life. Again, I have seen some let down from a higher heaven; and these were deprived of their wisdom until they no longer knew what their own heaven was. It is otherwise when, as is often done, angels are raised up by the Lord out of a lower heaven into a higher that they may behold its glory; for then they are prepared beforehand, and are encompassed by intermediate angels, through whom they have communication with those they come among. From all this it is plain that the three heavens are entirely distinct from each other.

Those, however, who are in the same heaven can affiliate with any who are there; but the delights of such affiliation are measured by the kinships of good they have come into; of which more will be said in the following chapters.

But although the heavens are so distinct that there can be no companionship between the angels of one heaven and the angels of another, still the Lord joins all the heavens together by both direct and mediate influx-direct from Himself into all the heavens, and mediate from one heaven into another. 37-1 He thus makes the three heavens to be one, and all to be in such connection from the First to the Last that nothing unconnected is possible. Whatever is not connected through intermediates with the First can have no permanent existence, but is dissipated and becomes nothing. 37-2.

Only he who knows how degrees are related to Divine order can comprehend how the heavens are distinct, or even what is meant by the internal and the external man. Most men in the world have no other idea of what is interior and what is exterior, or of what is higher and what is lower, than as something continuous, or coherent by continuity, from purer to grosser. But the relation of what is interior to what is exterior is discrete, not continuous. Degrees are of two kinds, those that are continuous and those that are not. Continuous degrees are related like the degrees of the waning of a light from its bright blaze to darkness, or like the degrees of the decrease of vision from objects in the light to those in the shade, or like degrees of purity in the atmosphere from bottom to top. These degrees are determined by distance. [2] On the other hand, degrees that are not continuous, but discrete, are distinguished like prior and posterior, like cause and effect, and like what produces and what is produced. Whoever looks into the matter will see that in each thing and all things in the whole world, whatever they are, there are such degrees of producing and compounding, that is, from one a second, and from that a third, and so on. [3] Until one has acquired for himself a perception of these degrees he cannot possibly understand the differences between the heavens, nor between the interior and exterior faculties of man, nor the differences between the spiritual world and the natural world, nor between the spirit of man and his body. So neither can he understand the nature and source of correspondences and representations, or the nature of influx. Sensual men do not apprehend these differences, for they make increase and decrease, even according to these degrees, to be continuous, and are therefore unable to conceive of what is spiritual otherwise than as a purer natural. And in consequence they remain outside of and a great way off from intelligence. 38-1

Finally, a certain arcanum respecting the angels of the three heavens, which has not hitherto come into any one's mind, because degrees have not been understood, may be related. In every angel and also in every man there is an inmost or highest degree, or an inmost or highest something, into which the Divine of the Lord primarily or proximately flows, and from which it disposes the other interiors in him that follow in accordance with the degrees of order. This inmost or highest degree may be called the entrance of the Lord to the angel or man, and His veriest dwelling-place in them. It is by virtue of this inmost or highest that a man is a man, and is distinguished from irrational animals, for these do not have it. From this it is that man, unlike the animals, is capable, in respect to all his interiors which pertain to his mind and disposition, of being raised up by the Lord to Himself, of believing in the Lord, of being moved by love to the Lord, and thereby beholding Him, and of receiving intelligence and wisdom, and speaking from reason. Also, it is by virtue of this that he lives to eternity. But what is arranged and provided by the Lord in this inmost does not distinctly flow into the perception of any angel, because it is above his thought and transcends his wisdom.

These now are the general truths respecting the three heavens; but in what follows each heaven will be particularly treated of.

VI. THE HEAVENS CONSIST OF INNUMERABLE SOCIETIES. The angels of each heaven are not together in one place, but are divided into larger and smaller societies in accordance with the differences of good of love and of faith in which they are, those who are in like good forming a single society. Goods in the heavens are in infinite variety, and each angel is as it were his own good. 41-1

Moreover, the angelic societies in the heavens are at a distance from each other as their goods differ in general and in particular. For in the spiritual world the only ground of distance is difference in the state of interiors, thus in the heavens difference in the states of love, those who differ much being far apart, and those who differ but little being but little apart, and likeness causing them to be together. 42-1

All who are in the same society are arranged in like manner in respect to each other; those who are more perfect, that is, who excel in good, thus in love, wisdom, and intelligence, being in the middle; those who are less pre-eminent being round about at a distance in accordance with the decrease of their perfection. The arrangement is like light diminishing from the middle to the circumference, those who are in the middle being in the greatest light, and those towards the circumference in less and less.

Like are drawn spontaneously as it were to their like; for with their like they are as if with their own and at home, but with others they are as if with strangers and abroad; also when with their like they are in their freedom, and consequently in every delight of life.

All this makes clear that all in the heavens are affiliated by good, and are distinguished according to the quality of the good. Nevertheless it is not the angels who thus affiliate themselves, but the Lord, from whom the good is. The Lord leads them, conjoins and separates them, and preserves them in freedom proportionate to their good. Thus He holds everyone in the life of his love and faith, of his intelligence and wisdom, and the resulting happiness. 45-1

Again, all who are in like good, even though they have never seen each other before, know each other, just as men in the world do their kinsmen, near relations, and friends; and for the reason that in the other life there are none but spiritual kinships, relationships, and friendships, thus such as spring from love and faith. 46-1 This it has sometimes been granted me to see, when I have been in the spirit, and thus withdrawn from the body, and in the society of angels. Some of those I then saw seemed as if I had known them from childhood, but others as if not known at all. Those whom I seemed to have known from childhood were such as were in a state similar to that of my spirit; but those who seemed unknown were in a dissimilar state.

All who form the same angelic society resemble each other in countenance in a general way, but not in particulars. How these general resemblances are related to differences in particulars can in some measure be seen from like things in the world. It is well known that with every race there is a certain general resemblance of face and eyes, by which it is known and distinguished from all other races. This is still more true of different families. In the heavens this is much more fully the case, because there all the interior affections appear in and shine forth from the face, for there the face is the external and representative form of those affections. No one there can have any other face than that of his own affection. It was also shown how this general likeness is varied in particulars with individuals in the same society. A face like an angel's appeared to me, and this was varied in accordance with such affections for good and truth as are in those who belong to a single society. These changes went on for a long time, and I noticed that the same face in general continued as a ground work, all besides being what was derived and produced from that. Thus by means of this face the affections of the whole society were exhibited, whereby the faces of those in it are varied. For, as has been said above, the faces of angels are the forms of their interiors, thus of the affections that belong to their love and faith.

From this it also comes to pass that an angel who excels in wisdom instantly sees the quality of another from his face. In heaven no one can conceal his interiors by his expression, or feign, or really deceive and mislead by craft or hypocrisy. There are hypocrites who are experts in disguising their interiors and fashioning their exteriors into the form of that good in which those are who belong to a society, and who thus make themselves appear angels of light; and these sometimes insinuate themselves into a society; but they cannot stay there long, for they begin to suffer inward pain and torture, to grow livid in the face, and to become as it were lifeless. These changes arise from the contrariety of the life that flows in and affects them. Therefore they quickly cast themselves down into hell where their like are, and no longer want to ascend. These are such as are meant by the man found among the invited guests at the feast not clothed with a wedding garment, who was cast out into outer darkness Matt. 22:11, seq.).

All the societies of heaven have communication with one another, though not by open interaction; for few go out of their own society into another, since going out of their own society is like going away from themselves or from their own life, and passing into another life which is less congenial. But all the societies communicate by an extension of the sphere that goes forth from the life of each. This sphere of the life is the sphere of the affections of love and faith. This sphere extends itself far and wide into the surrounding societies, and farther and wider in proportion as the affections are the more interior and perfect. 49-1 In the measure of that extension do the angels have intelligence and wisdom. Those that are in the inmost heaven and in the middle of it have extension into the entire heavens; thus there is a sharing of all in heaven with each one, and of each one with all. 49-2 But this extension will be considered more fully hereafter, where the form of heaven in accord with which the angelic societies are arranged, and also the wisdom and intelligence of angels, will be treated of, for in accordance with that form all extension of affections and thoughts proceeds.

It has been said above that in the heavens there are larger and smaller societies. The larger consist of myriads of angels, the smaller of some thousands, and the least of some hundreds. There are also some that dwell apart, house by house as it were, and family by family. Although these live in this scattered way, they are arranged in order like those who live in societies, the wiser in the middle and the more simple in the borders. Such are more closely under the Divine auspices of the Lord, and are the best of the angels.

Footnotes

1-1 The consummation of the age is the final period of the church (n. 4535, 10622).

1-2 The Lord's predictions in Matthew (24 and 25), respecting the consummation of the age and His coming, and the consequent successive vastation of the church and the final judgment, are explained in the prefaces to chapters 26-40 of Genesis (n. 3353-3356, 3486-3489, 3650-3655, 3751-3757, 3897-3901, 4056-4060, 4229-4231, 4332-4335, 4422-4424, 4635-4638, 4661-4664, 4807-4810, 4954-4959, 5063-5071).

1-3 Both in the wholes and in the particulars of the Word there is an internal or spiritual sense (n. 1143, 1984, 2135, 2333, 2395, 2495, 4442, 9048, 9063, 9086).

1-4 The Word is written solely by correspondences, and for this reason each thing and all things in it have a spiritual meaning (n. 1404, 1408, 1409, 1540, 1619, 1659, 1709, 1783, 2900, 9086).

1-5 In the Word the sun" signifies the Lord in respect to love, and in consequence love to the Lord (n. 1529, 1837, 2441, 2495, 4060, 4696, 7083, 10809).

1-6 In the Word the "moon" signifies the Lord in respect to faith, and in consequence faith in the Lord (n. 1529, 1530, 2495, 4060, 4696, 7083).

1-7 In the Word "stars" signify knowledges of good and truth (n. 2495, 2849, 4697).

1-8 "Tribes" signify all truths and goods in the complex, thus all things of faith and love (n. 3858, 3926, 4060, 6335).

1-9 The coming of the Lord signifies His presence in the Word, and revelation (n 3900, 4060).

1-10 In the Word clouds signify the Word in the letter or the sense of its letter (n. 4060, 4391, 5922, 6343, 6752, 8106, 8781, 9430, 10551, 10574).

1-11 In the Word "glory" signifies Divine truth as it is in heaven and as it is in the internal sense of the Word (n. 4809, 5922, 8267, 8427, 9429, 10574).

1-12 A "trumpet" or "horn" signifies Divine truth in heaven, and revealed from heaven (n. 8158, 8823, 8915); and "voice" has a like signification (n. 6771, 9926).

2-1 Christians were examined in the other life in regard to their idea of the one God and it was found that they held the idea of three Gods (n. 2329, 5256, 10736, 10738, 10821). A Divine trinity in the Lord is acknowledged in heaven (n. 14, 15, 1729, 2005, 5256, 9303).

3-1 A Divine that cannot be perceived by any idea cannot be received by faith (n. 4733, 5110, 5663, 6982, 6996, 7004, 7211, 9356, 9359, 9972, 10067,

10267).

5-1 The entire heaven is the Lord's (n. 2751, 7086). He has all power in the heavens and on the earths (n. 1607, 10089, 10827). As the Lord rules heaven He rules also all things that depend thereon, thus all things in the world (n. 2026, 2027, 4523, 4524). The Lord alone has power to remove the hells, to withhold from evil and hold in good, and thus to save (n. 10019).

8-1 The angels of heaven acknowledge all good to be from the Lord, and nothing from themselves, and the Lord dwells in them in His own and not in their own (n. 9338, 10125, 10151, 10157). Therefore in the Word by "angels" something of the Lord is meant (n. 1925, 2821, 3039, 4085, 8192, 10528). Furthermore, angels are called "gods" from the reception of the Divine from the Lord (n. 4295, 4402, 7268, 7873, 8192, 8301). Again, all good that is good, and all truth that is truth, consequently all peace, love, charity, and faith, are from the Lord (n. 1614, 2016, 2751, 2882, 2883, 2891, 2892, 2904). Also all wisdom and intelligence (n. 109, 112, 121, 124).

8-2 Those who are in heaven are said to be in the Lord (n. 3637, 3638).

9-1 Good from the Lord has the Lord inwardly in it, but good from one's own has not (n. 1802, 3951, 8480).

13-1 In the Word "fire" signifies heavenly love and infernal love (n. 934, 4906, 5215). "Holy and heavenly fire" signifies Divine love, and every affection that belongs to that love (n. 934, 6314, 6832). "Light" from fire signifies truth going forth from good of love; and light in heaven signifies Divine truth (n. 3195, 3485, 3636, 3643, 3993, 4302, 4413, 4415, 9548, 9684).

14-1 Love is the fire of life, and life itself is actually therefrom (n. 4906, 5071, 6032, 6314).

15-1 To love the Lord and the neighbor is to live according to the Lord's commandments (n. 10143, 10153, 10310, 10578, 10648).

15-2 To love the neighbor is not to love the person, but to love that in him from which he is what he is, that is, his truth and good (n. 5028. 10336). Those who love the person, and not that in him from which he is what he is, love evil and good alike (n. 3820). Charity is willing truths and being affected by truths for the sake of truths (n. 3876, 3877). Charity towards the neighbor is doing what is good, just, and right, in every work and in every function (n. 8120-8122).

17-1 Angels are forms of love and charity (n. 3804, 4735, 4797, 4985, 5199, 5530, 9879, 10177).

17-2 A spiritual sphere, which is a sphere of the life, overflows and pours forth from every man, spirit, and angel, and encompasses them (n. 4464, 5179, 7454, 8630). It flows from the life of their affection and consequent thought (n. 2489, 4464, 6206).

17-3 Spirits and angels turn themselves constantly to their loves, and those in the heavens turn themselves constantly to the Lord (n. 10130, 10189, 10420, 10702). Quarters in the other life are to each one in accordance with the direction of his face, and are thereby determined, otherwise than in the world (n. 10130, 10189, 10420, 10702).

18-1 Innumerable things are contained in love, and love gathers to itself all things that are in harmony with it (n. 2500, 2572, 3078, 3189, 6323, 7490, 7750).

20-1 There is infinite variety, and nowhere any thing the same as another (n. 7236, 9002). Also in the heavens there is infinite variety (n. 684, 690, 3744,

5598, 7236). Varieties in heaven are varieties of good (n. 3744, 4005, 7236, 7833, 7836, 9002). All societies in the heavens, and all angels in a society, are thereby distinguished from each other (n. 690, 3241, 3519, 3804, 3986, 4067, 4149, 4263, 7236, 7833, 7836). Nevertheless they are all made one by love from the Lord (n. 457, 3986).

21-1 Heaven as a whole is divided into two kingdoms, a celestial kingdom and a spiritual kingdom (n. 3887, 4138). The angels of the celestial kingdom receive the Divine of the lord in their voluntary part, thus more interiorly than the spiritual angels, who receive it in their intellectual part (n. 5113, 6367, 8521, 9936, 9995. 10124).

22-1 The heavens that constitute the celestial kingdom are called higher while those that constitute the spiritual kingdom are called lower (n. 10068).

22-2 Interior things are portrayed by higher things, and higher things signify interior things (n. 2148, 3084, 4599, 5146, 8325).

23-1 The good of the celestial kingdom is good of love to the Lord, and the good of the spiritual kingdom is good of charity towards the neighbor (n. 3691, 6435, 9468, 9680, 9683, 9780).

25-1 The celestial angels immeasurably surpass in wisdom the spiritual angels (n. 2718, 9995). The nature of the distinction between celestial angels and spiritual angels (n. 2088, 2669, 2708, 2715, 3235, 3240, 4788, 7068, 8521, 9277, 10295).

25-2 The celestial angels do not reason about truths of faith, because they perceive them in themselves; but the spiritual angels reason about them whether they are true or not (n. 202, 337, 597, 607, 784, 1121, 1384, 1898, 1919, 3246, 4448, 7680, 7877, 8780, 9277, 10786).

26-1 The Lord's influx is into good and through good into truth, and not the reverse; thus into the will and through that into the understanding, and not the reverse (n. 5482, 5649, 6027, 8685, 8701, 10153).

26-2 The will of man is the very being [esse] of his life, and the receptacle of the good of love, while his understanding is the outgo [existere] of his life therefrom, and the receptacle of the truth and good of faith (n. 3619, 5002, 9282). Thus the will's life is the chief life of man, and the life of the understanding goes forth therefrom (n. 585, 590, 3619, 7342, 8885, 9282, 10076, 10109, 10110). Whatever is received by the will comes to be the life, and is appropriated to man (n. 3161, 9386, 9393). Man is a man from his will and his understanding therefrom (n. 8911, 9069, 9071, 10076, 10109, 10110). Moreover, everyone who wills and understands rightly is loved and valued by others, while he that understands rightly and does not will rightly is rejected and despised (n. 8911, 10076). Also, after death man remains such as his will and his understanding therefrom have been, while the things that pertain to the understanding and not also to the will then vanish, because they are not in the man (n. 9069, 9071, 9282, 9386, 10153).

27-1 Between the two kingdoms there is communication and conjunction by mean's of angelic societies which are called celestial-spiritual (n. 4047, 6435, 8796, 8802). The influx of the Lord through the celestial kingdom into the spiritual (n. 3969, 6366).

30-1 All things of Divine order are brought together in man, and by creation man is Divine order in form (n. 3628, 4219, 4220, 4223, 4523, 4524, 5114, 5168,

6013, 6057, 6605, 6626, 9706, 10156, 10472). In man the internal man was formed after the image of heaven, and the external after the image of the world, and this is why man was called by the ancients a microcosm (n. 3628, 4523, 5115, 6013, 6057, 9279, 9706, 10156, 10472). Thus man is respect to his interiors is by creation a heaven in least form after the image of the greatest; and such also man becomes when he has been created anew or regenerated by the Lord (n. 911, 1900, 1928, 3624-3631, 3634, 3884, 4041, 4279, 4523, 4524, 4625, 6013, 6057, 9279, 9632).

31-1 There are three heavens, inmost, middle, and outmost, or third, second, and first (n. 684 9594, 10270). Goods therein also follow in triple order (n. 4938, 4939, 9992, 10005, 10017). The good of the inmost or third heaven is called celestial, the good of the middle or second is called spiritual, and the good of the outmost or first, spiritual-natural (n. 4279, 4286, 4938, 4939, 9992, 10005, 10017, 10068).

33-1 There are as many degrees of life in man as there are heavens, and these are opened after death in accordance with his life (n. 3747, 9594). Heaven is in man (n. 3884). Therefore he that has received heaven into himself in the world, comes into heaven after death in. 10717).

34-1 Interiors are more perfect because nearer to the Divine (n. 3405, 5146, 5147). In the internal there are thousands and thousands of things that appear in the external as one general thing (n. 5707). As far as man is raised from externals towards interiors, so far he comes into light and thus into intelligence and the elevation is like rising out of a cloud into clearness (n. 4598, 6183, 6313).

37-1 Influx from the Lord is direct from Himself and also mediate through on heaven into another, and in like manner into man's interiors (n. 6063, 6307, 6472, 9682, 9683). Direct influx of the Divine from the Lord (n. 6058, 6474-6478, 8717, 8728). Mediate influx through the spiritual world into the natural world (n. 4067, 6982, 6985, 6996).

37-2 All things spring from things prior to themselves, thus from a First, and in like inner subsist, because subsistence is unceasing springing forth; therefore nothing unconnected is possible (n. 3626-3628, 3648, 4523, 4524, 6040, 6056).

38-1 Things interior and things exterior are not continuous but distinct and discrete according to degrees, and each degree has its bounds (n. 3691, 5114, 5145, 8603, 10099). One thing is formed from another, and the things so formed are not continuously purer and grosser (n. 6326, 6465). Until the difference between what is interior and what is exterior according to such degrees is perceived, neither the internal and external man nor the interior and exterior heavens can be clearly understood (n. 5146, 6465, 10099, 10181).

41-1 There is infinite variety, and never any thing the same with any other (n. 7236, 9002). So in the heavens there is infinite variety (n. 684, 690, 3744, 5598, 7236). Varieties in the heavens, which are infinite, are varieties of good (n. 3744, 4005, 7236, 7833, 7836, 9002). These varieties exist through truths, which are manifold from which is each one's good (n. 3470, 3804, 4149, 6917, 7236). It is because of this that all the societies in the heavens, and all angels in a society, are distinct from each other (n. 690, 3241, 3519, 3804, 3986, 4067, 4149, 4263, 7236, 7833, 836). Nevertheless they all make one through love from the Lord (n. 457, 3986).

42-1 All the societies of heaven have a constant position in accordance with the differences of their state of life, thus in accordance with the differences of love and faith (n. 1274, 3638, 3639). Wonderful things in the other life, that is, in the spiritual world, respecting distance, situation, place space and time (n. 1273-1277).

45-1 All freedom pertains to love and affection, since what a man loves, that he does freely (n. 2870, 3158, 8987, 8990, 9555, 9591). Because freedom pertains to love everyone's life and delight is therefrom (n. 2873). Nothing appears as one's own, except what is from his freedom (n. 2880). The veriest freedom is to be led by the Lord, because one is thus led by the love of good and truth (n. 892, 905, 2872, 2886, 2890-2892, 9096, 9586-9591).

46-1 All nearness, relationship, connections, and as it were ties of blood, in heaven are from good and in accordance with its agreements and differences (n. 685, 917, 1394, 2739, 3612, 3815, 4121).

49-1 A spiritual sphere, which is the sphere of life flows out from every man, spirit, and angel, and encompasses them (n. 4464, 5179, 7454, 5630). It flows forth from the life of their affection and thought (n. 2459, 4464. 6206). These spheres extend themselves far into angelic societies in accordance with the quality and quantity of their good (n. 6598-6612, 8063, 5794, 5797).

49-2 In the heavens a sharing of all goods is possible because heavenly love shares with another everything that is its own (n. 549, 550, 1390, 1391, 1399, 10130, 10723).

Section 2

EACH SOCIETY IS A HEAVEN IN A SMALLER FORM, AND EACH ANGEL IN THE SMALLEST FORM. Each society is a heaven in a smaller form, and each angel in the smallest form, because it is the good of love and of faith that makes heaven, and this good is in each society of heaven and in each angel of a society. It does not matter that this good everywhere differs and varies, it is still the good of heaven; and there is no difference except that heaven has one quality here and another there. So when any one is raised up into any society of heaven he is said to come into heaven; and those who are there are said to be in heaven, and each one in his own. This is known to all in the other life; consequently those standing outside of or beneath heaven, when they see at a distance companies of angels, say that heaven is in this or that place. It is comparatively like civil and military officers and attendants in a royal palace or castle, who, although dwelling apart in their own quarters or chambers above and below, are yet in the same palace or castle, each in his own position in the royal service. This makes evident the meaning of the Lord's words, that In His Father's house are many abiding places (John 14:2); also what is meant by The dwelling-places of heaven, and the heavens of heavens, in the prophets.

That each society is a heaven in a smaller form can be seen from this also, that each society there has a heavenly form like that of heaven as a whole. In the whole heavens those who are superior to the rest are in the middle, with the less excellent round about in a decreasing order even to the borders (as stated in a preceding chapter, n. 43). It can be seen also from this, that the Lord directs all in the whole heaven as if they were a single angel; and the same is true of all in each society; and as a consequence an entire angelic society sometimes appears in angelic form like a single angel, as I have been permitted by the Lord to see. Moreover, when the Lord appears in the midst of the angels He does not appear as one surrounded by many, but the appearance is as a one, in an angelic form. This is why the Lord is called "an angel" in the Word, and why an entire society is so called. "Michael," "Gabriel," and "Raphael" are no other than angelic societies so named from their function. 52-1

As an entire society is a heaven in a smaller form, so an angel is a heaven in the smallest form. For heaven is not outside of the angel, but is within him, since the interior things which belong to his mind are arranged into the form of heaven, thus for the reception of all things of heaven that are outside of him. These also he receives according to the quality of the good that is in him from the Lord. It is from this that an angel is a heaven.

It can in no sense be said that heaven is outside of any one; it is within him. For it is in accordance with the heaven that is within him that each angel receives the heaven that is outside of him. This makes clear how greatly misled is he who believes that to come into heaven is simply to be taken up among angels, without regard to what one's interior life may be, thus that heaven is granted to each one by mercy apart from means; 54-1 when, in fact, unless heaven is within one, nothing of the heaven that is outside can flow in and be received There are many spirits who have this idea. Because of this belief they have been taken up into heaven; but when they came there, because their interior life was contrary to the angelic life, their intellectual faculties began to be blinded until they became like fools; and they began to be tortured in their voluntary faculties until they became like madmen. In a word, if those that have lived wickedly come into heaven they gasp for breath and writhe about, like fishes out of water in the air, or like animals in ether in an airpump when the air has been exhausted. From this it can be seen that heaven is not outside of a man, but within him. 54-2

As everyone receives the heaven that is outside of him in accordance with the quality of the heaven that is within him, so in like manner does everyone receive the Lord, since it is the Divine of the Lord that makes heaven. And for this reason when the Lord becomes manifestly present in any society His appearance there is in accord with the quality of the good in which the society is, thus not the same in one society as in another. This diversity is not in the Lord; it is in the angels who behold Him from their own good, and thus in accordance with their good. And they are affected by His appearance in accordance with the quality of their love, those who love Him inmostly being inmostly affected, and those who love Him less being less affected; while the evil who are outside of heaven are tortured by His presence. When the Lord is seen in any society He is seen as an angel, but is distinguished from others by the Divine that shines through.

Again, heaven is where the Lord is acknowledged, believed in, and loved. Variety in worship of the Lord from the variety of good in different societies is not harmful, but beneficial, for the perfection of heaven is therefrom. This can scarcely be made clear to the comprehension without employing terms that are in common use in the learned world, and showing by means of these how unity, that it may be perfect, must be formed from variety. Every whole exists from various parts, since a whole without constituents is not anything; it has no form, and therefore no quality. But when a whole exists from various parts, and the various parts are in a perfect form, in which each attaches itself like a congenial friend to another in series, then the quality is perfect. So heaven is a whole from various parts arranged in a most perfect form, for the heavenly form is the most perfect of all forms. That this is the ground of all perfection is evident from the nature of all beauty, agreeableness and delight, by which the senses and the mind are affected; for these qualities spring and flow from no other source than the concert and harmony of many concordant and congenial parts, either coexisting in order or following in order, and never from a whole without many parts. From this is the saying that variety gives delight; and the nature of variety, as is known, is what determines the delight. From all this it can be seen as in a mirror how perfection comes from variety even in heaven. For from the things that exist in the natural world the things of the spiritual world can be seen as in a mirror. 56-1

What has been said of heaven may be said also of the church, for the church is the Lord's heaven on earth. There are also many churches, each one of which is called a church, and so far as the good of love and faith reigns therein is a church. Here, too, the Lord out of various parts forms a unity, that is, one church out of many churches. 57-1 And the like may be said of the man of the church in particular that is said of the church in general, namely, that the church is within man and not outside of him; and that every man is a church in whom the Lord is present in the good of love and of faith. 57-2 Again, the same may be said of a man that has the church in him as of an angel that has heaven in him, namely, that he is a church in the smallest form, as an angel is a heaven in the smallest form; and furthermore that a man that has the church in him, equally with an angel, is a heaven. For man was created that he might come into heaven and become an angel; consequently he that has good from the Lord is a man-angel. 57-3 What man has in common with an angel and what he has in contrast with angels may be mentioned. It is granted to man, equally with the angel, to have his interiors conformed to the image of heaven, and to become, so far as he is in the good of love and faith, an image of heaven. But it is granted to man and not to angels to have his exteriors conform to the image of the world; and so far as he is in good to have the world in him subordinated to heaven and made to serve heaven. 57-4 And then the Lord is present in him both in the world and in heaven just as if he were in his heaven. For the Lord is in His Divine order in both worlds, since God is order. 57-5

Finally it should be said that he who has heaven in himself has it not only in the largest or most general things pertaining to him but also in every least or particular thing, and that these least things repeat in an image the greatest. This comes from the fact that everyone is his own love, and is such as his ruling love is. That which reigns flows into the particulars and arranges them, and everywhere induces a likeness of itself. 58-1 In the heavens love to the Lord is the ruling love, for there the Lord is loved above all things. Hence the Lord there is the All-in-all, flowing into all and each, arranging them, clothing them with a likeness of Himself, and making it to be heaven wherever He is. This is what makes an angel to be a heaven in the smallest form, a society to be a heaven in a larger form, and all the societies taken together a heaven in the largest form. That the Divine of the Lord is what makes heaven, and that He is the All-in-all, may be seen above (n. 7-12).

ALL HEAVEN IN THE AGGREGATE REFLECTS A SINGLE MAN. That heaven in its whole complex reflects a single man is an arcanum hitherto unknown in the world, but fully recognized in the heavens. To know this and the specific and particular things relating to it is the chief thing in the intelligence of the angels there, and on it many things depend which without it as their general principle would not enter distinctly and clearly into the ideas of their minds. Knowing that all the heavens with their societies reflect a single man they call heaven the Greatest Man and the Divine Man; 59-1—Divine because it is the Divine of the Lord that makes heaven (see above, n. 7-12).

That into such a form and image celestial and spiritual things are arranged and joined cannot be seen by those who have no right idea of spiritual and heavenly things. Such think that the earthy and material things of which man's outmost nature is composed are what makes the man; and that apart from these man is not a man. But let them know that it is not from these that man is a man, but from his ability to understand what is true and to will what is good. Such understanding and willing are the spiritual and celestial things of which man is made. Moreover, it is known that everyone's quality is determined by the quality of his understanding and will; and it can also be known that his earthly body is formed to serve the understanding and the will in the world, and to skillfully accomplish their uses in the outmost sphere of nature. For this reason the body by itself can do nothing, but is moved always in entire subservience to the bidding of the understanding and will, even to the extent that whatever a man thinks he speaks with his tongue and lips, and whatever he wills he does with his body and limbs, and thus the understanding and the will are what act, while the body by itself does nothing. Evidently, then, the things of the understanding and will are what make man; and as these act into the minutest particulars of the body, as what is internal into what is external, they must be in a like form, and on this account man is called an internal or spiritual man. Heaven is such a man in its greatest and most perfect form.

Such being the angelic idea of man, the angels give no thought to what a man does with his body, but only to the will from which the body acts. This they call the man himself, and the understanding they call the man so far as it acts in unison with the will. 61-1

The angels, it is true, do not see heaven in its whole complex in the human form, for heaven as a whole does not come within view of any angel; but remote societies, consisting of many thousands of angels, they sometimes see as a one in the human form; and from a society, as from a part, they draw their conclusion as to the general, which is heaven. For in the most perfect form generals are like the parts, and parts are like the generals, with simply such a difference as there is between like things of greater or less magnitude; consequently, the angels say that since the Divine from what is inmost or highest sees all things, so in the Lord's sight heaven as a whole must be in the human form.

Heaven being such, it is ruled by the Lord as a single man is ruled, thus as a one. For although man, as we know, consists of an innumerable variety of parts, not only as a whole but also in each part-as a whole, of members, organs, and viscera; and in each part, of series of fibers, nerves, and blood-vessels, thus of members within members, and of parts within parts-nevertheless, when he acts he acts as a single man. Such likewise is heaven under the auspices and direction of the Lord.

So many different things in man act as a one, because there is no least thing in him that does not do something for the general welfare and perform some use. The general performs a use for its parts, and the parts for the general, for the general is composed of the parts and the parts constitute the general; therefore they provide for each other, have regard for each other, and are joined together in such a form that each thing and all things have reference to the general and its good; thus it is that they act as one. [2] In the heavens there are like affiliations. Those there are conjoined according to uses in a like form; and consequently those who do not perform uses for the common good are cast out of heaven as something heterogeneous. To perform use is to will well to others for the sake of the common good; but to will well to others not for the sake of the common good but for the sake of self is not to perform use. These latter are such as love themselves supremely, while the former are such as love the Lord supremely. Thence it is that those who are in heaven act as a one; and this they do from the Lord, not from themselves, for they look to Him as the Only One, the source of all things, and they regard His kingdom as the general, the good of which is to be sought. This is what is meant by the Lord's words, Seek ye first the kingdom of God and His righteousness, and all things shall be added unto you (Matt. 6:33). "To seek His righteousness" means to seek His good. 64-1 [3] Those who in the world love their country's good more than their own, and their neighbor's good as their own, are they who in the other life love and seek the Lord's kingdom; for there the Lord's kingdom takes the place of country; and those who love doing good to others, not with self as an end but with good as an end, love the neighbor; for in heaven good is the neighbor. 64-2 All such are in the Greatest Man, that is, heaven.

As the whole heaven reflects a single man, and is a Divine spiritual man in the largest form, even in figure, so heaven like a man is arranged into members and parts, and these are similarly named. Moreover, angels know in what member this or that society is. This society, they say, is in a certain part or province of the head, that in a certain part or province of the breast, that in a certain part or province of the loins, and so on. In general, the highest or third heaven forms the head down to the neck; the middle or second heaven forms the breast down to the loins and knees; the lowest or first heaven forms the feet down to the soles, and also the arms down to the fingers. For the arms and hands belong to the lowest parts of man, although at the sides. From this again it is plain why there are three heavens.

The spirits that are beneath heaven are greatly astonished when they hear that heaven is not only above but below, for they have a like faith and opinion as men in the world, that heaven is nowhere but above, for they do not know that the arrangement of the heavens is like the arrangement of the members, organs, and viscera in man, some of which are above and some below; or like the arrangement of the parts in each of the members, organs, and viscera, some of which are within and some without. Hence their confused notions about heaven.

These things about heaven as the Greatest Man are set forth, because what follows in regard to heaven cannot be at all comprehended until these things are known, neither can there be any clear idea of the form of heaven, of the conjunction of the Lord with heaven, of the conjunction of heaven with man, of the influx of the spiritual world into the natural, or any idea at all of correspondence-subjects to be treated of in their proper order in what now follows. To throw some light on these subjects, therefore, the above has been premised.

EACH SOCIETY IN HEAVEN REFLECTS A SINGLE MAN. I have frequently been permitted to see that each society of heaven reflects a single man, and is in the likeness of a man. There was a society into which several had insinuated themselves who knew how to counterfeit angels of light. These were hypocrites. When these were being separated from the angels I saw that the entire society appeared at first like a single indistinct body, then by degrees in a human form, but still indistinctly, and at last clearly as a man. Those that were in that man and made up the man were such as were in the good of that society; the others who were not in the man and did not make up the man were hypocrites; these were cast out and the former were retained; and thus a separation was effected. Hypocrites are such as talk well and also do well, but have regard to themselves in everything. They talk as angels do about the Lord, heaven, love, and heavenly life, and also act rightly, so that they may appear to be what they profess to be. But their thinking is different; they believe nothing; and they wish good to none but themselves. Their doing good is for the sake of self, or if for the sake of others it is only for the appearance, and thus still for the sake of self.

I have also been permitted to see that an entire angelic society, where the Lord is visibly present, appears as a one in the human form. There appeared on high towards the east something like a cloud, from glowing white becoming red, and with little stars round about, which was descending; and as it gradually descended it became brighter, and at last appeared in a perfect human form. The little stars round about the cloud were angels, who so appeared by virtue of light from the Lord.

It must be understood that although all in a heavenly society when seen together as one appear in the likeness of a man; yet no one society is just such a man as another. Societies differ from one another like the faces of different individuals of the same family, for the reason given above (n. 47), that is, they differ in accordance with the varieties of good in which they are and which determines their form. The societies of the inmost or highest heaven, and in the center there, are those that appear in the most perfect and beautiful human form.

It is worthy of mention that the greater the number in any society in heaven and the more these make a one, the more perfect is its human form, for variety arranged in a heavenly form is what constitutes perfection, as has been shown above (n. 56), and number gives variety. Moreover, every society of heaven increases in number daily, and as it increases it becomes more perfect. Thus not only the society becomes more perfect, but also heaven in general, because it is made up of societies. As heaven gains in perfection by increase of numbers, it is evident how mistaken those are who believe that heaven may be closed by becoming full; for the opposite is true, that it will never be closed, but is perfected by greater and greater fullness. Therefore, the angels desire nothing so much as to have new angel guests come to them.

Each society, when it appears as one whole is in the form of a man, for the reason that heaven as a whole has that form (as has been shown in the preceding chapter); moreover, in the most perfect form, such as the form of heaven is, there is a likeness of the parts to the whole, and of lesser forms to the greatest. The lesser forms and parts of heaven are the societies of which it consists, which are also heavens in lesser form (see 51-58). This likeness is perpetual because in the heavens the goods of all are from a single love, that is, from a single origin. The single love, which is the origin of the good of all in heaven, is love to the Lord from the Lord. It is from this that the entire heaven in general, each society less generally, and each angel in particular, is a likeness of the Lord, as has been shown above (n. 58).

THEREFORE EVERY ANGEL IS IN A COMPLETE HUMAN FORM. In the two preceding chapters it has been shown that heaven in its whole complex, and likewise each society in heaven, reflects a single man. From the sequence of reasons there set forth it follows that this is equally true of each angel. As heaven is a man in largest form, and a society of heaven in a less form, so is an angel in least. For in the most perfect form, such as the form of heaven is, there is a likeness of the whole in the part and of the part in the whole. This is so for the reason that heaven is a common sharing, for it shares all it has with each one, and each one receives all he has from that sharing. Because an angel is thus a recipient he is a heaven in least form, as shown above in its chapter; and a man also, so far as he receives heaven, is a recipient, a heaven, and an angel (see above, n. 57). This is thus described in the Apocalypse:- He measured the wall of the holy Jerusalem, a hundred and forty and four cubits, the measure of a man, which is that of an angel (21:17). "Jerusalem" means here the Lord's church, and in a more eminent sense, heaven; 73-1 the "wall" means truth, which is a defence against the assault of falsities and evils; 73-2 "a hundred and forty and four" means all goods and truths in the complex; 73-3 "measure" means what a thing is, 73-4 a "man" means one in whom are goods and truths in general and in particular, thus in whom is heaven. And as it is from this that an angel is a man, it is said "the measure of a man, which is that of an angel." This is the spiritual meaning of these words. Without that meaning how could it be seen that "the wall of the Holy Jerusalem" is "the measure of a man, which is that of an angel?" 73-5

Let us now turn to experience. That angels are human forms, or men, has been seen by me a thousand times. I have talked with them as man with man, sometimes with one, sometimes with many together; and I have seen nothing whatever in their form different from the human form; and have occasionally been surprised to find them such. And that this might not be said to be a delusion or a vision of fancy, I have been permitted to see angels when fully awake or in possession of all my bodily senses, and in a state of clear perception. And I have often told them that men in the Christian world are in such blind ignorance in regard to angels and spirits as to believe them to be minds without form, even pure thoughts, of which they have no idea except as something ethereal in which there is some vitality. And as they thus ascribe to angels nothing human except a thinking faculty, they believe that having no eyes they do not see, having no ears they do not hear, and having no mouth or tongue they do not speak. [2] To this the angels replied that they are aware that such a belief is held by many in the world, and is prevalent among the learned, and to their surprise, even among the clergy. The reason, they said, is that the learned, who were the leaders and who first concocted such an idea of angels and spirits, conceived of them from the sense-conceptions of the external man; and those who think from these, and not from interior light and from the general idea implanted in everyone, must needs fabricate such notions, since the sense-conceptions of the external man take in only what belongs to nature, and nothing above nature, thus nothing whatever of the spiritual world. 74-1 From these leaders as guides this falsity of thought about angels extended to others who did not think from themselves but adopted the thoughts of their leaders; and those who first take their thoughts from others and make that thought their belief, and then view it with their own understanding, cannot easily recede from it, and are therefore in most cases satisfied with confirming it. [3] The angels said, furthermore, that the simple in faith and heart have no such idea about angels, but think of them as the men of heaven, and for the reason that they have not extinguished by learning what is implanted in them from heaven, and have no conception of anything apart from form. This is why angels in churches, whether sculptured or painted, are always depicted as men. In respect to this insight from heaven they said that it is the Divine flowing into such as are in the good of faith and life.

From all my experience, which is now of many years, I am able to say and affirm that angels are wholly men in form, having faces, eyes, ears, bodies, arms, hands, and feet; that they see and hear one another, and talk together, and in a word lack nothing whatever that belongs to men except that they are not clothed in material bodies. I have seen them in their own light, which exceeds by many degrees the noonday light of the world, and in that light all their features could be seen more distinctly and clearly than the faces of men are seen on the earth. It has also been granted me to see an angel of the inmost heaven. He had a more radiant and resplendent face than the angels of the lower heavens. I observed him attentively, and he had a human form in all completeness.

But it must be remembered that a man cannot see angels with his bodily eyes, but only with the eyes of the spirit within him, 76-1 because his spirit is in the spiritual world, and all things of the body are in the natural world. Like sees like from being like. Moreover, as the bodily organ of sight, which is the eye, is too gross, as everyone knows, to see even the smaller things of nature except through magnifying glasses, still less can it see what is above the sphere of nature, as all things in the spiritual world are. Nevertheless these things can be seen by man when he has been withdrawn from the sight of the body, and the sight of his spirit has been opened; and this can be effected instantly whenever it is the pleasure of the Lord that man should see these things; and in that case man does not know but what he is seeing them with his bodily eyes. Thus were angels seen by Abraham, Lot, Manoah, and the prophets; and thus, too, the Lord was seen by the disciples after the resurrection; and in the same way angels have been seen by me. Because the prophets saw in this way they were called "seers," and were said "to have their eyes opened" (1 Sam. 9:8; Num. 24:3); and enabling them to see thus was called "opening their eyes," as with Elisha's servant, of whom we read: Elisha prayed and said, Jehovah, I pray Thee open his eyes that he may see; and Jehovah opened the eyes of the young man and he saw, and behold the mountain was full of horses and chariots of fire round about Elisha (2 Kings 6:17).

Good spirits, with whom I have spoken about this matter, have been deeply grieved at such ignorance in the church about the condition of heaven and of spirits and angels; and in their displeasure they charged me to declare positively that they are not formless minds nor ethereal breaths, but are men in very form, and see, hear, and feel equally with those who are in this world.77-1

IT IS FROM THE LORD'S DIVINE HUMAN THAT HEAVEN AS A WHOLE AND IN PART REFLECTS MAN. That it is from the Lord's Divine Human that heaven as a whole and in part reflects man, follows as a conclusion from all that has been stated and shown in the preceding chapters, namely: (i) That the God of heaven is the Lord. (ii) It is the Divine of the Lord that makes heaven. (iii) Heaven consists of innumerable societies; and each society is a heaven in a smaller form, and each angel in the smallest form. (iv) All heaven in the aggregate reflects a single man. (v) Each society in the heavens reflects a single man. (vi) Therefore every angel is in a complete human form. All this leads to the conclusion that as it is the Divine that makes heaven, heaven must be human in form. That this Divine is the Lord's Divine Human can be seen still more clearly, because in a compendium, in what has been collected, brought together and collated from the Arcana Coelestia and placed as a supplement at the end of this chapter. That the Lord's Human is Divine, and that it is not true that His Human is not Divine, as those with in the church believe, may also be seen in the same extracts, also in the chapter on The Lord, in The New Jerusalem and its Heavenly Doctrine, at the end.

That this is true has been proved to me by much experience, about which something shall now be said. No angel in the heavens ever perceives the Divine as being in any other than a human form; and what is remarkable, those in the higher heavens are unable to think of the Divine in any other way. The necessity of thinking in this way comes from the Divine itself that flows in, and also from the form of heaven in harmony with which their thoughts spread forth. For every thought of an angel spreads forth into heaven; and the angels have intelligence and wisdom in the measure of that extension. It is in consequence of this that all in heaven acknowledge the Lord, because only in Him does the Divine Human exist. Not only have I been told all this by angels, but when elevated into the inner sphere of heaven I have been able to perceive it. From this it is evident that the wiser the angels are the more clearly they perceive this truth; and it is from this that the Lord is seen by them; for the Lord is seen in a Divine angelic form, which is the human form, by those who acknowledge and believe in a visible Divine Being, but not by those who believe in an invisible Divine. For the former can see their Divine Being, but the latter cannot.

Because the angels have no perception of an invisible Divine, which they call a Divine devoid of form, but perceive only a visible Divine in human form, they are accustomed to say that the Lord alone is man, and that it is from Him that they are men, and that each one is a man in the measure of his reception of the Lord. By receiving the Lord they understand receiving good and truth which are from Him, since the Lord is in His good and in His truth, and this they call wisdom and intelligence. Everyone knows, they say, that intelligence and wisdom make man, and not a face without these. The truth of this is made evident from the appearance of the angels of the interior heavens, for these, being in good and truth from the Lord and in consequent wisdom and intelligence, are in a most beautiful and most perfect human form; while the angels of the lower heavens are in human form of less perfection and beauty. On the other hand, those who are in hell appear in the light of heaven hardly as men, but rather as monsters, since they are not in good and truth but in evil and falsity, and consequently in the opposites of wisdom and intelligence. For this reason their life is not called life, but spiritual death.

Because heaven as a whole and in part, from the Lord's Divine Human, reflects a man, the angels say that they are in the Lord; and some say that they are in His body, meaning that they are in the good of His love. And this the Lord Himself teaches, saying, Abide in Me and I in you. As the branch cannot bear fruit of itself except it abide in the vine, so neither can ye, except ye abide in Me. For apart from Me ye can do nothing. Abide in My love. If ye keep My commandments ye shall abide in My love (John 15:4-10).

Because such a perception of the Divine exists in the heavens, to think of God as in a human form is implanted in every man who receives any influx from heaven. Thus did the ancients think of Him; and thus do the moderns think of Him both outside of the church and within it. The simple see Him in thought as the Ancient One in shining light. But this insight has been extinguished in all those that by self-intelligence and by a life of evil have rejected influx from heaven. Those that have extinguished it by self-intelligence prefer an invisible God; while those that have extinguished it by a life of evil prefer no God. Neither of these are aware that such an insight exists, because they do not have it; and yet it is the Divine heavenly itself that primarily flows into man out of heaven, because man is born for heaven, and no one without a conception of a Divine can enter heaven.

For this reason he that has no conception of heaven, that is, no conception of the Divine from which heaven is, cannot be raised up to the first threshold of heaven. As soon as such a one draws near to heaven a resistance and a strong repulsion are perceived; and for the reason that his interiors, which should be receptive of heaven, are closed up from their not being in the form of heaven, and the nearer he comes to heaven the more tightly are they closed up. Such is the lot of those within the church who deny the Lord, and of those who, like the Socinians, deny His Divinity. But the lot of those who are born out of the church, and who are ignorant of the Lord because they do not have the Word, will be described hereafter.

That the men of old time had an idea of the Divine as human is evident from the manifestation of the Divine to Abraham, Lot, Joshua, Gideon, Manoah and his wife, and others. These saw God as a man, but nevertheless adored Him as the God of the universe, calling Him the God of heaven and earth, and Jehovah. That it was the Lord who was seen by Abraham He Himself teaches in John (8:56); and that it was He who was seen by the rest is evident from His words: No one hath seen the Father, nor heard His voice, nor seen His form (John 1:18; 5:37).

But that God is man can scarcely be comprehended by those who judge all things from the sense-conceptions of the external man, for the sensual man must needs think of the Divine from the world and what is therein, and thus of a Divine and spiritual man in the same way as of a corporeal and natural man. From this he concludes that if God were a man He would be as large as the universe; and if He ruled heaven and earth it would be done through many others, after the manner of kings in the world. If told that in heaven there is no extension of space as in the world, he would not in the least comprehend it. For he that thinks only from nature and its light must needs think in accord with such extension as appears before his eyes. But it is the greatest mistake to think in this way about heaven. Extension there is not like extension in the world. In the world extension is determinate, and thus measurable; but in heaven it is not determinate, and thus not measurable. But extension in heaven will be further treated of hereafter in connection with space and time in the spiritual world. Furthermore, everyone knows how far the sight of the eye extends, namely, to the sun and to the stars, which are so remote; and whoever thinks deeply knows that the internal sight, which is of thought, has a still wider extension, and that a yet more interior sight must extend more widely still. What then must be said of Divine sight, which is the inmost and highest of all? Because thoughts have such extension, all things of heaven are shared with everyone there, so, too, are all things of the Divine which makes heaven and fills it, as has been shown in the preceding chapters.

Those in heaven wonder that men can believe themselves to be intelligent who, in thinking of God, think about something invisible, that is, inconceivable under any form; and that they can call those who think differently unintelligent and simple, when the reverse is the truth. They add, "Let those who thus believe themselves to be intelligent examine themselves, whether they do not look upon nature as God, some the nature that is before their eyes, others the invisible side of nature; and whether they are not so blind as not to know what God is, what an angel is, what a spirit is, what their soul is which is to live after death, what the life of heaven in man is, and many other things that constitute intelligence; when yet those whom they call simple know all these things in their way, having an idea of their God that He is the Divine in a human form, of an angel that he is a heavenly man, of their soul that is to live after death that it is like an angel, and of the life of heaven in man that it is living in accord with the Divine commandments." Such the angels call intelligent and fitted for heaven; but the others, on the other hand, they call not intelligent. EXTRACTS FROM THE ARCANA COELESTIA RELATING TO THE LORD AND HIS DIVINE HUMAN. [2] The Divine was in the Lord from very conception (n. 4641, 4963, 5041, 5157, 6716, 10125). The Lord alone had a Divine seed (n. 1438). His soul was Jehovah (n. 1999, 2004, 2005, 2018, 2025). Thus the Lord's inmost was the Divine Itself, while the clothing was from the mother (n. 5041). The Divine Itself was the Being [Esse] of the Lord's life, and from this the Human afterwards went forth and became the outgo [existere] from that Being [Esse] (n. 3194, 3210, 10269, 10738). [3] Within the church where the Word is and by it the Lord is known, the Lord's Divine ought not to be denied, nor the Holy that goes forth from Him (n. 2359). Those within the church who do not acknowledge the Lord have no conjunction with the Divine; but it is otherwise with those outside of the church (n. 10205). The essential of the church is to acknowledge the Lord's Divine and His union with the Father (n. 10083, 10112, 10370, 10730, 10738, 10816-10820). [4] The glorification of the Lord is treated of in the Word in many passages (n. 10828). And in the internal sense of the Word everywhere (n. 2249, 2523, 3245). The Lord glorified His Human, but not the Divine, since this was glorified in itself (n. 10057). The Lord came into the world to glorify His Human (n. 3637, 4287, 9315). The Lord glorified His Human by means of the Divine love that was in Him from conception (n. 4727). The Lord's life in the world was His love towards the whole human race (n. 2253). The Lord's love transcends all human understanding (n. 2077). The Lord saved the human race by glorifying His Human (n. 4180, 10019; 10152, 10655, 10659 10828). Otherwise the whole human race would have perished in eternal death (n. 1676). The state of the Lord's glorification and humiliation (n. 1785, 1999, 2159, 6866). Glorification in respect to the Lord is the uniting of His Human with the Divine; and to glorify is to make Divine (n. 1603, 10053,

10828). When the Lord glorified His Human He put off everything human that was from the mother, until at last He was not her son (n. 2159, 2574, 2649, 3036, 10830). [5] The Son of God from eternity was the Divine truth in heaven (n. 2628, 2798, 2803, 3195, 3704). When the Lord was in the world He made His Human Divine truth from the Divine good that was in Him (n. 2803, 3194, 3195, 3210, 6716, 6864, 7014, 7499, 8127, 8724, 9199). The Lord then arranged all things in Himself into a heavenly form, which is in accord with Divine truth (n. 1928, 3633). For this reason the Lord was called the Word, which is Divine truth (n. 2533, 2813, 2859, 2894, 3393, 3712). The Lord alone had perception and thought from Himself, and this was above all angelic perception and thought (n. 1904, 1914, 1919). The Divine truth which was Himself, the Lord united with Divine good which was in Himself (n. 10047, 10052, 10076). The union was reciprocal (n. 2004, 10067). [6] In passing out of the world the Lord also made His Human Divine good (n. 3194, 3210, 6864, 7499, 8724, 9199, 10076). This is what is meant by His coming forth from the Father and returning to the Father (n. 3194, 3210). Thus He became one with the Father (n. 2751, 3704, 4766). Since that union Divine truth goes forth from the Lord (n. 3704, 3712, 3969, 4577, 5704, 7499, 8127, 8241, 9199, 9398). How Divine truth goes forth, illustrated (n. 7270, 9407). It was from His own power that the Lord united the Human with the Divine (n. 1616, 1749, 1752, 1813, 1921, 2025, 2026, 2523, 3141, 5005, 5045, 6716). From this it is clear that the Lord's Human was not like the human of any other man, in that it was conceived from the Divine Itself (n. 10125, 10825, 10826). His union with the Father, from whom was His soul, was not as between two persons, but as between soul and body (n. 3737, 10824). [7] The most ancient people could not worship the Divine being [esse], but could worship only the Divine Outgo [existere], which is the Divine Human; therefore the Lord came into the world in order to become the Divine Existere from the Divine Esse (n. 4687, 5321). The ancients acknowledged the Divine because He appeared to them in a human form, and this was the Divine Human (n. 5110, 5663, 6845, 10737). The Infinite Being [Esse] could flow into heaven with the angels and with men only by means of the Divine Human (n. 1676, 1990, 2016, 2034). In heaven no other Divine than the Divine Human is perceived (n. 6475, 9303, 10067, 10267). The Divine Human from eternity was the Divine truth in heaven and the Divine passing through heaven; thus it was the Divine Outgo [existere] which afterwards in the Lord became the Divine Being [Esse] per se, from which is the Divine Existere in heaven (n. 3061, 6280, 6880, 10579). What the state of heaven was before the Lord's coming (n. 6371-6373). The Divine was not perceptible except when it passed through heaven (n. 6982, 6996, 7004). [8] The inhabitants of all the earth worship the Divine under a human form, that is, the Lord (n. 6700, 8541-8547, 10736-10738). They rejoice when they hear that God actually became Man (n. 9361). All who are in good and who worship the Divine under the human form, are received by the Lord (n. 9359). God cannot be thought of except in human form; and what is incomprehensible does not fall into any idea, so neither into belief (n. 9359, 9972). Man is able to worship that of which he has some idea, but not that of which he has no idea (n. 4733, 5110, 5663, 7211, 9356, 10067, 10267). Therefore the Divine is worshiped under a human form by most of the inhabitants of the entire globe, and this is the effect of influx from heaven (n.

10159). All who are in good in regard to their life, when they think of the Lord, think of the Divine Human, and not of the Human separate from the Divine; it is otherwise with those who are not in good in regard to their life (n. 2326, 4724, 4731, 4766, 8878, 9193, 9198). In the church at this day those that are in evil in regard to their life, and those that are in faith separate from charity, think of the Human of the Lord apart from the Divine, and do not even comprehend what the Divine Human is,-why they do not (n. 3212, 3241,4689, 4692, 4724, 4731, 5321, 6872, 8878, 9193, 9198). The Lord's Human is Divine because it is from the Being [Esse] of the Father, and this was His soul,—illustrated by a father's likeness in children (n. 10269, 10372, 10823). Also because it was from the Divine love, which was the very Being [Esse] of His life from conception (n. 6872). Every man is such as his love is, and is his love (n. 6872, 10177, 10284). The Lord made all His Human, both internal and external, Divine (n. 1603, 1815, 1902, 1926, 2083, 2093). Therefore, differently from any man, He rose again as to His whole body (n. 1729, 2083, 5078, 10825). [9] That the Lord's Human is Divine is acknowledged from His omnipresence in the Holy Supper (n. 2343, 2359). Also from His transfiguration before His three disciples (n. 3212). Also from the Word of the Old Testament, in that He is called God (n. 10154); and is called Jehovah (n. 1603, 1736, 1815, 1902, 2921, 3035, 5110, 6281, 6303, 8864, 9194, 9315). In the sense of the letter a distinction is made between the Father and the Son, that is, between Jehovah and the Lord, but not in the internal sense of the Word, in which the angels of heaven are (n. 3035). In the Christian world the Lord's Human has been declared not to be Divine; this was done in a council for the pope's sake, that he might be acknowledged as the Lord's vicar (n. 4738). [10] Christians were examined in the other life in regard to their idea of one God, and it was found they held an idea of three gods (n. 2329, 5256, 10736-10738, 10821). A Divine trinity or trine in one person, constituting one God, is conceivable, but not in three persons (n. 10738, 10821, 10824). A Divine trine in the Lord is acknowledged in heaven (n. 14, 15, 1729, 2004, 5256, 9303). The trine in the Lord is the Divine Itself, called the Father, the Divine Human, called the Son, and the Divine going forth, called the Holy Spirit and this Divine trine is a One (n. 2149, 2156, 2288, 2319, 2329, 2447, 3704, 6993, 7182, 10738, 10822, 10823). The Lord Himself teaches that the Father and He are One (n. 1729, 2004, 2005, 2018, 2025, 2751, 3704, 3736, 4766); also that the Holy Divine goes forth from Him and is His (n. 3969, 4673, 6788, 6993, 7499, 8127, 8302, 9199, 9228, 9229, 9264, 9407, 9818, 9820, 10330). [11] The Divine Human flows into heaven and makes heaven (n. 3038). The Lord is the all in heaven and is the life of heaven (n. 7211, 9128). In the angels the Lord dwells in what is His own (n. 9338, 10125, 10151, 10157). Consequently those who are in heaven are in the Lord (n. 3637, 3638). The Lord's conjunction with angels is measured by their reception of the good of love and charity from Him (n. 904, 4198, 4205, 4211, 4220, 6280, 6832, 7042, 8819, 9680, 9682, 9683, 10106, 10810). The entire heaven has reference to the Lord (n. 551, 552). The Lord is the common center of heaven (n. 3633, 3641). All in heaven turn themselves to the Lord, who is above the heavens (n. 9828, 10130, 10189). Nevertheless angels do not turn themselves to the Lord, but the Lord turns them to Himself (n. 10189). It is not a presence of angels with the Lord, but the Lord's presence with angels (n. 9415). In heaven there is no conjunction with the Divine Itself, but conjunction with the Divine Human (n. 4211, 4724, 5663). [12] Heaven corresponds to the Divine Human of the Lord; consequently heaven in general is as a single man, and for this reason heaven is called the Greatest Man (n. 2996, 2998, 3624-3649, 3741-3745, 4625). The Lord is the Only Man, and those only are men who receive the Divine from Him (n. 1894). So far as they receive are they men and images of Him (n. 8547). Therefore angels are forms of love and charity in human form, and this from the Lord (n. 3804, 4735, 4797, 4985, 5199, 5530, 9879, 10177). [13] The whole heaven is the Lord's (n. 2751, 7086). He has all power in the heavens and on earth (n. 1607, 10089, 10827). As the Lord rules the whole heaven He also rules all things depending thereon, thus all things in the world (n. 2025, 2026, 4523, 4524). The Lord alone has the power to remove the hells, to withhold from evils, and to hold in good, thus to save (n. 10019).

THERE IS A CORRESPONDENCE OF ALL THINGS OF HEAVEN WITH ALL THINGS OF MAN. What correspondence is is not known at the present day, for several reasons, the chief of which is that man has withdrawn himself from heaven by the love of self and love of the world. For he that loves self and the world above all things gives heed only to worldly things, since these appeal to the external senses and gratify the natural longings; and he does not give heed to spiritual things, since these appeal to the internal senses and gratify the mind, therefore he casts them aside, saying that they are too high for his comprehension. This was not so with the ancient people. To them the knowledge of correspondences was the chief of knowledges. By means of it they acquired intelligence and wisdom; and by means of it those who were of the church had communication with heaven; for the knowledge of correspondences is angelic knowledge. The most ancient people, who were celestial men, thought from correspondence itself, as the angels do. And therefore they talked with angels, and the Lord frequently appeared to them, and they were taught by Him. But at this day that knowledge has been so completely lost that no one knows what correspondence is. 87-1

Since, then, without a perception of what correspondence is there can be no clear knowledge of the spiritual world or of its inflow into the natural world, neither of what the spiritual is in its relation to the natural, nor any clear knowledge of the spirit of man, which is called the soul, and its operation into the body, neither of man's state after death, it is necessary to explain what correspondence is and the nature of it. This will prepare the way for what is to follow.

First, what correspondence is. The whole natural world corresponds to the spiritual world, and not merely the natural world in general, but also every particular of it; and as a consequence everything in the natural world that springs from the spiritual world is called a correspondent. It must be understood that the natural world springs from and has permanent existence from the spiritual world, precisely like an effect from its effecting cause. All that is spread out under the sun and that receives heat and light from the sun is what is called the natural world; and all things that derive their subsistence therefrom belong to that world. But the spiritual world is heaven; and all things in the heavens belong to that world.

Since man is both a heaven and a world in least form after the image of the greatest (see above, n. 57), there is in him both a spiritual and a natural world. The interior things that belong to his mind, and that have relation to understanding and will, constitute his spiritual world; while the exterior things that belong to his body, and that have relation to its senses and activities, constitute his natural world. Consequently, everything in his natural world (that is, in his body and its senses and activities), that has its existence from his spiritual world (that is, from his mind and its understanding and will) is called a correspondent.

From the human face it can be seen what correspondence is. In a face that has not been taught to dissemble, all the affections of the mind present themselves to view in a natural form, as in their type. This is why the face is called the index of the mind; that is, it is man's spiritual world presented in his natural world. So, too, what pertains to the understanding is presented in speech, and what pertains to the will is presented in the movements of the body. So whatever effects are produced in the body, whether in the face, in speech, or in bodily movements, are called correspondences.

All this shows also what the internal man is and what the external, namely, that the internal is what is called the spiritual man, and the external what is called the natural man; also that the one is distinct from the other as heaven is from the world; also that all things that take place and come forth in the external or natural man take place and come forth from the internal or spiritual man.

This much has been said about the correspondence of man's internal or spiritual with his external or natural; now the correspondence of the whole heaven with everything pertaining to man shall be treated of.

It has been shown that the entire heaven reflects a single man, and that it is in image a man and is therefore called the Greatest Man. It has also been shown that the angelic societies, of which heaven consists, are therefore arranged as the members, organs, and viscera are in man, that is, some are in the head, some in the breast, some in the arms, and some in each of their particulars (see above, n. 59-72); consequently the societies in any member there correspond to the like member in man; those in the head corresponding to the head in man, those in the breast to the breast in man, those in the arms to the arms in man; and so with all the rest. It is from this correspondence that man has permanent existence, for from heaven alone does man have permanent existence.

That heaven is divided into two kingdoms, one called the celestial kingdom and the other the spiritual kingdom, may be seen above in its own chapter. The celestial kingdom corresponds in general to the heart and all things of the heart in the whole body, and the spiritual kingdom to the lungs and to all things of the lungs in the whole body. Likewise in man heart and lungs form two kingdoms, the heart ruling there through the arteries and veins, and the lungs through the tendinous and motor fibers, both together in every exertion and movement. So in every man, in his spiritual world, which is called his spiritual man, there are two kingdoms, one of the will and the other of the understanding, the will ruling through affections for good, and the understanding through affections for truth; and these kingdoms correspond to the kingdoms of the heart and of the lungs in the body. It is the same in the heavens; the celestial kingdom is the voluntary part of heaven, and in it good of love reigns; the spiritual kingdom is the intellectual part of heaven, and in it truth reigns. These are what correspond to the functions of the heart and lungs in man. It is on account of this correspondence that in the Word the "heart" signifies the will and also good of love, and the "breath" of the lungs signifies the understanding and the truth of faith. For the same reason affections are ascribed to the heart, although they are neither in it nor from it. 95-1

The correspondence of the two kingdoms of heaven with the heart and lungs is the general correspondence of heaven with man. There is a less general correspondence with each one of his members, organs, and viscera; and what this is shall also be explained. In the Greatest Man, which is heaven, those that are in the head excel all others in every good, being in love, peace, innocence, wisdom, intelligence, and consequent joy and happiness. These flow into the head of man and the things belonging to the head and corresponding thereto. In the Greatest Man, or heaven, those that are in the breast are in the good of charity and of faith, and these flow into the breast of man and correspond to it. In the Greatest Man, or heaven, those that are in the loins and the organs devoted to generation are in marriage love. Those in the feet are in the lowest good of heaven, which is called spiritual natural good. Those in the arms and hands are in the power of truth from good. Those that are in the eyes are in understanding; those in the ears are in attention and obedience; those in the nostrils are in perception; those in the mouth and tongue are in the ability to converse from understanding and perception; those in the kidneys are in truths searching, separating, and correcting; those in the liver, pancreas, and spleen are in various purifications of good and truth; and so with the rest. All these flow into the like things of man and correspond to them. This inflow of heaven is into the functions and uses of the bodily members; and the uses, since they are from the spiritual world, take on a form by means of such things as are in the natural world, and thus present themselves in effect. From this is the correspondence.

For the same reason these same members, organs, and viscera have a like significance in the Word; for everything there has a meaning in accordance with correspondence. Thus the "head" signifies intelligence and wisdom; the "breast" charity; the "loins" marriage love; the "arms and hands" power of truth; the "feet" what is natural; the "eyes" understanding; the "nostrils" perception; the "ears" obedience, the "kidneys" the scrutiny of truth, and so on. 97-1 So, too, in the common speech of man it is said of one who is intelligent and wise that he has a good head; of one who is charitable that he is a bosom friend; of one who has clear perception that he is keen scented; of one who is intelligent that he is sharp sighted; of one who is powerful that he is long handed; of one who exercises his will from love that it is done from the heart. These and many other expressions in the speech of men are from correspondence, for they are from the spiritual world, although man is ignorant of it.

That there is such a correspondence of all things of heaven with all things of man has been made clear to me by much experience, by so much that I am as convinced of it as of any evident fact that admits of no doubt. But it is not necessary to describe all this experience here; nor would it be permissible on account of its abundance. It may be seen set forth in the Arcana Coelestia, where correspondences, representations, the influx of the spiritual world into the natural world, and the interaction between soul and body, are treated of. 98-1

But notwithstanding that all things of man's body correspond to all things of heaven, it is not in respect to his external form that man is an image of heaven, but in respect to his internal form; for man's interiors are what receive heaven, while his exteriors receive the world. So far, therefore, as his interiors receive heaven man is in respect to them a heaven in least form, after the image of the greatest. But so far as his interiors do not receive heaven he is not a heaven and an image of the greatest, although his exteriors, which receive the world, may be in a form in accordance with the order of the world, and thus variously beautiful. For the source of outward beauty which pertains to the body is in parents and formation in the womb, and it is preserved afterwards by general influx from the world. For this reason the form of one's natural man differs greatly from the form of his spiritual man. What the form of a man's spirit is I have been shown occasionally; and in some who were beautiful and charming in appearance the spirit was seen to be so deformed, black and monstrous that it might be called an image of hell, not of heaven; while in others not beautiful there was a spirit beautifully formed, pure, and angelic. Moreover, the spirit of man appears after death such as it has been in the body while it lived therein in the world.

But correspondence applies far more widely than to man; for there is a correspondence of the heavens with one another. To the third or inmost heaven the second or middle heaven corresponds, and to the second or middle heaven the first or outmost heaven corresponds, and this corresponds to the bodily forms in man called his members, organs, and viscera. Thus it is the bodily part of man in which heaven finally terminates, and upon which it stands as upon its base. But this arcanum will be more fully unfolded elsewhere.

Footnotes

52-1 In the Word the Lord is called an angel (n. 6280, 6831, 8192, 9303). A whole angelic society is called an angel, and Michael and Raphael are angelic societies, so called from their functions (n. 8192). The societies of heaven and the angels have no names, but are distinguished by the quality of their good, and by the idea of it (n. 1705, 1754).

54-1 Heaven is not granted from mercy apart from means, but in accordance with the life; yet everything of the life by which man is led to heaven by the Lord belongs to mercy; this is what is meant by mercy (n. 5057, 10659). If heaven were granted from mercy apart from means it would be granted to all (n. 2401). About some evil spirits cast down from heaven who believed that heaven was granted to everyone from mercy apart from means (n. 4226).

54-2 Heaven is in man (n. 3884).

56-1 Every whole is from the harmony and concert of many parts. Otherwise it has no quality (n. 457). From this the entire heaven is a whole (n. 457). And for the reason that all there have regard to one end, which is the lord (n. 9828).

57-1 If good were the characteristic and essential of the church, and not truth apart from good, the church would be one (n. 1255, 1316, 2952, 3267,

3445, 3451. 3452). From good all churches make one church before the Lord (n. 7396, 9276).

57-2 The church is in man, and not outside of him, and the church in general is made up of men that have the church in them (n. 3884 [6637]).

57-3 A man who is a church is a heaven in the smallest form after the image of the greatest, because his interiors, which belong to his mind, are arranged after the form of heaven, and consequently for reception of all things of heaven (n. 911, 1900, 1928, 3624-3631, 3634, 3884, 4041, 4279, 4523, 4524, 4625, 6013, 6057 9279, 9632).

57-4 Man has an internal and an external; hid internal is formed by creation after the image of heaven, and his external after the image of the world; and for this reason man was called by the ancients a microcosm (n. 3628, 4523, 4524, 5115, 5368, 6013, 6057, 9279, 9706, 10156, 10472). Therefore man was created to have the world in him serve heaven, and this takes place with the good; but it is the reverse with the evil, in whom heaven serves the world (n. 9278, 9283).

57-5 The Lord is order, since the Divine good and truth that go forth from the Lord make order (n. 1728, 1919, 2011, 2258, 5110, 5703, 8988, 10336, 10619). Divine truths are laws of order (n. 2447, 7995). So far as a man lives according to order, that is, so far as he lives in good in accordance with Divine truths, he is a man, and the church and heaven are in him (n. 4839, 6605, 8513, [8547]).

58-1 The ruling or dominant love with everyone is in each thing and all things of his life, thus in each thing and all things of his thought and will in. 6159, 7648, 8067, 8853). Man is such as is the ruling quality of his life in. 987, 1040, 1568, 3570,6571, 6935, 6938, 8853-8858, 10076, 10109, 10110, 10284). When love and faith rule they are in all the particulars of man's life, although he does not know it (n. 8854, 8864, 8865).

59-1 Heaven in the whole complex appears in form like a man, and for this reason heaven is called the Greatest Man (n. 2996, 2998, 3624-3649, 3741-3745, 4625).

61-1 The will of man is the very being [esse] of his life, and his understanding is the outgo [existere] of his life therefrom (n. 3619, 5002, 9282). The chief life of man is the life of his will, and from that the life of the understanding proceeds (n. 585, 590, 3619, 7342, 8885, 9282, 10076, 10109, 10110). Man is man by virtue of his will and his understanding therefrom (n. 8911, 9069, 9071, 10076, 10109, 10110).

64-1 In the Wood "righteousness" is predicated of good, and "judgment" of truth; therefore "to do righteousness and judgment" is to do what is good and true (n. 2235, 9857).

64-2 In the highest sense the Lord is the neighbor; consequently to love the Lord is to love that which is from Him, that is to love good and truth because the Lord is in everything that is from Him (n. 2425, 3419, 6706, 6711 6819, 6823, 8123). Therefore all good that is from the Lord is the neighbor, and to will and do that good is to love the neighbor (n. 5028, 10336)

73-1 "Jerusalem" means the church (n. 402, 3654, 9166)

73-2 The "wall" means truth defending against the assault of falsities and evils (n. 6419).

73-3 "Twelve" means all truths and goods in the complex (n. 577, 2089, 2129,

2130, 3272, 3858, 3913). Likewise "seventy-two," and "a hundred and forty-four," since this comes from twelve multiplied into itself (n. 7973). All numbers in the Word signify things (n. 482, 487, 647, 648, 755, 813, 1963, 1988, 2075, 2252, 3252, 4264, 4495, 5265). Multiplied numbers have a like signification as the simple numbers from which they arise by multiplication (n. 5291, 5335, 5708, 7973).

73-4 "Measure" in the Word signifies the quality of a thing in respect to truth and good (n. 3104, 9603).

73-5 In regard to the spiritual or internal sense of the Word see the explanation of The White Horse in the Apocalypse, and the Appendix to The Heavenly Doctrine.

74-1 Unless man is raised above the sense-conceptions of the external man he has vary little wisdom (n. 5089). The wise man thinks above these sense-conceptions (n. 5089, 5094). When man is raised above these, he comes into clearer light, and finally into heavenly light (n. 6183, 6313, 6315, 9407, 9730, 9922). Elevation and withdrawal from these was known to the ancients (n. 6313).

76-1 In respect to his interiors man is a spirit (n. 1594). And that spirit is the man himself, and it is from that spirit that the body lived (n. 447, 4622, 6054).

77-1 Inasmuch as each angel is a recipient of Divine order from the Lord, he is in a human form, perfect and beautiful in the measure of his reception (n. 322, 1880, 1881, 3633, 3804, 4622, 4735, 4797, 4985, 5199, 5530, 6054, 9879, 10177, 10594). It is by means of Divine truth that order exists; and Divine good is the essential of order (n. 2451, 3166, 4390, 4409, 5232, 7256, 10122, 10555).

87-1 How far the knowledge of correspondences excels other knowledges (n. 4280). The knowledge of correspondences was the chief knowledge of the ancient people; but at the present day it is wholly forgotten (n. 3021, 3419, 4280, 4749, 4844, 4964, 4966, 6004, 7729, 10252). The knowledge of correspondences flourished among the Eastern nations and in Egypt (5702, 6692, 7097, 7779, 9391, 10407).

95-1 The correspondence of the heart and lungs with the Greatest Man, which is heaven, from experience (n. 3883-3896), The heart corresponds to those in the celestial kingdom, and the lungs to those in the spiritual kingdom (n. 3885-3887). There is in heaven a pulse like that of the heart, and a respiration like that of the lungs but interior (n. 3884, 3885, 3887). There the pulse of the heart varies in conformity to states of love, and the respiration in conformity to states of charity and faith (n. 3886, 3887, 3889). In the Word the "heart" means the will, and "from the heart" means from the will (n. 2930, 7542, 8910, 9113, 10336). In the Word the "heart" also signifies love, and "from the heart" means from love (7542, 9050, 10336).

97-1 In the Word the "breast" signifies charity (n. 3934, 10081, 10087). The "loins" and organs of generation signify marriage love (n. 3021, 4280, 4462, 5050-5052). The "arms" and "hands" signify the power of truth (n. 878, 3091, 4931-4937, 6947, 7205, 10019). The "feet" signify the natural (n. 2162, 3147, 3761, 3986, 4280, 4938-4952). The "eye" signifies understanding (n. 2701, 4403-4421, 4523-4534, 6923, 9051, 10569). The "nostrils" signify perception (n. 3577, 4624, 4625, 4748, 5621, 8286, 10054, 10292). The "ears" signify obedience (n. 2542, 3869, 4523, 4653, 5017, 7216, 8361, 8990, 9311, 9397, 10061). The "kidneys" signify the scrutiny and correction of truth (n. 5380-5386, 10032).

98-1 The correspondence of all the members of the body with the Greatest Man, or heaven, in general and in particular, from experience (n. 3021, 3624-3649, 3741-3750, 3883-3895, 4039-4054, 4218-4228, 4318-4331, 4403-4421, 4523-4533, 4622-4633, 4652-4660, 4791-4805, 4931-4953, 5050-5061, 5171-5189, 5377-5396, 5552-5573, 5711-5727, 10030). The influx of the spiritual world into the natural world or of heaven into the world, and the influx of the soul into all things of the body, from experience (n. 6053-6058, 6189-6215, 6307-6326, 6466-6495, 6598-6626). The interaction between soul and body, from experience (n. 6053-6058, 6189-6215, 6307-6327, 6466-6495, 6598-6626).

Section 3

Especially it must be understood that all correspondence with heaven is with the Lord's Divine Human, because heaven is from Him, and He is heaven, as has been shown in previous chapters. For if the Divine Human did not flow into all things of heaven, and in accordance with correspondences into all things of the world, no angel or man could exist. From this again it is evident why the Lord became Man and clothed His Divine from first to last with a Human. It was because the Divine Human, from which heaven existed before the Lord's coming, was no longer sufficient to sustain all things, for the reason that man, who is the foundation of the heavens, had subverted and destroyed order. What the Divine Human was before the Lord's coming, and what the condition of heaven was at that time may be seen in the extracts appended to the preceding chapter.

Angels are amazed when they hear that there are men who attribute all things to nature and nothing to the Divine, and who also believe that their body, into which so many wonders of heaven are gathered, is a product of nature. Still more are they amazed that the rational part of man is believed to be from nature, when, if men will but lift their minds a little, they can see that such effects are not from nature but from the Divine; and that nature has been created simply for clothing the spiritual and for presenting it in a correspondent form in the outmost of order. Such men they liken to owls, which see in darkness, but in light see nothing.

THERE IS A CORRESPONDENCE OF HEAVEN WITH ALL THINGS OF THE EARTH. What correspondence is has been told in the preceding chapter, and it has there been shown that each thing and all things of the animal body are correspondences. The next step is to show that all things of the earth, and in general all things of the universe, are correspondences.

All things of the earth are distinguished into three kinds, called kingdoms, namely, the animal kingdom, the vegetable kingdom, and the mineral kingdom. The things of the animal kingdom are correspondences in the first degree, because they live; the things of the vegetable kingdom are correspondences in the second degree, because they merely grow; the things of the mineral kingdom are correspondences in the third degree, because they neither live nor grow. Correspondences in the animal kingdom are living creatures of various kinds, both those that walk and creep on the ground and those that fly in the air; these need not be specially named, as they are well known. Correspondences in the vegetable kingdom are all things that grow and abound in gardens, forests, fields, and meadows; these, too, need not be named, because they are well known. Correspondences in the mineral kingdom are metals more and less noble, stones precious and not precious, earths of various kinds, and also the waters. Besides these the things prepared from them by human activity for use are correspondences, as foods of every kind, clothing, dwellings and other buildings, with many other things.

Also the things above the earth, as the sun, moon, and stars, and those in the atmosphere, as clouds, mists, rain, lightning and thunder, are likewise correspondences. Things resulting from the presence and absence of the sun, as light and shade, heat and cold, are also correspondences, as well as those that follow in succession therefrom, as the seasons of the year, spring, summer, autumn, and winter; and the times of day, morning, noon, evening, and night.

In a word, all things that have existence in nature, from the least to the greatest thereof, are correspondences. 106-1 They are correspondences because the natural world with all things in it springs forth and subsists from the spiritual world, and both worlds from the Divine. They are said to subsist also, because everything subsists from that from which it springs forth, subsistence being a permanent springing forth; also because nothing can subsist from itself, but only from that which is prior to itself, thus from a First, and if separated from that it would utterly perish and vanish.

Everything in nature that springs forth and subsists in accordance with Divine order is a correspondence. Divine order is caused by the Divine good that flows forth from the Lord. It begins in Him, goes forth from Him through the heavens in succession into the world, and is terminated there in outmosts; and everything there that is in accordance with order is a correspondence. Everything there is in accordance with order that is good and perfect for use, because everything good is good in the measure of its use; while its form has relation to truth, truth being the form of good. And for this reason everything in the whole world and of the nature thereof that is in Divine order has reference to good and truth. 107-1

That all things in the world spring from the Divine, and are clothed with such things in nature as enable them to exist there and perform use, and thus to correspond, is clearly evident from the various things seen in both the animal and vegetable kingdoms. In both there are things that any one who thinks interiorly can see to be from heaven. For illustration a few things out of a countless number may be mentioned; and first some things from the animal kingdom. Many are aware what knowledge there is engrafted as it were in every animal. Bees know how to gather honey from flowers, to build cells out of wax in which to store their honey, and thus provide food for themselves and their families, even for a coming winter. That a new generation may be born their queen lays eggs, and the rest take care of them and cover them. They live under a sort of government which all know by instinct. They preserve the working bees and cast out the drones, depriving them of their wings; besides other wonderful things implanted in them from heaven for the sake of their use, their wax everywhere serving the human race for candles, their honey for adding sweetness to food. [2] Again, what wonders do we see in worms, the meanest creatures in the animal kingdom! They know how to get food from the juice of the leaves suited to them, and afterward at the appointed time to invest themselves with a covering and enter as it were into a womb, and thus hatch offspring of their own kind. Some are first turned into nymphs and chrysalides, spinning threads about themselves; and this travail being over they come forth clad with a different body, furnished with wings with which they fly in the air as in their heaven, and celebrate marriages and lay eggs and provide posterity for themselves. [3] Besides these special instances all creatures in general that fly in the air know the proper food for their nourishment, not only what it is but where to find it; they know how to build nests for themselves, one kind in one way and another kind in another way; how to lay their eggs in the nests, how to sit upon them, how to hatch their young and feed them, and to turn them out of their home when they are able to shift for themselves. They know, too, their enemies that they must avoid and their friends with whom they may associate, and this from early infancy; not to mention the wonders in the eggs themselves, in which all things lie ready in their order for the formation and nourishment of the chicks; besides numberless other things. [4] Who that thinks from any wisdom of reason will ever say that these instincts are from any other source than the spiritual world, which the natural serves in clothing what is from it with a body, or in presenting in effect what is spiritual in the cause? The beasts of the earth and the birds of the air are born into all this knowledge, while man, who is far superior to them, is not; for the reason that animals are in the order of their life, and have not been able to destroy what is in them from the spiritual world, because they have no rational faculty. Man, on the other hand, whose thought is from the spiritual world, having perverted what is in him from that world by a life contrary to order, which his rational faculty has favored, must needs be born into mere ignorance and afterwards be led back by Divine means into the order of heaven.

How the things in the vegetable kingdom correspond can be seen from many instances, as that little seeds grow into trees, put forth leaves, produce flowers, and then fruit, in which again they deposit seed, these things taking place in succession and existing together in an order so wonderful as to be indescribable in a few words. Volumes might be filled, and yet there would be still deeper arcana, relating more closely to their uses, which science would be unable to exhaust. Since these things, too, are from the spiritual world, that is, from heaven, which is in the human form (as has been shown above in its own chapter), so all the particulars in this kingdom have a certain relation to such things as are in man, as some in the learned world know. That all things in this kingdom also are correspondences has been made clear to me by much experience. Often when I have been in gardens and have been looking at the trees, fruits, flowers, and plants there, I have recognized their correspondences in heaven, and have spoken with those with whom these were, and have been taught whence and what they were.

But at the present day no one can know the spiritual things in heaven to which the natural things in the world correspond except from heaven, since the knowledge of correspondences is now wholly lost. But the nature of the correspondence of spiritual things with natural I shall be glad to illustrate by some examples. The animals of the earth correspond in general to affection, mild and useful animals to good affections, fierce and useless ones to evil affections. In particular, cattle and their young correspond to the affections of the natural mind, sheep and lambs to the affections of the spiritual mind; while birds correspond, according to their species, to the intellectual things of the natural or the spiritual mind. 110-1 For this reason various animals, as cattle and their young, rams, sheep, he-goats, and she-goats, he-lambs and she-lambs, also pigeons and turtledoves, were devoted to a sacred use in the Israelitish Church, which was a representative church, and sacrifices and burnt offerings were made of them. For they correspond in that use to spiritual things, and in heaven these were understood in accordance with the correspondences. Moreover, animals according to their kinds and species, because they have life, are affections; and the life of each one is solely from affection and in accordance with affection; consequently every animal has an innate knowledge that is in accord with its life's affection. Man is like an animal so far as his natural man is concerned, and is therefore likened to animals in common speech; for example, if he is gentle he is called a sheep or lamb, if fierce a bear or wolf, if cunning a fox or serpent, and so on.

There is a like correspondence with things in the vegetable kingdom. In general, a garden corresponds to the intelligence and wisdom of heaven; and for this reason heaven is called the Garden of God, and Paradise; 111-1 and men call it the heavenly paradise. Trees, according to their species, correspond to the perceptions and knowledges of good and truth which are the source of intelligence and wisdom. For this reason the ancient people, who were acquainted with correspondences, held their sacred worship in groves; 111-2 and for the same reason trees are so often mentioned in the Word, and heaven, the church, and man are compared to them; as the vine, the olive, the cedar, and others, and the good works done by men are compared to fruits. Also the food derived from trees, and more especially from the grain harvests of the field, corresponds to affections for good and truth, because these affections feed the spiritual life, as the food of the earth does the natural life; 111-3 and bread from grain, in a general sense, because it is the food that specially sustains life, and because it stands for all food, corresponds to an affection for all good. It is on account of this correspondence that the Lord calls Himself the bread of life; and that loaves of bread had a holy use in the Israelitish Church, being placed on the table in the tabernacle and called "the bread of faces;" also the Divine worship that was performed by sacrifices and burnt offerings was called "bread." Moreover, because of this correspondence the most holy act of worship in the Christian Church is the Holy Supper, in which bread is given, and wine. 111-4 From these few examples the nature of correspondence can be seen.

How conjunction of heaven with the world is effected by means of correspondences shall also be told in a few words. The Lord's kingdom is a kingdom of ends, which are uses; or what is the same thing, a kingdom of uses which are ends. For this reason the universe has been so created and formed by the Divine that uses may be every where clothed in such a way as to be presented in act, or in effect, first in heaven and afterwards in the world, thus by degrees and successively, down to the outmost things of nature. Evidently, then, the correspondence of natural things with spiritual things, or of the world with heaven, is through uses, and uses are what conjoin; and the form in which uses are clothed are correspondences and are conjunctions just to the extent that they are forms of uses. In the nature of the world in its threefold kingdom, all things that exist in accordance with order are forms of uses, or effects formed from use for use, and this is why the things in nature are correspondences. But in the case of man, so far as he is in accordance with Divine order, that is, so far as he is in love to the Lord and in charity towards the neighbor, are his acts uses in form, and correspondences, and through these he is conjoined to heaven. To love the Lord and the neighbor means in general to perform uses. 112-1

Furthermore, it must be understood that man is the means by which the natural world and the spiritual world are conjoined, that is, man is the medium of conjunction, because in him there is a natural world and there is a spiritual world (see above, n. 57); consequently to the extent that man is spiritual he is the medium of conjunction; but to the extent that a man is natural, and not spiritual, he is not a medium of conjunction. Nevertheless, apart from this mediumship of man, a Divine influx into the world and into the things pertaining to man that are of the world goes on, but not into man's rational faculty.

As all things that are in accord with Divine order correspond to heaven, so all things contrary to Divine order correspond to hell. All things that correspond to heaven have relation to good and truth; but those that correspond to hell have relation to evil and falsity.

Something shall now be said about the knowledge of correspondences and its use. It has been said above that the spiritual world, which is heaven, is conjoined with the natural world by means of correspondences; therefore by means of correspondences communication with heaven is granted to man. For the angels of heaven do not think from natural things, as man does; but when man has acquired a knowledge of correspondences he is able, in respect to the thoughts of his mind, to be associated with the angels, and thus in respect to his spiritual or internal man to be conjoined with them. That there might be such a conjunction of heaven with man the Word was written wholly by correspondences, each thing and all things in it being correspondent. 114-1 If man, therefore, had a knowledge of correspondences he would understand the spiritual sense of the Word, and from that it would be given him to know arcana of which he sees nothing in the sense of the letter. For there is a literal sense and there is a spiritual sense in the Word, the literal sense made up of such things as are in the world, and the spiritual sense of such things as are in heaven. And such a Word, in which everything down to the least jot is a correspondence, was given to men because the conjunction of heaven with the world is effected by means of correspondences. 114-2

I have been taught from heaven that the most ancient men on our earth, who were celestial men, thought from correspondences themselves, the natural things of the world before their eyes serving them as means of thinking in this way; and that they could be in fellowship with angels and talk with them because they so thought, and that thus through them heaven was conjoined to the world. For this reason that period was called the Golden Age, of which it is said by ancient writers that the inhabitants of heaven dwelt with men and associated with them as friends with friends. But after this there followed a period when men thought, not from correspondences themselves, but from a knowledge of correspondences, and there was then also a conjunction of heaven with man, but less intimate. This period was called the Silver Age. After this there followed men who had a knowledge of correspondences but did not think from that knowledge, because they were in natural good, and not, like those before them in spiritual good. This period was called the Copper Age. After this man gradually became external, and finally corporeal, and then the knowledge of correspondences was wholly lost, and with it a knowledge of heaven and of the many things pertaining to heaven. It was from correspondence that these ages were named from gold, silver, and copper, 115-1 and for the reason that from correspondence gold signifies celestial good in which were the most ancient people, silver spiritual good in which were the ancient people that followed, and copper natural good in which were the next posterity; while iron, from which the last age takes its name, signifies hard truth apart from good.

THE SUN IN HEAVEN. In heaven neither the sun of the world, nor anything from that sun, is seen, because it is wholly natural. For nature has its beginning from that sun, and whatever is produced by means of it is called natural. But the spiritual, to which heaven belongs, is above nature and wholly distinct from what is natural; and there is no communication between the two except by correspondences. What the distinction between them is may be understood from what has been already said about degrees (n. 38), and what the communication is from what has been said in the two preceding chapters about correspondences.

Although the sun of the world is not seen in heaven, nor anything from that sun, there is nevertheless a sun there, and light and heat, and all things that are in the world, with innumerable others, but not from a like origin; since the things in heaven are spiritual, and those in the world are natural. The sun of heaven is the Lord; the light there is the Divine truth and the heat the Divine good that go forth from the Lord as a sun. From this origin are all things that spring forth and are seen in the heavens. This light and heat and things existing therefrom in heaven will be treated of in the following chapters; in this chapter we will speak only of the sun there. In heaven the Lord is seen as a sun, for the reason that He is Divine love, from which all spiritual things, and by means of the sun of the world all natural things, have their existence. That love is what shines as a sun.

That the Lord is actually seen in heaven as a sun I have not only been told by angels, but it has occasionally been granted me to see it; and therefore what I have heard and seen respecting the Lord as a sun I shall be glad to tell in a few words. The Lord is seen as a sun, not in heaven, but high above the heavens; and not directly overhead or in the zenith, but before the faces of the angels at a middle height. He is seen at a considerable distance, in two places, one before the right eye and the other before the left eye. Before the right eye He is seen exactly like a sun, as it were, with a glow and size like that of the sun of the world. But before the left eye He is not seen as a sun, but as a moon, glowing white like the moon of our earth, and of like size, but more brilliant, and surrounded with many little moons, as it were, each of them of similar whiteness and splendor. The Lord is seen so differently in two places because every person sees the Lord in accordance with the quality of his reception of the Lord, thus He is seen in one way by those that receive Him with the good of love, and in another by those that receive Him with the good of faith. Those that receive Him with the good of love see Him as a sun, fiery and flaming, in accordance with their reception of Him; these are in His celestial kingdom; while those that receive Him with the good of faith see Him as a moon, white and brilliant in accordance with their reception of Him, and these are in His spiritual kingdom. 118-1 This is so because good of love corresponds to fire; therefore in the spiritual sense fire is love; and the good of faith corresponds to light, and in the spiritual sense light is faith. 118-2 And the Lord appears before the eyes because the interiors, which belong to the mind, see through the eyes, from good of love through the right eye, and from good of faith through the left eye; 118-3 since with angels and also with men all things at the right correspond to good from which truth is derived, and all at the left to truth that is from good. 118-4 Good of faith is in its essence truth from good.

This is why in the Word the Lord in respect to love is likened to the sun, and in respect to faith to the moon; also that the "sun" signifies love from the Lord to the Lord, and the "moon" signifies faith from the Lord in the Lord, as in the following passages: The light of the moon shall be as the light of the sun, and the light of the sun shall be sevenfold, as the light of seven days (Isa. 30:26). And when I shall extinguish thee I will cover the heavens and make the stars thereof dark; I will cover the sun with a cloud, and the moon shall not make her light to shine. All luminaries of light in the heavens will I make dark over thee, and I will set darkness upon thy land (Ezek. 32:7, 8). I will darken the sun in his going forth, and the moon shall not make her light to shine (Isa. 13:10) The sun and the moon shall be darkened, and the stars shall withdraw their shining. The sun shall be turned into darkness and the moon into blood (Joel 2:2, 10, 31; 3:16). The sun became black as sackcloth and hair, and the moon became as blood, and the stars fell unto the earth (Apoc. 6:12, 13). Immediately after the affliction of those days the sun shall be darkened, and the moon shall not give her light, and the stars shall fall from heaven (Matt. 24:29). And elsewhere. In these passages the "sun" signifies love, and the "moon" faith, and the "stars" knowledges of good and truth. 119-1 These are said to be darkened, to lose their light, and to fall from heaven, when they are no more. That the Lord is seen as a sun in heaven is evident also from His appearance when transfigured before Peter, James, and John, That His face did shine as the sun (Matt. 17:2). These disciples thus saw the Lord when they were withdrawn from the body, and were in the light of heaven. It was because of this correspondence that the ancient people, with whom was a representative church, turned the face to the sun in the east when they were in Divine worship; and for the same reason they gave to their temples an eastern aspect.

How great the Divine love is and what it is can be seen by comparison with the sun of the world, that it is most ardent, if you will believe it, much more ardent than that sun. For this reason the Lord as a sun does not flow without mediums into the heavens, but the ardor of His love is gradually tempered on the way. These temperings appear as radiant belts about the sun; furthermore, the angels are veiled with a thin adapting cloud to prevent their being harmed by the influx. 120-1 For this reason the heavens are more or less near in accordance with reception. As the higher heavens are in good of love they are nearest to the Lord as the sun; and as the lower heavens are in good of faith they are farther away from Him. But those that are in no good, like those in hell, are farthest away, at different distances in accordance with their opposition to good. 120-2

When, however, the Lord appears in heaven, which often occurs, He does not appear encompassed with a sun, but in the form of an angel, yet distinguished from angels by the Divine shining through from His face, since He is not there in person, for in person the Lord is constantly encompassed by the sun, but He is present by look. For it is a common occurrence in heaven for persons to appear to be present in a place where their look is fixed or is terminated, even when this place is far away from where they really are. This presence is called the presence of internal sight, which will be treated of further on. I have also seen the Lord out of the sun in an angelic form, at a height a little below the sun; also near by in a like form, with shining face, and once in the midst of angels as a flame-like radiance.

To the angels the sun of the world appears like a dense darkness opposite to the sun of heaven, and the moon like a darkness opposite to the moon of heaven, and this constantly; and for the reason that the world's fieriness corresponds to the love of self, and the light from it corresponds to what is false from that love; and the love of self is the direct opposite of the Divine love; and what is false from that love is the direct opposite of the Divine truth; and the opposite of the Divine love and the Divine truth is to the angels thick darkness. Therefore, in the Word, to worship the sun and moon of this world and bow down to them, signifies to love self and the falsities that spring from the love of self, and it is said that such would be cut off. (Deut. 4:19; 16:3-5; Jer. 8:1, 2; Ezek. 8:15, 16, 18; Apoc. 16:8; Matt. 13:6). 122-1

As it is from the Divine love that is in and from Him that the Lord appears in heaven like a sun, so all in the heavens are turned constantly to Him those in the celestial kingdom to Him as a sun and those in the spiritual kingdom to Him as a moon. But those that are in hell turn themselves to an opposite darkness and dense darkness, that is, they turn backwards, away from the Lord; and for the reason that all in the hells are in love of self and the world, thus antagonistic to the Lord. Those who turn themselves to the dense darkness that is in the place where this world's sun is are in the hells behind, and are called genii; while those that turn themselves to the darkness that is in the place of the moon are in the hells more in front, and are called spirits. This is why those in the hells are said to be in darkness, and those in the heavens in light, "darkness" signifying falsity from evil, and "light" truth from good. They so turn themselves because all in the other life look towards what rules in their interiors, thus to their loves; and with angels and spirits the interiors determine the face; and in the spiritual world quarters are not fixed, as in the natural world, but are determined by the face. In respect to his spirit man turns himself in like manner as a spirit does, backwards from the Lord if he is in love of self and the world, and towards the Lord if he is in love to the Lord and the neighbor. But of this man is ignorant, because he is in the natural world where quarters are determined by the rising and setting of the sun. But as this cannot be easily comprehended by men it will be elucidated hereafter when Quarters, Space, and Time in Heaven are treated of.

Because the Lord is the sun of heaven and everything that is from Him looks to Him, He is also the common center, the source of all direction and determination. 124-1 So, too, all things beneath are in His presence and under His auspices, both in the heavens and on the earths.

From all this what has been said and shown in previous chapters about the Lord may now be seen in clearer light, namely: That He is the God of heaven (n. 2-6). That it is His Divine that makes heaven (n. 7-12). That the Lord's Divine in heaven is love to Him and charity towards the neighbor (n. 13-19). That there is a correspondence of all things of the world with heaven, and through heaven with the Lord (n. 87-115). Also that the sun and moon of the world are correspondences (n. 105).

LIGHT AND HEAT IN HEAVEN. That there is light in the heavens those who think from nature alone cannot comprehend; and yet such is the light in the heavens that it exceeds by many degrees the noon-day light of the world. That light I have often seen, even during the evening and night. At first I wondered when I heard the angels say that the light of this world is little more than a shadow in comparison with the light of heaven; but having seen it I can testify that it is so. The brightness and splendor of the light of heaven are such as cannot be described. All things that I have seen in the heavens have been seen in that light, thus more clearly and distinctly than things in this world.

The light of heaven is not a natural light, like the light of the world, but a spiritual light, because it is from the Lord as a sun, and that sun is the Divine love (as has been shown in the foregoing chapter). That which goes forth from the Lord as a sun is called in the heavens Divine truth, but in its essence it is Divine good united to Divine truth. From this the angels have light and heat, light from Divine truth, and heat from Divine good. As the light of heaven, and the heat also, are from such a source, it is evident that they are spiritual and not natural. 127-1

The Divine truth is light to the angels because the angels are spiritual and not natural. Spiritual beings see from their sun, and natural beings from theirs. It is from Divine truth that angels have understanding, and their understanding is their inner sight, which flows into and produces their outer sight; therefore in heaven whatever is seen from the Lord as the sun is seen in light. 128-1 This being the source of light in heaven the light is varied there in accordance with the reception of Divine truth from the Lord; or what is the same, in accordance with the intelligence and wisdom in which the angels are, thus differently in the celestial kingdom and in the spiritual kingdom, and differently in each society. In the celestial kingdom the light appears flaming because the angels there receive light from the Lord as a sun; but in the spiritual kingdom the light is shining white, because the angels there receive light from the Lord as a moon (see above, n. 118). So, too, the light differs in different societies, and again in each society, those that are at the center being in greater light and those in the circumference in less light (see n. 43). In a word, the angels have light in the same degree in which they are recipients of Divine truth, that is, are in intelligence and wisdom from the Lord; 128-2 and this is why the angels of heaven are called angels of light.

As the Lord in the heavens is Divine truth, and the Divine truth there is light, so in the Word He is called Light, likewise all truth is from Him, as in the following passages: Jesus said, I am the light of the world; he that followeth Me shall not walk in darkness, but shall have the light of life (John 8:12). As long as I am in the world I am the light of the world (John 9:5). Jesus said, Yet a little while is the light with you. Walk while ye have the light, lest darkness overtake you. While ye have the light believe in the light, that ye may be sons of light. I have come a light into the world, that whosoever believeth in Me may not abide in darkness (John 12:35, 36, 46). Light has come into the world, but men have loved the darkness rather than the light (John 3:19). John says of the Lord: This is the true light which lighteneth every man (John 1:9). The people that sit in darkness have seen a great light, and to them that were sitting in the shadow of death light is sprung up (Matt. 4:16). I will give thee for a covenant of the people, for a light of the Gentiles (Isa. 13:6). I have established Thee for a light of the Gentiles that Thou mayest be My salvation unto the end of the earth (Isa. 19:6). The nations of them that are saved shall walk in His light (Apoc. 21:24). Send out Thy light and Thy truth; let them lead me (Psalm 43:3). In these and other passages the Lord is called light from Divine truth, which is from Him; and the truth itself is likewise called light. As light in the heavens is from the Lord as a sun, so when He was transfigured before Peter, James, and John: His face did shine as the sun, and His raiment was white as the light (Matt. 17:2). And His garments became shining, exceeding white as snow, so as no fuller on earth can whiten them (Mark 9:3; Matt. 17:2). The Lord's garments had this appearance because they represented Divine truth which is from Him in the heavens, "garments" also in the Word signifying truths, 129-1 consequently it is said in David: O Jehovah, Thou coverest Thyself with light as with a garment (Psalm 104:2).

That light in the heavens is spiritual and that this light is Divine truth may be inferred also from the fact that men as well as angels have spiritual light, and have enlightenment from that light so far as they are in intelligence and wisdom from Divine truth. Man's spiritual light is the light of his understanding, and the objects of that light are truths, which he arranges analytically into groups, forms into reason, and from them draws conclusions in series. 130-1 The natural man does not know that the light from which the understanding sees such things is a real light, for he neither sees it with his eyes nor perceives it by thought. And yet there are many who recognize this light, and distinguish it from the natural light in which those are who think naturally and not spiritually. Those think naturally who take account of the world only, and attribute all things to nature; while those think spiritually who take account of heaven and attribute all things to the Divine. It has often been granted me to perceive and also to see that there is a true light that enlightens the mind, wholly distinct from the light that is called natural light [lumen]. I have been raised up interiorly into that light by degrees; and as I was raised up my understanding became so enlightened as to enable me to perceive what I did not perceive before, and finally such things as I could not even comprehend by thought from natural light. Sometimes I felt indignant that I could not comprehend these things when they were so clearly and plainly perceived in the light of heaven. 130-2 Because there is a light that belongs to the understanding, the same things are said of it as of the eye, as that it sees and is in light when it perceives, and is in obscurity and shade when it does not perceive, and so on.

As the light of heaven is Divine truth, that light is also Divine wisdom and intelligence; therefore to be raised up into the light of heaven means the same as to be raised up into intelligence and wisdom and enlightened. For this reason the angels have light in just the same degree as they have intelligence and wisdom. Because the light of heaven is Divine wisdom, in that light the character of everyone is recognized. The interiors of everyone lie open to view in his face just as they are, with not the least thing hidden. And interior angels love to have all things that pertain to them lying open, since they will nothing but good. It is otherwise with those beneath heaven, who do not will what is good, and for that reason fear greatly to be seen in the light of heaven. And wonderful to tell, while those in hell appear to one another as men, in the light of heaven they appear as monsters, with a horrid face and body, the exact form of their own evil. 131-1 In respect to his spirit man appears, when seen by angels, in a like way; if good as a man, beautiful in accord with his good; if evil as a monster, ugly in accord with his evil. From this it is clear that in the light of heaven all things are made manifest, and for the reason that the light of heaven is Divine truth.

As Divine truth is light in the heavens, so all truths wherever they are, whether within an angel or outside of him, or whether within the heavens or outside of them, emit light. Nevertheless, truths outside of the heavens do not shine as truths within the heavens do. Truths outside of the heavens shine coldly, like something snowy, without heat, because they do not draw their essence from good, as truths within the heavens do; therefore that cold light vanishes as soon as the light of heaven falls on it, and if there is evil underneath it it is turned into darkness. This I have occasionally seen, with many other noteworthy things about the shining of truth, which must be omitted here.

Something shall now be said about the heat of heaven. That heat in its essence is love. It goes forth from the Lord as a sun, which is Divine love in the Lord and from the Lord, as has been shown in the preceding chapter. It is evident, therefore, that the heat of heaven, like the light of heaven, is spiritual, because from the same source. 133-1 There are two things that go forth from the Lord as a sun, Divine truth and Divine good; Divine truth is manifested in the heavens as light, and Divine good as heat; and yet Divine truth and Divine good are so united that they are not two, but one. Nevertheless, with angels they are separate, for there are angels that receive more of Divine good than of Divine truth, and there are those that receive more of Divine truth than of Divine good. Those who receive more of Divine good are in the Lord's celestial kingdom, and those who receive more of Divine truth are in His spiritual kingdom. Those that receive both in a like degree are the most perfect angels.

The heat of heaven, like the light of heaven, is everywhere different. It is different in the celestial kingdom from what it is in the spiritual kingdom, and it is different in each society therein. It differs both in degree and in quality. It is more intense and more pure in the Lord's celestial kingdom, because the angels there receive more of Divine good; and it is less intense and pure in His spiritual kingdom, because the angels there receive more of Divine truth. Also in each society the heat differs in accordance with reception. There is heat in the hells, but it is unclean heat. 134-1 The heat in heaven is what is meant by holy and heavenly fire, and the heat of hell by profane and infernal fire. Both mean love - heavenly fire meaning love to the Lord and love to the neighbor and every affection of those loves, and infernal fire meaning love of self and love of the world and every lust of those loves. That love is heat from a spiritual source is shown from one's growing warm with love; for in accordance with the strength and nature of his love a man is inflamed and grows warm; and the heat of his love is made manifest when it is opposed. From this also it is customary to speak of being inflamed, growing hot, burning, boiling, being on fire, both in regard to the affections of the love of good and the lusts of the love of evil.

Love going forth from the Lord as a sun is felt in heaven as heat, because the interiors of the angels are in a state of love from the Divine good that is from the Lord; and in consequence their exteriors which grow warm therefrom are in a state of heat. For this reason heat and love so correspond to each other in heaven that everyone there is in heat such as his love is, according to what has been said just above. This world's heat does not enter heaven at all, because it is too gross, and is natural, and not spiritual; but with men it is otherwise, because they are in both the spiritual world and the natural world. As to their spirits they grow warm in exact accordance with their loves; but as to the body they grow warm both from the heat of their spirit and from the heat of the world. The former flows into the latter, because they correspond. The nature of the correspondence of the two kinds of heat can be seen from animal life, in that the love of animals-the chief of which is the love of propagating offspring of their kind-bursts forth and becomes active in accordance with the presence and influence of heat from the sun of the world, which is the heat of the spring and the summer seasons. Those who believe that the world's heat flows in and excites these loves are greatly mistaken, for there can be no influx from the natural into the spiritual, but only from the spiritual into the natural. This influx is of Divine order, but the other would be contrary to Divine order. 135-1

Angels, like men, have understanding and will. The light of heaven constitutes the life of their understanding, because that light is Divine truth and Divine wisdom therefrom; and the heat of heaven constitutes the life of their will, because that heat is Divine good and Divine love therefrom. The veriest life of the angels is from heat, and from light only so far as heat is in it. That life is from heat is shown by the fact that when heat is taken away life perishes. The same is true of faith without love or of truth without good; since the truth that is called truth of faith is light, and the good that is called good of love is heat. 136-1 This is more clearly shown by the heat and light of the world, to which the heat and light of heaven correspond. By the world's heat when conjoined with light, as in spring and summer, all things on the earth are quickened and grow, but by light separate from heat nothing is quickened or grows, but everything lies torpid and dies. They are not conjoined in winter, when heat is absent though light remains. From this correspondence heaven is called paradise, since truth is there joined with good, or faith with love, as light is with heat in springtime on the earth. All this makes more clear the truth set forth in its own chapter (n. 13-19), that the Divine of the Lord in Heaven is love to Him and charity towards the neighbor.

It is said in John: In the beginning was the Word, and the Word was with God, and God was the Word. All things were made through Him, and without Him was not any thing made that hath been made. In Him was life, and the life was the light of men. He was in the world, and the world was made through Him. And the Word became flesh and dwelt among us, and we beheld His glory (1:1-14). Evidently the Lord is here meant by "the Word," for it is said that "the Word became flesh." But what is specifically meant by "the Word" is not known and shall therefore be explained. Here "the Word" means the Divine truth which is in the Lord and from the Lord; 137-1 and this is why it is also called "the Light," which is the Divine truth, as has been already shown in this chapter. That it was by means of Divine truth that all things were created and made shall now be explained. [2] In heaven Divine truth has all power, and apart from it there is no power whatever. 137-2 From the Divine truth angels are called powers, and are powers to the extent that they are recipients or receptacles of it. By means of it they prevail over the hells and over all that oppose them. A thousand enemies there cannot stand against a single ray of the light of heaven, which is Divine truth. As angels are angels by their reception of Divine truth it follows that the entire heaven is from no other source, since heaven consists of angels. [3] That there is such power in Divine truth those cannot believe that have no other idea of truth than that it is thought or speech, which has in it no power except as others do it from obedience. But Divine truth has power in itself, and such power that by means of it heaven was created and the world with all things therein. That there is such power in Divine truth may be shown by two comparisons-by the power of truth and good in man, and by the power of light and heat from the sun in the world. By the power of good and truth in man, in that everything that a man does he does from his understanding and will-from his will by means of good and from his understanding by means of truth; for all things in the will have relation to good and all things in the understanding have relation to truth. 137-3 Therefore it is from good and truth that man moves his whole body, and a thousand things therein rush with one accord to do their will and pleasure. This makes clear that the whole body is formed for subservience to good and truth, consequently is formed by good and truth. [4] By the power of heat and light from the sun in the world, in that all things that grow in the world, as trees, cereals, flowers, grasses, fruits, and seeds, come into existence wholly by means of the heat and light of the sun; which shows what power of producing there is in them. What, then, must be the power in Divine light, which is Divine truth, and in Divine heat, which is Divine good? Because heaven has its existence from these, so does the world have its existence therefrom, since the world has its existence by means of heaven, as has been already shown. From all this the meaning of these words can be seen that "all things were made through the Word, and without the Word was not anything made that has been made;" also that "the world was made through Him," that is, through Divine truth from the Lord. 137-4 For the same reason, in the Book of Creation, light is first spoken of, and then the things that are from light (Gen. 1:3, 4). For this reason also all things in the universe, both in heaven and in the world, have relation to good and truth and to their conjunction, in order to be any thing.

It must be understood that the Divine good and the Divine truth that are from the Lord as a sun in the heavens are not in the Lord, but are from the Lord. In the Lord there is only Divine love, which is the Being [Esse] from which the Divine good and the Divine truth spring. Outgo [existere] from being [esse] is meant by going forth [procedere]. This, too, can be made clear by comparison with the world's sun. The heat and light that are in the world are not in the sun, but are from the sun. In the sun there is fire only, and it is from this that heat and light spring and go forth.

Since the Lord as a sun is Divine love, and Divine love is Divine good itself, the Divine that goes forth from the Lord, which is His Divine in heaven, is called, for the sake of distinction, Divine truth, although it is in fact Divine good united to Divine truth. This Divine truth is what is called the Holy that goes forth from Him.

THE FOUR QUARTERS IN HEAVEN. Both in heaven and in the world there are four quarters, east, south, west, and north, determined in each world by its own sun; in heaven by the sun of heaven, which is the Lord, in the world by the sun of the world. And yet there are great differences between them. In the first place, in the world that is called the south where the sun is in its greatest altitude above the earth, north where it is in its opposite position beneath the earth, east where it rises at an equinox, and west where it then sets. Thus in the world it is from the south that all the quarters are determined. But in heaven that is called the east where the Lord is seen as a sun, opposite to this is the west, at the right is the south in heaven, and at the left the north; and this in whatever direction the face and the body are turned. Thus in heaven it is from the east that all the quarters are determined. That is called the east [oriens] where the Lord is seen as a sun, because all origin [origo] of life is from Him as a sun; moreover, so far as angels receive heat and light or love and intelligence from the Lord He is said to arise [exoriri] upon them. For the same reason the Lord is called the East [Oriens] in the Word. 141-1

Another difference is that to the angels the east is always before the face, the west behind, the south to the right, and the north to the left. But since this cannot be easily comprehended in the world, for the reason that men turn the face to every quarter, it shall be explained. The entire heaven turns itself to the Lord as to its common center; to that center do all the angels turn themselves. Also on the earth, as is well known, there is a directing of all things towards a common center; but there is this difference between this directing in the world and that in heaven, that in heaven the front parts are turned to the common center, but in the world the lower parts of the body. In the world this directing is called centripetal force, also gravitation. The interiors of angels are actually turned forwards; and since interiors manifest themselves in the face it is the face that determines the quarters. 142-1

It is still more difficult to comprehend in the world that in every turning of their face and body the angels have the east before the face, since man according as he turns, has every quarter before his face. This shall also be explained. Although angels, like men, turn and direct their faces and bodies in every direction, they nevertheless have the east always before their eyes. But the turnings of angels are unlike the turnings of men, because they are from a different origin. They appear alike, but they are not. The origin of these turnings is their ruling love, and from this all directions with angels and spirits are determined, for, as just said, their interiors are actually turned towards their common center, which in heaven is the Lord as a sun; consequently their ruling love is always before their face, because their love is always before their interiors, and the face has existence from the interiors, for it is their outward form; and in the heavens this love is the Lord as a sun because it is from Him that they have their love. 143-1 And as the Lord Himself is in angels in His love, it is the Lord who causes them to look to Him whithersoever they turn. This cannot be explained any farther now; but it will be made clearer to the understanding in subsequent chapters, especially where representations and appearances, and time and space in heaven, are treated of. That the angels have the Lord constantly before their faces it has been granted me to know and also to perceive from much experience; for whenever I have been in company with angels I have noticed the Lord's presence before my face, not actually seen, and yet perceptible in a light; and angels have often testified that this is so. As the Lord is constantly before the faces of the angels, so it is said in the world of those who believe in the Lord and love Him that they have God before their eyes and their face, and that they look to God, and see God. These expressions have their origin in the spiritual world, from which are many things in human speech, although their source is unknown to men.

This turning to the Lord is among the wonderful things in heaven. There may be many together in one place, some turning the face and body one way and some another, and yet all see the Lord before them, and have everyone has the south at his right, the north at his left, and the west behind him. Another wonderful thing is that, although the angels look only to the east they have also a look towards the other three quarters; but the look to these is from their interior sight, which pertains to their thought. And it is yet another wonderful thing that in heaven no one is ever permitted to stand behind another and look at the back of his head, for this would disturb the influx of good and truth from the Lord.

The Lord is seen by the angels, and the angels are seen by the Lord in another way. Angels see the Lord through their eyes; but the Lord sees the angels in the forehead, and this for the reason that the forehead corresponds to love, and it is through love that the Lord flows into their will, while it is through the understanding, to which the eyes correspond, that He causes Himself to be seen. 145-1

The quarters in the heavens that give form to the Lord's celestial kingdom differ from the quarters in the heavens that give form to His spiritual kingdom, for the reason that He is seen by the angels in His celestial kingdom as a sun, but by the angels in His spiritual kingdom as a moon; and where the Lord is seen is the east. The distance there between the position of the sun and that of the moon is thirty degrees, and there is a like difference in the position of the quarters. That heaven is divided into two kingdoms, called the celestial kingdom and the spiritual kingdom, may be seen in its own chapter (n. 20-28); and that the Lord is seen in the celestial kingdom as a sun, and in the spiritual kingdom as a moon (n. 118). But it does not follow that the quarters of heaven become confused on this account, for neither can the spiritual angels ascend among the celestial angels, nor the celestial descend among the spiritual, as may be seen above (n. 35).

This makes clear the nature of the Lord's presence in the heavens, that He is everywhere and with everyone in the good and truth that go forth from Him; consequently He is with angels in what is His own, as has been said above (n. 12). The perception of the Lord's presence is in their interiors; and it is from these that their eyes see, and it is by this continuity that they see the Lord outside of themselves. This shows what is meant by the Lord's being in them and they in Him, according to His own words: Abide in Me and I in you (John 15:4). He that eateth My flesh and drinketh My blood abideth in Me and I in him (John 6:56). "The Lord's flesh" signifies Divine good and "His blood" Divine truth. 147-1

All in the heavens have their own places of abode in accordance with the quarters. Those who are in the good of love dwell towards the east and west, those who are in clear perception of it towards the east, and those who are in obscure perception of it towards the west. Those who are in wisdom from the good of love dwell towards the south and north-those who are in the clear light of wisdom towards the south, and those who are in obscure light of it towards the north. The angels of the Lord's spiritual kingdom and those of His celestial kingdom dwell in a like order, but differently as their good of love and light of truth from good differ; for in the celestial kingdom the love is love to the Lord, and the light of truth therefrom is wisdom; while in the spiritual kingdom there is love towards the neighbor, which is called charity, and the light of truth therefrom is intelligence, which is also called faith (see above, n. 23). The quarters differ also in the two kingdoms by thirty degrees, as has been said just above (n. 146).

In like order the angels in each society in heaven dwell in relation to one another-towards the east there those who are in greater degree of love and charity, towards the west those who are in less degree; towards the south those who are in greater light of wisdom and intelligence, and towards the north those who are in less. This arrangement prevails because each society represents heaven, and is a heaven in a smaller form (see above, n. 51-58). The same arrangement prevails in their assemblies. They are brought into this order by virtue of the form of heaven, from which everyone knows his own place. The Lord also provides that there be in each society those of every kind, for the reason that in form heaven is every where like itself; and yet the arrangement of the whole heaven differs from the arrangement of a society as what is general from its parts, since the societies towards the east surpass those towards the west, and those towards the south surpass those towards the north.

Because of this the quarters in the heavens signify such things as pertain to those that dwell in them, - the east signifying love and its good clearly perceived, the west the same obscurely perceived, the south wisdom and intelligence in clear light, and the north the same in obscure light. And because of this signification of the quarters in heaven they have a like signification in the internal or spiritual sense of the Word, 150-1 since the internal or spiritual sense of the Word is in entire accord with what is in heaven.

Footnotes
106-1 All things that are in the world and its three kingdoms correspond to the heavenly things that are in heaven, that is, the things in the natural world correspond to the things in the spiritual world (n. 1632, 1881, 2758, 2760-2763, 2987-3003, 3213-3227, 3483, 3624-3649, 4044, 4053, 4116, 4366, 4939, 5116, 5377, 5428, 5477, 9280). By correspondences the natural world is conjoined to the spiritual world (n. 8615). For this reason all nature is a theatre representative of the Lord's kingdom (n. 2758, 2999, 3000, 3483, 4938, 4939, 8848, 9280).

107-1 Everything in the universe, both in heaven and in the world, that is in accordance with order, has reference to good and truth (n. 2451, 3166, 4390, 4409, 5232, 7256, 10122); and to the conjunction of these, in order to be any thing (n. 10555).

110-1 From correspondence animals signify affections; mild and useful animals good affections, fierce and useless ones evil affections (n. 41, 45, 46, 142, 143, 246, 714, 716, 719, 2179, 2180, 3519, 9280); illustrated by experience from the spiritual world (n. 3218, 5198, 9090). Influx of the spiritual world into the lives of animals in. 1633, 3646). Cattle and their young from correspondence signify affections of the natural mind (n. 2180, 2566, 9391, 10132, 10407). What sheep signify (n. 4169, 4809); and lambs (n. 3994, 10132). Flying creatures signify intellectual things (n. 40, 745, 776, 778, 866, 988, 991, 5149, 7441); with a difference according to their genera and species, from experience in the spiritual world (n. 3219).

111-1 From correspondence a garden and a paradise signify intelligence and wisdom (n. 100, 108); from experience (n. 3220). All things that have a correspondence have in the Word the same significance (n. 2896, 2987, 2989, 2990, 2991, 3002, 3225).

111-2 Trees signify perceptions and knowledges (n. 103, 2163, 2682, 2722, 2972, 7692). For this reason the ancient people held Divine worship in groves under trees according to their correspondence (n. 2722, 4552). Influx of heaven into subjects of the vegetable kingdom, as into trees and plants (n. 3648).

111-3 From correspondence foods signify such things as nourish the spiritual life (n. 3114, 4459, 4792, 4976, 5147, 5293, 5340, 5342, 5410, 5426, 5576, 5582, 5588, 5655, 5915, 6277, 8562, 9003).

111-4 Bread signifies every good that nourishes the spiritual life of man (n. 2165, 2177, 3478, 3735, 3813, 4211, 4217, 4735, 4976, 9323, 9545, 10686). Such was the signification of the loaves that were on the table in the tabernacle (n. 3478, 9545). Sacrifices in general were called bread (n. 2165). Bread includes all food (n. 2165). Thus it signifies all heavenly and spiritual food (n. 276, 680, 2165, 2177, 3478, 6118, 8410).

112-1 Every good has its delight as well as its quality from use and in accordance with use; therefore such as the use is, such is the good (n. 3049, 4984, 7038). Angelic life consists in the goods of love and charity, that is, in performing uses (n. 454). The Lord, and consequently the angels, look only, in regard to man, to ends, which are uses (n. 1317, 1645, 5854). The Lord's kingdom is a kingdom of uses that is, of ends (n. 454, 696, 1103, 3645, 4054, 7038). Serving the Lord is performing uses (n. 7038). Each thing and all things in man have been formed for use (n. 3626, 4104, 5189 9297; also from use, that is, the use is prior to the organic forms in man through which the use is performed, because use is from the inflowing of the Lord through heaven in. 4223, 4926). Moreover man's interiors, which constitute his mind, when he grows to maturity are formed from use and for use (n. 1964, 6815, 9297). Consequently man is such as are the uses with him (n. 1568, 3570, 4054, 6571, 6935, 6938, 10284). Uses are the ends for the sake of which (n. 3565, 4054, 4104, 6815). Use is the first and the last, thus the all of man (n. 1964).

114-1 The Word was written wholly by correspondences (n. 8615). By means, of the Word man has conjunction with heaven (n. 2899, 6943, 9396, 9400, 9401, 10375, 10452).

114-2 Concerning the spiritual sense of the Word see the little work on The White Horse referred to in the Apocalypse.

115-1 Gold from correspondence signifies celestial good (n. 113, 1551, 1552,

5658, 6914, 6917, 9510, 9874, 9881). Silver signifies spiritual good, that is, truth from a celestial origin (n. 1551, 1552, 2954, 5658). Copper signifies natural good (n. 425, 1551). Iron signifies truth in the outmost of order (n. 425, 426).

118-1 The Lord is seen in heaven as a sun, and is the sun of heaven (n. 1053, 3636, 3643, 4060). The Lord is seen as a sun by those who are in His celestial kingdom, where love to Him reigns, and as a moon by those who are in His spiritual kingdom, where charity to the neighbor and faith reign (n. 1521, 1529-1531, 1837, 4696). The Lord is seen as a sun at a middle height before the right eye, and an a moon before the left eye (n. 1053, 1521, 1529-1531, 3636, 3643, 4321, 5097, 7078, 7083, 7173, 7270, 8812, 10809). The Lord is seen as a sun and as a moon (n. 1531, 7173). The Lord's Divine Itself is far above His Divine in heaven (n. 7270, 8760).

118-2 "Fire" in the Word signifies love, both in a good sense and in a bad sense (n. 934, 4906, 5215). Holy or heavenly fire signifies the Divine Love (n. 934, 6314, 6832). Infernal fire signifies love of self and of the world and every lust of those loves (n. 1861, 5071, 6314, 6832, 7575, 10747). Love is the fire of life and life itself is really from it (n. 4906, 5071, 6032, 6314). "Light" signifies the truth of faith (n. 3195, 3485, 3636, 3643, 3993, 4302, 4413, 4415, 9548, 9684).

118-3 The sight of the left eye corresponds to truths of faith, and the sight of the right eye to their goods (n. 4410, 6923).

118-4 The things on man's right have relation to good from which is truth, and those on his left to truth from good (n. 9495, 9604).

119-1 "Stars" and "constellations" in the Word signify knowledges of good and truth (n. 2495, 2849, 4697).

120-1 What the Lord's Divine love is, and how great it is, illustrated by comparison with the fire of this world's sun (n. 6834, 6849, 8644). The Lord's Divine love is love toward the whole human race to save it (n. 1820, 1865, 2253, 6872). The love that first goes forth from the fire of the Lord's love does not enter heaven, but is seen as radiant belts about the sun (n. 7270). The angels are veiled with a corresponding thin cloud, to prevent their being harmed by the glow of burning love (n. 6849).

120-2 The Lord's presence with the angels is in proportion to their reception of good of love and faith from Him (n. 904, 4198, 4320, 6280, 6832, 7042, 8819, 9680, 9682, 9683, 10106, 10811). The Lord appears to each one in accordance with what he is (n. 1861, 3235, 4198, 4206). The hells are at a distance from the heavens because they cannot bear the presence of Divine love from the Lord (n. 4299, 7519, 7738, 7989, 8137, 8265, 9327). For this reason the hells are very far away from the heavens, and this is the "great gulf" (n. 9346, 10187).

122-1 The sun of the world is not seen by the angels, but in its place something dark behind, opposite to the sun of heaven or the Lord (n. 7078, 9755). In the opposite sense the sun signifies the love of self (n. 2441); and in this sense "to worship the sun" signifies to worship what is contrary to heavenly love or to the Lord (n. 2441, 10584). To those in the hells the sun of heaven is thick darkness (n. 2441).

124-1 The Lord is the common center to which all things of heaven turn (n. 3633, 3641).

127-1 All light in the heavens is from the Lord as a sun (n. 1053, 1521, 3195, 3341, 3636, 3643, 4415, 9548, 9684, 10809). The Divine truth that goes forth from the Lord appears in heaven as light, and furnishes all the light of heaven (n. 3195, 3222, 3223, 5400, 8644, 9399, 9548, 9684).

128-1 The light of heaven illumines both the sight and the understanding of angels and spirits (n. 2776, 3138).

128-2 The light in heaven is in harmony with the intelligence and wisdom of the angels (n. 1524, 1529, 1530, 3339). Differences of light in the heavens are as many as there are angelic societies; and as there are in the heavens endless varieties of good and truth, so are there of wisdom and intelligence (n. 684, 690, 3241, 3744, 3745, 4414, 5598, 7236, 7833, 7836).

129-1 In the Word "garments" signify truths, because truths clothe good (n. 1073, 2576, 5248, 5319, 5954, 9216, 9952, 10536). The Lord's garments when He was transfigured signified Divine truth going forth from His Divine love (n. 9212, 9216).

130-1 Man is rational because his understanding is illumined by the light of heaven (n. 1524, 3138, 3167, 4408, 6608, 8707, 9128, 9399, 10569). The understanding is enlightened because it is a recipient of truth (n. 6222, 6608, 10659). The understanding is enlightened to the extent that man receives truth in good from the lord (n. 3619). The understanding is such as are the truths from good by which it is formed (n. 10064). The understanding has light from heaven, as the sight has light from the world (n. 1524, 5114, 6608, 9128). The light of heaven from the Lord is always present with man, but it flows in only in the degree that man is in truth from good (n. 4060, 4214).

130-2 When man is raised up from the sensual he comes into a milder light, and at length into heavenly light (n. 6313, 6315, 9407). When man is raised up into intelligence there is an actual elevation into the light of heaven (n. 3190). How great a light was perceived when I was withdrawn from worldly ideas (n. 1526, 6608).

131-1 Those in the hells, in their own light, which is like the light from burning coals, appear to themselves as men but in the light of heaven they appear as monsters (n. 4531, 4533, 4674, 5057, 5058, 6605, 6626).

133-1 There are two sources of heat and also two sources of light, the sun of the world and the sun of heaven (n. 3338, 5215, 7324). Heat from the Lord as a sun is affection of love (n. 3636, 3643). Therefore spiritual heat in its essence is love (n. 2146, 3338, 3339, 6314).

134-1 There is heat in the hells, but it is unclean (n. 1773, 2757, 3340). The odor from it is like the odor from dung and excrement in the world and in the worst hells like the odor of dead bodies (n. 814, 815, 817, 819, 820, 943, 944, 5394).

135-1 There is spiritual influx, but not physical, that is, there is influx from the spiritual world into the natural, but not from the natural world into the spiritual (n. 3219, 5119, 5259, 5427, 5428, 5477, 6322, 9109, 9110, 9111).

136-1 Truths apart from good are not in themselves truths because they have no life; for truths have all their life from good (n. 9603). Thus truths apart from good are like a body without a soul (n. 3180, 9154). Truths apart from good are not accepted by the Lord (n. 4368). What truth apart from good, that is, what faith apart from love is, and what truth from good or faith from love is (n. 1949-1951, 1964, 5830, 5951). It amounts to the same thing whether you say truth or faith, or whether you say good or love, since truth is of faith and good is of love (n. 2839, 4352, 4353, 4997, 7178, 7623, 7624, 10367).

137-1 In the Sacred Scripture word signifies various things, namely, speech, thought of the mind, any thing that really exists, also something, and in the highest sense Divine truth, and the Lord (n. 9987). "Word" signifies Divine truth (n. 2803, 2894, 4692, 5075, 5272, 9383, 9987). "Word" signifies the Lord (n. 2533, 2859).

137-2 Divine truth going forth from the Lord has all power (n. 6948, 8200). Truth from good has all power in heaven (n. 3091, 3563, 6344, 6423, 8304, 9643, 10019, 10182). Angels are called powers, and are powers by the reception of Divine truth from the Lord (n. 9639). Angels are recipients of Divine truth from the Lord and therefore in the Word are sometimes called gods (n. 4295, 4402, 7873, 8192, 8301).

137-3 The understanding is a recipient of truth, and the will a recipient of good (n. 3623, 6125, 7503, 9300, 9930). Therefore all things in the understanding have relation to truths, whether they are really truths or are believed by man to be truths, and all things in the will in like manner have relation to goods (n. 803, 10122).

137-4 Divine truth going forth from the Lord is the only real thing (n. 6880, 7004, 8200). By means of Divine truth all things were created and made (n. 2803, 2884, 5272, 7678).

141-1 In the highest sense the Lord is the east [oriens], because He is the sun of heaven, which is always rising and never setting (n. 101, 5097, 9668).

142-1 In heaven all turn themselves to the Lord (n. 9828, 10130, 10189, 10420). Nevertheless, it is not the angels that turn themselves to the Lord, but the Lord turns the angels to Himself (n. 10189). It is not that the angels are present with the Lord, but the Lord is present with the angels (n. 9415).

143-1 In the spiritual world all constantly turn themselves to their loves; and the quarters there have their beginning in the face and are determined by it (n. 10130, 10189, 10420, 10702). The face is formed to a correspondence with the interiors (n. 4791-4805, 5695). Therefore the interiors shine forth from the face (n. 3527, 4066, 4796). With angels the face makes one with the interiors (n. 4796, 4797, 4799, 5695, 8250). The influx of the interiors into the face and its muscles (n. 3631, 4800).

145-1 The forehead corresponds to heavenly love; therefore in the Word the "forehead" signifies that love (n. 9936). The eye corresponds to the understanding, because the understanding is internal sight (n. 2701, 4410, 4526, 9051, 10569). For this reason "to lift up the eyes" and "to see" signifies to understand, perceive, and observe (n. 2789, 2829, 3198, 3202, 4083, 4086, 4339, 5684).

147-1 In the Word "the Lord's flesh" signifies His Divine Human, and the Divine good of His love (n. 3813, 7850, 9127, 10283). And "the Lord's blood" signifies Divine truth and the holy of faith (n. 4735, 4978, 6978, 7317, 7326, 7846, 7850, 7877, 9127, 9393, 10026, 10033, 10152, 10210).

150-1 In the Word the "east" signifies love clearly perceived (n. 1250, 3708); the "west" love obscurely perceived (n. 3708, 9653); the "south" a state of light, that is, of wisdom and intelligence (n. 1458, 3708, 5672); and the "north" that state in obscurity (n. 3708).

Section 4

The reverse is true of those in the hells. Those who are there do not look to the Lord as a sun nor as a moon; but they look backward away from the Lord to that dense darkness that is in the place of the sun of the world, and to the darkness that is in the place of the earth's moon. Those that are called genii look to that dense darkness that is in the place of the world's sun, and those called spirits look to the darkness that is in the place of the earth's moon. 151·1 It has been shown above (n. 122) that the world's sun and the earth's moon are not seen in the spiritual world, but in place of that sun a dense darkness over against the sun of heaven, and in place of that moon a darkness over against the moon of heaven. For this reason the quarters with those in the hells are opposite to the quarters of heaven. The east to them is where that dense darkness and darkness are, the west is where the sun of heaven is, the south is to their right, and the north to their left, and this also in every turning of their bodies. Nor can they face otherwise, because the whole bent and consequent determination of their interiors tends and strives that way. It has been shown above (n. 143) that the bent and consequent actual determination of the interiors of all in the other life are in harmony with their love. The love of those in the hells is the love of self and the world, and these loves are what are signified by the world's sun and the earth's moon (see n. 122); and these loves are opposite to love to the Lord and love towards the neighbor; 151·2 and this is the cause of their turning themselves backwards away from the Lord to this dense darkness. Moreover, those in the hells dwell likewise in accordance with their quarters, those who are in evil from love of self dwelling from their east to their west, and those who are in the falsities of evil from their south to their north. But more will be said about this below, where the hells are treated of.

When an evil spirit comes among good spirits the quarters are usually so confused that the good scarcely know where their east is. This I have sometimes seen take place, and have also heard about it from spirits who complained of it.

Evil spirits are sometimes seen turned towards the quarters of heaven; and they then have intelligence and perception of truth, but no affection for good; but as soon as they turn back to their own quarters they have no intelligence or perception of truth; and then they declare that the truths they heard and perceived are falsities and not truths, and they wish falsities to be truths. In respect to this turning I have been told that with the evil the intellectual part of the mind can be so turned, but not the voluntary part; and that this is provided by the Lord to the end that everyone may have the ability to see and acknowledge truths, but that no one can receive truths unless he is in good, since it is good, and never evil, that receives them; also that man has a like ability to the end that he may be made better by means of truths. Nevertheless, he is made better only so far as he is in good; consequently a man can in like manner be turned to the Lord; but if his life is evil he immediately turns himself back and confirms in himself the falsities of his evil, which are contrary to the truths he had understood and seen; and this takes place when he thinks in himself from his interior states.

CHANGES OF STATE OF THE ANGELS IN HEAVEN. By changes of state of angels their changes in respect to love and faith, and wisdom and intelligence therefrom, are meant, thus their changes in respect to states of life. States are predicated of life and of what belongs to life; and as angelic life is a life of love and faith, and of wisdom and intelligence therefrom, states are predicated of these and are called states of love and faith, and states of wisdom and intelligence. How with angels these states are changed shall now be told.

Angels are not constantly in the same state in respect to love, and in consequence in the same state in respect to wisdom; for all their wisdom is from their love and in accordance with their love. Sometimes they are in a state of intense love, sometimes in a state of love not so intense. The state decreases by degrees from its greatest degree to its least. When in their greatest degree of love they are in the light and warmth of their life, or in a clear and delightful state; but in their least degree they are in shade and cold, or in an obscure and undelightful state. From this last state they return again to the first, and so on, these alternations following one after another with variety. There is a sequence of these states like the varied states of light and shade, or of heat and cold, or like morning, noon, evening, and night, day after day in the world, with unceasing variety throughout the year. There is also a correspondence, morning corresponding to the state of their love in its clearness, noon to the state of their wisdom in its clearness, evening to the state of their wisdom in its obscurity, and night to a state of no love or wisdom. But it must be understood that there is no correspondence of night with the states of life of those in heaven, although there is what corresponds to the dawn that precedes morning; what corresponds to night is with those in hell. 155-1 From this correspondence "day" and "year" signify in the Word states of life in general; "heat" and "light" signify love and wisdom; "morning" the first and highest degree of love "noon" wisdom in its light; "evening" wisdom in its shade; "dawn" the obscurity that precedes the morning; and "night" the absence of love and wisdom. 155-2

Together with the state of the angels' interiors which pertain to their love and wisdom, the states of various things that are outside of them and that they see with their eyes are changed; for the things outside of them take on an appearance that is in accord with the things within them. But what things these are, and what kind of things they are, shall be told presently in the chapter on Representatives and Appearances in Heaven.

Every angel undergoes and passes through such changes of state, and also every society in general, and yet each one differently, for the reason that they differ in love and wisdom, those in the middle being in a more perfect state than those round about even to the circumference (see above, n. 43, 128). But it would be tedious to specify the differences, since the changes each one undergoes are in accord with the quality of his love and faith. From this it happens that while one may be in clearness and delight another may be in obscurity and lack of delight, and this at the same time within the same society. So, too, the state differs in different societies; it is different in the societies of the celestial kingdom from what it is in those of the spiritual kingdom. These differences in the changes of state are in general like the variations of the states of days in different climates on the earth, for with some it is morning when with others it is evening, and with some it is hot when with others it is cold.

I have been taught from heaven why there are such changes of state there. The angels said that there are many reasons-first, the delight of life and of heaven, which they have from love and wisdom from the Lord, would gradually lose its value if they were in it continually, as happens with those that are in allurements and pleasures without variety. A second reason is that angels, as well as men, have what is their own [proprium], which is loving self; and all that are in heaven are withheld from what is their own, and so far as they are withheld from it by the Lord are in love and wisdom; but so far as they are not withheld they are in the love of self; and because everyone loves what is his own and is drawn by it 158-1 they have changes of state or successive alternations. A third reason is that they are in this way perfected, for they thus become accustomed to being held in love to the Lord and withheld from love of self; also that by alternations between delight and lack of delight the perception and sense of good becomes more exquisite. 158-2 The angels added that their changes of state are not caused by the Lord, since the Lord as a sun is unceasingly flowing in with heat and light, that is, with love and wisdom; but the cause is in themselves, in that they love what is their own, and this continually leads them away. This was illustrated by comparison with the sun of the world, that the cause of the changes of state of heat and cold and of light and shade, year by year and day by day, is not in that sun, since it stands unchanged, but the cause is in the earth.

I have been shown how the Lord as a sun appears to the angels of the celestial kingdom in their first state, in their second state, and in their third state. I saw the Lord as a sun, at first glowing and brilliant with a splendor that cannot be described; and I was told that such is the appearance of the Lord as a sun to the angels in their first state. Afterwards there appeared a great obscure belt about the sun, and by this its first glow and brilliancy, which gave it such splendor, began to be dulled, and I was told that such is the appearance of the sun to them in their second state. Then the belt seemed by degrees to grow darker, and the sun to appear less glowing, and this by degrees until at length it took on a shining whiteness; and I was told that such is the appearance of the sun to them in their third state. After this, that shining whiteness was seen to move to the left towards the moon of heaven, and to add itself to her light; and in consequence the moon shone forth with unwonted splendor; and I was told that such is the fourth state of those in the celestial kingdom and the first state of those in the spiritual kingdom, and that in both kingdoms changes of state have such alternations; yet not in the whole kingdom at once, but in one society after another. Furthermore, I was told that these alternations are not fixed, but come upon them sooner or later without their knowledge. And it was added that the sun in itself is not thus changed or moved; but it takes on this appearance in accord with their successive progressions of state, since the Lord appears to everyone in accord with what his state is, thus glowing when one is in intense love and less glowing and finally shining white as his love subsides; and the quality of each one's state was represented by the obscure belt that induced upon the sun these apparent variations in its glow and light.

When angels are in the last of these states, which is when they are in what is their own, they begin to be sad. I have talked with them when they were in that state and have seen their sadness; but they said that they hoped to return soon to their former state, and thus into heaven again, as it were; for to them it is heaven to be withheld from what is their own.

There are also changes of state in the hells, but these will be described later when hell is treated of.

XVIII. TIME IN HEAVEN. Although there is a succession and a progression of all things in heaven, as in the world, yet angels have no notion or idea of time and space; and this so completely that they do not even know at all what time and space are. Time in heaven will here be considered, and space in its own chapter.

Angels do not know what time is, although with them there is a successive progression of all things, as there is in the world, and this so completely that there is no difference whatever; and the reason is that in heaven instead of years and days there are changes of state; and where there are years and days there are times, but where there are changes of state there are states.

In the world there are times because the sun of the world seemingly advances in succession from one degree to another, producing times that are called seasons of the year; and besides, it revolves about the earth, producing times that are called times of day; both of these by fixed alternations. With the sun of heaven it is different. This does not mark years and days by successive progressions and revolutions, but in its appearance it marks changes of state; and this, as has been shown in the preceding chapter, is not done by fixed alternations. Consequently no idea of time is possible to angels; but in its place they have an idea of state (see above n. 154).

As angels have no idea derived from time, such as men in the world have, so neither do they have any idea about time and what pertains to it. They do not even know what is meant by the terms of time, such as year, month, week, day, hour, to-day, to-morrow, yesterday. When angels hear these terms used by man (for angels are always associated with man by the Lord) in place of them they perceive state and what pertains to states. Thus the natural thought of man is turned into spiritual thought with angels. This is why times in the Word signify states, and the terms of time, as enumerated above, signify corresponding spiritual things. 165-1

The like is true of all things that exist from time, as the four seasons of the year, called spring, summer, autumn, and winter; the four periods of the day, morning, noon, evening, and night; and the four ages of man, infancy, youth, manhood, and old age; and all other things that either exist from time or have a succession in accordance with time. In thinking of these a man thinks from time, but an angel from state; and in consequence what there is in them from time with man is with the angels turned into an idea of state. Spring and morning are turned into an idea of the state of love and wisdom such as they are in angels in their first state; summer and noon are turned into an idea of love and wisdom such as they are in the second state; autumn and evening such as they are in the third state; night and winter into an idea of such a state as exists in hell. This is why these periods have a like significance in the Word (see above, n. 155). This makes clear how natural things in the thought of man become spiritual with the angels who are with man.

As angels have no notion of time so they have an idea of eternity different from that which men on the earth have. Eternity means to the angels infinite state, not infinite time. 167-1 I was once thinking about eternity, and was able, with the idea of time, to perceive what to eternity means, namely, without end, but not what from eternity means, thus not what God did from eternity before creation. When anxiety on this account arose in my mind I was raised up into the sphere of heaven, and thus into the perception that angels have in respect to eternity; and it was then made clear to me that eternity must be thought of, not from time but from state; and then the meaning of from eternity can be seen. This then happened to me.

When angels speak with men they never express themselves in natural ideas proper to man, all of which are from time, space, matter, and things analogous thereto, but in spiritual ideas, all of which are from states and their various changes within the angels and outside of them. Nevertheless, when these angelic ideas, which are spiritual, flow into men, they are turned in a moment and of themselves into natural ideas proper to man, that correspond perfectly to the spiritual ideas. Neither angels nor men know that this takes place; but such is all influx of heaven into man. Certain angels were permitted to enter more nearly into my thoughts, even into the natural thoughts in which there were many things from time and space; but as they then understood nothing they suddenly withdrew; and after they had withdrawn I heard them talking, and saying that they had been in darkness. [2] It has been granted me to know by experience how ignorant the angels are about time. There was a certain one from heaven who was able to enter into natural ideas, such as man has; and after he had done this I talked with him as man with man. At first he did not know what it was that I called time, and I was therefore obliged to tell him all about it, how the sun appears to be carried about our earth, and to produce years and days, and how years are thereby divided into four seasons, and also into months and weeks, and days into twenty-four hours; and how these times recur by fixed alternations, and how this is the source of times. On hearing this he was surprised, saying that he knew nothing about such things, but only what states are. [3] In speaking with him I added that it is known in the world, for men speak as if they knew that there is no time in heaven, saying of those who die that they "leave the things of time," and that they "pass out of time," meaning by this out of the world. I said also that some know that times in their origin are states, for they know that times are in exact accord with the states of their affections, short to those who are in pleasant and joyous states, long to those who are in unpleasant and sorrowful states, and various in a state of hope and expectation; and this therefore leads learned men to inquire what time and space are, and some know that time belongs to the natural man.

The natural man might think that he would be deprived of all thought if the ideas of time, space, and material things were taken away; for upon these all the thought of man rests. 169-1 But let him know that so far as thoughts partake of time, space, and matter they are limited and confined, but are unlimited and extended so far as they do not partake of these, since the mind is in that measure raised above bodily and worldly things. This is the source of wisdom to the angels; and such wisdom as is called incomprehensible, because it does not fall into ideas that are wholly made up of what is material.

REPRESENTATIVES AND APPEARANCES IN HEAVEN. The man who thinks from natural light alone is unable to comprehend that there is any thing in heaven like what is in the world; and for the reason that from natural light he has previously thought, and established himself in the idea, that angels are nothing but minds, and that minds are like ethereal breaths, having no senses like those of men, thus no eyes, and if no eyes no objects of sight; and yet the angels have every sense that a man has, and far more exquisite senses; and the light by which angels see is far brighter than the light by which man sees. That angels are men in the most complete form, and enjoy every sense, may be seen above (n. 73-77); and that the light in heaven is far brighter than the light in the world (n. 126-132).

The nature of the objects that are visible to angels in heaven cannot be described in a few words. For the most part they are like things on earth, but in form far more perfect, and in number more abundant. That such things exist in the heavens is evident from things seen by the prophets, -as by Ezekiel in relation to the new temple and the new earth (as described from chaps. 40 to 48); by Daniel (from chap. 7 to 12); by John (from the first chapter of the Apocalypse to the last); and by others, as described both in the historic and the prophetic part of the Word. These things were seen by them when heaven was open to them, and heaven is said to be opened when the interior sight, which is the sight of man's spirit, is opened. For what is in the heavens cannot be seen by the eyes of a man's body, but are seen by the eyes of his spirit; and when it seems good to the Lord these are opened, and man is then withdrawn from the natural light that he is in from the bodily senses and is raised up into spiritual light, which he is in from his spirit. In that light the things in heaven have been seen by me.

But although the things seen in heaven are in large part like those on the earth, in essence they are unlike them; for the things in heaven come forth from the sun of heaven, and those on the earth from the sun of the world. The things that come forth from the sun of heaven are called spiritual; those that come forth from the sun of the world are called natural.

The things that come forth in heaven do not come forth in the same manner as those on the earth. All things in heaven come forth from the Lord in correspondence with the interiors of the angels. For angels have both interiors and exteriors. All things in their interiors have relation to love and faith, thus to the will and understanding, since the will and understanding are their receptacles; while their exteriors correspond to their interiors. That exterior things correspond to interior things may be seen above (n. 87-115). This is illustrated by what has been said above about the heat and light of heaven, that angels have heat in accordance with the quality of their love, and light in accordance with the quality of their wisdom (n. 128-134). The like is true of all other things that present themselves to the senses of angels.

When I have been permitted to be in company with angels, the things there appeared precisely the same as those in the world; and so plainly that I would not have known that I was not in the world and in a king's palace. I also talked with the angels as man with man.

As all things that correspond to interiors also represent them they are called representatives; and as they differ in each case in accordance with the state of the interiors they are called appearances. Nevertheless, the things that appear before the eyes of angels in heaven and are perceived by their senses appear to their eyes and senses as fully living as things on earth appear to man, and even much more clearly, distinctly and perceptibly. Appearances from this source in heaven are called real appearances, because they have real existence. There are appearances also that are not real, which are things that become visible, but do not correspond to interiors. 175-1 These will be treated of further on.

To show what the things are that appear to the angels in accordance with correspondences, I will here mention one only for the sake of illustration. By those who are intelligent, gardens and parks full of trees and flowers of every kind are seen. The trees are planted in a most beautiful order, combined to form arbors with arched approaches and encircling walks, all more beautiful than words can describe. There the intelligent walk, and gather flowers and weave garlands with which they adorn little children. Moreover, there are kinds of trees and flowers there that are never seen and cannot exist on earth. The trees bear fruit that are in accordance with the good of love, in which the intelligent are. These things are seen by them because a garden or park and fruit trees and flowers correspond to intelligence and wisdom. 176-1 That there are such things in heaven is known also on the earth, but only to those who are in good, and who have not extinguished in themselves the light of heaven by means of natural light and its fallacies; for when such think about heaven they think and say that there are such things there as ear hath not heard and eye hath not seen.

THE GARMENTS WITH WHICH ANGELS APPEAR CLOTHED. Since angels are men, and live among themselves as men do on the earth, they have garments and dwellings and other such things, with the difference, however, that as they are in a more perfect state all things with them are in greater perfection. For as angelic wisdom surpasses human wisdom to such a degree as to be called ineffable, so is it with all things that are perceived and seen by angels, inasmuch as all things perceived and seen by them correspond to their wisdom (see above, n. 173).

The garments with which angels are clothed, like all other things with them, correspond; and because they correspond they have real existence (see above n. 175). Their garments correspond to their intelligence, and therefore all in the heavens appear clothed in accordance with their intelligence; and as one is more intelligent than another so the garments of one surpass those of another. The most intelligent have garments that blaze as if with flame, others have garments that glisten as if with light; the less intelligent have garments that are glistening white or white without the effulgence; and the still less intelligent have garments of various colors. But the angels of the inmost heaven are not clothed.

As the garments of angels correspond to their intelligence they correspond also to truth, since all intelligence is from Divine truth; and therefore it is the same thing whether you say that angels are clothed in accordance with intelligence or in accordance with Divine truth. The garments of some blaze as if with flame, and those of others glisten as if with light, because flame corresponds to good, and light corresponds to truth from good. 179-1 Some have garments that are glistening white and white without the effulgence, and others garments of various colors, because with the less intelligent the Divine good and truth are less effulgent, and are also received in various ways, 179-2 glistening white and white corresponding to truth, 179-3 and colors to its varieties. 179-4 Those in the inmost heaven are not clothed, because they are in innocence, and innocence corresponds to nakedness. 179-5

As in heaven the angels are clothed with garments, so when seen in the world they have appeared clothed with garments, as those seen by the prophets and those seen at the Lord's sepulchre: Whose appearance was as lightning, and their garments glistening and white (Matt. 28:3; Mark 16:5; Luke 24:4; John 20:12, 13); and those seen in heaven by John: Who had garments of fine linen and white (Apoc. 4:4; 19:14). And because intelligence is from Divine truth: The garments of the Lord, when He was transfigured, were radiant and glistening white like the light (Matt. 17:2; Mark 9:3; Luke 9:29). As light is Divine truth going forth from the Lord (see above, n. 129), so in the Word garments signify truths and intelligence from truths, as in the Apocalypse: Those that have not defiled their garments shall walk with Me in white, for they are worthy. He that overcometh shall be clothed in white garments (3:4, 5); Blessed is he that is awake and keepeth his garments (16:15). And of Jerusalem, which means a church that is in truth, 180-1 it is written in Isaiah: Awake, put on thy strength, O Zion; put on the garments of thy beauty, O Jerusalem (52:1). And in Ezekiel: Jerusalem, I girded thee about with fine linen, and covered thee with silk. Thy garments were of fine linen and silk (16:10, 13); besides many other passages. But he who is not in truths is said "not to be clothed with a wedding garment," as in Matthew: When the king came in he saw a man that had not on a wedding garment; and he said unto him, Friend, how camest thou in hither not having a wedding garment? Wherefore he was cast out into the outer darkness (22:11-13). The house of the wedding feast means heaven and the church because of the conjunction of the Lord with heaven and the church by means of His Divine truth; and for this reason the Lord is called in the Word the Bridegroom and Husband; and heaven, with the church, is called the bride and the wife.

That the garments of angels do not merely appear as garments, but are real garments, is evident from the fact that angels both see them and feel them, that they have many garments, and that they put them off and put them on, that they care for those that are not in use, and put them on again when they need them. That they are clothed with a variety of garments I have seen a thousand times. When I asked where they got their garments, they said from the Lord, and that they receive them as gifts, and sometimes they are clothed with them unconsciously. They said also that their garments are changed in accordance with their changes of state, that in the first and second state their garments are shining and glistening white, and in the third and fourth state a little less bright; and this likewise from correspondence, because their changes of state have respect to intelligence and wisdom (of which see above, n. 154, 161).

As everyone in the spiritual world has garments in accordance with his intelligence, that is, in accordance with truths which are the source of intelligence, so those in the hells, because they have no truths, appear clothed in garments, but in ragged, squalid, and filthy garments, each one in accordance with his insanity; and they can be clothed in no others. It is granted them by the Lord to be clothed, lest they be seen naked.

THE PLACES OF ABODE AND DWELLINGS OF ANGELS. As there are societies in heaven and the angels live as men, they have also places of abode, and these differ in accordance with each one's state of life. They are magnificent for those in higher dignity, and less magnificent for those in lower condition. I have frequently talked with angels about the places of abode in heaven, saying that scarcely any one will believe at the present day that they have places of abode and dwellings; some because they do not see them, some because they do not know that angels are men, and some because they believe that the angelic heaven is the heaven that they see with their eyes around them, and as this appears empty and they suppose that angels are ethereal forms, they conclude that they live in ether. Moreover, they do not comprehend how there can be such things in the spiritual world as there are in the natural world, because they know nothing about the spiritual. [2] The angels replied that they are aware that such ignorance prevails at this day in the world, and to their astonishment, chiefly within the church, and more with the intelligent than with those whom they call simple. They said also that it might be known from the Word that angels are men, since those that have been seen have been seen as men; and the Lord, who took all His Human with Him, appeared in like manner. It might be known also that as angels are men they have dwellings and places of abode, and do not fly about in air, as some think in their ignorance, which the angels call insanity, and that although they are called spirits they are not winds. This they said might be apprehended if men would only think independently of their acquired notions about angels and spirits, as they do when they are not bringing into question and submitting to direct thought whether it is so. For everyone has a general idea that angels are in the human form, and have homes which are called the mansions of heaven, which surpass in magnificence earthly dwellings; but this general idea, which flows in from heaven, at once falls to nothing when it is brought under direct scrutiny and inquiry whether it is so, as happens especially with the learned, who by their own intelligence have closed up heaven to themselves and the entrance of heavenly light. [3] The like is true of the belief in the life of man after death. When one speaks of it, not thinking at the same time about the soul from the light of worldly learning or from the doctrine of its reunion with the body, he believes that after death he is to live a man, and among angels if he has lived well, and that he will then see magnificent things and perceive joys; but as soon as he turns his thoughts to the doctrine of reunion with the body, or to his theory about the soul, and the question arises whether the soul be such, and thus whether this can be true, his former idea is dissipated.

But it is better to present the evidence of experience. Whenever I have talked with angels face to face, I have been with them in their abodes. These abodes are precisely like abodes on the earth which we call houses, but more beautiful. In them there are chambers, parlors, and bedrooms in great number; there are also courts, and there are gardens and flower beds and lawns round about. Where they live together their houses are near each other, arranged one next to the other in the form of a city, with avenues, streets, and public squares, exactly like cities on the earth. I have been permitted to pass through them, looking about on every side, and sometimes entering the houses. This occurred when my inner sight was opened, and I was fully awake. 184-1

I have seen palaces in heaven of such magnificence as cannot be described. Above they glittered as if made of pure gold, and below as if made of precious stones, some more splendid than others. It was the same within. Both words and knowledge are inadequate to describe the decorations that adorned the rooms. On the side looking to the south there were parks, where, too, everything shone, in some places the leaves glistening as if made of silver, and fruit as if made of gold; while the flowers in their beds formed rainbows with their colors. Beyond the borders, where the view terminated, were seen other palaces. Such is the architecture of heaven that you would say that art there is in its art; and no wonder, because the art itself is from heaven. The angels said that such things and innumerable others still more perfect are presented before their eyes by the Lord; and yet these things are more pleasing to their minds than to their eyes, because in everyone of them they see a correspondence, and through the correspondences what is Divine.

As to these correspondences I have also been told that not only the palaces and houses, but all things and each thing, both inside and outside of them, correspond to the interior things which they have from the Lord, the house itself in general corresponding to their good, the particular things inside of a house to the various things of which their good consists, 186-1 and the things outside to truths derived from good, and also to their perceptions and knowledges 186-2 and as these things correspond to the goods and truths they have from the Lord they correspond to their love, and to their wisdom and intelligence from love, since love belongs to good, wisdom to good and truth together, and intelligence to truth from good. These are what the angels perceive when they behold what is around them, and thus their minds are more delighted and moved by them than their eyes.

This makes clear why the Lord called Himself the temple at Jerusalem (John 2:19, 21), 187-1 namely, because the temple represented His Divine Human; also why the New Jerusalem was seen to be of pure gold, its gates of pearls, and its foundations of precious stones (Apoc. 21), namely, because the New Jerusalem signifies the church which was afterwards to be established, the twelve gates its truths leading to good, and the foundations the truths on which the church is founded. 187-2

The angels of whom the Lord's celestial kingdom consists dwell for the most part in elevated places that appear as mountains of soil; the angels of whom the Lord's spiritual kingdom consists dwell in less elevated places that appear like hills; while the angels in the lowest parts of heaven dwell in places that appear like ledges of stone. These things spring from correspondence, for interior things correspond to higher things, and exterior things to lower things; 1 and this is why in the Word "mountains" signify celestial love, "hills" spiritual love, and "rocks" faith. 188-1

There are also angels who do not live associated together, but apart, house by house. These dwell in the midst of heaven, since they are the best of angels.

The houses in which angels dwell are not erected, as houses in the world are, but are given to them gratuitously by the Lord, to everyone in accordance with his reception of good and truth. They also change a little in accordance with changes of the state of interiors of the angels (of which above, n. 154-160). Everything whatsoever that the angels possess they hold as received from the Lord; and everything they have need of is given them.

SPACE IN HEAVEN. All things in heaven appear, just as in the world, to be in place and in space, and yet the angels have no notion or idea of place and space. As this must needs sounds like a paradox, I will endeavor to present the matter in a clear light, as it is of great importance.

All changes of place in the spiritual world are effected by changes of state of the interiors, which means that change of place is nothing else than change of state. 192-1 In this way I have been taken by the Lord into the heavens and also to the earths in the universe; and it was my spirit that so journeyed, while my body remained in the same place. 192-2 Such are all movements of the angels; and in consequence they have no distances, and having no distances they have no spaces, but in place of spaces they have states and their changes.

As changes of place are thus effected it is evident that approaches are likenesses of state of the interiors, and separations are unlikenesses; and for this reason those are near each other who are in like states, and those are at a distance who are in unlike states; and spaces in heaven are simply the external conditions corresponding to the internal states. For the same reason the heavens are distinct from each other, also the societies of each heaven and the individuals in each society; and this is why also that the hells are entirely separated from the heavens, because they are in a contrary state.

For the same reason, again, any one in the spiritual world who intensely desires the presence of another comes into his presence, for he thereby sees him in thought, and puts himself in his state; and conversely, one is separated from another so far as he is averse to him. And since all aversion comes from contrariety of affection and from disagreement of thought, whenever in that world several are together in one place they are visible [to one another] so long as they agree, but vanish as soon as they disagree.

Again, when any one goes from one place to another, whether it be in his own city, or in courts or in gardens, or to others out of his own society, he arrives more quickly when he eagerly desires it, and less quickly when he does not, the way itself being lengthened and shortened in accordance with the desire, although it remains the same. This I have often seen to my surprise. All this again makes clear how distances, and consequently spaces, are wholly in accord with states of the interiors of the angels; 195-1 and this being so, no notion or idea of space can enter their thought, although there are spaces with them equally as in the world.

This can be illustrated by the thoughts of man, in that space does not pertain to thought, for whatever is thought of intently is set before one as present. Again, whoever reflects about it knows that his sight recognizes space only by intermediate objects on the earth that are seen at the same time, or by recalling what he already knows about the distance. This happens because of the continuity; and in what is continuous there is no appearance of distance except from things not continuous. This is even more true of the angels, because their sight acts as one with their thought, and their thought acts as one with their affection, and things appear near or remote, and also varied, in accordance with the states of their interiors, as has been said above.

It follows from this that in the Word places and spaces, and all things that in any way relate to space, signify such things as relate to states, such as distances, near, far off, ways, journeys, sojourning, miles and furlongs, plains, fields, gardens, cities and streets, motions, measures of various kinds, long, broad, high, and deep, and innumerable other things; for most things in man's thought from the world take on something from space and time. [2] I will mention here only what is signified in the Word by length, breadth, and height. In this world, that is called long or broad which is long or broad in relation to space, and the same is true of height. But in heaven, where there is no thought from space, length means a state of good, breadth a state of truth, and height the distinction between them in accordance with degrees (see n. 38). Such is the meaning of these three dimensions, because length in heaven is from east to west, and those that dwell there are in good of love; while breadth in heaven is from south to north, and those that dwell there are in truth from good (see n. 148); while height in heaven applies to both of these in respect to degrees. This is why length, breadth, and height have these significations in the Word, as in Ezekiel (from chap. 40 to 48), where the new temple and the new earth, with the courts, chambers, gates, doors, windows, and surroundings are described by measures giving the length, breadth, and height, by which a new church, and the goods and truths that are in it are signified. Otherwise to what purpose would be all those measures? [3] In like manner the New Jerusalem is described in the Apocalypse in these words: The city lieth foursquare, and the length thereof is as great as the breadth; and he measured the city with the reed, twelve thousand furlongs; the length, the breadth, and the height are equal (21:16). Because "the New Jerusalem" here signifies a new church these measures signify the things of the church, "length" its good of love, "breadth" truth from that good, "height" good and truth in respect to degrees, "twelve thousand furlongs" all good and truth in the complex. Otherwise, how could there be said to be a height of twelve thousand furlongs, the same as the length and the breadth? That "breadth" in the Word signifies truth is evident from David:- Jehovah, Thou hast not shut me up into the hand of the enemy, Thou hast made my feet to stand in a broad place (Psalm 31:8). Out of straitness I called upon Jah; He answereth me in a broad place (Psalm 118:5). Besides other passages (as in Isaiah 8:8; and in Habakkuk 1:6). So in all other cases.

From all this it can be seen that although there are spaces in heaven as in the world, still nothing there is reckoned in accordance with spaces but in accordance with states; and in consequence spaces there cannot be measured as in the world, but can be seen only from the state and in accordance with the state of the interiors there. 198-1

The primary and veriest cause of this is that the Lord is present with everyone in the measure of his love and faith, 199-1 and that it is in accordance with the Lord's presence that all things appear near or far away, for it is from this that all things in the heavens are determined. Also it is through this that angels have wisdom, for it is through this that they have extension of thought and through this a sharing of all things in the heavens; in a word, it is through this that they think spiritually, and not naturally like men.

THE FORM OF HEAVEN WHICH DETERMINES AFFILIATIONS AND

COMMUNICATIONS THERE. What the form of heaven is can be seen in some measure from what has been shown in the preceding chapters; as that heaven is like itself both in its greatest and in its least divisions (n. 72); that consequently each society is a heaven in a lesser form, and each angel in the least form (n. 51-58); that as the entire heaven reflects a single man, so each society of heaven reflects a man in a lesser form, and each angel in the least form (n. 59-77); that the wisest are at the center, and the less wise are round about even to the borders, and the like is true of each society (n. 43); and that those who are in the good of love dwell from the east to the west in heaven, and those who are in truths from good from the south to the north; and the same is true of each society (n. 148, 149). All this is in accord with the form of heaven; consequently it may be concluded from this what this form is in general. 200-1

Footnotes

151-1 Who and what those are who are called genii, and who and what those are who are called spirits (n. 947, 5035, 5977, 8593, 8622, 8625).

151-2 Those that are in the loves of self and of the world turn themselves backwards from the Lord (n. 10130, 10189, 10420, 10702). Love to the Lord and charity towards the neighbor make heaven, while love of self and love of the world make hell, because the two are opposite (n. 2041, 3610, 4225, 4776 6210, 7366, 7369, 7490, 8232, 8678, 10455, 10741-10745).

155-1 In heaven there is a state corresponding to the dawn that precedes morning, but no state corresponding to night (n. 6110). The "dawn" signifies a middle state between the last and the first (n. 10134).

155-2 Alternations of state in respect to enlightenment and perception occur in heaven, like the times of day in the world (n. 5672, 5962, 6110, 8426, 9213, 10605). In the Word "day" and "year" signify all states in general (n. 23, 487, 488, 493, 893, 2788, 3462, 4850, 10656). "Morning" signifies the beginning of a new state, and a state of love (n. 7218, 8426, 8427, 10114, 10134). "Evening" signifies a state of declining light and love (n. 10134, 10135). "Night" signifies a state of no love or faith (n. 221, 709, 2353, 6000, 6110, 7870, 7947).

158-1 Man's own [proprium] is loving self (n. 694, 731, 4317, 5660). The Lord cannot be present unless what is man's own is set aside (n. 1023, 1044). It is actually set aside when one is held in good by the Lord (n. 9334-9336, 9447, 9452-9454, 9938).

158-2 The angels are being perfected to eternity (n. 4803, 6648). In the heavens one state is never just like another, and from this there is an unceasing process of perfection (n. 10200).

165-1 Times in the Word signify states (n. 2788, 2837, 3254, 3356, 4814, 4901, 4916, 7218, 8070, 10133, 10605). Angels think apart from the idea of time and space (n. 3404); the reasons why (n. 1274, 1382, 3356, 4882, 4901, 6110, 7218, 7381). What a "year" signifies in the Word (n. 487, 488, 493, 893, 2906, 7828, 10209). What a "month" (n. 3814). What a "week" (n. 2044, 3845). What a "day" (n. 23, 487, 488, 6110, 7680, 8426, 9213, 10132, 10605). What "today" (n. 2838, 3998, 4304, 6165, 6984, 9939). What "to-morrow" (n. 3998, 10497). What "yesterday" (n. 6983, 7114, 7140).

167-1 Men have an idea of eternity associated with time, but angels apart from time (n. 1382, 3404, 8325).

169-1 Man does not think, as angels do, apart from the idea of time (n. 3404).

175-1 All things that are visible to the angels are representative (n. 1971, 3213-3226, 3342, 3457, 3475, 3485, 9481, 9457, 9576, 9577). The heavens are full of representatives (n. 1521, 1532, 1619). The representatives are more beautiful as they are more interior in the heavens (n. 3475). As the representatives there are from the light of heaven they are real appearances (n. 3485). The Divine influx is turned into representatives in the higher heavens, and therefrom in the lower heavens also (n. 2179, 3213, 9457, 9481, 9576, 9577). Those things are called representative that appear before the eyes of the angels in such form as are in nature, that is, such as are in the world (n. 9457). Internal things are thus turned into external (n. 1632, 2987-3002). What representatives in the heavens are; this made clear by various examples (n. 1521, 1532, 1619-1628, 1807, 1973, 1974, 1977, 1980, 1981, 2299, 2601, 2761, 2762, 3217, 3219, 3220, 3348, 3350, 5198, 9090, 10276). All things seen in the heavens are in accordance with correspondences and are called representatives (n. 3213-3226, 3342, 3475, 3485, 9481, 9457, 9576, 9577). All things that correspond also represent and likewise signify what they correspond to (n. 2896, 2987, 2989-2991, 3002, 3225).

176-1 A "garden" or "park" signifies intelligence and wisdom (n. 100, 108, 3220). What is meant by "the garden of Eden" and "the garden of Jehovah" (n. 99, 100, 1588). How magnificent the things seen in parks are in the other life (n. 1122, 1622, 2296, 4528, 4529). "Trees" signify perceptions and knowledges, from which wisdom and intelligence are derived (n. 103, 2163, 2682, 2722, 2972, 7692). "Fruits" signify goods of love and goods of charity (n. 3146, 7690, 9337).

179-1 From correspondence "garments" in the Word signify truths (n. 1073, 2576, 5319, 5954, 9212, 9216, 9952, 10536). For the reason that truths clothe good (n. 5248). A "covering" signifies something intellectual, because the intellect is the recipient of truth (n. 6378). "Shining garments of fine linen" signify truths from the Divine (n. 5319, 9469). "Flame" signifies spiritual good, and the light therefrom truth from that good (n. 3222, 6832).

179-2 Angels and spirits appear clothed with garments in accordance with their truths, thus in accordance with their intelligence (n. 165, 5248, 5954, 9212, 9216, 9814, 9952, 10536). The garments of some angels are resplendent, others are not (n. 5248).

179-3 In the Word "glistening white" and "white" signify truth because they are from light in heaven (n. 3301, 3993, 4007).

179-4 Colors in heaven are variegations of the light there (n. 1042, 1043, 1053, 1624, 3993, 4530, 4742, 4922). Colors signify various things pertaining to intelligence and wisdom (n. 4530, 4677, 4922, 9466). The precious stones in the Urim and Thummim signified, in accordance with their colors, all things of truth from good in the heavens (n. 9865, 9868, 9905). So far as colors partake of red they signify good; so far as they partake of white they signify truth (n. 9466).

179-5 All in the inmost heavens are innocences, and in consequence appear naked (n. 154, 165, 297, 2736, 3887, 8375, 9960). Innocence is presented in heaven as nakedness (n. 165, 8375, 9960). To the innocent and the chaste nakedness is no shame, because without offence (n. 165, 213, 8375).

180-1 "Jerusalem" signifies a church in which there is genuine doctrine (n. 402, 3654, 9166).

184-1 Angels have cities, palaces and houses (n. 940-942, 1116, 1626-1631, 4622).

186-1 "Houses," with their contents, signify the things in man that belong to his mind, thus his interiors (n. 710, 2233, 2331, 2559, 3128, 3538, 4973, 5023, 6639, 6690, 7353, 7848, 7910, 7929, 9150); consequently the things relating to good and truth (n. 2233, 2331, 2559, 4982, 7848, 7929). "Rooms" and "bed-chambers" signify interior things there (n. 3900, 5694, 7353). The "roof of a house" signifies what is inmost (n. 3652, 10184). A "house of wood" signifies what relates to good, and a "house of stone" what relates to truth (n. 3720).

186-2 A "garden" or "park" signifies intelligence and wisdom (n. 100, 108, 3220). What is meant by "the garden of Eden" and "the garden of Jehovah" (n. 99, 100, 1588). How magnificent the things seen in parks are in the other life (n. 1122, 1622, 2296, 4528, 4529). "Trees" signify perceptions and knowledges, from which wisdom and intelligence are derived (n. 103, 2163, 2682, 2722, 2972, 7692). "Fruits" signify goods of love and goods of charity (n. 3146, 7690, 9337).

187-1 In the highest sense "the house of God" signifies the Lord's Divine Human in respect to Divine good, and "the temple" the same in respect to Divine truth; and in a relative sense, heaven and the church in respect to good and truth (n. 3720).

187-2 "Jerusalem" signifies the church in which is genuine doctrine (n. 402, 3654, 9166). "Gates" signify introduction to the doctrine of the church, and through doctrine introduction into the church (n. 2943, 4477, 4478). "Foundation" signifies the truth on which heaven, the church, and doctrine are founded (n. 9643).

188-1

188-2 In the Word what is interior is expressed by what is higher and what is higher signifies what is interior (n. 2148, 3084, 4599, 5146, 8325). What is "high" signifies what is internal, and likewise heaven (n. 1735, 2148, 4210, 4599, 8153). 188-2 In heaven, mountains, hills, rocks, valleys, and lands are seen exactly the same as in the world (n. 10608). On the mountains angels who are in the good of love dwell, on the hills those who are in the good of charity, on the rocks those who are in the good of faith (n. 10438). Therefore in the Word "mountains" signify the good of love (n. 795, 4210, 6435, 8327, 8758, 10438, 10608). "Hills" signify the good of charity (n. 6435, 10438). "Rocks" signify the good and truth of faith (n. 8581, 10580). "Stone," of which rock consists, in like manner signifies the truth of faith (n. 114, 643, 1298, 3720, 6426, 8609, 10376). This is why "mountains" signify heaven (n. 8327, 8805, 9420). And "the summit of a mountain" signifies the highest part of heaven (n. 9422, 9434, 10608). Also why the ancients had their holy worship on mountains (n. 796, 2722).

192-1 In the Word places and spaces signify states (n. 2625, 2837, 3356, 3387, 7381, 10580); from experience (n. 1274, 1277, 1376-1381, 4321, 4882, 10146, 10580). Distance signifies difference of state of life (n. 9104, 9967). In the spiritual world movements and changes of place are changes of the state of life, because they originate in these (n. 1273-1275, 1377, 3356, 9440). The same is true of journeyings (n. 9440, 10734); illustrated by experience (n. 1273-1277, 5605). For this reason "to journey" signifies in the Word to live and progress in life; and "to sojourn has a like meaning (n. 3335, 4554, 4585, 4882, 5493, 5605, 5996, 8345, 8397, 8417, 8420, 8557). To go with the Lord means to live with Him (n. 10567).

192-2 Man may be led a long distance in respect to his spirit by means of changes of state, while his body remains in its place, also from experience (n. 9440, 9967, 10734). What it is to be "led by the spirit to another place" (n. 1884).

195-1 Places and spaces are presented to the sight in accordance with the states of the interiors of angels and spirits (n. 5605, 9440, 10146).

198-1 In the Word length signifies good (n. 1613, 9487). "Breadth" signifies truth (n. 1613, 3433, 3434, 4482, 9487, 10179). Height signifies good and truth in respect to their degrees (n. 9489, 9773, 10181).

199-1 The conjunction and presence of the Lord with the angels is according to their reception of love and charity from Him (n. 290, 681, 1954, 2658, 2886, 2888, 2889, 3001, 3741-3743, 4318 4319, 4524, 7211, 9128).

200-1 The entire heaven in respect to all angelic societies, is arranged by the Lord in accordance with His Divine order, since it is the Divine of the Lord with the angels that makes heaven (n. 3038, 7211, 9128, 9338, 10125, 10151, 10157). Concerning the heavenly form (n. 4040-4043, 6607, 9877).

Section 5

It is important to know what the form of heaven is, because not only is all affiliation there in accordance with it, but also all mutual communication, and in consequence of this all extension of thoughts and affections, and thus all the intelligence and wisdom of angels. From this it follows that each one there is wise just to the extent that he is in the form of heaven, and is thus a form of heaven. It makes no difference whether you say in the form of heaven, or in the order of heaven, since the form of any thing is from its order and in accordance with its order. 201-1

Let us consider first what is meant by being in the form of heaven. Man was created both in the image of heaven and in the image of the world; his internal in the image of heaven, and his external in the image of the world (see above, n. 57); and in the image means the same thing as in accordance with the form. But as man by the evils of his will and consequent falsities of thought has destroyed in himself the image of heaven, that is, the form of heaven, and in place of it has brought in the image and form of hell, his internal is closed up from his very birth; and this is why man is born into pure ignorance, while animals of every kind are not. And that man may have the image of heaven or form of heaven restored to him he must be taught the things that pertain to order; since form, as has been said, is in accord with order. The Word contains all the laws of Divine order, for its precepts are the laws of Divine order; therefore to the extent that man knows these and lives in accordance with them his internal is opened and the order or image of heaven is there formed anew. This makes clear what is meant by being in the form of heaven, namely, that it is to live in accordance with those things that are in the Word. 202-1

So far as any one is in the form of heaven he is in heaven, and is, in fact, a heaven in the least form (n. 57); consequently he is to the same extent in intelligence and wisdom; for as has been said above, all the thought of his understanding and all the affection of his will extend themselves on every side into heaven in accord with its form, and wonderfully communicate with the societies there, and these in turn with him. 203-1 [2] There are some who do not believe that thoughts and affections really extend themselves around about them, but believe that they are within them, because whatever they think they see within in themselves, and not as distant; but such are greatly mistaken. For as the sight of the eye has extension to remote objects, and is affected in accordance with the order of the things seen in that extension, so the interior sight, which is that of the understanding, has a like extension in the spiritual world, although not perceived by man, for the reason given above (n. 196). The only difference is that the sight of the eye is affected in a natural way, because it is affected by the things in the natural world, while the sight of the understanding is affected in a spiritual way, because by the things in the spiritual world, all of which have relation to good and truth; and man's ignorance of this is because of his not knowing that there is any light that enlightens the understanding; and yet without the light that enlightens the understanding man could not think at all (of which light see above, n. 126-132). [3] There was a certain spirit who believed that his thought was from himself, thus without any extension outside of himself and communication thereby with societies outside of him. That he might learn that this was not true his communication with neighboring societies was cut off, and in consequence, not only was he deprived of thought but he fell down as if lifeless, although tossing his arms about like a new-born infant. After a while the communication was restored to him, and then as it was gradually restored he returned into the state of his thought. [4] When other spirits had seen this they confessed that all thought and affection, and in consequence, everything of life, flow in in accordance with communication, since everything of man's life consists in his ability to think and be moved by affection, or what is the same, in his ability to understand and will. 203-2

But let it be understood that intelligence and wisdom vary with everyone in accordance with this communication, those whose intelligence and wisdom are formed out of genuine truths and goods having communication with societies in accordance with the form of heaven; while those whose intelligence and wisdom are not formed out of genuine truths and goods, and yet out of what is in accord therewith, have a broken and variously coherent communication, since it is not with societies that are in a series in which there is a form of heaven. On the other hand, those that are not in intelligence and wisdom, because they are in falsities from evil, have communication with societies in hell; and their extension is determined by the degree of their confirmation. Let it also be known that this communication with societies is not such a communication with them as is clearly perceptible to those there, but is a communication with what they really are, which is in them and flows from them. 204-1

There is an affiliation of all in heaven in accordance with spiritual relationships, that is, relationships of good and truth in their order. It is so in the whole heaven; so in each society, and so in each house. Because of this angels who are in like good and truth recognize each other, as relatives by blood and marriage do on the earth, precisely as if they had been acquainted from infancy. The good and truth in each angel, which constitute his wisdom and intelligence, are affiliated in like manner; they recognize each other in like manner, and as they recognize each other they join themselves together; 205-1 and in consequence those in whom truths and goods are thus joined in accordance with a form of heaven see things following one another in series, and how they cohere widely round about; but those in whom goods and truths are not conjoined in accordance with the form of heaven do not see this.

In each heaven there is such a form, and in accordance with it the angels have communication and extension of thoughts and affections, and thus in accordance with it they have intelligence and wisdom. But the communication of one heaven with another is different, that is, of the third or inmost with the second or middle, and of this with the first or outmost. But the communication between the heavens should not be called communication but influx. About this something shall now be said. That there are three heavens distinct from each other can be seen above in its own chapter (n. 29-40).

That between one heaven and another there is influx but not communication can be seen from their relative position. The third or inmost heaven is above, the second or middle heaven is below, and the first or outmost heaven is still lower. There is a like arrangement in all the societies in each heaven, for example, some dwell on elevated places that appear like mountains (n. 188); on the top of which those of the inmost heaven dwell; below these are the societies of the second heaven, below these again the societies of the outmost heaven. The same is true everywhere, both in elevated places and in those not elevated. A society of a higher heaven has no communication with a society of a lower except by correspondences (see above, n. 100); and communication by correspondences is what is called influx.

One heaven is joined with another, or a society of one heaven with the society of another, by the Lord alone, both by direct and by mediate influx, directly from Himself, and mediately through the higher heavens in order into the lower. 208-1 As the conjunction of the heavens by this inflowing is from the Lord alone there is a most careful precaution against any angel of a higher heaven looking down into a society of a lower heaven and talking with any one there; for the angel is thus immediately deprived of his intelligence and wisdom. The reason of this also shall be told. As there are three degrees of heaven, so each angel has three degrees of life, those in the inmost heaven having the third or inmost degree open, while the second and first degrees are closed; those in the middle heaven have the second degree opened and the first and third closed; and those in the lowest heaven have the first degree opened and the second and third closed. Consequently, as soon as an angel of the third heaven looks down into a society of the second heaven and talks with any one there his third degree is at once closed; and as his wisdom resides in that degree, if that is closed he is deprived of his wisdom, for he has none in the second or first degree. This is what is meant by the words of the Lord in Matthew: He that is on the housetop, let him not go down to take what is in his house; and he that is in the field, let him not turn back to take his garment (24:17, 18). And in Luke: In that day he that shall be on the housetop and his goods in the house, let him not go down to take them away; and he that is in the field let him not turn back. Remember Lot's wife (17:31, 32).

No influx is possible from the lower heavens into the higher, because this is contrary to order; but there is influx from the higher heavens into the lower. Moreover, the wisdom of the angels of a higher heaven surpasses the wisdom of the angels of a lower heaven as a myriad to one; and this is another reason why the angels of a lower heaven cannot converse with those of a higher heaven; and in fact when they look towards them they do not see them, the higher heaven appearing like a cloudy something over their heads. But the angels of a higher heaven can see those in a lower heaven, although if permitted to talk with them they would lose their wisdom, as has been said above.

The thoughts and affections as well as the speech of the angels of the inmost heaven are never perceived in the middle heaven, because they so transcend what is there. But when it pleases the Lord there is seen in the lower heavens from that source something like a flame, and from the thoughts and affections in the middle heaven there is seen in the outmost heaven something luminous, and sometimes a cloud glowing white and variegated. From that cloud, its ascent, descent, and form, what is being said there is in some measure known.

From all this it can be seen what the form of heaven is, namely, that it is the most perfect of all in the inmost heaven; in the middle heaven it is also perfect, but in a lower degree, and in the outmost heaven in a degree still lower; also that the form of one heaven has its permanent existence from another by means of influx from the Lord. But what communication by influx is cannot be understood unless it is known what degrees of height are, and how they differ from degrees of length and breadth. What these different degrees are may be seen above (n 38).

When it comes to the particulars of the form of heaven and how it proceeds and flows, this not even the angels can comprehend. Some conception of it can be gained from the form of all things in the human body, when this is scanned and investigated by an acute and wise man; for it has been shown above, in their respective chapters, that the entire heaven reflects a single man (see n. 59-72) and that all things in man correspond to the heavens (n. 87-102). How incomprehensible and inexplicable that form is is evident only in a general way from the nervous fibers, by which each part and all parts of the body are woven together. What these fibers are, and how they proceed and flow in the brain, the eye cannot at all perceive; for innumerable fibers are there so interwoven that taken together they appear like a soft continuous mass; and yet it is in accord with these that each thing and all things of the will and understanding flow with the utmost distinctness into acts. How again they interweave themselves in the body is clear from the various plexuses, such as those of the heart, the mesentery, and others; and also from the knots called ganglions, into which many fibers enter from every region and there intermingle, and when variously joined together go forth to their functions, and this again and again; besides like things in every viscus, member, organ, and muscle. Whoever examines these fibers and their many wonders with the eye of wisdom will be utterly bewildered. And yet the things seen with the eye are few, and those not seen are still more wonderful because they belong to an inner realm of nature. It is clearly evident that this form corresponds to the form of heaven, because all the workings of the understanding and the will are within it and are in accordance with it; for it is in accordance with this form that whatever a man wills passes spontaneously into act, and whatever he thinks spreads through the fibers from their beginnings even to their terminations, which is the source of sensations; and inasmuch as it is the form of thought and will, it is the form of intelligence and wisdom. Such is the form that corresponds to the form of heaven. And from this it can be known that such is the form in accordance with which every affection and thought of angels extends itself, and that so far as the angels are in that form they are in intelligence and wisdom. That this form of heaven is from the Divine Human of the Lord can be seen above (n. 78-86). All this has been said to make clear also that the heavenly form is such that even as to its generals it can never be completely known, thus that it is incomprehensible even to the angels, as has been said above.

GOVERNMENTS IN HEAVEN. As heaven is divided into societies, and the larger societies consist of some hundreds of thousands of angels (n. 50), and all within a society, although in like good, are not in like wisdom (n. 43), it must needs follow that governments exist there, since order must be observed, and all things of order must be guarded. But the governments in the heavens differ; they are of one sort in societies that constitute the Lord's celestial kingdom, and of another sort in the societies that constitute His spiritual kingdom; they differ also in accordance with the functions of the several societies. Nevertheless, no other government than the government of mutual love is possible in the heavens, and the government of mutual love is heavenly government.

Government in the Lord's celestial kingdom is called righteousness because all in that kingdom are in the good of love to the Lord from the Lord, and whatever is from that good is called righteous. Government there belongs to the Lord alone. He leads them and teaches them in the affairs of life. The truths that are called truths of judgment are written on their hearts; everyone knows them, perceives them, and sees them; 214-1 and in consequence matters of judgment there never come into question, but only matters of righteousness, which belong to the life. About these matters the less wise consult the more wise, and these consult the Lord and receive answers. Their heaven, that is, their inmost joy, is to live rightly from the Lord.

In the Lord's spiritual kingdom the government is called judgment; because those in that kingdom are in spiritual good, which is the good of charity towards the neighbor, and that good in its essence is truth; 215-1 and truth pertains to judgment, as good pertains to righteousness. 215-2 These, too, are led by the Lord, but mediately (n. 208); and in consequence they have governors, few or many according to the need of the society in which they are. They also have laws according to which they live together. The governors administer all things in accordance with the laws, which they understand because they are wise, and in doubtful matters they are enlightened by the Lord.

As government from good, which is the kind of government that exists in the Lord's celestial kingdom, is called righteousness; and government from truth, which is the kind of government that exists in the Lord's spiritual kingdom, is called judgment, so the terms "righteousness and judgment" are used in the Word when heaven and the church are treated of, "righteousness" signifying celestial good, and "judgment" spiritual good, which good, as has been said above, is in its essence truth, as in the following passages: Of peace there shall be no end upon the throne of David and upon His kingdom, to establish it and to uphold it in judgment and in righteousness from henceforth and even to eternity (Isaiah 9:7). By "David" here the Lord is meant; 216-1 and by "His kingdom" heaven, as is evident from the following passage: I will raise unto David a righteous Branch, and He shall reign as King, and shall deal intelligently and shall execute judgment and righteousness in the land (Jer. 23:5). Jehovah is exalted, for He dwelleth on high; He hath filled Zion with judgment and righteousness (Isaiah 33:5). "Zion" also means heaven and the church. 216-2 I, Jehovah, doing judgment and righteousness on the earth, for in these things I delight (Jer. 9:24). I will betroth thee unto Me forever, and I will betroth thee unto Me in righteousness and judgment (Hosea 2:19). O Jehovah, in the heavens Thy righteousness is like the mountains of God, and Thy judgments are like the great deep (Psalm 36:5, 6). They ask of Me the judgments of righteousness, they long for an approach unto God (Isaiah 58:2). So in other places.

In the Lord's spiritual kingdom there are various forms of government, differing in different societies, the variety being in accord with the functions performed by the societies; and the functions of these are in accord with the functions of all things in man to which they correspond. That these are various is well known, the heart having one function, the lungs another, the liver another, the pancreas and spleen another, and each sensory organ another. As in the body these organs perform various services, so there are various services pertaining to the societies in the Greatest Man, which is heaven for the societies there correspond to these organs. That there is a correspondence of all things of heaven with all things of man may be seen in its own chapter above (n. 87-102). But all these forms of government agree in this, that they look to the public good as their end, and in that good to the good of the individual. 217-1 And this is so because everyone in the whole heaven is under the auspices of the Lord, who loves all, and from Divine love ordains that there shall be a common good, from which each individual shall receive his own good. Each one, moreover, receives good according as he loves the common good; for so far as he loves the common good he loves all and everyone; and as that love is love of the Lord he is to that extent loved by the Lord, and good comes to him.

From all this it can be seen what the governors there are, namely, that they are such as are preeminent in love and wisdom, and therefore desire the good of all, and from wisdom know how to provide for the realization of that good. Such governors do not domineer or dictate, but they minister and serve (to serve meaning to do good to others from a love of the good, and to minister meaning to see to it that the good is done); nor do they make themselves greater than others, but less, for they put the good of society and of the neighbor in the first place, and put their own good last; and whatever is in the first place is greater and what is last is less. Nevertheless, the rulers have honor and glory; they dwell in the midst of the society, in higher position than the rest, and also in magnificent palaces; and this glory and honor they accept not for the sake of themselves but for the sake of obedience; for all there know that they have this honor and glory from the Lord, and on that account should be obeyed. This is what is meant by the Lord's words to His disciples Whosoever would become great among you let him be your minister; and whosoever would be first among you let him be your servant; as the Son of man came not to be ministered unto but to minister (Matt. 20:27, 28). He that is greatest among you let him be as the least, and he that is chief as he that doth minister (Luke 22:26).

Also in each house there is a like government in a lesser form. In every house there is a master and there are servants; the master loves the servants and the servants love the master, consequently they serve each other from love. The master teaches how they ought to live, and tells what is to be done; the servants obey and perform their duties. To perform use is the delight of everyone's life. This shows that the Lord's kingdom is a kingdom of uses.

Also in the hells there are governments, for without governments they could not be kept in restraint; but the governments there are opposite to the governments in the heavens; they are governments of the love of self. Everyone there wishes to dictate to others and to be over others. They hate those that do not favor them, and make them objects of their vengeance and fury, for such is the nature of the love of self. Therefore the more malignant are set over them as governors, and these they obey from fear. 220-1 But of this below, where the hells are treated of.

DIVINE WORSHIP IN HEAVEN. Divine worship in the heavens is not unlike in externals Divine worship on the earth, but in internals it is different. In the heavens, as on the earth, there are doctrines, preachings, and church edifices. In essentials the doctrines there are everywhere the same; but in the higher heavens they contain more interior wisdom than in the lower. The preachings are in harmony with the doctrines; and as they have houses and palaces (n. 183-190), so they have also church edifices, in which there is preaching. Such things exist in heaven, because the angels are being perfected continually in wisdom and love. For they possess, as men do, understanding and will; and both their understanding and their will are capable of being continually perfected, the understanding by means of truths of intelligence, and the will by means of the goods of love. 221-1

But essential Divine worship in the heavens does not consist in going to church and hearing preaching, but in a life of love, charity, and faith, in accordance with doctrine; preachings in churches serve solely as means of instruction in matters of life. I have talked with angels on this subject, and have told them that it is believed in the world that Divine worship consists solely in attending church, listening to the preaching, observing the sacrament of the Supper three or four times a year, and performing other acts of worship according to the requirements of the church; also devoting special times to prayers, and at such times, behaving devoutly. The angels said that these are outward acts that ought to be done, but are of no avail unless there is an internal from which they proceed, which is a life in accordance with the precepts that doctrine teaches.

That I might learn about their meeting in places of worship, I have been permitted at times to attend and to hear the preaching. The preacher stands in a pulpit at the east. Those who are in the light of wisdom more than others sit in front of him; those who are in less light sit to the right and left of these. There is a circular arrangement of the seats, so that all are in the preacher's view, no one so sitting at either side as to be out of his view. At the entrance, which is at the east of the building and on the left of the pulpit, those stand who are being initiated. No one is permitted to stand behind the pulpit; when there is any one there the preacher becomes confused. It is the same if any one in the congregation dissents; and for this reason the dissenter must needs turn away his face. The wisdom of the preachings is such as to be above all comparison with the preachings of this world, for those in the heavens are in interior light. The church edifices in the spiritual kingdom are apparently built of stone, and those in the celestial kingdom of wood; because stone corresponds to truth, and those who are in the spiritual kingdom are in truth, while wood corresponds to good, and those in the celestial kingdom are in good. 223-1 In that kingdom the sacred edifices are not called churches but houses of God. In that kingdom they are without magnificence; but in the spiritual kingdom they are more or less magnificent.

I have also talked with one of the preachers about the holy state in which those are who listen to the preaching in the churches. He said that everyone is pious, devout, and holy in harmony with his interiors, which pertain to love and faith, for holiness itself is in love and faith, because the Divine of the Lord is in them. He also said that he did not know what outward holiness is apart from love and faith; and when he thought about it he said that perhaps it is something counterfeiting holiness in outward appearance, either conventional or hypocritical; and that such holiness is kindled and sustained by spurious fire from the love of self and the world.

All the preachers are from the Lord's spiritual kingdom; none are from the celestial kingdom. They are from the spiritual kingdom because the angels there are in truths from good, and all preaching must be from truths. There are no preachers from the celestial kingdom because those who are there are in the good of love, and they see and perceive truths from good, but do not talk about them. But although the angels in the celestial kingdom perceive and see truths there are preachings there, since by means of preachings they are enlightened in the truths that they already know, and are perfected by many truths that they did not know before. As soon as they hear truths they acknowledge them and thus perceive them; and the truths they perceive they love, and by living in accordance with them they make them to be of their life, declaring that living in accordance with truths is loving the Lord. 225-1

All preachers are appointed by the Lord, and have therefrom a gift for preaching. No others are permitted to preach in the churches. They are not called priests, but preachers. They are not called priests because the celestial kingdom is the priesthood of heaven; for priesthood signifies the good of love to the Lord, and those in the celestial kingdom are in that good; while the spiritual kingdom is the kingship of heaven, for kingship signifies truth from good, and those in the spiritual kingdom are in that truth (see above, n. 24). 226-1

The doctrines with which their preachings are in accord all look to life as their end, and none look to faith separate from the life. The doctrine of the inmost heaven is more full of wisdom than the doctrine of the middle heaven, and this more full of intelligence than the doctrine of the outmost heaven; for in each heaven the doctrines are adapted to the perceptions of the angels. The essential of all doctrines is acknowledging the Divine Human of the Lord.

THE POWER OF THE ANGELS OF HEAVEN. That the angels possess power cannot be comprehended by those who know nothing about the spiritual world and its influx into the natural world. Such think that angels can have no power because they are spiritual and are even so pure and unsubstantial that no eye can see them. But those who look more interiorly into the causes of things take a different view. Such know that all the power that a man has is from his understanding and will (for apart from these he is powerless to move a particle of his body), and his understanding and will are his spiritual man. This moves the body and its members at its pleasure; for whatever it thinks the mouth and tongue speak, and whatever it wills the body does; and it bestows its strength at pleasure. As man's will and understanding are ruled by the Lord through angels and spirits, so also are all things of his body, because these are from the will and understanding; and if you will believe it, without influx from heaven man cannot even move a step. That this is so has been shown me by much experience. Angels have been permitted to move my steps, my actions, and my tongue and speech, as they pleased, and this by influx into my will and thought; and I have learned thereby that of myself I could do nothing. I was afterwards told by them that every man is so ruled, and that he can know this from the doctrine of the church and from the Word, for he prays that God may send His angels to lead him, direct his steps, teach him, and inspire in him what to think and what to say, and other like things; although he says and believes otherwise when he is thinking by himself apart from doctrine. All this has been said to make known what power angels have with man.

But so great is the power of angels in the spiritual world that if I should make known all that I have witnessed in regard to it it would exceed belief. Any obstruction there that ought to be removed because it is contrary to Divine order the angels cast down or overthrow merely by an effort of the will and a look. Thus I have seen mountains that were occupied by the evil cast down and overthrown, and sometimes shaken from end to end as in earthquakes; also rocks cleft asunder to their bottoms, and the evil who were upon them swallowed up. I have seen also hundreds of thousands of evil spirits dispersed by angels and cast down into hell. Numbers are of no avail against them; neither are devices, cunning, or combinations; for they see through them all, and disperse them in a moment. (But more may be seen on this subject in the account of The Destruction of Babylon.) Such power do angels have in the spiritual world. It is evident from the Word that they have like power in the natural world also when it is permitted; for instance, that they have given to destruction entire armies; and that they brought on a pestilence from which seventy thousand men died. Of this angel it is said: The angel stretched out his hand against Jerusalem to destroy it but Jehovah repented Him of the evil, and said to the angel that destroyed the people, It is enough, now stay thy hand. And David saw the angel that smote the people (2 Samuel 24:16, 17); besides other passages. Because the angels have such power they are called powers; as in David: Bless Jehovah, ye angels, mighty in power (Psalm 103:20).

But it must be understood that the angels have no power whatever from themselves, but that all their power is from the Lord; and that they are powers only so far as they acknowledge this. Whoever of them believes that he has power from himself instantly becomes so weak as not to be able to resist even a single evil spirit. For this reason angels ascribe no merit whatever to themselves, and are averse to all praise and glory on account of any thing they do, ascribing all the praise and glory to the Lord.

It is the Divine truth that goes forth from the Lord that has all power in the heavens, for the Lord in heaven is Divine truth united to Divine good (see n. 126-140). To the extent that angels are receptions of this truth they are powers. 231-1 Moreover each one is his own truth and his own good because each one is such as his understanding and will are. The understanding pertains to truth because everything of it is from truths, and the will pertains to good because everything of it is from goods; for whatever any one understands he calls truth, and whatever he wills he calls good. From this it is that everyone is his own truth and his own good. 231-2 Therefore so far as an angel is truth from the Divine and good from the Divine he is a power, because to that extent the Lord is in him. And as no one's good and truth are wholly like or the same as another's, since in heaven, as in the world, there is endless variety (n. 20), so the power of one angel is not like the power of another. Those who constitute the arms in the Greatest Man, or heaven, have the greatest power because such are more in truths than others, and into their truths good flows from the entire heaven. Moreover, the power of the whole man passes into the arms, and by means of these the whole body exercises its powers. It is for this reason that in the Word "arms" and "hand" signify powers. 231-3 Sometimes on this account a naked arm is seen in heaven so powerful as to be able to break in pieces everything in its way, even though it were a great rock on the earth. Once it was moved towards me, and I perceived that it was able to crush my bones to atoms.

It has been shown above (n. 137) that the Divine truth that goes forth from the Lord has all power, and that angels have power to the extent that they are receptions of Divine truth from the Lord. But angels are so far receptions of Divine truth as they are receptions of Divine good, for truths have all their power from good, and none apart from good. So, too, good has all its power through truths, and none apart from truths. Power springs from the conjunction of these two. The same is true of faith and love; for it is the same whether you say truth or faith, since everything of faith is truth; also it is the same whether you say good or love, since everything of love is good. 232-1 The great power that angels have by means of truths from good is shown also from this, that when an evil spirit is merely looked at by the angels he falls into a swoon, and does not appear like a man, and this until the angel turns away his eyes. Such an effect is produced by the look of the eyes of angels, because the sight of angels is from the light of heaven, and the light of heaven is Divine truth (see above, n. 126-132). Moreover, the eyes correspond to truths from good. 232-2

As truths from good have all power, so falsities from evil have no power at all; 233-1 and as all in hell are in falsities from evil they have no power against truth and good. But what power they have among themselves, and what power evil spirits have before they are cast into hell, will be told hereafter.

THE SPEECH OF ANGELS. Angels talk with each other just as men do in the world, and on various subjects, as on domestic matters, and on matters of the civil state, and of moral, and spiritual life. And there is no difference except that their talk is more intelligent than that of men, because it is from more interior thought. I have been permitted to associate with them frequently, and to talk with them as friend with friend, and sometimes as stranger with stranger; and as I was then in a state like theirs I knew no otherwise than that I was talking with men on the earth.

Angelic speech, like human speech, is distinguished into words; it is also audibly uttered and heard; for angels, like men, have mouth, tongue, and ears, and an atmosphere in which the sound of their speech is articulated, although it is a spiritual atmosphere adapted to angels, who are spiritual. In their atmosphere angels breathe and utter words by means of their breath, as men do In their atmosphere. 235-1

In the entire heaven all have the same language, and they all understand one another, to whatever society, near or remote, they belong. Language there is not learned but is instinctive with everyone, for it flows from their very affection and thought, the tones of their speech corresponding to their affections, and the vocal articulations which are words corresponding to the ideas of thought that spring from the affections; and because of this correspondence the speech itself is spiritual, for it is affection sounding and thought speaking. [2] Any one who gives any thought to it can see that all thought is from affection which pertains to love, and that the ideas of thought are the various forms into which the general affection is distributed; for no thought or idea is possible apart from affection-the soul and life of thought is from affection. This enables angels to know, merely from another's speech, what he is-from the tone what his affection is, and from the vocal articulations or words what his mind is. The wiser angels know what the ruling affection is from a single series of words, for that affection is what they chiefly attend to. [3] It is known that each individual has a variety of affections, one affection when in joy, another when in grief, another when in sympathy and compassion, another when in sincerity and truth, another when in love and charity, another when in zeal or in anger, another when in simulation and deceit, another when in quest of honor and glory, and so on. But the ruling affection or love is in all of these; and for this reason the wiser angels, because they perceive that love, know from the speech the whole state of another. [4] This it has been granted me to know from much experience. I have heard angels disclosing the character of another's life merely from hearing him speak. They also said that from any ideas of another's thought they could know all things of his life, because from those ideas they know his ruling love, in which are all things in their order. They know also that man's book of life is nothing else.

Angelic language has nothing in common with human languages except certain words that are the sounds of a specific affection; yet this is true not of the words themselves but of their sounds; on which subject something will be said in what follows That angelic language has nothing in common with human languages is evident from the fact that angels are unable to utter a single word of human language. This was tried but they could not do it, because they can utter nothing except what is in entire agreement with their affections; whatever is not in agreement is repugnant to their very life, for life belongs to affection, and their speech is from their life. I have been told that the first language of men on our earth coincided with angelic language because they had it from heaven; and that the Hebrew language coincides with it in some respects.

As the speech of angels corresponds to their affection, and their affection belongs to their love, and as the love of heaven is love to the Lord and love towards the neighbor (see above, n. 13-19), it is evident how choice and delightful their talk must be, affecting not the ears only but also the interiors of the mind of those who listen to it. There was a certain hard-hearted spirit with whom an angel spoke. At length he was so affected by what was said that he shed tears, saying that he had never wept before, but he could not refrain, for it was love speaking.

The speech of angels is likewise full of wisdom because it proceeds from their interior thoughts, and their interior thought is wisdom, as their interior affection is love, and in their speech their love and wisdom unite. For this reason their speech is so full of wisdom that they can express in a single word what man cannot express in a thousand words also the ideas of their thought include things that are beyond man's comprehension, and still more his power of expression. This is why the things that have been heard and seen in heaven are said to be ineffable, and such as ear hath never heard nor eye seen. [2] That this is true I have also been permitted to learn by experience. At times I have entered into the state in which angels are, and in that state have talked with them, and I then understood everything. But when I was brought back into my former state, and thus into the natural thought proper to man, and wished to recall what I had heard I could not; for there were thousands of things unadapted to the ideas of natural thought, and therefore inexpressible except by variegations of heavenly light, and thus not at all by human words. [3] Also the ideas of thought of the angels from which their words spring are modifications of the light of heaven, and the affections from which the tones of the words spring are variations of the heat of heaven, the light of heaven being Divine truth or wisdom, and the heat of heaven the Divine good or love (see above, n. 126-140); and the angels have their affection from the Divine love, and their thought from the Divine wisdom. 239-1

Because the speech of angels proceeds directly from their affection, and the ideas of their thought are the various forms into which their general affection is distributed (see above, n. 236), angels can express in a moment what a man cannot express in half an hour; also they can set forth in a few words what has been expressed in writing on many pages; and this, too, has been proved to me by much experience. 240-1 Thus the angels' ideas of thought and the words of their speech make one, like effecting cause and effect; for what is in the ideas of thought as cause is presented in the words as effect, and this is why every word comprehends in itself so many things. Also all the particulars of angelic thought, and thus of angelic speech, appear when presented to view like a thin wave or circumfluent atmosphere, in which are innumerable things in their order derived from angelic wisdom, and these enter another's thought and affect him. The ideas of thought of everyone, both angel and man, are presented to view in the light of heaven, whenever the Lord pleases. 240-2

The speech of angels of the Lord's celestial kingdom resembles the speech of the angels of His spiritual kingdom, but it is from more interior thought. Celestial angels are in good of love to the Lord, and therefore speak from wisdom; while spiritual angels are in the good of charity towards the neighbor, which in its essence is truth (n. 215), and therefore speak from intelligence, for wisdom is from good, and intelligence is from truth. For this reason the speech of celestial angels is like a gentle stream, soft, and as it were continuous; but the speech of spiritual angels is slightly vibratory and divided. The speech of celestial angels has much of the tones of the vowels u and o; while the speech of spiritual angels has much of the tones of e and i*; for the vowels stand for tone, and in the tone there is affection, the tone of the speech of angels corresponding to their affection, as has been said above (n. 236); while the vocal articulations, which are words, correspond to the ideas of thought which spring from affection. As the vowels are not essential to a language, but serve by means of tones to elevate the words to the various affections according to each one's state, so in the Hebrew tongue the vowels are not expressed, and are also variously pronounced. From this a man's quality in respect to his affection and love is known to the angels. Also in the speech of celestial angels there are no hard consonants, and it rarely passes from one consonant to another without the interposition of a word beginning with a vowel. This is why in the Word the particle "and" is so often interposed, as can be seen by those who read the Word in the Hebrew, in which this particle is soft, beginning and ending with a vowel sound. Again, in the Word, in Hebrew, it can in some measure be seen from the words used whether they belong to the celestial class or the spiritual class, that is, whether they involve good or truth. Those involving good partake largely of the sounds of u and o, and also somewhat of a, while those involving truth partake of the sounds of e and i. Because it is especially in tones that affections express themselves, so in human speech, when great subjects are discussed, such as heaven [caelum] and God [Deus], those words are preferred that contain the vowels u and o; and musical tones, whenever such themes are to be expressed, rise to the same fullness; but not when less exalted themes are rendered. By such means musical art is able to express affections of various kinds. * [As these vowels are pronounced in European language. - Tr.]

In angelic speech there is a kind of symphony that cannot be described; 242-1 which comes from the pouring forth and diffusion of the thoughts and affections from which speech flows, in accordance with the form of heaven, and all affiliation and all communication in heaven is in accordance with that form. That angels are affiliated in accordance with the form of heaven, and that their thoughts and affections flow in accordance with it may be seen above (n. 200-212).

Speech like that in the spiritual world is inherent in every man in his interior intellectual part; but man does not know this, because this speech does not with man, as with angels, fall into words analogous to affection; nevertheless this is what causes man, when he enters the other life, to come into the same speech as spirits and angels, and thus to know how to speak without instruction. 243-1 But more on this subject hereafter.

In heaven, as has been said above, all have one speech; but it is varied in this respect, that the speech of the wise is more interior and more full of variations of affections and ideas of thought, while the speech of the less wise is more external and less full; and the speech of the simple is still more external, consisting of words from which the meaning is to be gathered in the same way as when men are talking to one another. There is also speech by the face, terminating in something sonorous modified by ideas. Again, there is speech in which heavenly representatives are mingled with the ideas, and go forth from ideas to sight. There is also speech by gestures that correspond to affections, and represent things like those expressed by their words. There is speech by means of the generals of affections and the generals of thoughts. There is speech like thunder; besides other kinds.

The speech of evil and infernal spirits is likewise natural to them because it is from affections; but it is from evil affections and consequent filthy ideas, to which angels are utterly averse. Thus the modes of speaking in hell are opposite to those of heaven; and in consequence evil spirits cannot endure angelic speech, and angels cannot endure infernal speech. To the angels infernal speech is like a bad odor striking the nostrils. The speech of hypocrites, who are such as are able to feign themselves angels of light, resembles in respect to words the speech of angels, but in respect to affections and consequent ideas of thought it is the direct opposite. Consequently, when the inner nature of their speech is perceived as wise angels perceive it, it is heard as the gnashing of teeth, and strikes with horror.

THE SPEECH OF ANGELS WITH MAN. Angels who talk with man do not talk in their own language, nor in any language unknown to man, but in the man's own language, or in some other language with which he is acquainted. This is so because when angels speak with man they turn themselves to him and conjoin themselves with him; and this conjunction of angel with man causes the two to be in like thought; and as man's thought coheres to his memory, and this is the source of his speech, the two have the same language. Moreover, when an angel or a spirit comes to a man, and by turning to him is conjoined to him, he so enters into the entire memory of the man that he is scarcely conscious that he does not himself know whatever the man knows, including his languages. [2] I have talked with angels about this, and have said that perhaps they thought that they were addressing me in my mother tongue, since it is so perceived; and yet it was I and not they that spoke; and that this is evident from the fact that angels cannot utter a single word of human language (see n. 237); furthermore, human language is natural and they are spiritual, and spiritual beings cannot give expression to any thing in a natural way. To this they replied that they are aware that their conjunction with the man with whom they are speaking is with his spiritual thought; but because his spiritual thought flows into his natural thought, and his natural thought coheres to his memory, the language of the man and all his knowledge appear to them to be their own; and that this is so for this reason, that while it is the Lord's pleasure that there should be such a conjunction with and sort of insertion of man into heaven, yet the state of man is now such that there can no longer be such conjunction with angels, but only with spirits who are not in heaven. [3] When I talked about this with spirits also they were unwilling to believe that it is the man that speaks, insisting that they spoke in man, also that man's knowledge is their knowledge and not the man's knowledge, consequently that everything that man knows is from them. I tried to convince them by many proofs that this is not true, but in vain. Who are meant by spirits and who are meant by angels will be told further on when the world of spirits is treated of.

There is another reason why angels and spirits conjoin themselves so closely with man as not to know but that what is man's is their own, namely, that there is such conjunction between the spiritual world and the natural world in man that the two are seemingly one. But inasmuch as man has separated himself from heaven the Lord has provided that there should be angels and spirits with each individual, and that man should be ruled by the Lord through these. This is the reason for such close conjunction. It would have been otherwise if man had not separated himself; for in that case he might have been ruled by the Lord through the general influx from heaven, without spirits and angels being adjoined to him. But this subject will be specially considered in what follows when the conjunction of heaven with man is treated of.

The speech of an angel or spirit with man is heard by him as audibly as the speech of man with man, yet by himself only, and not by others who stand near; and for the reason that the speech of an angel or spirit flows first into a man's thought, and by an inner way into his organ of hearing, and thus moves it from within; while the speech of man with man flows first into the air and by an outward way into his organ of hearing, and moves it from without. Evidently, then, the speech of an angel or spirit with man is heard within him; but as the organs of hearing are thus equally moved, the speech is equally audible. That the speech of an angel or a spirit flows down from within even into the ear has been made clear to me by the fact that it flows also into the tongue, causing a slight vibration, but without any such motion as when the man himself by means of the tongue forms the sound of speech into words.

But at the present day to talk with spirits is rarely granted because it is dangerous; 249-1 for then the spirits know, what otherwise they do not know, that they are with man; and evil spirits are such that they hold man in deadly hatred, and desire nothing so much as to destroy him both soul and body, and this they do in the case of those who have so indulged themselves in fantasies as to have separated from themselves the enjoyments proper to the natural man. Some also who lead a solitary life sometimes hear spirits talking with them, and without danger; but that the spirits with them may not know that they are with man they are at intervals removed by the Lord; for most spirits are not aware that there is any other world than that in which they live, and therefore are unaware that there are men anywhere else; and this is why man is not permitted to speak with them in return. If he did they would know. Again, those who meditate much on religious subjects, and are so intent upon them as to see them as it were inwardly within themselves, begin to hear spirits speaking with them; for religious persuasions, whatever they are, when man dwells upon them by himself and does not adapt them to the various things of use in the world, penetrate to the interiors and rest there, and occupy the whole spirit of the man, and even enter into the spiritual world and act upon the spirits there. But such persons are visionaries and enthusiasts; and whatever spirit they hear they believe to be the Holy Spirit, when, in fact, such spirits are enthusiastic spirits. Such spirits see falsities as truths, and so seeing them they induce not themselves only but also those they flow into to believe them. Such spirits, however, have been gradually removed, because they began to lure others into evil and to gain control over them. Enthusiastic spirits are distinguished from other spirits by their believing themselves to be the Holy Spirit, and believing what they say to be Divine. As man honors such spirits with Divine worship they do not attempt to harm him. I have sometimes talked with them, and the wicked things they infused into their worshipers were then disclosed. They dwell together towards the left, in a desert place.

But to speak with the angels of heaven is granted only to those who are in truths from good, especially to those who are in the acknowledgment of the Lord and of the Divine in His Human, because this is the truth in which the heavens are. For, as it has been shown above, the Lord is the God of heaven (n. 2-6); it is the Divine of the Lord that makes heaven (n. 7-12); the Divine of the Lord in heaven is love to Him and charity towards the neighbor from Him (n. 13-19); the whole heaven in one complex reflects a single man; also every society of heaven; and every angel is in complete human form, and this from the Divine Human of the Lord (n. 59-86). All of which makes evident that only those whose interiors are opened by Divine Truths, even to the Lord, are able to speak with the angels of heaven, since it is into these truths with man that the Lord flows, and when the Lord flows in heaven also flows in. Divine truths open the interiors of man because man was so created as to be in respect to his internal man an image of heaven, and in respect to his external an image of the world

(n. 57); and the internal man is opened only by means of Divine truth going forth from the Lord, because that is the light of heaven and the life of heaven (n. 126-140).

Footnotes

201-1 The form of heaven is a form in accordance with the Divine order (n. 4040-4043, 6607, 9877).

202-1 Divine truths are the laws of order (n. 2447, 7995). Man is a man to the extent that he lives in accordance with order, that is, to the extent that he is in good in accordance with Divine truths (n. 4839, 6605, 6626). All things of Divine order are gathered up in man and he is from creation Divine order in form (n. 4219, 4220, 4222, 4223, 4523, 4524, 5114, 6013, 6057, 6605, 6626, 9706, 10156, 10472). Man is not born into good and truth, but into evil and falsity, that is, into the opposite of Divine order, and consequently into pure ignorance; and for this reason he must needs be born anew that is, be regenerated, which is effected by means of Divine truths from the Lord, that he may be introduced into order (n. 1047, 2307, 2308, 3518, 3812, 8480, 8550, 10283, 10284, 10286, 10731). When the Lord forms man anew, that is, regenerates him, He arranges all things in him in accordance with order, which means, into the form of heaven (n. 5700, 6690, 9931, 10303).

203-1 Everyone in heaven has communication of life, which may be called its extension into angelic societies round about, according to the quantity and quality of his good (n. 8794, 8797). Thoughts and affections have such extension (n. 2470, 6598-6613). They are united and separated in accordance with the ruling affections (n. 4111).

203-2 There is only one Life, from which all, both in heaven and in the world, live (n. 1954, 2021, 2536, 2658, 2886-2889, 3001, 3484, 3742, 5847, 6467). That life is from the Lord above (n. 2886-2889, 3344, 3484, 4319, 4320, 4524, 4882, 5986, 6325, 6468-6470, 9276, 10196). It flows into angels, spirits, and men, in a wonderful manner (n. 2886-2889, 3337, 3338, 3484, 3742). The Lord flows in from His Divine love, which is such that what is its own it wills should be another's (n. 3472, 4320). For this reason life appears to be in man, and not flowing in (n. 3742, 4320). Of the joy of angels, perceived and confirmed by what they told me, because of their not living from themselves but from the Lord (n. 6469). The evil are unwilling to be convinced that life flows in (n. 3743). Life from the Lord flows in also with the evil (n. 2706, 3743, 4417, 10196). But they turn good into evil, and truth into falsity; for such as man is such is his reception of life illustrated (n. 4319, 4320, 4417).

204-1 Thought pours itself into societies of spirits and of angels round about (n. 6600-6605). Still it does not move or disturb the thoughts of the societies (n. 6601, 6603).

205-1 Good recognizes its truth, and truth its good (n. 2429, 3101, 3102, 3161, 3179, 3180, 4358, 5704, 5835, 9637). In this way good and truth are conjoined (n. 3834, 4096, 4097, 4301, 4345, 4353, 4364, 4368, 5365, 7623-7627, 7752-7762, 8530, 9258, 10555). This is effected by influx from heaven (n. 9079).

208-1 There is direct influx from the Lord and mediate influx through heaven (n. 6063, 6307, 6472, 9682, 9683). There is a direct influx of the Lord into the minutest parts of all things (n. 6058, 6474-6478, 8717, 8728). Of the mediate influx of the Lord through the heavens (n. 4067, 6982, 6985, 6996).

214-1 The celestial angels do not think and speak from truths, as the spiritual angels do, because they have from the Lord a perception of all things of truth (n. 202, 597, 607, 784, 1121, 1384, 1398, 1442, 1919, 7680, 7877, 8780, 9277, 10336). In respect to truths the celestial angels say, Yea, yea, or Nay, nay; but the spiritual angels reason about them whether they are true or not (n. 2715, 3246, 4448, 9166, 10786, where the Lord's words, Let your speech be Yea, yea, Nay, nay; what is beyond these is from evil (Matt. 5:37). are explained).

215-1 Those in the spiritual kingdom are in truths, and those in the celestial kingdom are in good (n. 863, 875, 927, 1023, 1043, 1044, 1555, 2256, 4328, 4493, 5113, 9596) The good of the spiritual kingdom is the good of charity towards the neighbor and this good in its essence is truth (n. 8042, 10296).

215-2 In the Word "righteousness" is predicated of good, and "Judgment" of truth therefore "to do righteousness and judgment" means good and truth (n. 2235, 9857). "Great judgments" means the law of Divine order, thus Divine truths (n. 7206).

216-1 By "David" in the prophetic parts of the Word, the Lord is meant (n. 1888, 9954).

216-2 In the Word "Zion" means the church, and specifically the celestial church (n. 2362, 9055).

217-1 Every man and every community, also one's country and the church and in the universal sense the kingdom of the Lord, is a neighbor, and to do good to these from love of good in accordance with their state is to love the neighbor; that is, the neighbor is the good of these, which is the common good that must be consulted (n. 6818-6824, 8123). Civil good also, which is justice, is a neighbor (n. 2915, 4730, 8120-8123). Therefore charity towards the neighbor extends itself to all things and each thing of the life of man; and loving good and doing good from love of good and truth, and also doing what is just from a love of what is just in every function and in every work, is loving the neighbor (n. 2417, 8121-8124).

220-1 There are two kinds of rule, one from love towards the neighbor the other from love of self (n. 10814). From the rule that is from love towards the neighbor flow all goods and all happinesses (n. 10160, 10814). In heaven no one desires to rule from the love of self, but all desire to minister, which means to rule from love to the neighbor; this is the source of their great power (n. 5732). From rule from the love of self all evils flow in (n. 10038). When the loves of self and the world had begun to prevail men were compelled to subject themselves to governments as a means of security (n. 7364, 10160, 10814).

221-1 The understanding is receptive of truth, and the will of good (n. 3623, 6125, 7503, 9300, 9930). As all things have relation to truth and good, so everything of man's life has relation to understanding and will (n. 803, 10122). Angels are perfected to eternity (n. 4803, 6648).

223-1 "Stone" signifies truth (n. 114, 643, 1298, 3720, 6426, 8609, 10376). "Wood" signifies good (n. 643, 3720, 8354). For this reason the most ancient people, who were in celestial good, had sacred buildings of wood (n. 3720).

225-1 Loving the Lord and the neighbor is living in accordance with the Lord's commandments (n. 10143, 10153, 10310, 10578, 10645, 10683).

226-1 Priests represented the Lord in respect to the Divine good, kings in respect to Divine truth (n. 2015, 6148). Therefore, in the Word a "priest" signifies those who are in the good of love to the Lord, and the priesthood signifies that good (n. 9806, 9809). A "king" in the Word signifies those who are in Divine truth, and therefrom kingship signifies truth from good (n. 1672, 2015, 2069, 4575, 4581, 4966, 5044).

231-1 Angels are called powers and are powers from their reception of Divine truth from the Lord (n. 9639). Angels are recipients of Divine truth from the Lord and on this account are sometimes called "gods" in the Word (n. 4295, 4402, 7268, 7873, 8192, 8301, 9160)

231-2 A man or an angel is his own good and his own truth, thus his own love and his own faith (n. 10298, 10367). He is his own understanding and his own will, for everything of life is there from; the life of good is from the will, and the life of truth is from the understanding (n. 10076 10177 10264, 10284).

231-3 The correspondence of the hands, arms, and shoulders, with the Greatest man or heaven (n. 4931-4937). In the Word, "arms" and hands signify power (n. 878, 3091, 4932, 4933, 6947, 10019).

232-1 All power in heaven is the power of truth from good, thus of faith from loves (n. 3091, 3563, 6423, 8304, 9643, 10019, 10182). All power is from the Lord, because from Him is every truth of faith and every good of love (n. 9327, 9410). This power is meant by the keys given to Peter (n. 6344). It is Divine truth going forth from the Lord that has all power (n. 6948, 8200). This power of the lord is what is meant by "sitting at the right hand of Jehovah" (n. 3387, 4592, 4933, 7518, 7673, 8281, 9133). The right had means power (n. 10019).

232-2 The eyes correspond to truths from good (n.4403-4421, 4523-4534, 6923).

233-1 Falsity from evil has no power, because truth from food has all power (n 6784, 10481).

235-1 In the heavens there is respiration, but it is of an interior kind (n. 3884, 3885) from experience (n. 3884, 3885, 3891, 3893). There are differing respirations there, varying in accordance with their states (n. 1119, 3886, 3887, 3889, 3892, 3893). The evil are wholly unable to breathe in heaven, and they are suffocated if they go there (n. 3894).

239-1 The ideas of angels, from which they speak, are expressed by wonderful variegations of the light of heaven (n. 1646, 3343, 3993).

240-1 Angels can express by their speech in a moment more than a man can express by his in half an hour; and they can also express things that do not fall into the expressions of human speech (n. 1641-1643, 1645, 4609, 7089).

240-2 The innumerable things contained in one idea of thought (n. 1008, 1869, 4946, 6613-6618). The ideas of man's thought are opened in the other life, and what they are is presented to view to the life (n. 1869, 3310, 5510). What their appearance is (n. 6601, 8885). The ideas of angels of the inmost heaven present an appearance of flamy light (n. 6615). The ideas of angels of the outmost heaven present an appearance of thin white clouds (n. 6614). An angelic idea seen, from which there was a radiation towards the Lord (n. 6620). Ideas of thought extend themselves widely into the societies of angels round about (n. 6598-6613).

242-1 In angelic speech there is a symphony with harmonious cadence (n. 1648, 1649, 7191).

243-1 There is spiritual or angelic speech belonging to man, though he does not know it (n. 4104). The ideas of the internal man are spiritual, but during his life in the world man perceives them naturally, because he then thinks in what is natural (n. 10236, 10237, 10551). Man comes after death into his interior ideas (n. 3226, 3342, 3343, 10568, 10604). Those ideas then form his speech (n. 2470-2479).

249-1 Man is able to talk with spirits and angels; and the ancient people frequently talked with them (n. 67-69, 784, 1634, 1636, 7802). In some earths angels and spirits appear in human form and talk with the inhabitants (n. 10751, 10752). But on this earth at this day it is dangerous to talk with spirits, unless man is in true faith, and is led by the Lord (n. 784, 9438, 10751).

Section 6

The influx of the Lord Himself into man is into his forehead, and from that into the whole face, because the forehead of man corresponds to love, and the face corresponds to all his interiors. 251-1 The influx of spiritual angels into man is into his head every where, from the forehead and temples to the whole part that contains the cerebrum, because that region of the head corresponds to intelligence; but the influx of celestial angels is into that part of the head that contains the cerebellum, and is called the occiput, from the ears all around even to the neck, for that region corresponds to wisdom. All the speech of angels with man enters by these ways into his thought; and by this means I have perceived what angels they were that spoke with me.

Those who talk with the angels of heaven also see the things that exist in heaven, because they are then seeing in the light of heaven, for their interiors are in that light; also the angels through them see the things that are on the earth, 252-1 because in them heaven is conjoined to the world and the world is conjoined to heaven. For (as has been said above n. 246), when the angels turn themselves to man they so conjoin themselves to him as to be wholly unaware that what pertains to the man is not theirs-not only what pertains to his speech but also to his sight and hearing; while man, on the other hand, is wholly unaware that the things that flow in through the angels are not his. Such was the conjunction that existed between angels of heaven and the most ancient people on this earth, and for this reason their times were called the Golden Age. Because this race acknowledged the Divine under a human form, that is, the Lord, they talked with the angels of heaven as with their friends, and angels of heaven talked with them as with their friends; and in them heaven and the world made one. But after those times man gradually separated himself from heaven by loving himself more than the Lord and the world more than heaven, and in consequence began to feel the delights of the love of self and the world as separate from the delights of heaven, and finally to such an extent as to be ignorant of any other delight. Then his interiors that had been open into heaven were closed up, while his exteriors were open to the world; and when this takes place man is in light in regard to all things of the world, but in thick darkness in regard to all things of heaven.

Since those times it is only rarely that any one has talked with the angels of heaven; but some have talked with spirits who are not in heaven. This is so because man's interior and exterior faculties are such that they are turned either towards the Lord as their common center (n. 124), or towards self, that is, backwards from the Lord. Those that are turned towards the Lord are also turned towards heaven. But those that are turned towards self, are turned also towards the world. And to elevate these is a difficult matter; nevertheless the Lord elevates them as much as is possible, by turning the love about; which is done by means of truths from the Word.

I have been told how the Lord spoke with the prophets through whom the

Word was given. He did not speak with them as He did with the ancients, by an influx into their interiors, but through spirits who were sent to them, whom He filled with His look, and thus inspired with the words which they dictated to the prophets; so that it was not influx but dictation. And as the words came forth directly from the Lord, each one of them was filled with the Divine and contains within it an internal sense, which is such that the angels of heaven understand the words in a heavenly and spiritual sense, while men understand them in a natural sense. Thus has the Lord conjoined heaven and the world by means of the Word. How the Lord fills spirits with the Divine by His look has also been made clear. A spirit that has been filled by the Lord with the Divine does not know otherwise than that he is the Lord, and that it is the Divine that is speaking; and this continues until he has finished speaking. After that he perceives and acknowledges that he is a spirit, and that he spoke from the Lord and not from himself. Because this was the state of the spirits who spoke with the prophets they said that it was Jehovah that spoke; the spirits even called themselves Jehovah, as can be seen both from the prophetical and historical parts of the Word.

That the nature of the conjunction of angels and spirits with man may be understood I am permitted to mention some notable things by which it may be elucidated and verified. When angels and spirits turn themselves to man they do not know otherwise than that the man's language is their own and that they have no other language; and for the reason that they are there in the man's language, and not in their own, which they have forgotten. But as soon as they turn themselves away from the man they are in their own angelic and spiritual language, and know nothing about the man's language. I have had a like experience when in company with angels and in a state like theirs. I then talked with them in their language and knew nothing of my own, having forgotten it; but as soon as I ceased to be present with them I was in my own language. [2] Another notable fact is that when angels and spirits turn themselves to a man they are able to talk with him at any distance; they have talked with me at a considerable distance as audibly as when they were near. But when they turn themselves away from man and talk with each other man hears nothing at all of what they are saying, even if it be close to his ear. From this it was made clear that all conjunction in the spiritual world is determined by the way they turn. [3] Another notable fact is that many spirits together can talk with a man, and the man with them; for they send one of their number to the man with whom they wish to speak, and the spirit sent turns himself to the man and the rest of them turn to their spirit and thus concentrate their thoughts, which the spirit utters; and the spirit then does not know otherwise than that he is speaking from himself, and they do not know otherwise than that they are speaking. Thus also is the conjunction of many with one effected by turning. 255-1 But of these emissary spirits, who are also called subjects, and of communication by means of them, more will be said hereafter.

An angel or spirit is not permitted to speak with a man from his own memory, but only from the man's memory; for angels and spirits have a memory as well as man. If a spirit were to speak from his own memory with a man the man would not know otherwise than that the thoughts then in his mind were his own, although they were the spirit's thoughts. This would be like the recollection of something which the man had never heard or seen. That this is so has been given me to know from experience. This is the source of the belief held by some of the ancients that after some thousands of years they were to return into their former life, and into everything they had done, and in fact, had returned. This they concluded because at times there came to them a sort of recollection of things that they had never seen or heard. This came from an influx from the memory of spirits into their ideas of thought.

There are also spirits called natural and corporeal spirits. When these come to a man they do not conjoin themselves with his thought, like other spirits, but enter into his body, and occupy all his senses, and speak through his mouth, and act through his members, believing at the time that all things of the man are theirs. These are the spirits that obsess man. But such spirits have been cast into hell by the Lord, and thus wholly removed; and in consequence such obsessions are not possible at the present time. 257-1

WRITINGS IN HEAVEN. As the angels have speech, and their speech consists of words, they also have writings; and by writing as well as by speech they give expression to what is in their minds. At times I have had papers sent to me, traced with written words precisely like manuscripts in the world, and others like printed sheets; and I was able to read them in a like way, but was allowed to get from them only an idea here and there; for the reason that it is not in accordance with Divine order for man to be taught by writings from heaven; but he must be taught by means of the Word only; for it is only by means of the Word that there is communication and conjunction of heaven with the world, thus of the Lord with man. That papers written in heaven were seen also by the prophets is shown in Ezekiel: When I looked, behold a hand was put forth by a spirit unto me, and a roll of a book was therein which he unrolled in my sight; it was written on the front and on the back (2:9, 10). And in John: I saw upon the right hand of Him that sat on the throne a book written within and on the back, sealed up with seven seals (Apoc. 5:1).

The existence of writings in the heavens is a provision of the Lord for the sake of the Word; for the Word in its essence is Divine truth, and from it is all heavenly wisdom, both with men and with angels; for the Word was dictated by the Lord, and what is dictated by the Lord passes through all the heavens in order and terminates with man. Thereby it is adapted both to the wisdom of angels and the intelligence of men. Thereby, too, the angels have a Word, and read it the same as men do on the earth, and also draw from it their doctrinals, and preach from it (n. 221). It is the same Word; but its natural sense, which is the sense of the letter with us, does not exist in heaven, but only the spiritual sense, which is its internal sense. What this sense is can be seen in the small treatise on The White Horse spoken of in the Apocalypse.

A little paper was at one time sent to me from heaven, on which there were a few words only written in Hebrew letters, and I was told that every letter involved arcana of wisdom, and that these arcana were contained in the inflections and curvatures of the letters, and thus also in the sounds. This made clear to me what is signified by these words of the Lord: Verily I say unto you, until heaven and earth pass away, one iota or one tittle shall not pass away from the law (Matt. 5:18). That the Word in every tittle of it is Divine is known in the church; but just where the Divine lies hid in every tittle has not been known heretofore, and therefore shall be told. In the inmost heaven the writing consists of various inflected and circumflected forms, and the inflections and circumflections are in accordance with the forms of heaven. By means of these angels express the arcana of their wisdom, and also many things that they are unable to express in spoken words; and what is wonderful, the angels know this writing without training or a teacher, it being implanted in them like their speech (see n. 236); therefore this writing is heavenly writing. It is implanted because all extension of thoughts and affections and consequent communication of intelligence and wisdom of the angels proceeds in accordance with the form of heaven (n. 201); and for the same reason their writing flows into that form. I have been told that the most ancient people on this earth, before letters were invented, had such writing; and that it was transferred into the letters of the Hebrew language, and these letters in ancient times were all inflected, and none of them, as at present, were bounded by straight lines. Thus it is that in the Word Divine things and arcana of heaven are contained even in its iotas, points and tittles.

This writing in characters of a heavenly form is in use in the inmost heaven, the angels of which surpass all others in wisdom. By means of these characters they express the affections, from which thoughts flow and follow in order in accordance with the subject treated of. Consequently these writings, which I have also been permitted to see, involve arcana which thought cannot exhaust. But such writings do not exist in the lower heavens. The writings there resemble the writings in the world, having like characters, and yet they are not intelligible to man, because they are in angelic language; and angelic language is such that it has nothing in common with human languages (n. 237), since by the vowels they express affections, and by the consonants the ideas of thought from the affections, and by the words from these the sense of the matter (see above, n. 236, 241). Moreover, in this writing, which I have also seen, more is involved in a few words than a man can express in several pages. In this way they have the Word written in the lower heavens; but in the inmost heaven in heavenly characters.

It is a notable fact that the writings in the heavens flow naturally from their very thoughts, and this so easily that the thought puts itself forth, as it were, and the hand never hesitates in the choice of a word, because both the words they speak and those they write correspond to the ideas of their thought; and all correspondence is natural and spontaneous. There are also writings in the heavens that exist without the aid of the hand, from mere correspondence with the thoughts; but these are not permanent.

I have also seen writings from heaven made up of mere numbers set down in order and in a series, just as in writings made up of letters and words; and I have been taught that this writing is from the inmost heaven, and that their heavenly writing (spoken of above, n. 260, 261), when the thought from it flows down, is set forth before the angels of the lower heavens in numbers, and that this numerical writing likewise involves arcana, some of which can neither be comprehended by thought nor expressed by words. For all numbers correspond, and have a meaning, the same as words do, in accordance with the correspondence; 263-1 yet with the difference that in numbers generals are involved, and in words particulars; and as one general involves innumerable particulars, so more arcana are involved in numerical writing than in literal writing. From this I could see that in the Word numbers as well as words signify things. What the simple numbers signify, as 2, 3, 4, 5, 6, 7, 8, 9, 10, 12, and what the compound numbers, as 20, 30, 50, 70, 100, 144, 1000, 10,000, 12,000, and others, may be seen in the Arcana Celestia, where they are treated of. In this writing in heaven, a number is always prefixed on which those following in a series depend as on their subject; for that number is as it were an index to the matter treated of, and from it is the determination of the numbers that follow to the particular point.

Those who know nothing about heaven, and who are unwilling to have any other idea of it than as of something purely atmospherical, in which the angels fly about as intellectual minds, having no sense of hearing or seeing, are unable to conceive that the angels have speech and writing; for they place the existence of everything real in what is material; and yet the writings in heaven have as real an existence as those in the world, and the angels there have everything that is useful for life and useful for wisdom.

THE WISDOM OF THE ANGELS OF HEAVEN. The nature of angelic wisdom can scarcely be comprehended, because it so greatly transcends human wisdom that the two cannot be compared; and whatever is thus transcendent does not seem to be any thing. Moreover, some truths that must enter into a description of it are as yet unknown, and until these become known they exist in the mind as shadows, and thus hide the thing as it is in itself. Nevertheless, these truths can be known, and when known be comprehended, provided the mind takes any interest in them; for interest carries light with it because it is from love; and upon those who love the things pertaining to Divine and heavenly wisdom light shines forth from heaven and gives enlightenment.

What the wisdom of the angels is can be inferred from the fact that they are in the light of heaven, and the light of heaven in its essence is Divine truth or Divine wisdom; and this light enlightens at the same time their inner sight, or sight of the mind, and their outer sight, or sight of the eyes. (That the light of heaven is Divine truth or Divine wisdom may be seen above, n. 126-133.) The angels are also in heavenly heat, which in its essence is Divine good or Divine love, and from that they have an affection and longing to become wise. (That the heat of heaven is Divine good or Divine love may be seen above, n. 133-140.) That the angels are in wisdom, even to the extent that they may be called wisdoms, follows from the fact that their thoughts and affections all flow in accordance with the heavenly form, and this form is the form of Divine wisdom; also that their interiors, which are recipients of wisdom, are arranged in that form. (That the thoughts and affections of angels flow in accordance with the form of heaven, and consequently their intelligence and wisdom, may he seen above, n. 201-212.) [2] That the angels have supereminent wisdom is shown also by the fact that their speech is the speech of wisdom, for it flows directly and spontaneously from thought, and their thought from their affection, thus their speech is thought from affection in outward form; consequently there is nothing to withdraw them from the Divine influx, and nothing from without such as enters into the speech of man from other thoughts. (That the speech of angels is the speech of their thought and affection may be seen above, n. 234-235.) That the angels have such wisdom is in accord with the fact that all things that they behold with their eyes and perceive by their senses agree with their wisdom, since they are correspondences of it, and thus the objects perceived are representative forms of the things that constitute their wisdom. (That all things seen in the heavens are correspondences with the interiors of angels and representations of their wisdom may be seen above, n. 170-182.) [3] Furthermore, the thoughts of angels are not limited and contracted by ideas from space and time, as human thoughts are, for spaces and times belong to nature, and the things that belong to nature withdraw the mind from spiritual things, and deprive intellectual sight of its proper range. (That the ideas of angels are apart from time and space, and thus less limited than human ideas, may be seen above, n. 162-169 and 191-199.) Again, the thoughts of angels are neither brought down to earthly and material things, nor interrupted by anxieties about the necessities of life; thus they are not withdrawn by such things from the delights of wisdom, as the thoughts of men in the world are; for all things come to them gratuitously from the Lord; they are clothed gratuitously, are fed gratuitously, are housed gratuitously (n. 181-190), and besides this they receive delights and pleasures in the degree of their reception of wisdom from the Lord. These things have been said to make clear why it is that angels have so great wisdom. 266-1

Angels are capable of receiving such wisdom because their interiors are open; and wisdom, like every other perfection, increases towards the interiors, thus to the extent that interiors are opened. 267-1 In every angel there are three degrees of life, corresponding to the three heavens (see n. 29-40)- those in whom the first degree has been opened are in the first or outmost heaven; those in whom the second degree has been opened are in the second or middle heaven; while those in whom the third degree has been opened are in the third or inmost heaven. The wisdom of angels in the heavens is in accordance with these degrees. Therefore the wisdom of the angels of the inmost heaven immeasurably surpasses the wisdom of angels of the middle heaven, and the wisdom of these immeasurably surpasses the wisdom of angels of the outmost heaven (see above, n. 209, 210; and what degrees are, n. 38). There are such differences because the things which are in the higher degree are particulars, and those in the lower degree are generals, and generals are containants of particulars. Particulars compared with generals are as thousands or myriads to one; and such is the wisdom of the angels of a higher heaven compared with the wisdom of the angels of a lower heaven. In like manner the wisdom of the latter surpasses the wisdom of man, for man is in a bodily state and in those things that belong to the bodily senses, and man's bodily sense belongs to the lowest degree. This makes clear what kind of wisdom those possess who think from things of sense, that is, who are called sensual men, namely, that they have no wisdom, but merely knowledge. 267-2 But it is otherwise with men whose thoughts are raised above the things of sense, and especially with those whose interiors have been opened even into the light of heaven.

It can be seen how great the wisdom of angels is from the fact that in the heavens there is a communication of all things; intelligence and wisdom are communicated from one to another, and heaven is a common sharing of all goods; and this for the reason that heavenly love is such that it wishes what is its own to be another's; consequently no one in heaven perceives his own good in himself to be good unless it is also in another; and this is the source of the happiness of heaven. This the angels derive from the Lord, for such is His Divine love. That there is such a communication of all things in the heavens it has been permitted me to know by experience. Certain simple spirits were at one time taken up into heaven, and when there they entered into angelic wisdom, and then understood things that they were never before able to comprehend, and spoke things that they were unable to utter in their former state.

The wisdom of the angels is indescribable in words; it can only be illustrated by some general things. Angels can express in a single word what a man cannot express in a thousand words. Again, a single angelic word contains innumerable things that cannot be expressed in the words of human language; for in each of the things uttered by angels there are arcana of wisdom in continuous connection that human knowledges never reach. Again, what the angels fail to express in the words of their speech they make up by the tone, in which there is an affection for the things in their order; for (as has been said above, n. 236, 241) tones express affections, as words express ideas of thought from the affections; and for this reason the things heard in heaven are said to be ineffable. So, too, the angels are able to express in a few words every least thing written in an entire volume, and give to every word meanings that elevate the mind to interior wisdom; for their speech is such as to be in accord with their affections, and each word is in accord with their ideas; and their words are varied in infinite ways in accord with the series of things which in complex are in the thought. [2] Still again, the interior angels are able to perceive from the tone and from a few words the entire life of one speaking; for from the tone as varied by the ideas in the words they perceive his ruling love upon which, as it were, every particular of his life is inscribed. 269-1 All this makes clear the nature of angelic wisdom. In comparison with human wisdom it is as a myriad to one, or as the moving forces of the whole body, which are numberless, to the activities from them which appear to human sense as a single thing, or as the thousand particulars of an object seen under a perfect microscope to the one obscure thing seen by the naked eye. [3] Let me illustrate the subject by an example. An angel from his wisdom was describing regeneration, and brought forward arcana respecting it in their order even to some hundreds, filling each of them with ideas in which there were interior arcana, and this from beginning to end; for he explained how the spiritual man is conceived anew, is carried as it were in the womb, is born, grows up and is gradually perfected. He said that the number of arcana could be increased even to thousands, and that those told were only about the regeneration of the external man, while there were numberless more about the regeneration of the internal man. From these and other like things heard from the angels it has been made clear to me how great is their wisdom, and how great in comparison is the ignorance of man, who scarcely knows what regeneration is, and is ignorant of every least step of the process when he is being regenerated.

The wisdom of the angels of the third or inmost heaven shall now be described, and also how far it surpasses the wisdom of the angels of the first or outmost heaven. The wisdom of the angels of the third or inmost heaven is incomprehensible even to those who are in the outmost heaven, for the reason that the interiors of the angels of the third heaven have been opened to the third degree, while the interiors of angels of the first heaven have been opened only to the first degree; and all wisdom increases towards interiors and is perfected as these are opened (n. 208, 267). [2] Because the interiors of the angels of the third or inmost heaven have been opened to the third degree, Divine truths are as it were inscribed on them; for the interiors of the third degree are more in the form of heaven than the interiors of the second and first degrees, and the form of heaven is from the Divine truth, thus in accord with the Divine wisdom, and this is why the truth is as it were inscribed on these angels, or are as it were instinctive or inborn in them. Therefore as soon as these angels hear genuine Divine truths they instantly acknowledge and perceive them, and afterwards see them as it were inwardly in themselves. As the angels of that heaven are such they never reason about Divine truths, still less do they dispute about any truth whether it is so or not; nor do they know what it is to believe or to have faith. They say, "What is faith? for I perceive and see that a thing is so." This they illustrate by comparisons; for example, that it would be as when any one with a companion, seeing a house and the various things in it and around it, should say to his companion that he ought to believe that these things exist, and that they are such as he sees them to be; or seeing a garden and trees and fruit in it, should say to his companion that he ought to have faith that there is a garden and trees and fruits, when yet he is seeing them clearly with his eyes. For this reason these angels never mention faith, and have no idea what it is; neither do they reason about Divine truths, still less do they dispute about any truth whether it is so or not. 270-1 [3] But the angels of the first or outmost heaven do not have Divine truths thus inscribed on their interiors, because with them only the first degree of life is opened; therefore they reason about truths, and those who reason see almost nothing beyond the fact of the matter about which they are reasoning, or go no farther beyond the subject than to confirm it by certain considerations, and having confirmed it they say that it must be a matter of faith and must be believed. [4] I have talked with angels about this, and they said that the difference between the wisdom of the angels of the third heaven and the wisdom of the angels of the first heaven is like that between what is clear and what is obscure; and the former they compared to a magnificent palace full of all things for use, surrounded on all sides by parks, with magnificent things of many kinds round about them; and as these angels are in the truths of wisdom they can enter into the palace and behold all things, and wander about in the parks in every direction and delight in it all. But it is not so with those who reason about truths, especially with those who dispute about them, as such do not see truths from the light of truth, but accept truths either from others or from the sense of the letter of the Word, which they do not interiorly understand, declaring that truths must be believed, or that one must have faith, and are not willing to have any interior sight admitted into these things. The angels said that such are unable to reach the first threshold of the palace of wisdom, still less to enter into it and wander about in its grounds, for they stop at the first step. It is not so with those that are in truths themselves; nothing impedes these from going on and progressing without limit, for the truths they see lead them wherever they go, and into wide fields, for every truth has infinite extension and is in conjunction with manifold others. [5] They said still further that the wisdom of the angels of the inmost heaven consists principally in this, that they see Divine and heavenly things in every single object, and wonderful things in a series of many objects; for everything that appears before their eyes is a correspondent; as when they see palaces and gardens their view does not dwell upon the things that are before their eyes, but they see the interior things from which they spring, that is, to which they correspond, and this with all variety in accordance with the aspect of the objects; thus they see innumerable things at the same time in their order and connection; and this so fills their minds with delight that they seem to be carried away from themselves. That all things that are seen in the heavens correspond to the Divine things that are in the angels from the Lord may be seen above (n. 170-176).

Such are the angels of the third heaven because they are in love to the Lord, and that love opens the interiors of the mind to the third degree, and is a receptacle of all things of wisdom. It must be understood also that the angels of the inmost heaven are still being continually perfected in wisdom, and this differently from the angels of the outmost heaven. The angels of the inmost heaven do not store up Divine truths in the memory and thus make out of them a kind of science; but as soon as they hear them they perceive them and apply them to the life. For this reason Divine truths are as permanent with them as if they were inscribed on them, for what is committed in such a way to the life is contained in it. But it is not so with the angels of the outmost heaven. These first store up Divine truths in the memory and stow them away with their knowledge, and draw them out therefrom to perfect their understanding by them, and will them and apply them to the life, but with no interior perception whether they are truths; and in consequence they are in comparative obscurity. It is a notable fact that the angels of the third heaven are perfected in wisdom by hearing and not by seeing. What they hear from preachings does not enter into their memory, but enters directly into their perception and will, and comes to be a matter of life; but what they see with their eyes enters into their memory, and they reason and talk about it; which shows that with them the way of hearing is the way of wisdom. This, too, is from correspondence, for the ear corresponds to obedience, and obedience belongs to the life; while the eye corresponds to intelligence, and intelligence is a matter of doctrine. 271-1 The state of these angels is described in different parts of the Word, as in Jeremiah: I will put My law in their mind, and write it on their heart. They shall teach no more everyone his friend and everyone his brother, saying, Know ye Jehovah; for they shall all know Me, from the least of them even unto the greatest of them (31:33, 34). And in Matthew, Let your speech be Yea, yea, Nay, nay; what is more than these is from evil (5:37). "What is more than these is from evil" because it is not from the Lord; and inasmuch as the angels of the third heaven are in love to the Lord the truths that are in them are from the Lord. In that heaven love to the Lord is willing and doing Divine truth, for Divine truth is the Lord in heaven.

There is a still further reason, and this is in heaven the primary reason, why the angels are able to receive so great wisdom, namely, that they are without the love of self; for to the extent that any one is without the love of self he can become wise in Divine things. It is that love that closes up the interiors against the Lord and heaven, and opens the exteriors and turns them toward itself; and in consequence all in whom that love rules are in thick darkness in respect to the things of heaven, however much light they may have in worldly matters. The angels, on the other hand, are in the light of wisdom because they are without the love of self, for the heavenly loves in which they are, which are love to the Lord and love towards the neighbor, open the interiors, because these loves are from the Lord and the Lord Himself is in them. (That these loves constitute heaven in general, and form heaven in each one in particular, may be seen above, n. 13-19). As heavenly loves open the interiors to the Lord so all angels turn their faces towards the Lord (n. 142); because in the spiritual world the love turns the interiors of everyone to itself, and whichever way it turns the interiors it also turns the face, since the face there makes one with the interiors, for it is their outward form. Because the love turns the interiors and the face to itself, it also conjoins itself to them (love being spiritual conjunction), and shares its own with them. From that turning and consequent conjunction and sharing the angels have their wisdom. That all conjunction and all turning in the spiritual world are in accord may be seen above (n. 255).

Although the angels are continually perfected in wisdom, 273-1 their wisdom, even to eternity, cannot become so perfect that there can be any ratio between it and the Lord's Divine wisdom; for the Lord's Divine wisdom is infinite and the wisdom of angels finite; and between what is Infinite and what is finite no ratio is possible.

As it is wisdom that makes the angels perfect and constitutes their life, and as heaven with its goods flows into everyone in accordance with his wisdom, so all in heaven desire and hunger for wisdom much as a hungry man hungers for food. So, too, knowledge, intelligence, and wisdom are spiritual nutriment, as food is natural nutriment; and the one corresponds to the other.

The angels in the same heaven, or in the same society of heaven, are not all in like wisdom; their wisdom differs. Those at the center are in the greatest wisdom, and those round about even to the borders are in less wisdom. The decrease of wisdom in accord with the distance from the center is like the decrease of light verging to shade (see n. 43 and 128). Their light is in the same degree as their wisdom, since the light of heaven is the Divine wisdom, and everyone is in light in the measure of his reception of wisdom. Respecting the light of heaven and the varying kinds of reception of it see above (n. 126-132).

THE STATE OF INNOCENCE OF ANGELS IN HEAVEN. What innocence is and its nature few in the world know, and those who are in evil know nothing about it. It is, indeed, visible to the eyes, as seen in the face, speech and movements, particularly of children; and yet what innocence is, and especially that it is that in which heaven is stored up in man is unknown. In making this known let us proceed in order, and consider first the innocence of childhood, then the innocence of wisdom, and lastly the state of heaven in regard to innocence.

The innocence of childhood or of children is not genuine innocence, for it is innocence not in internal form but only in external form. Nevertheless one may learn from it what innocence is, since it shines forth from the face of children and from some of their movements and from their first speech, and affects those about them. It can be seen that children have no internal thought, for they do not yet know what is good and what is evil, or what is true and what is false, of which such thought consists. [2] Consequently they have no prudence from what is their own, no purpose or deliberation, thus no end that looks to evil; neither have they anything of their own acquired from love of self and the world; they do not attribute anything to themselves, regarding all that they have as received from their parents; they are content with the few and paltry things presented to them, and find delight in them; they have no solicitude about food and clothing, and none about the future; they do not look to the world and covet many things from it; they love their parents and nurses and their child companions with whom they play in innocence; they suffer themselves to be led; they give heed and obey. [3] And being in this state they receive everything as a matter of life; and therefore, without knowing why, they have becoming manners, and also learn to talk, and have the beginning of memory and thought, their state of innocence serving as a medium whereby these things are received and implanted. But this innocence, as has been said above, is external because it belongs to the body alone, and not to the mind; 277-1 for their minds are not yet formed, the mind being understanding and will and thought and affection therefrom. [4] I have been told from heaven that children are specially under the Lord's auspices, and that they receive influx from the inmost heaven, where there is a state of innocence that this influx passes through their interiors, and that in its passing through, their interiors are affected solely by the innocence; and for this reason innocence is shown in their faces and in some of their movements and becomes evident; and that it is this innocence by which parents are inmostly affected, and that gives rise to the love that is called storge.

The innocence of wisdom is genuine innocence, because it is internal, for it belongs to the mind itself, that is, to the will itself and from that to the understanding. And when there is innocence in these there is also wisdom, for wisdom belongs to the will and understanding. This is why it is said in heaven that innocence has its abode in wisdom, and that an angel has just so much of innocence as he has of wisdom. This is confirmed by the fact that those who are in a state of innocence attribute nothing of good to themselves, but regard all things as received and ascribe them to the Lord; that they wish to be led by Him and not by themselves; that they love everything that is good and find delight in everything that is true, because they know and perceive that loving what is good, that is, willing and doing it, is loving the Lord, and loving truth is loving the neighbor; that they live contented with their own, whether it be little or much, because they know that they receive just as much as is good for them-those receiving little for whom a little is useful, and those receiving much for whom much is useful; also that they do not themselves know what is good for them, the Lord alone knowing this, who looks in all things that He provides to what is eternal. [2] Neither are they anxious about the future; anxiety about the future they call care for the morrow, which they define as grief on account of losing or not receiving things that are not necessary for the uses of life. With companions they never act from an evil end but from what is good, just, and sincere. Acting from an evil end they call cunning, which they shun as the poison of a serpent, since it is wholly antagonistic to innocence. As they love nothing so much as to be led of the Lord, attributing all things they receive to

Him, they are kept apart from what is their own [proprium]; and to the extent that they are kept apart from what is their own the Lord flows into them; and in consequence of this whatever they hear from the Lord, whether through the Word or by means of preaching, they do not store up in the memory, but instantly obey it, that is, will it and do it, their will being itself their memory. These for the most part outwardly appear simple, but inwardly they are wise and prudent. These are meant by the Lord in the words, Be ye prudent as serpents and simple as doves (Matt. 10:16). Such is the innocence that is called the innocence of wisdom. [3] Because innocence attributes nothing of good to itself, but ascribes all good to the Lord, and because it thus loves to be led by the Lord, and is the source of the reception of all good and truth, from which wisdom comes,-because of this man is so created as to be during his childhood in external innocence, and when he becomes old in internal innocence, to the end that he may come by means of the former into the latter, and from the latter return into the former. For the same reason when a man becomes old he dwindles in body and becomes again like a child, but like a wise child, that is, an angel, for a wise child is in an eminent sense an angel. This is why in the Word, "a little child" signifies one who is innocent, and "an old man" signifies one who is wise in whom is innocence. 278-1

The same is true of everyone who is being regenerated. Regeneration, as regards the spiritual man, is re-birth. Man is first introduced into the innocence of childhood, which is that one knows no truth and can do no good from himself, but only from the Lord, and desires and seeks truth only because it is truth, and good only because it is good. As man afterwards advances in age good and truth are given him by the Lord. At first he is led into a knowledge of them, then from knowledge into intelligence, and finally from intelligence into wisdom, innocence always accompanying, which consists, as has been said, in his knowing nothing of truth, and being unable to do anything good from himself but only from the Lord. Without such a belief and such a perception of it no one can receive any thing of heaven. Therein does the innocence of wisdom chiefly consist.

As innocence consists in being led by the Lord and not by self, so all who are in heaven are in innocence; for all who are there love to be led by the Lord, knowing that to lead themselves is to be led by what is their own, and what is one's own is loving oneself, he that loves himself not permitting himself to be led by any one else. Therefore, so far as an angel is in innocence he is in heaven, in other words, is in Divine good and Divine truth, for to be in these is to be in heaven. Consequently the heavens are distinguished by degrees of innocence-those who are in the outmost or first heaven are in innocence of the first or outmost degree; those who are in the middle or second heaven are in innocence of the second or middle degree; while those who are in the inmost or third heaven are in innocence of the third or inmost degree, and are therefore the veriest innocences of heaven, for more than all others they love to be led by the Lord as little children by their father; and for the same reason the Divine truth that they hear immediately from the Lord or mediately through the Word and preaching they take directly into their will and do it, thus committing it to life. And this is why their wisdom is so superior to that of the angels of the lower heavens (see n. 270, 271). These angels of the inmost heaven, being such are nearest to the Lord from whom they receive innocence, and are so separated from what is their own that they live as it were in the Lord. Externally they appear simple, and before the eyes of the angels of the lower heavens they appear like children, that is, as very small, and not very wise, although they are the wisest of the angels of heaven; since they know that they have nothing of wisdom from themselves, and that acknowledging this is being wise. They know also that what they know is as nothing compared to what they do not know; and they say that knowing, acknowledging, and perceiving this is the first step towards wisdom. These angels have no clothing, because nakedness corresponds to innocence. 280-1

I have talked much with angels about innocence, and have been told that innocence is the being [esse] of all good, and that good is therefore so far good as it has innocence in it, consequently that wisdom is so far wisdom as it partakes of innocence; and the same is true of love, charity, and faith; 281-1 and therefore no one can enter heaven unless he possesses innocence; and this the Lord teaches when He says: Suffer little children to come unto Me, and forbid them not; for of such is the kingdom of the heavens. Verily I say unto you, Whoever shall not receive the kingdom of the heavens as a little child, he shall not enter into it (Mark 10:14, 16; Luke 18:16, 17), Here as elsewhere In the Word "little children" mean those who are innocent. A state of innocence is also described by the Lord in Matthew (6:25-34), but by correspondences only. Good is good so far as it has innocence in it, for the reason that all good is from the Lord, and innocence is a willingness to be led by the Lord. I have also been told that truth can be conjoined to good and good to truth only by means of innocence, and therefore an angel is not an angel of heaven unless he has innocence in him; for heaven is not in any one until good is conjoined to truth in him; and this is why the conjunction of truth and good is called the heavenly marriage, and the heavenly marriage is heaven. Again, I have been told that true marriage love derives its existence from innocence, because it derives its existence from the conjunction of good and truth, and the two minds of husband and wife are in that conjunction, and when that conjunction descends it presents the appearance of marriage love; for consorts are in mutual love, as their minds are. This is why in marriage love there is a playfulness like that of childhood and like that of innocence. 281-2

Because innocence With the angels of heaven is the very being [esse] of good, it is evident that the Divine good that goes forth from the Lord is innocence itself, for it is that good that flows into angels, and affects their inmosts, and arranges and fits them for receiving all the good of heaven. It is the same with children, whose interiors are not only formed by means of innocence flowing through them from the Lord, but also are continually being fitted and arranged for receiving the good of heavenly love, since the good of innocence acts from the inmost; for that good, as has been said, is the being [esse] of all good. From all this it can be seen that all innocence is from the Lord. For this reason the Lord is called in the Word a "lamb," a lamb signifying innocence. 282-1 Because innocence is the inmost in all the good of heaven, it so affects minds that when it is felt by any one-as when an angel of the inmost heaven approaches-he seems to himself to be no longer his own master and is moved and as it were carried away by such a delight that no delight of the world seems to be anything in comparison with it. This I say from having perceived it.

Everyone who is in the good of innocence is affected by innocence, and is affected to the extent that he is in that good; but those who are not in the good of innocence are not affected by innocence. For this reason all who are in hell are wholly antagonistic to innocence; they do not know what it is; their antagonism is such that so far as any one is innocent they burn to do him mischief; therefore they cannot bear to see little children; and as soon as they see them they are inflamed with a cruel desire to do them harm. From this it is clear that what is man's own, and therefore the love of self, is antagonistic to innocence; for all who are in hell are in what is their own, and therefore in the love of self. 283-1

THE STATE OF PEACE IN HEAVEN. Only those that have experienced the peace of heaven can have any perception of the peace in which the angels are. As man is unable, as long as he is in the body, to receive the peace of heaven, so he can have no perception of it, because his perception is confined to what is natural. To perceive it he must be able, in respect to thought, to be raised up and withdrawn from the body and kept in the spirit, and at the same time be with angels. In this way has the peace of heaven been perceived by me; and for this reason I am able to describe it, yet not in words as that peace is in itself, because human words are inadequate, but only as it is in comparison with that rest of mind that those enjoy who are content in God.

There are two inmost things of heaven, namely, innocence and peace. These are said to be inmost things because they proceed directly from the Lord. From innocence comes every good of heaven, and from peace every delight of good. Every good has its delight; and both good and delight spring from love, for whatever is loved is called good, and is also perceived as delightful. From this it follows that these two inmost things, innocence and peace, go forth from the Lord's Divine love and move the angels from what is inmost. That innocence is the inmost of good may be seen in the preceding chapter, where the state of innocence of the angels of heaven is described. That peace is the inmost of delight from the good of innocence shall now be explained.

The origin of peace shall be first considered. Divine peace is in the Lord; it springs from the union of the Divine Itself and the Divine Human in Him. The Divine of peace in heaven is from the Lord, springing from His conjunction with the angels of heaven, and in particular from the conjunction of good and truth in each angel. These are the origins of peace. From this it can be seen that peace in the heavens is the Divine inmostly affecting with blessedness everything good therefrom, and from this is every joy of heaven; also that it is in its essence the Divine joy of the Lord's Divine love, resulting from His conjunction with heaven and with everyone there. This joy, felt by the Lord in angels and by angels from the Lord, is peace. By derivation from this the angels have everything that is blessed, delightful, and happy, or that which is called heavenly joy. 286-1

Because these are the origins of peace the Lord is called "the Prince of peace," and He declares that from Him is peace and in Him is peace; and the angels are called angels of peace, and heaven is called a habitation of peace, as in the following passages: Unto us a Child is born, unto us a Son is given, and the government shall he upon His shoulder; and His name shall he called Wonderful, Counsellor, God, Mighty, Father of eternity, Prince of peace. Of the increase of His government and peace there shall be no end (Isa. 9:6, 7). Jesus said, Peace I leave with you, My peace I give unto you; not as the world giveth give I unto you (John 14:27). These things have I spoken unto you that in Me ye may have peace (John 16:33). Jehovah lift up His countenance upon thee and give thee peace (Num. 6:26). The angels of peace weep bitterly, the highways are wasted (Isa. 33:7, 8). The work of righteousness shall be peace; and My people shall dwell in a habitation of peace (Isa. 32:17, 18). [2] That it is Divine and heavenly peace that is meant in the Word by "peace" can be seen also from other passages where it is mentioned (As Isa. 52:7; 54:10; 59:8; Jer. 16:5; 25:37; 29:11; Hag. 2:9; Zech. 8:12; Psalm 37:37; and elsewhere.) Because "peace" means the Lord and heaven, and also heavenly joy and the delight of good, "Peace be with you" was an ancient form of salutation that is still in use; and it was ratified by the Lord in His saying to the disciples whom He sent forth: Into whatsoever house ye enter, first say, Peace be to this house; and if a son of peace be there, your peace shall rest upon it (Luke 10:5, 6). And when the Lord Himself appeared to the apostles, He said Peace be with you (John 20:19, 21, 26). [3] A state of peace is also meant in the Word where it is said that: Jehovah smelled an odor of rest (as Exod. 29:18, 25, 41; Lev. 1:9, 13, 17; 2:2, 9; 6:8, 14; 23:12, 13, 18; Num, 15:3, 7, 13; 28:6, 8, 13; 29:2, 6, 8, 13, 36). "Odor of rest" in the heavenly sense signifies a perception of peace. 287-1 As peace signifies the union of the Divine Itself and the Divine Human in the Lord, also the conjunction of the Lord with heaven and with the church, and with all who are in heaven, and with all in the church who receive Him, so the Sabbath was instituted as a reminder of these things, its name meaning rest or peace, and was the most holy representative of the church. For the same reason the Lord called Himself "the Lord of the Sabbath" (Matt. 12:8; Mark 2:27, 28; Luke 6:5).287-2

Because the peace of heaven is the Divine inmostly affecting with blessedness the veriest good in angels, it can be clearly perceived by them only in the delight of their hearts when they are in the good of their life, in the pleasure with which they hear truth that agrees with their good, and in gladness of mind when they perceive the conjunction of good and truth. From this it flows into all the acts and thoughts of their life, and there presents itself as joy, even in outward appearance. [2] But peace in the heavens differs in quality and quantity in agreement with the innocence of those who are there; since innocence and peace walk hand in hand; for every good of heaven, as said above, is from innocence, and every delight of that good is from peace. Evidently, then, the same that has been said in the foregoing chapter about the state of innocence in the heavens may be said here of the state of peace there, since innocence and peace are conjoined like good and its delight; for good is felt in its delight, and delight is known from its good. This being so, it is evident that angels of the inmost or third heaven are in the third or inmost degree of peace, because they are in the third or inmost degree of innocence; and that angels of the lower heavens are in a less degree of peace, because they are in a less degree of innocence (see above n. 280). [3] That innocence and peace go together like good and its delight can be seen in little children, who are in peace because they are in innocence, and because they are in peace are in their whole nature full of play. Yet the peace of little children is external peace; while internal peace, like internal innocence, is possible only in wisdom, and for this reason only in the conjunction of good and truth, since wisdom is from that conjunction. Heavenly or angelic peace is also possible in men who are in wisdom from the conjunction of good and truth, and who in consequence have a sense of content in God; nevertheless, while they live in the world this peace lies hidden in their interiors, but it is revealed when they leave the body and enter heaven, for their interiors are then opened.

As the Divine peace springs from the conjunction of the Lord with heaven, and specially from the conjunction of good and truth in each angel, so when the angels are in a state of love they are in a state of peace; for then good and truth are conjoined in them. (That the states of angels undergo successive changes may be seen above, n. 154-160.) The like is true also of a man who is being regenerated. As soon as good and truth come to be conjoined in him, which takes place especially after temptations, he comes into a state of delight from heavenly peace. 289-1 This peace may be likened to morning or dawn in spring time, when, the night being passed, with the rising of the sun all things of the earth begin to live anew, the fragrance of growing vegetation is spread abroad with the dew that descends from heaven, and the mild vernal temperature gives fertility to the ground and imparts pleasure to the minds of men, and this because morning or dawn in the time of spring corresponds to the state of peace of angels in heaven (see n. 155). 289-2

I have talked with the angels about peace, saying that what is called peace in the world is when wars and hostilities cease between kingdoms, and when enmities or hostilities cease among men; also that internal peace is believed to consist in rest of mind when cares are removed, especially in tranquility and enjoyment from success in affairs. But the angels said that rest of mind and tranquility and enjoyment from the removal of cares and success in affairs seem to be constituents of peace, but are so only with those who are in heavenly good, for only in that good is peace possible. For peace flows in from the Lord into the inmost of such, and from their inmost descends and flows down into the lower faculties, producing a sense of rest in the mind, tranquility of disposition, and joy therefrom. But to those who are in evil peace is impossible. 290-1 There is an appearance of rest, tranquility, and delight when things succeed according to their wishes; but it is external peace and not at all internal, for inwardly they burn with enmity, hatred, revenge, cruelty, and many evil lusts, into which their disposition is carried whenever any one is seen to be unfavorable to them, and which burst forth when they are not restrained by fear. Consequently the delight of such dwells in insanity, while the delight of those who are in good dwells in wisdom. The difference is like that between hell and heaven.

THE CONJUNCTION OF HEAVEN WITH THE HUMAN RACE. It is well known in the church that all good is from God, and that nothing of good is from man, consequently that no one ought to ascribe any good to himself as his own. It is also well known that evil is from the devil. Therefore those who speak from the doctrine of the church say of those who behave well, and of those who speak and preach piously, that they are led by God; but the opposite of those who do not behave well and who speak impiously. For this to be true man must have conjunction with heaven and with hell; and this conjunction must be with man's will and with his understanding; for it is from these that the body acts and the mouth speaks. What this conjunction is shall now be told.

With every individual there are good spirits and evil spirits. Through good spirits man has conjunction with heaven, and through evil spirits with hell. These spirits are in the world of spirits, which lies midway between heaven and hell. This world will be described particularly hereafter. When these spirits come to a man they enter into his entire memory, and thus into his entire thought, evil spirits into the evil things of his memory and thought, and good spirits into the good things of his memory and thought. These spirits have no knowledge whatever that they are with man; but when they are with him they believe that all things of his memory and thought are their own; neither do they see the man, because nothing that is in our solar world falls into their sight. 292-1 The Lord exercises the greatest care that spirits may not know that they are with man; for if they knew it they would talk with him, and in that case evil spirits would destroy him; for evil spirits, being joined with hell, desire nothing so much as to destroy man, not alone his soul, that is, his faith and love, but also his body. It is otherwise when spirits do not talk with man, in which case they are not aware that what they are thinking and also what they are saying among themselves is from man; for although it is from man that they talk with one another, they believe that what they are thinking and saying is their own, and everyone esteems and loves what is their own. In this way spirits are constrained to love and esteem man, although they do not know it. That such is the conjunction of spirits with man has become so well known to me from a continual experience of many years that nothing is better known to me.

The reason why spirits that communicate with hell are also associated with man is that man is born into evils of every kind, consequently his whole life is wholly from evil; and therefore unless spirits like himself were associated with him he could not live, nor indeed could he be withdrawn from his evils and reformed. He is therefore both held in his own life by means of evil spirits and withheld from it by means of good spirits; and by the two he is kept in equilibrium; and being in equilibrium he is in freedom, and can be drawn away from evils and turned towards good, and thus good can be implanted in him, which would not be possible at all if he were not in freedom; and freedom is possible to man only when the spirits from hell act on one side and spirits from heaven on the other, and man is between the two. Again, it has been shown that so far as a man's life is from what he inherits, and thus from self, if he were not permitted to be in evil he would have no life; also if he were not in freedom he would have no life; also that he cannot be forced to what is good, and that what is forced does not abide; also that the good that man receives in freedom is implanted in his will and becomes as it were his own. 293-1 These are the reasons why man has communication with hell and communication with heaven.

What the communication of heaven is with good spirits, and what the communication of hell is with evil spirits, and the consequent conjunction of heaven and hell with man, shall also be told. All spirits who are in the world of spirits have communication with heaven or with hell, evil spirits with hell, and good spirits with heaven. Heaven is divided into societies, and hell also. Every spirit belongs to some society, and continues to exist by influx from it, thus acting as one with it. Consequently as man is conjoined with spirits so is he conjoined with heaven or with hell, even with the society there to which he is attached by his affection or his love; for the societies of heaven are all distinguished from each other in accordance with their affections for good and truth, and the societies of hell in accordance with their affections for evil and falsity. (As to the societies of heaven see above, n. 41-45 also n. 148-151.)

The spirits associated with man are such as he himself is in respect to his affection or love; but the Lord associates good spirits with him, while evil spirits are invited by the man himself. The spirits with man, however, are changed in accordance with the changes of his affections; thus there are some spirits that are with him in early childhood, others in boyhood, others in youth and manhood, and others in old age. In early childhood those spirits are present who are in innocence and who thus communicate with the heaven of innocence, which is the inmost or third heaven; in boyhood those spirits are present who are in affection for knowing, and who thus communicate with the outmost or first heaven; in youth and manhood spirits are present who are in affection for what is true and good, and in consequent intelligence, and who thus communicate with the second or middle heaven; while in old age spirits are present who are in wisdom and innocence, and who thus communicate with the inmost or third heaven. But the Lord maintains this association with such as can be reformed and regenerated. It is otherwise with such as cannot be reformed or regenerated. While with these also good spirits are associated, that they may be thereby withheld from evil as much as possible, they are directly conjoined with evil spirits who communicate with hell, whereby they have such spirits with them as are like themselves. If they are lovers of self or lovers of gain, or lovers of revenge, or lovers of adultery, like spirits are present, and as it were dwell in their evil affections; and man is incited by these, except so far as he can be kept from evil by good spirits, and they cling to him, and do not withdraw, so far as the evil affection prevails. Thus it is that a bad man is conjoined to hell and a good man is conjoined to heaven.

Man is governed by the Lord through spirits because he is not in the order of heaven, for he is born into evils which are of hell, thus into the complete opposite of Divine order; consequently he needs to be brought back into order, and this can only be done mediately by means of spirits. It would be otherwise if man were born into the good that is in accord with the order of heaven; then he would be governed by the Lord not through spirits, but by means of the order itself, thus by means of general influx. By means of this influx man is governed in respect to whatever goes forth from his thought and will into act, that is, in respect to speech and acts; for both of these proceed in harmony with natural order, and therefore with these the spirits associated with man have nothing in common. Animals also are governed by means of this general influx from the spiritual world, because they are in the order of their life, and animals have not been able to pervert and destroy that order because they have no rational faculty. 296-1 What the difference between man and beasts is may be seen above (n. 39).

As to what further concerns the conjunction of heaven with the human race, let it be noted that the Lord Himself flows into each man, in accord with the order of heaven, both into his inmosts and into his outmosts, and arranges him for receiving heaven, and governs his outmosts from his inmosts, and at the same time his inmosts from his outmosts, thus holding in connection each thing and all things in man. This influx of the Lord is called direct influx; while the other influx that is effected through spirits is called mediate influx. The latter is maintained by means of the former. Direct influx, which is that of the Lord Himself, is from His Divine Human, and is into man's will and through his will into his understanding, and thus into his good and through his good into his truth, or what is the same thing, into his love and through his love into his faith; and not the reverse, still less is it into faith apart from love or into truth apart from good or into understanding that is not from will. This Divine influx is unceasing, and in the good is received in good, but not in the evil; for in them it is either rejected or suffocated or perverted; and in consequence they have an evil life which in a spiritual sense is death. 297-1

The spirits who are with man, both those conjoined with heaven and those conjoined with hell, never flow into man from their own memory and its thought, for if they should flow in from their own thought, whatever belonged to them would seem to man to be his (see above n. 256). Nevertheless there flows into man through them out of heaven an affection belonging to the love of good and truth, and out of hell an affection belonging to the love of evil and falsity. Therefore as far as man's affection agrees with the affection that flows in, so far that affection is received by him in his thought, since man's interior thought is wholly in accord with his affection or love; but so far as man's affection does not agree with that affection it is not received. Evidently, then, since thought is not introduced into man through spirits, but only an affection for good and an affection for evil, man has choice, because he has freedom; and is thus able by his thought to receive good and reject evil, since he knows from the Word what is good and what is evil. Moreover, whatever he receives by thought from affection is appropriated to him; but whatever he does not receive by thought from affection is not appropriated to him. All this makes evident the nature of the influx of good out of heaven with man, and the nature of the influx of evil out of hell.

I have also been permitted to learn the source of human anxiety, grief of mind, and interior sadness, which is called melancholy. There are spirits not as yet in conjunction with hell, because they are in their first state; these will be described hereafter when treating of the world of spirits. Such spirits love things undigested and pernicious, such as pertain to food becoming foul in the stomach; consequently they are present with man in such things because they find delight in them; and they talk there with one another from their own evil affection. The affection that is in their speech flows in from this source into man; and when this affection is the opposite of man's affection there arises in him sadness and melancholy anxiety; but when it agrees with it it becomes in him gladness and cheerfulness. These spirits appear near to the stomach, some to the left and some to the right of it, and some beneath and some above, also nearer and more remote, thus variously in accordance with their affections. That this is the source of anxiety of mind has been shown and proved to me by much experience. I have seen these spirits, I have heard them, I have felt the anxieties arising from them, and I have talked with them; when they have been driven away the anxiety ceased; when they returned the anxiety returned; and I have noted the increase and decrease of it according to their approach and removal. From this it has been made clear to me why some who do not know what conscience is, because they have no conscience, ascribe its pangs to the stomach. 299-1

The conjunction of heaven with man is not like the conjunction of one man with another, but the conjunction is with the interiors of man's mind, that is, with his spiritual or internal man; although there is a conjunction with his natural or external man by means of correspondences, which will be described in the next chapter where the conjunction of heaven with man by means of the Word will be treated of.

Footnotes

251-1 The "forehead" corresponds to heavenly love, and consequently in the Word signifies that love (n. 9936). The "face" corresponds to the interiors of man, which belong to thought and affection (n. 1568, 2988 2989, 3631, 4796, 4797, 4800, 5165, 5168, 5695, 9306). The face is formed to correspondence with the interiors (n. 4791-4805, 5695). Consequently the "face," in the Word, signifies the interiors (n. 1999, 2434, 3527, 4066, 4796).

252-1 Spirits are unable to see through man any thing that is in this solar world, but they have seen through my eyes; the reason (n. 1880).

255-1 Spirits sent from one society of spirits to other societies are called subjects (n. 4403, 5856). Communications in the spiritual world are effected by such emissary spirits (n. 4403, 5856, 5983). A spirit when he is sent forth, and serves as a subject thinks from those by whom he is sent forth and not from himself (n. 5985-5987).

257-1 External or bodily obsessions are not permitted at the present time, as they were formerly (n. 1983). But at present internal obsessions, which pertain to the mind, are permitted more than formerly (n. 1983, 4793). Man is inwardly obsessed when he has filthy and scandalous thoughts about God and the neighbor, and is withheld from making them known only by external consideration, which are fear of the loss of reputation, honor, gain and fear of the law and of loss of life (n. 5990). Of the devilish spirits who chiefly obsess the interiors of man (n. 4793). Of the devilish spirits who long to obsess the exteriors of man; that such are shut up in hell (n. 2752, 5990).

263-1 All numbers in the Word signify things (n. 482, 487, 647, 648, 755, 813, 1963, 1988, 2075, 2252, 3252, 4264, 6470, 6175, 9488, 9659, 10217, 10253). Shown from heaven (n. 4495, 5265). Composite numbers have the same signification as the simple numbers from which they result by multiplication (n. 5291, 5335, 5708, 7973). The most ancient people possessed heavenly arcana expressed in numbers forming a kind of computation of states of the church (n. 575).

266-1 The wisdom of angels, that it is incomprehensible and ineffable (n. 2795, 2796, 2802, 3314, 3404, 3405, 9094, 9176).

267-1 So far as man is raised up from outward towards inward things he comes into light, that is, into intelligence (n. 6183, 6313). There is an actual elevation (n. 7816, 10330). Elevation from outward to inward things is like elevation out of a mist into light (n. 4598). As outer things in man are farther removed from the Divine they are relatively obscure (n. 6451). Likewise relatively confused (n. 996, 3855). Inner things are more perfect because they are nearer to the Divine (n. 5146, 5147). In what is internal there are thousands and thousands of things that appear in what is external as one general thing (n. 5707). Consequently as thought and perception are more interior they are clearer (n. 5920).

267-2 The sensual is the outmost of man's life adhering to and inhering in his bodily part (n. 5077, 5767, 9212, 9216, 9331, 9730). He is called a sensual man who judges all things and draws all his conclusions from the bodily senses, and believes nothing except what he sees with his eyes and touches with his hands (n. 5094, 7693). Such a man thinks in externals, and not interiorly in himself (n. 5089, 5094, 6564, 7693). His interiors are so closed up that he sees nothing of spiritual truth in them (n. 6564, 6844, 6845). In a word, he is in gross natural light and thus perceives nothing that is from the light of heaven (n. 6201, 6310, 6564, 6598, 6612, 6614, 6622, 6624, 6844, 6845). Interiorly he is antagonistic to the things of heaven and the church (n. 6201, 6316, 6844, 6845, 6948, 6949). The learned who have confirmed themselves against the truths of the church come to be such (n. 6316). Sensual men are more cunning and malicious than others (n. 7693, 10236). They reason keenly and cunningly, but from the bodily memory, in which they place all intelligence (n. 195, 196, 5700, 10236). But they reason from the fallacies of the senses (n. 5084, 6948, 6949, 7693).

269-1 That which universally rules or is dominant in man is in every particular of his life, thus in each thing and all things of his thought and affection (n. 4459, 5949, 6159, 6571, 7648, 8067, 8853-8858). A man is such as his ruling love is (n. 917, 1040, 8858); illustrated by examples (n. 8854, 8857). That which rules universally constitutes the life of the spirit of man (n. 7648). It is his very will, his very love, and the end of his life, since that which a man will he loves, and that which he loves he has as an end (n. 1317, 1568, 1571, 1909, 3796, 5949, 6936). Therefore man is such as his will is, or such as his ruling love is, or such as the end of his life is (n. 1568, 1571, 3570, 4054, 6571, 6935, 6938, 8856, 10076, 10109, 10110, 10284).

270-1 The celestial angels know innumerable things, and are immeasurably wiser than the spiritual angels (n. 2718). The celestial angels do not think and talk from faith, as the spiritual angels do, for they have from the Lord a perception of all things that constitute faith (n. 202, 597, 607, 784, 1121, 1384, 1442, 1898, 1919, 7680, 7877, 8780, 9277, 10336). In regard to the truths of faith they say only "Yea, yea, or Nay, nay," while the spiritual angels reason about whether a thing is true (n. 2715, 3246, 4448, 9166, 10786, where the Lord's words, "Let your discourse be Yea, yea, Nay nay" (Matt. 5:37), are explained).

271-1 Of the correspondence of the ear and of hearing (n. 4652-4660). The ear corresponds to and therefore signifies perception and obedience (n. 2542, 3869, 4653, 5017, 7216, 8361, 9311, 9397, 10061). The ear signifies the reception of truths (n. 5471, 5475, 9926). The correspondence of the eye and its sight (n. 4403-4421, 4523-4534); from which the sight of the eye signifies the intelligence that belongs to faith, and also faith (n. 2701, 4410, 4526, 6923 9051, 10569).

273-1 Angels are perfected to eternity (n. 4803, 6648).

277-1 The innocence of children is not true innocence, but true innocence has its abode in wisdom (n. 1616, 2305, 2306, 3494, 4563, 4797, 5608, 9301, 10021) The good of childhood is not spiritual good, but it becomes such by the implantation of truth (n. 3504). Nevertheless the good of childhood is a medium whereby intelligence is implanted (n. 1616, 3183, 9301, 10110). Without the good of innocence in childhood man would be a wild man (n. 3494). Whatever the mind is imbued with in childhood appears natural (n. 3494).

278-1 In the Word "little children" signify innocence (n. 5608); likewise "sucklings" (n. 3183). An "old man" signifies one who is wise, and in an abstract sense wisdom (n. 3183, 6524). Man is so created that in proportion as he verges towards old age he may become like a little child, and that innocence may then be in his wisdom, and in that state he may pass into heaven and become an angel (n. 3183, 5608).

280-1 All in the inmost heaven are innocences (n. 154, 2736, 3887). Therefore they appear to others like children (n. 154). They are also naked (n. 165, 8375, 9960). Nakedness belongs to innocence (n. 165, 8375). Spirits have a custom of exhibiting innocence by laying aside their garments and presenting themselves naked (n. 165, 8375, 9960).

281-1 Every good of love and truth of faith, to be good and true must have innocence in it (n. 2526, 2780, 3111, 3994, 6013, 7840, 9262, 10134). Innocence is the essential of good and truth (n. 2780, 7840). No one is admitted into heaven unless he possesses something of innocence (4797).

281-2 True marriage love is innocence (n. 2736). Marriage love consists in willing what the other wills, thus mutually and reciprocally (n. 2731). They who are in marriage love dwell together in the inmosts of life (n. 2732). There is a union of the two minds, and thus from love they are a one (n. 10168, 10169). True marriage love derives its origin and essence from the marriage of good and truth (n. 2728, 2729). About angelic spirits who have a perception from the idea of the conjunction of good and truth whether anything of marriage exists (n. 10756). Marriage love is wholly like the conjunction of good and truth (n. 1904, 2173, 2508, 2729, 3103, 3132, 3155, 3179, 3180, 4358, 5807, 5835, 9206, 9207, 9495, 9637). Therefore in the Word "marriage" means the marriage of good and truth, such as there is in heaven and such as there will be in the church (n. 3132, 4434, 4835).

282-1 In the Word a "lamb" signifies innocence and its good. (n. 3994, 10132).

283-1 What is man's own is loving self more than God, and the world more than heaven, and making one's neighbor of no account as compared with oneself; thus it is the love of self and of the world (n. 694, 731, 4317, 5660). The evil are wholly antagonistic to innocence, even to the extent that they cannot endure its presence (n. 2126).

286-1 By peace in the highest sense the Lord is meant, because peace is from Him, and in the internal sense heaven is meant, because those are in a state of peace (n. 3780, 4681). Peace in the heavens is the Divine inmostly affecting with blessedness everything good and true there, and this peace is incomprehensible to man (n. 92, 3780, 5662, 8455, 8665). Divine peace is in good, but not in truth apart from good (n. 8722).

287-1 In the word an "odor" signifies the perception of agreeableness or disagreeableness, according to the quality of the love and faith of which it is predicated (n. 3577, 4626, 4628, 4748, 5621, 10292). An "odor of rest," in reference to Jehovah, means a perception of peace (n. 925, 10054). This is why frankincense, incense, and odors in oils and ointments, became representative (n. 925, 4748, 5621, 10177).

287-2 The "Sabbath" signifies in the highest sense the union of the Divine Itself and the Divine Human in the Lord; in the internal sense the conjunction of the Divine Human of the Lord with heaven and with the church; in general, the conjunction of good and truth, thus the heavenly marriage (n. 8495, 10356, 10730). Therefore "rest on the Sabbath day" signified the state of that union, because then the Lord had rest, and thereby there is peace and salvation in the heavens and on the earth; and in a relative sense it signified the conjunction of the Lord with man, because man then has peace and salvation (n. 8494, 8510, 10360, 10367, 10370, 10374, 10668, 10730).

289-1 The conjunction of good and truth in a man who is being regenerated is effected in a state of peace (n. 3696, 8517).

289-2 The state of peace in the heavens is like a state of dawn or springtime on the earth (n. 1726, 2780, 5662).

290-1 The lusts that originate in love of self and of the world wholly take away peace (n. 3170, 5662). There are some who think to find peace in restlessness, and in such things as are contrary to peace (n. 5662). Peace is possible only when the lusts of evil are removed (n. 5662).

292-1 There are angels and spirits with every man, and by means of them man has communication with the spiritual world (n. 697, 2796, 2886, 2887, 4047, 4048, 5846-5866, 5976-5993). Man without spirits attending him cannot live (n. 5993). Man is not seen by spirits, even as spirits are not seen by man (n. 5862). Spirits can see nothing in our solar world pertaining to any man except the one with whom they are speaking (n. 1880).

293-1 All freedom pertains to love and affection, since what a man loves, that he does freely (n. 2870, 3158, 8987, 8990, 9585, 9591). As freedom belongs to man's love, so it belongs to man's life (n. 2873). Nothing appears as man's own except what is from freedom (n. 2880). Man must have freedom that he may be reformed (n. 1937, 1947, 2876, 2881, 3145, 3146, 3158, 4031, 8700). Otherwise no love of good and truth can be implanted in man and be appropriated seemingly as his own (n. 2877, 2879, 2880, 2883, 8700). Nothing that comes from compulsion is conjoined to man (n. 2875, 8700). If man could be reformed by compulsion everyone would be reformed (n. 2881). Compulsion in reformation is harmful (n. 4031). What states of compulsion are (n. 8392).

296-1 The difference between men and beasts is, that men are capable of being raised up by the Lord to Himself, of thinking about the Divine, loving it, and being thereby conjoined to the Lord, from which they have eternal life; but it is otherwise with beasts (n. 4525, 6323, 9231). Beasts are in the order of their life, and are therefore born into things suitable to their nature, but man is not, and he must therefore be led into the order of his life by intellectual means (n. 637, 5850, 6323). According to general influx thought with man falls into speech and will into movements (n. 5862, 5990, 6192, 6211). The general influx of the spiritual world into the lives of beasts (n. 1633, 3646).

297-1 There is direct influx from the Lord, and also mediate influx through the spiritual world (n. 6063, 6307, 6472, 9682, 9683). The Lord's direct influx is into the least particulars of all things (n. 6058, 6474-6478, 8717, 8728). The Lord flows in into firsts and at the same time into lasts-in what manner (n. 5147, 5150, 6473, 7004, 7007, 7270). The Lord's influx is into the good in man, and through the good into truth and not the reverse (n. 5482, 5649, 6027, 8685, 8701, 10153). The life that flows in from the Lord varies in accordance with the state of man and in accordance with reception (n. 2069, 5986, 6472, 7343). With the evil the good that flows in from the Lord is turned into evil and the truth into falsity; from experience (n. 3642, 4632). The good and the truth therefrom that continually flow in from the Lord are received just to the extent that evil and falsity therefrom do not obstruct (n. 2411, 3142, 3147, 5828).

299-1 Those who have no conscience do not know what conscience is (n. 7490, 9121). There are some who laugh at conscience when they hear what it is (n. 7217). Some believe that conscience is nothing; some that it is something natural that is sad and mournful, arising either from causes in the body or from causes in the world; some that it is something that the common people get from their religion (n. 206, 831, 950; [TCR n. 665]). There is true conscience, spurious conscience, and false conscience (n. 1033). Pain of conscience is an anxiety of mind on account of what is unjust, insincere, or in any respect evil, which man believes to be against God and against the good of the neighbor (n. 7217). Those have conscience who are in love to God and in charity towards the neighbor, but those who are not so have no conscience (n. 831, 965, 2380, 7490).

Section 7

It will also be shown in the next chapter that the conjunction of heaven with the human race and of the human race with heaven is such that one has its permanent existence with the other.

I have talked with angels about the conjunction of heaven with the human race, saying that while the man of the church declares that all good is from God, and that angels are with man, yet few believe that angels are conjoined to man, still less that they are in his thought and affection. The angels replied that they knew that such a belief and such a mode of speaking still exist in the world, and especially, to their surprise, within the church, where the Word is present to teach men about heaven and its conjunction with man; nevertheless, there is such a conjunction that man is unable to think the least thing unless spirits are associated with him, and on this his spiritual life depends. They said that the cause of ignorance in this matter is man's belief that he lives from himself, and that he has no connection with the First Being [Esse] of life; together with his not knowing that this connection exists by means of the heavens; and yet if that connection were broken man would instantly fall dead. If man only believed, as is really true, that all good is from the Lord and all evil from hell, he would neither make the good in him a matter of merit nor would evil be imputed to him; for he would then look to the Lord in all the good he thinks and does, and all the evil that flows in would be cast down to hell from which it comes. But because man does not believe that anything flows into him either from heaven or from hell, and therefore supposes that all things that he thinks and wills are in himself and therefore from himself, he appropriates the evil to himself, and the good that flows in he defiles with merit.

CONJUNCTION OF HEAVEN WITH MAN BY MEANS OF THE WORD. Those who think from interior reason can see that there is a connection of all things through intermediates with the First, and that whatever is not in connection is dissipated. For they know, when they think about it, that nothing can have permanent existence from itself, but only from what is prior to itself, thus all things from a First; also that the connection with what is prior is like the connection of an effect with its effecting cause; for when the effecting cause is taken away from its effect the effect is dissolved and dispersed. Because the learned thought thus they saw and said that permanent existence is a perpetual springing forth; thus that all things have permanent existence from a First; and as they sprang from that First so they perpetually spring forth, that is, have permanent existence from it. But what the connection of everything is with that which is prior to itself, thus with the First which is the source of all things, cannot be told in a few words, because it is various and diverse. It can only be said in general that there is a connection of the natural world with the spiritual world, and that in consequence there is a correspondence of all things in the natural world with all things in the spiritual (see n. 103-115); also that there is a connection and consequently a correspondence of all things of man with all things of heaven (see n. 87-102).

Man is so created as to have a conjunction and connection with the Lord, but with the angels of heaven only an affiliation. Man has affiliation with the angels, but not conjunction, because in respect to the interiors of his mind man is by creation like an angel, having a like will and a like understanding. Consequently if a man has lived in accordance with the Divine order he becomes after death an angel, with the same wisdom as an angel. Therefore when the conjunction of man with heaven is spoken of his conjunction with the Lord and affiliation with the angels is meant; for heaven is heaven from the Lord's Divine, and not from what is strictly the angels' own [proprium]. That it is the Lord's Divine that makes heaven may be seen above (n. 7-12). [2] But man has, beyond what the angels have, that he is not only in respect to his interiors in the spiritual world, but also at the same time in respect to his exteriors in the natural world. His exteriors which are in the natural world are all things of his natural or external memory and of his thought and imagination therefrom; in general, knowledges and sciences with their delights and pleasures so far as they savor of the world, also many pleasures belonging to the senses of the body, together with his senses themselves, his speech, and his actions. And all these are the outmosts in which the Lord's Divine influx terminates; for that influx does not stop midway, but goes on to its outmosts. All this shows that the outmost of Divine order is in man; and being the outmost it is also the base and foundation. [3] As the Lord's Divine influx does not stop midway but goes on to its outmosts, as has been said, and as this middle part through which it passes is the angelic heaven, while the outmost is in man, and as nothing can exist unconnected, it follows that the connection and conjunction of heaven with the human race is such that one has its permanent existence from the other, and that the human race apart from heaven would be like a chain without a hook; and heaven without the human race would be like a house without a foundation. 304-1

But man has severed this connection with heaven by turning his exteriors away from heaven, and turning them to the world and to self by means of his love of self and of the world, thereby so withdrawing himself that he no longer serves as a basis and foundation for heaven; therefore the Lord has provided a medium to serve in place of this base and foundation for heaven, and also for the conjunction of heaven with man. This medium is the Word. How the Word serves as such a medium has been shown in many places in the Arcana Coelestia, all of which may be seen gathered up in the little work on The White Horse mentioned in the Apocalypse; also in the Appendix to the New Jerusalem and Its Heavenly Doctrine, from which some notes are here appended. 305-1

I have been told from heaven that the most ancient people, because their interiors were turned heavenwards, had direct revelation, and by this means there was at that time a conjunction of the Lord with the human race. After their times, however, there was no such direct revelation, but there was a mediate revelation by means of correspondences, inasmuch as all their Divine worship then consisted of correspondences, and for this reason the churches of that time were called representative churches. For it was then known what correspondence is and what representation is, and that all things on the earth correspond to spiritual things in heaven and in the church, or what is the same, represent them; and therefore the natural things that constituted the externals of their worship served them as mediums for thinking spiritually, that is, thinking with the angels. When the knowledge of correspondences and representations had been blotted out of remembrance a Word was written, in which all the words and their meanings are correspondences, and thus contain a spiritual or internal sense, in which are the angels; and in consequence, when a man reads the Word and perceives it according to the sense of the letter or the outer sense the angels perceive it according to the internal or spiritual sense; for all the thought of angels is spiritual while the thought of man is natural. These two kinds of thought appear diverse; nevertheless they are one because they correspond. Thus it was that when man had separated himself from heaven and had severed the bond the Lord provided a medium of conjunction of heaven with man by means of the Word.

How heaven is conjoined with man by means of the Word I will illustrate by some passages from it. "The New Jerusalem" is described in the Apocalypse in these words: I saw a new heaven and a new earth, and the first heaven and the first earth had passed away. And I saw the holy city New Jerusalem coming down from God out of heaven. The city was foursquare, its length as great as its breadth; and an angel measured the city with a reed, twelve thousand furlongs; the length, the breadth, and the height of it are equal. And he measured the wall thereof, an hundred and forty-four cubits, the measure of a man, that is, of an angel. The building of the wall was of jasper; but the city itself was pure gold, and like unto pure glass; and the foundations of the wall were adorned with every precious stone. The twelve gates were twelve pearls; and the street of the city was pure gold, as it were transparent glass (21:1, 2, 16-19, 21). When man reads these words he understands them merely in accordance with the sense of the letter, namely, that the visible heaven with the earth is to perish, and a new heaven is to come into existence; and upon the new earth the holy city Jerusalem is to descend, with all its dimensions as here described. But the angels that are with man understand these things in a wholly different way, that is, everything that man understands naturally they understand spiritually. [2] By "the new heaven and the new earth" they understand a new church; by "the city Jerusalem coming down from God out of heaven" they understand its heavenly doctrine revealed by the Lord; by " its length, breadth, and height, which are equal," and "twelve thousand furlongs," they understand all the goods and truths of that doctrine in the complex; by its "wall" they understand the truths protecting it; by "the measure of the wall, a hundred and forty-four cubits, which is the measure of a man, that is, of an angel," they understand all those protecting truths in the complex and their character; by its "twelve gates, which were of pearls," they understand introductory truths, "pearls" signifying such truths; by "the foundations of the wall, which were of precious stones," they understand the knowledge on which that doctrine is founded; by "the gold like unto pure glass," of which the city and its street were made, they understand the good of love which makes the doctrine and its truths transparent. Thus do the angels perceive all these things; and therefore not as man perceives them. The natural ideas of man thus pass into the spiritual ideas with the angels without their knowing anything of the sense of the letter of the

Word, that is, about "a new heaven and a new earth," "a new city Jerusalem," its "wall, the foundations of the wall, and its dimensions." And yet the thoughts of angels make one with the thoughts of man, because they correspond; they make one almost the same as the words of a speaker make one with the understanding of them by a hearer who attends solely to the meaning and not to the words. All this shows how heaven is conjoined with man by means of the Word: [3] Let us take another example from the Word: In that day there shall be a highway from Egypt to Assyria, and Assyria shall come into Egypt and Egypt into Assyria; and the Egyptians shall serve Assyria. In that day shall Israel be a third to Egypt and to Assyria, a blessing in the midst of the land, Which Jehovah of hosts shall bless, saying, Blessed be My people the Egyptian, and the Assyrian the work of My hands, and Israel Mine inheritance (Isaiah 19:23-25). What man thinks when these words are read, and what the angels think, can be seen from the sense of the letter of the Word and from its internal sense. Man from the sense of the letter thinks that the Egyptians and Assyrians are to be converted to God and accepted, and are then to become one with the Israelitish nation; but angels in accordance with the internal sense think of the man of the spiritual church who is here described in that sense, whose spiritual is "Israel," whose natural is the "Egyptian," and whose rational, which is the middle, is the "Assyrian." 307-1 Nevertheless, these two senses are one because they correspond; and therefore when the angels thus think spiritually and man naturally they are conjoined almost as body and soul are; in fact, the internal sense of the Word is its soul and the sense of the letter is its body. Such is the Word throughout. This shows that it is a medium of conjunction of heaven with man, and that its literal sense serves as a base and foundation.

There is also a conjunction of heaven by means of the Word with those who are outside of the church where there is no Word; for the Lord's church is universal, and is with all who acknowledge the Divine and live in charity. Moreover, such are taught after death by the angels and receive Divine truths; 308-1 on which subject more may be seen below, in the chapter on the heathen. The universal church on the earth in the sight of the Lord resembles a single man, just as heaven does (see n. 59-72); but the church where the Word is and where the Lord is known by means of it is like the heart and lungs in that man. It is known that all the viscera and members of the entire body draw their life from the heart and lungs through various derivations; and it is thus that those of the human race live who are outside of the church where the Word is, and who constitute the members of that man. Again, the conjunction of heaven with those who are at a distance by means of the Word may be compared to light radiating from a center all around. The Divine light is in the Word, and there the Lord with heaven is present, and from that presence those at a distance are in light; but it would be otherwise if there were no Word. This may be more clearly seen from what has been shown above respecting the form of heaven in accordance with which all who are in heaven have affiliation and communication. But while this arcanum may be comprehended by those who are in spiritual light, it cannot be comprehended by those who are only in natural light; for innumerable things are clearly seen by those who are in spiritual light that are not seen or are seen obscurely as a single thing by those who are only in natural light.

Unless such a Word had been given on this earth the man of this earth would have been separated from heaven; and if separated from heaven he would have ceased to be rational, for the human rational exists by an influx of the light of heaven. Again, the man of this earth is such that he is not capable of receiving direct revelation and of being taught about Divine truths by such revelation, as the inhabitants of other earths are, that have been especially described in another small work. For the man of this earth is more in worldly things, that is, in externals, than the men of other earths, and it is internal things that are receptive of revelation; if it were received in external things the truth would not be understood. That such is the man of this earth is clearly evident from the state of those who are within the church, which is such that while they know from the Word about heaven, about hell, about the life after death, still in heart they deny these things; although among them there are some who have acquired a pre-eminent reputation for learning, and who might for that reason be supposed to be wiser than others.

I have at times talked with angels about the Word, saying that it is despised by some on account of its simple style; and that nothing whatever is known about its internal sense, and for this reason it is not believed that so much wisdom lies hid in it. The angels said that although the style of the Word seems simple in the sense of the letter, it is such that nothing can ever be compared to it in excellence, since Divine wisdom lies concealed not only in the meaning as a whole but also in each word; and that in heaven this wisdom shines forth. They wished to declare that this wisdom is the light of heaven, because it is Divine truth, for that which shines in heaven is the Divine truth (see n. 132). Again, they said that without such a Word there would be no light of heaven with the men of our earth, nor would there be any conjunction of heaven with them; for there is conjunction only so far as the light of heaven is present with man, and that light is present only so far as Divine truth is revealed to man by means of the Word. This conjunction by means of the correspondence of the spiritual sense of the Word with its natural sense is unknown to man, because the man of this earth knows nothing about the spiritual thought and speech of angels, and how it differs from the natural thought and speech of men; and until this is known it cannot in the least be known what the internal sense is, and that such conjunction is therefore possible by means of that sense. They said, furthermore, that if this sense were known to man, and if man in reading the Word were to think in accordance with some knowledge of it, he would come into interior wisdom, and would be still more conjoined with heaven, since by this means he would enter into ideas like the ideas of the angels.

XXXV. HEAVEN AND HELL ARE FROM THE HUMAN RACE. In the Christian world it is wholly unknown that heaven and hell are from the human race, for it is believed that in the beginning angels were created and heaven was thus formed; also that the devil or Satan was an angel of light, but having rebelled he was cast down with his crew, and thus hell was formed. The angels never cease to wonder at such a belief in the Christian world, and still more that nothing is really known about heaven, when in fact that is the primary principle of all doctrine in the church. But since such ignorance prevails they rejoice in heart that it has pleased the Lord to reveal to mankind at this time many things about heaven and about hell, thereby dispelling as far as possible the darkness that has been daily increasing because the church has come to its end. [2] They wish for this reason that I should declare from their lips that in the entire heaven there is not a single angel who was created such from the beginning, nor in hell any devil who was created an angel of light and cast down; but that all, both in heaven and in hell, are from the human race; in heaven those who lived in the world in heavenly love and belief, in hell those who lived in infernal love and belief, also that it is hell taken as a whole that is called the Devil and Satan-the name Devil being given to the hell that is behind, where those are that are called evil genii, and the name Satan being given to the hell that is in front, where those are that are called evil spirits. 311-1 The character of these hells will be described in the following pages. [3] The angels said that the Christian world had gathered such a belief about those in heaven and those in hell from some passages in the Word understood according to the mere sense of the letter not illustrated and explained by genuine doctrine from the Word; although the sense of the letter of the Word until illuminated by genuine doctrine, draws the mind in different directions, and this begets ignorance, heresies, and errors. 311-2

The man of the church also derives this belief from his believing that no man comes into heaven or into hell until the time of the final judgment; and about that he has accepted the opinion that all visible things will perish at that time and new things will come into existence, and that the soul will then return into its body, and from that union man will again live as a man. This belief involves the other-that angels were created such from the beginning; for it is impossible to believe that heaven and hell are from the human race when it is believed that no man can go there until the end of the world. [2] But that men might be convinced that this is not true it has been granted me to be in company with angels, and also to talk with those who are in hell, and this now for some years, sometimes continuously from morning until evening, and thus be informed about heaven and hell. This has been permitted that the man of the church may no longer continue in his erroneous belief about the resurrection at the time of judgment, and about the state of the soul in the meanwhile, also about angels and the devil. As this belief is a belief in what is false it involves the mind in darkness, and with those who think about these things from their own intelligence it induces doubt and at length denial, for they say in heart, "How can so vast a heaven, with so many constellations and with the sun and moon, be destroyed and dissipated; and how can the stars which are larger than the earth fall from heaven to the earth; and can bodies eaten up by worms, consumed by corruption, and scattered to all the winds, be gathered together again to their souls; and where in the meantime is the soul, and what is it when deprived of the senses it had in the body?" [3] With many other like things, which being incomprehensible cannot be believed, and which destroy the belief of many in the life of the soul after death, and their belief in heaven and hell, and with these other matters pertaining to the faith of the church. That this belief has been destroyed is evident from its being said, "Who has ever come to us from heaven and told us that there is a heaven? What is hell? is there any? What is this about man's being tormented with fire to eternity? What is the day of judgment? has it not been expected in vain for ages?" with other things that involve a denial of everything. [4] Therefore lest those who think in this way-as many do who from their worldly wisdom are regarded as erudite and learned-should any longer confound and mislead the simple in faith and heart, and induce infernal darkness respecting God and heaven and eternal life, and all else that depends on these, the interiors of my spirit have been opened by the Lord, and I have thus been permitted to talk with all after their decease with whom I was ever acquainted in the life of the body-with some for days, with some for months, and with some for a year, and also with so many others that I should not exaggerate if I should say a hundred thousand; many of whom were in heaven, and many in hell. I have also talked with some two days after their decease, and have told them that their funeral services and obsequies were then being held in preparation for their interment; to which they replied that it was well to cast aside that which had served them as a body and for bodily functions in the world; and they wished me to say that they were not dead, but were living as men the same as before, and had merely migrated from one world into the other, and were not aware of having lost anything, since they had a body and its senses just as before, also understanding and will just as before, with thoughts and affections, sensations and desires, like those they had in the world. [5] Most of those who had recently died, when they saw themselves to be living men as before, and in a like state (for after death everyone's state of life is at first such as it was in the world, but there is a gradual change in it either into heaven or into hell), were moved by new joy at being alive, saying that they had not believed that it would be so. But they greatly wondered that they should have lived in such ignorance and blindness about the state of their life after death; and especially that the man of the church should be in such ignorance and blindness, when above all others in the whole world he might be clearly enlightened in regard to these things. 312-1 Then they began to see the cause of that blindness and ignorance, which is, that external things which are things, relating to the world and the body, had so occupied and filled their minds that they could not be raised into the light of heaven and look into the things of the church beyond its doctrinals; for when matters relating to the body and the world are loved, as they are at the present day, nothing but darkness flows into the mind when men go beyond those doctrines.

Very many of the learned from the Christian world are astonished when they find themselves after death in a body, in garments, and in houses, as in the world. And when they recall what they had thought about the life after death, the soul, spirits, and heaven and hell, they are ashamed and confess that they thought foolishly, and that the simple in faith thought much more wisely than they. When the minds of learned men who had confirmed themselves in such ideas and had ascribed all things to nature were examined, it was found that their interiors were wholly closed up and their exteriors were opened, that they looked towards the world and thus towards hell and not towards heaven. For to the extent that man's interiors are opened he looks towards heaven, but to the extent that his interiors are closed and his exteriors opened he looks towards hell, because the interiors of man are formed for the reception of all things of heaven, but the exteriors for the reception of all things of the world; and those who receive the world, and not heaven also, receive hell. 313-1

That heaven is from the human race can be seen also from the fact that angelic minds and human minds are alike, both enjoying the ability to understand, perceive and will, and both formed to receive heaven; for the human mind is just as capable of becoming wise as the angelic mind; and if it does not attain to such wisdom in the world it is because it is in an earthly body, and in that body its spiritual mind thinks naturally. But it is otherwise when the mind is loosed from the bonds of that body; then it no longer thinks naturally, but spiritually, and when it thinks spiritually its thoughts are incomprehensible and ineffable to the natural man; thus it becomes wise like an angel, all of which shows that the internal part of man, called his spirit, is in its essence an angel (see above, n. 57); 314-1 and when loosed from the earthly body is, equally with the angel, in the human form. (That an angel is in a complete human form may be seen above, n. 73-77.) When, however, the internal of man is not open above but only beneath, it is still, after it has been loosed from the body, in a human form, but a horrible and diabolical form, for it is able only to look downwards towards hell, and not upwards towards heaven.

Moreover, any one who has been taught about Divine order can understand that man was created to become an angel, because the outmost of order is in him (n. 304), in which what pertains to heavenly and angelic wisdom can be brought into form and can be renewed and multiplied. Divine order never stops midway to form there a something apart from an outmost, for it is not in its fullness and completion there; but it goes on to the outmost; and when it is in its outmost it takes on its form, and by means there collected it renews itself and produces itself further, which is accomplished through procreations. Therefore the seed-ground of heaven is in the outmost.

The Lord rose again not as to His spirit alone but also as to His body, because when He was in the world He glorified His whole Human, that is, made it Divine; for His soul which He had from the Father was of Itself the very Divine, while His body became a likeness of the soul, that is, of the Father, thus also Divine. This is why He, differently from any man, rose again as to both; 316-1 and this He made manifest to the disciples (who when they saw Him believed that they saw a spirit), by saying: See My hands and My feet, that it is I Myself; handle Me and see, for a spirit hath not flesh and bones as ye behold Me having (Luke 24:36-39); indicating thereby that He was a man both in respect to His spirit and in respect to His body.

That it might be made clear that man lives after death and enters in accordance with his life in the world either into heaven or into hell, many things have been disclosed to me about the state of man after death, which will be presented in due order in the following pages, where the world of spirits is treated of.

THE HEATHEN, OR PEOPLES OUTSIDE OF THE CHURCH, IN HEAVEN. There is a general opinion that those born outside of the church, who are called the nations, or heathen, cannot be saved, because not having the Word they know nothing about the Lord, and apart from the Lord there is no salvation. But that these also are saved this alone makes certain, that the mercy of the Lord is universal, that is, extends to every individual; that these equally with those within the church, who are few in comparison, are born men, and that their ignorance of the Lord is not their fault. Any one who thinks from any enlightened reason can see that no man is born for hell, for the Lord is love itself and His love is to will the salvation of all. Therefore He has provided a religion for everyone, and by it acknowledgment of the Divine and interior life; for to live in accordance with one's religion is to live interiorly, since one then looks to the Divine, and so far as he looks to the Divine he does not look to the world but separates himself from the world, that is, from the life of the world, which is exterior life. 318-1

That the heathen equally with Christians are saved any one can see who knows what it is that makes heaven in man; for heaven is within man, and those that have heaven within them come into heaven. Heaven with man is acknowledging the Divine and being led by the Divine. The first and chief thing of every religion is to acknowledge the Divine. A religion that does not acknowledge the Divine is no religion. The precepts of every religion look to worship; thus to the way in which the Divine is to be worshiped that the worship may be acceptable to Him; and when this has been settled in one's mind, that is, so far as one wills this or so far as he loves it, he is led by the Lord. Everyone knows that the heathen as well as Christians live a moral life, and many of them a better life than Christians. Moral life may be lived either out of regard to the Divine or out of regard to men in the world; and a moral life that is lived out of regard to the Divine is a spiritual life. In outward form the two appear alike, but in inward form they are wholly different; the one saves man, the other does not. For he who lives a moral life out of regard to the Divine is led by the Divine; while he who leads a moral life out of regard to men in the world is led by himself. [2] But this may be illustrated by an example. He that refrains from doing evil to his neighbor because it is antagonistic to religion, that is, antagonistic to the Divine, refrains from doing evil from a spiritual motive; but he that refrains from doing evil to another merely from fear of the law, or the loss of reputation, of honor, or gain, that is, from regard to self and the world, refrains from doing evil from a natural motive, and is led by himself. The life of the latter is natural, that of the former is spiritual. A man whose moral life is spiritual has heaven within him; but he whose moral life is merely natural does not have heaven within him; and for the reason that heaven flows in from above and opens man's interiors, and through his interiors flows into his exteriors; while the world flows in from beneath and opens the exteriors but not the interiors. For there can be no flowing in from the natural world into the spiritual, but only from the spiritual world into the natural; therefore if heaven is not also received, the interiors remain closed. All this makes clear who those are that receive heaven within them, and who do not. [3] And yet heaven is not the same in one as in another. It differs in each one in accordance with his affection for good and its truth. Those that are in an affection for good out of regard to the Divine, love Divine truth, since good and truth love each other and desire to be conjoined. 319-1 This explains why the heathen, although they are not in genuine truths in the world, yet because of their love receive truths in the other life.

A certain spirit from among the heathen who had lived in the world in good of charity in accordance with his religion, hearing Christian spirits reasoning about what must be believed, (for spirits reason with each other far more thoroughly and acutely than men, especially about what is good and true,) wondered at such contentions, and said that he did not care to listen to them, for they reasoned from appearances and fallacies; and he gave them this instruction: "If I am good I can know from the good itself what is true; and what I do not know I can receive."

I have been taught in many ways that the heathen who have led a moral life and have lived in obedience and subordination and mutual charity in accordance with their religion, and have thus received something of conscience, are accepted in the other life, and are there instructed with solicitous care by the angels in the goods and truths of faith; and that when they are being taught they behave themselves modestly, intelligently, and wisely, and readily accept truths and adopt them. They have not worked out for themselves any principles of falsity antagonistic to the truths of faith that will need to be shaken off, still less cavils against the Lord, as many Christians have who cherish no other idea of Him than that He is an ordinary man. The heathen on the contrary when they hear that God has become a Man, and has thus manifested Himself in the world, immediately acknowledge it and worship the Lord, saying that because God is the God of heaven and of earth, and because the human race is His, He has fully disclosed Himself to men. 321-1 It is a Divine truth that apart from the Lord there is no salvation; but this is to be understood to mean that there is no salvation except from the Lord. There are many earths in the universe, and all of them full of inhabitants, scarcely any of whom know that the Lord took on the Human on our earth. Yet because they worship the Divine under a human form they are accepted and led by the Lord. On this subject more may be seen in the little work on The Earths in the Universe.

Among the heathen, as among Christians, there are both wise and simple. That I might learn about them I have been permitted to speak with both, sometimes for hours and days. But there are no such wise men now as in ancient times, especially in the Ancient Church, which extended over a large part of the Asiatic world, and from which religion spread to many nations. That I might wholly know about them I have been permitted to have familiar conversation with some of these wise men. There was with me one who was among the wiser of his time, and consequently well known in the learned world, with whom I talked on various subjects, and had reason to believe that it was Cicero. Knowing that he was a wise man I talked with him about wisdom, intelligence, order, and the Word, and lastly about the Lord. [2] Of wisdom he said that there is no other wisdom than the wisdom of life, and that wisdom can be predicated of nothing else; of intelligence that it is from wisdom; of order, that it is from the Supreme God, and that to live in that order is to be wise and intelligent. As to the Word, when I read to him something from the prophets he was greatly delighted, especially with this, that every name and every word signified interior things; and he wondered greatly that learned men at this day are not delighted with such study. I saw plainly that the interiors of his thought or mind had been opened. He said that he was unable to hear more, as he perceived something more holy than he could bear, being affected so interiorly. [3] At length I spoke with him about the Lord, saying that while He was born a man He was conceived of God, and that He put off the maternal human and put on the Divine Human, and that it is He that governs the universe. To this he replied that he knew some things concerning the Lord, and perceived in his way that if mankind were to be saved it could not have been done otherwise. In the meantime some bad Christians infused various cavils; but to these he gave no attention, remarking that this was not strange, since in the life of the body they had imbibed unbecoming ideas on the subject, and until they got rid of these they could not admit ideas that confirmed the truth, as the ignorant can.

It has also been granted me to talk with others who lived in ancient times, and who were then among the more wise. At first they appeared in front at a distance, and were able then to perceive the interiors of my thoughts, thus many things fully. From one idea of thought they were able to discern the entire series and fill it with delightful things of wisdom combined with charming representations. From this they were perceived to be among the more wise, and I was told that they were some of the ancient people; and when they came nearer I read to them something from the Word, and they were delighted beyond measure. I perceived the essence of their delight and gratification, which arose chiefly from this, that all things and each thing they heard from the Word were representative and significative of heavenly and spiritual things. They said that in their time, when they lived in the world, their mode of thinking and speaking and also of writing was of this nature, and that this was their pursuit of wisdom.

But as regards the heathen of the present day, they are not so wise, but most of them are simple in heart. Nevertheless, those of them that have lived in mutual charity receive wisdom in the other life, and of these one or two examples may be cited. When I read the seventeenth and eighteenth chapters of Judges (about Micah, and how the sons of Dan carried away his graven image and teraphim and Levite) a heathen spirit was present who in the life of the body had worshiped a graven image. He listened attentively to the account of what was done to Micah, and his grief on account of his graven image which the Danites took away, and such grief came upon him and moved him that he scarcely knew, by reason of inward distress, what to think. Not only was this grief perceived, but also the innocence that was in all his affections. The Christian spirits that were present watched him and wondered that a worshiper of a graven image should have so great a feeling of sympathy and innocence stirred in him. Afterwards some good spirits talked with him, saying that graven images should not be worshiped, and that being a man he was capable of understanding this; that he ought, apart from a graven image, to think of God the Creator and Ruler of the whole heaven and the whole earth, and that God is the Lord. When this was said I was permitted to perceive the interior nature of his adoration, which was communicated to me; and it was much more holy than is the case of Christians, This makes clear that at the present day the heathen come into heaven with less difficulty than Christians, according to the Lord's words in Luke: Then shall they come from the east and the west, and from the north and the south, and shall recline in the kingdom of God. And behold, there are last who shall be first, and there are first who shall be last (13:29, 30). For in the state in which that spirit was he could be imbued with all things of faith and receive them with interior affection; there was in him the mercy of love, and in his ignorance there was innocence; and when these are present all things of faith are received as it were spontaneously and with joy. He was afterwards received among angels.

A choir at a distance was heard one morning, and from the choir's representations I was permitted to know that they were Chinese, for they exhibited a kind of woolly goat, then a cake of millet, and an ebony spoon, also the idea of a floating city. They desired to come nearer to me, and when they had joined me they said that they wished to be alone with me, that they might disclose their thoughts. But they were told that they were not alone, and that some were displeased at their wishing to be alone, although they were guests. When they perceived this displeasure they began to think whether they had transgressed against the neighbor, and whether they had claimed any thing to themselves that belonged to others. All thought in the other life being communicated I was permitted to perceive the agitation of their minds. It consisted of a recognition that possibly they had injured those who were displeased, of shame on that account, together with other worthy affections; and it was thus known that they were endowed with charity. Soon after I spoke with them, and at last about the Lord. When I called Him "Christ" I perceived a certain repugnance in them; but the reason was disclosed, namely, that they had brought this from the world, from their having learned that Christians lived worse lives than they did, and were destitute of charity. But when I called Him simply "Lord" they were interiorly moved. Afterwards, they were taught by the angels that the Christian doctrine beyond every other in the world prescribes love and charity, but that there are few who live in accordance with it. There are heathen who have come to know while they lived in the world, both from interaction and report, that Christians lead bad lives, are addicted to adultery, hatred, quarreling, drunkenness, and the like, which they themselves abhor because such things are contrary to their religion. These in the other life are more timid than others about accepting the truths of faith; but they are taught by the angels that the Christian doctrine, as well as the faith itself, teaches a very different life, but that the lives of Christians are less in accord with their doctrine than the lives of heathen. When they recognize this they receive the truths of faith, and adore the Lord, but less readily than others.

It is a common thing for heathen that have worshiped any god under an image or statue, or any graven thing to be introduced, when they come into the other life, to certain spirits in place of their gods or idols, in order that they may rid themselves of their fantasies. When they have been with these for some days, the fantasies are put away. Also those that have worshiped men are sometimes introduced to the men they have worshiped, or to others in their place - as many of the Jews to Abraham, Jacob, Moses, and David-but when they come to see that they are human the same as others, and that they can give them no help, they become ashamed, and are carried to their own places in accordance with their lives. Among the heathen in heaven the Africans are most beloved, for they receive the goods and truths of heaven more readily than others. They especially wish to be called obedient, but not faithful. They say that as Christians possess the doctrine of faith they may be called faithful; but not they unless they accept that doctrine, or as they say, have the ability to accept it.

I have talked with some who were in the Ancient Church. That is called the Ancient Church that was established after the deluge, and extended through many kingdoms, namely, Assyria, Mesopotamia, Syria, Ethiopia, Arabia, Libya,

Egypt, Philistia as far as Tyre and Zidon, and through the land of Canaan on both sides of the Jordan. 327-1 The men of this church knew about the Lord that He was to come, and were imbued with the goods of faith, and yet they fell away and became idolaters. These spirits were in front towards the left, in a dark place and in a miserable state. Their speech was like the sound of a pipe of one tone, almost without rational thought. They said they had been there for many centuries, and that they are sometimes taken out that they may serve others for certain uses of a low order. From this I was led to think about many Christians-who are inwardly though not outwardly idolaters, since they are worshipers of self and of the world, and in heart deny the Lord-what lot awaits such in the other life.

That the church of the Lord is spread over all the globe, and is thus universal; and that all those are in it who have lived in the good of charity in accordance with their religion; and that the church, where the Word is and by means of it the Lord is known, is in relation to those who are out of the church like the heart and lungs in man, from which all the viscera and members of the body have their life, variously according to their forms, positions, and conjunctions, may be seen above (n. 308).

LITTLE CHILDREN IN HEAVEN. It is a belief of some that only such children as are born within the church go to heaven, and that those born out of the church do not, and for the reason that the children within the church are baptized and by baptism are initiated into faith of the church. Such are not aware that no one receives heaven or faith through baptism; for baptism is merely for a sign and memorial that man should be regenerated, and that those born within the church can be regenerated because the Word is there, and in the Word are the Divine truths by means of which regeneration is effected, and there the Lord who regenerates is known. 329-1 Let them know therefore that every child, wherever he is born, whether within the church or outside of it, whether of pious parents or impious, is received when he dies by the Lord and trained up in heaven, and taught in accordance with Divine order, and imbued with affections for what is good, and through these with knowledges of what is true; and afterwards as he is perfected in intelligence and wisdom is introduced into heaven and becomes an angel. Everyone who thinks from reason can be sure that all are born for heaven and no one for hell, and if man comes into hell he himself is culpable; but little children cannot be held culpable.

When children die they are still children in the other life, having a like infantile mind, a like innocence in ignorance, and a like tenderness in all things. They are merely in the rudiments of a capacity to become angels, for children are not angels but become angels. For everyone passing out of this world enters the other in the same state of life, a little child in the state of a little child, a boy in the state of a boy, a youth, a man, an old man, in the state of a youth, a man, or an old man; but subsequently each one's state is changed. The state of little children surpasses the state of all others in that they are in innocence, and evil has not yet been rooted in them by actual life; and in innocence all things of heaven can be implanted, for it is a receptacle of the truth of faith and of the good of love.

The state of children in the other life far surpasses their state in the world, for they are not clothed with an earthly body, but with such a body as the angels have. The earthly body is in itself gross, and receives its first sensations and first motions not from the inner or spiritual world, but from the outer or natural world; and in consequence in this world children must be taught to walk, to guide their motions, and to speak; and even their senses, as seeing and hearing, must be opened by use. It is not so with children in the other life. As they are spirits they act at once in accordance with their interiors, walking without practice, and also talking, but at first from general affections not yet distinguished into ideas of thought; but they are quickly initiated into these also, for the reason that their exteriors are homogeneous with their interiors. The speech of angels (as may be seen above, n, 234-245) so flows forth from affection modified by ideas of thought that their speech completely conforms to their thoughts from affection.

As soon as little children are resuscitated, which takes place immediately after death, they are taken into heaven and confided to angel women who in the life of the body tenderly loved little children and at the same time loved God. Because these during their life in the world loved all children with a kind of motherly tenderness, they receive them as their own; while the children, from an implanted instinct, love them as their own mothers. There are as many children in each one's care as she desires from a spiritual parental affection. This heaven appears in front before the forehead, directly in the line or radius in which the angels look to the Lord. It is so situated because all little children are under the immediate auspices of the Lord; and the heaven of innocence, which is the third heaven, flows into them.

Little children have various dispositions, some that of the spiritual angels and some that of the celestial angels. Those who are of a celestial disposition are seen in that heaven to the right, and those of a spiritual disposition to the left. All children in the Greatest Man, which is heaven, are in the province of the eyes-those of a spiritual disposition in the province of the left eye, and those of a celestial disposition in the province of the right eye. This is because the angels who are in the spiritual kingdom see the Lord before the left eye, and those who are in the celestial kingdom before the right eye (see above, n. 118). This fact that in the Greatest Man or heaven children are in the province of the eyes is a proof that they are under the immediate sight and auspices of the Lord.

How children are taught in heaven shall also be briefly told. From their nurses they learn to talk. Their earliest speech is simply a sound of affection; this by degrees becomes more distinct as ideas of thought enter; for ideas of thought from affections constitute all angelic speech (as may be seen in its own chapter, n. 234-245). Into their affections, all of which proceed from innocence, such things as appear before their eyes and cause delight are first instilled; and as these things are from a spiritual origin the things of heaven at once flow into them, and by means of these heavenly things their interiors are opened, and they are thereby daily perfected. But when this first age is completed they are transferred to another heaven, where they are taught by masters; and so on.

Children are taught chiefly by representatives suited to their capacity. These are beautiful and full of wisdom from within, beyond all belief. In this way an intelligence that derives its soul from good is gradually instilled into them. I will here describe two representatives that I have been permitted to see, from which the nature of others may be inferred. First there was a representation of the Lord's rising from the sepulchre, and at the same time of the uniting of His Human with the Divine. This was done in a manner so wise as to surpass all human wisdom, and at the same time in an innocent infantile manner. An idea of a sepulchre was presented, and with it an idea of the Lord, but in so remote a way that there was scarcely any perception of its being the Lord, except seemingly afar off; and for the reason that in the idea of a sepulchre there is something funereal, and this was thus removed, afterwards they cautiously admitted into the sepulchre something atmospheric, with an appearance of thin vapor, by which with proper remoteness they signified spiritual life in baptism. Afterwards I saw a representation by the angels of the Lord's descent to those that are "bound," and of His ascent with these into heaven, and this with incomparable prudence and gentleness. In adaptation to the infantile mind they let down little cords almost invisible, very soft and tender, by which they lightened the Lord's ascent, always with a holy solicitude that there should be nothing in the representation bordering upon anything that did not contain what is spiritual and heavenly. Other representations are there given, whereby, as by plays adapted to the minds of children, they are guided into knowledges of truth and affections for good.

It was also shown how tender their understanding is. When I was praying the Lord's Prayer, and from their understanding they flowed into the ideas of my thought, their influx was perceived to be so tender and soft as to be almost solely a matter of affection; and at the same time it was observed that their understanding was open even from the Lord, for what flowed forth from them was as if it simply flowed through them. Moreover, the Lord flows into the ideas of little children chiefly from inmosts, for there is nothing, as with adults, to close up their ideas, no principles of falsity to close the way to the understanding of truth, nor any life of evil to close the way to the reception of good, and thereby to the reception of wisdom. All this makes clear that little children do not come at once after death into an angelic state, but are gradually brought into it by means of knowledges of good and truth, and in harmony with all heavenly order; for the least particulars of their nature are known to the Lord, and thus they are led, in accord with each and every movement of their inclination, to receive the truths of good and the goods of truth.
337.

I have also been shown how all things are instilled into them by delightful and pleasant means suited to their genius. I have been permitted to see children most charmingly attired, having garlands of flowers resplendent with most beautiful and heavenly colors twined about their breasts and around their tender arms; and once to see them accompanied by those in charge of them and by maidens, in a park most beautifully adorned, not so much with trees, as with arbors and covered walks of laurel, with paths leading inward; and when the children entered attired as they were the flowers over the entrance shone forth most joyously. This indicates the nature of their delights, also how they are led by means of pleasant and delightful things into the goods of innocence and charity, which goods the Lord continually instilled into these delights and pleasures.

It was shown me, by a mode of communication common in the other life, what the ideas of children are when they see objects of any kind. Each and every object seemed to them to be alive; and thus in every least idea of their thought there is life. And it was perceived that children on the earth have nearly the same ideas when they are at their little plays; for as yet they have no such reflection as adults have about what is inanimate.

It has been said above that children are of a genius either celestial or spiritual. Those of a celestial genius are easily distinguished from those of a spiritual genius. Their thought, speech, and action, is so gentle that hardly anything appears except what flows from a love of good to the Lord and from a love for other children. But those of a spiritual genius are not so gentle; but in everything with them there appears a sort of vibration, as of wings. The difference is seen also in their ill-feeling and in other things.

Many may suppose that in heaven little children remain little children, and continue as such among the angels. Those who do not know what an angel is may have had this opinion confirmed by paintings and images in churches, in which angels are represented as children. But it is wholly otherwise. Intelligence and wisdom are what constitute an angel, and as long as children do not possess these they are not angels, although they are with the angels; but as soon as they become intelligent and wise they become angels; and what is wonderful, they do not then appear as children, but as adults, for they are no longer of an infantile genius, but of a more mature angelic genius. Intelligence and wisdom produce this effect. The reason why children appear more mature, thus as youths and young men, as they are perfected in intelligence and wisdom, is that intelligence and wisdom are essential spiritual nourishment; 340-1 and thus the things that nourish their minds also nourish their bodies, and this from correspondence; for the form of the body is simply the external form of the interiors. But it should be understood that in heaven children advance in age only to early manhood, and remain in this to eternity. That I might be assured that this is so I have been permitted to talk with some who had been educated as children in heaven, and had grown up there; with some also while they were children, and again with the same when they had become young men; and I have heard from them about the progress of their life from one age to another.

That innocence is a receptacle of all things of heaven, and thus the innocence of children is a plane for all affections for good and truth, can be seen from what has been shown above (n. 276-283) in regard to the innocence of angels in heaven, namely, that innocence is a willingness to be led by the Lord and not by oneself; consequently so far as a man is in innocence he is separated from what is his own, and so far as one is separated from what is his own he is in what is the Lord's own. The Lord's own is what is called His righteousness and merit. But the innocence of children is not genuine innocence, because as yet it is without wisdom. Genuine innocence is wisdom, since so far as any one is wise he loves to be led by the Lord; or what is the same, so far as any one is led by the Lord he is wise. [2] Therefore children are led from the external innocence in which they are at the beginning, and which is called the innocence of childhood, to internal innocence, which is the innocence of wisdom. This innocence is the end that directs all their instruction and progress; and therefore when they have attained to the innocence of wisdom, the innocence of childhood, which in the meanwhile has served them as a plane, is joined to them. [3] The innocence of children has been represented to me as a wooden sort of thing, almost devoid of life, which becomes vivified as they are perfected by knowledges of truth and affections for good. Afterwards genuine innocence was represented by a most beautiful child, naked and full of life; for the really innocent, who are in the inmost heaven and thus nearest to the Lord, always appear before the eyes of other angels as little children, and some of them naked; for innocence is represented by nakedness unaccompanied by shame, as is said of the first man and his wife in Paradise (Gen. 2:25); so when their state of innocence perished they were ashamed of their nakedness, and hid themselves (chap. 3:7, 10, 11). In a word, the wiser the angels are the more innocent they are, and the more innocent they are the more they appear to themselves as little children. This is why in the Word "childhood" signifies innocence (see above, n. 278).

I have talked with angels about little children, whether they are free from evils, inasmuch as they have no actual evil as adults have; and I was told that they are equally in evil, and in fact are nothing but evil; 342-1 but, like all angels, they are so withheld from evil and held in good by the Lord as to seem to themselves to be in good from themselves. For this reason when children have become adults in heaven, that they may not have the false idea about themselves that the good in them is from themselves and not from the Lord, they are now and then let down into their evils which they inherited, and are left in them until they know, acknowledge and believe the truth of the matter. [2] There was one, the son of a king, who died in childhood and grew up in heaven, who held this opinion. Therefore he was let down into that life of evils into which he was born, and he then perceived from the sphere of his life that he had a disposition to domineer over others, and regarded adulteries as of no account; these evils he had inherited from his parents; but after he had been brought to recognize his real character he was again received among the angels with whom he had before been associated. [3] In the other life no one ever suffers punishment on account of his inherited evil, because it is not his evil, that is, it is not his fault that he is such; he suffers only on account of actual evil that is his, that is, only so far as he has appropriated to himself inherited evil by actual life. When, therefore, the children that have become adults are let down into the state of their inherited evil it is not that they may suffer punishment for it, but that they may learn that of themselves they are nothing but evil, and that it is by the mercy of the Lord that they are taken up into heaven from the hell in which they are, and that it is from the Lord that they are in heaven and not from any merit of their own; and therefore they may not boast before others of the good that is in them, since this is contrary to the good of mutual love, as it is contrary to the truth of faith.

Several times when a number of children that were in a purely infantile state have been with me in choirs, they were heard as a tender unarranged mass, that is, as not yet acting as one, as they do later when they have become more mature. To my surprise the spirits with me could not refrain from inducing them to talk. This desire is innate in spirits. But I noticed, each time, that the children resisted, unwilling to talk in this way. This refusal and resistance, which were accompanied by a kind of indignation, I have often perceived; and when an opportunity to talk was given them they would say nothing except that "It is not so." I have been taught that little children are so tempted in order that they may get accustomed to resisting, and may begin to resist falsity and evil, and also that they may learn not to think, speak, and act, from another, and in consequence may learn to permit themselves to be led by no one but the Lord.

From what has been said it can be seen what child education is in heaven, namely, that it is leading them by means of an understanding of truth and the wisdom of good into the angelic life, which is love to the Lord and mutual love, in which is innocence. But how different in many cases is the education of children on the earth can be seen from this example. I was in the street of a large city, and saw little boys fighting with each other; a crowd flocked around and looked on with much pleasure; and I was told that little boys are incited to such fights by their own parents. Good spirits and angels who saw this through my eyes so revolted at it that I felt their horror; and especially that parents should incite their children to such things, saying that in this way parents extinguish in the earliest age all the mutual love and all the innocence that children have from the Lord, and initiate them into the spirit of hatred and revenge; consequently by their own endeavors they shut their children out of heaven, where there is nothing but mutual love. Let parents therefore who wish well to their children beware of such things.

What the difference is between those who die in childhood and those who die in mature life shall also be told. Those dying in mature life have a plane acquired from the earthly and material world, and this they carry with them. This plane is their memory and its bodily natural affection. This remains fixed and becomes quiescent, but still serves their thought after death as an outmost plane, since the thought flows into it. Consequently such as this plane is, and such as the correspondence is between the things that are in it and the rational faculty, such is the man after death. But the children who die in childhood and are educated in heaven have no such plane, since they derive nothing from the material world and the earthly body; but they have a spiritual-natural plane. For this reason they cannot be in such gross affections and consequent thoughts, since they derive all things from heaven. Moreover, these children do not know that they were born in the world, but believe that they were born in heaven. Neither do they know about any other than spiritual birth, which is effected through knowledges of good and truth and through intelligence and wisdom, from which man is a man; and as these are from the Lord they believe themselves to be the Lord's own, and love to be so. Nevertheless it is possible for the state of men who grow up on the earth to become as perfect as the state of children who grow up in heaven, provided they put away bodily and earthly loves, which are the loves of self and the world, and receive in their place spiritual loves.

XXXVIII. THE WISE AND THE SIMPLE IN HEAVEN. It is believed that in heaven the wise will have more glory and eminence than the simple, because it is said in Daniel: They that are intelligent shall shine as with the brightness of the firmament, and they that turn many to righteousness as the stars for ever and ever (12:3). But few know who are meant by the "intelligent" and by those that "turn many to righteousness." The common belief is that they are such as are called the accomplished and learned, especially such as have taught in the church and have surpassed others in acquirements and in preaching, and still more such among them as have converted many to the faith. In the world all such are regarded as the intelligent; nevertheless such are not the intelligent in heaven that are spoken of in these words, unless their intelligence is heavenly intelligence. What this is will now be told.

Heavenly intelligence is interior intelligence, arising from a love for truth, not with any glory in the world nor any glory in heaven as an end, but with the truth itself as an end, by which they are inmostly affected and with which they are inmostly delighted. Those who are affected by and delighted with the truth itself are affected by and delighted with the light of heaven; and those who are affected by and delighted with the light of heaven are also affected by and delighted with Divine truth, and indeed with the Lord Himself; for the light of heaven is Divine truth, and Divine truth is the Lord in heaven (see above, n. 126-140). This light enters only into the interiors of the mind; for the interiors of the mind are formed for the reception of that light, and are affected by and delighted with that light as it enters; for whatever flows in and is received from heaven has in it what is delightful and pleasant. From this comes a genuine affection for truth, which is an affection for truth for truth's sake. Those who are in this affection, or what is the same thing, in this love, are in heavenly intelligence, and "shine in heaven as with the brightness of the firmament." They so shine because Divine truth, wherever it is in heaven, is what gives light (see above, n. 132); and the "firmament" of heaven signifies from correspondence the intellectual faculty, both with angels and men, that is in the light of heaven. [2] But those that love the truth, either with glory in the world or glory in heaven as an end, cannot shine in heaven, since they are delighted with and affected by the light of the world, and not with the very light of heaven; and the light of the world without the light of heaven is in heaven mere thick darkness. 347-1 For the glory of self is what rules, because it is the end in view; and when that glory is the end man puts himself in the first place, and such truths as can be made serviceable to his glory he looks upon simply as means to the end and as instruments of service. For he that loves Divine truths for the sake of his own glory regards himself and not the Lord in Divine truths, thereby turning the sight pertaining to his understanding and faith away from heaven to the world, and away from the Lord to himself. Such, therefore, are in the light of the world and not in the light of heaven. [3] In outward form or in the sight of men they appear just as intelligent and learned as those who are in the light of heaven, because they speak in a like manner; and sometimes to outward appearance they even appear wiser, because they are moved by love of self, and are skilled in counterfeiting heavenly affections; but in their inward form in which they appear before the angels they are wholly different. All this shows in some degree who those are that are meant by "the intelligent that will shine in heaven as with the brightness of the firmament." Who are meant by those that "turn many to righteousness," who will shine as the stars, shall now be told.

By those who "turn many to righteousness" are meant those who are wise, and in heaven those are called wise who are in good, and those are in good that apply Divine truths at once to the life; for as soon as Divine truth comes to be of the life it becomes good, since it comes to be of will and love, and whatever is of will and love is called good; therefore such are called wise because wisdom is of the life. But those that do not commit Divine truths at once to the life, but first to the memory, from which they afterwards draw them and apply them to the life, are called the "intelligent." What and how great the difference is between the wise and the intelligent in the heavens can be seen in the chapter that treats of the two kingdoms of heaven, the celestial and the spiritual (n. 20-28), and in the chapter that treats of the three heavens (n. 29-40). Those who are in the Lord's celestial kingdom, and consequently in the third or inmost heaven, are called "the righteous" because they attribute all righteousness to the Lord and none to themselves. The Lord's righteousness in heaven is the good that is from the Lord. 348-1 Such, then, are here meant by those that "turn to righteousness;" and such are meant also in the Lord's words, The righteous shall shine forth as the sun in the kingdom of their Father (Matt. 13:43). Such "shine forth as the Sun" because they are in love to the Lord from the Lord, and that love is meant by the "sun" (see above, n. 116-125). The light of such is flame-colored; and the ideas of their thought are so tinged with what is flaming because they receive the good of love directly from the Lord as the sun in heaven.

All who have acquired intelligence and wisdom in the world are received in heaven and become angels, each in accordance with the quality and degree of his intelligence and wisdom. For whatever a man acquires in the world abides, and he takes it with him after death; and it is further increased and filled out, but within and not beyond the degree of his affection and desire for truth and its good, those with but little affection and desire receiving but little, and yet as much as they are capable of receiving within that degree; while those with much affection and desire receive much. The degree itself of affection and desire is like a measure that is filled to the full, he that has a large measure receiving more, and he that has a small measure receiving less. This is so because man's love, to which affection and desire belong, receives all that accords with itself; consequently reception is measured by the love. This is what is meant by the Lord's words, To him that hath it shall be given, that he may have more abundantly (Matt. 13:12; 25:29). Good measure, pressed down, shaken together, and running over, shall be given into your bosom (Luke 6:38).

All are received into heaven who have loved truth and good for the sake of truth and good; therefore those that have loved much are called the wise, and those that have loved little are called the simple. The wise in heaven are in much light, the simple in less light, everyone in accordance with the degree of his love for good and truth. To love truth and good for the sake of truth and good is to will and do them; for those love who will and do, while those who do not will and do do not love. Such also love the Lord and are loved by the Lord, because good and truth are from the Lord. And inasmuch as good and truth are from the Lord the Lord is in good and truth; and He is in those who receive good and truth in their life by willing and doing. Moreover, when man is viewed in himself he is nothing but his own good and truth, because good is of his will and truth of his understanding, and man is such as his will and understanding are. Evidently, then, man is loved by the Lord just to the extent that his will is formed from good and his understanding from truth. Also to be loved by the Lord is to love the Lord, since love is reciprocal; for upon him who is loved the

Lord bestows ability to love.

Footnotes

304-1 Nothing springs from itself, but from what is prior to itself, thus all things from a First, and they also have permanent existence from Him from whom they spring forth, and permanent existence is a perpetual springing forth (n. 2886, 2888, 3627, 3628, 3648, 4523, 4524, 6040, 6056). Divine order does not stop midway, but terminates in an outmost, and that outmost is man, thus Divine order terminates in man (n. 634, 2853, 3632, 5897, 6239, 6451, 6465, 9215, 9216, 9824, 9828, 9836, 9905, 10044, 10329, 10335, 10548). Interior things flow into external things, even into the extreme or outmost in successive order, and there they spring forth and have permanent existence (n. 634, 6239, 6465, 9215, 9216). Interior things spring forth and have permanent existence in what is outmost in simultaneous order (n. 5897, 6451, 8603, 10099). Therefore all interior things are held together in connection from a First by means of a Last (n. 9828). Therefore "the First and the Last" signify all things and each thing, that is, the whole (n. 10044, 10329, 10335). Consequently in outmosts there is strength and power (n. 9836).

305-1 The Word in the sense of the letter is natural (n. 8783). For the reason that the natural is the outmost in which spiritual and heavenly things, which are interior things, terminate and on which they rest, like a house upon its foundation (n. 9430, 9433, 9824, 10044, 10436). That the Word may be such it is composed wholly of correspondences (n. 1404, 1408, 1409, 1540, 1619, 1659, 1709, 1783, 8615, 10687). Because the Word is such in the sense of the letter it is the continant of the spiritual and heavenly sense (n. 9407). And it is adapted both to men and to angels (n. 1769-1772, 1887, 2143, 2157, 2275, 2333, 2395, 2540, 2541, 2547, 2553, 7381, 8862, 10322). And it is what makes heaven and earth one (n. 2310, 2495, 9212, 9216, 9357, 9396, 10375). The conjunction of the Lord with man is through the Word, by means of the internal sense (n. 10375). There is conjunction by means of all things and each particular thing of the Word, and in consequence the Word is wonderful above all other writing (n. 10632-10634). Since the Word was written the Lord speaks with men by means of it (n. 10290). The church, where the Word is and the Lord is known by means of it, in relation to those who are out of the church where there is no Word and the Lord is unknown is like the heart and lungs in man in comparison with the other parts of the body, which live from them as from the fountains of their life (n. 637, 931, 2054, 2853). Before the Lord the universal church on the earth is as a single man (n. 7396, 9276). Consequently unless there were on this earth a church where the Word is, and where the Lord is known by means of it, the human race here would perish (n. 468, 637, 931, 4545, 10452).

307-1 In the Word "Egypt" and "Egyptian" signify the natural and its knowledge (n. 4967, 5079, 5080, 5095, 5160, 5460, 5799, 6015, 6147, 6252, 7355, 7648, 9340, 9391). "Assyria" signifies the rational (n. 119, 1186). "Israel" signifies the spiritual (n. 5414, 5801, 5803, 5806, 5812, 5817, 5819, 5826, 5833, 5879, 5951, 6426, 6637, 6862, 6868, 7035, 7062, 7198, 7201, 7215, 7223, 7957, 8234, 8805, 9340).

308-1 The church specifically is where the Word is and where the Lord is known by means of it, thus where Divine truths from heaven are revealed (n.

3857, 10761). The Lord's church is with all in the whole globe who live in good in accordance with the principles of their religion (n. 3263, 6637, 10765). All wherever they are who live in good in accordance with the principles of their religion and who acknowledge the Divine are accepted of the Lord (n. 2589-2604, 2861, 2863, 3263, 4190, 4197, 6700, 9256). And besides these all children wheresoever they are born (n. 2289-2309, 4792).

311-1 The hells taken together, or the infernals taken together, are called the Devil and Satan (n. 694). Those that have been devils in the world become devils after death (n. 968).

311-2 The doctrine of the church must be derived from the Word (n. 3464, 5402, 6822, 6832, 10763, 10765). Without doctrine the Word is not understood (n. 9025, 9409, 9424, 9430, 10324, 10431, 10582). True doctrine is a lamp to those who read the Word (n. 10400). Genuine doctrine must be from those who are enlightened by the Lord (n. 2510, 2516, 2519, 9424, 10105). Those who are in the sense of the letter without doctrine come into no understanding of Divine truths (n. 9409, 9410, 10582). And they are led away into many errors (n. 10431). The difference between those who teach and learn from the doctrine of the church derived from the Word and those who teach and learn from the sense of the letter alone (n. 9025).

312-1 There are few in Christendom at this day who believe that man rises again immediately after death (preface to Genesis, chap. 16 and n. 4622, 10758); but it is believed that he will rise again at the time of the final judgment, when the visible world will perish (n. 10595). The reason of this belief (n. 10595, 10758). Nevertheless man does rise again immediately after death, and then he is a man in all respects, and in every least respect (n. 4527, 5006, 5078, 8939, 8991, 10594, 10758). The soul that lives after death is the spirit of man, which in man is the man himself, and in the other life is in a complete human form (n. 322, 1880, 1881, 3633, 4622, 4735, 5883, 6054, 6605, 6626, 7021, 10594); from experience (n. 4527, 5006, 8939); from the Word (n. 10597). What is meant by the dead seen in the holy city (Matt. 27:53) explained (n. 9229). In what manner man is raised from the dead, from experience (n. 168-189). His state after his resurrection (n. 317-319, 2119, 5079, 10596). False opinions about the soul and its resurrection (n. 444, 445, 4527, 4622, 4658).

313-1 In man the spiritual world and the natural world are conjoined (n. 6057). The internal of man is formed after the image of heaven, but the external after the image of the world (n. 3628, 4523, 4524, 6013, 6057, 9706, 10156, 10472).

314-1 There are as many degrees of life in man as there are heavens, and they are opened after death in accordance with his life (n. 3747, 9594). Heaven is in man (n. 3884). Men who are living a life of love and charity have in them angelic wisdom, although it is for the time hidden, but they come into that wisdom after death (n. 2494). The man who receives from the Lord the good of love and of faith is called in the Word an angel (n. 10528).

316-1 Man rises again only as to his spirit (n. 10593, 10594). The Lord alone rose again in respect also to His body (n. 1729, 2083, 5078, 10825).

318-1 The heathen equally with the Christians are saved (n. 932, 1032, 1059, 2284, 2589, 2590, 3778, 4190, 4197). The lot of the nations and peoples outside of the church in the other life (n. 2589-2604). The church is specifically where the Word is, and by it the Lord is known (n. 3857, 10761). Nevertheless, those born where the Word is and where the Lord is known are not on that account of the church, but only those who live a life of charity and of faith (n. 6637, 10143, 10153, 10578, 10645, 10829). The Lord's church is with all in the whole world who live in good in accordance with their religion and acknowledge a Divine, and such are accepted of the Lord and come into heaven (n. 2589-2604, 2861, 2863, 3263, 4190, 4197, 6700, 9256).

319-1 Between good and truth there is a kind of marriage (n. 1904, 2173, 2508). Good and truth are in a perpetual endeavor to be conjoined, and good longs for truth and for conjunction with it (n. 9206, 9207, 9495). How the conjunction of good and truth takes place, and in whom (n. 3834, 3843, 4096, 4097, 4301, 4345, 4353, 4364, 4368, 5365, 7623-7627, 9258).

321-1 Difference between the good in which the heathen are and that in which Christians are (n. 4189, 4197). Truths with the heathen (n. 3263, 3778, 4190). The interiors cannot be so closed up with the heathen as with Christians (n. 9256). Neither can so thick a cloud exist with the heathen who live in mutual charity in accordance with their religion as with Christians who live in no charity; the reasons (n. 1059, 9256). The heathen cannot profane the holy things of the church as the Christians do, because they are ignorant of them (n. 1327, 1328, 2051). They have a fear of Christians on account of their lives (n. 2596, 2597). Those that have lived well in accordance with their religion are taught by angels and readily accept the truths of faith and acknowledge the Lord (n. 2049, 2595, 2598, 2600, 2601, 2603, 2861, 2863, 3263).

327-1 The first and Most Ancient Church on this earth was that which is described in the first chapters of Genesis, and that church above all others was celestial (n. 607, 895, 920, 1121-1124, 2896, 4493, 8891, 9942, 10545). What the celestial are in heaven (n. 1114-1125). There were various churches after the flood which are called ancient churches (n. 1125-1127, 1327, 10355). What the men of the Ancient Church were (n. 609, 895). The ancient churches were representative churches (n. 519, 521, 2896). In the Ancient Church there was a Word, but it has been lost (n. 2897). The character of the Ancient Church when it began to decline (n. 1128). The difference between the Most Ancient Church and the Ancient Church (n.597, 607, 640, 641, 765, 784, 895, 4493). The statutes, the judgments, and the laws, which were commanded in the Jewish Church, were in part like those in the Ancient Church (n. 4288, 4449, 10149). The God of the Most Ancient Church and of the Ancient Church was the Lord, and He was called Jehovah (n. 1343, 6846).

329-1 Baptism signifies regeneration by the Lord by means of the truths of faith from the Word (n. 4255, 5120, 9088, 10239, 10386-10388, 10392). Baptism is a sign that the man baptized is of the church in which the Lord, who regenerates, is acknowledged, and where the Word is from which are the truths of faith, by means of which regeneration is effected (n. 10386-10388). Baptism confers neither faith nor salvation, but it is a witness that those who are being regenerated will receive faith and salvation (n. 10391).

340-1 Spiritual food is knowledge, intelligence, and wisdom, thus the good and truth from which these are (n. 3114, 4459, 4792, 5147, 5293, 5340, 5342, 5410, 5426, 5576, 5582, 5588, 5655, 8562, 9003). Therefore in a spiritual sense everything that comes forth from the mouth of the Lord is food (n. 681). Because bread means all food in general it signifies every good, celestial and spiritual (n. 276, 680, 2165, 2177, 3478, 6118, 8410). And for the reason that these nourish the mind, which belongs to the internal man (n. 4459, 5293, 5576, 6277, 8410).

342-1 All kinds of men are born into evils of every kind, even to the extent that what is their own is nothing but evil (n. 210, 215, 731, 874-876, 987, 1047, 2307, 2308, 3518, 3701, 3812, 8480, 8550, 10283, 10284, 10286, 10731). Consequently man must needs be reborn, that is, regenerated (n. 3701). Man's inherited evil consists in his loving himself more than God, and the world more than heaven and in making his neighbor, in comparison with himself, of no account, except for the sake of self, that is, himself alone, thus it consists in the love of self and of the world (n. 694, 731, 4317, 5660). All evils are from the love of self and of the world, when those loves rule (n. 1307, 1308, 1321, 1594, 1691, 3413, 7255, 7376, 7488, 7490, 8318, 9335, 9348, 10038, 10742). These evils are contempt of others, enmity, hatred revenge, cruelty, deceit (n. 6667, 7370-7374, 9348, 10038, 10742). And from these evils comes all falsity (n. 1047, 10283, 10284, 10286). These loves, so far as the reins are given them, rush headlong; and the love of self aspires even to the throne of God (n. 7375, 8678).

347-1 The light of the world is for the external man, the light of heaven for the internal man (n. 3222-3224, 3337). The light of heaven flows into the natural light, and so far as the natural man receives the light of heaven he becomes wise (n. 4302, 4408). The things that are in the light of heaven can be seen in the light of heaven but not in the light of the world, which is called natural light (n. 9755). Therefore those who are solely in the light of the world do not perceive those things that are in the light of heaven (n. 3108). To the angels the light of the world is thick darkness (n. 1521, 1783, 1880).

348-1 The merit and righteousness of the Lord is the good that rules in heaven (n. 9486, 9983). He that is "righteous" or "made righteous" is one to whom the merit and righteousness of the Lord is ascribed; and he is "unrighteous" who holds to his own righteousness and merit (n. 5069, 9263). The quality of those in the other life who claim righteousness to themselves (n. 942, 2027). In the Word "righteousness" is predicated of good and judgment of truth; therefore "doing righteousness and judgment" is doing good and truth (n. 2235, 9857).

Section 8

It is believed in the world that those who have much knowledge, whether it be knowledge of the teachings of the church and the Word or of the sciences, have a more interior and keen vision of truth than others, that is, are more intelligent and wise; and such have this opinion of themselves. But what true intelligence and wisdom are, and what spurious and false intelligence and wisdom are, shall be told in what now follows. [2] True intelligence and wisdom is seeing and perceiving what is true and good, and thereby what is false and evil, and clearly distinguishing between them, and this from an interior intuition and perception. With every man there are interior faculties and exterior faculties; interior faculties belonging to the internal or spiritual man, and exterior faculties belonging to the exterior or natural man. Accordingly as man's interiors are formed and made one with his exteriors man sees and perceives. His interiors can be formed only in heaven, his exteriors are formed in the world. When his interiors have been formed in heaven the things they contain flow into his exteriors which are from the world, and so form them that they correspond with, that is, act as one with, his interiors; and when this is done man sees and perceives from what is interior. The interiors can be formed only in one way, namely, by man's looking to the Divine and to heaven, since, as has been said, the interiors are formed in heaven; and man looks to the Divine when he believes in the Divine, and believes that all truth and good and consequently all intelligence and wisdom are from the Divine; and man believes in the Divine when he is willing to be led by the Divine. In this way and none other are the interiors of man opened. [3] The man who is in that belief and in a life that is in accordance with his belief has the ability and capacity to understand and be wise; but to become intelligent and wise he must learn many things, both things pertaining to heaven and things pertaining to the world - things pertaining to heaven from the Word and from the church, and things pertaining to the world from the sciences. To the extent that man learns and applies to life he becomes intelligent and wise, for to that extent the interior sight belonging to his understanding and the interior affection belonging to his will are perfected. The simple of this class are those whose interiors have been opened, but not so enriched by spiritual, moral, civil and natural truths. Such perceive truths when they hear them, but do not see them in themselves. But the wise of this class are those whose interiors have been both opened and enriched. Such both see truths inwardly and perceive them. All this makes clear what true intelligence is and what true wisdom is.

Spurious intelligence and wisdom is failing to see and perceive from within what is true and what is good, and thereby what is false and what is evil, but merely believing that to be true and good and that to be false and evil which is said by others to be so, and then confirming it. Because such see truth from some one else, and not from the truth itself, they can seize upon and believe what is false as readily as what is true, and can confirm it until it appears true;

for whatever is confirmed puts on the appearance of truth; and there is nothing that can not be confirmed. The interiors of such are opened only from beneath; but their exteriors are opened to the extent that they have confirmed themselves. For this reason the light from which they see is not the light of heaven but the light of the world, which is called natural light [lumen]; and in that light falsities can shine like truths; and when confirmed they can even appear resplendent, but not in the light of heaven. Of this class those are less intelligent and wise who have strongly confirmed themselves, and those are more intelligent and wise who have less strongly confirmed themselves. All this shows what spurious intelligence and wisdom are. [2] But those are not included in this class who in childhood supposed what they heard from their masters to be true, if in a riper age, when they think from their own understanding, they do not continue to hold fast to it, but long for truth, and from that longing seek for it, and when they find it are interiorly moved by it. Because such are moved by the truth for the truth's sake they see the truth before they confirm it. 352-1 [3] This may be illustrated by an example. There was a discussion among spirits why animals are born into all the knowledge suited to their nature, but man is not; and the reason was said to be that animals are in the order of their life, and man is not, consequently man must needs be led into order by means of what he learns of internal and external things. But if man were born into the order of his life, which is to love God above all things and his neighbor as himself, he would be born into intelligence and wisdom, and as knowledges are acquired would come into a belief in all truth. Good spirits saw this at once and perceived it to be true, and this merely from the light of truth; while the spirits who had confirmed themselves in faith alone, and had thereby set aside love and charity, were unable to understand it, because the light of falsity which they had confirmed had made obscure to them the light of truth.

False intelligence and wisdom is all intelligence and wisdom that is separated from the acknowledgment of the Divine; for all such as do not acknowledge the Divine, but acknowledge nature in the place of the Divine, think from the bodily-sensual, and are merely sensual, however highly they may be esteemed in the world for their accomplishments and learning. 353-1 For their learning does not ascend beyond such things as appear before their eyes in the world; these they hold in the memory and look at them in an almost material way, although the same knowledges serve the truly intelligent in forming their understanding. By sciences the various kinds of experimental knowledge are meant, such as physics, astronomy, chemistry, mechanics, geometry, anatomy, psychology, philosophy, the history of kingdoms and of the literary world, criticism, and languages. [2] The clergy who deny the Divine do not raise their thoughts above the sensual things of the external man; and regard the things of the Word in the same way as others regard the sciences, not making them matters of thought or of any intuition by an enlightened rational mind; and for the reason that their interiors are closed up, together with those exteriors that are nearest to their interiors. These are closed up because they have turned themselves away from heaven, and have retroverted those faculties that were capable of looking heavenward, which are, as has been said above, the interiors of the human mind. For this reason they are incapable of seeing anything true or good, this being to them in thick darkness, while whatever is false and evil is in light. [3] And yet sensual men can reason, some of them more cunningly and keenly than any one else; but they reason from the fallacies of the senses confirmed by their knowledges; and because they are able to reason in this way they believe themselves to be wiser than others. 353-2 The fire that kindles with affection their reasonings is the fire of the love of self and the world. Such are those who are in false intelligence and wisdom, and who are meant by the Lord in Matthew: Seeing they see not, and hearing they hear not, neither do they understand (13:13-15). And again: These things are hid from the intelligent and wise, and revealed unto babes (11:25, 26).

It has been granted me to speak with many of the learned after their departure from the world; with some of distinguished reputation and celebrated in the literary world for their writings, and with some not so celebrated, although endowed with profound wisdom. Those that in heart had denied the Divine, whatever their professions may have been, had become so stupid as to have little comprehension even of anything truly civil, still less of anything spiritual. I perceived and also saw that the interiors of their minds were so closed up as to appear black (for in the spiritual world such things become visible), and in consequence they were unable to endure any heavenly light or admit any influx from heaven. This blackness which their interiors presented was more intense and extended with those that had confirmed themselves against the Divine by the knowledges they had acquired. In the other life such accept all falsity with delight, imbibing it as a sponge does water; and they repel all truth as an elastic bony substance repels what falls upon it. In fact, it is said that the interiors of those that have confirmed themselves against the Divine and in favor of nature become bony, and their heads down to the nose appear callous like ebony, which is a sign that they no longer have any perception. Those of this description are immersed in quagmires that appear like bogs; and there they are harassed by the fantasies into which their falsities are turned. Their infernal fire is a lust for glory and reputation, which prompts them to assail one another, and from an infernal ardor to torment those about them who do not worship them as deities; and this they do one to another in turns. Into such things is all the learning of the world changed that has not received into itself light from heaven through acknowledgment of the Divine.

That these are such in the spiritual world when they come into it after death may be inferred from this alone, that all things that are in the natural memory and are in immediate conjunction with the things of bodily sense (which is true of such knowledges as are mentioned above) then become quiescent; and only such rational principles as are drawn from these then serve for thought and speech. For man carries with him his entire natural memory, but its contents are not then under his view, and do not come into his thought as when he lived in the world. He can take nothing from that memory and bring it forth into spiritual light because its contents are not objects of that light. But those things of the reason and understanding that man has acquired from knowledges while living in the body are in accord with the light of the spiritual world; consequently so far as the spirit of man has been made rational in the world through knowledge and science it is to the same extent rational after being loosed from the body; for man is then a spirit, and it is the spirit that thinks in the body. 355-1

But in respect to those that have acquired intelligence and wisdom through knowledge and science, who are such as have applied all things to the use of life, and have also acknowledged the Divine, loved the Word, and lived a spiritual moral life (of which above, n. 319), to such the sciences have served as a means of becoming wise, and also of corroborating the things pertaining to faith. The interiors of the mind of such have been perceived by me, and were seen as transparent from light of a glistening white, flamy, or blue color, like that of translucent diamonds, rubies, and sapphires; and this in accordance with confirmations in favor of the Divine and Divine truths drawn from science. Such is the appearance of true intelligence and wisdom when they are presented to view in the spiritual world. This appearance is derived from the light of heaven; and that light is Divine truth going forth from the Lord, which is the source of all intelligence and wisdom (see above, n. 126-133). [2] The planes of that light, in which variegations like those of colors exist, are the interiors of the mind; and these variegations are produced by confirmations of Divine truths by means of such things as are in nature, that is, in the sciences. 356-1 For the interior mind of man looks into the things of the natural memory, and the things there that will serve as proofs it sublimates as it were by the fire of heavenly love, and withdraws and purifies them even into spiritual ideas. This is unknown to man as long as he lives in the body, because there he thinks both spiritually and naturally, and he has no perception of the things he then thinks spiritually, but only of those he thinks naturally. But when he has come into the spiritual world he has no perception of what he thought naturally in the world, but only of what he thought spiritually. Thus is his state changed. [3] All this makes clear that it is by means of knowledges and sciences that man is made spiritual, also that these are the means of becoming wise, but only with those who have acknowledged the Divine in faith and life. Such also before others are accepted in heaven, and are among those there who are at the center (n. 43), because they are in light more than others. These are the intelligent and wise in heaven, who "shine as with the brightness of the firmament" and "who shine as the stars," while the simple there are those that have acknowledged the Divine, have loved the Word, and have lived a spiritual and moral life, but the interiors of their minds have not been so enriched by knowledges and sciences. The human mind is like soil which is such as it is made by cultivation.

XXXIX. THE RICH AND THE POOR IN HEAVEN. There are various opinions about reception into heaven. Some are of the opinion that the poor are received and the rich are not; some that the rich and the poor are equally received; some that the rich can be received only by giving up their wealth and becoming like the poor; and proofs are found in the Word for all of these opinions. But those who make a distinction in regard to heaven between the rich and the poor do not understand the Word. In its interiors the Word is spiritual, but in the letter it is natural; consequently those who understand the Word only in accordance with its literal sense, and not according to any spiritual sense, err in many respects, especially about the rich and the poor; for example, that it is as difficult for the rich to enter into heaven as for a camel to pass through the eye of a needle; and that it is easy for the poor because they are poor, since it is said, Blessed are the poor, for theirs is the kingdom of the heavens (Matt. 5:3; Luke 6:20, 21). But those who know anything of the spiritual sense of the Word think otherwise; they know that heaven is for all who live a life of faith and love, whether rich or poor. But who are meant in the Word by "the rich" and who by "the poor" will be told in what follows. From much conversation and interaction with angels it has been granted me to know with certainty that the rich enter heaven just as easily as the poor, and that no man is shut out of heaven on account of his wealth, or received into heaven on account of his poverty. Both the rich and the poor are in heaven, and many of the rich in greater glory and happiness than the poor.

It should be said to begin with that a man may acquire riches and accumulate wealth as far as opportunity is given, if it is not done by craft or fraud; that he may enjoy the delicacies of food and drink if he does not place his life therein; that he may have a palatial dwelling in accord with his condition, have interaction with others in like condition, frequent places of amusement, talk about the affairs of the world, and need not go about like a devotee with a sad and sorrowful countenance and drooping head, but may be joyful and cheerful; nor need he give his goods to the poor except so far as affection leads him; in a word, he may live outwardly precisely like a man of the world; and all this will be no obstacle to his entering heaven, provided that inwardly in himself he thinks about God as he ought, and acts sincerely and justly in respect to his neighbor. For a man is such as his affection and thought are, or such as his love and faith are, and from these all his outward acts derive their life; since acting is willing, and speaking is thinking, acting being from the will, and speaking from the thought. So where it is said in the Word that man will be judged according to his deeds, and will be rewarded according to his works, it is meant that he will be judged and rewarded in accordance with his thought and affection, which are the source of his deeds, or which are in his deeds; for deeds are nothing apart from these, and are precisely such as these are. 358-1 All this shows that the man's external accomplishes nothing, but only his internal, which is the source of the external. For example: if a man acts honestly and refrains from fraud solely because he fears the laws and the loss of reputation and thereby of honor or gain, and if that fear did not restrain him would defraud others whenever he could; although such a man's deeds outwardly appear honest, his thought and will are fraud; and because he is inwardly dishonest and fraudulent he has hell in himself. But he who acts honestly and refrains from fraud because it is against God and against the neighbor would have no wish to defraud another if he could; his thought and will are conscience, and he has heaven in himself. The deeds of these two appear alike in outward form, but inwardly they are wholly unlike.

Since a man can live outwardly as others do, can grow rich, keep a plentiful table, dwell in an elegant house and wear fine clothing according to his condition and function, can enjoy delights and gratifications, and engage in worldly affairs for the sake of his occupation and business and for the life both of the mind and body, provided he inwardly acknowledges the Divine and wishes well to the neighbor, it is evident that to enter upon the way to heaven is not so difficult as many believe. The sole difficulty lies in being able to resist the love of self and the world, and to prevent their becoming dominant; for this is the source of all evils. 359-1 That this is not so difficult as is believed is meant by these words of the Lord: Learn of Me, for I am meek and lowly of heart, and ye shall find rest to your souls; for My yoke is easy and My burden is light (Matt. 11:29, 30). The Lord's yoke is easy and His burden light because a man is led by the Lord and not by self just to the extent that he resists the evils that flow forth from love of self and of the world; and because the Lord then resists these evils in man and removes them.

I have spoken with some after death who, while they lived in the world, renounced the world and gave themselves up to an almost solitary life, in order that by an abstraction of the thoughts from worldly things they might have opportunity for pious meditations, believing that thus they might enter the way to heaven. But these in the other life are of a sad disposition; they despise others who are not like themselves; they are indignant that they do not have a happier lot than others, believing that they have merited it; they have no interest in others, and turn away from the duties of charity by which there is conjunction with heaven. They desire heaven more than others; but when they are taken up among the angels they induce anxieties that disturb the happiness of the angels; and in consequence they are sent away; and when sent away they betake themselves to desert places, where they lead a life like that which they lived in the world. [2] Man can be formed for heaven only by means of the world. In the world are the outmost effects in which everyone's affection must be terminated; for unless affection puts itself forth or flows out into acts, which is done in association with others, it is suffocated to such a degree finally that man has no longer any regard for the neighbor, but only for himself. All this makes clear that a life of charity towards the neighbor, which is doing what is just and right in every work and in every employment, is what leads to heaven, and not a life of piety apart from charity; 360-1 and from this it follows that only to the extent that man is engaged in the employments of life can charity be exercised and the life of charity grow; and this is impossible to the extent that man separates himself from those employments. [3] On this subject I will speak now from experience. Of those who while in the world were employed in trade and commerce and became rich through these pursuits there are many in heaven, but not so many of those who were in stations of honor and became rich through those employments; and for the reason that these latter by the gains and honors that resulted from their dispensing justice and equity, and also by the lucrative and honorable positions bestowed on them were led into loving themselves and the world, and thereby separating their thoughts and affections from heaven and turning them to themselves. For to the extent that a man loves self and the world and looks to self and the world in everything, he alienates himself from the Divine and separates himself from heaven.

As to the lot of the rich in heaven, they live more splendidly than others. Some of them dwell in palaces within which everything is resplendent as if with gold and silver. They have an abundance of all things for the uses of life, but they do not in the least set their heart on these things, but only on uses. Uses are clearly seen as if they were in light, but the gold and silver are seen obscurely, and comparatively as if in shade. This is because while they were in the world they loved uses, and loved gold and silver only as means and instruments. It is the uses that are thus resplendent in heaven, the good of use like gold and the truth of use like silver. 361-1 Therefore their wealth in heaven is such as their uses were in the world, and such, too, are their delight and happiness. Good uses are providing oneself and one's own with the necessaries of life; also desiring wealth for the sake of one's country and for the sake of one's neighbor, whom a rich man can in many ways benefit more than a poor man. These are good uses because one is able thereby to withdraw his mind from an indolent life which is harmful, since in such a life man's thoughts run to evil because of the evil inherent in him. These uses are good to the extent that they have the Divine in them, that is, to the extent that man looks to the Divine and to heaven, and finds his good in these, and sees in wealth only a subservient good.

But the lot of the rich that have not believed in the Divine, and have cast out of their minds the things pertaining to heaven and the church, is the opposite of this. Such are in hell, where filth, misery, and want exist; and into these riches that are loved as an end are changed; and not only riches, but also their very uses, which are either a wish to live as they like and indulge in pleasures, and to have opportunity to give the mind more fully and freely to shameful practices, or a wish to rise above others whom they despise. Such riches and such uses, because they have nothing spiritual, but only what is earthly in them, become filthy; for a spiritual purpose in riches and their uses is like a soul in the body, or like the light of heaven in moist ground; and such riches and uses become putrid as a body does without a soul, or as moist ground does without the light of heaven. Such are those that have been led and drawn away from heaven by riches.

Every man's ruling affection or love remains with him after death, nor is it rooted out to eternity, since a man's spirit is wholly what his love is, and what is unknown, the body of every spirit and angel is the outward form of his love, exactly corresponding to his inward form, which is the form of his disposition and mind; consequently the quality of his spirit is known from his face, movements, and speech. While a man is living in the world the quality of the spirit would be known if he had not learned to counterfeit in his face, movements, and speech what is not his own. All this shows that man remains to eternity such as his ruling affection or love is. It has been granted me to talk with some who lived seventeen hundred years ago, and whose lives are well known from writings of that time, and it was found that the same love still rules them as when they were on the earth. This makes clear also that the love of riches, and of uses from riches, remains with everyone to eternity, and that it is exactly the same as the love acquired in the world, yet with the difference that in the case of those who devoted their riches to good uses riches are changed in the other world into delights which are in accord with the uses performed; while in the case of those who devoted their riches to evil uses riches are turned into mere filth, in which they then take the same delight as they did in the world in their riches devoted to evil uses. Such then take delight in filth because filthy pleasures and shameful acts, which had been the uses to which they had devoted their riches, and also avarice, which is a love of riches without regard to use, correspond to filth. Spiritual filth is nothing else.

The poor come into heaven not on account of their poverty but because of their life. Everyone's life follows him, whether he be rich or poor. There is no peculiar mercy for one in preference to another; 364-1 he that has lived well is received, while he that has not lived well is rejected. Moreover, poverty leads and draws man away from heaven just as much as wealth does. There are many among the poor who are not content with their lot, who strive after many things, and believe riches to be blessings; 364-2 and when they do not gain them are much provoked, and harbor ill thoughts about the Divine providence; they also envy others the good things they possess, and are as ready as any one to defraud others whenever they have opportunity, and to indulge in filthy pleasures. But this is not true of the poor who are content with their lot, and are careful and diligent in their work, who love labor better than idleness, and act sincerely and faithfully, and at the same time live a Christian life. I have now and then talked with those belonging to the peasantry and common people, who while living in the world believed in God and did what was just and right in their occupations. Since they had an affection for knowing truth they inquired about charity and about faith, having heard in this world much about faith and in the other life much about charity. They were therefore told that charity is everything that pertains to life, and faith everything that pertains to doctrine; consequently charity is willing and doing what is just and right in every work, and faith is thinking justly and rightly; and faith and charity are conjoined, the same as doctrine and a life in accordance with it, or the same as thought and will; and faith becomes charity when that which a man thinks justly and rightly he also wills and does, and then they are not two but one. This they well understood, and rejoiced, saying that in the world they did not understand believing to be anything else but living.

All this makes clear that the rich and the poor alike come into heaven, the one as easily as the other. The belief that the poor enter heaven easily and the rich with difficulty comes from not understanding the Word where the rich and the poor are mentioned. In the Word those that have an abundance of knowledges of good and truth, thus who are within the church where the Word is, are meant in the spiritual sense by the "rich;" while those who lack these knowledges, and yet desire them, thus who are outside of the church and where there is no Word, are meant by the "poor." [2] The rich man clothed in purple and fine linen, and cast into hell, means the Jewish nation, which is called rich because it had the Word and had an abundance of knowledges of good and truth therefrom, "garments of purple" signifying knowledges of good, and "garments of fine linen" knowledges of truth. 365-1 But the poor man who lay at the rich man's gate and longed to be fed with the crumbs that fell from the rich man's table, and who was carried by angels into heaven, means the nations that have no knowledges of good and truth and yet desired them (Luke 16:19-31). Also the rich that were called to a great supper and excused themselves mean the Jewish nation, and the poor brought in in their place mean the nations outside of the church (Luke 14:16-24). [3] By the rich man of whom the Lord says: It is easier for a camel to go through a needle's eye than for a rich man to enter into the kingdom of God (Matt. 19:24), the rich in both the natural sense and the spiritual sense are meant. In the natural sense the rich are those that have an abundance of riches and set their heart upon them; but in the spiritual sense they are those that have an abundance of knowledges and learning, which are spiritual riches, and who desire by means of these to introduce themselves into the things of heaven and the church from their own intelligence. And because this is contrary to Divine order it is said to be "easier for a camel to go through a needle's eye," a "camel" signifying in general in the spiritual sense the knowing faculty and things known, and a "needle's eye" signifying spiritual truth. 365-2 That such is the meaning of a "camel" and a "needle's eye" is not at present known, because the knowledge that teaches what is signified in the spiritual sense by the things said in the literal sense of the Word has not up to this time been disclosed. In every particular of the Word there is a spiritual sense and also a natural sense; for the Word was made to consist wholly of correspondences between natural and spiritual things in order that conjunction of heaven with the world, or of angels with men might thereby be effected, direct conjunction having ceased. This makes clear who in particular are meant in the Word by the "rich man." [4] That the "rich" in the Word mean in the spiritual sense those who are in knowledges of truth and good, and "riches" the knowledges themselves, which are spiritual riches, can be seen from various passages (as in Isa. 10:12-14; 30:6, 7; 45:3; Jer. 17:3; 48:7; 50:36, 37; 51:13; Dan. 5:2-4; Ezek. 26:7, 12; 27:1 to the end; Zech. 9:3, 4; Psalm 45:12; Hosea 12:9; Apoc. 3:17, 18; Luke 14:33; and elsewhere). Also that the "poor" in the spiritual sense signify those who do not possess knowledges of good and of truth, and yet desire them (Matt. 11:5; Luke 6:20, 21; 14:21; Isa. 14:30; 29:19; 41:17, 18; Zeph. 3:12, 13). All these passages may be seen explained in accordance with the spiritual sense in the Arcana Coelestia (n. 10227).

MARRIAGES IN HEAVEN. As heaven is from the human race, and angels therefore are of both sexes, and from creation woman is for man and man is for woman, thus the one belongs to the other, and this love is innate in both, it follows that there are marriages in heaven as well as on the earth. But marriages in heaven differ widely from marriages on the earth. Therefore what marriages in heaven are, and how they differ from marriages on the earth and wherein they are like them, shall now be told.

Marriage in heaven is a conjunction of two into one mind. It must first be explained what this conjunction is. The mind consists of two parts, one called the understanding and the other the will. When these two parts act as one they are called one mind. In heaven the husband acts the part called the understanding and the wife acts the part called the will. When this conjunction, which belongs to man's interiors, descends into the lower parts pertaining to the body, it is perceived and felt as love, and this love is marriage love. This shows that marriage love has its origin in the conjunction of two into one mind. This in heaven is called cohabitation; and the two are not called two but one. So in heaven a married pair is spoken of, not as two, but as one angel. 367-1

Moreover, such a conjunction of husband and wife in the inmosts of their minds comes from their very creation; for man is born to be intellectual, that is, to think from the understanding, while woman is born to be affectional, that is, to think from her will; and this is evident from the inclination or natural disposition of each, also from their form; from the disposition, in that man acts from reason and woman from affection; from the form in that man has a rougher and less beautiful face, a deeper voice and a harder body; while woman has a smoother and more beautiful face, a softer voice, and a more tender body. There is a like difference between understanding and will, or between thought and affection; so, too, between truth and good and between faith and love; for truth and faith belong to the understanding, and good and love to the will. From this it is that in the Word "youth" or "man" means in the spiritual sense the understanding of truth, and "virgin" or "woman" affection for good; also that the church, on account of its affection for good and truth, is called a "woman" and a "virgin;" also that all those that are in affection for good are called "virgins" (as in Apoc. 14:4). 368-1

Everyone, whether man or woman, possesses understanding and will; but with the man the understanding predominates, and with the woman the will predominates, and the character is determined by that which predominates. Yet in heavenly marriages there is no predominance; for the will of the wife is also the husband's will, and the understanding of the husband is also the wife's understanding, since each loves to will and to think like the other, that is mutually and reciprocally. Thus are they conjoined into one. This conjunction is actual conjunction, for the will of the wife enters into the understanding of the husband, and the understanding of the husband into the will of the wife, and this especially when they look into one another's faces; for, as has been repeatedly said above, there is in the heavens a sharing of thoughts and affections, more especially with husband and wife, because they reciprocally love each other. This makes clear what the conjunction of minds is that makes marriage and produces marriage love in the heavens, namely, that one wishes what is his own to be the others, and this reciprocally.

I have been told by angels that so far as a married pair are so conjoined they are in marriage love, and also to the same extent in intelligence, wisdom and happiness, because Divine truth and Divine good which are the source of all intelligence, wisdom, and happiness, flow chiefly into marriage love; consequently marriage love, since it is also the marriage of good and truth, is the very plane of Divine influx. For that love, as it is a conjunction of the understanding and will, is also a conjunction of truth and good, since the understanding receives Divine truth and is formed out of truths, and the will receives Divine good and is formed out of goods. For what a man wills is good to him, and what he understands is truth to him; therefore it is the same whether you say conjunction of understanding and will or conjunction of truth and good. Conjunction of truth and good is what makes an angel; it makes his intelligence, wisdom, and happiness; for an angel is an angel accordingly as good in him is conjoined with truth and truth with good; or what is the same, accordingly as love in him is conjoined with faith and faith with love.

The Divine that goes forth from the Lord flows chiefly into marriage love because marriage love descends from a conjunction of good and truth; for it is the same thing as has been said above, whether you say conjunction of understanding and will or conjunction of good and truth. Conjunction of good and truth has its origin in the Lord's Divine love towards all who are in heaven and on earth. From Divine love Divine good goes forth, and Divine good is received by angels and men in Divine truths. As truth is the sole receptacle of good nothing can be received from the Lord and from heaven by any one who is not in truths; therefore just to the extent that the truths in man are conjoined to good is man conjoined to the Lord and to heaven. This, then, is the very origin of marriage love, and for this reason that love is the very plane of Divine influx. This shows why the conjunction of good and truth in heaven is called the heavenly marriage, and heaven is likened in the Word to a marriage, and is called a marriage; and the Lord is called the "Bridegroom" and "Husband," and heaven and also the church are called the "bride" and the "wife." 371-1

Good and truth conjoined in an angel or a man are not two but one, since good is then good of truth and truth is truth of good. This conjunction may be likened to a man's thinking what he wills and willing what he thinks, when the thought and will make one, that is, one mind; for thought forms, that is, presents in form that which the will wills, and the will gives delight to it; and this is why a married pair in heaven are not called two, but one angel. This also is what is meant by the Lord's words: Have ye not read that He who made them from the beginning made them male and female, and said, For this cause shall a man leave father and mother and shall cleave to his wife, and they twain shall become one flesh? Therefore, they are no more twain, but one flesh. What, therefore, God hath joined together let not man put asunder. Not all can receive this word but they to whom it is given (Matt. 19:4-6, 11; Mark 10:6-9; Gen. 2:24). This is a description both of the heavenly marriage in which the angels are and of the marriage of good and truth, "man's not putting asunder what God has joined together" meaning that good is not to be separated from truth.

From all this the origin of true marriage love is made clear, namely, that it is formed first in the minds of those who are in marriage, and descends therefrom and is derived into the body, where it is perceived and felt as love; for whatever is felt and perceived in the body has its origin in the spiritual, because it is from the understanding and the will. The understanding and the will constitute the spiritual man. Whatever descends from the spiritual man into the body presents itself there under another aspect, although it is similar and accordant, like soul and body, and like cause and effect; as can be seen from what has been said and shown in the two chapters on Correspondences.

I heard an angel describing true marriage love and its heavenly delights in this manner: That it is the Lord's Divine in the heavens, which is Divine good and Divine truth so united in two persons, that they are not as two but as one. He said that in heaven the two consorts are marriage love, since everyone is his own good and his own truth in respect both to mind and to body, the body being an image of the mind because it is formed after its likeness. From this he drew the conclusion that the Divine is imaged in the two that are in true marriage love; and as the Divine is so imaged so is heaven, because the entire heaven is Divine good and Divine truth going forth from the Lord; and this is why all things of heaven are inscribed on marriage love with more blessings and delights than it is possible to number. He expressed the number by a term that involved myriads of myriads. He wondered that the man of the church should know nothing about this, seeing that the church is the Lord's heaven on the earth, and heaven is a marriage of good and truth. He said he was astounded to think that within the church, even more than outside of it, adulteries are committed and even justified; the delight of which in itself is nothing else in a spiritual sense, and consequently in the spiritual world, than the delight of the love of falsity conjoined to evil, which delight is infernal delight, because it is the direct opposite of the delight of heaven, which is the delight of the love of truth conjoined with good.

Everyone knows that a married pair who love each other are interiorly united, and that the essential of marriage is the union of dispositions and minds. And from this it can be seen that such as their essential dispositions or minds are, such is their union and such their love for each other. The mind is formed solely out of truths and goods, for all things in the universe have relation to good and truth and to their conjunction; consequently such as the truths and goods are out of which the minds are formed, exactly such is the union of minds; and consequently the most perfect union is the union of minds that are formed out of genuine truths and goods. Let it be known that no two things mutually love each other more than truth and good do; and therefore it is from that love that true marriage love descends. 375-1 Falsity and evil also love each other, but this love is afterwards changed into hell.

From what has now been said about the origin of marriage love one may conclude who are in that love and who are not; namely, that those are in marriage love who are in Divine good from Divine truths; and that marriage love is genuine just to the extent that the truths are genuine with which the good is conjoined. And as all the good that is conjoined with truths is from the Lord, it follows that no one can be in true marriage love unless he acknowledges the Lord and His Divine; for without that acknowledgment the Lord cannot flow in and be conjoined with the truths that are in man.

Evidently, then, those that are in falsities, and especially those that are in falsities from evil, are not in marriage love. Moreover, those that are in evil and in falsities therefrom have the interiors of their minds closed up; and in such, therefore, there can be no source of marriage love; but below those interiors, in the external or natural man separated from the internal, there can be a conjunction of falsity and evil, which is called infernal marriage. I have been permitted to see what this marriage is between those that are in the falsities of evil, which is called infernal marriage. Such converse together, and are united by a lustful desire, but inwardly they burn with a deadly hatred towards each other, too intense to be described.

Nor can marriage love exist between two partners belonging to different religions, because the truth of the one does not agree with the good of the other; and two unlike and discordant kinds of good and truth cannot make one mind out of two; and in consequence the love of such does not have its origin in any thing spiritual. If they live together in harmony it is solely on natural grounds. 378-1 And this is why in the heavens marriages are found only with those who are in the same society, because such are in like good and truth and not with those outside of the society. It may be seen above (n. 41, seq.) that all there in a society are in like good and truth, and differ from those outside the society. This was represented in the Israelitish nation by marriages being contracted within tribes, and particularly within families, and not outside of them.

Nor is true marriage love possible between one husband and several wives; for its spiritual origin, which is the formation of one mind out of two, is thus destroyed; and in consequence interior conjunction, which is the conjunction of good and truth, from which is the very essence of that love, is also destroyed. Marriage with more than one is like an understanding divided among several wills; or it is like a man attached not to one but to several churches, since his faith is so distracted thereby as to come to naught. The angels declare that marrying several wives is wholly contrary to Divine order, and that they know this from several reasons, one of which is that as soon as they think of marriage with more than one they are alienated from internal blessedness and heavenly happiness, and become like drunken men, because good is separated from its truth in them. And as the interiors of their mind are brought into such a state merely by thinking about it with some intention, they see clearly that marriage with more than one would close up their internal mind, and cause marriage to be displaced by lustful love, which love withdraws from heaven. 379-1 [2] They declare further that this is not easily comprehended by men because there are few who are in genuine marriage love, and those who are not in it know nothing whatever of the interior delight that is in that love, knowing only the delight of lust, and this delight is changed into what is undelightful after living together a short time; while the delight of true marriage love not only endures to old age in the world, but after death becomes the delight of heaven and is there filled with an interior delight that grows more and more perfect to eternity. They said also that the varieties of blessedness of true marriage love could be enumerated even to many thousands, not even one of which is known to man, or could enter into the comprehension of any one who is not in the marriage of good and truth from the Lord.

The love of dominion of one over the other entirely takes away marriage love and its heavenly delight, for as has been said above, marriage love and its delight consists in the will of one being that of the other, and this mutually and reciprocally. This is destroyed by love of dominion in marriage, since he that domineers wishes his will alone to be in the other, and nothing of the other's will to be reciprocally in himself, which destroys all mutuality, and thus all sharing of any love and its delight one with the other. And yet this sharing and consequent conjunction are the interior delight itself that is called blessedness in marriage. This blessedness, with everything that is heavenly and spiritual in marriage love, is so completely extinguished by love of dominion as to destroy even all knowledge of it; and if that love were referred to it would be held in such contempt that any mention of blessedness from that source would excite either laughter or anger. [2] When one wills or loves what the other wills or loves each has freedom, since all freedom is from love; but where there is dominion no one has freedom; one is a servant, and the other who rules is also a servant, for he is led as a servant by the lust of ruling. But all this is wholly beyond the comprehension of one who does not know what the freedom of heavenly love is. Nevertheless from what has been said above about the origin and essence of marriage love it can be seen that so far as dominion enters, minds are not united but divided. Dominion subjugates, and a subjugated mind has either no will or an opposing will. If it has no will it has also no love; and if it has an opposing will there is hatred in place of love. [3] The interiors of those who live in such marriage are in mutual collision and strife, as two opposites are wont to be, however their exteriors may be restrained and kept quiet for the sake of tranquillity. The collision and antagonism of the interiors of such are disclosed after their death, when commonly they come together and fight like enemies and tear each other; for they then act in accordance with the state of the interiors. Frequently I have been permitted to see them fighting and tearing one another, sometimes with great vengeance and cruelty. For in the other life everyone's interiors are set at liberty; and they are no longer restrained by outward bounds or by worldly considerations, everyone then being just such as he is interiorly.

To some a likeness of marriage love is granted. Yet unless they are in the love of good and truth there is no marriage love, but only a love which from several causes appears like marriage love, namely, that they may secure good service at home; that they may be free from care, or at peace, or at ease; that they may be cared for in sickness or in old age; or that the children whom they love may be attended to. Some are constrained by fear of the other consort, or by fear of the loss of reputation, or other evil consequences, and some by a controlling lust. Moreover, in the two consorts marriage love may differ, in one there may be more or less of it, in the other little or none; and because of this difference heaven may be the portion of one and hell the portion of the other.

[a.] In the inmost heaven there is genuine marriage love because the angels there are in the marriage of good and truth, and also in innocence. The angels of the lower heavens are also in marriage love, but only so far as they are in innocence; for marriage love viewed in itself is a state of innocence; and this is why consorts who are in the marriage love enjoy heavenly delights together, which appear before their minds almost like the sports of innocence, as between little children; for everything delights their minds, since heaven with its joy flows into every particular of their lives. For the same reason marriage love is represented in heaven by the most beautiful objects. I have seen it represented by a maiden of indescribable beauty encompassed with a bright white cloud. It is said that the angels in heaven have all their beauty from marriage love. Affections and thought flowing from that love are represented by diamond-like auras with scintillations as if from carbuncles and rubies, which are attended by delights that affect the interiors of the mind. In a word, heaven itself is represented in marriage love, because heaven with the angels is the conjunction of good and truth, and it is this conjunction that makes marriage love. 382. [b.] Marriages in heaven differ from marriages on the earth in that the procreation of offspring is another purpose of marriages on the earth, but not of marriages in heaven, since in heaven the procreation of good and truth takes the place of procreation of offspring. The former takes the place of the latter because marriage in heaven is a marriage of good and truth (as has been shown above); and as in that marriage good and truth and their conjunction are loved above all things so these are what are propagated by marriages in heaven. And because of this, in the Word births and generations signify spiritual births and generations, which are births and generations of good and truth; mother and father signify truth conjoined to good, which is what procreates; sons and daughters signify the truths and goods that are procreated; and sons-in-law and daughters-in-law conjunction of these, and so on. 382-1 All this makes clear that marriages in heaven are not like marriages on earth. In heaven marryings are spiritual, and cannot properly be called marryings, but conjunctions of minds from the conjunction of good and truth. But on earth there are marryings, because these are not of the spirit alone but also of the flesh. And as there are no marryings in heaven, consorts there are not called husband and wife; but from the angelic idea of the joining of two minds into one, each consort designates the other by a name signifying one's own, mutually and reciprocally. This shows how the Lord's words in regard to marrying and giving in marriage

(Luke 20:35, 36), are to be understood.

I have also been permitted to see how marriages are contracted in the heavens. As everywhere in heaven those who are alike are united and those who are unlike are separated, so every society in heaven consists of those who are alike. Like are brought to like not by themselves but by the Lord (see above, n. 41, 43, 44, seq.); and equally consort to consort whose minds can be joined into one are drawn together; and consequently at first sight they inmostly love each other, and see themselves to be consorts, and enter into marriage. For this reason all marriages in heaven are from the Lord alone. They have also marriage feasts; and these are attended by many; but the festivities differ in different societies.

Marriages on the earth are most holy in the sight of the angels of heaven because they are seminaries of the human race, and also of the angels of heaven (heaven being from the human race, as already shown under that head), also because these marriages are from a spiritual origin, namely, from the marriage of good and truth, and because the Lord's Divine flows especially into marriage love. Adulteries on the other hand are regarded by the angels as profane because they are contrary to marriage love; for as in marriages the angels behold the marriage of good and truth, which is heaven, so in adulteries they behold the marriage of falsity and evil, which is hell. If, then, they but hear adulteries mentioned they turn away. And this is why heaven is closed up to man when he commits adultery from delight; and when heaven is closed man no longer acknowledges the Divine nor any thing of the faith of church. 384-1 That all who are in hell are antagonistic to marriage love I have been permitted to perceive from the sphere exhaling from hell, which was like an unceasing endeavor to dissolve and violate marriages; which shows that the reigning delight in hell is the delight of adultery, and the delight of adultery is a delight in destroying the conjunction of good and truth, which conjunction makes heaven. From this it follows that the delight of adultery is an infernal delight directly opposed to the delight of marriage, which is a heavenly delight.

There were certain spirits who, from a practice acquired in the life of the body, infested me with peculiar craftiness, and this by a very gentle wave-like influx like the usual influx of well disposed spirits; but I perceived that there was craftiness and other like evils in them prompting them to ensnare and deceive. Finally, I talked with one of them who, I was told, had been when he lived in the world the leader of an army; and perceiving that there was a lustfulness in the ideas of his thought I talked with him about marriage, using spiritual speech with representatives, which fully expresses all that is meant and many things in a moment. He said that in the life of the body he had regarded adulteries as of no account. But I was permitted to tell him that adulteries are heinous, although to those like himself they do not appear to be such, and even appear permissible, on account of their seductive and enticing delights. That they are heinous he might know from the fact that marriages are the seminaries of the human race, and thus also the seminaries of the heavenly kingdom; consequently they must on no account be violated, but must be esteemed holy. This he might know from the fact, which he ought to know because of his being in the other life and in a state of perception, that marriage love descends from the Lord through heaven, and from that love, as from a parent, mutual love, which is the foundation of heaven is derived; and again from this, that if adulterers merely draw near to heavenly societies they perceive their own stench and cast themselves down therefrom towards hell. At least he must have known that to violate marriages is contrary to Divine laws, and contrary to the civil laws of all kingdoms, also contrary to the genuine light of reason, because it is contrary to both Divine and human order; not to mention other considerations. But he replied that he had not so thought in the life of the body. He wished to reason about whether it were so, but was told that truth does not admit of such reasonings; for reasonings defend what one delights in, and thus one's evils and falsities; that he ought first to think about the things that had been said because they are truths; or at least think about them from the principle well known in the world, that no one should do to another what he is unwilling that another should do to him; thus he should consider whether he himself would not have detested adulteries if any one had in that way deceived his wife, whom he had loved as everyone loves in the first period of marriage, and if in his state of wrath he had expressed himself on the subject; also whether being a man of talent he would not in that case have confirmed himself more decidedly than others against adulteries, even condemning them to hell.

I have been shown how the delights of marriage love advance towards heaven, and the delights of adultery towards hell. The advance of the delights of marriage love towards heaven is into states of blessedness and happiness continually increasing until they become innumerable and ineffable, and the more interiorly they advance the more innumerable and more ineffable they become, until they reach the very states of blessedness and happiness of the inmost heaven, or of the heaven of innocence, and this through the most perfect freedom; for all freedom is from love, thus the most perfect freedom is from marriage love, which is heavenly love itself. On the other hand, the advance of adultery is towards hell, and by degrees to the lowest hell, where there is nothing but what is direful and horrible. Such a lot awaits adulterers after their life in the world, those being meant by adulterers who feel a delight in adulteries, and no delight in marriages.

THE EMPLOYMENTS OF ANGELS IN HEAVEN. It is impossible to enumerate the employments in the heavens, still less to describe them in detail, but something may be said about them in a general way; for they are numberless, and vary in accordance with the functions of the societies. Each society has its peculiar function, for as societies are distinct in accordance with goods (see above, n. 41), so they are distinct in accordance with uses, because with all in the heavens goods are goods in act, which are uses. Everyone there performs a use, for the Lord's kingdom is a kingdom of uses. 387-1

In the heavens as on the earth there are many forms of service, for there are ecclesiastical affairs, there are civil affairs, and there are domestic affairs. That there are ecclesiastical affairs is evident from what has been said and shown above, where Divine worship is treated of (n. 221-227); civil affairs, where governments in heaven are treated of (n. 213-220); and domestic affairs, where the dwellings and homes of angels are treated of (n. 183-190); and marriages in heaven (n. 366-368); all of which show that in every heavenly society there are many employments and services.

All things in the heavens are organized in accordance with Divine order, which is everywhere guarded by the services performed by angels, those things that pertain to the general good or use by the wiser angels, those that pertain to particular uses by the less wise, and so on. They are subordinated just as uses are subordinated in the Divine order; and for this reason a dignity is connected with every function according to the dignity of the use. Nevertheless, an angel does not claim dignity to himself, but ascribes all dignity to the use; and as the use is the good that he accomplishes, and all good is from the Lord, so he ascribes all dignity to the Lord. Therefore he that thinks of honor for himself and subsequently for the use, and not for the use and subsequently for himself, can perform no function in heaven, because this is looking away backwards from the Lord, and putting self in the first place and use in the second. When use is spoken of the Lord also is meant, because, as has just been said, use is good, and good is from the Lord.

From this it may be inferred what subordinations in the heavens are, namely, that as any one loves, esteems, and honors the use he also loves, esteems, and honors the person with whom the use is connected; also that the person is loved, esteemed and honored in the measure in which he ascribes the use to the Lord and not to himself; for to that extent he is wise, and the uses he performs he performs from good. Spiritual love, esteem, and honor are nothing else than the love, esteem, and honor of the use in the person, together with the honor to the person because of the use, and not honor to the use because of the person. This is the way, moreover, in which men are regarded when they are regarded from spiritual truth, for one man is then seen to be like another, whether he be in great or in little dignity, the only perceptible difference being a difference in wisdom; and wisdom is loving use, that is, loving the good of a fellow citizen, of society, of one's country, and of the church. It is this that constitutes love to the Lord, because every good that is a good of use is from the Lord; and it constitutes also love towards the neighbor, because the neighbor means the good that is to be loved in a fellow citizen, in society, in one's country, and in the church, and that is to be done in their behalf. 390-1

As all the societies in the heavens are distinct in accordance with their goods (as said above, n. 41, seq.) so they are distinct in accordance with their uses, goods being goods in act, that is, goods of charity which are uses. Some societies are employed in taking care of little children; others in teaching and training them as they grow up; others in teaching and training in like manner the boys and girls that have acquired a good disposition from their education in the world, and in consequence have come into heaven. There are other societies that teach the simple good from the Christian world, and lead them into the way to heaven; there are others that in like manner teach and lead the various heathen nations. There are some societies that defend from infestations by evil spirits the newly arrived spirits that have just come from the world; there are some that attend upon the spirits that are in the lower earth; also some that attend upon spirits that are in the hells, and restrain them from tormenting each other beyond prescribed limits; and there are some that attend upon those who are being raised from the dead. In general, angels from each society are sent to men to watch over them and to lead them away from evil affections and consequent thoughts, and to inspire them with good affections so far as they will receive them in freedom; and by means of these they also direct the deeds or works of men by removing as far as possible evil intentions. When angels are with men they dwell as it were in their affections; and they are near to man just in the degree in which he is in good from truths, and are distant from him just in the degree in which his life is distant from good. 391-1 But all these employments of angels are employments of the Lord through the angels, for the angels perform them from the Lord and not from themselves. For this reason, in the Word in its internal sense "angels" mean, not angels, but something belonging to the Lord; and for the same reason angels are called "gods" in the Word. 391-2

These employments of the angels are their general employments; but each one has his particular charge; for every general use is composed of innumerable uses which are called mediate, ministering, and subservient uses, all and each coordinated and subordinated in accordance with Divine order, and taken together constituting and perfecting the general use, which is the general good.

Those are concerned with ecclesiastical affairs in heaven who in the world loved the Word and eagerly sought in it for truths, not with honor or gain as an end, but uses of life both for themselves and for others. These in heaven are in enlightenment and in the light of wisdom in the measure of their love and desire for use; and this light of wisdom they receive from the Word in heaven, which is not a natural Word, as it is in the world, but a spiritual Word (see above, n. 259.) These minister in the preaching office; and in accordance with Divine order those are in higher positions who from enlightenment excel others in wisdom. [2] Those are concerned with civil affairs who in the world loved their country, and loved its general good more than their own, and did what is just and right from a love for what is just and right. So far as these from the eagerness of love have investigated the laws of justice and have thereby become intelligent, they have the ability to perform such functions in heaven, and they perform these in that position or degree that accords with their intelligence, their intelligence being in equal degree with their love of use for the general good. [3] Furthermore, there are in heaven more functions and services and occupations than can be enumerated; while in the world there are few in comparison. But however many there may be that are so employed, they are all in the delight of their work and labor from a love of use, and no one from a love of self or of gain; and as all the necessaries of life are furnished them gratuitously they have no love of gain for the sake of a living. They are housed gratuitously, clothed gratuitously, and fed gratuitously. Evidently, then, those that have loved themselves and the world more than use have no lot in heaven; for his love or affection remains with everyone after his life in the world, and is not extirpated to eternity (see above, n. 563).

In heaven everyone comes into his own occupation in accordance with correspondence, and the correspondence is not with the occupation but with the use of each occupation (see above, n. 112); for there is a correspondence of all things (see n. 106). He that in heaven comes into the employment or occupation corresponding to his use is in much the same condition of life as when he was in the world; since what is spiritual and what is natural make one by correspondences; yet there is this difference, that he then comes into an interior delight, because into spiritual life, which is an interior life, and therefore more receptive of heavenly blessedness.

HEAVENLY JOY AND HAPPINESS. Hardly any one at present knows what heaven is or what heavenly joy is. Those who have given any thought to these subjects have had so general and so gross an idea about them as scarcely to amount to anything. From spirits that have come from the world into the other life I have been able to learn fully what idea they had of heaven and heavenly joy; for when left to themselves, as they were in the world, they think as they then did. There is this ignorance about heavenly joy for the reason that those who have thought about it have formed their opinion from the outward joys pertaining to the natural man, and have not known what the inner and spiritual man is, nor in consequence the nature of his delight and blessedness; and therefore even if they had been told by those who are in spiritual or inward delight what heavenly joy is, would have had no comprehension of it, for it could have fallen only into an idea not yet recognized, thus into no perception; and would therefore have been among the things that the natural man rejects. Yet everyone can understand that when a man leaves his outer or natural man he comes into the inner or spiritual man, and consequently can see that heavenly delight is internal and spiritual, not external and natural; and being internal and spiritual, it is more pure and exquisite, and affects the interiors of man which pertain to his soul or spirit. From these things alone everyone may conclude that his delight is such as the delight of his spirit has previously been and that the delight of the body, which is called the delight of the flesh, is in comparison not heavenly; also that whatever is in the spirit of man when he leaves the body remains after death, since he then lives a man-spirit.

All delights flow forth from love, for that which a man loves he feels to be delightful. No one has any delight from any other source. From this it follows that such as the love is such is the delight. The delights of the body or of the flesh all flow forth from the love of self and love of the world; consequently they are lusts and their pleasures; while the delights of the soul or spirit all flow forth from love to the Lord and love towards the neighbor, consequently they are affections for good and truth and interior satisfactions. These loves with their delights flow in out of heaven from the Lord by an inner way, that is, from above, and affect the interiors; while the former loves with their delights flow in from the flesh and from the world by an external way, that is, from beneath, and affect the exteriors. Therefore as far as the two loves of heaven are received and make themselves felt, the interiors of man, which belong to his soul or spirit and which look from the world heavenwards, are opened, while so far as the two loves of the world are received and make themselves felt, his exteriors, which belong to the body or flesh and look away from heaven towards the world, are opened. As loves flow in and are received their delights also flow in, the delights of heaven into the interiors and the delights of the world into the exteriors, since all delight, as has just been said above, belongs to love.

Heaven in itself is so full of delights that viewed in itself it is nothing else than blessedness and delight; for the Divine good that flows forth from the Lord's Divine love is what makes heaven in general and in particular with everyone there, and the Divine love is a longing for the salvation of all and the happiness of all from inmosts and in fullness. Thus whether you say heaven or heavenly joy it is the same thing.

The delights of heaven are both ineffable and innumerable; but he that is in the mere delight of the body or of the flesh can have no knowledge of or belief in a single one of these innumerable delights; for his interiors, as has just been said, look away from heaven towards the world, thus backwards. For he that is wholly in the delight of the body or of the flesh, or what is the same, in the love of self and of the world, has no sense of delight except in honor, in gain, and in the pleasures of the body and the senses; and these so extinguish and suffocate the interior delights that belong to heaven as to destroy all belief in them; consequently he would be greatly astonished if he were told that when the delights of honor and of gain are set aside other delights are given, and still more if he were told that the delights of heaven that take the place of these are innumerable, and are such as cannot be compared with the delights of the body and the flesh, which are chiefly the delights of honor and of gain. All this makes clear why it is not known what heavenly joy is.

One can see how great the delight of heaven must be from the fact that it is the delight of everyone in heaven to share his delights and blessings with others; and as such is the character of all that are in the heavens it is clear how immeasurable is the delight of heaven. It has been shown above (n. 268), that in the heavens there is a sharing of all with each and of each with all. Such sharing goes forth from the two loves of heaven, which are, as has been said, love to the Lord and love towards the neighbor; and to share their delights is the very nature of these loves. Love to the Lord is such because the Lord's love is a love of sharing everything it has with all, since it wills the happiness of all. There is a like love in everyone of those who love the Lord, because the Lord is in them; and from this comes the mutual sharing of the delights of angels with one another. Love towards the neighbor is of such a nature, as will be seen in what follows. All this shows that it is the nature of these loves to share their delights. It is otherwise with the loves of self and of the world. The love of self takes away from others and robs others of all delight, and directs it to itself, for it wishes well to itself alone; while the love of the world wishes to have as its own what belongs to the neighbor. Therefore these loves are destructive of the delights of others; or if there is any disposition to share, it is for the sake of themselves and not for the sake of others. Thus in respect to others it is the nature of those loves not to share but to take away, except so far as the delights of others have some relation to self. That the loves of self and of the world, when they rule, are such I have often been permitted to perceive by living experience. Whenever the spirits that were in these loves during their life as men in the world drew near, my delight receded and vanished; and I was told that at the mere approach of such to any heavenly society the delight of those in the society diminished just in the degree of their proximity; and what is wonderful, the evil spirits are then in their delight. All this indicates the state of the spirit of such a man while he is in the body, since it is the same as it is after it is separated from the body, namely, that it longs for or lusts after the delights or goods of another, and finds delight so far as it secures them. All this makes clear that the loves of self and of the world tend to destroy the joys of heaven, and are thus direct opposites of heavenly loves, which desire to share.

But it must be understood that the delight of those who are in the loves of self and of the world, when they draw near to any heavenly society, is the delight of their lust, and thus is directly opposite to the delight of heaven. And such enter into this delight of their lust in consequence of their taking away and dispelling heavenly delight in those that are in such delight. When the heavenly delight is not taken away or dispelled it is different, for they are then unable to draw near; for so far as they draw near they bring upon themselves anguish and pain; and for this reason they do not often venture to come near. This also I have been permitted to learn by repeated experience, something of which I would like to add. [2] Spirits who go from this world into the other life desire more than any thing else to get into heaven. Nearly all seek to enter, supposing that heaven consists solely in being admitted and received. Because of this desire they are brought to some society of the lowest heaven. But as soon as those who are in the love of self and of the world draw near the first threshold of that heaven they begin to be distressed and so tortured inwardly as to feel hell rather than heaven to be in them; and in consequence they cast themselves down headlong therefrom, and do not rest until they come into the hells among their like. [3] It has also frequently occurred that such spirits have wished to know what heavenly joy is, and having heard that it is in the interiors of angels, they have wished to share in it. This therefore was granted; for whatever a spirit who is not yet in heaven or hell wishes is granted if it will benefit him. But as soon as that joy was communicated they began to be so tortured as not to know how to twist or turn because of the pain. I saw them thrust their heads down to their feet and cast themselves upon the ground, and there writhe into coils like serpents, and this in consequence of their interior agony. Such was the effect produced by heavenly delight upon those who are in the delights of the love of self and of the world; and for the reason that these loves are directly opposite to heavenly loves, and when opposite acts against opposite such pain results. And since heavenly delight enters by an inward way and flows into the contrary delight, the interiors which are in the contrary delight are twisted backwards, thus into the opposite direction, and the result is such tortures. [4] They are opposite for the reason given above, that love to the Lord and love to the neighbor wish to share with others all that is their own, for this is their delight, while the loves of self and of the world wish to take away from others what they have, and take it to themselves; and just to the extent that they are able to do this they are in their delight. From this, too, one can see what it is that separates hell from heaven; for all that are in hell were, while they were living in the world, in the mere delights of the body and of the flesh from the love of self and of the world; while all that are in the heavens were, while they lived in the world, in the delights of the soul and spirit from love to the Lord and love to the neighbor; and as these are opposite loves, so the hells and the heavens are entirely separated, and indeed so separated that a spirit in hell does not venture even to put forth a finger from it or raise the crown of his head, for if he does this in the least he is racked with pain and tormented. This, too, I have frequently seen.

Footnotes

352-1 It is the part of the wise to see and perceive whether a thing is true before it is confirmed and not merely to confirm what is said by others (n. 1017, 4741, 7012, 7680, 7950). Only those can see and perceive whether a thing is true before it is confirmed who are affected by truth for the sake of truth and for the sake of life (n. 8521). The light of confirmation is not spiritual light but natural light, and is even sensual light which the wicked may have (n. 8780). All things, even falsities, may be so confirmed as to appear like truths (n. 2477, 2480, 5033, 6865, 8521).

353-1 The sensual is the outmost of man's life, clinging to and inhering in his bodily part (n. 5077, 5767, 9212, 9216, 9331, 9730). He is called a sensual man who forms all his judgments and conclusions from the bodily senses, and who believes nothing except what he sees with his eyes and touches with his hands (n. 5094, 7693). Such a man thinks in things outermost and not interiorly in himself (n. 5089, 5094, 6564, 7693). His interiors are so closed up that he sees nothing of Divine truth (n. 6564, 6844, 6845). In a word he is in gross natural light and thus perceives nothing that is from the light of heaven (n. 6201, 6310, 6564, 6598, 6612, 6614, 6622, 6624, 6844, 6845). Therefore he is inwardly opposed to all things pertaining to heaven and the church (n. 6201, 6310, 6844, 6845, 6948, 6949). The learned that have confirmed themselves against the truths of the church are sensual (n. 6316). A description of the sensual man (n. 10236).

353-2 Sensual men reason keenly and cunningly, since they place all intelligence in speaking from the bodily memory (n. 195, 196, 5700, 10236). But they reason from the fallacies of the senses (n. 5084, 6948, 6949, 7693). Sensual men are more cunning and malicious than others (n. 7693, 10236). By the ancients such were called serpents of the tree of knowledge (n. 195-197, 6398, 6949, 10313).

355-1 Knowledges belong to the natural memory that man has while he is in the body (n. 5212, 9922). Man carries with him after death his whole natural memory (n. 2475) from experience (n. 2481-2486). But he is not able, as he was in the world, to draw anything out of that memory, for several reasons (n. 2476, 2477, 2479).

356-1 Most beautiful colors are seen in heaven (n. 1053, 1624). Colors in heaven are from the light there, and are modifications or variegations of that light (n. 1042, 1043, 1053, 1624, 3993, 4530, 4742, 4922). Thus they are manifestations of truth from good, and they signify such things as pertain to intelligence and wisdom (n. 4530, 4677, 4922, 9466). EXTRACTS FROM THE ARCANA COELESTIA RESPECTING KNOWLEDGES. [In these extracts scientia, scientificum and cognitio are alike rendered knowledge, because any distinction between them intended by the author is not sufficiently obvious to be uniformly indicated in English. - Tr.] Man ought to be fully instructed in knowledges [scientiis et cognitionibus], since by means of them he learns to think [cogitare], afterwards to understand what is true and good, and finally to be wise (n. 129, 1450, 1451, 1453, 1548, 1802). Knowledges [scientifica] are the first things on which the life of man, civil, moral, and spiritual, is built and founded, and they are to be learned for the sake of use as an end (n. 1489, 3310). Knowledges [cognitiones] open the way to the internal man, and afterwards conjoin that man with the external in accordance with uses (n. 1563, 1616). The rational faculty has its birth by means of knowledges [scientias et cognitiones] (n. 1895, 1900, 3086). But not by means of knowledges [cognitiones] themselves, but by means of affection for the uses derived from them (n. 1895).

[2] There are knowledges [scientifica] that give entrance to Divine truths, and knowledges [scientifica] that do not (n. 5213). Empty knowledges [scientifica] are to be destroyed (n. 1489, 1492, 1499, 1581). Empty knowledges [scientifica] are such as have the loves of self and of the world as an end, and sustain those loves, and withdraw from love to God and love towards the neighbor, because such knowledges close up the internal man, even to the extent that man becomes unable to receive any thing from heaven (n. 1563, 1600). Knowledges [scientifica] are means to becoming wise and means to becoming insane and by them the internal man is either opened or closed, and thus the rational is either enriched or destroyed (n. 4156, 8628, 9922). [3] The internal man is opened and gradually perfected by means of knowledges [scientifica] if man has good use as an end, especially use that looks to external life (n. 3086). Then knowledges [scientificis], which are in the natural man, are met by spiritual and heavenly things from the spiritual man, and these adopt such of them as are suitable (n. 1495). Then the uses of heavenly life are drawn forth by the Lord and perfected and raised up out of the knowledges [scientificis] in the natural man by means of the internal man (n. 1895, 1896, 1900, 1901, 1902, 5871, 5874, 5901). While incongruous and opposing knowledges [scientifica] are rejected to the sides and banished (n. 5871, 5886, 5889). [4] The sight of the internal man calls forth from the knowledges [scientificis] of the external man only such things as are in accord with its love (n. 9394). As seen by the internal man what pertains to the love is at the center and in brightness, but what is not of the love is at the sides and in obscurity (n. 6068, 6084). Suitable knowledges [scientifica] are gradually implanted in man's loves and as it were dwell in them (n. 6325). If man were born into love towards the neighbor he would be born into intelligence, but because he is born into the loves of self and of the world he is born into total ignorance (n. 6323, 6325). Knowledge [scientia], intelligence, and wisdom are sons of love to God and of love towards the neighbor (n. 1226, 2049, 2116). [5] It is one thing to be wise, another thing to understand, another to know [scire], and another to do; nevertheless, in those that possess spiritual life these follow in order, and exist together in doing or deeds (n. 10331). Also it is one thing to know [scire], another to acknowledge, and another to have faith (n. 896). [6] Knowledges [scientifica], which pertain to the external or natural man, are in the light of the world, but truths that have been made truths of faith and of love, and have thus acquired life, are in the light of heaven (n. 5212). The truths that have acquired spiritual life are comprehended by means of natural ideas (n. 5510). Spiritual influx is from the internal or spiritual man into the knowledges [scientifica] that are in the external or natural man (n. 1940, 8005). Knowledges [scientifica] are receptacles, and as it were vessels, for the truth and good that belong to the internal man (n. 1469, 1496, 3068, 5489, 6004, 6023, 6052, 6071, 6077, 7770, 9922). Knowledges [scientifica] are like mirrors in which the truths and goods of the internal man appear as an image (n. 5201). There they are together as in their outmost (n. 5373, 5874, 5886, 5901, 6004, 6023, 6052, 6071). [7] Influx is not physical but spiritual, that is, influx is from the internal man into the external, thus into the knowledges of the external; and not from the external into the internal, thus not from the knowledges [scientificis] of the external into truths of faith (n. 3219, 5119, 5259, 5427, 5428, 5478, 6322, 9110). A beginning must be made from the truths of doctrine of the

church, which are from the Word, and those truths must first be acknowledged, and then it is permissible to consult knowledges [scientifica] (n. 6047). Thus it is permissible for those who are in an affirmative state in regard to truths of faith to confirm them intellectually by means of knowledges [scientifica], but not for those who are in a negative state (n. 2568, 2588, 4760, 6047). He that will not believe Divine truths until he is convinced by means of knowledges [scientificis] will never believe (n. 2094, 2832). To enter from knowledge [scientificis] into the truths of faith is contrary to order (n. 10236). Those who do so become demented respecting the things of heaven and the church (n. 128, 129, 130). They fall into the falsities of evil (n. 232, 233, 6047). In the other life when they think about spiritual matters they become as it were drunken (n. 1072). More respecting the character of such (n. 196). Examples showing that things spiritual cannot be comprehended when entered into through knowledges [scientifica] (n. 233, 2094, 2196, 2203, 2209). In spiritual things many of the learned are more demented than the simple, for the reason that they are in a negative state, which they confirm by means of the knowledges [scientifica] which they have continually and in abundance before their sight (n. 4760, 8629). [8] Those who reason from knowledges [scientificis] against the truths of faith reason keenly because they reason from the fallacies of the senses, which are engaging and convincing, because they cannot easily be dispelled (n. 5700). What things are fallacies of the senses, and what they are (n. 5084, 5094, 6400, 6948). Those that have no understanding of truth, and also those that are in evil, are able to reason about the truths and goods of faith, but are not able to understand them (n. 4214). Intelligence does not consist in merely confirming dogma but in seeing whether it is true or not before it is confirmed (n. 4741, 6047). [9] Knowledges [scientiae] are of no avail after death, but only that which man has imbibed in his understanding and life by means of knowledges [scientias] (n. 2480). Still all knowledge [scientifica] remains after death, although it is quiescent (n. 2476-2479, 2481-2486). [10] Knowledge [scientifica] with the evil are falsities, because they are adapted to evils, but with the good the same knowledges are truths, because applied to what is good (n. 6917). True knowledges [scientifica] with the evil are not true, however much they may appear to be true when uttered, because there is evil within them (n. 10331). [11] An example of the desire to know [sciendi], which spirits have (n. 1974). Angels have an illimitable longing to know [sciendi] and to become wise, since learning [scientia], intelligence, and wisdom are spiritual food (n. 3114, 4459, 4792, 4976, 5147, 5293, 5340, 5342, 5410, 5426, 5576, 5582, 5588, 5655, 6277, 8562, 9003). The knowledge [scientia] of the ancients was the knowledge [scientia] of correspondences and representations, by which they gained entrance into the knowledge [cognitionem] of spiritual things; but that knowledge [scientia] at this day is wholly lost (n. 4749, 4844, 4964, 4965). [12] For spiritual truths to be comprehended the following universals must be known [scientur]. (i) All things in the universe have relation to good and truth and to their conjunction that they may be anything, thus to love and faith and their conjunction. (ii) Man has understanding and will; and the understanding is the receptacle of truth and the will of good; and all things in man have relation to these two and to their conjunction, as all things have relation to truth and good and their conjunction. (iii) There is an internal man and an external man, which are as distinct from each other as heaven and the world are, and yet for a man to be truly a man, these must make one. (iv) The internal man is in the light of heaven, and the external man is in the light of the world; and the light of heaven is Divine truth itself, from which is all intelligence. (v) Between the things in the internal man and those in the external there is a correspondence, therefore the different aspect they present is such that they can be distinguished only by means of a knowledge [scientiam] of correspondences. Unless these and many other things are known [scientur], nothing but incongruous ideas of spiritual and heavenly truths can be conceived and formed; therefore without these universals the knowledges [scientifica et cognitiones] of the natural man can be of but little service to the rational man for understanding and growth. This makes clear how necessary knowledges [scientifica] are.

358-1 It is frequently said in the Word that man will be judged and will be rewarded according to his deeds and works (n. 3934). By "deeds and works" deeds and works in their internal form are meant, not in their external form, since good works in external form are likewise done by the wicked, but in internal and external form together only by the good (n. 3934, 6073). Works, like all activities, have their being and outgo [esse et existere] and their quality from the interiors of man, which pertain to his thought and will, since they proceed from these; therefore such as the interiors are such are the works (n. 3934, 8911, 10331). That is, such as the interiors are in regard to love and faith (n. 3934, 6073, 10331, 10332). Thus works contain love and faith, and are love and faith in effect (n. 10331). Therefore to be judged and rewarded in accordance with deeds and works, means in accordance with love and faith (n. 3147, 3934, 6073, 8911, 10331, 10332). So far as works look to self and the world they are not good, but they are good so far as they look to the Lord and the neighbor (n. 3147).

359-1 All evils are from the love of self and of the world (n. 1307, 1308, 1321, 1594, 1691, 3413, 7255, 7376, 7488, 7490, 8318, 9335, 9348, 10038, 10742). These are contempt of others, enmities, hatred, revenge, cruelty, deceit (n. 6667, 7370-7374, 9348, 10038, 10742). Into such loves man is born, thus in them are his inherited evils (n. 694, 4317, 5660).

360-1 Charity towards the neighbor is doing what is good, just, and right, in every work and every employment (n. 8120-8122). Thus charity towards the neighbor extends to all things and each thing that a man thinks, wills, and does (n. 8124). A life of piety apart from a life of charity is of no avail, but together they are profitable for all things (n. 8252, 8253).

361-1 Every good has its delight from use and in accordance with use (n. 3049, 4984, 7038); also its quality; and in consequence such as the use is such is the good (n. 3049). All the happiness and delight of life is from uses (n. 997). In general, life is a life of uses (n. 1964). Angelic life consists in the goods of love and charity, thus in performing uses (n. 454). The ends that man has in view, which are uses, are the only things that the Lord, and thus the angels, consider (n. 1317, 1645, 5844). The kingdom of the Lord is a kingdom of uses (n. 454, 696, 1103, 3645, 4054, 7038). Performing uses is serving the Lord (n. 7038). Everyone's character is such as are the uses he performs (n. 4054, 6315); illustrated (n. 7038).

364-1 There can be no mercy apart from means, but only mercy through means, that is, to those who live in accordance with the commandments of the Lord; such the Lord by His mercy leads continually in the world, and afterwards to eternity (n. 8700, 10659).

364-2 Dignities and riches are not real blessings, therefore they are granted both to the wicked and to the good (n. 8939, 10775, 10776). The real blessing is reception of love and faith from the Lord, and conjunction thereby, for this is the source of eternal happiness (n. 1420, 1422, 2846, 3017, 3406, 3504, 3514, 3530, 3565, 3584, 4216, 4981, 8939, 10495).

365-1 "Garments" signify truths, thus knowledges (n. 1073, 2576, 5319, 5954, 9212, 9216, 9952, 10536). "Purple" signifies celestial good (n. 9467). "Fine linen" signifies truth from a celestial origin (n. 5319, 9469, 9744).

365-2 A "camel" signifies in the Word the knowing faculty and knowledge in general (n. 3048, 3071, 3143, 3145). What is meant by "needlework, working with a needle," and therefore by a "needle" (n. 9688). To enter from knowledge into the truths of faith is contrary to Divine order (n. 10236). Those that do this become demented in respect to the thing of heaven and the church (n. 128-130, 232, 233, 6047). And in the other life, when they think about spiritual things they become as it were drunken (n. 1072). Further about such (n. 196). Examples showing that when spiritual things are entered into through knowledges they cannot be comprehended (n. 233, 2094, 2196, 2203, 2209). It is permissible to enter from spiritual truth into knowledges which pertain to the natural man, but not the reverse, because there can be spiritual influx into the natural, but not natural influx into the spiritual (n. 3219, 5119, 5259, 5427, 5428, 5478, 6322, 9110). The truths of the word and of the church must first be acknowledged, after which it is permissible to consider knowledges, but not before (n. 6047).

367-1 It is not known at this day what marriage love is, or whence it is (n. 2727). Marriage love is willing what another wills, thus willing mutually and reciprocally (n. 2731). Those that are in marriage love dwell together in the inmosts of life (n. 2732). It is such a union of two minds that from love they are one (n. 10168, 10169). For the love of minds, which is spiritual love, is a union (n. 1594, 2057, 3939, 4018, 5807, 6195, 7081-7086, 7501, 10130).

368-1 In the Word "young men" signify understanding of truth, or the intelligent (n. 7668). "Men" have the same signification (n. 158, 265, 749, 915, 1007, 2517, 3134, 3236, 4823, 9007). "Woman" signifies affection for good and truth (n. 568, 3160, 6014, 7337, 8994); likewise the church (n. 252, 253, 749, 770); "wife" has the same signification (n. 252, 253, 409, 749, 770); with what difference (n. 915, 2517, 3236, 4510, 4823). In the highest sense "husband and wife" are predicated of the Lord and of His conjunction with heaven and the church (n. 7022). A "virgin" signifies affection for good (n. 3067, 3110, 3179, 3189, 6729, 6742); likewise the church (n. 2362 3081, 3963, 4638, 6729, 6775, 6788).

371-1 The origin, cause, and essence of true marriage love is the marriage of good and truth; thus it is from heaven (n. 2728, 2729). Respecting angelic spirit, who have a perception whether there is anything of marriage from the idea of a conjunction of good and truth (n. 10756). It is with marriage love in every respect the same as it is with the conjunction of good and truth (n. 1904,

2173, 2429, 2508, 3101, 3102, 3155, 3179, 3180, 4358, 5807, 5835, 9206, 9495, 9637). How and with whom the conjunction of good and truth is effected (n. 3834, 4096, 4097, 4301, 4345, 4353, 4364, 4368, 5365, 7623-7627, 9258). Only those that are in good and truth from the Lord know what true marriage love is (n. 10171). In the Word "marriage" signifies the marriage of good and truth (n. 3132, 4434, 4835). The kingdom of the Lord and heaven are in true marriage love (n. 2737).

375-1 All things in the universe, both in heaven and in the world, have relation to good and truth (n. 2452, 3166, 4390, 4409, 5232, 7256, 10122). And to the conjunction of these (n. 10555). Between good and truth there is marriage (n. 1904, 2173, 2508). Good loves truth, and from love longs for truth and for the conjunction of truth with itself, and from this they are in a perpetual endeavor to be conjoined (n. 9206, 9207, 9495). The life of truth is from good (n. 1589, 1997, 2572, 4070, 4096, 4097, 4736, 4757, 4884, 5147, 9667). Truth is the form of good (n. 3049, 3180, 4574, 9154). Truth is to good as water is to bread (n. 4976).

378-1 Marriages between those of different religions are not permissible, because there can be no conjunction of like good and truth in the interiors (n. 8998).

379-1 As husband and wife should be one, and should live together in the inmost of life, and as they together make one angel in heaven, so true marriage love is impossible between one husband and several wives (n. 1907, 2740). To marry several wives at the same time is contrary to Divine order (n. 10837). That there is no marriage except between one husband and one wife is clearly perceived by those who are in the Lord's celestial kingdom (n. 865, 3246, 9002, 10172). For the reason that the angels there are in the marriage of good and truth (n. 3246). The Israelitish nation were permitted to marry several wives, and to add concubines to wives, but not Christians, for the reason that that nation was in externals separate from internals, while Christians are able to enter into internals, thus into the marriage of good and truth (n. 3246, 4837, 8809.)

382-1 Conceptions, pregnancies, births, and generations signify those that are spiritual, that is, such as pertain to good and truth, or to love and faith (n. 613, 1145, 1255, 2020, 2584, 3860, 3868, 4070, 4668, 6239, 8042, 9325, 10249). Therefore generation and birth signify regeneration and rebirth through faith and love (n. 5160, 5598, 9042, 9845). Mother signifies the church in respect to truth, and thus the truth of the church; father the church in respect to good, and thus the good of the church (n. 2691, 2717, 3703, 5581, 8897). Sons signify affections for truth, and thus truths (n. 489, 491, 533, 2623, 3373, 4257, 8649, 9807). Daughters signify affections for good, and the goods (n. 489-491, 2362, 3963, 6729, 6775, 6778, 9055). Son-in-law signifies truth associated with affection for good (n. 2389). Daughter-in-law signifies good associated with its truth (n. 4843).

384-1 Adulteries are profane (n. 9961, 10174). Heaven is closed to adulterers (n. 2750). Those that have experienced delight in adulteries cannot come into heaven (n. 539, 2733, 2747-2749, 2751, 10175). Adulterers are unmerciful and destitute of religion (n. 824, 2747, 2748). The ideas of adulterers are filthy (n. 2747, 2748). In the other life they love filth and are in filthy hells (n. 2755, 5394,

5722). In the Word adulteries signify adulterations of good, and whoredoms perversions of truth (n. 2466, 2729, 3399, 4865, 8904, 10648).

387-1 The Lord's kingdom is a kingdom of uses (n. 454, 696, 1103, 3645, 4054, 7038). Performing uses is serving the Lord (n. 7038). In the other life all must perform uses (n. 1103); even the wicked and infernal, but in what manner (n. 696). All are such as are the uses they perform (n. 4054, 6815); illustrated (n. 7038). Angelic blessedness consists in the goods of charity, that is, in performing uses (n. 454).

390-1 Loving the neighbor is not loving the person, but loving that which is in him and which constitutes him (n. 5025, 10336). Those who love the person, and not that which is in him, and which constitutes him, love equally an evil man and a good man (n. 3820); and do good alike to the evil and to the good; and yet to do good to the evil is to do evil to the good and that is not loving the neighbor (n. 3820, 6703, 8120). The judge who punishes the evil that they may be reformed, and may not contaminate or injure the good, loves his neighbor (n. 3820, 8120, 8121). Every individual and every community also one's country and the church, and in the most general sense the kingdom of the Lord, are the neighbor, and to do good to these from a love of good in accord with the quality of their state, is loving the neighbor; that is, the neighbor is their good, which is to be consulted (n. 6818-6824, 8123).

391-1 Of the angels that are with little children and afterwards with boys, and thus in succession (n. 2303). Man is raised from the dead by means of angels; from experiences (n. 168-189). Angels are sent to those who are in hell to prevent their tormenting each other beyond measure (n. 967). Of the services rendered by the angels to men on their coming into the other life (n. 2131). There are spirits and angels with all men and man is led by the Lord by means of spirits and angels (n. 50, 697, 2796, 2887, 2888, 5846-5866, 5976-5993, 6209). Angels have dominion over evil spirits (n. 1755).

391-2 In the Word by angels something Divine from the Lord is signified (n. 1925, 2821, 3039, 4085, 6280, 8192). In the Word angels are called "gods," because of their reception of Divine truth and good from the Lord (n. 4295, 4402, 8192, 8301).

Section 9

One who is in the love of self and love of the world perceives while he lives in the body a sense of delight from these loves and also in the particular pleasures derived from these loves. But one who is in love to God and in love towards the neighbor does not perceive while he lives in the body any distinct sense of delight from these loves or from the good affections derived from them, but only a blessedness that is hardly perceptible, because it is hidden away in his interiors and veiled by the exteriors pertaining to the body and dulled by the cares of the world. But after death these states are entirely changed. The delights of love of self and of the world are then turned into what is painful and direful, because into such things as are called infernal fire, and by turns into things defiled and filthy corresponding to their unclean pleasures, and these, wonderful to tell, are then delightful to them. But the obscure delight and almost imperceptible blessedness of those that had been while in the world in love to God and in love to the neighbor are then turned into the delight of heaven, and become in every way perceived and felt, for the blessedness that lay hidden and unrecognized in their interiors while they lived in the world is then revealed and brought forth into evident sensation, because such had been the delight of their spirit, and they are then in the spirit.

In uses all the delights of heaven are brought together and are present, because uses are the goods of love and charity in which angels are; therefore everyone has delights that are in accord with his uses, and in the degree of his affection for use. That all the delights of heaven are delights of use can be seen by a comparison with the five bodily senses of man. There is given to each sense a delight in accordance with its use; to the sight, the hearing, the smell, the taste, and the touch, each its own delight; to the sight a delight from beauty and from forms, to the hearing from harmonious sounds, to the smell from pleasing odors, to taste from fine flavors. These uses which the senses severally perform are known to those who study them, and more fully to those who are acquainted with correspondences. Sight has such a delight because of the use it performs to the understanding, which is the inner sight; the hearing has such a delight because of the use it performs both to the understanding and to the will through giving attention; the smell has such a delight because of the use it performs to the brain, and also to the lungs; the taste has such a delight because of the use it performs to the stomach, and thus to the whole body by nourishing it. The delight of marriage, which is a purer and more exquisite delight of touch, transcends all the rest because of its use, which is the procreation of the human race and thereby of angels of heaven. These delights are in these sensories by an influx of heaven, where every delight pertains to use and is in accordance with use.

There were some spirits who believed from an opinion adopted in the world that heavenly happiness consists in an idle life in which they would be served by others; but they were told that happiness never consists in abstaining from work and getting satisfaction therefrom. This would mean everyone's desiring the happiness of others for himself, and what everyone wished for no one would have. Such a life would be an idle not an active life, and would stupefy all the powers of life; and everyone ought to know that without activity of life there can be no happiness of life, and that rest from this activity should be only for the sake of recreation, that one may return with more vigor to the activity of his life. They were then shown by many evidences that angelic life consists in performing the good works of charity, which are uses, and that the angels find all their happiness in use, from use, and in accordance with use. To those that held the opinion that heavenly joy consists in living an idle life and drawing breaths of eternal joy in idleness, a perception was given of what such a life is, that they might become ashamed of the idea; and they saw that such a life is extremely sad, and that all joy thus perishing they would in a little while feel only loathing and disgust for it.

There were some spirits who thought themselves better instructed than others, and who said that they had believed in the world that heavenly joy would consist solely in praising and giving glory to God, and that this would be an active life. But these were told that praising and giving glory to God is not a proper active life, also that God has no need of praises and glorification, but it is His will that they should perform uses, and thus the good works that are called goods of charity. But they were unable to associate with goods of charity any idea of heavenly joy, but only of servitude, although the angels testified that this joy is most free because it comes from an interior affection and is conjoined with ineffable delight.

Almost all who enter the other life think that hell is the same to everyone, and heaven the same; and yet in both there are infinite varieties and diversities, and in no case is hell or heaven wholly the same to one as to another; as it is impossible that any one man, spirit or angel should ever be wholly like another even as to the face. At my mere thought of two being just alike or equal the angels expressed horror, saying that everyone thing is formed out of the harmonious concurrence of many things, and that the one thing is such as that concurrence is; and that it is thus that a whole society in heaven becomes a one, and that all the societies of heaven together become a one, and this from the Lord alone by means of love. 405-1 Uses in the heavens are likewise in all variety and diversity, and in no case is the use of one wholly the same as and identical with the use of another; so neither is the happiness of one the same as and identical with the happiness of another. Furthermore, the delights of each use are innumerable, and these innumerable delights are likewise various, and yet conjoined in such order that they mutually regard each other, like the uses of each member, organ, and viscus, in the body, and still more like the uses of each vessel and fiber in each member, organ and viscus; each and all of which are so affiliated as to have regard to another's good in their own good, and thus each in all, and all in each. From this universal and individual aspect they act as one.

I have talked at times with spirits that had recently come from the world about the state of eternal life, saying that it is important to know who the Lord of the kingdom is, and what kind and what form of government it has. As nothing is more important for those entering another kingdom in the world than to know who and what the king is, and what the government is, and other particulars in regard to the kingdom, so is it of still greater consequence in regard to this kingdom in which they are to live to eternity. Therefore they should know that it is the Lord who governs both heaven and the universe, for He who governs the one governs the other; thus that the kingdom in which they now are is the Lord's; and that the laws of this kingdom are eternal truths, all of which rest upon the law that the Lord must be loved above all things and the neighbor as themselves; and even more than this, if they would be like the angels they must love the neighbor more than themselves. On hearing this they could make no reply, for the reason that although they had heard in the life of the body something like this they had not believed it, wondering how there could be such love in heaven, and how it could be possible for any one to love his neighbor more than himself. But they were told that every good increases immeasurably in the other life, and that while they cannot go further in the life of the body than to love the neighbor as themselves, because they are immersed in what concerns the body, yet when this is set aside their love becomes more pure, and finally becomes angelic, which is to love the neighbor more than themselves. For in the heavens there is joy in doing good to another, but no joy in doing good to self unless with a view to its becoming another's, and thus for another's sake. This is loving the neighbor more than oneself. They were told that the possibility of such a love is shown in the world in the marriage love of some who have suffered death to protect a consort from injury, in the love of parents for their children, as in a mother's preferring to go hungry rather than see her child go hungry; in sincere friendship, in which one friend will expose himself to danger for another; and even in polite and pretended friendship that wishes to emulate sincere friendship, in offering the better things to those to whom it professes to wish well, and bearing such good will on the lips though not in the heart; finally, in the nature of love, which is such that its joy is to serve others, not for its own sake but for theirs. But all this was incomprehensible to those who loved themselves more than others, and in the life of the body had been greedy of gain; most of all to the avaricious.

There was one who in the life of the body had exercised power over others, and who had retained in the other life the desire to rule; but he was told that he was now in another kingdom, which is eternal, and that his rule on earth had perished, and that he was now where no one is esteemed except in accordance with his goodness and truth, and that measure of the Lord's mercy which he enjoyed by virtue of his life in the world; also that the same is true in this kingdom as on the earth, where men are esteemed for their wealth and for their favor with the prince, wealth here being good and truth, and favor with the prince the mercy bestowed on man by the Lord in accordance with his life in the world. Any wish to rule otherwise would make him a rebel, since he is in another's kingdom. On hearing these things he was ashamed.

I have talked with spirits who believed heaven and heavenly joy to consist in their being great; but such were told that in heaven he that is least is greatest, since he is called least who has, and wishes to have, no power or wisdom from himself, but only from the Lord, he that is least in that sense having the greatest happiness, and as he has the greatest happiness, it follows that he is greatest; for he has thereby from the Lord all power and excels all in wisdom. What is it to be the greatest unless to be the most happy? For to be the most happy is what the powerful seek through power and the rich through riches. It was further said that heaven does not consist in a desire to be least for the purpose of being greatest, for that would be aspiring and longing to be the greatest; but it consists in desiring from the heart the good of others more than one's own, and in serving others with a view to their happiness, not with recompense as an end, but from love.

Heavenly joy itself, such as it is in its essence, cannot be described, because it is in the inmost of the life of angels and therefrom in everything of their thought and affection, and from this in every particular of their speech and action. It is as if the interiors were fully opened and unloosed to receive delight and blessedness, which are distributed to every least fiber and thus through the whole. Thus the perception and sensation of this joy is so great as to be beyond description, for that which starts from the inmosts flows into every particular derived from the inmosts, propagating itself away with increase towards the exteriors. Good spirits who are not yet in that joy, because not yet raised up into heaven, when they perceive a sense of that joy from an angel from the sphere of his love, are filled with such delight that they come as it were into a delicious trance. This sometimes happens with those who desire to know what heavenly joy is.

When certain spirits wished to know what heavenly joy is they were allowed to feel it to such a degree that they could no longer bear it; and yet it was not angelic joy; it was scarcely in the least degree angelic, as I was permitted to perceive by sharing it, but was so slight as to be almost frigid; nevertheless they called it most heavenly, because to them it was an inmost joy. From this it was evident, not only that there are degrees of the joys of heaven, but also that the inmost joy of one scarcely reaches to the outmost or middle joy of another; also that when any one receives his own inmost joy he is in his heavenly joy, and cannot endure what is still more interior, for such a joy becomes painful to him.

Certain spirits, not evil, sinking into a quiescence like sleep, were taken up into heaven in respect to the interiors of their minds; for before their interiors are opened spirits can be taken up into heaven and be taught about the happiness of those there. I saw them in the quiescent state for about half an hour, and afterwards they relapsed into their exteriors in which they were before, and also into a recollection of what they had seen. They said that they had been among the angels in heaven, and had there seen and perceived amazing things, all of which were resplendent as if made of gold, silver, and precious stones, in exquisite forms and in wonderful variety; also that angels are not delighted with the outward things themselves, but with the things they represented, which were Divine, ineffable, and of infinite wisdom, and that these were their joy; with innumerable other things that could not be described in human language even as to a ten-thousandth part, or fall into ideas which partake of any thing material.

Scarcely any who enter the other life know what heavenly blessedness and happiness are, because they do not know what internal joy is, deriving their perception of it solely from bodily and worldly gladness and joy; and in consequence what they are ignorant of they suppose to be nothing, when in fact bodily and worldly joys are of no account in comparison. In order, therefore, that the well disposed, who do not know what heavenly joy is, may know and realize what it is, they are taken first to paradisal scenes that transcend every conception of the imagination. They then think that they have come into the heavenly paradise; but they are taught that this is not true heavenly happiness; and they are permitted to realize such interior states of joy as are perceptible to their inmost. They are then brought into a state of peace even to their inmost, when they confess that nothing of it is in the least expressible or conceivable. Finally they are brought into a state of innocence even to their inmost sense. Thus they are permitted to learn what true spiritual and heavenly good is.

But that I might learn the nature of heaven and heavenly joy I have frequently and for a long time been permitted by the Lord to perceive the delights of heavenly joys; but while I have been enabled to know by living experience what they are I am not at all able to describe them. Nevertheless, that some idea of them may be formed, something shall be said about them. Heavenly joy is an affection of innumerable delights and joys, which together present something general, and in this general, that is, this general affection, are harmonies of innumerable affections that come to perception obscurely, and not distinctly, because the perception is most general. Nevertheless I was permitted to perceive that there are innumerable things in it, in such order as cannot be at all described, those innumerable things being such as flow from the order of heaven. The order in the particulars of the affection even to the least, is such that these particulars are presented and perceived only as a most general whole, in accordance with the capacity of him who is the subject. In a word, each general affection contains infinite affections arranged in a most orderly form, with nothing therein that is not alive, and that does not affect all of them from the inmosts; for heavenly joys go forth from inmosts. I perceived also that the joy and ecstasy came as from the heart, diffusing most softly through all the inmost fibers, and from these into the bundles of fibers, with such an inmost sense of delight that the fiber seemed to be nothing but joy and ecstasy, and everything perceptive and sensitive therefrom seemed in like manner to be alive with happiness. Compared with these joys the joy of bodily pleasures is like a gross and pungent dust compared with a pure and most gentle aura. I have noticed that when I wished to transfer all my delight to another, a more interior and fuller delight continually flowed in in its place, and the more I wished this, the more flowed in; and this was perceived to be from the Lord.

Those that are in heaven are continually advancing towards the spring of life, with a greater advance towards a more joyful and happy spring the more thousands of years they live; and this to eternity, with increase according to the growth and degree of their love, charity, and faith. Women who have died old and worn out with age, if they have lived in faith in the Lord, in charity to the neighbor, and in happy marriage love with a husband, advance with the succession of years more and more into the flower of youth and early womanhood, and into a beauty that transcends every conception of any such beauty as is seen on the earth. Goodness and charity are what give this form and thus manifest their own likeness, causing the joy and beauty of charity to shine forth from every least particular of the face, and causing them to be the very forms of charity. Some who beheld this were struck with amazement. The form of charity that is seen in a living way in heaven, is such that it is charity itself that both forms and is formed; and this in such a manner that the whole angel is a charity, as it were, especially the face; and this is both clearly seen and felt. When this form is beheld it is beauty unspeakable, affecting with charity the very inmost life of the mind. In a word, to grow old in heaven is to grow young. Such forms or such beauties do those become in the other life who have lived in love to the Lord and in charity towards the neighbor. All angels are such forms in endless variety; and of these heaven is constituted.

XLIII. THE IMMENSITY OF HEAVEN. The immensity of the heaven of the Lord is evident from many things that have been said and shown in the foregoing chapters, especially from this, that heaven is from the human race (n. 311-317), both from those born within the church and from those born out of it (n. 318-328); thus it consists of all from the beginning of this earth that have lived a good life. How great a multitude of men there is in this entire world any one who knows anything about the divisions, the regions, and kingdoms of the earth may conclude. Whoever goes into a calculation will find that several thousands of men die every day, that is, some myriads of millions every year; and this from the earliest times, since which several thousands of years have elapsed. All of these after death have gone into the other world, which is called the spiritual world, and they are constantly going into it. But how many of these have become or are becoming angels of heaven cannot be told. This I have been told, that in ancient times the number was very great, because men then thought more interiorly and spiritually, and from such thought were in heavenly affection; but in the following ages not so many, because in the process of time man became more external and began to think more naturally, and from such thought to be in earthly affection. All of this shows how great heaven is even from the inhabitants of this earth alone.

The immensity of the heaven of the Lord is shown also by this, that all children, whether born within the church or out of it, are adopted by the Lord and become angels; and the number of these amounts to a fourth or fifth part of the whole human race on the earth. That every child, wherever born, whether within the church or out of it, whether of pious or impious parents, is received by the Lord when it dies, and is brought up in heaven, and is taught and imbued with affections for good, and through these with knowledges of truth, in accordance with Divine order, and as he becomes perfected in intelligence and wisdom is brought into heaven and becomes an angel, can be seen above (n. 329-345). From all this a conclusion may be formed of the multitude of angels of heaven, derived from this source alone, from the first creation to the present time.

Again, how immense the heaven of the Lord is can be seen from this, that all the planets visible to the eye in our solar system are earths, and moreover, that in the whole universe there are innumerable earths, all of them full of inhabitants. These have been treated of particularly in a small work on those earths from which I will quote the following passage: It is fully known in the other life that there are many earths inhabited by men from which spirits and angels come; for everyone there who desires from a love of truth and of use to do so is permitted to talk with spirits of other earths, and thus be assured that there is a plurality of worlds, and learn that the human race is not from one earth alone, but from innumerable earths. I have frequently talked about this with spirits of our earth, and was told that any intelligent person ought to know from many things that he does know that there are many earths inhabited by men; for it may be reasonably inferred that immense bodies like the planets, some of which exceed this earth in magnitude, are not empty masses created merely to be borne through space and to be carried around the sun, and to shine with their scanty light for the benefit of a single earth, but must have a more important use. He that believes, as everyone must believe, that the Divine created the universe for no other end than that the human race might exist, and heaven therefrom, for the human race is a seminary of heaven, must needs believe that wherever there is an earth there are men. That the planets visible to us because they are within the limits of our solar system are earths is evident from their being bodies of earthy matters, which is known from their reflecting the sun's light, and from their not appearing, when viewed through telescopes, like stars, sparkling with flame, but like earths varied with darker portions; also from their passing like our earth around the sun and following in the path of the zodiac, thus making years and seasons of the year, spring, summer, autumn, and winter, also revolving on their axes like our earth, making days and times of the day, morning, mid-day, evening, and night; also from some of them having moons, called satellites, that revolve around their earth at stated times, as the moon does around ours; while the planet Saturn, being at a greater distance from the sun, has also a large luminous belt which gives much light, though reflected, to that earth. Who that knows all this and thinks rationally can ever say that the planets are empty bodies? Moreover, I have said to spirits that man might believe that there are more earths in the universe than one, from the fact that the starry heaven is so immense, and the stars there so innumerable, and each of them in its place or in its system a sun, resembling our sun, although of a varying magnitude. Any one who duly weighs the subject must conclude that such an immense whole must needs be a means to an end that is the final end of creation; and this end is a heavenly kingdom in which the Divine may dwell with angels and men. For the visible universe or the heaven illumined by stars so numberless, which are so many suns, is simply a means for the existence of earths with men upon them from whom the heavenly kingdom is derived. From all this a rational man must needs conclude that so immense a means to so great an end could not have been provided merely for the human race on a single earth. What would this be for a Divine that is infinite, to which thousands and even myriads of earths, all of them full of inhabitants, would be little and scarcely anything? There are spirits whose sole pursuit is the acquisition of knowledges, because their delight is in this alone; and for this reason they are permitted to wander about, and even to pass out of our solar system into others, in acquiring knowledge. These spirits, who are from the planet Mercury, have told me that there are earths with men upon them not only in this solar system but also beyond it in the starry heaven in immense numbers. It was calculated that with a million earths in the universe, and on each earth three hundred millions of men, and two hundred generations in six thousand years, and a space of three cubic ells allowed to each man or spirit, the total number of so many men or spirits would not fill the space of this earth, and scarcely more than the space of one of the satellites about one of the planets - a space in the universe so small as to be almost invisible, since a satellite can scarcely be seen by the naked eye. What is this for the Creator of the universe, to whom it would not be sufficient if the whole universe were filled, since He is infinite? I have talked with angels about this, and they said that they had a similar idea of the fewness of the human race compared with the infinity of the Creator, although their thought is from states, not from spaces, and that in their thought earths amounting to as many myriads as could possibly be conceived of would still be nothing at all to the Lord. The earths in the universe, with their inhabitants, and the spirits and angels from them, are treated of in the above mentioned work. What is there related has been revealed and shown to me to the intent that it may be known that the heaven of the Lord is immense, and that it is all from the human race; also that our Lord is every where acknowledged as the God of heaven and earth.

Again, the immensity of the heaven of the Lord is shown in this, that heaven in its entire complex reflects a single Man, and corresponds to all things and each thing in man, and that this correspondence can never be filled out, since it is a correspondence not only with each of the members, organs, and viscera of the body in general, but also with all and each of the little viscera and little organs contained in these in every minutest particular, and even with each vessel and fiber; and not only with these but also with the organic substances that receive interiorly the influx of heaven, from which come man's interior activities that are serviceable to the operations of his mind; since everything that exists interiorly in man exists in forms which are substances, for anything that does not exist in a substance as its subject is nothing. There is a correspondence of all these things with heaven, as can be seen from the chapter treating of the correspondence of all things of heaven with all things of man (n. 87-102). This correspondence can never be filled out because the more numerous the angelic affiliations are that correspond to each member the more perfect heaven becomes; for every perfection in the heavens increases with increase of number; and this for the reason that all there have the same end, and look with one accord to that end. That end is the common good; and when that reigns there is, from the common good, good to each individual, and from the good of each individual there is good to the whole community. This is so for the reason that the Lord turns all in heaven to Himself (see above, n. 123), and thereby makes them to be one in Himself. That the unanimity and concord of many, especially from such an origin and held together by such a bond, produces perfection, everyone with a reason at all enlightened can see clearly.

I have also been permitted to see the extent of the inhabited and also of the uninhabited heaven; and the extent of the uninhabited heaven was seen to be so great that it could not be filled to eternity even if there were many myriads of earths, and as great a multitude of men on each earth as on ours. (On this also see the treatise on The Earths in the Universe, n. 168.)

That heaven is not immense, but it is of limited extent, is a conclusion that some have derived from certain passages in the Word understood according to the sense of its letter; for example, where it is said that only the poor are received into heaven, or only the elect, or only those within the church, and not those outside of it, or only those for whom the Lord intercedes; that heaven is closed when it is filled, and that this time is predetermined. But such are unaware that heaven is never closed, and that there is no time predetermined, or any limit of number; and that those are called the "elect" who are in a life of good and truth; 420-1 and those are called "poor" who are lacking in knowledges of good and truth and yet desire them; and such from that desire are also called hungry. 420-2 Those that have conceived an idea of the small extent of heaven from the Word not understood believe it to be in one place, where all are gathered together; when, in fact, heaven consists of innumerable societies (see above, n. 41-50). Such also have no other idea than that heaven is granted to everyone from mercy apart from means, and thus that there is admission and reception from mere favor; and they fail to understand that the Lord from mercy leads everyone who accepts Him, and that he accepts Him who lives in accordance with the laws of divine order, which are the precepts of love and of faith, and that the mercy that is meant is to be thus led by the Lord from infancy to the last period of life in the world and afterwards to eternity. Let them know, therefore, that every man is born for heaven, and that he is received that receives heaven in himself in the world, and he that does not receive it is shut out.

WHAT THE WORLD OF SPIRITS IS. The world of spirits is not heaven, nor is it hell, but it is the intermediate place or state between the two; for it is the place that man first enters after death; and from which after a suitable time he is either raised up into heaven or cast down into hell in accord with his life in the world.

The world of spirits is an intermediate place between heaven and hell and also an intermediate state of the man after death. It has been shown to me not only that it is an intermediate place, having the hells below it and the heavens above it, but also that it is in an intermediate state, since so long as man is in it he is not yet either in heaven or in hell. The state of heaven in man is the conjunction of good and truth in him; and the state of hell is the conjunction of evil and falsity in him. Whenever good in a man-spirit is conjoined to truth he comes into heaven, because that conjunction, as just said, is heaven in him; but whenever evil in a man-spirit is conjoined with falsity he comes into hell, because that conjunction is hell in him. That conjunction is effected in the world of spirits, man then being in an intermediate state. It is the same thing whether you say the conjunction of the understanding and the will, or the conjunction of good and truth.

Let something first be said about the conjunction of the understanding and the will, and its being the same thing as the conjunction of good and truth, that being the conjunction that is effected in the world of spirits. Man has an understanding and a will. The understanding receives truths and is formed out of them, and the will receives goods and is formed out of them; therefore whatever a man understands and thinks from his understanding he calls true, and whatever a man wills and thinks from his will he calls good. From his understanding man can think and thus perceive both what is true and what is good; and yet he thinks what is true and good from the will only when he wills it and does it. When he wills it and from willing does it, it is both in his understanding and in his will, consequently in the man. For neither the understanding alone nor the will alone makes the man, but the understanding and will together; therefore whatever is in both is in the man, and is appropriated to him. That which is in the understanding alone is in man, and yet not really in him; it is only a thing of his memory, or a matter of knowledge in his memory about which he can think when in company with others and outside of himself, but not in himself; that is, about which he can speak and reason, and can simulate affections and gestures that are in accord with it.

This ability to think from the understanding and not at the same time from the will is provided that man may be capable of being reformed; for reformation is effected by means of truths, and truths pertain to the understanding, as just said. For in respect to his will man is born into every evil, and therefore of himself wills good to no one but himself; and one who wills good to himself alone delights in the misfortunes that befall another, especially when they tend to his own advantage; for his wish is to divert to himself the goods of all others, whether honors or riches, and so far as he succeeds in this he inwardly rejoices. To the end that this will of man may be corrected and reformed, an ability to understand truths, and an ability to subdue by means of truths the affections of evil that spring from the will, are given to man. This is why man has this ability to think truths with his understanding, and to speak them and do them. But until man is such that he wills truths and does them from himself, that is, from the heart, he is not able to think truths from his will. When he becomes such, whatever he thinks from his understanding belongs to his faith, and whatever he thinks from his will belongs to his love; and in consequence his faith and his love, like his understanding and his will, are conjoined in him.

To the extent, therefore, that the truths of the understanding and the goods of the will are conjoined, that is, to the extent that a man wills truths and does them from his will, he has heaven in himself, since the conjunction of good and truth, as just said, is heaven. And on the other hand, just to the extent that the falsities of the understanding and the evils of the will are conjoined man has hell in himself, since the conjunction of falsity and evil is hell. But so long as the truths of the understanding and the goods of the will are not conjoined man is in an intermediate state. At the present time nearly everyone is in such a state that he has some knowledge of truths, and from his knowledge and understanding gives some thought to them, and conforms to them either much or little or not at all, or acts contrary to them from a love of evil and consequent false belief. In order, therefore, that man may have in him either heaven or hell, he is first brought after death into the world of spirits, and there with those who are to be raised up into heaven good and truth are conjoined, and with those who are to be cast down into hell evil and falsity are conjoined. For neither in heaven nor in hell is any one permitted to have a divided mind, that is, to understand one thing and to will another; but everyone must understand what he wills, and will what he understands. Therefore in heaven he who wills good understands truth, while in hell he who wills evil understands falsity. So in the intermediate state the falsities that the good have are put away, and truths that agree and harmonize with their good are given them; while the truths that the evil have are put away, and falsities that agree and harmonize with their evil are given them. This shows what the world of spirits is.

In the world of spirits there are vast numbers, because the first meeting of all is there, and all are there explored and prepared. The time of their stay in that world is not fixed; some merely enter it, and are soon either taken into heaven or are cast down into hell; some remain only a few weeks, some several years, but not more than thirty. These differences in the time they remain depend on the correspondence or lack of correspondence of man's interiors with his exteriors. How man is led in that world from one state into another and prepared shall now be told.

As soon as men after death enter the world of spirits the Lord clearly discriminates between them; and the evil are at once attached to the infernal society in which they were, as to their ruling love while in the world; and the good are at once attached to the heavenly society in which they were as to their love, charity and faith while in the world. But although they are thus divided, all that have been friends and acquaintances in the life of the body, especially wives and husbands, and also brothers and sisters, meet and converse together whenever they so desire. I have seen a father talking with six sons, whom he recognized, and have seen many others with their relatives and friends; but having from their life in the world diverse dispositions, after a short time they separate. But those who have passed from the world of spirits into heaven or into hell, unless they have a like disposition from a like love, no longer see or know each other. The reason that they see each other in the world of spirits, but not in heaven or in hell, is that those who are in the world of spirits are brought into one state after another, like those they experienced in the life of the body; but afterwards all are brought into a permanent state in accord with their ruling love, and in that state one recognizes another only by similarity of love; for then similarity joins and dissimilarity disjoins (see above, n. 41-50).

As the world of spirits is an intermediate state between heaven and hell with man, so it is an intermediate place with the hells below and the heavens above. All the hells are shut towards that world, being open only through holes and clefts like those in rocks and through wide openings that are so guarded that no one can come out except by permission, which is granted in cases of urgent necessity (of which hereafter). Heaven, too, is enclosed on all sides; and there is no passage open to any heavenly society except by a narrow way, the entrance to which is also guarded. These outlets and entrances are what are called in the Word the gates and doors of hell and of heaven.

The world of spirits appears like a valley between mountains and rocks, with windings and elevations here and there. The gates and doors of the heavenly societies are visible to those only who are prepared for heaven; others cannot find them. There is one entrance from the world of spirits to each heavenly society, opening through a single path which branches out in its ascent into several. The gates and doors of the hells also are visible only to those who are about to enter, to whom they are then opened. When these are opened gloomy and seemingly sooty caverns are seen tending obliquely downwards to the abyss, where again there are many doors. Through these caverns nauseous and fetid stenches exhale, which good spirits flee from because they abominate them, but evil spirits seek for them because they delight in them. For as everyone in the world has been delighted with his own evil, so after death he is delighted with the stench to which his evil corresponds. In this respect the evil may be likened to rapacious birds and beasts, like ravens, wolves, and swine, which fly or run to carrion or dunghills when they scent their stench. I heard a certain spirit crying out loudly as if from inward torture when struck by a breath flowing forth from heaven; but he became tranquil and glad as soon as a breath flowing forth from hell reached him.

With every man there are two gates; one that leads to hell and that is open to evils and their falsities; while the other leads to heaven and is open to goods and their truths. Those that are in evil and its falsity have the gate to hell opened in them, and only through chinks from above does something of light from heaven flow into them, and by that inflowing they are able to think, to reason, and to speak; but the gate to heaven is opened in those that are in good and its truth. For there are two ways that lead to the rational mind of man; a higher or internal way through which good and truth from the Lord enter, and a lower or external way through which evil and falsity enter from hell. The rational mind itself is at the middle point to which the ways tend. Consequently, so far as light from heaven is admitted man is rational; but so far as it is not admitted he is not rational, however rational he may seem to himself to be. This has been said to make known the nature of the correspondence of man with heaven and with hell. While man's rational mind is being formed it corresponds to the world of spirits, what is above it corresponding to heaven and what is below to hell. With those preparing for heaven the regions above the rational mind are opened, but those below are closed to the influx of evil and falsity; while with those preparing for hell the parts below it are opened, and the parts above it are closed to the influx of good and truth. Thus the latter can look only to what is below themselves, that is, to hell; while the former can look only to what is above themselves, that is, to heaven. To look above themselves is to look to the Lord, because He is the common center to which all things of heaven look; while to look below themselves is to look backwards from the Lord to the opposite center, to which all things of hell look and tend (see above, n. 123, 124).

In the preceding pages whenever spirits are mentioned those that are in the world of spirits are meant; but when angels are mentioned those that are in heaven are meant.

XLV. IN RESPECT TO HIS INTERIORS EVERY MAN IS A SPIRIT. Whoever duly considers the subject can see that as the body is material it is not the body that thinks, but the soul, which is spiritual. The soul of man, upon the immortality of which many have written, is his spirit, for this as to everything belonging to it is immortal. This also is what thinks in the body, for it is spiritual, and what is spiritual receives what is spiritual and lives spiritually, which is to think and to will. Therefore, all rational life that appears in the body belongs to the soul, and nothing of it to the body; for the body, as just said, is material, and the material, which is the property of the body, is added to and apparently almost joined to the spirit, in order that the spirit of man may be able to live and perform uses in the natural world, all things of which are material and in themselves devoid of life. And as it is the spiritual only that lives and not the material, it can be seen that whatever lives in man is his spirit, and that the body merely serves it, just as what is instrumental serves a moving living force. An instrument is said indeed to act, to move, or to strike; but to believe that these are acts of the instrument, and not of him who acts, moves, or strikes by means of the instrument, is a fallacy.

As everything in the body that lives, and that acts and feels from that life, belongs exclusively to the spirit, and nothing of it to the body, it follows that the spirit is the man himself; or what is the same thing, that a man viewed in himself is a spirit possessing a like form; for whatever lives and feels in man belongs to his spirit and everything in man, from his head to the sole of his foot, lives and feels; and in consequence when the body is separated from its spirit, which is what is called dying, man continues to be a man and to live. I have heard from heaven that some who die, while they are lying upon the bier, before they are resuscitated, continue to think even in their cold body, and do not know that they are not still alive, except that they are unable to move a particle of matter belonging to the body.

Unless man were a subject which is a substance that can serve a source and containant he would be unable to think and will. Any thing that is supposed to exist apart from a substantial subject is nothing. This can be seen from the fact that a man is unable to see without an organ which is the subject of his sight, or to hear without an organ which is the subject of his hearing. Apart from these organs, sight and hearing are nothing and have no existence. The same is true of thought, which is inner sight, and of perception, which is inner hearing; unless these were in substances and from substances which are organic forms and subjects, they would have no existence at all. All this shows that man's spirit as well as his body is in a form, and that it is in a human form, and enjoys sensories and senses when separated from the body the same as when it was in it, and that all the life of the eye and all the life of the ear, in a word, all the life of sense that man has, belongs not to his body but to his spirit, which dwells in these organs and in their minutest particulars. This is why spirits see, hear, and feel, as well as men. But when the spirit has been loosed from the body, these senses are exercised in the spiritual world, not in the natural world. The natural sensation that the spirit had when it was in the body it had by means of the material part that was added to it; but it then had also spiritual sensations in its thinking and willing.

All this has been said to convince the rational man that viewed in himself man is a spirit, and that the corporeal part that is added to the spirit to enable it to perform its functions in the natural and material world is not the man, but only an instrument of his spirit. But evidences from experience are preferable, because there are many that fail to comprehend rational deductions; and those that have established themselves in the opposite view turn such deductions into grounds of doubt by means of reasonings from the fallacies of the senses. Those that have established themselves in the opposite view are accustomed to think that beasts likewise have life and sensations and thus have a spiritual part, the same as man has, and yet that part dies with the body. But the spiritual of beasts is not the same as the spiritual of man is; for man has what beasts have not, an inmost, into which the Divine flows, raising man up to Itself, and thereby conjoining man to Itself. Because of this, man, in contrast with beasts, has the ability to think about God and about the Divine things of heaven and the church, and to love God from these and in these, and thus be conjoined to Him; and whatever can be conjoined to the Divine cannot be dissipated, but whatever cannot be conjoined is dissipated. The inmost that man has, in contrast with beasts, has been treated of above (n. 39), and what was there said will here be repeated, since it is important to have the fallacies dispelled that have been engendered in the minds of many who from lack of knowledge and trained intellect are unable to form rational conclusions on the subject. The words are these: I will mention a certain arcanum respecting the angels of the three heavens, which has not hitherto come into any one's mind, because degrees have not been understood. In every angel and in every man there is an inmost or highest degree, or an inmost or highest something, into which the Divine of the Lord first or most directly flows, and from which it disposes the other interiors in him that succeed in accordance with the degrees of order. This inmost or highest degree may be called the entrance of the Lord to the angel or man, and His veriest dwelling-place in them. It is by virtue of this inmost or highest that a man is a man, and distinguished from the animals, which do not have it. From this it is that man, unlike the animals, is capable, in respect to all his interiors which pertain to his mind and disposition, of being raised up by the Lord to Himself, of believing in the Lord, of being moved by love to the Lord, and thereby beholding Him, and of receiving intelligence and wisdom, and speaking from reason. Also it is by virtue of this that he lives to eternity. But what is arranged and provided by the Lord in this inmost does not distinctly fall into the perception of any angel, because it is above his thought and transcends his wisdom.

That in respect to his interiors man is a spirit I have been permitted to learn from much experience, which, to employ a common saying, would fill volumes if I were to describe it all. I have talked with spirits as a spirit, and I have talked with them as a man in the body; and when I talked with them as a spirit they knew no otherwise than that I myself was a spirit and in a human form as they were. Thus did my interiors appear before them, for when talking with them as a spirit my material body was not seen.

That in respect to his interiors man is a spirit can be seen from the fact that after his separation from the body, which takes place when he dies, man goes on living as a man just as before. That I might be convinced of this I have been permitted to talk with nearly everyone I had ever known in their life in the body; with some for hours, with some for weeks and months, and with some for years, and this chiefly that I might be sure of it and might testify to it.

To this may be added that every man in respect to his spirit, even while he is living in the body, is in some society with spirits, although he does not know it; if a good man he is by means of spirits in some angelic society; if an evil man in some infernal society; and after death he comes into that same society. This has been often told and shown to those who after death have come among spirits. Man, to be sure, does not appear in that society as a spirit while he is living in the world, for the reason that he then thinks naturally; but when one is thinking abstractly from the body, because he is then in the spirit, he sometimes appears in his society; and when seen he is easily distinguished from the spirits there, for he goes about meditating and in silence, not looking at others, and apparently not seeing them; and as soon as any spirit speaks to him he vanishes.

To make clear that man in respect to his interiors is a spirit I will relate from experience what happens when man is withdrawn from the body, and what it is to be carried away by the spirit to another place.

First, as to withdrawal from the body, it happens thus. Man is brought into a certain state that is midway between sleeping and waking, and when in that state he seems to himself to be wide awake; all the senses are as perfectly awake as in the completest bodily wakefulness, not only the sight and the hearing, but what is wonderful, the sense of touch also, which is then more exquisite than is ever possible when the body is awake. In this state spirits and angels have been seen to the very life, and have been heard, and what is wonderful, have been touched, with almost nothing of the body intervening. This is the state that is called being withdrawn from the body, and not knowing whether one is in the body or out of it. I have been admitted into this state only three or four times, that I might learn what it is, and might know that spirits and angels enjoy every sense, and that man does also in respect to his spirit when he is withdrawn from the body.

As to being carried away by the spirit to another place, I have been shown by living experience what it is, and how it is done, but only two or three times. I will relate a single instance. Walking through the streets of a city and through fields, talking at the same time with spirits, I knew no otherwise than that I was fully awake, and in possession of my usual sight. Thus I walked on without going astray, and all the while with clear vision, seeing groves, rivers, palaces, houses, men, and other objects. But after walking thus for some hours, suddenly I saw with my bodily eyes, and noted that I was in another place. Being greatly astonished I perceived that I had been in the same state as those who were said to have been led away by the spirit into another place. For in this state the distance, even though it be many miles, and the time, though it be many hours or days, are not thought of; neither is there any feeling of fatigue; and one is led unerringly through ways of which he himself is ignorant, even to the destined place.

But these two states of man, which are his states when he is in his interiors, or what is the same, when he is in the spirit, are extraordinary; but as they are states known about in the church, they were exhibited to me only that I might know what they are. But it has been granted to me now for many years to speak with spirits and to be with them as one of them, even in full wakefulness of the body.

That in respect to his interiors man is a spirit there are further evidences in what has been said and shown above (n. 311-317), where it is explained that heaven and hell are from the human race.

That man is a spirit in respect to his interiors means in respect to the things pertaining to his thought and will, for these are the interiors themselves that make man to be man, and such a man as he is in respect to these interiors.

XLVI. THE RESUSCITATION OF MAN FROM THE DEAD AND HIS ENTRANCE INTO ETERNAL LIFE. When the body is no longer able to perform the bodily functions in the natural world that correspond to the spirit's thoughts and affections, which the spirit has from the spiritual world, man is said to die. This takes place when the respiration of the lungs and the beatings of the heart cease. But the man does not die; he is merely separated from the bodily part that was of use to him in the world, while the man himself continues to live. It is said that the man himself continues to live since man is not a man because of his body but because of his spirit, for it is the spirit that thinks in man, and thought with affection is what constitutes man. Evidently, then, the death of man is merely his passing from one world into another. And this is why in the Word in its internal sense "death" signifies resurrection and continuation of life. 445-1

There is an inmost communication of the spirit with the breathing and with the beating of the heart, the spirit's thought communicating with the breathing, and its affection, which is of love, with the heart; 446-1 consequently when these two motions cease in the body there is at once a separation. These two motions, the respiration of the lungs and the beating of heart, are the very bond on the sundering of which the spirit is left to itself; and the body being then deprived of the life of its spirit grows cold and begins to decay. This inmost communication of the spirit of man is with the respiration and with the heart, because on these all vital motions depend, not only in general but in every particular. 446-2

After the separation the spirit of man continues in the body for a short time, but only until the heart's action has wholly ceased, which happens variously in accord with the diseased condition that causes death, with some the motion of the heart continuing for some time, with others not so long. As soon as this motion ceases the man is resuscitated; but this is done by the Lord alone. Resuscitation means the drawing forth of the spirit from the body, and its introduction into the spiritual world; this is commonly called the resurrection. The spirit is not separated from the body until the motion of the heart has ceased, for the reason that the heart corresponds to the affection of love, which is the very life of man, for it is from love that everyone has vital heat; 447-1 consequently as long as this conjunction continues correspondence continues, and thereby the life of the spirit in the body.

How this resuscitation is effected has both been told to me and shown to me in living experience. The actual experience was granted to me that I might have a complete knowledge of the process.

As to the senses of the body I was brought into a state of insensibility, thus nearly into the state of the dying; but with the interior life and thought remaining unimpaired, in order that I might perceive and retain in the memory the things that happened to me, and that happen to those that are resuscitated from the dead. I perceived that the respiration of the body was almost wholly taken away; but the interior respiration of the spirit went on in connection with a slight and tacit respiration of the body. Then at first a communication of the pulse of the heart with the celestial kingdom was established, because that kingdom corresponds to the heart in man. 449-1 Angels from that kingdom were seen, some at a distance, and two sitting near my head. Thus all my own affection was taken away although thought and perception continued. [2] I was in this state for some hours. Then the spirits that were around me withdrew, thinking that I was dead; and an aromatic odor like that of an embalmed body was perceived, for when the celestial angels are present everything pertaining to the corpse is perceived as aromatic, and when spirits perceive this they cannot approach; and in this way evil spirits are kept away from man's spirit when he is being introduced into eternal life. The angels seated at my head were silent, merely sharing their thoughts with mine; and when their thoughts are received the angels know that the spirit of man is in a state in which it can be drawn forth from the body. This sharing of their thoughts was effected by looking into my face, for in this way in heaven thoughts are shared. [3] As my thought and perception continued, that I might know and remember how resuscitation is effected, I perceived the angels first tried to ascertain what my thought was, whether it was like the thought of those who are dying, which is usually about eternal life; also that they wished to keep my mind in that thought. Afterwards I was told that the spirit of man is held in its last thought when the body expires, until it returns to the thoughts that are from its general or ruling affection in the world. Especially was I permitted to see and feel that there was a pulling and drawing forth, as it were, of the interiors of my mind, thus of my spirit, from the body; and I was told that this is from the Lord, and that the resurrection is thus effected.

The celestial angels who are with the one that is resuscitated do not withdraw from him, because they love everyone; but when the spirit comes into such a state that he can no longer be affiliated with celestial angels, he longs to get away from them. When this takes place angels from the Lord's spiritual kingdom come, through whom is given the use of light; for before this he saw nothing, but merely thought. I was shown how this is done. The angels appeared to roll off, as it were, a coat from the left eye towards the bridge of the nose, that the eye might be opened and be enabled to see. This is only an appearance, but to the spirit it seemed to be really done. When the coat thus seems to have been rolled off there is a slight sense of light, but very dim, like what is seen through the eyelids on first awakening from sleep. To me this dim light took on a heavenly hue, but I was told afterwards that the color varies. Then something is felt to be gently rolled off from the face, and when this is done spiritual thought is awakened. This rolling off from the face is also an appearance, which represents the spirit's passing from natural thought into spiritual thought. The angels are extremely careful that only such ideas as savor of love shall proceed from the one resuscitated. They now tell him that he is a spirit. When he has come into the enjoyment of light the spiritual angels render to the new spirit every service he can possibly desire in that state; and teach him about the things of the other life so far as he can comprehend them. But if he has no wish to be taught the spirit longs to get away from the company of the angels. Nevertheless, the angels do not withdraw from him, but he separates himself from them; for the angels love everyone, and desire nothing so much as to render service, to teach, and to lead into heaven; this constitutes their highest delight. When the spirit has thus withdrawn he is received by good spirits, and as long as he continues in their company everything possible is done for him. But if he had lived such a life in the world as would prevent his enjoying the company of the good he longs to get away from the good, and this experience is repeated until he comes into association with such as are in entire harmony with his life in the world; and with such he finds his own life, and what is surprising, he then leads a life like that which he led in the world.

Footnotes

405-1 One thing consists of various things, and receives thereby its form and quality and perfection in accordance with the quality of the harmony and concurrence (n. 457, 3241, 8003). There is an infinite variety and never any one thing the same as another (n. 7236, 9002). It is the same in the heavens (n. 3744, 4005, 7236, 7833, 7836, 9002). In consequence all the societies in the heavens and all the angels in a society are distinct from each other because they are in different goods and uses (n. 690, 3241, 3519, 3804, 3986, 4067, 4149, 4263, 7236, 7833). The Lord's Divine love arranges all into a heavenly form, and so conjoins them that they are as a single man (n. 457, 3986, 5598).

420-1 Those are the elect who are in a life of good and truth (n. 3755, 3900). Election and reception into heaven are not from mercy, as that term is understood, but are in accordance with the life (n. 5057, 5058). There is no mercy of the Lord apart from means, but only through means, that is, to those that live in accordance with His precepts; such the Lord from His mercy leads continually in the world, and afterwards to eternity (n. 8700, 10659).

420-2 By the "poor," in the Word, those are meant who are spiritually poor, that is, who are ignorant of truth and yet wish to he taught (n. 9209, 9253, 10227). Such are said to hunger and thirst, which is to desire knowledges of good and of truth, by which there is introduction into the church and into heaven (n. 4958, 10227).

445-1 In the Word "death" signifies resurrection, for when man dies his life still goes on (n. 3498, 3505, 4618, 4621, 6036, 6221).

446-1 The heart corresponds to the will, thus to the affection which belongs to the love, while the respiration of the lungs corresponds to the understanding, thus to the thought (n. 3888). From this the "heart" in the Word signifies the will and love (n. 7542, 9050, 10336). The "soul" signifies understanding, faith, and truth; therefore "from the soul and from the heart" signifies what is from the understanding, faith, and truth, and what is from the will, love, and good (n. 2930, 9050). The correspondence of the heart and lungs with the Greatest Man, or heaven (n. 3883-3895).

446-2 The beating of the heart and the respiration of the lungs reign in the body throughout, and flow mutually into every part (n. 3887, 3889, 3890).

447-1 Love is the being [esse] of the life of man (n. 5002). Love is spiritual heat, and therefore the very vital itself of man (n. 1589, 2146, 3338, 4906, 7081-7086, 9954, 10740). Affection is a continuation of love (n. 3938).

449-1 The heart corresponds to the Lord's celestial kingdom, the lungs to His spiritual kingdom (n. 3635, 3886, 3887).

Section 10

This opening state of man's life after death lasts only a few days. How he is afterwards led from one state to another, and finally either into heaven or into hell, will be told in what follows. This, too, I have been permitted to learn by much experience.

I have talked with some on the third day after their decease, when the process described above (n. 449, 450) had been completed, especially with three whom I had known in the world, to whom I mentioned that arrangements were now being made for burying their bodies; I said, for burying them; on hearing which they were smitten with a kind of surprise, saying that they were alive, and that the thing that had served them in the world was what was being buried. Afterwards they wondered greatly that they had not believed in such a life after death while they lived in the body, and especially that scarcely any within the church so believed. Those that have not believed in the world in any life of the soul after the life of the body are greatly ashamed when they find themselves to be alive. But those that have confirmed themselves in that disbelief seek affiliation with their like, and are separated from those that have had faith. Such are for the most part attached to some infernal society, because they have also denied the divine and have despised the truths of the church; for so far as any one confirms himself against the eternal life of his soul he confirms himself also against whatever pertains to heaven and the church.

MAN AFTER DEATH IS IN A COMPLETE HUMAN FORM It has already been shown in several previous chapters that the form of the spirit of man is the human form, that is, that the spirit is a man even in form, especially where it is shown that every angel has a complete human form (n. 73-77) that in respect to his interiors every man is a spirit (n. 432-444); and that the angels in heaven are from the human race (n. 311-317). [2] This can be seen still more clearly from the fact that it is by virtue of his spirit, and not by virtue of his body that man is a man, and that the bodily form is added to the spirit in accordance with the spirit's form, and not the reverse, for it is in accordance with its own form that the spirit is clothed with a body. Consequently the spirit of man acts into every part of the body, even the minutest, insomuch that if any part is not actuated by the spirit, or the spirit is not active in it, it does not live. Any one can see that this is true from this fact alone, that thought and will actuate all things and each thing of the body with such entire command that everything concurs, and any thing that does not concur is not a part of the body, but is cast out as something without life; and thought and will belong, not to the body, but to the spirit of man. [3] A spirit that has been loosed from the body or the spirit in another man, is not visible in the human form to man, because the body's organ of sight, or its eye, so far as it sees in the world, is a material organ, and what is material can see only what is material, while what is spiritual sees what is spiritual. When, therefore, the material part of the eye becomes darkened and is deprived of its cooperation with the spiritual, the eye sees spirits in their own form, which is the human form, not only the spirits that are in the spiritual world, but also the spirit of another man while it is yet in its body.

The form of the spirit is the human form because man is created in respect to his spirit in the form of heaven, for all things of heaven and of the order of heaven are brought together in the things that constitute the mind of man; 454-1 and from this comes his capacity to receive intelligence and wisdom. Whether you say the capacity to receive intelligence and wisdom or the capacity to receive heaven it is the same thing, as can be seen from what has been shown about the light and heat of heaven (n. 126-140); the form of heaven (n. 200-212); the wisdom of angels (n. 265-275); and in the chapter that the form of heaven as a whole and in part reflects a single man (n. 59-77); and this by virtue of the Divine Human of the Lord, which is the source of heaven and its form (n. 78-86).

That which has now been said can be understood by the rational man, for he can see it from the connection of causes and from truths in their order; but it is not understood by a man who is not rational, and for several reasons, the chief of which is that he has no desire to understand it because it is opposed to the falsities that he has made his truths; and he that is unwilling to understand for this reason has closed to his rational faculty the way to heaven, although that way can still be opened whenever the will's resistance ceases (see above, n. 424). That man is able to understand truths and be rational whenever he so wishes has been made clear to me by much experience. Evil spirits that have become irrational in the world by rejecting the Divine and the truths of the church, and confirming themselves against them, have frequently been turned by Divine power towards those who were in the light of truth, and they then comprehended all things as the angels did, and acknowledged them to be true, and also that they comprehended them all. But the moment these spirits relapsed into themselves, and turned back to the love of their will, they had no comprehension of truths and affirmed the opposite. [2] I have also heard certain dwellers in hell saying that they knew and perceived that which they did to be evil and that which they thought to be false; but that they were unable to resist the delight of their love, that is, their will, and that it is their will that drives their thought to see evil as good and falsity as truth. Evidently, then, those that are in falsity from evil have the ability to understand and be rational, but have no wish to; and they have no wish to for the reason that they have loved falsities more than truths, because these agree with the evils in which they are. To love and to will is the same thing, for what a man wills he loves, and what he loves he wills. [3] Because the state of men is such that they are able to understand truths if they wish to, I have been permitted to confirm spiritual truths, which are truths of heaven and the church, even by reasonings, and this in order that the falsities by which the rational mind in many has been closed up may be dispersed by reasonings, and thus the eye may perhaps in some degree be opened; for to confirm spiritual goods by reasonings is permitted to all that are in truths. Who could ever understand the Word from the sense of its letter, unless he saw from an enlightened reason the truths it contains? Is not this the source of so many heresies from the same Word? 455-1

That the spirit of man, when it has been loosed from the body, is still a man and in a like form, has been proved to me by the daily experience of many years;

for I have seen such and have listened to them a thousand times, and have talked with them about this fact, that men in the world do not believe them to be men, and that those that do believe this are regarded by the learned as simple. Spirits are grieved at heart that such ignorance still continues in the world, and above all within the church. [2] But this belief they said had emanated chiefly from the learned, who had thought about the soul from ideas derived from bodily sense; and from such ideas the only conception they formed of the soul was as being mere thought; and when this is regarded apart from any subject as its containant and source it is merely a fleeting breath of pure ether that must needs be dissipated when the body dies. But as the church believes from the Word in the immortality of the soul they are compelled to ascribe to it something vital, such as pertains to thought, but they deny to it any thing of sense, such as man possesses, until it has again been joined to the body. On this opinion the doctrine in regard to the resurrection is based, with the belief that the soul and body will be joined again at the time of the final judgment. For this reason when any one thinks about the soul in accordance with this doctrine and these conjectures, he has no conception that it is a spirit, and in a human form. And still further, scarcely any one at this day knows what the spiritual is, and still less that spiritual beings, as all spirits and angels are, have any human form. [3] Consequently, nearly all that go from this world are greatly surprised to find that they are alive, and are as much men as before, that they see, hear, and speak, and that their body enjoys the sense of touch as before, with no difference whatever (see above, n. 74). And when they cease to be astonished at themselves they are astonished that the church should know nothing about this state of men after death, thus nothing about heaven or hell, when in fact all that have ever lived in the world are in the other life and live as men. And as they wondered also why this had not been disclosed to man by visions, being an essential of the faith of the church, they were told from heaven that although this might have been done, since nothing is easier when it is the Lord's good pleasure, yet those that have confirmed themselves in the opposite falsities would not believe even if they themselves should behold it; also that there is danger in confirming any thing by visions when men are in falsities, for they would then first believe and afterwards deny, and thus would profane the truth itself, since to believe and afterwards deny is to profane; and those who profane truths are cast down into the lowest and most grievous of all the hells. 456-1 [4] This danger is what is meant by the Lord's words: He hath blinded their eyes and hardened their hearts lest they should see with their eyes, and understand with their heart, and should turn and I should heal them (John 12:40). And that those that are in falsities would not believe [even if visions were given] is meant by these words: Abraham said to the rich man in hell, They have Moses and the Prophets, let them hear them. But he said, Nay, father Abraham, but if one came to them from the dead they would be converted. But Abraham said to him, If they hear not Moses and the Prophets, neither will they believe though one should rise from the dead (Luke 16:29-31).

When the spirit of man first enters the world of spirits, which takes place shortly after his resuscitation, as described above, his face and his tone of voice resemble those he had in the world, because he is then in the state of his exteriors, and his interiors are not as yet uncovered. This is man's first state after death. But subsequently his face is changed, and becomes entirely different, resembling his ruling affection or ruling love, in conformity with which the interiors of his mind had been while he was in the world and his spirit while it was in the body. For the face of a man's spirit differs greatly from the face of his body. The face of his body is from his parents, but the face of his spirit is from his affection, and is an image of it. When the life of the spirit in the body is ended, and its exteriors are laid aside and its interiors disclosed, it comes into this affection. This is man's second state. I have seen some that have recently arrived from the world, and have recognized them from their face and speech; but seeing them afterwards I did not recognize them. Those that had been in good affections appeared with beautiful faces; but those that had been in evil affections with misshapen faces; for man's spirit, viewed in itself, is nothing but his affection; and the face is its outward form. Another reason why faces are changed is that in the other life no one is permitted to counterfeit affections that are not his own, and thus assume looks that are contrary to his love. All in the other life are brought into such a state as to speak as they think, and to manifest in their looks and gestures the inclinations of their will. And because of this the faces of all become forms and images of their affections; and in consequence all that have known each other in the world know each other in the world of spirits, but not in heaven nor in hell (as has been said above, n. 427). 457-1

The faces of hypocrites are changed more slowly than those of others, because by practice they had formed a habit of so managing their interiors as to imitate good affections; consequently for a long time they appear not unbeautiful. But as that which they had assumed is gradually put off, and the interiors of the mind are brought into accord with the form of their affections, they become after awhile more misshapen than others. Hypocrites are such as have been accustomed to talk like angels, but interiorly have acknowledged nature alone and not the Divine, and have therefore denied what pertains to heaven and the church.

It should be known that everyone's human form after death is the more beautiful in proportion as he has more interiorly loved Divine truths and lived according to them; for everyone's interiors are opened and formed in accordance with his love and life; therefore the more interior the affection is the more like heaven it is, and in consequence the more beautiful the face is. This is why the angels in the inmost heaven are the most beautiful, for they are forms of celestial love. But those that have loved Divine truths more exteriorly, and thus have lived in accordance with them in a more external way, are less beautiful; for exterior affections only shine forth from their faces; and through these no interior heavenly love shines, consequently nothing of the form of heaven as it is in itself. There is seen in the faces of such something comparatively obscure, not vivified by any thing of interior life shining through it. In a word, all perfection increases toward interiors and decreases toward exteriors, and as perfection increases and decreases so does beauty. I have seen angelic faces of the third heaven of such radiance that no painter with all his art could possibly give any such light to his colors as to equal a thousandth part of the brightness and life that shone forth from their countenances. But the faces of the angels of the lowest heaven may in some measure be equalled.

In conclusion I will mention a certain arcanum hitherto unknown to any one, namely, that every good and truth that goes forth from the Lord and makes heaven is in the human form; and this not only as a whole and in what is greatest, but also in every part and what is least; also that this form affects everyone who receives good and truth from the Lord, and causes everyone who is in heaven to be in the human form in accordance with his reception of good and truth. It is in consequence of this that heaven is like itself in general and in particular, and that the human form is the form of the whole, of every society, and of every angel (as has been shown in the four chapters from n. 59 to 86); to which let it be added that it is the form of the least things of thought derived from heavenly love with the angels. No man, however, can easily comprehend this arcanum; but it is clearly comprehended by the angels, because they are in the light of heaven.

AFTER DEATH MAN IS POSSESSED OF EVERY SENSE, AND OF ALL THE MEMORY, THOUGHT, AND AFFECTION, THAT HE HAD IN THE WORLD, LEAVING NOTHING BEHIND EXCEPT HIS EARTHLY BODY. It has been proved to me by manifold experience that when man passes from the natural world into the spiritual, as he does when he dies, he carries with him all his possessions, that is, everything that belongs to him as a man, except his earthly body. For when man enters the spiritual world or the life after death, he is in a body as he was in the world, with no apparent difference, since he neither sees nor feels any difference. But his body is then spiritual, and thus separated or purified from all that is earthly; and when what is spiritual touches or sees what is spiritual, it is just the same as when what is natural touches or sees what is natural. So when a man has become a spirit he does not know otherwise than that he is in the same body that he had in the world and thus does not know that he has died. [2] Moreover, a man's spirit enjoys every sense, both outer and inner, that he enjoyed in the world; he sees as before, he hears and speaks as before, smells and tastes, and when touched, he feels the touch as before; he also longs, desires, craves, thinks, reflects, is stirred, loves, wills, as before; and one who takes delight in studies, reads and writes as before. In a word, when a man passes from one life into the other, or from one world into the other, it is like passing from one place into another, carrying with him all things that he had possessed in himself as a man; so that by death, which is only the death of the earthly body, man cannot be said to have lost anything really his own. [3] Furthermore, he carries with him his natural memory, retaining everything that he has heard, seen, read, learned, or thought, in the world from earliest infancy even to the end of life; although the natural objects that are contained in the memory, since they cannot be reproduced in the spiritual world, are quiescent, just as they are when one is not thinking of them. Nevertheless, they are reproduced when the Lord so wills. But more will be said presently about this memory and its state after death. A sensual man finds it impossible to believe that such is the state of man after death, because he cannot comprehend it; for a sensual man must needs think naturally even about spiritual things; therefore, any thing that does not appeal to his senses, that is, that he does not see with his bodily eyes and touch with his hands (as is said of Thomas, John 20:25, 27, 29) he denies the existence of. (What the sensual man is may be seen above, n. 267 and notes.)

[a.] And yet there is a great difference between man's life in the spiritual world and his life in the natural world, in regard both to his outer senses and their affections and his inner senses and their affections. Those that are in heaven have more exquisite senses, that is, a keener sight and hearing, and also think more wisely than when they were in the world; for they see in the light of heaven, which surpasses by many degrees the light of the world (see above, n. 126); and they hear by means of a spiritual atmosphere, which likewise surpasses by many degrees the earthly atmosphere (n. 235). This difference in respect to the outward senses is like the difference between clear sunshine and dark cloudiness in the world, or between noonday light and evening shade. For the light of heaven, since it is Divine truth, enables the eyes of angels to perceive and distinguish most minute things. [2] Moreover, their outer sight corresponds to their inner sight or understanding; for with angels one sight so flows into the other as to act as one with it; and this gives them their great keenness of vision. In like manner, their hearing corresponds to their perception, which pertains both to the understanding and to the will, and in consequence they perceive in the tone and words of one speaking the most minute things of his affection and thought; in the tone what pertains to his affection, and in the words what pertains to his thought (see above, n. 234-245). But the rest of the senses with the angels are less exquisite than the senses of seeing and hearing, for the reason that seeing and hearing serve their intelligence and wisdom, and the rest do not; and if the other senses were equally exquisite they would detract from the light and joy of their wisdom, and would let in the delight of pleasures pertaining to various appetites and to the body; and so far as these prevail they obscure and weaken the understanding. This takes place in the world, where men become gross and stupid in regard to spiritual truths so far as they indulge the sense of taste and yield to the allurements of the sense of touch. [3] From what has already been said and shown in the chapter on the wisdom of the angels of heaven (n. 265-275), it can be seen that the inner senses also of the angels of heaven, which pertain to their thought and affection, are more exquisite and perfect than the senses they had in the world. But as regards the state of those that are in hell as compared with the state of those in the world there is also a great difference, for as great as is the perfection and excellence of the outer and inner senses of the angels in heaven, with those who are in hell the imperfection is equally great. But the state of these will be treated of hereafter. 462. [b.] That when a man leaves the world he takes with him all his memory has been shown to me in many ways, and many of the things I have seen and heard are worthy of mention, some of which I will relate in order. There were some who denied their crimes and villainies which they had perpetrated in the world; and in consequence, that they might not be believed innocent, all their deeds were disclosed and reviewed from their memory in order, from their earliest to their latest years; these were chiefly adulteries and whoredoms. [2] There were some who had deceived others by wicked arts and had committed thefts. The deceits and thefts of these were also enumerated in detail, many of which were known to scarcely any in the world except themselves. These deeds they confessed, because they were plainly set forth, with every thought, intention, pleasure, and fear which occupied their minds at the time. [3] There were others who had accepted bribes, and had rendered venal judgments, who were similarly explored from their memory and from it everything they had done from the beginning to the end of their office was reviewed. Every detail in regard to what and how much they had received, as well as the time, and their state of mind and intention, were brought to their recollection and made visibly clear to the number of many hundreds. This was done with several and what is wonderful, in some cases their memorandum-books, in which they had recorded these things, were opened and read before them page by page. [4] Others who had enticed maidens to shame or had violated chastity were called to a like judgment; and the details of their crimes were drawn forth from their memory and reviewed. The very faces of the maidens and women were also exhibited as if present, with the places, words and intentions, and this as suddenly as when a scene is presented to the sight, the exhibitions continuing sometimes for hours. [5] There was one who had made light of slandering others; and I heard his slanders recounted in order, and his defamations, with the very words, and the persons about whom and before whom they were uttered; all of which were produced and presented to the very life, although while he lived in the world he had most carefully concealed everything. [6] There was one who had deprived a relative of his inheritance under a fraudulent pretext; and he was in like manner convicted and judged; and what is wonderful, the letters and papers that passed between them were read in my hearing, and it was said that not a word was lacking. [7] The same person shortly before his death had also secretly poisoned his neighbor. This was disclosed in this way. He appeared to be digging a trench under his feet, from which a man came forth as out of a grave, and cried out to him, "What have you done to me?" Then everything was revealed, how the poisoner had talked with him in a friendly manner, and had held out the cup, also what he thought beforehand, and what happened afterwards. When all this had been disclosed he was sentenced to hell. [8] In a word, to each evil spirit all his evils, villainies, robberies, artifices, and deceits are made clear, and are brought forth from his very memory, and his guilt is fully established; nor is there any possible room for denial, because all the circumstances are exhibited together. Moreover, I have learned from a man's memory, when it was seen and inspected by angels, what his thoughts had been for a month, one day after another, and this without mistake, the thoughts being recalled just as they arose from day to day. [9] From these examples it can be seen that man carries with him all of his memory, and that nothing can be so concealed in the world as not to be disclosed after death, which is done in the presence of many, according to the Lord's words: There is nothing concealed that shall not be uncovered, and nothing secret that shall not be known; therefore what ye have spoken in the dark shall be heard in the light and what ye have spoken in the ear shall be proclaimed on the housetops (Luke 12:2, 3).

In disclosing his acts to a man after death, the angels to whom the office of searching is assigned look into his face, and their search extends through the whole body, beginning with the fingers of each hand, and thus proceeding through the whole. As I wondered at this the reason was given, namely, that as all things of the thought and will are inscribed on the brain, for their beginnings are there, so are they likewise inscribed on the whole body, since all things of thought and will extend from their beginnings into all things of the body and there terminate as in their outmosts; and this is why the things that are inscribed on the memory from the will and consequent thought are inscribed not only on the brain, but also upon the whole man, and there exist in order in accordance with the order of the parts of the body. It was thus made clear that man as a whole is such as he is in his will and its thought, even to the extent that an evil man is his own evil, and a good man his own good. 463-1 This shows what is meant by the book of man's life spoken of in the Word, namely, that all things that he has done and all things that he has thought are inscribed on the whole man, and when they are called forth from the memory they appear as if read in a book, and when the spirit is viewed in the light of heaven, they appear as in an image. To all this I would add something remarkable in regard to the continuance of the memory after death, by which I was assured that not only things in general but also the minutest particulars that have entered the memory remain and are never obliterated. I saw books there containing writings as in the world, and was told that they were from the memory of those who wrote, and that there was not a single word lacking in them that was in a book written by the same person in the world; and thus all the minutest particulars might be drawn from one's memory, even those that he had forgotten in the world. And the reason was given, namely, that man has an external and an internal memory, an external memory belonging to his natural man, and an internal memory belonging to his spiritual man; and that every least thing that a man has thought, willed, spoken, done or even heard and seen, is inscribed on his internal or spiritual memory; 463-2 and that what is there is never erased, since it is also inscribed on the spirit itself and on the members of its body, as has been said above; and that the spirit is thus formed in accordance with the thoughts and acts of its will. I know that this sounds like a paradox, and is therefore difficult to believe; but still it is true. Let no one believe, then, that there is any thing that a man has ever thought in himself or done in secret that can be concealed after death; but let him believe that all things and each single thing are then laid open as clear as day.

Although the external or natural memory remains in man after death, the merely natural things in it are not reproduced in the other life, but only the spiritual things adjoined to the natural by correspondences; but when these are present to the sight they appear in exactly the same form as they had in the natural world; for all things seen in the heavens have just the same appearance as in the world, although in their essence they are not natural but spiritual (as may be seen in the chapter on Representatives and Appearances in Heaven, n. 170-176). [2] But the external or natural memory in respect to the things in it that are derived from the material, and from time and space, and from other properties of nature, is not serviceable to the spirit in the way that it was serviceable to it in the world, for whenever man thinks in the world from his external sensual, and not at the same time from his internal or intellectual sensual, he thinks naturally and not spiritually; but in the other life when he is a spirit in the spiritual world he does not think naturally but spiritually, and to think spiritually is to think intellectually or rationally. For this reason the external or natural memory in respect to its material contents is then quiescent, and only those things that man has imbibed in the world by means of material things, and has made rational, come into use. The external memory becomes quiescent in respect to material things because these cannot then be brought forth, since spirits and angels speak from those affections and thoughts that are proper to their minds; and are therefore unable to give expression to any thing that is not in accord with their affections and thoughts as can be seen in what is said about the speech of angels in heaven and their speech with man (n. 234-257). [3] Because of this man after death is rational, not in the degree that he was skilled in languages and sciences in the world, but in the degree in which he became rational by means of these. I have talked with many who were believed in the world to be learned because they were acquainted with ancient languages, such as the Hebrew, Greek, and Latin, but had not cultivated their rational faculty by what is written in those languages. Some of them were seen to be just as simple as those who knew nothing of those languages, and some even stupid, and yet they retained the conceit of being wiser than others. [4] I have talked with some who had believed in the world that man is wise in the measure of the contents of his memory, and who had stored up many things in their memory, speaking almost solely from the memory, and therefore not from themselves but from others, and their rationality had not been at all perfected by means of the things in their memory. Some of these were stupid and some sottish, not in the least comprehending whether a truth is true or not, and seizing upon all falsities that are passed off for truths by those who called themselves learned; for from themselves they are unable to see any thing, whether it be true or not, and consequently are unable to see any thing rationally when listening to others. [5] I have also talked with some who had written much in the world on scientific subjects of every kind, and had thereby acquired a worldwide reputation for learning. Some of these, indeed, had the ability to reason about truths, whether they are true or not; and some, when they had turned to those who were in the light of truth, had some comprehension that truths are true, but still had no wish to comprehend them, and therefore when they were in their own falsities, and thus in themselves, denied them. Some had no more wisdom than the unlearned common people. Thus each differed from the other according as he had cultivated his rational faculty by means of the knowledges he had written about or collated. But those who were opposed to the truths of the church, and who thought from mere knowledges and confirmed themselves thereby in falsities, did not cultivate their rational faculty, but cultivated only an ability to reason, which in the world is believed to be rationality. But this ability is wholly different from rationality; it is an ability to prove any thing it pleases, and from preconceived principles and from fallacies to see falsities and not truths. Such persons can never be brought to acknowledge truths, since truths cannot be seen from falsities; but falsities may be seen from truths. [6] The rational faculty of man is like a garden or shrubbery, or like fresh ground; the memory is the soil, truths known and knowledges are the seeds, the light and heat of heaven cause them to grow; without light and heat there is no germination; so is it with the mind when the light of heaven, which is Divine truth, and the heat of heaven, which is Divine love, are not admitted; rationality is solely from these. It is a great grief to the angels that learned men for the most part ascribe all things to nature, and have thereby so closed up the interiors of their minds as to be unable to see any thing of truth from the light of truth, which is the light of heaven. In consequence of this such in the other life are deprived of their ability to reason that they may not disseminate falsities among the simple good and lead them astray; and are sent away into desert places.

A certain spirit was indignant because he was unable to remember many things that he knew in the life of the body, grieving over the lost pleasure which he had so much enjoyed, but he was told that he had lost nothing at all, that he still knew each and everything that he had known, although in the world where he now was no one was permitted to call forth such things from the memory, and that he ought to be satisfied that he could now think and speak much better and more perfectly than before, and that his rational was not now immersed as before in gross, obscure, material and corporeal things, which are of no use in the kingdom into which he had now come; also that he now possessed everything conducive to the uses of eternal life, and that this is the only way of becoming blessed and happy; and therefore it is the part of ignorance to believe that in this kingdom intelligence perishes with the removal or quiescence of the material things in the memory; for the real fact is that so far as the mind can be withdrawn from things of sense pertaining to the external man or the body, so far it is elevated to things spiritual and heavenly.

What these two memories are is sometimes presented to view in the other life in forms not elsewhere seen; for many things which in man take the form of ideas are there presented as objects of sight. The external memory there presents the appearance of a callus, the internal the appearance of a medullary substance like that in the human brain; and from this what they are can be known. With those that have devoted themselves in the life of the body to the cultivation of the memory alone, and have not cultivated their rational faculty, the callosity appears hard and streaked within as with tendons. With those that have filled the memory with falsities it appears hairy and rough, because of the confused mass of things in it. With those that have cultivated the memory with the love of self and the world as an end it appears glued together and ossified. With those that have wished to penetrate into Divine arcana by means of learning, especially of a philosophical kind, with an unwillingness to believe until convinced by such proofs, the memory appears like a dark substance, of such a nature as to absorb the rays of light and turn them into darkness. With those that have practiced deceit and hypocrisy it appears hard and bony like ebony, which reflects the rays of light. But with those that have been in the good of love and the truths of faith there is no such callous appearance, because their inner memory transmits the rays of light into the outer; and in its objects or ideas as in their basis or their ground, the rays terminate and find delightful receptacles; for the outer memory is the out most of order in which, when goods and truths are there, the spiritual and heavenly things are gently terminated and find their seat.

Men living in the world who are in love to the Lord and charity toward the neighbor have with them and in them angelic intelligence and wisdom, but it is then stored up in the inmosts of the inner memory; and they are not at all conscious of it until they put off corporeal things. Then the natural memory is laid asleep and they awake into their inner memory, and then gradually into angelic memory itself.

How the rational faculty may be cultivated shall also be told in a few words.

The genuine rational faculty consists of truths and not of falsities; whatever consists of falsities is not rational. There are three kinds of truths, civil, moral, and spiritual. Civil truths relate to matters of judgment and of government in kingdoms, and in general to what is just and equitable in them. Moral truths pertain to the matters of everyone's life which have regard to companionships and social relations, in general to what is honest and right, and in particular to virtues of every kind. But spiritual truths relate to matters of heaven and of the church, and in general to the good of love and the truth of faith. [2] In every man there are three degrees of life (see above, n. 267). The rational faculty is opened to the first degree by civil truths, to the second degree by moral truths, and to the third degree by spiritual truths. But it must be understood that the rational faculty that consists of these truths is not formed and opened by man's knowing them, but by his living according to them; and living according to them means loving them from spiritual affection; and to love truths from spiritual affection is to love what is just and equitable because it is just and equitable, what is honest and right because it is honest and right, and what is good and true because it is good and true; while living according to them and loving them from the bodily affection is loving them for the sake of self and for the sake of one's reputation, honor or gain. Consequently, so far as man loves these truths from a bodily affection he fails to become rational, for he loves, not them, but himself; and the truths are made to serve him as servants serve their Lord; and when truths become servants they do not enter the man and open any degree of life in him, not even the first, but merely rest in the memory as knowledges under a material form, and there conjoin themselves with the love of self, which is a bodily love. [3] All this shows how man becomes rational, namely, that he becomes rational to the third degree by a spiritual love of the good and truth which pertain to heaven and the church; he becomes rational to the second degree by a love of what is honest and right; and to the first degree by a love of what is just and equitable. These two latter loves also become spiritual from a spiritual love of good and truth, because that love flows into them and conjoins itself to them and forms in them as it were its own semblance.

Spirits and angels, equally with men, have a memory, whatever they hear, see, think, will and do, remaining with them, and thereby their rational faculty is continually cultivated even to eternity. Thus spirits and angels, equally with men, are perfected in intelligence and wisdom by means of knowledges of truth and good. That spirits and angels have a memory I have been permitted to learn by much experience, having seen everything that they have thought and done, both in public and in private, called forth from their memories when they were with other spirits; and I have seen those that were in some truth from simple good imbued with knowledges, and thereby with intelligence, and afterwards raised up into heaven. But it must be understood that such are not imbued with knowledges and thereby with intelligence beyond the degree of affection for good and for truth that they have attained to while in the world; for such and so much of affection as any spirit or angel had in the world remains with him; and this affection is afterwards perfected by being filled out, which goes on to eternity. For everything is capable of being filled out to eternity, since everything is capable of infinite variation, thus of enrichment by various things, and consequently of multiplication and fructification. To any thing good there is no limit because it is from the Infinite. That spirits and angels are being perfected unceasingly in intelligence and wisdom by means of knowledges of truth and good may be seen above, in the chapters on the wisdom of the angels of heaven (n. 265-275); on the heathen or people outside the church in heaven (n. 318-328); and on little children in heaven (n. 329-345); and that this is done to that degree of affection for good and for truth in which they had been in the world, and not beyond it, may be seen in n. 349.

MAN AFTER DEATH IS SUCH AS HIS LIFE HAD BEEN IN THE WORLD. Every Christian knows from the Word that one's own life awaits him after death; for it is there said in many passages that man will be judged and rewarded according to his deeds and works; and no one who thinks from good and from real truth can help seeing that he who lives well goes to heaven and that he who lives wickedly goes to hell. But the evil man is unwilling to believe that his state after death is according to his life in the world; he thinks, especially when he is sick, that heaven is granted to everyone out of pure mercy, whatever his life may have been, and that this is done in accordance with his faith, which he separates from life.

That man will be judged and rewarded according to his deeds and works is declared in many passages in the Word, some of which I will here quote: The Son of man shall come in the glory of His Father with His angels and then He will render unto everyone according to his works (Matt. 16:27). Blessed are the dead that die in the Lord; yea, saith the Spirit, that they may rest from their labors, for their works follow them (Apoc. 14:13). I will give to everyone according to his works (Apoc. 2:23). I saw the dead, small and great, standing before God; and the books were opened and the dead were judged out of the things that were written in the books according to their works. The sea gave up the dead that were in it, and death and hell gave up those that were in them, and they were judged everyone according to their works (Apoc. 20:12, 13). Behold I come, and My reward is with Me, to give to everyone according to his works (Apoc. 22:12). Everyone that heareth My words and doeth them I will liken to a prudent man; but everyone that heareth My words and doeth them not is likened to a foolish man (Matt. 7:24, 26). Not everyone that saith unto Me, Lord, Lord, shall enter into the kingdom of the heavens; but he that doeth the will of My Father who is in the heavens. Many will say unto Me in that day, Lord, Lord, have we not prophesied in Thy name, and through Thy name cast out demons, and in Thy name done many mighty works? But then will I confess to them, I know you not: depart from Me, ye workers of iniquity (Matt. 7:21-23). Then shall ye begin to say, We have eaten and drunk before Thee; Thou hast taught in our streets. But He will say, I tell you I know you not, ye workers of iniquity (Luke 13:25-27). I will recompense them according to their work and according to the doing of their hands (Jer. 25:14). Jehovah, whose eyes are open upon all the ways of men, to give to everyone according to his ways and according to the fruit of his works (Jer. 32:19). I will visit upon his ways and recompense to him his works (Hosea 4:9). Jehovah doeth with us according to our ways and according to our works (Zech. 1:6). In foretelling the last judgment the Lord recounts nothing but works, teaching that those that have done good works will enter into eternal life, and those that have done evil works will enter into damnation, as in Matthew (25:32-46), and in many other passages that treat of the salvation and condemnation of man. It is clear that works and deeds constitute the outward life of man, and that the quality of his inward life is made evident in them.

But by deeds and works, what they are inwardly is here meant, and not the way they outwardly appear; for everyone knows that every deed and work goes forth from the man's will and thought; otherwise it would be nothing but a movement like that of an automaton or image. Consequently, a deed or work viewed in itself is merely an effect that derives its soul and life from will and thought, even to the extent that it is nothing but will and thought in effect, and thus is will and thought in outward form. From this it follows that a deed or work is in quality such as are the will and thought that produce it. If the thought and will are good the deeds and works are good; but if the thought and will are evil the deeds and works are evil, although in outward form they appear alike. A thousand men may act alike, that is, may do like deeds, so alike in outward form as to be almost undistinguishable, and yet each one regarded in itself be different, because from an unlike will. [2] For example, when one acts honestly and justly with a companion, one person may do it for the purpose of appearing to be honest and just out of regard to himself and his own honor; another out of regard to the world and gain; a third out of regard to reward and merit; a fourth out of regard to friendship; a fifth from fear of the law and the loss of reputation or employment; a sixth that he may draw some one to his own side, even when he is in the wrong; a seventh that he may deceive; and others from other motives. In all these instances although the deeds are good in appearance, since it is a good thing to act honestly and justly with a companion, they are nevertheless evil, because they are done, not out of regard to honesty and justice and for the love of these, but out of regard to love of self and the world which are loved; and honesty and justice are made to serve that love as servants serve a lord, whom the lord despises and dismisses when they fail to serve him. [3] In outward form those act in a like way who act honestly and justly with a companion because they love what is honest and just. Some of these act from the truth of faith or from obedience, because the Word so commands; some from the good of faith or from conscience, because from a religious motive; some from good of charity towards the neighbor because his good should be regarded; some from the good of love to the Lord because good should be done for the sake of good, as also what is honest and just should be done for the sake of honesty and justice; and this they love because it is from the Lord, and because the Divine that goes forth from the Lord is in it, and consequently regarded in its very essence it is Divine. The deeds or works of such are inwardly good, and therefore are outwardly good also; for, as has been said above, deeds or works are precisely such in quality as the thought and will from which they proceed, and apart from thought and will they are not deeds and works, but only inanimate movements. All this explains what is meant in the Word by works and deeds.

As deeds and works are from the will and thought, so are they from the love and faith, consequently they are such as the love and faith are; for it is the same thing whether you say one's love or his will, and it is the same thing whether you say one's faith or his established thought; for that which a man loves he wills, and that which a man believes he thinks; and when a man loves what he believes he also wills it and as far as possible does it. Everyone may know that love and faith are within man's will and thought, and not outside of them, for love is what kindles the will, and the thought is what it enlightens in matters of faith; therefore only those that are able to think wisely are enlightened, and in the measure of their enlightenment they think what is true and will it, or what is the same, they believe what is true and love it. 473-1

But it must be understood that it is the will that makes the man, while thought makes the man only so far as it goes forth from the will; and deeds and works go forth from both; or what is the same, it is love that makes the man, and faith only so far as it goes forth from love; and deeds or works go forth from both. Consequently, the will or love is the man himself, for whatever goes forth belongs to that from which it goes forth. To go forth is to be brought forth and presented in suitable form for being perceived and seen. 474-1 All this makes clear what faith is when separated from love, namely, that it is no faith, but mere knowledge, which has no spiritual life in it; likewise what a deed or work is apart from love, namely, that it is not a deed or work of life, but a deed or work of death, which possesses an appearance of life from an evil love and a belief in what is false. This appearance of life is what is called spiritual death.

Again, it must be understood that in deeds or works the whole man is exhibited, and that his will and thought or his love and faith, which are his interiors, are not complete until they exist in deeds or works, which are his exteriors, for these are the outmosts in which the will and thought terminate, and without such terminations they are interminate, and have as yet no existence, that is, are not yet in the man. To think and to will without doing, when there is opportunity, is like a flame enclosed in a vessel and goes out; also like seed cast upon the sand, which fails to grow, and so perishes with its power of germination. But to think and will and from that to do is like a flame that gives heat and light all around, or like a seed in the ground that grows up into a tree or flower and continues to live. Everyone can know that willing and not doing, when there is opportunity, is not willing; also that loving and not doing good, when there is opportunity, is not loving, but mere thought that one wills and loves; and this is thought separate, which vanishes and is dissipated. Love and will constitute the soul itself of a deed or work, and give form to its body in the honest and just things that the man does. This is the sole source of man's spiritual body, or the body of his spirit; that is, it is formed solely out of the things that the man does from his love or will (see above, n. 463). In a word, all things of man and his spirit are contained in his deeds or works. 475-1

All this makes clear what the life is that awaits man after death, namely, that it is his love and his faith therefrom, not only in potency, but also in act; thus that it is his deeds or works, because in these all things of man's love and faith are contained.

It is man's ruling love that awaits him after death, and this is in no way changed to eternity. Everyone has many loves; but they are all related to his ruling love, and make one with it or together compose it. All things of the will that are in harmony with the ruling love are called loves, because they are loved. These loves are both inner and outer; some directly connected and some mediately; some nearer and some more remote; they are subservient in various ways. Taken together they constitute a kingdom, as it were, such being the order in which they are arranged in man, although man knows nothing whatever about that arrangement. And yet something of it is made manifest to him in the other life, for the spread of his thought and affection there is in accordance with the arrangement of his loves, his thought and affection extending into heavenly societies when the ruling love is made up of the loves of heaven, but into infernal societies when it is made up of the loves of hell. That all the thought and affection of spirits and of angels has extension into societies may be seen above, in the chapters on the wisdom of the angels of heaven, and on the form of heaven which determines affiliations and communications there.

But what has been said thus far appeals only to the thought of the rational man. That it may also be presented to the perception derived from the senses, I will add some experiences by which it may be illustrated and confirmed. First, Man after death is his own love or his own will. Second, Man continues to eternity such as his will or ruling love is. Third, The man who has heavenly and spiritual love goes to heaven, while the man who has corporeal and worldly love, and no heavenly and spiritual love, goes to hell. Fourth, Unless faith is from heavenly love it does not endure in man. Fifth, Love in act, that is, the life of man, is what endures.

(i) Man after death is his own love or his own will. This has been proved to me by manifold experience. The entire heaven is divided into societies according to differences of good of love; and every spirit who is taken up into heaven and becomes an angel is taken to the society where his love is; and when he arrives there he is, as it were, at home, and in the house where he was born; this the angel perceives, and is affiliated with those there that are like himself. When he goes away to another place he feels constantly a kind of resistance, and a longing to return to his like, thus to his ruling love. Thus are affiliations brought about in heaven; and in a like manner in hell, where all are affiliated in accordance with loves that are the opposites of heavenly loves. It has been shown above (n. 41-50 and 200-212) that both heaven and hell are composed of societies, and that they are all distinguished according to differences of love. [2] That man after death is his own love might also be seen from the fact that whatever does not make one with his ruling love is then separated and as it were taken away from him. From one who is good everything discordant or inharmonious is separated and as it were taken away, and he is thus let into his own love. It is the same with an evil spirit, with the difference that from the evil truths are taken away, and from the good falsities are taken away, and this goes on until each becomes his own love. This is effected when the man-spirit is brought into the third state, which will be described hereafter. When this has been done he turns his face constantly to his own love, and this he has continually before his eyes, in whatever direction he turns (see above, n. 123, 124). [3] All spirits, provided they are kept in their ruling love, can be led wherever one pleases, and are incapable of resistance, however clearly they may see that this is being done, and however much they may think that they will resist. They have often been permitted to try whether they could do anything contrary to their ruling love, but in vain. Their love is like a bond or a rope tied around them, by which they may be led and from which they cannot loose themselves. It is the same with men in the world who are also led by their love, or are led by others by means of their love; but this is more the case when they have become spirits, because they are not then permitted to make a display of any other love, or to counterfeit what is not their own. [4] All interaction in the other life proves that the spirit of man is his ruling love, for so far any one is acting or speaking in accord with the love of another, to the same extent is the other plainly present, with full, joyous, and lively countenance; but when one is speaking or acting contrary to another's love, to that extent the other's countenance begins to be changed, to be obscured and undiscernible, until at length he wholly disappears as if he had not been there. I have often wondered how this could be, for nothing of the kind can occur in the world; but I have been told that it is the same with the spirit in man, which when it turns itself away from another ceases to be within his view. [5] Another proof that a spirit is his ruling love is that every spirit seizes and appropriates all things that are in harmony with his love, and rejects and repudiates all that are not. Everyone's love is like a spongy or porous wood, which imbibes such fluids as promote its growth, and repels others. It is also like animals of every kind, which know their proper food and seek the things that agree with their nature, and avoid what disagrees; for every love wishes to be nourished on what belongs to it, evil love by falsities and good love by truths. I have sometimes been permitted to see certain simple good spirits desiring to instruct the evil in truths and goods; but when the instruction was offered them they fled far away, and when they came to their own they seized with great pleasure upon the falsities that were in agreement with their love. I have also seen good spirits talking together about truths, and the good who were present listened eagerly to the conversation, but the evil who were present paid no attention to it, as if they did not hear it. In the world of spirits ways are seen, some leading to heaven, some to hell, and each to some particular society. Good spirits go only in the ways that lead to heaven, and to the society there that is in the good of their love; and do not see the ways that lead elsewhere; while evil spirits go only in the ways that lead to hell, and to the society there that is in the evil of their love; and do not see the ways that lead elsewhere; or if they see them have no wish to enter them. In the spiritual world these ways are real appearances, which correspond to truths or falsities; and this is why ways have this signification in the Word. 479-1 By this evidence from experience what has previously been affirmed on the ground of reason is made more certain, namely, that every man after death is his own love and his own will. It is said one's own will because everyone's will is his love.

(ii) Man after death continues to eternity such as his will or ruling love is. This, too, has been confirmed by abundant experience. I have been permitted to talk with some who lived two thousand years ago, and whose lives are described in history, and thus known; and I found that they continued to be just the same as they were described, that is, in respect to the love out of which and according to which their lives were formed. There were others known to history, that had lived seventeen centuries ago, others that had lived four centuries ago, and three, and so on, with whom I was permitted to talk; and I found that the same affection still ruled in them, with no other difference than that the delights of their love were turned into such things as correspond. The angels declare that the life of the ruling love is never changed in any one even to eternity, since everyone is his love; consequently to change that love in a spirit is to take away or extinguish his life; and for the reason that man after death is no longer capable of being reformed by instruction, as in the world, because the outmost plane, which consists of natural knowledges and affections, is then quiescent and not being spiritual cannot be opened (see above, n. 464); and upon that plane the interiors pertaining to the mind and disposition rest as a house rests on its foundation; and on this account such as the life of one's love had been in the world such he continues to be to eternity. The angels are greatly surprised that man does not know that everyone is such as his ruling love is, and that many believe that they may be saved by mercy apart from means, or by faith alone, whatever their life may be; also that they do not know that Divine mercy works by means, and that it consists in man's being led by the Lord, both in the world and afterwards to eternity, and that those who do not live in evils are led by the Divine mercy; and finally that faith is affection for truth going forth from heavenly love, which is from the Lord.

(iii) The man who has heavenly and spiritual love goes to heaven; while the man who has corporeal and worldly love and no heavenly and spiritual love goes to hell. This has been made evident to me from all whom I have seen taken up into heaven or cast into hell. The life of those taken up into heaven had been derived from a heavenly and spiritual love, while the life of those cast into hell had been derived from a corporeal and worldly love. Heavenly love consists in loving what is good, honest, and just, because it is good, honest and just, and in doing this from love; and those that have this love have a life of goodness, honesty, and justice, which is the heavenly life. Those that love what is good, honest, and just, for its own sake, and who do this or live it, love the Lord above all things, because this is from Him; they also love the neighbor, because this is the neighbor who is to be loved. 481-1 But corporeal love is loving what is good, honest, and just, not for its own sake but for the sake of self, because reputation, honor, and gain can thus be acquired. Such, in what is good, honest, and just, do not look to the Lord and to the neighbor, but to self and the world, and find delight in fraud; and the goodness, honesty and justice that spring forth from fraud are evil, dishonesty, and injustice, and these are what are loved by such in their practice of goodness, honesty, and justice. [2] As the life of everyone is determined by these different kinds of love, as soon as men after death enter the world of spirits they are examined to discover their quality, and are joined to those that are in a like love; those that are in heavenly love to those that are in heaven, and those that are in corporeal love to those that are in hell; and after they have passed through the first and second state they are so separated as to no longer see or know each other; for each one becomes his own love, both in respect to his interiors pertaining to his mind, and in respect to his exteriors pertaining to his face, body, and speech; for everyone becomes an image of his own love, even in externals. Those that are corporeal loves appear gross, dusky, black and misshapen; while those that are heavenly loves appear fresh, bright, fair and beautiful. Also in their minds and thoughts they are wholly unlike, those that are heavenly loves being intelligent and wise, while those that are corporeal loves are stupid and as it were silly. [3] When it is granted to behold the interiors and exteriors of thought and affection of those that are in heavenly love, their interiors appear like light, and some like a flamy light, while their exteriors appear in various beautiful colors like rainbows. But the interiors of those that are in corporeal love appear as if black, because they are closed up; and the interiors of some who were interiorly in malignant deceit appear like a dusky fire. But their exteriors appear of a dirty color, and disagreeable to the sight. (The interiors and exteriors of the mind and disposition are made visible in the spiritual world whenever the Lord pleases.) [4] Those that are in corporeal love see nothing in the light of heaven; to them the light of heaven is thick darkness; but the light of hell, which is like light from burning coals, is to them as clear light. Moreover, in the light of heaven their inward sight is so darkened that they become insane; consequently they shun that light and hide themselves in dens and caverns, more or less deeply in accordance with the falsities in them derived from their evils. On the other hand those who are in heavenly love, the more interiorly and deeply they enter into the light of heaven, see all things more clearly and all things appear more beautiful to them, and they perceive truths more intelligently and wisely. [5] Again, it is impossible for those who are in corporeal love to live at all in the heat of heaven, for the heat of heaven is heavenly love; but they can live in the heat of hell, which is the love of raging against others that do not favor them. The delights of that love are contempt of others, enmity, hatred and revenge; and when they are in these delights they are in their life, and have no idea what it is to do good to others from good itself and for the sake of good itself, knowing only what it is to do good from evil and for the sake of evil. [6] Those who are in corporeal love are unable to breathe in heaven. When any evil spirit is brought into heaven he draws his breath like one struggling in a contest; while those that are in heavenly love have a freer respiration and a fuller life the more interiorly they are in heaven. All this shows that heaven with man is heavenly and spiritual love, because on that love all things of heaven are inscribed; also that hell in man is corporeal and worldly love apart from heavenly and spiritual love, because on such loves all things of hell are inscribed. Evidently, then, he whose love is heavenly and spiritual enters heaven, and he whose love is corporeal and worldly apart from heavenly and spiritual love enters hell.

(iv) Unless faith is from heavenly love it does not endure in man. This has been made clear to me by so much experience that if everything I have seen and heard respecting it were collected, it would fill a volume. This I can testify, that those who are in corporeal and worldly love apart from heavenly and spiritual love have no faith whatever, and are incapable of having any; they have nothing but knowledge or a persuasion that a thing is true because it serves their love. Some of those who claimed that they had faith were brought to those who had faith, and when they communicated with them they perceived that they had no faith at all; and afterwards they confessed that merely believing what is true and believing the Word is not faith, but that faith is loving truth from heavenly love, and willing and doing it from interior affection. Moreover, they were shown that their persuasion which they called faith was merely like the light of winter, in which light, because it has no heat in it, all things on the earth are bound up in frost, become torpid, and lie buried under the snow. As soon, therefore, as the light of persuasive faith in them is touched by the rays of the light of heaven it is not only extinguished but is turned into a dense darkness, in which no one can see himself; and at the same time their interiors are so obscured that they can understand nothing at all, and at length become insane from falsities. Consequently with such, all the truths that they have known from the Word and from the doctrine of the church, and have called the truths of their faith, are taken away; and they imbibe in their place every falsity that is in accord with the evil of their life. For they are all let down into their loves and into the falsities agreeing with them; and they then hate and abhor and therefore reject truths, because they are repugnant to the falsities of evil in which they are. From all my experience in what pertains to heaven and hell I can bear witness that all those who from their doctrine have professed faith alone, and whose life has been evil, are in hell. I have seen many thousands of them cast down to hell. (Respecting these see the treatise on The Last Judgment and the Destruction of Babylon.)

(v) Love in act, that is, the life of man, is what endures. This follows as a conclusion from what has just been shown from experience, and from what has been said about deeds and works. Love in act is work and deed.

It must be understood that all works and deeds pertain to moral and civil life, and therefore have regard to what is honest and right, and what is just and equitable, what is honest and right pertaining to moral life, and what is just and equitable to civil life. The love from which deeds are done is either heavenly or infernal. Works and deeds of moral and civil life, when they are done from heavenly love, are heavenly; for what is done from heavenly love is done from the Lord, and everything done from the Lord is good. But the deeds and works of moral and civil life when done from infernal love are infernal; for what is done from this love, which is the love of self and of the world, is done from man himself, and everything that is done from man himself is in itself evil; for man regarded in himself, that is, in regard to what is his own, is nothing but evil.484-1

THE DELIGHTS OF EVERY ONE'S LIFE ARE CHANGED AFTER DEATH INTO THINGS THAT CORRESPOND. It has been shown in the preceding chapter that the ruling affection or dominant love in everyone continues to eternity. It shall now be explained how the delights of that affection or love are changed into things that correspond. Being changed into corresponding things means into things spiritual that correspond to the natural. That they are changed into things spiritual can be seen from this, that so long as man is in his earthly body he is in the natural world, but when he leaves that body he enters the spiritual world and is clothed with a spiritual body. It has already been shown that angels, and men after death, are in a complete human form, and that the bodies with which they are clothed are spiritual bodies (n. 73-77 and 453-460); also what the correspondence is of spiritual things with natural (n. 87-115).

All the delights that a man has are the delights of his ruling love, for he feels nothing to be delightful except what he loves, thus especially that which he loves above all things. It means the same whether you say the ruling love or that which is loved above all things. These delights are various. In general, there are as many as there are ruling loves; consequently as many as there are men, spirits, and angels; for no one's ruling love is in every respect like that of another. For this reason no one has a face exactly like that of any other; for each one's face is an image of his mind; and in the spiritual world it is an image of his ruling love. In particular, everyone's delights are of infinite variety. It is impossible for any one delight to be exactly like another, or the same as another, either those that follow one after another or those that exist together at the same time, no one ever being the same as another. Nevertheless, the particular delights in everyone have reference to his one love, which is his ruling love, for they compose it and thus make one with it. Likewise all delights in general have reference to one universally ruling love, which in heaven is love to the Lord, and in hell is the love of self.

Only from a knowledge of correspondences can it be known what spiritual delights everyone's natural delights are changed into after death, and what kind of delights they are. In general, this knowledge teaches that nothing natural can exist without something spiritual corresponding to it. In particular it teaches what it is that corresponds, and what kind of a thing it is. Therefore, any one that has this knowledge can ascertain and know what his own state after death will be, if he only knows what his love is, and what its relation is to the universally ruling loves spoken of above, to which all loves have relation. But it is impossible for those who are in the love of self to know what their ruling love is, because they love what is their own, and call their evils goods; and the falsities that they incline to and by which they confirm their evils they call truths. And yet if they were willing they might know it from others who are wise, and who see what they themselves do not see. This however, is impossible with those who are so enticed by the love of self that they spurn all teaching of the wise. [2] On the other hand, those who are in heavenly love accept instruction, and as soon as they are brought into the evils into which they were born, they see them from truths, for truths make evils manifest. From truth which is from good any one can see evil and its falsity; but from evil none can see what is good and true; and for the reason that falsities of evil are darkness and correspond to darkness; consequently those that are in falsities from evil are like the blind, not seeing the things that are in light, but shunning them instead like birds of night. 487-1 But as truths from good are light, and correspond to light (see above, n. 126-134), so those that are in truths from good have sight and open eyes, and discern the things that pertain to light and shade. [3] This, too, has been proved to me by experience. The angels in heaven both see and perceive the evils and falsities that sometimes arise in themselves, also the evils and falsities in spirits in the world of spirits that are connected with the hells, although the spirits themselves are unable to see their own evils and falsities. Such spirits have no comprehension of the good of heavenly love, of conscience, of honesty and justice, except such as is done for the sake of self; neither what it is to be led by the Lord. They say that such things do not exist, and thus are of no account. All this has been said to the intent that man may examine himself and may recognize his love by his delights; and thus so far as he can make it out from a knowledge of correspondences may know the state of his life after death.

How the delights of everyone's life are changed after death into things that correspond can be known from a knowledge of correspondences; but as that knowledge is not as yet generally known I will try to throw some light on the subject by certain examples from experience. All who are in evil and who have established themselves in falsities in opposition to the truths of the church, especially those that have rejected the Word, flee from the light of heaven and take refuge in caves that appear at their openings to be densely dark, also in clefts of rocks, and there they hide themselves; and this because they have loved falsities and hated truths; for such caves and clefts of rocks, 488-1 well as darkness, correspond to falsities, as light corresponds to truths. It is their delight to dwell in such places, and undelightful to dwell in the open country. [2] Those that have taken delight in insidious and secret plots and in treacherous machinations do the same thing. They are also in such caves; and they frequent rooms so dark that they are even unable to see one another; and they whisper together in the ears in corners. Into this is the delight of their love changed. Those that have devoted themselves to the sciences with no other end than to acquire a reputation for learning, and have not cultivated their rational faculty by their learning, but have taken delight in the things of memory from a pride in such things, love sandy places, which they choose in preference to fields and gardens, because sandy places correspond to such studies. [3] Those that are skilled in the doctrines of their own and other churches, but have not applied their knowledge to life, choose for themselves rocky places, and dwell among heaps of stones, shunning cultivated places because they dislike them. Those that have ascribed all things to nature, as well as those that have ascribed all things to their own prudence, and by various arts have raised themselves to honors and have acquired wealth, in the other life devote themselves to the study of magic arts, which are abuses of Divine order, and find in these the chief delight of life. [4] Those that have adapted Divine truths to their own loves, and thereby have falsified them, love urinous things because these correspond to the delights of such loves. 488-2 Those that have been sordidly avaricious dwell in cells, and love swinish filth and such stenches as are exhaled from undigested food in the stomach. [5] Those that have spent their life in mere pleasures and have lived delicately and indulged their palate and stomach, loving such things as the highest good that life affords, love in the other life excrementitious things and privies, in which they find their delight, for the reason that such pleasures are spiritual filth. Places that are clean and free from filth they shun, finding them undelightful. [6] Those that have taken delight in adulteries pass their time in brothels, where all things are vile and filthy; these they love, and chaste homes they shun, falling into a swoon as soon as they enter them. Nothing is more delightful to them than to break up marriages. Those that have cherished a spirit of revenge, and have thereby contracted a savage and cruel nature, love cadaverous substances, and are in hells of that nature; and so on.

But the delights of life of those that have lived in the world in heavenly love are changed into such corresponding things as exist in the heavens, which spring from the sun of heaven and its light, that light presenting to view such things as have what is Divine inwardly concealed in them. The things that appear in that light affect the interiors of the minds of the angels, and at the same time the exteriors pertaining to their bodies; and as the Divine light, which is Divine truth going forth from the Lord, flows into their minds opened by heavenly love, it presents outwardly such things as correspond to the delights of their love. It has already been shown, in the chapter on representatives and appearances in heaven (n. 170-176), and in the chapter on the wisdom of the angels (n. 265-275), that the things that appear to the sight in the heavens correspond to the interiors of angels, or to the things pertaining to their faith and love and thus to their intelligence and wisdom. [2] Having already begun to establish this point by examples from experience, to make clearer what has been previously said on the ground of causes of things I will state briefly some particulars respecting the heavenly delightful things into which the natural delights of those that have lived in heavenly love in the world are changed. Those that have loved Divine truths and the Word from an interior affection, or from an affection for truth itself, dwell in the other life in light, in elevated places that appear like mountains, where they are continually in the light of heaven. They do not know what darkness is, like that of night in the world; they live also in a vernal temperature; there are presented to their view fields filled with grain and vine-yards; in their houses everything glows as if from precious stones; and looking through the windows is like looking through pure crystal. Such are the delights of their vision; but these same things are interiorly delightful because of their being correspondences of Divine heavenly things, for the truths from the Word which they have loved correspond to fields of grain, vineyards, precious stones, windows, and crystals. 489-1 [3] Those that have applied the doctrinals of the church which are from the Word immediately to life, are in the inmost heaven, and surpass all others in their delights of wisdom. In every object they see what is Divine; the objects they see indeed with their eyes; but the corresponding Divine things flow in immediately into their minds and fill them with a blessedness that affects all their sensations. Thus before their eyes all things seem to laugh, to play, and to live (see above, n. 270). [4] Those that have loved knowledges and have thereby cultivated their rational faculty and acquired intelligence, and at the same time have acknowledged the Divine-these in the other life have their pleasure in knowledges, and their rational delight changed into spiritual delight, which is delight in knowing good and truth. They dwell in gardens where flower beds and grass plots are seen beautifully arranged, with rows of trees round about, and arbors and walks, the trees and flowers changing from day to day. The entire view imparts delight to their minds in a general way, and the variations in detail continually renew the delight; and as everything there corresponds to something Divine, and they are skilled in the knowledge of correspondences, they are constantly filled with new knowledges, and by these their spiritual rational faculty is perfected. Their delights are such because gardens, flower beds, grass plots, and trees correspond to sciences, knowledges, and the resulting intelligence. 489-2 [5] Those that have ascribed all things to the Divine, regarding nature as relatively dead and merely subservient to things spiritual, and have confirmed themselves in this view, are in heavenly light; and all things that appear before their eyes are made by that light transparent, and in their transparency exhibit innumerable variegations of light, which their internal sight takes in as it were directly, and from this they perceive interior delights. The things seen within their houses are as if made of diamonds, with similar variegations of light. The walls of their houses, as already said, are like crystal, and thus also transparent; and in them seemingly flowing forms representative of heavenly things are seen also with unceasing variety, and this because such transparency corresponds to the understanding when it has been enlightened by the Lord and when the shadows that arise from a belief in and love for natural things have been removed. With reference to such things and infinite others, it is said by those that have been in heaven that they have seen what eye has never seen; and from a perception of Divine things communicated to them by those who are there, that they have heard what ear has never heard. [6] Those that have not acted in secret ways, but have been willing to have all that they have thought made known so far as civil life would permit, because their thoughts have all been in accord with what is honest and just from the Divine-these in heaven have faces full of light; and in that light every least affection and thought is seen in the face as in its form, and in their speech and actions they are like images of their affections. Such, therefore, are more loved than others. While they are speaking the face becomes a little obscured; but as soon as they have spoken, the things they have said become plainly manifest all at once in the face. And as all the objects that exist round about them correspond to their interiors, these assume such an appearance that others can clearly perceive what they represent and signify. Spirits that have found delight in clandestine acts, when they see such at a distance flee from them, and appear to themselves to creep away from them like serpents. [7] Those that have regarded adulteries as abominable, and have lived in a chaste love of marriage, are more than all others in the order and form of heaven, and therefore in all beauty, and continue unceasingly in the flower of youth. The delights of their love are ineffable, and increase to eternity; for all the delights and joys of heaven flow into that love, because that love descends from the conjunction of the Lord with heaven and with the church, and in general from the conjunction of good and truth, which conjunction is heaven itself in general, and with each angel in particular (see above, n. 366-386). What their outward delights are it is impossible to describe in human words. These are only a few of the things that have been told me about the correspondences of the delights of those that are in heavenly love.

All this makes evident that everyone's delights are changed after death into their correspondences, while the love itself continues to eternity. This is true of marriage love, of the love of justice, honesty, goodness and truth, the love of sciences and of knowledges, the love of intelligence and wisdom, and the rest. From these loves delights flow like streams from their fountain; and these continue; but when raised from natural to spiritual delights they are exalted to a higher degree.

THE FIRST STATE OF MAN AFTER DEATH. There are three states that man passes through after death before he enters either heaven or hell. The first state is the state of his exteriors, the second state the state of his interiors, and the third his state of preparation. These states man passes through in the world of spirits. There are some, however, that do not pass through them; but immediately after death are either taken up into heaven or cast into hell. Those that are immediately taken up into heaven are those that have been regenerated in the world and thereby prepared for heaven. Those that have been so regenerated and prepared that they need simply to cast off natural impurities with the body are at once taken up by the angels into heaven. I have seen them so taken up soon after the hour of death. On the other hand, those that have been inwardly wicked while maintaining an outward appearance of goodness, and have thus filled up the measure of their wickedness by artifices, using goodness as a means of deceiving-these are at once cast into hell. I have seen some such cast into hell immediately after death, one of the most deceitful with his head downward and feet upward, and others in other ways. There are some that immediately after death are cast into caverns and are thus separated from those that are in the world of spirits, and are taken out from these and put back again by turns. They are such as have dealt wickedly with the neighbor under civil pretences. But all these are few in comparison with those that are retained in the world of spirits, and are there prepared in accordance with Divine order for heaven or for hell.

In regard to the first state, which is the state of the exteriors, it is that which man comes into immediately after death. Every man, as regards his spirit, has exteriors and interiors. The exteriors of the spirit are the means by which it adapts the man's body in the world, especially the face, speech, and movements, to fellowship with others; while the interiors of the spirit are what belong to its own will and consequent thought; and these are rarely manifested in face, speech, and movement. For man is accustomed from childhood to maintain a semblance of friendship, benevolence, and sincerity, and to conceal the thoughts of his own will, thereby living from habit a moral and civil life in externals, whatever he may be internally. As a result of this habit man scarcely knows what his interiors are, and gives little thought to them.

The first state of man after death resembles his state in the world, for he is then likewise in externals, having a like face, like speech, and a like disposition, thus a like moral and civil life; and in consequence he is made aware that he is not still in the world only by giving attention to what he encounters, and from his having been told by the angels when he was resuscitated that he had become a spirit(n. 450). Thus is one life continued into the other, and death is merely transition.

The state of man's spirit that immediately follows his life in the world being such, he is then recognized by his friends and by those he had known in the world; for this is something that spirits perceive not only from one's face and speech but also from the sphere of his life when they draw near. Whenever any one in the other life thinks about another he brings his face before him in thought, and at the same time many things of his life; and when he does this the other becomes present, as if he had been sent for or called. This is so in the spiritual world because thoughts there are shared, and there is no such space there as in the natural world (see above, n. 191-199). So all, as soon as they enter the other life, are recognized by their friends, their relatives, and those in any way known to them; and they talk with one another, and afterward associate in accordance with their friendships in the world. I have often heard that those that have come from the world were rejoiced at seeing their friends again, and that their friends in turn were rejoiced that they had come. Very commonly husband and wife come together and congratulate each other, and continue together, and this for a longer or shorter time according to their delight in living together in the world. But if they had not been united by a true marriage love, which is a conjunction of minds by heavenly love, after remaining together for a while they separate. Or if their minds had been discordant and were inwardly adverse, they break forth into open enmity, and sometimes into combat; nevertheless they are not separated until they enter the second state, which will be treated of presently.

As the life of spirits recently from the world is not unlike their life in the natural world and as they know nothing about their state of life after death and nothing about heaven and hell except what they have learned from the sense of the letter of the Word and preaching from it, they are at first surprised to find themselves in a body and in every sense that they had in the world, and seeing like things; and they become eager to know what heaven is, what hell is, and where they are. Therefore their friends tell them about the conditions of eternal life, and take them about to various places and into various companies, and sometimes into cities, and into gardens and parks, showing them chiefly such magnificent things as delight the externals in which they are. They are then brought in turn into those notions about the state of their soul after death, and about heaven and hell, that they had entertained in the life of the body, even until they feel indignant at their total ignorance of such things, and at the ignorance of the church also. Nearly all are anxious to know whether they will get to heaven. Most of them believe that they will, because of their having lived in the world a moral and civil life, never considering that the bad and the good live a like life outwardly, alike doing good to others, attending public worship, hearing sermons, and praying; and wholly ignorant that external deeds and external acts of worship are of no avail, but only the internals from which the externals proceed. There is hardly one out of thousands who knows what internals are, and that it is in them that man must find heaven and the church. Still less is it known that outward acts are such as the intentions and thoughts are, and the love and faith in these from which they spring. And even when taught they fail to comprehend that thinking and willing are of any avail, but only speaking and acting. Such for the most part are those that go at this day from the Christian world into the other life.

Such, however, are explored by good spirits to discover what they are, and this in various ways; since in this the first state the evil equally with the good utter truths and do good acts, and for the reason mentioned above, that like the good they have lived morally in outward respects, since they have lived under governments, and subject to laws, and have thereby acquired a reputation for justice and honesty, and have gained favor, and thus been raised to honors, and have acquired wealth. But evil spirits are distinguished from good spirits chiefly by this, that the evil give eager attention to whatever is said about external things, and but little attention to what is said about internal things, which are the truths and goods of the church and of heaven. These they listen to, but not with attention and joy. The two classes are also distinguished by their turning repeatedly in specific directions, and following, when left to themselves, the paths that lead in those directions. From such turning to certain quarters and going in certain ways it is known by what love they are led.

All spirits that arrive from the world are connected with some society in heaven or some society in hell, and yet only as regards their interiors; and so long as they are in exteriors their interiors are manifested to no one, for externals cover and conceal internals, especially in the case of those who are in interior evil. But afterwards, when they come into the second state, their evils become manifest, because their interiors are then opened and their exteriors laid asleep.

This first state of man after death continues with some for days, with some for months, and with some for a year; but seldom with any one beyond a year; for a shorter or longer time with each one according to the agreement or disagreement of his interiors with his exteriors. For with everyone the exteriors and interior must make one and correspond. In the spiritual world no one is permitted to think and will in one way and speak and act in another. Everyone there must be an image of his own affection or his own love, and therefore such as he is inwardly such he must be outwardly; and for this reason a spirit's exteriors are first disclosed and reduced to order that they may serve the interiors as a corresponding plane.

THE SECOND STATE OF MAN AFTER DEATH. The second state of man after death is called the state of his interiors, because he is then let into the interiors of his mind, that is, of his will and thought; while his exteriors, which he has been in during his first state, are laid asleep. Whoever gives any thought to man's life and speech and action can see that everyone has exteriors and interiors, that is, exterior and interior thoughts and intentions. This is shown by the fact that in civil life one thinks about others in accordance with what he has heard and learned of them by report or conversation; but he does not talk with them in accordance with his thought; and if they are evil he nevertheless treats them with civility. That this is so is seen especially in the case of pretenders and flatterers, who speak and act in one way and think and will in a wholly different way; also in the case of hypocrites, who talk about God and heaven and the salvation of souls and the truths of the church and their country's good and their neighbor as if from faith and love, although in heart they believe otherwise and love themselves alone. [2] All this makes clear that there are two kinds of thought, one exterior and the other interior; and that there are those who speak from exterior thought, while from their interior thought they have other sentiments, and that these two kinds of thought are kept separate, since the interior is carefully prevented from flowing into the exterior and becoming manifest in any way. By creation man is so formed as to have his interior and exterior thought make one by correspondence; and these do make one in those that are in good, for such both think and speak what is good only. But in those that are in evil interior and exterior thought do not make one, for such think what is evil and say what is good. With such there is an inversion of order, for good with them is on the outside and evil within; and in consequence evil has dominion over good, and subjects it to itself as a servant, that it may serve it as a means for gaining its ends, which are of the same nature as their love. With such an end contained in the good that they seek and do, their good is evidently not good, but is infected with evil, however good it may appear in outward form to those not acquainted with their interiors. [3] It is not so with those that are in good. With such order is not inverted; but good from interior thought flows into exterior thought, and thus into word and act. Into this order man was created; and in heaven, and in the light of heaven, his interiors are in this order. And as the light of heaven is the Divine truth that goes forth from the Lord, and consequently is the Lord in heaven (n. 126-140), therefore such are led by the Lord. All this has been said to make known that every man has interior thought and exterior thought, and that these are distinct from each other. The term thought includes also the will, for thought is from the will, and thought apart from willing is impossible. All this makes clear what is meant by the state of man's exteriors and the state of his interiors.

When will and thought are mentioned will includes affection and love, and all the delight and pleasure that spring from affection and love, since all these relate to the will as to their subject; for what a man wills he loves and feels to be delightful or pleasurable; and on the other hand, what a man loves and feels to be delightful or pleasurable, that he wills. But by thought is then meant everything by which affection or love is confirmed, for thought is simply the will's form, or that whereby what is willed may appear in light. This form is made apparent through various rational analyses, which have their origin in the spiritual world and belong properly to the spirit of man.

Footnotes

454-1 Man is the being into whom are brought together all things of Divine order, and by creation he is Divine order in form (n. 4219, 4222, 4223, 4523, 4524, 5114, 6013, 6057, 6605, 6626, 9706, 10156, 10472). So far as a man lives in accordance with Divine order he is seen in the other life as a man, complete and beautiful (n. 4839, 6605, 6626).

455-1 The truths of doctrine of the church derived from the Word must be the starting-point, and these must first be acknowledged, and afterwards it is permissible to consult knowledges (n. 6047). Thus it is permissible for those that are in an affirmative state towards the truths of faith to confirm them rationally by knowledges, but it is not permissible for those who are in a negative state (n. 2568, 2588, 4760, 6047). It is in accordance with Divine order to enter rationally from spiritual truths into knowledges, which are natural truths, but not to enter from the latter into the former, because spiritual influx into natural things is possible, but not natural or physical influx into spiritual things (n. 3219, 5119, 5259, 5427, 5428, 5478, 6322, 9109, 9110).

456-1 Profanation is the mixing of good and evil and of truth and falsity in man (n. 6348). Only those can profane truth and good, or the holy things of the Word and the church, who first acknowledge them, and still more who live according to them, and who afterwards recede from the belief and reject it, and live for themselves and the world (n. 593, 1008, 1010, 1059, 3398, 3399, 3898, 4289, 4601, 10284, 10287). If man after repentance of heart relapses to former evils he profanes, and his latter state is then worse than his former (n. 8394). Those that have not acknowledged holy things, still less those that have no knowledge of them, cannot profane them (n. 1008, 1010, 1059, 9188, 10284). The heathen who are out of the church and do not have the Word cannot profane it (n. 1327, 1328, 2051, 2284). On this account interior truths were not disclosed to the Jews, for if they had been disclosed and acknowledged that people would have profaned them (n. 3398, 4289, 6963). The lot of profaners in the other life is the worst of all, because not only the good and truth they have acknowledged, but also their evil and falsity remain, and as these cling together, the life is rent asunder (n. 571, 582, 6348). Consequently most careful provision is made by the Lord to prevent profanation (n. 2426, 10287).

457-1 The face is so formed as to correspond with the interiors (n. 4791-4805, 5695). The correspondence of the face and its expressions with the affections of the mind (n. 1568, 2988, 2989, 3631, 4796, 4797, 4800, 5165, 5168,

5695, 9306). With the angels of heaven the face makes one with the interiors that belong to the mind (n. 4796-4799, 5695, 8250). Therefore in the Word the face signifies the interiors that belong to the mind, that is, to the affection and thought (n. 1999, 2434, 3527, 4066, 4796, 5102, 9306, 9546). In what manner the influx from the brain into the face has been changed in process of time and with it the face itself as regards its correspondence with the interiors (n. 4326, 8250).

463-1 A good man, spirit, or angel, is his own good and his own truth, that is, he is wholly such as his good and truth are (n. 10298, 10367). This is because good is what makes the will and truth the understanding; and the will and understanding make everything of life in man, spirit, or angel (n. 3332, 3623, 6065). It is the same thing to say that a man, spirit, or angel is his own love (n. 6872, 10177, 10284).

463-2 Man has two memories an outer and an inner, or a natural and a spiritual memory (n. 2469-2494). Man does not know that he has an inner memory (n. 2470, 2471). How far the inner memory surpasses the outer (n. 2473). The things contained in the outer memory are in the light of the world, but the things contained in the inner are in the light of heaven (n. 5212). It is from the inner memory that man is able to think and speak intellectually and rationally (n. 9394). All things and each thing that a man has thought, spoken, and done, and that he has seen and heard, are inscribed on the inner memory (n. 2474, 7398). That memory is the book of his life (n. 2474, 9386, 9841, 10505). In the inner memory are the truths that have been made truths of faith, and the goods that have been made goods of love (n. 5212, 8067). Those things that have become matters of habit and have come to be things of the life, and have thus disappeared from the outer memory, are in the inner memory (n. 9394, 9723, 9841). Spirits and angels speak from the inner memory and consequently have a universal language (n. 2472, 2476, 2490, 2493). The languages of the world belong to the outer memory (n. 2472, 2476).

473-1 As all things that exist according to order in the universe have relation to good and truth, so in man all things have relation to will and understanding (n. 803, 10122). For the reason that the will is a recipient of good and the understanding a recipient of truth (n. 3332, 3623, 5232, 6065, 6125, 7503, 9300, 9995). It amounts to the same whether you say truth or faith, for faith belongs to truth and truth belongs to faith; and it amounts to the same whether you say good or love for love belongs to good and good belongs to love (n. 4353, 4997, 7179, 10122, 10367). From this it follows that the understanding is a recipient of faith, and the will a recipient of love (n. 7179, 10122, 10367). And since the understanding of man is capable of receiving faith in God and the will is capable of receiving love to God, man is capable of being conjoined with God in faith and love, and he that is capable of being conjoined with God in love and faith can never die (n. 4525, 6323, 9231).

474-1 The will of man is the very being [esse] of his life, because it is the receptacle of love or good, and the understanding is the outgo [existere] of life therefrom, because it is the receptacle of faith or truth (n. 3619, 5002, 9282). Thus the life of the will is the chief life of man, and the life of the understanding proceeds therefrom (n. 585, 590, 3619, 7342, 8885, 9282, 10076, 10109, 10110). In the same way as light proceeds from fire or flame (n. 6032,

6314). From this it follows that man is man by virtue of his will and his understanding therefrom (n. 8911, 9069, 9071, 10076, 10109, 10110). Every man is loved and esteemed by others in accordance with the good of his will and of his understanding therefrom, for he that wills well and understands well is loved and esteemed; and he that understands well and does not will well is set aside and despised (n. 8911, 10076). After death man continues to be such as his will is, and his understanding therefrom (n, 9069, 9071, 9386, 10153). Consequently after death man continues to be such as his love is, and his faith therefrom; and whatever belongs to his faith and not also to his love then vanishes, because it is not in the man, thus not of the man (n. 553, 2364, 10153).

475-1 Interior things flow in successively into exterior things even down to the extreme or outmost, and there they come forth and have permanent existence (n. 634, 6451, 6465, 9215, 9216). They not only flow in, but in the outmost they form the simultaneous, in what order (n. 5897, 6451, 8603, 10099). Thereby all interior things are held together in connection, and have permanent existence (n. 9828). Deeds or works are the outmosts which contain the interiors (n. 10331). Therefore being recompensed and judged according to deeds and works is being recompensed and judged in accordance with all things of one's love and faith, or of his will and thought because these are the interiors contained in deeds and works (n. 3147, 3934, 6073, 8911, 10331, 10332).

479-1 A "way," a "path," a "road," a "street," and a "broad street," signify truths leading to good, or falsities leading to evil (n. 627, 2333, 10422). "To sweep [or prepare] a way" means to prepare for the reception of truths (n. 3142). "To make known the way" means, in respect to the Lord, to instruct in truths that lead to good (n. 10565).

481-1 In the highest sense, the Lord is the neighbor, because He is to be loved above all things; but loving the Lord is loving what is from Him, because He Himself is in everything that is from Him, thus it is loving what is good and true (n. 2425, 3419, 6706, 6711, 6819, 6823, 8123). Loving what is good and true which is from the Lord is living in accordance with good and truth, and this is loving the Lord (n. 10143, 10153, 10310, 10336, 10578, 10645). Every man and every society, also one's country and the church, and in a universal sense the Lord's kingdom, are the neighbor, and doing good to these from a love of good in accord with their state is loving the neighbor; that is, their good that should be consulted is the neighbor (n. 6818-6824, 8123). Moral good also, which is honesty, and civil good, which is justice, are the neighbor; and to act honestly and justly from the love of honesty and justice is loving the neighbor (n. 2915, 4730, 8120-8123). Thus charity towards the neighbor extends to all things of the life of man, and loving the neighbor is doing what is good and just, and acting honestly from the heart, in every function and in every work (n. 2417, 8121, 8124). The doctrine in the Ancient Church was the doctrine of charity, and from that they had wisdom (n. 2385, 2417, 3419, 3420, 4844, 6628).

484-1 Man's own consists in loving himself more than God, and the world more than heaven, and in making nothing of his neighbor in comparison with himself, thus it consists in the love of self and of the world (n. 694, 731, 4317). Man is born into this own, and it is dense evil (n. 210, 215, 731, 874-876, 987, 1047, 2307, 2308, 3518, 3701, 3812, 8480, 8550, 10283, 10284, 10286, 10732). From what is man's own not only every evil but also every falsity is derived (n.

1047, 10283, 10284, 10286). The evils that are from what is man's own are contempt for others, enmity, hatred, revenge, cruelty, deceit (n. 6667, 7370, 7373, 7374, 9348, 10038, 10742). So far as what is man's own rules, the good of love and the truth of faith are either rejected or suffocated or perverted (n. 2041, 7491, 7492, 7643, 8487, 10455, 10742). What is man's own is hell in him (n. 694, 8480). The good that man does from what is his own is not good, but in itself is evil (n. 8480).

487-1 From correspondence "darkness" in the Word signifies falsities, and "thick darkness" the falsities of evil (n. 1839, 1860, 7688, 7711). To the evil the light of heaven is thick darkness (n. 1861, 6832, 8197). Those that are in the hells are said to be in darkness because they are in falsities of evil; of such (n. 3340, 4418, 4531). In the Word "the blind" signify those that are in falsities and are not willing to be taught (n. 2383, 6990).

488-1 In the word a "hole" or "the cleft of a rock" signifies obscurity and falsity of faith (n. 10582). Because a "rock" signifies faith from the Lord (n. 8581, 10580); and a "stone" the truth of faith (n. 114, 643, 1298, 3720, 6426, 8609, 10376).

488-2 The defilements of truth correspond to urine (n. 5390).

489-1 In the Word a "field of corn" signifies a state of the reception and growth of truth from good (n. 9294). "Standing corn" signifies truth in conception (n. 9146), "Vineyards" signify the spiritual church and the truths of that church (n. 1069, 9139). "Precious stones" signify the truths of heaven and of the church transparent from good (n. 114, 9863, 9865, 9868, 9873, 9905). A "window" signifies the intellectual faculty which pertains to the internal sight (n. 655, 658, 3391).

489-2 A "garden," a "grove," and a "park," signify intelligence (n. 100, 108, 3220), This is why the ancients celebrated holy worship in groves (n. 2722, 4552). "Flowers" and "flower beds" signify truths learned and knowledges (n. 9553). "Herbs," "grasses," and "grass plots" signify truths learned (n. 7571). "Trees" signify perception and knowledges (n. 103, 2163, 2682, 2722, 2972, 7692).

Section 11

Let it be understood that man is wholly such as his interiors are, and not such as his exteriors are separate from his interiors. This is because his interiors belong to his spirit, and the life of his spirit is the life of man, for from it his body lives; and because of this such as a man's interiors are such he continues to be to eternity. But as the exteriors pertain to the body they are separated after death, and those of them that adhere to the spirit are laid asleep, and serve purely as a plane for the interiors, as has been shown above in treating of the memory of man which continues after death. This makes evident what is man's own and what is not his own, namely, that with the evil man nothing that belongs to his exterior thought from which he speaks, or to the exterior will from which he acts, is his own, but only that which belongs to his interior thought and will.

When the first state, which is the state of the exteriors treated of in the preceding chapter, has been passed through, the man-spirit is let into the state of his interiors, or into the state of his interior will and its thought, in which he had been in the world when left to himself to think freely and without restraint. Into this state he unconsciously glides, just as when in the world he withdraws the thought nearest to his speech, that is, from which he speaks, towards his interior thought and abides in the latter. Therefore in this state of his interiors the man-spirit is in himself and in his very life; for to think freely from his own affection is the very life of man, and is himself.

In this state the spirit thinks from his very will, thus from his very affection, or from his very love; and thought and will then make one, and one in such a manner that he seems scarcely to think but only to will. It is nearly the same when he speaks, yet with the difference that he speaks with a kind of fear that the thoughts of the will may go forth naked, since by his social life in the world this has come to be a part of his will.

All men without exception are let into this state after death, because it is their spirit's own state. The former state is such as the man was in regard to his spirit when in company; and that is not his own state. That this state, namely, the state of the exteriors into which man first comes after death (as shown in the preceding chapter) is not his own state, many things show, for example, that spirits not only think but also speak from their affection, since their speech is from their affection (as has been said and shown in the chapter on the speech of angels, n. 234-245). It was in this way that man had thought while in the world when he was thinking within himself, for at such times his thought was not from his bodily words, but he [mentally] saw the things, and in a minute of time saw more than he could afterwards utter in half an hour. Again that the state of the exteriors is not man's own state or the state of his spirit is evident from the fact that when he is in company in the world he speaks in accord with the laws of moral and civil life, and at such times interior thought rules the exterior thought, as one person rules another, to keep him from transgressing the limits of decorum and good manners. It is evident also from the fact that when a man thinks within himself, he thinks how he must speak and act in order to please and to secure friendship, good will, and favor, and this in extraneous ways, that is, otherwise than he would do if he acted in accordance with his own will. All this shows that the state of the interiors that the spirit is let into is his own state, and was his own state when he was living in the world as a man.

When the spirit is in the state of his interiors it becomes clearly evident what the man was in himself when he was in the world, for at such times he acts from what is his own. He that had been in the world interiorly in good then acts rationally and wisely, and even more wisely than in the world, because he is released from connection with the body, and thus from those earthly things that caused obscurity and interposed as it were a cloud. But he that was in evil in the world then acts foolishly and insanely, and even more insanely than in the world, because he is free and under no restraint. For while he lived in the world he was sane in outward appearance, since by means of externals he made himself appear to be a rational man; but when he has been stripped of his externals his insanities are revealed. An evil man who in externals takes on the semblance of a good man may be likened to a vessel shining and polished on the outside and covered with a lid, within which filth of all kinds is hidden, in accordance with the Lord's saying: Ye are like whited sepulchers, which outwardly appear beautiful, but inwardly are full of dead men's bones and of all uncleanness (Matt. 23:27).

All that have lived a good life in the world and have acted from conscience, who are such as have acknowledged the Divine and have loved Divine truths, especially such as have applied those truths to life, seem to themselves, when let into the state of their interiors, like one aroused from sleep into full wakefulness, or like one passing from darkness into light. They then think from the light of heaven, thus from an interior wisdom, and they act from good, thus from an interior affection. Heaven flows into their thoughts and affections with an interior blessedness and delight that they had previously had no knowledge of; for they have communication with the angels of heaven. They then acknowledge the Lord and worship Him from their very life, for being in the state of their interiors they are in their proper life (as has been said just above, n. 505); and as freedom pertains to interior affection they then acknowledge and worship the Lord from freedom. Thus, too, they withdraw from external sanctity and come into that internal sanctity in which worship itself truly consists. Such is the state of those that have lived a Christian life in accordance with the commandments in the Word. [2] But the state of those that have lived an evil life in the world and who have had no conscience, and have in consequence denied the Divine, is the direct opposite of this. For everyone who lives an evil life, inwardly in himself denies the Divine, however much he may suppose when in external thought that he acknowledges the Lord and does not deny Him; for acknowledging the Divine and living an evil life are opposites. When such in the other life enter into the state of their interiors, and are heard speaking and seen acting, they appear foolish; for from their evil lusts they burst forth into all sorts of abominations, into contempt of others, ridicule and blasphemy, hatred and revenge; they plot intrigues, some with a cunning and malice that can scarcely be believed to be possible in any man. For they are then in a state of freedom to act in harmony with the thoughts of their will, since they are separated from the outward conditions that restrained and checked them in the world. In a word, they are deprived of their rationality, because their reason while they were in the world did not have its seat in their interiors, but in their exteriors; and yet they seemed to themselves to be wiser than others. [3] This being their character, while in the second state they are let down by short intervals into the state of their exteriors, and into a recollection of their actions when they were in the state of their interiors; and some of them then feel ashamed, and confess that they have been insane; some do not feel ashamed; and some are angry because they are not permitted to remain permanently in the state of their exteriors. But these are shown what they would be if they were to continue in that state, namely, that they would attempt to accomplish in secret ways the same evil ends, and by semblances of goodness, honesty, and justice, would mislead the simple in heart and faith, and would utterly destroy themselves; for their exteriors would at length burn with the same fire as their interiors, and their whole life would be consumed.

When in this second state spirits become visibly just what they had been in themselves while in the world, what they then did and said secretly being now made manifest; for they are now restrained by no outward considerations, and therefore what they have said and done secretly they now say and endeavor to do openly, having no longer any fear of loss of reputation, such as they had in the world. They are also brought into many states of their evils, that what they are may be evident to angels and good spirits. Thus are hidden things laid open and secret things uncovered, in accordance with the Lord's words: There is nothing covered up that shall not be revealed, and hid that shall not be known. Whatsoever ye have said in the darkness shall be heard in the light, and what ye have spoken in the ear in the inner chambers shall be proclaimed on the housetops (Luke 12:2, 3). And elsewhere: I say unto you, that every idle word that men shall speak they shall give account thereof in the day of judgment (Matt. 12:36).

The nature of the wicked in this state cannot be described in a few words, for each one is insane in accord with his own lusts, and these are various; therefore I will merely mention some special instances from which conclusions may be formed respecting the rest. Those that have loved themselves above everything, and in their occupations and employments have looked to their own honor, and have performed uses and found delight in them not for the use's sake but for the sake of reputation, that they might because of them be esteemed more worthy than others, and have thus been fascinated by their reputation for honor, are more stupid in this second state than others; for so far as one loves himself he is separated from heaven, and so far as he is separated from heaven he is separated from wisdom. [2] But those that have not only been in self-love but have been crafty also, and have raised themselves to honors by means of crafty practices, affiliate themselves with the worst of spirits, and learn magic arts, which are abuses of Divine order, and by means of these they assail and infest all who do not honor them, laying snares, fomenting hatred, burning with revenge, and are eager to vent their rage on all who do not yield to them; and they rush into all these enormities so far as their fiendish companions favor them; and at length they meditate upon how they can climb up into heaven to destroy it, or be worshiped there as gods. To such length does their madness carry them. [3] Papists of this character are more insane than the rest, for they cherish the notion that heaven and hell are subject to their power, and that they can remit sins at pleasure, claiming to themselves all that is Divine, and calling themselves Christ. This persuasion is such with them that wherever it flows in it disturbs the mind and induces darkness even to pain. Such are nearly the same in both the first and the second state; but in the second they are without rationality. Of their insanities and their lot after this state some particulars will be given in the treatise on The Last Judgement and the Destruction of Babylon. [4] Those that have attributed creation to nature, and have therefore in heart if not with the lips denied the Divine, and thus all things of the church and of heaven, affiliate with their like in this second state, and call everyone a god who excels in craftiness, worshiping him even with Divine honors. I have seen such in an assembly adoring a magician, debating about nature, and behaving like fools, as if they were beasts under a human form, while among them there were some who in the world had been in stations of dignity, and some who had been esteemed learned and wise. So with others in other states. [5] From these few instances it may be inferred what those are who have the interiors of their minds closed heaven-wards, as is the case with all who have received no influx out of heaven through acknowledgment of the Divine and a life of faith. Everyone can judge from himself how he would act if, being such, he were left free to act with no fear of the law and no fear in regard to his life, and with no outward restraints, such as fear of injury to one's reputation or of loss of honor and gain and consequent pleasures. [6] Nevertheless, the insanity of such is restrained by the Lord that it may not rush beyond the limits of use; for even such spirits perform some use. In them good spirits see what evil is and its nature, and what man is when he is not led by the Lord. Another of their uses is their collecting together evil spirits like themselves and separating them from the good; and another, that the truths and goods that the evil had outwardly professed and feigned are taken away from them, and they are brought into the evils of their life and the falsities of their evil, and are thus prepared for hell. [7] For no one enters hell until he is in his own evil and the falsities of evil, since no one is permitted there to have a divided mind, that is, to think and speak one thing and to will another. Every evil spirit there must think what is false from evil, and speak from the falsity of evil, in both respects from the will, thus from his own essential love and its delight and pleasure, in the same way that he thought while in the world when he was in his spirit, that is, in the same way as he thought in himself when he thought from interior affection. The reason is that the will is the man himself, and not the thought except so far as it partakes of the will, the will being the very nature itself or disposition of the man. Therefore man's being let into his will is being let into his nature or disposition, and likewise into his life; for by his life man puts on a nature; and after death he continues to be such as the nature is that he has acquired by his life in the world; and with the evil this nature can no longer be amended and changed by means of the thought or by the understanding of truth.

When evil spirits are in this second state, as they rush into evils of every kind they are subjected to frequent and grievous punishments. In the world of spirits there are many kinds of punishment; and there is no regard for person, whether one had been in the world a king or a servant. Every evil carries its punishment with it, the two making one; therefore whoever is in evil is also in the punishment of evil. And yet no one in the other world suffers punishment on account of the evils that he had done in this world, but only on account of the evils that he then does; although it amounts to the same and is the same thing whether it be said that men suffer punishment on account of their evils in the world or that they suffer punishment on account of the evils they do in the other life, since everyone after death returns into his own life and thus into like evils; and the man continues the same as he had been in the life of the body (n. 470-484). Men are punished for the reason that the fear of punishment is the sole means of subduing evils in this state. Exhortation is no longer of any avail, neither is instruction or fear of the law and of the loss of reputation, since everyone then acts from his nature; and that nature can be restrained and broken only by punishments. But good spirits, although they had done evils in the world, are never punished, because their evils do not return. Moreover, I have learned that the evils they did were of a different kind or nature, not being done purposely in opposition to the truth, or from any other badness of heart than that which they received by inheritance from their parents, and that they were borne into this by a blind delight when they were in externals separate from internals.

Everyone goes to his own society in which his spirit had been in the world; for every man, as regards his spirit, is conjoined to some society, either infernal or heavenly, the evil man to an infernal society and the good man to a heavenly society, and to that society he is brought after death (see n. 438). The spirit is led to his society gradually, and at length enters it. When an evil spirit is in the state of his interiors he is turned by degrees toward his own society, and at length, before that state is ended, directly to it; and when that state is ended he himself casts himself into the hell where those are who are like himself. This act of casting down appears to the sight like one falling headlong with the head downwards and the feet upwards. The cause of this appearance is that the spirit himself is in an inverted order, having loved infernal things and rejected heavenly things. In this second state some evil spirits enter the hells and come out again by turns; but these do not appear to fall headlong as those do that are fully vastated. Moreover, the society itself in which they had been as regards their spirit while in the world is shown to them when they are in the state of their exteriors, that they may thus learn that even while in the life of the body they were in hell, although not in the same state as those that are in hell itself, but in the same state as those who are in the world of spirits. Of this state, as compared with those that are in hell, more will be said hereafter.

In this second state the separation of evil spirits from good spirits takes place. For in the first state they are together, since while a spirit is in his exteriors he is as he was in the world, thus the evil with the good and the good with the evil; but it is otherwise when he has been brought into his interiors and left to his own nature or will. The separation of evil spirits from good spirits is effected by various means; in general by their being taken about to those societies with which in their first state they had communication by means of their good thoughts and affections, thus to those societies that they had induced to believe by outward appearances that they were not evil. Usually they are led about through a wide circle, and everywhere what they really are is made manifest to good spirits. At the sight of them the good spirits turn away; and at the same time the evil spirits who are being led about turn their faces away from the good towards that quarter where their infernal society is, into which they are about to come. Other methods of separation, which are many, will not now be mentioned.

LIII. THIRD STATE OF MAN AFTER DEATH, WHICH IS A STATE OF INSTRUCTION FOR THOSE WHO ENTER HEAVEN. The third state of man after death, that is, of his spirit, is a state of instruction. This state is for those who enter heaven and become angels. It is not for those who enter hell, because such are incapable of being taught, and therefore their second state is also their third, ending in this, that they are wholly turned to their own love, thus to that infernal society which is in a like love. When this has been done they will and think from that love and as that love is infernal they will nothing but what is evil and think nothing but what is false; and in such thinking and willing they find their delights, because these belong to their love; and in consequence of this they reject everything good and true which they had previously adopted as serviceable to their love as means. [2] Good spirits, on the other hand, are led from the second state into the third, which is the state of their preparation for heaven by means of instruction. For one can be prepared for heaven only by means of knowledges of good and truth, that is, only by means of instruction, since one can know what spiritual good and truth are, and what evil and falsity are, which are their opposites, only by being taught. One can learn in the world what civil and moral good and truth are, which are called justice and honesty, because there are civil laws in the world that teach what is just, and there is interaction with others whereby man learns to live in accordance with moral laws, all of which have relation to what is honest and right. But spiritual good and truth are learned from heaven, not from the world. They can be learned from the Word and from the doctrine of the church that is drawn from the Word and yet unless man in respect to his interiors which belong to his mind is in heaven spiritual good and truth cannot flow into his life; and man is in heaven when he both acknowledges the Divine and acts justly and honestly for the reason that he ought so to act because it is commanded in the Word. This is living justly and honestly for the sake of the Divine, and not for the sake of self and the world, as ends. [3] But no one can so act until he has been taught, for example, that there is a God, that there is a heaven and a hell, that there is a life after death, that God ought to be loved supremely, and the neighbor as oneself, and that what is taught in the Word, ought to be believed because the Word is Divine. Without a knowledge and acknowledgment of these things man is unable to think spiritually; and if he has no thought about them he does not will them; for what a man does not know he cannot think, and what he does not think he cannot will. So it is when man wills these things that heaven flows into his life, that is, the Lord through heaven, for the Lord flows into the will and through the will into the thought, and through both into the life, and the whole life of man is from these. All this makes clear that spiritual good and truth are learned not from the world but from heaven, and that one can be prepared for heaven only by means of instruction. [4] Moreover, so far as the Lord flows into the life of any one He instructs him, for so far He kindles the will with the love of knowing truths and enlightens the thought to know them; and so far as this is done the interiors of man are opened and heaven is implanted in them; and furthermore, what is Divine and heavenly flows into the honest things pertaining to moral life and into the just things pertaining to civil life in man, and makes them spiritual, since man then does these things from the Divine, which is doing them for the sake of the Divine. For the things honest and just pertaining to moral and civil life which a man does from that source are the essential effects of spiritual life; and the effect derives its all from the effecting cause, since such as the cause is such is the effect.

Instruction is given by the angels of many societies, especially those in the northern and southern quarters, because those angelic societies are in intelligence and wisdom from a knowledge of good and truth. The places of instruction are towards the north and are various, arranged and distinguished according to the kinds and varieties of heavenly goods, that all and each may be instructed there according to their disposition and ability to receive; the places extending round about to a great distance. The good spirits who are to be instructed are brought by the Lord to these places when they have completed their second state in the world of spirits, and yet not all; for there are some that have been instructed in the world, and have been prepared there by the Lord for heaven, and these are taken up into heaven by another way-some immediately after death, some after a short stay with good spirits, where the grosser things of their thoughts and affections which they had contracted from honors and riches in the world are removed, and in that way they are purified. Some first endure vastations, which is effected in places under the soles of the feet, called the lower earth, where some suffer severely. These are such as had confirmed themselves in falsities and yet had led good lives, for when falsities have been confirmed they inhere with much force, and until they have been dispersed truths cannot be seen, and thus cannot be accepted. But vastations and how they are effected have been treated of in the Arcana Coelestia, from which the notes below have been collected. 513-1

All who are in places of instruction dwell apart; for each one is connected in regard to his interiors with that society of heaven which he is about to enter; thus as the societies of heaven are arranged in accord with the heavenly form (see above, n. 200-212), so are the places there where instruction is given; and for this reason when those places are viewed from heaven something like a heaven in a smaller form is seen. They are spread out in length from east to west, and in breadth from south to north; but the breadth appears to be less than the length. The arrangement in general is as follows. In front are those who died in childhood and have been brought up in heaven to the age of early youth; these after passing the state of their infancy with those having charge of them, are brought hither by the Lord and instructed. Behind these are the places where those are taught who died in adult age, and who in the world had an affection for truth derived from good of life. Again, behind these are those who in the world were connected with the Mohammedan religion, and lived a moral life and acknowledged one Divine, and the Lord as the very Prophet. When these withdraw from Mohammed, because he can give them no help, they approach the Lord and worship Him and acknowledge His Divinity, and they are then instructed in the Christian religion. Behind these more to the north are the places of instruction of various heathen nations who in the world have lived a good life in conformity with their religion, and have thereby acquired a kind of conscience, and have done what is just and right not so much from a regard to the laws of their government, as from a regard to the laws of religion, which they believed ought to be sacredly observed, and in no way violated by their doings. When these have been taught they are all easily led to acknowledge the Lord, because it is impressed on their hearts that God is not invisible, but is visible under a human form. These in number exceed all the rest, and the best of them are from Africa.

But all are not taught in the same way, nor by the same societies of heaven. Those that have been brought up from childhood in heaven, not having imbibed falsities from the falsities of religion or defiled their spiritual life with the dregs pertaining to honors and riches in the world, receive instruction from the angels of the interior heavens; while those that have died in adult age receive instruction mainly from angels of the lowest heaven, because these angels are better suited to them than the angels of the interior heavens, who are in interior wisdom which is not yet acceptable to them. But the Mohammedans receive instruction from angels who had been previously in the same religion and had been converted to Christianity. The heathen, too, are taught by their angels.

All teaching there is from doctrine drawn from the Word, and not from the Word apart from doctrine. Christians are taught from heavenly doctrine, which is in entire agreement with the internal sense of the Word. All others, as the Mohammedans and heathen, are taught from doctrines suited to their apprehension, which differ from heavenly doctrine only in this, that spiritual life is taught by means of moral life in harmony with the good tenets of their religion from which they had derived their life in the world.

Instruction in the heavens differs from instruction on earth in that knowledges are not committed to memory, but to life; for the memory of spirits is in their life, for they receive and imbibe everything that is in harmony with their life, and do not receive, still less imbibe, what is not in harmony with it; for spirits are affections, and are therefore in a human form that is similar to their affections. [2] Being such they are constantly animated by an affection for truth that looks to the uses of life; for the Lord provides for everyone's loving the uses suited to his genius; and that love is exalted by the hope of becoming an angel. And as all the uses of heaven have relation to the general use, which is the good of the Lord's kingdom, which in heaven is the fatherland, and as all special and particular uses are to be valued in proportion as they more closely and fully have regard to that general use, so all of these special and particular uses, which are innumerable, are good and heavenly; therefore in everyone an affection for truth is so conjoined with an affection for use that the two make one; and thereby truth is so implanted in use that the truths they acquire are truths of use. In this way are angelic spirits taught and prepared for heaven. [3] An affection for truth that is suited to the use is insinuated by various means, most of which are unknown in the world; chiefly by representatives of uses which in the spiritual world are exhibited in a thousand ways, and with such delights and pleasures that they permeate the spirit from the interiors of its mind to the exteriors of its body, and thus affect the whole; and in consequence the spirit becomes as it were his use; and therefore when he comes into his society, into which he is initiated by instruction, he is in his life by being in his use. 517-1 From all this it is clear that knowledges, which are external truths, do not bring any one into heaven; but the life itself, which is a life of uses implanted by means of knowledges.

There were some spirits who had convinced themselves, by thinking about it in the world, that they would go to heaven and be received before others because of their learning and their great knowledge of the Word and of the doctrines of their churches, believing that they were wise in consequence, and were such as are meant by those of whom it is said that They shall shine as the brightness of the firmament, and as the stars (Daniel 12:3). But these were examined to see whether their knowledges resided in the memory or in the life. Such of them as had a genuine affection of truth, that is, who had uses separated from what pertains to the body and the world as their end, which are essentially spiritual uses—these, when they had been instructed, were received into heaven; and it was then given them to know what it is that shines in heaven, namely, Divine truth (which is the light of heaven) in use, which is a plane that receives the rays of that light and turns them into various splendors. But those in whom knowledges resided merely in the memory, and who had acquired therefrom an ability to reason about truths and to prove what they had already accepted as principles, seeing such principles, after they had confirmed them, as truths, although they were falsities, these, as they were in no heavenly light, and yet were in a belief derived from the conceit that usually adheres to such intelligence that they were more learned than others, and would for that reason enter heaven and be served by the angels, in order that they might be withdrawn from their delusive faith, were taken up to the first or outmost heaven to be introduced into an angelic society. But at the very threshold their eyes began to be darkened by the inflowing of the light of heaven, and their understanding to be disturbed, and at length they began to gasp as if at the point of death; and as soon as they felt the heat of heaven, which is heavenly love, they began to be inwardly tormented. They were therefore cast down, and afterwards were taught that knowledges do not make an angel, but the life itself, which is gained by means of knowledges, for knowledges regarded in themselves are outside of heaven; but life acquired by means of knowledges is within heaven.

When spirits have been prepared for heaven by instruction in the places above described, which is effected in a short time on account of their being in spiritual ideas that comprehend many particulars together, they are clothed with angelic garments, which are mostly glowing white as if made of fine linen; and they are thus brought to the way that leads upwards towards heaven, and are delivered there to angel guards, and afterwards are received by other angels and introduced into societies and into many blessednesses there. After this each one is led by the Lord into his own society, which is also effected by various ways, sometimes by winding paths. The ways by which they are led are not known to any angel, but are known to the Lord alone. When they come to their own society their interiors are opened; and as these are in conformity with the interiors of the angels who are in that society they are immediately recognized and received with joy.

To this I will add a memorable fact respecting the ways that lead from these places to heaven, by which the newly arrived angels are introduced. There are eight ways, two from each place of instruction, one going up in an eastern direction the other towards the west. Those that enter the Lord's celestial kingdom are introduced by the eastern way, while those that enter the spiritual kingdom are introduced by the western way. The four ways that lead to the Lord's celestial kingdom appear adorned with olive trees and fruit trees of various kinds; but those that lead to the Lord's spiritual kingdom appear adorned with vines and laurels. This is from correspondence, because vines and laurels correspond to affection for truth and its uses, while olives and fruits correspond to affection for good and its uses.

NO ONE ENTERS HEAVEN BY MERCY APART FROM MEANS. Those that have not been instructed about heaven and the way to heaven, and about the life of heaven in man, suppose that being received into heaven is a mere matter of mercy, and is granted to those that have faith, and for whom the Lord intercedes; thus that it is an admission from mere favor; consequently that all men without exception might be saved if the Lord so pleased, and some even believe that all in hell might be so saved. But those who so think know nothing about man, that he is just such as his life is, and that his life is such as his love is, both in respect to the interiors pertaining to his will and understanding and in respect to the exteriors pertaining to his body; also that his bodily form is merely the external form in which the interiors exhibit themselves in effect; consequently that one's love is the whole man (see above, n. 363). Nor do they know that the body lives not from itself, but from its spirit, and that a man's spirit is his essential affection, and his spiritual body is nothing else than his affection in human form, and in such a form it appears after death (see above, n. 453-460). So long as man remains ignorant of all this he may be induced to believe that salvation involves nothing but the Divine good pleasure, which is called mercy and grace.

But first let us consider what the Divine mercy is. The divine mercy is pure mercy towards the whole human race, to save it; and it is also unceasing towards every man, and is never withdrawn from any one; so that everyone is saved who can be saved. And yet no one can be saved except by Divine means, which means the Lord reveals in the Word. The Divine means are what are called Divine truths, which teach how man must live in order to be saved. By these truths the Lord leads man to heaven, and by them He implants in man the life of heaven. This the Lord does for all. But the life of heaven can be implanted in no one unless he abstains from evil, for evil obstructs. So far, therefore, as man abstains from evil he is led by the Lord out of pure mercy by His Divine means, and this from infancy to the end of his life in the world and afterwards to eternity. This is what is meant by the Divine mercy. And from this it is evident that the mercy of the Lord is pure mercy, but not apart from means, that is, it does not look to saving all out of mere good pleasure, however they may have lived.

The Lord never does anything contrary to order, because He Himself is Order. The Divine truth that goes forth from the Lord is what constitutes order;

and Divine truths are the laws of order. It is in accord with these laws that the Lord leads man. Consequently to save man by mercy apart from means would be contrary to Divine order, and what is contrary to Divine order is contrary to the Divine. Divine order is heaven in man, and man has perverted this in himself by a life contrary to the laws of order, which are Divine truths. Into this order man is brought back by the Lord out of pure mercy by means of the laws of order; and so far as he is brought back into this order he receives heaven in himself; and he that receives heaven in himself enters heaven. This again makes evident that the Lord's Divine mercy is pure mercy, and not mercy apart from means. 523-1

If men could be saved by mercy apart from means all would be saved, even those in hell; in fact, there would be no hell, because the Lord is mercy itself, love itself, and goodness itself. Therefore it is inconsistent with His Divine to say that He is able to save all apart from means and does not save them. It is known from the Word that the Lord wills the salvation of all, and the damnation of no one.

Most of those who enter the other life from the Christian world bring with them this belief that they can be saved by mercy apart from means, and pray for that mercy; but when examined they are found to believe that entering heaven is merely gaining admission, and that those who are let in are in heavenly joy. They are wholly ignorant of what heaven is and what heavenly joy is, and consequently are told that the Lord denies heaven to no one, and that they can be admitted and can stay there if they desire it. Those who so desired were admitted; but as soon as they reached the first threshold they were seized with such anguish of heart from a draught of heavenly heat, which is the love in which angels are, and from an inflow of heavenly light, which is Divine truth, that they felt in themselves infernal torment instead of heavenly joy, and struck with dismay they cast themselves down headlong. Thus they were taught by living experience that it is impossible to grant heaven to any one from mercy apart from means.

I have occasionally talked with angels about this, and have told them that most of those in the world who live in evil, when they talk with others about heaven and eternal life, express no other idea than that entering heaven is merely being admitted from mercy alone. And this is believed by those especially who make faith the only medium of salvation. For such from the principles of their religion have no regard to the life and the deeds of love that make life, and thus to none of the other means by which the Lord implants heaven in man and renders him receptive of heavenly joy; and as they thus reject every actual mediation they conclude, as a necessary consequence of the principle, that man enters heaven from mercy alone, to which mercy God the Father is believed to be moved by the intercession of the Son. [2] To all this the angels said that they knew such a tenet follows of necessity from the assumption that man is saved by faith alone, and since that tenet is the head of all the rest, and since into it, because it is not true, no light from heaven can flow, this is the source of the ignorance that prevails in the church at this day in regard to the Lord, heaven, the life after death, heavenly joy, the essence of love and charity, and in general, in regard to good and its conjunction with truth, consequently in regard to the life of man, whence it is and what it is;

when it should be known that thought never constitutes any one's life, but the will and the consequent deeds; and that the life is from the thought only to the extent that the thought is derived from the will; neither is life from the faith except so far as the faith is derived from love. Angels are grieved that these persons do not know that faith alone is impossible in any one, since faith apart from its origin, which is love, is nothing but knowledge, and in some is merely a sort of persuasion that has the semblance of faith (see above, n. 482). Such a persuasion is not in the life of man, but outside of it, since it is separated from man unless it coheres with his love. [3] The angels said further that those who hold to this principle concerning the essential means of salvation in man must needs believe in mercy apart from means, for they perceive both from natural light and from the experience of sight that faith separate does not constitute the life of man, since those who lead an evil life are able to think and to be persuaded the same as others; and from this comes the belief that the evil as well as the good can be saved, provided that at the hour of death they talk with confidence about intercession, and about the mercy that is granted through that intercession. The angels declared that they had never yet seen any one who had lived an evil life received into heaven from mercy apart from means, whatever trust or confidence (which is preeminently meant by faith) he had exhibited in his talk in the world. [4] When asked about Abraham, Isaac, Jacob, David, and the apostles, whether they were not received into heaven from mercy apart from means, the angels replied that not one of them was so received, but everyone in accordance with his life in the world; that they knew where these were, and that they were no more esteemed there than others. They said that these persons are mentioned with honor in the Word for the reason that in the internal sense the Lord is meant by them - by Abraham, Isaac, and Jacob, the Lord in respect to the Divine and the Divine Human; by David the Lord in respect to the Divine royalty; and by the apostles the Lord in respect to Divine truths; also that when the Word is read by man the angels have no perception whatever of these men, for their names do not enter heaven; but they have instead a perception of the Lord as He has just been described; consequently in the Word that is in heaven (see above, n. 259) there are no such names mentioned, since that Word is the internal sense of the Word that is in the world. 526-1

I can testify from much experience that it is impossible to implant the life of heaven in those who in the world have lived a life opposite to the life of heaven. There were some who had believed that when after death they should hear Divine truths from the angels they would readily accept them and believe them, and consequently live a different life, and could thus be received into heaven. But this was tried with very many, although it was confined to those who held this belief, and was permitted in their case to teach them that repentance is not possible after death. Some of those with whom the experiment was made understood truths and seemed to accept them; but as soon as they turned to the life of their love they rejected them, and even spoke against them. Others were unwilling to hear them, and at once rejected them. Others wished to have the life of love that they had contracted from the world taken away from them, and to have the angelic life, or the life of heaven, infused in its place. This, too, was permitted to be done; but as soon as the life of their love was taken away they lay as if dead, with their powers gone. By these and other experiments the simple good were taught that no one's life can by any means be changed after death; and that an evil life can in no way be converted into a good life, or an infernal life into an angelic life, for every spirit from head to heel is such as his love is, and therefore such as his life is; and to convert his life into its opposite is to destroy the spirit completely. The angels declare that it would be easier to change a night-owl into a dove, or a horned-owl into a bird of paradise, than to change an infernal spirit into an angel of heaven. That man after death continues to be such as his life had been in the world can be seen above in its own chapter (n. 470-484). From all this it is evident that no one can be received into heaven from mercy apart from means.

IT IS NOT SO DIFFICULT TO LIVE THE LIFE THAT LEADS TO HEAVEN AS IS BELIEVED. There are some who believe that to live the life that leads to heaven, which is called the spiritual life, is difficult, because they have been told that man must renounce the world, must divest himself of the lusts called the lusts of the body and the flesh, and must live spiritually; and they understand this to mean that they must discard worldly things, which consist chiefly in riches and honors; that they must walk continually in pious meditation on God, salvation, and eternal life; and must spend their life in prayers and in reading the Word and pious books. Such is their idea of renouncing the world, and living in the spirit and not in the flesh. But that this is not at all true it has been given me to know by much experience and from conversation with the angels. I have learned, in fact, that those who renounce the world and live in the spirit in this manner acquire a sorrowful life that is not receptive of heavenly joy, since everyone's life continues the same after death. On the contrary, to receive the life of heaven a man must needs live in the world and engage in its business and employments, and by means of a moral and civil life there receive the spiritual life. In no other way can the spiritual life be formed in man, or his spirit prepared for heaven; for to live an internal life and not at the same time an external life is like dwelling in a house that has no foundation, that gradually sinks or becomes cracked and rent asunder, or totters till it falls.

When the life of man is scanned and explored by rational insight it is found to be threefold, namely, spiritual, moral, and civil, with these three lives distinct from each other. For there are men who live a civil life and not as yet a moral and spiritual life; and there are men who live a moral life and not as yet a spiritual life; and there are those who live a civil life, a moral life, and a spiritual life at the same time. These live the life of heaven; but the former live the life of the world separated from the life of heaven. This shows, in the first place, that the spiritual life is not a life separated from natural life or the life of the world, but is joined with it as the soul is joined with its body, and if it were separated it would be, as was said, like living in a house that has no foundation. For moral and civil life is the active plane of the spiritual life, since to will well is the province of the spiritual life, and to act well of the moral and civil life, and if the latter is separated from the former the spiritual life consists solely of thought and speech, and the will, left with no support, recedes; and yet the will is the very spiritual part of man.

That it is not so difficult as some believe to live the life that leads to heaven will now be shown. Who cannot live a civil and moral life? For everyone from his childhood is initiated into that life, and learns what it is by living in the world. Moreover, everyone, whether evil or good, lives that life; for who does not wish to be called honest, and who does not wish to be called just? Almost everyone practices honesty and justice outwardly, so far as to seem to be honest and just at heart, or to seem to act from real honesty and justice. The spiritual man ought to live in like manner, and can do so as easily as the natural man can, with this difference only, that the spiritual man believes in the Divine, and acts honestly and justly, not solely because to so act is in accord with civil and moral laws, but also because it is in accord with Divine laws. As the spiritual man, in whatever he is doing, thinks about Divine things, he has communication with the angels of heaven; and so far as this takes place he is conjoined with them; and thereby his internal man, which regarded in itself is the spiritual man, is opened. When man comes into this state he is adopted and led by the Lord, although himself unconscious of it, and then whatever he does that is honest and just pertaining to moral and civil life, is done from a spiritual motive; and doing what is honest and just from a spiritual motive is doing it from honesty and justice itself, or doing it from the heart. [2] His justice and honesty appear outwardly precisely the same as the justice and honesty of natural men and even of evil and infernal men; but in inward form they are wholly unlike. For evil men act justly and honestly solely for the sake of themselves and the world; and therefore if they had no fear of laws and penalties, or the loss of reputation, of honor, of gain, and of life, they would act in every respect dishonestly and unjustly, since they neither fear God nor any Divine law, and therefore are not restrained by any internal bond; consequently they would use every opportunity to defraud, plunder, and spoil others, and this from delight. That inwardly they are such can be clearly seen from those of the same character in the other life, while everyone's externals are taken away, and his internals in which he at last lives to eternity are opened (see above, n. 499-511). As such then act without external restraints, which are, as just said, fear of the law, of the loss of reputation, of honor, of gain, and of life, they act insanely, and laugh at honesty and justice. [3] But those who have acted honestly and justly from regard to Divine laws, when their externals are taken away and they are left to their internals, act wisely, because they are conjoined to the angels of heaven, from whom wisdom is communicated to them. From all this it can now be seen, in the first place, that when the internal man, that is, the will and thought, are conjoined to the Divine, the civil and moral life of the spiritual man may be wholly like the civil and moral life of the natural man (see above, n. 358-360).

Furthermore, the laws of spiritual life, the laws of civil life, and the laws of moral life are set forth in the ten commandments of the Decalogue; in the first three the laws of spiritual life, in the four that follow the laws of civil life, and in the last three the laws of moral life. Outwardly the merely natural man lives in accordance with the same commandments in the same way as the spiritual man does, for in like manner he worships the Divine, goes to church, listens to preachings, and assumes a devout countenance, refrains from committing murder, adultery, and theft, from bearing false witness, and from defrauding his companions of their goods. But all this he does merely for the sake of himself and the world, to keep up appearances; while inwardly such a person is the direct opposite of what he appears outwardly, since in heart he denies the Divine, in worship acts the hypocrite, and when left to himself and his own thoughts laughs at the holy things of the church, believing that they merely serve as a restraint for the simple multitude. [2] Consequently he is wholly disjoined from heaven, and not being a spiritual man he is neither a moral man nor a civil man. For although he refrains from committing murder he hates everyone who opposes him, and from his hatred burns with revenge, and would therefore commit murder if he were not restrained by civil laws and external bonds, which he fears; and as he longs to do so it follows that he is continually committing murder. Although he does not commit adultery, yet as he believes it to be allowable he is all the while an adulterer, since he commits adultery to the extent that he has the ability and as often as he has opportunity. Although he does not steal, yet as he covets the goods of others and does not regard fraud and wicked devices as opposed to what is lawful, in intent he is continually acting the thief. The same is true of the commandments relating to moral life, which forbid false witness and coveting the goods of others. Such is every man who denies the Divine, and who has no conscience derived from religion. That he is such is clearly evident from those of like character in the other life when their externals have been removed and they are let into their internals. As they are then separated from heaven they act in unity with hell, and in consequence are affiliated with those who are in hell. [3] It is not so with those who in heart have acknowledged the Divine, and in the actions of their lives have had respect to Divine laws, and have lived as fully in accord with the first three commandments of the Decalogue as they have in accordance with the others. When the externals of such are removed and they are let into their internals they are wiser than they were in the world; for entering into their internals is like entering from darkness into light, from ignorance into wisdom, and from a sorrowful life into a happy life, because they are in the Divine, thus in heaven. This has been said to make known what the one kind of man is and what the other is, although they have both lived the same external life.

Everyone may know that thoughts are led or tend in accord with the intentions, that is, in the directions that one intends; for thought is man's internal sight, and resembles the external sight in this, that to whatever point it is directed or aimed, thither it turns and there it rests. Therefore when the internal sight or the thought is turned towards the world and rests there, the thought in consequence becomes worldly; when it turns to self and self-honor it becomes corporeal; but when it is turned heavenwards it becomes heavenly. So, too, when turned heavenwards it is elevated; but when turned selfward it is drawn down from heaven and immersed in what is corporeal; and when turned towards the world it is also turned down-wards from heaven, and is spent upon those objects that are presented to the natural sight. [2] Man's love is what constitutes his intention and determines his internal sight or thought to its objects; thus the love of self fixes it upon self and its objects, the love of the world upon worldly objects, and the love of heaven upon heavenly objects; and when the love is known the state of the interiors which constitute the mind can be known, that is, the interiors of one who loves heaven are raised towards heaven and are opened above; while the interiors of one who loves the world or who loves himself are closed above and are opened outwardly. From this the conclusion follows that when the higher regions of the mind are closed above, man can no longer see the objects pertaining to heaven and the church, but those objects are in thick darkness to him; and what is in thick darkness is either denied or not understood. And this is why those that love themselves and the world above all things since the higher regions of their minds are closed, in heart deny Divine truths; and if from their memory they say anything about them they nevertheless do not understand them. Moreover, they regard them in the same way as they regard worldly and corporeal things. And being such they are able to direct the mind to those things only that enter through the senses of the body, and in these alone do they find delight. Among these are also many things that are filthy, obscene, profane and wicked; and these cannot be removed, because into the minds of such no influx from heaven is possible, since their minds, as just now said, are closed above. [3] Man's intention, by which his internal sight or thought is determined, is his will; for what a man wills he intends, and what he intends he thinks. Therefore when his intention is heavenward his thought is determined heavenward, and with it his whole mind, which is thus in heaven; and from heaven he beholds the things of the world beneath him like one looking down from the roof of a house. So the man that has the interiors of his mind open can see the evils and falsities that are in him, for these are beneath the spiritual mind. On the other hand, the man whose interiors are not open is unable to see his evils and falsities, because he is not above them but in them. From all this one may conclude whence man has wisdom and whence insanity, also what a man will be after death when he is left to will and think and to act and speak in accordance with his interiors. All this also has been said in order to make clear what constitutes a man's interior character, however he may seem outwardly to resemble others.

That it is not so difficult to live the life of heaven as some believe can now be seen from this, that when any thing presents itself to a man that he knows to be dishonest and unjust, but to which his mind is borne, it is simply necessary for him to think that it ought not to be done because it is opposed to the Divine precepts. If a man accustoms himself so to think, and from so doing establishes a habit of so thinking, he is gradually conjoined to heaven; and so far as he is conjoined to heaven the higher regions of his mind are opened; and so far as these are opened he sees whatever is dishonest and unjust, and so far as he sees these evils they can be dispersed, for no evil can be dispersed until it is seen. Into this state man is able to enter because of his freedom, for is not any one able from his freedom to so think? And when man has made a beginning the Lord quickens all that is good in him, and causes him not only to see evils to be evils, but also to refrain from willing them, and finally to turn away from them. This is meant by the Lord's words, My yoke is easy and My burden is light (Matt. 11:30). But it must be understood that the difficulty of so thinking and of resisting evils increases so far as man from his will does evils, for in the same measure he becomes accustomed to them until he no longer sees them, and at length loves them and from the delight of his love excuses them, and confirms them by every kind of fallacy, and declares them to be allowable and good. This is the fate of those who in early youth plunge into evils without restraint, and also reject Divine things from the heart.

The way that leads to heaven, and the way that leads to hell were once represented to me. There was a broad way tending towards the left or the north, and many spirits were seen going in it; but at a distance a large stone was seen where the broad way came to an end. From that stone two ways branched off, one to the left and one in the opposite direction to the right. The way that went to the left was narrow or straitened, leading through the west to the south, and thus into the light of heaven; the way that went to the right was broad and spacious, leading obliquely downwards towards hell. All at first seemed to be going the same way until they came to the large stone at the head of the two ways. When they reached that point they divided; the good turned to the left and entered the straitened way that led to heaven; while the evil, not seeing the stone at the fork of the ways fell upon it and were hurt; and when they rose up they ran on in the broad way to the right which went towards hell. [2] What all this meant was afterwards explained to me. The first way that was broad, wherein many both good and evil went together and talked with each other as friends, because there was no visible difference between them, represented those who externally live alike honestly and justly, and between whom seemingly there is no difference. The stone at the head of the two ways or at the corner, upon which the evil fell and from which they ran into the way leading to hell, represented the Divine truth, which is rejected by those who look towards hell; and in the highest sense this stone signified the Lord's Divine Human. But those who acknowledged the Divine truth and also the Divine of the Lord went by the way that led to heaven. By this again it was shown that in externals the evil lead the same kind of life as the good, or go the same way, that is, one as readily as the other; and yet those who from the heart acknowledge the Divine, especially those within the church who acknowledge the Divine of the Lord, are led to heaven; while those who do not are led to hell. [3] The thoughts of man that proceed from his intention or will are represented in the other life by ways; and ways are visibly presented there in exact accord with those thoughts of intention; and in accord with his thoughts that proceed from intention everyone walks. For this reason the character of spirits and their thoughts are known from their ways. This also makes clear what is meant by the Lord's words: Enter ye in through the narrow gate; for wide is the gate and broad is the way that leadeth to destruction, and many be they that enter in thereby; for straitened is the way and narrow the gate that leadeth to life, and few be they who find it (Matt. 7:13, 14). The way that leads to life is straitened not because it is difficult but because there are few who find it, as is said here. The stone seen at the corner where the broad and common way ended, and from which two ways were seen to lead in opposite directions, illustrated what is signified by these words of the Lord: Have ye not read what is written? The stone which the builders rejected was made the head of the corner. Whosoever shall fall upon that stone shall be broken (Luke. 20:17, 18). "Stone" signifies Divine truth, and "the stone of Israel" the Lord in respect to His Divine Human; the "builders" mean those who are of the church; "the head of the corner" is where the two ways are; "to fall" and "to be broken" is to deny and perish. 534-1

I have been permitted to talk with some in the other life who had withdrawn from worldly affairs that they might live in a pious and holy manner, also with some who had afflicted themselves in various ways, believing that they were thereby renouncing the world and subduing the lusts of the flesh. But as most of these have thus acquired a sorrowful life and had withdrawn from the life of charity, which life can be lived only in the midst of the world, they are incapable of being affiliated with angels, because the life of angels is a life of joy resulting from a state of blessedness, and consists in performing good deeds, which are works of charity. Moreover, those who have lived a life withdrawn from worldly employments are inflamed with the idea of their own merit, and are continually desiring heaven on that account, and thinking of heavenly joy as a reward, utterly ignorant of what heavenly joy is. When such are admitted into the company of angels and into their joy, which discards merit and consists in active labors and practical services, and in a blessedness resulting from the good thereby accomplished, they are astonished like one who has found out something quite foreign to his belief; and since they are not receptive of that joy they go away and ally themselves with spirits of their own kind that have lived in the world a life like their own. [2] But those who have lived an outwardly holy life, constantly attending church and praying and afflicting their souls, and at the same time have thought constantly of themselves that they would be esteemed and honored for all this above others, and finally after death would be accounted saints - such in the other life are not in heaven because they have done all this for the sake of themselves. And as they have defiled Divine truths by the self-love in which they have immersed them, some of them are so insane as to think themselves gods; and are consequently in hell among those like themselves. Some are cunning and deceitful, and are in the hells of the deceitful. These are such as by means of cunning arts and devices have maintained such pious conduct as induced the common people to believe that they possessed a Divine sanctity. [3] Of this character are many of the Roman Catholic saints. I have been permitted to talk with some of them, and their life was then plainly disclosed, such as it had been in the world and as it was afterwards. All this has been said to make known that the life that leads to heaven is not a life withdrawn from the world, but a life in the world; and that a life of piety separated from a life of charity, which is possible only in the world, does not lead to heaven; but a life of charity does; and a life of charity consists in acting honestly and justly in every employment, in every business, and in every work, from an interior, that is, from a heavenly, motive; and this motive is in that life whenever man acts honestly and justly because doing so is in accord with the Divine laws. Such a life is not difficult. But a life of piety separate from a life of charity is difficult; and as much as such a life is believed to lead towards heaven so much it leads away from heaven.535-1

THE LORD RULES THE HELLS. Above, in treating of heaven it has been everywhere shown (especially in n. 2-6) that the God of heaven is the Lord, thus that the whole government of the heavens is the Lord's government. And as the relation of heaven to hell and of hell to heaven is like the relation between two opposites which mutually act contrary to each other, and from the action and re-action of which an equilibrium results, which gives permanence to all things of their action and reaction, so in order that all things and each thing may be kept in equilibrium it is necessary that He who rules the one should rule the other; for unless the same Lord restrained the uprisings from the hells and checked insanities there the equilibrium would perish and everything with it.

But something about that equilibrium shall first be told. It is acknowledged that when two things mutually act against each other, and as much as one reacts and resists the other acts and impels, since there is equal power on either side, neither has any effect, and both can then be acted upon freely by a third. For when the force of the two is neutralized by equal opposition the force of a third has full effect, and acts as easily as if there were no opposition. [2] Such is the equilibrium between heaven and hell. Yet it is not an equilibrium like that between two bodily combatants whose strength is equal; but it is a spiritual equilibrium, that is, an equilibrium of falsity against truth and of evil against good. From hell falsity from evil continually exhales, and from heaven truth from good. It is this spiritual equilibrium that causes man to think and will in freedom; for whatever a man thinks and wills has reference either to evil and falsity therefrom or to good and truth therefrom. [3] Therefore when he is in that equilibrium he is in freedom either to admit or accept evil and its falsity from hell or to admit or accept good and its truth from heaven. Every man is held in this equilibrium by the Lord, because the Lord rules both heaven and hell. But why man is held in this freedom by such an equilibrium, and why evil and falsity are not taken away from him and good and truth implanted in him by Divine power will be told hereafter in its own chapter.

A perception of the sphere of falsity from evil that flows forth from hell has often been granted me. It was like a perpetual effort to destroy all that is good and true, combined with anger and a kind of fury at not being able to do so, especially an effort to annihilate and destroy the Divine of the Lord, and this because all good and truth are from Him. But out of heaven a sphere of truth from good was perceived, whereby the fury of the effort ascending from hell was restrained. The result of this was an equilibrium. This sphere from heaven was perceived to come from the Lord alone, although it appeared to come from the angels in heaven. It is from the Lord alone, and not from the angels, because every angel in heaven acknowledges that nothing of good and of truth is from himself, but all is from the Lord.

In the spiritual world truth from good is the source of all power, and falsity from evil has no power whatever. This is because the Divine Itself in heaven is Divine good and Divine truth, and all power belongs to the Divine. Falsity from evil is powerless because truth from good is the source of all power, and in falsity from evil there is nothing of truth from good. Consequently in heaven there is all power, and none in hell; for everyone in heaven is in truths from good, and everyone in hell is in falsities from evil. For no one is admitted into heaven until he is in truths from good, neither is any one cast down into hell until he is in falsities from evil, (That this is so can be seen in the chapters treating of the first, second, and third states of man after death, n. 491-520; and that all power belongs to truth from good can be seen in the chapter on the power of angels in heaven, n. 228-233.)

Such, then, is the equilibrium between heaven and hell. Those who are in the world of spirits are in that equilibrium, for the world of spirits is midway between heaven and hell. From the same source all men in the world are kept in a like equilibrium, since men in the world are ruled by the Lord by means of spirits in the world of spirits, as will be shown hereafter in its own chapter. No such equilibrium would be possible unless the Lord ruled both heaven and hell and regulated both sides. Otherwise falsities from evil would preponderate, and would affect the simple good who are in the outmosts regions of heaven, and who can be more easily perverted than the angels themselves; and thereby equilibrium would perish, and with it freedom in men.

Hell, like heaven, is divided into societies, and into as many societies as there are in heaven; for every society in heaven has a society opposite to it in hell, and this for the sake of equilibrium. But evils and falsities therefrom are what distinguish the societies in hell, as goods and truths therefrom are what distinguish the societies in heaven. That for every good there is an opposite evil, and for every truth an opposite falsity may be known from this, that nothing can exist without relation to its opposite, and what anything is in kind and degree can be known from its opposite, and from this all perception and sensation is derived. For this reason the Lord continually provides that every society in heaven shall have an opposite in some society of hell, and that there shall be an equilibrium between the two.

As hell is divided into the same number of societies as heaven, there are as many hells as there are societies of heaven; for as each society of heaven is a heaven in smaller form (see above, n. 51-58), so each society in hell is a hell in smaller form. As in general there are three heavens, so in general there are three hells, a lowest, which is opposite to the inmost or third heaven, a middle, which is opposite to the middle or second heaven, and a higher, which is opposite to the outmost or first heaven.

How the hells are ruled by the Lord shall be briefly explained. In general the hells are ruled by a general outflow from the heavens of Divine good and Divine truth whereby the general endeavor flowing forth from the hells is checked and restrained; also by a particular outflow from each heaven and from each society of heaven. The hells are ruled in particular by means of the angels, to whom it is granted to look into the hells and to restrain insanities and disturbances there; and sometimes angels are sent to them who moderate these insanities and disturbances by their presence. But in general all in the hells are ruled by means of their fears. Some are ruled by fears implanted in the world and still inherent in them; but as these fears are not sufficient, and gradually subside, they are ruled by fears of punishments; and it is especially by these that they are deterred from doing evil. The punishments in hell are manifold, lighter or more severe in accordance with the evils. For the most part the more wicked, who excel in cunning and in artifices, and who are able to hold the rest in subjection and servitude by means of punishments and consequent terror, are set over them; but these governors dare not pass beyond the limits prescribed to them. It must be understood that the sole means of restraining the violence and fury of those who are in the hells is the fear of punishment. There is no other way.

It has been believed heretofore in the world that there is one devil that presides over the hells; that he was created an angel of light; but having become rebellious he was cast down with his crew into hell. This belief has prevailed because the Devil and Satan, and also Lucifer, are mentioned by name in the Word, and the Word in those places has been understood according to the sense of the letter. But by "the devil" and "Satan" there hell is meant, "devil" meaning the hell that is behind, where the worst dwell, who are called evil genii; and

"Satan" the hell that is in front, where the less wicked dwell, who are called evil spirits; and "Lucifer" those that belong to Babel, or Babylon, who would extend their dominion even into heaven. That there is no one devil to whom the hells are subject is evident also from this, that all who are in the hells, like all who are in the heavens, are from the human race (see n. 311-317); and that those who have gone there from the beginning of creation to this time amount to myriads of myriads, and everyone of them is a devil in accord with his opposition to the Divine while he lived in the world (see above, n. 311, 312).

THE LORD CASTS NO ONE INTO HELL; THE SPIRIT CASTS HIMSELF DOWN. An opinion has prevailed with some that God turns away His face from man, casts man away from Himself, and casts him into hell, and is angry with him on account of his evil; and some believe also that God punishes man and does evil to him. In this opinion they establish themselves by the sense of the letter of the Word, where such things are declared, not knowing that the spiritual sense of the Word, by which the sense of the letter is made clear, is wholly different; and consequently that the genuine doctrine of the church, which is from the spiritual sense of the Word, teaches otherwise, namely, that God never turns away His face from man, and never casts man away from Himself, that He casts no one into hell and is angry with no one. 545-1 Everyone, moreover, whose mind is enlightened perceives this to be true when he reads the Word, from the simple truth that God is good itself, love itself, and mercy itself; and that good itself cannot do evil to any one, and love itself and mercy itself can not cast man away from itself, because this is contrary to the very essence of mercy and love, thus contrary to the Divine Itself. Therefore those who think from an enlightened mind clearly perceive, when they read the Word, that God never turns Himself away from man; and as He never turns Himself away from him He deals with him from goodness, love, and mercy, that is, wills good to him, loves him, and is merciful to him. And from this they see that the sense of the letter of the Word, in which such things are declared, has stored up within itself a spiritual sense, and that these expressions that are used in the sense of the letter in accommodation to man's apprehension and according to his first and general ideas are to be explained in accordance with the spiritual sense.

Those who are enlightened see further that good and evil are two opposites, and are therefore opposed as heaven and hell are, and that all good is from heaven and all evil from hell; and as it is the Divine of the Lord that makes heaven (n. 7-12), nothing but good flows into man from the Lord, and nothing but evil from hell; thus the Lord is continually withdrawing man from evil and leading him to good, while hell is continually leading man into evil. Unless man were between these two, he could have no thought nor any will, still less any freedom or any choice; for all these man has by virtue of the equilibrium between good and evil; consequently if the Lord should turn Himself away, leaving man to evil alone, man would cease to be man. All this shows that the Lord flows into every man with good, into the evil man as well as the good; but with the difference that the Lord is continually withdrawing the evil man from evil and is continually leading the good man to good; and this difference lies in the man himself, because he is the recipient.

From this it is clear that it is from hell that man does evil, and from the

Lord that he does good. But man believes that whatever he does he does from himself, and in consequence of this the evil that he does sticks to him as his own; and for this reason man is the cause of his own evil, and in no way the Lord. Evil in man is hell in him, for it is the same thing whether you say evil or hell. And since man is the cause of his own evil he is led into hell, not by the Lord but by himself. For so far is the Lord from leading man into hell that it is He who delivers man from hell, and this He does so far as man does not will and love to be in his own evil. All of man's will and love continues with him after death (n. 470-484). He who wills and loves evil in the world wills and loves the same evil in the other life, but he no longer suffers himself to be withdrawn from it. If, therefore, a man is in evil he is tied to hell, and in respect to his spirit is actually there, and after death desires nothing so much as to be where his evil is; consequently it is man who casts himself into hell after death, and not the Lord.

How this comes about shall also be explained. When man enters the other life he is received first by angels, who perform for him all good offices, and talk with him about the Lord, heaven, and the angelic life, and instruct him in things that are true and good. But if the man, now a spirit, be one who knew about these things in the world, but in heart denied or despised them, after some conversation he desires and seeks to get away from these angels. As soon as the angels perceive this they leave him. After some interaction with others he at length unites himself with those who are in evil like his own (see above, n. 445-452). When this takes place he turns himself away from the Lord and turns his face towards the hell to which he had been joined in the world, in which those abide who are in a like love of evil. All this makes clear that the Lord draws every spirit to Himself by means of angels and by means of influx from heaven; but those spirits that are in evil completely resist, and as it were tear themselves away from the Lord, and are drawn by their own evil, thus by hell, as if by a rope. And as they are so drawn, and by reason of their love of evil are eager to follow, it is evident that they themselves cast themselves into hell by their own free choice. Men in the world because of their idea of hell are unable to believe that this is so. In fact, in the other life before the eyes of those who are outside of hell it does not so appear; but only so to those who cast themselves into hell, for such enter of their own accord. Those who enter from a burning love of evil appear to be cast headlong, with the head downwards and the feet upwards. It is because of this appearance that they seem to be cast into hell by Divine power. (But about this more will be said below, n. 574.) From all this it can be seen that the Lord casts no one into hell, but everyone casts himself into hell, both while he is living in the world and also after death when he comes among spirits.

The Lord from His Divine Essence, which is goodness, love, and mercy, is unable to deal in the same way with every man, because evils and their falsities prevent, and not only quench His Divine influx but even reject it. Evils and their falsities are like black clouds which interpose between the sun and the eye, and take away the sunshine and the serenity of its light; although the unceasing endeavor of the sun to dissipate the opposing clouds continues, for it is operating behind them; and in the meantime transmits something of obscure light into the eye of man by various roundabout ways. It is the same in the spiritual world. The sun there is the Lord and the Divine love (n. 116-140); and the light there is the Divine truth (n. 126-140); black clouds there are falsities from evil; the eye there is the understanding. So far as any one in that world is in falsities from evil he is encompassed by such a cloud, which is black and dense according to the degree of his evil. From this comparison it can be seen that the Lord is unceasingly present with everyone, but that He is received variously.

Evil spirits are severely punished in the world of spirits in order that by means of punishments they may be deterred from doing evil. This also appears to be from the Lord; and yet nothing of punishment there is from the Lord, but is from the evil itself; since evil is so joined with its own punishment that the two cannot be separated. For the infernal crew desire and love nothing so much as doing evil, especially inflicting punishments and torment upon others; and they maltreat and inflict punishments upon everyone who is not protected by the Lord. When, therefore, evil is done from an evil heart, because it thereby discards all protection from the Lord, infernal spirits rush upon the one who does the evil, and inflict punishment. This may be partly illustrated by evils and their punishments in the world, where the two are also joined. For laws in the world prescribe a penalty for every evil; therefore he that rushes into evil rushes also into the penalty of evil. The only difference is that in the world the evil may be concealed; but in the other life it cannot be concealed. All this makes clear that the Lord does evil to no one; and that it is the same as it is in the world, where it is not the king nor the judge nor the law that is the cause of punishment to the guilty, because these are not the cause of the evil in the evil doer.

Footnotes

513-1 Vastations are effected in the other life, that is, those that pass into the other life from the world are vastated (n. 698, 7122, 7474, 9763). The well disposed are vastated in respect to falsities, while the evil are vastated in respect to truths (n, 7474, 7541, 7542). The well disposed undergo vastations that they also may be divested of what pertains to the earth and the world, which they had contracted while living in the world (n. 7186, 9763). Also that evils and falsities may be removed, and thus there may be room for the influx of goods and truths out of heaven from the Lord, and ability to accept these (n. 7122, 9330). Elevation into heaven is impossible until such things have been removed, because they obstruct heavenly things and are not in harmony with them (n. 6928, 7122, 7186, 7541, 7542, 9763). Those who are to be raised up into heaven are thus prepared for it (n. 4728, 7090). It is dangerous to come into heaven before being prepared (n. 537, 538). The state of enlightenment and the joy of those who come out of vastation and are raised up into heaven, and their reception there (n. 2699, 2701, 2704). The region where those vastations are effected is called the lower earth (n. 4728, 7090). That region is under the soles of the feet surrounded by the hells; its nature described (n. 4940-4951, 7090); from experience (n. 699). What the hells are which more than others infest and vastate (n. 7317, 7502, 7545). Those that have infested and vastated the well disposed are afterwards afraid of them, shun them, and turn away from them (n. 7768). These infestations and vastations are effected in different ways in accordance with the adhesion of evils and falsities, and they continue in accordance with their quality and quantity (n. 1106-1113). Some are quite willing to be vastated (n. 1107). Some are vastated by fears (n. 4942). Some by being infested with the evils they have done in the world, and with the falsities they have thought in the world, from which they have anxieties and pangs of conscience (n. 1106). Some by spiritual captivity, which is ignorance of truth and interception of truth, combined with a longing to know truths (n. 1109, 2694). Some by sleep; some by a middle state between wakefulness and sleep (n. 1108). Those that have placed merit in works seem to themselves to be cutting wood (n. 1110). Others in other ways, with great variety (n. 699).

517-1 Every good has both its delight and its quality from uses and in accordance with uses; therefore such as the good is such the use is (n. 3049, 4984, 7038). Angelic life consists in the goods of love and charity, thus in performing uses (n. 454). The Lord and therefore the angels, have regard to nothing in man but ends which are uses (n. 1317, 1645, 5854). The kingdom of the Lord is a kingdom of uses (n. 454, 696, 1103, 3645, 4054, 7038). Serving the Lord is performing uses (n. 7038). What man is, such are his uses (n. 1568, 3570, 4054, 6571, 6935, 6938, 10284).

523-1 Divine truth going forth from the Lord is the source of order, and Divine good is the essential of order (n. 1728, 2258, 8700, 8988). Thus the Lord is order (n. 1919, 2011, 5110, 5703, 10336, 10619). Divine truths are the laws of order (n. 2447, 7995). The whole heaven is arranged by the Lord in accordance with His Divine order (n. 3038, 7211, 9128, 9338, 10125, 10151, 10157). Therefore the form of heaven is a form in accord with the Divine order (n. 4040-4043, 6607, 9877). So far as a man is living in accordance with order, that is, so far as he is living in good in accordance with Divine truths, he is receiving heaven in himself (n. 4839). Man is the being in whom are brought together all things of Divine order, and by creation he is Divine order in form, because he is a recipient of Divine order (n. 3628, 4219, 4220, 4223, 4523, 4524, 5214, 6013, 6057, 6605, 6626, 9706, 10156, 10472). Man is not born into good and truth but into evil and falsity, thus not into Divine order but into the opposite of order, and for this reason he is born into pure ignorance; consequently it is necessary for him to be born anew, that is, to be regenerated, which is effected by the Lord by means of Divine truths, that be may be brought back into order (n. 1047, 2307, 2308, 3518, 8480, 8550, 10283, 10284, 10286, 10731). When the Lord forms man anew, that is, regenerates him, He arranges all things in him in harmony with order, that is, in the form of heaven (n. 5700, 6690, 9931, 10303). Evils and falsities are contrary to order; nevertheless those who are in them are ruled by the Lord not in accordance with order but from order (n. 4839, 7877, 10777). It is impossible for a man who lives in evil to be saved by mercy alone, for that would be contrary to Divine order (n. 8700).

526-1 In the internal sense of the Word by Abraham, Isaac, and Jacob, the Lord in respect to the Divine itself and the Divine Human is meant (n. 1893, 4615, 6098, 6185, 6276, 6804, 6847). In heaven Abraham is unknown (n. 1834, 1876, 3229). By David the Lord in respect to the Divine royalty is meant (n. 1888, 9954). The twelve apostles represented the Lord in respect to all things of the church, that is, all things pertaining to faith and love (n. 2129, 3354, 3488, 3858, 6397). Peter represented the lord in respect to faith, James in respect to charity, and John in respect to the works of charity (n. 3750, 10087). The twelve apostles sitting on twelve thrones and judging the twelve tribes of Israel, signified that the Lord will judge in accord with the truths and goods of faith and love (n. 2129, 6397). The names of persons and of places in the Word do not enter heaven, but are changed into things and states; and in heaven these names cannot even be uttered (n. 1876, 5225, 6516, 10216, 10282, 10432). Moreover, the angels think abstractedly from persons (n. 8343, 8985, 9907).

534-1 "Stone" signifies truth (n. 114, 643, 1298, 3720, 6426, 8609, 10376). For this reason the law was inscribed on tables of stone (n. 10376). "The stone of Israel" means the Lord in respect to the Divine truth and His Divine Human (n. 6426).

535-1 A life of piety separated from a life of charity is of no avail, but united with charity it is profitable for all things (n. 8252, 8253). Charity to the neighbor consists in doing what is good, just, and right in every work and in every employment (n. 8120-8122). Charity to the neighbor takes in all things and each thing that a man thinks, wills, and does (n. 8124). A life of charity is a life in accordance with the Lord's commandments (n. 3249). Living in accordance with the Lord's commandments is loving the Lord (n. 10143, 10153, 10310, 10578, 10645). Genuine charity claims no merit, because it is from interior affection and consequent delight (n. 2371, 2380, 2400, 3816, 3887, 6388-6393). Man continues to be after death such as was his life of charity in the world (n. 8256). Heavenly blessedness flows in from the Lord into a life of charity (n. 2363). Mere thinking admits no one into heaven; it must be accompanied by willing and doing good (n. 2401, 3459). Unless doing good is joined with willing good and thinking good there is no salvation nor any conjunction of the internal man with the external (n. 3987).

545-1 In the Word anger and wrath are attributed to the Lord, but they are in man, and it is so expressed because such is the appearance to man when he is punished and damned (n. 798, 5798, 6997, 8284, 8483, 8875, 9306, 10431). Evil also is attributed to the Lord, although nothing but good is from Him (n. 2447, 6071, 6991, 6997, 7533, 7632, 7679, 7926, 8227, 8228, 8632, 9306). Why it is so expressed in the Word (n. 6071, 6991, 6997, 7632, 7643, 7679, 7710, 7926, 8282, 9010, 9128). The Lord is pure mercy and clemency (n. 6997, 8875).

Section 12

ALL WHO ARE IN THE HELLS ARE IN EVILS AND IN FALSITIES THEREFROM DERIVED FROM THE LOVES OF SELF AND OF THE WORLD. All who are in the hells are in evils and in falsities therefrom, and no one there is in evils and at the same time in truths. In the world evil men for the most part have some knowledge of spiritual truths, which are the truths of the church, having been taught them from childhood and later by preaching and by reading the Word; and afterwards they have talked about them. Some have even led others to believe that they are Christians at heart because of their knowing how to talk with pretended affection in harmony with the truth, also how to act uprightly as if from spiritual faith. But those of this class whose interior thoughts have been hostile to these truths, and who have refrained from doing the evils that were in harmony with their thoughts only because of the civil laws, or with a view to reputation, honors, and gain, are all of them evil in heart, and are in truths and goods not in respect to their spirit but only in respect to their body; and consequently, when their externals are taken away from them in the other life, and their internals which pertain to their spirit are revealed, they are wholly in evils and falsities, and not at all in truths and goods; and it is thus made clear that truths and goods resided only in their memory merely as things known about, and that they brought them forth therefrom when talking, putting on a semblance of good seemingly from spiritual love and faith. When such are let into their internals and thus into their evils they are no longer able to speak what is true, but only what is false; since they speak from evils; for to speak what is true from evils is then impossible, since the spirit is nothing but his own evil, and from evil what is false goes forth. Every evil spirit is reduced to this state before he is cast into hell (see above, n. 499-512). This is called being vastated in respect to truths and goods. 551-1 Vastation is simply being let into one's internals, that is, into what is the spirit's own, or into the spirit itself (see above, n. 425).

When man after death comes into this state he is no longer a man-spirit, as he was in his first state (of which above, n. 491-498), but is truly a spirit; for he is truly a spirit who has a face and body that correspond to his internals which pertain to his mind, that is, has an external form that is a type or effigy of his internals. A spirit is such after he has passed through the first and second states spoken of above; consequently when he is looked upon his character is at once known, not only from his face and from his body, but also from his speech and movements; and as he is then in himself he can be nowhere else than where his like are. [2] For in the spiritual world there is a complete sharing of affections and their thoughts, and in consequence a spirit is conveyed to his like as if of himself, since it is done from his affection and its delight. In fact, he turns himself in that direction; for thus he inhales his own life or draws his breath freely, which he cannot do when he turns another way. It must be understood that this sharing with others in the spiritual world is effected in accordance with the turning of the face, and that each one has constantly before his face those who are in a love like his own, and this in every turning of the body (see above, n. 151) [3] In consequence of this all infernal spirits turn themselves away from the Lord toward the densely dark body and the dark body that are there in place of the sun and moon of this world, while all the angels of heaven turn themselves to the Lord as the sun of heaven and as the moon of heaven (see above, n. 123, 143, 144, 151). From all this it is clear that all who are in the hells are in evils and in falsities therefrom; also that they are turned to their own loves.

All spirits in the hells, when seen in any light of heaven, appear in the form of their evil; for everyone there is an image of his evil, since his interiors and his exteriors act as a one, the interiors making themselves visible in the exteriors, which are the face, body, speech and movements; thus the character of the spirit is known as soon as he is seen. In general evil spirits are forms of contempt of others and of menaces against those who do not pay them respect; they are forms of hatreds of various kinds, also of various kinds of revenge. Fierceness and cruelty from their interiors show through these forms. But when they are commended, venerated, and worshiped by others their faces are restrained and take on an expression of gladness from delight. [2] It is impossible to describe in a few words how all these forms appear, for no one is like another, although there is a general likeness among those who are in the same evil, and thus in the same infernal society, from which, as from a plane of derivation, the faces of all are seen to have a certain resemblance. In general their faces are hideous, and void of life like those of corpses; the faces of some are black, others fiery like torches, others disfigured with pimples, warts, and ulcers; some seem to have no face, but in its stead something hairy or bony; and with some only the teeth are seen; their bodies also are monstrous; and their speech is like the speech of anger or of hatred or of revenge; for what everyone speaks is from his falsity, while his tone is from his evil. In a word, they are all images of their own hell. [3] I have not been permitted to see what the form of hell itself in general is; I have only been told that as the entire heaven in one complex reflects a single man (n. 59-67), so the entire hell in one complex reflects a single devil, and might be exhibited in an image of a single devil (see above, n. 544). But the forms of particular hells or infernal societies I have often been permitted to see; for at their entrances, which are called the gates of hell, a monster commonly appears that represents in a general way the form of those within. The fierce passions of those who dwell there are represented at the same time in horrible and hideous ways that I forbear to describe. [4] But it must be understood that this is the way infernal spirits appear in the light of heaven, while among themselves they appear as men. This is of the Lord's mercy, that they may not appear as loathsome to one another as they appear before the angels. But this appearance is a fallacy, for as soon as any ray of light from heaven is let in, their human forms appear changed into monstrous forms, such as they are in themselves (as has been described above). For in the light of heaven everything appears as it is in itself. For this reason they shun the light of heaven and cast themselves down into their own light, which is like that from lighted coals, and in some cases like that from burning sulphur; but this light also is turned into mere thick darkness when any light from heaven flows in upon it. This is why the hells are said to be in thick darkness and in darkness; and why "thick darkness" and "darkness" signify falsities derived from evil, such as are in hell.

From an inspection of these monstrous forms of spirits in the hells (which, as I have said, are all forms of contempt of others and of menaces against those who do not pay them honor and respect, also forms of hatred and revenge against those who do not favor them), it became evident that in general they were all forms of the love of self and the love of the world; and that the evils of which these are the specific forms have their origin in these two loves. Moreover, I have been told from heaven, and it has been proved to me by much experience, that these two loves, the love of self and the love of the world, rule in the hells and constitute the hells as love to the Lord and love towards the neighbor rule in the heavens and constitute the heavens; also that the two loves that are the loves of hell and the two loves that are the loves of heaven are diametrically opposite to each other.

At first I wondered how it is that love of self and love of the world could be so diabolical, and how those who are in these loves could be such monsters in appearance; for in the world not much thought is given to love of self, but only to that elated state of mind in external matters which is called haughtiness, and that alone, being so apparent to the sight, is regarded as love of self. Furthermore, love of self, when it is not so displayed, is believed in the world to be the very fire of life by which man is stimulated to seek employment and to perform uses, and if he found no honor or glory in these his mind would grow torpid. It is asked, Who has ever done any worthy, useful, and distinguished deed except for the sake of being praised and honored by others, or regarded with esteem and honor by others? And can this be from any other source than the fire of love for glory and honor, consequently for self. For this reason, it is unknown in the world that love of self, regarded in itself, is the love that rules in hell and constitutes hell in man. This being so I will first describe what the love of self is, and then will show that all evils and their falsities spring from that love as their fountain.

The love of self is wishing well to oneself alone, and to others only for the sake of self, even to the church, one's country, or any human society. It consists also in doing good to all these solely for the sake of one's own reputation, honor, and glory; and unless these are seen in the uses he performs in behalf of others he says in his heart, How does it concern me? Why should I do this? What shall I get from it? and therefore he does not do it. Evidently, then, he who is in the love of self does not love the church or his country or society, nor any use, but himself alone. His delight is solely the delight of the love of self; and as the delight that comes forth from his love is what constitutes the life of man, his life is a life of self; and a life of self is a life from what is man's own, and what is man's own, regarded in itself, is nothing but evil. He who loves himself loves also those who belong to him, that is, in particular, his children and grandchildren, and in general, all who are at one with him, whom he calls his. To love these is to love himself, for he regards them as it were in himself, and himself in them. Among those whom he calls his are also all who commend, honor, and pay their court to him.

What love of self is can be seen by comparing it with heavenly love. Heavenly love consists in loving uses for the sake of uses, or goods for the sake of goods, which are done by man in behalf of the church, his country, human society, and a fellow-citizen; for this is loving God and loving the neighbor, since all uses and all goods are from God, and are the neighbor who is to be loved. But he who loves these for the sake of himself loves them merely as servants, because they are serviceable to him; consequently it is the will of one who is in self-love that the church, his country, human societies, and his fellow citizens, should serve him, and not he them, for he places himself above them and places them beneath himself. Therefore so far as any one is in love of self he separates himself from heaven, because he separates himself from heavenly love.

[a.] Furthermore, so far as any one is in heavenly love, which consists in loving uses and goods and being moved by delight of heart when doing them for the sake of the church, country, human society, and ones fellow-citizens, he is so far led by the Lord, because that love is the love in which the Lord is, and which is from Him. But so far as any one is in the love of self, which consists in performing uses and goods for the sake of himself, so far he is led by himself; and so far as any one is led by himself he is not led by the Lord. And from this it also follows that so far as any one loves himself he separates himself from the Divine, thus also from heaven. To be led by one's self is to be led by what is one's own; and what is man's own is nothing but evil; for man's inherited evil consists in loving self more than God, and the world more than heaven. 558-1 Whenever man looks to himself in the good that he does he is let into what is his own, that is, into his inherited evils for he then looks from good to himself and from himself to good, and therefore he presents an image of himself in his good, and not an image of the Divine. That this is so has also been proved to me by experience. There are evil spirits whose dwelling places are in the middle quarter between the north and the west, beneath the heavens, who are skilled in the art of leading well-disposed spirits into their nature [proprium] and thus into evils of various kinds. This they do by leading them into thoughts about themselves, either openly by praises and honors, or secretly by directing their affections to themselves; and so far as this is done they turn the faces of the well-disposed spirits away from heaven, and to the same extent they obscure their understanding and call forth evils from what is their own. 558-2 Man's own, which he derives by inheritance from his parents, is nothing but dense evil (n. 210, 215, 731, 876, 987, 1047, 2307, 2308, 3518, 3701, 3812, 8480, 8550, 10283, 10284, 10286, 10731). Man's own is loving self more than God, and the world more than heaven, and making nothing of one's neighbor in comparison with oneself, except for the sake of self, that is one's own self; thus it consists in love of self and of the world (n. 694, 731, 4317, 5660). All evils flow from the love of self and the love of the world when these predominate (n. 1307, 1308, 1321, 1594, 1691, 3413, 7255, 7376, 7488, 7489, 8318, 9335, 9348, 10038, 10742). These evils are contempt of others, enmity, hatred, revenge, cruelty, deceit (n. 6667, 7370, 7374, 9348, 10038, 10742). From these evils all falsity flows (n. 1047, 10283, 10284, 10286). 558. [b.] That the love of self is the opposite of love to the neighbor can be seen from the origin and essence of both. The love of the neighbor of one who is in the love of self begins with oneself, for he claims that everyone is neighbor to himself; and it goes forth from him as its center to all who make one with him, diminishing in accordance with the degree of their conjunction with him by love. All outside of this circle are regarded as of no account; and those who are opposed to those in the circle and to their evils are accounted as enemies, whatever their character may be, however wise, upright, honest, or just. But spiritual love to the neighbor begins with the Lord, and goes forth from Him as its center to all who are conjoined to Him by love and faith, going forth in accordance with the quality of their love and faith.

Again, love of self is such that so far as the reins are given it, that is, so far as external bonds are removed, which are fears of the law and its penalties, and of the loss of reputation, honor, gain, employment, and life, so far it rushes on until it finally longs to rule not only over the entire world but also over the entire heaven, and over the Divine Himself, knowing no limit or end. This propensity lurks hidden in everyone who is in love of self, although it is not manifest to the world, where it is held in check by such bonds as have been mentioned. Everyone can see examples of this in potentates and kings who are subject to no such restraints and bonds, but rush on and subjugate provinces and kingdoms so far as they are successful, and aspire to power and glory without limit; and still more strikingly in the Babylon of this day, which has extended its dominion into heaven, and has transferred to itself all the Divine power of the Lord, and continually lusts for more. That such men, when they have entered after death the other life, are directly opposed to the Divine and to heaven, and are on the side of hell, can be seen in the little work on The Last Judgment and the Destruction of Babylon.

Picture to yourself a society of such persons, all of whom love themselves alone and love others only so far as they make one with themselves, and you will see that their love is precisely like the love of thieves for each other, who embrace and call one another friends so long as they are acting together; but when they cease to act together and discard their subordination to one another, they rise up against and murder one another. When the interiors or the minds of such are explored they will be seen to be full of bitter hatred one against another, and at heart will laugh at all justice and honesty, and likewise at the Divine, which they reject as of no account. This is still more evident in the societies of such in the hells treated of below.

The interiors pertaining to the thoughts and affections of those who love themselves above all things are turned towards themselves and the world, and thus are turned away from the Lord and from heaven; and consequently they are obsessed with evils of every kind, and the Divine cannot flow in; for if it does flow in it is instantly submerged in thoughts of self, and is defiled, and is also mingled with the evils that flow from what is their own. This is why all such in the other life look backwards away from the Lord, and towards the densely dark body that is there in the place of the sun of the world, and is diametrically opposite to the sun of heaven, which is the Lord (see above, n. 123). "Thick darkness" signifies evil, and the "sun of the world" the love of self. 561-1

The evils of those who are in the love of self are, in general, contempt of others, envy, enmity against all who do not favor them, and consequent hostility, hatred of various kinds, revenge, cunning, deceit, unmercifulness, and cruelty; and in respect to religious matters there is not merely a contempt for the Divine and for Divine things, which are the truths and goods of the church, but also hostility to them. When man becomes a spirit this hostility is turned into hatred; and then he not only cannot endure to hear these truths and goods mentioned, he even burns with hatred against all who acknowledge and worship the Divine. I once talked with a certain spirit who in the world had been a man in authority, and had loved self to an unusual degree; and when he simply heard some one mention the Divine, and especially when he heard him mention the Lord, he was so excited by hatred arising from anger as to burn with the desire to kill; and when the reins of his love were loosened he wished to be the devil himself, that from his love of self he might continually infest heaven. This is the desire also of some of the Papist religion when they perceive in the other life that the Lord has all power and they have none.

Certain spirits were seen by me in the western quarter towards the south, who said that they had been in positions of great dignity in the world, and that they deserved to be more highly esteemed than others and to rule over others. Their interior character was explored by angels, and it was found that in their offices in the world they had not looked to uses but to themselves, and thus that they had set themselves before uses. But as they were very eager and importunate to be set over others they were allowed to associate with those who were consulting about matters of great importance; but it was perceived that they were unable to give any thought to the business under discussion, or to see matters as they are in themselves, or to speak with reference to the use of the thing, but were able to speak only with reference to self, and that they wished to act from what is pleasing on the ground of favor. They were therefore dismissed from that duty, and left to seek employment for themselves elsewhere. Therefore they went further into the western quarter, where they were received here and there, but everywhere were told that they thought only of themselves, and of no business except with reference to self, and for this reason were stupid and like merely sensual corporeal spirits. On this account wheresoever they went they were sent away. Some time afterwards they were seen reduced to a destitute state and asking alms. Thus it was made clear that those who are in the love of self, however from the fire of that love they may seem to speak in the world wisely, speak merely from the memory, and not from any rational light. Therefore in the other life, when they are no longer permitted to bring forth the things of the natural memory, they are more stupid than others, and for the reason that they are separated from the Divine.

There are two kinds of dominion, one of love towards the neighbor and the other of love of self. These two dominions in their essence are direct opposites. One who rules from love towards the neighbor wills good to all, and loves nothing so much as uses, that is, serving others; which is willing good to others and performing uses, either to the church, or to the country, or to society, or to a fellow citizen. This is his love and the delight of his heart. Moreover, so far as he is exalted to dignities above others he rejoices, not for the sake of the dignities but for the sake of the uses he is then able to perform in greater abundance and of a higher order. Such dominion exists in the heavens. [2] But one who rules from the love of self wills good to no one except himself; the uses he performs are for the sake of his own honor and glory, which to him are the only uses; his end in serving others is that he may himself be served, honored, and permitted to rule; he seeks dignities not for the sake of the good offices he may render to his country and the church, but that he may gain eminence and glory and thereby the delight of his heart. [3] Moreover this love of dominion continues with everyone after his life in the world. Those that have ruled from love towards the neighbor are entrusted with authority in the heavens; but then it is not they who rule, but the uses which they love; and when uses rule the Lord rules. But those who have ruled while in the world are in hell, and are there vile slaves. I have seen those who had power in the world, but who exercised dominion from love of self, cast out among the most vile, and some among those who are in excrementitious places.

But in respect to the love of the world: it is a love opposed to heavenly love in a less degree than love of self, because the evils hidden within it are lesser evils. The love of the world consists in one's desiring to secure to himself, by any kind of artifice, the wealth of others, and in setting his heart upon riches, and permitting the world to draw him and lead him away from spiritual love, which is love towards the neighbor, and thus from heaven and from the Divine. But this love is manifold. There is a love of wealth for the sake of being exalted to honors, when these alone are loved. There is a love of honors and dignities with a view to the increase of wealth. There is a love of wealth for the sake of various uses that give delight in the world. There is a love of wealth merely for the sake of wealth, which is a miserly love; and so on. The end for the sake of which wealth is sought is called its use; and it is the end or use that gives to love its quality; for the love is such as is the end in view, and all other things merely serve it as means.

WHAT HELL FIRE IS AND WHAT THE GNASHING OF TEETH IS. What eternal fire is, and what the gnashing of teeth is, which are mentioned in the Word in reference to those who are in hell, scarcely any one as yet has known, because the contents of the Word have been thought about only in a material way, and nothing has been known about its spiritual sense. So fire has been understood by some to mean material fire, by others to mean torment in general, by others remorse of conscience, and others have held that it is mentioned merely to excite terror in the wicked. Likewise some have supposed the gnashing of teeth to mean actual gnashing, and some only a horror, such as is excited when such a collision of teeth is heard. But any one who is acquainted with the spiritual meaning of the Word may know what eternal fire is, and what the gnashing of teeth is; for every expression and every meaning of the expressions in the Word contains a spiritual meaning, since the Word in its bosom is spiritual; and what is spiritual can be set before man only in natural forms of expression, because man is in the natural world and thinks from the things of that world. Therefore it shall now be told what is meant by "eternal fire" and "the gnashing of teeth" into which the spirits of evil men enter after death, or which their spirits, then in the spiritual world, endure.

There are two origins of heat, one the sun of heaven which is the Lord, and the other the sun of the world. The heat that is from the sun of heaven, that is, the Lord, is spiritual heat; and this in its essence is love (see above, n. 126-140); but the heat from the sun of the world is natural heat, and this in its essence is not love, but serves spiritual heat or love as a receptacle. Evidently love in its essence is heat, since it is love, in accord with its degree and quality, that gives heat to the mind, and thence to the body; and this man experiences as well in the winter as in the summer. The heating of the blood is from the same source. That the natural heat that springs from the sun of the world serves spiritual heat as a receptacle is evident from the heat of the body, which is excited by the heat of its spirit, and is a kind of substitute for that heat in the body. It is especially evident from the spring and summer heat in animals of every kind which then annually renew their loves. [2] It is not the natural heat that produces this effect, but it disposes their bodies to receive the heat that flows into them from the spiritual world; for the spiritual world flows into the natural as cause into effect. Whoever believes that natural heat produces these loves is much deceived, for influx is from the spiritual world into the natural world, and not from the natural world into the spiritual; and as all love belongs to the life itself it is spiritual. [3] Again, he who believes that any thing comes forth in the natural world without influx from the spiritual world is deceived, for what is natural comes forth and continues to exist only from what is spiritual. Furthermore, the subjects of the vegetable kingdom derive their germinations from influx out of the spiritual world. The natural heat of spring time and summer merely disposes the seeds into their natural forms by expanding and opening them so that influx from the spiritual world can there act as a cause. These things are mentioned to make clear that there are two kinds of heat, spiritual heat and natural heat; and that spiritual heat is from the sun of heaven and natural heat from the sun of the world, and that influx and consequent cooperation produce the effects that appear before the eyes in the world. 567-1

Spiritual heat in man is the heat of his life, because, as was said above, it is in its essence love. This heat is what is meant in the Word by "fire," love to the Lord and love towards the neighbor by "heavenly fire," and love of self and love of the world by "infernal fire."

Infernal fire or love springs from a like origin as heavenly fire or love, namely, the sun of heaven, or the Lord; but it is made infernal by those who receive it. For all influx from the spiritual world varies in accordance with reception, that is, in accordance with the forms into which it flows, just as it is with the heat and light from the sun of the world. The heat from that sun flowing into shrubberies and beds of flowers produces vegetation, and draws forth grateful and sweet odors; but the same heat flowing into excrementitious and decaying substances produces putrefactions, and draws forth rank and disgusting stenches. In like manner the light from the same sun produces in one subject beautiful and pleasing colors, in another unbeautiful and disagreeable colors. The same is true of the heat and light from the sun of heaven, which is love. When the heat, or love, from that sun flows into good, as it does in good men and angels, it makes their good fruitful; but when it flows into the evil it produces a contrary effect, for their evils either suffocate it or pervert it. In like manner when the light of heaven flows into the truths of good it imparts intelligence and wisdom; but when it flows into the falsities of evil it is turned into insanities and phantasies of various kinds. Thus in every instance the result is in accordance with reception.

As infernal fire is the love of self and of the world it is also every lust of these loves, since lust is love in its continuity, for what a man loves he continually lusts after. Infernal fire is also delight, since what a man loves and lusts after he perceives, when he obtains it, to be delightful. Man's delight of heart is from no other source. Infernal fire, therefore, is the lust and delight that spring from these two loves as their origins. The evils flowing from these loves are contempt of others, enmity, and hostility against those who do not favor them, envy, hatred, and revenge, and from these fierceness and cruelty; and in respect to the Divine they are denial and consequent contempt, derision, and detraction of the holy things of the church; and after death, when man becomes a spirit, these evils are changed to anger and hatred against these holy things (see above, n. 562). And as these evils breathe forth continually the destruction and murder of those whom they account as enemies, and against whom they burn with hatred and revenge, so it is the delight of their life to will to destroy and kill, and so far as they are unable to do this, to will to do mischief, to injure, and to exercise cruelty. [2] Such is the meaning of "fire" in the Word, where the evil and the hells are treated of, some passages from which I will here quote in the way of proof: Everyone is a hypocrite and an evil doer, and every mouth speaketh folly. For wickedness burneth as the fire; it devoureth the briers and thorns, and kindleth in the thickets of the forests, and they roll upward in the rising of smoke; and the people is become like food for fire; no man spareth his brother (Isa. 9:17-19). I will show wonders in the heavens, and in the earth blood and fire, and pillars of smoke; the sun shall be turned into darkness (Joel 2:30, 31). The land shall become burning pitch; it shall not be quenched night nor day; the smoke thereof shall go up forever (Isa. 34:9, 10). Behold the day cometh burning as a furnace, and all the proud and every worker of wickedness shall be stubble; and the day that cometh shall set them on fire (Mal. 4:1). Babylon is become a habitation of demons. They cried out as they saw the smoke of her burning. Her smoke goeth up unto the ages of the ages (Apoc. 18:2, 18; 19:3). He opened the pit of the abyss, and there went up a smoke out of the pit as the smoke of a great furnace; and the sun was darkened, and the air, by the smoke of the pit (Apoc. 9:2). Out of the mouth of the horses went forth fire and smoke and brimstone; by these was the third part of men killed, by the fire and by the smoke and by the brimstone (Apoc. 4:17, 18). If any one adores the beast he shall drink of the wine of the wrath of God mixed with unmixed wine in the cup of His anger, and shall be tormented with fire and brimstone (Apoc. 16:9, 10). The fourth angel poured out his bowl upon the sun; and it was given unto it to scorch men with fire; therefore men were scorched with great heat (Apoc. 16:8, 9). They were cast into a lake burning with fire and brimstone (Apoc. 19:20; 20:14, 15; 21:8). Every tree that bringeth not forth good fruit shall be hewn down and cast into the fire (Matt. 3:10; Luke 3:9). The Son of man shall send His angels, and they shall gather out of His kingdom all things that cause stumbling and them that do iniquity, and shall cast them into a furnace of fire (Matt. 13:41, 42, 50). The King shall say to them that are on the left hand, Depart from Me, ye cursed, into eternal fire, prepared for the devil and his angels (Matt. 25:41). They shall be sent into everlasting fire, into the hell of fire, where their worm shall not die, and the fire shall not be quenched (Matt. 18:8, 9; Mark 9:43-49). The rich man in hell said to Abraham that he was tormented in flame (Luke 16:24). In these and in many other passages "fire" means the lust pertaining to love of self and love of the world, and the "smoke" therefrom means falsity from evil.

As the lust of doing the evils that are from the love of self and of the world is meant by "infernal fire," and as such is the lust of all in the hells (as shown in the foregoing chapter) so when the hells are opened there is an appearance of fire with smoke, such as is seen in conflagrations, a dense fire from the hells where the love of self prevails, and a flaming fire from the hells where love of the world prevails. But when the hells are closed this fiery appearance is not seen, but in its place there is a kind of obscurity like a condensation of smoke; although the fire still rages within, as can be seen by the heat exhaling therefrom, which is like the heat from the burnt ruins after a fire, and in some places like the heat from a heated furnace, in others like the heat from a hot bath. When this heat flows into man it excites lusts in him, and in evil men hatred and revenge, and in the sick insanities. Such is the fire or such the heat that affects those who are in the above-mentioned loves, because in respect to their spirit they are attached to those hells, even while living in the body. But it must be understood that those who are in the hells are not in fire; the fire is an appearance; those there are conscious of no burning, but only of a warmth like that which they had felt when in the world. This appearance of fire is from correspondence, since love corresponds to fire, and all things seen in the spiritual world are seen in accordance with correspondences.

It must be noted that this infernal fire or heat is changed into intense cold when heat from heaven flows in; and those who are in it then shiver like those seized with chills and fever, and are inwardly distressed; and for the reason that they are in direct opposition to the Divine; and the heat of heaven (which is Divine love) extinguishes the heat of hell (which is the love of self), and with it the fire of their life; and this is the cause of such cold and consequent shivering and distress. This is accompanied by thick darkness and by infatuation and mutual blindness therefrom. But this rarely happens, and only when outbreaks that have increased beyond measure need to be repressed.

Since infernal fire means every lust for doing evil that flows forth from the love of self, this fire means also such torment as exists in the hells. For the lust from that love is a lust for injuring others who do not honor, venerate and worship oneself; and in proportion to the anger thereby excited, and the hatred and revenge from that anger, is there a lust for venting one's rage upon them. When such lust is active in everyone in a society, and is restrained by no external bond, such as the fear of the law, and of the loss of reputation, honor, gain, and life, everyone from the impulse of his own evil rushes upon another; and so far as he prevails subjugates the rest and subjects them to his dominion, and vents his rage with delight upon those who do not submit themselves. This delight is so intimately united with the delight of bearing rule that they exist in the same measure, since the delight of doing harm is contained in all enmity, envy, hatred, and revenge, which as said above, are the evils of that love. All the hells are such societies, and in consequence everyone there bears hatred in his heart against others, and from hatred bursts forth into cruelty so far as he has power. These cruelties and their torments are also meant by infernal fire, since they are the effects of lusts.

It has been shown above (n. 548) that an evil spirit casts himself into hell of his own accord. It shall now be told in a few words how this comes about, when yet there are in hell such torments. From every hell there exhales a sphere of the lusts of those who are in it. Whenever this sphere is perceived by one who is in a like lust he is affected at heart and filled with delight, for lust and its delight make one, since whatever one lusts after is delightful to him; and because of this a spirit turns himself hellwards, and from delight of heart lusts to go thither, since he does not yet know that such torments exist there, although he who knows it still lusts to go there. For no one in the spiritual world can resist his lust, because his lust belongs to his love, and his love belongs to his will, and his will belongs to his nature, and everyone there acts from his nature. [2] When, therefore, a spirit of his own accord and from his freedom drifts towards his hell and enters it, he is received at first in a friendly manner, which makes him believe that he has come among friends. But this continues for a few hours only. In the meanwhile he is explored in respect to his astuteness and consequent ability; and when this has been done they begin to infest him, and this by various methods, and with gradually greater severity and vehemence. This is accomplished by introducing him more interiorly and deeply into hell; for the more interior and deeper the hell the more malignant are the spirits. After these infestations they begin to treat him cruelly by punishments, and this goes on until he is reduced to the condition of a slave. [3] But rebellious movements are continually springing up there, since everyone wishes to be greatest, and burns with hatred against the others; and in consequence new uprisings occur, and thus one scene is changed into another, and those who are made slaves are delivered that they may assist some new devil to subjugate others; and again those who refuse to submit and render implicit obedience are tormented in various ways; and so on continually. Such torments are the torments of hell, which are called hell fire.

Gnashing of teeth is the continual contention and combat of falsities with each other, consequently of those who are in falsities, joined with contempt of others, with enmity, mockery, ridicule, blaspheming; and these evils burst forth into lacerations of various kinds; since everyone fights for his own falsity and calls it truth. These contentions and combats are heard outside of these hells like the gnashings of teeth; and are also turned into gnashings of teeth when truths from heaven flow in among them. In these hells are all who have acknowledged nature and have denied the Divine. In the deeper of these hells are those that have confirmed themselves in such denials. As such are unable to receive any thing of light from heaven, and are thus unable to see any thing inwardly in themselves, they are for the most part corporeal sensual spirits, who believe nothing except what they see with their eyes and touch with their hands. Therefore all the fallacies of the senses are truths to them; and it is from these that they dispute. This is why their contentions are heard as gnashings of teeth; for in the spiritual world all falsities give a grating sound, and the teeth correspond to the outmost things in nature and to the outmost things in man, which are corporeal sensual. 575-1 (That there is gnashing of teeth in the hells may be seen in Matthew 8:12; 13:42, 50; 22:13; 24:51; 25:30; Luke 13:28.)

THE MALICE AND HEINOUS ARTIFICES OF INFERNAL SPIRITS In what way spirits are superior to men everyone can see and comprehend who thinks interiorly and knows any thing of the operation of his own mind; for in his mind he can consider, evolve, and form conclusions upon more subjects in a single moment than he can utter or express in writing in half an hour. This shows the superiority of man when he is in his spirit, and therefore when he becomes a spirit. For it is the spirit that thinks, and it is the body by which the spirit expresses its thoughts in speech or writing. In consequence of this, when man after death becomes an angel he is in intelligence and wisdom ineffable in comparison with his intelligence and wisdom while he lived in the world; for while he lived in the world his spirit was bound to his body, and was thereby in the natural world; and therefore whatever he thought spiritually flowed into natural ideas, which are comparatively general, gross, and obscure, and which are incapable of receiving innumerable things that pertain to spiritual thought; and which infold spiritual thought in the obscurities that arise from worldly cares. It is otherwise when the spirit is released from the body and comes into its spiritual state, which takes place when it passes out of the natural world into the spiritual world to which it belongs. From what has already been said it is evident that the state of its thoughts and affections is then immeasurably superior to its former state. Because of this the thoughts of angels are ineffable and inexpressible, and are therefore incapable of entering into the natural thoughts of man; and yet every angel was born a man, and has lived as a man, and he then seemed to himself to be no wiser than any other like man.

In the same degree in which angels have wisdom and intelligence infernal spirits have malice and cunning; for the case is the same, since the spirit of man when released from the body is in his good or in his evil - if an angelic spirit in his good, and if an infernal spirit in his evil. Every spirit is his own good or his own evil because he is his own love, as has been often said and shown above. Therefore as an angelic spirit thinks, wills, speaks, and acts, from his good, an infernal spirit does this from his evil; and to think, will, speak, and act from evil itself, is to think, will, speak, and act from all things included in the evil. [2] So long as man lived in the body it was different, since the evil of the spirit was then under the restraints that every man feels from the law, from hope of gain, from honor, from reputation, and from the fear of losing these; and therefore the evil of his spirit could not then burst forth and show what it was in itself. Moreover, the evil of the spirit of man then lay wrapped up and veiled in outward probity, honesty, justice, and affection for truth and good, which such a man professes and counterfeits for the sake of the world; and under these semblances the evil has lain so concealed and obscured that he himself scarcely knew that his spirit contained so much malice and craftiness, that is, that in himself he was such a devil as he becomes after death, when his spirit comes into itself and into its own nature. [3] Such malice then manifests itself as exceeds all belief. There are thousands of evils that then burst forth from evil itself, among which are such as cannot be described in the words of any language. What they are has been granted me to know and also to perceive by much experience, since it has been granted me by the Lord to be in the spiritual world in respect to my spirit and at the same time in the natural world in respect to my body. This I can testify, that their malice is so great that it is hardly possible to describe even a thousandth part of it; and so great that if man were not protected by the Lord he could never be rescued from hell; for with every man there are spirits from hell as well as angels from heaven (see above, n. 292, 293); and yet the Lord cannot protect man unless he acknowledges the Divine and lives a life of faith and charity; for otherwise man turns himself away from the Lord and turns himself to infernal spirits, and thus his spirit becomes imbued with a malice like theirs. [4] Nevertheless, man is continually withdrawn by the Lord from the evils that he attaches and as it were attracts to himself by his affiliation with infernal spirits. If he is not withdrawn by the internal bonds of conscience, which he fails to receive if he denies a Divine, he is nevertheless withdrawn by external bonds, which are, as said above, fears in respect to the law and its penalties, and fears of the loss of gain and the deprivation of honor and reputation. In fact, such a man may be withdrawn from evils by means of the delights of his love and through fear of the loss or deprivation of those delights; but he cannot be led thereby into spiritual goods. For as soon as such a man is led into these he begins to give his thought to pretenses and devices by simulating or counterfeiting what is good, honest, and just, for the purpose of persuading and thus deceiving. Such cunning adjoins itself to the evil of his spirit and gives form to it, causing his evil to be of the same nature as itself.

Those are the worst of all who have been in evils from love of self and at the same time inwardly in themselves have acted from deceit; for deceit penetrates more deeply into the thoughts and intentions than other evils, and infects them with poison and thus wholly destroys the spiritual life of man. Most of these spirits are in the hells behind the back, and are called genii; and there they delight to make themselves invisible, and to flutter about others like phantoms secretly infusing evil into them, which they spread around like the poison of a viper. These are more direfully tormented than others. But those who are not deceitful, and who have not been so filled with malignant craftiness, and yet are in the evils derived from the love of self, are also in the hells behind, but in those less deep. On the other hand, those that have been in evils from the love of the world are in the hells in front, and are called spirits. These spirits are not such forms of evil, that is, of hatred and revenge, as those are who are in evils from the love of self; and therefore do not have such malice and cunning; and in consequence their hells are milder.

I have been permitted to learn by experience what kind of malice those possess who are called genii. Genii act upon and flow into the affections, and not the thoughts. They perceive and smell out the affections as dogs do wild beasts in the forest. Good affections, when they perceive them in another, they turn instantly into evil affections, leading and bending them in a wonderful manner by means of the other's delights; and this so secretly and with such malignant skill that the other knows nothing of it, for they most carefully guard against anything entering into the thought, as thereby they would be manifested. The seat of these in man is beneath the back part of the head. In the world they were such as deceitfully captivated the minds of others, leading and persuading them by the delights of their affections or lusts. But such spirits are not permitted by the Lord to come near to any man of whose reformation there is any hope; for they have the ability not only to destroy the conscience, but also to stir up in man his inherited evils, which otherwise lie hidden. Therefore to prevent man's being led into these evils, these hells, by the Lord's provision, are entirely closed up; and when any man of such a character comes after death into the other life, he is at once cast into their hell. When the deceit and craftiness of these spirits are clearly seen they appear as vipers.

The kind of malice infernal spirits possess is evident from their nefarious arts, which are so many that to enumerate them would fill a volume, and to describe them would fill many volumes. These arts are mostly unknown in the world. One kind relates to abuses of correspondences; a second to abuses of the outmosts of Divine order; a third to the communication and influx of thoughts and affections by means of turning towards another, fixing the sight upon another, and by the instrumentality of other spirits apart from themselves, and spirits sent out by themselves; a fourth to operations by phantasies; a fifth to a kind of casting themselves out beyond themselves and consequent presence elsewhere than where they are in the body; a sixth to pretenses, persuasion, and lies. The spirit of an evil man enters of itself into these arts when he is released from his body, for they are inherent in the nature of the evil in which he then is. By these arts they torment each other in the hells. But as all of these arts, except those that are effected by pretenses, persuasions, and lies, are unknown in the world, I will not here describe them in detail, both because they would not be comprehended, and because they are too abominable to be told.

The Lord permits torments in the hells because in no other way can evils be restrained and subdued. The only means of restraining and subduing evils and of keeping the infernal crew in bonds is the fear of punishment. It can be done in no other way; for without the fear of punishment and torment evil would burst forth into madness, and everything would go to pieces, like a kingdom on earth where there is no law and there are no penalties.

THE APPEARANCE, SITUATION, AND NUMBER OF THE HELLS. In the spiritual world, that is, in the world where spirits and angels are, the same objects appear as in the natural world, that is, where men are. In external appearance there is no difference. In that world plains and mountains, hills and rocks, and valleys between them are seen; also waters, and many other things that are seen on earth. And yet all these things are from a spiritual origin, and all are therefore seen by the eyes of spirits and angels, and not by the eyes of men, because men are in the natural world. Spiritual beings see such things as are from a spiritual origin, and natural beings such things as are from a natural origin. Consequently man with his eyes can in no way see the objects that are in the spiritual world unless he is permitted to be in the spirit, or after death when he becomes a spirit. On the other hand, an angel or a spirit is unable to see any thing at all in the natural world unless he is with a man who is permitted to speak with him. For the eyes of man are fitted to receive the light of the natural world, and the eyes of angels and spirits are fitted to receive the light of the spiritual world; although the eyes of the two are exactly alike in appearance. That the spiritual world is such the natural man cannot comprehend, and least of all the sensual man, who believes nothing except what he sees with his bodily eyes and touches with his hands, and therefore takes in by sight and touch. As his thought is from such things it is material and not spiritual. Such being the likeness between the spiritual world and the natural world, man can hardly believe after death that he is not in the world where he was born, and from which he has departed. For this reason death is called simply a translation from one world into another like it. (That the two worlds are thus alike can be seen above, where representatives and appearances in heaven have been treated of, n. 170-176.)

The heavens are in the higher parts of the spiritual world, the world of spirits in the lower parts, and under both are the hells. The heavens are visible to spirits in the world of spirits only when their interior sight is opened; although they sometimes see them as mists or as bright clouds. This is because the angels of heaven are in an interior state in respect to intelligence and wisdom; and for this reason they are above the sight of those who are in the world of spirits. But spirits who dwell in the plains and valleys see one another; and yet when they are separated there, which takes place when they are let into their interiors, the evil spirits do not see the good spirits; but the good spirits can see the evil spirits. Nevertheless, the good spirits turn themselves away from the evil spirits; and when spirits turn themselves away they become invisible. But the hells are not seen because they are closed up. Only the entrances, which are called gates, are seen when they are opened to let in other like spirits. All the gates to the hells open from the world of spirits, and none of them from heaven.

The hells are everywhere, both under the mountains, hills, and rocks, and under the plains and valleys. The openings or gates to the hells that are under the mountains, hills, and rocks, appear to the sight like holes and clefts in the rocks, some extended and wide, and some straitened and narrow, and many of them rugged. They all, when looked into, appear dark and dusky; but the infernal spirits that are in them are in such a luminosity as arises from burning coals. Their eyes are adapted to the reception of that light, and for the reason that while they lived in the world they were in thick darkness in respect to Divine truths, because of their denying them, and were in a sort of light in respect to falsities because of their affirming them. In this way did the sight of their eyes become so formed. And for the same reason the light of heaven is thick darkness to them, and therefore when they go out of their dens they see nothing. All this makes it abundantly clear that man comes into the light of heaven just to the extent that he acknowledges the Divine, and establishes in himself the things of heaven and the church; and that he comes into the thick darkness of hell just to the extent that he denies the Divine, and establishes in himself what is contrary to the truths of heaven and the church.

The openings or gates to the hells that are beneath the plains and valleys present to the sight different appearances. Some resemble those that are beneath the mountains, hills and rocks; some resemble dens and caverns, some great chasms and whirlpools; some resemble bogs, and some standing water. They are all covered, and are opened only when evil spirits from the world of spirits are cast in; and when they are opened there bursts forth from them either something like the fire and smoke that is seen in the air from burning buildings, or like a flame without smoke, or like soot such as comes from a burning chimney, or like a mist and thick cloud. I have heard that the infernal spirits neither see nor feel these things, because when they are in them they are as in their own atmosphere, and thus in the delight of their life; and this for the reason that these things correspond to the evils and falsities in which they are, fire corresponding to hatred and revenge, smoke and soot to the falsities therefrom, flame to the evils of the love of self, and a mist or thick cloud to falsities from that love.

I have also been permitted to look into the hells and to see what they are within; for when the Lord wills, the sight of a spirit or angel from above may penetrate into the lowest depths beneath and explore their character, notwithstanding the coverings. In this way I have been permitted to look into them. Some of the hells appeared to the view like caverns and dens in rocks extending inward and then downward into an abyss, either obliquely or vertically. Some of the hells appeared to the view like the dens and caves of wild beasts in forests; some like the hollow caverns and passages that are seen in mines, with caverns extending towards the lower regions. Most of the hells are threefold, the upper one appearing within to be in dense darkness, because inhabited by those who are in the falsities of evil; while the lower ones appear fiery, because inhabited by those who are in evils themselves, dense darkness corresponding to the falsities of evil, and fire to evils themselves. Those that have acted interiorly from evil are in the deeper hells, and those that have acted exteriorly from evil, that is, from the falsities of evil, are in the hells that are less deep. Some hells present an appearance like the ruins of houses and cities after conflagrations, in which infernal spirits dwell and hide themselves. In the milder hells there is an appearance of rude huts, in some cases contiguous in the form of a city with lanes and streets, and within the houses are infernal spirits engaged in unceasing quarrels, enmities, fightings, and brutalities; while in the streets and lanes robberies and depredations are committed. In some of the hells there are nothing but brothels, disgusting to the sight and filled with every kind of filth and excrement. Again, there are dark forests, in which infernal spirits roam like wild beasts and where, too, there are underground dens into which those flee who are pursued by others. There are also deserts, where all is barren and sandy, and where in some places there are ragged rocks in which there are caverns, and in some places huts. Into these desert places those are cast out from the hells who have suffered every extremity of punishment, especially those who in the world have been more cunning than others in undertaking and contriving intrigues and deceits. Such a life is their final lot.

As to the positions of the hells in detail, it is something wholly unknown even to the angels in heaven; it is known to the Lord alone. But their position in general is known from the quarters in which they are. For the hells, like the heavens, are distinguished by their quarters; and in the spiritual world quarters are determined in accordance with loves; for in heaven all the quarters begin from the Lord as the sun, who is the East; and as the hells are opposite to the heavens their quarters begin from the opposite point, that is, from the west. (On this see the chapter on the four quarters in heaven, n. 141-153.) [2] For this reason the hells in the western quarter are the worst of all, and the most horrible, becoming gradually worse and more horrible by degrees the more remote they are from the east. In the western hells are those who in the world were in the love of self, and in consequent contempt of others, and in enmity against those who did not favor them, also in hatred and revenge against those who did not render them respect and homage. In the most remote hells in that quarter are those that had belonged to the Catholic religion, so called, and that had wished to be worshiped as gods, and consequently had burned with hatred and revenge against all who did not acknowledge their power over the souls of men and over heaven. These continue to have the same disposition, that is, the same hatred and revenge against those who oppose them, that they had in the world. Their greatest delight is to practice cruelties; but in the other life this delight is turned against themselves; for in their hells, with which the western quarter is filled, one rages against everyone who detracts from his Divine power. (But more will be said about this in the treatise on The Last Judgment and the Destruction of Babylon.) [3] Nevertheless, no one can know how the hells in that quarter are arranged, except that the most dreadful hells of that kind are at the sides towards the northern quarter, and the less dreadful towards the southern quarter; thus the dreadfulness of the hells decreases from the northern quarter to the southern, and likewise by degrees towards the east. Towards the east are the dwelling places of the haughty, who have not believed in the Divine, and yet have not been in such hatred and revenge, or in such deceit, as those have who are in a greater depth in the western quarter. [4] In the eastern quarter there are at present no hells, those that were there having been transferred to the western quarter in front. In the northern and southern quarters there are many hells; and in them are those who while in the world were in love of the world, and in various kinds of evil therefrom, such as enmity, hostility, theft, robbery, cunning, avarice, and unmercifulness. The worst hells of this kind are in the northern quarter, the milder in the southern. Their dreadfulness increases as they are nearer to the western quarter, and also as they are farther away from the southern quarter, and decreases towards the eastern quarter and towards the southern quarter. Behind the hells that are in the western quarter there are dark forests, in which malignant spirits roam like wild beasts; and it is the same behind the hells in the northern quarter. But behind the hells in the southern quarter there are deserts, which have been described just above. This much respecting the situation of the hells.

In regard to the number of the hells, there are as many of them as there are angelic societies in the heavens, since there is for every heavenly society a corresponding infernal society as its opposite. That the heavenly societies are numberless, and are all distinguished in accordance with the goods of love, charity, and faith, may be seen in the chapter that treats of the societies of which the heavens consist (n. 41-50), and in the chapter on the immensity of heaven (n. 415-420). The like is true, therefore, of the infernal societies, which are distinguished in accordance with the evils that are the opposites of those goods. [2] Every evil, as well as every good, is of infinite variety. That this is true is beyond the comprehension of those who have only a simple idea regarding every evil, such as contempt, enmity, hatred, revenge, deceit, and other like evils. But let them know that each one of these evils contains so many specific differences, and each of these again so many specific or particular differences, that a volume would not suffice to enumerate them. The hells are so distinctly arranged in order in accordance with the differences of every evil that nothing could be more perfectly ordered or more distinct. Evidently, then, the hells are innumerable, near to and remote from one another in accordance with the differences of evils generically, specifically, and particularly. [3] There are likewise hells beneath hells. Some communicate with others by passages, and more by exhalations, and this in exact accordance with the affinities of one kind or one species of evil with others. How great the number is of the hells I have been permitted to realize from knowing that there are hells under every mountain, hill, and rock, and likewise under every plain and valley, and that they stretch out beneath these in length and in breadth and in depth. In a word, the entire heaven and the entire world of spirits are, as it were, excavated beneath, and under them is a continuous hell. Thus much regarding the number of the hells.

THE EQUILIBRIUM BETWEEN HEAVEN AND HELL. For any thing to have existence there must be an equilibrium of all things. Without equilibrium is no action and reaction; for equilibrium is between two forces, one acting and the other reacting, and the state of rest resulting from like action and reaction is called equilibrium. In the natural world there is an equilibrium in all things and in each thing. It exists in a general way even in the atmosphere, wherein the lower parts react and resist in proportion as the higher parts act and press down. Again, in the natural world there is an equilibrium between heat and cold, between light and shade, and between dryness and moisture, the middle condition being the equilibrium. There is also an equilibrium in all the subjects of the three kingdoms of nature, the mineral, the vegetable, and the animal; for without equilibrium in them nothing can come forth and have permanent existence. Everywhere there is a sort of effort acting on the one side and reacting on the other. [2] All existence or all effect is produced in equilibrium, that is, by one force acting and another suffering itself to be acted upon, or when one force by acting flows in, the other receives and harmoniously submits. In the natural world that which acts and reacts is called force, and also endeavor [or effort]; but in the spiritual world that which acts and reacts is called life and will. Life in that world is living force, and will is living effort; and the equilibrium itself is called freedom. Thus spiritual equilibrium or freedom has its outcome and permanence in the balance between good acting on the one side and evil reacting on the other side; or between evil acting on the one side and good reacting on the other side. [3] With the good the equilibrium is between good acting and evil reacting; but with the evil the equilibrium is between evil acting and good reacting. Spiritual equilibrium is between good and evil, because the whole life of man has reference to good and to evil, and the will is the receptacle. There is also an equilibrium between truth and falsity, but this depends on the equilibrium between good and evil. The equilibrium between truth and falsity is like that between light and shade, in that light and shade affect the objects of the vegetable kingdom only so far as heat and cold are in them. That light and shade themselves have no effect, but only the heat that acts through them, is evident from the fact that light and shade are the same in winter time and in spring time. This comparison of truth and falsity with light and shade is from correspondence, for truth corresponds to light, falsity to shade, and heat to the good of love; in fact, spiritual light is truth, spiritual shade is falsity, and spiritual heat is good of love (see the chapter where light and heat in heaven are treated of, n. 126-140).

There is a perpetual equilibrium between heaven and hell. From hell there continually breathes forth and ascends an endeavor to do evil, and from heaven there continually breathes forth and descends an endeavor to do good. In this equilibrium is the world of spirits; which world is intermediate between heaven and hell (see above, n. 421-431). The world of spirits is in this equilibrium because every man after death enters first the world of spirits, and is kept there in a state like that which he was in while in the world, and this would be impossible if there were not a perfect equilibrium there; for by means of this the character of everyone is explored, since they then remain in the same freedom as they had in the world. Spiritual equilibrium is freedom in man and spirit (as has been said just above, n. 589). What each one's freedom is the angels recognize by a communication of affections and thoughts therefrom; and it becomes visible to the sight of angelic spirits by the ways in which the spirits go. Good spirits there travel in the ways that go towards heaven, but evil spirits in the ways that go towards hell. Ways actually appear in that world; and that is the reason why ways in the Word signify the truths that lead to good, or in the opposite sense the falsities that lead to evil; and for the same reason going, walking, and journeying in the Word signify progressions of life. 590-1 Such ways I have often been permitted to see, also spirits going and walking in them freely, in accord with their affections and thoughts.

Evil continually breathes forth and ascends out of hell, and good continually breathes forth and descends out of heaven, because everyone is encompassed by a spiritual sphere; and that sphere flows forth and pours out from the life of the affections and the thoughts therefrom. 591-1 And as such a sphere flows forth from every individual, it flows forth also from every heavenly society and from every infernal society, consequently from all together, that is, from the entire heaven and from the entire hell. Good flows forth from heaven because all there are in good; and evil flows forth from hell because all there are in evil. The good that is from heaven is all from the Lord; for the angels in the heavens are all withheld from what is their own, and are kept in what is the Lord's own, which is good itself. But the spirits in the hells are all in what is their own, and everyone's own is nothing but evil; and because it is nothing but evil it is hell. 591-2 Evidently, then, the equilibrium in which angels are kept in the heavens and spirits in the hells is not like the equilibrium in the world of spirits. The equilibrium of angels in the heavens exists in the degree in which they have been willing to be in good, or in the degree in which they have lived in good in the world, and thus also in the degree in which they have held evil in aversion; but the equilibrium of spirits in hell exists in the degree in which they have been willing to be in evil, or have lived in evil in the world, and thus in heart and spirit have been opposed to good.

Unless the Lord ruled both the heavens and the hells there would be no equilibrium; and if there were no equilibrium there would be no heaven or hell; for all things and each thing in the universe, that is, both in the natural world and in the spiritual world, endure by means of equilibrium. Every rational man can see that this is true. If there were a preponderance on one part and no resistance on the other would not both perish? So would it be in the spiritual world if good did not react against evil and continually restrain its uprising; and unless this were done by the Divine Itself both heaven and hell would perish, and with them the whole human race. It is said unless the Divine Itself did this, because the self of everyone, whether angel, spirit, or man, is nothing but evil (see above, n. 591); consequently neither angels nor spirits are able in the least to resist the evils continually exhaling from the hells, since from self they all tend towards hell. It is evident, then, that unless the Lord alone ruled both the heavens and the hells no one could ever be saved. Moreover, all the hells act as one; for evils in the hells are connected as goods are in the heavens; and the Divine alone, which goes forth solely from the Lord, is able to resist all the hells, which are innumerable, and which act together against heaven and against all who are in heaven.

The equilibrium between the heavens and the hells is diminished or increased in accordance with the number of those who enter heaven and who enter hell; and this amounts to several thousands daily. The Lord alone, and no angel, can know and perceive this, and regulate and equalize it with precision; for the Divine that goes forth from the Lord is omnipresent, and sees everywhere whether there is any wavering, while an angel sees only what is near himself, and has no perception in himself of what is taking place even in his own society.

How all things are so arranged in the heavens and in the hells that each and all of those who are there may be in their equilibrium, can in some measure be seen from what has been said and shown above respecting the heavens and the hells, namely, that all the societies of heaven are distinctly arranged in accordance with goods and their kinds and varieties, and all the societies of hell in accordance with evils, and their kinds and varieties; and that beneath each society of heaven there is a society of hell corresponding to it from opposition, and from this opposing correspondence equilibrium results; and in consequence of this the Lord unceasingly provides that no infernal society beneath a heavenly society shall gain any preponderance, and as soon as it begins to do so it is restrained by various means, and is reduced to an exact measure of equilibrium. These means are many, only a few of which I will mention. Some of these means have reference to the stronger presence of the Lord; some to the closer communication and conjunction of one or more societies with others; some to the casting out of superabundant infernal spirits into deserts; some to the transference of certain spirits from one hell to another; some to the reducing of those in the hells to order, and this also is effected in various ways; some to the screening of certain hells under denser and thicker coverings, also letting them down to greater depths; besides other means; and still others that are employed in the heavens above the hells. All this has been said that it may in some measure be perceived that the Lord alone provides that there shall be an equilibrium everywhere between good and evil, thus between heaven and hell; for on such equilibrium the safety of all in the heavens and of all on the earth rests.

It should be known that the hells are continually assaulting heaven and endeavoring to destroy it, and that the Lord continually protects the heavens by withholding those who are in it from the evils derived from their self, and by holding them in the good that is from Himself. I have often been permitted to perceive the sphere that flows forth from the hells, which was wholly a sphere of effort to destroy the Divine of the Lord, and thus heaven. The ebullitions of some hells have also at times been perceived, which were efforts to break forth and to destroy. But on the other hand the heavens never assault the hells, for the Divine sphere that goes forth from the Lord is a perpetual effort to save all; and as those who are in the hells cannot be saved, (since all who are there are in evil and are antagonistic to the Divine of the Lord,) so as far as possible outrages in the hells are subdued and cruelties are restrained to prevent their breaking out beyond measure one against another. This also is effected by innumerable ways in which the Divine power is exercised.

There are two kingdoms into which the heavens are divided, the celestial kingdom and the spiritual kingdom (of which see above, n. 20-28). In like manner the hells are divided into two kingdoms, one of which is opposite to the celestial kingdom and the other opposite to the spiritual kingdom. That which is opposite to the celestial kingdom is in the western quarter, and those who are in it are called genii; and that which is opposite to the spiritual kingdom is in the northern and southern quarters, and those which are in it are called spirits. All who are in the celestial kingdom are in love to the Lord, and all who are in the hells opposite to that kingdom are in the love of self; while all who are in the spiritual kingdom are in love towards the neighbor, and all who are in the hells opposite to that kingdom are in love of the world. Evidently, then, love to the Lord and the love of self are opposites; and in like manner love towards the neighbor and love of the world are opposites. The Lord continually provides that there shall be no outflowing from the hells that are opposite the Lord's celestial kingdom towards those who are in the spiritual kingdom; for if this were done the spiritual kingdom would perish (for the reason given above, n. 678, 579). These are the two general equilibriums that are unceasingly maintained by the Lord.

BY MEANS OF THE EQUILIBRIUM BETWEEN HEAVEN AND HELL MAN IS IN FREEDOM. The equilibrium between heaven and hell has now been described, and it has been shown that it is an equilibrium between the good that is from heaven and the evil that is from hell, thus that it is a spiritual equilibrium, which in its essence is freedom. A spiritual equilibrium in its essence is freedom because it is an equilibrium between good and evil, and between truth and falsity, and these are spiritual. Therefore to be able to will either what is good or what is evil and to think either what is true or what is false, and to choose one in preference to the other, is the freedom which is here treated of. This freedom is given to every man by the Lord, and is never taken away; in fact, by virtue of its origin it is not man's but the Lord's, since it is from the Lord. Nevertheless, it is given to man with his life as if it were his; and this is done that man may have the ability to be reformed and saved; for without freedom there can be no reformation or salvation. With any rational intuition any one can see that it is a part of man's freedom to be able to think wrongly or rightly, sincerely or insincerely, justly or unjustly; also that he is free to speak and act rightly, honestly, and justly; but not to speak and act wrongly, insincerely, and unjustly, because of the spiritual, moral, and civil laws whereby his external is held in restraint. Evidently, then, it is man's spirit, which thinks and wills, that is in freedom, and not his external which speaks and acts, except in agreement with the above mentioned laws.

Man cannot be reformed unless he has freedom, for the reason that he is born into evils of every kind; and these must be removed in order that he may be saved; and they cannot be removed unless he sees them in himself and acknowledges them, and afterwards ceases to will them, and finally holds them in aversion. Not until then are they removed. And this cannot be done unless man is in good as well as in evil, since it is from good that he is able to see evils, while from evil he cannot see good. The spiritual goods that man is capable of thinking he learns from childhood by reading the Word and from preaching; and he learns moral and civil good from his life in the world. This is the first reason why man ought to be in freedom. [2] Another reason is that nothing is appropriated to man except what is done from an affection of his love. Other things may gain entrance, but no farther than the thought, not reaching the will; and whatever does not gain entrance into the will of man does not become his, for thought derives what pertains to it from memory, while the will derives what pertains to it from the life itself. Only what is from the will, or what is the same, from the affection of love, can be called free, for whatever a man wills or loves that he does freely; consequently man's freedom and the affection of his love or of his will are a one. It is for this reason that man has freedom, in order that he may be affected by truth and good or may love them, and that they may thus become as if they were his own [3] In a word, whatever does not enter into man's freedom has no permanence, because it does not belong to his love or will, and what does not belong to man's love or will does not belong to his spirit; for the very being [esse] of the spirit of man is love or will. It is said love or will, since a man wills what he loves. This, then, is why man can be reformed only in freedom. But more on the subject of man's freedom may be seen in the Arcana Coelestia in the passages referred to below.

In order that man may be in freedom, to the end that he may be reformed, he is conjoined in respect to his spirit both with heaven and with hell. For with every man there are spirits from hell and angels from heaven. It is by means of hell that man is in his own evil, while it is by means of angels from heaven that man is in good from the Lord; thus is he in spiritual equilibrium, that is, in freedom. That angels from heaven and spirits from hell are joined to every man may be seen in the chapter on the conjunction of heaven with the human race (n. 291-302).

It must be understood that the conjunction of man with heaven and with hell is not a direct conjunction with them, but a mediate conjunction by means of spirits who are in the world of spirits. These spirits, and none from hell itself or from heaven itself, are with man. By means of evil spirits in the world of spirits man is conjoined with hell, and by means of good spirits there he is conjoined with heaven. Because of this the world of spirits is intermediate between heaven and hell, and in that world is equilibrium itself. (That the world of spirits is intermediate between heaven and hell may be seen in the chapter on the world of spirits, n. 421-431; and that the essential equilibrium between heaven and hell is there may be seen in the preceding chapter, n. 589-596.) From all this the source of man's freedom is evident.

Footnotes
    551-1 Before the evil are cast down into hell they are devastated of truths and goods, and when these have been taken away they are of themselves carried into hell (n. 6977, 7039, 7795, 8210, 8232, 9330). The Lord does not devastate them, but they devastate themselves (n. 7643, 7926). Every evil has in it what is false; therefore those who are in evil are also in falsity, although some do not know it (n. 7577, 8094). Those who are in evil must needs think what is false when they think from themselves (n. 7437). All who are in hell speak falsities from hell (n. 1695, 7351, 7352, 7357, 7392, 7689).
    558-1 Evidently, then, the love of the neighbor that has its beginning in man is the opposite of the love to the neighbor that has its beginning in the Lord; and

the former proceeds from evil because it proceeds from what is man's own, while the latter proceeds from good because it proceeds from the Lord, who is good itself. Evidently, also, the love of the neighbor that proceeds from man and from what is his own is corporeal, while the love to the neighbor that proceeds from the Lord is heavenly. In a word, in the man in whom love of self prevails that love constitutes the head, and heavenly love constitutes the feet. On that love he stands; and if it does not serve him he tramples it under foot. This is the cause of the appearance that those who are cast down into hell fall with the head downward towards hell, and with the feet upwards towards heaven (see above, n. 548).

558-2 Those who do not know what it is to love the neighbor imagine every man to be a neighbor, and that good is to be done to everyone who is in need of help (n. 6704). They also believe that everyone is neighbor to himself, and thus that love to the neighbor begins with self (n. 6933). Those who love themselves above all things, that is, with whom self-love prevails, also make love to the neighbor to begin with themselves (n. 6710). In what manner everyone is neighbor to himself, explained (n. 6933-6938). But those who are Christians and who love God above all things make love to the neighbor to begin with the Lord, because He is to be loved above all things (n. 6706, 6711, 6819, 6824). The distinctions of neighbor are as many as the distinctions of good from the Lord, and there should be distinction in doing good to everyone in accordance with the quality of his state, and this is a matter of Christian prudence (n. 6707, 6709, 6711, 6818). These distinctions are innumerable, and for this reason the ancients, who knew what is meant by the neighbor, reduced the exercises of charity into classes, which they denoted by suitable names, and from this knew in what respect everyone was a neighbor, and in what manner good was to be done to everyone with prudence (n. 2417, 6628, 6705, 7259-7262). The doctrine in the ancient churches was the doctrine of charity towards the neighbor, and from this they had wisdom (n. 2417, 2385, 3419, 3420, 4844, 6628).

561-1 "The sun of the world" signifies the love of self (n. 2441). In this sense "to worship the sun" signifies to worship those things that are antagonistic to heavenly love and to the Lord (n. 2441, 10584). "The sun's growing hot" means an increasing lust of evil (n. 8487).

567-1 There is an influx from the spiritual world into the natural world (n. 6053-6058, 6189-6215, 6307-6327, 6466-6495, 6598-6626). There is also an influx into the lives of animals (n. 5850). And into the subjects of the vegetable kingdom (n. 3648). This influx is a continual endeavor to act in accordance with the Divine order (n. 6211 at the end).

575-1 The correspondence of the teeth (n. 5565-5568). Those who are purely sensual and have scarcely anything of spiritual light correspond to the teeth (n. 5565). In the Word a tooth signifies the sensual, which is the outmost of the life of man (n. 9052, 9062). Gnashing of teeth in the other life comes from those who believe that nature is everything and the Divine nothing (n. 5568).

590-1 In the word "to journey," as well as "to go," signifies progression of life (n. 3335, 4375, 4554, 4585, 4882, 5493, 5605, 5996, 8181, 8345, 8397, 8417, 8420, 8557). "To go (and to walk) with the Lord" means to receive spiritual life, and to live with Him (n. 10567). "To walk" means to live (n. 519, 1794, 8417, 8420).

591-1 A spiritual sphere, which is a sphere of life, flows forth and pours forth from every man, spirit, and angel, and encompasses him (n. 4464, 5179, 7454, 8630). It flows forth from the life of their affections and thoughts (n. 2489, 4464, 6206). The quality of spirits is recognized at a distance from their spheres (n. 1048, 1053, 1316, 1504). Spheres from the evil are the opposites of spheres from the good (n. 1695, 10187, 10312). Such spheres extend far into angelic societies in accordance with the quality and quantity of good (n. 6598-6613, 8063, 8794, 8797). And into infernal societies in accordance with the quality and quantity of evil (n. 8794).

591-2 Man's self is nothing but evil (n. 210, 215, 731, 874-876, 987, 1047, 2307, 2308, 3518, 3701, 3812, 8480, 8550, 10283, 10284, 10286, 10732). Man's self is hell in him (n. 684, 8480).

Section 13

Something more must be said about the spirits that are joined with man. An entire society can have communication with another society, or with an individual wherever he is; by means of a spirit sent forth from the society; this spirit is called the subject of the many. The same is true of man's conjunction with societies in heaven, and with societies in hell, by means of spirits from the world of spirits that are joined with man. (On this subject see also the Arcana Coelestia in the passages referred to below.)

Finally something must be said respecting man's intuition in regard to his life after death which is derived from the influx of heaven into man. There were some of the simple common people who had lived in the world in the good of faith who were brought back into a state like that in which they had been in the world, which can be done with any one when the Lord grants it; and it was then shown what opinion they had held about the state of man after death. They said that some intelligent persons had asked them in the world what they thought about their soul after the life on earth; and they replied that they did not know what the soul is. They were then asked what they believed about their state after death; and they said that they believed that they would live as spirits. Again they were asked what belief they had respecting a spirit; and they said that he is a man. They were asked how they knew this; and they said that they knew it because it is so. Those intelligent men were surprised that the simple had such a faith, which they themselves did not have. This is a proof that in every man who is in conjunction with heaven there is an intuition respecting his life after death. This intuition is from no other source than an influx out of heaven, that is, through heaven from the Lord by means of spirits from the world of spirits who are joined with man. This intuition those have who have not extinguished their freedom of thinking by notions previously adopted and confirmed by various arguments respecting the soul of man, which is held to be either pure thought, or some vital principle the seat of which is sought for in the body; and yet the soul is nothing but the life of man, while the spirit is the man himself; and the earthly body which he carries about with him in the world is merely an agent whereby the spirit, which is the man himself, is enabled to act fitly in the natural world.

What has been said in this work about heaven, the world of spirits, and hell, will be obscure to those who have no interest in learning about spiritual truths, but will be clear to those who have such an interest, and especially to those who have an affection for truth for the sake of truth, that is, who love truth because it is truth; for whatever is then loved enters with light into the mind's thought, especially truth that is loved, because all truth is in light. EXTRACTS FROM THE ARCANA COELESTIA RESPECTING THE FREEDOM OF MAN, INFLUX, AND THE SPIRITS THROUGH WHOM COMMUNICATIONS ARE EFFECTED. FREEDOM. All freedom pertains to love or affection, since whatever a man loves he does freely (n. 2870, 3158, 8987, 8990, 9585, 9591).

Since freedom pertains to love it is the life of everyone (n. 2873). Nothing appears to be man's own except what is from freedom (n. 2880). There is heavenly freedom and infernal freedom (n. 2870, 2873, 2874, 9589, 9590). [2] Heavenly freedom pertains to heavenly love, or the love of good and truth (n. 1947, 2870, 2872). And as the love of good and truth is from the Lord freedom itself consists in being led by the Lord (n. 892, 905, 2872, 2886, 2890-2892, 9096, 9586, 9587, 9589-9591). Man is led into heavenly freedom by the Lord through regeneration (n. 2874, 2875, 2882, 2892). Man must have freedom in order to be regenerated (n. 1937, 1947, 2876, 2881, 3145, 3146, 3158, 4031, 8700). In no other way can the love of good and truth be implanted in man, and appropriated by him seemingly as his own (n. 2877, 2879, 2880, 2888). Nothing is conjoined to man in a state of compulsion (n. 2875, 8700). If man could be reformed by compulsion all would be saved (n. 2881). In reformation compulsion is harmful (n. 4031). All worship from freedom is worship, but worship from compulsion is not worship (n. 1947, 2880, 7349, 10097). Repentance must be effected in a free state, and repentance effected in a state of compulsion is of no avail (n. 8392). States of compulsion, what they are (n. 8392). [3] It is granted to man to act from the freedom of reason, to the end that good may be provided for him, and this is why man has the freedom to think and will even what is evil, and to do it so far as the laws do not forbid (n. 10777). Man is kept by the Lord between heaven and hell, and thus in equilibrium, that he may be in freedom for the sake of reformation (n. 5982, 6477, 8209, 8987). What is implanted in freedom endures, but not what is implanted under compulsion (n. 9588). For this reason no one is ever deprived of his freedom (n. 2876, 2881). The Lord compels no one (n. 1937, 1947). Compelling one's self is from freedom, but not being compelled (n. 1937, 1947). A man ought to compel himself to resist evil (n. 1937, 1947, 7914). Also to do good as if from himself, and yet to acknowledge that it is from the Lord (n. 2883, 2891, 2892, 7914). Man has a stronger freedom in the temptation combats in which he conquers, since he then compels himself more interiorly to resist, although it appears otherwise (n. 1937, 1947, 2881). [4] Infernal freedom consists in being led by the loves of self and of the world and their lusts (n. 2870, 2873). Those who are in hell know no other freedom (n. 2871). Heavenly freedom is as far removed from infernal freedom as heaven is from hell (n. 2873, 2874). Infernal freedom, which consists in being led by the loves of self and of the world, is not freedom but servitude (n. 2884, 2890). For servitude is in being led by hell (n. 9586, 9589-9591) INFLUX. [5] All things that man thinks and wills flow into him from experience (n. 904, 2886-2888, 4151, 4319, 4320, 5846, 5848, 6189, 6191, 6194, 6197-6199, 6213, 7147, 10219). Man's capacity to give attention to subjects, to think, and to draw conclusions analytically, is from influx (n. 4319, 4320, 5288). Man could not live a single moment if influx from the spiritual world were taken away from him; from experience (n. 2887, 5849, 5854, 6321). The life that flows in from the Lord varies in accordance with the state of man and in accordance with reception (n. 2069, 5986, 6472, 7343). With those who are evil the good that flows in from the Lord is changed into evil, and the truth into falsity; from experience (n. 3642, 4632). The good and truth that continually flow in from the Lord are received just to the extent that they are not hindered by evil and falsity (n. 2411, 3142, 3147, 5828). [6] All good flows in from the Lord, and all evil from hell (n. 904,

4151). At the present day man believes that all things are in himself and are from himself, when in fact they flow in; and this he might know from the doctrine of the church, which teaches that all good is from God, and all evil from the devil (n. 4249, 6193, 6206). But if man's belief were in accord with this doctrine he would not appropriate evil to himself nor would he make good to be his own (n. 6206, 6324, 6325). How happy man's state would be if he believed that all good flows in from the Lord and all evil from hell. (n. 6325). Those who deny heaven or who know nothing about it do not know that there is any influx from heaven (n. 4322, 5649, 6193, 6479). What influx is, illustrated by comparisons (n. 6128, 6190, 9407). [7] Everything of life flows in from the first fountain of life, because that is the source of it; and it continually flows in thus everything of life is from the Lord (n. 3001, 3318, 3337, 3338, 3344, 3484, 3619, 3741-3743, 4318-4320, 4417, 4524, 4882, 5847, 5986, 6325, 6468-6470, 6479, 9276, 10196). Influx is spiritual and not physical, that is, influx is from the spiritual world into the natural, and not from the natural into the spiritual (n. 3219, 5119, 5259, 5427, 5428, 5477, 6322, 9110). Influx is through the internal man into the external, or through the spirit into the body, and not the reverse, because the spirit of man is in the spiritual world, and his body in the natural (n. 1702, 1707, 1940, 1954, 5119, 5259, 5779, 6322, 9380). The internal man is in the spiritual world and the external in the natural world (n. 978, 1015, 3628, 4459, 4523, 4524, 6057, 6309, 9701-9709, 10156, 10472). There is an appearance that there is an influx from the externals of man into internals, but this is a fallacy (n. 3721). With man there is influx into things rational, and through these into knowledges, and not the reverse (n. 1495, 1707, 1940). What the order of influx is (n. 775, 880, 1096, 1495, 7270). There is direct influx from the Lord, and likewise mediate influx through the spiritual world or heaven (n. 6063, 6307, 6472, 9682, 9683). The Lord's influx is into the good in man, and through good into truth, and not the reverse (n. 5482, 5649, 6027, 8685, 8701, 10153). Good gives the capacity to receive influx from the Lord, but truth without good does not (n. 8321). Nothing that flows into the thought is harmful, but only what flows into the will, since this is what is appropriated to man (n. 6308). [8] There is a general influx (n. 5850). This is a continual effort to act in accordance with order (n. 6211). This influx is into the lives of animals (n. 5850). Also into the subjects of the vegetable kingdom (n. 3648). It is in accord with this general influx that thought falls into speech with man, and will into acts and movements (n. 5862, 5990, 6192, 6211). SUBJECT SPIRITS. [9] Spirits sent forth from societies of spirits to other societies and to other spirits, are called "subjects" (n. 4403, 5856). Communications in the other life are effected by means of such emissary spirits (n. 4403, 5856, 5983). A spirit sent forth to serve as a subject does not think from himself, but thinks from those by whom he is sent forth (n. 5985-5987). Many particulars relating to such spirits (n. 5988, 5989). ??

Divine Love and Wisdom

Section 1

PART FIRST. LOVE IS THE LIFE OF MAN. Man knows that there is such a thing as love, but he does not know what love is. He knows that there is such a thing as love from common speech, as when it is said, he loves me, a king loves his subjects, and subjects love their king, a husband loves his wife, a mother her children, and conversely; also, this or that one loves his country, his fellow citizens, his neighbor; and likewise of things abstracted from person, as when it is said, one loves this or that thing. But although the word love is so universally used, hardly anybody knows what love is. And because one is unable, when he reflects upon it, to form to himself any idea of thought about it, he says either that it is not anything, or that it is merely something flowing in from sight, hearing, touch, or interaction with others, and thus affecting him. He is wholly unaware that love is his very life; not only the general life of his whole body, and the general life of all his thoughts, but also the life of all their particulars. This a man of discernment can perceive when it is said: If you remove the affection which is from love, can you think anything, or do anything? Do not thought, speech, and action, grow cold in the measure in which the affection which is from love grows cold? And do they not grow warm in the measure in which this affection grows warm? But this a man of discernment perceives simply by observing that such is the case, and not from any knowledge that love is the life of man.

What the life of man is, no one knows unless he knows that it is love. If this is not known, one person may believe that man's life is nothing but perceiving with the senses and acting, and another that it is merely thinking; and yet thought is the first effect of life, and sensation and action are the second effect of life. Thought is here said to be the first effect of life, yet there is thought which is interior and more interior, also exterior and more exterior. What is actually the first effect of life is inmost thought, which is the perception of ends. But of all this hereafter, when the degrees of life are considered.

Some idea of love, as being the life of man, may be had from the sun's heat in the world. This heat is well known to be the common life, as it were, of all the vegetations of the earth. For by virtue of heat, coming forth in springtime, plants of every kind rise from the ground, deck themselves with leaves, then with blossoms, and finally with fruits, and thus, in a sense, live. But when, in the time of autumn and winter, heat withdraws, the plants are stripped of these signs of their life, and they wither. So it is with love in man; for heat and love mutually correspond. Therefore love also is warm.

GOD ALONE, CONSEQUENTLY THE LORD, IS LOVE ITSELF, BECAUSE HE IS LIFE ITSELF AND ANGELS AND MEN ARE RECIPIENTS OF LIFE. This will be fully shown in treatises on Divine Providence and on Life; it is sufficient here to say that the Lord, who is the God of the universe, is uncreate and infinite, whereas man and angel are created and finite. And because the Lord is uncreate and infinite, He is Being [Esse] itself, which is called "Jehovah," and Life itself, or Life in itself. From the uncreate, the infinite, Being itself and Life itself, no one can be created immediately, because the Divine is one and indivisible; but their creation must be out of things created and finited, and so formed that the Divine can be in them. Because men and angels are such, they are recipients of life. Consequently, if any man suffers himself to be so far misled as to think that he is not a recipient of life but is Life, he cannot be withheld from the thought that he is God. A man's feeling as if he were life, and therefore believing himself to be so, arises from fallacy; for the principal cause is not perceived in the instrumental cause otherwise than as one with it. That the Lord is Life in Himself, He Himself teaches in John: As the Father hath life in Himself, so also hath He given to the Son to have life in Himself (5:26) He declares also that He is Life itself (John 11:25; 14:6). Now since life and love are one (as is apparent from what has been said above, n. 1, 2), it follows that the Lord, because He is Life itself, is Love itself.

But that this may reach the understanding, it must needs be known positively that the Lord, because He is Love in its very essence, that is, Divine Love, appears before the angels in heaven as a sun, and that from that sun heat and light go forth; the heat which goes forth therefrom being in its essence love, and the light which goes forth therefrom being in its essence wisdom; and that so far as the angels are recipients of that spiritual heat and of that spiritual light, they are loves and wisdoms; not loves and wisdoms from themselves, but from the Lord. That spiritual heat and that spiritual light not only flow into angels and affect them, but they also flow into men and affect them just to the extent that they become recipients; and they become recipients in the measure of their love to the Lord and love towards the neighbor. That sun itself, that is, the Divine Love, by its heat and its light, cannot create any one immediately from itself; for one so created would be Love in its essence, which Love is the Lord Himself; but it can create from substances and matters so formed as to be capable of receiving the very heat and the very light; comparatively as the sun of the world cannot by its heat and light produce germinations on the earth immediately, but only out of earthy matters in which it can be present by its heat and light, and cause vegetation. In the spiritual world the Divine Love of the Lord appears as a sun, and from it proceed the spiritual heat and the spiritual light from which the angels derive love and wisdom, as may be seen in the work on Heaven and Hell (n. 116-140).

Since, then, man is not life, but is a recipient of life, it follows that the conception of a man from his father is not a conception of life, but only a conception of the first and purest form capable of receiving life; and to this, as to a nucleus or starting-point in the womb, are successively added substances and matters in forms adapted to the reception of life, in their order and degree.

THE DIVINE IS NOT IN SPACE. That the Divine, that is, God, is not in space, although omnipresent and with every man in the world, and with every angel in heaven, and with every spirit under heaven, cannot be comprehended by a merely natural idea, but it can by a spiritual idea. It cannot be comprehended by a natural idea, because in the natural idea there is space;

since it is formed out of such things as are in the world, and in each and all of these, as seen by the eye, there is space. In the world, everything great and small is of space; everything long, broad, and high is of space; in short, every measure, figure and form is of space. This is why it has been said that it cannot be comprehended by a merely natural idea that the Divine is not in space, when it is said that the Divine is everywhere. Still, by natural thought, a man may comprehend this, if only he admit into it something of spiritual light. For this reason something shall first be said about spiritual idea, and thought therefrom. Spiritual idea derives nothing from space, but it derives its all from state. State is predicated of love, of life, of wisdom, of affections, of joys therefrom; in general, of good and of truth. An idea of these things which is truly spiritual has nothing in common with space; it is higher and looks down upon the ideas of space which are under it as heaven looks down upon the earth. But since angels and spirits see with eyes, just as men in the world do, and since objects cannot be seen except in space, therefore in the spiritual world where angels and spirits are, there appear to be spaces like the spaces on earth; yet they are not spaces, but appearances; since they are not fixed and constant, as spaces are on earth; for they can be lengthened or shortened; they can be changed or varied. Thus because they cannot be determined in that world by measure, they cannot be comprehended there by any natural idea, but only by a spiritual idea. The spiritual idea of distances of space is the same as of distances of good or distances of truth, which are affinities and likenesses according to states of goodness and truth.

From this it may be seen that man is unable, by a merely natural idea, to comprehend that the Divine is everywhere, and yet not in space; but that angels and spirits comprehend this clearly; consequently that a man also may, provided he admits into his thought something of spiritual light; and this for the reason that it is not his body that thinks, but his spirit, thus not his natural, but his spiritual.

But many fail to comprehend this because of their love of the natural, which makes them unwilling to raise the thoughts of their understanding above the natural into spiritual light; and those who are unwilling to do this can think only from space, even concerning God; and to think according to space concerning God is to think concerning the expanse of nature. This has to be premised, because without a knowledge and some perception that the Divine is not in space, nothing can be understood about the Divine Life, which is Love and Wisdom, of which subjects this volume treats; and hence little, if anything, about Divine Providence, Omnipresence, Omniscience, Omnipotence, Infinity and Eternity, which will be treated of in succession.

It has been said that in the spiritual world, just as in the natural world, there appear to be spaces, consequently also distances, but that these are appearances according to spiritual affinities which are of love and wisdom, or of good and truth. From this it is that the Lord, although everywhere in the heavens with angels, nevertheless appears high above them as a sun. Furthermore, since reception of love and wisdom causes affinity with the Lord, those heavens in which the angels are, from reception, in closer affinity with Him, appear nearer to Him than those in which the affinity is more remote. From this it is also that the heavens, of which there are three, are distinct from each other, likewise the societies of each heaven; and further, that the hells under them are remote according to their rejection of love and wisdom. The same is true of men, in whom and with whom the Lord is present throughout the whole earth; and this solely for the reason that the Lord is not in space.

GOD IS VERY MAN. In all the heavens there is no other idea of God than that He is a Man. This is because heaven as a whole and in part is in form like a man, and because it is the Divine which is with the angels that constitutes heaven and inasmuch as thought proceeds according to the form of heaven, it is impossible for the angels to think of God in any other way. From this it is that all those in the world who are conjoined with heaven think of God in the same way when they think interiorly in themselves, that is, in their spirit. From this fact that God is a Man, all angels and all spirits, in their complete form, are men. This results from the form of heaven, which is like itself in its greatest and in its least parts. That heaven as a whole and in part is in form like a man may be seen in the work on Heaven and Hell (n. 59-87); and that thoughts proceed according to the form of heaven (n. 203, 204). It is known from Genesis (1:26, 27), that men were created after the image and likeness of God. God also appeared as a man to Abraham and to others. The ancients, from the wise even to the simple, thought of God no otherwise than as being a Man; and when at length they began to worship a plurality of gods, as at Athens and Rome, they worshiped them all as men. What is here said may be illustrated by the following extract from a small treatise already published: The Gentiles, especially the Africans, who acknowledge and worship one God, the Creator of the universe, have concerning God the idea that He is a Man, and declare that no one can have any other idea of God. When they learn that there are many who cherish an idea of God as something cloud-like in the midst of things, they ask where such persons are; and on being told that they are among Christians, they declare it to be impossible. They are informed, however, that this idea arises from the fact that God in the Word is called "a Spirit," and of a spirit they have no other idea than of a bit of cloud, not knowing that every spirit and every angel is a man. An examination, nevertheless, was made, whether the spiritual idea of such persons was like their natural idea, and it was found not to be so with those who acknowledge the Lord interiorly as God of heaven and earth. I heard a certain elder from the Christians say that no one can have an idea of a Human Divine; and I saw him taken about to various Gentile nations, and successively to such as were more and more interior, and from them to their heavens, and finally to the Christian heaven; and everywhere their interior perception concerning God was communicated to him, and he observed that they had no other idea of God than that He is a man, which is the same as the idea of a Human Divine (C.L.J. n. 74).

The common people in Christendom have an idea that God is a Man, because God in the Athanasian doctrine of the Trinity is called a "Person." But those who are more learned than the common people pronounce God to be invisible; and this for the reason that they cannot comprehend how God, as a Man, could have created heaven and earth, and then fill the universe with His presence, and many things besides, which cannot enter the understanding so long as the truth that the Divine is not in space is ignored. Those, however, who go to the Lord alone think of a Human Divine, thus of God as a Man.

How important it is to have a correct idea of God can be known from the truth that the idea of God constitutes the inmost of thought with all who have religion, for all things of religion and all things of worship look to God. And since God, universally and in particular, is in all things of religion and of worship, without a proper idea of God no communication with the heavens is possible. From this it is that in the spiritual world every nation has its place allotted in accordance with its idea of God as a Man; for in this idea, and in no other, is the idea of the Lord. That man's state of life after death is according to the idea of God in which he has become confirmed, is manifest from the opposite of this, namely, that the denial of God, and, in the Christian world, the denial of the Divinity of the Lord, constitutes hell.

IN GOD-MAN ESSE AND EXISTERE 14-1 ARE ONE DISTINCTLY 14-2 Where there is Esse [being] there is Existere [taking form]; one is not possible apart from the other. For Esse is by means of Existere, and not apart from it. This the rational mind comprehends when it thinks whether there can possibly be any Esse [being] which does not Exist [take form], and whether there can possibly be Existere except from Esse. And since one is possible with the other, and not apart from the other, it follows that they are one, but one distinctly. They are one distinctly, like Love and Wisdom; in fact, love is Esse, and wisdom is Existere; for there can be no love except in wisdom, nor can there be any wisdom except from love; consequently when love is in wisdom, then it EXISTS. These two are one in such a way that they may be distinguished in thought but not in operation, and because they may be distinguished in thought though not in operation, it is said that they are one distinctly. 14-3 Esse and Existere in God-Man are also one distinctly like soul and body. There can be no soul apart from its body, nor body apart from its soul. The Divine soul of God-Man is what is meant by Divine Esse, and the Divine Body is what is meant by Divine Existere. That a soul can exist apart from a body, and can think and be wise, is an error springing from fallacies; for every man's soul is in a spiritual body after it has cast off the material coverings which it carried about in the world.

Esse is not Esse unless it Exists, because until then it is not in a form, and if not in a form it has no quality; and what has no quality is not anything. That which Exists from Esse, for the reason that it is from Esse, makes one with it. From this there is a uniting of the two into one; and from this each is the others mutually and interchangeably, and each is all in all things of the other as in itself.

From this it can be seen that God is a Man, and consequently He is God-Existing; not existing from Himself but in Himself. He who has existence in Himself is God from whom all things are.

IN GOD-MAN INFINITE THINGS ARE ONE DISTINCTLY. That God is infinite is well known, for He is called the Infinite; and He is called the Infinite because He is infinite. He is infinite not from this alone, that He is very Esse and Existere in itself, but because in Him there are infinite things. An infinite without infinite things in it, is infinite in name only. The infinite things in Him cannot be called infinitely many, nor infinitely all, because of the natural idea of many and of all; for the natural idea of infinitely many is limited, and the natural idea of infinitely all, though not limited, is derived from limited things in the universe. Therefore man, because his ideas are natural, is unable by any refinement or approximation, to come into a perception of the infinite things in God; and an angel, while he is able, because he is in spiritual ideas, to rise by refinement and approximation above the degree of man, is still unable to attain to that perception.

That in God there are infinite things, any one may convince himself who believes that God is a Man; for, being a Man, He has a body and every thing pertaining to it, that is, a face, breast, abdomen, loins and feet; for without these He would not be a Man. And having these, He also has eyes, ears, nose, mouth, and tongue; also the parts within man, as the heart and lungs, and their dependencies, all of which, taken together, make man to be a man. In a created man these parts are many, and regarded in their details of structure are numberless; but in God-Man they are infinite, nothing whatever is lacking, and from this He has infinite perfection. This comparison holds between the uncreated Man who is God and created man, because God is a Man; and He Himself says that the man of this world was created after His image and into His likeness (Gen. 1:26, 27).

That in God there are infinite things, is still more evident to the angels from the heavens in which they dwell. The whole heaven, consisting of myriads of myriads of angels, in its universal form is like a man. So is each society of heaven, be it larger or smaller. From this, too, an angel is a man, for an angel is a heaven in least form. (This is shown in the work Heaven and Hell, n. 51-86.) Heaven as a whole, in part, and in the individual, is in that form by virtue of the Divine which angels receive; for in the measure in which an angel receives from the Divine is he in complete form a man. From this it is that angels are said to be in God, and God in them; also, that God is their all. How many things there are in heaven cannot be told; and because the Divine is what makes heaven, and consequently these unspeakably many things are from the Divine, it is clearly evident that there are infinite things in Very Man, who is God.

From the created universe a like conclusion may be drawn when it is regarded from uses and their correspondences. But before this can be understood some preliminary illustrations must be given.

Because in God-Man there are infinite things which appear in heaven, in angel, and in man, as in a mirror; and because God-Man is not in space (as was shown above, n. 7-10), it can, to some extent, be seen and comprehended how God can be Omnipresent, Omniscient, and All-providing; and how, as Man, He could create all things, and as Man can hold the things created by Himself in their order to eternity.

That in God-Man infinite things are one distinctly, can also be seen, as in a mirror, from man. In man there are many and numberless things, as said above; but still man feels them all as one. From sensation he knows nothing of his brains, of his heart and lungs, of his liver, spleen, and pancreas; or of the numberless things in his eyes, ears, tongue, stomach, generative organs, and the remaining parts; and because from sensation he has no knowledge of these things, he is to himself as a one. The reason is that all these are in such a form that not one can be lacking; for it is a form recipient of life from God-Man (as was shown above, n. 4-6). From the order and connection of all things in such a form there comes the feeling, and from that the idea, as if they were not many and numberless, but were one. From this it may be concluded that the many and numberless things which make in man a seeming one, a Very Man who is God, are one distinctly, yea, most distinctly.

THERE IS ONE GOD-MAN, FROM WHOM ALL THINGS COME. All things of human wisdom unite, and as it were center in this, that there is one God, the Creator of the universe: consequently a man who has reason, from the general nature of his understanding, does not and cannot think otherwise. Say to any man of sound reason that there are two Creators of the universe, and you will be sensible of his repugnance, and this, perhaps, from the mere sound of the phrase in his ear; from which it appears that all things of human reason unite and center in this, that God is one. There are two reasons for this. First, the very capacity to think rationally, viewed in itself, is not man's, but is God's in man; upon this capacity human reason in its general nature depends, and this general nature of reason causes man to see as from himself that God is one. Secondly, by means of that capacity man either is in the light of heaven, or he derives the generals of his thought therefrom; and it is a universal of the light of heaven that God is one. It is otherwise when man by that capacity has perverted the lower parts of his understanding; such a man indeed is endowed with that capacity, but by the twist given to these lower parts, he turns it contrariwise, and thereby his reason becomes unsound.

Every man, even if unconsciously, thinks of a body of men as of one man; therefore he instantly perceives what is meant when it is said that a king is the head, and the subjects are the body, also that this or that person has such a place in the general body, that is, in the kingdom. As it is with the body politic, so is it with the body spiritual. The body spiritual is the church; its head is God-Man; and from this it is plain how the church thus viewed as a man would appear if instead of one God, the Creator and Sustainer of the universe, several were thought of. The church thus viewed would appear as one body with several heads; thus not as a man, but as a monster. If it be said that these heads have one essence, and that thus together they make one head, the only conception possible is either that of one head with several faces or of several heads with one face; thus making the church, viewed as a whole, appear deformed. But in truth, the one God is the head, and the church is the body, which acts under the command of the head, and not from itself; as is also the case in man; and from this it is that there can be only one king in a kingdom, for several kings would rend it asunder, but one is able to preserve its unity.

So would it be with the church scattered throughout the whole globe, which is called a communion, because it is as one body under one head. It is known that the head rules the body under it at will; for understanding and will have their seat in the head; and in conformity to the understanding and will the body is directed, even to the extent that the body is nothing but obedience. As the body can do nothing except from the understanding and will in the head, so the man of the church can do nothing except from God. The body seems to act of itself, as if the hands and feet in acting are moved of themselves; or the mouth and tongue in speaking vibrate of themselves, when, in fact, they do not in the slightest degree act of themselves, but only from an affection of the will and the consequent thought of the understanding in the head. Suppose, now, one body to have several heads and each head to be free to act from its own understanding and its own will, could such a body continue to exist? For among several heads singleness of purpose, such as results from one head would be impossible. As in the church, so in the heavens; heaven consists of myriads of myriads of angels, and unless these all and each looked to one God, they would fall away from one another and heaven would be broken up. Consequently, if an angel of heaven but thinks of a plurality of gods he is at once separated; for he is cast out into the outmost boundary of the heavens, and sinks downward.

Because the whole heaven and all things of heaven have relation to one God, angelic speech is such that by a certain unison flowing from the unison of heaven it closes in a single cadence - a proof that it is impossible for the angels to think otherwise than of one God; for speech is from thought.

Who that has sound reason can help seeing that the Divine is not divisible? also that a plurality of Infinites, of Uncreates, of Omnipotents, and of Gods, is impossible? Suppose one destitute of reason were to declare that a plurality of Infinites, of Uncreates, of Omnipotents, and of Gods is possible, if only they have one identical essence, and this would make of them one Infinite, Uncreate, Omnipotent, and God, would not the one identical essence be one identity? And one identity is not possible to several. If it should be said that one is from the other, the one who is from the other is not God in Himself; nevertheless, God in Himself is the God from whom all things are (see above, n. 16).

THE DIVINE ESSENCE ITSELF IS LOVE AND WISDOM Sum up all things you know and submit them to careful inspection, and in some elevation of spirit search for the universal of all things, and you cannot conclude otherwise than that it is Love and Wisdom. For these are the two essentials of all things of man's life; everything of that life, civil, moral, and spiritual, hinges upon these two, and apart from these two is nothing. It is the same with all things of the life of the composite Man, which is, as was said above, a society, larger or smaller, a kingdom, an empire, a church, and also the angelic heaven. Take away love and wisdom from these, and consider whether they be anything, and you will find that apart from love and wisdom as their origin they are nothing.

Love together with wisdom in its very essence is in God. This no one can deny; for God loves every one from love in Himself, and leads every one from wisdom in Himself. The created universe, too, viewed in relation to its order, is so full of wisdom coming forth from love that all things in the aggregate may be said to be wisdom itself. For things limitless are in such order, successively and simultaneously, that taken together they make a one. It is from this, and this alone, that they can be held together and continually preserved.

It is because the Divine Essence itself is Love and Wisdom that man has two capacities for life; from one of these he has understanding, from the other will. The capacity from which he has understanding derives everything it has from the influx of wisdom from God, and the capacity from which he has will derives everything it has from the influx of love from God. Man's not being truly wise and not loving rightly does not take away these capacities, but merely closes them up; and so long as they are closed up, although the understanding is still called understanding and the will is called will, they are not such in essence. If these two capacities, therefore, were to be taken away, all that is human would perish; for the human is to think and to speak from thought, and to will and to act from will. From this it is clear that the Divine has its seat in man in these two capacities, the capacity to be wise and the capacity to love (that is, that one may be wise and may love). That in man there is a possibility of loving [and of being wise], even when he is not wise as he might be and does not love as he might, has been made known to me from much experience, and will be abundantly shown elsewhere.

It is because the Divine Essence itself is Love and Wisdom, that all things in the universe have relation to good and truth; for everything that proceeds from love is called good, and everything that proceeds from wisdom is called truth. But of this more hereafter.

It is because the Divine Essence itself is Love and Wisdom, that the universe and all things in it, alive and not alive, have unceasing existence from heat and light; for heat corresponds to love, and light corresponds to wisdom; and therefore spiritual heat is love and spiritual light is wisdom. But of this, also, more hereafter.

From Divine Love and from Divine Wisdom, which make the very Essence that is God, all affections and thoughts with man have their rise-affections from Divine Love, and thoughts from Divine Wisdom; and each and all things of man are nothing but affection and thought; these two are like fountains of all things of man's life. All the enjoyments and pleasantnesses of his life are from these-enjoyments from the affection of his love, and pleasantnesses from the thought therefrom. Now since man was created to be a recipient, and is a recipient in the degree in which he loves God and from love to God is wise, in other words, in the degree in which he is affected by those things which are from God and thinks from that affection, it follows that the Divine Essence, which is the Creator, is Divine Love and Divine Wisdom.

DIVINE LOVE IS OF DIVINE WISDOM, AND DIVINE WISDOM IS OF DIVINE LOVE. In God-Man Divine Esse [Being] and Divine Existere [Taking Form] are one distinctly (as may be seen above, n. 14-16). And because Divine Esse is Divine Love, and Divine Existere is Divine Wisdom, these are likewise one distinctly. They are said to be one distinctly, because love and wisdom are two distinct things, yet so united that love is of wisdom, and wisdom is of love, for in wisdom love is, and in love wisdom Exists; and since wisdom derives its Existere from love (as was said above, n. 15), therefore Divine Wisdom also is Esse. From this it follows that love and wisdom taken together are the Divine Esse, but taken distinctly love is called Divine Esse, and wisdom Divine Existere. Such is the angelic idea of Divine Love and of Divine Wisdom.

Since there is such a union of love and wisdom and of wisdom and love in God-Man, there is one Divine Essence. For the Divine Essence is Divine Love because it is of Divine Wisdom and is Divine Wisdom, because it is of Divine Love. And since there is such a union of these, the Divine Life also is one. Life is the Divine essence. Divine Love and Divine Wisdom are a one because the union is reciprocal, and reciprocal union causes oneness. Of reciprocal union, however, more will be said elsewhere.

There is also a union of love and wisdom in every Divine work; from which it has perpetuity, yea, its everlasting duration. If there were more of Divine Love than of Divine Wisdom, or more of Divine Wisdom than of Divine Love, in any created work, it could have continued existence only in the measure in which the two were equally in it, anything in excess passing off.

The Divine Providence in the reforming, regenerating and saving of men, partakes equally of Divine Love and of Divine Wisdom. From more of Divine Love than of Divine Wisdom or from more of Divine Wisdom than of Divine Love, man cannot be reformed, regenerated and saved. Divine Love wills to save all, but it cam save only by means of Divine Wisdom; to Divine Wisdom belong all the laws through which salvation is effected; and these laws Love cannot transcend, because Divine Love and Divine Wisdom are one and act in unison.

In the Word, Divine Love and Divine Wisdom are meant by "righteousness" and "judgment," Divine Love by "righteousness," and Divine Wisdom by "judgment;" for this reason "righteousness" and "judgment" are predicated in the Word of God; as in David: Righteousness and judgment are the support of Thy Throne (Ps. 89:14). Jehovah shall bring forth righteousness as the light, and judgment as the noonday (Ps. 37:6). In Hosea: I will betroth thee unto Me for ever, in righteousness, and in judgment (2:18). In Jeremiah: I will raise unto David a righteous Branch, who shall reign as King and shall execute judgment and righteousness in the earth (23:5). In Isaiah: He shall sit upon the throne of David, and upon his kingdom, to establish it in judgment and in righteousness (9:7). Jehovah shall be exalted, because He hath filled the earth with judgment and righteousness (33:5). In David: When I shall have learned the judgments of Thy righteousness. Seven times a day do I praise Thee, because of the judgments of Thy righteousness (Ps. 119:7, 164). The same is meant by "life" and "light" in John: In Him was life, and the life was the light of men (1:4). By "life" in this passage is meant the Lord's Divine Love, and by "light" His Divine Wisdom. The same also is meant by "life" and "spirit" in John: Jesus said, The words which I speak unto you, they are spirit, and they are life (6:63).

In man love and wisdom appear as two separate things, yet in themselves they are one distinctly, because with man wisdom is such as the love is, and love is such as the wisdom is. The wisdom that does not make one with its love appears to be wisdom, but it is not; and the love that does not make one with its wisdom appears to be the love of wisdom, but it is not; for the one must derive its essence and its life reciprocally from the other. With man love and wisdom appear as two separate things, because with him the capacity for understanding may be elevated into the light of heaven, but not the capacity for loving, except so far as he acts according to his understanding. Any apparent wisdom, therefore, which does not make one with the love of wisdom, sinks back into the love which does make one with it; and this may be a love of unwisdom, yea, of insanity. Thus a man may know from wisdom that he ought to do this or that, and yet he does not do it, because he does not love it. But so far as a man does from love what wisdom teaches, he is an image of God.

DIVINE LOVE AND DIVINE WISDOM ARE SUBSTANCE AND ARE FORM. The idea of men in general about love and about wisdom is that they are like something hovering and floating in thin air or ether or like what exhales from something of this kind. Scarcely any one believes that they are really and actually substance and form. Even those who recognize that they are substance and form still think of the love and the wisdom as outside the subject and as issuing from it. For they call substance and form that which they think of as outside the subject and as issuing from it, even though it be something hovering and floating; not knowing that love and wisdom are the subject itself, and that what is perceived outside of it and as hovering and floating is nothing but an appearance of the state of the subject in itself. There are several reasons why this has not hitherto been seen, one of which is, that appearances are the first things out of which the human mind forms its understanding, and these appearances the mind can shake off only by the exploration of the cause; and if the cause lies deeply hidden, the mind can explore it only by keeping the understanding for a long time in spiritual light; and this it cannot do by reason of the natural light which continually withdraws it. The truth is, however, that love and wisdom are the real and actual substance and form that constitute the subject itself.

But as this is contrary to appearance, it may seem not to merit belief unless it be proved; and since it can be proved only by such things as man can apprehend by his bodily senses, by these it shall be proved. Man has five external senses, called touch, taste, smell, hearing and sight. The subject of touch is the skin by which man is enveloped, the very substance and form of the skin causing it to feel whatever is applied to it. The sense of touch is not in the things applied, but in the substance and form of the skin, which are the subject; the sense itself is nothing but an affecting of the subject by the things applied. It is the same with taste; this sense is only an affecting of the substance and form of the tongue; the tongue is the subject. It is the same with smell; it is well known that odor affects the nostrils, and that it is in the nostrils, and that the nostrils are affected by the odoriferous particles touching them. It is the same with hearing, which seems to be in the place where the sound originates; but the hearing is in the ear, and is an affecting of its substance and form; that the hearing is at a distance from the ear is an appearance. It is the same with sight. When a man sees objects at a distance, the seeing appears to be there; yet the seeing is in the eye, which is the subject, and is likewise an affecting of the subject. Distance is solely from the judgment concluding about space from things intermediate, or from the diminution and consequent indistinctness of the object, an image of which is produced interiorly in the eye according to the angle of incidence. From this it is evident that sight does not go out from the eye to the object, but that the image of the object enters the eye and affects its substance and form. Thus it is just the same with sight as with hearing; hearing does not go out from the ear to catch the sound, but the sound enters the ear and affects it. From all this it can be seen that the affecting of the substance and form which causes sense is not a something separate from the subject, but only causes a change in it, the subject remaining the subject then as before and afterwards. From this it follows that seeing, hearing, smell, taste, and touch, are not a something volatile flowing from their organs, but are the organs themselves, considered in their substance and form, and that when the organs are affected sense is produced.

It is the same with love and wisdom, with this difference only, that the substances and forms which are love and wisdom are not obvious to the eyes as the organs of the external senses are. Nevertheless, no one can deny that those things of wisdom and love, which are called thoughts, perceptions, and affections, are substances and forms, and not entities flying and flowing out of nothing, or abstracted from real and actual substance and form, which are subjects. For in the brain are substances and forms innumerable, in which every interior sense which pertains to the understanding and will has its seat. The affections, perceptions, and thoughts there are not exhalations from these substances, but are all actually and really subjects emitting nothing from themselves, but merely undergoing changes according to whatever flows against and affects them. This may be seen from what has been said above about the external senses. Of what thus flows against and affects more will be said below.

From all this it may now first be seen that Divine Love and Divine Wisdom in themselves are substance and form; for they are very Esse and Existere; and unless they were such Esse and Existere as they are substance and form, they would be a mere thing of reasoning, which in itself is nothing.

DIVINE LOVE AND DIVINE WISDOM ARE SUBSTANCE AND FORM IN ITSELF, THUS THE VERY AND THE ONLY. That Divine Love and Divine Wisdom are substance and form has been proved just above; and that Divine Esse [Being] and Existere [Taking Form] are Esse and Existere in itself, has also been said above. It cannot be said to be Esse and Existere from itself, because this involves a beginning, and a beginning from something within in which would be Esse and Existere in itself. But Very Esse and Existere in itself is from eternity. Very Esse and Existere in itself is also uncreated, and everything created must needs be from an Uncreate. What is created is also finite, and the finite can exist only from the Infinite.

He who by exercise of thought is able to grasp the idea of and to comprehend, Esse and Existere in itself, can certainly perceive and comprehend that it is the Very and the Only. That is called the Very which alone is; and that is called the Only from which every thing else proceeds. Now because the Very and the Only is substance and form, it follows that it is the very and only substance and form. Because this very substance and form is Divine Love and Divine Wisdom, it follows that it is the very and only Love, and the very and only Wisdom; consequently, that it is the very and only Essence, as well as the very and only Life: for Life is Love and Wisdom.

From all this it can be seen how sensually (that is, how much from the bodily senses and their blindness in spiritual matters) do those think who maintain that nature is from herself. They think from the eye, and are not able to think from the understanding. Thought from the eye closes the understanding, but thought from the understanding opens the eye. Such persons cannot think at all of Esse and Existere in itself, and that it is Eternal, Uncreate, and Infinite; neither can they think at all of life, except as a something fleeting and vanishing into nothingness; nor can they think otherwise of Love and Wisdom, nor at all that from these are all things of nature. Neither can it be seen that from these are all things of nature, unless nature is regarded, not from some of its forms, which are merely objects of sight, but from uses in their succession and order. For uses are from life alone, and their succession and order are from wisdom and love alone; while forms are only containants of uses. Consequently, if forms alone are regarded, nothing of life, still less anything of love and wisdom, thus nothing of God, can be seen in nature.

DIVINE LOVE AND DIVINE WISDOM MUST NECESSARILY HAVE

BEING [Esse] AND HAVE FORM [Existere] IN OTHERS CREATED BY ITSELF. It is the essential of love not to love self, but to love others, and to be conjoined with others by love. It is the essential of love, moreover, to be loved by others, for thus conjunction is effected. The essence of all love consists in conjunction; this, in fact, is its life, which is called enjoyment, pleasantness, delight, sweetness, bliss, happiness, and felicity. Love consists in this, that its own should be another's; to feel the joy of another as joy in oneself, that is loving. But to feel one's own joy in another and not the other's joy in oneself is not loving; for this is loving self, while the former is loving the neighbor. These two kinds of love are diametrically opposed to each other. Either, it is true, conjoins; and to love one's own, that is, oneself, in another does not seem to divide; but it does so effectually divide that so far as any one has loved another in this manner, so far he afterwards hates him. For such conjunction is by its own action gradually loosened, and then, in like measure, love is turned to hate.

Who that is capable of discerning the essential character of love cannot see this? For what is it to love self alone, instead of loving some one outside of self by whom one may be loved in return? Is not this separation rather than conjunction? Conjunction of love is by reciprocation; and there can be no reciprocation in self alone. If there is thought to be, it is from an imagined reciprocation in others. From this it is clear that Divine Love must necessarily have being (esse) and have form (existere) in others whom it may love, and by whom it may be loved. For as there is such a need in all love, it must be to the fullest extent, that is, infinitely in Love Itself.

With respect to God: it is impossible for Him to love others and to be loved reciprocally by others in whom there is anything of infinity, that is, anything of the essence and life of love in itself, or anything of the Divine. For if there were beings having in them anything of infinity, that is, of the essence and life of love in itself, that is, of the Divine, it would not be God loved by others, but God loving Himself; since the Infinite, that is, the Divine, is one only, and if this were in others, Itself would be in them, and would be the love of self Itself; and of that love not the least trace can possibly be in God, since it is wholly opposed to the Divine Essence. Consequently, for this relation to be possible there must be others in whom there is nothing of the Divine in itself. That it is possible in beings created from the Divine will be seen below. But that it may be possible, there must be Infinite Wisdom making one with Infinite Love; that is, there must be the Divine Love of Divine Wisdom, and the Divine Wisdom of Divine Love (concerning which see above, n. 35-39)

Upon a perception and knowledge of this mystery depend a perception and knowledge of all things of existence, that is, creation; also of all things of continued existence, that is, preservation by God; in other words, of all the works of God in the created universe; of which the following pages treat.

Footnotes

14-1 To be and to exist. Swedenborg seems to use this word "exist" nearly in the classical sense of springing or standing forth, becoming manifest, taking form. The distinction between esse and existere is essentially the same as between substance and form.

14-2 For the meaning of this phrase. "distincte unum," see below in this paragraph, also n. 17, 22, 34, 223, and DP 4.

14-3 It should be noticed that in Latin, distinctly is the adverb of the verb distinguish. If translated distinguishably, this would appear.

Section 2

But do not, I entreat you, confuse your ideas with time and with space, for so far as time and space enter into your ideas when you read what follows, you will not understand it; for the Divine is not in time and space. This will be seen clearly in the progress of this work, and in particular from what is said of eternity, infinity, and omnipresence.

ALL THINGS IN THE UNIVERSE WERE CREATED FROM THE DIVINE LOVE AND THE DIVINE WISDOM OF GOD-MAN. So full of Divine Love and Divine Wisdom is the universe in greatest and least, and in first and last things, that it may be said to be Divine Love and Divine Wisdom in an image. That this is so is clearly evident from the correspondence of all things of the universe with all things of man. There is such correspondence of each and every thing that takes form in the created universe with each and every thing of man, that man may be said to be a sort of universe. There is a correspondence of his affections, and thence of his thoughts, with all things of the animal kingdom; of his will, and thence of his understanding, with all things of the vegetable kingdom; and of his outmost life with all things of the mineral kingdom. That there is such a correspondence is not apparent to any one in the natural world, but it is apparent to every one who gives heed to it in the spiritual world. In that world there are all things that take form in the natural world in its three kingdoms, and they are correspondences of affections and thoughts, that is, of affections from the will and of thoughts from the understanding, also of the outmost things of the life, of those who are in that world, around whom all these things are Visible, presenting an appearance like that of the created universe, with the difference that it is in lesser form. From this it is very evident to angels, that the created universe is an image representative of God-Man, and that it is His Love and Wisdom which are presented, in an image, in the universe. Not that the created universe is God-Man, but that it is from Him; for nothing whatever in the created universe is substance and form in itself, or life in itself, or love and wisdom in itself, yea, neither is man a man in himself, but all is from God, who is Man, Wisdom and Love, also Form and Substance, in itself. That which has Being-in-itself is uncreate and infinite; but whatever is from Very Being, since it contains in it nothing of Being-in-itself, is created and finite, and this exhibits an image of Him from whom it has being and has form.

Of things created and finite Esse [Being] and Existere [Taking Form] can be predicated, likewise substance and form, also life, and even love and wisdom; but these are all created and finite. This can be said of things created and finite, not because they possess anything Divine, but because they are in the Divine, and the Divine is in them. For everything that has been created is, in itself, inanimate and dead, but all things are animated and made alive by this, that the Divine is in them, and that they are in the Divine.

The Divine is not in one subject differently from what it is in another, but one created subject differs from another; for no two things can be precisely alike, consequently each thing is a different continant. On this account, the Divine as imaged forth presents a variety of appearances. Its presence in opposites will be discussed hereafter.

ALL THINGS IN THE CREATED UNIVERSE ARE RECIPIENTS OF THE DIVINE LOVE AND THE DIVINE WISDOM OF GOD-MAN. It is well known that each and all things of the universe were created by God; hence the universe, with each and every thing pertaining to it, is called in the Word the work of the hands of Jehovah. There are those who maintain that the world, with everything it includes, was created out of nothing, and of that nothing an idea of absolute nothingness is entertained. From absolute nothingness, however, nothing is or can be made. This is an established truth. The universe, therefore, which is God's image, and consequently full of God, could be created only in God from God; for God is Esse itself, and from Esse must be whatever is. To create what is, from nothing which is not, is an utter contradiction. But still, that which is created in God from God is not continuous from Him; for God is Esse in itself, and in created things there is not any Esse in itself. If there were in created things any Esse in itself, this would be continuous from God, and that which is continuous from God is God. The angelic idea of this is, that what is created in God from God, is like that in man which has been derived from his life, but from which the life has been withdrawn, which is of such a nature as to be in accord with his life, and yet it is not his life. The angels confirm this by many things which have existence in their heaven, where they say they are in God, and God is in them, and still that they have, in their esse, nothing of God which is God. Many things whereby they prove this will be presented hereafter; let this serve for present information.

Every created thing, by virtue of this origin, is such in its nature as to be a recipient of God, not by continuity, but by contiguity. By the latter and not the former comes its capacity for conjunction. For having been created in God from God, it is adapted to conjunction; and because it has been so created, it is an analogue, and through such conjunction it is like an image of God in a mirror.

From this it is that angels are angels, not from themselves, but by virtue of this conjunction with God-Man; and this conjunction is according to the reception of Divine Good and Divine Truth, which are God, and which seem to proceed from Him, though really they are in Him. This reception is according to their application to themselves of the laws of order, which are Divine truths, in the exercise of that freedom of thinking and willing according to reason, which they possess from the Lord as if it were their own. By this they have a reception, as if from themselves, of Divine Good and of Divine Truth, and by this there is a reciprocation of love; for, as was said above, love is impossible unless it is reciprocal. The same is true of men on the earth. From what has been said it can now first be seen that all things of the created universe are recipients of the Divine Love and the Divine Wisdom of God-Man.

It cannot yet be intelligibly explained how all other things of the universe which are unlike angels and men, that is, the things below man in the animal kingdom, and the things below these in the vegetable kingdom, and the things still below these in the mineral kingdom, are also recipients of the Divine Love and of the Divine Wisdom of God-Man; for many things need to be said first about degrees of life, and degrees of the recipients of life. Conjunction with these things is according to their uses; for no good use has any other origin than through a like conjunction with God, but yet different according to degrees. This conjunction in its descent becomes successively such that nothing of freedom is left therein, because nothing of reason, and therefore nothing of the appearance of life; but still they are recipients. Because they are recipients, they are also re-agents; and forasmuch as they are re-agents, they are containants. Conjunction with uses which are not good will be discussed when the origin of evil has been made known.

From the above it can be seen that the Divine is in each and every thing of the created universe, and consequently that the created universe is the work of the hands of Jehovah, as is said in the Word; that is, the work of Divine Love and Divine Wisdom, for these are meant by the hands of Jehovah. But though the Divine is in each and all things of the created universe there is in their esse nothing of the Divine in itself; for the created universe is not God, but is from God; and since it is from God, there is in it an image of Him like the image of a man in a mirror, wherein indeed the man appears, but still there is nothing of the man in it.

I heard several about me in the spiritual world talking together, who said that they were quite willing to acknowledge that the Divine is in each and every thing of the universe, because they behold therein the wonderful works of God, and these are the more wonderful the more interiorly they are examined. And yet, when they were told that the Divine is actually in each and every thing of the universe, they were displeased; which is a proof that although they assert this they do not believe it. They were therefore asked whether this cannot be seen simply from the marvelous power which is in every seed, of producing its own vegetable form in like order, even to new seeds; also because in every seed an idea of the infinite and eternal is presented; since there is in seeds an endeavor to multiply themselves and to fructify infinitely and eternally? Is not this evident also in every living creature, even the smallest? In that there are in it organs of sense, also brains, a heart, lungs, and other parts; with arteries, veins, fibers, muscles, and the activities proceeding therefrom; besides the surpassing marvels of animal nature, about which whole volumes have been written. All these wonderful things are from God; but the forms with which they are clothed are from earthy matters, out of which come plants, and in their order, men. Therefore it is said of man, That he was created out of the ground, and that he is dust of the earth, and that the breath of lives was breathed into him Genesis 2:7. From which it is plain that the Divine is not man's own, but is adjoined to him.

ALL CREATED THINGS HAVE RELATION IN A KIND OF IMAGE TO MAN. This can be seen from each and all things of the animal kingdom, from each and all things of the vegetable kingdom, and from each and all things of the mineral kingdom. A relation to man in each and all things of the animal kingdom is evident from the following. Animals of every kind have limbs by which they move, organs by which they feel, and viscera by which these are exercised; these they have in common with man. They have also appetites and affections similar to man's natural appetites and affections; and they have inborn knowledges corresponding to their affections, in some of which there appears a resemblance to what is spiritual, which is more or less evident in beasts of the earth, and birds of the air, and in bees, silk-worms, ants, etc. From this it is that merely natural men consider the living creatures of this kingdom to be like themselves, except in the matter of speech. A relation to man arising out of each and all things of the vegetable kingdom is evident from this: they spring forth from seed, and thereafter proceed step by step through their periods of growth; they have something akin to marriage, followed by prolification; their vegetative soul is use, and they are forms thereof; besides many other particulars which have relation to man. These also have been described by various authors. A relation to man deducible from each and every thing of the mineral kingdom is seen only in an endeavor to produce forms which exhibit such a relation (which forms, as said above, are each and all things of the vegetable kingdom), and in an endeavor to perform uses thereby. For when first a seed falls into the bosom of the earth, she cherishes it, and out of herself provides it with nourishment from every source, that it may shoot up and present itself in a form representative of man. That such an endeavor exists also in its solid parts is evident from corals at the bottom of the seas and from flowers in mines, where they originate from minerals, also from metals. This endeavor towards vegetating, and performing uses thereby, is the outmost derivation from the Divine in created things.

As there is an endeavor of the minerals of the earth towards vegetation, so there is an endeavor of the plants towards vivification: this accounts for insects of various kinds corresponding to the odors emanating from plants. This does not arise from the heat of this world's sun, but from life operating through that heat according to the state of its recipients (as will be seen in what follows).

That there is a relation of all things of the created universe to man may be known from the foregoing statements, yet it can be seen only obscurely; whereas in the spiritual world this is seen clearly. In that world, also, there are all things of the three kingdoms, and in the midst of them the angel; he sees them about him, and also knows that they are representations of himself; yea, when the inmost of his understanding is opened he recognizes himself in them, and sees his image in them, hardly otherwise than as in a mirror.

From these and from many other concurring facts which there is not time to adduce now, it may be known with certainty that God is a Man; and that the created universe is an image of Him; for there is a general relation of all things to Him, as well as a particular relation of all things to man.

THE USES OF ALL CREATED THINGS ASCEND BY DEGREES FROM LAST THINGS TO MAN, AND THROUGH MAN TO GOD THE CREATOR, FROM WHOM THEY ARE. Last things, as was said above, are each and all things of the mineral kingdom, which are materials of various kinds, of a stony, saline, oily, mineral, or metallic nature, covered over with soil formed of vegetable and animal matters reduced to the finest dust. In these lie concealed both the end and the beginning of all uses which are from life. The end of all uses is the endeavor to produce uses, and the beginning is the acting force from that endeavor. These pertain to the mineral kingdom. Middle things are each and all things of the vegetable kingdom, such as grasses and herbs of every kind, plants and shrubs of every kind, and trees of every kind. The uses of these are for the service of each and all things of the animal kingdom, both imperfect and perfect. These they nourish, delight, and vivify; nourishing the bellies of animals with their vegetable substances, delighting the animal senses with taste, fragrance, and beauty, and vivifying their affections. The endeavor towards this is in these also from life. First things are each and all things of the animal kingdom. Those are lowest therein which are called worms and insects, the middle are birds and beasts, and the highest, men; for in each kingdom there are lowest, middle and highest things, the lowest for the use of the middle, and the middle for the use of the highest. Thus the uses of all created things ascend in order from outmost things to man, who is first in order.

In the natural world there are three degrees of ascent, and in the spiritual world there are three degrees of ascent. All animals are recipients of life. The more perfect are recipients of the life and the three degrees of the natural world, the less perfect of the life of two degrees of that world, and the imperfect of one of its degrees. But man alone is a recipient of the life both of the three degrees of the natural world and of the three degrees of the spiritual world. From this it is that man can be elevated above nature, while the animal cannot. Man can think analytically and rationally of the civil and moral things that are within nature, also of the spiritual and celestial things that are above nature, yea, he can be so elevated into wisdom as even to see God. But the six degrees by which the uses of all created things ascend in their order even to God the Creator, will be treated of in their proper place. From this summary, however, it can be seen that there is an ascent of all created things to the first, who alone is Life, and that the uses of all things are the very recipients of life; and from this are the forms of uses.

It shall also be stated briefly how man ascends, that is, is elevated, from the lowest degree to the first. He is born into the lowest degree of the natural world; then, by means of knowledges, he is elevated into the second degree; and as he perfects his understanding by knowledges he is elevated into the third degree, and then becomes rational. The three degrees of ascent in the spiritual world are in man above the three natural degrees, and do not appear until he has put off the earthly body. When this takes place the first spiritual degree is open to him, afterwards the second, and finally the third; but this only with those who become angels of the third heaven; these are they that see God. Those become angels of the second heaven and of the last heaven in whom the second degree and the last degree can be opened. Each spiritual degree in man is opened according to his reception of Divine Love and Divine Wisdom from the Lord. Those who receive something thereof come into the first or lowest spiritual degree those who receive more into the second or middle spiritual degree, those who receive much into the third or highest degree. But those who receive nothing thereof remain in the natural degrees, and derive from the spiritual degrees nothing more than an ability to think and thence to speak, and to will and thence to act, but not with intelligence.

Of the elevation of the interiors of man, which belong to his mind, this also should be known. In everything created by God there is reaction. In Life alone there is action; reaction is caused by the action of Life. Because reaction takes place when any created thing is acted upon, it appears as if it belonged to what is created. Thus in man it appears as if the reaction were his, because he has no other feeling than that life is his, when yet man is only a recipient of life. From this cause it is that man, by reason of his hereditary evil, reacts against God. But so far as man believes that all his life is from God, and that all good of life is from the action of God, and all evil of life from the reaction of man, so far his reaction comes to be from [God's] action, and man acts with God as if from himself. The equilibrium of all things is from action and simultaneous reaction, and in equilibrium everything must be. These things have been said lest man should believe that he himself ascends toward God from himself, and not from the Lord.

THE DIVINE, APART FROM SPACE, FILLS ALL SPACES OF THE UNIVERSE. There are two things proper to nature - space and time. From these man in the natural world forms the ideas of his thought, and thereby his understanding. If he remains in these ideas, and does not raise his mind above them, he is in no wise able to perceive things spiritual and Divine, for these he involves in ideas drawn from space and time; and so far as that is done the light [lumen] of his understanding becomes merely natural. To think from this lumen in reasoning about spiritual and Divine things, is like thinking from the thick darkness of night about those things that appear only in the light of day. From this comes naturalism. But he who knows how to raise his mind above ideas of thought drawn from space and time, passes from thick darkness into light, and has discernment in things spiritual and Divine, and finally sees the things which are in and from what is spiritual and Divine; and then from that light he dispels the thick darkness of the natural lumen, and banishes its fallacies from the middle to the sides. Every man who has understanding is able to transcend in thought these properties of nature, and actually does so; and he then affirms and sees that the Divine, because omnipresent, is not in space. He is also able to affirm and to see the things that have been adduced above. But if he denies the Divine Omnipresence, and ascribes all things to nature, then he has no wish to be elevated, though he can be.

All who die and become angels put off the two above- mentioned properties of nature, namely, space and time; for they then enter into spiritual light, in which objects of thought are truths, and objects of sight are like those in the natural world, but are correspondent to their thoughts. The objects of their thought which, as just said, are truths, derive nothing at all from space and time; and though the objects of their sight appear as if in space and in time, still the angels do not think from space and time. The reason is, that spaces and times there are not fixed, as in the natural world, but are changeable according to the states of their life. In the ideas of their thought, therefore, instead of space and time there are states of life, instead of spaces such things as have reference to states of love, and instead of times such things as have reference to states of wisdom. From this it is that spiritual thought, and spiritual speech therefrom, differ so much from natural thought and natural speech therefrom, as to have nothing in common except as regards the interiors of things, which are all spiritual. Of this difference more will be said elsewhere. Now, because the thoughts of angels derive nothing from space and time, but everything from states of life, when it is said that the Divine fills spaces angels evidently cannot comprehend it, for they do not know what spaces are; but when, apart from any idea of space, it is said that the Divine fills all things, they clearly comprehend it.

To make it clear that the merely natural man thinks of spiritual and Divine things from space, and the spiritual man apart from space, let the following serve for illustration. The merely natural man thinks by means of ideas which he has acquired from objects of sight, in all of which there is figure partaking of length, breadth, and height, and of shape determined by these, either angular or circular. These [conceptions] are manifestly present in the ideas of his thought concerning things visible on earth; they are also in the ideas of his thought concerning those not visible, such as civil and moral affairs. This he is unconscious of; but they are nevertheless there, as continuations. With a spiritual man it is different, especially with an angel of heaven, whose thought has nothing in common with figure and form that derives anything from spiritual length, breadth, and height, but only with figure and form derived from the state of a thing resulting from the state of its life. Consequently, instead of length of space he thinks of the good of a thing from good of life; instead of breadth of space, of the truth of a thing from truth of life; and instead of height, of the degrees of these. Thus he thinks from the correspondence there is between things spiritual and things natural. From this correspondence it is that in the Word "length" signifies the good of a thing, "breadth" the truth of a thing, and "height" the degrees of these. From this it is evident that an angel of heaven, when he thinks of the Divine Omnipresence, can by no means think otherwise than that the Divine, apart from space, fills all things. And that which an angel thinks is truth, because the light which enlightens his understanding is Divine Wisdom.

This is the basis of thought concerning God; for without it, what is to be said of the creation of the universe by God-Man, of His Providence, Omnipotence, Omnipresence and Omniscience, even if understood, cannot be kept in mind; since the merely natural man, even while he has these things in his understanding, sinks back into his life's love, which is that of his will; and that love dissipates these truths, and immerses his thought in space, where his lumen, which he calls rational, abides, not knowing that so far as he denies these things, he is irrational. That this is so, may be confirmed by the idea entertained of this truth, that GOD is a MAN. Read with attention, I pray you, what has been said above (n. 11-13) and what follows after, and your understanding will accept it. But when you let your thought down into the natural lumen which derives from space, will not these things be seen as paradoxes? and if you let it down far, will you not reject them? This is why it is said that the Divine fills all spaces of the universe, and why it is not said that God-Man fills them. For if this were said, the merely natural lumen would not assent. But to the proposition that the Divine fills all space, it does assent, because this agrees with the mode of speech of the theologians, that God is omnipresent, and hears and knows all things. (On this subject, more may be seen above, n. 7-10.).

THE DIVINE IS IN ALL TIME, APART FROM TIME. As the Divine, apart from space, is in all space, so also, apart from time, is it in all time. For nothing which is proper to nature can be predicated of the Divine, and space and time are proper to nature. Space in nature is measurable, and so is time. This is measured by days, weeks, months, years, and centuries; days are measured by hours; weeks and months by days; years by the four seasons; and centuries by years. Nature derives this measurement from the apparent revolution and annual motion of the sun of the world. But in the spiritual world it is different. The progressions of life in that world appear in like manner to be in time, for those there live with one another as men in the world live with one another; and this is not possible without the appearance of time. But time there is not divided into periods as in the world, for their sun is constantly in the east and is never moved away; for it is the Lord's Divine Love that appears to them as a sun. Wherefore they have no days, weeks, months, years, centuries, but in place of these there are states of life, by which a distinction is made which cannot be called, however, a distinction into periods, but into states. Consequently, the angels do not know what time is, and when it is mentioned they perceive in place of it state; and when state determines time, time is only an appearance. For joyfulness of state makes time seem short, and joylessness of state makes time seem long; from which it is evident that time in the spiritual world is nothing but quality of state. It is from this that in the Word, "hours," "days," "weeks," "months," and "years," signify states and progressions of state in series and in the aggregate; and when times are predicated of the church, by its "morning" is meant its first state, by "mid-day" its fullness by "evening" its decline, and by "night" its end. The four seasons of the year "spring," "summer," "autumn," and "winter," have a like meaning.

From the above it can be seen that time makes one with thought from affection; for from that is the quality of man's state. And with progressions of time, in the spiritual world, distances in progress through space coincide; as may be shown from many things. For instance, in the spiritual world ways are actually shortened or are lengthened in accordance with the longings that are of thought from affection. From this, also, comes the expression, "spaces of time." Moreover, in cases where thought does not join itself to its proper affection in man, as in sleep, the lapse of time is not noticed.

Now as times which are proper to nature in its world are in the spiritual world pure states, which appear progressive because angels and spirits are finite, it may be seen that in God they are not progressive because He is Infinite, and infinite things in Him are one (as has been shown above, n. 17-22). From this it follows that the Divine in all time is apart from time.

He who has no knowledge of God apart from time and is unable from any perception to think of Him, is thus utterly unable to conceive of eternity in any other way than as an eternity of time; in which case, in thinking of God from eternity he must needs become bewildered; for he thinks with regard to a beginning, and beginning has exclusive reference to time. His bewilderment arises from the idea that God had existence from Himself, from which he rushes headlong into an origin of nature from herself; and from this idea he can be extricated only by a spiritual or angelic idea of eternity, which is an idea apart from time; and when time is separated, the Eternal and the Divine are the same, and the Divine is the Divine in itself, not from itself. The angels declare that while they can conceive of God from eternity, they can in no way conceive of nature from eternity, still less of nature from herself and not at all of nature as nature in herself. For that which is in itself is the very Esse, from which all things are; Esse in itself is very life, which is the Divine Love of Divine Wisdom and the Divine Wisdom of Divine Love. For the angels this is the Eternal, an

Eternal as removed from time as the uncreated is from the created, or the infinite from the finite, between which, in fact, there is no ratio.

THE DIVINE IN THINGS GREATEST AND LEAST IS THE SAME. This follows from the two preceding articles, that the Divine apart from space is in all space, and apart from time is in all time. Moreover, there are spaces greater and greatest, and lesser and least; and since spaces and times, as said above, make one, it is the same with times. In these the Divine is the same, because the Divine is not varying and changeable, as everything is which belongs to nature, but is unvarying and unchangeable, consequently the same everywhere and always.

It seems as if the Divine were not the same in one person as in another; as if, for instance, it were different in the wise and in the simple, or in an old man and in a child. But this is a fallacy arising from appearance; the man is different, but the Divine in him is not different. Man is a recipient, and the recipient or receptacle is what varies. A wise man is a recipient of Divine Love and Divine Wisdom more adequately, and therefore more fully, than a simple man; and an old man who is also wise, more than a little child or boy; yet the Divine is the same in the one as in the other. It is in like manner a fallacy arising from appearance, that the Divine is different with angels of heaven from what it is with men on the earth, because the angels of heaven are in wisdom ineffable, while men are not; but the seeming difference is not in the Lord but in the subjects, according to the quality of their reception of the Divine.

That the Divine is the same in things greatest and least, may be shown by means of heaven and by means of an angel there. The Divine in the whole heaven and the Divine in an angel is the same; therefore even the whole heaven may appear as one angel. So is it with the church, and with a man of the church. The greatest form receptive of the Divine is the whole heaven together with the whole church; the least is an angel of heaven and a man of the church. Sometimes an entire society of heaven has appeared to me as one angel-man; and it was told that it may appear like a man as large as a giant, or like a man as small as an infant; and this, because the Divine in things greatest and least is the same.

The Divine is also the same in the greatest and in the least of all created things that are not alive; for it is in all the good of their use. These, moreover, are not alive for the reason that they are not forms of life but forms of uses; and the form varies according to the excellence of the use. But how the Divine is in these things will be stated in what follows, where creation is treated of.

Put away space, and deny the possibility of a vacuum, and then think of Divine Love and of Divine Wisdom as being Essence itself, space having been put away and a vacuum denied. Then think according to space; and you will perceive that the Divine, in the greatest and in the least things of space, is the same; for in essence abstracted from space there is neither great nor small, but only the same.

Something shall now be said about vacuum. I once heard angels talking with Newton about vacuum, and saying that they could not tolerate the idea of a vacuum as being nothing, for the reason that in their world which is spiritual, and which is within or above the spaces and times of the natural world, they equally feel, think, are affected, love, will, breathe, yea, speak and act, which would be utterly impossible in a vacuum which is nothing, since nothing is nothing, and of nothing not anything can be affirmed. Newton said that he now knew that the Divine, which is Being itself, fills all things, and that to him the idea of nothing as applied to vacuum is horrible, because that idea is destructive of all things; and he exhorts those who talk with him about vacuum to guard against the idea of nothing, comparing it to a swoon, because in nothing no real activity of mind is possible.

PART SECOND. DIVINE LOVE AND DIVINE WISDOM APPEAR IN THE SPIRITUAL WORLD AS A SUN. There are two worlds, the spiritual and the natural. The spiritual world does not draw anything from the natural, nor the natural world from the spiritual. The two are totally distinct, and communicate only by correspondences, the nature of which has been abundantly shown elsewhere. To illustrate this by an example: heat in the natural world corresponds to the good of charity in the spiritual world, and light in the natural world corresponds to the truth of faith in the spiritual world; and who does not see that heat and the good of charity, and that light and the truth of faith, are wholly distinct? At first sight they appear as distinct as two entirely different things. They so appear when one inquires what the good of charity has in common with heat, or the truth of faith with light; when in fact, spiritual heat is that good, and spiritual light is that truth. Although these things are in themselves so distinct, they make one by correspondence. They make one in this way: when man reads, in the Word, of heat and light, the spirits and angels who are with the man perceive charity instead of heat, and faith instead of light. This example is adduced, in order that it may be known that the two worlds, the spiritual and the natural, are so distinct as to have nothing in common with each other; yet are so created as to have communication, yea, conjunction by means of correspondences.

Since these two worlds are so distinct, it can be seen very clearly that the spiritual world is under another sun than the natural world. For in the spiritual world, must as in the natural, there is heat and light; but the heat there, as well as the light, is spiritual; and spiritual heat is the good of charity, and spiritual light is the truth of faith. Now since heat and light can originate only in a sun, it is evident that the spiritual world has a different sun from the natural world; and further, that the sun of the spiritual world in its essence is such that spiritual heat and light can come forth from it; whereas the sun of the natural world in its essence is such that natural heat can come forth from it. Everything spiritual has relation to good and truth, and can spring from no other source than Divine Love and Divine Wisdom; for all good is of love and all truth is of wisdom; that they have no other origin any discerning man can see.

That there is any other sun than that of the natural world has hitherto been unknown. The reason is, that the spiritual of man has so far passed over into his natural, that he does not know what the spiritual is, and thus does not know that there is a spiritual world, the abode of spirits and angels, other than and different from the natural world. Since the spiritual world has lain so deeply hidden from the knowledge of those who are in the natural world, it has pleased the Lord to open the sight of my spirit, that I might see the things which are in that world, just as I see those in the natural world, and might afterwards describe that world; which has been done in the work Heaven and Hell, in one chapter of which the sun of the spiritual world is treated of. For that sun has been seen by me; and it appeared of the same size as the sun of the natural world; also fiery like it, but more glowing. It has also been made known to me that the whole angelic heaven is under that sun; and that angels of the third heaven see it constantly, angels of the second heaven very often, and angels of the first or outmost heaven sometimes. That all their heat and all their light, as well as all things that are manifest in that world, are from that sun will be seen in what follows.

That sun is not the Lord Himself, but is from the Lord. It is the Divine Love and the Divine Wisdom proceeding from Him that appear as a sun in that world. And because Love and Wisdom in the Lord are one (as shown in Part I.), that sun is said to be Divine Love; for Divine Wisdom is of Divine Love, consequently is Love.

Since love and fire mutually correspond, that sun appears before the eyes of the angels as fiery; for angels cannot see love with their eyes, but they see in the place of love what corresponds to it. For angels, equally with men, have an internal and an external; it is their internal that thinks and is wise, and that wills and loves; it is their external that feels, sees, speaks and acts. All their externals are correspondences of internals; but the correspondences are spiritual, not natural. Moreover, Divine love is felt as fire by spiritual beings. For this reason "fire," when mentioned in the Word, signifies love. In the Israelitish Church, "holy fire" signified love; and this is why, in prayers to God, it is customary to ask that "heavenly fire," that is Divine Love, "may kindle the heart."

With such a difference between the spiritual and the natural (as shown above, n. 83), nothing from the sun of the natural world, that is, nothing of its heat and light, nor anything pertaining to any earthly object, can pass over into the spiritual world. To the spiritual world the light of the natural world is thick darkness, and its heat is death. Nevertheless, the heat of the world can be vivified by the influx of heavenly heat, and the light of the world can be illumined by the influx of heavenly light. Influx is effected by correspondences; and it cannot be effected by continuity.

OUT OF THE SUN THAT TAKES FORM [existit] FROM THE DIVINE LOVE AND THE DIVINE WISDOM, HEAT AND LIGHT GO FORTH. In the spiritual world where angels and spirits are there are heat and light, just as in the natural world where men are; moreover in like manner as heat, the heat is felt and the light is seen as light. Still the heat and light of the spiritual world and of the natural world are (as said above) so entirely different as to have nothing in common. They differ one from the other as what is alive differs from what is dead. The heat of the spiritual world in itself is alive; so is the light; but the heat of the natural world in itself is dead; so is its light. For the heat and light of the spiritual world go forth from a sun that is pure love, while the heat and light of the natural world go forth from a sun that is pure fire; and love is alive, and the Divine Love is Life itself; while fire is dead, and solar fire is death itself, and may be so called because it has nothing whatever of life in it.

Since angels are spiritual they can live in no other than spiritual heat and light, while men can live in no other than natural heat and light; for what is spiritual accords with what is spiritual, and what is natural with what is natural. If an angel were to derive the least particle from natural heat and light he would perish; for it is totally discordant with his life. As to the interiors of the mind every man is a spirit. When he dies he withdraws entirely from the world of nature, leaving behind him all its belongings, and enters a world where there is nothing of nature. In that world he lives so separated from nature that there is no communication whatever by continuity, that is, as between what is purer and grosser, but only like that between what is prior and posterior; and between such no communication is possible except by correspondences. From this it can be seen that spiritual heat is not a purer natural heat, or spiritual light a purer natural light, but that they are altogether of a different essence; for spiritual heat and light derive their essence from a sun which is pure Love, and this is Life itself; while natural heat and light derive their essence from a sun which is pure fire, in which (as said above) there is absolutely nothing of life.

Such being the difference between the heat and light of the two worlds, it is very evident why those who are in the one world cannot see those who are in the other world. For the eyes of man, who sees from natural light, are of the substance of his world, and the eyes of an angel are of the substance of his world; thus in both cases they are formed for the proper reception of their own light. From all this it can be seen from how much ignorance those think who, because they cannot see angels and spirits with their eyes, are unwilling to believe them to be men.

Hitherto it has not been known that angels and spirits are in a totally different light and different heat from men. It has not been known even that another light and another heat are possible. For man in his thought has not penetrated beyond the interior or purer things of nature. And for this reason many have placed the abodes of angels and spirits in the ether, and some in the stars - thus within nature, and not above or outside of it. But, in truth, angels and spirits are entirely above or outside of nature, and are in their own world, which is under another sun. And since in that world spaces are appearances (as was shown above), angels and spirits cannot be said to be in the ether or in the stars; in fact, they are present with man, conjoined to the affection and thought of his spirit; since man is a spirit, and because of that thinks and wills; consequently the spiritual world is wherever man is, and in no wise away from him. In a word, every man as regards the interiors of his mind is in that world, in the midst of spirits and angels there; and he thinks from its light, and loves from its heat.

THE SUN OF THE SPIRITUAL WORLD IS NOT GOD, BUT IS A PROCEEDING FROM THE DIVINE LOVE AND DIVINE WISDOM OF GOD-MAN; SO ALSO ARE THE HEAT AND LIGHT FROM THAT SUN. By that sun which is before the eyes of the angels, and from which they have heat and light, is not meant the Lord Himself, but the first proceeding from Him, which is the highest [degree] of spiritual heat. The highest [degree] of spiritual heat is spiritual fire, which is Divine Love and Divine Wisdom in their first correspondence. On this account that sun appears fiery, and to the angels is fiery, but not to men. Fire which is fire to men is not spiritual, but natural; and between the two fires there is a difference like the difference between what is alive and what is dead. Therefore the spiritual sun by its heat vivifies spiritual beings and renews spiritual objects. The natural sun does the same for natural beings and natural objects; yet not from itself, but by means of an influx of spiritual heat, to which it renders aid as a kind of substitute.

This spiritual fire, in which also there is light in its origin, becomes spiritual heat and light, which decrease in their going forth. This decrease is effected by degrees, which will be treated of in what follows. The ancients represented this by circles glowing with fire and resplendent with light around the head of God, as is common also at the present day in paintings representing God as a Man.

That love begets heat, and wisdom light, is manifest from actual experience. When man loves he grows warm, and when he thinks from wisdom he sees things as it were in light. And from this it is evident that the first proceeding of love is heat, and that the first proceeding of wisdom is light. That they are also correspondences is obvious; for heat takes place [existit] not in love itself, but from love in the will, and thence in the body; and light takes place not in wisdom, but in the thought of the understanding, and thence in the speech. Consequently love and wisdom are the essence and life of heat and light. Heat and light are what proceed, and because they are what proceed, they are also correspondences.

That spiritual light is altogether distinct from natural light, any one may know if he observes the thoughts of his mind. For when the mind thinks, it sees its objects in light, and they who think spiritually see truths, and this at midnight just as well as in the daytime. For this reason light is predicated of the understanding, and the understanding is said to see; thus one sometimes declares of something which another says that he sees (that is, understands) that it is so. The understanding, because it is spiritual, cannot thus see by natural light, for natural light does not inhere in man, but withdraws with the sun. From this it is obvious that the understanding enjoys a light different from that of the eye, and that this light is from a different origin.

Let every one beware of thinking that the sun of the spiritual world is God Himself. God Himself is a Man. The first proceeding from His Love and Wisdom is that fiery spiritual [substance] which appears before the angels as a sun. When, therefore, the Lord manifests Himself to the angels in person, He manifests Himself as a Man; and this sometimes in the sun, sometimes outside of it.

It is from this correspondence that in the Lord the Lord is called not only a "sun" but also "fire" and "light." And by the "sun" is meant Himself as to Divine Love and Divine Wisdom together; by "fire" Himself in respect to Divine Love, and by "light" Himself in respect to Divine Wisdom.

SPIRITUAL HEAT AND LIGHT IN PROCEEDING FROM THE LORD AS A SUN, MAKE ONE, JUST AS HIS DIVINE LOVE AND DIVINE WISDOM MAKE ONE. How Divine Love and Divine Wisdom in the Lord make one has been explained in Part I.; in like manner heat and light make one, because they proceed from these, and the things which proceed make one by virtue of their correspondence, heat, corresponding to love, and light to wisdom. From this it follows that as Divine Love is Divine Esse [Being] and Divine Wisdom is Divine Existere [Taking form] (as shown above, n. 14-16), so spiritual heat is thy Divine proceeding from Divine Esse, and spiritual light is the Divine proceeding from Divine Existere. And as by that union Divine Love is of Divine Wisdom, and Divine Wisdom is of Divine Love (as shown above, n. 35-39), so spiritual heat is of spiritual light, and spiritual light is of spiritual heat And because there is such a union it follows that heat and light, in proceeding from the Lord as a sun, are one. It will be seen, however, in what follows, that they are not received as one by angels and men.

The heat and light that proceed from the Lord as a sun are what in an eminent sense are called the spiritual, and they are called the spiritual in the singular number, because they are one; when, therefore, the spiritual is mentioned in the following pages, it is meant both these together. From that spiritual it is that the whole of that world is called spiritual. Through that spiritual, all things of that world derive their origin, and also their name. That heat and that light are called the spiritual, because God is called Spirit, and God as Spirit is the spiritual going forth. God, by virtue of His own very Essence, is called Jehovah; but by means of that going forth He Vivifies and enlightens angels of heaven and men of the church. Consequently, vivification and enlightenment are said to be effected by the Spirit of Jehovah.

Section 3

That heat and light, that is, the spiritual going forth from the Lord as a Sun, make one, may be illustrated by the heat and light that go forth from the sun of the natural world. These two also make one in their going out from that sun. That they do not make one on earth is owing not to the sun, but to the earth. For the earth revolves daily round its axis, and has a yearly motion following the ecliptic, which gives the appearance that heat and light do not make one. For in the middle of summer there is more of heat than of light, and in the middle of winter more of light than of heat. In the spiritual world it is the same, except that there is in that world no daily or yearly motion of the earth; but the angels turn themselves, some more, some less, to the Lord; those who turn themselves more, receive more from heat and less from light, and those who turn themselves less to the Lord receive more from light and less from heat. From this it is that the heavens, which consist of angels, are divided into two kingdoms, one called celestial, the other spiritual. The celestial angels receive more from heat, and the spiritual angels more from light. Moreover, the lands they inhabit vary in appearance according to their reception of heat and light. If this change of state of the angels is substituted for the motion of the earth, the correspondence is complete.

In what follows it will be seen, also, that all spiritual things that originate through the heat and light of their sun, make one in like manner when regarded in themselves, but when regarded as proceeding from the affections of the angels do not make one. When heat and light make one in the heavens, it is with the angels as if it were spring; but when they do not make one, it is either like summer or like winter - not like the winter in the frigid zones, but like the winter in the warmer zone. Thus reception of love and wisdom in equal measure is the very angelic state, and therefore an angel is an angel of heaven according to the union in him of love and wisdom. It is the same with the man of the church, when love and wisdom, that is, charity and faith, make one in him.

THE SUN OF THE SPIRITUAL WORLD APPEARS AT A MIDDLE ALTITUDE, FAR OFF FROM THE ANGELS, LIKE THE SUN OF THE NATURAL WORLD FROM MEN. Most people take with them out of the world an idea of God, as being above the head, on high, and an idea of the Lord, as living in heaven among the angels. They take with them this idea of God because, in the Word, God is called the "Most High," and is said to "dwell on high;" therefore in prayer and worship men raise their eyes and hands upwards, not knowing that by "The Most High" is signified the inmost. They take with them the idea of the Lord as being in heaven among the angels, because men think of Him as they think of another man, some thinking of Him as they think of an angel, not knowing that the Lord is the Very and Only God who rules the universe, who if He were among the angels in heaven, could not have the universe under His gaze and under His care and government. And unless He shone as a sun before those who are in the spiritual world, angels could have no light; for angels are spiritual, and therefore no other than spiritual light is in accord with their essence. That there is light in the heavens, immensely exceeding the light on earth, will be seen below where degrees are discussed.

As regards the sun, therefore, from which angels have light and heat, it appears above the lands on which the angels dwell, at an elevation of about forty-five degrees, which is the middle altitude; it also appears far off from the angels like the sun of the world from men. The sun appears constantly at that altitude and at that distance, and does not move from its place. Hence it is that angels have no times divided into days and years, nor any progression of the day from morning, through midday to evening and into night; nor any progression of the year from spring, through summer to autumn, into winter; but there is perpetual light and perpetual spring; consequently, with the angels, as was said above, in place of times there are states.

The sun of the spiritual world appears at a middle altitude chiefly for the following reasons: First, the heat and light which proceed from that sun are thus at their medium intensity, consequently are equally proportioned and thus properly attempered. For if the sun were to appear above the middle altitude more heat than light would be perceived, if below it more light than heat; as is the case on earth when the sun is above or below the middle of the sky; when above, the heat increases beyond the light, when below, the light increases beyond the heat; for light remains the same in summer and in winter, but heat increases and diminishes according to the degree of the sun's altitude. Secondly, the sun of the spiritual world appears in a middle altitude above the angelic heaven, because there is thus a perpetual spring in all the angelic heavens, whereby the angels are in a state of peace; for this state corresponds to springtime on earth. Thirdly, angels are thus enabled to turn their faces constantly to the Lord, and behold Him with their eyes. For at every turn of their bodies, the angels have the east, thus the Lord, before their faces. This is peculiar to that world, and would not be the case if the sun of that world were to appear above or below the middle altitude, and least of all if it were to appear overhead in the zenith.

If the sun of the spiritual world did not appear far off from the angels, like the sun of the natural world from men, the whole angelic heaven, and hell under it, and our terraqueous globe under these, would not be under the view, the care, the omnipresence, omniscience, omnipotence, and providence of the Lord; comparatively as the sun of our world, if it were not at such a distance from the earth as it appears, could not be present and powerful in all lands by its heat and light, and therefore could not render its aid, as a kind of substitute, to the sun of the spiritual world.

It is very necessary to be known that there are two suns, one spiritual, the other natural; a spiritual sun for those who are in the spiritual world, and a natural sun for those who are in the natural world. Unless this is known, nothing can be properly understood about creation and about man, which are the subjects here to be treated of. Effects may, it is true, be observed, but unless at the same time the causes of effects are seen, effects can only appear as it were in the darkness of night.

THE DISTANCE BETWEEN THE SUN AND THE ANGELS IN THE SPIRITUAL WORLD IS AN APPEARANCE ACCORDING TO RECEPTION BY THEM OF DIVINE LOVE AND DIVINE WISDOM. All fallacies which prevail with the evil and the simple arise from appearances which have been confirmed. So long as appearances remain appearances, they are apparent truths, according to which every one may think and speak; but when they are accepted as real truths, which is done when they are confirmed, then apparent truths become falsities and fallacies. For example: It is an appearance that the sun is borne around the earth daily, and follows yearly the path of the ecliptic. So long as this appearance is not confirmed it is an apparent truth, according to which any one may think and speak; for he may say that the sun rises and sets and thereby causes morning, midday, evening, and night; also that the sun is now in such or such a degree of the ecliptic or of its altitude, and thereby causes spring, summer, autumn, and winter. But when this appearance is confirmed as the real truth, then the confirmer thinks and utters a falsity springing from a fallacy. It is the same with innumerable other appearances, not only in natural, civil, and moral, but also in spiritual affairs.

It is the same with the distance of the sun of the spiritual world, which sun is the first proceeding of the Lord's Divine Love and Divine Wisdom. The truth is that there is no distance, but that the distance is an appearance according to the reception of Divine Love and Wisdom by the angels in their degree. That distances, in the spiritual world, are appearances may be seen from what has been shown above (as in n. 7-9, That the Divine is not in space; and in n. 69-72, That the Divine, apart from space, fills all spaces). If there are no spaces, there are no distances, or, what is the same, if spaces are appearances, distances also are appearances, for distances are of space.

The sun of the spiritual world appears at a distance from the angels, because they receive Divine Love and Divine Wisdom in the measure of heat and light that is adequate to their states. For an angel, because created and finite, cannot receive the Lord in the first degree of heat and light, such as is in the sun; if he did he would be entirely consumed. The Lord, therefore, is received by angels in a degree of heat and light corresponding to their love and wisdom. The following may serve for illustration. An angel of the lowest heaven cannot ascend to the angels of the third heaven; for if he ascends and enters their heaven, he falls into a kind of swoon, and his life as it were, strives with death; the reason is that he has a less degree of love and wisdom, and the heat of his love and the light of his wisdom are in the same degree as his love and wisdom. What, then, would be the result if an angel were even to ascend toward the sun, and come into its fire? On account of the differences of reception of the Lord by the angels, the heavens also appear separate from one another. The highest heaven, which is called the third, appears above the second, and the second above the first; not that the heavens are apart, but they appear to be apart, for the Lord is present equally with those who are in the lowest heaven and with those who are in the third heaven. That which causes the appearance of distance is not in the Lord but in the subjects, that is, the angels.

That this is so can hardly be comprehended by a natural idea, because in such there is space, but by a spiritual idea, such as angels have, it can be comprehended, because in such there is no space. Yet even by a natural idea this much can be comprehended, that love and wisdom (or what is the same, the Lord, who is Divine Love and Divine Wisdom) cannot advance through spaces, but is present with each one according to reception. That the Lord is present with all, He teaches in Matthew (28:20), and that He makes His abode with those who love Him, in John (14:23).

As this has been proved by means of the heavens and the angels, it may seem a matter of too exalted wisdom; but the same is true of men. Men, as to the interiors of their minds, are warmed and illuminated by that same sun. They are warmed by its heat and illuminated by its light in the measure in which they receive love and wisdom from the Lord. The difference between angels and men is that angels are under the spiritual sun only, but men are not only under that sun, but also under the sun of this world; for men's bodies can begin and continue to exist only under both suns; but not so the bodies of angels, which are spiritual.

ANGELS ARE IN THE LORD, AND THE LORD IN THEM; AND BECAUSE ANGELS ARE RECIPIENTS, THE LORD ALONE IS HEAVEN. Heaven is called "the dwelling-place of God," also "the throne of God," and from this it is believed that God is there as is a king in his kingdom. But God (that is, the Lord) is in the sun above the heavens, and by His presence in heat and light, is in the heavens (as is shown in the last two paragraphs). But although the Lord is present in heaven in that manner, still He is there as He is in Himself. For (as shown just above, n. 108-112) the distance between the sun and heaven is not distance, but appearance of distance; and since that distance is only an appearance it follows that the Lord Himself is in heaven, for He is in the love and wisdom of the angels of heaven; and since He is in the love and wisdom of all angels, and the angel constitute heaven, He is in the whole heaven.

The Lord not only is in heaven, but also is heaven itself; for love and wisdom are what make the angel, and these two are the Lord's in the angels; from which it follows that the Lord is heaven. For angels are not angels from what is their own; what is their own is altogether like what is man's own, which is evil. An angel's own is such because all angels were once men, and this own clings to the angels from their birth. It is only put aside, and so far as it is put aside the angels receive love and wisdom, that is, the Lord, in themselves. Any one, if he will only elevate his understanding a little, can see that the Lord can dwell in angels, only in what is His, that is, in what is His very own, which is love and wisdom, and not at all in the selfhood of angels, which is evil. From this it is, that so far as evil is put away so far the Lord is in them, and so far they are angels. The very angelic of heaven is Love Divine and Wisdom Divine. This Divine is called the angelic when it is in angels. From this, again, it is evident that angels are angels from the Lord, and not from themselves; consequently, the same is true of heaven.

But how the Lord is in an angel and an angel in the Lord cannot be comprehended, unless the nature of their conjunction is known. Conjunction is of the Lord with the angel and of the angel with the Lord; conjunction, therefore, is reciprocal. On the part of the angel it is as follows. The angel, in like manner as man, has no other perception than that he is in love and wisdom from himself, consequently that love and wisdom are, as it were, his or his own.

Unless he so perceived there would be no conjunction, thus the Lord would not be in him, nor he in the Lord. Nor can it be possible for the Lord to be in any angel or man, unless the one in whom the Lord is, with love and wisdom, has a perception and sense as if they were his. By this means the Lord is not only received, but also, when received, is retained, and likewise loved in return. And by this, also, the angel is made wise and continues wise. Who can wish to love the Lord and his neighbor, and who can wish to be wise, without a sense and perception that what he loves, learns, and imbibes is, as it were, his own? Who otherwise can retain it in himself? If this were not so, the inflowing love and wisdom would have no abiding-place, for it would flow through and not affect; thus an angel would not be an angel, nor would man be a man; he would be merely like something inanimate. From all this it can be seen that there must be an ability to reciprocate that there may be conjunction.

It shall now be explained how it comes that an angel perceives and feels as his, and thus receives and retains that which yet is not his; for, as was said above, an angel is not an angel from what is his, but from those things which he has from the Lord. The essence of the matter is this:- Every angel has freedom and rationality; these two he has to the end that he may be capable of receiving love and wisdom from the Lord. Yet neither of these, freedom nor rationality, is his, they are the Lord's in him. But since the two are intimately conjoined to his life, so intimately that they may be said to be joined into it, they appear to be his own. It is from them that he is able to think and will, and to speak and act; and what he thinks, wills, speaks, and does from them, appears as if it were from himself. This gives him the ability to reciprocate, and by means of this conjunction is possible. Yet so far as an angel believes that love and wisdom are really in him, and thus lays claim to them for himself as if they were his, so far the angelic is not in him, and therefore he has no conjunction with the Lord; for he is not in truth, and as truth makes one with the light of heaven, so far he cannot be in heaven; for he thereby denies that he lives from the Lord, and believes that he lives from himself, and that he therefore possesses Divine essence. In these two, freedom and rationality, the life which is called angelic and human consists. From all this it can be seen that for the sake of conjunction with the Lord, - the angel has the ability to reciprocate, but that this ability, in itself considered, is not his but the Lord's. From this it is, that if he abuses his ability to reciprocate, by which he perceives and feels as his what is the Lord's, which is done by appropriating it to himself he falls from the angelic state. That conjunction is reciprocal, the Lord Himself teaches (John 14:20-24; 154-6); also that the conjunction of the Lord with man and of man with the Lord, is in those things of the Lord that are called His words (John 15:7).

Some are of the opinion that Adam was in such liberty or freedom of choice as to be able to love God and be wise from himself, and that this freedom of choice was lost in his posterity. But this is an error; for man is not life, but is a recipient of life (see above, n. 4-6, 54-60); and he who is a recipient of life cannot love and be wise from anything of his own; consequently, when Adam willed to be wise and to love from what was his own he fell from wisdom and love, and was cast out of Paradise.

What has just been said of an angel is likewise true of heaven, which consists of angels, since the Divine in greatest and least things is the same (as was shown above n. 77-82). What is said of an angel and of heaven is likewise true of man and the church, for the angel of heaven and the man of the church act as one through conjunction; in fact, a man of the church is an angel, in respect to the interiors which are of his mind. By a man of the church is meant a man in whom the church is.

IN THE SPIRITUAL WORLD THE EAST IS WHERE THE LORD APPEARS AS A SUN, AND FROM THAT THE OTHER QUARTERS ARE DETERMINED. The sun of the spiritual world and its essence, also its heat and light, and the presence of the Lord thereby, have been treated of; a description is now to be given of the quarters in the spiritual world. That sun and that world are treated of, because God and love and wisdom are treated of; and to treat of those subjects except from their very origin would be to proceed from effects, not from causes. Yet from effects nothing but effects can be learned; when effects alone are considered no cause is brought to light; but causes reveal effects. To know effects from causes is to be wise; but to search for causes from effects is not to be wise, because fallacies then present themselves, which the investigator calls causes, and this is to turn wisdom into foolishness. Causes are things prior, and effects are things posterior; and things prior cannot be seen from things posterior, but things posterior can be seen from things prior. This is order. For this reason the spiritual world is here first treated of, for all causes are there; and afterwards the natural world, where all things that appear are effects.

120.

The quarters in the spiritual world shall now be spoken of. There are quarters there in like manner as in the natural world, but like that world itself, they are spiritual; while the quarters in the natural world, like that world itself, are natural; the difference between them therefore is so great that they have nothing in common. In each world there are four quarters, which are called east, west, south, and north. In the natural world, these four quarters are constant, determined by the sun on the meridian; opposite this is north, on one side is east, on the other, west. These quarters are determined by the meridian of each place; for the sun's station on the meridian at each point is always the same, and is therefore fixed. In the spiritual world it is different. The quarters there are determined by the sun of that world, which appears constantly in its own place, and where it appears is the east; consequently the determination of the quarters in that world is not from the south, as in the natural world, but from the east, opposite to this is west, on one side is south, and on the other, north. But that these quarters are not determined by the sun, but by the inhabitants of that world, who are angels and spirits, will be seen in what follows.

As these quarters, by virtue of their origin, which is the Lord as a sun, are spiritual, so the dwelling-places of angels and spirits, all of which are according to these quarters, are also spiritual. They are spiritual, because angels and spirits have their places of abode according to their reception of love and wisdom from the Lord. Those in a higher degree of love dwell in the east; those in a lower degree of love in the west; those in a higher degree of wisdom, in the south; and those in a lower degree of wisdom, in the north. From this it is that, in the Word, by "the east," in the highest sense, is meant the Lord, and in a relative sense love to Him; by the "west," a diminishing love to Him; by the "south" wisdom in light; and by the "north" wisdom in shade; or similar things relatively to the state of those who are treated of.

Since the east is the point from which all quarters in the spiritual world are determined, and by the east, in the highest sense, is meant the Lord, and also Divine Love, it is evident that the source from which all things are, is the Lord and love to Him, and that one is remote from the Lord in the measure in which he is not in that love, and dwells either in the west, or in the south, or in the north, at distances corresponding to the reception of love.

Since the Lord as a sun is constantly in the east, the ancients, with whom all things of worship were representative of spiritual things, turned their faces to the east in their devotions; and that they might do the like in all worship, they turned their temples also in that direction. From this it is that, at the present day, churches are built in like manner.

THE QUARTERS IN THE SPIRITUAL WORLD ARE NOT FROM THE LORD AS A SUN, BUT FROM THE ANGELS ACCORDING TO RECEPTION. It has been stated that the angels dwell separate from each other; some in the eastern quarter, some in the western, some in the southern, and some in the northern; and that those who dwell in the eastern quarter are in a higher degree of love; those in the western, in a lower degree of love; those in the southern, in the light of wisdom; and those in the northern, in the shade of wisdom. This diversity of dwelling-places appears as though it were from the Lord as a sun, when, in fact it is from the angels. The Lord is not in a greater and lesser degree of love and wisdom, that is, as a sun He is not in a greater or lesser degree of heat and light with one than with another, for He is everywhere the same. But He is not received by one in the same degree as by another; and this makes them appear to themselves to be more or less distant from one another, and also variously as regards the quarters. From this it follows that quarters - in the spiritual world are nothing else than various receptions of love and wisdom, and thence of heat and light from the Lord as a sun. That this is so is plain from what was shown above (n. 108-112), that in the spiritual world distances are appearances.

As the quarters are various receptions of love and wisdom by angels, the variety from which that appearance springs shall now be explained. The Lord is in the angel, and the angel in the Lord (as was shown in a preceding article). But on account of the appearance that the Lord as a sun is outside of the angel, there is also the appearance that the Lord sees him from the sun, and that he sees the Lord in the sun. This is almost like the appearance of an image in a mirror. Speaking, therefore, according to that appearance, it may be said that the Lord sees and looks at each one face to face, but that angels, on their part, do not thus behold the Lord. Those who are in love to the Lord from the Lord see Him directly in front; these, therefore, are in the east and the west; but those who are more in wisdom see the Lord obliquely to the right, and those who are less in wisdom obliquely to the left; therefore the former are in the south, and the latter in the north. The view of these is oblique because love and wisdom (as has been said before), although they proceed from the Lord as one, are not received as one by angels; and the wisdom which is in excess of the love, while it appears as wisdom, is not wisdom, because in the overplus of wisdom there is no life from love. From all this it is evident whence comes the diversity of reception according to which angels appear to dwell according to quarters in the spiritual world.

That this variety of reception of love and wisdom is what gives rise to the quarters in the spiritual world can be seen from the fact that an angel changes his quarter according to the increase or decrease of love with him; from which it is evident that the quarter is not from the Lord as a sun, but from the angel according to reception. It is the same with man as regards his spirit. In respect to his spirit, he is in some quarter of the spiritual world, whatever quarter of the natural world he may be in, for quarters in the spiritual world, as has been said above, have nothing in common with quarters in the natural world. Man is in the latter as regards his body, but in the former as regards his spirit.

In order that love and wisdom may make one in an angel or in a man, there are pairs in all the things of his body. The eyes, ears, and nostrils are pairs; the hands, loins, and feet are pairs; the brain is divided into two hemispheres, the heart into two chambers, the lungs into two lobes, and in like manner the other parts. Thus in angel and man there is right and left; and all their right parts have relation to the love from which wisdom comes; and all the left parts, to the wisdom which is from love; or, what is the same, all the right parts have relation to the good from which truth comes; and all the left parts, to the truth that is from good. Angel and man have these pairs in order that love and wisdom, or good and truth, may act as one, and as one, may have regard to the Lord. But of this more in what follows.

From all this it can be seen in what fallacy and consequent falsity those are, who suppose that the Lord bestows heaven arbitrarily, or arbitrarily grants one to become wise and loving more than another, when, in truth, the Lord is just as desirous that one may become wise and be saved as another. For He provides means for all; and every one becomes wise and is saved in the measure in which he accepts these means, and lives in accordance with them. For the Lord is the same with one as with another; but the recipients, who are angels and men, are unlike by reason of unlike reception and life. That this is so can be seen from what has just been said of spiritual quarters, and of the dwelling-places of the angels in accordance with them; namely, that this diversity is not from the Lord but from the recipients.

ANGELS TURN THEIR FACES CONSTANTLY TO THE LORD AS A SUN, AND THUS HAVE THE SOUTH TO THE RIGHT, THE NORTH TO THE LEFT, AND THE WEST BEHIND THEM. All that is here said of angels, and of their turning to the Lord as a sun, is to be understood also of man, as regards his spirit. For man in respect to his mind is a spirit, and if he be in love and wisdom, is an angel; consequently, after death, when he has put off his externals, which he had derived from the natural world, he becomes a spirit or an angel. And because angels turn their faces constantly toward the sun in the east, thus toward the Lord, it is said also of any man who is in love and wisdom from the Lord, that "he sees God," that "he looks to God," that "he has God before his eyes," by which is meant that he lives as an angel does. Such things are spoken of in the world, because they actually take place [existunt] both in heaven and in the spirit of man. Who does not look before himself to God when he prays, to whatever quarter his face may be turned?

Angels turn their faces constantly to the Lord as a sun, because they are in the Lord, and the Lord in them; and the Lord interiorly leads their affections and thoughts, and turns them constantly to Himself; consequently they cannot do otherwise than look towards the east where the Lord appears as a sun; from which it is evident that angels do not turn themselves to the Lord, but the Lord turns them to Himself. For when angels think interiorly of the Lord, they do not think of Him otherwise than as being in themselves. Real interior thought does not cause distance, but exterior thought, which acts as one with the sight of the eyes; and for the reason that exterior thought, but not interior, is in space; and when not in space, as in the spiritual world, it is still in an appearance of space. But these things can be little understood by the man who thinks about God from space. For God is everywhere, yet not in space. Thus He is both within and without an angel; consequently an angel can see God, that is, the Lord, both within himself and without himself; within himself when he thinks from love and wisdom, without himself when he thinks about love and wisdom. But these things will be treated of in detail in treatises on The Lord's Omnipresence, Omniscience, and Omnipotence. Let every man guard himself against falling into the detestable false doctrine that God has infused Himself into men, and that He is in them, and no longer in Himself; for God is everywhere, as well within man as without, for apart from space He is in all space (as was shown above, n. 7-10, 69-72); whereas if He were in man, He would be not only divisible, but also shut up in space; yea, man then might even think himself to be God. This heresy is so abominable, that in the spiritual world it stinks like carrion.

The turning of angels to the Lord is such that at every turn of their bodies they look toward the Lord as a sun in front of them. An angel may turn himself round and round, and thereby see the various things that are about him, still the Lord as a sun appears constantly before his face. This may seem wonderful, yet it is the truth. It has also been granted me to see the Lord thus as a sun. I see Him now before my face; and for several years I have so seen Him, to whatever quarter of the world I have turned.

Since the Lord as a sun, consequently the east, is before the faces of all angels of heaven, it follows that to their right is the south; to their left the north; and behind them the west; and this, too, at every turn of the body. For, as was said before, all quarters in the spiritual world are determined from the east; therefore those who have the east before their eyes are in these very quarters, yea, are themselves what determine the quarters; for (as was shown above, n. 124-128) the quarters are not from the Lord as a sun, but from the angels according to reception.

Now since heaven is made up of angels, and angels are of such a nature, it follows that all heaven turns itself to the Lord, and that, by means of this turning, heaven is ruled by the Lord as one man, as in His sight it is one man. That heaven is as one man in the sight of the Lord may be seen in the work Heaven and Hell (n. 59-87). Also from this are the quarters of heaven.

Since the quarters are thus inscribed as it were on the angel, as well as on the whole heaven, an angel, unlike man in the world, knows his own home and his own dwelling-place wherever he goes. Man does not know his home and dwelling-place from the spiritual quarter in himself, because he thinks from space, thus from the quarters of the natural world, which have nothing in common with the quarters of the spiritual world. But birds and beasts have such knowledge, for it is implanted in them to know of themselves their homes and dwelling-places, as is evident from abundant observation; a proof that such is the case in the spiritual world; for all things that have form [existunt] in the natural world are effects, and all things that have form in the spiritual world are the causes of these effects. There does not take place [existit] a natural that does not derive its cause from a spiritual.

ALL INTERIOR THINGS OF THE ANGELS, BOTH OF MIND AND BODY, ARE TURNED TO THE LORD AS A SUN. Angels have understanding and will, and they have a face and body. They have also the interior things of the understanding and will, and of the face and body. The interiors of the understanding and will are such as pertain to their interior affection and thought; the interiors of the face are the brains; and the interiors of the body are the viscera, chief among which are the heart and lungs. In a word, angels have each and all things that men on earth have; it is from these things that angels are men. External form, apart from these internal things, does not make them men, but external form together with, yea, from, internals - for otherwise they would be only images of man, in which there would be no life, because inwardly there would be no form of life.

It is well known that the will and understanding rule the body at pleasure, for what the understanding thinks, the mouth speaks, and what the will wills, the body does. From this it is plain that the body is a form corresponding to the understanding and will. And because form also is predicated of understanding and will, it is plain that the form of the body corresponds to the form of the understanding and will. But this is not the place to describe the nature of these respective forms. In each form there are things innumerable; and these, in each of them, act as one, because they mutually correspond. It is from this that the mind (that is, the will and understanding) rules the body at its pleasure, thus as entirely as it rules its own self. From all this it follows that the interiors of the mind act as a one with the interiors of the body, and the exteriors of the mind with the exteriors of the body. The interiors of the mind, likewise the interiors of the body, will be considered further on, when degrees of life have been treated of.

Since the interiors of the mind make one with the interiors of the body, it follows that when the interiors of the mind turn themselves to the Lord as a sun, those of the body turn themselves in like manner; and because the exteriors of both, of mind as well as body, depend upon their interiors, they also do the same. For what the external does, it does from internals, the general deriving all it has from the particulars from which it is. From this it is evident that as an angel turns his face and body to the Lord as a sun, all the interiors of his mind and body are turned in the same direction. It is the same with man, if he has the Lord constantly before his eyes, which is the case if he is in love and wisdom. He then looks to the Lord not only with eyes and face, but also with all the mind and all the heart, that is, with all things of the will and understanding, together with all things of the body.

This turning to the Lord is an actual turning, a kind of elevation; for there is an uplifting into the heat and light of heaven, which takes place by the opening of the interiors; when these are opened, love and wisdom flow into the interiors of the mind, and the heat and light of heaven into the interiors of the body. From this comes the uplifting, like a rising out of a cloud into clear air, or out of air into ether. Moreover, love and wisdom, with their heat and light, are the Lord with man; and He, as was said before, turns man to Himself. It is the reverse with those who are not in love and wisdom, and still more with those who are opposed to love and wisdom. Their interiors, both of mind and body, are closed; and when closed, the exteriors re-act against the Lord, for such is their inherent nature. Consequently, such persons turn themselves backward from the Lord; and turning oneself backward is turning to hell.

This actual turning to the Lord is from love together with Wisdom; not from love alone, nor from wisdom alone; for love alone is like esse [being] without its existere [taking form] since love has its form in wisdom; and wisdom without love is like existere without its esse, since wisdom has its form from love. Love is indeed possible without wisdom; but such love is man's, and not the Lord's. Wisdom alone is possible without love; but such wisdom, although from the Lord, has not the Lord in it; for it is like the light of winter, which is from the sun; still the sun's essence, which is heat, is not in it.

EVERY SPIRIT, WHATEVER HIS QUALITY, TURNS IN LIKE MANNER TO HIS RULING LOVE. It shall first be explained what a spirit is, and what an angel is. Every man after death comes, in the first place, into the world of spirits, which is midway between heaven and hell, and there passes through his own times, that is, his own states, and becomes prepared, according to his life, either for heaven or for hell. So long as one stays in that world he is called a spirit. He who has been raised out of that world into heaven is called an angel; but he who has been cast down into hell is called either a satan or a devil. So long as these continue in the world of spirits, he who is preparing for heaven is called an angelic spirit; and he who is preparing for hell, an infernal spirit; meanwhile the angelic spirit is conjoined with heaven, and the infernal spirit with hell. All spirits in the world of spirits are adjoined to men; because men, in respect to the interiors of their minds, are in like manner between heaven and hell, and through these spirits they communicate with heaven or with hell according to their life. It is to be observed that the world of spirits is one thing, and the spiritual world another; the world of spirits is that which has just been spoken of; but the spiritual world includes that world, and heaven and hell.

Since the subject now under consideration is the turning of angels and spirits to their own loves by reason of these loves, something shall be said also about loves. The whole heaven is divided into societies according to all the differences of loves; in like manner hell, and in like manner the world of spirits. But heaven is divided into societies according to the differences of heavenly loves; hell into societies according to the differences of infernal loves; and the world of spirits, according to the differences of loves both heavenly and infernal. There are two loves which are the heads of all the rest, that is, to which all other loves are referable; the love which is the head of all heavenly loves, or to which they all relate, is love to the Lord; and the love which is the head of all infernal loves, or to which they all relate, is the love of rule springing from the love of self. These two loves are diametrically opposed to each other.

Since these two loves, love to the Lord and love of rule springing from love of self, are wholly opposed to each other, and since all who are in love to the Lord turn to the Lord as a sun (as was shown in the preceding article), it can be seen that all who are in the love of rule springing from love of self, turn their backs to the Lord. They thus face in opposite directions, because those who are in love to the Lord love nothing more than to be led by the Lord, and will that the Lord alone shall rule; while those who are in the love of rule springing from love of self, love nothing more than to be led by themselves, and will that themselves alone may rule. This is called a love of rule springing from love of self, because there is a love of rule springing from a love of performing uses, which is a spiritual love, because it makes one with love towards the neighbor. Still this cannot be called a love of rule, but a love of performing duties.

Every spirit, of whatever quality, turns to his own ruling love, because love is the life of every one (as was shown in Part I., n. 1-3); and life turns its receptacles, called members, organs, and viscera, thus the whole man, to that society which is in a love similar to itself, thus where its own love is.

Since the love of rule springing from love of self is wholly opposed to love to the Lord, the spirits who are in that love of rule turn the face backwards from the Lord, and therefore look with their eyes to the western quarters of the spiritual world; and being thus bodily in a reversed position, they have the east behind them, the north at their right, and the south at their left. They have the east behind them because they hate the Lord; they have the north at their right, because they love fallacies and falsities therefrom; and they have the south at their left, because they despise the light of wisdom. They may turn themselves round and round, and yet all things which they see about them appear similar to their love. All such are sensual-natural; and some are of such a nature as to imagine that they alone live, looking upon others as images. They believe themselves to be wise above all others, though in truth they are insane.

In the spiritual world ways are seen, laid out like ways in the natural world; some leading to heaven, and some to hell; but the ways leading to hell are not visible to those going to heaven, nor are the ways leading to heaven visible to those going to hell. There are countless ways of this kind; for there are ways which lead to every society of heaven and to every society of hell. Each spirit enters the way which leads to the society of his own love, nor does he see the ways leading in other directions. Thus it is that each spirit, as he turns himself to his ruling love, goes forward in it.

DIVINE LOVE AND DIVINE WISDOM PROCEEDING FROM THE LORD AS A SUN AND PRODUCING HEAT AND LIGHT IN HEAVEN, ARE THE PROCEEDING DIVINE, WHICH IS THE HOLY SPIRIT. In The Doctrine of the New Jerusalem concerning the Lord it has been shown, that God is one in person and essence in whom there is a trinity, and that that God is the Lord; also, that the trinity in Him is called Father, Son, and Holy Spirit; and that the Divine from which, (Creative Divine) is called the Father; the Human Divine, the Son; and the proceeding Divine, the Holy Spirit. This is called the "proceeding Divine," but no one knows why it is called proceeding. This is not known, because until now it has been unknown that the Lord appears before the angels as a sun, from which sun proceeds heat which in its essence is Divine Love, and also light which in its essence is Divine Wisdom. So long as these things were unknown, it could not be known that the proceeding Divine is not a Divine by itself; consequently the Athanasian doctrine of the trinity declares that there is one person of the Father, another of the Son, and another of the Holy Spirit. Now, however, when it is known that the Lord appears as a sun, a correct idea may be had of the proceeding Divine, which is called the Holy Spirit, that it is one with the Lord, but proceeds from Him, as heat and light from a sun. For the same reason angels are in Divine heat and Divine light just so far as they are in love and wisdom. Without knowing that the Lord appears as a sun in the spiritual world, and that His Divine thus proceeds, it can in no way be known what is meant by "proceeding," whether it means simply communicating those things which are the Father's and the Son's, or simply enlightening and teaching. But inasmuch as it has been known that God is one, and that He is omnipresent, it is not in accord with enlightened reason to recognize the proceeding Divine as a Divine per se, and to call it God, and thus divide God.

It has been shown above that God is not in space, and that He is thereby omnipresent; also that the Divine is the same everywhere, but that there is an apparent variety of it in angels and men from variety of reception. Now since the proceeding Divine from the Lord as a sun is in light and heat, and light and heat flow first into universal recipients, which in the world are called atmospheres, and these are the recipients of clouds, it can be seen that according as the interiors pertaining to the understanding of man or angel are veiled by such clouds, is he a receptacle of the proceeding Divine. By clouds are meant spiritual clouds, which are thoughts. These, if from truths, are in accordance, but if from falsities, are at variance with Divine Wisdom; consequently, in the spiritual world thoughts from truths, when presented to the sight, appear as shining white clouds, but thoughts from falsities as black clouds. From all this it can be seen that the proceeding Divine is indeed in every man, but is variously veiled by each.

As the Divine Itself is present in angel and man by spiritual heat and light, those who are in the truths of Divine Wisdom and in the goods of Divine Love, when affected by these, and when from affection they think from them and about them, are said to grow warm with God; and this sometimes becomes so evident as to be perceived and felt, as when a preacher speaks from zeal. These same are also said to be enlightened by God, because the Lord, by His proceeding Divine, not only kindles the will with spiritual heat, but also enlightens the understanding with spiritual light.

From the following passages in the Word it is plain that the Holy Spirit is the same as the Lord, and is truth itself, from which man has enlightenment: Jesus said, When the spirit of truth is come, He will guide you into all truth; He shall not speak of Himself; but whatsoever He shall have heard, that shall He speak (John 16:13). He shall glorify Me; for He shall receive of Mine, and shall show it unto you (John 16:14, 15). That He will be with the disciples and in them (John 14:17; 15:26). Jesus said, The words that I speak unto you, they are spirit and they are life (John 6:63). From these passages it is evident that the Truth itself which proceeds from the Lord, is called the Holy Spirit; and because it is in light, it enlightens.

Enlightenment, which is attributed to the Holy Spirit, is indeed in man from the Lord, yet it is effected by spirits and angels as media. But the nature of that mediation cannot yet be described; only it may be said that angels and spirits can in no way enlighten man from themselves, because they, in like manner as man, are enlightened by the Lord; and as they are enlightened in like manner, it follows that all enlightenment is from the Lord alone. It is effected by angels or spirits as media, because the man when he is enlightened is placed in the midst of such angels and spirits as, more than others, receive enlightenment from the Lord alone.

Section 4

THE LORD CREATED THE UNIVERSE AND ALL THINGS OF IT BY MEANS OF THE SUN WHICH IS THE FIRST PROCEEDING OF DIVINE LOVE AND DIVINE WISDOM. By "the Lord" is meant God from eternity, that is, Jehovah: who is called Father and Creator, because He is one with Him, as has been shown in The Doctrine of the New Jerusalem concerning the Lord; consequently in the following pages, where also creation is treated of, He is called the Lord

That all things in the universe were created by Divine Love and Divine Wisdom was fully shown in Part I., (particularly in n. 52, 53); here now it is to be shown that this was done by means of the sun, which is the first proceeding of Divine Love and Divine Wisdom. No one who is capable of seeing effects from causes, and afterwards by causes effects in their order and sequence, can deny that the sun is the first of creation, for all the things that are in its world have perpetual existence from it; and because they have perpetual existence from it, their existence was derived from it. The one involves and is proof of the other; for all things are under the sun's view, since it is determined that they should be, and to hold under its view is to determine perpetually; therefore it is said that subsistence is perpetual existence. If, moreover, any thing were to be withdrawn entirely from the sun's influx through the atmospheres, it would instantly be dissipated; for the atmospheres, which are purer and purer, and are rendered active in power by the sun, hold all things in connection. Since, then, the perpetual existence of the universe, and of every thing pertaining to it, is from the sun, it is plain that the sun is the first of creation, from which [is all else]. The sun is spoken of as creating, but this means the Lord, by means of the sun; for the sun also was created by the Lord.

There are two suns through which all things were created by the Lord, the sun of the spiritual world and the sun of the natural world. All things were created by the Lord through the sun of the spiritual world, but not through the sun of the natural world, since the latter is far below the former; it is in middle distance; above it is the spiritual world and below it is the natural world. This sun of the natural world was created to render aid, as a kind of substitute; this aid will be spoken of in what follows.

The universe and all things thereof were created by the Lord, the sun of the spiritual world serving as a medium, because that sun is the first proceeding of Divine Love and Divine Wisdom, and from Divine Love and Divine Wisdom all things are (as was pointed out above, n. 52-82). In every thing created, greatest as well as least, there are these three, end, cause and effect. A created thing in which these three are not, is impossible. In what is greatest, that is, in the universe, these three exist in the following order; in the sun, which is the first proceeding of Divine Love and Divine Wisdom, is the end of all things; in the spiritual world are the causes of all things; in the natural world are the effects of all things. How these three are in things first and in things last shall be shown in what follows. Since, then, no created thing is possible in which these three are not, it follows that the universe and all things of it were created by the Lord through the sun, wherein is the end of all things.

Creation itself cannot be brought within man's comprehension unless space and time are removed from thought; but if these are removed, it can be comprehended. Removing these if you can, or as much as you can, and keeping the mind in ideas abstracted from space and time, you will perceive that there is no difference between the maximum of space and the minimum of space; and then you cannot but have a similar idea of the creation of the universe as of the creation of the particulars therein; you will also perceive that diversity in created things springs from this, that there are infinite things in God-Man, consequently things without limit in the sun which is the first proceeding from Him; these countless things take form, as in an image, in the created universe. From this it is that no one thing can anywhere be precisely the same as another. From this comes that variety of all things which is presented to sight, in the natural world, together with space, but in the spiritual world with appearance of space; and it is a variety both of generals and of particulars. These are the things that have been pointed out in Part I., where it is shown that in God-Man infinite things are one distinctly (n. 17-22); that all things in the universe were created by Divine Love and Divine Wisdom, n. 52, 53); that all things in the created universe are recipients of the Divine Love and of the Divine Wisdom of God-Man (n. 54-60); that the Divine is not in space (n. 7-10); that the Divine apart from space fills all spaces (n. 66 - 72); that the Divine is the same in things greatest and least (n. 77-82).

The creation of the universe, and of all things of it, cannot be said to have been wrought from space to space, or from time to time, thus progressively and successively, but from eternity and from infinity; not from eternity of time, because there is no such thing, but from eternity not of time, for this is the same with the Divine; nor from infinity of space, because again there is no such thing, but from infinity not of space, which also is the same with the Divine. These things, I know, transcend the ideas of thoughts that are in natural light, but they do not transcend the ideas of thoughts that are in spiritual light, for in these there is nothing of space and time. Neither do they wholly transcend ideas that are in natural light; for when it is said that infinity of space is not possible, this is affirmed by every one from reason. It is the same with eternity, for this is infinity of time. If you say "to eternity," it is comprehensible from time; but "from eternity" is not comprehensible, unless time is removed.

THE SUN OF THE NATURAL WORLD IS PURE FIRE, CONSEQUENTLY DEAD; NATURE ALSO IS DEAD, BECAUSE IT DERIVES ITS ORIGIN FROM THAT SUN. Creation itself cannot be ascribed in the least to the sun of the natural world, but must be wholly ascribed to the sun of the spiritual world; because the sun of the natural world is altogether dead; but the sun of the spiritual world is living; for it is the first proceeding of Divine Love and Divine Wisdom; and what is dead does not act at all from itself, but is acted upon; consequently to ascribe to it anything of creation would be like ascribing the work of an artificer to the tool which is moved by his hands. The sun of the natural world is pure fire from which everything of life has been withdrawn; but the sun of the spiritual world is fire in which is Divine Life. The angelic idea of the fire of the sun of the natural world, and of the fire of the sun of the spiritual world, is this; that in the fire of the sun of the spiritual world the Divine Life is within, but in the fire of the sun of the natural world it is without. From this it can be seen that the actuating power of the natural sun is not from itself, but from a living force proceeding from the sun of the spiritual world; consequently if the living force of that sun were withdrawn or taken away, the natural sun would have no vital power. For this reason the worship of the sun is the lowest of all the forms of God-worship, for it is wholly dead, as the sun itself is, and therefore in the Word it is called "abomination."

As the sun of the natural world is pure fire, and therefore dead, the heat proceeding from it is also dead, likewise the light proceeding from it is dead; so also are the atmospheres, which are called ether and air, and which receive in their bosom and carry down the heat and light of that sun; and as these are dead so are each and all things of the earth which are beneath the atmospheres, and are called soils, yet these, one and all, are encompassed by what is spiritual, proceeding and flowing forth from the sun of the spiritual world. Unless they had been so encompassed, the soils could not have been stirred into activity, and have produced forms of uses, which are plants, nor forms of life, which are animals; nor could have supplied the materials by which man begins and continues to exist.

Now since nature begins from that sun, and all that springs forth and continues to exist from it is called natural, it follows that nature, with each and every thing pertaining thereto, is dead. It appears in man and animal as if alive, because of the life which accompanies and actuates it.

Since these lowest things of nature which form the lands are dead, and are not changeable and varying according to states of affections and thoughts, as in the spiritual world, but unchangeable and fixed, therefore in nature there are spaces and spatial distances. There are such things, because creation has there terminated, and abides at rest. From this it is evident that spaces are a property of nature; and because in nature spaces are not appearances of spaces according to states of life, as they are in the spiritual world, these also may be called dead.

Since times in like manner are settled and constant, they also are a property of nature; for the length of a day is constantly twenty-four hours, and the length of a year is constantly three hundred and sixty-five days and a quarter. The very states of light and shade, and of heat and cold, which cause these periods to vary, are also regular in their return. The states which recur daily are morning, noon, evening, and night; those recurring yearly are spring, summer, autumn, and winter. Moreover, the annual states modify regularly the daily states. All these states are likewise dead because they are not states of life, as in the spiritual world; for in the spiritual world there is continuous light and there is continuous heat, the light corresponding to the state of wisdom, and the heat to the state of love with the angels; consequently the states of these are living.

From all this the folly of those who ascribe all things to nature can be seen. Those who have confirmed themselves in favor of nature have brought such a state on themselves that they are no longer willing to raise the mind above nature; consequently their minds are shut above and opened below. Man thus becomes sensual-natural, that is, spiritually dead; and because he then thinks only from such things as he has imbibed from his bodily senses, or through the senses from the world, he at heart even denies God. Then because conjunction with heaven is broken, conjunction with hell takes place, the capacity to think and will alone remaining; the capacity to think, from rationality, and the capacity to will, from freedom; these two capacities every man has from the Lord, nor are they taken away. These two capacities devils have equally with angels; but devils devote them to insane thinking and evil doing, and angels to becoming wise and doing good.

WITHOUT A DOUBLE SUN, ONE LIVING AND THE OTHER DEAD, NO CREATION IS POSSIBLE. The universe in general is divided into two worlds, the spiritual and the natural. In the spiritual world are angels and spirits, in the natural world men. In external appearance these two worlds are entirely alike, so alike that they cannot be distinguished; but as to internal appearance they are entirely unlike. The men themselves in the spiritual world, who (as was said above) are called angels and spirits, are spiritual, and, being spiritual, they think spiritually and speak spiritually. But the men of the natural world are natural, and therefore think naturally and speak naturally; and spiritual thought and speech have nothing in common with natural thought and speech. From this it is plain that these two worlds, the spiritual and the natural, are entirely distinct from each other, so that they can in no respect be together.

Now as these two worlds are so distinct, it is necessary that there should be two suns, one from which all spiritual things are, and another from which all natural things are. And as all spiritual things in their origin are living, and all natural things from their origin are dead, and these origins are suns, it follows that the one sun is living and the other dead; also, that the dead sun itself was created by the Lord through the living sun.

A dead sun was created to this end, that in outmosts all things may be fixed, settled, and constant, and thus there may be forms of existence which shall be permanent and durable. In this and in no other way is creation founded. The terraqueous globe, in which, upon which, and about which, things exist, is a kind of base and support; for it is the outmost work [ultimum opus], in which all things terminate, and upon which they rest. It is also a kind of matrix, out of which effects, which are ends of creation, are produced, as will be shown in what follows.

That all things were created by the Lord through the living sun, and nothing through the dead sun, can be seen from this, that what is living disposes what is dead in obedience to itself, and forms it for uses, which are its ends; but not the reverse. Only a person bereft of reason and who is ignorant of what life is, can think that all things are from nature, and that life even comes from nature. Nature cannot dispense life to anything, since nature in itself is wholly inert. For what is dead to act upon what is living, or for dead force to act upon living force, or, what is the same, for the natural to act upon the spiritual, is entirely contrary to order, therefore so to think is contrary to the light of sound reason. What is dead, that is, the natural, may indeed in many ways be perverted or changed by external accidents, but it cannot act upon life; on the contrary life acts into it, according to the induced change of form. It is the same with physical influx into the spiritual operations of the soul; this, it is known, does not occur, for it is not possible.

THE END OF CREATION HAS FORM [existat] IN OUTMOSTS, WHICH END IS THAT ALL THINGS MAY RETURN TO THE CREATOR AND THAT THERE MAY BE CONJUNCTION. In the first place, something shall be said about ends. There are three things that follow in order, called first end, middle end, and last end; they are also called end, cause, and effect. These three must be together in every thing, that it may be anything. For a first end without a middle end, and at the same time a last end, is impossible; or, what is the same, an end alone, without a cause and an effect is impossible. Equally impossible is a cause alone without an end from which and an effect in which it is, or an effect alone, that is, an effect without its cause and end. That this is so may be comprehended if it be observed that an end without an effect, that is, separated from an effect, is a thing without existence, and therefore a mere term. For in order that an end may actually be an end it must be terminated, and it is terminated in its effect, wherein it is first called an end because it is an end. It appears as if the agent or the efficient exists by itself; but this so appears from its being in the effect; but if separated from the effect it would instantly vanish. From all this it is evident that these three, end, cause, and effect, must be in every thing to make it anything.

It must be known further, that the end is everything in the cause, and also everything in the effect; from this it is that end, cause, and effect, are called first end, middle end, and last end. But that the end may be everything in the cause, there must be something from the end [in the cause] wherein the end shall be; and that the end may be everything in the effect, there must be something from the end through the cause [in the effect] wherein the end shall be. For the end cannot be in itself alone, but it must be in something having existence from it, in which it can dwell as to all that is its own, and by acting, come into effect, until it has permanent existence. That in which it has permanent existence is the last end, which is called effect.

These three, namely, end, cause, and effect, are in the created universe, both in its greatest and least parts. They are in the greatest and least parts of the created universe, because they are in God the Creator, who is the Lord from eternity. But since He is Infinite, and in the Infinite in finite things are one distinctly (as was shown above, n. 17-22), therefore also these three in Him, and in His infinites, are one distinctly. From this it is that the universe which was created from His Esse, and which, regarded as to uses, is His image, possesses these three in each and all of its parts.

The universal end, that is, the end of all things of creation, is that there may be an eternal conjunction of the Creator with the created universe; and this is not possible unless there are subjects wherein His Divine can be as in Itself, thus in which it can dwell and abide. In order that these subjects may be dwelling-places and mansions of Him, they must be recipients of His love and wisdom as of themselves; such, therefore, as will elevate themselves to the Creator as of themselves, and conjoin themselves with Him. Without this ability to reciprocate no conjunction is possible. These subjects are men, who are able as of themselves to elevate and conjoin themselves. That men are such subjects, and that they are recipients of the Divine as of themselves, has been pointed out above many times. By means of this conjunction, the Lord is present in every work created by Him; for everything has been created for man as its end;

consequently the uses of all created things ascend by degrees from outmosts to man, and through man to God the Creator from whom [are all things] (as was shown above, n. 65-68).

To this last end creation progresses continually, through these three, namely, end, cause, and effect, because these three are in the Lord the Creator (as was said just above); and the Divine apart from space is in all space (n. 69-72); and is the same in things greatest and least (77 - 82); from which it is evident that the created universe, in its general progression to its last end, is relatively the middle end. For out of the earth forms of uses are continually raised by the Lord the Creator, in their order up to man, who as to his body is also from the earth. Thereafter, man is elevated by the reception of love and wisdom from the Lord; and for this reception of love and wisdom, all means are provided; and he has been so made as to be able to receive, if he will. From what has now been said it can be seen, though as yet only in a general manner, that the end of creation takes form [existat] in outmost things; which end is, that all things may return to the Creator, and that there may be conjunction.

That these three, end, cause, and effect, are in each and every thing created, can also be seen from this, that all effects, which are called last ends, become anew first ends in uninterrupted succession from the First, who is the Lord the Creator, even to the last end, which is the conjunction of man with Him. That all last ends become anew first ends is plain from this, that there can be nothing so inert and dead as to have no efficient power in it. Even out of sand there is such an exhalation as gives aid in producing, and therefore in effecting something.

PART THIRD. IN THE SPIRITUAL WORLD THERE ARE ATMOSPHERES, WATERS AND LANDS, JUST AS IN THE NATURAL WORLD; ONLY THE FORMER ARE SPIRITUAL, WHILE THE LATTER ARE NATURAL. It has been said in the preceding pages, and shown in the work Heaven and Hell, that the spiritual world is like the natural world, with the difference only that each and every thing of the spiritual world is spiritual, and each and every thing of the natural world is natural. As these two worlds are alike, there are in both, atmospheres, waters, and lands, which are the generals through and from which each and all things take their form [existunt] with infinite variety.

As regards the atmospheres, which are called ethers and airs, they are alike in both worlds, the spiritual and the natural, with the difference only that they are spiritual in the spiritual world, and natural in the natural world. The former are spiritual, because they have their form from the sun which is the first proceeding of the Divine Love and Divine Wisdom of the Lord, and from Him receive within them the Divine fire which is love, and the Divine light which is wisdom, and carry these down to the heavens where the angels dwell, and cause the presence of that sun there in things greatest and least. The spiritual atmospheres are divided substances, that is, least forms, originating from the sun. As these each singly receive the sun, its fire, distributed among so many substances, that is, so many forms, and as it were enveloped by them, and tempered by these envelopments, becomes heat, adapted finally to the love of angels in heaven and of spirits under heaven. The same is true of the light of that sun. In this the natural atmospheres are like spiritual atmospheres, that they also are divided substances or least forms originating from the sun of the natural world; these also each singly receive the sun and store up its fire in themselves, and temper it, and carry it down as heat to the earth, where men dwell. The same is true of natural light.

The difference between spiritual and natural atmospheres is that spiritual atmospheres are receptacles of Divine fire and Divine light, thus of love and wisdom, for they contain these interiorly within them; while natural atmospheres are receptacles, not of Divine fire and Divine light, but of the fire and light of their own sun, which in itself is dead, as was shown above; consequently there is nothing interiorly in them from the sun of the spiritual world, although they are environed by spiritual atmospheres from that sun. That this is the difference between spiritual and natural atmospheres has been learned from the wisdom of angels.

That there are atmospheres in the spiritual, just as in the natural world, can be seen from this, that angels and spirits breathe, and also speak and hear - just as men do in the natural world; and respiration, speech, and hearing are all effected by means of a lowest atmosphere, which is called air; it can be seen also from this, that angels and spirits, like men in the natural world, have sight, and sight is possible only by means of an atmosphere purer than air; also from this, that angels and spirits, like men in the natural world, think and are moved by affection, and thought and affection are not possible except by means of still purer atmospheres; and finally from this, that all parts of the bodies of angels and spirits, external as well as internal, are held together in connection by atmospheres, the external by air and the internal by ethers. Without the surrounding pressure and action of these atmospheres the interior and exterior forms of the body would evidently dissolve away. Since angels are spiritual, and each and all things of their bodies are held together in connection, form, and order by means of atmospheres, it follows that these atmospheres are spiritual; they are spiritual, because they arise from the spiritual sun which is the first proceeding of the Lord's Divine Love and Divine Wisdom.

That there are also waters and lands in the spiritual as well as in the natural world, with the difference that these waters and lands are spiritual, has been said above and has been shown in the work Heaven and Hell; and because these are spiritual, they are moved and modified by the heat and light of the spiritual sun, the atmospheres therefrom serving as mediums, just as the waters and lands in the natural world are moved and modified by the heat and light of the sun of their world, its atmospheres serving as mediums.

Atmospheres, waters, and lands are here specified, because these three are generals, through and from which each and all things have their form [existunt] in infinite variety. The atmospheres are the active forces, the waters are the mediate forces, and the lands are the passive forces, from which all effects have existence. These three forces are such in their series solely by virtue of life that proceeds from the Lord as a sun, and that makes them active.

THERE ARE DEGREES OF LOVE AND WISDOM, CONSEQUENTLY DEGREES OF HEAT AND LIGHT ALSO DEGREES, OF ATMOSPHERES. The things which follow cannot be comprehended unless it be known that there are degrees, also what they are, and what their nature is, because in every created thing, thus in every form, there are degrees. This Part of Angelic

Wisdom will therefore treat of degrees. That there are degrees of love and wisdom can be clearly seen from the fact that there are angels of the three heavens. The angels of the third heaven so far excel the angels of the second heaven in love and wisdom, and these, the angels of the lowest heaven, that they cannot be together. The degrees of love and wisdom distinguish and separate them. It is from this that angels of the lower heavens cannot ascend to angels of higher heavens, or if allowed to ascend, they do not see the higher angels or anything that is about them. They do not see them because the love and wisdom of the higher angels is of a higher degree, transcending the perception of the lower angels. For each angel is his own love and his own wisdom; and love together with wisdom in its form is a man, because God, who is Love itself and Wisdom itself, is a Man. It has sometimes been permitted me to see angels of the lowest heaven who have ascended to the angels of the third heaven; and when they had made their way thither, I have heard them complaining that they did not see any one, and all the while they were in the midst of the higher angels. Afterwards they were instructed that those angels were invisible to them because their love and wisdom were imperceptible to them, and that love and wisdom are what make an angel appear as a man.

That there must be degrees of love and wisdom is still more evident when the love and wisdom of angels are compared with the love and wisdom of men. It is well known that the wisdom of angels, when thus compared, is ineffable; also it will be seen in what follows that to men who are in natural love, this wisdom is incomprehensible. It appears ineffable and incomprehensible because it is of a higher degree.

Since there are degrees of love and wisdom, there are also degrees of heat and light. By heat and light are meant spiritual heat and light, such as angels in the heavens have, and such as men have as to the interiors of their minds; for men have a heat of love similar to that of the angels, and a similar light of wisdom. In the heavens, such and so much love as the angels have, such and so much is their heat; and the same is true of their light as compared with their wisdom; the reason is, that with them love is in the heat, and wisdom in the light (as was shown above). It is the same with men on earth, with the difference, however, that angels feel that heat and see that light, but men do not, because they are in natural heat and light; and while they are in the natural heat and light spiritual heat is not felt except by a certain enjoyment of love, and spiritual light is not seen except by a perception of truth. Now since man, so long as he is in natural heat and light, knows nothing of the spiritual heat and light within him, and since knowledge of these can be obtained only through experience from the spiritual world, the heat and light in which the angels and their heavens are, shall here be especially spoken of. From this and from no other source can enlightenment on this subject be had.

But degrees of spiritual heat cannot be described from experience, because love, to which spiritual heat corresponds, does not come thus under ideas of thought; but degrees of spiritual light can be described, because light pertains to thought, and therefore comes under ideas of thought. Yet degrees of spiritual heat can be comprehended by their relation to the degrees of light, for the two are in like degree. With respect then to spiritual light in which angels are, it has been granted me to see it with my eyes. With angels of the higher heavens, the light is so glistening white as to be indescribable, even by comparison with the shining whiteness of snow, and so glowing as to be indescribable even by comparison with the beams of this world's sun. In a word, that light exceeds a thousand times the noonday light upon earth. But the light with angels of the lower heavens can be described in a measure by comparisons, although it still exceeds the most intense light of our world. The light of angels of the higher heavens is indescribable, because their light makes one with their wisdom; and because their wisdom, compared to the wisdom of men, is ineffable, thus also is their light. From these few things it can be seen that there must be degrees of light; and because wisdom and love are of like degrees, it follows that there must be like degrees of heat.

Since atmospheres are the receptacles and containants of heat and light, it follows that there are as many degrees of atmospheres as there are degrees of heat and light; also that there are as many as there are degrees of love and wisdom. That there are several atmospheres, and that these are distinct from each other by means of degrees, has been manifested to me by much experience in the spiritual world; especially from this, that angels of the lower heavens are not able to breathe in the region of higher angels, and appear to themselves to gasp for breath, as living creatures do when they are raised out of air into ether, or out of water into air. Moreover, spirits below the heavens appear in a kind of cloud. That there are several atmospheres, and that they are distinct from each other by means of degrees, may be seen above (n. 176).

DEGREES ARE OF A TWOFOLD KIND, DEGREES OF HEIGHT AND DEGREES OF BREADTH. A knowledge of degrees is like a key to lay open the causes of things, and to give entrance into them. Without this knowledge, scarcely anything of cause can be known; for without it, the objects and subjects of both worlds seem to have but a single meaning, as if there were nothing in them beyond that which meets the eye; when yet compared to the things which lie hidden within, what is thus seen is as one to thousands, yea, to tens of thousands. The interiors which are not open to view can in no way be discovered except through a knowledge of degrees. For things exterior advance to things interior and through these to things inmost, by means of degrees; not by continuous degrees but by discrete degrees. "Continuous degrees" is a term applied to the gradual lessenings or decreasings from grosser to finer, or from denser to rarer; or rather, to growths and increasings from finer to grosser, or from rarer to denser; precisely like the gradations of light to shade, or of heat to cold. But discrete degrees are entirely different: they are like things prior, subsequent and final; or like end, cause, and effect. These degrees are called discrete, because the prior is by itself; the subsequent by itself; and the final by itself; and yet taken together they make one. There are atmospheres, from highest to lowest, that is, from the sun to the earth, called ethers and airs that are separated into such degrees; they are like simples, collections of simples, and again collections of these, which taken together are called a composite. Such degrees are discrete [or separate], because each has a distinct existence, and these degrees are what are meant by "degrees of height;" but the former degrees are continuous, because they increase continuously and these degrees are what are meant by "degrees of breadth."

Each and all things that have existence in the spiritual world and in the natural world, have conjoint existence from discrete degrees and from continuous degrees together, that is, from degrees of height and from degrees of breadth. The dimension which consists of discrete degrees is called height, and the dimension that consists of continuous degrees is called breadth; their position relatively to the sight of the eye does not alter the designation. Without a knowledge of these degrees nothing can be known of how the three heavens differ from each other; nor can anything be known of the differences of love and wisdom of the angels there; nor of the differences of heat and light in which they are; nor of the differences of atmospheres which environ and contain these. Nor without a knowledge of these degrees can anything be known of the differences among the interior powers of the minds of men, thus nothing of their state as regards reformation and regeneration; nor anything of the differences among the exterior powers of the bodies both of angels and men; and nothing whatever can be known of the distinction between spiritual and natural, thus nothing of correspondence. Nor, indeed, can anything be known of any difference between the life of men and that of beasts, or between the more perfect and the less perfect animals; neither of the differences among the forms of the vegetable kingdom, nor among the matters of the mineral kingdom. From which it can be seen that they who are ignorant of these degrees are unable to see causes from anything of judgment; they see only effects, and from these judge of causes, which is done for the most part by an induction that is continuous with effects. But causes produce effects not continuously but discretely; for cause is one thing, and effect is another. The difference between the two is like the difference between prior and subsequent, or between that which forms and that which is formed.

That it may be still better comprehended what discrete degrees are, what their nature is, and how they differ from continuous degrees, the angelic heavens may serve as an example. There are three heavens, and these are separated by degrees of height; therefore the heavens are one below another, nor do they communicate with each other except by influx, which proceeds from the Lord through the heavens in their order to the lowest; and not contrariwise. Each heaven by itself, however, is divided not by degrees of height but by degrees of breadth. Those who are in the middle, that is, at the center, are in the light of wisdom; but those who are around about, even to the boundaries, are in the shade of wisdom. Thus wisdom grows less and less even to ignorance, as light decreases to shade, which takes place continuously. It is the same with men. The interiors belonging to their minds are separated into as many degrees as the angelic heavens; and these degrees are one above another; therefore the interiors of men which belong to their minds are separated by discrete degrees, that is, degrees of height. Consequently a man may be in the lowest degree, then in a higher, and also in the highest degree, according to the degree of his wisdom; moreover, when he is in the lowest degree only, the higher degree is shut, - but is opened as he receives wisdom from the Lord. There are also in a man, as in heaven, continuous degrees, that is degrees of breadth. A man is like the heavens because as regards the interiors of his mind, he is a heaven in least form, in the measure in which he is in love and wisdom from the Lord. That man as regards the interiors of his mind is a heaven in least form may be seen in the work Heaven and Hell (n. 51-58.)

From all this it can be seen, that one who knows nothing about discrete degrees, that is, degrees of height, can know nothing about the state of man as regards his reformation and regeneration, which are effected through the reception of love and wisdom of the Lord, and then through the opening of the interior degrees of his mind in their order. Nor can he know anything about influx from the Lord through the heavens nor anything about the order into which he was created. For if anyone thinks about these, not from discrete degrees or degrees of height but from continuous degrees or degrees of breadth, he is not able to perceive anything about them from causes, but only from effects; and to see from effects only is to see from fallacies, from which come errors, one after another; and these may be so multiplied by inductions that at length enormous falsities are called truths.

I am not aware that anything has been known hitherto about discrete degrees or degrees of height, only continuous degrees or degrees of breadth have been known; yet nothing of the real truth about cause can become known without a knowledge of degrees of both kinds. These degrees therefore shall be treated of throughout this Part; for it is the object of this little work to uncover causes, that effects may-be seen from them, and thus the darkness may be dispelled in which the man of the church is in respect to God and the Lord, and in respect to Divine things in general which are called spiritual things. This I may mention, that the angels are in grief for the darkness on the earth; saying that they see light hardly anywhere, and that men eagerly lay hold of fallacies and confirm them, thereby multiplying falsities upon falsities; and to confirm fallacies men search out, by means of reasonings from falsities and from truths falsified, such things as cannot be controverted, owing to the darkness in respect to causes and the ignorance respecting truths. The angels lament especially over confirmations respecting faith separate from charity and justification thereby; also over men's ideas about God, angels and spirits, and their ignorance of what love and wisdom are.

DEGREES OF HEIGHT ARE HOMOGENEOUS, AND ONE IS FROM THE OTHER IN SUCCESSION LIKE END, CAUSE, AND EFFECT. As degrees of breadth, that is continuous degrees, are like gradations from light to shade, from heat to cold, from hard to soft, from dense to rare, from thick to thin, and so forth; and as these degrees are known from sensuous and ocular experience, while degrees of height, or discrete degrees, are not, the latter kind shall be treated of especially in this Part; for without a knowledge of these degrees, causes cannot be seen. It is known indeed that end, cause, and effect follow in order, like prior, subsequent, and final; also that the end begets the cause, and, through the cause, the effect, that the end may have form; also about these many other things are known; and yet to know these things, and not to see them in their applications to existing things is simply to know abstractions, which remain in the memory only so long as the mind is in analytical ideas from metaphysical thought. From this it is that although end, cause, and effect advance according to discrete degrees, little if anything is known in the world about these degrees. For a mere knowledge of abstractions is like an airy something which flies away; but when abstractions are applied to such things as are in the world, they become like what is seen with the eyes on earth, and remains in the memory.

All things which have existence in the world, of which threefold dimension is predicated, that is, which are called compounds, consist of degrees of height, that is, discrete degrees; as examples will make clear. It is known from ocular experience, that every muscle in the human body consists of minute fibers, and these put together into little bundles form larger fibers, called motor fibers, and groups of these form the compound called a muscle. It is the same with nerves; in these from minute fibers larger fibers are compacted, which appear as filaments, and these grouped together compose the nerve. The same is true of the rest of the combinations, bundlings and groupings out of which the organs and viscera are made up; for these are compositions of fibers and vessels variously put together according to like degrees. It is the same also with each and every thing of the vegetable and mineral kingdoms. In woods there are combinations of filaments in threefold order. In metals and stones there are groupings of parts, also in threefold order. From all this the nature of discrete degrees can be seen, namely, that one is from the other, and through the second there is a third which is called the composite; and that each degree is discreted from the others.

From these examples a conclusion may be formed respecting those things that are not visible to the eye, for with those it is the same; for example, with the organic substances which are the receptacles and abodes of thoughts and affections in the brains; with atmospheres; with heat and light; and with love and wisdom. For atmospheres are receptacles of heat and light; and heat and light are receptacles of love and wisdom; consequently, as there are degrees of atmospheres, there are also like degrees of heat and light, and of love and wisdom; for the same principle applies to the latter as to the former.

That these degrees are homogeneous, that is, of the same character and nature, appears from what has just been said. The motor fibers of muscles, least, larger, and largest, are homogeneous. Woody filaments, from the least to the composite formed of these, are homogeneous. So likewise are parts of stones and metals of every kind. The organic substances which are receptacles and abodes of thoughts and affections, from the most simple to their general aggregate which is the brain, are homogeneous. The atmospheres, from pure ether to air, are homogeneous. The degrees of heat and light in series, following the degrees of atmospheres, are homogeneous, therefore the degrees of love and wisdom are also homogeneous. Things which are not of the same character and nature are heterogeneous, and do not harmonize with things homogeneous; thus they cannot form discrete degrees with them, but only with their own, which are of the same character and nature and with which they are homogeneous.

That these things in their order are like ends, causes, and effects, is evident; for the first, which is the least, effectuates its cause by means of the middle, and its effect by means of the last.

It should be known that each degree is made distinct from the others by coverings of its own, and that all the degrees together are made distinct by means of a general covering; also, that this general covering communicates with interiors and inmosts in their order. From this there is conjunction of all and unanimous action.

THE FIRST DEGREE IS THE ALL IN EVERYTHING OF THE

SUBSEQUENT DEGREES. This is because the degrees of each subject and of each thing are homogeneous; and they are homogeneous because produced from the first degree. For their formation is such that the first, by bundlings or groupings, in a word, by aggregations of parts, produces the second, and through this the third; and discretes each from the other by a covering drawn around it; from which it is clear that the first degree is chief and singly supreme in the subsequent degrees; consequently that in all things of the subsequent degrees, the first is the all.

When it is said that degrees are such in respect to each other, the meaning is that substances are such in their degrees. This manner of speaking by degrees is abstract, that is, universal, which makes the statement applicable to every subject or thing which is in degrees of this kind.

This can be applied to all those things which have been enumerated in the preceding chapter, to the muscles, the nerves, the matters and parts of both the vegetable and mineral kingdoms, to the organic substances that are the subjects of thoughts and affections in man, to atmospheres, to heat and light, and to love and wisdom. In all these, the first is singly supreme in the subsequent things; yea, it is the sole thing in them, and because it is the sole thing in them, it is the all in them. That this is so is clear also from these well-known truths; that the end is the all of the cause, and through the cause is the all of the effect; and thus end, cause, and effect are called first, middle, and last end. Further, that the cause of the cause is also the cause of the thing caused; and that there is nothing essential in causes except the end, and nothing essential in movement excepting effort [conatus]; also, that the substance that is substance in itself is the sole substance.

From all this it can clearly be seen that the Divine, which is substance in itself, that is, the one only and sole substance, is the substance from which is each and every thing that has been created; thus that God is the All in all things of the universe, according to what has been shown in Part First, as follows. Divine Love and Divine Wisdom are substance and form (n. 40-43); Divine Love and Divine Wisdom are substance and form in itself, therefore the Very and the Only (n. 44-46); all things in the universe were created by Divine Love and Divine Wisdom (n. 52-60); consequently the created universe is His image (n. 61-65); the Lord alone is heaven where angels are (n. 113-118).

ALL PERFECTIONS INCREASE AND ASCEND ALONG WITH DEGREES AND ACCORDING TO THEM. That degrees are of two kinds, degrees of breadth and degrees of height has been shown above (n. 185-188); also that degrees of breadth are like those of light verging to shade, or of wisdom verging to ignorance; but that degrees of height are like end, cause and effect, or like prior, subsequent and final. Of these latter degrees it is said that they ascend or descend, for they are of height; but of the former that they increase or decrease for they are of breadth. These two kinds of degrees differ so much that they have nothing in common; they should therefore be perceived as distinct, and by no means be confounded.

All perfections increase and ascend along with degrees and according to them, because all predicates follow their subjects, and perfection and imperfection are general predicates; for they are predicated of life, of forces and of forms. Perfection of life is perfection of love and wisdom; and because the will and understanding are receptacles of love and wisdom, perfection of life is also perfection of will and understanding, consequently of affections and thoughts; and because spiritual heat is the containant of love, and spiritual light is the containant of wisdom, perfection of these may also be referred to perfection of life. Perfection of forces is perfection of all things that are actuated and moved by life, in which, however, there is no life. Atmospheres as to their active powers are such forces; the interior and exterior organic substances with man, and with animals of every kind, are such forces; all things in the natural world that are endowed with active powers both immediately and mediately from its sun are such forces. Perfection of forms and perfection of forces make one, for as the forces are, such are the forms; with the difference only, that forms are substances but forces are their activities; therefore like degrees of perfection belong to both. Forms that are not at the same time forces are also perfect according to degrees.

Section 5

The perfection of life, forces, and forms that increase or decrease according to degrees of breadth, that is, continuous degrees, will not be discussed here, because there is a knowledge of these degrees in the world; but only the perfections of life, forces, and forms that ascend or descend according to degrees of height, that is, discrete degrees; because these degrees are not known in the world. Of the mode in which perfections ascend and descend according to these degrees little can be learned from things visible in the natural world, but this can be seen clearly from things visible in the spiritual world. From things visible in the natural world it is merely found that the more interiorly they are looked into the more do wonders present themselves; as, for instance, in the eyes, ears, tongue; in muscles, heart, lungs, liver, pancreas, kidneys, and other viscera; also, in seeds, fruits and flowers; and in metals, minerals and stones. That wonders increase in all these the more interiorly they are looked into is well known; yet it has become little known thereby that the objects are interiorly more perfect according to degrees of height or discrete degrees. This has been concealed by ignorance of these degrees. But since these degrees stand out conspicuously in the spiritual world (for the whole of that world from highest to lowest is distinctly discreted into these degrees), from that world knowledge of these degrees can be drawn; and afterwards conclusions may be drawn therefrom respecting the perfection of forces and forms that are in similar degrees in the natural world.

In the spiritual world there are three heavens, arranged according to degrees of height. In the highest heavens are angels superior in every perfection to the angels in the middle heaven; and in the middle heaven are angels superior in every perfection to the angels in the lowest heaven. The degrees of perfections are such, that angels of the lowest heaven cannot attain to the first threshold of the perfections of the angels of the middle heaven, nor these to the first threshold of the perfections of the angels of the highest heaven. This seems incredible, yet it is a truth. The reason is that they are consociated according to discrete, not according to continuous degrees. I have learned from observation that the difference between the affections and thoughts, and consequently the speech, of the angels of the higher and the lower heavens, is such that they have nothing in common; and that communication takes place only through correspondences, which have existence by immediate influx of the Lord into all the heavens, and by mediate influx through the highest heaven into the lowest. Such being the nature of these differences, they cannot be expressed in natural language, therefore not described; for the thoughts of angels, being spiritual, do not fall into natural ideas. They can be expressed and described only by angels themselves, in their own languages, words, and writings, and not in those that are human. This is why it is said that in the heavens unspeakable things are heard and seen. These differences may be in some measure comprehended when it is known that the thoughts of angels of the highest or third heaven are thoughts of ends; the thoughts of angels of the middle or second heaven thoughts of causes, and the thoughts of angels of the lowest or first heaven thoughts of effects. It must be noted, that it is one thing to think from ends, and another to think about ends; that it is one thing to think from causes, and another to think about causes; and that it is one thing to think from effects, and another to think about effects. Angels of the lower heavens think about causes and about ends, but angels of the higher heavens from causes and from ends; and to think from these is a mark of higher wisdom, but to think about these is the mark of lower wisdom. To think from ends is of wisdom, to think from causes is of intelligence, and to think from effects is of knowledge. From all this it is clear that all perfection ascends and descends along with degrees and according to them.

Since the interior things of man, which are of his will and understanding, are like the heavens in respect to degrees (for man, as to the interiors of his mind, is a heaven in least form), their perfections also are like those of the heavens. But these perfections are not apparent to any one so long as he lives in the world, because he is then in the lowest degree; and from the lowest degree the higher degrees cannot be known; but they are known after death, because man then enters into that degree which corresponds to his love and wisdom, for he then becomes an angel, and thinks and speaks things ineffable to his natural man; for there is then an elevation of all things of his mind, not in a single, but in a threefold ratio. Degrees of height are in threefold ratio, but degrees of breadth are in single ratio. But into degrees of height none ascend and are elevated except those who in the world have been in truths, and have applied them to life.

It seems as if things prior must be less perfect than things subsequent, that is, things simple than things composite; but things prior out of which things subsequent are formed, that is, things simple out of which things composite are formed, are the more perfect. The reason is that the prior or the simpler are more naked and less covered over with substances and matters devoid of life, and are, as it were, more Divine, consequently nearer to the spiritual sun where the Lord is; for perfection itself is in the Lord, and from Him in that sun which is the first proceeding of His Divine Love and Divine Wisdom, and from that in those things which come immediately after; and thus in order down to things lowest, which are less perfect as they are farther removed. Without such preeminent perfection in things prior and simple, neither man nor any kind of animal could have come into existence from seed, and afterwards continue to exist; nor could the seeds of trees and shrubs vegetate and bear fruit. For the more prior anything prior is, or the more simple anything simple is, the more exempt is it from injury, because it is more perfect.

IN SUCCESSIVE ORDER THE FIRST DEGREE MAKES THE HIGHEST, AND THE THIRD THE LOWEST; BUT IN SIMULTANEOUS ORDER THE FIRST DEGREE MAKES THE INNERMOST, AND THE THIRD THE OUTERMOST. There is successive order and simultaneous order. The successive order of these degrees is from highest to lowest, or from top to bottom. The angelic heavens are in this order; the third heaven there is the highest, the second is the middle, and the first is the lowest; such is their relative situation. In like successive order are the states of love and wisdom with the angels there, also states of heat and light, and of the spiritual atmospheres. In like order are all the perfections of the forms and forces there. When degrees of height, that is, discrete degrees, are in successive order, they may be compared to a column divided into three stories, through which ascent and descent are made. In the upper rooms are things most perfect and most beautiful; in the middle rooms, things less perfect and beautiful; in the lowest, things still less perfect and beautiful. But simultaneous order, which consists of like degrees, has another appearance. In it, the highest things of successive order, which are (as was said above) the most perfect and most beautiful, are in the inmost, the lower things are in the middle, and the lowest in the circumference. They are as if in a solid body composed of these three degrees: in the middle or center are the finest parts, round about this are parts less fine, and in the extremes which constitute the circumference are the parts composed of these and which are therefore grosser. It is like the column mentioned just above subsiding into a plane, the highest part of which forms the innermost of the plane, the middle forms the middle, and the lowest the outermost.

As the highest of successive order becomes the innermost of simultaneous order, and the lowest becomes the outermost, so in the Word, "higher" signifies inner, and "lower" signifies outer. "Upwards" and "downwards," and "high" and "deep" have a like meaning.

In every outmost there are discrete degrees in simultaneous order. The motor fibers in every muscle, the fibers in every nerve, also the fibers and the little vessels in all viscera and organs, are in such an order. Innermost in these are the most simple things, which are the most perfect; the outermost is a composite of these. There is a like order of these degrees in every seed and in every fruit, also in every metal and stone; their parts, of which the whole is composed, are of such a nature. The innermost, the middle, and the outermost elements of the parts exist in these degrees, for they are successive compositions, that is, bundlings and massings together from simples that are their first substances or matters.

In a word, there are such degrees in every outmost, thus in every effect. For every outmost consists of things prior and these of their firsts. And every effect consists of a cause, and this of an end; and end is the all of cause, and cause is the all of effect (as was shown above); and end makes the inmost, cause the middle, and effect the outmost. The same is true of degrees of love and wisdom, and of heat and light, also of the organic forms of affections and thoughts in man (as will be seen in what follows). The series of these degrees in successive order and in simultaneous order has been treated of also in The Doctrine of the New Jerusalem Concerning the Sacred Scripture (n. 38, and elsewhere), where it is shown that there are like degrees in each and all things of the Word.

THE OUTMOST DEGREE IS THE COMPLEX, CONTAINANT AND BASE OF THE PRIOR DEGREES. The doctrine of degrees which is taught in this Part, has hitherto been illustrated by various things which exist in both worlds; as by the degrees of the heavens where angels dwell, by the degrees of heat and light with them, and by the degrees of atmospheres, and by various things in the human body, and also in the animal and mineral kingdoms. But this doctrine has a wider range; it extends not only to natural, but also to civil, moral, and spiritual things, and to each and all their details. There are two reasons why the doctrine of degrees extends also to such things. First, in every thing of which anything can be predicated there is the trine which is called end, cause, and effect, and these three are related to one another according to degrees of height. And secondly things civil, moral, and spiritual are not something abstract from substance, but are substances. For as love and wisdom are not abstract things, but substance (as was shown above, n. 40-43), so in like manner are all things that are called civil, moral, and spiritual. These may be thought of abstractly from substances, yet in themselves they are not abstract; as for example, affection and thought, charity and faith, will and understanding; for it is the same with these as with love and wisdom, in that they are not possible outside of subjects which are substances, but are states of subjects, that is, substances. That they are changes of these, presenting variations, will be seen in what follows. By substance is also meant form, for substance is not possible apart from form.

From its being possible to think of will and understanding, of affection and thought, and of charity and faith, abstractly from the substances which are their subjects, and from their having been so thought of, it has come to pass, that a correct idea of these things, as being states of substances or forms, has perished. It is altogether as with sensations and actions, which are not things abstract from the organs of sensation and motion. Abstracted, that is, separate, from these they are mere figments of reason; for they are like sight apart from an eye, hearing apart from an ear, taste apart from a tongue, and so forth.

Since all things civil, moral, and spiritual advance through degrees, just as natural things do, not only through continuous but also through discrete degrees; and since the progressions of discrete degrees are like progressions of ends to causes, and of causes to effects, I have chosen to illustrate and confirm the present point, that the outmost degree is the complex, containant, and base of prior degrees, by the things above mentioned, that is, by what pertains to love and wisdom, to will and understanding, to affection and thought, and to charity and faith.

That the outmost degree is the complex, containant, and base of prior degrees, is clearly seen from progression of ends and causes to effects. That the effect is the complex, containant, and base of causes and ends can be comprehended by enlightened reason; but it is not so clear that the end with all things thereof, and the cause with all things thereof, are actually in the effect, and that the effect is their full complex. That such is the case can be seen from what has been said above in this Part, particularly from this, that one thing is from another in a threefold series, and that the effect is nothing else than the end in its outmost. And since the outmost is the complex, it follows that it is the containant and also the base.

As regards love and wisdom:-Love is the end, wisdom the instrumental cause, and use is the effect; and use is the complex, containant, and base of wisdom and love; and use is such a complex and such a containant, that all things of love and all things of wisdom are actually in it; it is where they are all simultaneously present. But it should be borne in mind that all things of love and wisdom, which are homogeneous and concordant, are present in use, according to what is said and shown above (in chapter, n. 189-194).

Affection, thought, and action are also in a series of like degrees, because all affection has relation to love, thought to wisdom, and action to use. Charity, faith, and good works are in a series of like degrees, for charity is of affection, faith of thought, and good works of action. Will, understanding, and doing are also in a series of like degrees; for will is of love and so of affection, understanding is of wisdom and so of faith, and doing is of use and so of work; as, then, all things of wisdom and love are present in use, so all things of thought and affection are present in action, all things of faith and charity in good works, and so forth; but all are homogeneous, that is, concordant.

That the outmost in each series, that is to say, use, action, work, and doing, is the complex and containant of all things prior, has not yet been known. There seems to be nothing more in use, in action, in work, and in doing than such as there is in movement; yet all things prior are actually present in these, and so fully that nothing is lacking. They are contained therein like wine in its cask, or like furniture in a house. They are not apparent, because they are regarded only externally; and regarded externally they are simply activities and motions. It is as when the arms and hands are moved, and man is not conscious that a thousand motor fibers concur in every motion of them, and that to the thousand motor fibers correspond thousands of things of thought and affection, by which the motor fibers are excited. As these act deep within, they are not apparent to any bodily sense. This much is known, that nothing is done in or through the body except from the will through the thought; and because both of these act, it must needs be that each and all things of the will and thought are present in the action. They cannot be separated; consequently from a man's deeds or works others judge of the thought of his will, which is called his intention. It has been made known to me that angels, from a man's deed or work alone, perceive and see every thing of the will and thought of the doer; angels of the third heaven perceiving and seeing from his will the end for which he acts, and angels of the second heaven the cause through which the end operates. It is from this that works and deeds are so often commanded in the Word, and that it is said that a man is known by his works.

It is according to angelic wisdom that unless the will and understanding, that is, affection and thought, as well as charity and faith, clothe and wrap themselves in works or deeds, whenever possible, they are only like something airy which passes away, or like phantoms in air which perish; and that they first become permanent in man and a part of his life, when he practices and does them. The reason is that the outmost is the complex, containant, and base of things prior. Such an airy nothing and such a phantom is faith separated from good works; such also are faith and charity without their exercise, with this difference only, that those who hold to faith and charity know what is good and can will to do it, but not so those who are in faith separated from charity.

THE DEGREES OF HEIGHT ARE IN FULLNESS AND IN POWER IN THEIR OUTMOST DEGREE. In the preceding chapter it is shown that the outmost degree is the complex and containant of prior degrees. From this it follows that prior degrees are in their fullness in their outmost degree, for they are in their effect, and every effect is the fullness of causes.

That these ascending and descending degrees, also called prior and subsequent, likewise degrees of height or discrete degrees, are in their power in their outmost degree, may be confirmed by all those things that have been adduced in the preceding chapters as confirmations from objects of sense and perception. Here, however, I choose to confirm them only by the conatus, forces and motions in dead and in living subjects. It is known that conatus does nothing of itself, but acts through forces corresponding to it, thereby producing motion; consequently that conatus is the all in forces, and through forces is the all in motion; and since motion is the outmost degree of conatus, through motion conatus exerts its power. Conatus, force, and motion are no otherwise conjoined than according to degrees of height, conjunction of which is not by continuity, for they are discrete, but by correspondences. For conatus is not force, nor is force motion, but force is produced by conatus, because force is conatus made active, and through force motion is produced; consequently there is no power in conatus alone, nor in force alone, but in motion, which is their product. That this is so may still seem doubtful, because not illustrated by applications to sensible and perceptible things in nature; nevertheless, such is the progression of conatus, force, and motion into power.

But let application of this be made to living conatus, and to living force, and to living motion. Living conatus in man, who is a living subject, is his will united to his understanding; living forces in man are the interior constituents of his body, in all of which there are motor fibers interlacing in various ways; and living motion in man is action, which is produced through these forces by the will united to the understanding. For the interior things pertaining to the will and understanding make the first degree; the interior things pertaining to the body make the second degree; and the whole body, which is the complex of these, makes the third degree. That the interior things pertaining to the mind have no power except through forces in the body, also that forces have no power except through the action of the body itself, is well known. These three do not act by what is continuous, but by what is discrete; and to act by what is discrete is to act by correspondences. The interiors of the mind correspond to the interiors of the body, and the interiors of the body correspond to the exteriors, through which actions come forth; consequently the two prior degrees have power through the exteriors of the body. It may seem as if conatus and forces in man have some power even when there is no action, as in sleep and in states of rest, but still at such times the determinations of conatus and forces are directed into the general motor organs of the body, which are the heart and the lungs; but when their action ceases the forces also cease, and, with the forces, the conatus.

Since the powers of the whole, that is, of the body, are determined chiefly into the arms and hands, which are outmosts, "arms" and "hands," in the Word, signify power, and the "right hand" signifies superior power. And such being the evolution and putting forth of degrees into power, the angels that are with man and in correspondence with all things belonging to him, know merely from such action as is effected through the hands, what a man is in respect to his understanding and will, also his charity and faith, thus in respect to the internal life pertaining to his mind and the external life derived therefrom in the body. I have often wondered that the angels have such knowledge from the mere action of the body through the hands; but that it is so has been shown to me repeatedly by living experience, and it has been said that it is from this that inductions into the ministry are performed by the laying on of the hands, and that "touching with the hand" signifies communicating, with other like things. From all this the conclusion is formed, that the all of charity and faith is in works, and that charity and faith without works are like rainbows about the sun, which vanish away and are dispersed by a cloud. On this account "works" and "doing works" are so often mentioned in the Word, and it is said that a man's salvation depends upon these; moreover, he that doeth is called a wise man, and he that doeth not is called a foolish man. But it should be remembered that by "works" here are meant uses actually done; for the all of charity and faith is in uses and according to uses. There is this correspondence of works with uses, because the correspondence is spiritual, but it is carried out through substances and matters, which are subjects.

Two arcana, which are brought within reach of the understanding by what precedes, may here be revealed. The First Arcanum is that the Word is in its fullness and in its power in the sense of the letter. For there are three senses in the Word, according to the three degrees; the celestial sense, the spiritual sense, and the natural sense. Since these senses are in the Word according to the three degrees of height, and their conjunction is effected by correspondences, the outmost sense, which is the natural and is called the sense of the letter, is not only the complex, containant and base of the corresponding interior senses, but moreover in the outmost sense the Word is in its fullness and in its power. This is abundantly shown and proved in The Doctrine of the New Jerusalem Concerning the Sacred Scripture (n. 27-35, 36-49, 50-61, 62-69). The Second Arcanum is that the Lord came into the world, and took upon Him the Human, in order to put Himself into the power of subjugating the hells, and of reducing all things to order both in the heavens and on the earth. This Human He put on over His former Human. This Human which He put on in the world was like the human of a man in the world. Yet both Humans are Divine, and therefore infinitely transcend the finite humans of angels and men. And because He fully glorified the natural Human even to its outmosts, He rose again with the whole body, differently from any man. Through the assumption of this Human the Lord put on Divine Omnipotence not only for subjugating the hells, and reducing the heavens to order, but also holding the hells in subjection to eternity, and saving mankind. This power is meant by His "sitting at the right hand of the power and might of God." Because the Lord, by the assumption of a natural Human, made Himself Divine Truth in outmosts, He is called "the Word," and it is said that "the Word was made flesh;" moreover, Divine Truth in outmosts is the Word in the sense of the letter. This the Lord made Himself by fulfilling all things of the Word concerning Himself in Moses and the Prophets. For while every man is his own good and his own truth, and man is man on no other ground, the Lord, by the assumption of a natural Human, is Divine Good itself and Divine Truth itself, or what is the same, He is Divine Love itself and Divine Wisdom itself, both in Firsts and in Lasts. Consequently the Lord, since His advent into the world, appears as a sun in the angelic heavens, in stronger radiance and in greater splendor than before His advent. This is an arcanum which is brought within the range of the understanding by the doctrine of degrees. The Lord's omnipotence before His advent into the world will be treated of in what follows.

THERE ARE DEGREES OF BOTH KINDS IN THE GREATEST AND IN

THE LEAST OF ALL CREATED THINGS. That the greatest and the least of all things consist of discrete and continuous degrees, that is, of degrees of height and of breadth, cannot be illustrated by examples from visible objects, because the least things are not visible to the eyes, and the greatest things which are visible seem undistinguished into degrees; consequently this matter does not allow of demonstration otherwise than by universals. And since angels are in wisdom from universals, and from that in knowledge of particulars, it is allowed to bring forward their statements concerning these things.

The statements of angels on this subject are as follows: There can be nothing so minute as not to have in it degrees of both kinds; for instance, there can be nothing so minute in any animal, or in any plant, or in any mineral, or in the ether or air, as not to have in it degrees of both kinds, and since ether and air are receptacles of heat and light, and spiritual heat and spiritual light are the receptacles of love and wisdom, there can be nothing of heat and light or of love and wisdom so minute as not to have in it degrees of both kinds. Angels also declare that the minutest thing of an affection and the minutest thing of a thought, nay, the minutest thing of an idea of thought, consists of degrees of both kinds, and that a minute thing not consisting of these degrees would be nothing; for it would have no form, thus no quality, nor any state which could be changed and varied, and by this means have existence. Angels confirm this by the truth, that infinite things in God the Creator, who is the Lord from eternity, are one distinctly; and that there are infinite things in His infinites; and that in things infinitely infinite there are degrees of both kinds, which also in Him are one distinctly; and because these things are in Him, and all things were created by Him, and things created repeat in an image the things which are in Him, it follows that there cannot be the least finite in which there are not such degrees. These degrees are equally in things least and greatest, because the Divine is the same in things greatest and in things least. That in God-Man infinite things are one distinctly, see above (n. 17-22); and that the Divine is the same in things greatest and in things least (n. 77-82); which positions are further illustrated (n. 155, 169, 171).

There cannot be the least thing of love and wisdom, or the least thing of affection and thought, or even the least thing of an idea of thought, in which there are not degrees of both kinds, for the reason that love and wisdom are substance and form (as shown above, n. 50-53), and the same is true of affection and thought; and because there can be no form in which these degrees are not (as was said above), it follows that in these there are like degrees; for to separate love and wisdom, or affection and thought, from substance in form, is to annihilate them, since they are not possible outside of their subjects; for they are states of their subjects perceived by man varyingly, which states present them to view.

The greatest things in which there are degrees of both kinds, are the universe in its whole complex, the natural world in its complex, and the spiritual world in its complex; every empire and every kingdom in its complex; also, all civil, moral and spiritual concerns of these in their complex; the whole animal kingdom, the whole vegetable kingdom, and the whole mineral kingdom, each in its complex; all atmospheres of both worlds taken together, also their heats and lights. Likewise things less general, as man in his complex;

every animal in its complex, every tree and every shrub in its complex; as also every stone and every metal in its complex. The forms of these are alike in this, that they consist of degrees of both kinds; the reason is that the Divine, by which they were created, is the same in things greatest and least (as was shown above, n.77-82). The particulars and the veriest particulars of all these are like generals and the largest generals in this, that they are forms of both kinds of degrees.

On account of things greatest and least being forms of both kinds of degrees, there is connection between them from first to last; for likeness conjoins them. Still, there can be no least thing which is the same as any other; consequently all particulars are distinct from each other, likewise all veriest particulars. In any form or in different forms there can be no least thing the same as any other, for the reason that in greatest forms there are like degrees, and the greatest are made up of leasts. From there being such degrees in things greatest, and perpetual differences in accordance with these degrees, from top to bottom and from center to circumference, it follows that their lesser or least constituents, in which there are like degrees, can no one of them be the same as any other.

It is likewise a matter of angelic wisdom that from this similitude between generals and particulars, that is, between things greatest and least in respect to these degrees, comes the perfection of the created universe; for thereby one thing regards another as its like, with which it can be conjoined for every use, and can present every end in effect.

But these things may seem paradoxical, because they are not explained by application to visible things; yet things abstract, being universals, are often better comprehended than things applied, for these are of perpetual variety, and variety obscures.

Some contend that there can be a substance so simple as not to be a form from lesser forms, and out of that substance, through a process of massing, substantiated or composite things arise, and finally substances called material. But there can be no such absolutely simple substances. For what is substance without form? It is that of which nothing can be predicated; and out of mere being of which nothing can be predicated, no process of massing can make anything. That there are things innumerable in the first created substance of all things, which are things most minute and simple, will be seen in what follows, where forms are treated of.

IN THE LORD THE THREE DEGREES OF HEIGHT ARE INFINITE AND UNCREATE, BUT IN MAN THE THREE DEGREES ARE FINITE AND CREATED. In the Lord the three degrees of height are infinite and uncreate, because the Lord is Love itself and Wisdom itself (as has been already shown); and because the Lord is Love itself and Wisdom itself, He is also Use itself. For love has use for its end, and brings forth use by means of wisdom; for without use love and wisdom have no boundary or end, that is, no home of their own, consequently they cannot be said to have being and have form unless there be use in which they may be. These three constitute the three degrees of height in subjects of life. These three are like first end, middle end which is called cause, and last end which is called effect. That end, cause and effect constitute the three degrees of height has been shown above and abundantly proved.

That in man there are these three degrees can be seen from the elevation of his mind even to the degrees of love and wisdom in which angels of the second and third heavens are; for all angels were born men; and man, as regards the interiors pertaining to his mind, is a heaven in least form; therefore there are in man, by creation, as many degrees of height as there are heavens. Moreover, man is an image and likeness of God; consequently these three degrees have been inscribed on man, because they are in God-Man, that is, in the Lord. That in the Lord these degrees are infinite and uncreate, and in man finite and created, can be seen from what was shown in Part First; namely, from this, that the Lord is Love and Wisdom in Himself; and that man is a recipient of love and wisdom from the Lord; also, that of the Lord nothing but what is infinite can be predicated, and of man nothing but what is finite.

These three degrees with the angels are called Celestial, Spiritual, and Natural; and for them the celestial degree is the degree of love, the spiritual the degree of wisdom, and the natural the degree of uses. These degrees are so called because the heavens are divided into two kingdoms, one called the celestial, the other the spiritual, to which is added a third kingdom wherein are men in the world, and this is the natural kingdom. Moreover, the angels of whom the celestial kingdom consists are in love; the angels, of whom the spiritual kingdom consists are in wisdom; while men in the world are in uses; therefore these kingdoms are conjoined. How it is to be understood that men are in uses will be shown in the next Part.

It has been told me from heaven, that in the Lord from eternity, who is Jehovah, before His assumption of a Human in the world, the two prior degrees existed actually, and the third degree potentially, as they do also with angels; but that after the assumption of a Human in the world, He put on over these the third degree, called the natural, thereby becoming Man, like a man in the world; but with the difference, that in the Lord this degree, like the prior degrees, is infinite and uncreate, while in angel and in man they are all finite and created. For the Divine which, apart from space, had filled all spaces (n. 69-72), penetrated even to the outmosts of nature; yet before the assumption of the Human, the Divine influx into the natural degree was mediate through the angelic heavens, but after the assumption it was immediate from Himself. This is the reason why all churches in the world before His Advent were representative of spiritual and celestial things, but after His Advent became spiritual-natural and celestial-natural, and representative worship was abolished. This also was the reason why the sun of the angelic heaven, which, as was said above, is the first proceeding of His Divine Love and Divine Wisdom, after the assumption of the Human shone out with greater effulgence and splendor than before the assumption. And this is what is meant by these words in Isaiah: In that day the light of the moon shall be as the light of the sun, and the light of the sun shall be sevenfold, as the light of seven days (30:26). This is said of the state of heaven and of the church after the Lord's coming into the world. Again, in the Apocalypse: The countenance of the Son of man was as the sun shineth in his strength (1:16); and elsewhere (as in Isaiah 60:20; 2 Sam. 23:3, 4; Matt. 17:1, 2). The mediate enlightenment of men through the angelic heaven, which existed before the coming of the Lord, may be compared to the light of the moon, which is the mediate light of the sun; and because after His coming this was made immediate, it is said in Isaiah, That the light of the moon shall be as the light of the sun (30:26); and in David: In His days shall the righteous flourish, and abundance of peace until there is no longer any moon (72:7). This also is said of the Lord.

The reason why the Lord from eternity, that is, Jehovah, put on this third degree by the assumption of a Human in the world, was that He could enter into this degree only by means of a nature like human nature, thus only by means of conception from His Divine and by birth from a virgin; for in this way He could put off a nature which, although a receptacle of the Divine, is in itself dead, and could put on the Divine. This is meant by the Lord's two states in the world, which are called the state of exinanition and the state of glorification, which are treated of in The Doctrine of the New Jerusalem Concerning the Lord.

Of the threefold ascent of the degrees of height this much has been said in general; but these degrees cannot here be discussed in detail, because (as was said in the preceding chapter) there must be these three degrees in things greatest and things least; this only need be said, that there are such degrees in each and all things of love, and therefrom in each and all things of wisdom, and from both of these in each and all things of use. In the Lord all these degrees are infinite; in angel and man they are finite. But how there are these three degrees in love, in wisdom, and in uses cannot be described and unfolded except in series.

THESE THREE DEGREES OF HEIGHT ARE IN EVERY MAN FROM BIRTH, AND CAN BE OPENED SUCCESSIVELY; AND, AS THEY ARE OPENED, MAN IS IN THE LORD AND THE LORD IN MAN. That there are three degrees of height in every man, has not until now become known for the reason that these degrees have not been recognized, and so long as they remained unnoticed, none but continuous degrees could be known; and when none but continuous degrees are known, it may be supposed that love and wisdom increase in man only by continuity. But it should be known, that in every man from his birth there are three degrees of height, or discrete degrees, one above or within another; and that each degree of height, or discrete degree, has also degrees of breadth, or continuous degrees, according to which it increases by continuity. For there are degrees of both kinds in things greatest and least of all things (as was shown above, n. 222-229); for no degree of one kind is possible without degrees of the other kind.

These three degrees of height are called natural, spiritual, and celestial (as was said above, n. 232). When man is born he comes first into the natural degree, and this grows in him, by continuity, according to his knowledges and the understanding acquired by means of knowledges even to the highest point of understanding, which is called the rational. Yet not by this means is the second degree opened, which is called the spiritual. That degree is opened by means of a love of uses in accordance with the things of the understanding, although by a spiritual love of uses, which is love towards the neighbor. This degree may grow in like manner by continuous degrees to its height, and it grows by means of knowledges of truth and good, that is, by spiritual truths. Yet even by such truths the third degree which is called the celestial is not opened; for this degree is opened by means of the celestial love of use, which is love to the Lord; and love to the Lord is nothing else than committing to life the precepts of the Word, the sum of which is to flee from evils because they are hellish and devilish, and to do good because it is heavenly and Divine. In this manner these three degrees are successively opened in man.

So long as man lives in the world he knows nothing of the opening of these degrees within him, because he is then in the natural degree, which is the outmost, and from this he then thinks, wills, speaks, and acts; and the spiritual degree, which is interior, communicates with the natural degree, not by continuity but by correspondences, and communication by correspondences is not sensibly felt. But when man puts off the natural degree, which he does at death, he comes into that degree which has been opened within him in the world; he in whom the spiritual degree has been opened coming into that degree, and he within whom the celestial degree has been opened coming into that degree. He who comes into the spiritual degree after death no longer thinks, wills, speaks, and acts naturally, but spiritually; and he who comes into the celestial degree thinks, wills, speaks, and acts according to that degree. And as there can be communication between the three degrees only by correspondences, the differences of love, wisdom, and use, as regards these degrees are such as to have no common ground by means of anything continuous. From all this it is plain that man has three degrees of height that may be successively opened in him.

Since there are in man three degrees of love and wisdom, and therefore of use, it follows that there must be in him three degrees, of will, of understanding, and of result therefrom, thus of determination to use; for will is the receptacle of love, understanding the receptacle of wisdom, and result is use from these. From this it is evident that there are in every man a natural, a spiritual, and a celestial will and understanding, potentially by birth and actually when they are opened. In a word the mind of man, which consists of will and understanding, is from creation and therefore from birth, of three degrees, so that man has a natural mind, a spiritual mind, and a celestial mind, and can thereby be elevated into and possess angelic wisdom while he lives in the world; but it is only after death, and then only if he becomes an angel, that he enters into that wisdom, and his speech then becomes ineffable and incomprehensible to the natural man. I knew a man of moderate learning in the world, whom I saw after death and spoke with in heaven, and I clearly perceived that he spoke like an angel, and that the things he said would be inconceivable to the natural man; and for the reason that in the world he had applied the precepts of the Word to life and had worshiped the Lord, and was therefore raised up by the Lord into the third degree of love and wisdom. It is important that this elevation of the human mind should be known about, for upon it depends the understanding of what follows.

There are in man from the Lord two capacities whereby he is distinguished from beasts. One of these is the ability to understand what is true and what is good; this is called rationality, and is a capacity of his understanding. The other is an ability to do what is true and good; this is called freedom, and is a capacity of his will. For man by virtue of his rationality is able to think whatever he pleases, either with or against God, either with or against the neighbor; he is also able to will and to do what he thinks; but when he sees evil and fears punishment, he is able, by virtue of his freedom, to abstain from doing it. By virtue of these two capacities man is man, and is distinguished from beasts. Man has these two capacities from the Lord, and they are from Him every moment; nor are they taken away, for if they were, man's human would perish. In these two capacities the Lord is with every man, good and evil alike; they are the Lord's abode in the human race; from this it is that all men live for ever, both the good and evil. But the Lord's abode in man is nearer as by the agency of these capacities man opens the higher degrees, for by the opening of these man comes into higher degree of love and wisdom, thus nearer to the Lord. From this it can be seen that as these degrees are opened, man is in the Lord and the Lord in him.

It is said above, that the three degrees of height are like end, cause, and effect, and that love, wisdom, and use follow in succession according to these degrees; therefore a few things shall be said here about love as being end, wisdom as being cause, and use as being effect. Whoever consults his reason, if it is enlightened, can see that the end of all things of man is his love; for what he loves that he thinks, decides upon, and does, consequently that he has for his end. Man can also see from his reason that wisdom is cause; since he, that is, his love, which is his end, searches in his understanding for its means through which to attain its end, thus consulting its wisdom, and these means constitute the instrumental cause. That use is effect is evident without explanation. But one man's love is not the same as another's, neither is one man's wisdom the same as another's; so it is with use. And since these three are homogeneous (as was shown above, n. 189-194), it follows that such as is the love in man, such is the wisdom and such is the use. Wisdom is here spoken of, but by it what pertains to man's understanding is meant.

SPIRITUAL LIGHT FLOWS IN WITH MAN THROUGH DEGREES, BUT NOT SPIRITUAL HEAT, EXCEPT SO FAR AS MAN FLEES FROM EVILS AS SINS AND LOOKS TO THE LORD. It is evident from what has been shown above that from the sun of heaven, which is the first proceeding of Divine Love and Divine Wisdom (treated of in Part Second), light and heat proceed - light from its wisdom, and heat from its love; also that light is the receptacle of wisdom, and heat of love; also that so far as man comes into wisdom he comes into that Divine light, and so far as he comes into love he comes into that Divine heat. From what has been shown above it is also evident that there are three degrees of light and three degrees of heat, that is, three degrees of wisdom and three degrees of love, and that these degrees have been formed in man in order that he may be a receptacle of the Divine Love and the Divine Wisdom, thus of the Lord. It is now to be shown that spiritual light flows in through these three degrees in man, but not spiritual heat, except so far as man shuns evils as sins and looks to the Lord - or, what is the same, that man is able to receive wisdom even to the third degree, but not love, unless he flees from evils as sins and looks to the Lord; or what is still the same, that man's understanding can be raised into wisdom, but not his will, except so far as he flees from evils as sins.

That the understanding can be raised into the light of heaven, that is, into angelic wisdom, while the will cannot be raised into the heat of heaven, that is, into angelic love, unless man flees from evils as sins and looks to the Lord, has been made plainly evident to me from experience in the spiritual world. I have frequently seen and perceived that simple spirits, who knew merely that God is and that the Lord was born a man, and who knew scarcely anything else, clearly apprehended the arcana of angelic wisdom almost as the angels do; and not these simple ones alone, but many also of the infernal crew. These, while they listened, understood, but not when they thought within themselves; for while they listened, light entered from above, and when they thought within themselves, no light could enter except that which corresponded to their heat or love; consequently when they had listened to and perceived these arcana, as soon as they turned their ears away they remembered nothing, those belonging to the infernal crew even rejecting these things with disgust and utterly denying them, because the fire of their love and its light, being delusive, induced darkness, by which the heavenly light entering from above was extinguished.

The same thing happens in the world. A man not altogether stupid, and who has not confirmed himself in falsities from the pride of self-intelligence, hearing others speak on some exalted matter, or reading something of the kind, if he is in any affection of knowing, understands these things and also retains them, and may afterwards confirm them. A bad man as well as a good man may do this. Even a bad man, though in heart he denies the Divine things pertaining to the church, can still understand them, and also speak of and preach them, and in writing learnedly prove them; but when left to his own thought, from his own infernal love he thinks against them and denies them. From which it is obvious that the understanding can be in spiritual light even when the will is not in spiritual heat; and from this it also follows that the understanding does not lead the will, or that wisdom does not beget love, but only teaches and shows the way, - teaching how a man ought to live, and showing the way in which he ought to go. It further follows that the will leads the understanding, and causes it to act as one with itself; also that whatever in the understanding agrees with the love which is in the will, the love calls wisdom. In what follows it will be seen that the will does nothing by itself apart from the understanding, but does all that it does in conjunction with the understanding; moreover, that it is the will that by influx takes the understanding into partnership with itself, and not the reverse.

The nature of the influx of light into the three degrees of life in man which belong to his mind, shall now be shown. The forms which are receptacles of heat and light, that is, of love and wisdom in man, and which (as was said) are in threefold order or of three degrees, are transparent from birth, transmitting spiritual light as crystal glass transmits natural light; consequently in respect to wisdom man can be raised even into the third degree. Nevertheless these forms are not opened except when spiritual heat conjoins itself to spiritual light, that is, love to wisdom; by such conjunction these transparent forms are opened according to degrees. It is the same with light and heat from the sun of the world in their action on plants on the earth. The light of winter, which is as bright as that of summer, opens nothing in seed or in tree, but when vernal heat conjoins itself to that light then the heat opens them. There is this similarity because spiritual light corresponds to natural light, and spiritual heat to natural heat.

This spiritual heat is obtained only by fleeing from evils as sins, and at the same time looking to the Lord; for so long as man is in evils he is also in the love of them, for he lusts after them; and the love of evil and the lust, abide in a love contrary to spiritual love and affection; and such love or lust can be removed only by fleeing from evils as sins; and because man cannot flee from evils from himself, but only from the Lord. He must look to the Lord. So when he flees from evils from the Lord, the love of evil and its heat are removed, and the love of good and its heat are introduced in their stead, whereby a higher degree is opened; for the Lord flowing in from above opens that degree, and then conjoins love, that is, spiritual heat, to wisdom or spiritual light, from which conjunction man begins to flourish spiritually, like a tree in spring-time.

By the influx of spiritual light into all three degrees of the mind man is distinguished from beasts; and, as contrasted with beasts, he can think analytically, and see both natural and spiritual truth; and when he sees them he can acknowledge them, and thus be reformed and regenerated. This capacity to receive spiritual light is what is meant by rationality (referred to above), which every man has from the Lord, and which is not taken away from him, for if it were taken away he could not be reformed. From this capacity, called rationality, man, unlike the beasts, is able not only to think but also to speak from thought; and afterwards from his other capacity, called freedom (also referred to above), he is able to do those things that he thinks from his understanding. As these two capacities, rationality and freedom, which are proper to man, have been treated of above (n. 240), no more will be said about them here.

UNLESS THE HIGHER DEGREE WHICH IS THE SPIRITUAL IS OPENED IN MAN, HE BECOMES NATURAL AND SENSUAL. It was shown above that there are three degrees of the human mind, called natural, spiritual, and celestial, and that these degrees may be opened successively in man; also, that the natural degree is first opened; afterwards, if man flees from evil as sins and looks to the Lord, the spiritual degree is opened; and lastly, the celestial. Since these degrees are opened successively according to man's life, it follows that the two higher degrees may remain unopened, and man then continues in the natural degree, which is the outmost. Moreover, it is known in the world that there is a natural and a spiritual man, or an external and an internal man; but it is not known that a natural man becomes spiritual by the opening of some higher degree in him, and that such opening is effected by a spiritual life, which is a life conformed to the Divine precepts; and that without a life conformed to these man remains natural.

There are three kinds of natural men; the first consists of those who know nothing of the Divine precepts; the second, of those who know that there are such precepts, but give no thought to a life according to them; and the third, of those who despise and deny these precepts. In respect to the first class, which consists of those who know nothing of the Divine precepts, since they cannot be taught by themselves they must needs remain natural. Every man is taught respecting the Divine precepts, not by immediate revelations, but by others who know them from religion, on which subject see The Doctrine of the New Jerusalem Concerning the Sacred Scriptures (n. 114-118). Those of the second class, who know that there are Divine precepts but give no thought to a life according to them, also remain natural, and care about no other concerns than those of the world and the body. These after death become mere menials and servants, according to the uses which they are able to perform for those who are spiritual; for the natural man is a menial and servant, and the spiritual man is a master and lord. Those of the third class, who despise and deny the Divine precepts, not only remain natural, but also become sensual in the measure of their contempt and denial. Sensual men are the lowest natural men, who are incapable of thinking above the appearances and fallacies of the bodily senses. After death they are in hell.

As it is unknown in the world what the spiritual man is, and what the natural, and as by many he who is merely natural is called spiritual, and conversely, these subjects shall be separately discussed, as follows: (1) What the natural man is, and what the spiritual man. (2) The character of the natural man in whom the spiritual degree is opened. (3) The character of the natural man in whom the spiritual degree is not opened and yet not closed. (4) The character of the natural man in whom the spiritual degree is entirely closed. (5) Lastly, The nature of the difference between the life of a man merely natural and the life of a beast.

Section 6

1) What the natural man is, and what the spiritual man. Man is not man from face and body, but from understanding and will; therefore by the natural man and the spiritual man is meant that man's understanding and will are either natural or spiritual. The natural man in respect to his understanding and will is like the natural world, and may be called a world or microcosm; and the spiritual man in respect to his understanding and will is like the spiritual world, and may be called a spiritual world or heaven. From which it is evident that as the natural man is in a kind of image a natural world, so he loves those things which are of the natural world; and that as the spiritual man is in a kind of image a spiritual world, so he loves those things which are of that world, or of heaven. The spiritual man indeed loves the natural world also but not otherwise than as a master loves his servant through whom he performs uses. Moreover, according to uses the natural man becomes like the spiritual, which is the case when the natural man feels from the spiritual the delight of use; such a natural man may be called spiritual-natural. The spiritual man loves spiritual truths; he not only loves to know and understand them, but also wills them; while the natural man loves to speak of those truths and also do them. Doing truths is performing uses. This subordination is from the conjunction of the spiritual world and the natural world; for whatever appears and is done in the natural world derives its cause from the spiritual world. From all this it can be seen that the spiritual man is altogether distinct from the natural, and that there is no other communication between them than such as there is between cause and effect.

(2) The character of the natural man in whom the spiritual degree is opened. This is obvious from what has been said above; to which it may be added, that a natural man is a complete man when the spiritual degree is opened in him, for he is then consociated with angels in heaven and at the same time with men in the world, and in regard to both, lives under the Lord's guidance. For the spiritual man imbibes commands from the Lord through the Word, and executes them through the natural man. The natural man who has the spiritual degree opened does not know that he thinks and acts from his spiritual man, for it seems as if he did this from himself, when yet he does not do it from himself but from the Lord. Nor does the natural man whose spiritual degree has been opened know that by means of his spiritual man he is in heaven, when yet his spiritual man is in the midst of angels of heaven, and sometimes is even visible to them; but because he draws himself back to his natural man, after a brief stay there he disappears. Nor does the natural man in whom the spiritual degree has been opened know that his spiritual mind is being filled by the Lord with thousands of arcana of wisdom, and with thousands of delights of love, and that he is to come into these after death, when he becomes an angel. The natural man does not know these things because communication between the natural man and the spiritual man is effected by

correspondences; and communication by correspondences is perceived in the understanding only by the fact that truths are seen in light, and is perceived in the will only by the fact that uses are performed from affection.

(3) *The character of the natural man in whom the spiritual degree is not opened, and yet not closed.* The spiritual degree is not opened, and yet not closed, in the case of those who have led somewhat of a life of charity and yet have known little of genuine truth. The reason is, that this degree is opened by conjunction of love and wisdom, or of heat with light; love alone or spiritual heat alone not opening it, nor wisdom alone or spiritual light alone, but both in conjunction. Consequently, when genuine truths, out of which wisdom or light arises, are unknown, love is inadequate to open that degree; it only keeps it in the possibility of being opened; this is what is meant by its not being closed. Something like this is seen in the vegetable kingdom, in that heat alone does not cause seeds and trees to vegetate, but heat in conjunction with light effects this. It is to be known that all truths are of spiritual light and all goods are of spiritual heat, and that good opens the spiritual degree by means of truths; for good, by means of truths, effects use, and uses are goods of love, which derive their essence from a conjunction of good and truth. The lot, after death, of those in whom the spiritual degree is not opened and yet not closed, is that since they are still natural and not spiritual, they are in the lowest parts of heaven, where they sometimes suffer hard times; or they are in the outskirts in some higher heaven, where they are as it were in the light of evening; for (as was said above) in heaven and in every society there the light decreases from the middle to the outskirts, and those who above others are in Divine truths are in the middle, while those who are in few truths are in the outskirts. Those are in few truths who from religion know only that there is a God, and that the Lord suffered for them, and that charity and faith are essentials of the church, not troubling themselves to know what faith is or what charity is; when yet faith in its essence is truth, and truth is manifold, and charity is all the work of his calling which man does from the Lord; he does this from the Lord when he flees from evils as sins. It is just as was said above, that the end is the all of the cause, and the effect the all of the end by means of the cause; the end is charity or good, the cause is faith or truth, and effects are good works or uses; from which it is plain that from charity no more can be carried into works than the measure in which charity is conjoined with the truths which are called truths of faith. By means of these truths charity enters into works and qualifies them.

(4) *The character of the natural man in whom the spiritual degree is entirely closed.* The spiritual degree is closed in those who are in evils as to life, and still more in those who from evils are in falsities. It is the same as with the fibril of a nerve, which contracts at the slightest touch of any thing heterogeneous; so every motive fiber of a muscle, yea, the muscle itself, and even the whole body shrinks from the touch of whatever is hard or cold. So also the substances or forms of the spiritual degree in man shrink from evils and their falsities, because these are heterogeneous. For the spiritual degree, being in the form of heaven, admits nothing but goods, and truths that are from good; these are homogeneous to it; but evils, and falsities that are from evil, are heterogeneous to it. This degree is contracted, and by contraction closed, especially in those who in the world are in love of ruling from love of self,

because this love is opposed to love to the Lord. It is also closed, but not so much, in those who from love of the world are in the insane greed of possessing the goods of others. These loves shut the spiritual degree, because they are the origins of evils. The contraction or closing of this degree is like the twisting back of a spiral in the opposite direction; for which reason, that degree after it is closed, turns back the light of heaven; consequently there is thick darkness there instead of heavenly light, and truth which is in the light of heaven, becomes nauseous. In such persons, not only does the spiritual degree itself become closed, but also the higher region of the natural degree which is called the rational, until at last the lowest region of the natural degree, which is called the sensual, alone stands open; this being nearest to the world and to the outward senses of the body, from which such a man afterwards thinks, speaks, and reasons. The natural man who has become sensual through evils and their falsities, in the spiritual world in the light of heaven does not appear as a man but as a monster, even with nose drawn back (the nose is drawn in because the nose corresponds to the perception of truth); moreover, he cannot bear a ray of heavenly light. Such have in their caverns no other light than what resembles the light from live coals or from burning charcoal. From all this it is evident who and of what character are those in whom the spiritual degree is closed.

(5) The nature of the difference between the life of a natural man and the life of a beast. This difference will be particularly discussed in what follows, where Life will be treated of. Here it may be said only that the difference is that man has three degrees of mind, that is, three degrees of understanding and will, which degrees can be opened successively; and as these are transparent, man can be raised as to his understanding into the light of heaven and see truths, not only civil and moral, but also spiritual, and from many truths seen can form conclusions about truths in their order, and thus perfect the understanding to eternity. But beasts do not have the two higher degrees, but only the natural degrees, and these apart from the higher degrees have no capacity to think on any subject, civil, moral, or spiritual. And since the natural degrees of beasts are incapable of being opened, and thereby raised into higher light, they are unable to think in successive order, but only in simultaneous order, which is not thinking, but acting from a knowledge corresponding to their love. And because they are unable to think analytically, and to view a lower thought from any higher thought, they are unable to speak, but are able only to utter sounds in accordance with the knowledge pertaining to their love. Yet the sensual man, who is in the lowest sense natural, differs from the beast only in this, that he can fill his memory with knowledges, and think and speak therefrom; this power he gets from a capacity proper to every man, of being able to understand truth if he chooses; it is this capacity that makes the difference. Nevertheless many, by abuse of this capacity, have made themselves lower than beasts.

THE NATURAL DEGREE OF THE HUMAN MIND REGARDED IN ITSELF IS CONTINUOUS, BUT BY CORRESPONDENCE WITH THE TWO HIGHER DEGREES IT APPEARS WHEN IT IS ELEVATED AS IF IT WERE DISCRETE. Although this is hardly comprehensible, by those who have as yet no knowledge of degrees of height, it must nevertheless be revealed, because it is a part of angelic wisdom; and while the natural man is unable to think about this wisdom in the same way as angels do, nevertheless it can be comprehended by his understanding, when it has been raised into the degree of light in which angels are; for his understanding can be elevated even to that extent, and enlightened according to its elevation. But this enlightenment of the natural mind does not ascend by discrete degrees; but increases in a continuous degree, and as it increases, that mind is enlightened from within by the light of the two higher degrees. How this occurs can be comprehended from a perception of degrees of height, as being one above another, while the natural degree, which is the lowest, is a kind of general covering to the two higher degrees. Then, as the natural degree is raised up towards a degree of the higher kind, the higher acts from within upon the outer natural and illuminates it. This illumination is effected, indeed, from within, by the light of the higher degrees, but the natural degree which envelops and surrounds the higher receives it by continuity, thus more lucidly and purely in proportion to its ascent; that is, from within, by the light of the higher degrees, the natural degree is enlightened discretely, but in itself is enlightened continuously. From this it is evident that so long as man lives in the world, and is thereby in the natural degree, he cannot be elevated into very wisdom, such as the angels have, but only into higher light, even up to angels, and can receive enlightenment from their light that flows in from within and illuminates. But these things cannot as yet be more clearly described; they can be better comprehended from effects; for effects present causes in themselves in clear light, and thus illustrate them, when there is some previous knowledge of causes.

    The effects are these: (1) The natural mind may be raised up to the light of heaven in which angels are, and may perceive naturally, thus not so fully, what the angels perceive spiritually; nevertheless, man's natural mind cannot be raised into angelic light itself. (2) By means of his natural mind, raised to the light of heaven, man can think, yea, speak with angels; but the thought and speech of the angels then flow into the natural thought and speech of the man, and not conversely; so that angels speak with man in a natural language, which is the man's mother tongue. (3) This is effected by a spiritual influx into what is natural, and not by any natural influx into what is spiritual. (4) Human wisdom, which so long as man lives in the natural world is natural, can by no means be raised into angelic wisdom, but only into some image of it. The reason is, that elevation of the natural mind is effected by continuity, as from shade to light, or from grosser to purer. Still the man in whom the spiritual degree has been opened comes into that wisdom when he dies; and he may also come into it by a suspension of bodily sensations, and then by an influx from above into the spiritual parts of his mind. (5) Man's natural mind consists of spiritual substances together with natural substances; thought comes from its spiritual substances, not from its natural substances; these recede when the man dies, while its spiritual substances do not. Consequently, after death, when man becomes a spirit or angel, the same mind remains in a form like that which it had in the world. (6) The natural substances of that mind, which recede (as was said) by death, constitute the cutaneous covering of the spiritual body which spirits and angels have. By means of such covering, which is taken from the natural world, their spiritual bodies maintain existence; for the natural is the outmost containant: consequently there is no spirit or angel who was not born a man. These arcana of angelic wisdom are here adduced that the quality of the natural mind in man may be known, which subject is further treated of in what follows.

Every man is born into a capacity to understand truths even to the inmost degree in which the angels of the third heaven are; for the human understanding, rising up by continuity around the two higher degrees, receives the light of their wisdom, in the manner stated above (n. 256). Therefore man has the ability to become rational according to his elevation; if raised to the third degree he becomes rational from that degree, if raised to the second degree he becomes rational from that degree, if not raised he is rational in the first degree. It is said that he becomes rational from those degrees, because the natural degree is the general receptacle of their light. The reason why man does not become rational to the height that he might is, that love, which is of the will, cannot be raised in the same manner as wisdom, which is of the understanding. Love, which is of the will, is raised only by fleeing from evils as sins, and then by goods of charity, which are uses, which the man thereafter performs from the Lord. Consequently, when love, which is of the will, is not at the same time raised, wisdom, which is of the understanding, however it may have ascended, falls back again down to its own love. Therefore, if man's love is not at the same time raised into the spiritual degree, he is rational only in the lowest degree. From all this it can be seen that man's rational is in appearance as if it were of three degrees, a rational from the celestial, a rational from the spiritual, and a rational from the natural; also that rationality, which is the capacity whereby man is elevated, is still in man whether he be elevated or not.

It has been said that every man is born into that capacity, namely, rationality, but by this is meant every man whose externals have not been injured by some accident, either in the womb, or by some disease after birth, or by a wound inflicted on the head, or in consequence of some insane love bursting forth, and breaking down restraints. In such the rational cannot be elevated; for life, which is of the will and understanding, has in such no bounds in which it can terminate, so disposed that it can produce outmost acts according to order; for life acts in accordance with outmost determinations, though not from them. That there can be no rationality with infants and children, may be seen below (n. 266, at the end).

THE NATURAL MIND, SINCE IT IS THE COVERING AND CONTAINANT OF THE HIGHER DEGREES OF THE HUMAN MIND, IS REACTIVE; AND IF THE HIGHER DEGREES ARE NOT OPENED IT ACTS AGAINST THEM, BUT IF THEY ARE OPENED IT ACTS WITH THEM. It has been shown in the preceding chapter that as the natural mind is in the outmost degree, it envelops and encloses the spiritual mind and the celestial mind, which, in respect to degrees, are above it. It is now to be shown that the natural mind reacts against the higher or interior minds. It reacts because it covers, includes, and contains them, and this cannot be done without reaction; for unless it reacted, the interior or enclosed parts would become loosened and press outward and thus fall apart, just as the viscera, which are the interiors of the body, would push forth and fall asunder if the coverings which are about the body did not react against them; so, too, unless the membrane investing the motor fibers of a muscle reacted against the force of these fibers in their activities, not only would action cease, but all the inner tissues would be let loose. It is the same with every outmost degree of the degrees of height; consequently with the natural mind with respect to higher degrees; for, as was said above, there are three degrees of the human mind, the natural, the spiritual, and the celestial, and the natural mind is in the outmost degree. Another reason why the natural mind reacts against the spiritual mind is, that the natural mind consists not only of substances of the spiritual world but also of substances of the natural world (as was said above, n. 257), and substances of the natural world of their very nature react against the substances of the spiritual world; for substances of the natural world are in themselves dead, and are acted upon from without by substances of the spiritual world; and substances which are dead, and which are acted upon from without, by their nature resist, and thus by their nature react. From all this it can be seen that the natural man reacts against the spiritual man, and that there is combat. It is the same thing whether the terms "natural and spiritual man" or "natural and spiritual mind" are used.

From this it is obvious that when the spiritual mind is closed the natural mind continually acts against the things of the spiritual mind, fearing lest anything should flow in therefrom to disturb its own states. Everything that flows in through the spiritual mind is from heaven, for the spiritual mind in its form is a heaven; while everything that flows into the natural mind is from the world, for the natural mind in its form is a world. From which it follows that when the spiritual mind is closed, the natural mind reacts against all things of heaven, giving them no admission except so far as they are serviceable to it as means for acquiring and possessing the things of the world. And when the things of heaven are made to serve the natural mind as means to its own ends, then those means, though they seem to be heavenly, are made natural; for the end qualifies them, and they become like the knowledges of the natural man, in which interiorly there is nothing of life. But as things heavenly cannot be so joined to things natural that the two act as one, they separate, and, with men merely natural, things heavenly arrange themselves from without, in a circuit about the natural things which are within. From this it is that a merely natural man can speak and preach about heavenly things, and even simulate them in his actions, though inwardly he thinks against them; the latter he does when alone, the former when in company. But of these things more in what follows.

By virtue of the reaction which is in him from birth the natural mind, or man, when he loves himself and the world above all things, acts against the things that are of the spiritual mind or man. Then also he has a sense of enjoyment in evils of every kind, as adultery, fraud, revenge, blasphemy, and other like things; he then also acknowledges nature as the creator of the universe; and confirms all things by means of his rational faculty; and after confirmation he either perverts or suffocates or repels the goods and truths of heaven and the church, and at length either shuns them or turns his back upon them or hates them. This he does in his spirit, and in the body just so far as he dares to speak with others from his spirit without fear of the loss of reputation as a means to honor and gain. When man is such, he gradually shuts up the spiritual mind closer and closer. Confirmations of evil by means of falsities especially close it up; therefore evil and falsity when confirmed cannot be uprooted after death; they are only uprooted by means of repentance in the world.

But when the spiritual mind is open the state of the natural mind is wholly different. Then the natural mind is arranged in compliance with the spiritual mind, and is subordinated to it. For the spiritual mind acts upon the natural mind from above or within, and removes the things therein that react, and adapts to itself those that act in harmony with itself, whereby the excessive reaction is gradually taken away. It is to be noted, that in things greatest and least of the universe, both living and dead, there is action and reaction, from which comes an equilibrium of all things; this is destroyed when action overcomes reaction, or the reverse. It is the same with the natural and with the spiritual mind. When the natural mind acts from the enjoyments of its love and the pleasures of its thought, which are in themselves evils and falsities, the reaction of the natural mind removes those things which are of the spiritual mind and blocks the doors lest they enter, and it makes action to come from such things as agree with its reaction. The result is an action and reaction of the natural mind opposite to the action and reaction of the spiritual mind, whereby there is a closing of the spiritual mind like the twisting back of a spiral. But when the spiritual mind is opened, the action and reaction of the natural mind are inverted; for the spiritual mind acts from above or within, and at the same time it acts from below or from without, through those things in the natural mind which are arranged in compliance with it; and it twists back the spiral in which the action and reaction of the natural mind lie. For the natural mind is by birth in opposition to the things belonging to the spiritual mind; an opposition derived, as is well known, from parents by heredity. Such is the change of state which is called reformation and regeneration. The state of the natural mind before reformation may be compared to a spiral twisting or bending itself downward; but after reformation it may be compared to a spiral twisting or bending itself upwards; therefore man before reformation looks downwards to hell, but after reformation looks upwards to heaven.

THE ORIGIN OF EVIL IS FROM THE ABUSE OF THE CAPACITIES PROPER TO MAN, THAT ARE CALLED RATIONALITY AND FREEDOM. By rationality is meant the capacity to understand what is true and thereby what is false, also to understand what is good and thereby what is evil; and by freedom is meant the capacity to think, will and do these things freely. From what precedes it is evident, and it will become more evident from what follows, that every man from creation, consequently from birth, has these two capacities, and that they are from the Lord; that they are not taken away from man; that from them is the appearance that man thinks, speaks, wills, and acts as from himself; that the Lord dwells in these capacities in every man, that man by virtue of that conjunction lives to eternity; that man by means of these capacities can be reformed and regenerated, but not without them; finally, that by them man is distinguished from beasts.

That the origin of evil is from the abuse of these capacities will be explained in the following order: (1) A bad man equally with a good man enjoys these two capacities. (2) A bad man abuses these capacities to confirm evils and falsities, but a good man uses them to confirm goods and truths. (3) Evils and falsities confirmed in man are permanent, and come to be of his love, consequently of his life. (4) Such things as have come to be of the love and life are engendered in offspring. (5) All evils, both engendered and acquired, have their seat in the natural mind.

(1) A bad man, equally with a good man enjoys these two capacities. It was shown in the preceding chapter that the natural mind, as regards the understanding, can be elevated even to the light in which angels of the third heaven are, and can see truths, acknowledge them, and then give expression to them. From this it is plain that since the natural mind can be elevated, a bad man equally with a good man enjoys the capacity called rationality; and because the natural mind can be elevated to such an extent, it follows that a bad man can also think and speak about heavenly truths. Moreover, that he is able to will and to do them, even though he does not will and do them, both reason and experience affirm. Reason affirms it: for who cannot will and do what he thinks? His not willing and doing it is because he does not love to will and do it. This ability to will and to do is the freedom which every man has from the Lord; but his not willing and doing good when he can, is from a love of evil, which opposes; but this love he is able to resist, and many do resist it. Experience in the spiritual world has often corroborated this. I have listened to evil spirits who inwardly were devils, and who in the world had rejected the truths of heaven and the church. When the affection for knowing, in which every man is from childhood, was excited in them by the glory that, like the brightness of fire, surrounds each love, they perceived the arcana of angelic wisdom just as clearly as good spirits do who inwardly were angels. Those diabolical spirits even declared that they were able to will and act according to those arcana, but did not wish to. When told that they might will them, if only they would flee from evils as sins, they said that they could even do that, but did not wish to. From this it was evident that the wicked equally with the good have the capacity called freedom. Let any one look within himself, and he will observe that it is so. Man has the power to will, because the Lord, from whom that capacity comes, continually gives the power; for, as was said above, the Lord dwells in every man in both of these capacities, and therefore in the capacity, that is, in the power, of being able to will. As to the capacity to understand, called rationality, this man does not have until his natural mind reaches maturity; until then it is like seed in unripe fruit, which cannot be opened in the soil and grow up into a shrub. Neither does this capacity exist in those mentioned above (n. 259).

(2) A bad man abuses these capacities to confirm evils and falsities, but a good man uses them to confirm goods and truths. From the intellectual capacity called rationality, and from the voluntary capacity called freedom, man derives the ability to confirm whatever he wishes; for the natural man is able to raise his understanding into higher light to any extent he desires; but one who is in evils and in falsities therefrom, raises it no higher than into the upper regions of his natural mind, and rarely as far as the border of the spiritual mind; for the reason that he is in the delights of the love of his natural mind, and when he raises the understanding above that mind, the delight of his love perishes; and if it is raised still higher, and sees truths which are opposed to the delights of his life or to the principles of his self-intelligence, he either falsifies those truths or passes them by and contemptuously leaves them behind, or retains them in the memory as means to serve his life's love, or the pride of his self-intelligence.

That the natural man is able to confirm whatever he wishes is plainly evident from the multitude of heresies in the Christian world, each of which is confirmed by its adherents. Who does not know that evils and falsities of every kind can be confirmed ? It is possible to confirm, and by the wicked it is confirmed within themselves, that there is no God, and that nature is everything and created herself; that religion is only a means for keeping simple minds in bondage; that human prudence does everything, and Divine providence nothing except sustaining the universe in the order in which it was created; also that murders, adulteries, thefts, frauds, and revenge are allowable, as held by Machiavelli and his followers. These and many like things the natural man is able to confirm, and even to fill volumes with the confirmations; and when such falsities are confirmed they appear in their delusive light, but truths in such obscurity as to be seen only as phantoms of the night. In a word, take what is most false and present it as a proposition, and ask an ingenious person to prove it, and he will do so to the complete extinction of the light of truth; but set aside his confirmations, return and view the proposition itself from your own rationality, and you will see its falsity in all its deformity. From all this it can be seen that man is able to abuse these two capacities, which he has from the Lord, to confirm evils and falsities of every kind. This no beast can do, because no beast enjoys these capacities. Consequently, a beast is born into all the order of its life, and into all the knowledge of its natural love, but man is not.

(3) Evils and falsities confirmed in man are permanent, and come to be of his love and life. Confirming evil and falsity is nothing else than putting away good and truth, and if persisted in, is their rejection; for evil removes and rejects good, and falsity truth. For this reason confirming evil and falsity is a closing up of heaven, - for every good and truth flows in from the Lord through heaven, - and when heaven is closed, man is in hell, and in a society therein which a like evil prevails and a like falsity; from which hell he cannot afterwards be delivered. It has been granted me to speak with some who ages ago confirmed themselves in the falsities of their religion, and I saw that they remained in the same falsities, in the same way as they were in them in the world. The reason is, that all things in which a man confirms himself come to be of his love and life. They come to be of his love because they come to be of his will and understanding; and will and understanding constitute the life of every one; and when they come to be of man's life, they come to be not only of his whole mind but also of his whole body. From this it is evident that a man who has confirmed himself in evils and falsities is such from head to foot, and when he is wholly such, by no turning or twisting back can he be reduced to an opposite state, and thus withdrawn from hell. From all this, and from what precedes in this chapter, it can be seen what the origin of evil is.

(4) Such things as have come to be of the love, and consequently of the life, are engendered in offspring. It is known that man is born into evil, and that he derives it by inheritance from parents; though by some it is believed that he inherits it not from his parents, but through parents from Adam; this, however, is an error. He derives it from the father, from whom he has a soul that is clothed with a body in the mother. For the seed, which is from the father, is the first receptacle of life, but such a receptacle as it was with the father; for the

seed is in the form of his love, and each one's love is, in things greatest and least, similar to itself; and there is in the seed a conatus to the human form, and by successive steps it goes forth into that form. From this it follows that evils called hereditary are from fathers, thus from grandfathers and great-grandfathers, successively transmitted to offspring. This may be learned also from observation, for as regards affections, there is a resemblance of races to their first progenitor, and a stronger resemblance in families, and a still stronger resemblance in households; and this resemblance is such that generations are distinguishable not only by the disposition, but even by the face. But of this ingeneration of the love of evil by parents in offspring more will be said in what follows, where the correspondence of the mind, that is, of the will and understanding, with the body and its members and organs will be fully treated of. Here these few things only are brought forward, that it may be known that evils are derived from parents successively, and that they increase through the accumulations of one parent after another, until man by birth is nothing but evil; also that the malignity of evil increases according to the degree in which the spiritual mind is closed up, for in this manner the natural mind also is closed above; finally, that there is no recovery from this in posterity except through their fleeing from evils as sins by the help of the Lord. In this and in no other way is the spiritual mind opened, and by means of such opening the natural mind is brought back into correspondent form.

(5) All evils and their falsities, both engendered and acquired, have their seat in the natural mind. Evils and their falsities have their seat in the natural mind, because that mind is, in form or image, a world; while the spiritual mind in its form or image is a heaven, and in heaven evil cannot be entertained. The spiritual mind, therefore, is not opened from birth, but is only in the capability of being opened. Moreover, the natural mind derives its form in part from substances of the natural world; but the spiritual mind from substances of the spiritual world only; and this mind is preserved in its integrity by the Lord, in order that man may be capable of becoming a man; for man is born an animal, but he becomes a man. The natural mind, with all its belongings, is coiled into gyres from right to left, but the spiritual mind into gyres from left to right; the two thus curving in directions contrary to each other - a proof that evil has its seat in the natural mind, and that of itself it acts against the spiritual mind. Moreover, the gyration from right to left is turned downward, thus towards hell, but the gyration from left to right tends upward, thus toward heaven. This was made evident to me by the fact that an evil spirit can gyrate his body only from right to left, not from left to right; while a good spirit can gyrate his body from right to left only with difficulty, but with ease from left to right. Gyration follows the flow of the interiors, which belong to the mind.

EVILS AND FALSITIES ARE IN COMPLETE OPPOSITION TO GOODS AND TRUTHS, BECAUSE EVILS AND FALSITIES ARE DIABOLICAL AND INFERNAL, WHILE GOODS AND TRUTHS ARE DIVINE AND HEAVENLY. That evil and good are opposites, also the falsity of evil and the truth of good, every one acknowledges when he hears it. Still those who are in evil do not feel, and therefore do not perceive, otherwise than that evil is good; for evil gives enjoyment to their senses, especially sight and hearing, and from that gives enjoyment also to their thoughts, and thus their perceptions. While, therefore, the evil acknowledge that evil and good are opposites, still, when they are in evil, they declare from their enjoyment of it that evil is good, and good evil. For example:-One who abuses his freedom to think and to do what is evil calls that freedom, while its opposite, namely, to think the good which in itself is good, he calls bondage; when, in fact, the latter is to be truly free, and the former to be in bondage. He who loves adulteries calls it freedom to commit adultery, but not to be allowed to commit adultery he calls bondage; for in lasciviousness he has a sense of enjoyment, but of the contrary in chastity. He who is in the love of ruling from love of self feels in that love an enjoyment of life surpassing other enjoyments of every kind; consequently, everything belonging to that love he calls good, and everything contrary to it he declares to be evil; when yet the reverse is true. It is the same with every other evil. While every one, therefore, acknowledges that evil and good are opposites, those who are in evils cherish a reverse conception of such opposition, and only those who are in good have a right conception of it. No one so long as he is in evil can see good, but he who is in good can see evil. Evil is below as in a cave, good is above as on a mountain.

Now as many do not know what the nature of evil is, and that it is entirely opposite to good, and as this knowledge is important, the subject shall be considered in the following order: (1) The natural mind that is in evils and in falsities therefrom is a form and image of hell. (2) The natural mind that is a form and image of hell descends through three degrees. (3) The three degrees of the natural mind that is a form and image of hell, are opposite to the three degrees of the spiritual mind which is a form and image of heaven. (4) The natural mind that is a hell is in every respect opposed to the spiritual mind that is a heaven.

(1) The natural mind that is in evils and in falsities therefrom is a form and image of hell. The nature of the natural mind in man in its substantial form cannot here be described, that is, its nature in its own form woven out of the substances of both worlds, in the brains where that mind in its first principles, has its seat. The universal idea of that form will be given in what follows, where the correspondence of the mind and body is to be treated of. Here somewhat only shall be said of its form as regards the states and their changes, whereby perceptions, thoughts, intentions, volitions, and their belongings are manifested; for, as regards these states and changes, the natural mind that is in evils and their falsities is a form and image of hell. Such a form supposes a substantial form as a subject; for without a substantial form as a subject, changes of state are impossible, just as sight is impossible without an eye, or hearing without an ear. In regard, then, to the form or image wherein the natural mind images hell, that form or image is such that the reigning love with its lusts, which is the universal state of that mind, is like what the devil is in hell; and the thoughts of the false arising out of that reigning love are, as it were, the devil's crew. By "the devil" and by "his crew" nothing else is meant in the Word. Moreover, the case is similar, since in hell there is a love of ruling from love of self, a reigning love, called there the "devil;" and the affections of the false, with the thoughts arising out of that love, are called "his crew." It is the same in every society of hell, with differences resembling the differences of species in a genus. And the natural mind that is in evils and in falsities therefrom is in a similar form; consequently, a natural man who is of this

character comes, after death, into a society of hell similar to himself, and then, in each and every particular, he acts in unison with it; for he thus enters into his own form, that is, into the states of his own mind. There is also another love, called "satan," subordinate to the former love that is called the devil; it is the love of possessing the goods of others by every evil device. Cunning villainies and subtleties are its crew. Those who are in this hell are generally called satans; those in the former, devils; and such of them as do not act in a clandestine way there do not disown their name. From this it is that the hells, as a whole, are called the Devil and Satan. The two hells are generically divided in accordance with these two loves, because all the heavens are divided into two kingdoms, the celestial and the spiritual, in accordance with two loves; and the devil - hell corresponds, by opposites, to the celestial kingdom, and the satan - hell corresponds, by opposites, to the spiritual kingdom. That the heavens are divided into two kingdoms, the celestial and the spiritual, may be seen in the work Heaven and Hell (n. 20-28). The reason why a natural mind of such a character is in form a hell, is that every spiritual form is like itself both in what is greatest and in what is least; therefore every angel is, in lesser form, a heaven, as is also shown in the work on Heaven and Hell (n. 51-58); from which it follows that every man or spirit who is a devil or a satan is, in lesser form, a hell.

(2) The natural mind that is a form or image of hell descends through three degrees It may be seen above (n. 222-229) that both in the greatest and in the least of all things there are degrees of two kinds, namely, degrees of height and degrees of breadth. This is also true of the natural mind in its greatest and its least parts. Degrees of height are what are now referred to. The natural mind, by its two capacities called rationality and freedom, is in such a state as to be capable of ascending through three degrees, or of descending through three degrees; it ascends by goods and truths, and descends by evils and falsities. When it ascends, the lower degrees which tend to hell are shut, and when it descends, the higher degrees which tend to heaven are shut; for the reason that they are in reaction. These three degrees, higher and lower, are neither open nor shut in man in earliest infancy, for he is then ignorant both of good and truth and of evil and falsity; but as he lets himself into one or the other, the degrees are opened and shut on the one side or the other. When they are opened towards hell, the reigning love, which is of the will, obtains the highest or inmost place; the thought of the false, which is of the understanding from that love, obtains the second or middle place; and the result of the love through the thought, or of the will through the understanding, obtains the lowest place. The same is true here as of degrees of height treated of above; they stand in order as end, cause, and effect, or as first end, middle end, and last end. The descent of these degrees is towards the body, consequently in the descent they wax grosser, and become material and corporeal. If truths from the Word are received in the second degree to form it, these truths are falsified by the first degree, which is the love of evil, and become servants and slaves. From this it can be seen what the truths of the church from the Word become with those who are in the love of evil, or whose natural mind is in form a hell, namely, that they are profaned because they serve the devil as means; for the love of evil reigning in the natural mind that is a hell, is the devil, as was said above.

(3) The three degrees of the natural mind that is a form and image of hell, are opposite to the three degrees of the spiritual mind which is a form and image of heaven. It has been shown above that there are three degrees of the mind, called natural, spiritual, and celestial, and that the human mind, made up of these degrees, looks towards heaven, and turns itself about in that direction. From this it can be seen that the natural mind, looking downwards and turning itself about towards hell, is made up in like manner of three degrees, and that each degree of it is opposite to a degree of that mind which is a heaven. That this is so has been made very clear to me by things seen in the spiritual world; namely, that there are three heavens, and these distinct according to three degrees of height; that there are three hells, and these also distinct according to three degrees of height or depth; that the hells are opposed to the heavens in each and every particular; also that the lowest hell is opposite to the highest heaven, and the middle hell to the middle heaven, and the uppermost hell to the lowest heaven. It is the same with the natural mind that is in the form of hell; for spiritual forms are like themselves in things greatest and least. The heavens and hells are thus opposite, because their loves are opposed. In the heavens, love to the Lord, and consequent love to the neighbor, constitute the inmost degree; in the hells, love of self and love of the world constitute the inmost degree. In the heavens, wisdom and intelligence, springing from their loves, constitute the middle degree; in the hells folly and insanity, springing from their loves and appearing like wisdom and intelligence, constitute the middle degree. In the heavens, the results from the two other degrees, either laid up in the memory as knowledges, or determined into actions in the body, constitute the lowest degree; in the hells, the results from the two other degrees, which have become either knowledges or acts, constitute the outermost degree. How the goods and truths of heaven are turned, in the hells, into evils and falsities, thus into what is opposite, may be seen from this experience: I heard that a certain Divine truth flowed down out of heaven into hell, and that in its descent by degrees it was converted on the way into what is false, until at the lowest hell, it became the exact opposite of that truth; from which it was manifest that the hells according to degrees are in opposition to the heavens in regard to all goods and truths, these becoming evils and falsities by influx into forms turned the reverse way; for all inflowing, it is well known, is perceived and felt according to recipient forms and their states. This conversion into the opposite was made further evident to me from this experience: it was granted me to see the hells as they are placed relatively to the heavens; and those who were there appeared inverted, the head downward and the feet upward; but it was said that they nevertheless appear to themselves to be upright on their feet; comparatively like the antipodes. By these evidences from experience, it can be seen that the three degrees of the natural mind, which is a hell in form and image, are opposite to the three degrees of the spiritual mind which is a heaven in form and image.

(4) The natural mind that is a hell is in complete opposition to the spiritual mind which is a heaven. When the loves are opposite all things of perception become opposites; for out of love, which makes the very life of man, everything else flows like streams from their source; the things not from that source separating in the natural mind from those which are. Whatever springs from

man's reigning love is in the middle, and other things are at the sides. If these latter are truths of the church from the Word, they are transferred from the middle further away to the sides, and are finally exterminated; and then the man, that is, the natural mind, perceives evil as good, and sees falsity as truth; and conversely. This is why he believes perfidy to be wisdom, insanity to be intelligence, cunning to be prudence, and evil devices to be ingenuity; moreover, he makes nothing of Divine and heavenly things pertaining to the church and worship, while he regards bodily and worldly things as of the greatest worth. He thus inverts the state of his life, making what is of the head to be of the sole of the foot, and trampling upon it; and making what is of the sole of the foot to be of the head. Thus from being alive he becomes dead. One is said to be alive whose mind is a heaven, and one is said to be dead whose mind is a hell.

ALL THINGS OF THE THREE DEGREES OF THE NATURAL MIND ARE INCLUDED IN THE DEEDS THAT ARE DONE BY THE ACTS OF THE BODY. By the knowledge of degrees, which is set forth in this Part, the following arcanum is disclosed: all things of the mind, that is, of the will and understanding of man, are in his acts or deeds, included therein very much as things visible and invisible are in a seed or fruit or egg. Acts or deeds by themselves appear outwardly as these do, but in their internals there are things innumerable, such as the concurring forces of the motor fibers of the whole body and all things of the mind that excite and determine these forces, all of which, as shown above, are of three degrees. And since all things of the mind are in these, so also are things of the will, that is, all the affections of man's love, which make the first degree; all things of the understanding, that is, all thoughts from his perception, which makes the second degree; and all things of the memory, that is, all ideas of the thought nearest to speech, taken from the memory, which compose the third degree. Out of these things determined into act, deeds come forth, in which, seen in external form, prior things are not visible although they are actually therein. That the outmost is the complex, containant, and base of things prior may be seen above (n. 209-216); and that degrees of height are in fullness in their outmost (n. 217-221).

The acts of the body when viewed by the eye, appear thus simple and uniform, as seeds, fruits, and eggs do, in external form, or as nuts and almonds in their shells, yet they contain in themselves all the prior things from which they exist, because every outmost is sheathed about and is thereby rendered distinct from things prior. So is each degree enveloped by a covering, and thereby separated from other degrees; consequently things of the first degree are not perceived by the second, nor those of the second by the third. For example: The love of the will, which is the first degree of the mind, is not perceived in the wisdom of the understanding, which is the second degree of the mind, except by a certain enjoyment in thinking of the matter. Again, the first degree, which is, as just said, the love of the will, is not perceived in the knowledge of the memory, which is the third degree, except by a certain pleasure in knowing and speaking. From all this it follows that every deed, or bodily act, includes all these things, although externally it appears simple, and as if it were a single thing.

This is corroborated by the following: The angels who are with man perceive separately the things that are from the mind in the act, the spiritual angels perceiving those things therein that are from the understanding, and the celestial angels those things therein that are from the will. This appears incredible, but it is true. It should be known, however, that the things of the mind pertaining to any subject that is under consideration, or before the mind, are in the middle, and the rest are round about these according to their affinities therewith. The angels declare that a man's character is perceived from a single deed, but in a likeness of his love, which varies according to its determinations into affections, and into thoughts therefrom. In a word, before the angels every act or deed of a spiritual man is like a palatable fruit, useful and beautiful, which when opened and eaten yields flavor, use, and delight. That the angels have such a perception of the acts and deeds of men may also be seen above (n. 220).

It is the same with man's speech. The angels recognize a man's love from his tone in speaking, his wisdom from his articulation, and his knowledge from the meaning of the words. They declare, moreover, that these three are in every word, because the word is a kind of resultant, involving tone, articulation, and meaning. It was told me by angels of the third heaven that from each successive word that a man speaks in discourse they perceive the general state of his disposition, and also some particular states. That in each single word of the Word there is something spiritual from the Divine wisdom, and something celestial from the Divine love; and that these are perceived by angels when the Word is devoutly read by man, has been abundantly shown in The Doctrine of the New Jerusalem Concerning the Sacred Scripture.

The conclusion is, that in the deeds of a man whose natural mind descends through three degrees into hell there are all his evils and his falsities of evil; and that in the deeds of a man whose natural mind ascends into heaven there are all his goods and truths; and that both are perceived by the angels from the mere speech and act of man. From this it is said in the Word that a man "shall be judged according to his deeds," and that he shall render an account of his words.

PART FOURTH. THE LORD FROM ETERNITY, WHO IS JEHOVAH, CREATED THE UNIVERSE AND ALL THINGS THEREOF FROM HIMSELF, AND NOT FROM NOTHING. It is known throughout the world, and acknowledged by every wise man from interior perception, that God, who is the Creator of the universe, is One; and it is known from the Word that God the Creator of the universe is called "Jehovah," which is from the verb to be, because He alone is. That the Lord from eternity is that Jehovah is shown by many statements from the Word in The Doctrine of the New Jerusalem Concerning the Lord. Jehovah is called the Lord from eternity, since Jehovah assumed a Human that He might save men from hell; He then commanded His disciples to call Him Lord. Therefore in the New Testament Jehovah is called "the Lord;" as can be seen from this: Thou shalt love Jehovah thy God with all thy heart and with all thy soul (Deut. 5:5); but in the New Testament: Thou shalt love the Lord thy God with all thy heart and with all thy soul (Matt. 22:35). It is the same in other passages in the Gospels, taken from the Old Testament.

Every one who thinks from clear reason sees that the universe was not created out of nothing, for he sees that not anything can be made out of nothing;

since nothing is nothing, and to make anything out of nothing is a contradiction, and a contradiction is contrary to the light of truth, which is from Divine Wisdom; and whatever is not from Divine Wisdom is not from Divine Omnipotence. Every one who thinks from clear reason sees also that all things have been created out of a Substance that is Substance in itself for that is Esse itself, out of which every thing that is can take form; and since God alone is Substance in itself, and therefore Esse itself, it is evident that from this source alone is the formation of things. Many have seen this, because reason causes them to see it; and yet they have not dared to confirm it, fearing lest they might thereby be led to think that the created universe is God, because from God, or that nature is from itself, and consequently that the inmost of nature is what is called God. For this reason, although many have seen that the formation of all things is from God alone and out of his Esse, yet they have not dared to go beyond their first thought on the subject, lest their understanding should become entangled in a so-called Gordian knot, beyond the possibility of release. Such release would be impossible, because their thought of God, and of the creation of the universe by God, has been in accordance with time and space, which are properties of nature; and from nature no one can have any perception of God and of the creation of the universe; but every one whose understanding is in any interior light can have a perception of nature and of its creation out of God, because God is not in time and space. That the Divine is not in space may be seen above (n. 7-10); that the Divine apart from space fills all the spaces of the universe (n. 69-72); and that the Divine apart from time is in all time (n. 73-76). In what follows it will be seen that although God has created the universe and all things thereof out of Himself, yet there is nothing whatever in the created universe that is God; and other things besides, which will place this matter in its proper light.

Part First of this Work treated of God, that He is Divine Love and Divine Wisdom; that He is life, and that He is substance and form, which is the very and only Esse. Part Second treated of the spiritual sun and its world, and of the natural sun and its world, and of the creation of the universe with all things thereof from God by means of these two suns. Part Third treated of degrees in which are each and all things that have been created. Part Fourth will now treat of the creation of the universe from God. All these subjects are now explained, because the angels have lamented before the Lord, that when they look upon the world they see nothing but darkness, and among men no knowledge of God, of heaven, or of the creation of nature, for their wisdom to rest upon.

THE LORD FROM ETERNITY, THAT IS, JEHOVAH, COULD NOT HAVE CREATED THE UNIVERSE AND ALL THINGS THEREOF UNLESS HE WERE A MAN. Those who have a corporeal natural idea of God as a Man, are wholly unable to comprehend how God as a Man could have created the universe and all things thereof; for they think within themselves, How can God as a Man wander all over the universe from space to space, and create? Or how can He, from His place, speak the word, and as soon as it is spoken, creation follow? When it is said that God is a Man, such ideas present themselves to those whose conception of the God-Man is like their conception of a man in the world, and who think of God from nature and its properties, which are time and space. But those whose conception of God-Man is not drawn from their conception of a man in the world, nor from nature and its space and time, clearly perceive that unless God were a man the universe could not have been created. Bring your thought into the angelic idea of God as being a Man, putting away, as much as you can, the idea of space, and you will come near in thought to the truth. In fact, some of the learned have a perception of spirits and angels as not in space, because they have a perception of the spiritual as apart from space. For the spiritual is like thought, which although it is in man, man is nevertheless able by means of it to be present as it were elsewhere, in any place however remote. Such is the state of spirits and angels, who are men even as regards their bodies. In whatever place their thought is, there they appear, because in the spiritual world spaces and distances are appearances, and make one with the thought that is from their affection. From all this it can be seen that God, who appears as a sun far above the spiritual world, and to whom there can belong no appearance of space, is not to be thought of from space. And it can then be comprehended that He created the universe out of Himself, and not out of nothing; also that His Human Body cannot be thought great or small, that is, of any one stature, because this also pertains to space; consequently that in things first and last, and in things greatest and least, He is the same; and still further, that the Human is the inmost in every created thing, though apart from space. That the Divine is the same in things greatest and least may be seen above (n. 77-82); and that the Divine apart from space fills all spaces (n. 69-72). And because the Divine is not in space, it is not continuous [nec est continuum], as the inmost of nature is.

That God unless He were a Man could not have created the universe and all things thereof, may be clearly apprehended by any intelligent person from this, that he cannot deny that in God there is Love and Wisdom, mercy and clemency, and also goodness itself and truth itself, inasmuch as these are from God. And because he cannot deny this, neither can he deny that God is a Man; for abstractly from man not one of these is possible; for man is their subject, and to separate them from their subject is to say that they are not. Think of wisdom, and place it outside of man - is it anything? Can you conceive of it as something ethereal, or as something flaming? You cannot; unless perchance you conceive of it as being within these; and if within these, it must be wisdom in a form such as man has; it must be wholly in the form of man, not one thing can be lacking if wisdom is to be in that form. In a word, the form of wisdom is man; and because man is the form of wisdom, he is also the form of love, mercy, clemency, good and truth, because these make one with wisdom. That love and wisdom are not possible except in a form, see above (n. 50-53).

That love and wisdom are man is further evident from the fact that the angels of heaven are men in beauty in the measure in which they are in love and its wisdom from the Lord. The same is evident from what is said of Adam in the Word, that he was created into the likeness and into the image of God (Gen. 1:26), because into the form of love and wisdom. Every man on earth is born into the human form as regards his body, for the reason that his spirit, which is also called his soul, is a man; and this is a man because it is receptive of love and wisdom from the Lord; and so far as these are received by the spirit or soul of man, so far it becomes a man after the death of the material body which it had drawn about it; and so far as these are not received it becomes a monster, which derives something of manhood from the ability to receive.

Because God is a Man, the whole angelic heaven in the aggregate resembles a single man, and is divided into regions and provinces according to the members, viscera, and organs of man. Thus there are societies of heaven which constitute the province of all things of the brain, of all things of the facial organs, and of all things of the viscera of the body; and these provinces are distinct from each other, just as those organs are in man; moreover, the angels know in what province of Man they are. The whole heaven is in this image, because God is a Man. God is also heaven, because the angels, who constitute heaven, are recipients of love and wisdom from the Lord, and recipients are images. That heaven is in the form of all things of man is shown in the Arcana Coelestia, at the end of various chapters.

All this makes evident how empty are the ideas of those who think of God as something else than a Man, and of the Divine attributes as not being in God as a Man, since these separated from man are mere figments of reason. That God is very Man, from whom every man is a man according to his reception of love and wisdom, may be seen above (n. 11-13). This truth is here corroborated on account of what follows, that the creation of the universe by God, because He is a Man, may be perceived.

THE LORD FROM ETERNITY, THAT IS, JEHOVAH, BROUGHT FORTH FROM HIMSELF THE SUN OF THE SPIRITUAL WORLD, AND FROM THAT CREATED THE UNIVERSE AND ALL THINGS THEREOF. The sun of the spiritual world was treated of in Part Second of this work, and the following propositions were there established:-Divine Love and Divine Wisdom appear in the spiritual world as a sun (n. 83-88). Spiritual heat and spiritual light go forth from that sun (n. 89-92). That sun is not God, but is a Proceeding from the Divine Love and Divine Wisdom of God-Man; so also are the heat and light from that sun (n. 93-98). The sun of the spiritual world is at a middle altitude, and appears far off from the angels like the sun of the natural world from men (n. 103-107). In the spiritual world the east is where the Lord appears as a sun, and from that the other quarters are determined (n. 119-123, 125-128). Angels turn their faces constantly to the Lord as a sum (n. 129-134, 135-139). The Lord created the universe and all things thereof by means of the sun, which is the first proceeding of Divine Love and Divine Wisdom (n. 151-156). The sun of the natural world is mere fire, and nature, which derives its origin from that sun, is consequently dead; and the sun of the natural world was created in order that the work of creation might completed and finished (n. 157-162). Without a double sun, one living and the other dead, no creation is possible (n. 163-166).

This also, among other things, is shown in Part Second:-that the spiritual sun is not the Lord, but is a Proceeding from His Divine Love and His Divine Wisdom. It is called a proceeding, because the sun was brought forth out of Divine Love and Divine Wisdom which are in themselves substance and form, and it is by means of this that the Divine proceeds. But as human reason is such as to be unwilling to yield assent unless it sees a thing from its cause, and therefore has some perception of how it is, - thus in the present case, how the sun of the spiritual world, which is not the Lord, but a proceeding from Him, was brought forth - something shall be said on this subject. In regard to this matter I have conversed much with the angels. They said that they have a clear perception of it in their own spiritual light, but that they cannot easily present it to man, in his natural light, owing to the difference between the two kinds of light and the consequent difference of thought. The matter, however, may be likened, they said, to the sphere of affections and of thoughts therefrom which encompasses each angel, whereby his presence is made evident to others near and far. But that encompassing sphere, they said, is not the angel himself; it is from each and everything of his body, wherefrom substances are constantly flowing out like a stream, and what flows out surrounds him; also that these substances, contiguous to his body, as they are constantly moved by his life's two fountains of motion, the heart and the lungs, arouse the same activities in the atmospheres, and thereby produce a perception as of his presence with others; therefore that it is not a separate sphere of affections and of thoughts therefrom that goes forth and is continuous from him, although it is so called, since the affections are mere states of the mind's forms in the angel. They said, moreover, that there is such a sphere about every angel, because there is one about the Lord, and that the sphere about the Lord is in like manner from Him, and that that sphere is their sun, that is, the sun of the spiritual world.

A perception has often been granted me of such a sphere around each angel and spirit, and also a general sphere around many in a society. I have also been permitted to see it under various appearances, in heaven sometimes appearing like a thin flame, in hell like gross fire, also sometimes in heaven like a thin and shining white cloud, and in hell like a thick and black cloud. It has also been granted me to perceive these spheres as various kinds of odors and stenches. By these experiences I was convinced that a sphere, consisting of substances set free and separated from- their bodies, encompasses every one in heaven and every one in hell.

It was also perceived that a sphere flows forth, not only from angels and spirits but also from each and all things that appear in the spiritual world, - from trees and from their fruits, from shrubs and from their flowers, from herbs, and from grasses, even from the soils and from their very particles. From which it was patent that both in the case of things living and things dead this is a universal law, That each thing is encompassed by something like that which is within it, and that this is continually exhaled from it. It is known, from the observation of many learned men, that it is the same in the natural world - that is, that there is a wave of effluvia constantly flowing forth out of man, also out of every animal, likewise out of tree, fruit, shrub, flower, and even out of metal and stone. This the natural world derives from the spiritual, and the spiritual world from the Divine.

Because those things that constitute the sun of the spiritual world are from the Lord, but are not the Lord, they are not life in itself, but are devoid of life in itself; just as those things that flow forth from angel or man, and constitute spheres around him are not the angel or the man, but are from him, and devoid of his life. These spheres make one with the angel or man no otherwise than that they are concordant; and this they are because taken from the forms of their bodies, which in them were forms of their life. This is an arcanum which angels, with their spiritual ideas, are able to see in thought and also express in speech, but men with their natural ideas are not; because a thousand spiritual ideas make one natural idea, and one natural idea cannot be resolved by man into any spiritual idea, much less into so many. The reason is that these ideas differ according to degrees of height, which were treated of in Part Third.

That there is such a difference between the thoughts of angels and the thoughts of men was made known to me by this experience: The angels were asked to think spiritually on some subject, and afterwards to tell me what they had thought. This they did; but when they wished to tell me they could not, and said that these things could not be expressed in words. It was the same with their spiritual language and their spiritual writing; there was not a word of spiritual language that was like any word of natural language; nor was there anything of spiritual writing like natural writing, except the letters, each of which contained an entire meaning. But what is wonderful, they said that they seemed to themselves to think, speak, and write in the spiritual state in the same manner that man does in the natural state, when yet there is no similarity. From this it was plain that the natural and the spiritual differ according to degrees of height, and that they communicate with each other only by correspondences.

THERE ARE IN THE LORD THREE THINGS THAT ARE THE LORD, THE DIVINE OF LOVE, THE DIVINE OF WISDOM, AND THE DIVINE OF USE; AND THESE THREE ARE PRESENTED IN APPEARANCE OUTSIDE OF THE SUN OF THE SPIRITUAL WORLD, THE DIVINE OF LOVE BY HEAT, THE DIVINE OF WISDOM BY LIGHT AND THE DIVINE OF USE BY THE ATMOSPHERE WHICH IS THEIR CONTAINANT. That heat and light go forth out of the sun of the spiritual world, heat out of the Lord's Divine Love, and light out of His Divine Wisdom, may be seen above (n. 89-92, 99-102, 156-150). Now it will be shown that the third which goes forth out of that sun is the atmosphere, which is the containant of heat and light, and that this goes forth out of the Lord's Divine which is called Use.

Any one who thinks with any enlightenment can see that love has use for an end and intends it, and brings it forth by means of wisdom; for love can bring forth no use of itself, but only by wisdom as a medium. What, in fact, is love unless there be something loved? That something is use; and because use is that which is loved, and is brought forth by means of wisdom, it follows that use is the containant of wisdom and love. That these three, love, wisdom and use follow in order according to degrees of height, and that the outmost degree is the complex, containant, and base of the prior degrees has been shown (n. 209-216, and elsewhere). From all this it can be seen that these three, the Divine of Love, the Divine of Wisdom, and the Divine of Use, are in the Lord, and are the Lord in essence.

That man, as regards both his exteriors and his interiors, is a form of all uses, and that all the uses in the created universe correspond to those uses in him, will be fully shown in what follows; it need only be mentioned here, that it may be known that God as a Man is the form itself of all uses, from which form all uses in the created universe derive their origin, thus that the created universe, viewed as to uses, is an image of Him. Those things are called uses which from God-Man, that is, from the Lord, are by creation in order; but those things which are from what is man's own are not called uses; since what is man's own is hell, and whatever is therefrom is contrary to order.

Now since these three, love, wisdom, and use, are in the Lord, and are the Lord; and since the Lord is everywhere, for He is omnipresent; and since the Lord cannot make Himself present, such as He is in Himself and such as He is in His own sun, to any angel or man, He therefore presents Himself by means of such things as can be received, presenting Himself, as to love by heat, as to wisdom by light, and as to use by an atmosphere. The Lord presents Himself as to use by an atmosphere, because an atmosphere is a containant of heat and light, as use is the containant of love and wisdom. For light and heat going forth from the Divine Sun cannot go forth in nothing, that is, in vacuum, but must go forth in a containant which is a subject. This containant we call an atmosphere; and this encompasses the sun, receiving the sun in its bosom, and bearing it to heaven where angels are, and then to the world where men are, thus making the Lord's presence everywhere manifest.

That there are atmospheres in the angelic world, as well as in the natural world, has been shown above (n. 173-178, 179-183). It was there declared that the atmospheres of the spiritual world are spiritual, and the atmospheres of the natural world are natural. It can now be seen, from the origin of the spiritual atmosphere most closely encompassing the spiritual sun, that everything belonging to it is in its essence such as the sun is in its essence. The angels, by means of their spiritual ideas, which are apart from space, elucidate this truth as follows: There is only one substance from which all things are, and the sun of the spiritual world is that substance; and since the Divine is not in space, and is the same in things greatest and least, this is also true of that sun which is the first going forth of God-Man; furthermore, this one only substance, which is the sun, going forth by means of atmospheres according to continuous degrees or degrees of breadth, and at the same time according to discrete degrees or degrees of height presents the varieties of all things in the created universe. The angels declared that these things are totally incomprehensible, unless spaces be removed from the ideas; and if not removed, appearances must needs induce fallacies. But so long as the thought is held that God is the very Esse from which all things are, fallacies cannot enter.

Section 7

It is evident, moreover, from angelic ideas, which are apart from space, that in the created universe nothing lives except God-Man, that is, the Lord, neither is anything moved except by life from Him, nor has being except through the sun from Him; so that it is a truth, that in God we live, and move, and have our being.

THE ATMOSPHERES, OF WHICH THERE ARE THREE BOTH IN THE SPIRITUAL AND IN THE NATURAL WORLD, IN THEIR OUTMOSTS CLOSE INTO SUBSTANCES AND MATTERS SUCH AS ARE IN LANDS. It has been shown in Part Third (n. 173-176), that there are three atmospheres both in the spiritual and in the natural world, which are distinct from each other according to degrees of height, and which, in their progress toward lower things, decrease [in activity] according to degrees of breadth. And since atmospheres in their progress toward lower things decrease [in activity], it follows that they constantly become more compressed and inert, and finally, in outmosts, become so compressed and inert as to be no longer atmospheres, but substances at rest, and in the natural world, fixed like those in the lands that are called matters. As such is the origin of substances and matters, it follows, first, that these substances and matters also are of three degrees; secondly, that they are held together in mutual connection by encompassing atmospheres; thirdly, that they are fitted for the production of all uses in their forms.

That such substances or matters as are in earths, were brought forth by the sun through its atmospheres any one will readily acknowledge who reflects that there are continual mediations from the First to outmosts, and that nothing can take form except from what is prior to itself, and so finally from the First. The First is the sun of the spiritual world, and the First of that sun is God-Man, or the Lord. Now as atmospheres are those prior things, whereby the spiritual sun manifests itself in outmosts, and as these prior things continually decrease in activity and expansion down to the outmosts, it follows that when their activity and expansion come to an end in outmosts they become substances, and matters such as are in lands, which retain within them, from the atmospheres out of which they originated, an effort and conatus to bring forth uses. Those who do not evolve the creation of the universe and all things thereof by continuous mediations from the First [Being], can but hold hypotheses, disjoined and divorced from their causes, which, when surveyed by a mind with an interior perception of things, do not appear like a house, but like heaps of rubbish.

From this universal origin of all things in the created universe, every particular thereof has a similar order; in that these also go forth from their first to outmosts which are relatively in a state of rest, that they may terminate and become permanent. Thus in the human body fibers proceed from their first forms until at last they become tendons; also fibers with vessels proceed from their first forms until they become cartilages and bones; upon these they may rest and become permanent. Because of such a progression of fibers and vessels in man from firsts to outmosts, there is a similar progression of their states, which are sensations, thoughts, and affections. These, also, from their firsts, where they are in light, proceed through to outmosts, where they are in shade; or from their firsts, where they are in heat, to outmosts where they are not in heat. With such a progression of these there is also a like progression of love and of all things thereof, and of wisdom and all things thereof. In a word, such is the progression of all things in the created universe. This is the same as was shown above (n. 222-229), that there are degrees of both kinds in the greatest and least of all created things. There are degrees of both kinds even in the least things of all, because the spiritual sun is the sole substance from which all things are (according to the spiritual ideas of the angels, n. 300).

IN THE SUBSTANCES AND MATTERS OF WHICH LANDS ARE FORMED THERE IS NOTHING OF THE DIVINE IN ITSELF, BUT STILL THEY ARE FROM THE DIVINE IN ITSELF. From the origin of lands (treated of in the preceding chapter), it can be seen, that in their substances and matters there is nothing of the Divine in itself, but that they are devoid of all-that is Divine in itself. For they are, as was said, the endings and closings of the atmospheres, whose heat has died away into cold, whose light into darkness, and whose activity into inertness. Nevertheless, by continuation from the substance of the spiritual sun, they have brought with them what there was in that substance from the Divine, which (as said above, n. 291-298), was the sphere encompassing God-Man, or the Lord. From that sphere, by continuation from the sun through the atmospheres as mediums have arisen the substances and matters of which the lands are formed.

The origin of lands from the spiritual sun through the atmospheres, as mediums, can no otherwise be described by expressions flowing out of natural ideas, but may by expressions flowing out of spiritual ideas, because these are apart from space, and for this reason, they do not fall into any expressions of natural language. That spiritual thoughts, speech, and writings differ so entirely from natural thoughts, speech, and writings, that they have nothing in common, and have communication only by correspondences, may be seen above (n. 295). It may suffice, therefore, if the origin of lands be perceived in some measure naturally.

ALL USES, WHICH ARE ENDS OF CREATION ARE IN FORMS, WHICH FORMS THEY TAKE FROM SUBSTANCES AND MATTERS SUCH AS ARE IN LANDS. All things treated of hitherto, as the sun, atmospheres, and lands, are only means to ends. The ends of creation are those things that are produced by the Lord as a sun, through the atmospheres, out of lands; and these ends are called uses. In their whole extent these are all things of the vegetable kingdom, all things of the animal kingdom, and finally the human race, and the angelic heaven which is from it. These are called uses, because they are recipients of Divine Love and Divine Wisdom also because they have regard to God the Creator from whom they are, and thereby conjoin Him to His great work; by which conjunction it comes that, as they spring forth from Him, so do they have unceasing existence from Him. They are said to have regard to God the Creator from whom they are, and to conjoin Him to His great work, but this is to speak according to appearance. It is meant that God the Creator causes them to have regard and to conjoin themselves to Him as it were of themselves; but how they have regard and thereby conjoin will be declared in what follows. Something has been said before on these subjects in their place, as that Divine Love and Divine Wisdom must necessarily have being and form in other things created by themselves (n. 37-51); that all things in the created universe are recipients of Divine Love and Divine Wisdom (n. 55-60); that the uses of all created things ascend by degrees to man, and through man to God the Creator from whom they are (n. 65-68).

Who does not see clearly that uses are the ends of creation, when he considers that from God the Creator nothing can have form, and therefore nothing can be created, except use; and that to be use, it must be for the sake of others; and that use for the sake of self is also for the sake of others, since a use for the sake of self looks to one's being in a state to be of use to others? Whoso considers this is also able to see, that use which is use cannot spring from man, but must be in man from that Being from whom everything that comes forth is use, that is, from the Lord.

But as the forms of uses are here treated of, the subject shall be set forth in the following order: (1) In lands there is a conatus to produce uses in forms, that is, forms of uses. (2) In all forms of uses there is a kind of image of the creation of the universe. (3) In all forms of uses there is a kind of image of man. (4) In all forms of uses there is a kind of image of the Infinite and the Eternal.

(1) In lands there is a conatus to produce uses in forms, that is, forms of uses. That there is this conatus in lands, is evident from their source, since the substances and matters of which lands consist are endings and closings of atmospheres which proceed as uses from the spiritual sun (as may be seen above, n. 305, 306). And because the substances and matters of which lands consist are from that source, and their aggregations are held in connection by the pressure of the surrounding atmospheres, it follows that they have from that a perpetual conatus to bring forth forms of uses. The very quality that makes them capable of bringing forth they derive from their source, as being the outmosts of atmospheres, with which they are constantly in accord. Such a conatus and quality are said to be in lands, but it is meant that they are present in the substances and matters of which lands consist, whether these are in the lands or in the atmospheres as exhalations from the lands. That atmospheres are full of such things is well known. That there is such a conatus and such quality in the substances and matters of lands is plain from the fact that seeds of all kinds, opened by means of heat even to their inmost core, are impregnated by the most subtle substances (which can have no other than a spiritual origin), and through this they have power to conjoin themselves to use, from which comes their prolific principle. Then through conjunction with matters from a natural origin they are able to produce forms of uses, and thereafter to deliver them as from a womb, that they may come forth into light, and thus sprout up and grow. This conatus is afterwards continuous from the lands through the root even to outmosts, and from outmosts to firsts, wherein use itself is in its origin. Thus uses pass into forms; and forms, in their progression from firsts to outmosts and from outmosts to firsts, derive from use (which is like a soul) that each and every thing of the form is of some use. Use is said to be like a soul, since its form is like a body. It also follows that there is a conatus more interior,

that is, the conatus to produce uses for the animal kingdom through vegetable growths, since by these animals of every kind are nourished. It further follows that in all these there is an inmost conatus, the conatus to perform use to the human race. From all this these things follow: (1) that there are outmosts, and in outmosts are all prior things simultaneously in their order, according to what has been frequently explained above; (2) that as there are degrees of both kinds in the greatest and least of all things (as was shown above, n. 222-229), so there are likewise in this conatus; (3) that as all uses are brought forth by the Lord out of outmosts, so in outmosts there must be a conatus to uses.

Still none of these are living conatus, for they are the conatus of life's outmost forces; within which forces there exists, from the life out of which they spring, a striving to return at last to their origin through the means afforded. In outmosts, atmospheres become such forces; and by these forces, substances and matters, such as are in the lands, are molded into forms and held together in forms both within and without. But the subject is too large to allow a more extended explanation here.

The first production from these earthy matters, while they were still new and in their simple state, was production of seed; the first conatus therein could not be any other.

(2) In all forms of uses there is a kind of image of creation. Forms of uses are of a threefold kind; forms of uses of the mineral kingdom, forms of uses of the vegetable kingdom, and forms of uses of the animal kingdom. The forms of uses of the mineral kingdom cannot be described, because they are not visible to the eye. The first forms are the substances and matters of which the lands consist, in their minutest divisions; the second forms are aggregates of these, and are of infinite variety; the third forms come from plants that have fallen to dust, and from animal remains, and from the continual evaporations and exhalations from these, which are added to lands and make their soil. These forms of the mineral kingdom in three degrees represent creation in an image in this, that, made active by the sun through the atmospheres and their heat and light, they bring forth uses in forms, which uses were creative ends. This image of creation lies deeply hidden within their conatus (of which see above, n. 310).

In the forms of uses of the vegetable kingdom an image of creation appears in this, that from their firsts they proceed to their outmosts, and from outmosts to firsts. Their firsts are seeds, their outmosts are stalks clothed with bark; and by means of the bark which is the outmost of the stalk, they tend to seeds which, as was said, are their firsts. The stalks clothed with layers of bark represent the globe clothed with lands, out of which come the creation and formation of all uses. That vegetation is effected through the outer and inner barks and coatings, by a climbing up, by means of the coverings of the roots (which are continued around the stalks and branches), into the beginnings of the fruit, and in like manner through the fruits into the seeds, is known to many. An image of creation is displayed in forms of uses in the progress of the formation of uses from firsts to outmosts, and from outmosts to firsts; also in this, that in the whole progression there lies the end of producing fruit and seeds, which are uses. From what has been said above it is plain, that the progression of the creation of the universe was from its First (which is the Lord encircled by the sun) to outmosts which are lands, and from these through uses to its First, that is, the Lord; also that the ends of the whole creation were uses.

It should be known that to this image of creation the heat, light, and atmospheres of the natural world contribute nothing whatever. It is only the heat, light, and atmospheres of the sun of the spiritual world that do this, bringing that image with them, and clothing it with the forms of uses of the vegetable kingdom. The heat, light, and atmospheres of the natural world simply open the seeds, keep their products in a state of expansion, and clothe them with the matters that give them fixedness. And this is done not by any forces from their own sun (which viewed in themselves are null), but by forces from the spiritual sun, by which the natural forces are unceasingly impelled to these services. Natural forces contribute nothing whatever towards forming this image of creation, for the image of creation is spiritual. But that this image may be manifest and perform use in the natural world, and may stand fixed and be permanent, it must be materialized, that is, filled in with the matters of that world.

In the forms of uses of the animal kingdom there is a similar image of creation, in that the animal body, which is the outmost thereof, is formed by a seed deposited in a womb or an ovum, and this body, when mature, brings forth new seed. This progression is similar to the progression of the forms of uses of the vegetable kingdom: seeds are the beginnings; the womb or the ovum is like the ground; the state before birth is like the state of the seed in the ground while it takes root; the state after birth until the animal becomes prolific is like the growth of a tree until it reaches its state of fruit-bearing. From this parallelism it is plain that there is a likeness of creation in the forms of animals as well as in the forms of plants, in that there is a progression from firsts to outmosts, and from outmosts to firsts. A like image of creation exists in every single thing there is in man; for there is a like progression of love through wisdom into uses, consequently a like progression of the will through the understanding into acts, and of charity through faith into deeds. Will and understanding, also charity and faith, are the firsts as their source; acts and deeds are the outmosts; from these, by means of the enjoyments of uses, a return is made to their firsts, which, as was said, are the will and understanding, or charity and faith. That the return is effected by means of the enjoyments of uses is very evident from the enjoyments felt in those acts and deeds which are from any love, in that they flow back to the first of the love from which they spring and that thereby conjunction is effected. The enjoyments of acts and deeds are what are called the enjoyments of uses. A like progression from firsts to outmosts, and from outmosts to firsts, is exhibited in the forms most purely organic of affections and thoughts in man. In his brains there are those star-like forms called the cineritious substances; out of these go forth fibers through the medullary substance by the neck into the body; passing through to the outmosts of the body, and from outmosts returning to their firsts. This return of fibers to their firsts is made through the blood vessels. There is a like progression of all affections and thoughts, which are changes and variations of state of those forms or substances, for the fibers issuing out of those forms or substances are comparatively like the atmospheres from the spiritual sun, which are containants of heat and light; while bodily acts are like the things produced from the lands by means of atmospheres, the enjoyments of their uses returning to the source from which they sprang. But that the progression of these is such, and that within this progression there is an image of creation, can hardly be comprehended fully by the understanding, both because thousands and myriads of forces operating in act appear as one, and because the enjoyments of uses do not appear as ideas in the thought, but only affect without distinct perception. On this subject see what has been declared and explained above, as follows: The uses of all created things ascend by degrees of height to man, and through man to God the Creator from whom they are (n. 65-68). The end of creation takes form in outmosts, which end is that all things may return to the Creator and that there may be conjunction (n. 167-172). But these things will appear in still clearer light in the following Part, where the correspondence of the will and understanding with the heart and lungs will be treated of.

(3) In all forms of uses there is a kind of image of man. This has been shown above (n. 61-64). That all uses, from firsts to outmosts and from outmosts to firsts, have relation to all parts of man and have correspondence with them, consequently that man is, in a kind of image, a universe, and conversely that the universe viewed as to uses is in image a man, will be seen in the following chapter.

(4) In all forms of uses there is a kind of image of the Infinite and the Eternal. The image of the Infinite in these forms is plain from their conatus and power to fill the spaces of the whole world, and even of many worlds, to infinity. For a single seed produces a tree, shrub, or plant, which fills its own space; and each tree, shrub, or plant produces seeds, in some cases thousands of them, which, when sown and grown up, fill their own spaces; and if from each seed of these there should proceed as many more, reproduced again and again, in the course of years the whole world would be filled; and if the production were still continued many worlds would be filled; and this to infinity. Estimate a thousand seeds from one, and multiply the thousand by a thousand ten times, twenty times, even to a hundred times, and you will see. There is a like image of the Eternal in these forms; seeds are propagated from year to year, and the propagations never cease; they have not ceased from the creation of the world till now, and will not cease to eternity. These two are standing proofs and attesting signs that all things of the universe have been created by an Infinite and Eternal God. Beside these images of the Infinite and Eternal, there is another image of the Infinite and Eternal in varieties, in that there can never be a substance, state, or thing in the created universe the same as or identical with any other, neither in atmospheres, nor in lands, nor in the forms arising out of these. Thus not in any of the things which fill the universe can any thing the same be produced to eternity. This is plainly to be seen in the variety of the faces of human beings; no one face can be found throughout the world which is the same as another, nor can there be to all eternity, consequently not one mind, for the face is the type of the mind.

ALL THINGS OF THE CREATED UNIVERSE, VIEWED IN REFERENCE TO USES REPRESENT MAN IN AN IMAGE, AND THIS TESTIFIES THAT GOD IS A MAN By the ancients man was called a microcosm, from his representing the macrocosm, that is, the universe in its whole complex; but it is not known at the present day why man was so called by the ancients, for no more of the universe or macrocosm is manifest in him than that he derives nourishment and bodily life from its animal and vegetable kingdoms, and that he is kept in a living condition by its heat, sees by its light, and hears and breathes by its atmospheres. Yet these things do not make man a microcosm, as the universe with all things thereof is a macrocosm. The ancients called man a microcosm, or little universe, from truth which they derived from the knowledge of correspondences, in which the most ancient people were, and from their communication with angels of heaven; for angels of heaven know from the things which they see about them that all things of the universe, viewed as to uses, represent man as an image.

But the truth that man is a microcosm, or little universe, because the created universe, viewed as to uses is, in image, a man, cannot come into the thought and from that into the knowledge of any one on earth from the idea of the universe as it is viewed in the spiritual world; and therefore it can be corroborated only by an angel, who is in the spiritual world, or by some one to whom it has been granted to be in that world, and to see things which are there. As this has been granted to me, I am able, from what I have seen there, to disclose this arcanum.

It should be known that the spiritual world is in external appearance, wholly like the natural world. Lands, mountains, hills, valleys, plains, fields, lakes, rivers, springs of water are to be seen there, as in the natural world; thus all things belonging to the mineral kingdom. Paradises, gardens, groves, woods, and in them trees and shrubs of all kinds bearing fruit and seeds; also plants, flowers, herbs, and grasses are to be seen there; thus all things pertaining to the vegetable kingdom. There are also to be seen there, beasts, birds, and fishes of every kind; thus all things pertaining to the animal kingdom. Man there is an angel or spirit. This is premised that it may be known that the universe of the spiritual world is wholly like the universe of the natural world, with this difference only, that things in the spiritual world are not fixed and settled like those in the natural world, because in the spiritual world nothing is natural but every thing is spiritual.

That the universe of that world represents man in an image can be clearly seen from this, that all things just mentioned (n. 321) appear to the life, and take form about the angel, and about the angelic societies, as if they were produced or created by them; they are about them permanently, and do not pass away. That they are as if they were produced or created by them is seen by their no longer appearing when the angel goes away, or when the society passes to another place; also when other angels come in place of these the appearance of all things about them is changed - in the paradises the trees and fruits are changed, in the flower gardens the flowers and seeds, in the fields the herbs and grasses, also the kinds of animals and birds are changed. Such things take form and are changed in this manner, because all these things take form according to the affections and consequent thoughts of the angels, for they are correspondences. And because things that correspond make one with that to which they correspond they are an image representative of it. The image itself is not seen when these things are viewed in their forms, it is seen only when they are viewed in respect to uses. It has been granted me to perceive that angels, when their eyes were opened by the Lord, and they saw these things from the correspondence of uses, recognized and saw themselves therein.

Inasmuch as these things which have existence about the angels, corresponding to their affections and thoughts, represent a universe, in that there are lands, plants, and animals, and these constitute an image representative of the angel, it is evident why the ancients called man a microcosm.

That this is so has been abundantly confirmed in the Arcana Coelestia, also in the work Heaven and Hell, and occasionally in the preceding pages where correspondence is treated of. It has been there shown also that nothing is to be found in the created universe which has not a correspondence with something in man, not only with his affections and their thoughts, but also with his bodily organs and viscera; not with these however as substances, but as uses. From this it is that in the Word, where the church and the man of the church are treated of, such frequent mention is made of trees, such as "olives," "vines," and "cedars;" of "gardens," "groves" and "woods;" and of the "beasts of the earth," "birds of the air," and "fish of the sea." They are there mentioned because they correspond, and by correspondence make one, as was said above; consequently, when such things are read in the Word by man, these objects are not perceived by angels, but the church or the men of the church in respect to their states are perceived instead.

Since all things of the universe have relation in an image to man, the wisdom and intelligence of Adam are described by the "garden of Eden," wherein were all kinds of trees, also rivers, precious stones, and gold, and animals to which he gave names; by all of which are meant such things as were in Adam, and constitute that which is called man. Nearly the same things are said of Ashur, by whom the church in respect to intelligence is signified (Ezek. 31:3-9); and of Tyre, by which the church in respect to knowledges of good and truth is signified (Ezek. 28:12, 13).

From all this it can be seen that all things in the universe, viewed from uses, have relation in an image to man, and that this testifies that God is a man. For such things as have been mentioned above take form about the angelic man, not from the angels, but from the Lord through the angels. For they take their form from the influx of the Lord's Divine Love and Divine Wisdom into the angel, who is a recipient, and before whose eyes all this is brought forth like the creation of a universe. From this they know there that God is a Man, and that the created universe, viewed in its uses, is an image of God.

ALL THINGS CREATED BY THE LORD ARE USE; THEY ARE USES IN THE ORDER, DEGREE, AND RESPECT IN WHICH THEY HAVE RELATION TO MAN, AND THROUGH MAN TO THE LORD, FROM WHOM [THEY ARE]. In respect to this it has been shown above: That from God the Creator nothing can take form except uses (n. 308); that the uses of all created things ascend by degrees from outmost things to man, and through man to God the Creator, from whom they are (n. 65-68); that the end of creation takes form in outmosts, which end is, that all things may return to God the Creator, and that there may be conjunction (n. 167-172); that things are uses so far as they have regard to the Creator (n. 307); that the Divine must necessarily have being and form in other things created by itself (n. 47-51); that all things of the universe are recipients according to uses, and this according to degrees (n. 58);

that the universe, viewed from uses, is an image of God (n. 59); and many other things. From all which this- truth is plain, that all things created by the Lord are uses, and that they are uses in that order, degree, and respect in which they have relation to man, and through man to the Lord from whom [they are]. It remains now that some things should be said in detail respecting uses.

By man, to whom uses have relation, is meant not alone an individual but an assembly of men, also a society smaller or larger, as a commonwealth, kingdom, or empire, or that largest society, the whole world, for each of these is a man. Likewise in the heavens, the whole angelic heaven is as one man before the Lord, and equally every society of heaven; from this it is that every angel is a man. That this is so may be seen in the work Heaven and Hell (n. 68-103). This makes clear what is meant by man in what follows.

The end of the creation of the universe clearly shows what use is. The end of the creation of the universe is the existence of an angelic heaven; and as the angelic heaven is the end, man also or the human race is the end, since heaven is from that. From which it follows that all created things are mediate ends, and that these are uses in that order, degree, and respect in which they have relation to man, and through man to the Lord.

Inasmuch as the end of creation is an angelic heaven out of the human race, and thus the human race itself, all other created things are mediate ends, and these, as having relation to man, with a view to his conjunction with the Lord, refer themselves to these three things in him, his body, his rational, and his spiritual. For man cannot be conjoined to the Lord unless he be spiritual, nor can he be spiritual unless he be rational, nor can he be rational unless his body is in a sound state. These three are like a house; the body like the foundation, the rational like the superstructure, the spiritual like those things which are in the house, and conjunction with the Lord like dwelling in it. From this can be seen in what order, degree, and respect uses (which are the mediate ends of creation) have relation to man, namely, (1) for sustaining his body, (2) for perfecting his rational, (3) for receiving what is spiritual from the Lord.

Uses for sustaining the body relate to its nourishment, its clothing, its habitation, its recreation and enjoyment, its protection and the preservation of its state. The uses created for the nourishment of the body are all things of the vegetable kingdom suitable for food and drink, as fruits, grapes, grain, pulse, and herbs; in the animal kingdom all things which are eaten, as oxen, cows, calves, deer, sheep, kids, goats, lambs, and the milk they yield; also fowls and fish of many kinds. The uses created for the clothing of the body are many other products of these two kingdoms; in like manner, the uses for habitation, also for recreation, enjoyment, protection, and preservation of state. These are not mentioned because they are well known, and their mere enumeration would fill pages. There are many things, to be sure, which are not used by man; but what is superfluous does not do away with the use, but ensures its continuance. Misuse of uses is also possible, but misuse does not do away with use, even as falsification of truth does not do away with truth except with those who falsify it.

Uses for perfecting the rational are all things that give instruction about the subjects above mentioned, and are called sciences and branches of study, pertaining to natural, economical, civil and moral affairs, which are learned either from parents and teachers, or from books, or from interaction with others, or by reflection on these subjects by oneself. These things perfect the rational so far as they are uses in a higher degree, and they are permanent as far as they are applied to life. Space forbids the enumeration of these uses, by reason both of their multitude and of their varied relation to the common good.

Uses for receiving the spiritual from the Lord, are all things that belong to religion and to worship therefrom; thus all things that teach the acknowledgment and knowledge of God and the knowledge and acknowledgment of good and truth and thus eternal life, which are acquired in the same way as other learning, from parents, teachers, discourses, and books, and especially by applying to life what is so learned; and in the Christian world, by doctrines and discourses from the Word, and through the Word from the Lord. These uses in their full extent may be described under the same heads as the uses of the body, as nourishment, clothing, habitation, recreation and enjoyment, and preservation of state, if only they are applied to the soul; as nutrition to goods of love, clothing to truths of wisdom, habitation to heaven, recreation and enjoyment to felicity of life and heavenly joy, protection to safety from infesting evils, and preservation of state to eternal life. All these things are given by the Lord according to the acknowledgment that all bodily things are also from the Lord, and that a man is only as a servant and house-steward appointed over the goods of his Lord.

That such things have been given to man to use and enjoy, and that they are free gifts, is clearly evident from the state of angels in the heavens, who have, like men on earth, a body, a rational, and a spiritual. They are nourished freely, for food is given them daily; they are clothed freely, for garments are given them; their dwellings are free, for houses are given them; nor have they any care about all these things; and so far as they are rational-spiritual do they have enjoyment, protection, and preservation of state. The difference is that angels see that these things, - because created according to the state of their love and wisdom, - are from the Lord (as was shown in the preceding chapter, n. 322); but men do not see this, because their harvest returns yearly, and is not in accord with the state of their love and wisdom, but in accord with the care bestowed by them.

These things are called uses, because through man they have relation to the Lord; nevertheless, they must not be said to be uses from man for the Lord's sake, but from the Lord for man's sake, inasmuch as in the Lord all uses are infinitely one, but in man there are no uses except from the Lord; for man cannot do good from himself, but only from the Lord, and good is what is called use. The essence of spiritual love is doing good to others, not for the sake of self but for the sake of others; infinitely more is this the essence of Divine Love. It is like the love of parents for their children, in that parents do good to their children from love, not for their own sake but for their children's sake. This is especially manifest in a mothers love for her offspring. Because the Lord is to be adored, worshiped and glorified, He is supposed to love adoration, worship, and glory for His own sake; but He loves these for man's sake, because by means of them man comes into a state in which the Divine can flow in and be perceived; since by means of them man puts away that which is his own, which hinders influx and reception, for what is man's own, which is self-love, hardens the heart and shuts it up. This is removed by man's acknowledging that from himself comes nothing but evil and from the Lord nothing but good; from this acknowledgment there is a softening of the heart and humiliation, out of which flow forth adoration and worship. From all this it follows, that the use which the Lord performs for Himself through man is that Man may be able to do good from love, and since this is the Lord's love, its reception is the enjoyment of His love. Therefore, let no one believe that the Lord is with those who merely worship Him, He is with those who do His commandments, thus who perform uses; with such He has His abode, but not with the former. (See what was said above on this subject, n. 47-49.)

EVIL USES WERE NOT CREATED BY THE LORD, BUT ORIGINATED TOGETHER WITH HELL. All good things that take form in act are called uses; and all evil things that take form in act are also called uses, but evil uses, while the former are called good uses. Now, since all good things are from the Lord and all evil things from hell, it follows that none but good uses were created by the Lord, and that evil uses arose out of hell. By the uses specially treated of in this chapter are meant all those things which are to be seen upon the earth, as animals of every kind and plants of every kind. Such things of both kingdoms as are useful to man are from the Lord, but those which are harmful to man are from hell. By uses from the Lord are likewise meant all things that perfect the rational of man, and cause him to receive the spiritual from the Lord; but by evil uses are meant all things that destroy the rational, and make man unable to become spiritual. Those things that are harmful to man are called uses because they are of use to the evil in doing evil, and also are serviceable in absorbing malignities and thus also as remedies. "Use" is employed in both senses, as love is when we speak of good love and evil love; moreover, everything that love does it calls use.

That good uses are from the Lord, and evil uses from hell, will be shown in the following order. (1) What is meant by evil uses on the earth. (2) All things that are evil uses are in hell, and all things that are good uses are in heaven. (3) There is unceasing influx from the spiritual world into the natural world. (4) Those things that are evil uses are effected by the operation of influx from hell, wherever there are such things as correspond thereto. (5) This is done by the lowest spiritual separated from what is above it. (6) There are two forms into which the operation by influx takes place, the vegetable and the animal. (7) Both these forms receive the ability to propagate their kind and the means of propagation.

(1) What is meant by evil uses on the earth. By evil uses on earth are meant all noxious things in both the animal and vegetable kingdom, also in the mineral kingdom. It is needless to enumerate all the noxious things in these kingdoms, for to do so would merely heap up names, and doing this without indicating the noxious effect that each kind produces would not contribute to the object which this work has in view. For the sake of information a few examples will suffice:-In the animal kingdom there are poisonous serpents, scorpions, crocodiles, great snakes, horned owls, screech owls, mice, locusts, frogs, spiders; also flies, drones, moths, lice, mites; in a word, creatures that destroy grasses, leaves, fruits, seed, food, and drink, and are harmful to beast and man. In the vegetable kingdom there are all hurtful, virulent, and

poisonous herbs, with leguminous plants and shrubs of like character; and in the mineral kingdom all poisonous earths. From these few examples it can be seen what is meant by evil uses on earth; for evil uses are all things that are opposite to good uses (of which, in the preceding paragraph, n. 336).

(2) All things that are evil uses are in hell, and all things that are good uses are in heaven. Before it can be seen that all evil uses that take form on earth are not from the Lord but from hell, something must be premised concerning heaven and hell, without a knowledge of which evil uses as well as good may be attributed to the Lord, and it may be believed that they are together from creation; or they may be attributed to nature, and their origin to the sun of nature. From these two errors man cannot be delivered, unless he knows that nothing whatever takes form in the natural world that does not derive its cause and therefore its origin from the spiritual world, and that good is from the Lord, and evil from the devil, that is, from hell. By the spiritual world is meant both heaven and hell. In heaven are to be seen all those things that are good uses (of which in a preceding article, n. 336). In hell are to be seen all those that are evil uses (see just above, n. 338, where they are enumerated). These are wild creatures of every kind, as serpents, scorpions, great snakes, crocodiles, tigers, wolves, foxes, swine, owls of different kinds, bats, rats, and mice, frogs, locusts, spiders, and noxious insects of many kinds; also hemlocks and aconites, and all kinds of poisons, both of herbs and of earths; in a word, everything hurtful and deadly to man. Such things appear in the hells to the life precisely like those on and in the earth. They are said to appear there; yet they are not there as on earth, for they are mere correspondences of lusts that swarm out of their evil loves, and present themselves in such forms before others. Because there are such things in the hells, these abound in foul smells, cadaverous, stercoraceous, urinous, and putrid, wherein the diabolical spirits there take delight, as animals do in rank stenches. From this it can be seen that like things in the natural world did not derive their origin from the Lord, and were not created from the beginning, neither did they spring from nature through her sun, but are from hell. That they are not from nature through her sun is plain, for the spiritual inflows into the natural, and not the reverse. And that they are not from the Lord is plain, because hell is not from Him, therefore nothing in hell corresponding to the evils of its inhabitants is from Him.

(3) There is unceasing influx out of the spiritual world into the natural world. He who does not know that there is a spiritual world, or that it is distinct from the natural world, as what is prior is distinct from what is subsequent, or as cause from the thing caused, can have no knowledge of this influx. This is the reason why those who have written on the origin of plants and animals could not do otherwise than ascribe that origin to nature; or if to God, then in the sense that God had implanted in nature from the beginning a power to produce such things, - not knowing that no power has been implanted in nature, since nature, in herself, is dead, and contributes no more to the production of these things than a tool does, for instance, to the work of a mechanic, the tool acting only as it is continually moved. It is the spiritual, deriving its origin from the sun where the Lord is, and proceeding to the outmosts of nature, that produces the forms of plants and animals, exhibiting the marvels that exist in both, and filling the forms with matters from the earth, that they may become fixed and

enduring. But because it is now known that there is a spiritual world, and that the spiritual is from the spiritual sun, in which the Lord is and which is from the Lord, and that the spiritual is what impels nature to act, as what is living impels what is dead, also that like things exist in the spiritual world as in the natural world, it can now be seen that plants and animals have had their existence only from the Lord though that world, and through that world they have perpetual existence. Thus there is unceasing influx from the spiritual world into the natural. That this is so will be abundantly corroborated in the next chapter. Noxious things are produced on earth through influx from hell, by the same law of permission whereby evils themselves from hell flow into men. This law will be set forth in the Angelic Wisdom Concerning the Divine Providence.

(4) Those things that are evil uses are effected by the operation of influx from hell, wherever there are such things as correspond thereto. The things that correspond to evil uses, that is, to hurtful plants and noxious animals, are cadaverous, putrid, excrementitious, stercoraceous, rancid, and urinous matters; consequently, in places where these are, such herbs and such animalcules spring forth as are mentioned above; and in the torrid zone, like things of larger size, as serpents, basilisks, crocodiles, scorpions, rats, and so forth. Every one knows that swamps, stagnant ponds, dung, fetid bogs, are full of such things; also that noxious insects fill the atmosphere in clouds, and noxious vermin walk the earth in armies, and consume its herbs to the very roots. I once observed in my garden, that in the space of a half yard, nearly all the dust was turned into minute insects, for when it was stirred with a stick, they rose in clouds. That cadaverous and putrid matters are in accord with these noxious and useless little things, and that the two are homogeneous, is evident from mere observation; and it is still more clearly seen from the cause, which is, that like stenches and fumes exist in the hells, where such little things are likewise to be seen. Those hells are therefore named accordingly; some are called cadaverous, some stercoraceous, some urinous, and so on. But all these hells are covered over, that those vapors may not escape from them. For when they are opened a very little, which happens when novitiate devils enter, they excite vomiting and cause headache, and such as are also poisonous induce fainting. The very dust there is also of the same nature, wherefore it is there called damned dust. From this it is evident that there are such noxious insects wherever there are such stenches, because the two correspond.

It now becomes a matter of inquiry whether such things spring from eggs conveyed to the spot by means of air, or rain, or water oozing through the soil, or whether they spring from the damp and stenches themselves. That these noxious animalcules and insects mentioned above are hatched from eggs which have been carried to the spot, or which have lain hidden everywhere in the ground since creation, is opposed to all observation. For worms spring forth in minute seeds, in the kernels of nuts, in wood, in stones, and even from leaves, and upon plants and in plants there are lice and grubs which are accordant with them. Of flying insects, too, there are such as appear in houses, fields, and woods, which arise in like manner in summer, with no oviform matters sufficient to account for them; also such as devour meadows and lawns, and in some hot localities fill and infest the air; besides those that swim and fly unseen in filthy waters, wines becoming sour, and pestilential air. These facts of observation support those who say that the odors, effluvia, and exhalations emitted from plants, earths, and ponds, are what give the initiative to such things. That when they have come forth, they are afterwards propagated either by eggs or offshoots, does not disprove their immediate generation; since every living creature, along with its minute viscera, receives organs of generation and means of propagation (see below, n. 347). In agreement with these phenomena is the fact heretofore unknown that there are like things also in the hells.

That the hells mentioned above have not only communication but conjunction with such things in the earths may be concluded from this, that the hells are not distant from men, but are about them, yea, are within those who are evil; thus they are contiguous to the earth; for man, in regard to his affections and lusts, and consequent thoughts, and in regard to his actions springing from these, which are good or evil uses, is in the midst either of angels of heaven or of spirits of hell; and as such things as are on the earth are also in the heavens and hells, it follows that influx therefrom directly produces such things when the conditions are favorable. All things, in fact, that appear in the spiritual world, whether in heaven or in hell, are correspondences of affections or lusts, for they take form there in accordance with these; consequently when affections or lusts, which in themselves are spiritual, meet with homogeneous or corresponding things in the earths, there are present both the spiritual that furnishes a soul, and the material that furnishes a body. Moreover, within everything spiritual there is a conatus to clothe itself with a body. The hells are about men, and therefore contiguous to the earth, because the spiritual world is not in space, but is where there is a corresponding affection.

I heard two presidents of the English Royal Society, Sir Hans Sloane and Martin Folkes, conversing together in the spiritual world about the existence of seeds and eggs, and about productions from them in the earths. The former ascribed them to nature, and contended that nature was endowed from creation with a power and force to produce such effects by means of the sun's heat. The other maintained that this force is in nature unceasingly from God the Creator. To settle the discussion, a beautiful bird appeared to Sir Hans Sloane, and he was asked to examine it to see whether it differed in the smallest particle from a similar bird on earth. He held it in his hand, examined it, and declared that there was no difference. He knew indeed that it was nothing but an affection of some angel represented outside of the angel as a bird, and that it would vanish or cease with its affection. And this came to pass. By this experience Sir Hans Sloane was convinced that nature contributes nothing whatever to the production of plants and animals, that they are produced solely by what flows into the natural world out of the spiritual world. If that bird, he said, were to be infilled, in its minutest parts, with corresponding matters from the earth, and thus fixed, it would be a lasting bird, like the birds on the earth; and that it is the same with such things as are from hell. To this he added that had he known what he now knew of the spiritual world, he would have ascribed to nature no more than this, that it serves the spiritual, which is from God, in fixing the things which flow in unceasingly into nature.

(5) This is effected by the lowest spiritual separated from what is above it. It was shown in Part Third that the spiritual flows down from its sun even to

the outmosts of nature through three degrees, which are called the celestial, the spiritual, and the natural; that these three degrees are in man from creation, consequently from birth; that they are opened according to man's life; that if the celestial degree which is the highest and inmost is opened, man becomes celestial; if the spiritual degree which is the middle is opened, he becomes spiritual; but if only the natural degree which is the lowest and outermost is opened, he becomes natural; that if man becomes natural only, he loves only corporeal and worldly things; and that so far as he loves these, so far he does not love celestial and spiritual things, and does not look to God, and so far he becomes evil. From all this it is evident that the lowest spiritual, which is called the spiritual-natural, can be separated from its higher degrees, and is separated in such men as hell consists of. This lowest spiritual can separate itself from its higher parts, and look to hell, in men only; it cannot be so separated in beasts, or in soils. From which it follows that these evil uses mentioned above are effected on the earth by this lowest spiritual separated from what is above it, such as it is in those who are in hell. That the noxious things on the earth have their origin in man, thus from hell, may be shown by the state of the land of Canaan, as described in the Word; in that when the children of Israel lived according to the commandments, the earth yielded its increase, likewise the flocks and herds; but when they lived contrary to the commandments the ground was barren, and as it is said, accursed; instead of harvests it yielded thorns and briars, the flocks and herds miscarried, and wild beasts broke in. The same may be inferred from the locusts, frogs, and lice in Egypt.

(6) There are two forms into which the operation by influx takes place, the vegetable and the animal form. That there are only two universal forms produced out of the earth is known from the two kingdoms of nature, called the animal and the vegetable kingdoms, also that all the subjects of either kingdom possess many things in common. Thus the subjects of the animal kingdom have organs of sense and organs of motion and members and viscera that are actuated by brains, hearts, and lungs. So the subjects of the vegetable kingdom send down a root into the ground, and bring forth stem, branches, leaves, flowers, fruits, and seeds. Both the animal and the vegetable kingdoms, as regards the production of their forms, derive their origin from spiritual influx and operation out of the sun of heaven where the Lord is, and not from the influx and operation of nature out of her sun; from this they derive nothing except their fixation, as was said above. All animals, great and small, derive their origin from the spiritual in the outmost degree, which is called the natural; man alone from all three degrees, called the celestial, spiritual, and natural. As each degree of height or discrete degree decreases from its perfection to its imperfection, as light to shade, by continuity, so do animals; there are therefore perfect, less perfect, and imperfect animals. The perfect animals are elephants, camels, horses, mules, oxen, sheep, goats, and others which are of the herd or the flock; the less perfect are birds; and the imperfect are fish and shell-fish; these, as being the lowest of that degree, are as it were in shade, while the former are in light. Yet animals, since they live only from the lowest spiritual degree, which is called the natural, can look nowhere else than towards the earth and to food there, and to their own kind for the sake of propagation; the soul of all these is natural affection and appetite. The subjects

of the vegetable kingdom comprise, in like manner, the perfect, less perfect, and imperfect; the perfect are fruit trees, the less perfect are vines and shrubs, and the imperfect are grasses. But plants derive from the spiritual out of which they spring that they are uses, while animals derive from the spiritual out of which they spring that they are affections and appetites, as was shown above.

(7) Each of these forms receives with its existence the means of propagation. In all products of the earth, which pertain, as was said above, either to the vegetable or to the animal kingdom, there is a kind of image of creation, and a kind of image of man, and also a kind of image of the infinite and the eternal; this was shown above (n. 313-318); also that the image of the infinite and the eternal is clearly manifest in the capacity of all these for infinite and eternal propagation. They all, therefore, receive means of propagation; the subjects of the animal kingdom through seed, in the egg or in the womb or by spawning; and the subjects of the vegetable kingdom through seeds in the ground. From which it can be seen that although the more imperfect and the noxious animals and plants originate through immediate influx out of hell, yet afterwards they are propagated mediately by seeds, eggs, or grafts; consequently, the one position does not annul the other.

That all uses, both good and evil, are from a spiritual origin, thus from the sun where the Lord is, may be illustrated by this experience. I have heard that goods and truths have been sent down through the heavens by the Lord to the hells, and that these same, received by degrees to the lowest deep, were there turned into evils and falsities, which are the opposite of the goods and truths sent down. This took place because recipient subjects turn all things that inflow into such things as are in agreement with their own forms, just as the white light of the sun is turned into ugly colors or into black in those objects whose substances are interiorly of such a form as to suffocate and extinguish the light, and as stagnant ponds, dung-hills, and dead bodies turn the heat of the sun into stenches. From all this it can be seen that even evil uses are from the spiritual sun, but that good uses are changed in hell into evil uses. It is evident, therefore, that the Lord has not created and does not create any except good uses, but that hell produces evil uses.

THE VISIBLE THINGS IN THE CREATED UNIVERSE BEAR WITNESS THAT NATURE HAS PRODUCED AND DOES PRODUCE NOTHING, BUT THAT THE DIVINE OUT OF ITSELF, AND THROUGH THE SPIRITUAL WORLD, HAS PRODUCED AND DOES PRODUCE ALL THINGS. Speaking from appearances, most men say that the sun by heat and light produces whatever is to be seen in plains, fields, gardens, and forests; also that the sun by its heat hatches worms from eggs, and makes prolific the beasts of the earth and the fowls of the air; and that it even gives life to man. Those who speak from appearances only may speak in this way without ascribing these things to nature, because they are not thinking about the matter; as there are those who speak of the sun as rising and setting, and causing days and years, and being now at this or that altitude; such persons speak from appearances, and in doing so, do not ascribe such effects to the sun, because they are not thinking of the sun's fixity or the earth's revolution. But those who confirm themselves in the idea that the sun produces the things that appear upon the earth by means of its heat and light, end by ascribing all things to nature, even the creation of the universe, and become naturalists and, at last, atheists. These may continue to say that God created nature and endowed her with the power of producing such things, but this they say from fear of losing their good name; and by God the Creator they still mean nature, and some mean the innermost of nature, and then the Divine things taught by the church they regard as of no account.

There are some who are excusable for ascribing certain visible things to nature, for two reasons. First, because they have had no knowledge of the sun of heaven, where the Lord is, or of influx therefrom, or of the spiritual world and its state, or even of its presence with man, and therefore had no other idea than that the spiritual is a purer natural; consequently, that angels are in the ether or in the stars; and that the devil is either man's evil or if an actual existence, that he is in the air or the abyss; also that the souls of men, after death, are either in the interior of the earth, or in an undetermined somewhere till the day of judgment; and other like things deduced by fancy out of ignorance of the spiritual world and its sun. Secondly, they are excusable, because they are unable to see how the Divine could produce everything that appears on the earth, where there are not only good things but also evil things; and they are afraid to confirm themselves in such an idea, lest they ascribe the evil things also to God, and form a material conception of God, and make God and nature one, and thus confound the two. For these two reasons those are excusable who have believed that nature produces the visible world by a power implanted in her by creation. But those who have made themselves atheists by confirmations in favor of nature are not excusable, because they might have confirmed themselves in favor of the Divine. Ignorance indeed excuses, but does not remove, falsity - which has been confirmed, for such falsity coheres with evil, thus with hell. Consequently, those same persons who have confirmed themselves in favor of nature to such an extent as to separate the Divine from nature, regard nothing as sin, because all sin is against the Divine, and this they have separated, and thus have rejected it; and those who in spirit regard nothing as sin, after death when they become spirits, since they are in bonds to hell, rush into wickednesses which are in accord with the lusts to which they have given rein.

Section 8

Those who believe in a Divine operation in all the details of nature, are able by very many things they see in nature to confirm themselves in favor of the Divine, as fully as others confirm themselves in favor of nature, yea, more fully. For those who confirm themselves in favor of the Divine give attention to the wonders which are displayed in the production both of plants and animals. In the production of plants, how out of a little seed cast into the ground there goes forth a root, and by means of the root a stem, and branches, leaves, flowers, and fruits in succession, even to new seeds; just as if the seed knew the order of succession, or the process by which it is to renew itself. Can any reasonable person think that the sun, which is mere fire, has this knowledge, or that it is able to empower its heat and light to effect these results, or is able to fashion these wonderful things in plants, and to contemplate use? Any man of elevated reason who sees and weighs these things, cannot think otherwise than that they come from Him who has infinite reason, that is, from God. Those who acknowledge the Divine also see and think this, but those who do not acknowledge the Divine do not see or think this because they do not wish to; thus they sink their rational into the sensual, which draws all its ideas from the lumen which is proper to the bodily senses and which confirms their illusions, saying, Do you not see the sun effecting these things by its heat and light? What is a thing that you do not see? Is it anything? Those who confirm themselves in favor of the Divine give attention to the wonders which are displayed in the production of animals; to mention here only, in reference to eggs, how the chick in its seed or beginning lies hidden therein, with everything requisite till it is hatched, also with everything pertaining to its subsequent development, until it becomes a bird or winged thing of the same form as its parent. And if one observes the living form, it is such as to fill any one with astonishment who thinks deeply, seeing that in the minutest as in the largest living creatures, even in the invisible, as in the visible, there are the organs of sense, namely, sight, hearing, smell, taste, and touch; and organs of motion which are muscles, for they fly and walk; also viscera surrounding the heart and lungs, which are set in action by brains. That even the commonest insects enjoy such organisms is shown in their anatomy as described by some writers, and especially by Swammerdam, in his Biblia Naturae. Those who ascribe everything to nature, see all these things, but they merely perceive that they exist, and say that nature produces them. They say this because they have turned their minds away from thinking about the Divine; and those who have done this are unable, when they see the wonderful things in nature, to think rationally, still less spiritually; but they think sensually and materially; and then they think in nature from nature, and not above nature, just as those do who are in hell. They differ from beasts only in having the power to think rationally, that is, in being able to understand, and therefore to think otherwise, if they choose.

Those who have averted themselves from thinking about the Divine when observing the wonderful things in nature, and who thereby become sensual, do not reflect that the sight of the eye is so gross as to see many little insects as an obscure speck, when yet each one of these is organized to feel and to move, and is accordingly furnished with fibers and vessels, also with a minute heart, pulmonary tubes, viscera, and brains; also that these organs are woven out of the purest substances in nature, their tissues corresponding to that somewhat of life by which their minutest parts are separately moved. When the sight of the eye is so gross that many such creatures, with innumerable particulars in each, appear to it as an obscure speck, and yet those who are sensual think and judge by that sight, it is clear how dulled their minds are, and therefore what thick darkness they are in concerning spiritual things.

Any one who chooses may confirm himself in favor of the Divine from things seen in nature, and whoever thinks about God in reference to life does so confirm himself; as when he observes the birds of the air, how each species knows its food and where to find it, recognizes its kind by sound and sight, and which among other kinds are its friends and which its enemies; how also they mate, have knowledge of the sexual relation, skillfully build nests, lay eggs therein, sit upon these, know the period of incubation, and this having elapsed, bring forth their young, love them most tenderly, cherish them under their wings, bring them food and feed them, until they can do for themselves, perform the same offices, and bring forth a family to perpetuate their kind. Any one who is willing to reflect on the Divine influx through the spiritual world into the natural can see such influx in these things, and if he will, can say from his heart, Such knowledges cannot flow into these creatures out of the sun through its rays of light, for the sun, from which nature derives its origin and essence, is mere fire, consequently its rays of light are wholly dead; and thus he may conclude that such things are from the influx of Divine Wisdom into the outmosts of nature.

Any one may confirm himself in favor of the Divine from things visible in nature, when he sees larvae, from the delight of some impulse, desiring and longing to change their terrestrial state to a certain likeness of the heavenly state, and for this purpose creeping into corners, and putting themselves as it were into a womb in order to be born again, and there becoming chrysalises, aurelias, caterpillars, nymphs, and at length butterflies; and having undergone this metamorphosis, and each after its kind been decked with beautiful wings, they ascend into the air as into their heaven, and there disport themselves joyfully, form marriage unions, lay eggs, and provide for themselves a posterity, nourished meanwhile with pleasant and sweet food from flowers. Who that confirms himself in favor of the Divine from the visible things in nature can help seeing a kind of image of man's earthly state in these as larvae, and in them as butterflies an image of the heavenly state? Those who confirm themselves in favor of nature see the same things, but because in heart they have rejected the heavenly state of man they call them merely natural instincts.

Any one may confirm himself in favor of the Divine from things seen in nature by giving attention to what is known about bees: that they know how to collect wax and suck honey from herbs and flowers, and to build cells like little houses, and set them in the form of a city, with streets through which to come in and go out; that they scent at long distances the flowers and herbs from which they collect wax for their houses and honey for food, and laden with these fly back in a direct line to their hive; thus providing themselves with food and habitation for the coming winter, as if they had foresight and knowledge of it. They also set over them a mistress as queen, out of whom a posterity may be propagated; and for her they build a sort of a palace over themselves with guards around it; and when her time of bringing forth is at hand, she goes attended by her guards from cell to cell, and lays her eggs, which the crowd of followers smear over to protect them from the air, from which a new progeny springs forth for them. When this progeny becomes mature enough to do the same, it is driven from the hive. The expelled swarm first collects, and then in a close body, to preserve its integrity, flies away in quest of a home for itself. Moreover, in the autumn the useless drones are led out and are deprived of their wings to prevent their returning and consuming the food for which they have not labored; not to mention other particulars. From all this it can be seen that bees, because of their use to the human race, have from influx from the spiritual world, a form of government similar to that among men on earth, and even like that of angels in heaven. Can any man of unimpaired reason fail to see that these doings of the bees are not from the natural world? What has that sun, from which nature springs, in common with a government that vies with and resembles the government of heaven? From these things and others very similar to them in the brute creation, the confessor and worshiper of nature confirms himself in favor of nature, while the confessor and worshiper of God confirms himself from the same things in favor of the Divine; for the spiritual man sees in them spiritual things and the natural man natural things, thus each according to his character. As for myself, such things have been proofs to me of an influx of the spiritual into the natural, that is, of the spiritual world into the natural world, thus of an influx from the Lord's Divine Wisdom. Consider, moreover, whether you can think analytically concerning any form of government, or any civil law, or moral virtue, or spiritual truth, unless the Divine out of His wisdom flows in through the spiritual world? For myself, I could not and cannot. For having now observed that influx perceptibly and sensibly for about nineteen years continually, I speak as an eye-witness.

Can anything natural regard use as an end and dispose uses into series and forms? No one can do this unless he be wise; and no one but God, whose wisdom is infinite, can so give order and form to the universe. Who else or what else is able to foresee and provide all things needful for the food and clothing of man, - food from the fruits of earth and from animals, and clothing from the same? How marvelous that so insignificant a creature as the silk-worm should clothe in silk and splendidly adorn both women and men, from queens and kings to maidservants and menservants, and that insignificant insects like the bees should supply wax for the candles by which temples and palaces are made brilliant. These and many other things are manifest proofs that the Lord from Himself by means of the spiritual world, brings about everything that comes into existence in nature.

To this must be added that those who have confirmed themselves in favor of nature, from the visible things of the world, until they have become atheists, have been seen by me in the spiritual world; and in the spiritual light their understanding appeared open below, but closed above, because in thought they had looked downward toward the earth, and not upward toward heaven. Above their sensual, which is the bottom of the understanding, appeared something like a veil; which in some flashed with hellish fire, in some was black like soot, and in some livid like a corpse. Therefore let every one beware of confirmations in favor of nature; let him confirm himself in favor of the Divine; there is no lack of materiaL

PART FIFTH. TWO RECEPTACLES AND ABODES FOR HIMSELF, CALLED WILL AND UNDERSTANDING, HAVE BEEN CREATED AND FORMED BY THE LORD IN MAN; THE WILL FOR HIS DIVINE LOVE, AND THE UNDERSTANDING FOR HIS DIVINE WISDOM. The Divine Love and Divine Wisdom of God the Creator, who is the Lord from eternity, and also the creation of the universe, have been treated of; something shall now be said of the creation of man. We read (in Gen. 1:26) that man was created "in the image of God, after His likeness." By "image of God" is there meant the Divine Wisdom, and by "likeness" of God the Divine Love; since wisdom is nothing but an image of love, for in wisdom love presents itself to be seen and recognized, and because it is seen and recognized in wisdom, wisdom is an image of it. Moreover love is the esse of life, and wisdom is the existere of life therefrom. In angels the likeness and image of God clearly appear, since love from within shines forth in their faces, and wisdom in their beauty, and their beauty is a form of their love. I have seen and know.

Man cannot be an image of God, after His likeness, unless God is in him and is his life from the inmost. That God is in man and, from the inmost, is his life, follows from what has been shown above (n. 4-6), that God alone is life, and that men and angels are recipients of life from Him. Moreover, that God is in man and that He makes His abode with him, is known from the Word; for which reason it is customary for preachers to declare that men ought to prepare themselves to receive God, that He may enter into them, and be in their hearts, that they may be His dwelling-place. The devout man says the same in his prayers, and some speak more openly respecting the Holy Spirit, which they believe to be in them when they are in holy zeal, and from that zeal they think, speak, and preach. That the Holy Spirit is the Lord, and not a God who is a person by Himself, has been shown in The Doctrine of the New Jerusalem Concerning the Lord (n. 51-53). For the Lord declares: In that day ye shall know that ye are in Me, and I in you (John 14:20; so also in chap. 15:4, 5; and chap. 17:23).

Now because the Lord is Divine Love and Divine Wisdom, and these two essentially are Himself, it is necessary, in order that He may abide in man and give life to man, that He should create and form in man receptacles and abodes for Himself; the one for love and the other for wisdom. These receptacles and abodes in man are called will and understanding; the receptacle and abode of love is called the will, and the receptacle and abode of wisdom is called the understanding. That these two are the Lord's in man, and that from these two man has all his life, will be seen in what follows.

That every man has these two, will and understanding, and that they are distinct from each other, as love and wisdom are distinct, is known and is not known in the world. It is known from common perception, but it is not known from thought and still less from thought when written out; for who does not know from common perception that the will and the understanding are two distinct things in man? For every one perceives this when he hears it stated, and may himself say to another, This man means well, but does not understand clearly; while that one's understanding is good, but his will is not; I like the man whose understanding and will are both good; but I do not like him whose understanding is good and his will bad. Yet when he thinks about the will and the understanding he does not make them two and distinguish them, but confounds them, since his thought then acts in common with the bodily sight. When writing he apprehends still less that will and understanding are two distinct things, because his thought then acts in common with the sensual, that is, with what is the man's own. From this it is that some can think and speak well, but cannot write well. This is common with women. It is the same with many other things. Is it not known by everyone from common perception that a man whose life is good is saved, but that a man whose life is bad is condemned? Also that one whose life is good will enter the society of angels, and will there see, hear, and speak like a man? Also that one who from justice does what is just and from what is right does right, has a conscience? But if one lapses from common perception, and submits these things to thought, he does not know what conscience is; or that the soul can see, hear, and speak like a man; or that the good of life is anything except giving to the poor. And if from thought you write about these things, you confirm them by appearances and fallacies, and by words of sound but of no substance. For this reason many of the learned who have thought much, and especially who have written much, have weakened and obscured, yea, have destroyed their common perception; while the simple see more clearly what is good and true than those who think themselves their superiors in wisdom. This common perception comes by influx from heaven, and descends into thought even to sight; but thought separated from common perception falls into imagination from the sight and from what is man's own. You may observe that this is so. Tell some truth to any one that is in common perception, and he will see it; tell him that from God and in God we are and live and are moved, and he will see it; tell him that God dwells with man in love and in wisdom, and he will see it; tell him further that the will is the receptacle of love, and the understanding of wisdom, and explain it a little, and he will see it; tell him that God is Love itself and Wisdom itself, and he will see it; ask him what conscience is, and he will tell you. But say the same things to one of the learned, who has not thought from common perception, but from principles or from ideas obtained from the world through sight, and he will not see. Then consider which is the wiser.

WILL AND UNDERSTANDING, WHICH ARE THE RECEPTACLES OF LOVE AND WISDOM, ARE IN THE BRAINS, IN THE WHOLE AND IN EVERY PART OF THEM, AND THEREFROM IN THE BODY, IN THE WHOLE AND IN EVERY PART OF IT. This shall be shown in the following order: (1) Love and wisdom, and will and understanding therefrom, make the very life of man. (2) The life of man in its first principles is in the brains, and in its derivatives in the body. (3) Such as life is in its first principles, such it is in the whole and in every part. (4) By means of first principles life is in the whole from every part, and in every part from the whole. (5) Such as the love is, such is the wisdom, consequently such is the man.

(1) Love and wisdom, and will and understanding therefrom, make the very life of man. Scarcely any one knows what life is. When one thinks about life, it seems as if it were a fleeting something, of which no distinct idea is possible. It so seems because it is not known that God alone is life, and that His life is Divine Love and Divine Wisdom. From this it is evident that in man life is nothing else than love and wisdom, and that there is life in man in the degree in which he receives these. It is known that heat and light go forth from the sun, and that all things in the universe are recipients and grow warm and bright in the degree in which they receive. So do heat and light go forth from the sun where the Lord is; the heat going forth therefrom is love, and the light wisdom (as shown in Part Second). Life, therefore, is from these two which go forth from the Lord as a sun. That love and wisdom from the Lord is life can be seen also from this, that man grows torpid as love recedes from him, and stupid as wisdom recedes from him, and that were they to recede altogether he would become extinct. There are many things pertaining to love which have received other names because they are derivatives, such as affections, desires, appetites, and their pleasures and enjoyments; and there are many things pertaining to wisdom, such as perception, reflection, recollection, thought, intention to an end; and there are many pertaining to both love and wisdom, such as consent, conclusion, and determination to action; besides others. All of these, in fact, pertain to both, but they are designated from the more prominent and nearer of the two. From these two are derived ultimately sensations, those of sight, hearing, smell, taste, and touch, with their enjoyments and pleasures. It is according to appearance that the eye sees; but it is the understanding that sees through the eye; consequently seeing is predicated also of the understanding. The appearance is that the ear hears; but it is the understanding that hears through the ear; consequently hearing is predicated also of attention and giving heed, which pertain to the understanding. The appearance is that the nose smells, and the tongue tastes but it is the understanding that smells and also tastes by virtue of its perception; therefore smelling and tasting are predicated also of perception. So in other cases. The sources of all these are love and wisdom; from which it can be seen that these two make the life of man.

Everyone sees that the understanding is the receptacle of wisdom, but few see that the will is the receptacle of love. This is because the will does not act at all by itself, but only through the understanding; also because the love of the will, in passing over into the wisdom of the understanding, is first changed into affection, and thus passes over; and affection is not perceived except by something pleasant in thinking, speaking, and acting, which is not noticed. Still it is evident that love is from the will, for the reason that everyone wills what he loves, and does not will what he does not love.

(2) The life of man in its first principles is in the brains, and in its derivatives in the body. In first principles means in its firsts, and in derivatives means in what is brought forth and formed from its firsts. By life in first principles is meant will and understanding. These two are what are in their first principles in the brains, and in their derivatives in the body. It is evident that the first principles or firsts of life are in the brains: (1) From the feeling itself; since man perceives, when he exerts his mind and thinks, that he thinks

in the brain. He draws in as it were the sight of the eye, contracts the forehead, and perceives the mental process to be within, especially inside the forehead and somewhat above it. (2) From man's formation in the womb; in that the brain or head is first developed, and continues for some time larger than the body. (3) In that the head is above and the body below; and it is according to order for the higher to act upon the lower, and not the reverse. (4) In that, when the brain is injured in the womb or by a wound or by disease, or by excessive application, thought is weakened and sometimes the mind becomes deranged. (5) In that all the external senses of the body sight, hearing, smell, and taste, with touch (the universal sense) as also speech, are in the front part of the head, which is called the face, and communicate immediately through fibers with the brains, and derive therefrom their sensitive and active life. (6) It is from this that affections, which are of love, appear imaged forth in the face, and that thoughts, which are of wisdom, are revealed in a kind of sparkle of the eyes. (7) Anatomy teaches that all fibers descend from the brains through the neck into the body, and that none ascend from the body through the neck into the brains. And where the fibers are in their first principles or firsts, there life is in its first principles or firsts. Will any one venture to deny that life has its origin where the fibers have their origin? (8) Ask any one of common perception where his thought resides or where he thinks, and he will say, In the head. Then appeal to some one who has assigned the seat of the soul to some gland or to the heart or somewhere else, and ask him where affection and thought therefrom are in their firsts, whether they are not in the brain? and he will answer, No, or that he does not know. The cause of this ignorance may be seen above (n. 361).

(3) Such as life is in its first principles, such it is in the whole and in every part. That this may be perceived, it shall now be told where in the brains these first principles are, and how they become derivative. Anatomy shows where in the brains these first principles are; it teaches that there are two brains; that these are continued from the head into the spinal column; that they consist of two substances, called cortical substance and medullary substance; that cortical substance consists of innumerable gland-like forms, and medullary substance of innumerable fiber-like forms. Now as these little glands are heads of fibrils, they are also their first principles. For from these, fibers begin and thereupon go forth, gradually bundling themselves into nerves. These bundles or nerves, when formed, descend to the organs of sense in the face, and to the organs of motion in the body, and form them. Consult any one skilled in the science of anatomy, and you will be convinced. This cortical or glandular substance constitutes the surface of the cerebrum, and also the surface of the corpora striata, from which proceeds the medulla oblongata; it also constitutes the middle of the cerebellum, and the middle of the spinal marrow. But medullary or fibrillary substance everywhere begins in and proceeds from the cortical; out of it nerves arise, and from them all things of the body. That this is true is proved by dissection. They who know these things, either from the study of anatomical science or from the testimony of those who are skilled in the science, can see that the first principles of life are in the same place as the beginnings of the fibers, and that fibers cannot go forth from themselves, but must go forth from first principles. These first principles, that is, beginnings, which appear as little glands, are almost countless; their multitude may be compared to the

multitude of stars in the universe; and the multitude of fibrils coming out of them may be compared to the multitude of rays going forth from the stars and bearing their heat and light to the earth. The multitude of these little glands may also be compared to the multitude of angelic societies in the heavens, which also are countless, and, I have been told, are in like order as the glands. Also the multitude of fibrils going out from these little glands may be compared to the spiritual truths and goods which in like manner flow down from the angelic societies like rays. From this it is that man is like a universe, and like a heaven in least form (as has been frequently said and shown above). From all which it can now be seen that such as life is in first principles, such it is in derivatives; or such as it is in its firsts in the brains, such it is in the things arising therefrom in the body.

(4) By means of first principles life is in the whole from every part, and in every part from the whole. This is because the whole, which is the brain and the body together, is originally made up of nothing but fibers proceeding from their first principles in the brains. It has no other origin, as is evident from what has been shown just above (n. 366); consequently, the whole is from every part; and by means of these first principles life is in every part from the whole, because the whole dispenses to each part its task and needs, thereby making it to be a part in the whole. In a word, the whole has existence from the parts, and the parts have permanent existence from the whole. That there is such reciprocal communion, and conjunction thereby, is clear from many things in the body. For the same order prevails there as in a state, commonwealth, or kingdom; the community has its existence from the individuals which are its parts, and the parts or individuals have permanent existence from the community. It is the same with every thing that has form, most of all in man.

(5) Such as the love is, such is the wisdom, consequently such is the man. For such as the love and wisdom are, such are the will and understanding, since the will is the receptacle of love, and the understanding of wisdom, as has been shown above; and these two make the man and his character. Love is manifold, so manifold that its varieties are limitless; as can be seen from the human race on the earths and in the heavens. There is no man or angel so like another that there is no difference. Love is what distinguishes; for every man is his own love. It is supposed that wisdom distinguishes; but wisdom is from love; it is the form of love; love is the esse of life, and wisdom is the existere of life from that esse. In the world it is believed that the understanding makes the man; but this is believed because the understanding can be elevated, as was shown above, into the light of heaven, giving man the appearance of being wise; yet so much of the understanding as transcends, that is to say, so much as is not of the love, although it appears to be man's and therefore to determine man's character, is only an appearance. For so much of the understanding as transcends is, indeed, from the love of knowing and being wise, but not at the same time from the love of applying to life what man knows and is wise in. Consequently, in the world it either in time passes away or lingers outside of the things of memory in its mere borders as something ready to drop off; and therefore after death it is separated, no more of it remaining than is in accord with the spirit's own love. Inasmuch as love makes the life of man, and thus the man himself, all societies of heaven, and all angels in societies, are arranged according to affections

belonging to love, and no society nor any angel in a society according to anything of the understanding separate from love. So likewise in the hells and their societies, but in accordance with loves opposite to the heavenly loves. From all this it can be seen that such as the love is such is the wisdom, and consequently such is the man.

It is acknowledged, indeed, that man is such as his reigning love is, but only in respect to his mind and disposition, not in respect to his body, thus not wholly. But it has been made known to me by much experience in the spiritual world, that man from head to foot, that is, from things primary in the head to the outmosts in the body, is such as his love is. For all in the spiritual world are forms of their own love; the angels forms of heavenly love, the devils of hellish love; the devils deformed in face and body, but the angels beautiful in face and body. Moreover, when their love is assailed their faces are changed, and if much assailed they wholly disappear. This is peculiar to that world, and so happens because their bodies make one with their minds. The reason is evident from what has been said above, that all things of the body are derivatives, that is, are things woven together by means of fibers out of first principles, which are receptacles of love and wisdom. Howsoever these first principles may be, their derivatives cannot be different; therefore wherever first principles go their derivatives follow, and cannot be separated. For this reason he who raises his mind to the Lord is wholly raised up to Him, and he who casts his mind down to hell is wholly cast down thither; consequently the whole man, in conformity to his life's love, comes either into heaven or into hell. That man's mind is a man because God is a Man, and that the body is the mind's external, which feels and acts, and that they are thus one and not two, is a matter of angelic wisdom.

It is to be observed that the very forms of man's members, organs, and viscera, as regards the structure itself, are from fibers that arise out of their first principles in the brains; but these become fixed by means of such substances and matters as are in earths, and from earths in air and in ether. This is effected by means of the blood. Consequently, in order that all parts of the body may be maintained in their formation and rendered permanent in their functions, man requires to be nourished by material food, and to be continually renewed.

THERE IS A CORRESPONDENCE OF THE WILL WITH THE HEART, AND OF THE UNDERSTANDING WITH THE LUNGS. This shall be shown in the following series: (1) All things of the mind have relation to the will and understanding, and all things of the body to the heart and lungs. (2) There is a correspondence of the will and understanding with the heart and lungs, consequently a correspondence of all things of the mind with all things of the body. (3) The will corresponds to the heart. (4) The understanding corresponds to the lungs. (5) By means of this correspondence many arcana relating to the will and understanding, thus also to love and wisdom, may be disclosed. (6) Man's mind is his spirit, and the spirit is the man, while the body is the external by means of which the mind or spirit feels and acts in its world. (7) The conjunction of man's spirit with his body is by means of the correspondence of his will and understanding with his heart and lungs, and their separation is from non-correspondence.

(1) All things of the mind have relation to the will and understanding, and

all things of the body to the heart and lungs. By the mind nothing else is meant than the will and understanding, which in their complex are all things that affect man and all that he thinks, thus all things of man's affection and thought. The things that affect man are of his will, and the things that he thinks are of his understanding. That all things of man's thought are of his understanding is known, since he thinks from the understanding; but it is not so well known that all things of man's affection are of his will, this is not so well known because when man is thinking he pays no attention to the affection, but only to what he is thinking; just as when he hears a person speaking, he pays no attention to the tone of the voice but only to the language. Yet affection is related to thought as the tone of the voice is to the language; consequently the affection of the one speaking is known by the tone, and his thought by the language. Affection is of the will, because all affection is of love, and the will is the receptacle of love, as was shown above. He that is not aware that affection is of the will confounds affection with understanding, for he declares it to be one with thought, yet they are not one but act as one. That they are confounded is evident from the common expression, I think I will do this, meaning, I will to do it. But that they are two is also evident from a common expression, I wish to think about this matter; and when one thinks about it, the affection of the will is present in the thought of the understanding, like the tone in speech, as was said before. That all parts of the body have relation to the heart and lungs is known, but that there is a correspondence of the heart and lungs with the will and understanding is not known. This subject will therefore be treated in what follows.

Because the will and understanding are the receptacles of love and wisdom, these two are organic forms, or forms organized out of the purest substances; for such they must be to be receptacles. It is no objection that their organization is imperceptible to the eye; it lies beyond the reach of vision, even when this is increased by the microscope. The smallest insects are also too small to be seen, yet they have organs of sense and motion, for they feel, walk, and fly. That they have brains, hearts, pulmonary pipes, and viscera, acute observers have discovered from their anatomy by means of the microscope. Since minute insects themselves are not visible, and still less so their component viscera, and since it is not denied that they are organized even to each single particle in them, how can it be said that the two receptacles of love and wisdom, called will and understanding, are not organic forms? How can love and wisdom, which are life from the Lord, act upon what is not a subject, or upon what has no substantial existence? Without organic forms, how can thought inhere; and from thought inherent in nothing can one speak? Is not the brain, where thought comes forth, complete and organized in every part? The organic forms themselves are there visible even to the naked eye; and the receptacles of the will and understanding, in their first principles, are plainly to be seen in the cortical substance, where they are perceptible as minute glands (On which see above, n. 366). Do not, I pray, think of these things from an idea of vacuum. Vacuum is nothing, and in nothing nothing takes place, and from nothing nothing comes forth. (On the idea of vacuum, see above, n. 82.)

(2) There is a correspondence of the will and understanding with the heart and lungs, consequently a correspondence of all things of the mind with all

things of the body. This is new: it has hitherto been unknown because it has not been known what the spiritual is, and how it differs from the natural; therefore it has not been known what correspondence is; for there is a correspondence between things spiritual and things natural, and by means of correspondence they are conjoined. It is said that heretofore there has been no knowledge of what the spiritual is, or of what its correspondence with the natural is and therefore what correspondence is; yet these might have been known. Who does not know that affection and thought are spiritual, therefore that all things of affection and thought are spiritual? Who does not know that action and speech are natural, therefore that all things of action and speech are natural: who does not know that affection and thought, which are spiritual, cause man to act and to speak? From this who cannot see what correspondence is between things spiritual and things natural? Does not thought make the tongue speak, and affection together with thought make the body act? There are two distinct things: I can think without speaking, and I can will without acting; and the body, it is known, neither thinks nor wills, but thought falls into speech, and will descends into action. Does not affection also beam forth from the face, and there exhibit a type of itself? This everyone knows. Is not affection, regarded in itself, spiritual, and the change of countenance, called the expression, natural? From this who might not conclude that there is correspondence; and further, a correspondence of all things of the mind with all things of the body; and since all things of the mind have relation to affection and thought, or what is the same, to the will and understanding, and all things of the body to the heart and lungs, - that there is a correspondence of the will with the heart and of the understanding with the lungs? Such things have remained unknown, though they might have been known, because man has become so external as to be unwilling to acknowledge anything except the natural. This has become the joy of his love, and from that the joy of his understanding; consequently it has become distasteful to him to raise his thought above the natural to anything spiritual separate from the natural; therefore, from his natural love and its delights, he can think of the spiritual only as a purer natural, and of correspondence only as a something flowing in by continuity; yea, the merely natural man cannot think of anything separate from the natural; any such thing to him is nothing. Again, these things have not heretofore been seen and known, because everything of religion, that is, everything called spiritual, has been banished from the sight of man by the dogma of the whole Christian world, that matters theological, that is, spiritual, which councils and certain leaders have decreed, are to be believed blindly because (as they say) they transcend the understanding. Some, therefore, have imagined the spiritual to be like a bird flying above the air in an ether to which the sight of the eye does not reach; when yet it is like a bird of paradise, which flies near the eye, even touching the pupil with its beautiful wings and longing to be seen. By the sight of the eye intellectual vision is meant.

The correspondence of the will and understanding with the heart and lungs cannot be abstractly proved, that is, by mere reasonings, but it may be proved by effects. It is much the same as it is with the causes of things which can be seen rationally, yet not clearly except by means of effects; for causes are in effects, and by means of effects make themselves visible; and until causes are thus made visible, the mind is not assured respecting them. In what follows, the effects of this correspondence will be described. But lest any one should fall into ideas of this correspondence imbibed from hypotheses about the soul, let him first read over carefully the propositions in the preceding chapter, as follows: Love and wisdom, and the will and understanding therefrom, make the very life of man (n. 363, 365). The life of man is in first principles in the brains, and in derivatives in the body (n. 365). Such as life is in first principles, such it is in the whole and in every part (n. 366). By means of these first principles life is in the whole from every part, and in every part from the whole (n. 367). Such as the love is, such is the wisdom, consequently such is the man (n. 368).

It is permitted to introduce here, in the way of evidence, a representation of the correspondence of the will and understanding with the heart and lungs which was seen in heaven among the angels. By a wonderful flowing into spiral movements, such as no words can express, the angels formed the likeness of a heart and the likeness of lungs, with all the interior structures therein; and in this they were falling in with the flow of heaven, for heaven from the inflowing of love and wisdom from the Lord strives to come into such forms. They thus represented the conjunction of the heart and lungs, and at the same time the correspondence of these with the love of the will and with the wisdom of the understanding. This correspondence and union they called the heavenly marriage; saying that in the whole body, and in its several members, organs, and viscera, it is the same as in the things belonging to the heart and lungs; also that where the heart and lungs do not act, each in its turn, there can be no motion of life from any voluntary principle, and no sensation of life from any intellectual principle.

Inasmuch as the correspondence of the heart and lungs With the will and understanding is treated of in what now follows, and upon this correspondence is based that of all parts of the body, namely, the members, the organs of the senses, and the viscera throughout the body, and inasmuch as the correspondence of natural things with spiritual has been heretofore unknown, and yet is amply shown in two works, one of which treats of Heaven and Hell and the other, the Arcana Coelestia, of the spiritual sense of the Word in Genesis and Exodus, I will here point out what has been written and shown in those two works respecting correspondence. In the work on Heaven and Hell: The correspondence of all things of heaven with all things of man (n. 87-102). The correspondence of all things of heaven with all things on earth (n. 103-115). In the Arcana Coelestia, the work on the spiritual sense of the Word in Genesis and Exodus: The correspondence of the face and its expressions with the affections of the mind (n. 1568, 2988, 2989, 3631, 4796, 4797, 4800, 5165, 5168, 5695, 9306). The correspondence of the body, its gestures and actions, with things intellectual and things voluntary (n. 2988, 3632, 4215). The correspondence of the senses in general (n. 4318-4330). The correspondence of the eyes and of their sight (n. 4403-4420). The correspondence of the nostrils and of smell (n. 4624-4634). The correspondence of the ear, and of hearing (n. 4652-4660). The correspondence of the tongue and of taste (n. 4791-4805). The correspondence of the hands, arms, shoulders and feet (n. 4931-4953). The correspondence of the loins and organs of generation (n. 5050-5062). Thy correspondence of the internal viscera of the body, especially of the stomach, thymus gland, the receptacle and ducts of the chyle and lacteals, and of the mesentery (n. 5171-5180, 5181, 5189). The correspondence of the spleen (n. 9698). The correspondence of the peritonaeum, kidneys and bladder (n. 5377-5385). The correspondence of the liver, and of the hepatic, cystic and pancreatic ducts (n. 5183-5185). The correspondence of the intestines (n. 5392-5395, 5379). The correspondence of the bones (n. 5560-5564). The correspondence of the skin (n. 5552-5559). The correspondence of heaven with man (n. 911, 1900, 1982, 2996-2998, 3624-3649, 3741-3745, 3884, 4051, 4279, 4403, 4423, 4524, 4525, 6013, 6057, 9279, 9632). All things that exist in the natural world and in its three kingdoms correspond to all things which appear in the spiritual world (n. 1632, 1831, 1881, 2758, 2990-3003, 3213-3227, 3483, 3624-3649, 4044, 4053, 4116, 4366, 4939, 5116, 5377, 5428, 5477, 8211 9280). All things that appear in the heavens are correspondences (n. 1521, 1532, 1619-1625, 1807, 1808, 1971, 1974, 1977, 1980, 1981, 2299, 2601, 3213-3226, 3349, 3350, 3475-3585, 3748, 9481, 9570, 9576, 9577). The correspondence of the sense of the letter of the Word and of its spiritual sense is treated of in the Arcana Coelestia throughout; and on this subject see also the Doctrine of the New Jerusalem concerning the Sacred Scripture (n. 5-26, 27-65).

(3) The will corresponds to the heart. This can not be seen so clearly taken by itself as when the will is considered in its effects (as was said above). Taken by itself it can be seen by this, that all affections, which are of love, induce changes in the heart's pulsations, as is evident from the pulse of the arteries, which act synchronously with the heart. The heart's changes and pulsations in accordance with the love's affections are innumerable. Those felt by the finger are only that the beats are slow or quick, high or low, weak or strong, regular or irregular, and so on; thus that there is a difference in joy and in sorrow, in tranquillity of mind and in wrath, in fearlessness and in fear, in hot diseases and in cold, and so on. Because the two motions of the heart, systolic and diastolic, change and vary in this manner according to the affections of each one's love, many of the ancient and after them some modern writers have assigned the affections to the heart, and have made the heart their dwelling-place. From this have come into common language such expressions as a stout heart, a timid heart, a joyful heart, a sad heart, a soft heart, a hard heart, a great heart, a weak heart, a whole heart, a broken heart, a heart of flesh, a heart of stone; likewise being gross, or soft, or tender in heart; giving the heart to a thing, giving a single heart, giving a new heart, laying up in the heart, receiving in the heart, not reaching the heart, hardening one's heart, a friend at heart; also the terms concord, discord, folly [vecordia], and other similar terms expressive of love and its affections. There are like expressions in the Word, because the Word was written by correspondences. Whether you say love or will it is the same, because the will is the receptacle of love, as was explained above.

It is known that there is vital heat in man and in every living creature; but its origin is not known. Every one speaks of it from conjecture, consequently such as have known nothing of the correspondence of natural things with spiritual have ascribed its origin, some to the sun's heat, some to the activity of the parts, some to life itself; but as they have not known what life is, they have been content with the mere phrase. But any one who knows that there is a correspondence of love and its affections with the heart and its derivations may know that the origin of vital heat is love. For love goes forth as heat from the spiritual sun where the Lord is, and moreover is felt as heat by the angels. This spiritual heat which in its essence is love, is what inflows by correspondence into the heart and its blood, and imparts heat to it, and at the same time vivifies it. That a man grows hot, and, as it were, is fired, according to his love and the degree of it, and grows torpid and cold according to its decrease, is known, for it is felt and seen; it is felt by the heat throughout the body, and seen by the flushing of the face; and on the other hand, extinction of love is felt by coldness in the body, and is seen by paleness in the face. Because love is the life of man, the heart is the first and the last of his life; and because love is the life of man, and the soul maintains its life in the body by means of the blood, in the Word blood is called the soul (Gen. 9:4; Levit. 17:14). The various meanings of soul will be explained in what follows.

The redness, also, of the blood is from the correspondence of the heart and the blood with love and its affection; for in the spiritual world there are all kinds of colors, of which red and white are the fundamental, the rest deriving their varieties from these and from their opposites, which are a dusky fire color and black. Red there corresponds to love, and white to wisdom. Red corresponds to love because it originates in the fire of the spiritual sun, and white corresponds to wisdom because it originates in the light of that sun. And because there is a correspondence of love with the heart, the blood must needs be red, and reveal its origin. For this reason in the heavens where love to the Lord reigns the light is flame-colored, and the angels there are clothed in purple garments; and in the heavens where wisdom reigns the light is white, and the angels there are clothed in white linen garments.

The heavens are divided into two kingdoms, one called celestial, the other spiritual; in the celestial kingdom love to the Lord reigns, and in the spiritual kingdom wisdom from that love. The kingdom where love reigns is called heaven's cardiac kingdom, the one where wisdom reigns is called its pulmonic kingdom. Be it known, that the whole angelic heaven in its aggregate represents a single man, and before the Lord appears as a single man; consequently its heart makes one kingdom and its lungs another. For there is a general cardiac and pulmonic movement throughout heaven, and a particular movement therefrom in each angel. The general cardiac and pulmonic movement is from the Lord alone, because love and wisdom are from Him alone. For these two movements are in the sun where the Lord is and which is from the Lord, and from that in the angelic heavens and in the universe. Banish spaces and think of omnipresence, and you will be convinced that it is so. That the heavens are divided into two kingdoms, celestial and spiritual, see the work on Heaven and Hell (n. 20-28); and that the whole angelic heaven in the aggregate represents a single man (n. 59-67).

(4) The understanding corresponds to the lungs. This follows from what has been said of the correspondence of the will with the heart; for there are two things, will and understanding, which reign in the spiritual man, that is, in the mind, and there are two things, heart and lungs, which reign in the natural man, that is, in the body; and there is correspondence (as was said above) of all things of the mind with all thinks of the body; from which it follows that as the

will corresponds to the heart, so the understanding corresponds to the lungs. Moreover, that the understanding corresponds to the lungs any one may observe in himself, both from his thought and from his speech. (1) From thought: No one is able to think except with the concurrence and concordance of the pulmonary respiration; consequently, when he thinks tacitly he breathes tacitly, if he thinks deeply he breathes deeply; he draws in the breath and lets it out, contracts and expands the lungs, slowly or quickly, eagerly, gently, or intently, all in conformity to his thought, thus to the influx of affection from love; yea, if he hold the breath entirely he is unable to think, except in his spirit by its respiration, which is not manifestly perceived. (2) From speech: Since not the least vocal sound flows forth from the mouth without the concurrent aid of the lungs, - for the sound, which is articulated into words, all comes forth from the lungs through the trachea and epiglottis, - therefore, according to the inflation of these bellows and the opening of the passage the voice is raised even to a shout, and according to their contraction it is lowered; and if the passage is entirely closed speech ceases and thought with it.

Since the understanding corresponds to the lungs and thought therefrom to the respiration of the lungs, in the Word, "soul" and "spirit" signify the understanding; for example: Thou shalt love the Lord thy God with all thy heart and with all thy soul (Matt. 22:37). God will give a new heart and a new spirit (Ezek. 36:26; Psalm 51:10). That "heart" signifies the love of the will was shown above; therefore "soul" and "spirit" signify the wisdom of the understanding. That the spirit of God, also called the Holy Spirit, means Divine Wisdom, and therefore Divine Truth which is the light of men, may be seen in The Doctrine of the New Jerusalem concerning the Lord (n. 50, 51), therefore, The Lord breathed on His disciples, and said, Receive ye the Holy Spirit John 20:22); for the same reason it is said that: Jehovah God breathed into the nostrils of Adam the breath of lives, and he was made into a living soul (Gen. 2:7); also He said to the prophet: Prophesy upon the breath, and say unto the wind, Come from the four winds, O breath, and breathe upon these slain, that they may live (Ezek. 37:9); likewise in other places; therefore the Lord is called "the breath of the nostrils," and "the breath of life." Because respiration passes through the nostrils, perception is signified by them; and an intelligent man is said to be keen-scented, and an unintelligent man to be dull-scented. For the same reason, spirit and wind in the Hebrew, and in some other languages, are the same word; for the word spirit is derived from a word that means breathing; and therefore when a man dies he is said to give up the ghost [anima]. It is for the same reason that men believe the spirit to be wind, or an airy something like breath breathed out from the lungs, and the soul to be of like nature. From all this it can be seen that to "love God with all the heart and all the soul" means to love Him with all the love and with all the understanding, and to "give a new heart and a new spirit" means to give a new will and a new understanding. Because "spirit" signifies understanding, it is said of Bezaleel: That he was filled with the spirit of wisdom, of intelligence, and of knowledge (Exod. 31:3); and of Joshua: That he was filled with the spirit of wisdom (Deut. 34:9); and Nebuchadnezzar says of Daniel: That an excellent spirit of knowledge, of intelligence, and of wisdom, was in him (Dan. 5:11, 12, 14); and it is said in Isaiah: They that err in spirit shall learn intelligence (29:24); likewise in many other places.

Since all things of the mind have relation to the will and understanding, and all things of the body to the heart and lungs, there are in the head two brains, distinct from each other as will and understanding are distinct. The cerebellum is especially the organ of the will, and the cerebrum of the understanding. Likewise the heart and lungs in the body are distinct from the remaining parts there. They are separated by the diaphragm, and are enveloped by their own covering, called the pleura, and form that part of the body called the chest. In the other parts of the body, called members, organs, and viscera, there is a joining together of the two, and thus there are pairs; for instance, the arms, hands, loins, feet, eyes, and nostrils; and within the body the kidneys, ureters, and testicles; and the viscera which are not in pairs are divided into right and left. Moreover, the brain itself is divided into two hemispheres, the heart into two ventricles, and the lungs into two lobes; the right of all these having relation to the good of truth, and the left to the truth of good, or, what is the same, the right having relation to the good of love from which is the truth of wisdom, and the left having relation to the truth of wisdom which is from the good of love. And because the conjunction of good and truth is reciprocal, and by means of that conjunction the two become as it were one, therefore the pairs in man act together and conjointly in functions, motions, and senses.

(5) By means of this correspondence many arcana relating to the will and understanding, thus also to love and wisdom, may be disclosed. In the world it is scarcely known what the will is or what love is, for the reason that man is not able, by himself, to love, and from love to will, although he is able as it were by himself to exercise intelligence and thought; just as he is not able of himself to cause the heart to beat, although he is able of himself to cause the lungs to respire. Now because it is scarcely known in the world what the will is or what love is, but it is known what the heart and the lungs are, - for these are objects of sight and can be examined, and have been examined and described by anatomists, while the will and the understanding are not objects of sight, and cannot be so examined - therefore when it is known that these correspond, and by correspondence act as one, many arcana relating to the will and understanding may be disclosed that could not otherwise be disclosed; those for instance relating to the conjunction of the will with the understanding, and the reciprocal conjunction of the understanding with the will; those relating to the conjunction of love with wisdom, and the reciprocal conjunction of wisdom with love; also those relating to the derivation of love into affections, and to the consociation of affections, to their influx into perceptions and thoughts, and finally their influx according to correspondence into the bodily acts and senses. These and many other arcana may be both disclosed and illustrated by the conjunction of the heart and lungs, and by the influx of the blood from the heart into the lungs, and reciprocally from the lungs into the heart, and therefrom through the arteries into all the members, organs and viscera of the body.

(6) Man's mind is his spirit, and the spirit is the man, while the body is an external by means of which the mind or spirit feels and acts in its world. That man's mind is his spirit, and that the spirit is the man, can hardly enter the faith of those who have supposed the spirit to be wind, and the soul to be an airy something like breath breathed out from the lungs. For they say, How can the

spirit, when it is spirit, be the man, and how can the soul, when it is soul, be the man? They think in the same way of God because He is called a Spirit. This idea of the spirit and the soul has come from the fact that spirit and wind in some languages are the same word; also, that when a man dies, he is said to give up the ghost or spirit; also, that life returns, after suffocation or swooning, when the spirit or breath of the lungs comes back. Because in these cases nothing but the breath or air is perceived, it is concluded from the eye and bodily sense that the spirit and soul of man after death is not the man. From this corporeal conclusion about the spirit and soul, various hypotheses have arisen, and these have given birth to a belief that man after death does not become a man until the day of the last judgment, and that meanwhile his spirit remains somewhere or other awaiting reunion with the body, according to what has been shown in the Continuation concerning the Last Judgment (n. 32-38). Because man's mind is his spirit, the angels, who also are spirits, are called minds.

Man's mind is his spirit, and the spirit is the man, because by the mind all things of man's will and understanding are meant, which things are in first principles in the brains and in derivatives in the body; therefore in respect to their forms they are all things of man. This being so, the mind (that is, the will and understanding) impels the body and all its belongings at will. Does not the body do whatever the mind thinks and wills? Does not the mind incite the ear to hear, and direct the eye to see, move the tongue and the lips to speak, impel the hands and fingers to do whatever it pleases, and the feet to walk whither it will? Is the body, then, anything but obedience to its mind; and can the body be such unless the mind is in its derivatives in the body? Is it consistent with reason to think that the body acts from obedience simply because the mind so wills? in which case they should be two, the one above and the other below, one commanding, the other obeying. As this is in no way consistent with reason, it follows that man's life is in its first principles in the brains, and in its derivatives in the body (according to what has been said above, n. 365); also that such as life is in first principles, such it is in the whole and in every part (n. 366); and by means of these first principles life is in the whole from every part, and in every part from the whole (n. 367). That all things of the mind have relation to the will and understanding, and that the will and understanding are the receptacles of love and wisdom from the Lord, and that these two make the life of man, has been shown in the preceding pages.

From what has now been said it can also be seen that man's mind is the man himself. For the primary texture of the human form, that is, the human form itself with each and every thing thereof, is from first principles continued from the brain through the nerves, in the manner described above. It is this form into which man comes after death, who is then called a spirit or an angel, and who is in all completeness a man, but a spiritual man. The material form that is added and superinduced in the world, is not a human form by itself, but only by virtue of the spiritual form, to which it is added and superinduced that man may be enabled to perform uses in the natural world, and also to draw to himself out of the purer substances of the world a fixed continant of spiritual things, and thus continue and perpetuate life. It is a truth of angelic wisdom that man's mind, not alone in general, but in every particular, is in a perpetual conatus toward the human form, for the reason that God is a Man.

That man may be man there must be no part lacking, either in head or in body, that has existence in the complete man; since there is nothing therein that does not enter into the human form and constitute it; for it is the form of love and wisdom, and this, in itself considered, is Divine. In it are all terminations of love and wisdom, which in God-Man are infinite, but in His image, that is, in man, angel, or spirit, are finite. If any part that has existence in man were lacking, there would be lacking something of termination from the love and wisdom corresponding to it, whereby the Lord might be from firsts in outmosts with man, and might from His Divine Love through His Divine Wisdom provide uses in the created world.

(7) The conjunction of man's spirit with his body is by means of the correspondence of his will and understanding with his heart and lungs, and their separation is from non- correspondence. As it has heretofore been unknown that man's mind, by which is meant the will and understanding, is his spirit, and that the spirit is a man; and as it has been unknown that man's spirit, as well as his body, has a pulse and respiration, it could not be known that the pulse and respiration of the spirit in man flow into the pulse and respiration of his body and produce them. Since, then, man's spirit, as well as his body, enjoys a pulse and respiration, it follows that there is a like correspondence of the pulse and respiration of man's spirit with the pulse and respiration of his body, - for, as was said, his mind is his spirit, - consequently, when the two pairs of motions cease to correspond, separation takes place, which is death. Separation or death ensues when from any kind of disease or accident the body comes into such a state as to be unable to act in unison with its spirit, for thus correspondence perishes, and with it conjunction; not, however, when respiration alone ceases, but when the heart's pulsation ceases. For so long as the heart is moved, love with its vital heat remains and preserves life, as is evident in cases of swoon and suffocation, and in the condition of fetal life in the womb. In a word, man's bodily life depends on the correspondence of its pulse and respiration with the pulse and respiration of his spirit; and when that correspondence ceases, the bodily life ceases, and his spirit departs and continues its life in the spiritual world, which is so similar to his life in the natural world that he does not know that he has died. Men generally enter the spiritual world two days after the death of the body. For I have spoken with some after two days.

That a spirit, as well as a man on earth in the body enjoys a pulse and a respiration, can only be proved by spirits and angels themselves, when privilege is granted to speak with them. This privilege has been granted to me. When questioned about the matter they declared that they are just as much men as those in the world are, and possess a body as well as they, but a spiritual body, and feel the beat of the heart in the chest, and the beat of the arteries in the wrist, just as men do in the natural world. I have questioned many about the matter, and they all gave like answer. That man's spirit respires within his body has been granted me to learn by personal experience. On one occasion angels were allowed to control my respiration, and to diminish it at pleasure, and at length to withdraw it, until only the respiration of my spirit remained, which I then perceived by sense. A like experience was granted me when permitted to learn the state of the dying (as may be seen in the work on Heaven and Hell, n. 449). I have sometimes been brought into the respiration of my spirit only, which I have then sensibly perceived to be in accord with the common respiration of heaven. Also many times I have been in a state like that of angels, and also raised up into heaven to them, and being then out of the body in spirit, I talked with angels with a respiration in like manner as in the world. From this and other personal evidence it has been made clear to me that man's spirit respires, not only in the body but also after it has left the body; that the respiration of the spirit is so silent as not to be perceptible to man; and that it inflows into the manifest respiration of the body almost as cause flows into effect, or thought into the lungs and through the lungs into speech. From all this it is also evident that conjunction of spirit and body in man is by means of the correspondence of the cardiac and pulmonic movement in both.

These two movements, the cardiac and the pulmonic, derive their origin and persistence from this, that the whole angelic heaven, in general and in particular, is in these two movements of life; and the whole angelic heaven is in these movements because the Lord pours them in from the sun, where He is, and which is from Him; for these two movements are maintained by that sun from the Lord. It is evident that such is their origin since all things of heaven and all things of the world depend on the Lord through that sun in a connection, by virtue of form, like a chain-work from the first to outmosts, also since the life of love and wisdom is from the Lord, and all the forces of the universe are from life. That the variation of these movements is according to the reception of love and wisdom, also follows.

More will be said in what follows of the correspondence of these movements, as what the nature of that correspondence is in those who respire with heaven, and what it is in those who respire with hell; also what it is in those who speak with heaven, but think with hell, thus what it is with hypocrites, flatterers, deceivers, and others.

FROM THE CORRESPONDENCE OF THE HEART WITH THE WILL AND OF THE LUNGS WITH THE UNDERSTANDING, EVERYTHING MAY BE KNOWN THAT CAN BE KNOWN ABOUT THE WILL AND UNDERSTANDING, OR ABOUT LOVE AND WISDOM, THEREFORE ABOUT THE SOUL OF MAN. Many in the learned world have wearied themselves with inquiries respecting the soul; but as they knew nothing of the spiritual world, or of man's state after death, they could only frame theories, not about the nature of the soul, but about its operation on the body. Of the nature of the soul they could have no idea except as something most pure in the ether, and of its containing form they could have no idea except as being ethereal. But knowing that the soul is spiritual, they dared not say much about the matter openly, for fear of ascribing to the soul something natural. With this conception of the soul, and yet knowing that the soul operates on the body, and produces all things in it that relate to its sensation and motion, they have wearied themselves, as was said, with inquiries respecting the operation of the soul on the body. This has been held by some to be effected by influx, and by some to be effected by harmony. But as this investigation has disclosed nothing in which the mind anxious to see the real truth can acquiesce, it has been granted me to speak with angels, and to be enlightened on the subject by their wisdom; the fruits of which are as follows: Man's soul, which lives after death, is his spirit, and is in complete form a man; the soul of this form is the will and understanding, and the soul of these is love and wisdom from the Lord; these two are what constitute man's life, which is from the Lord above; yet for the sake of man's reception of Him, He causes life to appear as if it were man's; but that man may not claim life for himself as his, and thus withdraw himself from this reception of the Lord, the Lord has also taught that everything of love, which is called good, and everything of wisdom, which is called truth, is from Him, and nothing of these from man; and as these two are life, that everything of life which is life is from Him.

Since the soul in its very esse is love and wisdom, and these two in man are from the Lord, there are created in man two receptacles, which are also the abodes of the Lord in man; one for love, the other for wisdom, the one for love called the will, the other for wisdom called the understanding. Now since Love and Wisdom in the Lord are one distinctly (as may be seen above, n. 17-22), and Divine Love is of His Divine Wisdom, and Divine Wisdom is of His Divine Love (n. 34-39), and since these so go forth from God-Man, that is, from the Lord, therefore these two receptacles and abodes of the Lord in man, the will and understanding, are so created by the Lord as to be distinctly two, and yet make one in every operation and every sensation; for in these the will and understanding cannot be separated. Nevertheless, to enable man to become a receptacle and an abode of the Lord, it is provided, as necessary to this end, that man's understanding can be raised above his proper love into some light of wisdom in the love of which the man is not, and that he can thereby see and be taught how he must live if he would come also into that higher love, and thus enjoy eternal happiness. But by the misuse of this power to elevate the understanding above his proper love, man has subverted in himself that which might have been the receptacle and abode of the Lord (that is, of love and wisdom from the Lord), by making the will an abode for the love of self and the world, and the understanding an abode for whatever confirms those loves. From this it has come that these two abodes, the will and understanding, have become abodes of infernal love, and by confirmations in favor of these loves, abodes of infernal thought, which in hell is esteemed as wisdom.

The reason why the love of self and love of the world are infernal loves, and yet man has been able to come into them and thus subvert the will and understanding within him, is as follows: the love of self and the love of the world by creation are heavenly loves; for they are loves of the natural man serviceable to spiritual loves, as a foundation is to a house. For man, from the love of self and the world, seeks the welfare of his body, desires food, clothing, and habitation, is solicitous for the welfare of his family, and to secure employment for the sake of use, and even, in the interest of obedience, to be honored according to the dignity of the affairs which he administers, and to find delight and refreshment in worldly enjoyment; yet all this for the sake of the end, which must be use For through these things man is in a state to serve the Lord and to serve the neighbor. When, however, there is no love of serving the Lord and serving the neighbor, but only a love of serving himself by means of the world, then from being heavenly that love becomes hellish, for it causes a man to sink his mind and disposition in what is his own, and that in itself is wholly evil.

Now that man may not by the understanding be in heaven while by the will he is in hell, as is possible, and may thereby have a divided mind, after death everything of the understanding which transcends its own love is removed; whereby it comes that in everyone the will and understanding finally make one. With those in heaven the will loves good and the understanding thinks truth; but with those in hell the will loves evil and the understanding thinks falsity. The same is true of man in this world when he is thinking from his spirit, as he does when alone; yet many, so long as they are in the body, when they are not alone think otherwise. They then think otherwise because they raise their understanding above the proper love of their will, that is, of their spirit. These things have been said, to make known that the will and understanding are two distinct things, although created to act as one, and that they are made to act as one after death, if not before.

Now since love and wisdom, and therefore will and understanding, are what are called the soul, and how the soul acts upon the body, and effects all its operations, is to be shown in what follows, and since this may be known from the correspondence of the heart with the will, and of the lungs with the understanding, by means of that correspondence what follows has been disclosed: (1) Love or the will is man's very life. (2) Love or the will strives unceasingly towards the human form and all things of that form. (3) Love or the will is unable to effect anything by its human form without a marriage with wisdom or the understanding. (4) Love or the will prepares a house or bridal chamber for its future wife, which is wisdom or the understanding. (5) Love or the will also prepares all things in its human form, that it may act conjointly with wisdom or the understanding. (6) After the nuptials, the first conjunction is through affection for knowing, from which springs affection for truth. (7) The second conjunction is through affection for understanding, from which springs perception of truth. (8) The third conjunction is through affection for seeing truth, from which springs thought. (9) Through these three conjunctions love or the will is in its sensitive life and in its active life. (10) Love or the will introduces wisdom or the understanding into all things of its house. (11) Love or the will does nothing except in conjunction with wisdom or the understanding. (12) Love or the will conjoins itself to wisdom or the understanding, and causes wisdom or the understanding to be reciprocally conjoined to it. (13) Wisdom or the understanding, from the potency given to it by love or the will, can be elevated, and can receive such things as are of light out of heaven, and perceive them. (14) Love or the will can in like manner be elevated and can perceive such things as are of heat out of heaven, provided it loves its consort in that degree. (15) Otherwise love or the will draws down wisdom or the understanding from its elevation, that it may act as one with itself. (16) Love or the will is purified by wisdom in the understanding, if they are elevated together. (17) Love or the will is defiled in the understanding and by it, if they are not elevated together. (18) Love, when purified by wisdom in the understanding, becomes spiritual and celestial. (19) Love, when defiled in the understanding and by it, becomes natural and sensual. (20) The capacity to understand called rationality, and the capacity to act called freedom, still remain. (21) Spiritual and celestial love is love towards the neighbor and love to the Lord; and natural and sensual love is love of the world and love of self.

(22) It is the same with charity and faith and their conjunction as with the will and understanding and their conjunction.

(1) Love or the will is man's very life. This follows from the correspondence of the heart with the will (considered above, n. 378-381). For as the heart acts in the body, so does the will act in the mind; and as all things of the body depend for existence and motion upon the heart, so do all things of the mind depend for existence and life upon the will. It is said, upon the will, but this means upon the love, because the will is the receptacle of love, and love is life itself (see above, n. 1-3), and love, which is life itself, is from the Lord alone. By the heart and its extension into the body through the arteries and veins it can be seen that love or the will is the life of man, for the reason that things that correspond to each other act in a like manner, except that one is natural and the other spiritual. How the heart acts in the body is evident from anatomy, which shows that wherever the heart acts by means of the vessels put forth from it, everything is alive or subservient to life; but where the heart by means of its vessels does not act, everything is lifeless. Moreover, the heart is the first and last thing to act in the body. That it is the first is evident from the fetus, and that it is the last is evident from the dying, and that it may act without the cooperation of the lungs is evident from cases of suffocation and swooning; from which it can be seen that the life of the mind depends solely upon the will, in the same way as the substitute life of the body depends on the heart alone; and that the will lives when thought ceases, in the same way as the heart lives when breathing ceases. This also is evident from the fetus, from the dying, and from cases of suffocation and swooning. From which it follows that love or the will is man's very life.

(2) Love or the will strives unceasingly towards the human form and all things of that form. This is evident from the correspondence of heart and will. For it is known that all things of the body are formed in the womb, and that they are formed by means of fibers from the brains and blood vessels from the heart, and that out of these two the tissues of all organs and viscera are made; from which it is evident that all things of man have their existence from the life of the will, which is love, from their first principles, out of the brains, through the fibers; and all things of his body out of the heart through the arteries and veins. From this it is clearly evident that life (which is love and the will therefrom), strives unceasingly towards the human form. And as the human form is made up of all the things there are in man, it follows that love or the will is in a continual conatus and effort to form all these. There is such a conatus and effort towards the human form, because God is a Man, and Divine Love and Divine Wisdom is His life, and from His life is everything of life. Any one can see that unless Life which is very Man acted into that which in itself is not life, the formation of anything such as exists in man would be impossible, in whom are thousands of thousands of things that make a one, and that unanimously aspire to an image of the Life from which they spring, that man may become a receptacle and abode of that Life. From all this it can be seen that love, and out of the love the will, and out of the will the heart, strive unceasingly towards the human form.

Section 9

(3) Love or the will is unable to effect anything by its human form without a marriage with wisdom or the understanding. This also is evident from the correspondence of the heart with the will. The embryo man lives by the heart, not by the lungs. For in the fetus the blood does not flow from the heart into the lungs, giving it the ability to respire; but it flows through the foramen ovale into the left ventricle of the heart; consequently the fetus is unable to move any part of its body, but lies enswathed, neither has it sensation, for its organs of sense are closed. So is it with love or the will, from which the fetus lives indeed, though obscurely, that is, without sensation or action. But as soon as the lungs are opened, which is the case after birth, he begins to feel and act, and likewise to will and think. From all this it can be seen, that love or the will is unable to effect anything by means of its human form without a marriage with wisdom or the understanding.

(4) Love or the will prepares a house or bridal chamber for its future wife, which is wisdom or the understanding. In the created universe and in each of its particulars there is a marriage of good and truth; and this is so because good is of love and truth is of wisdom, and these two are in the Lord, and out of Him all things are created. How this marriage has existence in man can be seen mirrored in the conjunction of the heart with the lungs; since the heart corresponds to love or good, and the lungs to wisdom or truth (see above, n. 378-381, 382-385). From that conjunction it can be seen how love or the will betroths to itself wisdom or the understanding, and afterwards weds it, that is, enters into a kind of marriage with it. Love betroths to itself wisdom by preparing for it a house or bridal chamber, and marries it by conjoining it to itself by affections, and afterwards lives wisely with it in that house. How this is cannot be fully described except in spiritual language, because love and wisdom, consequently will and understanding, are spiritual; and spiritual things can, indeed, be expressed in natural language, but can be perceived only obscurely, from a lack of knowledge of what love is, what wisdom is, what affections for good are, and what affections for wisdom, that is, affections for truth, are. Yet the nature of the betrothal and of the marriage of love with wisdom, or of will with understanding, can be seen by the parallel that is furnished by their correspondence with the heart and lungs. What is true of these is true of love and wisdom, so entirely that there is no difference whatever except that one is natural and the other spiritual. Thus it is evident from the heart and lungs, that the heart first forms the lungs, and afterwards joins itself to them; it forms the lungs in the fetus, and joins itself to them after birth. This the heart does in its abode which is called the breast, where the two are encamped together, separated from the other parts of the body by a partition called the diaphragm and by a covering called the pleura. So it is with love and wisdom or with will and understanding.

(5) Love or the will prepares all things in its own human form, that it may

act conjointly with wisdom or the understanding. We say, will and understanding, but it is to be carefully borne in mind that the will is the entire man; for it is the will that, with the understanding, is in first principles in the brains, and in derivatives in the body, consequently in the whole and in every part (see above, n. 365-367). From this it can be seen that the will is the entire man as regards his very form, both the general form and the particular form of all parts; and that the understanding is its partner, as the lungs are the partner of the heart. Beware of cherishing an idea of the will as something separate from the human form, for it is that same form. From this it can be seen not only how the will prepares a bridal chamber for the understanding, but also how it prepares all things in its house (which is the whole body) that it may act conjointly with the understanding. This it prepares in such a way that as each and every thing of the body is conjoined to the will, so is it conjoined to the understanding; in other words, that as each and everything of the body is submissive to the will, so is it submissive to the understanding. How each and every thing of the body is prepared for conjunction with the understanding as well as with the will, can be seen in the body only as in a mirror or image, by the aid of anatomical knowledge, which shows how all things in the body are so connected, that when the lungs respire each and every thing in the entire body is moved by the respiration of the lungs, and at the same time from the beating of the heart. Anatomy shows that the heart is joined to the lungs through the auricles, which are continued into the interiors of the lungs; also that all the viscera of the entire body are joined through ligaments to the chamber of the breast; and so joined that when the lungs respire, each and all things, in general and in particular, partake of the respiratory motion. Thus when the lungs are inflated, the ribs expand the thorax, the pleura is dilated, and the diaphragm is stretched wide, and with these all the lower parts of the body, which are connected with them by ligaments therefrom, receive some action through the pulmonic action; not to mention further facts, lest those who have no knowledge of anatomy, on account of their ignorance of its terms should be confused in regard to the subject. Consult any skillful and discerning anatomist whether all things in the entire body, from the breast down be not so bound together, that when the lungs expand by respiration, each and all of them are moved to action synchronous with the pulmonic action. From all this the nature of the conjunction prepared by the will between the understanding and each and every thing of the human form is now evident. Only explore the connections well and scan them with an anatomical eye; then, following the connections, consider their cooperation with the breathing lungs and with the heart; and finally, in thought, substitute for the lungs the understanding, and for the heart the will, and you will see.

(6) After the nuptials, the first conjunction is through affection for knowing, from which springs affection for truth. By the nuptials is meant man's state after birth, from a state of ignorance to a state of intelligence, and from this to a state of wisdom. The first state which is one of pure ignorance, is not meant here by nuptials, because there is then no thought from the understanding, and only an obscure affection from the love or will. This state is initiatory to the nuptials. In the second state, which belongs to man in childhood, there is, as we know, an affection for knowing, by means of which the infant child learns to

speak and to read, and afterwards gradually learns such things as belong to the understanding. That it is love, belonging to the will, that effects this, cannot be doubted; for unless it were effected by love or the will it would not be done. That every man has, after birth, an affection for knowing, and through that acquires the knowledge by which his understanding is gradually formed, enlarged, and perfected, is acknowledged by every one who thoughtfully takes counsel of experience. It is also evident that from this comes affection for truth; for when man, from affection for knowing, has become intelligent, he is led not so much by affection for knowing as by affection for reasoning and forming conclusions on subjects which he loves, whether economical or civil or moral. When this affection is raised to spiritual things, it becomes affection for spiritual truth. That its first initiatory state was affection for knowing, may be seen from the fact that affection for truth is an exalted affection for knowing; for to be affected by truths is the same as to wish from affection to know them, and when found, to drink them in from the joy of affection. (7) The second conjunction is through affection for understanding, from which springs perception of truth. This is evident to any one who is willing by rational insight to examine the matter. From rational insight it is clear that affection for truth and perception of truth are two powers of the understanding, which in some persons harmonize as one, and in others do not. They harmonize as one in those who wish to perceive truths with the understanding, but do not in those who only wish to know truths. It is also clear that every one is in perception of truth so far as he is in an affection for understanding; for if you take away affection for understanding truth, there will be no perception of truth; but give the affection for understanding truth, and there will be perception of truth according to the degree of affection for it. No man of sound reason ever lacks perception of truth, so long as he has affection for understanding truth. That every man has a capacity to understand truth, which is called rationality, has been shown above. (8) The third conjunction is through affection for seeing truth, from which springs thought. That affection for knowing is one thing, affection for understanding another, and affection for seeing truth another, or that affection for truth is one thing, perception of truth another, and thought another, is seen but obscurely by those who cannot perceive the operations of the mind as distinct, but is seen clearly by those who can. This is obscurely seen by those who do not perceive the operations of the mind as distinct, because with those who are in affection for truth and in perception of truth, these operations are simultaneous in the thought, and when simultaneous they cannot be distinguished. Man is in manifest thought when his spirit thinks in the body, which is especially the case when he is in company with others; but when he is in affection for understanding, and through that comes into perception of truth, he is then in the thought of his spirit, which is meditation. This passes, indeed, into the thought of the body, but into silent thought; for it is above bodily thought, and looks upon what belongs to thought from the memory as below itself, drawing therefrom either conclusions or confirmations. But real affection for truth is perceived only as a pressure of will from something pleasurable which is interiorly in meditation as its life, and is little noticed. From all this it can now be seen that these three, affection for truth, perception of truth, and thought, follow in order from love, and that they have existence only in the understanding. For when love enters into the understanding, which it does when their conjunction is accomplished, it first brings forth affection for truth, then affection for understanding that which it knows, and lastly, affection for seeing in the bodily thought that which it understands; for thought is nothing but internal sight. It is true that thought is the first to be manifest, because it is of the natural mind; but thought from perception of truth which is from affection for truth is the last to be manifest; this thought is the thought of wisdom, but the other is thought from the memory through the sight of the natural mind. All operations of love or the will not within the understanding have relation not to affections for truth, but to affections for good.

That these three from the will's love follow in order in the understanding can, indeed, be comprehended by the rational man but yet cannot be clearly seen and thus so proved as to command belief. But as love that is of the will acts as one with the heart by correspondence, and wisdom that is of the understanding acts as one with the lungs (as has been shown above) therefore what has been said (in n. 404) about affection for truth, perception of truth, and thought, can nowhere be more clearly seen and proved than in the lungs and the mechanism thereof. These, therefore, shall be briefly described. After birth, the heart discharges the blood from its right ventricle into the lungs; and after passing through these it is emptied into the left ventricle: thus the heart opens the lungs. This it does through the pulmonary arteries and veins. The lungs have bronchial tubes which ramify, and at length end in air-cells, into which the lungs admit the air, and thus respire. Around the bronchial tubes and their ramifications there are also arteries and veins called the bronchial, arising from the vena azygos or vena cava, and from the aorta. These arteries and veins are distinct from the pulmonary arteries and veins. From this it is evident that the blood flows into the lungs by two ways, and flows out from them by two ways. This enables the lungs to respire non-synchronously with the heart. That the alternate movements of the heart and the alternate movements of the lungs do not act as one is well known. Now, inasmuch as there is a correspondence of the heart and lungs with the will and understanding (as shown above), and inasmuch as conjunction by correspondence is of such a nature that as one acts so does the other, it can be seen by the flow of the blood out of the heart into the lungs how the will flows into the understanding, and produces the results mentioned just above (n. 404) respecting affection for and perception of truth, and respecting thought. By correspondence this and many other things relating to the subject, which cannot be explained in a few words, have been disclosed to me. Whereas love or the will corresponds to the heart, and wisdom or the understanding to the lungs, it follows that the blood vessels of the heart in the lungs correspond to affections for truth, and the ramifications of the bronchia of the lungs to perceptions and thoughts from those affections. Whoever will trace out all the tissues of the lungs from these origins, and disclose the analogy with the love of the will and the wisdom of the understanding, will be able to see in a kind of image the things mentioned above (n. 404), and thereby attain to a confirmed belief. But since a few only are familiar with the anatomical details respecting the heart and lungs, and since confirming a thing by what is unfamiliar induces obscurity, I omit further demonstration of the analogy.

(9) Through these three conjunctions love or the will is in its sensitive life

and in its active life. Love without the understanding, or affection which is of love without thought, which is of the understanding, can neither feel nor act in the body; since love without the understanding is as it were blind, and affection without thought is as it were in thick darkness, for the understanding is the light by which love sees. The wisdom of the understanding, moreover, is from the light that proceeds from the Lord as a sun. Since, then, the will's love, without the light of the understanding, sees nothing and is blind, it follows that without the light of the understanding even the bodily senses would be blind and blunted, not only sight and hearing, but the other senses also, - the other senses, because all perception of truth is a property of love in the understanding (as was shown above), and all the bodily senses derive their perception from their mind's perception. The same is true of every bodily act; for action from love without understanding is like man's action in the dark, when he does not know what he is doing; consequently in such action there would be nothing of intelligence and wisdom. Such action cannot be called living action, for action derives its esse from love and its quality from intelligence. Moreover, the whole power of good is by means of truth; consequently good acts in truth, and thus by means of truth; and good is of love, and truth is of the understanding. From all this it can be seen that love or the will through these three conjunctions (see above, n. 404) is in its sensitive life and in its active life.

That this is so can be proved to the life by the conjunction of the heart with the lungs, because the correspondence between the will and the heart, and between the understanding and the lungs, is such that just as the love acts with the understanding spiritually, so does the heart act with the lungs naturally: from this, what has been said above can be seen as in an image presented to the eye. That man has neither any sensitive life nor any active life, so long as the heart and the lungs do not act together, is evident from the state of the fetus or the infant in the womb, and from its state after birth. So long as man is a fetus, that is, in the womb, the lungs are closed, wherefore he has no feeling nor any action; the organs of sense are closed up, the hands are bound, likewise the feet; but after birth the lungs are opened, and as they are opened man feels and acts; the lungs are opened by means of the blood sent into them from the heart. That man has neither sensitive life nor active life without the co-operation of the heart and the lungs, is evident also in swoons, when the heart alone acts, and not the lungs, for respiration then ceases; in this case there is no sensation and no action, as is well known. It is the same with persons suffocated, either by water or by anything obstructing the larynx and closing the respiratory passage; it is well-known that the man then appears to be dead, he feels nothing and does nothing; and yet he is alive in the heart; for he returns to both his sensitive and his active life as soon as the obstructions to the lungs are removed. The blood, it is true, circulates in the meantime through the lungs, but through the pulmonary arteries and veins, not through the bronchial arteries and veins, and these last are what give man the power of breathing. It is the same with the influx of love into the understanding.

(10) Love or the will introduces wisdom or the understanding into all things of its house. By the house of love or the will is meant the whole man as to all things of his mind; and as these correspond to all things of the body (as shown above), by the house is meant also the whole man as to all things of his body,

called members, organs, and viscera. That the lungs are introduced into all these things just as the understanding is introduced into all things of the mind, can be seen from what has been shown above, namely, that love or the will prepares a house or bridal chamber for its future wife, which is wisdom or the understanding (n. 402); and that love or the will prepares all things in its own human form, that is, in its house, that it may act conjointly with wisdom or the understanding (n. 403). From what is there said, it is evident that each and all things in the whole body are so connected by ligaments issuing from the ribs, vertebrae, sternum, and diaphragm, and from the peritonaeum which depends on these, that when the lungs respire all are likewise drawn and borne along in alternate movements. Anatomy shows that the alternate waves of respiration even enter into the very viscera to their inmost recesses; for the ligaments above mentioned cleave to the sheaths of the viscera, and these sheaths, by their extensions, penetrate to their innermost parts, as do the arteries and veins also by their ramifications. From this it is evident that the respiration of the lungs is in entire conjunction with the heart in each and every thing of the body; and in order that the conjunction may be complete in every respect, even the heart itself is in pulmonic motion, for it lies in the bosom of the lungs and is connected with them by the auricles, and reclines upon the diaphragm, whereby its arteries also participate in the pulmonic motion. The stomach, too, is in similar conjunction with the lungs, by the coherence of its oesophagus with the trachea. These anatomical facts are adduced to show what kind of a conjunction there is of love or the will with wisdom or the understanding, and how the two in consort are conjoined with all things of the mind; for the spiritual and the bodily conjunction are similar.

(11) Love or the will does nothing except in conjunction with wisdom or the understanding. For as love has no sensitive nor any active life apart from the understanding; and as love introduces the understanding into all things of the mind (as was shown above, n. 407, 408), it follows that love or the will does nothing except in conjunction with the understanding. For what is it to act from love without the understanding? Such action can only be called irrational; for the understanding teaches what ought to be done and how it ought to be done. Apart from the understanding love does not know this; consequently such is the marriage between love and the understanding, that although they are two, they act as one. There is a like marriage between good and truth, for good is of love and truth is of the understanding. In every particular thing of the universe as created by the Lord there is such a marriage, their use having relation to good, and the form of their use to truth. From this marriage it is that in each and every thing of the body there is a right and a left, the right having relation to the good from which truth proceeds, and the left to truth from good, thus to their conjunction. From this it is that there are pairs in man; there are two brains, two hemispheres of the brain, two ventricles of the heart, two lobes of the lungs, two eyes, ears, nostrils, arms, hands, loins, feet, kidneys, testicles, etc.; and where there are not pairs, there is a right and a left side, all this for the reason that good looks to truth that it may take form, and truth looks to good that it may have being. It is the same in the angelic heavens and in their several societies. On this subject more may be seen above (n. 401), where it is shown that love or the will is unable to effect anything by its human form

without a marriage with wisdom or the understanding. Conjunction of evil and falsity, which is opposite to the conjunction of good and truth, will be spoken of elsewhere.

(12) Love or the will conjoins itself to wisdom or the understanding, and causes wisdom or the understanding to be reciprocally conjoined to it. That love or the will conjoins itself to wisdom or the understanding is plain from their correspondence with the heart and lungs. Anatomical observation shows that the heart is in its life's motion when the lungs are not yet in motion; this it shows by cases of swooning and of suffocation, also by the fetus in the womb and the chick in the egg. Anatomical observation shows also that the heart, while acting alone, forms the lungs and so adjusts them that it may carry on respiration in them; also that it so forms the other viscera and organs that it may carry on various uses in them, the organs of the face that it may have sensation, the organs of motion that it may act, and the remaining parts of the body that it may exhibit uses corresponding to the affections of love. From all this it can now for the first time be shown that as the heart produces such things for the sake of the various functions which it is afterwards to discharge in the body, so love, in its receptacle called the will, produces like things for the sake of the various affections that constitute its form, which is the human form (as was shown above). Now as the first and nearest of love's affections are affection for knowing, affection for understanding, and affection for seeing what it knows and understands, it follows, that for these affections love forms the understanding and actually enters into them when it begins to feel and to act and to think. To this the understanding contributes nothing, as is evident from the analogy of the heart and lungs (of which above). From all this it can be seen, that love or the will conjoins itself to wisdom or the understanding, and not wisdom or the understanding to love or the will; also from this it is evident that knowledge, which love acquires to itself by the affection for knowing, and perception of truth, which it acquires by the affection for understanding, and thought which it acquires by the affection for seeing what it knows and understands, are not of the understanding but of love. Thoughts, perceptions, and knowledges therefrom, flow in, it is true, out of the spiritual world, yet they are received not by the understanding but by love, according to its affections in the understanding. It appears as if the understanding received them, and not love or the will, but this is an illusion. It appears also as if the understanding conjoined itself to love or the will, but this too, is an illusion; love or the will conjoins itself to the understanding, and causes the understanding to be reciprocally conjoined to it. This reciprocal conjunction is from love's marriage with wisdom, wherefrom a conjunction seemingly reciprocal, from the life and consequent power of love, is effected. It is the same with the marriage of good and truth; for good is of love and truth is of the understanding. Good does everything and it receives truth into its house and conjoins itself with it so far as the truth is accordant. Good can also admit truths which are not accordant; but this it does from an affection for knowing, for understanding, and for thinking its own things, whilst it has not as yet determined itself to uses, which are its ends and are called its goods. Of reciprocal conjunction, that is, the conjunction of truth with good, there is none whatever. That truth is reciprocally conjoined is from the life belonging to good. From this it is that

every man and every spirit and angel is regarded by the Lord according to his love or good, and no one according to his intellect, or his truth separate from love or good. For man's life is his love (as was shown above), and his life is qualified according as he has exalted his affections by means of truth, that is, according as he has perfected his affections by wisdom. For the affections of love are exalted and perfected by means of truths, thus by means of wisdom. Then love acts conjointly with its wisdom, as though from it; but it acts from itself through wisdom, as through its own form, and this derives nothing whatever from the understanding, but everything from a kind of determination of love called affection.

All things that favor it love calls its goods, and all things that as means lead to goods it calls its truths; and because these are means they are loved and come to be of its affection and thus become affections in form; therefore truth is nothing else than a form of the affection that is of love. The human form is nothing else than the form of all the affections of love; beauty is its intelligence, which it procures for itself through truths received either by sight or by hearing, external and internal. These are what love disposes into the form of its affections; and these forms exist in great variety; but all derive a likeness from their general form, which is the human. To the love all such forms are beautiful and lovely, but others are unbeautiful and unlovely. From this, again, it is evident that love conjoins itself to the understanding, and not the reverse, and that the reciprocal conjunction is also from love. This is what is meant by love or the will causing wisdom or the understanding to be reciprocally conjoined to it.

What has been said may be seen in a kind of image and thus corroborated by the correspondence of the heart with love and of the lungs with the understanding (of which above). For if the heart corresponds to love, its determinations, which are arteries and veins, correspond to affections, and in the lungs to affections for truth; and as there are also other vessels in the lungs called air vessels, whereby respiration is carried on, these vessels correspond to perceptions. It must be distinctly understood that the arteries and veins in the lungs are not affections, and that respirations are not perceptions and thoughts, but that they are correspondences, that is, they act correspondently or synchronously; likewise that the heart and the lungs are not the love and understanding, but correspondences: and inasmuch as they are correspondences the one can be seen in the other. Whoever from anatomy has come to understand the whole structure of the lungs can see clearly, when he compares it with the understanding, that the understanding does not act at all by itself, does not perceive nor think by itself, but acts wholly by affections which are of love. These, in the understanding, are called affection for knowing, for understanding, and for seeing truth (which have been treated of above). For all states of the lungs depend on the blood from the heart and from the vena cava and aorta; and respirations, which take place in the bronchial branches, proceed in accordance with the state of those vessels; for when the flow of the blood stops, respiration stops. Much more may be disclosed by comparing the structure of the lungs with the understanding, to which the lungs correspond; but as few are familiar with anatomical science, and to try to demonstrate or prove anything by what is unknown renders it obscure, it is not well to say more on this subject. By what I know of the structure of the lungs I am fully convinced that love through its affections conjoins itself to the understanding, and that the understanding does not conjoin itself to any affection of love, but that it is reciprocally conjoined by love, to the end that love may have sensitive life and active life. But it must not be forgotten that man has a twofold respiration, one of the spirit and another of the body; and that the respiration of the spirit depends on the fibers from the brains, and the respiration of the body on the blood-vessels from the heart, and from the vena cava and aorta. It is evident, moreover, that thought produces respiration; it is evident, also, that affection, which is of love, produces thought, for thought without affection is precisely like respiration without a heart, a thing impossible. From this it is clear that affection, which is of love, conjoins itself to thought, which is of the understanding (as was said above), in like manner as the heart does in the lungs.

(13) Wisdom or the understanding, from the potency given to it by love, can be elevated and can receive such things as are of light out of heaven, and perceive them. That man has the ability to perceive arcana of wisdom when he hears them, has been shown above in many places. This capacity of man is called rationality. It belongs to every man by creation. It is the capacity to understand things interiorly, and to decide what is just and right, and what is good and true; and by it man is distinguished from beasts. This, then, is what is meant when it is said, that the understanding can be elevated and receive things that are of light out of heaven, and perceive them. That this is so can also be seen in a kind of image in the lungs, for the reason that the lungs correspond to the understanding. In the lungs it can be seen from their cellular substance, which consists of bronchial tubes continued down to the minutest air-cells, which are receptacles of air in respirations; these are what the thoughts make one with by correspondence. This cell-like substance is such that it can be expanded and contracted in a twofold mode, in one mode with the heart, in the other almost separate from the heart. In the former, it is expanded and contracted through the pulmonary arteries and veins, which are from the heart alone; in the latter, through the bronchial arteries and veins, which are from the vena cava and aorta, and these vessels are outside of the heart. This takes place in the lungs for the reason that the understanding is capable of being raised above its proper love, which corresponds to the heart, and to receive light from heaven. Still, when the understanding is raised above its proper love, it does not withdraw from it, but derives from it what is called the affection for knowing and understanding, with a view to somewhat of honor, glory, or gain in the world; this clings to every love as a surface, and by it the love shines on the surface; but with the wise, the love shines through. These things respecting the lungs are brought forward to prove that the understanding can be elevated and can receive and perceive things that are of the light of heaven; for the correspondence is plenary. To see from correspondence is to see the lungs from the understanding, and the understanding from the lungs, and thus from both together to perceive proof.

(14) Love or the will can in like manner be elevated and can receive such things as are of heat out of heaven provided it loves wisdom, its consort, in that degree. That the understanding can be elevated into the light of heaven, and

from that light draw forth wisdom, has been shown in the preceding chapter and in many places above; also that love or the will can be elevated as well, provided it loves those things that are of the light of heaven or that are of wisdom, has also been shown in many places. Yet love or the will cannot be thus elevated through anything of honor, glory, or gain as an end, but only through a love of use, thus not for the sake of self, but for the sake of the neighbor; and because this love is given only by the Lord out of heaven, and is given by the Lord when man flees from evils as sins, therefore it is that love or the will can be elevated by these means, and cannot without these means. But love or the will is elevated into heaven's heat, while the understanding is elevated into its light. When both are elevated, a marriage of the two takes place there, which is called celestial marriage, because it is a marriage of celestial love and wisdom; consequently it is said that love also is elevated if it loves wisdom, its consort, in that degree. The love of wisdom, that is, the genuine love of the human understanding is love towards the neighbor from the Lord. It is the same with light and heat in the world. Light exists without heat and with heat; light is without heat in winter time, and with heat in summer time; and when heat is with light all things flourish. The light with man that corresponds to the light of winter is wisdom without its love; and the light with man that corresponds to the light of summer is wisdom with its love.

This conjunction and disjunction of wisdom and love can be seen effigied, as it were, in the conjunction of the lungs with the heart. For the heart can be conjoined to the clustering vesicles of the bronchia by blood sent out from itself, and also by blood sent out not from itself but from the vena cava and the aorta. Thereby the respiration of the body can be separated from the respiration of the spirit; but when blood from the heart alone acts the respirations cannot be separated. Now since thoughts act as one with respirations by correspondence it is plain, from the twofold state of the lungs in respirations, that man is able to think and from thoughts to speak and act in one way when in company with others, and to think and from thought to speak and act in another way when not in company, that is, when he has no fear of loss of reputation; for he can then think and speak against God, the neighbor, the spiritual things of the church, and against moral and civil laws; and he can also act contrary to them, by stealing, by being revengeful, by blaspheming, by committing adultery. But in company with others, where he is afraid of losing reputation, he can talk, preach and act precisely like a spiritual, moral and civil man. From all this it can be seen that love or the will as well as the understanding can be elevated and can receive such things as are of the heat or love of heaven, provided it loves wisdom in that degree, and if it does not love wisdom, that it can as it were be separated.

(15) Otherwise love or the will draws down wisdom, or the understanding, from its elevation, that it may act as one with itself. There is natural love and there is spiritual love. A man who is in natural and in spiritual love both at once, is a rational man; but one who is in natural love alone, although able to think rationally, precisely like a spiritual man, is not a rational man; for although he elevates his understanding even to heavenly light, thus to wisdom, yet the things of wisdom, that is, of heavenly light, do not belong to his love. His love, it is true, effects the elevation, but from desire for honor, glory and gain.

But when he perceives that he gains nothing of the kind from that elevation (as is the case when he thinks with himself from his own natural love), then he does not love the things of heavenly light or wisdom; consequently he then draws down the understanding from its height, that it may act as one with himself. For example: when the understanding by its elevation is in wisdom, then the love sees what justice is, what sincerity is, what chastity is, even what genuine love is. This the natural love can see by its capacity to understand and contemplate things in heavenly light; it can even talk and preach about these and explain them as at once moral and spiritual virtues. But when the understanding is not elevated, the love, if it is merely natural, does not see these virtues, but instead of justice it sees injustice, instead of sincerity deceit, instead of chastity lewdness, and so on. If it then thinks of the things it spoke of when its understanding was in elevation, it can laugh at them and speak of them merely as serviceable to it in captivating the souls of men. From all this it can be seen how it is to be understood that love, unless it loves wisdom, its consort, in that degree, draws wisdom down from its elevation, that it may act as one with itself. That love is capable of elevation if it loves wisdom in that degree, can be seen above (n. 414).

Now as love corresponds to the heart, and the understanding to the lungs, the foregoing statements may be corroborated by their correspondence; as, for instance, how the understanding can be elevated above its own love even into wisdom; and how, if that love is merely natural, the understanding is drawn down by it from that elevation. Man has a twofold respiration; one of the body, the other of the spirit. These two respirations may be separated and they may be conjoined; with men merely natural, especially with hypocrites, they are separated, but rarely with men who are spiritual and sincere. Consequently a merely natural man and hypocrite, whose understanding has been elevated, and in whose memory therefore various things of wisdom remain, can talk wisely in company by thought from the memory; but when not in company, he does not think from the memory, but from his spirit, thus from his love. He also respires in like manner, inasmuch as thought and respiration act correspondently. That the structure of the lungs is such that they can respire both by blood from the heart and by blood from outside of the heart has been shown above.

It is the common opinion that wisdom makes the man; therefore when any one is heard to talk and teach wisely he is believed to be wise; yea, he himself believes it at the time, because when he talks or teaches in company he thinks from the memory, and if he is a merely natural man, from the surface of his love, which is a desire for honor, glory, and gain; but when the same man is alone he thinks from the more inward love of his spirit, and then not wisely, but sometimes insanely. From all this it can be seen that no one is to be judged of by wise speaking, but by his life; that is, not by wise speaking separate from life, but by wise speaking conjoined to life. By life is meant love. That love is the life has been shown above.

(16) Love or the will is purified in the understanding, if they are elevated together. From birth man loves nothing but self and the world, for nothing else appears before his eyes, consequently nothing else occupies his mind. This love is corporeal-natural, and may be called material love. Moreover, this love has

become impure by reason of the separation of heavenly love from it in parents. This love could not be separated from its impurity unless man had a power to raise his understanding into the light of heaven, and to see how he ought to live in order that his love, as well as his understanding, may be elevated into wisdom. By means of the understanding, love, that is, the man, sees what the evils are that defile and corrupt the love; he also sees that if he flees from those evils as sins and turns away from them, he loves the things that are opposite to those evils; all of which are heavenly. Then also he perceives the means by which he is enabled to flee from and turn away from those evils as sins. This the love, that is, the man, sees, by the exercise of his power to elevate his understanding into the light of heaven, which is the source of wisdom. Then so far as love gives heaven the first place and the world the second, and at the same time gives the Lord the first place and self the second, so far love is purged of its uncleanness and is purified; in other words, is raised into the heat of heaven, and conjoined with the light of heaven in which the understanding is; and the marriage takes place that is called the marriage of good and truth, that is, of love and wisdom. Any one can comprehend intellectually and see rationally, that so far as he flees from and turns away from theft and cheating, so far he loves sincerity, rectitude and justice; so far as he flees and turns away from revenge and hatred, so far he loves the neighbor; and so far as he flees and turns away from adulteries, so far he loves chastity; and so on. And yet scarcely any one knows what there is of heaven and the Lord in sincerity, rectitude, justice, love towards the neighbor, chastity, and other affections of heavenly love, until he has removed their opposites. When he has removed the opposites, then he is in those affections, and therefrom recognizes and sees them. Previously there is a kind of veil interposed, that does, indeed, transmit to love the light of heaven; yet inasmuch as the love does not in that degree love its consort, wisdom, it does not receive it, yea, may even contradict and rebuke it when it returns from its elevation. Still man flatters himself that the wisdom of his understanding may be made serviceable as a means to honor, glory, or gain. Then man gives self and the world the first place, and the Lord and heaven the second, and what has the second place is loved only so far as it is serviceable, and if it is not serviceable it is disowned and rejected; if not before death, then after it. From all this the truth is now evident, that love or the will is purified in the understanding if they are elevated together.

The same thing is imaged in the lungs, whose arteries and veins correspond to the affections of love, and whose respirations correspond to the perceptions and thoughts of the understanding, as has been said above. That the heart's blood is purified of undigested matters in the lungs, and nourishes itself with suitable food from the inhaled air, is evident from much observation. (1) That the blood is purified of undigested matter in the lungs, is evident not only from the influent blood, which is venous, and therefore filled with the chyle collected from food and drink, but also from the moisture of the outgoing breath and from its odor as perceived by others, as well as from the diminished quantity of the blood flowing back into the left ventricle of the heart. (2) That the blood nourishes itself with suitable food from the inhaled air is evident from the immense volumes of odors and exhalations continually flowing forth from fields, gardens, and woods; from the immense supply of salts of various kinds in the water that rises from the ground and from rivers and ponds, and from the immense quantity of exhalations and effluvia from human beings and animals with which the air is impregnated. That these things flow into the lungs with the inhaled air is undeniable: it is therefore undeniable also that from them the blood draws such things as are useful to it; and such things are useful as correspond to the affections of its love. For this reason there are, in the vesicles or innermost recesses of the lungs, little veins in great abundance with tiny mouths that absorb these suitable matters; consequently, the blood that flows back into the left ventricle of the heart is changed into arterial blood of brilliant hue. These facts prove that the blood purifies itself of heterogeneous things and nourishes itself with homogeneous things. That the blood in the lungs purifies and nourishes itself correspondently to the affections of the mind is as yet unknown; but in the spiritual world it is very well known, for angels in the heavens find delight only in the odors that correspond to the love of their wisdom, while the spirits in hell find delight only in the odors that correspond to a love opposed to wisdom; these are foul odors, but the former are fragrant. It follows that men in the world impregnate their blood with similar things according to correspondence with the affections of their love; for what the spirit of a man loves, his blood according to correspondence craves and by respiration attracts. From this correspondence it results that man as regards his love is purified if he loves wisdom, and is defiled if he does not love it. Moreover, all purification of man is effected by means of the truths of wisdom, and all pollution of man is effected by means of falsities that are opposite to the truths of wisdom.

(17) Love or the will is defiled in the understanding and by it, if they are not elevated together. This is because love, if not elevated, remains impure (as stated above, n. 419, 420); and while it remains impure it loves what is impure, such as revenges, hatreds, deceits, blasphemes, adulteries, for these are then its affections that are called lusts, and it rejects what belongs to charity, justice, sincerity, truth, and chastity. Love is said to be defiled in the understanding, and by it; in the understanding, when love is affected by these impure things; by the understanding, when love makes the things of wisdom to become its servants, and still more when it perverts, falsifies, and adulterates them. Of the corresponding state of the heart, or of its blood in the lungs, there is no need to say more than has been said above (n. 420), except that instead of the purification of the blood its defilement takes place; and instead of the nutrition of the blood by fragrant odors its nutrition is effected by stenches, precisely as it is respectively in heaven and in hell.

(18) Love, when purified by wisdom in the understanding, becomes spiritual and celestial. Man is born natural, but in the measure in which his understanding is raised into the light of heaven, and his love conjointly is raised into the heat of heaven, he becomes spiritual and celestial; he then becomes like a garden of Eden, which is at once in vernal light and vernal heat. It is not the understanding that becomes spiritual and celestial, but the love; and when the love has so become, it makes its consort, the understanding, spiritual and celestial. Love becomes spiritual and celestial by a life according to the truths of wisdom which the understanding teaches and requires. Love imbibes these truths by means of its understanding, and not from itself; for love cannot

elevate itself unless it knows truths, and these it can learn only by means of an elevated and enlightened understanding; and then so far as it loves truths in the practice of them so far it is elevated; for to understand is one thing and to will is another; or to say is one thing and to do is another. There are those who understand and talk about the truths of wisdom, yet neither will nor practise them. When, therefore, love puts in practice the truths of light which it understands and speaks, it is elevated. This one can see from reason alone; for what kind of a man is he who understands the truths of wisdom and talks about them while he lives contrary to them, that is, while his will and conduct are opposed to them? Love purified by wisdom becomes spiritual and celestial, for the reason that man has three degrees of life, called natural, spiritual, and celestial (of which in the Third Part of this work), and he is capable of elevation from one degree into another. Yet he is not elevated by wisdom alone, but by a life according to wisdom, for a man's life is his love. Consequently, so far as his life is according to wisdom, so far he loves wisdom; and his life is so far according to wisdom as he purifies himself from uncleannesses, which are sins; and so far as he does this does he love wisdom.

That love purified by the wisdom in the understanding becomes spiritual and celestial cannot be seen so clearly by their correspondence with the heart and lungs, because no one can see the quality of the blood by which the lungs are kept in their state of respiration. The blood may abound in impurities, and yet not be distinguishable from pure blood. Moreover, the respiration of a merely natural man appears the same as the respiration of a spiritual man. But the difference is clearly discerned in heaven, for there every one respires according to the marriage of love and wisdom; therefore as angels are recognized according to that marriage, so are they recognized according to their respiration. For this reason it is that when one who is not in that marriage enters heaven, he is seized with anguish in the breast, and struggles for breath like a man in the agonies of death; such persons, therefore throw themselves headlong from the place, nor do they find rest until they are among those who are in a respiration similar to their own; for then by correspondence they are in similar affection, and therefore in similar thought. From all this it can be seen that with the spiritual man it is the purer blood, called by some the animal spirit, which is purified; and that it is purified so far as the man is in the marriage of love and wisdom. It is this purer blood which corresponds most nearly to that marriage; and because this blood inflows into the blood of the body, it follows that the latter blood is also purified by means of it. The reverse is true of those in whom love is defiled in the understanding. But, as was said, no one can test this by any experiment on the blood; but he can by observing the affections of love, since these correspond to the blood.

(19) Love, when defiled in the understanding and by it, becomes natural, sensual, and corporeal. Natural love separated from spiritual love is the opposite of spiritual love; because natural love is love of self and of the world, and spiritual love is love to the Lord and love to the neighbor; and love of self and the world looks downward and outward, and love to the Lord looks upward and inward. Consequently when natural love is separated from spiritual love it cannot be elevated above what is man's own, but remains immersed in it, and so far as it loves it, is glued to it. Then if the understanding ascends, and sees

by the light of heaven such things as are of wisdom, this natural love draws down such wisdom, and joins her to itself in what is its own; and there either rejects the things of wisdom or falsifies them or encircles itself with them, that it may talk about them for reputation's sake. As natural love can ascend by degrees and become spiritual and celestial, in the same way it can descend by degrees and become sensual and corporeal, and it does descend so far as it loves dominion from no love of use, but solely from love of self. It is this love which is called the devil. Those who are in this love are able to speak and act in the same manner as those who are in spiritual love; but they do this either from memory or from the understanding elevated by itself into the light of heaven. Nevertheless, what they say and do is comparatively like fruit that appears beautiful on the surface but is wholly rotten within; or like almonds which from the shell appear sound but are wholly worm-eaten within. These things in the spiritual world are called fantasies, and by means of them harlots, there called sirens, make themselves appear handsome, and adorn themselves with beautiful garments; but when the fantasy is dissipated the sirens appear like ghosts, and are like devils who make themselves angels of light. For when that corporeal love draws its understanding down from its elevation, as it does when man is alone and thinks from his own love, then he thinks against God in favor of nature, against heaven in favor of the world, and against the truths and goods of the church in favor of the falsities and evils of hell; thus against wisdom. From this the character of those who are called corporeal men can be seen: for they are not corporeal in understanding, but corporeal in love; that is, they are not corporeal in understanding when they converse in company, but are so when they hold converse with themselves in spirit; and being such in spirit, therefore after death they become, both in love and in understanding, spirits that are called corporeal. Those who in the world had been in a supreme love of ruling from the love of self, and had also surpassed others in elevation of understanding, then appear in body like Egyptian mummies, and in mind gross and silly. Who in the world at the present day is aware that this love in itself is of such a nature? Yet a love of ruling from love of use is possible, but only from love of use for the sake of the common good, not for the sake of self. It is difficult, however, for man to distinguish the one love from the other, although the difference between them is like that between heaven and hell. The differences between these two loves of ruling may be seen in the work on Heaven and Hell (n. 551-565).

(20) The capacity to understand called rationality and the capacity to act called freedom, still remain. These two capacities belonging to man have been treated of above (n. 264-267). Man has these two capacities that he may from being natural become spiritual, that is, may be regenerated. For, as was said above, it is man's love that becomes spiritual, and is regenerated; and it cannot become spiritual or be regenerated unless it knows, by means of its understanding, what evil is and what good is, and therefore what truth is and what falsity is. When it knows this it can choose either one or the other; and if it chooses good it can, by means of its understanding, be instructed about the means by which to attain to good. All the means by which man is enabled to attain good are provided. It is by rationality that man is able to know and understand these means, and by freedom that he is able to will and to do them.

There is also a freedom to will to know, to understand, and to think these means. Those who hold from church doctrine that things spiritual or theological transcend the understanding, and are therefore to be believed apart from the understanding know nothing of these capacities called rationality and freedom. These cannot do otherwise than deny that there is a capacity called rationality. Those, too, who hold from church doctrine that no one is able to do good from himself, and consequently that good is not to be done from any will to be saved, cannot do otherwise than deny, from a principle of religion, the existence of both these capacities which belong to man. Therefore, those who have confirmed themselves in these things, after death, in agreement with their faith, are deprived of both these capacities; and in place of heavenly freedom, in which they might have been, are in infernal freedom, and in place of angelic wisdom from rationality, in which they might have been, are in infernal insanity; and what is wonderful, they claim that both these capacities have place in doing what is evil and thinking what is false, not knowing that the exercise of freedom in doing what is evil is slavery, and that the exercise of the reason to think what is false is irrational. But it is to be carefully noted that these capacities, freedom and rationality, are neither of them man's, but are of the Lord in man, and that they cannot be appropriated to man as his; nor indeed, can they be given to man as his, but are continually of the Lord in man, and yet are never taken away from man; and this because without them man cannot be saved, for without them he cannot be regenerated (as has been said above). For this reason man is instructed by the church that from himself he can neither think what is true nor do what is good. But inasmuch as man perceives no otherwise than that he thinks from himself what is true and does from himself what is good, it is very evident that he ought to believe that he thinks as if from himself what is true, and does as if from himself what is good. For if he does not believe this, either he does not think what is true nor do what is good, and therefore has no religion, or he thinks what is true and does what is good from himself, and thus ascribes to himself that which is Divine. That man ought to think what is true and do good as if from himself, may be seen in the Doctrine of Life for the New Jerusalem, from beginning to end.

(21) Spiritual and celestial love is love toward the neighbor and love to the Lord; and natural and sensual love is love of the world and love of self. By love toward the neighbor is meant the love of uses, and by love to the Lord is meant the love of doing uses (as has been shown before). These loves are spiritual and celestial, because loving uses and doing them from a love of them, is distinct from the love of what is man's own; for whoever loves uses spiritually looks not to self, but to others outside of self for whose good he is moved. Opposed to these loves are the loves of self and of the world, for these look to uses not for the sake of others but for the sake of self; and those who do this invert Divine order, and put self in the Lord's place, and the world in the place of heaven; as a consequence they look backward, away from the Lord and away from heaven, and looking backward away from these is looking to hell. (More about these loves may be seen above, n. 424.) Yet man does not feel and perceive the love of performing uses for the sake of uses as he feels and perceives the love of performing uses for the sake of self; consequently when he is performing uses he does not know whether he is doing them for the sake of uses or for the sake

of self. But let him know that he is performing uses for the sake of uses in the measure in which he flees from evils; for so far as he flees from evils, he performs uses not for himself, but from the Lord. For evil and good are opposites; so far as one is not in evil he is in good. No one can be in evil and in good at the same time, because no one can serve two masters at the same time. All this has been said to show that although man does not sensibly perceive whether the uses which he performs are for the sake of use or for the sake of self, that is, whether the uses are spiritual or merely natural, still he can know it by this, whether or not he considers evils to be sins. If he regards them as sins, and for that reason abstains from doing them, the uses which he does are spiritual. And when one who does this flees from sins from a feeling of aversion, he then begins to have a sensible perception of the love of uses for the sake of uses, and this from spiritual enjoyment in them.

(22) It is the same with charity and faith and their conjunction as with the will and understanding and their conjunction. There are two loves, according to which the heavens are distinct, celestial love and spiritual love. Celestial love is love to the Lord, and spiritual love is love towards the neighbor. These loves are distinguished by this, that celestial love is the love of good, and spiritual love the love of truth; for those who are in celestial love perform uses from love of good, and those in spiritual love from love of truth. The marriage of celestial love is with wisdom, and the marriage of spiritual love with intelligence; for it is of wisdom to do good from good, and it is of intelligence to do good from truth, consequently celestial love does what is good, and spiritual love does what is true. The difference between these two loves can be defined only in this way, that those who are in celestial love have wisdom inscribed on their life, and not on the memory, for which reason they do not talk about Divine truths, but do them; while those who are in spiritual love have wisdom inscribed on their memory, therefore they talk about Divine truths, and do them from principles in the memory. Because those who are in celestial love have wisdom inscribed on their life, they perceive instantly whether whatever they hear is true or not; and when asked whether it is true, they answer only, It is, or It is not. These are they who are meant by the words of the Lord: Let your speech be Yea, yea, Nay, nay (Matt. 5:37). And because they are such, they are unwilling to hear anything about faith, saying, What is faith? is it not wisdom? and what is charity? is it not doing ? And when told that faith is believing what is not understood, they turn away, saying, The man is crazy. These are they who are in the third heaven, and who are the wisest of all. Such have they become who in the world have applied the Divine truths which they have heard immediately to the life by turning away from evils as infernal, and worshiping the Lord alone. These, since they are in innocence, appear to others as infants; and since they never talk about the truths of wisdom and there is nothing of pride in their discourse, they also appear simple. Nevertheless, when they hear any one speaking, they perceive from the tone all things of his love, and from the speech all things of his intelligence. These are they who are in the marriage of love and wisdom from the Lord; and who represent the heart region of heaven, mentioned above.

Those, however, who are in spiritual love, which is love towards the neighbor, do not have wisdom inscribed on their life, but intelligence; for it is of wisdom to do good from affection for good, while it is of intelligence to do good from affection for truth (as has been said above). Neither do these know what faith is. When faith is mentioned they understand truth, and when charity is mentioned they understand doing the truth; and when told that they must believe, they call it empty talk, and ask, Who does not believe what is true? This they say because they see truth in the light of their own heaven; therefore, to believe what they do not see they call either simplicity or foolishness. These are they who constitute the lung region of heaven, also mentioned above.

But those who are in spiritual-natural love have neither wisdom nor intelligence inscribed on their life, but only something of faith out of the Word, so far as this has been conjoined with charity. Inasmuch as these do not know what charity is, or whether faith be truth, they cannot be among those in the heavens who are in wisdom and intelligence, but among those who are in knowledge only. Yet such of them as have fled from evil as sins are in the outmost heaven, and are in a light there like the light of the moon by night; while those who have not confirmed themselves in a faith in what is unknown, but have cherished a kind of affection for truth are instructed by angels, and according to their reception of truths and a life in agreement therewith, are raised into the societies of those who are in spiritual love and therefore in intelligence. Those become spiritual, the rest becoming spiritual-natural. But those who have lived in faith separate from charity are removed, and sent away into deserts, because they are not in any good, thus not in any marriage of good and truth, in which all are who are in the heavens.

All that has been said of love and wisdom in this Part may be said of charity and faith, if by charity spiritual love is understood, and by faith the truth whereby there is intelligence. It is the same whether the terms will and understanding, or love and intelligence be used, since the will is the receptacle of love, and the understanding of intelligence.

To this I will add the following notable experience:-In heaven all who perform uses from affection for use, because of the communion in which they live are wiser and happier than others; and with them performing uses is acting sincerely, uprightly, justly, and faithfully in the work proper to the calling of each. This they call charity; and observances pertaining to worship they call signs of charity, and other things they call obligations and favors; saying that when one performs the duties of his calling sincerely, uprightly, justly, and faithfully, the good of the community is maintained and perpetuated, and that this is to "be in the Lord," because all that flows in from the Lord is use, and it flows in from the parts into the community, and flows out from the community to the parts. The parts there are angels, and the community is a society of them.

WHAT MAN'S BEGINNING IS FROM CONCEPTION. What man's beginning or primitive form is in the womb after conception no one can know, because it cannot be seen; moreover, it is made up of spiritual substance, which is not visible by natural light. Now because there are some in the world who are eager to investigate even the primitive form of man, which is seed from the father, from which conception is effected, and because many of these have fallen into the error of thinking that man is in his fullness from his first, which is the rudiment, and is afterwards perfected by growth, it has been disclosed to me what that rudiment or first is in its form. It has been disclosed to me by angels, to whom it was revealed by the Lord; and because they had made it a part of their wisdom, and it is the joy of their wisdom to communicate to others what they know, permission having been granted, they presented before my eyes in the light of heaven a type of man's initial form, which was as follows: There appeared as it were a tiny image of a brain with a delicate delineation of something like a face in front, with no appendage. This primitive form in the upper convex part was a structure of contiguous globules or spherules, and each spherule was a joining together of those more minute, and each of these in like manner of those most minute. It was thus of three degrees. In front, in the flat part, a kind of delineation appeared for a face. The convex part was covered round about with a very delicate skin or membrane which was transparent. The convex part, which was a type of the brain in least forms, was also divided into two beds, as it were, just as the brain in its larger form is divided into hemispheres. It was told me that the right bed was the receptacle of love, and the left the receptacle of wisdom; and that by wonderful interweavings these were like consorts and partners. It was further shown in the light of heaven, which fell brightly on it, that the structure of this little brain within, as to position and movement, was in the order and form of heaven, and that its outer structure was in direct opposition to that order and form. After these things were seen and pointed out, the angels said that the two interior degrees, which were in the order and form of heaven, were the receptacles of love and wisdom from the Lord; and that the exterior degree, which was in direct opposition to the order and form of heaven, was the receptacle of hellish love and insanity; for the reason that man, by hereditary corruption, is born into evils of every kind, and these evils reside there in the outermosts; and that this corruption is not removed unless the higher degrees are opened, which, as was said, are the receptacles of love and wisdom from the Lord. And as love and wisdom are very man, for love and wisdom in their essence are the Lord, and this primitive form of man is a receptacle, it follows that in that primitive form there is a continual effort towards the human form, which also it gradually assumes.

Divine Providence

The reader will find in this book a firm assurance of God's care of mankind as a whole and of each human being. The assurance is rested in God's infinite love and wisdom, the love pure mercy, the wisdom giving love its ways and means. It is further grounded in an interpretation of the universe as a spiritual-natural world, an interpretation fully set forth in the earlier book, Divine Love and Wisdom, on which the present work draws heavily. As there is a world of the spirit, no view of providence can be adequate which does not take that world into account. For in that world must be channels for the outreach of God's care to the human spirit. There also any eternal goal--such as a heaven from the human race--must exist. A view of providence limited to the horizons of the passing existence can hardly resemble the care which the eternal God takes of men and women who, besides possessing perishable bodies, are themselves creatures of the spirit and immortal. The full title of the book, Angelic Wisdom about Divine Providence, implies that its author, in an other-world experience, had at hand the knowledge which men and women in heaven have of God's care. Who should know the divine guidance if not the men and women in heaven who have obviously enjoyed it? "The laws of divine providence, hitherto hidden with angels in their wisdom, are to be revealed now"(n. 70).

As it is presented in this book, providence seeks to engage man in its purposes, and to enlist all his faculties, his freedom and reason, his will and understanding, his prudence and enterprise. It acts first of all on his volitions and thinking, to align them with itself. That it falls directly on history, its events and our circumstances, is a superficial view. It is man's inner life which first feels the omnipresent divine influence and must do so. If we cannot be lifted to our best selves and if our aims and outlook cannot be modified for the better, how shall the world be bettered which we affect to handle? Paramount in God's presence with all men, if only in their possibilities, is His providential care.

This care, to which man's inner life is open, is alert every moment, not occasional. It is gentle and not tyrannical, constantly respecting man's freedom and reason, otherwise losing him as a human being. It has set this and other laws for itself which it pursues undeviatingly. The larger part of the book is an exposition of these laws in the conviction that by them the nature of providence is best seen. Is it not to be expected in a universe which has its laws, and in which impersonal forces are governed by laws, that the Creator of all should pursue laws in His concern with the lives of conscious beings? To fit a world of laws must not the divine care have its laws, too? Adjustment of thought about divine providence to scientific thought is not the overriding necessity, for scientific thought must keep adjusting to laws which it discerns in the physical world. In consonance, religious thought seeks to learn the lawful order in the guidance of the human spirit.

Do not each and all things in tree or shrub proceed constantly and wonderfully from purpose to purpose according to the laws of their order of things? Why should not the supreme purpose, a heaven from the human race, proceed in similar fashion? Can there be anything in its progress which does not proceed with all constancy according to the laws of divine providence? (n 332)

Respecting the laws of providence, it is to be noted that there are more laws than those, five in number, which are stated at the heads of as many chapters in the book. Further laws are embodied in other chapters. At n. 249(2) we are told that further laws were presented in nn. 191-213, 214-220, and 221-233. In fact, at n. 243. there is a reference to laws which follow in even later chapters. In nn. 191-213 the law, partly stated in the heading over the chapter, comes to full sight particularly at n. 210(2), namely, that providence, in engaging human response, shall align human prudence with itself, so that providence becomes one's prudence (n. 311e). In nn. 214-220 the law is that providence employ the temporal goals of distinction and wealth towards its eternal goals, and perpetuate standing and wealth in a higher form, for a man will then have sought them not for themselves and handled them for the use they can be. To keep a person from premature spiritual experience, nn. 221-233, is obviously a law of providence, guarding against relapse and consequent profanation of what had become sacred to him.

The paradox of divine foreknowledge and human freedom, regularly discussed in studies of providence, receives an explanation which becomes more and more enlightening in the course of the book. The paradox, probably nowhere else discussed, of man's thinking and willing to all appearance all by himself, and of the fact that volition and thought come to him from beyond him, receives a similar, cumulative answer. The tension between the divine will and human self-will is a subject that pervades the book; to that subject the profoundest insights into the hidden activity of providence and into human nature are brought. On the question, "Is providence only general or also detailed?" the emphatic answer is that it cannot be general unless it takes note of the least things. On miracle and on chance conclusions unusual in religious thought meet the reader. The inequalities, injustices and tragedies in life which raise doubts of the divine care are faced in a long chapter after the concept of providence has been spread before the reader. What would be the point in considering them before what providence is has been considered? Against what manner of providence are the arguments valid? A chapter such as this, on doubts of providence and on the mentality which cherishes them, becomes a monograph on the subject, as the chapter on premature spiritual experience, with the risk of relapse and profanation, becomes a monograph on kinds of profanation.

Coming by revelation and by a lengthy other-world experience on Swedenborg's part (in which he learned of the incorrectness of some of his own beliefs, nn. 279(2), 290) the book, like others of his, nevertheless has for an outstanding feature a steady address to the reason. The profoundest truths of the spiritual life, among them the nature of God and the laws and ways of providence, are not beyond grasp by the reason. Sound reason Swedenborg credits with lofty insights.

Divine Providence is a book to be studied, and not merely read, and studied slowly. By its own way of proceeding, it extends an invitation to read, not straight through, but something like a chapter at a time. In a new chapter

Swedenborg will recall for the reader what was said in the preceding chapter, as though the reader had mean-while laid the book down. The revelator proceeds at a measured pace, carries along the whole body of his thought, and places each new point in this larger context, where it receives its precise significance and its full force. It is an accumulation of thought and not a repetition of statements merely that one meets. "What has been written earlier cannot be as closely connected with what is written later as it will be if the same things are recalled and placed with both in view" (n. 193 (1)).

THE TRANSLATION

This volume has been translated afresh from the Latin; it is not a revision of any earlier edition. Greater readableness has been striven for. In the past, it is generally recognized, Latin sentence structure and word order were clung to unnecessarily. "The defects in previous translations of Swedenborg have arisen mainly from too close an adherence to cognate words and to the Latin order of words and phrases." So wrote the Rev. John C. Ager in 1899 in his translator's note in the Library Edition of Divine Providence. Why, indeed, should English not be allowed its own sentence structure and word order? In addition, in this translation, long sentences, readily followed in an inflected language like Latin, have been broken up into short ones. English also uses fewer particles of logical relation than are at home in Latin. There is more paragraphing, aiding the eye, which both British and American translators have been doing for some years. Latin has neither a definite article nor an indefinite article, and a translator into English must decide when to use either or neither. The definite article, the present translator thinks, has been overused, perhaps in a dogmatic tendency to be as precise as can be. When, for instance, one is admitted into "truths of faith" he is certainly not admitted into "the truths of faith," as though he could comprehend them all. The very title of the book changes the impression which it makes as the definite article is inserted or omitted in it. "The divine providence" seems to single out a theological concept; "divine providence" seems more likely to lead the thought to God's actual care.

Swedenborg has his carefully chosen terms, of course, like "proprium," which are best kept, although in the present translation that term is sometimes rendered by an explanatory word and one which, in the particular context, is an equivalent. The verb "appropriate" presents a difficulty, but has been kept, partly because of the noun "proprium." One could translate rather wordily "make"--something good or evil--"one's own." The English word now means "take exclusive possession of," which one can hardly do of good or evil. Assimilation is the thought and the act, and with that in mind the verb "appropriate" and the noun "appropriation" can be retained. The unusual locution "affection of truth" or "of good," which Mr. Ager abandoned, translating "for truth" and "for good," has been returned to. Much is implied in that phrase which is not to be found in the other wording, namely, that we are affected by truth and by good, and that there is an influx of these into the human spirit. Similarly meaningful is another unusual way of speaking in English, of a person's being "in" faith or "in" charity, where we say that he has faith or exercises charity. The thought is that faith and charity, truth and goodness beckon to us, to be welcomed and entered into.

Latin sometimes has a number of words for an idea or an entity, and the English has not, but when English has the richer vocabulary, why not avail oneself of the variety possible? The Latin word "finis," for example, used in so many connections, can be rendered by one word in one connection and by another in another connection. The "goal" or the "object" of providence is plainer than the "end" of providence. The "close" of life is common speech. "Meritorious" has been kept in our translations, for in a restricted field of traditional theology it does mean that virtue, for example, earns a reward. To most readers the word will be misleading, for they will understand it in its usual meaning, that some act is well-deserving. The former is Swedenborg's meaning, which is that an act is done to earn merit, or is considered to have earned merit. We translate variously according to context to make that meaning clear (nn. 321(11), 326(8), 90).

As it is what Swedenborg has written that is to be translated, the Scripture passages which he quotes are translated without an effort to follow the Authorized Version, which he did not know. This is also done when he refers to the book which stands last in our Bibles; the name he knew it by, the Apocalypse, is retained.

Section 1

DIVINE PROVIDENCE IS GOVERNMENT BY THE LORD'S DIVINE LOVE AND WISDOM

To understand what divine providence is--namely, government by the Lord's divine love and wisdom--one needs to know what was said and shown earlier about divine love and wisdom in the treatise about them: "In the Lord divine love is of divine wisdom, and divine wisdom of divine love" (nn. 34-39); "Divine love and wisdom cannot but be in, and be manifested in, all else, created by them" (nn. 47-51); "All things in the universe were created by them" (nn. 52, 53, 151-156); "All are recipients of that love and wisdom" (nn. 55-60); "The Lord appears before the angels as a sun, the heat proceeding from it being love, and the light wisdom" (nn. 83-88, 89-92, 93-98, 296-301); "Divine love and wisdom, proceeding from the Lord, make one" (nn. 99-102); "The Lord from eternity, who is Jehovah, created the universe and everything in it from Himself, and not from nothing" (nn. 282-284, 290-295). This is to be found in the treatise entitled Angelic Wisdom about Divine Love and Wisdom.

Putting with these propositions the description of creation in that treatise, one may indeed see that what is called divine providence is government by the Lord's divine love and wisdom. In that treatise, however, creation was the subject, and not the preservation of the state of things after creation--yet this is the Lord's government. We now treat of this, therefore, and in the present chapter, of the preservation of the union of divine love and wisdom or of divine good and truth in what was created, which will be done in the following order: i. The universe, with each and all things in it, was created from divine love by divine wisdom. ii Divine love and wisdom proceed as one from the Lord. iii. This one is in some image in every created thing. iv. It is of the divine providence that every created thing, as a whole and in part, should be such a one, and if it is not, should become such a one. v. Good of love is good only so far as it is united to truth of wisdom, and truth of wisdom truth only so far as it is united to good of love. vi. Good of love not united to truth of wisdom is not good in itself but seeming good, and truth of wisdom not united to good of love is not truth in itself but seeming truth. vii. The Lord does not suffer anything to be divided; therefore it must be either in good and at the same time in truth, or in evil and at the same time in falsity. viii. That which is in good and at the same time in truth is something; that which is in evil and at the same time in falsity is not anything. ix. The Lord's divine providence causes evil and the attendant falsity to serve for equilibrium, contrast, and purification, and so for the conjunction of good and truth in others.

(i) The universe, with each and all things in it, was created from divine love by divine wisdom. In the work Divine Love and Wisdom we showed that the Lord from eternity, who is Jehovah, is in essence divine love and wisdom, and that He created the universe and all things in it from Himself. It follows that the universe, with each and all things in it, was created from divine love by means of divine wisdom. We also showed in that treatise that love can do nothing without wisdom, and wisdom nothing without love. For love apart from wisdom, or the will apart from understanding, cannot think anything, indeed cannot see, feel or say anything, so cannot do anything. Likewise, wisdom apart from love, or understanding apart from will, cannot think, see, feel, or speak, therefore cannot do, anything. For if love is removed from wisdom or understanding, there is no willing and thus no doing. If this is true of man, for him to do anything, it was much more true of God--who is love itself and wisdom itself--when He created and made the world and all that it contains.

[2] That the universe, with each and all things in it, was created from divine love by divine wisdom may also be established from objects to be seen in the world. Take a particular object, examine it with some wisdom, and you will be convinced. Take the seed, fruit, flower or leaf of a tree, muster your wisdom, examine the object with a strong microscope, and you will see marvels. Even more wonderful are the more interior things which you do not see. Note the unfolding order in the growth of a tree from seed to new seed; reflect on the continuous effort in all stages after self-propagation--the end to which it moves is seed in which its reproductive power arises anew. If then you will think spiritually, as you can if you will, will you not see wisdom in all this? Furthermore, if you can think spiritually enough, you will see that this energy does not come from the seed, nor from the sun of the world, which is only fire, but is in the seed from God the Creator whose wisdom is infinite, and is from Him not only at the moment of creation but ever after, too. For maintenance is perpetual creation, as continuance is perpetual coming to be. Else it is quite as work ceases when you withdraw will from action, or as utterance fails when you remove thought from speech, or as motion ceases when you remove impetus; in a word, as an effect perishes when you remove the cause.

[3] Every created thing is endowed with energy, indeed, but this does nothing of itself but from Him who implanted it. Examine any other earthly object, like a silkworm, bee or other small creature. View it first naturally, then rationally, and at length spiritually, and if you can think deeply, you will be astounded at all you see. Let wisdom speak in you, and you will exclaim in astonishment, "Who does not see the divine in such things? They are all of divine wisdom." Still more will you exclaim, if you note the uses of all created things, how they mount in regular order even to the human being, and from man to the Creator whence they are, and that the connection, and if you will acknowledge it, the preservation also of them all, depend on the conjunction of the Creator with man. That divine love created all things, but nothing apart from the divine wisdom, will be seen in what follows.

(ii) Divine love and wisdom proceed as one from the Lord. This, too, is plain from what was shown in the work Divine Love and Wisdom, especially in the propositions: "Esse and existere are distinguishably one in the Lord" (nn. 14-17); "Infinite things are distinguishably one in Him" (nn. 17-22); "Divine love is of divine wisdom, and divine wisdom of divine love" (nn. 34-39); "Love not married to wisdom cannot effect anything" (nn. 401-403); "Love does nothing except in union with wisdom" (nn. 409, 410); "Spiritual heat and light, proceeding from the Lord as a sun, make one as divine love and wisdom make one in Him" (nn. 99-102). The truth of the present proposition is plain from these propositions, demonstrated in that treatise. But as it is not known how two distinct things can act as one, I wish now to show that there is no "one" apart from form, and that the form itself makes it a unit; then, that a form makes a "one" the more perfectly as the elements entering into it are distinctly different and yet united.

[2] There is no "one" apart from form, and the form itself makes it a unit. Everyone who brings his mind to bear on the matter can see clearly that there is no "one" apart from form, and if a thing exists at all, it is a form. For what exists at all derives from form what is known as its character and its predicates, its changes of state, also its relevance, and so on. A thing without form has no way of affecting us, and what has no power of affecting, has no reality. It is form which enables to all this. And as all things have a form, then if the form is perfect, all things in it regard each other mutually, as link does link in a chain. It follows that it is form which makes a thing a unit and thus an entity of which character, state, affection or anything else can be predicated; each is predicated of it according to the perfection of the form.

[3] Such a unit is every object which meets the eye in the world. Such, too, is everything not seen with the eye, whether in interior nature or in the spiritual world. The human being is such a unit, human society is, likewise the church, and in the Lord's view the whole angelic heaven, too; in short, all creation in general and in every particular. For each and all things to be forms, He who created all things must be form itself, and all things made must be from that form. This, therefore, was also demonstrated in the work Divine Love and Wisdom, as that "Divine love and wisdom are substance and form" (nn. 40-43); "Divine love and wisdom are form itself, thus the one Self and the single independent existence" (nn. 44-46); "Divine love and wisdom are one in the Lord" (nn. 14-17, 18-22), "and proceed as one from Him" (nn. 99-102, and elsewhere).

[4] A form makes a one the more perfectly as the elements entering into it are distinctly different and yet united. This hardly falls into a comprehension not elevated, for the appearance is that a form cannot make a one except as its elements are quite alike. I have spoken with angels often on the subject. They said that this is a secret perceived clearly by their wiser men, obscurely by the less wise. They said it is the truth that a form is the more perfect as its constituents are distinctly different and yet severally united. They established the fact from the societies which in the aggregate constitute the form of heaven, and from the angels of a society, for as these are different and free and love their associates from themselves and from their own affection, the form of the society is more perfect. They also illustrated the fact from the marriage of good and truth, in that the more distinguishably two these are, the more perfectly do they make a one; similarly, of love and wisdom. The indistinguishable is confusion, they said, whence comes imperfection of form.

[5] In various ways they went on to establish the manner in which perfectly distinct things are united and thus make a one, especially by what is in the human body, in which are innumerable things quite distinct and yet united, held distinct by coverings and united by ligaments. It is so with love, they said, and all its things, and wisdom and all its things, for love and wisdom are not perceived except as one. See further on the subject in Divine Love and Wisdom (nn. 14-22) and in the work Heaven and Hell (nn. 56 and 489). This has been

adduced as part of angelic wisdom.

(iii) This "one" is in some image in every created thing. It can be seen from what was demonstrated throughout the treatise Divine Love and Wisdom and especially at nn. 47-51, 55-60, 282-284, 290-295, 313-318, 319-326, 349-357, that divine love and wisdom which are one in the Lord and proceed as one from Him, are in some image in each created thing. It was shown that the divine is in every created thing because God the Creator, who is the Lord from eternity, produced the sun of the spiritual world from Himself, and all things of the universe through that sun. That sun, which is from Him and in which He is, is therefore not only the first but the sole substance from which are all things. As this is the one substance, it is in everything made, but with endless variety in accord with uses.

[2] In the Lord, then, are divine love and wisdom, and in the sun from Him divine fire and radiance, and from the sun spiritual heat and light; and in each instance the two make one. It follows that this oneness is in every created thing. All things in the world are referable, therefore, to good and truth, in fact to the conjunction of them. Or, what is the same, they are referable to love and wisdom and to the union of these; for good is of love and truth of wisdom, love calling all its own, "good," and wisdom calling all its own, "truth." It will be seen in what follows that there is a conjunction of these in each created thing.

Many avow that there is a single substance which is also the first, from which are all things, but what that substance is, is not known. The belief is that it is so simple nothing is more so, and that it can be likened to a point without dimensions, and that dimensional forms arose out of an infinite number of such points. But this is a fallacy, springing from an idea of space. To such an idea there seems to be such a least thing. The truth is that the simpler and purer a thing is, the more replete it is and the more complete. This is why the more interiorly a thing is examined, the more wonderful, perfect, and well formed are the things seen in it, and in the first substance the most wonderful, perfect and fully formed of all. For the first substance is from the spiritual sun, which, as we said, is from the Lord and in which He is. That sun is therefore the sole substance and, not being in space, is all in all, and is in the greatest and least things of the created universe.

[2] As that sun is the first and sole substance from which all things are, it follows that in it are infinitely more things than can possibly appear in substances arising from it, called substantial and lastly material. This infinity cannot appear in derivative substances because these descend from that sun by degrees of two kinds in accord with which perfections decline. For that reason, as we said above, the more interiorly a thing is regarded, the more wonderful, perfect and well formed are the things seen. This has been said to establish the fact that the divine is in some image in every created thing, but is less and less manifest with the descent over degrees, and still less when a lower degree, parted from the higher by being closed, is also choked with earthy matter. These concepts cannot but seem obscure unless one has read and understood what was shown in the treatise Divine Love and Wisdom about the spiritual sun (nn. 83-172), about degrees (nn. 173-281) and about the creation of the world (nn. 282-357).

(iv) It is of the divine providence that every created thing as a whole and in part should be such a one or should become such a one, or that there be in it something of the divine love and wisdom, or what is the same, that there be good and truth in it, or a union of them. (Inasmuch as good is of love and truth is of wisdom, as was said above (n. 5), in what follows we shall at times say good and truth instead of love and wisdom, and marriage of good and truth instead of union of love and wisdom.)

It is evident from the preceding proposition that divine love and wisdom, which are one in the Lord and proceed as one from Him, are in some image in everything created by Him. Something shall be said now specifically of the "one" or the union called the marriage of good and truth. 1. This marriage is in the Lord Himself--for, as we said, divine love and wisdom in Him are one. 2. This marriage is from Him, for in all that proceeds from Him love and wisdom are fully united. The two proceed from Him as a sun, divine love as heat, and divine wisdom as light. 3. These are received as two, indeed, by angels, likewise by men of the church, but are made one in them by the Lord. 4. In view of this influx of love and wisdom as one from the Lord with angels of heaven and men of the church, and in view of their reception of it, the Lord is spoken of in the Word as bridegroom and husband, and heaven and the church are called bride and wife. 5. An image and a likeness of the Lord are therefore to be found in heaven and in the church in general, and in an angel of heaven and a man of the church in particular, so far as they are in that union or in the marriage of good and truth. For good and truth in the Lord are one, indeed are the Lord. 6. Love and wisdom in heaven and in the church as a whole, and in an angel of heaven and a man of the church, are one when will and understanding, thus when good and truth, make one; or what is still the same, when doctrine from the Word and life according to doctrine make one. 7. How the two make one in man and in all that pertains to him was shown, moreover, in Part V of the treatise Divine Love and Wisdom, where the creation of man, and especially the correspondence of will and understanding with heart and lungs, were treated of (nn. 358-432).

How good and truth, however, make one in what is below or outside man, in both the animal and the vegetable kingdom, shall be told from time to time in what follows. Three points are premised. First, in the universe and in each and all things of it as created by the Lord, there was a marriage of good and truth. Second, after creation this marriage was severed in man. Third, it is the work of divine providence to unite what was severed, and so to restore the marriage of good and truth. As all three points were established by many things in the work Divine Love and Wisdom, there is no need to substantiate them further. Anyone can see from reason, moreover, that if there was a marriage of good and truth in each created thing and later it was severed, the Lord must be working constantly to restore it, and that the restoration of it, and hence the conjunction of the created world with the Lord through man, are of divine providence.

(v) Good of love is good only so far as it is united to truth of wisdom, and truth of wisdom is truth only so far as it is united to good of love. Good and truth have this from their origin, the one and the other originating in the Lord, who is good itself and truth itself and in whom the two are one. Hence in angels in heaven and men on earth, good is not good basically except so far as it is joined to truth, and truth is not truth basically except so far as it is joined to good. Granted that all good and truth are from the Lord, then inasmuch as good makes one with truth and truth with good in Him, good to be good in itself and truth to be truth in itself must make one in the recipient, that is, the angel in heaven or the man on earth.

It is indeed known that all things in the world are referable to good and truth. For by good is meant what universally embraces and involves all things of love; and by truth what universally embraces and involves all things of wisdom. Still it is not known that good is nothing except when it is joined to truth, and truth nothing unless it is joined to good. Good apart from truth and truth apart from good still seem to be something; yet they are not. For love (to which all that is called good pertains) is the esse of a thing, and wisdom (to which all things called truths pertain) is a thing's existere from that esse (as was shown in the treatise Divine Love and Wisdom, nn. 14-16). Therefore, as esse is nothing apart from existere, or existere apart from esse, good is nothing apart from truth or truth from good. What, again, is good which has no relation to anything? Can it be called good if it is without affection and perception?

[2] That which is associated with good, permitting it to affect and to be perceived and felt, is referable to truth, since it has relation to what is in the understanding. Tell someone, not that a given thing is good, but simply say "good"--is good anything? It becomes something from what is perceived along with it. This is united with good only in the understanding, and all understanding has relation to truth. It is the same with willing. Apart from knowing, perceiving and thinking what one wills, to will is nothing actual; together with them it becomes something. All volition is of love and is referable to good; and all knowing, perceiving and thinking is of the understanding, and is referable to truth. It is clear, then, that to will is nothing actual, but to will this or that means something.

[3] So also with a use, inasmuch as a use is a good. Unless a use is addressed to something which makes one with it, it is not a use, and thus not anything. A use derives its something from the understanding, and what is thence conjoined or adjoined to it, has relation to truth. So a use gets its character.

[4] From these few things it is plain that good is nothing apart from truth, nor truth anything apart from good. But if good together with truth and truth together with good are something, evil with falsity and falsity with evil are not, for the latter are opposite to the former and the opposition destroys--that is, destroys the something. But of this in what follows.

Marriage of good and truth may, however, be found either in a cause or from the cause in an effect. In a cause the marriage of good and truth is one of will and understanding, or of love and wisdom. Such a marriage is in all that a man wills and thinks and in all his ensuing determinations and purposes. This marriage enters into and in fact produces the effect. But in producing the effect, good and truth seem distinct, for then the simultaneous turns successive. When, for example, a man wills and thinks about food, clothing, shelter, business or employment, or about his relationship to others, first he wills and thinks or comes to his conclusions and intentions all at the same time; but when these are determined to effects, truth follows on good, though in will and thought they continue to make one. In the effects the uses pertain to love or good, and the ways of performing the uses pertain to understanding or truth. Anyone can confirm these general truths by particular instances provided he perceives what is referable respectively to good of love and to truth of wisdom, and also how differently it is referable in cause and in effect.

We have said often that love constitutes man's life. This does not mean, however, love separate from wisdom or good from truth in the cause, for love separate or good separate is not an actuality. The love which makes man's inmost life--the life he has from the Lord--is therefore love and wisdom together; neither is the love which makes his life as a recipient being separate in the cause, but only in the effect. For love cannot be understood except from its quality, which is wisdom; and the quality or wisdom can exist only from its own esse, which is love; thence it is that they are one; it is the same with good and truth. Since truth is from good as wisdom is from love, it is the two taken together that are called good or love. For love has wisdom for its form, and good for its form truth, and form is the source, and the one source, of quality. It is plain from all this that good is good only so far as it has become one with its truth, and truth truth only so far as it has become one with its good.

14.

(vi) Good of love not united to truth of wisdom is not good in itself but seeming good; and truth of wisdom not conjoined with good of love is not truth in itself but seeming truth. The fact is that no good, in itself good, can exist unless joined with its truth, and no truth, in itself truth, can exist unless it has become joined with its good. And yet good separate from truth is possible, and truth separate from good. They are found in hypocrites and flatterers, in evil persons of every sort, and in such as are in natural but not spiritual good. These can all do well by church, country, society, fellow-citizens, the needy, the poor, and widows and orphans. They can also comprehend truths, from understanding think them, and from thought speak and teach them. But the goods and truths are not interiorly such, that is, basically goods and truths, but only outwardly and seemingly such. For such good and truth look to self and the world, not to good itself and truth itself; they are not from good and truth; they are of the mouth and body only, therefore, and not of the heart.

[2] They may be likened to gold or silver which is spread on dross, rotten wood or mire. When uttered the truths may be likened to a breath exhaled and gone, or to a delusive light which dies away, though they appear outwardly like genuine truths. They are seeming truths in those who utter them; to those hearing and assenting, and unaware of this, they may be altogether different. For everyone is affected by what is external according to his internal. A truth, by whomsoever uttered, enters another's hearing and is taken up by his mind in keeping with the state or character of his mind.

Of those in natural good by inheritance, but in no spiritual good, nearly the same is true as of those described above. The internal of every good or truth is spiritual. The spiritual dispels falsities and evils, but the natural left to itself favors them. To favor evil and falsity does not accord with doing good.

Good can be separated from truth, and truth from good, and then still appear as good or truth, for the reason that the human being has a capacity to act which is called liberty, and a capacity of understanding called rationality. By abuse of these powers a man can appear in externals other than he is in internals; an evil man can do good and speak truth, and a devil feign himself an angel of light. But on this see the following propositions in the treatise Divine Love and Wisdom: "The origin of evil is in the abuse of faculties proper to man, called liberty and rationality" (nn. 246-270); "These two faculties are to be found with the evil as well as with the good" (n. 425); "Love not married to wisdom, and good not married to truth, can effect nothing" (n. 401); "Love does nothing except in conjunction with wisdom or understanding, and it brings wisdom or the understanding reciprocally into conjunction with itself" (nn. 410-412); "From power given it by love, wisdom or understanding can be elevated and can perceive and receive the things of light from heaven" (n. 413); "Love can be raised similarly to receive the things of heat from heaven if it loves its mate, wisdom, in that degree" (nn. 414, 415); "Else love pulls wisdom or the understanding down from its elevation to act at one with itself" (nn. 416-418); "If the two are elevated, love is purified in the understanding" (nn. 419-421); "Purified by wisdom in the understanding, love becomes spiritual and celestial, but defiled in the understanding it become sensuous and corporeal" (nn. 422-424); "What is true of love and wisdom and their union is true of charity and faith and their conjunction" (nn. 427-430). What charity in heaven is, see n. 431.

(vii) The Lord does not suffer anything to be divided; it must be either in good and at the same time in truth, or in evil and at the same time in falsity. The Lord's divine providence has for its goal, and to this end it labors, that man shall be in good and at the same time in truth. For then he is his own good and love and his own truth and wisdom; thereby the human being is human, for he is then an image of the Lord. But while he lives in the world he can be in good and at the same time in falsity, likewise in evil and at the same time in truth, indeed in evil and at the same time in good, and thus be double. As the cleavage destroys the Lord's image in him and thus the man, the Lord's divine providence takes care in every least act that this division shall not be. And as it is better for man to be in evil and at the same time in falsity than to be in good and at the same time in evil, the Lord permits it, not as one willing it, but as one unable to resist because of the end sought, which is salvation.

[2] A man can be simultaneously in evil and in truth and the Lord be unable to prevent it in view of the end, which is salvation, for the reason that man's understanding can be raised into the light of wisdom and see truths, or acknowledge them when he hears them, while his love remains below. Thus a man can be in heaven as to understanding, while as to his love he is in hell. This is not denied him, because the two faculties of liberty and rationality, by virtue of which he is a human being and distinguished from beasts and by which alone he can be regenerated and thus saved, cannot be taken away. By means of them, he can act according to wisdom and at the same time according to an unwise love. From wisdom above he can view the love below and also the thoughts, intentions and affections, therefore the evils and falsities as well as the goods and truths of his life and doctrine, without a knowledge and recognition of which he cannot be reformed. We spoke of the two faculties before and shall say more in what follows. What has been said explains how man can be simultaneously in good and truth, or in evil and falsity, or in mixtures of them.

In this world a man can hardly come into one or the other conjunction or union, that is, of good and truth or of evil and falsity, for during his life in the world he is kept in a state of reformation or regeneration. After death, however, every man comes into the one union or the other, because he can then no longer be reformed or regenerated. He remains such as his life was in the world, that is, such as his reigning love was. If therefore his was a life of an evil love, all the truth acquired by him in the world from teacher, pulpit or Word is taken away. On the removal of it, he absorbs the falsity agreeing with his evil as a sponge does water. On the other hand, if his was the life of a good love, all the falsity is removed which he may have picked up in the world by hearing or from reading but did not confirm in himself, and in its place truth congruous with his good is given him. This is meant by the Lord's words:

Take ... the talent from him, and give it to him that has ten talents. For to everyone who has, shall be given until he abounds but from him who has not, even what he has shall be taken away (Mt 25:28, 29; 13:12; Mk 4:25; Lu 8:18; 19:24-26).

After death everyone must be either in good and at the same time in truth or in evil and at the same time in falsity, for the reason that good and evil cannot be united, nor can good and the falsity of evil, nor evil and the truth of good. For these are opposites, and opposites contend until one destroys the other. Those who are at the same time in evil and in good are meant in the Apocalypse in these words of the Lord to the church of the Laodiceans:

I know your works, that you are neither cold nor hot; would that you were cold or hot; but because you are lukewarm, I will spue you out of my mouth (3:15, 16):

also in these words of the Lord:

No man can serve two masters, for either he will hate the one and love the other, or cleave to the one and not heed the other (Mt 6:24).

(viii) That which is in good and at the same time in truth is something; that which is in evil and at the same time in falsity is not anything. See above (n. 11) that what is in good and at the same time in truth is something. It follows that what is at once evil and false is not anything. By not being anything is meant that it is without power and without spiritual life. Those at once in evil and in falsity (all of whom are in hell) have power indeed among themselves, for an evil man can do evil and does so in a thousand ways. Yet he can do evil to the evil only by reason of their evil; he cannot harm the good at all; if, as sometimes happens, he does, it is by conjunction with their evil.

[2] In this way temptations arise; they are infestations by evil spirits who are with a man; so combats ensue by which the good are freed from their evils. Since the wicked have no power, all hell in the Lord's sight is not only nothing, but nothing at all in point of power, as I have seen proved by much experience. But it is remarkable that the evil all deem themselves powerful, and the good all think themselves powerless. This is because the evil ascribe everything to their own power or shrewdness and malice, and nothing to the Lord; whereas the good ascribe nothing to their own prudence, but all to the Lord who is almighty. Evil and falsity together are not anything for the further reason that they have no spiritual life. The life of the infernals is therefore called death, not life. Since life holds everything, death has nothing.

Men in evil and at the same time in truths may be likened to eagles flying aloft which, deprived of their wings, fall. For after death, on becoming spirits, men do the like who have understood and spoken and taught truths and yet have not looked to God in their lives. By means of things of the understanding they raise themselves aloft and even enter heaven at times and feign themselves angels of light. But when they are deprived of truths and are cast out, they fall down to hell. Eagles also signify rapacious men with intellectual acumen, and wings signify spiritual truths. Such, we said, are those who have not looked to God in their lives. To look to God in life means simply to think that a given evil is a sin against God, and for that reason not to commit it.

(ix) The Lord's divine providence causes evil and its falsity to serve for equilibrium, contrast, and purification, and so for the conjunction of good and truth in others. It is obvious from the preceding that the Lord's divine providence continually operates in order that truth may be united in man with good and good with truth, because that union is the church and heaven. For that union is in the Lord and in all that proceeds from Him. From that union, heaven and the church are called a marriage, and the kingdom of God is likened in the Word to a marriage. Again, the Sabbath signified that union and was the holiest observance in the worship of the Israelitish Church. From that union also there is a marriage of good and truth in the Word and in each and all things of it (on this see Doctrine of the New Jerusalem about Sacred Scripture, nn. 80-90). The marriage of good and truth is from the marriage of the Lord with the church, and this in turn from the marriage of love and wisdom in Him, for good is of love, and truth of wisdom. It is plain, then, that it is the constant aim of divine providence to unite good to truth and truth to good in a man, for so he is united to the Lord.

But many have severed and do sever this marriage, especially by separating faith from charity (for faith is of truth and truth is of faith, and charity is of good and good is of charity), and in so doing they conjoin evil and falsity in themselves and thus come into and continue in the opposite to good and truth. The Lord therefore provides that they shall nevertheless serve for uniting good and truth in others, through equilibrium, contrast and purification.

Conjunction of good and truth in others is provided by the Lord through equilibrium between heaven and hell. From hell evil and at the same time falsity constantly exhale, and from heaven good and at the same time truth. In equilibrium between them, and so in freedom to think, will, speak and act in which he can be reformed, every man is kept while he lives in the world. On the spiritual equilibrium from which the human being has freedom, see the work Heaven and Hell, nn. 589-596, 597-603.

Conjunction of good and truth is provided by the Lord through contrast. For the nature of good is not known except by contrast with what is less good and by its contrariety to evil. All perceptiveness and sensitivity arise so; their quality is thence. All pleasantness is perceived and felt over against the less pleasant and the unpleasant; all the beautiful by reference to the less beautiful and the unbeautiful; similarly all good of love by reference to lesser good and to evil; all truth of wisdom by a sense of lesser truth and of falsity. Everything inevitably varies from greatest to least, and with the same variation in its opposite and with equilibrium between them, there is contrast degree by degree, and the perception and sensation of a thing increase or diminish. But be it known that an opposite may either lower or exalt perceptions and sensitivities. It lowers them when it mingles in and exalts them when it does not mingle in, for which reason the Lord separates good and evil with man that they shall not mingle, as exquisitely as He does heaven and hell.

Conjunction of good and truth in others is provided by the Lord through purification in two ways; one through temptations, and the other through fermentations. Spiritual temptations are nothing else than combats against the evils and falsities exhaled from hell and affecting man. By these combats a man is purified from evils and falsities, and good and truth are united in him. Spiritual fermentations take place in many ways, and in heaven as well as on earth; but in the world it is not known what they are or how they come about. For evils and their falsities, let into societies, act as ferments do in meal or in must, separating the heterogeneous and conjoining the homogeneous until there is clarity and purity. Such fermentations are meant in the Lord's words:

The kingdom of heaven is like leaven which a woman took and hid in three measures of meal until the whole was leavened (Mt 13:33; Lu 12:21).

The Lord provides these uses through the united evil and falsity of those in hell. The Lord's kingdom, which extends over hell as well as over heaven, is a kingdom of uses. It is the Lord's providence that there shall be no creature and no thing whereby a use is not performed.

Section 2

THE LORD'S DIVINE PROVIDENCE HAS FOR ITS OBJECT A HEAVEN FROM THE HUMAN RACE

Heaven does not consist of angels created such to begin with, nor does hell come from any devil created an angel of light and cast down from heaven. Both heaven and hell are from mankind, heaven consisting of those in the love of good and consequent understanding of truth, and hell of those in the love of evil and consequent understanding of falsity. This has been made known and sure to me by long-continued intercourse with angels and spirits. See what was said on the subject in the work Heaven and Hell (nn. 311-316); also in the little work The Last Judgment (nn. 14-27), and in Continuation about the Last Judgment and the Spiritual World (throughout).

[2] As heaven is from mankind and is an abiding with the Lord to eternity, it must have been the Lord's purpose in creation; being the purpose in creation, it is the purpose of His providence. The Lord created the world not for His own sake but for the sake of those with whom He would be in heaven. Spiritual love by nature desires to give its own to another, and so far as it can do so is in its esse, peace, and blessedness. Spiritual love derives this from the Lord's divine love which is such infinitely. It follows that the divine love and hence divine providence has for its object a heaven consisting of human beings who have become or are becoming angels, on whom the Lord can bestow all the blessings and felicities of love and wisdom and do so from Himself in men. It must be in this way, for the Lord's image and likeness are in men from creation, the image in them wisdom and the likeness love. Furthermore, the Lord in them is love united to wisdom and wisdom united to love or (what is the same) is good united to truth and truth united to good (this union was treated of in the preceding chapter).

[3] What heaven is in general or with a number, and in particular or with an individual, is not known. Nor is it known what heaven is in the spiritual world and what it is in the natural world. Yet this knowledge is important, for heaven is the purpose of providence. I therefore desire to set the subject in some light in this order:

i. Heaven is conjunction with the Lord. ii. By creation the human being is such that he can be conjoined more and more closely to the Lord. iii. The more closely one is conjoined to the Lord the wiser one becomes. iv. The more closely one is conjoined to the Lord the happier one becomes. v. The more closely one is conjoined to the Lord the more distinctly does he seem to himself to be his own, and the more plainly does he recognize that he is the Lord's.

(i) Heaven is conjunction with the Lord. Heaven is heaven, not from the angels but from the Lord. For the love and wisdom in which angels are and which make heaven are not theirs, but the Lord's, indeed are the Lord in them. And as love and wisdom are the Lord's, and are the Lord in heaven, and make the life of angels, it is plain that their life is the Lord's, indeed is the Lord. The angels themselves avow that they live from the Lord. Hence it is evident that heaven is conjunction with the Lord. But conjunction with Him is various and one man's heaven is not another's; therefore heaven is also according to the conjunction with the Lord. In the following proposition it will be seen that conjunction is more and more close or more and more remote.

[2] Here let something be said about how the conjunction takes place and what the nature of it is. It is a conjunction of the Lord with the angels and of the angels with Him, therefore is reciprocal. The Lord flows into the life's love of the angels, and they receive Him in wisdom, thus in turn conjoining themselves with Him. It must be said, however, that it seems to the angels that they conjoin themselves to the Lord by wisdom; actually the Lord conjoins them to Himself by their wisdom, for the wisdom is also from the Lord. It is the same thing if we say that the Lord conjoins Himself to the angels by good and they in turn conjoin themselves to the Lord by truth, for all good is of love, and truth, of wisdom.

[3] This reciprocal conjunction is an arcanum, however, which few can understand unless it is explained. I want therefore to unfold it so far as it can be done by things within one's grasp. We showed in the treatise Divine Love and Wisdom (nn. 404, 405) how love unites itself with wisdom, namely, through affection for knowing from which comes an affection for truth, through affection for understanding from which comes perception of truth, and through affection for seeing what is known and understood, from which comes thought. Into all these affections the Lord flows, for they are all derivatives of one's life's love, and the angels receive the influx in perception of truth and in thought, for in these the influx becomes apparent to them, but not in the affections.

[4] As the perceptions and thoughts appear to the angels to be their own, although they arise from affections which are from the Lord, the appearance is that the angels reciprocally conjoin themselves to the Lord, when nevertheless the Lord conjoins them to Himself. The affection itself produces the perceptions and thoughts, for the affection, which is of love, is their soul. Apart from affection no one can perceive or think anything, and every one perceives and thinks according to his affection. It is evident that the reciprocal conjunction of the angels with the Lord is not from them, but as it were from them. Such, too, is the conjunction of the Lord with the church and of the church with Him, a union called celestial and spiritual marriage.

All conjunction in the spiritual world is effected by intent regard. When anyone there thinks of another with a desire to speak with him, the other is at once present, and the two come face to face. Likewise, when one thinks of another from an affection of love; by this affection, however, there is conjunction, but by the other only presence. This is peculiar to the spiritual world; for there all are spiritual beings. It is otherwise in the natural world where all are physical beings. In the natural world something similar takes place in the affections and thoughts of the spirit; but as there is space here, while in the spiritual world space is appearance only, what takes place here in one's spirit occurs outwardly there.

[2] We have said so much to make known how conjunction of the Lord with angels and their seemingly reciprocal conjunction with Him is effected. All angels turn the face to the Lord; He regards them in the forehead, and they

regard Him with the eyes. The reason is that the forehead corresponds to love and its affections, and the eyes correspond to wisdom and its perceptions. Still the angels do not of themselves turn the face to the Lord, but He faces them toward Himself, doing so by influx into their life's love, by this entering the perceptions and thoughts, and so turning the angels to Him.

[3] There is such a circuit from love to thoughts and under love's impulse from thoughts to love in all the mind's activity. It may be called the circling of life. On these subjects see some things also in the treatise Divine Love and Wisdom: as that "Angels constantly turn the face to the Lord as a sun" (nn. 129-134); "All the interiors of both the mind and the bodies of the angels are likewise turned to the Lord as a sun" (nn. 135-139); "Every spirit, whatever his character, turns himself likewise to his ruling love" (nn. 140-145); "Love conjoins itself to wisdom and causes wisdom to be conjoined reciprocally with it" (nn. 410-412); "Angels are in the Lord and He in them; and as the angels are only recipients, the Lord alone is heaven" (nn. 113-118).

The Lord's heaven in the natural world is called the church; an angel of this heaven is a man of the church who is conjoined to the Lord; on departure from this world he also becomes an angel of the spiritual heaven. What was said of the angelic heaven is evidently to be understood, then, of the human heaven also which is called the church. The reciprocal conjunction with the Lord which makes heaven in the human being is revealed by the Lord in these words in John:

Abide in Me, and I in you; ... he who abides in Me, and I in him, bears much fruit; for without Me ye can do nothing (15:4, 5, 7).

It is plain from this that the Lord is heaven not only in general with all in heaven, but in particular with each one there. For each angel is a heaven in least form; of as many heavens as there are angels, does heaven in general consist. In substantiation see Heaven and Hell (nn. 51-58). Since this is so, let no one cherish the mistaken idea, which first visits the thought of so many, that the Lord dwells in heaven among the angels or is among them like a king in his kingdom. To the sight He is above them in the sun there; He is in them in their life of love and wisdom.

(ii) By creation the human being is such that he can be conjoined more and more closely to the Lord. This becomes evident from what was shown about degrees in the treatise Divine Love and Wisdom, Part III, especially in the propositions: "By creation there are three discrete degrees or degrees of height in the human being" (nn. 230-235); "These three degrees are in man from birth, and as they are opened, the man is in the Lord, and the Lord in him" (nn. 236-241); "All perfection increases and mounts with and according to the degrees" (nn. 199-204). Evidently, then, man is such by creation that he can be conjoined with the Lord more and more closely according to these degrees.

[2] But one must know well what degrees are and that there are two kinds --discrete degrees or degrees of height, and continuous degrees or degrees of breadth; also how they differ. It must be known, too, that every human being has by creation and hence from birth three discrete degrees or degrees of height, and that he comes at birth into the first degree, called natural, and can grow in this degree continuously until he becomes rational. He comes into the second degree, called spiritual, if he lives according to spiritual laws of order, which are

divine truths. He can also come into the third degree, called celestial, if he lives according to the celestial laws of order, which are divine goods.

[3] These degrees are opened in a person by the Lord according to his life and actually opened in the world, but not perceptibly and sensibly until after his departure from the world. As they are opened and later perfected a man is conjoined to the Lord more and more closely. This conjunction can grow to eternity in nearness to God and does so with the angels. And yet no angel can attain or touch the first degree of the Lord's love and wisdom, for the Lord is infinite and an angel is finite, and between infinite and finite no ratio obtains. Man's state and the state of his elevation and nearness to the Lord cannot be understood without a knowledge of these degrees; they have been specifically treated of, therefore, in the treatise Divine Love and Wisdom, nn. 173-281, which see.

We shall say briefly how man can be more and more closely conjoined to the Lord, and then how the conjunction seems closer and closer. How man is more and more closely conjoined to the Lord: this is effected not by knowledge alone, nor by intelligence alone, nor even by wisdom alone, but by a life conjoined to them. A man's life is his love, and love is manifold. In general there are love of good and love of evil. Love of evil is love of committing adultery, taking revenge, defrauding, blaspheming, depriving others of their possessions. In thinking and doing such things the love of evil finds its pleasure and joy. Of this love there are as many derivatives, which are affections, as there are evils in which it can find expression. And there are as many perceptions and thoughts of this love as there are falsities favoring and confirming such evils. The falsities make one with the evils as understanding makes one with will; they are mutually inseparable; the one is of the other.

[2] Inasmuch as the Lord flows into one's life's love and by its affections into the perceptions and thoughts, and not the other way about, as we said above, it follows that the Lord can conjoin Himself more closely to a man only as the love of evil is removed along with its affections, which are lusts. These lusts reside in the natural man. What a man does from the natural man he feels that he does of himself. For his part, therefore, a man should remove the evils of that love; so far as he does, the Lord comes nearer and conjoins Himself to him. Anyone can see from reason that lusts with their pleasures block and close the door to the Lord and cannot be cast out by the Lord as long as the man himself keeps the door shut and presses and pushes from outside to keep it from being opened. It is plain from the Lord's words in the Apocalypse that a man must himself open the door:

Behold, I stand at the door and knock; if anyone hears My voice and opens the door, I will come in to him, and sup with him, and he with Me (3:20).

[3] Plainly, then, so far as one shuns evils as diabolical and as obstacles to the Lord's entrance, he is more and more closely conjoined to the Lord, and he the most closely who abhors them as so many dusky and fiery devils. For evil and the devil are one and the same, and the falsity of evil and satan are one and the same. As the Lord's influx is into the love of good and into its affections and by these into the perceptions and thoughts, which have it from the good in which a man is that they are truths, so the influx of the devil, that is of hell, is into the love of evil and its affections, which are lusts, and by these into the

perceptions and thoughts, which have it from the evil in which the man is that they are falsities.

[4] How the conjunction seems closer and closer. The more the evils in the natural man are removed by shunning and turning away from them, the more closely a man is conjoined to the Lord. Love and wisdom, which are the Lord Himself, are not in space, as affection which is of love, and thought which is of wisdom, have nothing in common with space. In the measure of the conjunction by love and wisdom, therefore, the Lord seems nearer; and, contrariwise, in the measure of the rejection of love and wisdom, more distant. There is no space in the spiritual world; distance and presence there are appearances according to similarity or dissimilarity of the affections. For, as we said, affections which are of love, and thoughts which are of wisdom, in themselves spiritual, are not in space (on this see what was shown in the treatise Divine Love and Wisdom, nn. 7-10, 69-72, and elsewhere).

[5] The Lord's conjunction with a man in whom evils have been put away is meant by the Lord's words:

The pure in heart shall see God (Mt 5:8);

and by the words:

He who has my commandments and does them ... with him will I make an abode (Jn 14:21, 23).

"To have the commandments" is to know and "to do them" is to love, for it is also said: "he who does my commandments, he it is that loves Me."

(iii) The more closely one is conjoined to the Lord the wiser one becomes. As there are three degrees of life in man by creation and so from birth (see just above, n. 32), there are specifically three degrees of wisdom in him. These degrees it is that are opened in man according to conjunction, that is, according to love, for love is conjunction itself. Love's ascent by degrees, however, is only obscurely perceived by man; but wisdom's ascent is clearly perceived by those who know and see what wisdom is. The degrees of wisdom are perceived because love by its affections enters the perceptions and thoughts, and these present themselves to the internal mental sight, which corresponds to the external bodily sight. Thus wisdom appears, but not the affection of love which produces it. It is the same with all a man's deeds; he is aware how the body does them, but not how the soul does them. So he perceives how he meditates, perceives and thinks, but not how the soul of these mental activities, which is an affection of good and truth, produces them.

[2] There are three degrees of wisdom: natural, spiritual, and celestial. Man is in the natural degree of wisdom during his life in the world. This degree can be perfected in him to its height, but even so cannot pass into the spiritual degree, for the latter is not continuous with it, but conjoined to it by correspondences. After death man is in the spiritual degree of wisdom. This degree also is such that it can be perfected to its height, and yet cannot pass into the celestial degree of wisdom, because neither is this continuous with the spiritual but conjoined to it by correspondences. Plainly, then, wisdom can be raised threefold, and in each degree can be perfected but only to its peak.

[3] One who understands the elevation and perfecting of these degrees can see to an extent why angelic wisdom is said to be ineffable. So ineffable, indeed, is it, that a thousand ideas in the thought of angels in their wisdom can present

only a single idea in the thought of men in their wisdom, the other nine hundred and ninety-nine ideas being unutterable, because they are supernatural. Many a time have I been given to know this by living experience. But, as was said, no one can enter into the ineffable wisdom of the angels except by and according to conjunction with the Lord, for He alone opens spiritual and celestial degrees, and only in those who are wise from Him. Those are wise from the Lord who cast the devil, that is, evil, out of themselves.

But let no one believe that he has wisdom because he knows many things, perceives them in some light, and is able to talk intelligently about them, unless his wisdom is conjoined to love. For it is love that through its affections produces wisdom. Not conjoined to love, wisdom is like a meteor vanishing in the air and like a falling star. Wisdom united to love is like the abiding light of the sun and like a fixed star. A man has the love of wisdom when he is averse to the diabolical crew, that is, to the lusts of evil and falsity.

Wisdom that comes to perception is perception of truth from being affected by it, especially perception of spiritual truth. For there is civil, moral, and spiritual truth. Those who have some perception of spiritual truth from affection by it also have perceptions of moral and civil truth, for the affection of spiritual truth is the soul of those perceptions. I have spoken with angels at times about wisdom who said that wisdom is conjunction with the Lord because He is wisdom itself, and that the man who rejects hell comes into this conjunction and comes into it so far as he rejects hell. They said that they picture wisdom to themselves as a magnificent and highly ornate palace into which one mounts by twelve steps. No one arrives at even the first step, they said, except from the Lord by conjunction with Him; and according to the measure of conjunction one ascends; also as one ascends, one perceives that no man is wise from himself but from the Lord. Furthermore, they said that the things in which one is wise are to those in which one is not wise like a few drops of water to a large lake. By the twelve steps into the palace of wisdom are meant goods united to truths and truths united to goods.

(iv) The more closely one is conjoined to the Lord the happier one becomes. The like can be said of degrees of happiness as was said (nn. 32 and 34) of degrees of life and of wisdom according to conjunction with the Lord. Happiness, that is, blessedness and joy, also are heightened as the higher degrees of the mind, called spiritual and celestial, are opened with man. After his life in the world these degrees grow to eternity.

No one who is in the pleasures of the lusts of evil can know anything of the joys of the affections of good in which the angelic heaven is. These pleasures and joys are opposites in internals and hence inwardly in externals, though superficially they may differ little. Every love has its enjoyments; the love of evil with those in lusts also has, such as the love of committing adultery, of taking revenge, of defrauding, of stealing, of acting cruelly, indeed, in the worst men, of blaspheming the holy things of the church and of inveighing against God. The fountainhead of those enjoyments is the love of ruling from self-love. They come of lusts which obsess the interiors of the mind, from these flow into the body, and excite uncleannesses there which titillate the fibers. The physical pleasure springs from the pleasure which the mind takes in lusts.

[2] After death everyone comes to know in the spiritual world what the

uncleannesses are which titillate the body's fibers in such persons and comes to know the nature of them. In general they are things cadaverous, excrementitious, filthy, malodorous, and urinous; for their hells teem with such uncleannesses. These are correspondences, as may be seen in the treatise Divine Love and Wisdom (nn. 422-424). After one has entered hell, however, these filthy delights are turned into wretchedness. This has been told in order that it may be understood what heaven's felicity is and its nature, of which we are now to speak; for a thing is known from its opposite.

It is impossible to describe in words the blessedness, satisfaction, joy and pleasure, in short, the felicity of heaven, so sensibly perceived there. What is perceived solely by feeling, cannot be described, for it does not fall into ideas of thought nor, therefore, into words. For the understanding sees only and sees what is of wisdom or truth, but not what is of love or good. Those felicities are therefore inexpressible, but still they ascend in like degree with wisdom. They are infinitely various, and each is ineffable. I have heard this, also perceived it.

[2] These felicities enter when a man, of himself and yet from the Lord, casts out the lusts of the love of evil and falsity. For these felicities are the happinesses of the affections of good and truth, the opposites of the lusts of the love of evil and falsity. Those happinesses begin from the Lord, thus from the inmost, diffuse themselves thence into things lower even to lowermost things, and thus fill the angel, making him a body of delight. Such happinesses are to be found in infinite variety in every affection of good and truth, and eminently in the affection of wisdom.

There is no comparing the joys of the lusts of evil and the joys of the affections of good. Inwardly in the former is the devil, in the latter the Lord. If comparisons are to be ventured, the pleasures of the lusts of evil can only be compared to the lewd pleasures of frogs in stagnant ponds or to those of snakes in filth, while the pleasures of the affections of good must be likened to the delights which the mind takes in gardens and flower beds. For things like those which affect frogs and snakes affect those in the hells who are in lusts of evil; and things like those which affect the mind in gardens and flower beds affect those in the heavens who are in affections of good. For, as was said above, corresponding uncleannesses affect the evil, and corresponding cleannesses the good.

Plainly, then, the more closely one is conjoined with the Lord the happier one is. This happiness rarely shows itself in the world, however; for man is then in a natural state, and the natural does not communicate with the spiritual by continuity, but by correspondence. The communication is felt only in a certain repose and peace of mind, especially after struggles against evil. But when a person puts off the natural state and enters the spiritual state, as he does on leaving the world, the happiness described above gradually manifests itself.

(v) The more closely one is conjoined to the Lord the more distinctly does he seem to himself to be his own, and the more plainly does he recognize that he is the Lord's. The appearance is that the more closely one is conjoined to the Lord the less one is one's own. This appearance prevails with all the evil. It also prevails with those who from religion believe that they are not under the yoke of the law and that no one can of himself do good. All these inevitably think that to be free only to do good and not to think and will evil is not to be one's own.

Inasmuch as a man who is conjoined to the Lord does not will and cannot think or will evil, they conclude from the look that this is not to be one's own. Yet that is the opposite of the truth.

There is infernal freedom, and there is heavenly freedom. Thinking and willing evil and also speaking and doing it so far as civil and moral laws do not prevent, is from infernal freedom. But thinking and willing good and speaking and doing it so far as opportunity offers, is from heavenly freedom. A man perceives as his own what he thinks, wills, speaks and does in freedom. The freedom anyone has always comes from his love. The man in an evil love cannot but deem infernal freedom to be real freedom, and a man in love of the good perceives that heavenly freedom is real freedom; consequently each regards the opposite of his freedom as bondage. No one can deny that one or the other must be freedom, for two kinds of freedom opposed to each other cannot both be freedom. Furthermore it cannot be denied that to be led by good is freedom and to be led by evil is bondage. For to be led by good is to be led by the Lord, but to be led by evil is to be led by the devil.

[2] Inasmuch as all he does in freedom appears to a man to be his own, coming as it does from what he loves, and to act from one's love, as was said, is to act freely, it follows that conjunction with the Lord causes a man to seem free and also his own, and the more closely he is conjoined to the Lord, to seem so much freer and so much more his own. He seems the more distinctly his own because it is the nature of the divine love to want its own to be another's, that is, to be the angel's or the man's. All spiritual love is such, preeminently the Lord's. The Lord, moreover, never coerces anyone. For nothing to which one is coerced seems one's own, and what seems not one's own cannot be done from one's love or be appropriated to one as one's own. Man is always led in freedom by the Lord, therefore, and reformed and regenerated in freedom. On this much more will be said in what follows; also see some things above, n. 4.

The reason why the more distinctly a man seems to be his own the more plainly he sees that he is the Lord's, is that the more closely he is conjoined to the Lord the wiser he becomes (as was shown, nn. 34-36), and wisdom teaches and recognizes this. The angels of the third heaven, as the wisest angels, perceive this and call it freedom itself; but to be led by themselves they call bondage. They give as the reason for this that the Lord does not flow immediately into the perceptions and thoughts of wisdom, but into the affections of the love of good and by these into the former, and this influx they perceive in the affection by which they have wisdom. Hence, they say, all that they think from wisdom seems to be from themselves, thus seemingly their own, and this gives reciprocal conjunction.

As the Lord's divine providence has for its object a heaven from mankind, it has for its object the conjunction of the human race with Him (see nn. 28-31). It also has for its object that man should be more and more closely conjoined to Him (nn. 32, 33); for thus man possesses a more interior heaven. Further, it has for its object that by the conjunction man should become wiser (nn. 34-36) and happier (nn. 37-41), for he has heaven by and according to wisdom, and happiness by wisdom, too. Finally, providence has for its object that man shall seem more distinctly his own, yet recognize the more clearly that he is the Lord's (nn. 42-44). All these are of the Lord's divine providence, for all are heaven and heaven is its object.

Section 3

IN ALL THAT IT DOES THE LORD'S DIVINE PROVIDENCE LOOKS TO WHAT IS INFINITE AND ETERNAL

Christendom knows that God is infinite and eternal. The doctrine of the Trinity which is named for Athanasius says that God the Father is infinite, eternal and omnipotent, so also God the Son, and God the Holy Spirit, and that nevertheless there are not three who are infinite, eternal and omnipotent, but One. As God is infinite and eternal, only what is infinite and eternal can be predicated of Him. What infinite and eternal are, finite man cannot comprehend and yet can comprehend. He cannot comprehend them because the finite is incapable of what is infinite; he can comprehend them because there are abstract ideas by which one can see that things are, though not what they are. Of the infinite such ideas are possible as that God or the Divine, being infinite, is esse itself, is essence and substance itself, wisdom and love themselves or good and truth themselves, thus is the one Self, indeed is veritable Man; there is such an idea, too, in speaking of the infinite as "all," as that infinite wisdom is omniscience and infinite power omnipotence.

[2] Still these ideas turn obscure to thought and may meet denial for not being comprehended, unless what one's thought gets from nature is removed from the idea, especially what it gets from the two properties of nature, space and time. For these are bound to restrict the ideas and to make abstract ideas seem to be nothing. But if such things can be removed in a man, as they are in an angel, what is infinite can be comprehended by the means just mentioned. Then also it will be grasped that the human being is something because he was created by infinite God who is all; also that he is a finite substance, having been created by infinite God who is substance itself; further that man is wisdom inasmuch as he was created by infinite God who is wisdom itself; and so on. For were infinite God not all, and were He not substance and wisdom themselves, man would not be anything actual, thus would either be nothing or exist only in idea, as those visionaries think who are called idealists.

[3] It is plain from what was shown in the treatise Divine Love and Wisdom that the divine essence is love and wisdom (nn. 28-39); that divine love and wisdom are substance itself and form itself, the one Self and the sole underived being (nn. 40-46); and that God created the universe and its contents from Himself, and not from nothing (nn. 282-284). It follows that every creature and above all the human being and the love and wisdom in him, are real, and do not exist only in idea. For were God not infinite, the finite would not be; were the infinite not all, no particular thing would be; and had not God created all things from Himself, nothing whatever would be. In a word, we are because God is.

We are considering divine providence and at this point how it regards what is infinite and eternal in all that it does. This can be clearly told only in some order. Let this be the order:

i. The infinite and eternal in itself is the same as the Divine. ii. What is infinite and eternal in itself cannot but look to what is infinite and eternal from itself in finite things. iii. Divine providence looks to the infinite and eternal from itself in all that it does, especially in saving mankind. iv. An image of the infinite and eternal offers in an angelic heaven formed from a redeemed mankind. v. The heart of divine providence is to look to what is infinite and eternal by fashioning an angelic heaven, for it to be like one human being before the Lord, an image of Him.

(i) The infinite and eternal in itself is the same as the Divine. This is plain from what was shown in many places in the work Divine Love and Wisdom. The concept comes from the angelic idea. By the infinite, angels understand nothing else than the divine esse and by the eternal the divine existere. But men can see and cannot see that what is infinite and eternal in itself is the Divine. Those can see this who do not think of the infinite from space and of the eternal from time; those cannot see it who think of infinite and eternal in terms of space and time. Those, therefore, can see it who think at some elevation, that is, inwardly in the rational mind; those cannot who think in a lower, that is, more external way.

[2] Those by whom it can be seen reflect that a spatial infinite is an impossibility, so likewise a temporal eternity or an eternity from which the world has been. The infinite has no first or final limit or boundaries. They also reflect that there cannot be another infinite from it, for "from it" implies a boundary or beginning, or a prior source. They therefore think that it is meaningless to speak of an infinite and eternal from itself, for that is like talking of an esse from itself, which is a contradiction. An infinite from itself could only be an infinite from an infinite, and esse from itself only esse from esse. Such an infinite or esse would either be the same with the infinite or be finite. From these and like considerations, inwardly seen in the rational mind, it is plain that there is what is infinite in itself and eternal in itself, and that they are the Divine whence are all things.

I know that many will say to themselves, "How can anybody grasp anything inwardly and rationally apart from space and time, and think that it not only exists, but is also the all and the self from which are all things?" But think deeply whether love or any affection of love, or wisdom or any perception of wisdom, yes, whether thought is in space and time, and you will grasp the fact that they are not. The Divine, therefore, being love itself and wisdom itself, cannot be conceived of in space and time; neither, then, can the infinite. To see this more clearly ponder whether thought is in time and space. Suppose thought is sustained for ten or twelve hours; may not the length of time seem like one or two hours? May it not seem like one or two days? The seeming duration is according to the state of affection from which the thought springs. If the affection is a joyous one, in which time is not noticed, thought over ten or twelve hours seems as though it were one or two hours. The contrary is true if the affection is a sorrowful one, in which one watches the passage of time. It is evident from this that time is only an appearance according to the state of affection from which the thought springs. The same is true of one's thought of the distance on a walk or a journey.

Since angels and spirits are affections of love and thoughts thence they are not in space or time, either, but only in an appearance of them. Space and time appear to them in keeping with the states of their affections and their thoughts thence. When one of them, therefore, thinks with affection of another, intently desiring to see or speak with him, the other is at once present.

[2] Hence, too, present with every man are spirits who are in an affection like his--evil spirits with a man in an affection of similar evil, and good spirits with the man in an affection of similar good. They are as fully present as though he was one of their society. Space and time have nothing to do with their presence, for affection and thought therefrom are not in space and time, and spirits and angels are affections and thoughts therefrom.

[3] I have been given to know this by living experience over many years. For I have spoken with many on their death, some in different kingdoms of Europe, and some in different kingdoms of Asia and Africa, and all were near me. If space and time existed for them, a journey and time to make it would have intervened.

[4] Indeed, every man knows this by some instinct in him or in his mind, as has been verified to me by the fact that nobody has thought of distances when I have reported that I had spoken with some person who died in Asia, Africa or Europe, for example with Calvin, Luther, or Melancthon, or with some king, governor or priest in a far region. The thought occurred to no one, "How could he speak with those who had lived there, and how could they come and be present with him, when lands and seas lay between?" So it was plain to me that in thinking of those in the spiritual world a man does not think of space and time. For those there, however, there is an appearance of time and space; see the work Heaven and Hell, nn. 162-169, 191-199.

From these considerations it may now be plain that the infinite and eternal, thus the Lord, are to be thought of apart from space and time and can be so thought of; plain, likewise, that they are so thought of by those who think interiorly and rationally; and plain that the infinite and eternal are identical with the Divine. So think angels and spirits. In thought withdrawn from space and time, divine omnipresence is comprehended, and divine omnipotence, also the Divine from eternity, but these are not at all grasped by thought to which an idea of space and time adheres. Plain it is, then, that one can conceive of God from eternity, but never of nature from eternity. So one can think of the creation of the world by God, but never of its creation from nature, for space and time are proper to nature, but the Divine is apart from them. That the Divine is apart from space and time may be seen in the treatise Divine Love and Wisdom (nn. 7-10, 69-72, 73-76, and other places).

(ii) What is infinite and eternal in itself cannot but look to what is infinite and eternal from itself in finite things. By what is infinite and eternal in itself the Divine itself is meant, as was shown in the preceding section. By finite things are meant all things created by the Lord, especially men, spirits, and angels. By looking to the infinite and eternal from itself is meant to look to the Divine, that is to Himself, in these, as a person beholds his image in a mirror. This was shown in several places in the treatise Divine Love and Wisdom, particularly where it was demonstrated that in the created universe there is an image of the human being and that this is an image of the infinite and eternal (nn. 317, 318), that is, of God the Creator, namely, the Lord from eternity. But be it known that the Divine-in-itself is in the Lord; whereas the divine-from-itself is the divine from the Lord in things created.

But for better comprehension let this be illustrated. The Divine can look only to the divine, and can do so only in what has been created by it. This is evident from the fact that no one can regard another except from what is his own in himself. One who loves another regards him from his own love; a wise man regards another from his own wisdom. He can note whether the other loves him or not, is wise or not; but this he does from the love and wisdom in himself. Therefore he unites himself with the other so far as the other loves him as he loves the other, or so far as the other is wise as he is wise; for thus they make one.

[2] It is the same with the Divine-in-itself. For the Divine cannot look to itself from another, that is, from man, spirit, or angel. For there is nothing in them of the Divine-in-itself from which are all things, and to look to the Divine from another in whom there is nothing of the Divine would be to look to the Divine from what is not divine, which is an impossibility. Hence the Lord is so conjoined to man, spirit, or angel that all which is referable to the Divine is not from them but from the Lord. For it is known that all good and truth which anyone has are not from him but from the Lord; indeed that no one can name the Lord or speak His names Jesus and Christ except from Him.

[3] Consequently the infinite and eternal, which is the same as the Divine, looks to all things in finite beings infinitely and conjoins itself with them in the degree in which they receive love and wisdom. In a word, the Lord can have His abode and dwell with man and angel only in His own, and not in what is solely theirs, for this is evil; if it is good, it is still finite, which in and of itself is

incapable of the infinite. Plainly, the finite cannot possibly look to what is infinite, but the infinite can look to the infinite-from-itself in finite beings.

It seems as if the infinite could not be conjoined to the finite because no ratio is possible between them and because the finite cannot compass the infinite. Conjunction is possible, nevertheless, both because the Infinite created all things from Himself (as was shown in the work Divine Love and Wisdom, nn. 282-284), and because the Infinite cannot but look in things finite to what is infinite from Him, and this infinite-from-Him in finite beings can appear as if it were in them. Thereby a ratio is possible between finite and infinite, not from the finite, indeed, but from the infinite in the finite. Thereby, too, the finite is capable of the infinite, not the finite being in himself, but as if in himself from the infinite-from-itself in him. But of this more in what follows.

(iii) Divine providence looks to the infinite and eternal from itself in all that it does, especially in saving mankind. The infinite and eternal in itself is the Divine itself, or the Lord in Himself; the infinite and eternal from itself is the proceeding Divine or the Lord in others created by Him, thus in men and angels. This Divine is identical with divine providence, for by the divine from Himself the Lord provides that all things shall be held together in the order in which and into which they were created. This the Divine in the act of proceeding accomplishes and consequently all this is divine providence.

That divine providence in all that it does looks to what is infinite and eternal from itself is evident from the fact that every created thing proceeds from a first, which is the infinite and eternal, to things last, and from things last to the first whence it is (as was shown in the work Divine Love and Wisdom, in the part in which the creation of the world is treated of). But the first whence anything is, is inmostly in all the progression, and therefore the proceeding Divine or divine providence in all that it does has in view some image of the infinite and eternal. It does so in all things, in some obviously so that it is perceptible, in others not. It makes that image evident to perception in the variety, and in the fructification and multiplication, of all things.

[2] An image of the infinite and eternal is apparent in the variety of all things, in that no one thing is the same as another nor can be to eternity. The eye beholds this in the variety of human faces ever since creation; in the variety of minds, of which faces are types; and in the variety of affections, perceptions and thoughts, for of these the mind consists. In all heaven, therefore, no two angels or spirits are the same, nor can be to eternity. The same is true of every object to be seen in either the natural or the spiritual world. Plainly, the variety is infinite and eternal.

[3] An image of the infinite and eternal is manifest in the fructification and multiplication of all things, in the vegetable kingdom in the capacity implanted in seeds, and in the animal kingdom in reproduction, especially in the family of fishes. Were the seeds to bear fruit and the animals to multiply in the measure of ability, they would fill all the world, even the universe, in a generation. Obviously there is latent in that ability an endeavor after self-propagation to infinity. And as fructification and multiplication have not failed from the beginning of creation and never will, plainly there is in that ability an endeavor after self-propagation to eternity also.

The like is true of human beings as to their affections, which are of love, and their perceptions, which are of wisdom. The variety of either is infinite and eternal; so, too, is their fructification and multiplication, which is spiritual. No person enjoys an affection and perception so like another's as to be identical with it, nor ever will. Affections, moreover, may be fructified and perceptions multiplied without end. Knowledge, it is well known, is inexhaustible. This capacity of fructification and multiplication without end or to infinity and eternity exists in natural things with men, in spiritual with the spiritual angels, and in celestial with the celestial angels. Affections, perceptions and knowledges have this endless capacity not only in general, but in every least particular. They have it because they exist from the infinite and eternal in itself through what is infinite and eternal from itself. But as the finite has in it nothing of the Divine, nothing of the kind, not the least, is in the human being as his own. Man or angel is finite and only a receptacle, by itself dead. Whatever is living in him is from the proceeding Divine, joined to him by contact, and appearing in him as if it were his. The truth of this will be seen in what follows.

Divine providence regards what is infinite and eternal from itself especially in saving mankind because its object is a heaven from mankind (as was shown, nn. 27-45), and therefore it is man's reformation and regeneration or salvation to which it especially looks, since heaven consists of the saved or regenerate. To regenerate man, moreover, is to unite good and truth or love and wisdom in him, as they are united in the Lord's proceeding Divine; to this especially, therefore, providence looks in saving the race. The image of the infinite and eternal is not to be found elsewhere in man than in the marriage of good and truth. This marriage the proceeding Divine effects. Men filled by the proceeding Divine, which is called the Holy Spirit, have prophesied, as we know from the Word; men enlightened by it see divine truths in heaven's light; above all, angels sensibly perceive the presence, influx and conjunction, though they are aware that the conjunction is no more than can be termed adjunction.

It has not been known that divine providence in all its procedure with man looks to his eternal state. It can look to nothing else because the Divine is infinite and eternal, and the infinite and eternal or the Divine is not in time; therefore all future things are present to it. It follows that there is eternity in all that the Divine does. But those who think from time and space perceive this with difficulty, not only because they love temporal things, but also because they think from what is on hand in the world and not from what is at hand in heaven; this is as remote to them as the ends of the earth. Those, however, who are in the Divine, inasmuch as they think from the Lord, think from what is eternal as well as from what is at present, asking themselves, "What is that which is not eternal? Is not the temporal relatively nothing and does it not become nothing when it is past?" The eternal is not so; it alone is; its esse has no end. To think thus is to think both from the present and the eternal, and when a man not only thinks so but lives so, the proceeding Divine with him or divine providence looks in all its procedure to the state of his eternal life in heaven and guides to it. In what follows it will be seen that the Divine looks to the eternal in everybody, in an evil as well as in a good person.

(iv) An image of the infinite and eternal offers in an angelic heaven. Among things we need to know about is the angelic heaven. Everyone who has any religion thinks about heaven and wishes to go there. Yet heaven is granted only to those who know the way to it and walk in that way. We can know the way to an extent by knowing the character of those who constitute heaven and by knowing that no one becomes an angel or comes into heaven unless he brings with him from the world what is angelic. In what is angelic there is a knowledge of the way from walking in it, and a walking in the way through a knowledge of it. In the spiritual world, moreover, there are actually ways leading to every society of heaven or of hell. Each sees his own way as if for himself. He does so because a way is there for every love; the love discloses the way and takes a man to his fellows. No one sees other ways than the way of his love. Plain it is from this that angels are nothing but heavenly loves; otherwise they would not have seen the ways tending to heaven. This will be plainer still when heaven is described.

Every man's spirit is affection and thought therefrom. And as all affection is of love, and thought is of the understanding, every spirit is his own love and his own understanding therefrom. When a man is thinking solely from his own spirit, therefore, as he does in private meditation at home, he thinks from the affection belonging to his love. It is clear, then, that when a man becomes a spirit, as he does after death, he is the affection of his own love and has no other thought than that of his affection. If his love has been one of evil, he is an evil affection, which is a lust; if his love has been one of good, he is a good affection. Everyone has a good affection so far as he has shunned evils as sins, and an evil affection so far as he has not shunned evils as sins. As all spirits and angels, then, are affections, the whole angelic heaven is nothing but the love of all the affections of good and the attendant wisdom of all the perceptions of truth. Since all good and truth are from the Lord and He is love itself, the angelic heaven is an image of Him. Furthermore, as divine love and wisdom are human in form, it also follows that the angelic heaven must be in that form. Of this we shall say more in the following section.

The angelic heaven is an image of the infinite and eternal, then, because it is an image of the Lord, who is infinite and eternal. The image of His infinity and eternity is manifest in heaven's being constituted of myriads and myriads of angels, and in its consisting of as many societies as there are general affections of heavenly love; manifest, again, in every angel's being distinctly his own affection; manifest further in that the form of heaven--a unit in the divine sight just as man is a unit--is assembled from so many affections, general and particular; also manifest in that this form is perfected to eternity with the increase in numbers, the greater the number of those entering into the form of the divine love which is the form of forms, the more perfect the resulting unity. It is plain from all this that the angelic heaven presents an image of the infinite and eternal.

From the knowledge of heaven to be had from this brief description it is evident that it is an affection of the love of good that makes heaven in a man. But who knows this today? Who knows even what an affection of the love of good is, or that these affections are innumerable, in fact, infinite? For, as was said, each angel is his own particular affection; and the form of heaven is the form of all the affections of the divine love there. Only one Being can combine all affections into this form--only He who is love and wisdom itself and who is at once infinite and eternal. For throughout that form is what is infinite and eternal; the infinite is in its unity and the eternal in its perpetuity; were they removed the form would instantly collapse. Who else can combine affections into a form? Who else can bring about this unity? The unity can be accomplished only in an idea of the total, and the total realized only in thought for each single part. Myriads on myriads compose that form; annually myriads enter it and will do so to eternity. All infants enter it and all adults who are affections of the love of good. Again from all this the image of the infinite and eternal in the angelic heaven is to be seen.

(v) The heart of divine providence is to look to what is infinite and eternal by fashioning an angelic heaven for it to be like one human being before the Lord, an image of Him. See in the work Heaven and Hell (nn. 59-86) that heaven as a whole is like one man in the Lord's sight; that each society of heaven also is; that as a result each angel is a human being in perfect form; and that this is because God the Creator, who is the Lord from eternity, is Man; also (nn. 87-102) that as a result there is a correspondence of all things of heaven with all things in the human being. The entire heaven as one man has not been seen by me, for only the Lord can so behold it; but that an entire society, whether large or small, can appear as one man, I have seen. I was then told that the largest society of all, which is heaven in its entirety, so appears, but to the Lord alone; and that this causes every angel to be in full form a human being.

As all heaven is like one man in the Lord's view, it is divided into as many general societies as there are organs, viscera and members in man, and each general society into as many less general or particular societies as there are larger divisions in each of the viscera and organs. This makes evident what heaven is. Because the Lord is very Man and heaven is His image, to be in heaven is called "being in the Lord." See in the work Divine Love and Wisdom that the Lord is very Man (nn. 11-13, 285-289).

From all this the arcanum, well called angelic, can in a measure be seen, that each affection of good and at the same time of truth is human in form. For whatever proceeds from the Lord gets from His divine love that it is an affection of good and from His divine wisdom that it is an affection of truth. An affection of truth proceeding from the Lord appears in angel and man as perception and consequent thought of truth. For we are aware of perception and thought, but little aware of the affection whence they are, although all come as one from the Lord.

Man, then, is by creation a heaven in least form and hence an image of the Lord; heaven consists of as many affections as there are angels; and each affection in its form is man. It must then be the constant striving of divine providence that a man may become a heaven in form and an image of the Lord, and as this is effected by means of an affection of the good and true, that he may become such an affection. This is therefore the unceasing effort of divine providence. But its inmost aim is that a man may be here or there in heaven or in the divine heavenly man, for so he is in the Lord. But this is accomplished with those whom the Lord can lead to heaven. As He foresees who can be led He also provides continually that a man may become amenable; for thus everyone who suffers himself to be led to heaven is prepared for his own place there.

We have said that heaven is divided into as many societies as there are organs, viscera and members in man; and in these no part can be in any place but its own. As angels are the parts in the divine heavenly man, and none become angels who were not men in the world, the man who suffers himself to be led to heaven is continually prepared by the Lord for his own place there. This is done by the affection of good and truth which corresponds with that place. To this place every angel-man is also assigned on his departure from the world. This is the inmost of divine providence touching heaven.

On the other hand, a man who does not permit himself to be led to heaven and allotted a place there is prepared for his own place in hell. Of himself a man tends constantly to the depths of hell but is continually withheld by the Lord. He who cannot be withheld is prepared for a given place in hell, to which he is assigned on departure from the world. This place is opposite one in heaven; for hell is the opposite of heaven. So, as the angel-man according to his affection of good and truth is allotted his place in heaven, the devil-man according to his affection of evil and falsity is allotted his in hell. The two opposites, set exactly over against each other, are kept in connection. This is the inmost of divine providence touching hell.

Section 4

THERE ARE LAWS OF PROVIDENCE THAT ARE UNKNOWN TO MEN

Men know there is divine providence, but not what its nature is. This is not known because its laws are arcana, hitherto hidden in the wisdom of angels. These laws are to be revealed now in order that what belongs to the Lord may be ascribed to Him, and nothing ascribed to man that is not man's. For very many in the world attribute everything to themselves and their prudence, and what they cannot so attribute they call fortuitous and accidental, not knowing that human prudence is nothing and that "fortuitous" and "accidental" are idle words.

[2] We say that the laws of divine providence are arcana "hidden until now in the wisdom of the angels." They have been hidden because the understanding has been closed in Christendom in religion's name on divine things, and has been rendered so dull and averse in these matters that man has not been able because he has not been willing, or has not been willing because he has not been able, to understand anything about providence beyond the mere fact that it exists, or to do more than argue whether it exists or not, also whether it is only general or also detailed. Closed up on divine things in the name of religion, understanding could advance no further.

[3] But it is acknowledged in the church that man cannot of himself do good which is in itself good or of himself think truth which is in itself truth. This acknowledgment is at one with divine providence; these are interdependent beliefs. Lest therefore one be affirmed and the other denied and both fail, what divine providence is must by all means be revealed. It cannot be revealed unless the laws by which the Lord oversees and governs the volitions and thoughts of the human being are disclosed. The laws enable one to know the nature of providence, and only one who knows its nature can acknowledge providence, for then he beholds it. The laws of divine providence, hitherto hidden with angels in their wisdom, are therefore to be revealed now.

Section 5

IT IS A LAW OF DIVINE PROVIDENCE THAT MAN SHALL ACT FROM FREEDOM ACCORDING TO REASON

As is known, man is free to think and will as he wishes, but not to speak whatever he thinks or to do whatever he wills. The freedom meant here, therefore, is spiritual freedom and natural freedom only as they make one; for thinking and willing are spiritual, and speaking and acting are natural. The two are readily distinguishable in man, for he can think what he does not utter and will what he does not do; plainly, spiritual and natural are discriminated in him. He can pass from the former to the latter therefore only on a decision to do so--a decision which can be likened to a door that must first be unfastened and opened. This door, it is true, stands open, as it were, in those who think and will from reason in accord with the civil laws of the land and the moral laws of society, for they speak what they think and do what they will to do. But in those who think and will contrary to those laws, the door stands shut, as it were. One who watches his volitions and subsequent deeds knows that such a decision intervenes, sometimes more than once in a single utterance or action. This we have premised for it to be understood that by acting from freedom according to reason is meant to think and will freely and thence to speak and do freely what is according to reason.

Since few know, however, that the law above can be a law of divine providence, principally because a man is also free then to think evil and falsity (still divine providence is continually leading him to think and will what is good and true), for clearer perception we must proceed step by step and shall do so in this order:

i. The human being has reason and freedom or rationality and liberty, and has these two faculties from the Lord. ii. Whatever a man does in freedom, whether with reason or not, provided it is according to his reason, seems to him to be his. iii. Whatever a man does in freedom according to his thought, is appropriated to him as his and remains. iv. A man is reformed and regenerated by the Lord by means of the two faculties and cannot be reformed and regenerated without them. v. A man can be reformed and regenerated by means of the two faculties so far as he can be led by them to acknowledge that all truth and good which he thinks and does are from the Lord and not from himself. vi. The conjunction of the Lord with man, and man's reciprocal conjunction with the Lord, is effected by means of these two faculties. vii. In all the procedure of His divine providence the Lord safeguards the two faculties in man unimpaired and as sacred. viii. It is therefore of the divine providence that man shall act in freedom according to reason.

(i) The human being has reason and freedom or rationality and liberty, and has these two faculties from the Lord. Man has a faculty of understanding, which is rationality, and a faculty of thinking, willing, speaking and doing what he understands, which is liberty; and he has these two faculties from the Lord (see the work Divine Love and Wisdom, nn. 264-270, 425, and above, nn. 43, 44). But many doubts may arise about either of the two faculties when thought is given to them; therefore I want to say something at this point just about man's freedom to act according to reason.

[2] First, it should be known that all freedom is of love, so much so that love and freedom are one. As love is man's life, freedom is of his life, too. For man's every enjoyment is from some love of his and has no other source, and to act from the enjoyment of one's love is to act in freedom. Enjoyment leads a man as the current bears an object along on a stream. But loves are many, some harmonious, others not; therefore freedoms are many. In general there are three: natural, rational, and spiritual freedom.

[3] Natural freedom is man's by heredity. In it he loves only himself and the world: his first life is nothing else. From these two loves, moreover, all evils arise and thus attach to love. Hence to think and will evil is man's natural freedom, and when he has also confirmed evils in himself by reasonings, he does them in freedom according to his reason. Doing them is from his faculty called liberty, and confirming them from his faculty called rationality.

[4] For example, it is from the love into which he is born that he desires to commit adultery, to defraud, to blaspheme, to take revenge. Confirming these evils in himself and by this making them allowable, he then, from his love's enjoyment in them, thinks and wills them freely and as if according to reason, and so far as civil laws do not hinder, speaks and does them. It is of the Lord's divine providence that man is allowed to do so, for freedom or liberty is his. This natural freedom is man's by nature because by heredity, and those are in this freedom who have confirmed it in themselves by reasonings from enjoyment in self-love and love of the world.

[5] Rational freedom is from the love of good repute for the sake of standing or gain. The delight of this love is to seem outwardly a moral person. Loving this reputation, the man does not defraud, commit adultery, take revenge, or blaspheme; and making this his reasoned course, he also does in freedom according to reason what is sincere, just, chaste, and friendly; indeed from reason can advocate such conduct. But if his rational is only natural and not spiritual, his freedom is only external and not internal. He does not love these goods inwardly at all, but only outwardly for reputation's sake, as we said. The good deeds he does are therefore not in themselves good. He can also say that they should be done for the sake of the general welfare, but he speaks out of no love for that welfare, but from love of his own standing or gain. His freedom therefore derives nothing from love of the public good, nor does his reason, which complies with his love. This rational freedom, therefore, is inwardly natural freedom. The Lord's divine providence leaves everyone this freedom too.

[6] Spiritual freedom is from love of eternal life. Into this love and its enjoyment only he comes who regards evils as sins and therefore does not will them, and who also looks to the Lord. Once a man does this he is in this freedom. One can refuse to will and do evils for the reason that they are sins, only from an interior or higher freedom, belonging to his interior or higher love. This freedom does not seem at first to be freedom, yet it is. Later it does seem freedom, and the man acts in real freedom according to true reason, thinking, willing, speaking and doing the good and the true. This freedom grows as

natural freedom decreases and serves it; and it unites with rational freedom and purifies it.

[7] Anyone can come into this freedom if he is willing to think that there is a life eternal, and that the joy and bliss of life in time and for a time is like a passing shadow to the joy and bliss of life in eternity and for eternity. A man can think so if he will, for he has rationality and liberty, and the Lord, from whom he has the two faculties, constantly enables him to do so.

(ii) Whatever a man does in freedom, whether with reason or not, provided it is according to his reason, seems to him to be his. Nothing makes so clear what rationality and liberty are, which are proper to the human being, as to compare man and beast. Beasts do not have any rationality or faculty of understanding, or any liberty or faculty of willing freely. They do not have understanding or will, therefore, but instead of understanding they have knowledge and instead of will affection, both of these natural. Not having the two faculties, animals do not have thought, but instead an internal sight which makes one with their external sight by correspondence.

[2] Every affection has its mate, its consort, so to speak. An affection of natural love has knowledge, one of spiritual love has intelligence, and one of celestial love, wisdom. Without its mate or consort an affection is nothing, but is like esse apart from existere or substance without form, of which nothing can be predicated. Hence there is in every created thing something referable to the marriage of good and truth, as we have shown several times. In beasts it is a marriage of affection and knowledge; the affection is one of natural good, and the knowledge is knowledge of natural truth.

[3] Affection and knowledge in beasts act altogether as one. Their affection cannot be raised above their knowledge, nor the knowledge above the affection; if they are raised, they are raised together. Nor have animals a spiritual mind into which, or into the heat and light of which, they can be raised. Thus they have no faculty of understanding or rationality, or faculty of freely willing or liberty, and nothing more than natural affection with its knowledge. Their natural affection is that of finding food and shelter, of propagating, of avoiding and guarding against injury, together with the knowledge needed for this. As this is their kind of existence, they cannot think, "I will this but not that," or "I know this but not that," still less, "I understand this" or "I love that." They are borne along by affection and its knowledge without rationality and liberty. It is not from the natural world that they are borne along so, but from the spiritual world. Nothing can exist in the natural world that does not have its connection with the spiritual world: thence is every cause that accomplishes an effect. On this see also some things below (n. 96).

It is otherwise with man, who has affections not only of natural love, but also of spiritual and celestial loves. For man's mind is of three degrees, as was shown in Part III of the treatise Divine Love and Wisdom. Man can be raised therefore from natural knowledge into spiritual intelligence and on into celestial wisdom. From the two, intelligence and wisdom, he can look to the Lord, be conjoined with Him, and thereby live to eternity. This elevation as to affection would not be possible did he not from rationality have the power to raise the understanding, and from liberty the power to will this.

[2] By means of the two faculties man can think in himself about what he

perceives outside him through the senses, and can also think on high about what he thinks below. Anyone can say, "I have thought and I think so and so," "I have willed and I will so and so," "I understand that this is a fact," "I love this for what it is," and so on. Obviously, man thinks above his thought, and sees it, as it were, below him. This comes to him from rationality and liberty; from rationality he can think on high, and from liberty he can will so to think. Unless he had liberty to think so, he would not have the will, nor the thought from it.

[3] Those, therefore, who will to understand only what is of the world and nature and not what moral and spiritual good and truth are, cannot be raised from knowledge into intelligence, still less into wisdom, for they have stifled those faculties. They render themselves no longer men except that they can understand if they wish, and can also will, by virtue of the implanted rationality and liberty; from the two capacities it is that one can think and from thought speak. In other respects, they are not men but beasts, and some, in their abuse of those faculties, are worse than beasts.

From an unclouded rationality anyone can see or grasp that without the appearance that it is his own a man cannot be in any affection to know or to understand. Every joy and pleasure, thus everything of the will, is from an affection of some love. Who can wish to know or to understand anything except that an affection of his takes pleasure in it? Who can feel this pleasure unless what he is affected by seems to be his? Were it not his, but another's altogether, that is, if another from his affection should infuse something into his mind when he himself felt no affection for knowing or grasping it, would he receive it? Indeed, could he receive it? Would he not be like one called a dullard or a clod?

[2] It should be manifest then that although everything that a man perceives, thinks, knows and, according to perception, wills and does, flows into him, nevertheless it is of the Lord's divine providence that it seems to be the man's. Otherwise, as we said, a man would not receive anything and so could be given no intelligence or wisdom. It is known that all good and truth are the Lord's and not man's, and yet appear to be man's. As good and truth so appear, so do all things of the church and of heaven, and all things of love and wisdom, and all things of charity and faith; yet none of them is man's. No one can receive them from the Lord unless it seems to him that he perceives them for himself. Plainly, the truth of the matter is that whatever a man does in freedom, whether with reason or not, provided only that it accords with his reason, seems to him to be his.

Who cannot from his faculty called rationality understand that a given good is serviceable to society, and a given evil harmful to society? That, for example, justice, sincerity, the chastity of marriage are serviceable to it, and injustice, insincerity, and misconduct with the wives of others, harmful? Consequently that these evils are in themselves injuries, and those goods in themselves benefits? Who then cannot make this a matter of his reason if only he will? He has rationality and he has liberty; the two faculties are bared, show, take charge and enable him to perceive and do in the measure that he avoids those evils because they are evils. So far as a man does this he looks on those goods as a friend looks on friends.

[2] By his faculty called rationality a man can conclude from this what goods

are useful to society in the spiritual world and what evils are hurtful there, if instead of evils he sees sins and instead of goods works of charity. This he can also make a matter of his reason if he will, since he has liberty and rationality. His rationality and liberty emerge, become manifest, take charge and give him perception and power so far as he shuns evils as sins. So far as he does this he regards the goods of charity as neighbor regards neighbor in mutual love.

[3] For the sake of reception and union the Lord wills that whatever a man does freely according to reason shall seem to him to be his; this agrees with reason itself. It follows that a man can from his reason will something on the ground that it means his eternal happiness and can perform it by the Lord's divine power, implored by him.

(iii) Whatever a man does in freedom according to his thought is appropriated to him as his and remains. The reason is that a man's own and his freedom make one. His proprium is of his life, and what he does from his life he does in freedom. His proprium is also of his love, for love is one's life, and what he does from his life's love he does in freedom. We speak of his acting in freedom "according to his thought" because what is of his life or love he also thinks and confirms by thought, and what is so confirmed he does in freedom then according to thought. What a man does, he does from the will by the understanding; freedom is of the will and thought is of the understanding.

[2] A man can also act freely contrary to reason, likewise not freely in accord with reason: then nothing is appropriated to him--what he does is only of the mouth and body, not of the spirit or heart; only what is of the spirit and heart, when it is also of the mouth and body, is appropriated. The truth of this can be illustrated by many things, but this is not the place.

[3] By being appropriated to man is meant entering his life and becoming part of it, consequently becoming his own. It will be seen in what follows that there is nothing, however, which is man's very own; it only seems to him as if it were. Only this now: all the good a man does in freedom according to reason is appropriated to him as if it were his because it seems to be his in that he thinks, wills, speaks and does it. Good is not man's, however, but the Lord's with man (above, n. 76). How evil is appropriated to man will appear in a section of its own.

We said that what a man does in freedom in accord with his thought also remains. For nothing that a man has appropriated to himself can be eradicated; it has been made part of his love and at the same time of his reason, or of his will and at the same time of his understanding, and so of his life. It can be put aside indeed, but not cast out; put aside, it is borne from center to periphery, where it stays; this is what we mean by its remaining.

[2] If, for example, in boyhood or youth, a man appropriated an evil to himself by doing it with enjoyment from love of it--a fraud, blasphemy, revenge, or fornication--having done it freely with the assent of thought, he made it his; but if later he repents, shuns it and considers it a sin to be averse from, and so desists from it freely according to reason, then the opposite good is appropriated to him. Good then takes the center and removes evil to the periphery, farther according to his aversion and abhorrence for it. Still the evil cannot be so thrust out that one can say it is extirpated; it may indeed in that removal seem extirpated. What occurs is that the man is withheld from the evil by the Lord

and held in good. This can happen with all inherited evil and all a man's actual evil.

[3] I have seen this verified by the experience of some in heaven who thought they were without evil, being held in good as they were by the Lord. Lest they should believe that the good in which they were was their own, they were let down from heaven and let into their evils until they acknowledged that of themselves they were in evil, and in good only from the Lord. Upon this acknowledgment they were returned to heaven.

[4] Be it known, therefore, that goods are appropriated to man only in that they are constantly with him from the Lord, and that as a man acknowledges this the Lord grants that good shall seem to be the man's, that is, that it shall seem to him that he loves the neighbor or has charity, believes or has faith, does good and understands truth, thus is wise, of himself. From this an enlightened person may see the nature and the strength of the appearance in which the Lord wills man to be. The Lord wills it for salvation's sake, for without that appearance no one can be saved. Also see what was shown above on the subject (nn. 42-45).

Nothing that a person only thinks, not even what he thinks to will, is appropriated to him unless he also wills it so that he does it when opportunity offers. For when a man then does it, he does it from the will by the understanding or from affection of the will by thought of the understanding. If it is something thought only, it cannot be appropriated, for the understanding does not conjoin itself to the will, or the thought of the understanding to the affection of the will, but the latter with the former, as we have shown many times in the treatise Divine Love and Wisdom, Part V. This is meant by the Lord's words,

Not that which enters the mouth renders a man unclean, but that which goes forth from the heart by the mouth renders a man unclean (Mt 15:11, 17, 18, 19).

In the spiritual sense thought is meant by "mouth," for thought is spoken by it; affection which is of love is meant by "heart"; if the man thinks and speaks from this he makes himself unclean. In Luke 6:45 also by "heart" an affection of love or of the will is meant, and by "mouth" the thought of the understanding.

Evils which a man believes are allowable, though he does not do them, are also appropriated to him, for the licitness in thought is from the will, as there is assent. When a man deems an evil allowable he loosens the internal bond on it and is kept from doing it only by external bonds, which are fears. As his spirit favors the evil, he commits it when external bonds are removed as allowable, and meanwhile is committing it in spirit. But on this see Doctrine of Life for the New Jerusalem, nn. 108-113.

(iv) A man is reformed and regenerated by the Lord by means of the two faculties and cannot be reformed or regenerated without them. The Lord teaches that,

Unless one is born anew, he cannot see the kingdom of God (Jn 3:3,5,7).

Few know what it is to be born anew or regenerated. For most do not know what love and charity are, therefore what faith is, either. One who does not know what love and charity are cannot know what faith is because charity and faith make one as good and truth do, and as affection which is of the will, and thought which is of the understanding, do. On this union see the treatise Divine Love and Wisdom, nn. 427-431; also Doctrine for the New Jerusalem, nn. 13-24; and above, nn. 3-20.

No one can enter the kingdom of God unless he has been born anew for the reason that by heredity from his parents he is born into evils of every kind, with the capacity of becoming spiritual through removal of the evils; unless he becomes spiritual, then, he cannot enter heaven. To become spiritual from being natural is to be born again or regenerated. Three things need to be considered if one is to know how man is regenerated: the nature of his first state, which is one of damnation; the nature of his second state, which is one of reformation; and the nature of his third state, which is one of regeneration.

[2] Man's first state, which is one of damnation, is every one's state by heredity from his parents. For man is born thereby into self-love and love of the world, and from these as fountains into evils of every kind. By the enjoyments of those loves he is led, and they keep him from knowing that he is in evil, for the enjoyment of any love is felt to be good. Unless he is regenerated, therefore, a man knows no otherwise than that to love himself and the world above all things is good itself, and to rule over others and possess their riches is the supreme good. So comes all evil. For only oneself is regarded with love. If another is regarded with love it is as devil loves devil or thief thief when they are in league.

[3] Those who confirm these loves with themselves and the evils flowing from them, from enjoyment in them, remain natural and become sensuous-corporeal, and in their own thinking, which is that of their spirit, are insane. And yet, as long as they are in the world they can speak and act rationally and wisely, for they are human beings and so have rationality and liberty, though they still do this from self-love and love of the world. After death and on becoming spirits, they can enjoy nothing that they did not enjoy in the world. Their enjoyment is that of an infernal love and is turned into the unpleasant, sorrowful and dreadful, meant in the Word by torment and hell-fire. Plain it is, then, that man's first state is one of damnation and that they are in it who do not suffer themselves to be regenerated.

[4] Man's second state--of reformation--is his state when he begins to think of heaven for the joy there, thus of God from whom he has heaven's joy. But at first the thought comes from the enjoyment of self-love; to him heaven's joy is that enjoyment. While the enjoyments of that love and of the evils flowing from it rule, moreover, he cannot but think that to gain heaven is to pour out prayers, hear sermons, observe the Supper, give to the poor, help the needy, make offerings to churches, contribute to hospitals, and the like. In this state a man is persuaded that merely to think about what religion teaches, whether this is called faith or called faith and charity, is to be saved. He is so minded because he gives no thought to the evils in the enjoyments of which he is. While those enjoyments remain, the evils do. The enjoyments of the evils are from the lust for them which continually inspires them and, when no fear restrains, brings them to pass.

[5] While evils remain in the lusts of love for them and so in one's enjoyments, there is no faith, piety, charity or worship except in externals, which seem real in the world's sight, but are not. They may be likened to waters

flowing from an impure fountain, which one cannot drink. While a man is such that he thinks about heaven and God from religion but gives no thought to evils as sins, he is still in the first state. He comes into the second state, which is one of reformation, when he begins to think that there is such a thing as sin and still more when he thinks that a given evil is a sin, explores it somewhat in himself, and does not will it.

[6] Man's third state, which is one of regeneration, sets in and continues from the former. It begins when a man desists from evils as sins, progresses as he shuns them, and is perfected as he battles against them. Then as he conquers from the Lord he is regenerated. The order of his life is changed; from natural he becomes spiritual; the natural separated from the spiritual is in disorder and the spiritual is in order. The regenerated man acts from charity and makes what is of his faith a part of his charity. But he becomes spiritual only in the measure in which he is in truths. Everyone is regenerated by means of truths and of a life in accord with them; by truths he knows life and by his life he does the truths. So he unites good and truth, which is the spiritual marriage in which heaven is.

Man is reformed and regenerated by means of the two faculties called rationality and liberty, and cannot be reformed or regenerated without them, because it is by means of rationality that he can understand and know what is evil and what is good, and hence what is false and true, and by means of liberty that he can will what he understands and knows. But while the enjoyment of an evil love rules him he cannot will good and truth freely or make them a matter of his reason, and therefore cannot appropriate them to him. For, as was shown above, what a man does in freedom from reason is appropriated to him as his, and unless it is so appropriated, he is not reformed and regenerated. He acts from the enjoyment of a love of good and truth for the first time when the enjoyment of love for the evil and false has been removed. Two opposite kinds of enjoyments of love at one and the same time are impossible. To act from the enjoyment of love is to act freely and is also to act according to reason, inasmuch as the reason favors the love.

Because an evil man as well as a good man has rationality and liberty, the evil man as well as the good can understand truth and do good. The evil man cannot do this in freedom according to reason, while a good man can; for the evil man is in the enjoyment of a love of evil, the good man in the enjoyment of a love of good. The truth which an evil man understands and the good he does are therefore not appropriated to him, as they are to the good man, and aside from appropriation there is no reformation or regeneration. With the evil man evils with their falsities occupy the center, as it were, and goods with their truths the circumference, but goods with their truths the center with the good man and evils with their falsities the periphery. In each case what is at the center is diffused to the circumference, as heat is from a fiery center and cold from an icy one. Thus with the wicked the good at the circumference is defiled by evils at the center, and with the good evils at the circumference grow mild from the good at the center. For this reason evils do not condemn a regenerating man, nor do goods save the unregenerate.

(v) A man can be reformed and regenerated by means of the two faculties so far as he can be led by them to acknowledge that all truth and good which he thinks and does are from the Lord and not from himself. What reformation and regeneration are has been told just above, likewise that man is reformed and regenerated by means of the two faculties of rationality and liberty. Because it is done by those faculties, something more is to be said of them. From rationality a man can understand and from liberty he can will, doing each as of himself. Yet he does not have the ability to will good in freedom and to do it in accord with reason unless he is regenerated. An evil man can will only evil in freedom and do it according to his thinking, which by confirmations he has made to be his reasoning. For evil can be confirmed as well as good, but is confirmed by fallacies and appearances which then become falsities; evil so confirmed seems to accord with reason.

Anyone thinking from interior understanding can see that the power to will and the power to understand are not from man, but from Him who has power itself, that is, power in its essence. Only think whence power is. Is it not from Him who has it in its full might, that is, who possesses it in and from Himself? Power in itself, therefore, is divine. All power must have a supply on which to draw and direction from an interior or higher self. Of itself the eye cannot see, nor the ear hear, nor the mouth speak, nor the hand do; there must be supply and direction from the mind. Nor can the mind of itself think or will this or that unless something more interior or higher determines the mind to it. The same is true of the power to understand and the power to will. These are possible only from Him who has in Himself the power of willing and understanding.

[2] It is plain, then, that the two faculties called rationality and liberty are from the Lord and not from man. Man can therefore will or understand something only as if of himself, and not of himself. Anyone can confirm the truth of this for himself who knows and believes that the will to good and the understanding of truth are wholly from the Lord, and not from man. The Word teaches that man can take nothing of himself and do nothing of himself (Jn 3:27; 15:5).

As all willing is from love and all understanding is from wisdom, the ability to will is from divine love, and the ability to understand is from divine wisdom; thus both are from the Lord who is divine love itself and divine wisdom itself. Hence to act in freedom according to reason has no other source. Everyone acts in freedom because, like love, freedom cannot be separated from willing. But there is interior and exterior willing, and a man can act upon the exterior without acting at the same time on the interior willing; so hypocrite and flatterer act. Exterior willing, however, is still from freedom, being from a love of appearing other than one is, or from love of an evil which the person intends in the love of his inner will. An evil man, however, as has been said, cannot in freedom according to reason do anything but evil; he cannot do good in freedom according to reason; he can do good, to be sure, but not in the inner freedom which is his own, from which the outer freedom has its character of not being good.

A person can be reformed and regenerated, we have said, in the measure in which he is led by the two faculties to acknowledge that all good and truth which he thinks and does are from the Lord and not from himself. A man can make this acknowledgment only by means of the two faculties, because they are from the Lord and are the Lord's in him, as is plain from what has been said.

Man can make this acknowledgment, therefore, only from the Lord and not from himself; he can make it as if of himself; this the Lord gives everyone to do. He may believe that it is of himself, but when wiser acknowledge that it is not of himself. Otherwise the truth he thinks and the good he does are not in themselves truth and good, for the man and not the Lord is in them. Good in which the man is and which is done by him for salvation's sake is self-righteous, but not that in which the Lord is.

Few can grasp with understanding that acknowledgment of the Lord, and acknowledgment that all good and truth are from Him, cause one to be reformed and regenerated. For a person may think, "What does the acknowledgment effect when the Lord is omnipotent and wills the salvation of all? This He wills and can accomplish if only He is moved to mercy." One is not thinking then from the Lord, nor from the interior sight of the understanding, that is, from enlightenment. Let me say briefly what the acknowledgment accomplishes.

[2] In the spiritual world where space is appearance only, wisdom brings about presence and love union, or the contrary happens. One can acknowledge the Lord from wisdom, and one can acknowledge Him from love. The acknowledgment of Him from wisdom (viewed in itself this is only knowledge) is made by doctrine; acknowledgment from love is made in a life according to doctrine. This effects union, the other, presence. Those, therefore, who reject instruction about the Lord remove themselves from Him, and as they also refuse life they part from Him. Those who do not reject instruction, but do refuse life, are present but still separated--like friends who converse but do not love each other, or like two one of whom speaks as a friend with the other, although as his enemy he hates him.

[3] The truth of this is commonly recognized in the idea that one who teaches and lives well is saved but not one who teaches well but lives wickedly, and in the idea that one who does not acknowledge God cannot be saved. This makes plain what kind of religion it is only to think about the Lord from faith, so called, and not to do something from charity. Therefore the Lord says,

Why do you call Me Lord, Lord, and do not do what I say? Everyone who comes to Me and hears my words and does them ... is like a house-builder who has placed the foundation on a rock, but the man who hears and does not do, is like a man building a house on the ground without a foundation (Lu 6:46-49).

(vi) The conjunction of the Lord with man and man's reciprocal conjunction with the Lord is effected by these two faculties. Conjunction with the Lord and regeneration are one and the same thing, for a man is regenerated in the measure that he is conjoined with the Lord. All that we have said above about regeneration can be said therefore of the conjunction, and all we said about conjunction can be said about regeneration. The Lord Himself teaches in John that there is a conjunction of the Lord with man and a reciprocal conjunction of man with the Lord.

Abide in Me, and I in you. . . . He that abides in Me and I in him, brings forth much fruit (15:4, 5).

In that day you will know that you are in Me and I in you (14:20).

[2] From reason alone anyone can see that there is no conjunction of minds unless it is reciprocal, and that what is reciprocal conjoins. If one loves another

without being loved in return, then as he approaches, the other withdraws; but if he is loved in return, as he approaches, the other does also, and there is conjunction. Love also wills to be loved; this is implanted in it; and so far as it is loved in return it is in itself and in its delight. Thence it is plain that if the Lord loves man and is not in turn loved by man, the Lord advances but man withdraws; thus the Lord would be constantly willing to meet with man and enter him, but man would be turning back and departing. So it is with those in hell, but with those in heaven there is mutual conjunction.

[3] Since the Lord wills conjunction with man for salvation's sake, He also provides something reciprocal with man. This consists in the fact that the good a man wills and does in freedom and the truth he thinks and speaks from the will according to reason seem to be from himself, and that the good in his will and the truth in his understanding seem to be his--indeed they seem to the man to be from himself and to be as completely his as though they really were; there is no difference; does anyone perceive otherwise by any sense? See above (nn. 74-77) on the appearance as of self, and (nn. 78-81) on appropriation as of oneself. The only difference is the acknowledgment which a man ought to make, that he does good and thinks truth not of himself but from the Lord, and hence that the good he does and the truth he thinks are not his. So to think from some love of the will because it is the truth makes conjunction; for then a man looks to the Lord and the Lord looks on the man.

I have been granted both to hear and see in the spiritual world what the difference is between those who believe that all good is from the Lord and those who believe that good is from themselves. Those who believe that good is from the Lord turn their faces to Him and receive the enjoyment and blessedness of good. Those who think that good is from themselves look to themselves and think they have merit. Looking to themselves, they perceive only the enjoyment of their own good which is the enjoyment not of good but of evil, for man's own is evil, and enjoyment of evil perceived as good is hell. Those who have done good but believed it was of themselves, and who after death do not receive the truth that all good is from the Lord, mingle with infernal spirits and finally join them. Those who receive that truth, however, are reformed, though no others receive it than those who have looked to God in their life. To look to God in one's life is nothing else than to shun evils as sins.

The Lord's conjunction with man and man's reciprocal conjunction with the Lord is effected by loving the neighbor as one's self and the Lord above all. To love the neighbor as one's self consists simply in not acting insincerely or unjustly with him, not hating him or avenging one's self on him, not cursing and defaming him, not committing adultery with his wife, and not doing other like things to him. Who cannot see that those who do such things do not love the neighbor as themselves? Those, however, who do not do such things because they are evils to the neighbor and at the same time sins against the Lord, deal sincerely, justly, amicably and faithfully by the neighbor; as the Lord does likewise, reciprocal conjunction takes place. And when conjunction is reciprocal, whatever a man does to the neighbor he does from the Lord, and what he does from the Lord is good. The neighbor to him then is not the person, but the good in the person. To love the Lord above all is to do no evil to the Word, for the Lord is in the Word, or to the holy things of the church, for He is in these, too, and to do no evil to the soul of another, for everyone's soul is in the Lord's hand. Those who shun these evils as monstrous sins against the Lord love Him above all else. None can do this except those who love the neighbor as themselves, for the two loves are conjoined.

In view of the fact that there is a conjunction of the Lord with man and of man with the Lord, there are two tables of the Law, one for the Lord and the other for man. So far as man as of himself keeps the laws of his table, the Lord enables him to observe the laws of the Lord's table. A man, however, who does not keep the laws of his table, which are all referable to love for the neighbor, cannot do the laws of the Lord's table, which are all referable to love for the Lord. How can a murderer, thief, adulterer, or false witness love God? Does reason not insist that to be any of these and to love God is a contradiction? Is not the devil such? Must he not hate God? But a man can love God when he abhors murder, adultery, theft and false witness, for then he turns his face away from the devil to the Lord; turning his face to the Lord he is given love and wisdom--these enter him by the face, and not by the back of the neck. As conjunction is accomplished only so, the two tables are called a covenant, and a covenant exists between two.

(vii) In all the procedure of His divine providence the Lord safeguards the two faculties in man unimpaired and as sacred. The reasons are that without those two faculties man would not have understanding and will and thus would not be human; likewise that without them he could not be conjoined to the Lord and so be reformed and regenerated; and because without them he would not have immortality and eternal life. The truth of this can be seen from what has been said about the two faculties, liberty and rationality, but not clearly seen unless the reasons just given are brought forward as conclusions. They are, therefore to be clarified.

[2] Without those two faculties man would not have understanding and will and thus would not be human. Man has will only in that he can will freely as of himself, and to will freely as of oneself is from the faculty called liberty, steadily imparted by the Lord. Man has understanding only in that he can understand as of himself whether a thing is of reason or not, and so to understand is from the other faculty, called rationality, steadily imparted to him by the Lord. These faculties unite in man as will and understanding do, for because a man can will, he can also understand; willing is impossible without understanding; understanding is its partner and mate apart from which it cannot exist. With the faculty called liberty there is therefore given the faculty called rationality. If, too, you take willing away from understanding, you understand nothing.

[3] In the measure that you will, you can understand provided the helps, called knowledges, are present or available, for these are like tools to a workman. We say, in the measure you will you can understand, meaning, so far as you love to understand, for will and love act as one. This seems like a paradox, but it appears so to those who do not love or hence will to understand. They say they cannot understand, but in the following section we shall tell who cannot understand, and who can hardly understand.

[4] It is plain without confirmation that unless man had will from the faculty called liberty, and understanding from the faculty called rationality, he

would not be human. Beasts do not have these faculties. Beasts seem to be able to will and to understand, but cannot do so. They are led and moved to do what they do solely by a natural affection, in itself desire, which has knowledge for its mate. Something civil and moral there is in their knowledge, but it does not transcend the knowledge, for they have nothing spiritual enabling them to perceive or to think analytically of what is moral. They can indeed be taught to do something, but this is natural only, is assimilated to their knowledge and at the same time to their affection, and reproduced through sight or hearing, but never becomes with them anything of thought, still less of reason. On this see some things above, n. 74.

[5] Without those two faculties man could not be con-joined to the Lord or reformed and regenerated. This has been shown above. The Lord resides with men, whether evil or good, in these two faculties and conjoins Himself by them to every man. Hence an evil man as well as a good man can understand and has the will of good and the understanding of truth potentially--that he does not possess them actually is owing to abuse of those faculties. The Lord resides in those faculties in everyone by the influx of His will, namely, to be received by man and to have an abode with him, and to give him the felicities of eternal life; all this is of the Lord's will, being of His divine love. It is this will of the Lord which causes what a man thinks, speaks, wills and does, to seem to be his own.

[6] That the influx of the Lord's will effects this can be confirmed by much in the spiritual world. Sometimes the Lord fills an angel with His divine so that the angel does not know but that he is the Lord. Thus inspired were the angels who appeared to Abraham, Hagar, and Gideon, and who therefore spoke of themselves as Jehovah; of whom the Word tells. So also one spirit may be filled by another so that he does not know but that he is the other; I have seen this often. In heaven it is general knowledge that the Lord operates all things by willing, and that what He wills takes place.

From all this it is plain that it is by those two faculties that the Lord conjoins Himself to man and causes the man to be reciprocally conjoined. We told above and shall say more below about how man is reciprocally conjoined by the two faculties and how, consequently, he is reformed and regenerated by means of them.

[7] Without those two faculties man would not have immortality or eternal life. This follows from what has been said: that by the two faculties there is conjunction with the Lord and also reformation and regeneration. By conjunction man has immortality, and through reformation and regeneration he has eternal life. As every man, evil as well as good, is conjoined to the Lord by the two faculties every man has immortality. Eternal life, or the life of heaven, however, only that man has with whom there is reciprocal conjunction from inmosts to outmosts.

The reasons may now be clear why the Lord, in all the procedure of His divine providence, safeguards the two faculties in man unimpaired and as sacred.

(viii) It is therefore [a law] of divine providence that man shall act in freedom from reason. To act in freedom according to reason, to act from liberty and rationality, and to act from will and understanding, are the same. But it is one thing to act in freedom according to reason, or from liberty and rationality, and another thing to act from freedom itself according to reason itself or from liberty and rationality themselves. The man who does evil from love of evil and confirms it in himself acts indeed from freedom according to reason, but his freedom is not in itself freedom or very freedom, but an infernal freedom which in itself is bondage, and his reason is not in itself reason, but is either spurious or false or plausible through confirmations. Still, either is of divine providence. For if freedom to will evil and do it as of the reason through confirmation of it were taken from the natural man, liberty and rationality and at the same time will and understanding would perish, and he could not be withdrawn any longer from evils, be reformed or united with the Lord, and live to eternity. The Lord therefore guards man's freedom as a man does the apple of his eye. Through that freedom the Lord steadily withdraws man from evils and so far as He can do this implants goods, thus gradually putting heavenly freedom in place of infernal freedom.

We said above that every man has the faculty of volition called liberty and the faculty of understanding called rationality. Those faculties, moreover, it should be known, are as it were inherent in man, for humanness itself is in them. But as was just said, it is one thing to act from freedom in accord with reason, and another thing to act from freedom itself and according to reason itself. Only those do the latter who have suffered themselves to be regenerated by the Lord; others act in freedom according to thought which they make seem like reason. Unless he was born foolish or supremely stupid, every person can attain to reason itself and by it to liberty itself. Many reasons why all do not do so will be disclosed in what follows. Here we shall only tell to whom freedom itself or liberty itself, and at the same time reason itself or rationality itself cannot be given and to whom they can hardly be given.

[2] True liberty and rationality cannot be given to those foolish from birth or to those who become foolish later, while they remain so. Nor can they be given to those born stupid and dull or to any made so by the torpor of idleness, or by a disease which perverts or entirely closes the interiors of the mind, or by love of a bestial life.

[3] Genuine liberty and rationality cannot be given to those in Christendom who utterly deny the Divine of the Lord and the holiness of the Word, and have kept that denial confirmed to life's close. For this is meant by the sin against the Holy Spirit which is not forgiven in this world or in the world to come (Mt 12:31, 32).

[4] Liberty itself and rationality itself cannot be given to those who ascribe all things to nature and nothing to the Divine, and have made this a conviction by reasonings from visible things; for these are atheists.

[5] True liberty and rationality can hardly be given to those who have confirmed themselves much in falsities of religion; for a confirmer of falsity is a denier of truth. But they can be given to those, in whatever religion, who have not so confirmed themselves. On this see what is adduced in Doctrine for the New Jerusalem about Sacred Scripture, nn. 91-97.

[6] Infants and children cannot attain to essential liberty and rationality before they grow up. For the interiors of the mind of man are opened gradually, and meanwhile are like seeds in unripe fruit, without ground in which to sprout.

We have said that true liberty and rationality cannot be given to those who have denied the Divine of the Lord and the holiness of the Word; to those who have confirmed themselves in favor of nature and against the Divine; and hardly to those who have strongly confirmed themselves in falsities of religion; still none of these have destroyed the faculties themselves. I have heard atheists, who had become devils and satans, understand arcana of wisdom quite as well as angels, but only while they heard them from others; on returning into their own thought, they did not understand them, for the reason that they did not will to do so. They were shown that they could also will this, did not the love and enjoyment of evil turn them away. This they understood, too, when they heard it. Indeed they asserted that they could but did not will to be able to do so, for then they could not will what they did will, namely, evil from enjoyment in the lust of it. I have often heard such astonishing things in the spiritual world. I am fully persuaded therefore that every man has liberty and rationality, and that every man can attain true liberty and rationality if he shuns evils as sins. But the adult who has not come into true liberty and rationality in the world can never do so after death, for the state of his life remains to eternity what it was in the world.

Section 6

IT IS A LAW OF DIVINE PROVIDENCE THAT MAN SHALL REMOVE EVILS AS SINS IN THE EXTERNAL MAN OF HIMSELF, AND ONLY SO CAN THE LORD REMOVE THE EVILS IN THE INTERNAL MAN AND AT THE SAME TIME IN THE EXTERNAL

Anyone can see from reason alone that the Lord who is good itself and truth itself cannot enter man unless the evils and falsities in him are removed. For evil is opposed to good, and falsity to truth, and two opposites cannot mingle, but as one approaches the other, combat arises which lasts until one gives way to the other; what gives way departs and the other takes its place. Heaven and hell, or the Lord and the devil, are in such opposition. Can anyone reasonably think that the Lord can enter where the devil reigns, or heaven be where hell is? By the rationality with which every sane person is endowed, who cannot see that for the Lord to enter, the devil must be cast out, or for heaven to enter, hell must be removed?

[2] This opposition is meant by Abraham's words from heaven to the rich man in hell:

Between us and you a great gulf is fixed, so that those who would cross from us to you cannot, nor those over there cross to us (Lu 16:26).

Evil is itself hell, and good is itself heaven, or what is the same, evil is itself the devil, and good itself the Lord. A person in whom evil reigns is a hell in least form, and one in whom good reigns is a heaven in least form. How, then, can heaven enter hell when a gulf is fixed between them so great that there is no crossing from one to the other? It follows that hell must by all means be removed for the Lord to enter with heaven.

But many, especially those who have confirmed themselves in faith severed from charity, do not know that they are in hell when they are in evils. In fact, they do not know what evils are, giving them no thought. They say that they are not under the yoke of the law and so the law does not condemn them; likewise, that as they cannot contribute to their salvation, they cannot remove any evil of themselves and furthermore cannot do any good of themselves. It is these who neglect to give some thought to evil and therefore keep on in evil. They are meant by the Lord under "goats" in Matthew 25:32, 33; 41-46, as may be seen in Doctrine of the New Jerusalem on Faith, nn. 61-68; to them it is said in verse 41, "Depart from Me, you accursed, into everlasting fire prepared for the devil and his angels."

[2] Persons who give no thought to the evils in them, and who do not examine themselves and then desist from the evils, cannot but be ignorant what evil is, and cannot but love it then from delighting in it. For one who is ignorant of it loves it, and one who fails to give it thought, goes on in it, blind to it. Thought sees good and evil as the eye sees beauty and ugliness. One who thinks and wills evil is in evil, and so is a person who thinks that it does not come to God's sight, or if it does is forgiven by Him; he supposes then that he is without evil. If such persons refrain from doing evil, they do so not because it is a sin against God, but for fear of the law and for their reputation's sake. In spirit they still do evil, for it is man's spirit that thinks and wills. As a result, what a man thinks in his spirit in the world, he commits when he becomes a spirit on his departure from the world.

[3] In the spiritual world, into which everyone comes after death, the question is not asked what your belief has been or your doctrine, but what your life has been. Was it such or such? For, as is known, such as one's life is, such is one's belief, yes, one's doctrine. For life fashions a doctrine and a belief for itself.

From all this it is plain that it is a law of divine providence that evils be removed by man, for without the removal of them the Lord cannot be conjoined to man and from Himself lead man to heaven. But it is not known that man ought to remove evils in the external man as of himself and that unless he does so the Lord cannot remove the evils in his internal man. This is to be presented, therefore, to the reason in light of its own in this order:

i. Every man has an external and an internal of thought. ii. His external of thought is in itself such as his internal is. iii. The internal cannot be purified from the lusts of evil as long as the evils in the external man have not been removed, for these impede. iv. Only with the man's participation can evils in the external man be removed by the Lord. v. Therefore a man ought to remove evils from the external man as of himself. vi. The Lord then purifies him from the lusts of evil in the internal man and from the evils themselves in the external. vii. The continuous effort of the Lord in His divine providence is to unite man to Himself and Himself to man, in order to be able to bestow the felicities of eternal life on him, which can be done only so far as evils, along with their lusts, are removed.

(i) Every man has an external and an internal of thought. By external and internal of thought the same is meant here as by external and internal man, and by this nothing else is meant than external and internal of will and understanding, for will and understanding constitute man, and as they both manifest themselves in thoughts, we speak of external and internal of thought. And as it is man's spirit and not his body which wills and understands and consequently thinks, external and internal are external and internal of his spirit. The body's activity in speech or deed is only an effect from the external and internal of man's spirit, for the body is so much obedience.

As he grows older, every person has an external and an internal of thought, or an external and an internal of will and understanding or of his spirit, identical with external and internal man. This is evident to anyone who observes another's thoughts and intentions as they are revealed in speech or deed, or who observes his own when he is in company and when he is by himself. For from the external thought one can talk amicably with another and yet in internal thought be hostile. From external thought and from its affection, too, a man can talk about love for the neighbor and for God when in his internal thought he cares nothing for the neighbor and does not fear God. From external thought together with its affection he can talk about the justice of civil laws, the virtues of the moral life, and matters of doctrine and the spiritual life, and yet in private and from his internal thought and its affection speak against the civil laws, the moral virtues, and matters of doctrine and spiritual life. So those do who are in lusts of evil but want to appear to the world not to be in them.

[2] Many also, as they listen to others, think to themselves, "Do those speaking think inwardly in themselves as they think in utterance? Are they to be believed or not? What do they intend?" Flatterers and hypocrites notoriously possess a twofold thought. They can be self-restrained and guard against the interior thought's being disclosed, and some can hide it more and more deeply and bar the door against its appearing. That a man possesses external and internal thought is also plain in that from his interior thought he can behold the exterior thought, can reflect on it, too, and judge whether or not it is evil. The human mind is such because of the two faculties, called liberty and rationality, which one has from the Lord. Unless he possessed internal and external of thought from these faculties, a man could not perceive and see an evil in himself and be reformed. In fact, he could not speak but only make sounds like a beast.

The internal of thought comes out of the life's love, its affections and the perceptions from them. The external of thought is from what is in the memory, serving the life's love for confirmation and as means to its end. From childhood to early manhood a person is in the external of thought from an affection for knowledge, which is then his internal; from the life's love born in one from parents something of lust and hence of disposition issues, too. Later, however, his life's love is as he lives, and its affections and the perceptions from them make the internal of his thought. From his life's love comes a love of means; the enjoyments of these means and the information drawn thereby from the memory make his external of thought.

(ii) Man's external of thought is in itself such as his internal is. We showed earlier that from head to foot a man is what his life's love is. Something must be said about his life's love, for until this is done nothing can be said about the affections which together with perceptions make the internal of man, or about the enjoyments of the affections together with thoughts which make his external. Loves are many, but two--heavenly love and infernal love--are like lords or kings. Heavenly love is love to the Lord and the neighbor; infernal love is love of self and the world. These are opposite to each other as heaven and hell are. For a man in love of self and the world wishes well only to himself; a man in love to the Lord and the neighbor wishes well to all. These two are the loves of man's life, though with much variety. Heavenly love is the life's love of those whom the Lord leads, and infernal love the life's love of those whom the devil leads.

[2] No one's life's love can be without derivatives, called affections. The derivatives of infernal love are affections of evil and falsity --lusts, properly speaking; and those of heavenly love are affections of good and truth--loves, strictly. Affections, or strictly lusts, of infernal love are as numerous as evils are, and affections, or properly loves, of heavenly love are as many as there are goods. Love dwells in its affections like a lord in his domain and a king in his realm; its domain or realm is over the things of the mind, that is, of the will and understanding and thence of the body. By its affections and the perceptions from them and by its enjoyments and the thoughts therefrom, the life's love of man rules him completely, the internal of the mind by the affections and perceptions from them, and the external by the enjoyments of the affections and of the thoughts from them.

The manner of this rule may be seen to some extent from comparisons. Heavenly love with its affections of good and truth and the perceptions from them, together with the enjoyments of such affections and the thoughts from these, may be compared to a tree, notable for its branches, leaves and fruit. The life's love is the tree; the branches with their leaves are the affections of good and truth with their perceptions; and the fruits are the enjoyments of the affections with their thoughts. Infernal love, however, with its affections or lusts of evil and falsity, together with the enjoyments of the lusts and the thinking from those enjoyments, may be compared to a spider and the web spun about it. The love itself is the spider; the lusts of evil and falsity together with their subtle cunning are the net of threads nearest the spider's post; and the enjoyments of the lusts together with their crafty schemes are the more remote threads where flies are snared on the wing, enveloped and eaten.

These comparisons may help one to see the connection of all things of the will and understanding or of man's mind with his life's love, and yet not to see it rationally. Rationally it may be seen in this way. Everywhere there are three which make one, called end, cause and effect. Here the life's love is end; the affections with their perceptions are cause; and the enjoyments of the affections and consequent thoughts are effect. For as an end passes into effect through a cause, love passes by its affections to its enjoyments and by its perceptions to its thoughts. The effects are in the enjoyments of the mind and the thoughts thence when the enjoyments are from the will and the thoughts from the attendant understanding, that is, when all fully agree. The effects are then part of man's spirit and although they do not come into bodily act are still a deed there when there is this agreement. At the same time they are in the body, dwelling there with man's life's love and longing for the deed, which occurs when nothing hinders. The same is true of lusts of evil and evil deeds with those who make evils allowable in spirit.

[2] As an end unites itself with a cause and by the cause with an effect, the

life's love unites itself with the internal of thought and by this with its external. It is plain then that man's external of thought is in itself what his internal is, for an end imparts all of itself to the cause and through the cause to the effect. Nothing essential is present in an effect which is not in the cause and through the cause in the end, and as the end is what essentially enters cause and effect, these are called "mediate end" and "final end" respectively.

Sometimes the external of thought seems to be different in itself from the internal. This is because the life's love with its internals about it sets a vicar under it called the love of means, and directs it to watch and guard against anything of its lusts appearing. This vicar, with the cunning of its chief, the life's love, therefore speaks and acts in accordance with the laws of a kingdom, the ethical demands of reason, and the spiritual requirements of the church, so cunningly, too, and cleverly that no one sees that persons are other than they say and act, and finally the persons themselves, so disguised, scarcely know otherwise. Such are all hypocrites. Such are priests, also, who at heart care nothing for the neighbor and do not fear God, yet preach about love of the neighbor and of God. Such are judges who judge by gifts and friendships while affecting zeal for justice and speaking with reason about judgment. Such are traders who at heart are insincere and fraudulent while dealing honestly for the sake of profit. Such are adulterers when, from the rationality every man possesses, they talk about the chastity of marriage; and so on.

[2] The same persons, when they strip the love of means, the vicar of their life's love, of the purple and linen which they have thrown around it and put its house dress on it, then think exactly the contrary, and exchanging thought with their best friends who are in a similar life's love, they speak so. It may be believed that when they have spoken so justly, honestly and piously from the love of means, the character of the internal of thought was not in the external of their thought; yet it was; hypocrisy is in them, and love of self and the world is in them, the cunning of which aims to capture a reputation for the sake of standing or gain through just the outward appearance. This, the nature of the internal, is in the external of their thought when they speak and act so.

With those in a heavenly love, however, internal and external of thought or internal and external man make one when they speak, and they are aware of no difference. Their life's love, with its affections of good and the perceptions of truth from these, is like a soul in what they think and then say and do. If they are priests, they preach out of love to the neighbor and to the Lord; if judges, they judge from justice itself; if tradesmen, they deal with honesty; if they are husbands, they love the partner with true chastity; and so on. Their life's love also has a love of the means for vicar, which it teaches and leads to act with prudence and clothes with garments of a zeal for both truths of doctrine and goods of life.

(iii) The internal cannot be purified from the lusts of evil as long as evils in the external man are not removed, for these impede. This follows from what has been said above, that the external of man's thought is in itself what the internal of his thought is and that they cohere as what is not only in the other but also from the other; one cannot be removed, therefore, unless the other is at the same time. This is true of any external which is from an internal, and of anything subsequent from what is prior, and of every effect from a cause.

[2] As lusts together with slynesses make the internal of thought with evil persons, and the enjoyments of the lusts together with scheming make the external of thought in them, and the two are joined into one, it follows that the internal cannot be purified from the lusts as long as the evils in the external man are not removed. It should be known that man's internal will is in the lusts; his internal understanding in the slynesses; his external will in the enjoyments of the lusts; and his external understanding in the sly scheming. Anyone can see that lusts and their enjoyments make one, that slynesses and scheming also do, and that the four are one series and as it were make a single bundle. From this again it is evident that the internal, consisting of lusts, cannot be cast out except on the removal of the external, consisting of evils. Lusts produce evils by their enjoyments, and when evils are deemed allowable, as they are when will and understanding agree on it, the enjoyments and the evils make one. It is well known that assent is deed; this is also what the Lord said:

If anyone looks on the woman of another to lust after her, he has already committed adultery with her in his heart (Mt 5:28). 111-1

The same is true of all other evils.

From this it may now be evident that for a person to be purified from the lusts of evil, evils must by all means be removed from the external man, for the lusts have no way out before. If no outlet exists, they remain within and breathe out enjoyments and so incite man to consent, thus to deed. Lusts enter the body by the external of thought; when there is consent, therefore, in the external of thought they are instantly in the body; the enjoyment felt is bodily. See in the treatise Divine Love and Wisdom (nn. 362-370) that the body, thus the whole man, is what the mind is. This can be illustrated by comparisons, and by examples.

[2] By comparisons: lusts with their enjoyments can be compared to a fire which blazes the more, the more it is nursed; the freer its way the more widely it spreads until in a city it consumes houses and in a woods the trees. In the Word, moreover, lusts are compared to fire, and the evils from them to a conflagration. The lusts of evil with their enjoyments also appear as fires in the spiritual world; hellfire is nothing else. Lusts may also be compared to floods and inundations as dikes or dams give way. They may also be likened to gangrene and abscesses which bring death to the body as they run their course or are not healed.

[3] By examples: it is obvious that when evils are not removed in the external man, the lusts with their enjoyments grow and flourish. The more he steals the more a thief lusts to steal until he cannot stop; so with a defrauder, the more he defrauds; it is the same with hatred and vengeance, luxury and intemperance, whoredom and blasphemy. It is notorious that the love of ruling from the love of self increases when left unbridled; so also the love of possessing things from love of the world; they seem to have no limit or end. Plain it is then that so far as evils are not removed in the external man, lusts for them intensify; also that in the degree that evils are given free rein, the lusts increase.

A person does not see the lusts of his evil; he sees their enjoyments, to be sure, but still he reflects little on them, for they divert thought and drive off reflection. Unless he learned from elsewhere that they are evils he would call them goods and give them expression freely according to his thought's reasoning; doing so, he appropriates them to himself. So far as he confirms them as allowable he enlarges the court of his ruling love, which is his life's love. Lusts constitute its court, being its ministers and retinue, as it were, by which it governs the exteriors of its realm. But such as is the king, such are the ministers and retinue, and such is the kingdom. If the king is diabolic, his ministers and the retinue are insanities, and the people of his realm are falsities of every kind. The ministers (who are called wise although they are insane) cause these falsities to appear as truths by reasonings from fallacies and by fantasies and cause them to be acknowledged as truths. Can such a state in a man be changed except by the evils being removed in the external man? Then the lusts which cling to the evils are also removed. Otherwise no outlet offers for the lusts; they are shut in like a besieged city or like an indurated ulcer.

(iv) Only with man's participation can evils in the external man be removed by the Lord. In all Christian churches it is an accepted point of doctrine that before coming to the Holy Communion a person should examine himself, see and confess his sins, and do penitence, desisting from his sins and rejecting them because they are from the devil; and that otherwise the sins are not forgiven him and he is damned. The English, despite the fact that they are in the doctrine of faith alone, nevertheless in the exhortation to the Holy Communion openly teach self-examination, acknowledgment, confession of sins, penitence and renewal of life, and warn those who do not do these things with the words that otherwise the devil will enter into them as he did into Judas, fill them with all iniquity, and destroy both body and soul. Germans, Swedes and Danes, who are also in the doctrine of faith alone, teach the same in the exhortation to the Holy Communion, also warning that otherwise the communicants will make themselves liable to infernal punishments and eternal damnation for mixing sacred and profane together. These words are read out by the priest in a deep voice to all who are about to observe the Holy Supper, and are listened to by them in full acknowledgment that they are true.

[2] Nevertheless, after hearing a sermon on the same day about faith alone and to the effect that the law does not condemn them because the Lord has fulfilled it for them, and that of themselves they cannot do any good which is not self-righteous and thus that one's works have nothing saving in them, only faith alone has, these same persons return home completely forgetting their earlier confession and rejecting it so far as they think along the lines of the sermon. But which is true, the latter or the former? Contrary to each other, both cannot be true. Which is? That there can be no forgiveness of sins, thus no salvation but only eternal damnation, apart from self-examination, the knowledge and acknowledgment, confession and breaking off of sins, that is, apart from repentance? Or that such things effect nothing towards salvation inasmuch as full satisfaction for all the sins of men has been made by the Lord through the passion of the cross for those who have faith, and that those in faith alone with trust that it is so and with confidence in the imputation of the Lord's merit, are sinless and appear before God like men with shining faces for having washed?

[3] It is plain from this that the religion common to all churches in

Christendom is that one shall examine himself, see and acknowledge his sins and then desist from them, and that otherwise there is no salvation, but damnation. This, moreover, is divine truth itself, as is plain from passages in the Word in which man is bidden to do penitence, as from the following:

John said, Do ... fruits worthy of repentance ... this moment the axe is at the root of the tree; every tree not giving good fruit will be cut down and cast into the fire (Lu 3:8, 9).

Jesus said, Unless you do repentance, you shall all ... perish (Lu 13:3,5).

Jesus preached the gospel of the kingdom of God; ... do repentance, and believe the gospel (Mk 1:14, 15).

Jesus sent out the disciples who on going out were to preach that men should repent (Mk 6:12).

Jesus told the apostles that they were to preach repentance and the remission of sins to all peoples (Lu 24:27).

John preached the baptism of repentance for the remission of sins (Mk 1:4; Lu 3:3).

Think about this also with some degree of understanding; if you have religion, you will see that repentance of one's sins is the way to heaven, that faith apart from repentance is not faith, and that those in no faith for lack of repenting are in the way to hell.

Those in faith severed from charity who have confirmed themselves in it by Paul's saying to the Romans that a man is justified by faith without the works of the law (3:28) worship that saying quite like men who worship the sun. They become like those who fix their gaze steadily on the sun with the result that the blurred vision sees nothing in normal light. For they fail to see what is meant in the passage by "works of the law," namely, the rituals described by Moses in his books, called "law" in them everywhere, and not the precepts of the Decalog. Lest it be thought these are meant, Paul explains, saying at that point,

Do we not then make the law void through faith? Far from it, rather we establish the law (verse 31 of the same chapter).

Those who have confirmed themselves by that saying in faith severed from charity, looking on it as on the sun, do not see the passages in which Paul lists the laws of faith and that these are the very works of charity. What indeed is faith without its laws? Nor do they see the passages in which he lists evil works, declaring that those who do them cannot enter heaven. What blindness has been brought about by this one passage badly understood!

Evils in the external man cannot be removed without man's cooperation for the reason that it is by divine providence that whatever a man hears, sees, thinks, wills, speaks and does shall seem to him to be his own doing. Apart from that appearance (as was shown above, nn. 71-95 ff.) there would be no reception of divine truth on man's part, nor determination to do what is good, nor any appropriation of love and wisdom or of charity and faith, hence no conjunction with the Lord, no reformation therefore or regeneration, and thus no salvation. Without that appearance, repentance for sins would clearly be impossible and in fact faith would; without that appearance, likewise, man is not man but is devoid of rational life like the beasts. Let him who will, consult his reason whether it appears otherwise than that man thinks from himself about good and truth, spiritual as well as moral and civil; then accept the doctrine that all good and truth are from the Lord and none from man. Must he not then acknowledge as a consequence that man is to do good and think truth of himself, yet always acknowledge that these are from the Lord? And acknowledge further that man is to remove evils of himself, but still acknowledge that he does so from the Lord?

Many are unaware that they are in evils since they do not do them outwardly, fearing the civil law and the loss of reputation. Thus by custom and habit they practice to avoid evils as detrimental to their standing and interests. But if they do not shun evils on religious principle, because they are sins and against God, the lusts of evil with their enjoyments remain in them like impure waters stopped up or stagnant. Let them probe their thoughts and intentions and they will come on the lusts provided they know what sins are.

[2] Many such, who have confirmed themselves in faith separated from charity and who believe that the law does not condemn, pay no attention to sins. Some doubt there are sins, or if so, that they exist in God's sight, having been pardoned. Such also are natural moralists, who believe that civil and moral life with its prudence accomplishes all things and divine providence nothing. Such are those, also, who strive with great care after a reputation and a name for honesty and sincerity for the sake of standing and preferment. But those who are such and who at the same time have spurned religion become lustful spirits after death, appearing to themselves like men indeed, but to others at a distance like priapi; and they see in the dark and not at all in the light, like night-owls.

Proposition v, that a man ought to remove evils from the external man of himself, is substantiated then. Further explanation may be seen in Doctrine of Life for the New Jerusalem under three propositions: 1. No one can flee evils as sins so as to be averse to them inwardly except by combats against them (nn. 92-100); 2. A man ought to shun evils as sins and fight against them as of himself (nn. 101-107); and 3. If he shuns evils for any other reason than that they are sins, he does not shun them, but only keeps them from appearing to the world.

(vi) The Lord then purifies man from the lusts of evil in the internal man and from the evils themselves in the external. The Lord purifies man from the lusts of evil only when man as of himself removes the evils because He cannot do so before. For the evils are in the external man and the lusts in the internal man, and they cling together like roots and a trunk. Unless the evils are removed, therefore, no outlet offers; they block the way and shut the door, which the Lord can open only with a man's participation, as was shown just above. When the man as of himself opens the door, the Lord then roots out the lusts.

[2] A second reason why the Lord cannot do so sooner is that He acts upon man's inmost and by that on all that follows even to outmosts where man himself is. While outmosts, therefore, are kept closed by man, no purification can take place, but only that activity of the Lord in interiors which is His activity in hell, of which the man who is in lusts and at the same time in evils is a form--an activity which is solely provision lest one thing destroy another and lest good and truth be violated. It is plain from words of the Lord in the Apocalypse that He constantly urges and prompts man to open the door to Him:

Behold, I stand at the door, and knock; if anyone hears my voice and opens the door, I will come in to him, and sup with him, and he with Me (3:20).

Man knows nothing at all of the interior state of his mind or internal man, yet infinite things are there, not one of which comes to his knowledge. His internal of thought or internal man is his very spirit, and in it are things as infinite and innumerable as there are in his body, in fact, more numerous. For his spirit is man in its form, and all things in it correspond to all things of his body. Now, just as man knows nothing by any sensation about how his mind or soul operates on all things of the body as a whole or severally, so he does not know, either, how the Lord works on all things of his mind or soul, that is, of his spirit. The divine activity is unceasing; man has no part in it; still the Lord cannot purify a man from any lust of evil in his spirit or internal man as long as the man keeps the external closed. Man keeps his external closed by evils, each of which seems to him to be a single entity, although in each are infinite things. When a man removes what seems a single thing, the Lord removes infinite things in it. So much is implied in the Lord's purifying man from the lusts of evil in the internal man and from the evils themselves in the external.

Many believe that a person is purified from evils merely by believing what the church teaches; some, by doing good; others by knowing, speaking and teaching what is of the church; others by reading the Word and books of devotion; others by going to church, hearing sermons and especially by observing the Holy Supper; still others, by renouncing the world and devoting oneself to piety; others still by confessing oneself guilty of all sins; and so on. And yet none of these things purifies man at all unless he examines himself, sees his sins, acknowledges them, condemns himself on account of them, and repents by desisting from them, and does all this as of himself, yet with the acknowledgment in heart that he does so from the Lord.

[2] Until this is done, the things mentioned above do not avail, being either self-righteous or hypocritical. Such persons appear to the angels in heaven either like pretty courtesans smelling badly of their corruption, or like unsightly women painted to appear handsome, or like masked clowns and mimics in the theater, or like apes in men's clothes. But when evils have been removed, then all that has just been mentioned becomes the expression of love in such persons, and they appear as beautiful human beings to the sight of the angels in heaven and as partners and companions of theirs.

But it should be rightly known that in repenting a man ought to look to the Lord alone. He cannot be purified if he looks to God the Father alone, or to the Father for the sake of the Son, or to the Son as a man only. For there is one God and the Lord is He, for His Divine and Human is one Person, as we have shown in Doctrine of the New Jerusalem about the Lord. In order that the intending penitent may look to Him alone, the Lord instituted the Holy Supper, which confirms the remission of sins in those who repent, and does so because everyone is kept looking to the Lord alone in it.

(vii) The perpetual effort of the Lord in His divine providence is to conjoin man with Himself and Himself with man, in order to be able to bestow the felicities of eternal life on him, which can be done only so far as evils with their lusts have been removed. It was shown above (nn. 27-45) that it is the unceasing effort of the Lord in His divine providence to conjoin man to Himself and Himself to man; that this conjunction is what is called reformation and regeneration; and that by it man has salvation. Who does not see that conjunction with God is life eternal and salvation? Everyone sees this who believes that men by creation are images and likenesses of God (Ge 1:26, 27) and who knows what an image and likeness of God is. [2] What man of sound reason, thinking from his rationality and wanting to think in freedom, can believe that there are three Gods equal in essence and that divine being or essence can be divided? One can conceive and comprehend a Trine in the one God, however, just as soul, body and outgoing life in angel and man are comprehensible. As this Trine in One exists only in the Lord, conjunction must be with Him. Use your power of reason together with your liberty of thought, and you will see this truth in its own light; but admit first that God is, and heaven, and eternal life.

[3] As, then, God is one, and the human being was made by creation an image and likeness of Him, and inasmuch as by infernal love and its lusts and enjoyments man has come into a love of all evils and thus destroyed the image and likeness of God in him, it follows that it is the continuous effort of the Lord's divine providence to conjoin man to Himself and Himself to man and thus make him an image of Himself. It also follows that this is to the end that the Lord may be able to bestow on him the felicities of eternal life, for such is divine love.

[4] He cannot bestow them, however, nor make man an image of Himself, unless man removes sins in the external man as of himself, because the Lord is not only divine love but also divine wisdom, and divine love does nothing except by its divine wisdom and in consonance with it. It is according to divine wisdom that man cannot be conjoined to the Lord and thus reformed, regenerated and saved unless he is allowed to act in freedom according to reason, for so man is man. Whatever is according to the Lord's divine wisdom is also of His divine providence.

To this let me append two arcana of angelic wisdom showing further what divine providence is like. One is that the Lord never acts on one thing by itself in man, but on all things at the same time, and the other is that He acts at once from inmosts and outmosts. He never acts on some one thing by itself but on all things together because all things in man are in such connection and from this in such form that they act not as a number but as one. We know that there is such connectedness and by it such organization in man's body. The human mind is in similar form as a result of the connection of all things, for the mind is the spiritual man and truly the man. Hence man's spirit or the mind in the body in its entire form is man. Consequently man is man after death equally as he was in the world with the sole difference that he has thrown off the clothing which made up his body in the world.

[2] As the human form, then, is such that all its parts form a community which acts as a whole, some one thing cannot be moved out of place or altered in state except with adaptation of the rest, for if it were, the form which acts as a whole would suffer. Hence it is plain that the Lord never acts on any one thing without acting on all. So He acts on the total angelic heaven since in His view it is like one man; so He acts on each angel, for each angel is heaven in least form; so He acts also on each man, most nearly on all things of man's mind and by these on all things of his body; for man's mind is his spirit and in the

measure of conjunction with the Lord is an angel, and the body is obedience.

[3] It is to be well noted, however, that the Lord does act on each particular thing in man singly, singularly so, when acting on all things in man's organization; even so He does not alter the state of any part or of any one thing except suitably to the whole form. But more will be said of this in following numbers where we shall show that divine providence is general because it extends to particulars, and particular because it is general.

[4] The Lord acts from inmosts and outmosts at the same time because only in this way are all things held in connection, for the intermediate things depend one upon another from inmosts to outmosts and are assembled in outmosts (it was shown in Part III of the treatise Divine Love and Wisdom that all things from the inmost onward are present simultaneously in what is outmost). For this reason the Lord from eternity or Jehovah came into the world and assumed and bore human nature in outmosts. He could thus be at once from firsts in lasts, and from firsts by lasts govern the whole world and so save whom He could save according to the laws of His divine providence, which are also the laws of His divine wisdom. For it is true, as Christendom knows, that no mortal could have been saved had the Lord not come into the world (see Doctrine for the New Jerusalem on Faith, n. 35). For the same reason the Lord is called "The First and the Last."

These angelic arcana have been premised in order that it may be comprehended how the Lord's divine providence operates to unite man to Him and Himself to man. It does not act upon a particular thing by itself in man, but on all things together and from man's inmost and outmosts simultaneously. Man's inmost is his life's love; the outmosts are in the external of thought; what is intermediate is in the internal of thought (what external and internal are like with the wicked was shown earlier); from which is plain again that the Lord cannot act by inmosts and outmosts simultaneously except together with man, for in the outmosts man and the Lord are together. Wherefore, as the man acts in outmosts, which are in his determination, being within the range of his freedom, so the Lord acts from man's inmosts and in what follows from them to the outmosts. Man does not know at all what is in the inmosts and in what follows to the outmosts, therefore is unaware of how the Lord acts there or what He effects there. But as all these things cohere as one with the outmosts, man does not need to know more than that he should shun evils as sins and look to the Lord. Only so can his life's love, which by birth is infernal, be removed by the Lord and a heavenly life's love be implanted in its place.

When a heavenly life's love has been implanted by the Lord in place of an infernal life's love, affections of good and truth are implanted in place of lusts of evil and falsity; enjoyments of affections of good are implanted instead of enjoyments of lusts of evil and falsity, and goods of heavenly love in place of evils of infernal love; prudence is implanted in place of cunning, wise thinking in place of malevolent. So a man is born again and becomes a new man. What goods replace evils you may see in Doctrine of Life for the New Jerusalem, nn. 67-73, 74-79, 80-86, 87-91; likewise that so far as man shuns and is averse to evils as sins so far he loves truths of wisdom, nn. 32-41, and has faith and is spiritual, nn.42-52.

From the exhortations read aloud in all Christian churches before Holy

Communion we showed that it is the common religion of all Christendom that a man should examine himself, see his sins, avow them, confess them before God, and desist from them; and that this is repentance, remission of sins and hence salvation. This is also evident from the Creed named after Athanasius and received throughout Christendom which concludes with the words:

The Lord will come to judge the living and the dead; at whose coming those who have done good will enter into life eternal, and those who have done evil, into everlasting fire.

Who does not know from the Word that everyone is allotted a life after death according to his deeds? Open the Word, read it, and you will see this clearly, but the while remove the thoughts from faith and justification by faith alone. The few passages following are testimony that the Lord teaches so everywhere in His Word:

Every tree which does not yield good fruit shall be cut down and cast into the fire. By their fruits therefore shall you know them (Mt 7:19, 20).

Many will say to Me in that day, Lord ... have we not prophesied in your name, ... and in your name done many mighty things? But I shall confess to them then, I know you not, depart from Me, you who work iniquity (Mt 7:22, 23).

Everyone who hears my words and does them I shall liken to a prudent man who built a house on a rock: ... but everyone who hears my words but does not do them shall be likened to a foolish man who built his house on the ground without a foundation (Mt 7:24, 26; Lu 6:46-49).

[2] The Son of man will come in the glory of His Father ... and render then to everyone according to his deeds (Mt 16:27).

The kingdom of God shall be taken away from you, and given to a people bringing forth its fruits (Mt 21:43).

Jesus said, These are My mother and brothers who hear the Word of God and do it (Lu 8:21).

Then shall you begin to stand ... and knock at the door, saying, Lord, ... open to us, but replying He will say to them, I know not whence you are; depart from Me, all you workers of iniquity (Lu 13:25-27).

Those who have done good shall go out into the resurrection of life, but those who have done evil into the resurrection of judgment (Jn 5:29).

[3] We know ... that God does not hear sinners, but if a man worships God and does His will, him He hears (Jn 9:31).

If you know these things, blessed are you if you do them (13:17).

He who has My commandments and does them, he it is who loves Me, ... and I will love him, ... and I will come to him, and make an abode with him (14:15, 21-24).

You are My friends, if you do whatsoever I command you.... I have chosen you ... that you may bear fruit and that your fruit may remain (15:14, 16).

[4] The Lord said to John, Write to the angel of the Ephesian church, I know your works: ... I have against you that you have left an earlier charity; ... repent, and do the former works; else ... I shall remove your candlestick from its place (Apoc 2:1, 2, 4, 5).

To the angel of the church of the Smyrneans write, I know your works (2:8, 9).

To the angel of the church in Pergamos write, ... I know your works, repent (2:12, 13, 16).

To the angel of the church in Thyatira write, ... I know your works and charity, ... and your later works are more than the first (2:18, 19).

To the angel of the church in Sardis write, ... I know your works, that you have a name that you are alive, but you are dead; ... I have not found your works perfect before God; ... repent (3:1-3).

To the angel of the church in Philadelphia write, I know your works (3:7, 8).

To the angel of the church of the Laodiceans write, I know your works; ... repent (3:14, 15, 19).

I heard a voice from heaven saying, Write, blessed are the dead who die in the Lord from now on; ... their works follow them (14:13).

A book was opened, which is the book of life, and the dead were judged, ... all according to their works (20:12, 13).

Lo, I come quickly, and My reward is with Me, to give to everyone according to his work (22:12).

These are passages in the New Testament;

[5] there are still more in the Old, from which I shall quote only this one:

Stand in the gate ... of Jehovah, and proclaim this word there: Thus says Jehovah Zebaoth the God of Israel, Make your ways good, and your works; ... put not your trust in lying words, saying, The temple, the temple, the temple of Jehovah is this. ... Thieving and killing and committing adultery and swearing falsely ... will you then come to stand before Me in this house which is called by My name and say, We are delivered? When you do those abominable things? Has not this house been made a den of robbers? Even I, lo, I have seen it, is the word of Jehovah (Je 7:2-4, 9-11).

Section 7

IT IS A LAW OF DIVINE PROVIDENCE THAT MAN SHALL NOT BE COMPELLED BY EXTERNAL MEANS TO THINK AND WILL, THUS TO BELIEVE AND LOVE WHAT PERTAINS TO RELIGION, BUT BRING HIMSELF AND AT TIMES COMPEL HIMSELF TO DO SO

This law of divine providence follows from the preceding two, namely: man is to act in freedom according to reason (nn. 71-99); and is to do this of himself and yet from the Lord, thus as of himself (nn. 100-128). Inasmuch as being compelled is not to act in freedom according to reason and also not to act of oneself, but to act from what is not freedom and from someone else, this law of divine providence follows in due order on the first two. Everyone knows that no one can be forced to think what he is unwilling to think or to will what he decides not to will, thus to believe what he does not believe, least of all what he wills not to believe, or to love what he does not love and still less what he wills not to love. For the spirit or mind of man enjoys complete freedom in thinking, willing, believing and loving. It does so by influx which is not coercive from the spiritual world (for the human spirit or mind is in that world); and not by influx from the natural world, received only when the two agree.

[2] A man can be driven to say that he thinks and wills, believes and loves what is religious, but if this is not a matter of his affection and reasoning or does not become so, he does not think, will, believe or love it. A man may also be compelled to speak in favor of religion and to act according to it, but he cannot be compelled to think in its favor from any faith or to will in its favor out of love for it. In countries in which justice and judgment are guarded, one is indeed compelled not to speak or act against religion, but still no one can be compelled to think and will in its favor. For everyone has freedom to think and to will along with, and in favor of, hell or along with, and in favor of, heaven. Reason, however, teaches what either course is like and what lot awaits it, and by reason the will has the choice and decision.

[3] Plainly, then, what is external cannot coerce what is internal; nevertheless it happens sometimes, but that it works harm will be shown in this order:

i. No one is reformed by miracles and signs, for they coerce. ii. No one is reformed by visions and communication with the dead, for they coerce. iii. No one is reformed by threats and penalties, as these coerce. iv. No one is reformed in states of no rationality or no freedom. v. Self-compulsion is not contrary to rationality and freedom. vi. The external man is to be reformed through the internal, and not the other way about.

(i) No one is reformed by miracles and signs, for they coerce. We have shown above that man has an internal and an external of thought, and that the Lord acts into the external by the internal in man and so teaches and leads him; also that it is of the Lord's divine providence that man is to act in freedom according to reason. Either action would perish in man if miracles were done and he were driven by them to believe. That this is so can be seen rationally in this way: undeniably miracles induce belief and powerfully persuade a person that what the miracle-doer says and teaches is true, and at first this engages man's external of thought, virtually holding it spellbound. But one is deprived by this of the two faculties called rationality and liberty, thus cannot act in freedom according to reason, nor can the Lord then inflow into the external of man's thought through the internal save only to leave man to confirm from his rationality what has been made a matter of his belief by the miracle.

[2] The state of man's thought is such that from the internal of thought he can see a piece in the external of his thought as in a mirror--for as was said above, one can behold one's own thought, which is possible only from more interior thought. Beholding the item as in a mirror he can turn it this way and that and shape it to look attractive to him. If there is truth in it, it may be likened to an attractive and animated maiden or youth. But if a man cannot turn it this way and that and shape it, but only believe it persuaded of it by a miracle, then if there is truth in it, it may be likened to a maiden or youth carved in stone or wood, in which is nothing alive. It may also be compared to an object which is constantly in view and looked at alone, keeps one from seeing what is to either side and behind it. It can also be compared to a continual sound in the ear, which does away with perceiving the harmony of many sounds. Such are the blindness and deafness induced on the mind by miracles. It is the same with anything confirmed but not regarded from rationality before it is confirmed.

Plain it is from this that a faith induced by miracles is not faith, but persuasion. For it has nothing rational in it, still less anything spiritual, as it is only external without an internal. This is true of everything a man does from such persuasive faith, whether he is acknowledging God, worshiping Him at home or in church, or doing good deeds. When only a miracle leads a person to acknowledgment of God and to adoration and piety, he acts from the natural and not the spiritual man. For a miracle infuses belief by an external and not an internal way, thus from the world and not from heaven. The Lord enters man by an internal way, by the Word and by doctrine and preaching from it. As miracles close this way, no miracles are done today.

That miracles are of this nature can be clearly established from those performed in the presence of the people of Judah and Israel. Although they beheld many miracles in the land of Egypt and later at the Red Sea and others in the Wilderness and particularly on Mt. Sinai when the Law was promulgated, nevertheless, in a month's time while Moses tarried on that mountain, they made themselves a golden calf and hailed it as Jehovah who had led them out of the land of Egypt (Ex 32:4-6). Again, it is plain from the miracles done later in the land of Canaan; nevertheless the people fell away time and again from the prescribed worship. It is equally plain from the miracles which the Lord did before their eyes when He was in the world; yet they crucified Him.

[2] Miracles were done among the Jews and Israelites because they were altogether external men and had been brought into the land of Canaan merely to represent a church and its eternal verities by the externalities of worship--something a bad man as well as a good man can do. For the externals

are rituals which with that people signified spiritual and celestial things. Indeed Aaron, although he made the golden calf and ordered worship of it (Ex 32:2-5, 35), could still represent the Lord and His work of salvation. As the people could not be brought by the internal things of worship to represent them, they were brought to do so by miracles--in fact, were driven and forced to it.

[3] They could not be led by internals of worship because they did not acknowledge the Lord although the entire Word which they had treats of Him alone. One who does not acknowledge the Lord cannot receive anything internal in worship. But miracles ceased after the Lord had manifested Himself and was received and acknowledged as eternal God in the churches.

The effect of miracles on the good and on the evil differs, however. The good do not desire miracles, but believe those in the Word. If they hear of some miracle, they regard it only as a slight indication confirming their faith; for they draw their thought from the Word and thus from the Lord, and not from a miracle. It is different with the evil. They can be driven and compelled, of course, to belief, to worship, too, and to piety, but only for a little while. For their evils are enclosed, and the lusts of those evils and the enjoyments of the lusts continually press against the outward worship and piety; and in order that the evils may come out of their confinement and burst forth, the wicked ponder the miracle, finally call it ridiculous and a ruse or a natural phenomenon, and so return to their evils. One who returns to his evils after having worshiped profanes the truths and goods of worship, and the lot of profaners after death is the worst of all fates. They are meant by the Lord's words in Matthew (12:43-45) about those whose last state is worse than the first. Besides, if miracles were to be done for those who have no faith from the miracles in the Word, they would have to be done constantly and before their eyes. It may be plain from all this why miracles are not done at this day.

(ii) No one is reformed by visions or by communication with the dead, for they coerce. Visions are of two kinds, divine and diabolic. Divine visions are effected by representations in heaven; diabolic by magic in hell. There are also phantasmal visions, which are illusions of an estranged mind. Divine visions, produced as we said by representative things in heaven, are such as the prophets had who at the time were not in the body but in the spirit, for visions cannot appear to anyone in bodily wakefulness. When these came to the prophets, therefore, it is remarked that they were "in the spirit," as is plain from the following:

Ezekiel said, The Spirit picked me up and carried me to Chaldea to the captivity in a vision of God, in the spirit of God; so the vision rose over me which I saw (11:1, 24).

Again that the Spirit bore him between earth and heaven and brought him to Jerusalem in visions of God (8:3, 4).

He was likewise in visions of God or in the spirit when he saw four beasts which were cherubim (1 and 10).

So, too, when he saw a new temple and a new earth, and an angel measuring them (40-48).

That he was in "visions of God" then, he says at 40:2, 26, and that he was "in the spirit" at 43:5.

[2] Zechariah was in a similar state when he saw

a horseman among myrtle trees (1:8 ff)
four horns (1:18) and a man with a measuring line in his hand (2:1ff)
a candlestick and two olive trees (4:1 ff)
a flying roll and an ephah (5:1, 6)
four chariots coming out between two mountains, and horses (8:1 ff).
In a like state was Daniel when he saw
four beasts coming up from the sea (7:1 ff)
a combat between a ram and a he-goat (8:1 ff).

That he saw these things "in the vision of his spirit" is stated at 7:1, 2, 7, 13; 8:2; 10:1, 7, 8, and that the angel Gabriel was seen by him in a "vision" at 9:21.

[3] John was also in the vision of the spirit when he beheld what he has described in the Apocalypse, as when he saw
seven candlesticks and the Son of man in the midst of them (1:12-16)
a throne in heaven, and One sitting on the throne, and around it four beasts, which were cherubim (4)
the book of life taken by the Lamb (5)
horses coming out from the book (6)
seven angels with trumpets (8)
the pit of the abyss opened, and locusts coming out a dragon, and its battle with Michael (12)
two beasts, rising, one from the sea and the other from the land (13)
a woman seated on a scarlet beast (17)
Babylon destroyed (18)
a white horse, and One seated on it (19)
a new heaven and a new earth, and the holy Jerusalem descending from heaven (21)
the river of the water of life (22).

That he saw these "in the vision of the spirit" is said 1:10; 4:2; 5:1; 6:1; 21:1, 2.

[4] Such were the visions which appeared from heaven to the sight of the spirit of these men, but not to their bodily sight. Such visions do not occur at this day because if they did, they would not be understood inasmuch as they are produced by representations the details of which signify internal things of the church and arcana of heaven. Daniel also foretold (9:24) that they would cease when the Lord came into the world.

Diabolic visions, however, have occurred at times, incited by fanatical and visionary spirits who in their delirium called themselves the Holy Spirit. But those spirits have now been gathered together by the Lord and cast into a hell separate from the hells of others. There are also phantasmal visions which are merely the illusions of an estranged mind.

All this makes clear that no one can be reformed by any visions other than those in the Word.

The fact that no one is reformed by communication with the dead is plain from the Lord's words about the rich man in hell and Lazarus in Abraham's bosom.

For the rich man said, I ask you, father Abraham, to send Lazarus to my father's house, for I have five brothers, to testify to them lest they also come into this place of torment. Abraham said to him, They have Moses and the prophets;

let them hear them. But he said, No, father Abraham, but if some one will go to them from the dead, they will repent. He replied, If they do not hear Moses and the prophets, they will not be persuaded either if one should arise from the dead (Lu 16:27-31).

Communication with the dead would have the same result as miracles (of which just above), namely, that a man would be influenced and driven into worship for a short time. But as this deprives a man of rationality and at the same time shuts his evils in, as was said above, the captivation or the inward bond is undone, and the imprisoned evils break out, with blasphemy and profanation; this last occurs, however, only when spirits introduce something dogmatic from religion, which is never done by a good spirit, still less by an angel of heaven.

Nevertheless, speech with spirits--rarely with angels of heaven--is possible and has been granted to many for ages. When it is granted, spirits speak with a man in his native tongue and briefly. And those who speak with the Lord's permission never say anything that takes away the freedom of the reason, nor do they instruct, for the Lord alone teaches man, doing so by means of the Word to the man's enlightenment (of this in numbers to come). I have been given to know this in my own experience. I have spoken with spirits and angels for many years now. No spirit has dared and no angel has wished to tell me, still less to instruct me, about things in the Word or about any of its doctrine. The Lord alone has taught me, who revealed Himself to me and afterwards continued to appear to me as He does now, as the Sun in which He is, as He appears to the angels, and He has enlightened me.

(iii) No one is reformed by threats or penalties, as these coerce. It is known that the external cannot compel the internal, but the internal can compel the external; also that the internal refuses to be coerced by the external and turns away. It is likewise known that external enjoyments entice the assent and love of the internal; and it may also be known that there is a forced internal and a free internal. But all this, though known, needs to be lighted up, for much on being heard is perceived at once to be so, because it is truth and hence is affirmed, but if it is not confirmed by reasons, it can be weakened by arguments from fallacies and finally denied. What we have said is known, is therefore to be taken up afresh and established rationally.

[2] First: The external cannot compel the internal, but the internal can compel the external. Who can be forced to believe or love? One can no more be compelled to believe than he can be compelled to think that something is so when he thinks it is not so, or to love than to will something that he does not will; belief attaches to thought, and love to the will. The internal can be compelled, however, by what is external not to speak improperly against the laws of a kingdom, the morals of life or the sanctities of the church. The internal can be compelled to this by threats and penalties and is compelled and should be. But this is not the specifically human internal, but one which the human being shares with beasts; they can also be compelled. The human internal resides above this animal internal. Here the human internal which cannot be coerced is meant.

[3] Second: The internal refuses to be coerced by the external and turns away. The reason is that the internal wills to be in freedom and loves freedom.

For, as was shown, freedom attaches to man's love and life. When the internal feels it is being subjected to compulsion, therefore, it withdraws as it were into itself, averts itself, and regards the compulsion as its enemy. For the love which makes man's life is irritated and causes him to think that he is then not himself and has no life of his own. The internal of the human being is of this nature by the law of the Lord's divine providence that he shall act from freedom in accord with reason.

[4] Plainly, then, it does harm to compel men to divine worship by threats and penalties. Some permit themselves to be forced to religion, some do not. Many who do are adherents of Catholicism; but this is the case with those in whom there is nothing internal in worship, but all is external. Among those who do not allow themselves to be coerced are many of the English nation, and as a result there is what is internal in their worship and what is external is from the internal. Their interiors in respect to religion appear in the light of the spiritual world like bright clouds, but those of the former like dark clouds. The one and the other appearance is to be seen in that world, and one who wishes may see it when he enters that world on death. Furthermore, enforced worship shuts one's evils in, which are hidden then like fire in wood under ashes which keeps stirring and spreading until it bursts into flame. But worship, not enforced but spontaneous, does not shut evils in; these are therefore like a fire that flares up and goes out. Thence it is plain that the internal refuses to be forced by the external and turns away. The internal can compel the external because it is like a master and the external like a servant.

[5] Third: External enjoyments entice assent and love from the internal. Enjoyments are of two kinds, of the understanding or of the will. Enjoyments of the understanding are also enjoyments of wisdom, and those of the will also enjoyments of love; for wisdom belongs to the understanding and love to the will. Enjoyments of the body or of the senses, which are external pleasures, act as one with the internal enjoyments, which are enjoyments of the understanding and the will. Therefore, just as the internal is so averse to compulsion by the external as to turn away, it looks so kindly on enjoyment in the external that it turns to it. Assent follows on the part of the understanding, and love on the part of the will.

[6] In the spiritual world all children are introduced by the Lord into angelic wisdom and through this into heavenly love by delightful and charming means, first by pretty things in the home and the charms of a garden; then by representations of spiritual things affecting the interiors of their minds with pleasure; and finally by truths of wisdom and goods of love. Thus they are steadily led by enjoyments in due order, first by the enjoyments of a love of the understanding and of its wisdom, and then by the enjoyments of the love of the will which is their life's love, to which all else that has entered through enjoyment is kept subordinate.

[7] This is done because the will and understanding must all be formed by what is external before they are formed by what is internal, for they are formed first by what enters by the physical senses, chiefly the sight and the hearing; then when a first will and understanding have been formed, the internal of thought regards them as the externals of its thinking, and either joins itself to them or separates itself from them, as they are or are not enjoyable to it.

[8] It should be well understood, however, that the internal of the understanding does not unite itself to the internal of the will, but it is the latter that unites itself to the former and causes reciprocal union. This is done by the internal of the will, not at all by the internal of the understanding. Hence it is that man cannot be reformed by faith alone, but by the love of the will which makes a faith for itself.

[9] Fourth: There is a forced internal and a free one. A forced internal is found in those who are in external worship only and in none that is internal. Their internal consists of thinking and willing what the external is coerced to. Such are persons who worship living or dead men or idols, or who rest their faith on miracles. No internal is possible with them which is not at the same time external. And yet a forced internal is possible with persons in internal worship; it may be forced by fear or compelled by love. That forced by fear is found in those who worship for fear of the torment and fire of hell. This internal is not the internal of thought of which we have treated, however, but an external of thought called internal here because it partakes of thought. The internal of thought of which we have treated cannot be forced by any fear; it can be compelled by love and by fear of failing to love. In the true sense fear of God is nothing else. To be compelled by love and by the fear of failing in it is self-compulsion, and self-compulsion, it will be seen in what follows, is not contrary to freedom and rationality.

It is plain then what forced worship and unforced worship are like. Forced worship is corporeal, inanimate, obscure and sad--corporeal because it is of the body and not of the mind; inanimate because it has no life in it; obscure for lack of understanding in it; and sad because it does not have the joy of heaven in it. But worship not forced and real is spiritual, living, seeing and joyful--spiritual, because spirit from the Lord is in it; living, because life from Him is in it; seeing because wisdom from Him is in it; and joyful because heaven from Him is in it.

(iv) No one is reformed in states of no liberty or rationality. We showed above that only what a man does in freedom according to reason is made his. This is because freedom belongs to the will and reason to the understanding; acting in freedom in accord with reason a man acts from the will by the understanding and what is done in the union of the two is appropriated. Now, since the Lord wills that a man be reformed and regenerated in order that eternal life or the life of heaven may be his, and none can be reformed or regenerated unless good is appropriated to his will and truth to his understanding as if they were his, and only that can be appropriated which is done in freedom of the will and in accord with the reason of the understanding, no one is reformed in states of no freedom or rationality. There are many such states, but they may be summarized as states of fear, misfortune, mental illness, physical disease, ignorance, and intellectual blindness. Something will be said of each.

No one is reformed in a state of fear because fear takes away freedom and reason or liberty and rationality. Love opens the mind's interiors but fear closes them, and when they are closed man thinks little and only what comes to the lower mind or to the senses. All fears that assail the lower mind have this effect.

[2] We showed above that man has an internal and an external of thought. Fear can never invade the internal of thought; this is always in freedom, being

in a man's life-love. But it can invade the external of thought. When it does, the internal of thought is closed and thereupon man can no longer act in freedom in accord with his reason, nor be reformed.

[3] The fear which invades the external of thought and closes the internal is chiefly fear of losing standing or profit. Fear of civil penalties or of outward ecclesiastical penalties does not close the internal, for the laws respecting them pronounce penalties only on those who speak and act contrary to the civil requirements of the kingdom and the spiritual of the church, but not on those who think contrary to them.

[4] Fear of infernal punishment invades the external of thought, to be sure, but only for some moments, hours or days; it is soon restored to its freedom by the internal of thought, which is man's spirit and life-love and is called thought of the heart.

[5] Fear of losing one's standing or wealth, however, does invade man's external of thought, and when it does, closes the internal of thought above to influx from heaven and makes it impossible for man to be reformed. This is because everyone's life-love from birth is love of self and the world, and self-love is at one with the love of position, and love of the world with the love of wealth. When a man has position or wealth, therefore, for fear of losing them he strengthens the means at hand--whether civil or churchly and in either case means to power--which serve him for position and wealth. The man who does not yet have standing or wealth but aspires to them, does the same, but for fear he will lose the reputation they give.

[6] It was said that this fear seizes on the external of thought and closes the internal above to heaven's inflowing. The internal is said to be closed when it makes one completely with the external, as it is then not in itself but in the external.

[7] But as the loves of self and the world are infernal loves and the fountain-heads of all evils, it is plain what the internal of thought in itself is like with men in whom those loves reign and are their life's loves, namely, that it is full of lusts of evils of every kind.

[8] This men do not know who fear loss of place and opulence and are strongly persuaded of their special religion, most particularly if this promises that they may be worshiped as holy and also as governors of hell; they can blaze, as it were, with zeal for the salvation of souls and yet this is from infernal fire. As this fear especially takes away rationality itself and liberty itself, which have a heavenly origin, plainly it makes against the possibility that a man may be reformed.

No one is reformed in a state of misfortune if he thinks about God and implores help only then, for it is a coerced state; wherefore, on coming into a free state he returns to his former state when he thought little if at all about God. It is different with those who feared God in a state of freedom previously. For by "fearing God" is meant fearing to offend Him, and by "offending Him" to sin, and this comes not from fear but from love. Does not one who loves another fear to hurt him? And the more he loves him, the more he fears hurting him? Lacking this fear, love is insipid and superficial, of the mind only and not of the will. By states of misfortune states of despair in danger are meant, in battles, for example, duels, shipwreck, falls, fires, threatening or unexpected loss of property, also of office or standing, and similar mishaps. To think about God only then is not to think from God but from self. For then the mind is as it were imprisoned in the body, so is not in freedom nor possessed then of rationality, and without these reformation is impossible.

No one is reformed in a state of mental illness because such illness takes away rationality and thus the liberty of acting in accord with reason. The whole mind is sick and not sane; the sane mind is rational, but not a sick one. Such disorders are melancholy, a spurious or a false conscience, fantasies of different kinds, mental grief over misfortune, anxiety and anguish of the mind over a bodily defect. Sometimes these are regarded as temptations, but they are not. Genuine temptations have spiritual objects in view and in them the mind is wise, but these states are concerned with natural objects and in them the mind is disordered.

No one is reformed in a state of bodily sickness because his reason is not then in a state of freedom; the state of the mind depends on that of the body. When the body is sick, the mind is also, if for no other reason because it is withdrawn from the world. Withdrawn from the world it thinks indeed about God but not from Him, for it is not possessed of freedom of the reason. Man has this freedom in being midway between heaven and the world, thus can think from heaven and from the world, likewise from heaven about the world and from the world about heaven. So when he is ill and thinks about death and the state of his soul after death, he is not in the world but is withdrawn in spirit. In this state by itself no one can be reformed, but he can be strengthened in it if he was reforming before he fell ill.

[2] It is similar with those who renounce the world and all occupation in it and give themselves only to thoughts about God, heaven and salvation; on this further elsewhere. If those of whom we were speaking have not been reformed before their illness, then if they die they become such as they were before their illness. It is vain, therefore, to suppose that one can repent or receive some faith in illness; for no deed accompanies the repentance, and there is no charity in the faith; each is oral only and not at all from the heart.

No one is reformed in a state of ignorance, for all reformation is by truths and a life according to them. Therefore those who do not know truths cannot be reformed, but if they long for them with affection for them, after they die they undergo reformation in the spiritual world.

Nor can one be reformed in a state of blindness of the understanding. These also have no knowledge of truths or consequently of life, for the understanding must teach truths and the will must do them; when the will does what the understanding teaches, a man has life in accord with truths. When the understanding is blind, however, the will also is indifferent and acts in freedom according to one's reason only to do the evil confirmed in the understanding, and the confirmation is falsity. Besides ignorance, a religion which teaches a blind faith also blinds the understanding; so does a false doctrine. For just as truths open the understanding, falsities close it. They close it above and open it below, and opened only below, the understanding cannot see truths but only confirm what a man wills, falsity especially. The understanding is also blinded by lusts of evil. As long as the will is in these, it moves the understanding to confirm them, and so far as they are confirmed, the will cannot be in affections of good, from these see truths, and so be reformed.

[2] Take, for instance, one who is in the lust of adultery: his will, which is in the enjoyment of his love, moves his understanding to confirm it, saying, "What is adultery? Is there any evil in it? Does not the like occur between husband and wife? Cannot offspring be born of it, too? Cannot a woman receive more than one without harm? How does anything spiritual enter into this?" So thinks the understanding which is then the courtesan of the will. So stupid is it made by debauchery with the will that it is unable to see that marital love is spiritual and heavenly love itself, a reflection of the love between the Lord and the church from which it is derived; is in itself sacred and chastity itself, purity and innocence; causes men to be forms of love, since partners can love each other from inmosts and so form themselves into loves; nor can it see that adultery destroys this form and with it the Lord's image; and what is abhorrent, that the adulterer mingles his life with that of the husband in the wife, for a man's life is in the seed.

[3] Because this is profane, hell is called adultery, and heaven on the other hand is called marriage. Furthermore, the love of adultery communicates with the lowest hell, but true marital love with the inmost heaven; the reproductive organs of both sexes also correspond to societies of the inmost heaven. These things are adduced so that it may be known how blinded the understanding is when the will is in the lust of evil, and that no one can be reformed in a state of blindness of the understanding.

(v) *Self-compulsion is not contrary to rationality and liberty.* We have shown that man has an internal and an external of thought; that they are distinguishable as prior and subsequent or higher and lower; and that being so distinct they can act separately and also jointly. They act separately when a man speaks and acts from the external of his thought otherwise than he thinks and wills inwardly; they act jointly when he speaks and acts as he thinks and wills. The latter is common with the sincere, the former with the insincere.

[2] Inasmuch as the internal and the external of the mind are so distinct, the internal can even fight with the external and by combat drive it to compliance. Conflict arises when the man deems evils to be sins and resolves to desist from them. When he desists, a door is opened and the lusts of evil which have occupied the internal of thought are cast out by the Lord and affections of good are implanted in their place. This occurs in the internal of thought. But the enjoyments of evil lust which occupy the external of thought cannot be cast out at the same time; conflict arises therefore between the internal and the external of thought. The internal wants to cast out those enjoyments because they are enjoyments of evil and do not agree with the affections of good in which the internal now is, and wants to introduce in their place enjoyments of good which do agree. These are what are called goods of charity. From the disagreement comes the conflict which, if it grows severe, is called temptation.

[3] Now as man is man by virtue of the internal of his thought, for this is his very spirit, obviously he compels himself when he compels the external of his thought to comply or to receive the enjoyments of his affections or the goods of charity. Plainly this is not contrary to rationality and liberty but in accord with them; rationality starts the combat and liberty follows it up; liberty itself resides

with rationality in the internal man and from that in the external.

[4] Accordingly, when the internal conquers, which it does when it has reduced the external to compliance and obedience, man is given liberty itself and rationality itself by the Lord, for he is delivered by the Lord then from infernal freedom which in itself is enslavement, is brought into heavenly freedom which is freedom in itself, and is given association with angels. The Lord Himself teaches (John 8:31-36) that those who are in sins are enslaved and that He delivers those who receive truth from Him through the Word.

Let an example serve for illustration. A man who has taken pleasure in defrauding and deceiving sees and inwardly acknowledges it to be sin and resolves to desist from it; with this a battle begins of his internal with the external. The internal man is in an affection for honesty, but the external still in the enjoyment of defrauding. This enjoyment, utterly opposed to enjoyment in honesty, does not give way unless forced to do so and can be forced to do so only by combat with it. When the fight is won, the external man comes into the enjoyment of a love of honesty, which is charity. Then the pleasure of defrauding gradually turns unpleasant to him. It is the same with all other sins, with adultery and whoredom, revenge and hatred, blasphemy and lying. The most difficult battle of all is with the love of ruling from self-love. A person who subdues this love, easily subdues all other evil loves, for this is their summit.

Let it be told briefly how the Lord casts out lusts of evil occupying the internal man from birth and in their place bestows affections of good when a man on his part removes the evils as sins. It was shown earlier that man possesses a natural, a spiritual and a celestial mind, that he is only in the natural mind as long as he is in lusts of evil and their enjoyments, and that during this time the spiritual mind is closed. But as soon as a man on self-examination confesses evils to be sins against God because they are contrary to divine laws and accordingly resolves to desist from them, the Lord opens the spiritual mind, enters the natural by affections of truth and good, enters the reason, and by the reason puts into order what is disordered below in the natural. It is this that strikes the man as a battle, and strikes those who have indulged much in enjoyments of evil as temptation, for when the order of its thinking is inverted the lower mind suffers pain.

Inasmuch as the battle is against what is in the man himself and what he feels to be his, and no one can fight against himself except from a more interior self and from freedom in it, it follows that the internal man fights against the external and does so from freedom, and compels the external to obey. This, then, is compelling oneself, and, clearly, it is not contrary to liberty and rationality, but in accord with them.

Everyone desires to be free, moreover, and to be rid of the unfree or servitude. The boy under a master wishes to be his own master and thus free; so every man-servant under his master or maid under her mistress. Every girl wishes to leave the paternal home and marry, to do freely in a home of her own; and every boy who desires to work, enter business, or hold some position wishes to be released from his subordination to others and to be at his own disposal. All of these who serve willingly in order to be free compel themselves, and in doing so act from freedom according to reason but from an inner freedom, by which outward freedom is regarded as servant. We add this to confirm the fact that self-compulsion is not contrary to rationality and liberty.

One reason why man does not wish in like manner to come out of spiritual servitude into spiritual freedom is that he does not know what either is; he does not have the truths to teach this, and without them spiritual servitude is believed to be freedom and spiritual freedom to be servitude. A second reason is that the religion of Christendom has closed the understanding, and "faith alone" has sealed it shut. Each has built an iron wall around itself in the dogma that theological matters transcend and cannot be approached by the reason, but are for the blind and not the seeing. So truths that would teach what spiritual liberty is have been hidden. A third reason is that few examine themselves and see their sins, and one who does not see and quit them is in the freedom that sins have, which is infernal freedom, in itself enslavement. To view heavenly freedom, which is genuine freedom, from that freedom is like trying to see daylight in pitch darkness or sunshine from under a black cloud. So it happens that it is not known what heavenly freedom is, or that the difference between it and infernal freedom is like the difference between what is living and what is dead.

(vi) The external man is to be reformed by the internal, and not the other way about. By internal and external man the same is meant as by external and internal of thought, of which frequently before. The external must be reformed by the internal because the internal flows into the external and not the reverse. The learned world knows that what is spiritual flows into what is natural and not the reverse, for reason dictates it; the church knows that the internal man must first be cleansed and made new and the external by it then, because the Lord teaches it. He does so in the words:

Woe to you . . . hypocrites, for you make the outside of the cup and platter clean, but the inside is full of extortion and excess. Blind Pharisee, cleanse first the inside of the cup and platter that the outside may also be made clean (Mt 23:25, 26).

We have shown in a number of places in the treatise Divine Love and Wisdom that reason dictates this. For what the Lord teaches He grants man to see rationally. This a man does in two ways: in one, he sees in himself that something is so upon hearing it; in the other, he grasps it by reasons for it. Seeing in oneself takes place in the internal man, and understanding through reasoning in the external man. Who does not perceive it within himself when he hears that the internal man is to be purified first and the external by it? But one who does not receive the general idea of this by influx from heaven may go astray when he consults the external of this thought; from it alone no one sees but that outward works of charity and piety are saving apart from the internal. It is so in other things, as that sight and hearing flow into thought, and smell and taste into perception, that is, that the external flows into the internal, when the contrary is true. The appearance that what is seen and heard flows into the thought is a fallacy, for the understanding does the seeing in the eye and the hearing in the ear, and not the other way about. So it is in all else.

Footnotes

111-1 The Greek is simply "on a woman" and does not have the word here rendered "of another." Though Swedenborg quotes the verse several times in his works he seems not to have checked as he usually did beyond the rendering of the Schmidius Latin Bible which he used.

But something should be said here on how the internal man is reformed and by it the external. The internal man is not reformed solely by knowing, understanding and being wise, consequently not by thinking only; but by willing what these teach. When a person knows, understands and has the wisdom to see that heaven and hell exist and that all evil is from hell and all good from heaven, and if he then does not will evil because it is from hell but good because it is from heaven, he has taken the first step in reformation and is on the threshold from hell to heaven. When he advances farther and resolves to desist from evils, he is at the second step in reformation and is out of hell but not yet in heaven; this he beholds above him. There must be this internal for man to be reformed, but he is not reformed unless the external is reformed as well as the internal. The external is reformed by the internal when the external desists from the evils which the internal sets its will against because they are infernal, and still further reformed when the external shuns and fights against the evils. Thus the internal provides the will, the external the deed. For unless a man does the deed he wills, inwardly he does not will it, and finally he wills not to do it.

[2] One can see from these few considerations how the external man is reformed by the internal. This is also meant by the Lord's words to Peter:

Jesus said, If I do not wash you, you have no part with Me. Peter said to Him, not my feet only but my hands and head. Jesus said to him, he who has been washed has no need except to have his feet washed, and is entirely clean (Jn 13:8-10).

By "washing" spiritual washing is meant, which is purification from evils; by "washing head and hands" purifying the internal man is meant, and by "washing the feet" purifying the external. That when the internal man has been purified, the external must be, is meant by this: "He who has been washed has no need except to have his feet washed." That all purification from evils is the Lord's doing, is meant by this, "If I do not wash you, you have no part with Me." We have shown in many places in Arcana Caelestia that with the Jews washing represented purification from evils, that this is signified by "washing" in the Word, and that purification of the natural or external man is signified by the "washing of feet."

Since man has an internal and an external and each must be reformed for the man to be reformed, and since no one can be reformed unless he examines himself, sees and admits his evils, and then quits them, not only the external is to be examined, but the internal as well. If a man examines only the external he sees only what he has committed to deed, and that he has not murdered or committed adultery or stolen or borne false witness, and so on. He examines bodily evils and not those in his spirit; yet evils of the spirit are to be examined if one is to be capable of reformation. Man lives as a spirit after death and all the evils in his spirit persist. The spirit is examined only when a man attends to his thoughts, above all to his intentions, for these are thoughts from the will. There the evils exist at their source and roots, that is, in their lusts and enjoyments. Unless they are seen and acknowledged, a man is still in evils though he may not have committed them outwardly. That to think with intention is to will and do, is plain from the Lord's words:

If any one has looked on another's woman to lust after her, he has already committed adultery with her in his heart (Mt 5:28). 152-1

Such self-examination is of the internal man, and from it the external man is truly examined.

I have often marveled that although all Christendom knows that evils must be shunned as sins and otherwise are not forgiven, and that if they are not forgiven there is no salvation, yet scarcely one person among thousands understands this. Inquiry was made about this in the spiritual world, and it was found to be so. Anyone in Christendom knows it from the exhortations, read out to those who attend the Holy Supper, in which it is publicly stated; and yet when asked whether they know it, they reply that they do not know it and have not known it. The reason is that they have paid no attention to it, and most say they have thought only about faith and salvation by faith alone. I have also marveled that "faith alone" has closed their eyes so that those who have confirmed themselves in it do not see anything in the Word when they read it about love, charity and works. It is as though they spread "faith" all over the Word, as red lead is spread over writing so that nothing underneath shows; if anything does show, it is absorbed by faith and declared to be faith.

Section 8

IT IS A LAW OF DIVINE PROVIDENCE THAT MAN SHALL BE LED AND TAUGHT BY THE LORD OUT OF HEAVEN BY MEANS OF THE WORD AND DOCTRINE AND PREACHING FROM IT, AND THIS TO ALL APPEARANCE AS OF HIMSELF

The appearance is that man is led and taught by himself; in reality he is led and taught by the Lord alone. Those who confirm the appearance in themselves and not the reality at the same time are unable to remove evils from themselves as sins, but those who confirm the appearance and at the same time the reality can do so; for evils are removed as sins apparently by the man, but really by the Lord. The latter can be reformed, but the former cannot.

[2] All who confirm the appearance in themselves and not the reality also, are idolaters inwardly, for they are worshipers of self and the world. If they have no religion they become worshipers of nature and thus atheists; if they have some religion they become worshipers of men and of images. Such are meant now in the first commandment of the Decalog under those who worship other gods. Those, however, who confirm in themselves the appearance and also the reality become worshipers of the Lord, for He raises them out of what is their own, in which the appearance is, conducts them into the light in which the reality is and which is the reality, and gives them to perceive inwardly that they are not led and taught by themselves but by Him.

[3] The rational capacity of the two may seem much the same to many, but it differs. In those who are at once in the appearance and the reality, it is a spiritual reasoning ability, but in those in the appearance but not at the same time in the reality it is a natural reasoning ability; this can be likened to a garden in winter light, and the spiritual reasoning capacity to a garden in springtime light. But If these things more in what follows, in this order:

i. Man is led and taught by the Lord alone. ii. He is led and taught by the Lord alone through and from the angelic heaven. iii. He is led by the Lord through influx and taught through enlightenment. iv. Man is taught by the Lord through the Word and doctrine and preaching from it, thus immediately by Him alone. v. Man is led and taught in externals by the Lord to all appearance as of himself.

(i) Man is led and taught by the Lord alone. This flows as a general consequence from all that was demonstrated in the treatise Divine Love and Wisdom; from what was said in Part I about the Lord's divine love and wisdom; in Part II about the sun of the spiritual world and the sun of the natural world; in Part III about degrees; in Part IV about the creation of the universe; and in Part V about the creation of the human being.

Man is led and taught by the Lord alone in that he lives from the Lord alone; for his life's will is led, and his life's understanding is taught. But this is contrary to the appearance, for it seems to man that he lives of himself, and yet the truth is that he lives from the Lord and not from himself. Man cannot, however, be given a sense-perception of this while he is in the world (the appearance that he lives of himself is not taken away, for without it man is not man). This must be established by reasons, therefore, which are then to be confirmed from experience and finally from the Word.

That the human being has life from the Lord alone and not of himself is established by these considerations: 1. There is an only essence, substance and form from which all the essences, substances, and forms exist that have been created. 2. The one essence, substance and form is divine love and wisdom from which is all that is referable to love and wisdom in man. 3. It is also good itself and truth itself to which all things are referable. 4. Likewise it is life, from which is the life of all and all things of life. 5. Again the only One and very Self is omnipresent, omniscient and omnipotent. 6. This only One and very Self is the Lord-from-eternity or Jehovah.

[2] 1. There is an only essence, substance and form from which all the essences, substances, and forms exist that have been created. This was demonstrated in the treatise Divine Love and Wisdom (nn.44-46). In Part II it was shown that the sun of the angelic heaven, which is from the Lord and in which He is, is the one sole substance and form from which all that has been created exists, also that nothing can exist or come into existence except from it. In Part III it was shown that all things arise from that sun by derivations according to degrees.

[3] Who does not perceive by the reason and acknowledge that there is some one essence from which is all essence, or one being from which is all being? What can exist apart from being, and what can being be from which is all other being except being itself? Being itself is also unique and is being in itself. Since this is so (and anyone perceives and acknowledges it by reason, or if not, can do so), what else follows than that this Being, the Divine itself, Jehovah, is all in all in what is or comes to be?

[4] It is the same if we say there is an only substance from which all things are, and as there is no substance without form there is a single form from which all things are. We have shown in the treatise mentioned above that the sun of the angelic heaven is that substance and form, also shown how that essence, substance and form is varied in things created.

[5] 2. The one essence, substance and form is divine love and wisdom from which is all that is referable to love and wisdom in man. This also was fully demonstrated in the treatise Divine Love and Wisdom. Whatever appears to live in man is referable to will and understanding in him; any-one can perceive by the reason and acknowledge that these two constitute his life. What else is "This I will," or "This I understand," or "I love this," or "I think this"? And as man wills what he loves, and thinks what he understands, all things of the will relate to love and those of the understanding to wisdom. As no one has love or wisdom from himself but only from Him who is love itself and wisdom itself, they are from the Lord-from-eternity or Jehovah. If they were not, man would be love itself and wisdom itself, thus God-from-eternity, at which the human reason itself is horrified. Can anything exist except from a prior self? Or the prior self exist except from one prior to it? And finally from a first or from underived being?

[6] 3. It is also good itself and truth itself, to which all things are referable. Everyone possessed of reason agrees and acknowledges that God is good itself and truth itself, likewise that all good and truth are from Him, therefore that any good and truth can come only from good itself and truth itself. All this is acknowledged by every rational person when he first hears it. When it is said, then, that everything of the will and understanding, of love and wisdom, or of affection and thought in a man who is led by the Lord relates to good and truth,

it follows that all that such a man wills and understands or loves and has for his wisdom, or is affected by and thinks, is from the Lord. Hence anyone in the church knows that whatever good and truth a man has in himself is not good and truth except as it is from the Lord. Since this is true, all that such a man wills and thinks is from the Lord. It will be seen in following numbers that an evil man can will and think from no other source.

[7] 4. *The one essence, substance and form is likewise life, from which is the life of all and all things of life.* This we have shown in many places in the treatise *Divine Love and Wisdom.* At the first hearing the human reason also agrees and acknowledges that all man's life is that of the will and understanding, for if these are taken away he ceases to live, or what is the same, that all his life is one of love and thought, for if these are taken away he does not live. Inasmuch as all of the will and understanding or all of love and thought in man is from the Lord, all of his life, as we said above, is from Him.

[8] 5. *This only One and very Self is omnipresent, omniscient and omnipotent.* This also every Christian acknowledges from his doctrine and every gentile from his religion. In consequence, wherever he is, a man thinks that God is there and that he prays to God at hand; thinking and praying so, men cannot but think that God is everywhere, that is, omnipresent; likewise omniscient and omnipotent. Everyone praying to God, therefore, implores Him from the heart to lead him because He can lead him; thus he acknowledges the divine omnipresence, omniscience and omnipotence, doing so in turning his face to the Lord; thereupon the truth flows in from the Lord.

[9] 6. *This only One and very Self is the Lord-from-eternity or Jehovah.* In *Doctrine of the New Jerusalem about the Lord* it was shown that God is one in essence and in person and that He is the Lord, and that the Divine itself, called Jehovah Father, is the Lord-from-eternity; that the Divine Human is the Son conceived by His Divine from eternity and born in the world; and that the proceeding Divine is the Holy Spirit. He is called "very Self" and "only One" because, as was said, the Lord-from-eternity or Jehovah is life itself, being love itself and wisdom itself or good itself and truth itself, from which are all things. That the Lord created all things from Himself and not from nothing may be seen in the treatise *Divine Love and Wisdom* nn. 282-284, 349-357. So the truth that the human being is led and taught by the Lord alone is established by reasons.

This same truth is established in angels not only by reasons but also by living perceptions, especially with angels of the third heaven. They perceive the influx of divine love and wisdom from the Lord. Perceiving it and in their wisdom aware that love and wisdom are life, they declare that they live from the Lord and not of themselves, and not only say so but love and will it so. Yet they are in the full appearance that they live of themselves, yes, more strongly in the appearance than other angels. For as was shown above (nn. 42-45) the more nearly one is united with the Lord, the more distinctly does he seem to himself to be his own, and the more plainly is he aware that he is the Lord's. For many years now it has been granted me to be in a similar simultaneous perception and appearance, and I am fully convinced that I will and think nothing from myself but that it only appears to be from myself; it has also been granted to love and will it so. The same truth may be established by much else from the spiritual world, but these two references must suffice now.

It is plain from the following passages in the Word that life is the Lord's alone.

I am the resurrection and the life; he who believes in Me, though he die, shall live (Jn 11:25).

I am the way and the truth and the life (Jn 14:6).

The Word was God ... and in Him was life; and the life was the light of men (Jn 1:1, 4).

"The Word" in this passage is the Lord.

As the Father has life in Himself, so has he given the Son to have life in Himself (Jn 5:26).

From the following it is clear that man is led and taught by the Lord alone: Without Me you can do nothing (Jn 15:5).

A man cannot receive anything unless it is given him from heaven (Jn 3:27).

A man cannot make one hair white or black (Mt 5:36).

By "hair" in the Word the least of all is signified.

It will be shown in what follows in an article of its own that the life of the wicked has the same source; now this will merely be illustrated by a comparison. Heat and light flow in from the sun of the world alike to trees bearing bad fruit and to trees bearing good fruit, and they are alike quickened and grow. The forms into which the heat flows make the difference, not the heat in itself. It is the same with light, which is turned into various colors according to the forms into which it flows. The colors are beautiful and gay or ugly and sombre, and yet it is the same light. It is so with the influx of spiritual heat which in itself is love, and with spiritual light which in itself is wisdom, from the sun of the spiritual world. The forms into which they flow cause diversity, but not in itself that heat which is love or that light which is wisdom. The forms into which these flow are human minds. It is clear from these considerations that man is led and taught by the Lord alone.

What the life of animals is, however, was shown above (nn. 74, 96), namely that it is a life of merely natural affection with its attendant knowledge, and a mediated life corresponding to the life of human beings in the spiritual world.

(ii) Man is led and taught by the Lord alone through the angelic heaven and from it. We say "through" the angelic heaven and from it, but that He does so "through" the angelic heaven is the apparent fact, while "from it" is the reality. The Lord seems to lead and teach through the angelic heaven because He appears above that heaven as a sun, but the reality is that He does so from heaven because He is in heaven as the soul is in man. For the Lord is omnipresent and not in space, as was shown above. Therefore distance is an appearance according to conjunction with Him, and the conjunction is according to the reception of love and wisdom from Him. Since no one can be conjoined to the Lord as He exists in Himself He appears to angels at a distance as a sun; nevertheless He is in the angelic heaven as the soul is in man. He is similarly in every society of heaven and in every angel, for man's soul is not only the soul of man as a whole but also of every part of him.

[2] It is according to the appearance that the Lord governs all heaven and through it the world from the sun which is from Him and in which He is (about the sun see Part II of the treatise Divine Love and Wisdom), and everyone is

allowed to speak according to the appearance, cannot, in fact, do otherwise. Everyone who is not in wisdom itself is also allowed to think that the Lord rules each and all things from His sun and rules the world through the angelic heaven. Angels of the lower heavens think from the appearance, but those of the higher heavens speak indeed in keeping with the appearance but think from the reality, namely, that the Lord rules the universe from the angelic heaven, that is, from Himself.

[3] One can illustrate by the sun of the world that simple and wise speak alike but do not think alike. All speak from the appearance that the sun rises and sets. Despite speaking so the wise think it stands still, which is again the reality, as the other is the appearance. The same thing can be illustrated from appearances in the spiritual world, for space and distance appear there but are dissimilarities of affections and of resulting thoughts. The same is true of the Lord's appearing in His sun.

We shall say briefly how the Lord leads and teaches everyone from the angelic heaven. In the treatise Divine Love and Wisdom and above in the present treatise, also in the work Heaven and Hell, published in London in the year 1758, it has been made known from things seen and heard that the angelic heaven appears before the Lord as one man, and each society of heaven likewise, and it is from this that each angel or spirit is a human being in complete form. It was also shown in the treatises mentioned that heaven is not heaven from anything belonging to the angels but from their reception of divine love and wisdom from the Lord. Hence it may be evident that the Lord rules the whole angelic heaven as one man, and since heaven is itself man, it is the very image and likeness of the Lord and the Lord rules it as the soul rules its body. Since all mankind is ruled by the Lord, it is ruled by the Lord not through heaven, but from heaven, consequently by Him, for He is heaven, as we have said.

This is an arcanum of angelic wisdom, however, and therefore cannot be comprehended by man unless his spiritual mind has been opened; for such a man, who is united with the Lord, is an angel. From what has preceded he can comprehend the following:

1. Men as well as angels are in the Lord and the Lord in them according to their conjunction with Him, or, what is the same, according to their reception of love and wisdom from Him. 2. Each of them has a place allotted to him in the Lord, thus in heaven, according to the nature of the conjunction or the reception of Him. 3. Each in his place has a state of his own distinct from that of others and draws his portion from what is had in common according to his situation, function and need, quite as each part does in the human body. 4. Everyone is brought into his place by the Lord according to his life. 5. Every human being is introduced from infancy into this divine man whose soul and life is the Lord, and within it and not outside of it is led and taught from His divine love according to His divine wisdom; but as a man is not deprived of freedom, he can be led and taught only in the measure of his receptiveness as of himself. 6. Those who are receptive are conducted to their places through an infinite maze by winding paths, much as the chyle is carried through the mesentery and the lacteal vessels there to its cistern, and from this into the blood by the thoracic duct, and so to its place. 7. Those who are not receptive are parted from those

within the divine man, as excrement and urine are removed from man.

These are arcana of angelic wisdom which man can comprehend to some extent; there are many more which he cannot.

(iii) Man is led by the Lord through influx and taught through enlightenment. Man is led through influx by the Lord because "being led" and "flowing in" are spoken of love and the will; and he is taught by the Lord through enlightenment because "being taught" and "enlightened" are spoken of wisdom and the understanding. It is known that every person is led by himself from his own love and according to it by others, and not by his understanding. He is led by his understanding and according to it only as his love or his will prompts the understanding, and then it can be said that his understanding is led also. Even then the understanding is not led, but the will which prompts it.

The term "influx" is used because it is commonly said that the soul flows into the body; influx is spiritual and not physical, as we showed above, and man's soul or life is his love or will. For another reason, influx is comparatively like the flow of the blood into the heart and from the heart into the lungs. We showed in the treatise Divine Love and Wisdom that the heart corresponds to the will and the lungs correspond to the understanding, and that the conjunction of the will with the understanding is like the flowing of the blood from the heart to the lungs.

Man is taught, however, through enlightenment; being taught and being enlightened are said of the understanding. For the understanding or man's internal sight is enlightened by spiritual light quite as the eye or man's external sight is by natural light. The two are also taught similarly; the internal sight, however, which is that of the understanding, by spiritual objects, and the external sight or the sight of the eye by natural objects. There is spiritual light and natural light, one like the other in outward appearance, but dissimilar in internal appearance. For natural light comes from the sun of the natural world and so is in itself dead, but spiritual light, which is from the sun of the spiritual world, is in itself living. This light, not nature's, enlightens the human intellect. Natural and rational light comes from it and not from nature's light, and is here called natural and rational because it is spiritual-natural.

[2] There are three degrees of light in the spiritual world: celestial, spiritual and spiritual-natural. Celestial light is a flaming, ruddy light and is the light of those who are in the third heaven; spiritual light is a gleaming white light and is the light of those in the middle heaven; and spiritual-natural light is like daylight in our world. This is the light of those who are in the lowest heaven and of those in the world of spirits, which is intermediate between heaven and hell; with the good in that world it is like the light of summer on earth and with the evil like winter's light.

It should be known, however, that light in the spiritual world has nothing in common with light in the natural world; they are as different as what is living and what is lifeless. It is plain, then, from what has been said that it is spiritual light and not the natural light before our eyes that enlightens the understanding. Man does not know this, not having known anything hitherto about spiritual light. In the work Heaven and Hell we have shown (nn. 126-140) that spiritual light has its origin in divine wisdom and truth.

Having spoken about the light of heaven, we should say something about the light of hell. This also is of three degrees. The light in the lowest hell is like that from fiery coals; in the middle hell like that from the flame of a hearth; and in the highest hell like that from candles and to some like moonlight at night. All this is spiritual light and not natural, for all natural light is dead and extinguishes the understanding. As has been shown, those in hell possess the faculty of understanding called rationality; rationality itself comes from spiritual light and not from natural light. The spiritual light which they have in rationality is turned, however, into infernal light, as the light of day is into the dark of night.

[2] Nevertheless, all those in the spiritual world, whether in the heavens or the hells, see in their own light as clearly as man sees in his by day. This is because everyone's eyesight is formed to receive the light in which it finds itself. Thus the eyesight of the angels of heaven is formed to receive the light in which they see, and the sight of the spirits of hell is formed to receive their light; this is comparatively like that of birds of night and bats, which see objects at night and in the evening as clearly as other birds see them by day, for their eyes are formed to receive their light.

[3] The difference between the one light and the other appears very clearly, however, to those who look from one to the other. When, for instance, an angel of heaven looks into hell he sees only thick darkness, and when a spirit of hell looks into heaven he sees only thick darkness there. For heavenly wisdom is like thick darkness to those in hell; in turn, infernal insanity is like thick darkness to those in heaven. It is plain from all this that such as a man's understanding is, such is the light he has, and that after death everyone comes into his own light, for he sees in no other. In the spiritual world, moreover, where all are spiritual even to the body, the eyes of all are formed to see by their own light. Everyone's life-love fashions an understanding for itself and thus a light, also, for love is like the fire of life and from this comes the light of life.

As few know anything about the enlightenment in which the understanding of a man is who is taught by the Lord, something will be said of it. There is inner and outer enlightenment from the Lord, and inner and outer enlightenment from oneself. Inner enlightenment from the Lord consists in man's perceiving on first hearing something whether it is true or not; outer enlightenment consists in thought from this. Inner enlightenment from oneself is simply from confirmation and outer enlightenment merely from information. We will say something of each.

[2] By inner enlightenment from the Lord a rational person perceives about many things the moment he hears them whether they are true or not; for example, that love is the life of faith or that faith lives by love. By interior enlightenment a person also perceives that a man wills what he loves and does what he wills, consequently that to love is to do; again, that a man wills and does whatever he believes from love, and therefore to have faith is also to do; and that the impious man cannot have love for God or faith then in Him. By inner enlightenment a rational man also perceives the following truths at once on hearing them: God is one; He is omnipresent; all good is from Him; all things have relation to good and truth; all good is from good itself and all truth from truth itself. A man perceives these and other similar truths inwardly in himself

on hearing them and does so because he possesses a rationality which is in heaven's enlightening light.

[3] Outer enlightenment is enlightenment of one's thought from this inner enlightenment. One's thought is in this enlightenment so far as it remains in the perception it has from inner enlightenment and so far as it possesses knowledge of good and truth, for it gets from this knowledge reasons confirming it. Thought from outer enlightenment sees a matter on both sides; on the one, it sees reasons which confirm it, and on the other, the appearances that weaken it; it dispels these and assembles the reasons.

[4] Inner enlightenment from oneself, however, is quite different. By it one regards a matter on one side only, and having confirmed it sees it in light apparently like that just spoken of, but it is a wintry light. For example, a judge who judges unjustly in view of gifts or gain, once he has confirmed the judgment by law and reason sees in it nothing but justice. Some judges see the injustice but not wanting to see it, they keep it out of sight and blind themselves and so do not see. The same is true of a judge who renders judgments out of friendship, or to gain favor, or on account of relationship.

[5] Such persons act in the same way in anything they have from a man in authority or from the mouth of a celebrity or have hatched from self-intelligence; they are blind reasoners, for they see from the falsities which they confirm; falsity closes the sight, just as truth opens it. They do not see any truth in the light of truth nor justice from a love for it but from the light of confirmation, which is an illusory light. They appear in the spiritual world like headless faces or like faces resembling human faces on wooden heads, and are called reasoning animals for rationality is potential in them. Those have outer enlightenment from themselves who think and speak solely from information impressed on the memory; of themselves they can hardly confirm anything.

Such are the differences in enlightenment and consequently in perception and thought. There is actual enlightenment by spiritual light, but it is not manifest to one in the natural world because natural light has nothing in common with spiritual light. This enlightenment has sometimes been manifested to me in the spiritual world, however, visible in those enlightened by the Lord as a luminosity around the head, aglow with the color of the human face. With those in enlightenment from themselves the luminosity was not around the head but around the mouth and over the chin.

Besides these kinds of enlightenment there is another in which it is revealed to one in what faith, intelligence and wisdom he is; he perceives this in himself, such is the revelation. He is admitted into a society where there is genuine faith and true intelligence and wisdom. There his interior rationality is opened, from which he sees the nature of his own faith, intelligence and wisdom, even to avowing it. I have seen some as they returned and heard them confessing that they had no faith although in the world they had believed they had much faith and markedly more than others; they said the same of their intelligence and wisdom. Some were in faith alone and in no charity, and some in self-intelligence.

(iv) Man is taught by the Lord through the Word and doctrine and preaching from it, thus immediately by the Lord alone. We said and showed above that man is led and taught by the Lord alone, and from heaven but not through heaven or any angel there. As it is by the Lord alone, it is done immediately and not mediately. How this takes place will be told now.

It was shown in Doctrine of the New Jerusalem about the Sacred Scripture that the Lord is the Word and that all the doctrine of the church is to be drawn from the Word. Inasmuch as the Lord is the Word the man who is taught from the Word is taught by the Lord alone. This is comprehended with difficulty and will be clarified in this order:

1. The Lord is the Word because the Word is from Him and about Him. 2. Also because the Word is divine truth together with divine good. 3. To be taught from the Word is to be taught from Him, therefore. 4. That this is done mediately through preaching does not take away its immediacy.

[2] First: The Lord is the Word because it is from Him and about Him. No one in the church denies that the Word is from the Lord, but that it is about Him alone, while not denied, is not known. This was shown in Doctrine of the New Jerusalem about the Lord, nn. 1-7, 37-44, and in Doctrine of the New Jerusalem about the Sacred Scripture, nn. 62-69, 80-90, 98-100. Inasmuch as the Word is from the Lord alone and treats of Him alone, a man is taught by the Lord when he is taught from the Word, for it is the divine Word. Who can communicate what is divine and implant it in the heart except the Divine Himself from whom it is and of whom it treats? Therefore, in speaking of His union with His disciples He says that they are to abide in Him and His words in them (Jn 15:7), that His words are spirit and life (Jn 6:63), and that He makes His abode with those who keep His words (Jn 14:20-24). To think from the Lord therefore is to think from the Word, and as it were, through the Word. It was shown in Doctrine of the New Jerusalem about the Sacred Scripture from beginning to end that all things of the Word have communication with heaven, and as the Lord is heaven, this means that all things of the Word have communication with the Lord Himself. The angels of heaven indeed have communication; this, too, is from the Lord.

[3] Second: The Lord is the Word because it is divine truth together with divine good. The Lord teaches that He is the Word by these words in John:

In the beginning was the Word, and the Word was with God, and the Word was God . . . and the Word was made flesh and dwelt among us (1:1, 14).

This passage has been understood hitherto to mean only that God teaches men through the Word and has been explained as an hyperbole, with the implication that the Lord is not the Word itself. This is because expositors did not know that the Word is divine truth together with divine good or, what is the same, divine wisdom together with divine love. That these are the Lord Himself was shown in the treatise Divine Love and Wisdom, Part I, and that they are the Word in Doctrine of the New Jerusalem about the Sacred Scripture, nn. 1-86.

[4] We will say briefly in what way the Lord is divine truth together with divine good. Each human being is human not because of face and body but from the good of his love and the truths of his wisdom; and because a man is a man from these, he is also his own good and his own truth or his own love and his own wisdom; without these he is not a human being. But the Lord is good itself and truth itself or, what is the same, love itself and wisdom itself; and these are the Word which in the beginning was with God and was God and which was

made flesh.

[5] Third: To be taught from the Word, then, is to be taught by the Lord Himself. For it means that one is taught from good itself and truth itself or from love itself and wisdom itself, and, as we have said, these are the Word. But everyone is taught according to an understanding agreeing with his love; what goes beyond this does not remain. All who are taught by the Lord in the Word are instructed in a few truths while in the world but in many when they become angels. For the interiors of the Word, which are divine spiritual and divine celestial, are implanted at the time, but are not consciously possessed until a man on his death is in heaven where he is in angelic wisdom which, compared with human wisdom, thus his earlier wisdom, is ineffable. That divine spiritual and divine celestial things which constitute angelic wisdom are present in each and all things of the Word see Doctrine of the New Jerusalem about the Sacred Scripture, nn. 5-26.

[6] Fourth: That this teaching is done mediately through preaching does not take away the immediacy. Inevitably the Word is taught mediately by parents, teachers, preachers, books and particularly by reading. Still it is not taught by them but by the Lord through them. Preachers, aware of this, say that they speak not from themselves but from the spirit of God and that all truth like all good is from God. They can speak it and bring it to the understanding of many, but not to anyone's heart; and what is not in the heart passes away from the understanding; by "heart" a man's love is meant. From this it is plain that man is led and taught by the Lord alone and immediately by Him when he is taught from the Word. This is a supreme arcanum of angelic wisdom.

We have shown in Doctrine of the New Jerusalem about the Sacred Scripture (nn. 104-113) that those outside the church who do not have the Word still have light by means of it. Man has light by means of the Word and from the light has understanding, and both the wicked and the good have understanding. It follows that from light in its origin there is light in its derivatives which are perceptions and thoughts on whatever subject. The Lord says that without Him men can do nothing (Jn 15:5); that a man can receive nothing unless it is given him from heaven (Jn 3:27); and that the Father in the heavens makes His sun to rise on the evil and the good, and sends rain on the just and on the unjust (Mt 5:45). In the Word in its spiritual sense by "sun" here, as elsewhere, is meant the divine good of divine love and by "rain" the divine truth of divine wisdom. These are extended to the evil and the good, to the unjust and the just, for if they were not, no one would possess perception and thought. It was shown above that there is only one Life from which all have life. But perception and thought are part of life; they are therefore from the same fountain from which life springs. It has been shown many times before that all the light which forms the understanding is from the sun of the spiritual world, which is the Lord.

(v) Man is led and taught in externals by the Lord to all appearance as of himself. This is so of man's externals, but not inwardly. No one knows how the Lord leads and teaches man inwardly, just as no one knows how the soul operates so that the eye sees, the ear hears, the tongue and mouth speak, the heart circulates the blood, the lungs breathe, the stomach digests, the liver and the pancreas distribute, the kidneys secrete, and much else. These processes do not come to man's perception or sensation. The same is true of what the Lord does in the infinitely more numerous interior substances and forms of the mind. The Lord's activity in these is not apparent to man, but many of the effects are, as well as some of the causes producing the effects. It is in the externals that man and the Lord are together, and as the externals make one with the internals, cohering as they do in one series, no disposition can be made by the Lord except in keeping with the disposition made in the externals with man's participation.

[2] Everyone knows that man thinks, wills, speaks and acts to all appearance as of himself, and everyone can see that without this appearance man would have no will and understanding, thus no affection and thought, also no reception of any good and truth from the Lord. It follows that without this appearance there would be no rational conception of God, no charity and no faith, consequently no reformation and regeneration, and therefore no salvation. Plainly, this appearance is granted to man by the Lord for the sake of all these uses and particularly that he may have the power to receive and reciprocate so that the Lord may be united to him and he to the Lord, and that through this conjunction the human being may live forever. This is "appearance" as it is meant here.

Section 9

IT IS A LAW OF DIVINE PROVIDENCE THAT MAN SHALL NOT PERCEIVE OR FEEL ANY OF THE ACTIVITY OF DIVINE PROVIDENCE, AND YET SHOULD KNOW AND ACKNOWLEDGE PROVIDENCE

The natural man who does not believe in divine providence thinks to himself, "What can divine providence be when the wicked are promoted to honors and gain wealth more than the good, and many such things go better with those who do not believe in divine providence than with the good who believe in it? Indeed, infidels and the impious can inflict injuries, loss, misfortune and sometimes death on the believing and pious, doing so, too, by cunning and malice." He thinks therefore, "Do I not see in full daylight, as it were, in actual experience that crafty schemes prevail over fidelity and justice if only a man can make them seem trustworthy and just by a clever artfulness? What is left except necessities, consequences and the fortuitous in which there is no semblance of divine providence? Does not nature have its necessities, and are not consequences causes arising from natural or civil order, while the fortuitous comes, does it not, from unknown causes or from none?" So the natural man thinks to himself who attributes all things to nature and nothing to God, for one who ascribes nothing to God ascribes nothing to divine providence either; God and divine providence make one.

[2] But the spiritual man speaks and thinks within himself quite otherwise. Although he does not perceive the course of divine providence by any thought or feel it from any sight of it, he still knows and acknowledges providence. Inasmuch as the appearances and resulting fallacies just mentioned have blinded the understanding, and this can receive sight only when the fallacies which have induced the blindness and the falsities which have induced the darkness are dispelled, and since this can be done only by truths which have the power to dispel falsities, these truths are to be disclosed, and for distinctness let it be in this order:

i. If man perceived or felt the activity of divine providence he would not act in freedom according to reason, nor would anything appear to be his own doing. It would be the same if he foreknew events. ii. If man saw divine providence plainly, he would inject himself into the order and tenor of its course, and pervert and destroy them. iii. If man beheld divine providence plainly he would either deny God or make himself god. iv. Man can see divine providence on the back and not in the face; also in a spiritual, not a natural state.

(i) If man perceived or felt the activity of divine providence he would not act in freedom according to reason, nor would anything appear to be his own doing. It would be the same if he foreknew events. In given articles we made evident to the understanding that it is a law of providence that man should act in freedom according to reason; also that all which a man wills, thinks, speaks and does shall seem to be his own doing; that without this appearance a man would have nothing of his own nor be his own man. He would thus have no selfhood and nothing could be imputed to him, and in that case whether he did good or evil would not matter, and whether he believed in God or was under the persuasion of hell would be immaterial; in a word, he would not be a human being.

[2] We have now to show that man would have no liberty to act according to reason and there would be no appearance of self-activity if he perceived or felt the activity of divine providence, for if he did he would also be led by it. The Lord leads all men by His divine providence and man only seemingly leads himself, as was shown above. If, therefore, man had a lively perception or sense of being led, he would not be conscious of living life and would be moved to make sounds and act much like a graven image. If he were still conscious of living he would be led like one bound in manacles and fetters or like a yoked animal. Who does not see that man would have no freedom then? And without freedom he would be without reason, for one thinks from and in freedom; whatever he does not so think seems to him to be not from himself but from someone else. Indeed if you consider this interiorly you will perceive that he would not possess thought, still less reason, and hence would not be a human being.

The Lord's divine providence is constantly seeking to withdraw man from evils. If a man perceived or felt this constant activity and yet was not led like one bound, would he not struggle against it continually and then either quarrel with God or mingle himself in divine providence? If he did the latter he would also make himself God; if he did the former he would free himself from constraint and deny God. Manifestly two forces would constantly be acting then against each other, the force of evil from man and the force of good from the Lord. When two opposites act against each other, one of them conquers or they both perish. In this instance if one conquers they both perish. For the evil, which is man's, does not let in good from the Lord in a moment, nor does good from the Lord cast out evil from man in a moment; if either was done in a moment no life would be left to man. These and many other harmful results would follow if man manifestly perceived or felt the operation of divine providence. This will be demonstrated clearly by examples in what follows.

Man is not given a foreknowledge of events for the same reason, namely, that he may be able to act in freedom according to reason. It is well known that man wants what he loves effected, and he guides himself to this end by reasoning. It is also known that what a man meditates in his reason comes from his love of giving it effect through thought. If, then, he knew the effect or the eventuality by divine prediction, his reason would become inactive and with it his love; for love along with reasoning ends with the effect, to begin anew. It is reason's very enjoyment to envision with love the effect in thought, not after it is attained but before it is, not in the present but as future. So man has what is called hope, which rises and declines in the reason as he beholds or awaits the event. The enjoyment is fulfilled in the event and then is forgotten along with thought about the event. The same thing would occur with an event that was foreknown.

[2] The human mind dwells always in the trine called end, cause and effect. If one of these is lacking, the mind is not possessed of its life. An affection of the will is the initiating end; the thought of the understanding is the efficient cause;

and bodily action, utterance or external sensation is the effect from the end by means of the thought. Anyone sees that the human mind is not possessed of its life when it is only in an affection of the will and in naught besides, or when it is only in an effect. The mind has no life from one of these separately, therefore, but from the three together. The life of the mind would diminish and depart if an event were foretold.

As a foreknowledge of future events takes away humanness itself, which is action in freedom in accord with one's reason, no one is given to know the future; but everyone is allowed to form conclusions by the reason about the future; the reason is then fully in its own life. Accordingly man does not know his lot after death or know any event until he is on it. For if he knew, he would no longer think from his inner self how he should act or live so as to meet it, but would think only from his exterior self that he was meeting it. This state closes the interiors of his mind where the two faculties of his life, liberty and reason, especially reside. A desire to know the future is born with most persons but has its origin in a love of evil. It is taken away, therefore, from those who believe in divine providence; and trust that the Lord disposes their lot is given them. Therefore they do not desire to know it beforehand lest they inject themselves in some way into divine providence. The Lord teaches this in many sayings in Luke (12:14-48).

[2] Much from the world of the spirit can confirm that this is a law of divine providence. On entering that world after death most persons desire to know their lot. The answer they receive is that if they have lived well their lot is in heaven and if wickedly it is in hell. But as all, including the wicked, fear hell they ask what they should do and believe to get into heaven. They are answered that they are to do and believe as they will, but know that one does not do good or believe truth in hell, only in heaven. "As you can, seek what is good and true, thinking truth and doing good." Everyone is thus left to act in freedom according to reason in the spiritual world as he is in the natural world; but as one has acted in this world he acts in that, for everyone's life remains to him and so his lot awaits him, for this is his life's lot.

(ii) If man saw divine providence plainly he would inject himself into the order and tenor of its course and pervert and destroy them. To bring this distinctly to the perception of the rational man and also of the natural man, it will be illustrated by examples in this order:

1. External things are so connected with internal things that they make one in all that is done. 2. The human being joins the Lord only in some external things and if he did in internal things also, he would pervert and destroy the whole order and tenor of the course of divine providence.

As we said, these points will be illustrated by examples.

[2] First: External things are so connected with internal things that they make one in all that is done. Let this be illustrated by examples from several things in man's body. Everywhere in it are things external and internal. The external are called skins, membranes and coverings; the internal are forms variously composed and woven of nerve fibres and blood vessels. The covering over these enters into them by extensions from itself even to the inmost, so that the external or the covering unites with the internals or the organic forms of fibres and vessels. It follows that the internals act and are acted on as the

external acts or is acted on. For they are all constantly bound up together.

[3] Take such a common covering in the body as the pleura, for example, which covers the chest cavity and the heart and lungs. Examine it in an anatomical view, or if you do not know anatomy consult anatomists, and you will learn that this general covering by various circumvolutions and finer and finer extensions from itself enters into the inmost parts of the lungs, even into the smallest bronchial branches and into the sacs themselves which are the beginnings of the lungs, not to mention its subsequent progress by the trachea into the larynx and toward the tongue. From this it is plain that there is a constant connection of the outmost with inmosts; the interiors from the inmosts on therefore act and are acted upon as the external acts or is acted on. For this reason when that outmost covering, the pleura, is congested, inflamed or ulcerated, the lungs labor from their inmost parts; if the disease grows worse, all action of the lungs ceases and the man dies.

[4] The same is true everywhere else in the body. For instance it is true of the peritoneum, the general covering of all the abdominal viscera, also of the coverings on such organs severally as the stomach, liver, pancreas, spleen, intestines, mesentery, kidneys, and the organs of generation in both sexes. Choose any one of these viscera, examine it yourself or consult those skilled in the science, and you will see or hear. Take the liver, for example; you will find there is a connection between the peritoneum and that organ and by its covering with its inmost parts. For the covering puts out constant extensions from itself and insertions towards the interiors and thus continues to inmosts and as a result the whole is bound together. The entire form acts or is acted upon in such manner as the covering acts or is acted upon. The same is true of the rest of the organs. For what is general and what is particular or the universal and the singular in a form act together by a marvelous connection.

[5] You will see below that what occurs in natural forms and their processes, which relate to motion and actions, occurs similarly in spiritual forms and in the changes and variations of their state, which relate to activities of the will and the understanding. Inasmuch as man joins the Lord in certain external activities and no one is deprived of the liberty of acting according to reason, the Lord can act in internals only as, together with man, He does in externals. If man does not shun and turn away from evils as sins, therefore, the external and at the same time the internal of his thought and will are infected and destroyed, comparatively as the pleura is by the disease in it called pleurisy, of which the body dies.

[6] Second: If man were in internals at the same time he would pervert and destroy the whole order and tenor of divine providence. Examples from the human body will illustrate this also. If man knew all the workings of the two brains into the fibres, of the fibres into the muscles and of the muscles into actions, and by this knowledge were to have the disposition of them as he disposes his deeds, would he not pervert and destroy all?

[7] If man knew how the stomach digests, and how the surrounding organs take their portion, work the blood and distribute it where needed for life, and if he had the disposing of these as he has of external activities, such as eating and drinking, would he not pervert and destroy all? When he cannot handle the external, seemingly a single thing, without destroying it by luxury and

intemperance, what would he do if he had the disposal of the internals, infinite in number? Lest man enter into them by any volition and have control of them, things internal are therefore taken entirely away from the will except for the muscles, which are a covering; moreover, how these act is not known, only that they do.

[8] The same can be said of other organs. To give examples: if man had the disposing of the interiors of the eye for seeing, those of the ear for hearing, or the tongue for tasting, those of the skin for feeling, those of the heart for systolic action, of the lungs for breathing, of the mesentery to distribute the chyle, or of the kidneys for secretion, the interiors of the organs of generation for propagation, or those of the womb for perfecting an embryo, and so on, would he not pervert and destroy the ordered course of the divine providence in them in innumerable ways? As we know, man is in externals, for example sees with the eye, hears with the ear, tastes with the tongue, feels with the skin, breathes with the lungs, impregnates a wife, and so on. Is it not enough for him to know the externals and dispose them for health of body and mind? When he cannot do this, what would happen if he disposed internals also? It may be plain from this that if man saw divine providence plainly, he would inject himself into the order and tenor of its course and pervert and destroy them.

The like occurs in the spiritual things of the mind to what occurs in the natural things of the body for the reason that all things of the mind correspond to all things of the body. For the same reason the mind actuates the body in externals and generally does so completely. It moves the eyes to see, the ears to hear, the mouth and tongue to eat and drink, also to speak, the hands to do, the feet to walk, the generative organs to propagate. The mind not only moves the externals in these ways but the internals, too, in their whole series, outmosts from inmosts and inmosts from outmosts. Thus while moving the mouth to speak, it moves lungs, larynx, glottis, tongue and lips at the same time, each separately to its especial function, and the face suitably also.

[2] It is clear then that the same can be said of the spiritual forms of the mind as was said of the natural forms of the body, and the same can be said of the spiritual activities of the mind as was said of the natural activities of the body. Consequently the Lord orders the internals as a man does the externals, in one way if the man orders the externals of himself and in another if he orders them under the Lord and at the same time as of himself. The mind of man is also in its total organization a man, for it is his spirit which appears after death altogether as a human being as in the world; hence there are similar things in mind and body. Thus what has been said about the conjunction of externals with internals in the body is to be understood of the conjunction of externals with internals in the mind, with the sole difference that the latter is spiritual and the former is natural.

(iii) If man beheld divine providence plainly he would either deny God or make himself god. The merely natural man says to himself, "What is divine providence? Is it anything else or more than an expression which people get from a priest? Who sees anything of it? Is it not by prudence, wisdom, cunning and malice that all things are done in the world? Is not all else necessity or consequence? And does not much happen by chance? Does divine providence lie concealed in this? How can it do so in deceptions and schemes? Yet it is said that divine providence effects all things. Then let me see it and I will believe in it. Can one believe in it until he sees it?"

[2] So speaks the merely natural man, but the spiritual man speaks differently. Acknowledging God he also acknowledges divine providence and sees it, too. He cannot make it manifest, however, to anyone whose thought is on nature only and from nature, for such a person cannot raise his mind above nature, see anything of divine providence in its phenomena, or come to conclusions about providence from nature's laws, which are also laws of divine wisdom. If, therefore, he beheld divine providence plainly, he would sink it in nature and thus not only enshroud it in fallacies but profane it. Instead of acknowledging it he would deny it, and one who denies divine providence in his heart denies God also.

[3] Either one thinks that God governs all things or that nature does. He who thinks that God does thinks that they are ruled by love itself and wisdom itself, thus by life itself; but he who thinks that nature governs all, thinks that all things are ruled by nature's heat and light, although these in themselves are dead, coming as they do from a dead sun. Does not what is itself alive govern what is lifeless? Can what is dead govern anything? If you think that what is lifeless can give life to itself, you are mad; life must come from life.

It does not seem likely that if a man saw divine providence and its activity plainly he would deny God; it would seem that he could not but acknowledge it and thus acknowledge God. Yet the contrary is true. Divine providence never acts in keeping with the love of man's will, but constantly against it. For the human being by force of his hereditary evil is ever panting for the lowest hell, but the Lord in His providence is constantly leading him away and withdrawing him from it, first to a milder hell, then away from hell, and finally to Himself in heaven. This activity of divine providence is perpetual. If, then, man saw or felt this withdrawing and leading away, he would be angered, consider God his enemy, and deny Him on account of the evil of his selfhood. In order that man may not know of it, therefore, he is held in freedom and thereby does not know but that he leads himself.

[2] But let examples serve for illustration. By heredity man wants to become great and also rich. In the measure in which these loves are not checked he wants to become still greater and richer and finally the greatest and richest; even so he would not rest, but would want to become greater than God Himself and possess heaven itself. This lust is hidden deep in hereditary evil and consequently in man's life and in the nature of his life. Divine providence does not remove this evil in a moment; if it were removed in a moment man would cease to live; but divine providence removes it quietly and gradually without man's knowing of it. It does this by letting man act according to the thinking which he deems rational; then by various means, rational and also civil and moral, it leads him away and withdraws him so far as he can be withdrawn in freedom. Nor can evil be removed from anyone unless it comes out and is seen and acknowledged; it is like a wound which heals only when opened.

[3] If, therefore, man knew and saw that the Lord in His divine providence works in this way against his life's love, the source of his highest enjoyment, he could not but go in the opposite direction, be enraged, rebel, say harsh things, and finally, on account of his evil, brush aside the activity of divine providence,

denying it and so denying God. He would do this especially if he saw success thwarted or saw himself lowered in standing or deprived of wealth.

[4] But it is to be known that the Lord in no wise leads man away from seeking position and acquiring wealth, but leads him away from the lust of seeking position solely for the sake of eminence or for his own sake, and also from acquiring wealth for its own sake or just to have it. Leading the man away, He introduces him into the love of uses so that he may regard eminence not for his own sake but for the sake of uses, thus as attached to uses and only so to himself, and not as attached to him and then to the uses; the same applies to wealth. At many places in the Word the Lord Himself teaches that He continually humbles the proud and exalts the humble; what He teaches in it is also of His divine providence.

Any other evil in which man is by heredity is dealt with in like manner, such as adultery, fraud, vengeance, blasphemy and other similar evils, none of which can be removed except as freedom to think and will them is left to man for him to remove them as if of himself. Nevertheless he can do this only as he acknowledges divine providence and prays that it may be done by it. Apart from this freedom and from divine providence at the same time, the evils would be like poison shut in and not driven out, which would spread quickly and consign all parts to death, or would be like disease of the heart itself, from which the whole body soon dies.

The truth of what has been said cannot be better known than from human lives after death in the spiritual world. Very many who had become great or wealthy in the natural world and in their eminence or riches had regarded themselves alone, at first speak of God and divine providence as though they had acknowledged them at heart, but seeing divine providence clearly then and their final lot under it, namely, for them to enter hell, they unite with devils there and not only deny God then but also blaspheme Him. Finally they reach such madness that they acknowledge the more powerful among devils as their gods and desire nothing more ardently than to become gods themselves.

Man would go contrary to God and also deny Him if he saw the activities of God's divine providence plainly, for the reason that man is in the enjoyment of self-love and this enjoyment constitutes his very life. Therefore when man is held in the enjoyment of his life he is in his freedom, for freedom and the enjoyment make one. If, then, he should perceive that he is continually being led away from his enjoyment, he would be enraged as against one who wanted to destroy his life and would hold him to be an enemy. Lest it happen, the Lord in His divine providence does not appear manifestly, but leads man by it as silently as a hidden stream or favorable current does a vessel. Consequently man does not know but that he is steadily in his own, for his freedom and his proprium make one. Hence it is plain that freedom appropriates to him what divine providence introduces, which would not take place if providence were manifest. To be appropriated means to become of one's life.

(iv) Man can see divine providence on the back and not in the face; also in a spiritual state but not in a natural. To see divine providence on the back but not in the face means after it acts and not before. To see it in a spiritual state and not in a natural is to see it from heaven and not from the world. All who receive influx from heaven and acknowledge divine providence, especially those who have become spiritual through reformation, on beholding events taking a wonderful course see providence as it were from an interior acknowledgment and confess it. These do not wish to see it in the face, that is, before it eventuates, fearing that their volition may intrude on something of its order and tenor.

[2] It is otherwise with those who do not admit any influx from heaven but only from the world, especially with those who have become natural by confirming appearances in themselves. They do not see anything of divine providence on the back, that is, after it eventuates, but wish to behold it in the face or before it eventuates; and as divine providence works by means, and these are provided through man or the world, they attribute providence, whether they look it in the face or on the back, to man or to nature, and so confirm themselves in the denial of it. They make this ascription of it because their understanding is closed above, that is, to heaven, and open only below, that is, to the world; one cannot see divine providence in a worldly outlook, only in a heavenly. I have wondered sometimes whether they would acknowledge divine providence if their understanding was opened above and they were to see as in the light of day that nature in itself is dead, and human intelligence in itself nothing, and that it is by influx that either appears to have being. I perceived that those who have confirmed themselves in favor of nature and of human prudence would not make the acknowledgment because the natural light flowing in from below would immediately extinguish the spiritual light flowing in from above.

The man who has become spiritual by acknowledgment of God, and wise by rejection of the proprium, sees divine providence in the world as a whole and in each and all things in it. Looking at natural things, he sees it; at civil things, he sees it; at spiritual things, he sees it; and in things simultaneous as well as successive. He sees it in ends, causes, effects, uses, forms, things great and small. Above all he sees it in the salvation of men, as that Jehovah gave the Word, taught men by it about God and about heaven and hell and eternal life, and Himself came into the world to redeem men and save them. Man sees these and many other things and divine providence in them from spiritual light in natural light.

[2] The merely natural man, however, sees none of these things. He is like a man who sees a magnificent temple and hears a preacher enlightened in divine things, but once home asserts that he saw only a stone building and heard nothing but sounds made. Again, he is like a near-sighted man who steps into a garden remarkable for fruits of every sort and who reports on getting home that he saw only woods and trees. Moreover, when such persons, having become spirits after death, are taken up into the angelic heaven where all objects are in forms representative of love and wisdom, they see none of them, not even that they exist. I have seen this happen with a number who denied the Lord's divine providence.

Many constant things exist, created that inconstant things may exist. Such constants are the ordained changes in the rising and setting of sun, moon and stars; their obscurations by interpositions called eclipses; the heat and light from them; the seasons of the year, called spring, summer, autumn and winter; the times of the day, morning, noon, evening and night; also atmospheres, waters and lands, viewed in themselves; the vegetative force in the plant kingdom, that and the reproductive in the animal kingdom; likewise what is constantly produced when these forces are set in action in accord with the laws of order. These and many more things existing from the creation are provided so that infinitely varying things may exist, for what varies can exist only in what is constant, fixed and certain.

[2] Examples will illustrate this. The varieties of vegetation would not be possible unless sunrise and sunset and the resulting heat and light were constant. Harmonies are infinitely varied, and would not exist unless the atmospheres were constant in their laws and the ear in its form. Varieties of vision, which are also infinite, would not exist unless the ether in its laws and the eye in its organization were constant; equally so, colors, unless light was constant. The same is true of thoughts, words and actions, which are of infinite variety too; they could not exist, either, unless the organic forms of the body were constant. Must not a house be steady for a variety of things to be done in it by a person? So must a temple be for the various acts of worship, preaching, instruction and devout meditation to be possible in it. So in much else.

[3] As for the varieties found in the constant, fixed and certain, they go on to infinity and have no end; no one thing in the whole universe or in any part of it is ever precisely the same as another, nor can be in the progress of things to eternity. Who disposes these varieties which proceed to infinity and eternity so that they have order unless it is He who created what is constant to the end that they may exist in it? And who can dispose the infinite varieties of life among men but He who is life itself, that is, love itself and wisdom itself? Except by His divine providence, which is like a continual creation, can the infinite affections of men and their thoughts thence and thus the men themselves be disposed so as to make one? Evil affections and the thoughts from them to make one devil which is hell, and good affections and the thoughts from them one Lord in heaven? We have said and shown several times before that the whole angelic heaven is like one man in the Lord's sight, an image and likeness of Him, and all hell over against it like one monstrous man. This has been said because some natural men seize on arguments for their madness in favor of nature and of one's own prudence from even the constant and fixed which must exist for the variable to exist in it.

Section 10

THERE IS NO SUCH THING AS ONE'S OWN PRUDENCE; THERE ONLY APPEARS TO BE AND IT SHOULD SO APPEAR; BUT DIVINE PROVIDENCE IS UNIVERSAL BY BEING IN THE LEAST THINGS

That there is no such thing as one's own prudence is contrary to appearances and therefore to the belief of many. Because it is, one who believes, on the strength of the appearance, that human prudence does all things, cannot be convinced except by reasons to be had from a more profound investigation and to be gathered from causes. The appearance is an effect, and causes disclose how it arises. By way of introduction something will be said about the common faith on the subject. Contrary to the appearance the church teaches that love and faith are not from man but from God, so also wisdom and intelligence, therefore prudence also, and in general all good and truth. When this teaching is accepted, one must also agree that there is no such thing as one's own prudence, but there only appears to be. Prudence comes only from intelligence and wisdom and both of these only from the understanding and its grasp of truth and good. All this is accepted and believed by those who acknowledge divine providence, but not by those who only acknowledge human prudence.

[2] Now, either what the church teaches is true, that all wisdom and prudence are from God, or what the world teaches, that they are from man. Can these views be reconciled in any other way than this, that what the church teaches is the truth, and what the world teaches is the appearance? For the church establishes its teaching from the Word, but the world its teaching from the proprium; and the Word is God's, and the proprium is man's. Because prudence is from God and not from man a Christian in his devotions, prays God to lead his thoughts, purposes and actions, and also adds that by himself he cannot. Again, seeing someone doing good, he says the person has been led to it by God; and so about much else. Can anyone speak so unless he inwardly believes it? To believe it inwardly comes from heaven. But when a man deliberates and gathers arguments in favor of human prudence he can believe the contrary, and this is from the world. The internal faith prevails with those who acknowledge God in their hearts; the external faith with those who do not acknowledge Him at heart, however much they may with the lips.

We said that a person who believes, on the strength of the appearance, that human prudence does all things, can be convinced only by reasons to be had from a more profound investigation and gathered from causes. In order, then, that the reasons gathered from causes may be plain to the understanding, let them be put forward in due order as follows:

i. All man's thoughts are from affections of his life's love; there are and can be no thoughts apart from them. ii. The affections of the life's love are known to the Lord alone. iii. Through His divine providence the Lord leads the affections of the life's love of man and at the same time the thoughts, too, from which human prudence comes. iv. By His divine providence the Lord assembles the affections of all mankind into one form--the human form. v. Heaven and hell, which are from mankind, are therefore in such a form. vi. Those who have acknowledged nature alone and human prudence alone make up hell, and those who have acknowledged God and His divine providence make up heaven. vii. All this can be effected only as it appears to man that he thinks from himself and disposes by himself.

(i) All man's thoughts are from affections of his life's love; there are and can be no thoughts apart from them. It has been shown above in this treatise and also in the one entitled Angelic Wisdom about Divine Love and Wisdom, Parts I and V particularly, what the life's love and the affections and the thoughts from them are essentially, and what the sensations and actions arising from them in the body are. Inasmuch as these are the causes from which human prudence issues as an effect, something needs to be said about them here also. For what has been written earlier elsewhere cannot be as closely connected with what is written later as it will be if the same things are recalled and placed with both in view.

[2] Earlier in this treatise, and in that just mentioned about Divine Love and Wisdom, it was shown that in the Lord are divine love and wisdom; that these two are life itself; that from the two man has will and understanding, will from the divine love and understanding from the divine wisdom; that heart and lungs in the body correspond to these two; that this may make plain that as the pulsation of the heart along with the respiration of the lungs rules the whole man as to the body, so the will together with the understanding rules him as to his mind; that thus there are two principles of life in everyone, one natural and the other spiritual, and that the natural principle of life is the heartbeat, and the spiritual is the will of the mind; that each adjoins a consort to itself with which it cohabits and performs the functions of life; and that the heart joins the lungs to itself, and the will the understanding to itself.

[3] Now, as the soul of the will is love, and the soul of the understanding is wisdom, both of them from the Lord, love is the life of everyone and is such life as it has in union with wisdom; or what is the same, the will is the life of everyone and is such life as it has in conjunction with the understanding. More on the subject may be seen above in this treatise and especially in Angelic Wisdom about Divine Love and Wisdom, Parts I and V.

It was also demonstrated in the treatises mentioned that the life's love produces subordinate loves from itself, called affections; that these are exterior and interior; and that taken together they make one dominion or kingdom as it were, in which the life's love is lord or king. It was also shown that these subordinate loves or affections adjoin consorts to themselves, each its own, the interior affections consorts called perceptions, and the exterior consorts called knowledges, and each cohabits with its consort and performs the functions of its life. In each instance, it was shown, the union is like that of life's very being with life's coming forth, which is such that the one is nothing without the other; for what is life's being unless it is active and what is life's activity if it is not from life's very being? The conjunction in life, it was likewise shown, is like that of sound and harmony, of sound and utterance, too, in general like that of the heart's pulsation and the respiration of the lungs, a union, again, such that one without the other is nothing and each becomes something in union with the other. Union must either be in them or come about by them.

[2] Consider, for example, sound. One who thinks that sound is something if there is nothing distinctive in it is much mistaken. It also corresponds to affection in man, and as something distinctive is always in it the affection of a person's love is known from the sound of his voice in speaking, and his thought is known from the varied sounds which speech is. Hence the wiser angels perceive just from the sound of his voice a man's life's love together with some of the affections which are its derivatives. This has been remarked that it may be known that no affection is possible without its thought, and no thought without its affection. More on the subject can be seen above in this treatise and in Angelic Wisdom about Divine Love and Wisdom.

Inasmuch as the life's love has its enjoyment, and its wisdom its pleasure, and likewise every affection, which is essentially a lesser love derived from the life's love like a stream from its source or a branch from a tree or an artery from the heart, therefore every affection has its enjoyment and the perception or thought from it its pleasure. Consequently these enjoyments and pleasures make man's life. What is life without joy and pleasure? It is not animated at all, but inanimate. Reduce enjoyment and pleasure and you grow cold and torpid; take them away and you expire and die. Vital heat comes from the enjoyments of the affections and the pleasures of the perceptions and thoughts.

[2] As every affection has its enjoyment and the thought thence its pleasure, it may be plain whence good and truth are and what they are essentially. Whatever is the enjoyment of one's affection is one's good, and one's truth is what is pleasant to the thought from that affection. For everyone calls that good which he feels in the love of his will to be enjoyable, and calls that truth which he then perceives in the wisdom of his understanding to be pleasant. The enjoyable and the pleasant both flow out from the life's love as water does from a spring or blood from the heart; together they are like an element or the atmosphere in which man's whole mind is.

[3] The two, enjoyment and pleasure, are spiritual in the mind and natural in the body, and in each make man's life. From this it is plain what it is in man that is called good, and what it is that is called truth; likewise what it is in man that is called evil and false; whatever destroys the enjoyment of his affection is evil to him, and what destroys the pleasure of his thought thence is false to him. It is plain, moreover, that evil on account of the enjoyment in it and falsity on account of the pleasure in it may be called good and truth and believed to be good and truth. Goods and truths are indeed changes and variations of state in the forms of the mind, but they are perceived and have life only through the enjoyments and pleasures they have to give. This is noted to make known what affection and thought are in their life.

Inasmuch as it is not the body but man's mind that thinks and that does so from the enjoyment of one's affection, and inasmuch as man's mind is his spirit which lives after death, man's spirit is nothing else than affection and thought therefrom. It is altogether plain from spirits and angels in the spiritual world that thought cannot exist apart from affection, for they all think from the affections of their life's love; the enjoyments of these affections attend each as his atmosphere, and all are united by these spheres exhaled from the affections by their thoughts. The character of each one is known also by the sphere of his life. It may be seen from this that all thought is from an affection and is the form of that affection. The same applies to the relationship between will and understanding, good and truth, and charity and faith.

(ii) The affections of the life's love of man are known to the Lord alone. Man knows his thoughts and his intentions in them because he sees them in himself, and as all prudence is from them, he sees this, too, within him. Then if his life's love is self-love, he comes to take pride in his own intelligence, ascribes prudence to himself, gathers arguments in support of it, and thus recedes from acknowledging divine providence. Much the same happens if love of the world is his life's love, but he does not then recede to the same extent. It is plain from this that these two loves ascribe all things to man and to his prudence and when interiorly examined ascribe nothing to God and to His providence. When persons who do this happen to hear that the reality is that there is no such thing as human prudence, but that divine providence alone governs all things, they laugh at this if they are outright atheists; if they hold something of religion in remembrance and are told that all wisdom is from God, they assent on first hearing it, but inwardly in their spirit deny it. Such especially are priests who love themselves more than God, and the world more than heaven, or what is the same, worship God for position's or riches' sake, and yet have been preaching that charity and faith, all good and truth, all wisdom, too, and in fact prudence are from God and none of them from man.

[2] In the spiritual world I once heard two priests debating with a certain royal ambassador about human prudence whether it is from God or from man, and the debate was heated. The three believed alike at heart, namely, that human prudence does all and divine providence nothing, but the priests in their theological zeal at the moment asserted that there was nothing of wisdom and prudence from man. When the ambassador retorted that there was nothing of thought then, either, they said "yes, nothing of thought." But as angels perceived that the three believed alike, they bade the ambassador, "Put on priestly robes, believe yourself to be a priest, and then speak." He robed himself, believed he was a priest, and thereupon declared in a deep voice that never could there be wisdom or prudence in man save from God. He defended this with the customary eloquence filled with rational arguments. Then the two priests were told, "Put off your robes, put on those of political ministers, and believe that that is what you are." They did so, thought then from their interior selves, and gave voice to the arguments they had entertained inwardly before in favor of human prudence and against divine providence. Upon this the three, believing alike, became warm friends and set out together on the path of one's own prudence, which leads to hell.

It was shown above that man can have no thought except from some affection of his life's love and that the thought is nothing other than the form of the affection. Now, man sees his thought but cannot see his affection, which he feels; it is therefore from sight which dwells on the appearance, and not from affection which does not come into sight but into feeling, that he concludes that one's own prudence does all things. For affection shows itself only in a certain enjoyment of thought and in pleasure ever reasoning about it. This pleasure and enjoyment make one with the thought in those who, from self-love or love of the world, believe in one's own prudence. The thought glides along in its enjoyment like a ship in a river current to which the skipper does not attend, attending only to the sails he spreads.

Man can indeed reflect on what his external affection finds enjoyable when it is also an enjoyment of a bodily sense, but he still does not reflect that that enjoyment comes from the enjoyment of his affection in thought. For example, when a lecher sees a lewd woman his eyes light with a lascivious fire and from this he feels a physical pleasure; he does not, however, feel his affection's enjoyment or that of the lust in his thought, only a strong desire more nearly physical. The same is true of the robber in a forest at sight of travelers and of the pirate at sea on sighting vessels, and so on. Obviously a man's enjoyments govern his thoughts, and the thoughts are nothing apart from them; but he thinks he has only the thoughts, when nevertheless these are affections put into forms by his life's love so that they appear in the light; for all affection has heat for its element and thought has light.

[2] The external affections of thought manifest themselves in bodily sensation, and sometimes in the thought of the mind, but the internal affections of the thought from which the external exist never make themselves manifest to man. Of these he knows no more than a rider asleep in a carriage does of the road or than one feels the rotation of the earth. Now, when man knows nothing of the things beyond number that take place in the interiors of his mind, and the few external things which come to the sight of his thought are produced from the interiors, and the interiors are governed by the Lord alone through His divine providence and the few external by the Lord also together with man, how can anyone assert that one's own prudence does all things? Were you to see just one idea laid open, you would see astounding things, more than tongue can tell.

[3] It is clear from the endless things in the body that there are so many things in the mind's interiors that the number cannot be given, and nothing of them comes to sight or sense except only a much simplified action. Yet to the action thousands of motor or muscular fibres contribute, and thousands of nerve fibres, thousands of blood-vessels, thousands of cells in the lungs which must cooperate in every action, thousands in the brains and in the spinal cord, and many more things still in the spiritual man which is the human mind, in which all things are forms of affections and of perceptions and thoughts from the affections. Does not the soul, which disposes the interiors, dispose the actions also which spring from them? Man's soul is nothing else than the love of his will and the resulting love of his understanding; such as this love is the whole man is, becoming so according to the disposition he makes of his externals in which he and the Lord are together. Therefore, if he attributes all things to himself and to nature, self-love becomes the soul; but if he attributes all things to the Lord, love to the Lord becomes the soul; this love is heavenly, the other infernal.

Inasmuch as the enjoyments of his affections, from inmosts down through interiors to exteriors and finally to outermost things in the body, bear man along as wave and wind bear a ship; and inasmuch as nothing of this is apparent to man except what takes place in the outermost things of the mind and the body, how can he claim for himself what is divine on the strength merely of the fact that those few outermost things seem to be his own? Even less should he claim what is divine for himself, knowing from the Word that a man can receive nothing of himself unless it is given by heaven; and knowing from reason that this appearance has been granted him in order to live as a human being, see what is good and evil, choose between them, and appropriate his choice to himself that he may be united reciprocally with the Lord, be reformed, regenerated and saved, and live forever. It has been stated and shown above that this appearance has been granted to man in order that he may act in freedom according to reason, thus as of himself, and not drop his hands and await influx. From all this it follows that proposition iii to be demonstrated has been confirmed: Through His divine providence the Lord leads the affections of the life's love of man and at the same time the thoughts, too, from which human prudence comes.

Footnotes
152-1 See footnote at n. 111.

iv) By His divine providence the Lord assembles the affections of all mankind into one form--the human form. In a subsequent paragraph it will be seen that this is the universal effort of divine providence. Those who ascribe everything to nature deny God at heart, and those who ascribe everything to human prudence, at heart deny divine providence; the one cannot be separated from the other. Yet both groups for their reputation's sake and for fear of losing it profess in words that divine providence is universal, but say its details fall to man and in their aggregate are grasped by human prudence.

[2] But consider: what is universal providence when the details are taken from it? Is it anything but just an expression? For that is called universal which consists of the total of details as what is general does of particulars. If, then, you remove details, what is the universal except something empty, thus like a surface with nothing underneath or an aggregate without content? If it should be said that divine providence is a universal government but nothing is governed but only held in connection and items of the government are handled by others, can this be called a universal government? No king has such a government. For if a king gave his subjects the government of everything in his kingdom, he would no longer be king, but would only be called king; he would have the standing in name only and not in fact. In the case of such a king one cannot speak of government, still less of universal government.

[3] God's providence is called man's prudence. As universal prudence cannot be said of a king who has only kept the name so that the kingdom may be called a kingdom and be held together, so one cannot speak of universal providence if human beings provide everything by their own prudence. The same is true of the terms "universal providence" and "universal government" in reference to nature when they mean that God created the universe but endowed nature to produce everything from herself. What is "universal providence" then but a metaphysical term, and nothing but a term? Many of those who attribute everything produced to nature and everything accomplished to human prudence and yet profess orally that God created nature, regard divine providence as an empty expression. But the reality is that divine providence is in the least things of nature and of human prudence also and is thereby universal.

The Lord's divine providence is universal by being in the least things in that He created the universe in order that an infinite and eternal creation might come about from Him, and it does as He forms a heaven from mankind which in His sight is like one humanity, His image and likeness. We showed above (nn. 27-45) that heaven formed of human beings is such in His sight; that this was the purpose of creation; and that the divine regards what is infinite and eternal in all that it does (nn. 46-69). The infinite and eternal to which the Lord looks in forming His heaven from mankind is the growth of it to infinity and eternity and thus His dwelling constantly in the purpose of His creation. This infinite and eternal creation the Lord provided for in creating the universe and He pursues it steadily in His divine providence.

[2] Can anyone who knows and believes from the church's doctrine 202-1 that God is infinite and eternal be so lacking in reason that he does not agree on hearing it that God can then regard only what is infinite and eternal in the great work of His creation? To what else can He look from His infinite being?

To what else in mankind of which He forms His heaven? What else can divine providence then have for its end than the reformation and salvation of mankind? No one can be reformed by himself through his prudence; he is reformed by the Lord through His divine providence. Consequently, unless the Lord leads man every least moment the man lapses from the way of reformation and perishes.

[3] Every change or variation in the state of the human mind means a change or variation in a series of things present and to come; what then of progress to eternity? The situation is like that of an arrow shot from a bow, which if it deviated from the target in the least on being aimed would deviate widely at a thousand feet or more. The like would happen if the Lord did not lead the states of the human mind every least moment. The Lord does so according to the laws of His divine providence; it is according to them that it seems to man he leads himself; but the Lord foresees how he leads himself and constantly acts in adaptation. In what follows it will be seen that laws of tolerance are also laws of divine providence, that every man can be reformed and regenerated, and that no other predestination is possible.

Since every man lives forever after death and is allotted a place either in heaven or in hell according to his life, and heaven and hell must each be in a form to act as a unit, as we said before, and since no one can be allotted a place in that form other than his own, humanity in all the world is under the Lord's guidance and everyone is led by the Lord from infancy to the close of life in the least things, and his place is foreseen and provided.

[2] Clearly then, the Lord's divine providence is universal by being in the least things, and it is an infinite and eternal creation that He has provided for Himself in creating the world. Man does not espy this universal providence, and if he did, it would look to him like scattered heaps and collections of material for building a house such as passersby see, while the Lord beholds rather a magnificent palace, constantly building and enlarging.

(v) Heaven and hell are in the form described. That heaven is in the human form has been made known in the work Heaven and Hell, published in London in 1758 (nn. 59-102), also in the treatise Divine Love and Wisdom, and here and there in the present treatise. I therefore omit further confirmation. Hell is said to be in the human form also, but it is in a monstrous human form, like that of the devil, by whom hell in its entirety is meant. Hell is in the human form inasmuch as those who are in it were born human beings too; they also possess the two human faculties of liberty and rationality, though they have misused liberty by willing and doing evil, and rationality by thinking and confirming evil.

(vi) Those who have acknowledged nature alone and human prudence alone make up hell, and those who have acknowledged God and His divine providence make up heaven. All who lead an evil life, inwardly acknowledge nature and human prudence alone. This acknowledgment lies hidden in all evil, however the evil may be veiled by good and truth, which are borrowed raiment, or like wreaths of perishable flowers, put around the evil lest it appear in its nakedness. That all who lead an evil life, inwardly acknowledge nature and human prudence alone is not known because of this general covering hiding it from view. The source and cause of their acknowledgment, however, may make clear that they acknowledge nature and one's own prudence. We shall say, therefore, whence man's own prudence is and what it is; then whence divine providence is and what it is; next who they are respectively, and of what character, who acknowledge divine providence and who acknowledge man's own prudence; and lastly show that those who acknowledge divine providence are in heaven and that those who acknowledge man's own prudence are in hell.

Whence man's own prudence is and what it is. It is from man's proprium, which is his nature and is called his soul from his parent. This proprium is self-love and the accompanying love of the world, or it is love of the world and the accompanying self-love. Self-love by nature regards self only and others as cheap or of no account. If it regards any it does so as long as they honor and do it homage. Inmostly in that love, like the endeavor in seed to fructify and propagate, there lies hidden the desire to become great and if possible a king and then possibly a god. A devil is such, for he is self-love itself; he adores himself and favors no one unless he also adores him; another devil like himself he hates, because he in turn wants alone to be adored. Since no love is possible without its consort and the consort of love or of the will in man is called the understanding, when self-love breathes itself into its consort, the understanding, it becomes pride there, which is the pride of self-intelligence, and from this comes man's own prudence.

[2] Inasmuch as self-love wants to be the one lord of the world and thus a god, the lusts of evil which are derived from it have their life from it, so have the perceptions of the lusts, which are schemes; likewise the enjoyments of the lusts, which are evils, and the thoughts of the lusts, which are falsities. All these are like slaves and ministers of their lord, responding to his every nod, unaware that they do not act but are acted upon; they are actuated by self-love through the pride of self-intelligence. Hence man's own prudence because of its origin lies concealed in every evil.

[3] The acknowledgment of nature alone is also hidden in it, for self-love has closed the window overhead through which heaven is plain and the side windows, too, in order not to see or hear that the Lord alone governs all things, that nature in herself is lifeless, and that man's proprium is infernal and consequently love of it is diabolical. With the windows shuttered, self-love is in darkness, builds itself a hearth fire at which it sits with its consort, and the two reason amicably in favor of nature as against God and in favor of man's own prudence as against divine providence.

Whence and what divine providence is. It is the divine activity in the man who has removed self-love. For, as was said, self-love is the devil, and lusts with their enjoyments are the evils of his kingdom, which is hell. On the removal of self-love the Lord enters with the affections of neighborly love, opening the overhead window and then the side windows, thus enabling man to see that there is a heaven, a life after death and eternal happiness. By the spiritual light and at the same time the spiritual love which then flow in, the Lord causes him to acknowledge that God governs all things by His divine providence.

Who and of what nature those in each group are. Those who acknowledge God and His divine providence are like the angels of heaven, who are averse to being led by themselves and love to be led by the Lord. It is a sign that they are led by the Lord that they love the neighbor. Those, however, who acknowledge nature and one's own prudence are like the spirits of hell, who are averse to being led by the Lord and love to be led by themselves. If they were powerful persons in a kingdom or prelates in the church they want to dominate all things. If they were judges, they pervert judgment and exercise power over the laws. If they were learned, they apply scientific information to confirm nature and man's proprium. If they were merchants they act like robbers, and if husbandmen like thieves. All are enemies of God and scoffers at divine providence.

It is amazing that when heaven is opened to such men and they are told that they are insane, and this is made plain to their very perception by influx and enlightenment, still they angrily shut heaven away from them and look to the earth beneath which is hell. This is done with such men while they are still outside hell. It makes plain how mistaken those are who think, "If I see heaven and hear angels speaking with me, I shall acknowledge." Their understanding makes the acknowledgment, but if the will does not at the same time, they still do not acknowledge. For the love of the will inspires in the understanding what it wills (it is not the other way about); indeed, it destroys everything in the understanding which is not from itself.

All this can be effected only as it appears to man that he thinks from himself and disposes by himself. In what precedes we have shown fully that unless it seemed to man that he lives of himself and thus thinks and wills, speaks and acts of himself, he would not be man. Consequently, unless he could in his own prudence make the disposition of all pertaining to his function and life, he could not be led and guided by divine providence. He would be like one with his hands hanging limp, his mouth open, his eyes shut, holding his breath in expectation of influx. He would divest himself of the human which he has from the perception and sensation that he thinks, wills, speaks and acts as it were of himself. At the same time he would divest himself of the two faculties, liberty and rationality, distinguishing him from the beasts. Above in this treatise and in the treatise Divine Love and Wisdom it was shown that without this appearance a man would not have the power to receive or reciprocate nor have immortality then.

[2] If then you desire to be led by divine providence, use prudence as a servant and minister that faithfully dispenses his master's goods. This prudence is the talent given to the servants to trade with, of which they were to give account (Lu 19:13-28; Mt 25:14-31). It seems to man to be his own, and he believes it is his own as long as he holds shut up within him the bitterest enemy God and divine providence have, the love of self. This dwells in the interiors of every man by birth; if you do not recognize it (and it wishes not to be recognized), it dwells securely and guards the door lest man open the door and the Lord cast it out. The door is opened by man through shunning evils as sins as if of himself with the acknowledgment that he does so from the Lord. With this prudence divine providence acts as one.

Divine providence operates so secretly that scarcely anyone is aware it exists in order that man may not perish. For man's proprium, which is his will, never acts at one with divine providence, against which it has an inborn enmity. The proprium is the serpent which seduced the race's parents of which it is said,

I will put enmity between you and the woman, and between your seed and her Seed, and It shall bruise your head (Ge 3:15).

The serpent is evil of every sort; its head is self-love. The seed of the woman is the Lord, and the enmity set is between the love of man's proprium and the Lord, thus between man's own prudence and the Lord's divine providence. For man's own prudence is constantly exalting that head, and divine providence is constantly abasing it.

[2] If man felt this, he would be enraged and wrought-up against God and would perish. While he does not feel it, he may be enraged and wrought-up against others or himself or against fortune without perishing. Therefore the Lord leads man by His divine providence in freedom always, and the freedom seems to man to be utterly his own. To lead a man freely in opposition to himself is like raising a heavy and resisting weight from the ground by means of screws through the power of which weight and resistance are not felt. And it is as though someone is unknowingly with an enemy who means to kill him and a friend leads him away quietly and only afterwards tells him the enemy's intention.

Who does not talk of fortune? Who does not acknowledge it by speaking of it and know something of it by experience? Yet who knows what it is? One cannot deny that it is something, for it exists and occurs, and a thing cannot exist and occur without being caused; but the cause of this something, fortune, is not known. Lest fortune be denied merely because the cause is unknown, consider dice or playing cards and play yourself or ask the players; do any deny that fortune exists? For they play with it and it plays with them surprisingly. Who can repulse it if it opposes him? Does it not laugh then at prudence and wisdom? When you shake the dice or shuffle the cards, does fortune not seem to know and direct the turns and twists of the wrists in favor of one player rather than another for some cause? Can the cause have any other source than divine providence in outermost things where it works along with human prudence in a wonderful way, constant or changeful, concealing itself at the same time?

[2] We know that pagans of old acknowledged Fortune and built a temple to her, as Italians did at Rome. It has been granted me to learn many things which I am not permitted to make public about this fortune, which, as was said, is divine providence in outmosts. These made it plain to me that fortune is not an illusion of the mind nor a sport of nature nor something without a cause, for this has no reality, but is visible evidence that divine providence is over the least things in human thought and action. As divine providence occurs in these least things which are insignificant and trifling, why should it not in the significant and important matters of peace and war in the world and of salvation and life in heaven?

I know, however, that human prudence bears the rational faculty its way more than divine providence does its way, for the latter does not show itself and the former does. It can be accepted more readily that there is only one life, namely God, and that all men are recipients of life from Him, as we have shown many times, yet this amounts to saying that prudence is from Him, for prudence is part of life. What man, speaking in favor of nature and of human prudence in his reasoning, is not speaking from the natural or external man? And what man, speaking in favor of divine providence and of God in his reasoning, is not speaking from the spiritual or internal man? But, "Pray, write two books," I say to the natural man, "and fill them with plausible, likely and lifelike reasons which in your judgment are solid ones, the one book in favor of one's own prudence, and the other in favor of nature. Then hand them to any angel. I know he will write down on them these few words: 'All this is appearance and fallacy.'"

Section 11

DIVINE PROVIDENCE LOOKS TO WHAT IS ETERNAL, AND TO THE TEMPORAL ONLY AS THIS ACCORDS WITH THE ETERNAL

That divine providence looks to what is eternal and to the temporal only so far as this makes one with the eternal, will be demonstrated in this order:

i. The temporal has to do with distinction and wealth, thus with standing and gain, in the world. ii. The eternal has to do with spiritual standing and abundance, of love and wisdom, in heaven. iii. The temporal and the eternal are separated by man, but are united by the Lord. iv. The uniting of temporal and eternal is the Lord's divine providence.

(i) The temporal has to do with distinction and wealth, thus with standing and gain, in the world. Many things are temporal, but they are all related to distinction and wealth. By the temporal is meant all that either perishes in time or at least comes to an end with man's life in the world. By the eternal is meant all that does not perish or come to an end in time and thus not with life in the world. Since, as we said, all that is temporal concerns distinction and wealth, it is important to know the following: what, and whence, distinction and wealth are; the nature of the love of them for themselves and the nature of the love of them for the sake of use; that these two loves are distinct from each other, as hell and heaven are; and that man hardly knows the difference between them. But of these points one by one.

[2] First: What, and whence, distinction and wealth are. Distinction and wealth in the most ancient times were quite different from what they gradually became later. Distinction in those times existed only in the relation of parents and children and was one of love, a love full of respect and veneration, accorded the parents not because of birth from them, but because of the instruction and wisdom received from them, which was a second birth of the children, in itself spiritual, being of their spirit. This was the sole distinction in most ancient days because tribes, families, and households dwelt separately and not like today under governments. The distinction attached to the head of the family. Men of old called the times golden ages.

[3] But after those times the love of ruling, just out of enjoyment of that love, crept in by stages, and as enmity and hostility did so at the same time towards those who were unwilling to submit, tribes, families, and households congregated of necessity in communities and set over themselves one whom they called judge at first, then prince, and finally king and emperor. They also began to protect themselves by towers, earthworks and walls. The lust of ruling spread like a contagion to many from the judge, prince, king or emperor as from the head into the body, and as a result degrees of distinction arose and prestige according to them, and self-love also and pride in one's own prudence.

[4] The same thing happened with the love of riches. In the most ancient

days when tribes and families lived by themselves, there was no other love of riches than to possess the necessaries of life which they provided for themselves from flocks and herds and from the lands, fields and gardens which supplied their food. Suitable houses, furnished with useful articles of every kind, and clothing were also among their necessities of life. Parents, children and male and female servants, making up the household, engaged in the care and labor for all these necessities.

[5] But after the love of dominion entered and destroyed this state of society, the love of having means beyond what was needed crept in also and grew to the extreme of wanting to possess the wealth of all other men. The two loves are like blood relatives, for one who wants to rule over all things, also wants to possess all things; for then all others become servants, and they alone masters. This is clearly evident from those in the papist world who have exalted their dominion even into heaven, to the Lord's throne, on which they have placed themselves, and who at the same time seek the wealth of the whole earth and want to enlarge their treasury endlessly.

[6] Second: The nature of the love of distinction and wealth for their own sake and for usefulness' sake respectively. The love of distinction and standing for their own sake is self-love--strictly, the love of ruling from self-love; and the love of riches and wealth for their own sake is love of the world--more precisely, the love of possessing the goods of others by whatever device. But the love of distinction and riches for usefulness' sake is love of the use, which is the same as love to the neighbor; for that for the sake of which a man acts is the purpose from which he acts, and is first or primary, and all else is means and secondary.

[7] As for the love of distinction and standing, identical with self-love and strictly with the love of ruling from self-love, it is the love of the proprium; and man's proprium is all evil. Hence it is said that man is born into all evil and that what he has by heredity is nothing but evil. What he has by heredity is his proprium in which he is and into which he comes through self-love and especially through the love of ruling from self-love; for one who is in that love regards only himself and thus immerses his thoughts and affections in his proprium. Hence a love of evil-doing is present in self-love. The reason is that he does not love the neighbor but only himself; and one who loves himself only, sees others as outsiders or as mean or nothing worth, despises them, and does not hesitate to do them injury.

[8] For this reason one who is in the love of ruling from the love of self thinks nothing of defrauding his neighbor, committing adultery with his wife, slandering him, breathing vengeance on him even to the death, treating him cruelly, and other such deeds. This a man gets from the fact that the devil himself, with whom he is conjoined and by whom he is led, is nothing else than the love of ruling from self-love. One who is led by the devil, that is, by hell, is led into all these evils and is constantly led by enjoyments of these evils. Hence all who are in hell want to do evil to all, but those in heaven want to do well by all. From this opposition there results the intermediate state in which man is and in it is in equilibrium, as it were, so that he can turn towards hell or towards heaven. So far as he favors the evils of self-love he turns towards hell, and so far as he removes them from him he turns towards heaven.

[9] It has been granted me to feel the nature and also the strength of the

enjoyment of ruling from the love of self. I was let into it that I might know. It was such as to exceed all worldly enjoyments. It was an enjoyment of the whole mind from its inmosts to its outmosts, but felt in the body only as pleasure and gratification, making the chest swell. It was also granted me to perceive that there issued from this enjoyment as from their fountainhead the enjoyments of evils of all kinds, such as adultery, revenge, fraud, slander, and evil-doing in general. There is a similar enjoyment in the love of possessing the wealth of others by whatever ruse, and from this love in the lusts derived from it; yet not the same degree of enjoyment unless this love is conjoined with self-love. As for distinction and riches sought not for themselves but for usefulness' sake, this is not love of them but love of uses; distinction and wealth serve it as means. This love is heavenly. But of it more in what follows.

[10] Third: These two loves are distinct from each other, as heaven and hell are. This is plain from what has just been said, to which I will add the following. All who are in the love of ruling from self-love, whoever they are and whether they are great or small, are in hell in spirit. They are also in the love of all evils. If they do not commit them, still in their spirit they believe that they are allowable, and when honor, standing, or fear of the law do not deter, they commit them physically. What is more, the love of ruling from self-love hides hatred of God deeply within itself, consequently of divine things which are of the church and especially of the Lord. If such men acknowledge God it is with the lips only, and if they acknowledge the divine things of the church, it is for fear of losing standing. This love hides hatred of the Lord deeply within it because deep in it is the desire to be God, for it worships and adores itself alone. Hence if anyone honors it, even to saying that it possesses divine wisdom and is the god of the world, it loves him with all the heart.

[11] It is otherwise with the love of distinction and wealth for usefulness' sake; this love is heavenly, for, as was said, it is the same as love of the neighbor. By uses goods are meant, and by doing uses doing good is meant, and by doing uses or good, serving and helping others is meant. Although those doing so may possess distinction and wealth, they regard these only as means for doing uses, thus for serving and helping. They are meant in these words of the Lord:

Whoever would be great among you, must be your minister; and whoever would . . . be first, must be your servant (Mt 20:26, 27).

It is these also whom the Lord entrusts with ruling in heaven. For ruling is to them the means of doing uses or good, thus of serving; and when uses or good deeds are their purpose and their love, they do not rule; the Lord does, from whom is all that is good.

[12] Fourth: Man hardly knows the difference between the two loves. For most men of distinction and wealth also perform uses, yet do not know whether they do so for their own sake or for the sake of usefulness. They know this the less because love of self and the world has more fire and ardor for doing uses than have those who are not in love of self and the world. The former do uses, however, for the sake of fame or gain, thus for their own benefit; but the latter, doing so for the sake of usefulness and what is beneficial, act not from themselves but from the Lord.

[13] The difference between the two loves can scarcely be recognized by

man, for he is ignorant whether he is being led by the devil or by the Lord. Led by the devil he does uses for his own sake or the world's; led by the Lord, he does them for the sake of the Lord and of heaven. All who shun evils as sins do uses from the Lord; all who do not shun evils as sins do uses from the devil, for evil is the devil, and use or good is the Lord. Only so is the difference in question recognizable. Outwardly the two loves look the same; inwardly they are wholly unlike. One is like gold with dross in it, the other like gold with pure gold in it. One is like artificial fruit, looking outwardly like the fruit of a tree, but is colored wax with dust or pitch in it; the other is like noble fruit, flavorsome and fragrant, with seeds in it.

(ii) The eternal has to do with spiritual standing and wealth, of love and wisdom, in heaven. As the natural man calls the enjoyments of self-love, which are also the enjoyments of the lusts of evil, good, and confirms that they are goods, he calls distinction and wealth divine blessings. But when the natural man sees the wicked as well as the good raised to distinction and prospered, and still more when he beholds the good despised and poorly off and the wicked honored and affluent, he thinks to himself, "Why is this? It cannot be by divine providence. For if providence governed everything, it would lavish distinction and wealth on the good and inflict contempt and poverty on the wicked, and thus drive the wicked to acknowledge there is a God and divine providence."

[2] But unless he is enlightened by the spiritual man, that is, is at the same time spiritual, the natural man does not see that distinction and wealth can be blessings but also curses, and that when they are from God they are blessings, and when they are from the devil they are curses. It is well known, moreover, that the devil bestows distinction and wealth; it is on this account that he is called the prince of the world. As it is not known when distinction and wealth are blessings and when they are curses, let it be told in this order: 1. Distinction and wealth are blessings and are curses. 2. When they are blessings they are spiritual and eternal; when they are curses they are temporal and ephemeral. 3. Distinction and wealth which are curses, compared with those which are blessings, are as nothing compared with everything or as that which has no existence in itself compared with that which has.

The three points are now each to be clarified. 1. Distinction and wealth are blessings and are curses. Common experience attests that both the pious and the impious, or the just and the unjust, that is, the wicked and the good, gain distinction and wealth, and yet it is undeniable that the impious and unjust, that is, the wicked, enter hell, and the pious and just, that is, the good, enter heaven. As this is true, distinction and wealth or standing and means are either blessings or curses, blessings with the good and curses with the evil. It was shown in the work Heaven and Hell, published in London in the year 1758, that rich and poor and great and small are found in both heaven and hell (nn. 357-365). It is plain from this that distinction and wealth with those now in heaven were blessings in the world, and with those now in hell were curses in the world.

[2] If he will think about the matter with reason, anyone can know when distinction and wealth are blessings or curses, namely, that they are blessings with those who do not set their heart on them, and curses with those who do. One sets the heart on them in loving oneself in them, and one does not set the

heart on them when he loves uses and not himself in them. Above (n. 215) we told what the difference between the two loves, and the nature of it, is. It is to be added that distinction and wealth seduce some and not others. They do so when they excite the loves in man's proprium, that is, self-love, which is the love found in hell and is called the devil (as remarked above), and they do not seduce if they do not excite that love.

[3] Both the wicked and the good come to distinction and are prospered in means because the wicked as well as the good perform uses. The wicked perform uses for the sake of their personal standing and gain; the good do so for the sake of the standing and profit of the work which they do. The good regard the standing and profit of their work as principal causes of action, and personal standing and gain as instrumental causes; but the wicked regard their personal standing and gain as the main incentives and the standing and gain of their work as the instrumental. Yet who does not see that a person, whatever his function or standing, is to serve the affairs which he administers, and not they him? Who does not see that a judge is to serve justice, a magistrate the common welfare, a king his kingdom, and that it is not to be the other way around? According to the laws of a kingdom, a man is invested therefore with distinction and standing in keeping with the eminence of the work he does. Moreover, who does not see that the difference between the two loves is like that between what is principal and what is instrumental? One who ascribes to himself personally the eminence of a position appears in the spiritual world, when this inversion is pictured, as himself inverted, feet up and head down.

[4] Second: When distinction and wealth are blessings they are spiritual and eternal, but when they are curses they are temporal and ephemeral. There are distinction and wealth in heaven as there are in the world. For governments and hence administrations and functions exist there, trade also and hence wealth, for there are societies and communities. All heaven is divided into two kingdoms, one called the celestial kingdom and the other the spiritual kingdom. Each kingdom is divided into innumerable societies, larger and smaller, all of which with all in them are arranged according to differences of love and of wisdom thence, the societies of the celestial kingdom according to differences of celestial love, which is love to the Lord, and the societies of the spiritual kingdom according to differences of spiritual love, which is love to the neighbor. Inasmuch as there are such societies, and all who are in them were men in the world and hence retain the loves they cherished in the world, with the one difference that they are spiritual beings now, and that distinction and wealth are spiritual in the spiritual kingdom and celestial in the celestial kingdom, therefore those have greater distinction and abundance than others who have greater love and wisdom. And to them distinction and wealth in the world were blessings.

[5] The nature of spiritual distinction and wealth may then be plain--they attach to one's function and not to one's person. The distinguished person in the spiritual world indeed enjoys magnificence and glory like those of kings on earth, yet does not regard the distinction itself as anything but rather the uses in the administration and discharge of which he is engaged. Each also receives the honors of his high post but ascribes them not to himself but to the uses, and as all uses are from the Lord, he ascribes the honors to the Lord as their source.

Such are the spiritual distinction and wealth which are eternal.

[6] It is quite otherwise with those to whom eminence and wealth were curses in the world. Having attributed these to themselves and not to uses, and not wanting the uses to control them but wanting to control the uses, which they regarded as uses only as they served their own standing and honor, they are in hell and are base slaves, despised and wretched. Their distinction and wealth are gone, therefore are called temporal and fleeting. The Lord teaches about both sorts in the words:

Do not lay up treasures for yourselves on earth, where moth and rust corrupt and thieves break through and steal; but lay up treasures for yourselves in heaven, where neither moth nor rust corrupts and where thieves do not break through and steal; for where your treasure is . . . your heart also is (Mt 6:19-21).

[7] Third: The distinction and wealth which are curses, compared with those which are blessings, are as nothing compared with everything or as that which has no existence in itself compared with that which has. Everything that perishes and comes to nothing is inwardly nothing in itself. Outwardly, indeed, it is something and appears to be much and to some everything while it lasts; but inwardly in itself it is not. It is like a surface with nothing beneath or like an actor in kingly robes when the play is over. But what remains to eternity is something in itself perpetually, thus everything, and it truly is, for it does not cease to be.

(iii) The temporal and the eternal are separated by man, but are united by the Lord. For all that is man's is temporal, and he may therefore be called temporal, but all things that are the Lord's are eternal, and so the Lord is called eternal. Temporal things are such as come to an end and perish, eternal things are such as do not. Anyone can see that the two can be united only by the infinite wisdom of the Lord, thus by Him and not by man. To make it known, however, that the two are separated by man and united by the Lord, this is to be demonstrated in the following order:

1. What temporal things are and what eternal are. 2. The human being is in himself temporal and the Lord in Himself eternal, and only the temporal can proceed from man, and only the eternal from the Lord. 3. Temporal things separate eternal things from themselves, while eternal things join temporal things to themselves. 4. The Lord joins man to Himself by means of appearances. 5. He does so by correspondences also.

These points will be clarified and established one by one. First: What temporal things are and what eternal are. The temporal are all things that are proper to nature and from nature proper to man. Space and time especially are proper to nature, both of them having a limit or termination. Things thence derived and proper to man are all things of his own will and understanding, thus of his affection and thought and especially of his prudence; it is well known that these are finite and limited. Eternal things, however, are all that are proper to the Lord and from Him seemingly proper to man. What is proper to the Lord is all of it infinite and eternal, thus timeless, endless and without limit; what is seemingly proper to man thence is also infinite and eternal; but nothing of this is actually proper to man, but the Lord's alone in him.

[2] Second: The human being is in himself temporal and the Lord in Himself

eternal, and only the temporal can proceed from man, and from the Lord only the eternal. Man, we said, is in himself temporal and the Lord in Himself eternal. Since only what is in a person can proceed from him, nothing can proceed from man except what is temporal, and nothing from the Lord except what is eternal. For the infinite cannot proceed from the finite; that it can is a contradiction. The infinite, however, can proceed from the finite, still not from the finite but from the infinite by the finite. In turn, what is finite cannot proceed from the infinite; this is also a contradiction; it can be produced from the infinite and this is creation and not proceeding. On this subject see Angelic Wisdom about Divine Love and Wisdom, from beginning to end. If then the finite proceeds from the Lord, as it does in many ways with man, it proceeds not from the Lord but from man, and can be said to do so from the Lord by man, because it so appears.

[3] This may be clarified by these words of the Lord:

Let your communication be, Yea, yea, Nay, nay, what is more than these comes of evil (Mt 5:37).

Such is the speech of all in the third heaven. For they never reason about divine things whether a thing is so or not, but see in themselves from the Lord whether or not it is. To reason about divine things whether they are so or not comes from the reasoner's not seeing them from the Lord, but wanting to see them from himself, and what one sees from oneself is evil. But still the Lord desires man to think and speak about things divine, also to reason about them, in order that he may see whether or not they are so. Such thought, speech and reasoning may be said to be from the Lord in man provided the end is to see the truth, although they are from the man until he sees and acknowledges the truth. Meanwhile it is from the Lord alone that he can think, speak and reason; for he does so from the two faculties, called liberty and rationality, which are his from the Lord alone.

[4] Third: Temporal things separate eternal things from themselves, while eternal things join temporal things to themselves. That temporal things separate eternal things from themselves means that man, who is temporal, does so from the temporal in himself; and that eternal things join temporal things to themselves means that the Lord, who is eternal, does so from what is eternal in Himself, as was said above. In what precedes we showed that there is a conjunction of the Lord with man and a conjunction in turn of man with the Lord, but the reciprocal conjunction of man with the Lord is not man's doing but the Lord's; also that man's will goes counter to the Lord's will or, what is the same, man's own prudence goes counter to divine providence. From these circumstances it follows that man puts the eternal things of the Lord aside by force of the temporal things in him, but the Lord joins His eternal things to man's temporal, that is, Himself to man and man to Him. As these points have been treated many times in what precedes, there is no need to confirm them further.

[5] Fourth: The Lord joins man to Himself by means of appearances. For it is an appearance that of himself man loves the neighbor, does good, and speaks truth. Unless this appeared to man to be so, he would not love the neighbor, do good, or speak truth, and therefore would not be conjoined with the Lord. Since love, good and truth are from the Lord, plainly the Lord joins man to Himself

by means of the appearance. This appearance, and the Lord's conjunction with man and man's with the Lord, have been treated above at length.

[6] Fifth: The Lord unites man to Himself by means of correspondences. He does this by means of the Word, the sense of the letter of which consists wholly of correspondences. In Doctrine of the New Jerusalem about Sacred Scripture, from beginning to end, it was shown that by means of that sense there is a conjunction of the Lord with man and a reciprocal conjunction of man with the Lord.

(iv) The conjunction of the temporal and the eternal in man is the Lord's divine providence. As this cannot come at once to the perception of the understanding or before being reduced to order and then unfolded and demonstrated according to that order, let this be the order in considering it:

1. It is by divine providence that man puts off the natural and temporal through death and puts on the spiritual and eternal. 2. Through His divine providence the Lord joins Himself with natural things by means of spiritual and to temporal by means of eternal in accordance with uses. 3. The Lord joins Himself to uses by means of correspondences, and so by means of appearances according as man confirms these. 4. This conjunction of temporal and eternal is divine providence.

All this will be placed in clearer light by explanation.

[2] First: It is of divine providence that man puts off the natural and temporal through death and puts on the spiritual and eternal. Natural and temporal things are the outermost and lowest things which man first enters, as he does on being born, to the end that he may be introduced then into interior and higher things; for the outmost and lowest things are containants, and these are in the natural world. For this reason no angel or spirit was created such at once, but all were born as men first and then were introduced into interior and higher things. Thus they have an outmost and lowest which in itself is fixed and stable, within and by which the interiors can be held in connection.

[3] Man first puts on the grosser substances of nature; his body consists of them; but he puts these off by death, retaining the purer substances of nature nearest to the spiritual, which then are his containants. Moreover, all interior or higher things are together in the outmost and lowermost, as was shown earlier in passages on the subject. Every activity of the Lord is therefore from topmost and outmost simultaneously and so is in fullness. But as the farthest and outmost things of nature as they are in themselves cannot receive the spiritual and eternal things for which the human mind was formed, and yet man was born to become spiritual and live forever, man puts them off and retains only those interior natural things which suit and harmonize with the spiritual and celestial and serve to contain them. This is effected by the rejection of the temporal and natural outmosts, which is the death of the body.

[4] Second: Through His divine providence the Lord joins Himself with natural things by means of spiritual things and to temporal by means of eternal in accordance with uses. Natural and temporal things are not only those proper to nature, but also those proper to men in the natural world. At death man puts off both of these and puts on the spiritual and eternal things corresponding to them. That he puts these on according to uses has been shown in much that precedes. The natural things proper to nature relate in general to time and

space and in particular to things visible on earth. These man leaves behind at death and instead receives spiritual things which are similar in outward aspect or appearance but not in their inward aspect and actual essence. This also was considered above.

[5] Temporal things proper to men in the natural world in general are related to distinction and wealth and in particular to human needs such as food, clothing and habitation. These are also put off at death and left behind; things are put on and received that are similar in outward aspect or appearance but not in their internal aspect and essence. All these get their inward aspect and essence from the uses made of temporal things in the world. Uses are the goods which are called goods of charity. It is evident, then, that the Lord through His divine providence unites spiritual and eternal things to natural and temporal things according to uses.

[6] Third: The Lord joins Himself to uses by means of correspondences, and thus by means of appearances according as man confirms these. As this must seem obscure to those who have not yet acquired a clear idea of correspondence and appearance, what these are must be illustrated by examples and explained. All the sayings of the Word are outright correspondences of spiritual and celestial things, and being correspondences are also appearances, that is, are all divine goods of divine love and divine truths of divine wisdom which in themselves are naked, but are clothed upon by the Word's literal meaning. They therefore appear as a man would clothed, if his clothing corresponded to the state of his love and wisdom. Obviously, then, if one confirms appearances in himself, he mistakes the clothing for the man, whereupon appearance becomes fallacy. It is otherwise if he seeks truths and sees them in the appearances.

[7] Inasmuch as all uses or truths and goods of charity, which a man renders to the neighbor may be rendered either according to the appearance or according to the verities of the Word, he is in fallacies if he renders them according to the appearances he has confirmed, but renders them as he should if he does so in accord with the verities. This may make plain what is meant when the Lord is said to join Himself to uses through correspondences and thus through appearances according to the confirmation of these by man.

[8] Fourth: This conjunction of temporal and eternal is divine providence. This is to be illustrated by two instances in order to bring it before the understanding in some light. The one instance is that of eminence and standing, and the other that of riches and wealth. These are all natural and temporal in outward form but spiritual and eternal in inward form. Distinction with its standing is natural and temporal when a man has regard in them only to himself personally and not to the common welfare and to the uses. For he is bound then to think inwardly that the community exists for his sake and not he for its sake. It is like a king's thinking that the kingdom and all its members exist for his sake, and not he for the sake of kingdom and people.

[9] The identical distinction, however, along with the standing it brings, is spiritual and eternal when man considers that he exists for the sake of the common well-being and for uses, and not these for his sake. Doing this, he is in the truth and essence of the distinction and of the standing it brings. But doing as described above, he is in the correspondence and appearance; if then he confirms these, he is in fallacies and has conjunction with the Lord only as those

have who are in falsities and evils therefrom, for fallacies are falsities with which evils unite themselves. Such men have indeed done uses and good but from themselves and not from the Lord, thus have put themselves in the Lord's place.

[10] The same is true of riches and wealth; for these also are natural and temporal, and spiritual and eternal. They are natural and temporal with those who have regard only to them and to themselves in them and who find all their pleasure and enjoyment in them. But they are spiritual and eternal with those who regard good uses in them and take an interior pleasure and enjoyment in uses. The outward pleasure and enjoyment in such men also becomes spiritual, and the temporal becomes eternal. They are therefore in heaven after death and in palaces there, the useful designs of which are resplendent with gold and precious stones. They look on these things, however, as the shining and translucent external of inward things, namely, of uses, in which they take a pleasure and enjoyment which are the happiness and joy of heaven. The opposite is the lot of those who have looked on riches and wealth just for the sake of riches and wealth and for their own sake, thus on the externalities and on nothing inward; thus on appearance and not on the essential reality. When they put off the externalities, as they do on dying, they come into their internals, and as these are not spiritual, they cannot but be infernal; they must be one or the other and cannot be spiritual and infernal at the same time. The lot of these men then is poverty instead of riches and wretchedness instead of wealth.

[11] By uses not only the necessities of life are meant, such as food, raiment and habitation for oneself and one's own, but also the good of one's country, community and fellow-citizens. Business is such a good when it is the end-love and money is a mediate, subservient love, as it is only when the businessman shuns and is averse to fraud and bad practices as sin. It is otherwise when money is the end-love and business the mediate, subservient love. For this is avarice, which is a root of evils (on this see Lu 12:15 and the parable on it, verses 16-21).

Section 12

MAN IS NOT ADMITTED INWARDLY INTO TRUTHS OF FAITH AND GOODS OF CHARITY EXCEPT AS HE CAN BE KEPT IN THEM TO THE CLOSE OF LIFE

It is well known in Christendom that the Lord wills the salvation of all, and also is almighty. From this many conclude that He can save everyone and saves those who implore His mercy, especially those who implore it by the formula of the received faith that God the Father may be merciful for the sake of the Son, particularly if they pray at the same time that they may receive this faith. That it is quite otherwise, however, will be seen in the last chapter of this treatise where it will be explained that the Lord cannot act contrary to the laws of His divine providence because that would be acting against His divine love and wisdom, thus against Himself. There, too, it will be seen that such immediate mercy is impossible, for man's salvation is effected by means, and he can be led in accordance with these means only by Him who wills the salvation of all and is at the same time almighty, thus by the Lord. These means are what are called laws of divine providence. Among them is this, that man is not admitted inwardly into truths of wisdom and goods of love except as he can be kept in them to the close of life. To make this plain to the reason, it is to be explained in this order:

i. Man may be admitted into wisdom about spiritual things and also into love of them and still not be reformed. ii. If he recedes from them afterwards and turns to what is the contrary, he profanes holy things. iii. There are many kinds of profanation, but this kind is the worst of all. iv. The Lord therefore does not admit man interiorly into truths of wisdom and at the same time into goods of love except as man can be kept in them to the very close of life.

(i) Man may be admitted into wisdom about spiritual things and also into love of them and still not be reformed. This is because he possesses rationality and liberty; by rationality he can be raised into an almost angelic wisdom, and by liberty into love not unlike angelic love. But such as the love is, such is the wisdom; if the love is celestial and spiritual, the wisdom becomes so, but if the love is diabolical and infernal, the wisdom is likewise. Outwardly, and so to others, it may seem to be celestial and spiritual, but in inward form, namely in its essence, it is diabolical and infernal; not as manifested, but as it is within one. That it is of this nature men do not see, for they are natural, see and hear naturally, and the outward form is natural; but angels do see it, for they are spiritual, see and hear spiritually, and the inward form is spiritual.

[2] From this it is plain that man can be admitted into wisdom about spiritual things and also into love of them and still not be reformed; he is admitted only into a natural love of them, not into a spiritual. This is for the reason that man can admit himself into a natural love, but the Lord alone can admit him into a spiritual love, and those admitted into this are reformed, but those admitted only into the natural love are not. For the most part the latter

are hypocrites, and many are of the Order of Jesuits who inwardly do not believe in the divine at all, but play outwardly with divine things like actors.

It has been granted me by much experience in the spiritual world to know that man possesses in himself the faculty of apprehending arcana of wisdom like the angels themselves. For I have seen fiery devils who not only understood arcana of wisdom when they heard them, but who spoke them, too, out of their rationality. But the moment they returned to their diabolical love they did not understand them, but in place of them the contrary, which was insanity, and this they called wisdom. In fact, I was allowed to hear them laugh at their insanity when they were in a state of wisdom, and at wisdom when they were in an insane state. One who has been of this character in the world, on becoming a spirit after death is usually brought into states of wisdom and insanity by turns, for him to distinguish the one from the other. But although such men see from the wisdom that they are insane, when the choice is given them, as it is to each, they betake themselves into the state of insanity, love it and feel hatred for the state of wisdom. The reason is that their inward nature has been diabolical and their outward seemingly divine. They are meant by devils who affect to be angels of light, and by the man in the house of the nuptials who was not dressed in a wedding garment and was cast into outer darkness (Mt 22:11-13).

Who cannot see that it is the internal from which the external exists and that consequently the external has its essence from the internal? And who does not know by experience that the external can appear out of accord with the essence it has from the internal? It does so obviously with hypocrites, flatterers and dissemblers. That a person can outwardly feign to be other than himself is manifest from actors and mimics. They know how to represent kings, emperors and even angels in tone of voice, speech, face and gesture as though they were really such, when they are nevertheless only actors. We allude to this because man can similarly act the deceiver in spiritual things as well as civil and moral, and that many do is well known.

[2] When the internal in its essence is infernal, and the external in its form appears to be spiritual and yet has its essence, as we said, from the internal, the question arises where in the external that essence is hidden. It does not show in gesture, voice, speech or face, yet is interiorly hidden in all four. That it is, is plain from the same in the spiritual world. For when man passes from the natural world to the spiritual, as he does at death, he leaves his externals behind along with his body and retains his internals, which he has stored up in his spirit. If his internal was infernal, he then appears as a devil, such as he was as to his spirit during life in the world. Who does not acknowledge that everyone leaves external things behind with the body and enters into internal things on becoming a spirit?

[3] To this I will add that in the spiritual world there is a communication of affections and of thoughts from them, which results in no one's being able to speak except as he thinks; likewise, everyone changes facial expression and reflects his affection, and thus shows in his face what he is. Hypocrites are allowed sometimes to speak otherwise than they think, but the tone of the voice sounds utterly out of harmony with their interior thoughts, and they are recognized by the discord. It may be evident from this that the internal lies

hidden in the tone of voice, the speech, the face and gesture of the external, and that it is not perceived by men in the world, but plainly by angels in the spiritual world.

It is plain from this that while he lives in the natural world man may be admitted into wisdom about spiritual things and into love of them also, and that this happens or can happen with the merely natural as well as with those who are spiritual, with this difference, however, that the latter are reformed by these means and the former are not. It may seem, also, that the former love wisdom, but they do so only as an adulterer loves a noble woman, that is, as mistress, speaking caressingly to her and giving her beautiful garments, but saying of her privately to himself, "She is only a vile harlot whom I will make believe that I love because she gratifies my lust; if she should not, I would cast her away." The internal man of the unreformed lover of wisdom is this adulterer; his external man is the woman.

(ii) If man recedes from these later and turns to what is contrary, he profanes holy things. There are many kinds of profanation of what is holy, of which in the following section, but this is the gravest of all. Those who profane in this way become no longer human beings after death; they live indeed, but are continually in wild fantasies. They seem to themselves to soar aloft and while they remain there they sport with fantasies which they see as realities. No longer human, they are referred to not as "he" or "she" but "it." In fact, when they come to view in heaven's light they look like skeletons, some like skeletons of the color of bone, others like fiery skeletons, and still others like charred ones. The world does not know that profaners of this kind become like this after death, and the reason is that the cause is unknown. The real cause is that when man first acknowledges and believes divine things and then lapses and denies them, he mixes the holy with the profane. Once they are mixed, they cannot be separated without destroying the whole. That these things may be perceived more clearly, they are to be disclosed in due order as follows: 1. Whatever a man thinks, speaks and does from the will, whether good or evil, is appropriated to him and remains. 2. The Lord in His divine providence constantly foresees and disposes that evil shall be by itself and good by itself, and thus may be separated. 3. This cannot be done, however, if man first acknowledges and lives according to truths of faith and afterwards recedes and denies them. 4. Then he mixes good and evil to the point that they cannot be separated. 5. Since good and evil in anyone must be separated, and in such a person cannot be, he is destroyed in all that is truly human.

These are the causes that lead to such enormity, but as they are obscure as a result of ignorance of them, they are to be explained so that they will be plain to the understanding. 1. Whatever man thinks, speaks and does from the will, whether good or evil, is appropriated to him and remains. This was explained above (nn. 78-81); for man has an external or natural memory and an internal or spiritual memory. On the latter memory are written each and all things that he thought, spoke or did from his will in the world, so fully that nothing is lacking. This memory is his book of life, which is opened after death and according to which he is judged. Much more about this memory is reported from experience in the work Heaven and Hell (nn. 461-465).

[2] 2. The Lord in His divine providence constantly foresees and disposes

that evil shall be by itself and good by itself, and thus may be separated. Everyone is both in evil and in good, for he is in evil from himself and in good from the Lord; he cannot live without being in both. If he were in himself alone and thus in evil alone, he would not possess anything living; nor would he if he were in the Lord alone and thus in good alone. In the latter case he would be like one suffocated and gasping for breath or like one dying in agony; in the former case he would be devoid of life, for evil apart from good is dead. Therefore everyone is in both, with the difference that in the one instance he is inwardly in the Lord and outwardly as if in himself, and in the other inwardly in himself and outwardly as if in the Lord. The latter man is in evil, the former in good, and yet each is in good and evil both. The wicked man is in both because he is in the good of civil and moral life and outwardly, in some measure, in the good of spiritual life, too, besides being kept by the Lord in rationality and liberty, making it possible for him to be in good. This is the good by means of which everyone, even a wicked man, is led by the Lord. It may then be seen that the Lord keeps evil and good apart, so that one is interior and the other exterior, and thus provides against their being mingled.

[3] 3. This cannot be done, however, if man first acknowledges and lives according to truths of faith and then later recedes and denies them. This is plain from what has just been said, that all which a man thinks, speaks and does from the will is appropriated to him and remains; and that the Lord in His divine providence constantly foresees and disposes that good shall be by itself and evil by itself, and so can be separated. They are also separated by the Lord after death. Those who are inwardly evil and outwardly good are deprived of the good and left to their evil. The reverse occurs with the inwardly good who outwardly like other men have acquired wealth, sought distinction, delighted in the mundane, and indulged some lusts. Good and evil have not been commingled by them, however, but are separate, like internal and external; they have resembled the evil in many ways outwardly but not inwardly. Evil is separate from good in the evil, too, who have appeared outwardly like the good for piety, worship, speech and deeds, although wicked inwardly. With those, however, who have first acknowledged and lived by truths of faith and then lived contrary to them and rejected them and particularly if they have denied them, good and evil are no longer separate, but mixed. Such a person has appropriated both good and evil to himself, and thus combined and mixed them.

[4] 4. He then mixes good and evil to a point where they cannot be separated. This follows from what has just been said. And if evil cannot be separated from good and good from evil, a person can be neither in heaven nor in hell. Everyone must be in one or the other; he cannot be in both; for so he would be now in heaven and now in hell; and in heaven he would act in hell's favor and in hell act in heaven's favor. He would thus destroy the life of all around him, heavenly life among the angels and infernal life among the devils; as a result everyone's life would perish. For everyone must live his own life; no one lives a life foreign to his own, still less one opposed to it. Hence, in every man after death, when he becomes a spirit or a spiritual being, the Lord separates good from evil and evil from good, good from evil in those who are inwardly in evil, and evil from good in those inwardly in good. This accords with His own words:

To every one who has, shall be given, that he may abound, and from him who has not, shall even what he has be taken away (Mt 13:12; 25:29; Mk 4:25; Lu 8:18; 19:26).

[5] Fifth: Since good and evil in anyone must be separated and in such a person cannot be, he is destroyed in all that is truly human. As was shown earlier, everyone has what is truly human from rationality, in that he can see and know what is true and good if he wishes, and from liberty, enabling him to will, think, speak and do it. But this liberty has been destroyed along with their rationality in those who have commingled good and evil in themselves, for they cannot from good see evil, nor from evil recognize good; the two make one in them. Hence they no longer possess rationality in any efficacy or power, nor any liberty. For this reason they are like the sheerest wild fantasies, as we said above, and no longer look like men but like bones covered with skin, and therefore when mentioned are referred to not as "he" or "she" but "it." Such is the lot of those who have commingled sacred and profane in the manner we have described. There are several kinds of profanation which are not of this character, however; of them in a later section.

No one can profane holy things in the way described who is ignorant of them. For one who is ignorant of them cannot acknowledge them and then deny them. Those, therefore, who are outside Christendom and know nothing of the Lord or of redemption and salvation at His hands do not profane the holiness of this in not accepting it or even by speaking against it. The Jews do not profane its sanctity, for from infancy they have no desire to receive and acknowledge it. It would be otherwise if they received and acknowledged it and afterwards denied it. This seldom occurs, however; for many among them acknowledge it outwardly but deny it inwardly and are like hypocrites. But those who first accept and acknowledge and later lapse and deny, are the ones who profane holy things by mingling them with profane.

[2] It is beside the point here that holy things are accepted and acknowledged in infancy and childhood, as they are by every Christian. For what pertains to faith and charity is not accepted and acknowledged at that age from any rationality and liberty, that is, in the understanding from the will, but only by the memory and from confidence in the teacher; and if the life is in accord it is so by blind obedience. If, however, on coming into the exercise of his rationality and freedom, which one does gradually in growing up to youth and manhood, a man acknowledges truths and lives by them only later to deny them, he does mingle the holy with the profane and (as was said above) from being human becomes a monster. On the other hand, if a man is in evil after attaining rationality and freedom, that is, after becoming his own master, even in his early manhood, but later acknowledges truths of faith and lives by them and remains in them also to the close of life, he does not commingle the holy and the profane. The Lord then severs the evils of his earlier life from the good of his later life, as is done with all who repent. Of this more will be said in what follows.

(iii) There are many kinds of profanation of what is holy, but this kind is the worst of all. In the widest sense by profanation all impiety is meant, and by profaners, therefore, all the impious who at heart deny God, the holiness of the Word, and consequently the spiritual things of the church which are essentially holy, and who also speak of them impiously. We are not now treating of such profaners but of those who profess God, uphold the holiness of the Word, and acknowledge the spiritual things of the church (yet most persons do so with the lips only). These commit profanation for the reason that holiness from the Word is in them and with them, and this which is in them, part of their understanding and will, they profane. But in the impious who deny the Divine and divine things, there is nothing holy which they can profane; they are profaners, of course, but still not profane as the others are.

The profanation of what is holy is meant in the second precept of the Decalog, "You shall not profane the name of your God," and that it ought not to be profaned is meant in the Lord's Prayer by "Hallowed be Thy name." Hardly anyone in Christendom understands what is meant by God's name. The reason for this is that in the spiritual world names are not what they are in this world; everyone has a name in accord with the character of his love and wisdom. As soon as he enters a society or into fellowship with others he is named according to his character. This can be done in spiritual language, which is such that it can give a name to everything, for each letter in the alphabet signifies some one thing, and the several letters combined in a word, making a person's name, involve the whole state of the subject. This is among the wonders in the spiritual world.

[2] From this it is plain that by "the name of God" in the Word, God with all the divine in Him and proceeding from Him is signified. And as the Word is the divine proceeding, it is God's name, and as all the divine things which are called the spiritual things of the church are from the Word, they, too, are God's name. It may be seen then what is meant in the second commandment of the Decalog by

You shall not profane the name of God (Ex 20:7);

and in the Lord's Prayer by

Hallowed be Thy name (Mt 6:9).

The name of God and of the Lord has a like signification in many passages in the Word of either Testament, as in Mt 7:22; 10:22; 18:5, 20; 19:29; 21:9; 24:9, 10; Jn 1:12; 2:23; 3:17, 18; 12:13, 28; 14:14-16; 16:23, 24, 26, 27; 17:6; 20:31; besides other passages, and in very many in the Old Testament.

[3] One who knows this significance of "name" can know what is signified by these words of the Lord:

Whoever receives a prophet in the name of a prophet will receive a prophet's reward; whoever receives a righteous man in the name of a righteous man will receive a righteous man's reward ... and whoever will give one of these little ones to drink a cup of cold water only in the name of a disciple ... shall not lose a reward (Mt 10:41, 42).

One who understands by the name of a prophet, of a righteous man and of a disciple only a prophet, a righteous man and a disciple knows only the sense of the letter in that passage. Nor does he know what is signified by a prophet's reward, a righteous man's reward, or by the reward given a disciple for a cup of cold water, when yet by the name and reward of a prophet the state and happiness of those who are in divine truths is meant; by the name and reward of a righteous man is meant the state and happiness of those in divine goods; by a disciple is meant the state of those who are in a measure of the spiritual things of the church, and by a cup of cold water is meant a measure of truth.

[4] That the nature of a state of love and wisdom or of good and truth is meant by "name" is also made evident by these words of the Lord:

He who enters in by the door is the shepherd of the sheep; the porter opens to him, and the sheep hear his voice; he calls his own sheep by name, and leads them out (Jn 10:2, 3).

To "call the sheep by name" is to teach and lead everyone who is in the good of charity according to the state of his love and wisdom; by the "door" the Lord is meant, as verse 9 makes plain:

I am the door; if a man enters by Me, he will be saved (Jn 10:9).

It is clear from this that for one to be saved the Lord Himself is to be approached; one who does so is a "shepherd of the sheep" and one who does not is a "thief" and a "robber" (so the first verse of the chapter).

Profanation of what is holy is predicated of those who know truths of faith and goods of charity from the Word and also acknowledge them in some measure, not of those who do not know them, nor of those who impiously reject them altogether. Therefore what now follows is said of the former, not of the latter; by the former many kinds of profanation, lighter and graver, are committed, but they may be summed up in the seven following.

A first kind of profanation on their part is making jokes from the Word or about the Word, or of and about the divine things of the church. Some do this from a bad habit, picking names or expressions from the Word and mingling them with unseemly and sometimes filthy speech. This cannot be done without some contempt being added for the Word. Yet the Word in each and all things is divine and holy; every expression in it stores in its bosom something divine and by means of it gives communication with heaven. This kind of profanation is lighter or more grave according to one's acknowledgment of the sacredness of the Word and to the unseemliness of the comment into which it is brought by those who jest about it.

[2] A second kind of profanation by those under discussion is that while they understand and acknowledge divine truths, they live contrary to them. Those who only understand profane more lightly, and those who also acknowledge profane more seriously; for the understanding only teaches quite as a preacher does, but does not of itself unite with the will, but acknowledgment does, for one cannot acknowledge anything without the consent of the will. Still this union with the will varies and the profanation is according to the measure of it in living contrary to acknowledged truths. Thus if one acknowledges that revenge and hatred, adultery and fornication, fraud and deceit, blasphemy and lying are sins against God and yet commits them, he is therefore in the more grievous of this kind of profanation. For the Lord says:

The servant who knows his lord's will and does not do it, shall be beaten with many strokes (Lu 12:47).

And again,

If you were blind, you would not have sin, but you say, We see; therefore your sin remains (Jn 9:41).

But it is one thing to acknowledge apparent truths and another to acknowledge genuine truths. Those who acknowledge genuine truths and yet do not live by them appear in the spiritual world to be without the light and warmth of life in voice and speech, as though they were so much inertness.

[3] A third kind of profanation is committed by those who apply the sense of the letter of the Word to confirm evil loves and false principles. This is because the confirmation of falsity is the denial of truth, and the confirmation of evil is a rejection of good. In its bosom the Word is nothing but divine truth and good. But this does not appear in the lowest sense or sense of the letter in genuine truths, except where the Lord and the very way of salvation are taught, but in clothed truths, called appearances of truth.

That sense can therefore be seized upon to confirm heresies of many kinds. But one who confirms evil loves does violence to divine goods, and one who confirms false principles does violence to divine truths. The latter violence is called falsification of truth and the former adulteration of good; both are meant by "bloods" 231-1 in the Word. For a spiritual holiness, which is also the spirit of truth proceeding from the Lord, is in every particular of the sense of the letter of the Word. This holiness is injured when the Word is falsified and adulterated. It is plain that this is profanation.

[4] A fourth kind of profanation is committed by those who utter pious and holy things and also counterfeit affections of a love for them in tone and manner, and yet at heart do not believe and love them. Most of these are hypocrites and Pharisees who are deprived after death of all truth and good and thereupon are sent into outer darkness. Those who have confirmed themselves by this kind of profanation against the Divine and against the Word and thus against the spiritual things of the Word, sit in outer darkness dumb, unable to speak, wanting to babble pious and holy things as they did in the world, but unable to do so. For in the spiritual world everyone is compelled to speak as he thinks. A hypocrite, however, wants to speak otherwise than he thinks, but there is impediment in the tongue as a result of which he can only mumble. Hypocrisies are lighter or more grave in the measure of the confirmation against God and of the outward rationalizing in favor of God.

[5] A fifth kind of profanation is committed by those who ascribe to themselves what is divine. These are meant by Lucifer in Isaiah 14; and by Lucifer Babylon is meant, as is plain from verses 4 and 24 of that chapter, where the fate, too, of such profaners is described. The same profaners are also meant and described in the Apocalypse (chapter 17) under the harlot seated on the scarlet beast. Babylon and Chaldea are mentioned at many places in the Word; by Babylon profanation of good is meant and by Chaldea profanation of truth; the one and the other committed by those who ascribe to themselves what is divine.

[6] A sixth kind of profanation is committed by those who acknowledge the Word but deny the divine of the Lord. In the world they are called Socinians and some Arians. The lot of both is that they invoke the Father and not the Lord and keep praying the Father, some of them for the sake of the Son, that they may be admitted to heaven, but in vain, until they lose hope of salvation. They are then sent down to hell among deniers of God. They are meant by those who blaspheme the Holy Spirit and who will not be forgiven in this world or that to come (Mt 12:32). For God is one in person and essence, in Him is the Trinity, and this God is the Lord. Since the Lord is heaven also and thus those in heaven are in the Lord, those who deny the divine of the Lord cannot be

admitted to heaven and be in the Lord. It was shown above that the Lord is heaven and that those in heaven are therefore in Him.

[7] The seventh kind of profanation is committed by those who first acknowledge and live by divine truths and then recede from them and deny them. This is the worst kind of profanation because holy things are mixed by them with profane to the point where they cannot be separated. Yet they must be separated for one to be either in heaven or in hell, and as this cannot be accomplished with them, all that is human, either of the understanding or of the will, is rooted out, and they become, as we said, no longer human beings. Almost the same occurs with those who acknowledge the divine things of the Word and of the church at heart but immerse them entirely in their proprium, which is a love of ruling over all things, of which much has been said before. After death, when they become spirits, they do not want to be led by the Lord but by themselves. When loose rein is given their love, they want to rule not only over heaven but over the Lord, too; and as they cannot do this, they deny the Lord and become devils. It should be known that the life's love, which is one's reigning love, remains with everyone after death and cannot be taken away.

[8] Profaners of this class are meant by the lukewarm, of whom it is written in the Apocalypse:

I know your works, that you are neither cold nor hot; would that you were cold or hot; but because you are lukewarm, and neither cold nor hot, I will spue you out of my mouth (3:14, 15, 16).

This manner of profanation is also described by the Lord in Matthew:

When the unclean spirit goes out from a man, he walks through dry places, seeking rest but finds none. Then he says, I will return to the house whence I came out. When he returns and finds it empty, swept and garnished for him, he goes and gathers to him seven other spirits worse than himself, and they enter and dwell there; and the last state of the man is worse than the first (12:43-45).

The conversion of the man is described by the unclean spirit's going out of him; his reverting to his former evils when things good and true have been cast out, is described by the return of the unclean spirit with seven worse than himself into the house garnished for him; and the profanation of the holy by what is profane is described by the last state of that man being worse than the first. The same is meant by this passage in John,

Jesus said to the man healed in the pool of Bethesda: Sin no more, lest something worse befall you (5:14).

[9] That the Lord provides that man shall not acknowledge truths inwardly and afterwards leave them and become profane, is meant by these words:

He has blinded their eyes and hardened their heart, that they should not see with their eyes and understand with their heart, and be converted, and I should heal them (Jn 12:40).

"Lest they should be converted, and I should heal them" signifies lest they should acknowledge truths and then depart from them and thus become profane. For the same reason the Lord spoke in parables, as He Himself says (Mt 13:13). The Jews were forbidden to eat fat and blood (Lev 3:17, 7:13, 25); this signifies that they were not to profane holy things, for "fat" signifies divine good and "blood" divine truth. In Matthew the Lord teaches that once converted a man must continue in good and truth to the close of life:

Jesus said: Whosoever perseveres to the end, shall be saved (10:20; similarly Mk 13:13).

(iv) The Lord therefore does not admit man interiorly into truths of wisdom and at the same time into goods of love except as man can be kept in them to the close of life. To demonstrate this we must proceed by steps for two reasons; one, because it concerns human salvation, and the other, because a knowledge of the laws of permission (to be considered in the next chapter) depends on a knowledge of this law. It concerns human salvation, because, as has just been said, one who first acknowledges what is divine in Word and church and subsequently departs from them profanes what is holy most grievously. In order, then, that this arcanum of divine providence may be revealed so that the rational man can see it in his own light, it is to be unfolded as follows:

1. Evil and good cannot exist together in man's interior being, consequently neither can the falsity of evil and the truth of good. 2. Good and the truth of good can be introduced into man's interior being only so far as evil and the falsity of evil there have been removed. 3. If good with its truth were introduced there before or further than evil with its falsity is removed, man would depart from the good and go back to his evil. 4. When man is in evil many truths may be introduced into his understanding and kept in memory, and yet not be profaned. 5. But the Lord in His divine providence takes the greatest care that they are not received from the understanding by the will sooner or more largely than man as of himself removes evil in the external man. 6. Should it welcome them sooner or in larger measure, the will would adulterate good and the understanding would falsify truth by mingling them with evils and falsities. 7. The Lord therefore admits man inwardly into truths of wisdom and goods of love only so far as man can be kept in them to the close of life.

In order, then, that this arcanum of divine providence may be disclosed so that the rational man will see it in his light, the points made will be explained one by one. 1. Evil and good cannot exist together in man's interior being, consequently neither can the falsity of evil and the truth of good. By man's interiors the internal of his thought is meant. Of this he knows nothing until he comes into the spiritual world and its light, which happens on death. In the natural world it can be known only by the enjoyment of his love in the external of his thought, and from evils themselves as he examines them in himself. For the internal of thought in man is so closely connected with the external of thought that they cannot be separated (of this more may be seen above). We say "good and truth of good," and "evil and falsity of evil" because good cannot exist apart from its truth nor evil apart from its falsity. They are bedfellows or partners, for the life of good is from its truth and the life of truth is from its good; the same is to be said of evil and its falsity.

[2] The rational man can see without explanation that evil with its falsity and good with its truth cannot exist in man's interiors at the same time. For evil is the opposite of good and good the opposite of evil; two opposites cannot coexist. Implanted in all evil, moreover, is a hatred for good, and implanted in all good the love of protecting itself against evil and removing it from itself. Consequently one cannot be where the other is. If they were together conflict and combat would start and destruction ensue, as the Lord teaches also in these

words:

> Every kingdom divided against itself is desolated, and every city or house divided against itself does not stand ... Whoever is not with me is against me, and whoever does not gather with me disperses (Mt 25:30);

and in another place,

> No one can serve two masters at the same time: for either he will hate the one and love the other ... (Mt 6:24).

Two opposites are impossible in one substance or form without its being torn apart and destroyed. If one should advance and approach the other, they would keep apart like two enemies, one retiring to his camp or fort, and the other posting himself outside. This happens with evil and good in a hypocrite; he harbors both, but the evil is inside and the good outside and so the two are separate and not mingled. It is plain then that evil with its falsity and good with its truth cannot coexist.

[3] 2. Good and the truth of good can be introduced into man's interiors only so far as evil and the falsity of evil there have been removed. This is a necessary consequence from what has preceded, for as evil and good cannot exist together, good cannot be introduced before evil has been removed. We say man's "interiors" and mean by these the internal of thought; and in these, now being considered, either the Lord or the devil must be present. The Lord is there after reformation and the devil before reformation. So far as man suffers himself to be reformed, therefore, the devil is cast out, but so far as he does not suffer himself to be reformed the devil remains. Anyone can see that the Lord cannot enter as long as the devil is there, and he is there as long as man keeps the door closed where man acts together with the Lord. The Lord teaches in the Apocalypse that He enters when that door is opened by man's mediation:

> I stand at the door, and knock; if anyone hears my voice, and opens the door, I will come in to him, and sup with him, and he with Me (3:20).

The door is opened by man's removing evil, fleeing and turning away from it as infernal and diabolical. Whether one says "evil" or "the devil," it is one and the same, in turn whether one says "good" or "the Lord," for within all good is the Lord and within all evil is the devil. From these considerations the truth of this proposition is plain.

[4] 3. If good with its truth were introduced before or further than evil with its falsity is removed, man would depart from the good and go back to his evil. This is because evil would be the stronger, and what is stronger conquers, eventually if not then. As long as evil is stronger, good cannot be introduced into the inner chambers but only into the entry hall; for evil and good, as we said, cannot exist together, and what is in the entry hall is removed by its enemy in the chamber. Thus good is receded from and evil is returned to, which is the worst kind of profanation.

[5] Furthermore, it is the enjoyment of man's life to love himself and the world above all else. This enjoyment cannot be removed in a moment, but only gradually. In the measure in which it remains in man, evil is stronger in him and can be removed only as self-love becomes a love of uses, or as the love of ruling is not for its own sake but for the sake of uses. Uses then make the head, and self-love or the love of ruling is at first the body under the head and finally the feet, on which to walk. Who does not see that good should be the head, and

that when it is, the Lord is there? Good and use are one. Who does not see that when evil is the head, the devil is there? As civil and moral good and, in its external form, spiritual good, too, are still to be received, who does not see that these then constitute the feet and the soles of the feet, and are trodden on?

[6] Inasmuch, then, as man's state of life is to be inverted so that what is uppermost may be lowermost, and the inversion cannot be instantaneous, for the chief enjoyment of his life, coming of self-love and the love of ruling, can be diminished and turned into a love of uses only gradually, the Lord cannot introduce good sooner or further than this evil is removed; done earlier or further, man would recede from good and return to his evil.

[7] 4. When man is in evil many truths may be introduced into his understanding and kept in memory, and still not be profaned. This is because the understanding does not flow into the will, but the will into the understanding. As the understanding does not flow into the will, many truths can be received by the understanding and held in memory and still not be mingled with the evil in the will, and the holy thus not profaned. Moreover, it is incumbent on everyone to learn truths from the Word or from preaching, to lay them up in the memory and to think about them. For by truths held in the memory and entering into the thought, the understanding is to teach the will, that is, the man, what he should do. This is therefore the chief means of reformation. Truths that are only in the understanding and thence in the memory are not in man but outside him.

[8] Man's memory may be compared to the ruminatory stomach of certain animals in which they put their food; as long as it is there, it is not in but outside their body; as they draw it thence and consume it, it becomes part of their life, and their body is nourished. The food in man's memory is not material but spiritual, namely truths, rightly knowledges; so far as he takes them thence by thinking, which is like ruminating, his spiritual mind is nourished. It is the will's love that has the desire and the appetite, so to speak, and that causes them to be taken thence and to be nourishing. If that love is evil, it desires or has an appetite for what is unclean, but if good, for what is clean, and sets aside, rejects and casts out what is unsuitable; this is done in various ways.

[9] 5. But the Lord in His divine providence takes the greatest care that truths are not received from the understanding by the will sooner or more largely than man as of himself removes evil in his external man. For what is from the will enters man, is appropriated to him, and becomes part of his life, and in that life, which is man's from the will, evil and good cannot exist together, for so he would perish. The two may, however, be in the understanding, where they are called falsities of evil and truths of good, and without being mingled; else man could not behold evil from good or know good from evil; but there they are distinguishable and separated like the inner and outer sections of a house. When a wicked man thinks and speaks what is good, he is thinking and speaking externally to himself, but inwardly when he thinks and speaks what is evil; his speech, therefore, when he speaks what is good, comes off a wall, as it were. It can be likened to fruit fair outside but wormy and decayed inside, or to the shell, especially, of a serpent's egg.

[10] 6. Should the will welcome truths sooner or in larger measure, it would adulterate good and the understanding would falsify truth by mingling them

with evils and falsities. When the will is in evil, it adulterates good in the understanding, and good adulterated in the understanding is evil in the will, for it confirms that evil is good and good is evil. So evil deals with all good, which is its opposite. Evil also falsifies truth, for truth of good is the opposite of the falsity of evil; this is done in the understanding by the will, and not by the understanding alone. Adulterations of good are depicted in the Word by adulteries and falsifications of truth by whoredoms. These adulterations and falsifications are effected by reasonings from the natural man which is in evil, and also by confirmations of appearances in the sense of the letter of the Word.

[11] The love of self, the head of all evils, surpasses other loves in the ability to adulterate goods and falsify truths, and it does this by misuse of the rationality which every man, wicked as well as good, enjoys from the Lord. By confirmations it can in fact make evil look exactly like good and falsity like truth. What can it not do when it can prove by a thousand arguments that nature created itself and then created human beings, animals and plants of every kind, and also prove that by influx from within itself nature causes men to live, to think analytically and to understand wisely? Self-love excels in ability to prove whatever it desires because a certain glamour of varicolored light overlays it. This glamour is the vainglory of that love in being wise and thus also of being eminent and dominant.

[12] And yet, when self-love has proved such things, it becomes so blind that it sees man only as a beast, and that man and beast both think, and if a beast could also speak, conceives it would be man in another form. If it were induced by some manner of persuasion to believe that something of the human being survives death, it then is so blind as to believe that the beast also survives; and that the something which lives after death is only a subtle exhalation of life, like a vapor, constantly falling back to its corpse, or is something vital without sight, hearing or speech, and so is blind, deaf and dumb, soaring about and cogitating. Self-love entertains many other insanities with which nature, in itself dead, inspires its fantasy. Such is the effect of self-love, which regarded in itself is love of the proprium. Man's proprium, in respect of its affections which are all natural, is not unlike the life of a beast, and in respect of its perceptions, inasmuch as they spring from these affections, is not unlike a bird of night. One who constantly immerses his thoughts in his proprium, therefore, cannot be raised out of natural light into spiritual light and see anything of God, heaven or eternal life. Since the love of the proprium is of this nature and yet excels in the ability to confirm whatever it pleases, it has a similar ability to adulterate the goods of the Word and falsify its truths, even while it is constrained by some necessity to confess them.

[13] 7. The Lord therefore does not admit man inwardly into truths of wisdom and goods of love except as man can be kept in them to the close of life. The Lord does this lest man fall into that most serious kind of profanation of which we have treated in this chapter. In view of that peril the Lord also tolerates evils of life and many heresies in worship, the tolerance of which will be the subject of the following chapter.

Section 13

LAWS ON PERMISSION ARE ALSO LAWS OF DIVINE PROVIDENCE

There are no laws of permission per se or apart from the laws of divine providence; rather they are the same. Hence to say that God permits something does not mean that He wills it, but that He cannot avert it in view of the end, which is salvation. Whatever is done for the sake of that end is in accord with the laws of divine providence. For divine providence, as was said, constantly travels in a different direction from that of man's will and against his will, always intent on its objective. At each moment of its activity or at each step in its progress, as it perceives man straying from that end, it directs, turns and disposes him according to its laws, leading him away from evil and to good. It will be seen in what follows that this cannot be done without the tolerance of evil. Furthermore, nothing can be permitted for no cause, and the cause can only be in some law of divine providence, explaining why it is permitted.

One who does not acknowledge divine providence at all does not acknowledge God at heart, but nature instead of God, and human prudence instead of divine providence. This does not appear to be so because man can think and speak in two ways. He can think and speak in one way from his inner self and in another from his outer self. This capability is like a hinge that lets a door swing either way, in one direction as one enters, in the other as one leaves; or like a sail which can take a ship one way or the other as the skipper spreads it. Those who have confirmed themselves in favor of human prudence to the denial of divine providence see nothing else as long as they are in this way of thinking, no matter what they see, hear or read, nor can they, for they accept nothing from heaven but only from themselves. As they draw their conclusions from appearances and fallacies alone and see nothing else, they can swear that prudence is all. If they also recognize nature only, they become enraged at defenders of divine providence, except that they think when these are priests they are simply pursuing their teaching and office.

We will enumerate now some things that are tolerated and yet are in accord with laws of divine providence, by which, however, the merely natural man confirms himself in favor of nature and against God and in favor of human prudence and against divine providence. For instance he reads in the Word that:

1. Adam, wisest of men, and his wife allowed themselves to be led astray by the serpent, and God did not avert this in His divine providence. 2. Their first son, Cain, killed his brother Abel, and God did not speak to him and dissuade him but only afterwards cursed him. 3. The Israelites worshiped a golden calf in the wilderness and acknowledged it as the god that had brought them out of Egypt, yet Jehovah saw this from Mt. Sinai near by and did not warn against it. 4. David numbered the people and as a consequence a pestilence befell them in which so many thousands of them perished; God sent the prophet Gad to him not before but after the deed and denounced punishment. 5. Solomon was

allowed to establish idolatrous worship. 6. After him many kings were allowed to profane the temple and the sacred things of the church. 7. And finally that nation was permitted to crucify the Lord.

One who hails nature and human prudence sees nothing but what contradicts divine providence in these and many other passages of the Word. He can use them as arguments in denial of providence, if not in his outward thought nearest to speech, still in his inner thought, remote from it.

Every worshiper of self and nature confirms himself against divine providence:

1. When he sees such numbers of wicked in the world and so many of their impieties and how some glory in them, and sees the men go unpunished by God. 2. He confirms himself the more against divine providence when he sees plots, schemes and frauds succeed even against the devout, just and sincere, and injustice triumph over justice in the courts and in business. 3. He confirms himself especially on seeing the impious advanced to honors and becoming leaders in the state or in the church, abounding, too, in riches and living in luxury and magnificence, and on the other hand sees worshipers of God despised and poor. 4. He also confirms himself against divine providence when he reflects that wars are permitted and the slaughter of so many in them and the looting of so many cities, nations and families. 5. Furthermore, he reflects that victories are on the side of prudence and not always on the side of justice, and that it is immaterial whether a commander is upright or not.

Besides many other things of the kind, all of which are permissions according to laws of divine providence.

The same natural man confirms himself against divine providence when he observes how religion is circumstanced in various nations.

1. Some are totally ignorant of God; some worship the sun and moon; others idols and monstrous graven images, dead men also. 2. He notes especially that the Mohammedan religion is accepted by so many empires and kingdoms. 3. He notes that the Christian religion is found only in a very small part of the habitable globe, called Europe, and is divided there. 4. Also that some in Christendom arrogate divine power to themselves, want to be worshiped as gods, and invoke the dead. 5. And there are those who place salvation in certain phrases which they are to think and speak and not at all in good works which they are to do; likewise there are few who live their religion. 6. Besides there are heretical ideas; these have been many and some exist today, like those of the Quakers, Moravians and Anabaptists, besides others. 7. Judaism also persists.

As a result, one who denies divine providence concludes that religion in itself is nothing, but still is needed to serve as a restraint.

To these more arguments can be added today by which those who think interiorly in favor of nature and of human prudence alone can still further confirm themselves. For example:

1. All Christendom has acknowledged three Gods, not knowing that God is one in essence and in person and that He is the Lord. 2. It has not been known before this that there is a spiritual sense in each particular of the Word from which it derives its holiness. 3. Again, Christians have not known that to avoid evils as sins is the Christian religion itself. 4. It has also been unknown that the

human being lives as such after death.

For men may ask themselves and one another, "Why does divine providence, if it exists, reveal such things for the first time now?"

All the points listed in nn. 236-239 have been put forward in order that it may be seen that each and all things which take place in the world are of divine providence; consequently divine providence is in the least of man's thoughts and actions and thereby is universal. But this cannot be seen unless the points are taken up one by one; therefore they will be explained briefly in the order in which they were listed, beginning with n. 236.

The wisest of human beings, Adam and his wife, allowed themselves to be led astray by the serpent, and God in His divine providence did not avert this. This is because by Adam and his wife the first human beings created in the world are not meant, but the people of the Most Ancient Church, whose new creation or regeneration is described thus: their creation anew or regeneration in Genesis 1 by the creation of heaven and earth; their wisdom and intelligence by the Garden of Eden; and the end of that church by their eating of the tree of knowledge. For the Word in its bosom is spiritual, containing arcana of divine wisdom, and in order to contain them has been composed throughout in correspondences and representations. It is plain then that the men of that church, who at first were the wisest of men but finally became the worst through pride in their own intelligence, were led astray not by a serpent but by self-love, meant in Genesis by "the serpent's head," which the Seed of the woman, namely, the Lord, was to trample.

[2] Who cannot see from reason that other things are meant than those recorded literally like history? For who can understand that the world could be created as there described? The learned therefore labor over the explanation of the things in the first chapter, finally confessing that they do not understand them. So of the two trees placed in the garden or paradise, one of life and the other of knowledge, the latter as a stumbling-block. Again, that just by eating of this tree they transgressed so greatly that not only they but their posterity--the whole human race--became subject to damnation; further, how any serpent could lead them astray; besides other things, as that the woman was created out of a rib of her husband; that they recognized their nakedness after the fall and covered it with fig leaves; that coats of skin were given them to cover the body; and that cherubim with a flaming sword were stationed to guard the way to the tree of life.

[3] All this is representative, describing the establishment, state, alteration and finally destruction of the Most Ancient Church. The arcana involved, contained in the spiritual sense which fills the details, may be seen explained in Arcana Caelestia, on Genesis and Exodus, published at London. There it may also be seen that by the tree of life the Lord is meant as to His divine providence, and by the tree of knowledge man is meant as to his own prudence.

Their first son, Cain, killed his brother Abel, and God did not speak to him and dissuade him, but only afterwards cursed him. As the Most Ancient Church is meant by Adam and his wife, as we have just said, the two essentials of a church, love and wisdom or charity and faith are meant by their first sons, Cain and Abel. Love and charity are meant by Abel, and wisdom and faith and in particular wisdom separate from love, and faith separate from charity, are meant by Cain. Wisdom as well as faith when separate is of such a nature that it not only rejects love and charity, but also destroys them and thus kills its brother. It is well known in Christendom that faith apart from charity does so; see Doctrine of the New Jerusalem about Faith.

[2] The curse on Cain portends the spiritual state into which those come after death who separate faith from charity or wisdom from love. But lest wisdom or faith should perish, a mark was put on Cain lest he be slain, for love cannot exist without wisdom, nor charity without faith. As almost the same thing is represented by this as by eating of the tree of knowledge, it follows next after the account of Adam and his wife. Moreover, those in faith separate from charity are in intelligence of their own; those who are in charity and thence in faith are in intelligence from the Lord, thus in divine providence.

The Israelites worshiped a golden calf in the wilderness and acknowledged it as the god that had brought them out of Egypt, yet Jehovah saw this from Mt. Sinai near by and did not warn against it. This occurred in the desert of Sinai near the mountain. It is in accordance with all the laws of divine providence recounted so far and with those to follow that Jehovah did not restrain the Israelites from that atrocious worship. This evil was permitted them that they might not all perish. For the children of Israel were brought out of Egypt to represent the Lord's church; they could not represent it unless the Egyptian idolatry was first rooted out of their hearts. This could not be done unless it was left to them to act upon what was in their hearts and then to remove it on being severely punished. What further is signified by that worship, by the threat that they would be entirely rejected, and by the possibility that a new nation might be raised from Moses, may be seen in Arcana Caelestia on Exodus 32, where these things are spoken of.

David numbered the people and as a consequence a pestilence befell them in which so many thousands of them perished; God sent the prophet Gad to him not before but after the deed and denounced punishment. One who confirms himself against divine providence may have various thoughts about this also and ponder especially why David was not admonished first and why the people were so severely punished for the king's transgression. That he was not warned first is in accord with the laws of divine providence already adduced, especially with the two explained at nn. 129-153 and 154-174. The people were so severely punished for the king's transgression and seventy thousand smitten by the pestilence not on account of the king but on account of themselves, for we read

The anger of Jehovah kindled still more against Israel; therefore He incited David against them saying, Go, number Israel and Judah (2 Sa 24:1).

Solomon was allowed to establish idolatrous forms of worship. For he was to represent the Lord's kingdom or church in all varieties of religion in the world. For the church established with the Israelitish and Jewish nation was a representative church; all of its judgments and statutes represented the spiritual things of a church, which are its internals. The people represented the church, the king the Lord, David the Lord to come into the world, Solomon the Lord after His coming. As the Lord after the glorification of His humanity had all power over heaven and earth (as He said, Mt 28:18), Solomon as representative of Him appeared in glory and magnificence, was wise beyond all earthly kings, and also built the temple. Moreover, he permitted and set up the forms of worship of many nations, by which the various religions of the world were represented. His wives, who numbered seven hundred and his concubines who numbered three hundred (1 Kgs 11:13), had a similar signification, for "wife" in the Word signifies the church and "concubine" a form of religion. Hence it may be evident why it was granted Solomon to build the temple, by which the Divine Humanity of the Lord (Jn 2:19, 21) is signified and the church, too; and why he was allowed to establish idolatrous forms of worship and to take so many wives. See Doctrine of the New Jerusalem about the Lord (nn. 43, 44) that in many places in the Word the Lord who was to come into the world is meant by David.

After Solomon many kings were allowed to profane the temple and the sacred things of the church. This was because the people represented the church and the king was their head. The Israelitish and Jewish nation was of such a nature that they could not represent the church for long, for at heart they were idolaters; they therefore relapsed gradually from representative worship, perverting all things of the church, even to devastating it finally. This was represented by the profanations of the temple by the kings and by the people's idolatries; the full devastation of the church was represented by the destruction of the temple, the carrying off of Israel, and the captivity of Judah in Babylon. Such was the cause of this toleration; and what is done for some cause is done under divine providence according to one of its laws.

That nation was permitted to crucify the Lord. This was because the church with that nation was entirely devastated and had become such that they not only did not know or acknowledge the Lord, but hated Him. Still, all that they did to Him was according to laws of His divine providence. See in Doctrine of the New Jerusalem about the Lord (nn. 12-14) and in Doctrine of the New Jerusalem about Faith (nn. 34, 35) that the passion of the cross was the last temptation or battle by which the Lord fully conquered the hells and fully glorified His Humanity.

So far the points listed at n. 236 have been explained, involving passages in the Word by which the naturally minded reasoner may confirm himself against divine providence. For, as was said, whatever such a man sees, hears or reads he can make into an argument against providence. Few persons, however, confirm themselves against divine providence from incidents in the Word, but many do so from things before their eyes, listed at n. 237. These are to be explained now in like manner.

Every worshiper of self and of nature confirms himself against divine providence when he sees so many impious in the world and so many of their impieties and how some glory in them, yet sees the impious go unpunished by God. All impieties and all gloryings in them are permissions, of which the causes are laws of divine providence. Each human being can freely, indeed very freely, think what he wills, against God as well as in favor of God. One who thinks against God is rarely punished in the natural world, for he is always in a state to be reformed then, but is punished in the spiritual world, which is done after death, for then he can no longer be reformed.

[2] That laws of divine providence are the causes of tolerance is clear from the laws set forth above, if you will recall and examine them. They are: that man shall act in freedom according to reason (of this law above, nn. 71-79); that

he shall not be forced by external means to think and will, thus to believe and love what is of religion, but bring himself and sometimes compel himself to do so (nn. 129-153); that there is no such thing as one's own prudence, but there only appears to be and it should so appear, but divine providence is universal from being in the least things (nn. 191-213); divine providence looks to what is eternal, and to the temporal only as this makes one with the eternal (nn. 214-220); man is not admitted inwardly into truths of faith and goods of charity except as he can be kept in them to the close of life (nn. 221-233).

[3] That the laws of divine providence are the causes of tolerance will also be evident from the following, for one thing from this: evils are tolerated because of the end, which is salvation. Again from this: that divine providence is continual with the wicked as well as with the good. And finally from this: the Lord cannot act contrary to the laws of His divine providence because to do so would be to act contrary to His divine love and wisdom, thus contrary to Himself. Brought together, these laws can make the causes manifest why impieties are tolerated by the Lord and are not punished while they exist in the thought only and rarely, too, while they exist in intention, thus in the will but not in act. Yet its own punishment follows every evil; it is as if its punishment were inscribed on an evil, and the impious man suffers it after death.

[4] These considerations also explain the next point, listed at n. 237: The worshiper of self and of nature confirms himself still more against divine providence when he sees plots, schemes and frauds succeed even against the devout, just and sincere, and injustice triumph over justice in the courts and in business. All the laws of divine providence have requirements; and as they are the causes why such things are permitted, it is plain that for man to live as a human being and be reformed and saved, these things can be removed from him by the Lord only through means. The Word and, in particular, the precepts of the Decalog are the means with those who acknowledge all kinds of murder, adultery, theft and false witness to be sins. With those who do not acknowledge such things as sins, they are removed by means of the civil laws and fear of their penalties and by means also of the moral laws and fear of disrepute and consequent loss of standing and wealth. By the latter means the Lord leads the evil, but only away from doing such things, not from thinking and willing them. But by the former means He leads the good, not only away from doing them, but from thinking and willing them, too.

The worshiper of self and of nature confirms himself against divine providence on seeing the impious advanced to honors and becoming leaders in the state and in the church, abounding, too, in riches and living in luxury and magnificence, and on the other hand sees worshipers of God despised and poor. A worshiper of self and of nature believes that standing and riches are the greatest and the one felicity possible, thus felicity itself. If he has some thought of God as a result of worship begun in childhood, he calls them divine blessings, and as long as he is not elated by them he thinks that there is a God and worships Him. But in the worship there lurks a desire, of which he is unaware then, to be advanced by God to still higher standing and to still greater wealth. If he attains them, his worship tends more and more to externalities until it slips away and at last he makes little account of God and denies Him. The same thing occurs if he is cast down from the standing and loses the riches on which he has set his heart. What, then, are standing and riches to the wicked but stumbling blocks?

[2] To the good they are not, for these do not set their heart on them, but on the uses or goods for rendering which standing and wealth serve as means. Hence only a worshiper of self and of nature can confirm himself against divine providence because the impious are advanced to honors and become leaders in the state and in the church. Moreover, what is greater or less standing, or greater or less wealth? Is this not in itself imaginary? Is one person more blessed and happier than another for it? Is a great man's standing, or even a king's or an emperor's, not regarded in a year's time as a commonplace, no longer exalting his heart with joy but quite possibly becoming worthless to him? Have those with standing a larger measure of happiness than those with little standing or even the least standing, like farmers and their hands? May not these enjoy more happiness when it is well with them and they are content with their lot? What is more unquiet at heart, more often provoked, or more violently enraged than self-love? It happens as often as it is not honored to suit the haughtiness of its heart or as something does not succeed at its beck and wish. What, then, is standing except an idea, unless it attaches to the office or the use? Can the idea exist in any other thought than thought about self and the world, and does it not really mean that the world is all and eternity nothing?

[3] Something shall be said now why divine providence permits the impious at heart to be promoted to standing and to acquire wealth. The impious or the evil can render services as well as the pious or good, indeed with more fire, for they regard themselves in the use and their standing as the use. As self-love mounts, therefore, the lust of doing service for one's glory is fired. There is no such fire with the devout or good unless it is kindled incidentally to their standing. Therefore the Lord governs the impious at heart who have standing by their desire for a name and arouses them to perform uses to the community or their country, their society or city, and their fellow citizen or neighbor. With such persons this is the Lord's government which is called divine providence, for the Lord's kingdom is one of uses, and where only a few perform uses for uses' sake providence brings it about that worshipers of self are raised to higher offices, in which each is incited by his love to do good.

[4] Suppose an infernal kingdom in the world (though there is none) where self-love alone rules, which is itself the devil, would not everyone perform uses with the zeal of self-love and for the enhancement of his glory more than in another kingdom? The public good is borne on the lips of them all, but their own benefit in the heart. And as each relies on what rules him in order to become greater, and aspires to be greatest, how can he see that God exists? A smoke like that of a conflagration envelops him through which no spiritual truth can pass with its light. I have seen that smoke around the hells of such men. Light a lamp and inquire how many in present-day kingdoms aspire to eminence who are not loves of self and the world. Will you find fifty in a thousand who are loves of God, among whom, moreover, only a few aspire to eminence? Since so few are loves of God and so many are loves of self and the world and since the latter perform more uses by their ardor, how can one confirm himself against divine providence because the evil surpass the good in eminence and opulence?

[5] This is borne out also by these words of the Lord:

The lord praised the unjust steward because he had acted prudently; for the sons of this age are more prudent in their generation than the sons of light in their generation. So I say to you, Make friends for yourselves of the unjust mammon that when you fail they may receive you into eternal habitations (Lu 16:8, 9).

The meaning in the sense of the letter is plain. But in the spiritual sense by the "mammon of injustice" are meant knowledges of good and truth which the evil possess and employ solely to acquire standing and wealth for themselves. It is of these knowledges that the good or the children of light are to make friends for themselves and it is these knowledges that will conduct them into eternal homes. The Lord also teaches that many are loves of self and the world, and few are loves of God, in these words:

Wide is the gate, and broad is the way, which leads to destruction, and many there be who enter it, but narrow and strait is the way which leads to life, and there are few who find it (Mt 7:13, 14).

It may be seen above (n. 217) that eminence and riches are either curses or blessings, and with whom they are the one or the other.

Footnotes

202-1 It is the doctrine of all churches in Christendom that God the Father, God the Son and God the Holy Spirit is infinite, eternal, uncreated and omnipotent, as may be seen in the Athanasian Creed.

231-1 Plural in the Hebrew, especially of blood that has been shed. "Both" is emphatic here, and for the significance of the plural see Arcana Caelestia, n. 374e and Apocalypse Explained, n. 329(27).

The worshiper of self and of nature confirms himself against divine providence when he reflects that wars are permitted and the slaughter in them of so many men and the plundering of their wealth. It is not by divine providence that wars occur, for they entail murder, plunder, violence, cruelty, and other terrible evils which are diametrically opposed to Christian charity. Yet they cannot but be permitted because the life's love of mankind, since the time of the most ancient people, meant by Adam and his wife (n. 241), has become such that it wants to rule over others and finally over all, and also to possess the wealth of the world and finally all wealth. These two loves cannot be kept in fetters, for it is according to divine providence that everyone is allowed to act in freedom in accordance with reason, as may be seen above (nn. 71-97); and apart from permissions man cannot be led from evil by the Lord and consequently cannot be reformed and saved. For unless evils were allowed to break out, man would not see them, therefore would not acknowledge them, and thus could not be induced to resist them. Evils cannot be repressed, therefore, by any act of providence; if they were, they would remain shut in, and like a disease such as cancer and gangrene, would spread and consume everything vital in man.

[2] For from birth man is like a little hell between which and heaven there is perpetual discord. No one can be withdrawn from his hell by the Lord unless he sees he is in it and desires to be led out of it. This cannot be done apart from tolerations the causes of which are laws of divine providence. As a result, minor and major wars occur, the minor between owners of estates and their neighbors, and the major between sovereigns of kingdoms and their neighbors. Except for size the only difference is that the minor conflicts are held within limits by a country's laws and the major by the law of nations; each may wish to transgress its laws, but the minor cannot, and while the major can, still the possibility has limits.

[3] Hidden in the stores of divine wisdom are several causes why the major wars of kings and rulers, involving murder, looting, violence and cruelty as they do, are not prevented by the Lord, either at their beginning or during their course, only finally when the power of one or the other has been so reduced that he is in danger of annihilation. Some of the causes have been revealed to me and among them is this: all wars, although they are civil in character, represent in heaven states of the church and are correspondences. The wars described in the Word were all of this character; so are all wars at this day. Those in the Word are the wars which the children of Israel waged with various nations, Amorites, Moabites, Philistines, Syrians, Egyptians, Chaldeans and Assyrians. Moreover, it was when the children of Israel, who represented the church, departed from their precepts and statutes and fell into evils represented by other peoples (for each nation with which the children of Israel waged war represented a particular evil), that they were punished by that nation. For instance, when they profaned the sanctities of the church by foul idolatries they were punished by the Assyrians and Chaldeans because Assyria and Chaldea signify the profanation of what is holy. What was signified by the wars with the Philistines may be seen in Doctrine of the New Jerusalem about Faith (nn. 50-54).

[4] Wars at the present day, wherever they may occur, represent similar things. For all things which occur in the natural world correspond to spiritual

things in the spiritual world, and all spiritual things are related to the church. It is not known in the world which kingdoms in Christendom represent the Moabites, the Ammonites, the Syrians, the Philistines, the Chaldeans and the Assyrians or others, with whom the children of Israel waged war; yet there are nations that do so. Moreover, the condition of the church on earth and what the evils are into which it falls and for which it is punished by wars, cannot be seen at all in the natural world, for only externals are manifest here and these do not constitute the church. This is seen, however, in the spiritual world where internal conditions appear and in these the church itself consists. There all are united according to their various states. Conflicts between them correspond to wars, which on both sides are governed by the Lord correspondentially in accordance with His divine providence.

[5] The spiritual man acknowledges that wars on earth are ruled by the Lord's divine providence. The natural man does not, except that at a celebration of a victory he may thank God on his knees for having given the victory, and except for a few words on going into battle. But when he returns into himself he ascribes the victory either to the prudence of the general or to some counsel or incident in the midst of the fighting which escaped notice and yet decided the victory.

[6] It may be seen above (n. 212) that divine providence, which is called fortune, is in the least things, even in trivial ones, and if you acknowledge divine providence in these you will certainly do so in the issues of war. Success and happy conduct of war, moreover, are in common parlance called the fortune of war, and this is divine providence, to be found especially in a general's judgments and plans, although he may at the time and also afterwards ascribe all to his own prudence. This he may do if he will, for he has full freedom to think in favor of divine providence or against it, indeed in favor of God or against Him; but let him know that no judgment or plan is from himself; it comes either from heaven or from hell, from hell by permission, from heaven by providence.

A worshiper of self and of nature confirms himself against divine providence when he thinks, as he sees it, that victories are on the side of prudence and not always on the side of justice, and that it is immaterial whether a commander is upright or not. Victories seem to be on the side of prudence and not always on the side of justice, because man judges by the appearance and favors one side more than the other and can by reasoning confirm what he favors. Nor does he know that the justice of a cause is spiritual in heaven and natural in the world, as was said just above, and that the two are united in a connection of things past and of things to come, known only to the Lord.

[2] It is immaterial whether the commander is an upright man or not because, as was established above (n. 250), the evil as well as the good perform uses, and by their zeal more ardently than the good. This is so especially in war because the evil man is more crafty and cunning in devising schemes than a good man, and in his love of glory takes pleasure in killing and plundering those whom he knows and declares to be the enemy. The good man has prudence and zeal for defense and rarely for attacking. This is much the same as it is with spirits of hell and angels of heaven; the spirits of hell attack and the angels of heaven defend themselves. Hence comes this conclusion that it is

allowable for one to defend his country and his fellow-citizens against invading enemies even by iniquitous commanders, but not allowable to make oneself an enemy without cause. To have the seeking of glory for cause is in itself diabolical, for it comes of self-love.

The points made above (n. 237) by which the merely natural man confirms himself against divine providence have now been explained. The points which follow (n. 238) about the varieties of religion in many nations, which also serve the merely natural man for arguments against divine providence, are to be clarified next. For the merely natural man says in his heart, How can so many discordant religions exist instead of one world-wide and true religion when (as was shown above, nn. 27-45) divine providence has a heaven from mankind for its purpose? But pray, listen: all human beings who are born, however numerous and of whatever religion, can be saved if only they acknowledge God and live according to the precepts of the Decalog, which forbid committing murder, adultery, theft, and false witness because to do such things is contrary to religion and therefore contrary to God. Such persons fear God and love the neighbor. They fear God inasmuch as they think that to do such things is to act against God, and they love the neighbor because to murder, commit adultery, steal, bear false witness and covet the neighbor's house or wife is to act against one's neighbor. Heeding God in their lives and doing no evil to the neighbor, they are led by the Lord, and those whom He leads are also taught about God and the neighbor in accordance with their religion, for those who live in this way love to be taught, but those living otherwise have no such desire. Loving to be taught, they are also instructed by angels after death when they become spirits, and willingly receive such truths as the Word contains. Something about them may be seen in Doctrine of the New Jerusalem about Sacred Scripture (nn. 91-97 and 104-113).

The merely natural man confirms himself against divine providence when he observes the religious conditions in various nations and notes that some people are totally ignorant of God, some worship the sun and moon, and some worship idols and graven images. Those who argue from these facts against divine providence are ignorant of the arcana of heaven; these arcana are innumerable and man is acquainted with hardly any of them. Among them is this: man is not taught from heaven directly but mediately (this may be seen treated above, nn. 154-174). Because he is taught mediately, and the Gospel could not through the medium of missionaries reach all who dwell in the world, but religion could be spread in various ways to inhabitants of the remote corners of the earth, this has been effected by divine providence. For a knowledge of religion does not come to a man from himself, but through another who has either learned it from the Word or by tradition from others who have learned it, for instance that God is, heaven and hell exist, there is a life after death, and God must be worshiped for man to be blessed.

[2] See in Doctrine of the New Jerusalem about Sacred Scripture (nn. 101-103) that religion spread throughout the world from the Ancient Word and afterwards from the Israelitish Word, and (nn. 114-118) that unless there had been a Word no one could have known about God, heaven and hell, life after death, and still less about the Lord. Once a religion is established in a nation the Lord leads that nation according to the precepts and tenets of its own

religion, and He has provided that there should be precepts in every religion like those in the Decalog, that God should be worshiped, His name not be profaned, a holy day be observed, that parents be honored, murder, adultery and theft not be committed, and false witness not be spoken. A nation that regards these precepts as divine and lives according to them in religion's name is saved, as was just said (n. 253). Most nations remote from Christendom regard these laws not as civil but as divine, and hold them sacred. See in Doctrine of the New Jerusalem [about Life] from the Precepts of the Decalog, from beginning to end, that a man is saved by a life according to these precepts.

[3] Also among the arcana of heaven is this: in the Lord's sight the angelic heaven is like one man whose soul and life is the Lord. In each particular of his form this divine man is man, not only as to the external members and organs but as to the more numerous internal members and organs, also as to the skins, membranes, cartilages and bones; but in that man all these, both external and internal, are not material but spiritual. Further, the Lord has provided that those who cannot be reached by the Gospel but only by some form of religion shall also have a place in this divine man, that is, in heaven, by constituting the parts called skins, membranes, cartilages and bones, and like others should be in heavenly joy. For it does not matter whether their joy is that of the angels of the highest heaven or of the lowest heaven, for everyone entering heaven comes into the highest joy of his own heart; joy higher still he does not endure; he would suffocate in it.

[4] A peasant and a king may serve for comparison. A peasant may reach the height of joy when he steps out in a new suit of homespun wool or seats himself at a table with pork, a piece of beef, cheese, beer and fiery wine on it. He would feel constricted at heart if he was clothed like a king in purple, silk, gold and silver, or if a table was set for him on which were delicacies and costly viands of many kinds with noble wine. It is plain from this that the last as well as the first find heavenly happiness, each in his measure, those outside Christendom also, therefore, provided they shun evils as sins against God because these are contrary to religion.

[5] Few are entirely ignorant of God. If they have lived a moral life they are instructed after death by angels and receive what is spiritual in their moral life (see Doctrine of the New Jerusalem about Sacred Scripture, n. 116). The same is true of those who worship sun and moon, believing that God is there. They know no better, therefore it is not imputed to them as a sin, for the Lord says,

If you were blind (that is, if you did not know), you would have no sin (Jn 9:41).

But there are many who worship idols and graven images even in the Christian world. This, to be sure, is idolatrous, yet not with all. There are those for whom graven images serve as a means of exciting thought about God, for by an influx from heaven one who acknowledges God desires to see Him, and these, unable to raise the mind above the sensuous as those do who are inwardly spiritual, rouse it by means of statue or image. Those who do so and do not worship the image itself as God are saved if they also live by the precepts of the Decalog from religious principle.

[6] It is plain, then, that as the Lord desires the salvation of all, He has also provided that everyone who lives well may have a place in heaven. See in the

work Heaven and Hell, published at London, 1758 (nn. 59-102), in Arcana Caelestia (nn. 5552-5569) and above (nn. 201-204) that heaven in the Lord's sight is like one man; that heaven accordingly corresponds to each and all things in man; and that there are also those who represent skin, membranes, cartilages and bones.

The merely natural man confirms himself against divine providence when he sees the Mohammedan religion accepted by so many empires and kingdoms. The fact that this form of religion is accepted by more kingdoms than Christianity is may be a stumbling-block to those who give thought to divine providence and at the same time believe that no one can be saved unless he has been born a Christian, thus where the Word is, by which the Lord is known. That form of religion is no stumbling-block, however, to those who believe that all things are of divine providence. These ask in what the providence consists and find it is in this, that Mohammedanism, acknowledges the Lord as Son of God, the wisest of men and a very great prophet who came into the world to teach men; most Mohammedans consider Him to be greater than Mohammed.

[2] That form of religion was called forth in the divine providence to destroy the idolatries of many nations. To make this fully known we will pursue some order; first, something on the origin of idolatries. Previously to that form of religion the worship of idols was general in the world. This was because the churches before the Lord's advent were all representative churches. The Israelitish church was of this character. In it the tabernacle, Aaron's garments, the sacrifices, all things of the temple in Jerusalem, the statutes also, were representative. Moreover, the ancients had a knowledge of correspondences, which is the knowledge of representations--it was the chief knowledge of their wise men. This knowledge was cultivated especially in Egypt and was the origin of Egyptian hieroglyphics. By that knowledge the ancients knew what animals of every kind signified and what trees of every kind signified, as they did what mountains, hills, rivers and fountains signified, as well as sun, moon and stars. As all their worship was representative, consisting of sheer correspondences, they worshiped on mountains and hills and in groves and gardens, regarded fountains as sacred, and in adoration of God faced the rising sun. Furthermore, they made graven images of horses, oxen, calves and lambs, and of birds, fish and serpents, and placed them in their houses and elsewhere, arranged according to the spiritual things of the church to which they corresponded or which they represented. They placed similar objects in their temples, too, to put them in mind of the holy things they signified.

[3] Later, when the knowledge of correspondences had been lost, their posterity began to worship the graven images themselves, as holy in themselves, not knowing that their forefathers had seen no holiness in them, but only that they represented holy things by correspondences and thus signified them. So arose the idolatries which filled the whole world, Africa and Europe as well as Asia with its adjacent islands. In order that all these idolatries might be uprooted, of the Lord's divine providence it was brought about that a new religion, adapted to the genius of Orientals, should start up, in which there would be something from each Testament of the Word, and which would teach that the Lord had come into the world and was a very great prophet, wisest of all, and Son of God. This was done through Mohammed, from

whom the religion is called the Mohammedan religion.

[4] Of the Lord's divine providence this religion was raised up and, as we said, adapted to the genius of Orientals, in order that it might destroy the idolatries of so many peoples and give them some knowledge of the Lord before they passed into the spiritual world. This religion would not have been accepted by so many kingdoms or had the power to uproot idolatries, had it not suited and met the ideas and thinking of them all. It did not acknowledge the Lord as God of heaven and earth, for the Orientals acknowledged God the Creator of the universe, but could not comprehend that He came into the world and assumed human nature, quite as Christians do not comprehend this, who therefore separate His divine from His humanity in their thinking and place His divine near the Father in heaven and His humanity they know not where.

[5] Hence it may be seen that the Mohammedan religion arose under the Lord's divine providence and that all adherents of it who acknowledge the Lord as Son of God and live according to the precepts of the Decalog, which they also have, shunning evils as sins, come into a heaven called the Mohammedan heaven. This heaven, like others, is divided into three, the highest, middle and lowest. Those who acknowledge the Lord to be one with the Father and thus the one God are in the highest heaven; in the next heaven are those who renounce a plurality of wives and live with one; and in the lowest are those who are being initiated. More about this religion may be seen in Continuation about the Last Judgment and the Spiritual World (nn. 68-72), where the Mohammedans and Mohammed are treated of.

The merely natural man confirms himself against divine providence when he sees that the Christian religion exists only in a small part of the habitable world, called Europe, and there is divided. The Christian religion exists only in the small part of the habitable world called Europe because it was not adapted to the genius of Orientals as was a mixed one like the Mohammedan religion, as was just shown; and an unadapted religion is not received. For example, a religion which ordains that it is unlawful to take more than one wife is not received but rejected by those who for ages have been polygamists. This is true of other ordinances of the Christian religion.

[2] Nor is it material whether a smaller or a larger part of the world has received this religion, as long as there are people with whom the Word is. For those who are outside the church and do not possess the Word still have light from it, as was shown in Doctrine of the New Jerusalem about Sacred Scripture, nn. 104-113. It is a marvel that where the Word is reverently read and the Lord is worshiped from it, He is present with heaven. The reason is that He is the Word and the Word is divine truth which makes heaven. The Lord therefore says:

Where two or three are gathered in my name, there am I in the midst of them (Mt 18:20).

Europeans can bring this about with the Word in many parts of the habitable globe, for they trade the world over and read or teach the Word everywhere. This seems like fiction and yet is true.

[3] The Christian religion is divided because it is from the Word and the Word is written in sheer correspondences and these in large part are appearances of truth in which, nevertheless, genuine truths lie concealed. As

a church's doctrine is to be drawn from the sense of the letter of the Word which is of this character, disputes, controversies and dissensions were bound to arise over the understanding of the Word, but not over the Word itself or the Divine itself of the Lord. For it is acknowledged everywhere that the Word is holy and that the Lord possesses the divine, and these two are essentials of the church. Those, therefore, who deny the Divine of the Lord and are called Socinians have been excommunicated from the church, and those who deny the holiness of the Word are not regarded as Christians.

[4] To this let me add a remarkable item about the Word from which one may conclude that inwardly the Word is divine truth itself and inmostly the Lord. When a spirit opens the Word and touches his face or dress with it, just from the contact his face or garment shines as brightly as the moon or a star, in the sight of all, too, whom he meets. It is evidence that there is nothing holier in the world than the Word.

That the Word is written throughout in correspondences may be seen in Doctrine of the New Jerusalem about Sacred Scripture, nn. 5-26; that the church's doctrine is to be drawn from the sense of the letter of the Word and confirmed thereby, nn. 50-61; that heresies can be wrested from the sense of the letter of the Word, but that it is harmful to confirm them, nn. 91-97; that the church is from the Word and is such as is its understanding of the Word, nn. 76-79.

The merely natural man confirms himself against divine providence because in many kingdoms where the Christian religion is accepted there are those who arrogate divine power to themselves, want to be worshiped as gods, and also invoke dead men. To be sure, they say that they have not arrogated divine power to themselves and do not wish to be worshiped as gods. Yet they say that they can open and close heaven, remit and retain sins, and so save and condemn men, and this is what is divine itself. Divine providence has no other purpose than reformation and hence salvation; this is its unceasing activity with everyone. And salvation can be effected only by acknowledgment of the divine of the Lord and by confidence that He brings salvation as man lives according to His commandments.

[2] Who cannot see that the usurpation of divine power is the Babylon described in the Apocalypse and the Babel spoken of here and there in the Prophets? It is also Lucifer in Isaiah 14, as is plain from verses 4 and 22 of that chapter, where are the words:
 You shall speak this parable about the king of Babel (verse 4);
 (Then), I will cut off the name and remnant of Babel (verse 22);
 it is plain from this that this Babel is Lucifer, of whom it is said:
 How you have fallen from heaven, O Lucifer, son of the morning! ... For you have said in your heart, I will ascend into heaven, I will exalt my throne above the stars of God; I will also sit on the mount of the congregation, at the sides of the north; I will ascend above the heights of the clouds; I will be like the Most High (Isa 14:12-14).

It is well known that the same persons invoke the dead and pray to them for help. We make the assertion because such invocation was established by a papal bull, confirming the decree of the Council of Trent, in which it is openly said that the dead are to be invoked. Yet who does not know that only God is to be invoked, and not any dead person?

[3] It shall be told now why the Lord has permitted such things. Can one deny that He has done so for the sake of the end in view, namely salvation? For men know that there is no salvation without the Lord. Therefore it was necessary that the Lord should be preached from the Word and that the Christian Church should be established by this means. This could be done, however, only by leaders who would act with zeal and no others offered than those who burned with zeal out of self-love. At first this fire aroused them to preach the Lord and teach the Word. From this their first state Lucifer is called "the son of the morning" (14:12). But as they saw that they could dominate by means of the sanctities of the Word and the church, the self-love by which they were first aroused to preach the Lord broke out from within and finally exalted itself to such a height that they transferred all the Lord's divine power to themselves, leaving Him none.

[4] This could not be prevented by the Lord's divine providence, for if it had been they would have declared that the Lord is not God and that the Word is not sacred and would have made themselves Socinians and Arians, so would have destroyed the whole church. But, whatever its rulers are, the church continues among the people submissive to them. For all in this religion who approach the Lord and shun evils as sins are saved; therefore many heavenly societies are formed from them in the spiritual world. It has also been provided that there should be a nation among them that has not bowed to the yoke of such domination and that regards the Word as holy; this noble nation is the French nation.

[5] But what was done? When self-love exalted its dominion even to the Lord's throne, removing Him and setting itself on it, that love, which is Lucifer, could not but have profaned all things of the Word and the church. Lest this should happen, the Lord in His divine providence took care that they should recede from worship of Him, invoke the dead, pray to graven images of the dead, kiss their bones and kneel at their tombs, should ban the reading of the Word, appoint holy worship in masses not understood by the common people, and sell salvation for money. For if they had not done this, they would have profaned the sanctities of the Word and the church. For, as was shown in the preceding section, only those profane holy things who know them.

[6] Lest, too, they should profane the most Holy Supper it is of the Lord's divine providence that they divide it, giving the bread to the people and drinking the wine themselves. For the wine of the Supper signifies holy truth and the bread holy good; but divided the wine signifies truth profaned and the bread good adulterated. It is also of the Lord's divine providence that they should render the Holy Supper corporeal and material and give it the prime place in religion. Anyone who gives these particulars his attention and reflects on them in some enlightenment of his mind can see the amazing action of divine providence for the protection of the sanctities of the church and for the salvation of all who can be saved and are ready to be snatched from the fire, so to speak, from which they must be snatched.

The merely natural man confirms himself against divine providence because some among those who profess the Christian religion place salvation in certain phrases which they are to think and speak and not at all in good works which they are to do. We showed in Doctrine of the New Jerusalem about Faith that these are such as make faith alone saving and not the life of charity, thus such as separate faith from charity. It was also shown that these are meant in the Word by "Philistines," "dragon" and "goats."

[2] That such doctrine has been permitted is also of divine providence lest the divine of the Lord and the sanctity of the Word should be profaned. The divine of the Lord is not profaned when salvation is placed in these words: That God the Father may have mercy for the sake of the Son, who suffered the Cross and made satisfaction for us. For men do not then address the divine of the Lord but have in mind His human nature, which they do not acknowledge to be divine. Nor do they profane the Word, for they do not attend to the passages in which love, charity, deeds and works are mentioned. All this, they say, is involved in the faith expressed in the saying quoted. Those who confirm this tell themselves, "The law does not condemn me, neither then does evil, and good does not save because good done by me is not good." They are therefore like those who do not know any truth from the Word and consequently cannot profane it. Only those confirm the faith expressed in that saying who from self-love are in the pride of their own intelligence. Nor are these Christians at heart; they only desire to be looked on as such.

[3] It shall now be shown that the Lord's divine providence is nevertheless acting constantly to save those with whom faith separated from charity has become an article of religion. Although this faith has become an article of their religion, by the Lord's divine providence each knows that it is not faith that saves, but a life of charity with which faith makes one. For all churches in which that religion is accepted also teach that there is no salvation unless man examines himself, sees and acknowledges his sins, repents, desists from them, and begins a new life. This is read out with much zeal in the presence of all who come to the Holy Supper. In addition they are told that unless they do so, they mingle the holy with the profane and cast themselves into eternal condemnation. Indeed, in England they are told that unless they do so the devil will enter them as he did Judas and destroy them soul and body. It is plain, then, that everyone in the churches in which faith alone is accepted is nevertheless taught that evils are to be shunned as sins.

[4] Furthermore, everyone who is born a Christian is aware that evils are to be shunned as sins because the Decalog is put into the hands of every boy and girl and is taught by parents and teachers. The citizens of a kingdom and especially the common people are examined by the priest on the Decalog alone, which is recited from memory, for what they know of the Christian religion, and are also admonished to do what is commanded in it. At such times they are not told by the priest that they are not under the yoke of that law, or that they cannot do what is commanded because they cannot do anything good of themselves. Again, the Athanasian Creed has been accepted throughout the Christian world and what is said at its close is also acknowledged, namely, that the Lord will come to judge the living and the dead, and then those who have done good will enter everlasting life and those who have done evil will enter everlasting fire.

[5] In Sweden, where the religion of faith alone has been received, it is also

plainly taught that faith is impossible apart from charity or good works. This is pointed out in an Appendix on things to be remembered, inserted in all copies of the Psalms, and called "Impediments or Stumbling Blocks of the Impenitent" (Obotferdigas Foerhinder), where are these words,

Those who are rich in good works thereby show that they are rich in faith, because when faith is saving it acts through charity. For justifying faith is never found alone and separate from good works, quite as no good tree is without fruit, nor the sun without light and heat, nor water without moisture.

[6] These items have been adduced to make known that although a religious formula about faith alone has been accepted, nevertheless goods of charity, which are good works, are taught everywhere and that this is by the Lord's divine providence, lest the common people be led astray by the formula. I have heard Luther, with whom I have spoken at times in the spiritual world, execrate faith alone and heard him say that when he established it he was warned by an angel of the Lord not to do it; but that he thought to himself that if he did not reject works, separation from Catholicism would not be accomplished. Therefore, contrary to the warning, he established that faith.

The merely natural man confirms himself against divine providence in that there have been so many heresies in Christendom and still are, such as Quakerism, Moravianism, Anabaptism, and more. For he may think to himself, If divine providence is universal in the least things and has the salvation of all for its object, it would have seen to it that one true religion should exist on the globe, not one divided and, still less, one torn by heresies. But use reason and think more deeply if you can. Can man be saved without being reformed first? For he is born into love of self and the world, and as these loves do not have any love of God and the neighbor in them except for the sake of self, he is also born into evils of every kind. Is there love or mercy in those loves? Does the man make anything of defrauding or defaming or hating another even to death, or of committing adultery with his wife, or of being cruel to him out of revenge, the while having the desire in mind to get the upper hand of all and to possess the goods of all others, thus regarding others in comparison with himself as insignificant and of little worth? To be saved, must he not first be led away from these evils and thus be reformed? As has been shown above in many places, this can be accomplished only in accordance with many laws of divine providence. For the most part these laws are unknown and yet they come of divine wisdom and at the same time of divine love, and the Lord cannot act contrary to them, for to do so would result in destroying man, not in saving him.

[2] Look over the laws which have been set forth, bring them together, and you will see. According to those laws there is no direct influx from heaven but one mediated by the Word, doctrine and preaching; and since the Word, to be divine, had to be composed wholly in correspondences, inevitably there are dissensions and heresies. The tolerance of them is also in accord with the laws of divine providence. Furthermore, when the church itself has taken for essentials what pertains only to the understanding, that is, to doctrine, and not what pertains to the will, that is, to life, and what pertains to life is not made the essentials of a church, then man is in complete darkness for understanding and wanders like one blind, striking against things constantly and falling into pits. For the will must see in the understanding and not the understanding in

the will, or what is the same, the life and its love must lead the understanding to think, speak and act, and not the reverse. Were the reverse true, the understanding might out of an evil and even diabolical love seize on what comes by the senses and demand that the will do it. What has been said may show whence dissensions and heresies come.

[3] Yet it has been provided that everyone, in whatever heresy he may be intellectually, may still be reformed and saved if he shuns evils as sins and does not confirm heretical falsities in himself. For by shunning evils as sins the will is reformed and through it the understanding is, which emerges for the first time then out of obscurity into light. There are three essentials of the church: acknowledgment of the divine of the Lord, acknowledgment of the holiness of the Word, and the life which is called charity. Everyone's faith is according to the life which is charity; from the Word he has a rational perception of what life should be; and from the Lord he has reformation and salvation. Had these three been regarded as the church's essentials, intellectual differences would not have divided it but only varied it as light varies colors in beautiful objects and as various insignia of royalty give beauty to a king's crown.

The merely natural man confirms himself against divine providence in that Judaism still continues. That is, after all these centuries the Jews have not been converted although they live among Christians and do not, in keeping with prophecies in the Word, confess the Lord and acknowledge Him to be the Messiah, who, as they think, was to lead them back to the land of Canaan; but they steadfastly persist in denying Him and yet it is well with them. Those who take this view, however, and thus call divine providence in question, do not know that by Jews in the Word all who are of the church and acknowledge the Lord are meant, and by the land of Canaan, into which it is said that they are to be led, the Lord's church is meant.

[2] But the Jews persist in denying the Lord because they are such that, if they received and acknowledged the divine of the Lord and the holy things of His church, they would profane them. Therefore the Lord said of them:

He has blinded their eyes, and hardened their heart; that they should not see with their eyes, nor understand with their heart, and be converted, and I should heal them (Jn 12:40; Mt 13:14; Mk 4:12; Lu 8:10; Isa 6:9, 10).

It is said, "lest they should be converted, and I should heal them" because if they had been converted and healed they would have committed profanation, and according to the law of divine providence treated above (nn. 221-233) no one is admitted interiorly into truths of faith and goods of charity by the Lord except so far as he can be kept in them to the close of life; were he admitted, he would profane what is holy.

[3] This nation has been preserved and dispersed over much of the earth for the sake of the Word in its original language, which they hold more sacred than Christians do. The Lord's divine is in every particular of the Word, for it is divine truth joined with divine good coming from the Lord. By it the Lord is united with the church, and heaven is present, as was shown in Doctrine of the New Jerusalem about Sacred Scripture (nn. 62-69). The Lord and heaven are present wherever the Word is read as sacred. This is the end which divine providence has pursued in the preservation and in the dispersal of the Jews over much of the world. On the nature of their lot after death see Continuation

about the Last Judgment and the Spiritual World (nn. 79-82).

These then are the objections listed above at n. 238 by which the natural man confirms himself against divine providence, or may do so. Still other objections, listed at n. 239, may serve the natural man for arguments against divine providence; they may occur to the minds of others, too, and excite doubts. They are the following.

Doubt may be raised against divine providence in that the whole of Christendom worships one God under three persons, that is, three Gods, and has not known hitherto that God is one in person and in essence, in whom is the Trinity, and that this God is the Lord. One who reasons about divine providence may ask, Are not three persons three Gods if each person by himself is God? Who can think of it otherwise? In fact, who does? Athanasius himself could not; therefore it is said in the Creed which bears his name:

Although in Christian verity we ought to acknowledge each Person as God and Lord, yet by Christian faith it is not allowable to affirm or to name three Gods or three Lords.

This can only mean that we ought to acknowledge three Gods and Lords, but it is not allowable to affirm or name three Gods and three Lords.

[2] Who can possibly have a perception of one God unless He is one in person? If it is said that such a concept is possible if one thinks of the three as having one essence, does one, indeed can one, have any other idea than that they are thus of one mind and agree, and yet are three Gods? Thinking more deeply, one asks oneself, How can the divine essence, which is infinite, be divided? Further, how can divine essence from eternity beget another and produce still another who proceeds from them both? It may be said that it is to be believed and not thought about; but who does not think about what he is told must be believed? How else can there be any acknowledgment which in its essence is faith? Was it not because of the concept of God as three persons that Socinianism and Arianism arose, which prevail in the hearts of more persons than you suppose? Belief in one God and that this God is the Lord makes the church, for in Him is the divine trinity. The truth of this may be seen in Doctrine of the New Jerusalem about the Lord, from beginning to end.

[3] But what is thought of the Lord today? Is it not thought that He is God and Man, God from Jehovah the Father of whom He was conceived and Man from the Virgin Mary from whom He was born? Who thinks that God and Man in Him, or His Divine and His Human, are one person, and are one as soul and body are? Does anyone know this? Ask the learned in the church and they will say that they have not known it. Yet it is part of the doctrine of the church received throughout Christendom, as follows:

Our Lord Jesus Christ, the Son of God, is God and Man; and although He is God and Man yet there are not two, but there is one Christ. He is one because the divine took to itself the human; indeed He is altogether one, for He is one Person, since as soul and body make one man, so God and Man is one Christ.

This comes from the Faith or Creed of Athanasius. The learned have not known it because on reading this they have thought of the Lord not as God but only as Man.

[4] When they are asked if they know from whom the Lord was conceived, whether from God the Father or from His own Divine, they reply that He was

conceived from God the Father, for this is according to Scripture. Are the Father and He not one then, like soul and body? Who can think that He was conceived from two Divines, and if from His own that this was His Father? If you ask them further what their idea of the Lord's Divine and of His Human is, they will say that His Divine is from the essence of the Father and His Human from the essence of His mother, and that His Divine is with the Father. Then, when they are asked where His Human is, they have no answer, for they separate His Divine and His Human in their thinking and make His Divine equal to the Divine of the Father and His Human like the human of another man, unaware that in doing this they separate soul and body; nor do they see the flaw in this, that then a rational man would have been born from a mother alone.

[5] As a result of the fixed idea that the Lord's humanity was like that of another man, it has come about that a Christian can with difficulty be led to think of a Divine Human, even when it is said that the Lord's soul or life from conception was and is Jehovah Himself. Now sum up the reasons and consider whether there is any other God of the universe than the Lord alone, in whom is the Divine itself, Source of all, called the Father; the Divine Human, called the Son; and the proceeding Divine, called the Holy Spirit; and thus that God is one in person and essence, and that this God is the Lord.

[6] You may persist and remark that the Lord Himself spoke of three in Matthew:

Go and make disciples of all nations, baptizing them in the name of the Father, the Son and the Holy Spirit (28:19).

But it is plain from the preceding verse and the one following that the Lord said this in order to make it known that the Divine Trinity was in Him, now glorified. For in the preceding verse He said that all power in heaven and on earth was given Him, and in the following verse that He would be with men to the end of the age, speaking of Himself alone and not of three.

[7] Now, why did divine providence permit Christians to worship the one God under three persons, that is, worship three Gods, and not know until now that God is one in essence and person, in whom is the Trinity and that this God is the Lord? Man and not the Lord was the cause. The Lord had taught it plainly in His Word, as is clear from all the passages cited in Doctrine of the New Jerusalem about the Lord, and has also taught it in the doctrine of all the churches, in which it is said that His Divine and His Human are not two but one Person united like soul and body.

[8] The first reason why men divided the Divine and the Human and made the Divine equal to the Divine of Jehovah the Father and the Human equal to the human of another man, was that the church after its rise fell away into Babylonianism. This took to itself the Lord's divine power, and in order that it should be called human and not divine power made the Lord's human like that of another man. When later the church was reformed and faith alone was received as the one means of salvation--faith that God the Father has mercy for the sake of the Son--the Lord's Human could be viewed in no other way. For no one can approach the Lord and acknowledge Him at heart as God of heaven and earth unless he lives by His precepts. In the spiritual world, where everyone is bound to speak as he thinks, no one can so much as mention the name Jesus if he has not lived as a Christian in the world; this is by divine providence lest His

name be profaned.

To make what has just been said clearer I will add what was set forth in Doctrine of the New Jerusalem about the Lord (towards the end, nn. 60, 61), which is as follows:

"That God and Man in the Lord, according to the Creed, are not two but one Person, altogether one as soul and body are, appears clearly in many sayings of the Lord, as that the Father and He are one; that all things of the Father are His and all His the Father's; that He is in the Father and the Father in Him; that all things are given into His hand; that He has all power; that He is God of heaven and earth; that one who believes on Him has eternal life; and that the wrath of God abides on one who does not believe on Him; and further, that both the Divine and the Human were taken up into heaven; and that as to both He sits at the right hand of God, that is, is almighty; besides the numerous passages in the Word about His Divine Human which were quoted abundantly above. They all testify that God is one both in person and in essence, and in Him is the Trinity, and that this God is the Lord.

[2] "These things about the Lord are published now for the first time because it is foretold in the Apocalypse, chapters 21 and 22, that at the end of the former church a new church is to be established in which this will be the chief doctrine. This church is meant in those chapters by the New Jerusalem into which only one who acknowledges the Lord alone as God of heaven and earth can enter; this church is therefore called 'the Lamb's wife'. I can also report that all heaven acknowledges the Lord alone and that one who does not is not admitted to heaven, for heaven is heaven from the Lord. This very acknowledgment made in love and faith causes men to be in the Lord and Lord in them, as He teaches in John:

In that day you will know that I am in my Father, and you in me and I in you (14:20);

again in the same:

Abide in me, and I in you; ... I am the vine, and you are branches; he who abides in me and I in him, bears much fruit; for without me you can do nothing; unless a man abides in me, he is cast out (15:4-6, also 17:22, 23).

[3] "This has not been seen from the Word before, because if it had been, it would not have been received. For the last judgment had not been accomplished yet, and prior to it the power of hell prevailed over the power of heaven. Man is in the midst between heaven and hell; had this been seen before, therefore, the devil, that is, hell, would have plucked it from men's hearts and furthermore would have profaned it. The predominance of hell was completely broken by the last judgment which has been accomplished now; since that judgment, thus today, every man who wishes enlightenment and wisdom is able to have it."

A doubt may be raised against divine providence in that it has been unknown hitherto that in each particular of the Word there is a spiritual meaning from which it has its holiness. One may raise this doubt about divine providence, asking, "why has this been revealed for the first time now, and why has it been revealed through any one at all and not through a church leader?" But it is at the Lord's good pleasure whether it should be a leader or a leader's servant; He knows the one and the other. However, that sense of the Word has not been disclosed before because 1. If it had been, the church would have profaned it and thereby profaned the holiness itself of the Word. 2. Neither were the genuine truths, in which the spiritual sense of the Word resides, revealed by the Lord until the last judgment was accomplished, and a new church, meant by the Holy Jerusalem, was about to be established by the Lord. These reasons will be examined separately.

[2] 1. The spiritual sense of the Word was not disclosed earlier because if it had been, the church would have profaned it and thereby would have profaned the holiness itself of the Word. Not long after it was established, the church was turned into Babylon, and later into Philistia. Babylon acknowledges the Word, to be sure, and yet esteems it lightly, asserting that the Holy Spirit inspires its own highest judgment just as much as it did the prophets. They acknowledge the Word for the vicarship founded on the Lord's words to Peter, but esteem it lightly because it does not accord with their teaching. It is therefore taken from the people also and hidden in monasteries where few read it. If, therefore, the spiritual sense of the Word had been revealed, in which the Lord is present together with all angelic wisdom, the Word would have been profaned not only, as it is now, in its lowermost expression in the sense of the letter, but in its inmosts, too.

[3] Philistia, by which faith separated from charity is meant, would have profaned the spiritual sense of the Word also, because, as we have shown before, it puts salvation in certain formulas which are to be thought and spoken, and not in good works which are to be done. It thus makes saving what is not saving and also removes the understanding from what is to be believed. What would they do with the light in which the spiritual sense of the Word is? Would that not be turned into darkness? When the natural sense is, why not the spiritual sense? Does any one of them who has confirmed himself in faith separate from charity and in justification by this faith alone, want to know what good of life is, what love to the Lord and towards the neighbor is, what charity is and what the goods of charity are, what good works are and what it is to do them, or in fact what faith is essentially and what genuine truth is, constituting it? They compose volumes, establish in them only what they call faith, and declare that all the things just mentioned are present in that faith. It is clear from this that if the spiritual sense of the Word had been revealed earlier, it would come to pass according to the Lord's words in Matthew:

If your eye is evil, your whole body will be full of darkness. If then the light that is in you is darkness, how great is that darkness (6:23).

In the spiritual sense of the Word by "eye" the understanding is meant.

[4] 2. Neither were the genuine truths in which the spiritual sense of the Word resides, revealed by the Lord until after the last judgment was accomplished, and a new church, meant by the Holy Jerusalem, was about to be established by the Lord. The Lord foretold in the Apocalypse that after the last judgment was effected genuine truths were to be revealed, a new church was to be established, and the spiritual sense of the Word would be disclosed. In the small work, The Last Judgment, and later in the Continuation of that work, it was shown that the last judgment has been accomplished and that this is meant by the heaven and earth which would pass away (Apoc 21:1). That genuine truths are then to be revealed is foretold in these words in the Apocalypse:

And he that sat upon the throne said, Behold, I make all things new (11:5; also 19:17, 18; 21:18-21; 22:1, 2).

At 19:11-16 it was predicted that the spiritual sense of the Word was to be revealed; it is meant by "the white horse" on which He who sat was called the Word of God and was Lord of lords and King of kings (on this see the little work The White Horse). That by the Holy Jerusalem a new church is meant which was to be established then by the Lord may be seen in Doctrine of the New Jerusalem about the Lord (nn. 62-65).

[5] It is clear, then, that the spiritual sense of the Word was to be revealed for a new church which should acknowledge and worship the Lord alone, hold His Word sacred, love divine truths and reject faith separated from charity. More about this sense of the Word may be seen in Doctrine of the New Jerusalem about Sacred Scripture (nn. 5-26 and following numbers); what the spiritual sense of the Word is (nn. 5-26); that a spiritual sense exists in all of the Word in general and in detail (nn. 9-17); that by virtue of the spiritual sense the Word is divinely inspired and holy in every expression (nn. 18, 19); that until now the spiritual sense has been unknown, and why it was not revealed before (nn. 20-25); and that henceforth that sense will be open only to one who is in genuine truths from the Lord (n. 26).

[6] It may be evident from these propositions that it is by the Lord's divine providence that the spiritual sense has lain concealed from the world until the present day and been kept meanwhile in heaven with the angels, who draw their wisdom from it. This sense was known and treasured among ancient peoples who lived before Moses, but when their descendants converted the correspondences, of which their Word and hence their religion solely consisted, into various idolatries, and the Egyptians converted them into magic, by the Lord's divine providence this sense was closed up, first with the Israelites and then with Christians for the reasons given above, and is now opened for the first time for the Lord's new church.

Doubt may arise against divine providence in that it has been unknown hitherto that to shun evils as sins is the Christian religion itself. That this is the Christian religion itself was shown in Doctrine of Life for the New Jerusalem, from beginning to end; and as faith separated from charity is the one obstacle to its being received, that also was treated of. We say that it has not been known that to shun evils as sins is the Christian religion itself, for it is unknown to nearly everyone; yet everyone does know it, as may be seen above (n. 258). Nearly all are ignorant of it because faith separate has obliterated knowledge of it. For this faith declares that it alone saves and not any good work, that is, any good of charity; also that men are no longer under the yoke of the law, but are free. Those who have frequently heard such teaching no longer give thought to any evil of life or any good of life. Everyone, moreover, is inclined by nature to embrace such teaching, and once he has done so he no longer thinks about the state of his life. This is why it is not known that shunning evils as sins is the Christian religion itself.

[2] That this is unknown was disclosed to me in the spiritual world. I have asked more than a thousand newcomers from the world whether they knew that to shun evils as sins is religion itself. They said that they did not and that it was a new idea which they had not heard before, but had heard that they

cannot of themselves do good and that they are not under the yoke of the law. When I inquired whether they knew that a man must examine himself, see his sins, repent and begin a new life and that otherwise sins are not remitted, and if sins are not remitted, men are not saved; and when I reminded them that this was read out in a deep voice to them each time they observed the Holy Supper, they replied that they paid no attention to that but only to this, that they have remission of sins by the sacrament of the Supper and that faith effects the rest without their knowing it.

[3] I asked again, Why have you taught your children the Decalog? Was it not that they might know what evils are sins to be shunned? Was it only that they might know and believe, but do nothing? Why is it said that this is new? To this they could only reply that they know and yet do not know, and that they never think of the sixth 265-1 commandment when they commit adultery, or about the seventh when they steal or defraud secretly, and so on, and still less that such acts are contrary to divine law, thus contrary to God.

[4] When I recalled to them many things from the teachings of the churches and from the Word confirming the fact that to avoid and be averse to evils as sins is the Christian religion's very self and that one who does so has faith, they fell silent. They were convinced of it, however, when they saw that all were examined as to their life and judged according to their deeds, and no one was judged according to faith apart from life, for everyone has faith according to his life.

[5] Christendom in large part has not known this because by a law of divine providence everyone is left to act in freedom according to reason (on this, above, nn. 71-91 and nn. 101-128); and by another law no one is taught directly from heaven but by means of the Word and by doctrine and preaching from it; there are besides all the laws on permission which are also laws of divine providence. On these see above, n. 258.

A doubt may be raised against divine providence in that it has not been known before that a man lives as a human being after death and that this has not been disclosed before. It has been unknown because with those who do not shun evils as sins the belief lies hidden that man does not live after death. It is of no moment therefore to them whether one says that man lives after death or will rise again on the day of the last judgment. If belief in resurrection happens to visit one, he tells himself, "I shall fare no worse than others; if I go to hell I shall have the company of many and also if I pass to heaven." Yet all in whom there is any religion have an implanted recognition that they will live as human beings after death. Only those infatuated with their own intelligence think that they survive as souls but not as human beings.

It may be seen from the following that anyone in whom is any religion has an implanted recognition that he lives after death as a human being:

1. Who thinks otherwise when he is dying? 2. What eulogizer, mourning the dead, does not exalt them to heaven and place them among the angels conversing with them and sharing their joy? Some men are deified. 3. Who among the common people does not believe that when he dies, if he has lived well he will enter a heavenly paradise, be arrayed in white, and enjoy eternal life? 4. What priest does not speak so to the dying? And when he speaks so he believes it, provided he does not think of the last judgment at the time. 5. Who

does not believe that his little ones are in heaven and that after death he will see his wife, whom he has loved? Who thinks that they are spectres, still less souls or minds hovering in the universe? 6. Who contradicts when something is said about the lot or state of those who have passed from time into eternal life? I have told many what the state or lot of various persons is and have never heard anyone protest that their lot is not yet determined but will be at the time of the judgment. 7. When one sees angels in paintings or statuary does he not recognize them as such? Who thinks then that they are bodiless spirits or airy entities or clouds, as do some of the erudite? 8. Papists believe that their saints are human beings in heaven and others elsewhere are; so do Mohammedans of their dead; more than others Africans do, and many other peoples do. Why then do not Reformed Christians believe it, who know it from the Word? 9. Moreover, as a result of the recognition implanted in everyone, some men aspire to the immortality of renown. The recognition is given that turn in them and makes heroes and brave men of them in war. 10. Inquiry was made in the spiritual world whether this knowledge is implanted in all men; it was found that it is in a spiritual idea attached to their internal thought, not in a natural idea attached to their external thought.

It is plain from all this that doubt should not be thrown on the Lord's divine providence on the supposition that only now has it been disclosed that the human being continues such after death. It is only the sensuous in man that wants to see and touch what is to be credited. One who does not raise his thinking above it is in the dark of night about the state of his own life.

Section 14

EVILS ARE TOLERATED IN VIEW OF THE END, WHICH IS SALVATION

If man were born into the love for which he was created, he would not be in evil, in fact would not know what evil is. For one who has not been in evil and is not in it, cannot know what it is; told that this or that is evil, he would not believe it. This is the state of innocence in which Adam and his wife Eve were; that state was signified by the nakedness of which they were not ashamed; the knowledge of evil subsequent to the fall is meant by eating of the tree of the knowledge of good and evil. The love for which the human being was created is love to the neighbor, to wish him as well as one does oneself and even better. He is in the enjoyment of this love when he serves his neighbor quite as parents do their children. This is truly human love, for in it is what is spiritual, distinguishing it from the natural love of brute animals. Were man born into this love, he would not be born into the darkness of ignorance as everyone is now, but into some light of the knowledge and hence of the intelligence soon to be his. To be sure, he would creep on all fours at first but come erect on his feet by an implanted striving. However much he might resemble a quadruped, he would not face down to the ground but forward to heaven and come erect so that he could look up.

When love of the neighbor was turned into self-love, however, and this love increased, human love was turned into animal love, and man, from being man, became a beast, with the difference that he could think about what he sensed physically, could rationally discriminate among things, be taught, and become a civil and moral person and finally a spiritual being. For, as was said, man possesses what is spiritual and is distinguished by it from the brute animal. By it he can know what civil evil and good are, also what moral evil and good are, and if he so wills, what spiritual evil and good are also. When love for the neighbor was turned into self-love, however, man could no longer be born into the light of knowledge and intelligence but was born into the darkness of ignorance, being born on the lowest level of life, called corporeal-sensuous. From this he could be led into the interiors of the natural mind by instruction, the spiritual always attending on this. Why one is born on the lowest level of life known as corporeal-sensuous, therefore into the darkness of ignorance, will be seen in what follows.

[2] Anyone can see that love of the neighbor and self-love are opposites. Neighborly love wishes well to all from itself, but self-love wishes everyone to wish it well; neighborly love wants to serve everyone, but self-love wants all to serve it; love of the neighbor regards everyone as brother and friend, while love of self regards everyone as its servant, and if one does not serve it, as its enemy; in short, it regards only itself and others scarcely as human beings, esteeming them at heart less than one's horses and dogs. Thinking so meanly of others, it thinks nothing of doing evil to them; hence come hatred and vengeance,

adultery and whoredom, theft and fraud, lying and defamation, violence and cruelty, and similar evils. Such are the evils in which man is by birth. That they are tolerated in view of the end, which is salvation, is to be shown in this order:

i. Everyone is in evil and must be led away from it to be reformed. ii. Evils cannot be removed unless they appear. iii. So far as they are removed they are remitted. iv. The toleration of evil is therefore for the sake of the end in view, namely, salvation.

(i) Everyone is in evil and must be led away from it to be reformed. The church knows that there is hereditary evil in man and that as a result he is in the lust of many evils. Thence it is that he cannot do good of himself, for evil does only such good as has evil in it; the evil inwardly in it is that one does good for one's own sake and thus only for the sake of appearances. It is known that hereditary evil comes from one's parents. It is said to come from Adam and his wife, but this is an error; for everyone is born into hereditary evil from his parent, and the parent from his parent, and so on; thus it is transmitted from one to another, is augmented and becomes an accumulation, and is passed to one's progeny. There is therefore nothing sound in man but all is evil. Who feels that it is evil to love himself above others? Who, then, knows that this is an evil, though it is the head of evils?

[2] Inheritance from parents, grandparents and great-grandparents is plain from much which is known in the world, from the fact, for instance, that households, families and even nations are distinguishable by the face; the face is also a type of the mind which in turn accords with the affections of one's love. Sometimes, too, the features of a grandfather recur in a grandson or a great-grandson. From the face alone I know whether a person is a Jew or not; likewise of what stock certain persons are; others no doubt know also. If the affections which spring from love are thus derived from parents and transmitted by them, evils are, for these spring from affections. But it shall be told how the resemblance comes about.

[3] Everyone's soul comes from his father and is only clothed with the body by one's mother. That the soul is from the father follows not only from what has been said above, but from many other indications, too; also from this, that the child of a black man or Moor by a white or European woman is black, and vice versa; and especially in that the soul is in the seed, for impregnation is by the seed, and the seed is what is clothed with a body by the mother. The seed is the primal form of the love in which the father is--the form of his ruling love with its nearest derivatives or the inmost affections of that love.

[4] These affections are enveloped in everyone with the honesties of moral life and with the goodnesses partly of civil and partly of spiritual life, which are the external of life even with the evil. An infant is born into this external life and is therefore lovable, but coming to boyhood and adolescence he passes from that external to the inner life and at length to his father's ruling love. If this has been evil and not been moderated and bent by various means by his teachers, it becomes his ruling love as it was his father's. Still the evil is not eradicated, but put aside; of this in what follows. Plainly, then, everyone is in evil.

277r. It is plain without explanation that man must be led away from evil in order to be reformed. For one who is in evil in the world is in evil after he has left the world. Not removed in the world, evil cannot be removed afterwards.

Where a tree falls, it lies. So, too, when a man dies his life remains such as it has been. Everyone is judged according to his deeds, not that these are recounted, but he returns to them and acts as before. Death is a continuation of life with the difference that man cannot then be reformed. For reformation is effected in full, that is, in what is inmost and outmost, and what is outmost is reformed suitably to what is inmost only while man is in the world. It cannot be reformed afterwards because as it is carried along by the man after death it falls quiescent and conforms to his inner life, that is, they act as one.

(ii) Evils cannot be removed unless they appear. This does not mean that man must do evils in order for them to appear, but that he must examine himself, his thoughts as well as his deeds, and see what he would do if he did not fear the laws and disrepute--see especially what evils he deems allowable in his spirit and does not regard as sins, for these he still does. To enable him to examine himself, man has been given understanding, and an understanding separate from his will, in order that he may know, comprehend and acknowledge what is good and what is evil, likewise see the character of his will or what it loves and desires. To see this his understanding has been given higher and lower or interior and exterior thought, so as to see from the higher or interior what his will prompts in the lower or exterior thinking: he sees this quite as he does his face in a mirror. When he does and knows what is sin, he is able, on imploring the Lord's help, not to will it but to shun it, then to act contrary to it, if not freely, then by overcoming it through fighting it, and finally to become averse to it and abominate it. Then first does he perceive and also sense that evil is evil and good is good. This, now, is self-examination--to see one's evils, acknowledge them, confess them and thereupon desist from them.

[2] But as few know that this is the Christian religion itself, and these alone have charity and faith and are led by the Lord and do good from Him, something will be said of those who fail to examine themselves but still think that they possess religion. They are 1. Those who confess themselves guilty of all sins but do not search out any one sin in themselves. 2. Those who neglect the search on religious principle. 3. Those who in absorption with the mundane give no thought to sins and hence do not know them. 4. Those who favor them and therefore cannot know them. 5. With all these, sins do not appear and therefore cannot be removed. 6. Finally, the reason, so far unknown, will be made plain why evils cannot be removed apart from their being searched out, appearing, being acknowledged, confessed and resisted.

. But these points will be considered one by one, for they are fundamentals of the Christian religion on man's part.

First, of those who confess themselves guilty of all sins, but do not search out any one sin in themselves. They say, "I am a sinner. I was born in sin. From head to foot there is nothing sound in me. I am nothing but evil. Good God, be gracious to me, pardon, cleanse and save me. Make me to walk in purity and in a right path"; and more of the kind. And yet the man does not examine himself and hence does not know any evil, and no one can shun what he is ignorant of, still less fight against it. After his confessions he also thinks that he is clean and washed, when nevertheless he is unclean and unwashed from the head to the sole of the foot. For the confession of all sins is the lulling of them all to sleep and finally blindness to them. It is like a generality devoid of anything specific, which amounts to nothing.

[2] Second: Those who omit the search in consequence of their religion. They are especially those who separate charity from faith. They say to themselves, "Why should I search out evil or good? Why evil, when it does not condemn me? Why good, when it does not save me? Faith alone, thought and uttered with trust and confidence, justifies and purifies from all sin, and when once I am justified, I am whole in the sight of God. I am indeed in evil, but God wipes it away the moment it is committed and it no longer appears"; and much else. But who does not see, if he opens his eyes, that these are empty words, without reality because nothing of good is in them? Who cannot think and speak so, with trust and confidence, too, even when he is thinking of hell and eternal condemnation? Does he want to know anything further about either truth or good? Of truth he says, "What is truth except that which confirms this faith?" and of good, "What is good except what is in me from this faith? And that it may be in me I will not do it as from myself, for that would be self-righteous and what is self-righteous is not good." So he neglects all until he does not know what evil is; what then is he to search out and see in himself? Is it not his state then that a pent-up fire of lusts of evil consumes the interiors of his mind and lays them waste even to the entrance? He is on guard only at the door to keep the fire from appearing. After death the door is opened and the fire appears for all to see.

[3] Third: Those absorbed with the mundane give no thought to sins, hence do not know of any. These love the world above all things and welcome no truth that would lead them away from any falsity in their religion. They tell themselves, "What is this to me? It is not to my way of thinking." So they reject truth on hearing it and if they listen to it smother it. They do much the same on hearing sermons; they retain some sayings but not any of the substance. Dealing in this way with truths they do not know what good is, for truth and good act as one; and from good which is not linked with truth one does not recognize evil except as one calls it good also, which is done by rationalizing from falsities. It is these who are meant by the seed which fell among thorns, of whom the Lord said:

Other seeds fell among thorns; and the thorns sprang up and choked them ... These are they who hear the Word, but the cares of this world and the deceitfulness of riches choke the Word so that it become unfruitful (Mt 13:7, 22; Mk 4:7, 18, 19; Lu 8:7, 14).

[4] Fourth: Those who favor sins and therefore cannot know them. These acknowledge God and worship Him with the usual ceremonials and assure themselves that a given evil, which is a sin, is not a sin. For they color it with fallacies and appearances and thus hide its enormity. Then they indulge it and make it their friend and familiar. We say that those who acknowledge God do this, for others do not regard an evil as a sin, for one sins against God. But let examples illustrate this. A man makes an evil not to be a sin when in coveting wealth he makes some kinds of fraud allowable by reasoning which he devises. So does the man who confirms himself in plundering those who are not his enemies in a war.

[5] Fifth: Sins do not appear in these men, therefore cannot be removed. All evil which does not come to sight nurses itself; it is like fire in wood under ashes

or like matter in an unopened wound; for all evil which is repressed increases and does not stop until it destroys all. Lest evil be repressed, therefore, everyone is allowed to think in favor of God or against God and in favor of the sanctities of the church or against them, without being punished for it in the world. Of this the Lord says in Isaiah:

From the sole of the foot even to the head there is no soundness; wound, and scar, and fresh bruise; they have not been pressed out, nor bound up, nor softened with oil.... Wash you, make you clean, remove the evil of your doings from before my eyes; cease to do evil, learn to do good.... Then if your sins have been as scarlet, they shall be white as snow; if they have been red like crimson, they shall be like wool.... But if you refuse and rebel, you shall be devoured by the sword (Isa 1:6, 16, 17, 18, 20).

To be devoured by the sword signifies to perish by falsity of evil.

[6] Sixth: The cause, hidden so far, why evils cannot be removed apart from their being searched out, appearing, being acknowledged, confessed and resisted. In preceding pages we have mentioned the fact that all heaven is arranged in societies according to affections of good, and all hell in societies according to the lusts of evil opposite to the affections of good. Each person as to his spirit is in some society, in a heavenly one if in an affection of good, but in an infernal one if in some lust of evil. While living in the world man does not know this and yet as to his spirit he is in some society; otherwise he cannot live; and by it he is governed by the Lord. If he is in an infernal society, he cannot be led out of it by the Lord except according to the laws of divine providence, among which is this also, that a man shall see that he is there, want to leave, and make the effort himself to do so. One can do this while in the world but not after death, for then he remains forever in the society in which he put himself in the world. It is for this reason that man is to examine himself, see and avow his sins, do repentance, and thereupon persevere to the close of life. I might substantiate this to full belief by much experience, but this is not the place to document the experience.

(iii) So far as evils are removed they are remitted. It is an error of the age to believe

1. That evils are separated and in fact cast out from man when they are remitted; and 2. That the state of man's life can be changed in a moment, even to its opposite, so that from wicked he becomes good, and consequently can be led from hell and be transported straightway to heaven, and this by the Lord's sheer mercy. 3. But those who believe and suppose so, do not know at all what evil and good are and nothing at all about the state of man's life. 4. Moreover, they are wholly unaware that affections, which are of the will, are nothing other than changes and variations of the state of the purely organic substances of the mind; and that thoughts, which are of the understanding, also are; and that memory is the permanent state of these changes.

When one knows these things, one can see clearly that an evil can be removed only by successive stages, and that the remission of an evil is not complete removal of it. But all this has been said in summary form and unless the items are demonstrated may be assented to and yet not comprehended. What is not comprehended is as indistinct as a wheel spun around by the hand. The points made above are therefore to be demonstrated one by one in the order in which they were set forth.

[2] First: It is an error of the age to believe that evils are separated and in fact cast out when they are remitted. It has been granted me to learn from heaven that no evil into which man is born and which he has made actual in him is separated from him, but is removed so as not to appear. Earlier I shared the belief of most persons in the world that when evils are remitted they are cast out and are washed and wiped away as dirt is from the face by water. It is not like this with evils or sins. They all remain. When they are remitted on repentance, they are thrust from the center to the sides. What is in the center, being directly under view, appears as in the light of day, and what is to one side is in shadow and at times in the darkness of night. Inasmuch as evils are not separated but only removed, that is, thrust to one side, and as man can go from The center to the periphery, he can return, as it may happen, to his evils, which he supposed had been cast out. For the human being is such that he can go from one affection to another and sometimes to the opposite, and thus from one center into another; the affection in which he is at the time makes the center, for he is then in the enjoyment and light of it.

[3] Some who are raised after death into heaven by the Lord, for they have lived well, have carried with them, however, the belief that they are clean and rid of sins, therefore are not in a state of guilt. In accord with their belief they are clothed at first in white garments, for white garments signify a state purified from evils. But after a time they begin to think, as they did in the world, that they are washed, as it were, from all evil, and to glory that they are no longer sinners like other men. This can hardly be kept from being an elation of mind and a contempt of others in comparison with oneself. In order, therefore, that they may be delivered from their imaginary belief, they are sent down from heaven and let back into the evils which they pursued in the world; they are also shown that they are in hereditary evils of which they had not known. When they have been led in this way to realize that their evils have not been separated from them but only put aside, thus that in themselves they are impure, indeed nothing but evil, and that they are withheld from evils and held in goods by the Lord, and that this only seems to be their doing, they are raised again into heaven by the Lord.

[4] Second: It is an error of the age to believe that the state of man's life can be changed in a moment, so that from wicked he can become good, and consequently can be led from hell and transported at once to heaven, and this by the Lord's direct mercy. Those who separate charity and faith and place salvation in faith alone, commit this error. For they suppose that merely to think and speak formulas of that faith, if it is done with trust and confidence, justifies and saves one. Many think it is done instantly, too, and if not previously, can be done in the last hour of one's life. These are bound to believe that the state of man's life can be changed in a moment and that he can be saved by direct mercy. But in the last chapter of this treatise it will be seen that the Lord's mercy is mediated, that man cannot become good in a moment from being wicked, and can be led from hell and transported to heaven only by the continual activity of divine providence from infancy to the very close of life. Here it need only be said that all the laws of divine providence have the salvation and reformation of the human being for their object, in other words,

the inversion of his state, which by nativity is infernal, into the opposite, which is heavenly. This can only be done progressively as man recedes from evil and its enjoyment and comes into good and its enjoyment.

[5] Third: Those who believe in an instantaneous change do not know at all what evil and good are. For they do not know that evil is the enjoyment of the lust of acting and thinking contrary to divine order, and good is the enjoyment of the affection for acting and thinking in accord with divine order. They do not know, either, that myriads of lusts enter into and compose each individual evil and myriads of affections enter into and compose each individual good, and that these myriads are in such order and connection in man's interiors that it is impossible to change one without changing all at the same time. Those who are ignorant of this may believe or suppose that evil, which seems to them to be a single entity, can be easily removed, and that good, which also seems to be a single entity, can be introduced in its place. Not knowing what evil and good are, they cannot but suppose that there is such a thing as instantaneous salvation and such a thing as direct mercy. That these are not possible will be seen in the last chapter of this treatise.

[6] Fourth: Those who believe in instantaneous salvation and unmediated mercy do not know that affections, which are of the will, are nothing other than changes of state in the purely organic substances of the mind; that thoughts, which are of the understanding, are nothing other than changes and variations in the form of those substances; and that memory is the persisting state of the changes and variations. Everyone acknowledges, on its being said, that affections and thoughts exist only in substances and their forms, which are the subjects; existing in the brain which is full of substances and forms, they are called purely organic forms. No one who thinks rationally can help laughing at the fancies of some that affections and thoughts do not have substantive bases, but are exhalations given shape by heat and light, like images apparently in the air or ether. For thought can no more exist apart from a substantial form than sight can apart from its form, the eye, or hearing apart from its form, the ear, or taste apart from its form, the tongue. If you examine the brain, you will see innumerable substances and fibres, also, and see, too, that everything in it is organized. What more is needed than this ocular proof?

[7] But one may ask, What are affection and thought then? A conclusion can be reached from each and all things in the body. In it are many viscera, each fixed in its place, and all performing their several functions by changes and variations of state and form. It is well known that they are engaged in their own activities--the stomach, the intestines, the kidneys, the liver, the pancreas, the spleen, the heart and the lungs, each in its particular activity. All the activities are maintained from within, and to be actuated from within means that it is by changes and variations of state and form. It may be plain then that the activities of the purely organic substances of the mind are similar, the one difference being that those of the organic substances of the body are natural, but of the mind are spiritual; plainly, also, the two make one by correspondences.

[8] The nature of the changes and variations of state and form in the organic substances of the mind, which are affections and thoughts, cannot be shown to the eye. It may, however, be seen as in a mirror by the changes of state in the

lungs on speaking and singing. There is correspondence, moreover; for the sound of the voice in speaking and singing, and the articulations of the sound which are the words of speech and the modulations of song, are produced by means of the lungs; sound corresponds to affection, and speech to thought. Sound and speech are produced also from affection and thought. This is done by changes and variations in the state and form of the organic substances of the lungs, and from the lungs through the trachea or windpipe in the larynx and glottis, and then in the tongue, and finally in the lips. The first changes and variations in the state and form of the sound occur in the lungs, the second in trachea and larynx, the third in the glottis by the different openings of its orifice, the fourth in the tongue by its various positions against palate and teeth, and the fifth in the lips by the various modifications of form in them. It may be evident, then, that these consecutive changes and variations in the state of organic forms produce the sounds and their articulations which are speech and song. Inasmuch, then, as sound and speech are produced from no other source than the affections and thoughts of the mind (for they exist from them and are never apart from them), clearly the affections of the will are changes and variations in the state of the purely organic substances of the mind, and the thoughts of the understanding are changes and variations in the form of those substances, quite like those in the substances of the lungs.

[9] Since affections and thoughts are simply changes of state in the forms of the mind, memory is nothing other than the permanent state of those changes. For all changes and variations of state in organic substances are such that once they are habitual they become permanent. So the lungs are habituated to produce certain sounds in the trachea, to vary them in the glottis, articulate them by the tongue, and modify them by the mouth; once these organic activities have become habitual, they are settled in the organs and can be reproduced. These changes and variations are infinitely more perfect in the organs of the mind than in those of the body, as is evident from what was said in the treatise Divine Love and Wisdom (nn. 199-204), where we showed that all perfections increase and ascend by and according to degrees. More on this will be seen below (n. 319).

It is also an error of the age to suppose that when sins are remitted they are taken away. This is the error of those who believe that their sins are pardoned by the sacrament of the Holy Supper although they have not removed them from themselves by repentance. Those also commit this error who believe that they are saved by faith alone; those also who believe that they are saved by papal dispensations. All these believe in unmediated mercy and instant salvation. But when the statement is reversed it becomes truth, that is, when sins are removed they are also remitted. For repentance precedes pardon, and aside from repentance there is no pardon. Therefore the Lord bade His disciples:

That they should preach repentance for the remission of sins (Lu 24:27, 47), and John preached

The baptism of repentance for the remission of sins (Lu 3:3).

The Lord remits the sins of all; He does not accuse and impute; but He can take sins away only in accordance with laws of His divine providence. For when Peter asked how often he was to forgive a brother sinning against him, whether seven times, the Lord said to him:

That he should forgive not only seven times, but seventy times seven (Mt 18:21, 22).

What then will the Lord not do, who is mercy itself?

(iv) Thus the permission of evil is for the sake of the end, namely, salvation. It is well known that man has full liberty to think and will but not to say and do whatever he thinks and wills. He may think as an atheist, deny God and blaspheme the sanctities of Word and church. He may even want to destroy them utterly by word and deed, but this is prevented by civil, moral and ecclesiastical laws. He therefore cherishes this impiety and wickedness inwardly by thinking, willing and even intending to do it, but not doing it actually. The man who is not an atheist also has full liberty to think many evil things, things fraudulent, lascivious, revengeful and otherwise insane; he also does them at times. Who can believe that unless man had full liberty, he not only could not be saved but would even perish utterly?

[2] Now let us have the reason for this. Everyone from birth is in evils of many kinds. They are in his will, and what is in the will is loved. For what a man wills inwardly he loves, what he loves he wills, and the will's love flows into the understanding where it makes its pleasure felt and thereupon enters the thoughts and intentions. If, therefore, he were not allowed to think in accord with the love in his will, which is hereditarily implanted in him, that love would remain shut in and never be seen by him. A love of evil which does not become apparent is like an enemy in ambush, like matter in an ulcer, like poison in the blood, or corruption in the breast, which cause death when they are kept shut in. But when a person is permitted to think the evils of his life's love, even to intend doing them, they are cured by spiritual means as diseases are by natural means.

[3] It will be told now what man would be like if he were not permitted to think in accord with the enjoyment of his life's love. No longer would he be man, for he would lose his two faculties called liberty and rationality in which humanness itself consists. The enjoyment of those evils would occupy the interiors of his mind to such an extent that it would burst open the door. He could then only speak and commit the evils; his unsoundness would be manifest not only to himself but to the world; and at length he would not know how to cover his shame. In order that he may not come into this state, he is permitted to think and to will the evils of his inherited nature but not to say and commit them. Meanwhile he is learning civil, moral and spiritual things. These enter his thoughts and remove the unsoundness and he is healed by the Lord by means of them, only to the extent, however, of knowing how to guard the door unless he also acknowledges God and implores His aid for power to resist the unsoundness. Then, so far as he resists it, he does not let it into his intentions and eventually not even into his thoughts.

[4] Since man is free to think as he pleases to the end that his life's love may emerge from its hiding-place into the light of his understanding, and since he would not otherwise know anything of his own evil and consequently would not know how to shun it, it is also true that it would increase in him so much that recovery would become impossible in him and hardly be possible in his children, were he to have children, for a parent's evil is transmitted to his offspring. The

Lord, however, provides that this may not occur.

The Lord could heal the understanding in every man and thus cause him to think not evil but good, and this by means of fears of different kinds, miracles, conversations with the dead, or visions and dreams. But to heal the understanding alone is to heal man only outwardly, for understanding with its thought is the external of man's life while the will with its affection is the internal. The healing of the understanding alone would therefore be like palliative healing in which the interior malignity, closed in and kept from issuing, would destroy first the near and then the remote parts till all would become mortified. The will itself must be healed, not by the influx of the understanding into it, for that is impossible, but by means of instruction and exhortation from the understanding. Were the understanding alone healed, man would become like a dead body embalmed or covered by fragrant spices and roses which would soon get such a foul odor from the body that they could not be brought near anyone's nostrils. So heavenly truths in the understanding would be affected if the evil love of the will were shut in.

Man is permitted, as was said, to think evils even to intending them in order that they may be removed by means of what is civil, moral and spiritual. This is done when he considers that they are contrary to what is just and equitable, to what is honest and decorous and to what is good and true, contrary therefore to the peace, joy and blessedness of life. By these three means the Lord heals the love of man's will, in fear at first, it is true, but with love later. Still the evils are not separated from the man and cast out, but only removed in him and put to the side. When they are and good has the center, evils do not appear, for whatever has the central place is squarely under view and is seen and perceived. It should be known, however, that even when good occupies the center man is not for that reason in good unless the evils at the side tend downward or outward. If they look upward or inward they have not been removed, but are still trying to return to the center. They tend downward and outward when man shuns his evils as sins and still more when he holds them in aversion, for then he condemns them, consigns them to hell, and makes them face that way.

Man's understanding is the recipient of both good and evil and of both truth and falsity, but not his will. His will must be either in evil or in good; it cannot be in both, for it is the man himself and in it is his life's love. But good and evil are separate in the understanding like what is internal and what is external. Thus man may be inwardly in evil and outwardly in good. Still, when he is being reformed, the two meet, and conflict and combat ensue. This is called temptation when it is severe, but when it is not severe a fermentation like that of wine or strong drink occurs. If good conquers, evil with its falsity is carried to the side, as lees, to use an analogy, fall to the bottom of a vessel. The good is like wine that becomes generous on fermentation and like strong drink which becomes clear. But if evil conquers, good with its truth is borne to the side and becomes turbid and noisome like unfermented wine or unfermented strong drink. Comparison is made with ferment because in the Word, as at Hosea 7:4, Luke 12:1 and elsewhere, "ferment" signifies falsity of evil.

Section 15

DIVINE PROVIDENCE ATTENDS THE EVIL AND THE GOOD ALIKE

In every person, good or bad, there are two faculties one of which makes the understanding and the other the will. The faculty making the understanding is the ability to understand and think, therefore is called rationality. The faculty making the will is the ability to do this freely, that is, to think and consequently to speak and act also, provided that it is not contrary to reason or rationality; for to act freely is to act as often as one wills and according as one wills. The two faculties are constant and are present from first to last in each and all things which a man thinks and does. He has them not from himself, but from the Lord. It follows that the Lord's presence in these faculties is also in the least things, indeed the very least, of man's understanding and thought, of his will and affection too, and thence of his speech and action. If you remove these faculties from even the very least thing, you will not be able to think or utter it as a human being.

[2] It has already been shown abundantly that the human being is a human being by virtue of the two faculties, enabled by them to think and speak, and to perceive goods and understand truths, not only such as are civil and moral but also such as are spiritual, and made capable, too, of being reformed and regenerated; in a word, made capable of being conjoined to the Lord and thereby of living forever. It was also shown that not only good men but evil also possess the two faculties. These faculties are in man from the Lord and are not appropriated to him as his, for what is divine cannot be appropriated but only adjoined to him and thus appear to be his, and this which is divine with the human being is in the least things pertaining to him. It follows that the Lord governs the least things in an evil man as well as in a good man. This government of His is what is called divine providence.

Inasmuch as it is a law of divine providence that man shall act from freedom according to reason, that is, from the two faculties, liberty and rationality; and a law of divine providence that what he does shall appear to be from himself and thus his own; and also a law that evils must be permitted in order that man may be led out of them, it follows that man can abuse these faculties and in freedom according to reason confirm whatever he pleases. He can make reasonable whatever he will, whether it is reasonable in itself or not. Some therefore ask, "What is truth? Can I not make true whatever I will?" Does not the world do so? Anybody can do it by reasoning. Take an utter falsity and bid a clever man confirm it, and he will. Tell him, for instance, to show that man is a beast, or that the soul is like a small spider in its web and governs the body as that does by threads, or tell him that religion is nothing but a restraining bond, and he will prove any one of these propositions until it appears to be truth. What is more easily done? For he does not know what appearance is or what falsity is which in blind faith is taken for truth.

[2] Hence it is that a man cannot see this truth, namely, that divine

providence is in the very least things of the understanding and the will, or what is the same, in the very least things of the thoughts and affections of every person, wicked or good. He is perplexed especially because it seems then that evils are also from the Lord, but it will be seen in what follows that nevertheless there is not a particle of evil from the Lord but that evil is from man in that he confirms in him the appearance that he thinks, wills, speaks and acts of himself. In order that these things may be seen clearly, they will be demonstrated in this order:

i. Divine providence is universal in the least things with the evil as well as the good, and yet is not in one's evils. ii. The evil are continually leading themselves into evils, but the Lord is continually leading them away from evils. iii. The evil cannot be fully withdrawn from evil and led in good by the Lord so long as they believe their own intelligence to be everything and divine providence nothing. iv. The Lord rules hell through opposites; and rules the evil who are in the world, in hell as to their interiors, but not as to their exteriors.

(i) Divine providence is universal in the least things with the evil as well as the good, and yet is not in one's evils. It was shown above that divine providence is in the least things of man's thoughts and affections. This means that man can think and will nothing from himself, but that everything he thinks and wills and consequently says and does, is from influx. If it is good, it is from influx out of heaven, and if evil, from influx out of hell; or what is the same, the good is from influx from the Lord and the evil from man's proprium. I know that it is difficult to grasp this, because what flows in from heaven or from the Lord is distinguished from what flows in from hell or from man's proprium, and yet divine providence is said to be in the least of man's thoughts and affections, even so far that he can think and will nothing from himself. It appears like a contradiction to say that he can also think and will from hell and from his proprium. Yet it is not, and this will be seen in what follows, after some things have been premised which will clarify the matter.

All the angels of heaven confess that no one can think from himself but does so from the Lord, while all the spirits of hell say that no one can think from any other than himself. These spirits have been shown many times that no one of them thinks or can think from himself, but that thought flows in; it was in vain, however; they would not accept the idea. But experience will teach, first, that everything of thought and affection even with spirits of hell flows in from heaven, but that the inflowing good is turned into evil there and truth into falsity, thus everything into its opposite. This was shown in this way: a truth from the Word was sent down from heaven, was received by those uppermost in hell, and by them sent to lower hells, and on to the lowest. On the way it was turned by stages into falsity and finally into falsity the direct opposite of the truth. Those with whom it was so changed thought the falsity of themselves seemingly and knew no otherwise; still it was truth, flowing down from heaven on the way to the lowest hell, which was thus falsified and perverted. I have heard of this several times. The same thing occurs with good; as it flows down from heaven, it is changed step by step into the evil opposite to it. Hence it was plain that truth and good, proceeding from the Lord and received by those who are in falsity and evil, are completely altered and so transformed that their first form is lost. The like happens in every evil person, for as to his spirit he is in hell.

I have often been shown that no one in hell thinks from himself but through others around him, and these do not, but through others still. Thoughts and affections make their way from one society to another, but no one is aware that they do not originate with himself. Some who believed that they thought and willed of themselves were dispatched to another society and held there, and communication was cut off with the societies around to which their thoughts usually extended. Then they were told to think differently from the spirits of this society, and compel themselves to think to the contrary; they confessed that they could not.

[2] This was done with a number and with Leibnitz, too, who was also convinced that no one thinks from himself, but from others, nor do these think from themselves, but all think by an influx from heaven, and heaven by an influx from the Lord. Some, pondering this, said that it was amazing, and that hardly anyone can be led to credit it, for it is utterly contrary to the appearance, but that they still could not deny it, for it was fully demonstrated. Nevertheless, astonished as they were, they said that they are not in fault then in thinking evil; also that it seems then as if evil is from the Lord; and, again, that they do not understand how the one Lord can cause all to think so diversely. The three points will be explained in what follows.

To the experiences cited this is also to be added. When it was granted me by the Lord to speak with spirits and angels, the foregoing arcanum was at once disclosed to me. For I was told from heaven that like others I believed that I thought and willed from myself, when in fact nothing was from myself, but if it was good, it was from the Lord, and if evil from hell. That this was so, was shown me to the life by various thoughts and affections which were induced on me, and gradually I was given to perceive and feel it. Therefore, as soon as an evil afterwards entered my will or a falsity into my thought, I investigated the source of it. I inquired from whom it came. This was disclosed to me, and I was also allowed to speak with those spirits, refute them, and compel them to withdraw, thus to take back their evil and falsity and keep it to themselves, and no longer infuse anything of the kind into my thought. This has occurred a thousand times. I have remained in this state for many years, and still do. Yet I seem to myself to think and will from myself like others, with no difference, for of the Lord's providence it should so appear to everyone, as was shown above in the section on it. Newly arriving spirits wonder at this state of mine, seeing as they do only that I do not think and will from myself, and am therefore like some empty thing. But I disclosed the arcanum to them, and added that I also think more interiorly, and perceive whether what flows into my exterior thought is from heaven or from hell, reject the latter and welcome the former, yet seem to myself, like them, to be thinking and willing from myself.

It is not unknown in the world that all good is from heaven and all evil from hell; it is known to everyone in the church. Who that has been inaugurated into the church's priesthood does not teach that all good is from God, and that man can receive nothing of himself except it be given him from heaven? And also that the devil infuses evils into the thoughts and leads astray and incites one to commit evils? Therefore a priest who believes that he preaches out of a holy zeal, prays that the Holy Spirit may teach him, and guide his thoughts and utterances. Some say that they have sensibly perceived being acted upon, and when a sermon is praised, reply piously that they have spoken not from themselves but from God. Therefore when they see someone speak and act well, they remark he was led to do so by God; on the other hand, seeing someone speak and act wickedly, they remark he was led to do so by the devil. That there is talk of the kind in the church is known, but who believes that it is so?

Everything that a man thinks and wills, and consequently speaks and does, flows in from the one Fountain of life, and yet that one Fountain of life, namely, the Lord, is not the cause of man's thinking what is evil and false. This may be clarified by these facts in the world of nature. Heat and light proceed from the sun of the world. They flow into all visible subjects and objects, not only into subjects that are good and objects that are beautiful, but also into subjects that are evil and objects that are ugly, producing varying effects in them. They flow not only into trees that bear good fruit but into trees that bear bad fruit, and into the fruits themselves, quickening their growth. They flow into good seed and into weeds, into shrubs which have a good use and are wholesome, and into shrubs that have an evil use and are poisonous. Yet it is the same heat and the same light; there is no cause of evil in them; the cause is in the recipient subjects and objects.

[2] The same warmth that hatches eggs in which a screech-owl, a horned owl, and a viper lie acts as it does when it hatches those in which a dove, a bird of paradise and a swan lie. Put eggs of both sorts under the hen and they will be hatched by her warmth, which in itself is innocent of harm. What has the heat in common then with what is evil and noxious? The heat flowing into a marsh or a dung-hill or into decaying or dead matter acts in the same way as it does when it flows into things flavorsome and fragrant, lush and living. Who does not see that the cause is not in the heat but in the recipient subject? The same light gives pleasing colors in one object and displeasing colors in another; indeed, it grows brighter in white objects and becomes dazzling, and dims in those verging on black and becomes dusky.

[3] There is what is similar in the spiritual world. There are heat and light in it from its sun, which is the Lord, and they flow from the sun into their subjects and objects. Now the subjects and objects are angels and spirits, in particular their volitional and mental life, and the heat is divine love going forth, and the light is divine wisdom going forth. The light and heat are not the cause of the different reception of them by one and another. For the Lord says,

He makes the sun to rise on the evil and the good, and sends rain on the just and the unjust (Mt 5:45).

In the highest spiritual sense by the "sun" the divine love is meant, and by the "rain" the divine wisdom.

Let me add to this the view of the angels on will and understanding in man. This is that there cannot be a grain of will or of prudence in man that is his own. They say that if there were, neither heaven nor hell would continue in existence, and all mankind would perish. The reason they give is that myriads of human beings, as many as have been born since the creation of the world, constitute heaven and hell, of which the one is under the other in such an order that each is a unit, heaven one comely humanity, and hell one monstrous humanity. If the individual had a grain of will and intelligence of his very own, that unity could not exist, but would be torn apart. Upon this that divine form would perish, which can arise and remain only as the Lord is all in all and men are nothing besides. A further reason, they say, is that to think and will actually from one's own being is the divine itself, and to think and will from God, is the truly human. The very divine cannot be appropriated to anyone, for then man would be God. Bear the above in mind, and if you wish you will have confirmation of it by angels when on death you come into the spiritual world.

It was stated above (n. 289) that when some were convinced that no one thinks from himself but from others, nor the others from themselves, but all by influx through heaven from the Lord, they remarked in their astonishment that then they are not in fault when they do evil, also that then it seems evil comes from the Lord, nor do they comprehend how the Lord can cause them all to think so differently. Since these three notions cannot but flow into the thoughts of those who regard effects only from effects and not from causes, they need to be taken up and explained by what causes them.

[2] First: They are not in fault then in doing evil. For if all that a person thinks flows into him from others, the fault seems to be theirs from whom it comes. Yet the fault is the recipient's, for he receives what inflows as his own and neither knows nor wants to know otherwise. For everyone wants to be his own, to be led by himself, and above all to think and will from himself; this is freedom itself, which appears as the proprium in which every person is. If he knew, therefore, that what he thinks and wills flows in from another, it would seem to him that he was bound and captive and no longer master of himself. All enjoyment in his life would thus perish, and finally his very humanness would perish.

[3] I have often seen this evidenced. It was granted some spirits to perceive and sense that they were being led by others. Thereupon they were so enraged that they were reduced almost to mental impotence. They said that they would rather be kept bound in hell than not to be allowed to think as they willed and to will as they thought. This they called being bound in their very life, which was harder and more intolerable than to be bound bodily. Not being allowed to speak and act as they thought and willed, they did not call being bound. For the enjoyment of civil and moral life, which consists in speaking and acting, itself restrains and at the same time mitigates that.

[4] Inasmuch as man does not want to know that he is led to think by others, but wants to think from himself and believes that he does so, it follows that he himself is in fault, nor can he throw off the blame so long as he loves to think what he thinks. If he does not love it, he breaks his connection with those from whom his thought flows. This occurs when he knows the thought is evil, therefore determines to avoid it and desist from it. He is then also taken by the Lord from the society in that evil and transferred to a society free of it. If, however, he recognizes the evil and does not shun it, fault is imputed to him, and he is responsible for the evil. Therefore, whatever a man believes that he does from himself is said to be done from the man, and not from the Lord.

[5] Second: It then seems as if evil is from the Lord. This may be thought to be the conclusion from what was shown above (n. 288), namely, that good flowing in from the Lord is turned into evil and truth into falsity in hell. But who cannot see that evil and falsity do not come of good and truth, therefore not

from the Lord, but from the recipient subject or object which is in evil and falsity and which perverts and inverts what flows into it, as was amply shown above (n. 292). The source of evil and falsity in man has been pointed out frequently in the preceding pages. Moreover, an experiment was made in the spiritual world with those who believed that the Lord could remove evils in the wicked and introduce good instead, thus move the whole of hell into heaven and save all. That this is impossible, however, will be seen towards the end of this treatise, where instantaneous salvation and unmediated mercy are to be treated of.

[6] Third: They do not comprehend how the one Lord can cause all to think so diversely. The Lord's divine love is infinite, likewise His divine wisdom. An infinity of love and wisdom proceeds from Him, flows in with all in heaven, thence with all in hell, and from heaven and hell with all in the world. Thinking and willing therefore cannot lack in anyone, for what is infinite is limitless. The infinite things that issue from the Lord flow in not only universally but also in least things. For the divine is universal by being in least things, and the divine in least things constitutes what is called universal, as was shown above, and the divine in something least is still infinite. Hence it may be evident that the one Lord causes each person to think and will according to the person's nature and does so in accordance with laws of His providence. It was shown above (nn. 46-69) and also in the treatise Divine Love and Wisdom (nn. 17-22), that everything in the Lord, or proceeding from Him, is infinite.

(ii) *The evil are continually leading themselves into evils, but the Lord is continually leading them away from evils.* The nature of divine providence with the good is more readily comprehended than its nature with the evil. As the latter is now under consideration, it will be set forth in this order:

1. In every evil there are innumerable things. 2. An evil man of himself continually leads himself more and more deeply into his evils. 3. Divine providence with the evil is a continual tolerance of evil, to the end that there may be a continual withdrawal from it. 4. Withdrawal from evil is effected by the Lord in a thousand most secret ways.

In order, then, that divine providence with the evil may be seen clearly and therefore understood, the propositions just stated are to be explained in the order in which they were presented.

First: *In every evil there are innumerable things.* To man's sight an evil appears to be a single thing. Hatred does, and revenge, theft and fraud, adultery and whoredom, pride and presumption, and the rest. It is unknown that in every evil there are innumerable things, exceeding in number the fibres and vessels in the human body. For an evil man is a hell in least form, and hell consists of myriads and myriads of spirits, each of whom is in form like a man, but a monstrous one, in whom all the fibres and vessels are inverted. A spirit himself is an evil which appears to him as one thing, but in it are innumerable things, as numerous as the lusts of that evil. For everyone, from head to foot, is his own evil or his own good. Since an evil man is such, plainly he is one evil composed of countless different evils, all severally evils, and called lusts of evil. It follows that all these, one after another, must be cured and changed by the Lord for man to be reformed, and that it can be done only by the Lord's divine providence, step by step from man's first years to his last.

[2] Every lust of evil, when it is visually presented, appears in hell like some noxious creature, a serpent, a cockatrice, a viper, a horned owl, a screech-owl, or some other; so do the lusts of evil in an evil man appear when he is viewed by angels. All these forms of lust must be changed one by one. The man himself, who appears as to his spirit like a monstrous man or devil, must be changed to appear like a comely angel, and each lust of evil changed to appear like a lamb or sheep or pigeon or turtle dove, as affections of good in angels appear in heaven when they are visually represented. Changing a serpent into a lamb, or a cockatrice into a sheep, or an owl into a dove, can be done only gradually, by uprooting evil together with its seed and implanting good seed in its place. This can only be done, however, comparatively as is done in the grafting of trees, of which the roots with some of the trunk remain, but the engrafted branch turns the sap drawn through the old root into sap that produces good fruit. The branch to be engrafted in this instance is to be had only from the Lord, who is the tree of life; this is also in keeping with the Lord's words in John 15:1-7.

[3] Second: An evil man from himself continually leads himself more deeply into his evils. He does so "from himself" because all evil is from man, for, as was said, he turns good, which is from the Lord, into evil. He leads himself more and more deeply into evil for the reason, essentially, that as he wills and commits evil, he enters more and more interiorly and also more and more deeply into infernal societies. Hence the enjoyment of evil increases, too, and occupies his thoughts until he feels nothing more agreeable. One who has entered more interiorly and deeply into infernal societies becomes like one bound by chains. So long as he lives in the world, however, he does not feel his chains; they seem to be made of soft wool or smooth silken threads. He loves them, for they titillate; but after death, from being soft, those chains become hard, and from being pleasant become galling.

[4] That the enjoyment of evil grows is known from thefts, robberies, plunderings, revenge, tyranny, lucre, and other evils. Who does not feel a heightening of enjoyment in them as he succeeds in them and practices them uninhibited? A thief, we know, feels such enjoyment in thefts that he cannot desist from them, and, a wonder, he loves one stolen coin more than ten that are given him. It would be similar with adultery, had it not been provided that the power to commit this evil decreases with the abuse, but with many there still remains the enjoyment of thinking and talking about it, and if nothing more, there is still the lust of touch.

[5] It is not known, however, that this heightening of enjoyment comes from a man's entering into infernal societies more and more interiorly and deeply as he perpetrates evils from the will as well as from thought. If the evils are only in the thoughts, and not in the will, he is not yet in an infernal society having that evil; he enters it when the evils are also in the will. Then, if he also thinks the evil is contrary to the precepts of the Decalog and regards these precepts as divine, he commits the evil of set purpose and by so doing plunges to a depth from which he can be brought out only by active repentance. It is to be understood that everyone as to his spirit is in the spiritual world, in one of its societies, an evil man in an infernal society and a good man in a heavenly society; sometimes, when in deep meditation one also appears there. Moreover, as sound and, along with it, speech spread on the air in the natural world,

affection and thought with it spread among societies in the spiritual world; there is correspondence, too, affection corresponding to sound and thought to speech.

[7] Third: Divine providence with the evil is a continual tolerance of evil, to the end that there may be a continual withdrawal from it. Divine providence with evil men is continual permission because only evil can issue from their life. For whether he is in good or in evil, man cannot be in both at once, nor by turns in one and the other unless he is lukewarm. Evil of life is not introduced into the will and through this into the thought by the Lord but by man, and this is named permission.

[8] Inasmuch as everything which an evil man wills and thinks is by permission, the question arises, what in this case divine providence is, which is said to be in the least things with every person, evil or good. It consists in this, that it exercises tolerance continually for the sake of its objective, and permits what helps to the end and nothing more. It constantly observes the evils that issue by permission, separates and purifies them, and rejects what is unsuitable and discharges it by unknown ways. This is done principally in man's interior will and through it in his interior thought. Divine providence also sees to it constantly that what must be rejected and discharged is not received again by the will, since all that is received by the will is appropriated to the man; what is received by the thought, but not by the will, is set aside and banished. Such is the constant divine providence with the evil; as was said, it is a continual tolerance of evil to the end that there may be continual withdrawal from it.

[9] Of these activities man knows scarcely anything, for he does not perceive them. The chief reason why he does not, is that the evils come from the lusts of his life's love, and are not felt to be evils but enjoyments, to which one does not give thought. Who gives thought to the enjoyments of his love? His thought floats along in them like a skiff carried along by the current of a stream; and he perceives a fragrant air which he inhales with a deep breath. Only in one's external thought does one have a sense of the enjoyments, but even in it he pays no attention to them unless he knows well that they are evil. More will be said on this in what follows.

[10] Fourth: Withdrawal from evil is effected by the Lord in a thousand most secret ways. Only some of these have been disclosed to me, and only the most general ones. For instance, the enjoyments of lusts, of which man knows nothing, are let by clusters and bundles into the interior thoughts of his spirit and thence into his exterior thoughts, where they appear in a feeling of pleasure, delight or longing, and mingle with his natural and sensuous enjoyments. There the means to separation and purification and the ways of withdrawal and unburdening are to be found. The means are chiefly the enjoyments of meditation, thought and reflection on ends that are uses. Such ends are as numerous as the particulars and details of one's business or occupation. Just as numerous are the enjoyments of reflection on such an end as that one shall appear to be a civil and moral and also a spiritual person, no matter what interposes which is unenjoyable. These enjoyments, being those of one's love in the external man, are the means to the separation, purification, expulsion and withdrawal of the enjoyments of the lusts in the internal man.

[11] Take, for example, an unjust judge who regards gain or friendship as

the end or use of his office. Inwardly he is constantly in those ends, but outwardly must act as one learned in the law and just. He is constantly in the enjoyment of meditation, thought, reflection and intent to bend and turn a decision and adapt and adjust it so that it may still seem to be in conformity with the laws and resemble justice. He does not know that his inward enjoyment consists in craftiness, defrauding, deceit, clandestine theft, and many other evils, and that this enjoyment, made up of so many enjoyments of the lusts of evil, governs each and all things of his external thought, in which he enjoys appearing just and sincere. Into the external enjoyment the internal enjoyment is let down, the two are mingled as food is in the stomach, and thereupon the internal enjoyments are separated, purified, and withdrawn. Still this is true only of the more grievous enjoyments of the lusts of evil.

[12] For in an evil man the only separation, purification and withdrawal possible is of the more grievous evils from the less grievous.

In a good man, however, separation, purification and withdrawal is possible not only of the more grievous evils but also of the less grievous. This is effected by the enjoyments of the affections of what is good and true, and of what is just and sincere, affections into which one comes so far as he regards evils as sins and therefore avoids and is averse to them, and still more as he fights against them. It is by these means that the Lord purifies all who are saved. He purifies them by external means also, such as fame and standing and sometimes wealth, but put into these means by the Lord are the enjoyments of affections of good and truth, by which they are directed and fitted to become enjoyments of love for the neighbor.

[13] If one saw the enjoyments of the lusts of evil assembled in some form, or perceived them distinctly by some sense, he would see and perceive that they are too numerous for definition. For hell in its entirety is nothing but the form of all the lusts of evil, and no one lust in it is quite similar to or the same as another, nor can be to eternity. Of these countless lusts man knows scarcely anything, and even less how they are connected with one another. Yet the Lord in His divine providence continually allows them to come forth, for them to be drawn away, and this is done in perfect order and sequence. For the evil man is a hell in miniature, and the good man a heaven in miniature.

[14] The withdrawal from evils, which the Lord effects in a thousand highly secret ways, may best be seen and concluded about from the secret activities of the soul in the body. Man knows that he examines the food he is about to eat, perceives what it is by its odor, hungers for it, tastes it, chews it, and by the tongue rolls it down into the esophagus and so into the stomach. But then there are the hidden activities of the soul of which he knows nothing, for he has no sensation of them. The stomach rolls about the food it receives, opens and breaks it up by solvents, that is, digests it, and offers fit portions to the little mouths opening in it and to veins which imbibe it. Some it sends to the blood, some to the lymphatic vessels, some to the lacteal vessels of the mesentery, and some down to the intestines. Then the chyle, conveyed through the thoracic duct from its cistern in the mesentery, is carried to the vena cava, and so to the heart. From the heart it is carried into the lungs, from them through the left ventricle of the heart into the aorta, and from this by its branches to viscera throughout the body and also to the kidneys. In each organ separation and

purification of the blood are effected and removal of the heterogeneous, not to mention how the heart sends its blood up to the brain after purification in the lungs, which is done by the arteries called carotids, and how the brain returns the blood, now vivified, to the vena cava just above where the thoracic duct brings in the chyle, and so back again to the heart.

[15] These and countless other activities are secret operations of the soul in the body. Man has no sense of them, and unless he is acquainted with the science of anatomy, knows nothing of them. Yet similar activities take place in the interiors of the human mind. Nothing can take place in the body except from the mind, for man's mind is his spirit, and his spirit is equally man; the sole difference being that what is done in the body is done naturally, while what is done in the mind is done spiritually; there is all similarity. Plainly, then, divine providence operates with every man in a thousand hidden ways, and its incessant care is to cleanse him, since its purpose is to save him. Plainly, too, nothing more is incumbent on man than to remove evils in the outward man; the Lord sees to the rest, when He is implored.

(iii) The evil cannot be fully withdrawn from evil and led in good by the Lord so long as they believe their own intelligence to be everything and divine providence nothing. It would seem that man could withdraw himself from evil provided he thought that this or that was contrary to the common good, or to what is useful, or to national or international law, and this an evil as well as a good man can do if by birth or through practice he is such that he can think clearly within himself, analysing and reasoning. But even then he is not capable of withdrawing himself from evil. The faculty of understanding and of perceiving, even abstractly, has indeed been given everyone by the Lord, to the evil as well as to the good, as has been shown above in many places, and yet man cannot deliver himself from evil by means of this faculty. For evil comes of the will, and the understanding influences the will only with light, enlightening and instructing. If the heat of the will, that is, man's love, is hot with the lust of evil, it is cold towards the affection of good, therefore does not receive the light but either repels or extinguishes it, or by some fabricated falsity turns it into evil. The light is then like winter light, which is as clear as the light in summer and remains as clear even when it flows into frozen trees. But this can be seen better in the following order:

1. When the will is in evil, one's own intelligence sees only falsity, and neither desires to see, nor can see, anything else. 2. If then one's own intelligence is confronted with truth, it either turns away from it or falsifies it. 3. Divine providence continually causes man to see truth, and also gives him affection for perceiving and receiving it. 4. Through this means man is withdrawn from evil, not by himself, but by the Lord.

For these things to be made apparent to the rational man, whether he is evil or good, thus whether he is in the light of winter or in the light of summer (for colors appear the same in them), they are to be explained in due order.

First: When the will is in evil, one's own intelligence sees only falsity, and neither desires nor is able to see anything else. This has often been demonstrated in the spiritual world. Everyone, on becoming a spirit, which takes place after death when he puts off the material body and puts on the spiritual, is introduced by turns into the two states of his life, the external and the internal. In the external state he speaks and acts rationally, quite as a rational and wise man does in the world; he can also instruct others in much that pertains to moral and civil life, and if he has been a preacher he can also give instruction in the spiritual life. But when he is brought from this external state into his internal state, and the external is put to sleep and the internal awakes, the scene changes if he is evil. From being rational he becomes sensuous, and from being wise he becomes insane. For he thinks then from the evil of his will and its enjoyments, thus from his own intelligence, and sees only falsity and does nothing but evil, believing that evil is wisdom and that cunning is prudence. From his own intelligence he believes himself to be a deity and with all his mind sucks up nefarious ways.

[2] I have often seen instances of such insanity. I have also seen spirits introduced into these alternating states two or three times within an hour, and it was granted them to see and also acknowledge their insanities. Nevertheless they were unwilling to remain in a rational and moral state, but voluntarily returned to their internal sensuous and insane state. They loved this more than the other because the enjoyment of their life's love was in it. Who can believe that an evil man is such beneath his outward appearance and that he undergoes such a transformation when he enters on his internal state? This one experience makes plain the nature of one's own intelligence when one thinks and acts from the evil of one's will. It is otherwise with the good. When they are admitted from their external state into their internal state, they become still wiser and still more moral.

[3] Second: If then one's own intelligence is confronted with truth, it either turns away from it or falsifies it. The human being has a volitional and an intellectual proprium. The volitional proprium is evil, and the intellectual proprium is falsity derived from evil; the latter is meant by "the will of man" and the former by "the will of the flesh" in John 1:13. The volitional proprium is in essence self-love, and the intellectual proprium is the pride coming of that love. The two are like married partners, and their union is called the marriage of evil and falsity. Into this union each evil spirit is admitted before he enters hell; he then does not know what good is; he calls his evil good, because that is what he feels to be enjoyable. He also turns away from truth then and has no desire to see it, because he sees the falsity which accords with his evil as the eye beholds what is beautiful, and hears it as the ear hears what is harmonious.

[4] Third: Divine providence continually causes man to see truth and also gives him affection for perceiving and receiving it. For divine providence acts from within and flows thence into the exteriors, that is, flows from what is spiritual into what is in the natural man, by the light of heaven enlightening his understanding and by the heat of heaven quickening his will. The light of heaven in essence is divine wisdom, and the heat of heaven in essence is divine love. From divine wisdom nothing can flow but truth, and from divine love nothing but good. With good the Lord bestows an affection in the understanding for seeing and also perceiving and receiving truth. Man thus becomes man not only in external aspect but in internal aspect, too. Everyone desires to appear a rational and spiritual man, and knows he so desires in order that others may believe him to be truly man. If then he is rational and spiritual in external form only, and not at the same time in his internal form, is he man? Is he different

from a player on the stage or from an ape with an almost human face? May one not know from this that only he is a human being who is inwardly what he desires others to think he is? One who acknowledges the one fact must admit the other. Man's own intelligence can induce the human form only on externals, but divine providence induces it on internals and thence on externals. When it has been so induced, a man does not only appear to be a man; he is one.

[5] Fourth: Through this means man is withdrawn from evil, not by himself, but by the Lord. When divine providence gives man to see truth and to be affected by it, he can be withdrawn from evil for the reason that truth points the way and dictates; doing what truth dictates, the will unites with truth and within itself turns it into good, for it becomes something one loves, and what is loved is good. All reformation is effected through truth, not without it, for without truth the will continues in its evil, and should it consult the understanding, is not instructed, rather the evil is confirmed by falsities.

[6] With regard to intelligence, this seems to the good man as well as to an evil man to be his and proper to him. Like an evil man, he is also bound to act from intelligence as if it were his own. But one who believes in divine providence is withdrawn from evil, and one who does not believe in it is not withdrawn; he believes who acknowledges that evil is sin and desires to be withdrawn from it, and he does not believe who does not so acknowledge and desire. The difference between the two kinds of intelligence is like that between what is believed to exist in itself and what is believed not to exist in itself but to appear as if it did. It is also like the difference between an external without an internal similar to it and an external with a similar internal. Thus it is like the difference between impersonations of kings, princes or generals by mimes and actors through word and bearing, and actual kings, princes or generals. The latter are such in fact as well as outwardly, but the former only outwardly, and when the exterior is laid off, are known only as comedians, actors or players.

(iv) The Lord governs hell by means of opposites, and those in the world who are evil He governs in hell as to their interiors but not as to their exteriors. One who does not know the character of heaven and hell cannot know at all that of man's mind; his mind is his spirit which survives death. For the mind or spirit of man is altogether in form what heaven or hell is. The only difference is that one is vast and the other very small, or one is archetype and the other a copy. As to his mind or spirit, accordingly, the human being is either heaven or hell in least form, heaven if he is led by the Lord, and hell if he is led by his proprium. Inasmuch as it has been granted me to know what heaven and hell are, and it is important to know what the human being is in respect to his mind or spirit, I will describe both heaven and hell briefly.

All who are in heaven are nothing other than affections of good and thoughts thence of truth, and all who are in hell are nothing other than lusts of evil and imaginations thence of falsity. These are so arranged respectively that the lusts of evil and the imaginings of falsity in hell are precisely opposite to the affections of good and the thoughts of truth in heaven. Therefore hell is under heaven and diametrically opposite, that is, the two are like two men lying in opposite directions, or standing, invertedly, like men at the antipodes, only the soles of their feet meeting and their heels hitting. At times hell also appears to be so situated or inverted relatively to heaven, for the reason that those in hell make lusts of evil the head and affections of good the feet, while those in heaven make affections of good the head and lusts of evil the soles of the feet; hence the mutual opposition. When it is said that in heaven there are affections of good and thoughts of truth from them, and in hell lusts of evil and imaginations of falsity from them, the meaning is that there are spirits and angels who are such. For everyone is his affection or his lust, an angel of heaven his affection and a spirit of hell his lust.

Footnotes
265-1 Swedenborg follows the numbering of the Commandments customary with Lutherans, as with Roman Catholics.

The angels of heaven are affections of good and thoughts thence of truth because they are recipients of divine love and wisdom from the Lord; for all affections of good are from the divine love and all thoughts of truth are from the divine wisdom. But the spirits of hell are lusts of evil and the imaginations thence of falsity because they are in self-love and their own intelligence, and all lusts of evil come of self-love and imaginations of falsity from one's own intelligence.

The ordering of affections in heaven and of lusts in hell is marvelous, and is known to the Lord alone. They are each distinguished into genera and species, and are so conjoined as to make a unit. As they are distinguished into genera and species, they are distinguished into larger and smaller societies, and as they are so conjoined as to make a unit, they are conjoined as all things in man are. Hence in its form heaven is like a comely man, whose soul is divine love and wisdom, thus the Lord, and hell in its form is like a monstrous man, his soul self-love and self-intelligence, thus the devil. No devil is sole lord there; self-love is so called.

But that the nature of heaven and of hell respectively may be better known, instead of affections of good let enjoyments of good be understood, and enjoyments of evil instead of lusts of evil, for no affections or lusts are without their enjoyments, and enjoyments make one's life. These enjoyments are distinguished and conjoined as we said affections of good and lusts of evil are. The enjoyment of his affection fills and surrounds each angel, the enjoyment common to a society of heaven fills and surrounds each society, and the enjoyment of all the angels together or the most widely shared enjoyment fills and envelops heaven as a whole. Similarly, the pleasure of his lust fills and envelops each spirit of hell, a common enjoyment every society in hell, and the enjoyment of all or the most widely shared enjoyment fills and envelops all hell. Since, as was said, the affections of heaven and the lusts of hell are diametrically opposite to each other, plainly a heavenly joy is so unenjoyable to hell that it is unbearable, and in turn an infernal joy is so unenjoyable to heaven that it is unbearable, too. Hence the antipathy, aversion and separateness.

As these enjoyments constitute the life of each individual and of all in general, they are not sensed by those in them, but the opposite enjoyments are sensed when brought near, especially if they are turned into odors; for every enjoyment corresponds to an odor and in the spiritual world may be converted into it. Then the general enjoyment in heaven is sensed as the odor of a garden, varied according to the fragrance of flowers and fruits; the general enjoyment in hell is sensed as the odor of stagnant water, into which filth of various sorts has been thrown, the odor varied according to the stench of the things decaying and reeking in it. While I have been given to know how the enjoyment of a particular affection of good is sensed in heaven, and the enjoyment of some lust of evil in hell, it would take too long to relate it here.

I have heard many newcomers from the world complain that they had not known that their destiny would be according to the affections of their love. To these, they said, they had given no thought in the world, much less to the enjoyments of the affections, for they loved what they found enjoyable. They had believed that each person's lot would be according to his thoughts from his intelligence, especially according to thoughts of piety and of faith. But they were answered, that they could have known, if they wished, that evil of life is unacceptable to heaven and displeasing to God, but acceptable to hell and pleasing to the devil, and the other way about, that good of life is acceptable to heaven and pleasing to God, but unacceptable to hell and displeasing to the devil; consequently that evil in itself is malodorous and good is fragrant. As they might have known this if they wished, why did they not shun evils as infernal and diabolical, but indulge in them merely because they were enjoyable? Aware now that the enjoyments of evil smell so foully, they might also know that those full of them cannot enter heaven. Upon this reply they betook themselves to those who were in similar enjoyments, for only there could they breathe.

From the idea of heaven and hell just given, it may be evident what the nature of man's mind is. For, as was said, man's mind or spirit is either a heaven or a hell in least form, that is, his interiors are nothing other than affections and thoughts thence, distinguished into genera and species, like the larger and smaller societies of heaven or hell, and so connected as to act as a unit. The Lord governs them as He does heaven or hell. That the human being is either heaven or hell in least form may be seen in the work Heaven and Hell, published at London in 1758.

Now to the subject proposed, that the Lord governs hell by means of opposites, and those in the world who are evil He governs in hell as to their interiors but not as to their exteriors. On the first point, that the Lord governs hell through opposites, it was shown above (nn. 288, 289) that the angels of heaven are not in love and wisdom, or in the affection of good and thence in thought of truth from themselves, but from the Lord, likewise that good and truth flow from heaven into hell where good is turned into evil and truth into falsity because the interiors of the minds of those in heaven and in hell respectively are turned in opposite directions. Inasmuch then as all things in hell are the opposite of all things in heaven, the Lord governs hell by means of opposites.

[2] The second point, that the Lord governs in hell those in the world who are evil. This is for the reason that the human being as to his spirit is in the spiritual world and in some society there, in an infernal society if he is evil, in a heavenly one if he is good. For his mind, which in itself is spiritual, cannot be anywhere but among spiritual beings, of whom he becomes one after death. This has also been stated and demonstrated above. A man is not there, however, in the same way as a spirit is who has been assigned to the society, for man is constantly in a state to be reformed, and therefore, if he is evil, is transferred by the Lord from one infernal society to another according to his life and the changes in it. But if he permits himself to be reformed, he is led out of hell and elevated to heaven, and there, too, he is carried from one society to another until his death, after which this does not take place as he is then no longer in a state to be reformed, but remains in the state which is his from his life. When a person dies, therefore, he is assigned his place.

[3] Thirdly, the Lord governs the evil who are in the world in this way as to their interiors, but in another way as to their exteriors. The Lord governs the interiors of man's mind in the manner just stated, but governs the exteriors in the world of spirits, which is between heaven and hell. The reason is that

commonly man is different in externals from what he is in internals. He can feign outwardly to be an angel of light and yet inwardly be a spirit of darkness. His external is therefore governed in one way, and his internal in another; as long as he is in the world, his external is governed in the world of spirits, and his internal in either heaven or hell. On death one also enters the world of spirits first, therefore, and comes into his external, which he puts off there; having put it off, he is conducted to the place assigned as his. What the world of spirits is and its nature may be seen in the work Heaven and Hell, published at London in 1758, nn. 421-535.

Section 16

DIVINE PROVIDENCE APPROPRIATES NEITHER EVIL NOR GOOD TO ANYONE, BUT ONE'S OWN PRUDENCE APPROPRIATES BOTH

Almost everyone believes that man thinks and wills, hence speaks and acts, from himself. Who of himself can believe otherwise? For the appearance that he does is so strong that it differs not at all from actually thinking, willing, speaking and acting from oneself, which is impossible. In Angelic Wisdom about Divine Love and Wisdom it was shown that there is only one life and that men are recipients of life; also that the human will is the receptacle of love, and the human understanding the receptacle of wisdom; love and wisdom are the one life. It was also demonstrated that by creation and steadily therefore by divine providence this life appears in the human being quite as though it sprang from him and hence was his own, but that this is the appearance so that man can be a receptacle. It was also shown above (nn. 288-294) that no one thinks from himself but from others, nor the others from themselves, but all from the Lord, an evil person as well as a good person. We showed further that this is well known in Christendom, especially to those who not only say but also believe that all good and truth, all wisdom and thus all faith and charity are from the Lord, also that all evil and falsity are from the devil or hell.

[2] One can only conclude from all this that everything which a man thinks and wills flows into him. And since all speech flows from thought as an effect from its cause, and all action flows similarly from the will, it follows that everything which one speaks and does also flows in, albeit derivatively or indirectly. It is undeniable that all which one sees, hears, smells, tastes or feels flows in; why not then what he thinks and wills? Can there be any difference other than this, that entities in the natural world flow into the organs of the external senses or of the body, while entities in the spiritual world flow into the organic substances of the internal senses or of the mind? Hence as the organs of the external senses or of the body are receptacles of natural objects, so the organic substances of the internal senses or of the mind are receptacles of spiritual objects. As this is man's situation, what then is his proprium? It cannot consist in his being such or such a receptacle, for then it would only be the man's manner of reception, not the life's proprium. No one understands by proprium anything else than that he lives of himself and consequently thinks and wills of himself; but that there is no such proprium and indeed cannot be with anyone follows from what was said above.

But let me relate what I have heard from some in the spiritual world. They were of those who believe that one's own prudence is everything and divine providence nothing. I remarked that man has no proprium unless you want to call it his proprium that he is such or such a subject or organ or form. This is not the proprium that is meant, however, for it is only descriptive of the nature of man. No man, I said, has any proprium as the word is commonly understood. At this those who ascribed everything to their own prudence and who may be called the very picture of proprietorship, flared up so that flames seemed to come from their nostrils as they said, "You speak paradox and insanity! Would man not be an empty nothing then? Or an idea or fancy? Or a graven image or statue?"

[2] To this I could only reply that it is paradox and insanity to believe that man has life of himself, and that wisdom and prudence, likewise the good of charity and the truth of faith, do not flow in from God but are in man. To attribute them to oneself every wise person calls insane and also paradoxical. Those who attribute them to themselves are like tenants of another's house and property who persuade themselves by living there that it is their own; or like stewards and administrators who consider all that their master owns to be theirs; or like servants in business to whom their master gave talents and pounds to trade with, but who rendered no account to him but kept all as theirs and thus behaved like robbers.

[3] It may be said of such that they are insane, indeed are nothing and empty, likewise are idealists, since they do not have in them from the Lord good which is the esse itself of life, thus do not have truth, either. They are also called "dead" therefore and "nothing and empty" (Isa 40:17, 23), and elsewhere "makers of images," "graven images" and "statues." More about them in what follows, to be done in this order:

i. What one's own prudence is, and what prudence not one's own is. ii. By his own prudence man persuades himself and confirms in himself that all good and truth are from him and in him; similarly all evil and falsity. iii. All that a man is persuaded of and confirms remains with him as his own. iv. If man believed, as is the truth, that all good and truth are from the Lord, and all evil and falsity from hell, he would not appropriate good to himself and consider it merited, nor appropriate evil to himself and make himself responsible for it.

(i) *What one's own prudence is, and what prudence not one's own is.* Those are in prudence of their own who confirm appearances in themselves and make them truths, especially the appearance that one's own prudence is all and divine providence nothing--unless it is something universal, which it cannot be without singulars to constitute it, as was shown above. They are also in fallacies, for every appearance confirmed as truth becomes a fallacy, and so far as they confirm themselves by fallacies they become naturalists and to that extent believe nothing that they cannot perceive by one of the bodily senses, particularly that of sight, for this especially acts as one with thought. They finally become sensuous. If they confirm themselves in favor of nature instead of God, they close the interiors of their mind, interpose a veil as it were, and then do their thinking below it and not at all above it. Such sense-ridden men were called serpents of the tree of knowledge by the ancients. It is also said of them in the spiritual world that as they confirm themselves they at length close the interiors of their mind "to the nose," for the nose signifies perception of truth, of which they have none. What their nature is will be told now.

[2] They are more cunning and crafty than others and are ingenious reasoners. They call cunning and craftiness intelligence and wisdom, nor do they know otherwise. They look on those who are not like themselves as simple and stupid, especially those who worship God and acknowledge divine providence. In respect of the interior principles of their minds, of which they

know little, they are like those called Machiavellians, who make murder, adultery, theft and false witness, viewed in themselves, of no account; if they reason against them it is only out of prudence not to appear to be of that nature.

[3] Of man's life in the world they think it is like that of a beast, and of his life after death that it is like a vital vapor which, rising from the body or the grave, sinks back again and dies. From this madness comes the notion that spirits and angels are airy entities, and with those who have been enjoined to believe in everlasting life that the souls of men also are. They therefore do not see, hear or speak, but are blind, deaf and dumb, and only cogitate in their particle of air. The sense-ridden ask, "How can the soul be anything else? The external senses died with the body, did they not? They cannot be resumed before the soul is reunited with the body." Inasmuch as they could comprehend the state of the soul after death only sensuously and not spiritually, they have fixed upon the state described; otherwise their belief in everlasting life would have perished. Above all, they confirm self-love in themselves, calling it the fire of life and the incentive to various uses in the kingdom. Being of this nature, they are their own idols, and their thoughts, being fallacies and from fallacies, are images of falsity. Indulging in the enjoyments of lusts, they are satans and devils; those who confirm lusts of evil in themselves are satans, and those who live them are called devils.

[4] It has also been granted me to know the nature of the most crafty sensuous men. Their hell is deep down at the back, and they want to be inconspicuous. Therefore they appear to hover about there like spectres, which are their fantasies, and they are called genii. Some were sent out from that hell once for me to learn what they are like. They immediately addressed themselves to my neck below the occiput and thus entered my affections, not wanting to enter my thoughts, which they adroitly avoided. They altered my affections one by one with a mind to bend them imperceptibly into their opposites, which are lusts of evil; and as they did not touch my thought at all they would have bent and inverted my affections without my knowledge, had not the Lord prevented it.

[5] Such do they become who do not believe that there can be any divine providence, and who search only for cupidities and cravings in others and thus lead them along until they dominate them. They do this so secretly and artfully that one does not know it, and they remain the same on death; therefore they are cast down into that hell as soon as they enter the spiritual world. Seen in heaven's light they appear to be without a nose, and it is remarkable that although they are so crafty they are more sense-ridden than others.

[6] The ancients called a sensuous man a serpent, and such a man is more cunning and crafty and a more ingenious reasoner than others; therefore it is said,

The serpent was more crafty than any beast of the field (Ge 3:1), and the Lord said:

Be prudent as serpents and simple as doves (Mt 10:16).

The dragon, too, called "that old serpent" and the "devil" and "satin," is described as

Having seven heads and ten horns, and on his heads seven crowns (Apoc 12:3, 9).

Craftiness is signified by the seven heads; the power to persuade by fallacies is meant by the ten horns; and holy things of the Word and the church which have been profaned are signified by the seven crowns.

From the description of one's own prudence and of those who are in it, the nature of prudence not one's own and of those who are in it may be seen. Those have prudence not their own who do not confirm in themselves that intelligence and wisdom are from man. They ask, "How can anyone be wise of himself or do good of himself?" When they speak so, they see in themselves that it is so, for they think interiorly. They also believe that others think similarly, especially the learned, for they are unaware that any-one can think only exteriorly.

[2] They are not in fallacies by any confirmation of appearances. They know and perceive, therefore, that murder, adultery, theft and false witness are sins and accordingly shun them on that account. They also know that wickedness is not wisdom and cunning is not intelligence. When they hear ingenious reasoning from fallacies they wonder and smile to themselves. This is because with them there is no veil between interiors and exteriors, or between the spiritual and the natural things of the mind, as there is with the sensuous. They therefore receive influx from heaven by which they see these things.

[3] They speak more simply and sincerely than others and place wisdom in life and not in talk. Relatively they are like lambs and sheep while those who are in their own prudence are like wolves and foxes. Or they are like those living in a house who see the sky through the windows while those who are in prudence of their own are like persons living in the basement of a house who can look out through the windows only on what is down on the ground. Again they are like persons standing on a mountain who see those who are in prudence of their own as wanderers in valleys and forests.

[4] Hence it may be plain that prudence not one's own is prudence from the Lord, in externals appearing similar to prudence of one's own, but totally unlike it in internals. In internals prudence not one's own appears in the spiritual world as man, while prudence which is one's own appears like a statue, which seems living only because those who are in such prudence still possess rationality and freedom or the capacity to understand and to will, hence to speak and act, and by means of these faculties can make it appear that they also are men. They are such statues because evils and falsities have no life; only goods and truths do. By their rationality they know this, for if they did not they would not feign goods and truths; hence in their simulation of them they possess a vital humanness.

[5] Who does not know that a man is what he is inwardly? Consequently that he is a man who is inwardly what he wishes to appear to be outwardly, while he is a copy who is a man outwardly only and not inwardly. Think, as you speak, in favor of God and religion, of righteousness and sincerity, and you will be a man, and divine providence will be your prudence; you will perceive in others that one's own prudence is insanity.

(ii) By his own prudence man persuades himself and confirms in himself that all good and truth are from him and in him; similarly all evil and falsity. Rest the argument on the parallel between natural good and truth and spiritual good and truth. Ask what truth and good are to the sight of the eye. Is not what is called beautiful truth to it, and what is called enjoyable good to it? For enjoyment is felt in beholding what is beautiful. What are truth and good to the hearing? Is not what is called harmonious truth to it, and what is called pleasing good to it? For pleasure is felt in hearing harmonies. It is the same with the other senses. What natural good and truth are is plain, then. Consider now what spiritual good and truth are. Is spiritual truth anything other than beauty and harmony in spiritual matters and objects? And is spiritual good anything other than the enjoyment and pleasure of perceiving the beauty and harmony?

[2] Let us see now whether anything different is to be said of the one from what is said of the other, that is, of the spiritual from what is said of the natural. Of the natural we say that what is beautiful and enjoyable to the eye flows in from objects, and what is harmonious and pleasing to the ear flows in from musical instruments. Is something different to be said in relation to the organic substances of the mind? Of these it is said that the enjoyable and pleasing are in them, while it is said of eye and ear that they flow in. If you inquire why it is said that they flow in, the one answer possible is that distance appears between the objects and the organs. But when one asks why it is said that in the other case they are indwelling, the one possible answer is that no distance appears between the two. Consequently, it is the appearance of distance that results in believing one thing about what one thinks and perceives, and another thing about what one sees and hears. But this becomes baseless when one reflects that the spiritual is not in space as the natural is. Think of sun or moon, or of Rome or Constantinople: do you not think of them apart from distance (provided the thought is not joined to the experience gained by sight or hearing)? Why then persuade yourself that because there is no appearance of distance in thought, that good and truth, as also evil and falsity, are indwelling, and do not flow in?

[3] Let me add to this an experience which is common in the spiritual world. One spirit can infuse his thoughts and affections into another, and the other not know that it is not his own thinking and affection. This is called in that world thinking from and in another. I have witnessed it a thousand times and also done it a hundred times; and it seemed to occur at a considerable distance. As soon as the spirits learned that another was introducing the thoughts and affections, they were indignant and turned away, recognizing then, however, that to the internal thought or sight no distance is apparent unless it is disclosed, as it may be, to the external sight or the eye; as a result it is believed that there is influx.

[4] I will add to this experience an everyday experience of mine. Evil spirits have often put into my thoughts evils and falsities which seemed to me to be in me and to originate from me, or seemed to be my own thought. Knowing them to be evils and falsities, I searched out the spirits who had introduced them, and they were detected and driven off. They were at a great distance from me.

It may be manifest from these things that all evil with its falsity flows in from hell and all good with its truth flows in from the Lord, and that both appear to be in man.

The nature of men who are in prudence of their own, and the nature of those in prudence not their own and hence in the divine providence, is depicted in the Word by Adam and his wife Eve in the Garden of Eden where were two trees, one of life and the other of the knowledge of good and evil, and by their eating of the latter tree. It may be seen above (n. 241) that in the internal or spiritual sense of the Word by Adam and Eve, his wife, the Most Ancient Church of the Lord on this earth is meant and described, which was more noble and heavenly than subsequent churches.

[2] Following is what is signified by other particulars. The wisdom of the men of that church is signified by the Garden of Eden; the Lord in respect to divine providence is signified by the tree of life, and man in respect to his own prudence is meant by the tree of knowledge; his sensuous life and his proprium, which in itself is self-love and pride in one's own intelligence, and thus is the devil and satan, is signified by the serpent; and the appropriation of good and truth with the thought that they are not from the Lord and are not the Lord's, but are from man and are his, is signified by eating of the tree of knowledge. Inasmuch as good and truth are what is divine with man (for everything of love is meant by good, and everything of wisdom by truth), if man claims them as his, he cannot but believe that he is as God. Therefore the serpent said:

In the day you eat of it, your eyes will be opened, and you will be as God, knowing good and evil (Ge 3:5).

So do those in hell believe, who are in self-love and thence in the pride of their own intelligence.

[3] Condemnation of self-love and self-intelligence is meant by the condemnation of the serpent; the condemnation of the volitional proprium is meant by the condemnation of Eve and the condemnation of the intellectual proprium by the condemnation of Adam; sheer falsity and evil are signified by the thorn and thistle which the earth would produce for Adam; the loss of wisdom is signified by the expulsion from the Garden; the Lord's care lest holy things of the Word and the church be violated is meant by guarding the way to the tree of life; moral truths, veiling men's self-love and conceit, are signified by the fig leaves with which Adam and Eve covered their nakedness; and appearances of truth, in which alone they were, are signified by the coats of skin with which they were later clothed. Such is the spiritual understanding of these particulars. Let him who wishes remain in the sense of the letter, only let him know that it is so understood in heaven.

The nature of those who are infatuated with their own intelligence can be seen from their fancies in matters of interior judgment, as, for example, about influx, thought and life. Their thinking about influx is inverted. They think that the sight of the eye flows into the internal sight of the mind or into the understanding, and that the hearing of the ear flows into the internal hearing, which also is the understanding. They do not perceive that the understanding from the will flows into the eye and the ear, and not only constitutes those senses but also employs them as its instruments in the natural world. As this is not according to the appearance, they do not perceive even if it is only said that the natural does not flow into the spiritual, but the spiritual into the natural. They still think, "What is the spiritual except a finer natural?" And again, "When the eye beholds something beautiful or the ear hears something melodious, of course the mind, which is understanding and will, is delighted." They do not know that the eye does not see of itself, nor the tongue taste, nor the nose smell, nor the skin feel of itself, but that it is the man's mind or spirit which has the perceptions in the sensation and which is affected according to its nature by the sensation. Indeed, the mind or spirit does not sense things of itself, but does so from the Lord; to think otherwise is to think from appearances, and if these are confirmed, from fallacies.

[2] Regarding thought, they say that it is something modified in the air, varied according to topic, and widened by cultivation; thus that the ideas in thoughts are images appearing, meteor-like, in the air; and that the memory is a tablet on which they are imprinted. They do not know that thought goes on in purely organic substances just as much as sight and hearing do. Only let them examine the brain, and they will see that it is full of such substances; injure them and you will become delirious; destroy them and you will die. But what thought and memory are see above at n. 279 end.

[3] Regarding life, they know it only as an activity of nature, which makes itself felt in different ways, as a live body bestirs itself organically. If it is remarked that nature is alive then, they deny this, and say it enables to life. If one asks, "Is life not dissipated then on the death of the body?" they reply that life remains in a particle of air called the soul. Asked "What then is God? Is He not life itself?" they keep silence and do not want to utter what they think. Asked, "Would you grant that divine love and wisdom are life itself?" they answer, "What are love and wisdom?" For in their fallacies they do not see what these are or what God is.

These things have been adduced that it may be seen how man is infatuated by prudence of his own because he draws all conclusions then from appearances and thus from fallacies.

By one's own prudence one is persuaded and confirmed that all good and truth are from man and in man, because a man's own prudence is his intellectual proprium, flowing in from self-love, which is his volitional proprium; proprium inevitably makes everything its own; it cannot be raised above doing so. All who are led by the Lord's divine providence are raised above the proprium and then see that all good and truth are from the Lord, indeed see that what in the human being is from the Lord is always the Lord's and never man's. He who believes otherwise is like one who has his master's goods in his care and claims them himself or appropriates them--he is no steward, but a thief. As man's proprium is nothing but evil, he also immerses the goods in his evil, by which they are destroyed like pearls thrown into dung or into acid.

(iii) All that a man is persuaded of and confirms remains with him as his own. Many believe that no truth can be seen by man without confirmations of it, but this is false. In civic and economic matters in a kingdom or republic what is useful and good can be seen only with some knowledge of its numerous statutes and ordinances; in judicial matters only with knowledge of the law; and in natural subjects, like physics, chemistry, anatomy, mechanics and others, only on acquaintance with those sciences. But in purely rational, moral and spiritual matters, truths appear in light of their own, if man has become somewhat rational, moral and spiritual through a suitable education. This is because everyone as to his spirit, which is what thinks, is in the spiritual world and is one among those there, consequently is in spiritual light, which enlightens the interiors of his understanding and, as it were, dictates. For spiritual light in essence is the divine truth of the Lord's divine wisdom. Thence it is that man can think analytically, form conclusions about what is just and right in matters of judgment, see what is honorable in moral life and good in spiritual life, and see many truths, which are darkened only by the confirmation of falsities. Man sees them almost as readily as he sees another's disposition from his face or perceives his affections from the sound of his voice, with no further knowledge than is implanted in one. Why should not man in some measure see from influx the interiors of his life, which are spiritual and moral, when there is no animal that does not know by influx all things necessary to it, which are natural? A bird knows how to build its nest, lay its eggs, hatch its young and recognize its food, besides other wonders which are named instinct.

How this state is changed, however, by confirmations and consequent persuasions will be told now in this order:

1. There is nothing that cannot be confirmed, and falsity is confirmed more readily than truth. 2. Truth does not appear when falsity has been confirmed, but falsity is apparent from confirmed truth. 3. The ability to confirm whatever one pleases is not intelligence but only ingenuity, to be found in the worst of men. 4. Confirmation may be mental and not at the same time volitional, but all volitional confirmation is also mental. 5. Confirmation of evil both volitional and intellectual causes man to believe that one's own prudence is everything and divine providence nothing, but not confirmation solely intellectual. 6. Everything confirmed by the will and at the same time by the understanding, remains to eternity, but not what has been confirmed only by the understanding.

[2] Touching the first, that there is nothing that cannot be confirmed, and that falsity is confirmed more readily than truth. What, indeed, cannot be confirmed when atheists confirm that God is not the Creator of the universe but that nature is her own creator; that religion is only a restraint and is for simple and common folks; that man is like the beast and dies like one; that adultery and secret theft, fraud and deceitful schemes are allowable, and that cunning is intelligence and wickedness is wisdom. Everyone confirms his heresy. Volumes are filled with confirmations of the two heresies prevalent in Christendom. Assemble ten heresies, however abstruse, ask an ingenious man to confirm them, and he will confirm them all. If you regard them then solely from the confirmations of them, will you not be seeing falsities as truth? Since all that is false lights up in the natural man from its appearances and fallacies, but truth lights up only in the spiritual man, plainly falsity can be confirmed more readily than truth.

[3] For it to be known that everything false and everything evil can be confirmed even to the point that what is false seems true and what is evil seems to be good, take for example the confirmation that light is darkness and darkness is light. A man may ask: "What is light 'in itself'? Is not light only something which appears in the eye according to the eye's condition? What is light when the eye is closed? Do not bats and owls have eyes to see light as darkness and darkness as light? I have heard it said that some persons see in like manner, and that infernal spirits, despite being in darkness, see one another. Does one not have light in his dreams in the middle of the night? Is darkness not light, therefore, and light darkness?" It can be replied, "What of that? Light is light as truth is truth, and darkness is darkness as falsity is

falsity."

[4] Take a further example: confirmation that the crow is white. May its blackness not be said to be only a shading which is not the real fact? Its feathers are white inside, its body, too; and these are the stuff of which the bird is made. As its blackness is a shading, the crow turns white as it grows old--some such have been seen. What is black in itself but white? Pulverize black glass and you will see that the powder is white. When you call the crow black, therefore, you are speaking of the shadow and not of the reality. The reply can be, "What of it? All birds should be called white then."

Contrary as they are to sound reason, these arguments have been recited to show that it is possible to confirm falsity that is directly opposite to truth and evil that is directly opposite to good.

[5] Second: Truth does not appear when falsity has been confirmed, but falsity is apparent from truth confirmed. All falsity is in darkness and all truth in light. In darkness nothing is seen, nor indeed is it known what anything is except by contact with it, but it is different in the light. In the Word falsities are therefore called darkness, and those who are in falsities are said to walk in darkness and in the shadow of death. In turn, truths are called light in it, and those who are in truths are said to walk in the light and to be the children of light.

[6] There is much to show that when falsity has been confirmed, truth does not appear, but when truth has been confirmed, falsity is apparent. For instance, who would see a spiritual truth unless the Word taught it? Would there not be darkness that could be dispelled only by the light in which the Word is, and only with one who wishes to be enlightened? What heretic can see his falsities unless he welcomes the genuine truth of the church? Until then he does not see them. I have talked with those who confirmed themselves in faith apart from charity and who were asked whether they saw the frequent mention in the Word of love and charity, works and deeds, and keeping the Commandments, and the declaration that the man who keeps the Commandments is blessed and wise, but the man who does not is foolish. They said that on reading these things they saw them only as matters of faith, and passed them by with their eyes closed, so to speak.

[7] Those who have confirmed themselves in falsities are like men who see streaks on a wall, and at twilight fancy that they see the figure of a horseman or just of a man, a visionary image which is dissipated when the daylight floods in. Who can sense the spiritual uncleanness of adultery except one who is in the cleanliness of chastity? Who can feel the cruelty of vengeance except one who is in good from love to the neighbor? What adulterer or what avenger does not sneer at those who call enjoyment in such acts as theirs infernal but the enjoyments of marital love and neighborly love heavenly? And so on.

[8] Third: The ability to confirm whatever one pleases is not intelligence but only ingenuity, to be found in the worst of men. Some show the greatest dexterity in confirmation, who know no truth and yet can confirm both truth and falsity. Some of them remark, "What is truth? Is there such a thing? Is not that true which I make true?" In the world they are believed to be intelligent, and yet they are only daubing a wall. 318-1 Only those are intelligent who perceive truth to be truth and who confirm it by verities constantly perceived.

Little difference may be seen between the latter and the former because one cannot distinguish between the light of confirmation and the light of the perception of truth. Those in the light of confirmation seem also to be in the light of the perception of truth. Yet the difference is like that between illusory light and genuine. In the spiritual world illusory light is such that it turns into darkness when genuine light flows in. There is such illusory light with many in hell; on being brought out into genuine light they see nothing at all. It is evident, then, that to be able to confirm whatever one pleases is only ingenuity, which the worst of men may have.

[9] Fourth: Confirmation may be mental and not at the same time volitional, but all volitional confirmation is also mental. Let an example serve to illustrate this. Those who confirm faith separate from charity and yet live the life of charity, and in general those who confirm a falsity of doctrine and yet do not live according to it, are in intellectual confirmation but not at the same time volitional. On the other hand, those who confirm falsity of doctrine and live according to it are in volitional and at the same time in intellectual confirmation. For the understanding does not flow into the will, but the will into the understanding. Hence it is plain what falsity of evil is, and what falsity not of evil is. Falsity which is not of evil can be conjoined with good, but falsity of evil cannot be. For falsity which is not of evil is falsity in the understanding but not in the will, while falsity of evil is falsity in the understanding which comes of evil in the will.

[10] Fifth: Confirmation of evil, both volitional and intellectual, but not confirmation only intellectual, causes man to believe that his own prudence is everything and divine providence nothing. Many confirm their own prudence in themselves on the strength of appearances in the world, and yet do not deny divine providence; theirs is only intellectual confirmation. But in others, who deny divine providence at the same time, there is volitional confirmation; this, together with persuasion, is found chiefly in worshipers of nature and also in worshipers of self.

[11] Sixth: Everything confirmed by the will and at the same time by the understanding remains to eternity, but not what is confirmed only by the understanding. For what pertains to the understanding alone is not within man but outside him; it is only in the thought. Nothing enters man and is appropriated to him except what is received by the will; then it comes to be of his life's love. This, it will be shown in the next number, remains to eternity.

Everything confirmed by both the will and the understanding remains to eternity because everyone is his own love, and love attaches to the will; also because everyone is his own good or his own evil, for that is called good or evil which belongs to the love. Since man is his own love he is also the form of his love, and may be called the organ of his life's love. It was stated above (n. 279) that the affections of man's love and his resulting thoughts are changes and variations of the state and form of the organic substances of his mind. What these changes and variations are and their nature will be explained now. Some idea of them may be obtained from the alternating expansions and compressions or dilations and contractions in the heart and lungs, called in the heart systole and diastole, and in the lungs respirations. These are reciprocal extensions and retractions or expansions and contractions of their lobes. Such are the changes and variations in the state of the heart and lungs. Such changes and variations occur in the other viscera of the body and in their parts, too, by which the blood and the animal juices are received and transmitted.

[2] Similar changes and variations take place in the organic forms of the mind, which, as we showed above, are the substances underlying man's affections and thoughts. There is a difference. Their expansions and compressions or reciprocal activities in comparison have so much greater perfection that they cannot be described in words of natural language, but only in words of spiritual language, which can sound only as saying that the changes and variations are vortical gyrations in and out, after the manner of perpetually winding spirals wonderfully massed into forms receptive of life.

[3] Now to tell the nature of these purely organic substances and forms in the evil and in the good respectively: in the good the spiral forms travel forward, in the evil backward; the forward-traveling are turned to the Lord and receive influx from Him; the retrogressive are turned towards hell and receive influx from hell. It should be known that in the measure in which they turn backward these forms are open behind and closed in front; and on the other hand in the measure in which they turn forward, they are open in front and closed behind.

[4] This can make plain what kind of form or organ an evil man is and what kind of form or organ a good man is, and that they are turned in opposite directions. As the turning once established cannot be twisted back it is plain that man remains to eternity such as he is at death. The love of man's will is what effects this turning, or is what either converts or inverts, for, as was said above, each person is his own love. Hence, on death, everyone goes the way of his love, the man in a good love to heaven, and the man in an evil love to hell, nor does he rest except in that society where his ruling love is. Marvelous it is that each knows the way; it is as though he scents it.

(iv) If man believed, as is the truth, that all good and truth are from the Lord and all evil and falsity from hell, he would not appropriate good to himself and consider it merited, nor evil and make himself responsible for it. This is contrary to the belief of those who have confirmed in themselves the appearance that wisdom and prudence come from man and do not flow in according to the state of the organization of the mind, treated of above (n. 319). It must therefore be demonstrated, and to be done clearly, it will be done in this order:

1. One who confirms in himself the appearance that wisdom and prudence are from man and thus in him as his, must take the view that otherwise he would not be a man, but either a beast or a statue; yet the contrary is true. 2. To believe and think, as is the truth, that all good and truth are from the Lord and all evil and falsity from hell, seems impossible, yet is truly human and hence angelic. 3. So to believe and think is impossible to those who do not acknowledge the divine of the Lord and that evils are sins, but possible for those who make these two acknowledgments. 4. Those who make the two acknowledgments alone reflect on the evils in themselves, and so far as they flee them and are averse to them, they send them back to hell from which they come. 5. So divine providence appropriates neither evil nor good to anyone, but one's own prudence appropriates both.

These propositions will be explained in the order proposed. First: One who confirms in himself the appearance that wisdom and prudence are from man and thus in him as his, must take the view that otherwise he would not be a man, but either a beast or a statue; yet the contrary is true. It comes from a law of divine providence that man is to think as it were from himself and act prudently as of himself, but still acknowledge that he does so from the Lord. It follows that one who thinks and acts prudently as of himself and acknowledges at the same time that he does so from the Lord, is a man, but that person is not who confirms in himself the idea that all he thinks and does is from himself. Neither is he a man who, knowing that wisdom and prudence are from God, keeps awaiting influx. This man becomes like a statue, the other like a beast. One who waits for influx is obviously like a statue; he is sure to stand or sit motionless, his hands dropped, his eyes closed or, if open, unblinking, and neither thinking nor breathing. What life has he then?

[2] Plainly, too, one who believes that everything he thinks and does is from himself is not unlike a beast. For he thinks only from the natural mind which man has in common with beasts, and not from the spiritual, rational mind which is the truly human mind; for this mind acknowledges that God alone thinks from Himself and that man does so from God. Therefore one who thinks only from the natural mind knows no difference between man and animal except that man speaks and a beast makes sounds, and he believes they die alike.

[3] Something further is to be said about those who await influx. They receive none, except for a few who desire it with the whole heart. These at times receive some response through a living perception in thought or by tacit utterance but rarely by an explicit one, and this then is that they should think and act as they determine and are able, and that one who acts wisely is wise and one who acts foolishly is foolish. They are never instructed what to believe or do, in order that human rationality and liberty may not perish, that is, in order that everyone shall act in freedom according to reason in all appearance as of himself. Those who are told by influx what they are to believe or do are not being instructed by the Lord, nor by any angel of heaven, but by some spirit, an Enthusiast, Quaker or Moravian, and are being misled. All influx from the Lord is effected by enlightenment of the understanding and by an affection of truth, and passes by the latter into the former.

[4] Second: To believe and think, as is the truth, that all good and truth are from the Lord and all evil and falsity from hell, seems impossible, yet is truly human and hence angelic. To believe and think that all good and truth are from God seems possible, if no more is said, for it falls in with a theological belief contrary to which it is not allowable to think. But to believe and think also that all evil and falsity are from hell seems impossible, for in that belief man would not think at all. But man still thinks as from himself though it is from hell, for the Lord grants to everyone that his thought, wherever it is from, shall appear to be his own in him. Else man would not live as a human being, nor could he be led out of hell and brought into heaven, that is, be reformed, as we have shown many times.

[5] Therefore the Lord also grants man to know and consequently to think that when he is in evil he is in hell, and that if he thinks evil he thinks from hell. He likewise grants him to think of the means by which he can escape from

hell and not think from hell, but enter heaven and in heaven think from the Lord, and He grants man the freedom to choose. From all this it may be seen that man can think evil and falsity as if from himself and also think that this or that is evil or false; consequently that it is only an appearance that he does so of himself, an appearance without which he would not be man. To think from truth is what is human itself and consequently angelic itself; it is a truth that man does not think from himself, but is granted by the Lord to think from himself to all appearance.

[6] Third: So to believe and think is impossible to those who do not acknowledge the divine of the Lord and that evils are sins, but possible to those who make the two acknowledgments. It is impossible to those who do not acknowledge the divine of the Lord, for the Lord alone gives man to think and will; and those who do not acknowledge the divine of the Lord, being separated from Him believe that they think for themselves. It is impossible also to those who do not acknowledge evils to be sins, for they think then from hell, and in hell everyone supposes that he thinks from himself. That it is possible, however, to those who make the two acknowledgments can be seen from what was set forth fully above (nn. 288-294).

[7] Fourth: Only those who live in the two acknowledgments reflect on the evils in themselves, and so far as they shun and are averse to them, they send them back to hell from which they come. All know or can know that evil is from hell and good is from heaven. Who then cannot know that so far as man shuns and is averse to evil he shuns and is averse to hell? He can know then, too, that so far as he shuns and is averse to evil, he wills and loves what is good, and consequently is so far released from hell by the Lord and led to heaven. Every rational person may see these things provided he knows that heaven and hell exist, where good and evil have their respective origins. If, now, he reflects on the evils in him, which is the same thing as examining himself, and shuns them, he disengages himself from hell, puts it behind him, and brings himself into heaven, where he beholds the Lord before him. Man does this, we say, but he does it as of himself and from the Lord now. When a man acknowledges this truth out of a good heart and in a devout faith, it lies inwardly hidden in all that he thinks and does afterwards as of himself. It is like the prolific force in a seed which remains in it even until new seed is produced, and like the pleasure in one's appetite for food the wholesomeness of which one has learned; in a word, like heart and soul in all he thinks and does.

[8] Fifth: So divine providence appropriates neither evil nor good to anyone, but one's own prudence appropriates both. This follows from all that has been said. Good is the objective of divine providence; it purposes good in all its activity, therefore. Accordingly, it does not appropriate good to anyone, for then this would become self-righteous; nor does it appropriate evil to anyone, for so it would make him responsible for evil. But man does both by his proprium, for this is nothing but evil. The proprium of the will is self-love and that of the understanding is the pride of self-intelligence, and of these comes man's own prudence.

Section 17

EVERY MAN CAN BE REFORMED, AND THERE IS NO PREDESTINATION [as commonly understood]

Sound reason dictates that all are predestined to heaven and none to hell, for all are born human beings and consequently God's image is in them. God's image in them consists in their ability to understand truth and to do good. The ability to understand truth comes from the divine wisdom, and the ability to do good from the divine love. This ability, which is God's image, remains in any sane person and is not eradicated. Hence it is that he can become a civil and moral man, and one who is civil and moral can also become spiritual, for the civil and moral is a receptacle of what is spiritual. He is called a civil man who knows and lives according to the laws of the kingdom of which he is a citizen; he is called a moral man who makes those laws his ethics and his virtues and from reason lives by them.

[2] Let me say how civil and moral life is the receptacle of spiritual life. Live these laws not only as civil and moral laws but also as divine laws, and you will be a spiritual man. There is hardly a nation so barbarous that it has not by law prohibited murder, adultery, theft, false witness and damage to what is another's. The civil and moral man keeps these laws that he may be, or seem to be, a good citizen. If he does not consider them divine laws also he is only a civil and moral natural man, but if he considers them divine also, he becomes a civil and moral spiritual man. The difference is that the latter is a good citizen both of an earthly kingdom and of a heavenly, while the former is a good citizen only of the earthly kingdom and not of the heavenly. They are distinguishable by the good they do. The good done by civil and moral natural men is not in itself good, for man and the world are in it; the good done by civil and moral spiritual men is in itself good, because the Lord and heaven are in it.

[3] From all this it may be seen that every person, because he is born able to become a civil and moral natural being, is also born able to become a civil and moral spiritual man. He has only to acknowledge God and not commit evils because they are against God, but do good because good is siding with God. Then spirit enters into his civil and moral actions and they live; otherwise there is no spirit in them and hence they are not living. Therefore the natural man, however much he acts like a civil and moral being, is spoken of as dead, but the spiritual man is spoken of as living.

[4] Of the Lord's divine providence every nation has some religion, and primary in every religion is the acknowledgment that God is, else it is not called a religion. Every nation that lives its religion, that is, does not do evil because this is contrary to its God, receives something spiritual in its natural life. Who, on hearing a Gentile say he will not do this or that evil because it is contrary to his God, does not say to himself, "Is this person not saved? It seems, it cannot be otherwise." Sound reason tells him this. On the other hand, hearing a Christian say, "I make no account of this or that evil. What does it mean to say

that it is contrary to God?" one says to himself, "This man is not saved, is he? It would seem, he cannot be." Sound reason dictates this also.

[5] Should someone say, "I was born a Christian, have been baptized, have known the Lord, read the Word, observed the Sacrament of the Supper," what does this amount to when he does not count as sins murder, or the revenge breathing it, adultery, stealing, false witness, or lying, and different sorts of violence? Does such a person think of God or of eternal life? Does he think they exist? Does sound reason not dictate that such a man cannot be saved? This has been said of a Christian, for a Gentile in his life gives more thought to God from religion than a Christian does. But more is to be said on these points in what follows in this order:

i. The goal of creation is a heaven from mankind. ii. Of divine providence, therefore, every man can be saved, and those are saved who acknowledge God and live rightly. iii. Man himself is in fault if he is not saved. iv. Thus all are predestined to heaven, and no one to hell.

(i) The goal of creation is a heaven from mankind. It has been shown above and in the work, Heaven and Hell (London, 1758), that heaven consists solely of those who have been born as human beings. Since heaven consists of no others, it follows that the purpose of creation is a heaven from mankind. This has been shown above (nn. 27-45), it is true, but will be seen more clearly still with explanation of the following:

1. Everyone is created to live forever. 2. Everyone is created to live forever in a blessed state. 3. Thus every person has been created to enter heaven. 4. The divine love cannot but will this, and the divine wisdom cannot but provide it.

One can see from these points that divine providence is none other than predestination to heaven and cannot be altered into anything else. We must now demonstrate, therefore, in the order proposed, that the goal of creation is a heaven from the human race. First: Everyone has been created to live to eternity. In the treatise Divine Love and Wisdom, Parts III and V, it was shown that there are three degrees of life in man, called natural, spiritual and celestial, that they are actually in everyone, and that in animals there is only one degree of life, which is like the lowest degree in man, called the natural. The result is that by the elevation of his life to the Lord man is in such a state above that of animals that he can comprehend what is of divine wisdom, and will what is of divine love, in other words, receive what is divine; and he who can receive what is divine, so as to see and perceive it within him, cannot but be united with the Lord and by the union live to eternity.

[2] What would the Lord do with all the created universe if He had not also created images and likenesses of Himself to whom He could communicate His divine? What would He exist for, otherwise, except to make this and not that or bring something into existence but not something else, and this merely to be able to contemplate from afar only incidents and constant changes as on a stage? What would there be divine in these unless they were for the purpose of serving subjects who would receive the divine more intimately and see and sense it? The divine is of an inexhaustible glory and would not keep it to itself, nor could. For love wants to communicate its own to another, indeed to impart all it can of itself. Must not divine love do this, then, being infinite? Can it impart and then take away? Would that not be to give what will perish, what

in itself is nothing, coming to nothing when it perishes? What really is is not in it. But divine love imparts what really is or what does not cease to be, and this is eternal.

[3] In order that a man may live forever, what is mortal with him is taken away. This mortal of his is his material body, which is taken away by its death. His immortal, which is his mind, is thus laid bare and he becomes a spirit in human form; his mind is this spirit. Ancient sages and wise men perceived that man's mind cannot die. They asked how the mind could die when it is capable of wisdom. Few today know the interior idea they had in this. It was the idea, slipping into their general perception from heaven, that God is wisdom itself, of which man partakes, and God is immortal or eternal.

[4] Since it has been granted me to speak with angels, I will say something from experience. I have spoken with those who lived many ages ago, with some who lived before the Flood and some who lived after it, with some who lived at the time of the Lord and with one of His apostles, and with many who lived in the centuries since. They all seemed like men of middle age and said that they do not know what death can be unless it is condemnation. Further, all who have lived well, on coming into heaven, come into the state of early manhood in the world and continue in it to eternity, even those who had been old and decrepit in the world. Women, too, although they had become shrunken and old, return into the bloom and beauty of their youth.

[5] That man lives after death to eternity is manifest from the Word, where life in heaven is called eternal life, as in Mt 19:29, 25:46; Mk 10:17; Lu 10:25, 18:30; Jn 3:15, 16, 36, 5:24, 25, 39, 6:27, 40, 68, 12:50; also called simply life (Mt 18:8, 9; Jn 5:40, 20:31). The Lord also told His disciples,

Because I live, you will live also (Jn 14:19),

and concerning resurrection said that

God is God of the living and not God of the dead, and that they cannot die any more (Lu 20:38, 36).

[6] Second: Everyone is created to live forever in a blessed state. This naturally follows. He who wills that man shall live forever also wills that he shall live in a blessed state. What would eternal life be without this? All love desires the good of another. The love of parents desires the good of their children, the love of the bridegroom and the husband desires the good of the bride and the wife, and love in friendship desires the good of one's friends. What then must divine love desire! What is good but enjoyment, and divine good but eternal blessedness? All good is so named for its enjoyableness or blessedness. True, anything one is given or possesses is also called good, but again, unless it is enjoyable, it is a barren good, not in itself good. Clearly, then, eternal life is also eternal blessedness. This state of man is the aim of creation; that only those who come into heaven are in that state is not the Lord's fault but man's. That man is in fault will be seen in what follows.

[7] Third: Thus every person has been created to come into heaven. This is the goal of creation, but not all enter heaven because they become imbued with the enjoyments of hell, the opposite of heavenly blessedness. Those who are not in the blessedness of heaven cannot enter heaven, for they cannot endure doing so. No one who comes into the spiritual world is refused ascent into heaven, but when one ascends who is in the enjoyment of hell his heart pounds, his

breathing labors, his life ebbs, he is in anguish and torment and writhes like a snake placed near a fire. This happens because opposites act against each other.

[8] Nevertheless, having been born human beings, consequently with the faculties of thought and volition and hence of speech and action, they cannot die, but they can live only with those in a similar enjoyment of life and are sent to them, those in enjoyments of evil to their like, as those in enjoyments of good are to their like. Indeed, everyone is granted the enjoyment of his evil provided that he does not molest those who are in the enjoyment of good. Still, as evil is bound to molest good, for inherently it hates good, those who are in evil are removed lest they inflict injury and are cast down to their own places in hell, where their enjoyment is turned into joylessness.

[9] But this does not alter the fact that by creation and hence by birth man is such that he can enter heaven. For everyone who dies in infancy enters heaven, is brought up there and instructed as one is in the world, and by the affection of good and truth is imbued with wisdom and becomes an angel. So could the man become who is brought up and instructed in the world; the same is in him as in an infant. On infants in the spiritual world see the work Heaven and Hell, London, 1758 (nn. 329-345).

[10] This does not take place, however, with many in the world because they love the first level of their life, called natural, and do not purpose to withdraw from it and become spiritual. The natural degree of life, in itself regarded, loves only self and the world, for it keeps close to the bodily senses, which are to the fore, also, in the world. But the spiritual degree of life regarded in itself loves the Lord and heaven, and self and the world, too, but God and heaven as higher, paramount and controlling, and self and the world as lower, instrumental and subservient.

[11] Fourth: Divine love cannot but will this, and divine wisdom cannot but provide it. It was fully shown in the treatise Divine Love and Wisdom that the divine essence is divine love and wisdom, and it was also demonstrated there (nn. 358-370) that in every human embryo the Lord forms two receptacles, one of the divine love and the other of the divine wisdom, the former for man's future will and the latter for his future understanding, and that in this way the Lord has endowed each human being with the faculty of willing good and the faculty of understanding truth.

[12] Inasmuch as man is endowed from birth with these two faculties by the Lord, and the Lord then is in them as in what is His own with man, it is manifest that His divine love cannot but will that man should come into heaven and His divine wisdom cannot but provide for this. But since it is of the Lord's divine love that man should feel heavenly blessedness in himself as his own, and this cannot be unless man is kept in the appearance that he thinks, wills, speaks and acts of himself, the Lord can therefore lead man only according to the laws of His divine providence.

(ii) Of divine providence, therefore, every man can be saved, and those are saved who acknowledge God and live rightly. It is plain from what has been demonstrated above that every human being can be saved. Some persons suppose that the Lord's church is to be found only in Christendom, because only there is the Lord known and the Word possessed. Still many believe that the Lord's church is general, that is, extends and is scattered throughout the world, existing thus with those who do not know the Lord or possess the Word. They say that those men are not in fault and are without means to overcome their ignorance. They believe that it is contrary to God's love and mercy that any should be born for hell who are equally human beings.

[2] Inasmuch as many Christians, if not all, have faith that the church is common to many--it is in fact called a communion--there must be some very widely shared things of the church that enter all religions and that constitute this communion. These most widely shared factors are acknowledgment of God and good of life, as will be seen in this order:

1. Acknowledgment of God effects a conjunction of God and man; denial of God causes disjunction. 2. Each one acknowledges God and is conjoined with Him in accord with the goodness of his life. 3. Goodness of life, or living rightly, is shunning evils because they are contrary to religion, thus to God. 4. These are factors common to all religions, and by them anyone can be saved.

To clarify and demonstrate these propositions one by one. First: Acknowledgment of God brings conjunction of God and man; denial of God results in disjunction. Some may think that those who do not acknowledge God can be saved equally with those who do, if they lead a moral life. They ask, "What does acknowledgment accomplish? Is it not merely a thought? Can I not 'acknowledge God when I learn for certain that God there is? I have heard of Him but not seen Him. Let me see Him and I will believe." Such is the language of many who deny God when they have an opportunity to argue with one who acknowledges God. But that an acknowledgment of God conjoins and denial disjoins will be clarified by some things made known to me in the spiritual world. In that world when anyone thinks of another and desires to speak with him, the other is at once present. The explanation is that there is no distance in the spiritual world such as there is in the natural, but only an appearance of distance.

[2] A second phenomenon: as thought from some acquaintance with another causes his presence, love from affection for another causes conjunction with him. So spirits move about, converse as friends, dwell together in one house or in one community, meet often, and render one another services. The opposite happens, also; one who does not love another and still more one who hates another does not see or encounter him; the distance between them is according to the degree in which love is wanting or hatred is present. Indeed, one who is present and recalls his hatred, vanishes.

[3] From these few particulars it may be evident whence presence and conjunction come in the spiritual world. Presence comes with the recollection of another with a desire to see him, and conjunction comes of an affection which springs from love. This is true also of all things in the human mind. There are countless things in the mind, and its least parts are associated and conjoined in accord with affections or as one thing attracts another.

[4] This is spiritual conjunction and it is the same in things large and things small. It has its origin in the conjunction of the Lord with the spiritual world and the natural world in general and in detail. It is manifest from this that in the measure in which one knows the Lord and thinks of Him from knowledge of Him, in that measure the Lord is present, and in the measure in which one acknowledges Him from an affection of love, in that measure the Lord is united

with him. On the other hand, in the measure of one's ignorance of the Lord, in that measure He is absent; and so far as one denies Him, so far is He separated from one.

[5] The result of conjunction is that the Lord turns man's face towards Himself and thereupon leads him; the disjunction results in hell's turning man's face to it and it leads him. Therefore all the angels of heaven turn their faces towards the Lord as the Sun, and all the spirits of hell avert their faces from the Lord. It is plain from this what the acknowledgment of God and the denial of God each accomplish. Those who deny God in the world deny Him after death also; they have become organized as described above (n. 319); the organization induced in the world remains to eternity.

[6] Second: Everyone acknowledges God and is conjoined with Him according to the goodness of his life. All who know something of religion can know God; from information or from the memory they can also speak about God, and some may also think about Him from the understanding. But this only brings about presence if a man does not live rightly, for despite it all he can turn away from God and towards hell, and this takes place if he lives wickedly. Only those who live rightly can acknowledge God with the heart, and these the Lord turns away from hell and towards Himself according to the goodness of their life. For these alone love God; for in doing what comes from Him they love what is divine. The precepts of His law are divine things from Him. They are God because He is His own proceeding divine. As this is to love God, the Lord says:

He who keeps my commandments is he who loves me . . . But he who does not keep my commandments does not love me (Jn 14: 21, 24).

[7] Here is the reason why there are two tables of the Decalog, one having reference to God and the other to man. God works unceasingly that man may receive what is in His table, but if man does not do what he is bidden in his own table he does not receive with acknowledgment of heart what is in God's table, and if he does not receive this he is not conjoined. The two tables were joined, therefore, to be one and are called the tables of the covenant; covenant means conjunction. One acknowledges God and is conjoined to Him in accord with the goodness of his life because this good is like the good in the Lord and consequently comes from the Lord. So when man is in the good of life there is conjunction. The contrary takes place with evil of life; it rejects the Lord.

[8] Third: Goodness of life, or living rightly, is shunning evils because they are contrary to religion, thus to God. That this is good of life or living rightly is fully shown in Doctrine of Life for the New Jerusalem, from beginning to end. To this I will only add that if you do good aplenty, build churches for instance, adorn them and fill them with offerings, spend money lavishly on hospitals and hostels, give alms daily, aid widows and orphans, diligently observe the sanctities of worship, indeed think and speak and preach about them as from the heart, and yet do not shun evils as sins against God, all those good deeds are not goodness. They are either hypocritical or done for merit, for evil is still deep in them. Everyone's life pervades all that he does. Goods become good only by the removal of evil from them. Plainly, then, shunning evils because they are contrary to religion and thus to God is living rightly.

[9] Fourth: These are factors common to all religions, and anyone can be saved by them. To acknowledge God, and to refrain from evil because it is

contrary to God, are the two acts that make religion to be religion. If one is lacking, it cannot be called religion, for to acknowledge God and to do evil is a contradiction; so it is, too, to do good and yet not acknowledge God; one is impossible apart from the other. The Lord has provided that there should be some religion almost everywhere and that these two elements should be in it, and has also provided that everyone who acknowledges God and refrains from doing evil because it is against God shall have a place in heaven. For heaven as a whole is like one man whose life or soul is the Lord. In that heavenly man are all things to be found in a natural man with the difference which obtains between the heavenly and the natural.

[10] It is a matter of common knowledge that in the human being there are not only forms organized of blood vessels and nerve fibres, but also skins, membranes, tendons, cartilages, bones, nails and teeth. These have a smaller measure of life than those organized forms, which they serve as ligaments, coverings or supports. For all these entities to be in the heavenly humanity, which is heaven, it cannot be made up of human beings all of one religion, but of men of many religions. Therefore all who make these two universals of the church part of their lives have a place in this heavenly man, that is, heaven, and enjoy happiness each in his measure. More on the subject may be seen above (n. 254).

[11] That these two are primary in all religion is evident from the fact that they are the two which the Decalog teaches. The Decalog was the first of the Word, promulgated by Jehovah from Mount Sinai by a living voice, and also inscribed on two tables of stone by the finger of God. Then, placed in the ark, the Decalog was called Jehovah, and it made the holy of holies in the tabernacle and the shrine in the temple of Jerusalem; all things in each were holy only on account of it. Much more about the Decalog in the ark is to be had from the Word, which is cited in Doctrine of Life for the New Jerusalem (nn. 53-61). To that I will add this. From the Word we know that the ark with the two tables in it on which the Decalog was written was captured by the Philistines and placed in the temple of Dagon in Ashdod; that Dagon fell to the ground before it, and afterward his head, together with the palms of the hands, torn from his body, lay on the temple threshold; that the people of Ashdod and Ekron to the number of many thousands were smitten with hemorrhoids and their land was ravaged by mice; that on the advice of the chiefs of their nation, the Philistines made five golden hemorrhoids, five golden mice and a new cart, and on this placed the ark with the golden hemorrhoids and mice beside it; with two cows that lowed before the cart along the way, they sent the ark back to the children of Israel and by them cows and cart were offered in sacrifice (1 Sa 5 and 6).

[12] To state now what all this signified: the Philistines signified those who are in faith separated from charity; Dagon signified that religiosity; the hemorrhoids by which they were smitten signified natural loves which when severed from spiritual love are unclean, and the mice signified the devastation of the church by falsification of truth. The new cart on which the Philistines sent back the ark signified a new but still natural doctrine (chariot in the Word signifies doctrine from spiritual truths), and the cows signified good natural affections. Hemorrhoids of gold signified natural loves purified and made good, and the golden mice signified an end to the devastation of the church by means

of good, for in the Word gold signifies good. The lowing of the kine on the way signified the difficult conversion of the lusts of evil of the natural man into good affections. That cows and cart were offered up as a burnt offering signified that so the Lord was propitiated.

[13] This is how what is told historically is understood spiritually. Gather all into a single conception and make the application. That those who are in faith severed from charity are represented by the Philistines, see Doctrine of the New Jerusalem about Faith (nn. 49-54), and that the ark was the most holy thing of the church because of the Decalog enclosed in it, see Doctrine of Life for the New Jerusalem (nn. 53-61).

(iii) Man himself is in fault if he is not saved. As soon as he hears it any rational man acknowledges the truth that evil cannot issue from good nor good from evil, for they are opposites; consequently only good comes of good and only evil of evil. When this truth is acknowledged this also is: that good can be turned into evil not by a good but by an evil recipient; for any form changes into its own nature what flows into it (see above, n. 292). Inasmuch as the Lord is good in its very essence or good itself, plainly evil cannot issue from Him or be produced by Him, but good can be turned into evil by a recipient subject whose form is a form of evil. Such a subject is man as to his proprium. This constantly receives good from the Lord and constantly turns it into the nature of its own form, which is one of evil. It follows that man is in fault if he is not saved. Evil is indeed from hell but as man receives it from hell as his and appropriates it to himself, it is the same whether one says that evil is from man or from hell. But whence there is an appropriation of evil until finally religion perishes will be told in this order:

1. Every religion declines and comes to an end in the course of time. 2. It does so through the inversion of God's image in man. 3. This takes place through a continual increase of hereditary evil over the generations. 4. Nevertheless the Lord provides that everyone may be saved. 5. It is also provided that a new church shall succeed in place of the former devastated church.

These points are to be demonstrated in the order given. First: Every religion declines and comes to an end in the course of time. There have been several churches on this earth, one after another, for wherever mankind is, a church is. For, as was shown above, heaven, which is the goal of creation, is from mankind, and no one can enter heaven unless he is in the two universal marks of the church which, as was shown just above (n. 326), are the acknowledgment of God and living aright. It follows that there have been churches on this earth from the most ancient times to the present. These churches are described in the Word, but not historically except the Israelitish and Jewish church. There were churches before it which are only described in the Word under the names of nations and persons and in a few items about them.

[2] The first, the Most Ancient Church, is described under the names of Adam and his wife Eve. The next church, to be called the Ancient Church, is described by Noah, his three sons and their posterity. This church was widespread and extended over many of the kingdoms of Asia: the land of Canaan on both sides of the Jordan, Syria, Assyria and Chaldea, Mesopotamia, Egypt, Arabia, Tyre and Sidon. These had the Ancient Word (Doctrine of the

New Jerusalem about Sacred Scripture, nn. 101-103). That this church existed in those kingdoms is evident from various things recorded about them in the prophetical parts of the Word. This church was markedly altered by Eber, from whom arose the Hebrew church, in which worship by sacrifices was first instituted. From the Hebrew church the Israelitish and Jewish church was born and solemnly established for the sake of the Word which was composed in it.

[3] These four churches are meant by the statue seen by Nebuchadnezzar in a dream, the head of which was of pure gold, the breast and arms of silver, the belly and thighs of brass, and the legs and feet of iron and clay (Da 2:32, 33). Nor is anything else meant by the golden, silver, copper and iron ages mentioned by ancient writers. Needless to say, the Christian church succeeded the Jewish. It can be seen from the Word that all these churches declined in the course of time, eventually coming to an end, called their consummation.

[4] The consummation of the Most Ancient Church, brought about by the eating of the tree of knowledge, meaning by the pride of one's own intelligence, is depicted by the Flood. The consummation of the Ancient Church is depicted in the various devastations of nations mentioned in the historical as well as the prophetical Word and especially by the expulsion of the nations from the land of Canaan by the children of Israel. The consummation of the Israelitish and Jewish church is understood by the destruction of the temple at Jerusalem and by the carrying away of the people of Israel into permanent captivity and of the Jewish nation to Babylon, and finally by the second destruction of the temple and of Jerusalem at the same time, and by the dispersion of that nation. This consummation is foretold in many places in the Prophets and in Daniel 9:24-27. The gradual devastation of the Christian church even to its end is pictured by the Lord in Matthew (24), Mark (13) and Luke (21), but the end itself in the Apocalypse. Hence it may be manifest that in the course of time a church declines and comes to an end; so does a religion.

[5] Second: Every religion declines and comes to an end through the inversion of God's image in man. It is known that the human being was created in the image and after the likeness of God (Ge 1:26), but let us say what the image and the likeness of God are. God alone is love and wisdom; man was created to be a receptacle of both love and wisdom, his will to be a receptacle of divine love and his understanding a receptacle of the divine wisdom. These two receptacles, it was shown above, are in man from creation, constitute him, and are formed in everyone in the womb. Man's being an image of God thus means that he is a recipient of the divine wisdom, and his being a likeness of God means that he is a recipient of the divine love. Therefore the receptacle called the understanding is an image of God, and the receptacle called the will is a likeness of God. Since, then, man was created and formed to be a receptacle, it follows that he was created and formed that his will might receive love from God and his understanding wisdom from God. He receives these when he acknowledges God and lives according to His precepts, receiving them in lesser or larger measure as by religion he has some knowledge of God and of His precepts, consequently according to his knowledge of truths. For truths teach what God is and how He is to be acknowledged, also what His precepts are and how man is to live according to them.

[6] The image and likeness of God have not been destroyed in man, but

seem to have been; they remain inherent in his two faculties called liberty and rationality, of which we have treated above at many places. They seem to have been destroyed when man made the receptacle of divine love, namely, his will, a receptacle of self-love, and the receptacle of divine wisdom, namely, his understanding, a receptacle of his own intelligence. Doing this, he inverted the image and likeness of God and turned these receptacles away from God and towards himself. Consequently they have become closed above and open below, or closed in front and open behind, though by creation they were open in front and closed behind. When they have been opened and closed contrariwise, the receptacle of love, the will, receives influx from hell or from one's proprium; so does the receptacle of wisdom, the understanding. Hence worship of men arose in the churches instead of the worship of God, and worship by doctrines of falsity instead of worship by doctrines of truth, the latter arising from man's own intelligence, and the former from love of self. Thence it is evident that religion falls away in the course of time and is ended by the inversion of God's image in man.

[7] Third: This takes place as a result of a continual increase of hereditary evil over the generations. It was said and explained above that hereditary evil does not come from Adam and his wife Eve by their having eaten of the tree of knowledge, but is derived and transmitted successively from parents to offspring. Thus it grows by continual increase from generation to generation. When evil increases so among many, it spreads to many more, for in all evil there is a lust to lead astray, in some burning with anger against goodness--hence a contagion of evil. When the contagion reaches leaders, rulers and the prominent in the church, religion has become perverted, and the means of restoring it to health, namely truths, become corrupted by falsifications. As a result there is a gradual devastation of good and desolation of truth in the church on to its end.

[8] Fourth: Nevertheless the Lord provides that everyone may be saved. He provides that there shall be religion everywhere and in it the two essentials for salvation, acknowledgment of God and ceasing from evil because it is contrary to God. Other things, which pertain to the understanding and hence to the thinking, called matters of faith, are provided everyone in accord with his life, for they are accessory to life and if they have been given precedence, do not become living until they are subsidiary. It is also provided that those who have lived rightly and acknowledged God are instructed by angels after death. Then those who were in the two essentials of religion while in the world accept such truths of the church as are in the Word, and acknowledge the Lord as God of heaven and of the church. This last they receive more readily than do Christians who have brought with them from the world an idea of the Lord's human nature parted from His divine. It is also provided by the Lord that all are saved who die as infants, no matter where they have been born.

[9] Furthermore, every person is given the opportunity after death of amending his life if possible. All are instructed and led by the Lord by means of angels. Knowing now that they live after death and that heaven and hell exist, they at first receive truths. But those who did not acknowledge God and shun evils as sins when in the world soon show a distaste for truths and draw back, and those who acknowledged truths with the lips but not with the heart

are like the foolish virgins who had lamps but no oil and begged oil of others, also went off and bought some, but still were not admitted to the wedding. "Lamps" signify truths of faith and "oil" signifies the good of charity. It may be evident then that divine providence sees to it that everyone can be saved and that man is himself in fault if he is not saved.

[10] Fifth: It is also provided that a new church shall succeed in place of a former devastated church. It has been so from the most ancient days that on the devastation of a church a new one followed. The Ancient Church succeeded the Most Ancient; the Israelitish or Jewish Church followed the Ancient; after this came the Christian Church. And this, it is foretold in the Apocalypse, will be followed by a new church, signified in that book by the New Jerusalem descending from heaven. The reason why a new church is provided by the Lord to follow in place of a former devastated church may be seen in Doctrine of the New Jerusalem about Sacred Scripture (nn. 104-113).

(iv) Thus all are predestined to heaven, and no one to hell. In the work Heaven and Hell (London, 1758) we showed at nn. 545-550 that the Lord casts no one into hell; the spirit himself does this. So it happens with every evil and impious person after death and also while he is in the world, with the difference that while he is in the world he can be reformed and can embrace and avail himself of the means of salvation, but not after departure from the world. The means of salvation are summed up in these two: that evils are to be shunned because they are contrary to the divine laws in the Decalog and that it be acknowledged that God exists. Everyone can do both if he does not love evils. For the Lord is constantly flowing into his will with power for shunning evils and into his understanding with power to think that God there is. But no one can do the one without doing the other; the two are joined together like the two tables of the Decalog, one relating to God and the other to man. In accordance with what is in His table the Lord enlightens and empowers everyone, but man receives power and enlightenment so far as he does what he is bidden in his table. Until then the two tables appear to be laid face to face and to be sealed, but as man acts on the biddings in his table they are unsealed and opened out.

[2] Today is not the Decalog like a small, closed book or document, opened only in the hands of children and the young? Tell someone farther along in years, "Do not do this because it is contrary to the Decalog" and who gives heed? He may give heed if you say, "Do not do this because it is contrary to divine laws," and yet the precepts of the Decalog are the divine laws themselves. Experiment was made with a number in the spiritual world, who at mention of the Decalog or Catechism rejected it with contempt. This is because in the second table, which is man's, the Decalog teaches that evils are to be shunned, and one who does not do so, whether from impiety or from the religious tenet that deeds effect nothing, only faith does, hears mention of the Decalog or Catechism with disdain, as though it was a child's book he heard mentioned, no longer of use to adults.

[3] These things have been said in order that it may be known that a knowledge of the means by which one can be saved is not lacking to anyone, nor power if he wants to be saved. It follows that all are predestined to heaven and no one to hell. Since, however, a belief in a predestination not to salvation but to damnation has prevailed with some, and this belief is damaging and cannot

be broken up unless one's reason sees the insanity and cruelty in it, it is to be dealt with in this order:

1. Predestination except to heaven is contrary to divine love and its infiniteness. 2. Predestination other than to heaven is contrary to divine wisdom and its infiniteness. 3. That only those born in the church are saved is an insane heresy. 4. That any of mankind are condemned by predestination is a cruel heresy.

That it may be apparent how damaging the belief is in predestination as this is commonly understood, these four arguments are to be taken up and confirmed. First: Predestination except to heaven is contrary to divine love and its infiniteness. In the treatise Divine Love and Wisdom we demonstrated that Jehovah or the Lord is divine love, is infinite, and is the esse of all life; also that the human being was created in God's image after God's likeness. As everyone is formed in the womb by the Lord into that image and after that likeness, as was also shown, the Lord is the heavenly Father of all human beings and they are His spiritual children. So Jehovah or the Lord is called in the Word, and so human beings are. Therefore He says:

Do not call your father on earth your father, for One is your Father, who is in the heavens (Mt 23:9).

This means that He alone is the Father with reference to the life in us, and the earthly father is father of the covering on life, which is the body. In heaven, therefore, no one but the Lord is called Father. And from many passages in the Word it is clear that those who do not pervert that life are said to be His sons and to be born from Him.

[2] Plainly, then, the divine love is in every man, an evil man as well as a good man, and the Lord who is divine love cannot act otherwise than a father on earth does with his children, infinitely more lovingly because divine love is infinite. Furthermore, He cannot withdraw from anyone because everyone's life is from Him. He appears to withdraw from those who are evil, but it is they who withdraw, while He still in love leads them. Thus the Lord says:

Ask, and it shall be given you; seek and you will find; knock and it shall be opened to you ... What man of you, if his son shall ask bread, will give him a stone? If you, then, who are evil, know how to give good things to your children, how much more shall your Father, who is in heaven, give good things to those who ask Him (Mt 7:7-11),

and in another place,

He makes His sun to rise on the evil and the good, and sends rain on the just and unjust (Mt 5:45).

It is also known in the church that the Lord desires the salvation of all and the death of no one. It may be seen from all this that predestination except to heaven is contrary to divine love.

[3] Second: Predestination other than to heaven is contrary to divine wisdom, which is infinite. By its divine wisdom divine love provides the means by which every man can be saved. To say that there is any predestination except to heaven is therefore to say that divine love cannot provide means to salvation, when yet the means exist for all, as was shown above, and these are of divine providence which is boundless. The reason that there are those who are not saved is that divine love desires man to feel the felicity and blessedness

of heaven for himself, else it would not be heaven to him, and this can be effected only as it seems to man that he thinks and wills of himself. For without this appearance nothing would be appropriated to him nor would he be a human being. To this end divine providence exists, which acts by divine wisdom out of divine love.

[4] But this does not do away with the truth that all are predestined to heaven and no one to hell. Were the means to salvation lacking, it would; but, as was demonstrated above, the means to salvation have been provided for everyone, and heaven is such that all of whatever religion who live rightly have a place in it. Man is like the earth which produces fruits of every kind, a power the earth has as the earth. That it also produces evil fruits does not do away with its capability of producing good fruits; it would if it could only produce evil fruits. Or, again, man is like an object which variegates the rays of light in it. If the object gives only unpleasing colors, the light is not the cause, for its rays can be variegated to produce pleasing colors.

[5] Third: That only those who have been born in the church are saved is an insane heresy. Those born outside the church are human beings equally with those born within it; they have the same heavenly origin, and like them they are living and immortal souls. They also have some religion by virtue of which they acknowledge God's existence and that they should live aright. One who acknowledges God and lives aright becomes spiritual in his measure and is saved, as we showed above. It may be protested that they have not been baptized, but baptism does not save any who are not washed spiritually, that is, regenerated, of which baptism is a sign and reminder.

[6] It is also objected that the Lord is not known to them and that there is no salvation without Him. But salvation does not come to a person because the Lord is known to him, but because he lives according to the Lord's precepts. Moreover, the Lord is known to everyone who acknowledges God, for He is God of heaven and earth, as He Himself teaches (Mt 28:18 and elsewhere). Furthermore, those outside the church have a clearer idea about God as Man than Christians have, and those who have a concept of God as Man and live rightly are accepted by the Lord. They also acknowledge God as one in person and essence, differently from Christians. They also give thought to God in their lives, for they regard evils as sins against God, and those who do this regard God in their lives. Christians have precepts of religion from the Word, but few draw precepts of life from it.

[7] Roman Catholics do not read the Word, and the Reformed who are in faith apart from charity do not attend to those utterances in it which concern life, only to those which concern faith, and yet the Word as a whole is nothing else than a doctrine of life. Christianity obtains only in Europe; Mohammedanism and Gentilism are found in Asia, the Indies, Africa and America, and the people in these parts of the globe are ten times more numerous than those in the Christian part, and in this part few put religion in life. What then is more mad than to believe that only these latter are saved and the former condemned, and that a man has heaven on the strength of his birth and not on the strength of his life? So the Lord says:

I say to you, many will come from the east and the west, and recline with Abraham, Isaac and Jacob in the kingdom of heaven; but the children of the kingdom shall be cast out (Mt 8:11, 12).

[8] Fourth: That any of mankind are condemned by predestination is a cruel heresy. For it is cruel to believe that the Lord, who is love itself and mercy itself, suffers so vast a throng of persons to be born for hell or so many myriads of myriads to be born condemned and doomed, that is, to be born devils and satans, and that He does not provide out of His divine wisdom that those who live aright and acknowledge God should not be cast into everlasting fire and torment. The Lord is still the Creator and the Savior of all men and wills the death of no one. It is cruel therefore to believe and think that a vast multitude of nations and peoples under His auspices and care should be handed over as prey to the devil by predestination.

Section 17

THE LORD CANNOT ACT CONTRARY TO THE LAWS OF DIVINE PROVIDENCE BECAUSE TO DO SO WOULD BE TO ACT CONTRARY TO HIS DIVINE LOVE AND WISDOM, THUS CONTRARY TO HIMSELF

It was shown in Angelic Wisdom about Divine Love and Wisdom that the Lord is divine love and wisdom, and that these are being itself and life itself from which everything is and lives. It was also shown that they proceed from Him, so that the proceeding divine is the Lord Himself. Paramount in what proceeds is divine providence, for this is constantly in the end for which the universe was created. The operation and progress of the end through means is what is called divine providence.

[2] Inasmuch as the proceeding divine is the Lord Himself and paramount in it is divine providence, to act contrary to the laws of His divine providence is to act contrary to Himself. One can also say that the Lord is providence just as one says that God is order, for divine providence is the divine order with reference primarily to the salvation of men. As order does not exist without laws, for they constitute it, and each law derives from order that it, too, is order, it follows that God, who is order, is also the law of His order. Similarly it is to be said of divine providence that as the Lord is providence Himself, He is also the law of His providence. Hence it is clear that the Lord cannot act contrary to the laws of His divine providence because to do so would be to act contrary to Himself.

[3] Furthermore, there is no activity except on a subject and on the subject by means; action is impossible except on a subject and on it by means. Man is the subject of divine providence; divine truths by which he has wisdom, and divine goods by which he has love, are the means; and by these means divine providence pursues its purpose, which is the salvation of man. For he who wills the purpose, wills the means. Therefore when he who wills the purpose pursues it, he does so through means. But these things will become plainer on being examined in this order:

i. The activity of divine providence to save man begins at his birth and continues to the close of his life and afterwards to eternity. ii. The activity of divine providence is maintained steadily out of pure mercy through means. iii. Instantaneous salvation by direct mercy is impossible. iv. Instantaneous salvation by direct mercy is the flying fiery serpent in the church.

(i) The activity of divine providence to save man begins at his birth and continues to the close of his life and afterwards to eternity. It was shown above that a heaven from mankind is the very purpose of the creation of the universe; that this purpose in its operation and progress is the divine providence for the salvation of man; and that all which is external to man and available to him for use is a secondary end in creation--in brief, all that is to be found in the three kingdoms, animal, vegetable and mineral. When all this constantly proceeds according to laws of divine order fixed at the first of creation, how can the primary end, which is the salvation of the human race, fail to proceed constantly according to laws of its order, which are the laws of divine providence?

[2] Observe just a fruit tree. It springs up first as a slender shoot from a tiny seed, grows gradually into a stalk, spreads branches which become covered with leaves, and then puts forth flowers and bears fruit, in which it deposits fresh seed to provide for its perpetuation. This is also true of every shrub and of every herb of the field. Do not each and all things in tree or shrub proceed constantly and wonderfully from purpose to purpose according to the laws of their order of things? Why should not the supreme end, a heaven from the human race, proceed in similar fashion? Can there be anything in its progress which does not proceed with all constancy according to the laws of divine providence?

[3] As there is a correspondence of man's life with the growth of a tree, let us draw the parallel or make the comparison. His infancy is relatively like the tender shoot of the tree sprouting from seed out of the ground; his childhood and youth are like the shoot grown to a stalk with its small branches; the natural truths with which everyone is imbued at first are like the leaves with which the branches are covered ("leaves" signify precisely this in the Word); man's first steps in the marriage of good and truth or the spiritual marriage are like the blossoms which the tree puts forth in the springtime; spiritual truths are the petals in these blossoms; the earliest signs of the spiritual marriage are like the start of fruit; spiritual goods, which are goods of charity, are like the fruit (they are also signified in the Word by "fruits"); the procreations of wisdom from love are like the seed and by them the human being becomes like a garden or paradise. Man is also described in the Word by a tree, and his wisdom from love by a garden; nothing else is meant by the Garden of Eden.

[4] True, man is a corrupt tree from the seed, but still a grafting or budding with shoots taken from the Tree of Life is possible, by which the sap drawn from the old root is turned into sap producing good fruit. The comparison was drawn for it to be known that when the progression of divine providence is so constant in the growth and rebirth of trees, it surely must be constant in the reformation and rebirth of human beings, who are of much more value than trees; so the Lord's words:

Are not five sparrows sold for two farthings, yet not one of them is forgotten by God? But even the hairs of your head are all numbered; fear not therefore; you are of more value than many sparrows. Which of you moreover can by taking thought add a cubit to his stature? ... if then you are unable to do what is least, why do you take thought for the rest? Consider the lilies, how they grow ... If then God so clothed the grass, which is in the field today and is cast into an oven tomorrow, how much more will he clothe you, O men of little faith? (Lu 12: 6, 7, 25-28).

The activity of divine providence for man's salvation is said to begin with his birth and continue to the close of his life. For this to be understood, it should be known that the Lord sees what a man's nature is and foresees what he wills to be and thus what he will be. For him to be man and thus immortal, his freedom of will cannot be taken away. The Lord therefore foresees his state after death and provides for it from the man's birth to the close of his life. With the evil He makes the provision by permitting and withdrawing from evils, in the case of the good by leading to good. Divine providence is thus continually acting for man's salvation, but more cannot be saved than are willing to be saved, and those are willing who acknowledge God and are led by Him. Those are not willing who do not acknowledge God and who lead themselves. The latter give no thought to eternal life and to salvation, the former do. The Lord sees the unwillingness but still He leads such men, and does so in accordance with the laws of His divine providence, contrary to which he cannot act, for to act contrary to them would be to act contrary to His divine love and wisdom, and this is to act contrary to Himself.

[2] Inasmuch as the Lord foresees the states of all after death, and also foresees the places in hell of those who do not desire to be saved and the places in heaven of those who do desire to be saved, it follows that He provides their places for the evil by the permitting and withdrawing of which we spoke, and their places for the good by leading them. Unless this was done steadily from birth to the close of life neither heaven nor hell would remain standing, for apart from this foresight and providence neither would be anything but confusion. It may be seen above (nn. 202, 203) that everyone has his place provided for him by the Lord through this foresight.

[3] A comparison may throw light on this. If a javelin thrower or a marksman should aim at a target, from which a line was drawn straight back for a mile and should err in aim by only a finger's breadth, the missile or the bullet at the end of the mile would have deviated very far from the line. So would it be if the Lord did not, at every moment and even the least fraction of a moment, look to what is eternal in foreseeing and making provision for one's place after death. But this the Lord does: the entire future is present to Him, and the entire present is to Him eternal. That divine providence looks in all it does to what is infinite and eternal, may be seen above, nn. 46-49, 214 ff.

As was said also, the activity of divine providence continues to eternity, for every angel is being perfected in wisdom to eternity, each, however, according to the degree of affection of good and truth in which he was when he left this world. It is this degree that is perfected to eternity; what is beyond that is outside the angel and not in him, and what is external to him cannot be perfected in him. This perfecting is meant by the "Good measure, pressed down and shaken together and running over" which will be given into the bosom of those who forgive and give to others (Lu 6:37, 38), that is, those who are in the good of charity.

(ii) The activity of divine providence is maintained steadily out of pure mercy through means. Divine providence has means and methods. Its means are the things by which man becomes man and is perfected in will and understanding; its methods are the ways this is accomplished. The means by which man becomes man and is perfected in understanding are collectively called truths. In the thought they become ideas, are called objects of the memory, and in themselves are forms of knowledge from which information comes. All these means, viewed in themselves, are spiritual, but as they exist in what is natural, they seem by reason of their covering or clothing to be natural and some of them seem to be material. They are infinite in number and variety, and more or less simple or composite, and also more or less imperfect or perfect. There are means for forming and perfecting natural civil life;

likewise for forming and perfecting rational moral life; as there are for forming and perfecting heavenly spiritual life.

[2] These means advance, one kind after another, from infancy to the last of man's life, and thereafter to eternity. As they come along and mount, the earlier ones become means to the later, entering into all that is forming as mediate causes. From these every effect or conclusion is efficacious and therefore becomes a cause. In turn what is later becomes means; and as this goes on to eternity, there is nothing farthest on or final to make an end. For as what is eternal is without end, so a wisdom that increases to eternity is without end. If there were an end to wisdom for a wise man, the enjoyment of his wisdom would perish, which consists in the perpetual multiplication and fructification of wisdom. His life's enjoyment would also perish; in its place an enjoyment of glory would succeed, in which by itself there is no heavenly life. The wise man then becomes no longer like a youth but like an old man, and at length like a decrepit one.

[3] Although a wise man's wisdom increases forever in heaven, angelic wisdom cannot approximate the divine wisdom so much as to touch it. It is relatively like what is said of a straight line drawn about a hyperbola, always approaching but never touching it, and like what is said about squaring a circle. Hence it may be plain what is meant by the means by which divine providence acts in order that man may be man and be perfected in understanding, and that these means are called by the common term truths. There are an equal number of means by which man is formed and perfected as to his will. These are called collectively goods. By them man comes to have love, by the others wisdom. The conjunction of love and wisdom makes the man, for what he is is in keeping with the nature of this conjunction. This conjunction is what is called the marriage of good and truth.

The methods by which divine providence acts on and through the means to form and perfect the human being are also infinite in number and variety. They are as numerous as the activities of divine wisdom from divine love to save man, and therefore as numerous as the activities of divine providence in accordance with its laws, treated of above. That these methods are most secret was illustrated above by the activities of the soul in the body, of which man knows so little it is scarcely anything--how, for instance, eye, ear, nose, tongue and skin sense things; how the stomach digests; how the mesentery elaborates the chyle and the liver the blood; how the pancreas and the spleen purify the blood, the kidneys separate it from impure humors, the heart collects and distributes it, and the lungs purify it and pass it on; how the brain refines the blood and vivifies it anew; besides innumerable other things which are all secret, and of which one can scarcely know. Clearly, the hidden activities of divine providence can be entered into even less; it is enough to know its laws.

Divine providence acts in all things out of pure mercy. For the divine essence is itself pure love; this love acts through divine wisdom and its activity is what is called divine providence. This pure love is pure mercy because 1. It is active with all men the world over, who are such that they can do nothing of themselves. 2. It is active with the evil and unjust and the good and just alike. 3. It leads the former in hell and rescues them from it. 4. It strives with them there perpetually and fights for them against the devil, that is, against the evils of hell. 5. To this end pure love came into the world and endured temptations even to the last of them, which was the passion of the Cross. 6. It acts continually with the unclean to make them clean and with the unsound to make them sound in mind. Thus it labors incessantly out of pure mercy.

(iii) *Instantaneous salvation by direct mercy is impossible.* We have just shown that the activity of divine providence to save man begins at his birth and continues to the close of his life and afterwards to eternity; also that this activity is continually pursued out of pure mercy through means. It follows that there is neither instantaneous salvation nor unmediated mercy. But as many, not thinking from the understanding about things of the church or of religion, believe that they are saved by immediate mercy and hence that salvation is instantaneous, and yet this is contrary to the truth and in addition is a pernicious belief, it is important that it be considered in due order:

1. Belief in instantaneous salvation by direct mercy has been assumed from man's natural state. 2. This belief comes from ignorance of the spiritual state, which is completely different from the natural state. 3. The doctrines of all churches in Christendom, viewed interiorly, are opposed to instantaneous salvation by direct mercy, but external men of the church nevertheless maintain the belief.

[2] First: *Belief in instantaneous salvation by direct mercy has been assumed from man's natural state.* From his state the natural man does not know otherwise than that heavenly joy is like worldly joy and that it flows in and is received in the same way; that, for example, it is like a poor man's becoming rich and from a sad state of poverty coming into a happy one of plenty, or like a lowly person's being raised to honors and passing thus from contempt to renown; or like one's going from a house of mourning to happy nuptials. As these states can be changed in a day and as there is a like idea of man's state after death, it is plain whence it comes that instantaneous salvation by direct mercy is believed in.

[3] In the world, moreover, many can join in one group or in one civic community and enjoy the same things, yet all differ in mind; this is true of the natural state. The reason is that the external of one person can be accommodated to that of another, no matter how unlike their internals are. From this natural situation it is also concluded that salvation is merely admission among angels in heaven, and that admission is by direct mercy. It is also believed, therefore, that heaven can be given to the evil as well as to the good, and that their association then is similar to that in the world, with the difference that it is filled with joy.

[4] Second: *This belief comes from ignorance of the spiritual state, which is altogether different from the natural state.* The spiritual state, which is man's state after death, has been treated of in many places above. It has been shown that everyone is his own love, that no one can live with others than those who are in a like love, and that if he comes among others he cannot breathe his own life. For this reason everyone comes after death into a society of his own people, that is, who are in a like love, and recognizes them as relatives and friends, and what is remarkable, on meeting and seeing them it is as if he had known them from infancy. Spiritual relationship and friendship bring this about. What is more, in a society no one can dwell in any other house than his own. Everyone

in a society has his own home, which he finds prepared for him as soon as he enters the society. He may be in close company with others outside his home, but he cannot dwell elsewhere. Again, in somebody else's apartment one can sit only in his own place; seated elsewhere he becomes frustrated and mute. And it is remarkable that on entering he knows his own place. This is as true in temples he enters and in any companies in which people gather.

[5] It is plain from this that the spiritual state is altogether different from the natural state, and is such that no one can be anywhere but where his ruling love is to be found. For there the enjoyment of one's life is, and everyone desires to be in the enjoyment of his life. A man's spirit cannot be anywhere else because that enjoyment constitutes his life, his very breathing, in fact, and his heartbeat. It is different in the natural world; there man's external is taught from infancy to simulate in look, speech and bearing other enjoyments than those of his internal man. Accordingly, no conclusion can be formed about man's state after death from his state in the natural world. For after death everyone's state is spiritual and is such that he cannot be anywhere except in the enjoyment of his love, an enjoyment that he has acquired in the natural world by his life.

[6] Hence it is quite plain that no one who is in the enjoyment of hell can be admitted into the enjoyment of heaven, commonly called heavenly happiness, or what is the same, no one who is in the enjoyment of evil can be admitted into the enjoyment of good. This can be concluded still more plainly from the fact that after death no one is denied going up to heaven; he is shown the way, has the opportunity given him, and is admitted, but as soon as he enters heaven and inhales its enjoyment, he begins to feel constricted in his chest and racked at heart, and falls into a swoon, in which he writhes as a snake does brought near a fire. Then with his face turned away from heaven and towards hell, he flees headlong and does not stop until he is in a society of his own love. Hence it may be plain that no one reaches heaven by direct mercy. Consequently, just to be admitted is not enough, as many in the world suppose. Nor is there any instantaneous salvation, for this presupposes unmediated mercy.

[7] When some who had believed in the world in instantaneous salvation by direct mercy became spirits, they wanted their infernal enjoyment or enjoyment of evil changed by both divine omnipotence and divine mercy into heavenly enjoyment or enjoyment in the good. As they ardently desired this, permission was given for it to be done by angels, who proceeded to remove their infernal enjoyment. But as this was the enjoyment of their life's love and consequently their life, they thereupon lay as if dead, devoid of all feeling and movement; nor could any life be breathed into them except their own, because all things of mind and body which had been turned backward could not be reversed. They were therefore revived by letting in the enjoyment of their life's love. They said afterwards that in that state they had experienced something dreadful and horrible, which they did not care to divulge. There is a saying in heaven, therefore, that it is easier to change an owl into a turtle-dove or a serpent into a lamb than an infernal spirit into an angel of heaven.

[8] Third: The doctrines of all churches in Christendom, viewed interiorly, are opposed to instantaneous salvation by direct mercy, but still some external men of the church maintain the idea. Viewed interiorly, the doctrines of all the

churches teach life. Is there a church whose doctrine does not teach that man ought to examine himself, see and acknowledge his sins, confess them, repent and then live a new life? Who is admitted to Holy Communion without this admonition and precept? Inquire and you will be assured of it. Is there a church whose doctrine is not based on the precepts of the Decalog? The precepts of the Decalog are precepts of life. What man of the church, in whom there is anything of the church, does not, on hearing it, acknowledge that he who lives rightly is saved and he who lives wickedly is condemned? In the Athanasian Creed, which is also the doctrine received in the whole Christian world, it is therefore said:

The Lord will come to judge the quick and the dead; and then those who have done good will enter into eternal life, and those who have done evil into everlasting fire.

[9] It is clear, then, that the doctrines of all churches, when viewed interiorly, teach life, and teaching life they teach that salvation is according to the life. Man's life is not breathed into him in a moment but is formed gradually, and it is reformed as the man shuns evils as sins, consequently as he learns what sin is, recognizes and acknowledges it, does not will it but desists from it, and also learns the helps that come with a knowledge of God. By all these means man's life is formed and reformed, and they cannot be given on the instant. For hereditary evil, in itself infernal, has to be removed, and good, in itself heavenly, implanted in its place. Because of his hereditary evil man may be compared to an owl as to the understanding and to a serpent as to the will, but when he has been reformed, he may be compared to a dove as to the understanding and to a sheep as to the will. Instantaneous reformation and hence salvation would be like changing an owl at once into a dove or a serpent at once into a sheep. Who that knows anything about man's life does not see the impossibility of this? Salvation is impossible unless the owl and serpent nature is removed and the nature of the dove and sheep implanted instead.

[10] Moreover, it is common knowledge that every intelligent person can become more intelligent than he is, and every wise man wiser than he is, and that intelligence and wisdom in man may increase and do so in some men from infancy to the close of life, and that man is thus continually perfected. Why should not spiritual intelligence and wisdom increase as well? These rise by two degrees above natural intelligence and wisdom, and as they ascend become angelic intelligence and wisdom, which are ineffable. These in turn increase to eternity with the angels. Who cannot understand, if he will, that what is being perfected to eternity cannot possibly be made perfect in an instant?

Thence it is evident now that all who give thought to salvation for their life's sake do not think of an instantaneous salvation by immediate mercy. Their thought is about the means to salvation, on and by which the Lord acts in accord with the laws of His divine providence, and thus by which man is led by the Lord out of pure mercy. Those, however, who do not think of salvation for their life's sake presume an instantaneousness in salvation and an immediacy in mercy, as do those who, separating faith from charity (charity is life), presume that faith can be instantaneous, at the final hour of death, if not earlier. Those do this, too, who believe remission of sins without any repentance to be absolution from sins and thus salvation, when attending the Holy Supper. So again those do who trust to indulgences of monks, their prayers for the dead, and the dispensations they grant by the authority which they claim over the souls of men.

(iv) Instantaneous salvation by unmediated mercy is the flying fiery serpent in the church. By a flying fiery serpent evil aglow with infernal fire is meant, as it is by the flying fiery serpent in Isaiah:

Rejoice not, all Philistia, that the rod which smote you is broken, for out of the serpent's root shall come forth a basilisk, whose fruit is a flying fiery serpent (14:29).

Evil of the kind is flying about in the church when belief is put in instantaneous salvation by immediate mercy, for this 1. abolishes religion; 2. induces security; and 3. charges condemnation to the Lord.

[2] First: It abolishes religion. Two things are the essentials and at the same time the universals of religion, namely, acknowledgment of God, and repentance. Neither has meaning for those who believe that they are saved out of mercy alone no matter how they live. What need then to do more than cry, "Have mercy on me, O God"? In all else pertaining to religion they are in darkness, even loving the darkness. In regard to the first essential of the church, which is an acknowledgment of God, they only think, "What is God? Who has seen Him?" If told that God is, and is one, they say that He is one; if told there are three, they also say there are three, but the three must be called one. Such is their acknowledgment of God.

[3] Touching the church's second essential, namely, repentance, they give this no thought, nor thought to any sin, and finally do not know that there is such a thing as sin. Then they hear and drink in with pleasure that the law does not condemn them because a Christian is not under its yoke. If only you say, "Have mercy on me, O God, for the sake of the Son," you will be saved. This is repentance in their life. If, however, you take away repentance, or what is the same thing, separate life from religion, what is left except the words, "Have mercy on me"? They are therefore sure to maintain that salvation is instantaneous, accomplished by these words, even if uttered at the hour of death, if not before. What does the Word become to them then but an obscure and cryptic utterance issuing from a tripod in a cave, or like an incomprehensible response from the oracle of an idol? In a word, if you remove repentance, that is, sever life from religion, what is human nature then but evil aglow with infernal fire or a flying fiery serpent in the church? For without repentance man is in evil, and evil is hell.

[4] Second: By the belief in instantaneous salvation out of pure mercy alone security of life is induced. Security of life arises either from the belief of the impious man that there is no life after death, or from the belief of one who separates life from salvation. Although the latter may believe in eternal life, he still thinks, "whether I live rightly or wickedly, I can be saved, for salvation is by outright mercy, and God's mercy is universal, for He does not desire the death of anyone." If it occurs to him that mercy should be implored in the words of the traditional faith, he can think that this can be done, if not earlier, just before death. Everyone who feels this security, makes light of adultery, fraud, injustice, acts of violence, blasphemy and revenge, and gives a free rein to body and spirit for committing all these evils; nor does he know what spiritual evil, or the lust of evil, is. Should he hear something about it from the Word, it is like

something falling on ebony and rebounding, or falling into a ditch and being swallowed up.

[5] Third: By this belief condemnation is charged to the Lord. If the Lord can save anybody out of pure mercy, who is not going to conclude that if man is not saved, it is not he but the Lord who is in fault? If it is asserted that faith is the medium of salvation, what man cannot have this faith? For it is only a thought, and this can be imparted, along with confidence, in any state of the spirit withdrawn from the mundane. Man may also declare "I cannot acquire this faith of myself." Hence if it is not vouchsafed him and he is condemned, what else can he think except that the Lord is in fault who could have given him the faith but would not? Would this not amount to calling the Lord unmerciful? Moreover, in the fervor of his belief he may ask, "How can God see so many condemned in hell when He can save them all in an instant from pure mercy?" And more such things, which can only be called an atrocious indictment of the Divine. From the above it may be evident that belief in instantaneous salvation out of sheer mercy is the flying fiery serpent in the church.

[6] Excuse the addition of what follows to fill the remainder of the sheet.

Certain spirits were permitted to ascend from hell who said to me, "You have written much from the Lord; write something from us, too." I asked, "What shall I write?" They said, "Write that every spirit, good or evil, has his own enjoyment; a good spirit is in the enjoyment of his good, and an evil spirit in the enjoyment of his evil." I then asked, "What is your enjoyment?" They answered that it was the enjoyment of committing adultery, stealing, defrauding and lying. Again I inquired, "What is the nature of those enjoyments?" They replied, "By others they are perceived as offensive odors from excrement and as the putrid smell from dead bodies and as the reeking stench from stagnant urine." I then said, "Do you find them enjoyable?" "Most enjoyable," they said. I remarked, "Then you are like unclean beasts which live in such filth." They replied to this, "If we are, we are; but such things are delightful to our nostrils."

[7] I asked, "What more shall I write from you?" They said, "Write this. Everyone is allowed to be in his own enjoyment, even the most unclean, as it is called, provided he does not infest good spirits and angels, but as we could not but infest them, we were driven off and cast into hell, where we suffer fearful things." I asked, "Why did you infest the good?" They replied that they could not help it; a fury seems to seize them when they see an angel and feel the divine sphere around him. Then I said, "So you are also like savage beasts!" On hearing this, a fury came over them which appeared like the fire of hate, and lest they inflict some injury, they were drawn back into hell. On enjoyments sensed as odors or as stenches in the spiritual world, see above (nn. 303-305, 324).

Footnotes

318-1 Cf. Ezekiel 13:10, 11 and Arcana Caelestia n. 739(2), Apocalypse Explained nn. 237(5) and 644(25). Tr.